The New Walford
Guide to Reference Resources

Volume 2
Social Sciences

facet publishing

© CILIP: the Chartered Institute of Library and Information Professionals 2008

Published by
Facet Publishing
7 Ridgmount Street
London WC1E 7AE
www.facetpublishing.co.uk
Facet Publishing is wholly owned by CILIP: the Chartered Institute of Library and Information Professionals.

This book is the second volume of a series that succeeds *Walford's guide to reference material*, published in eight editions between 1959 and 2000 by Library Association Publishing.

British Library Cataloguing in Publication Data
A catalogue record for this book is available from the British Library.

ISBN 978-1-85604-498-1
First published 2008

Text design by Studio 183
Database management and typesetting by York & Timberlake Partnership
Printed and made in Great Britain by MPG Books Ltd, Bodmin, Cornwall

Contents

Contents

Preface

In this second volume of *The New Walford* (TNW), we have continued the process of re-engineering 'Walford' for the 21st century network society. TNW is not conceptualized primarily as a tool to establish details of specific reference resources. All of us these days – or, at least, all who might also have access to this work – can readily use the web to do that. Rather, TNW Vol 2 principally is a carefully structured guide to examples of the various types of reference resource germane to communication in the social sciences. It is as much an encyclopedia as a resource discovery tool: of especial value – we trust – to students, information professionals and others new to some aspect of social science, and wanting an entrée to its literature.

Naturally, we have aimed to give a faithful description of the content and characteristics of the items chosen for citation. But not only subsequently will new editions have appeared, imprints changed, URLs moved, organizations discontinued, and so on; also, completely new resources will have arisen, supplementing or in some cases supplanting existing artefacts as the instruments of choice. So what we have here – as with any print tool – is a snapshot, the details planned to be accurate as at mid-2007.

Not surprisingly, we have toyed with the idea of updating the entries within this volume (and within the first volume of the series) online; or, indeed, of providing a web-searchable version of the whole of each volume's data. But further thought has convinced us that we should eschew such an approach. This, partly because there are already a number of well established generic web-based resource discovery tools for which TNW would be but a partial competitor (including, of course, Google itself!). Partly also, because we feel it very unlikely that we would be able to find enough information specialists willing and able optimally to maintain the currency of the online content, given the overall time, effort and funds that could reasonably be dedicated to the project. In our experience, so frequently human-intermediated web-based companions to, or versions of, print-based tools in the event turn out to be unsustainable. After the initial enthusiasm and flurry of activity, one soon finds the 'last updated date' on the website (if such be admitted) to be long ago. We would not want that.

But the main reason for retaining TNW as a print-on-paper work is that we still believe in the value of books to portray the richness and complexity of a subject's information landscape; and, more importantly still, to encourage the reader to pause and reflect. Despite the continuing advances in the relevant technologies, being able to hold in one's hand an easily browsable, well presented collection of descriptions of a subject's leading reference resources provides an experience and a perspective which we believe still cannot be matched online. The ideal of course is to have the best of both worlds: to have access to those resources which work best in print (such as TNW), alongside those which work best online. And that in turn is why from the outset of our design for *The New Walford* we wanted to ensure that we covered both types of reference resource herein: each genre complementing the other.

I need to thank all those who have directly or indirectly contributed to this volume: the readers and reviewers whose response to Volume 1 encouraged us to continue with our work; the Subject Specialists; the Facet Publishing team; Stephen York and the technical team putting the volume together; and, most critically, those in the background providing that intangible support that is so important in any significant venture of this type.

Ray Lester
Chair, TNW Editorial Board

Quick-start guide

How TNW is organized

Entries are hierarchically classified by subject area to four levels:

- At the highest level are the *Subject Parts*, in the order Psychology, Sociology & Social Work; Politics, Law & Government; Finance, Industry & Business; Education & Sport; and Media & Information.
- At the next level are the thirteen *Subject Groupings*, three each in Psychology, Sociology & Social Work, Politics, Law & Government and Finance, Industry & Business and two each in Education & Sport and Media & Information.
- Each Grouping is then sub-divided into around one hundred *Subject Fields*.
- In many of the Subject Groupings, where the subject demands more detailed categorization, subject fields have themselves been further subdivided in *Subject Subfields*.
- There are also two generic collections of entries: one at the start, describing resources covering the whole of Social Sciences (and, in some cases, *all* disciplines); and one at the other end, highlighting tools that are especially valuable for information professionals.

Within this structure, descriptions of resources are allocated to one of the subject areas and then placed within one of thirteen *Resource Categories*:

[1] Introductions to the subject
[2] Dictionaries, thesauri, classifications
[3] Laws, standards, codes
[4] Official & quasi-official bodies
[5] Research centres & institutes
[6] Associations & societies
[7] Libraries, archives & museums
[8] Portal & task environments
[9] Discovering print & electronic resources
[10] Digital data, image & text collections
[11] Directories & encyclopedias
[12] Handbooks & manuals
[13] Keeping up to date

For around a quarter of the resources, we have appended descriptions of associated or related resources (for example, additional items from the same producer or alternative views of the subject).

We do not duplicate or cross-reference entries within the set of resource categories for a specific subject area: if a resource description could equally well be placed within two (or more) categories, it will usually appear in the category earliest in the sequence. However, we do frequently cross-reference (but not duplicate) resource descriptions between different subject areas. In a few special instances, mainly in the section on Law, the same resource has been given an entry in several subject subfields, where a part of that resource is in itself an important authority in the narrow focus of the subfield; for similar reasons the key resource Intute has its own entry in several of TNW's subject sections.

Entries, including cross-referenced entries, appear alphanumerically by title within each resource category. Where a resource has a particular area or country focus that is not apparent from its title, we have added a geographical indicator.

The Table of Contents lists all the subject parts, groupings and fields, as well as the two generic sections, in the order in which they appear in the volume.

The Topic Index provides alphabetical access to the subject headings used for the subject fields and groupings. It also lists more detailed and alternative subject headings to the ones chosen for the subject fields, indicating where commonly sought topics are located within our subject structure (for example, 'Memory' takes you to entries located in Cognitive Psychology & Cognitive Science).

The Title/Author Index lists the titles and authors for all resources listed, including both main entries and associated resources. For organizations, we have also often provided cross-references for commonly-used acronyms or alternative forms of an organization's name and for English translations of names of resources in a foreign language, and cross-references linking parent and subordinate bodies.

How to find resources

- If you are looking for a known item, consult the Title/Author Index under the title of the work or the name of the author or organization associated with the resource.
- If you are looking for resources about a subject, browse the entries for the relevant subject part/grouping/field, using the Topic Index to target your search as necessary.

Information & Library Sciences

subject grouping heading

subject field heading

Information Society

subject subfield heading

resource category heading

Information Policy

Introductions to the subject

title of resource

geographical indicator

entry number

5441 Copyright: interpreting the law for libraries, archives and information services [UK]

resource author

G.P. Cornish 4th edn, Facet Publishing, 2004, 207pp. £29.95. ISBN 9781856045087.

price*

URL and type of website

www.facetpublishing.co.uk/cornish [COMPANION]

explanatory detail of contents

User-friendly, well established text explaining the provisions of the UK Copyright Act and supporting legislation in quick and easy question-and-answer form. There is a detailed index and appendices lay out the statutory declaration forms and provide helpful lists of addresses and selected further sources of information.

main resource

review of resource

'As Victorian travelers once carried their Baedekers, MLIS students will now cart their Cornish ...' (*Journal of the American Society for Information Science*)

bibliographical note

Previously published as Copyright for librarians

■ **Practical copyright for information professionals: the CILIP handbook S. Norman** Facet Publishing, 2004, 194pp. £29.95. ISBN 9781856044905. Basic guide covering all the key areas.

additional resource

* Resources from primarily US-based publishers have been given US$ prices; from those primarily based in the UK (or Europe) UK£ (or €) prices

Topic Index entries

Title/Author Index entries for main and additional resources

Editorial Board and Subject Specialists

Editorial Board

Dr Ray Lester (chair)
SOCIAL SCIENCE (GENERIC), EDUCATION & LEARNING, MEDIA & COMMUNICATIONS, TOOLS FOR INFORMATION PROFESSIONALS
Ray Lester graduated in chemistry, took a PhD in chemical pathology, and then worked at the multinational company Unilever as an information scientist/systems analyst. He was a subject specialist in several academic libraries before becoming Head of the Library at the London Business School. Subsequently he became Director of Information Systems at LBS in charge of all of the School's IT, library, audio-visual and telephone services, before taking up the post of Head of Information Services at The Natural History Museum, with a remit to manage the institution's IT, library, archive, publishing, and collections databasing services, and to chair its Information Strategy Group. Dr Lester also served on the boards of SCONUL and the Research Libraries Group.

Dr Peter Clinch
LAW, GOVERNMENT
Peter Clinch read law at Keele University, trained as a town planner at the University of London and practised within a local authority before changing careers into library and information work. He qualified from Sheffield University and worked again within local government, providing an information service to the officers of the authority. In 1978 he moved into academic library and information work, where he has been ever since, gradually focusing more and more on law libraries, their services and how to teach legal research. His PhD dissertation was on the development of the law reporting system in England and Wales. He has written two books on using a law library, one for law students, the other for librarians. In 1999 he was commissioned by the UK Centre for Legal Education to write the definitive guide to teaching legal research, which was published in a revised, second edition in 2005. He is the author of many journal articles and is in frequent demand as a consultant to UK and overseas universities setting up new or wishing to appraise existing provision for law library and information services.

Heather Dawson
SOCIOLOGY, POLITICS
Heather Dawson is a subject liaison Librarian at the LSE Library. Since 1997 she has also worked as the Government and Politics section editor for the Intute information gateway (www.intute.ac.uk), where she has been kept busy writing politics and international relations tutorials for the virtual training suite as well as maintaining catalogue records and writing a regular blog on elections. She is also one of the founder members of the ALISS Social Science Librarians group (www.alissnet.org.uk) where she helps maintain a website containing current awareness news for UK social science information professionals.

Helen Edwards
Helen Edwards has a BA in English from Queen Mary College, University of London and a Postgraduate Diploma in Librarianship from the Polytechnic of North London. She worked at King's College London and the University of Sussex libraries before moving to the London Business School, where she is currently Head of Information Services, responsible for the library and enterprise application development. Projects include the School's Portal, the gateway to a wide range of information sources and services for students, staff and alumni of the School, and the library's BestofBiz business information site. She is the President of the European Business Schools Librarians' Group.

Susan Tarrant
PSYCHOLOGY
Susan Tarrant first qualified as a librarian and later studied for a psychology degree with the Open University. She has previously worked in a polytechnic and a medical library, and since 1988 has been the subject librarian for psychology at the Senate House Library, University of London (formerly University of London Library) which also houses the library collections of the British Psychological Society.

Subject Specialists

Pat Budgen
SPORT
Pat Budgen works for Intute Social Sciences, covering the areas of Hospitality, Leisure, Sport and Tourism, and based at the University of Birmingham. Prior to this, she worked in a similar role for Altis, one of the Resource Discovery Network subject hubs which merged in 2006 to form Intute, both JISC-funded services. Her previous experience includes indexing the Sports Documentation Monthly Bulletin, later the Sport and Leisure Index, produced by the former Centre for Sports Science and History (CENSSAH) at the University of Birmingham. She is a history graduate and member of CILIP, with an MA in Librarianship from the University of Sheffield.

Peter Chapman
INDUSTRIES & UTILITIES
Peter Chapman read History at the University of Hull, and studied Librarianship at the Polytechnic of North London and Leeds Polytechnic (receiving an MA from the latter institution). He has been an active user of

electronic information sources since the early days of online databases, and is now an independent consultant specializing in website optimization. His interest in business information sources developed from his use of databases to assist business journalists, which led him to write columns for UKOLOG and 'In a Nutshell'. Whilst researching his subject area, he was impressed by the efforts of the British Library to make a multitude of business information sources available to the widest range of users.

Professor Sheila Corrall
INFORMATION & LIBRARY SCIENCES

Sheila Corrall is Professor of Librarianship & Information Management and Head of the Department of Information Studies at the University of Sheffield. Before moving to her current role, Sheila spent 25 years as an information specialist, library manager and strategic director in the public sector and universities, most recently as Director of Academic Services at the University of Southampton. She has served on many national committees and working groups and has also been active as a consultant, trainer and writer on professional and management topics. She was the first President of the Chartered Institute of Library and Information Professionals (CILIP).

Jonathan Cowley
FINANCE, ACCOUNTANCY & TAXATION

Jonathan Cowley is a corporate information specialist at London Business School Library. He read Geography at the University of Nottingham, and gained a Master's degree in Information Science from City University in 2004. His Master's dissertation examined the impact of the Freedom of Information Act on UK higher education institutions. He has previously worked in libraries at De Montfort University, the University of Leicester, University College London and Birkbeck, University of London.

Tracey Ellis
BUSINESS & MANAGEMENT

Tracey Ellis is a librarian at the London Business School, where she has worked for the past four years.

Her current role as Bibliographic Services Librarian entails all aspects of acquisitions, cataloguing and classification of the library's specialist monograph collection. She has been a qualified librarian since 1999, working mainly in an academic setting, plus two years at the Office for National Statistics.

Gwyneth Price
EDUCATION & LEARNING

Gwyneth Price read Ancient History and Archaeology at the University of Birmingham before studying for a PGCE and teaching in secondary schools for seven years. Her involvement in running a school library led to a career change, a Master's degree in Library and Information Studies and a move to the Institute of Education, University of London, where Gwyneth is currently employed as Student Services Librarian. Gwyneth is a Fellow of the Centre for Distance Education at the University of London and is particularly interested in information literacy and the uses of social software in learning and teaching.

Angela Upton
SOCIAL WORK & SOCIAL CARE

Angela Upton has a BA in English from the University of Sussex and went on to do a Postgraduate Diploma in Library and Information Studies at the Polytechnic of North London. She worked in the Library at the National Institute for Social Work, where she was responsible for library services and for selecting, abstracting and keywording books and other material for the social care database Caredata. She now works at the Social Care Institute for Excellence, where she manages the organization's Intranet and is responsible for selecting books and other material for the successor to Caredata, Social Care Online.

Thanks also to **Gill Dwyer** (London Business School), **Wendy Buckle** and **Lynne Seddon** (Cranfield University), and **Stephen Tapril** (University of Sheffield Department of Information Studies) for their input, and to **Jean Walford** for her continuing interest in the project.

Introduction

This Introduction covers:

- Introducing TNW
- What's new about TNW?
- The new information universe
- Selection and description of resources
- Organization and arrangement of entries

Introducing TNW

The second volume of *The New Walford* (TNW) is a guide to reference resources in the Social Sciences. It provides a collection of resources aimed particularly at helping people to research unfamiliar subject areas. It offers comprehensive coverage of the range of resources available in the networked world, but is necessarily selective in the set of items chosen for each subject field. Our aim is to get you started, to help you navigate uncharted territory and find the right types of resources to meet your needs.

This new guide builds on the reputation and concept of the classic *Walford's guide to reference material*, but we have made radical changes to the design, focus and layout. The internet and the world wide web have had a dramatic impact on the quantity and quality of information resources. The new information universe is diverse and complex with its mix of established and emergent media.

What's *new* about TNW?

TNW has been completely 're-engineered' for the hybrid information world. There are seven key changes from 'The Old Walford'.

- *Focus on the newcomer* – TNW has been specially designed to help the less-experienced user of Social Science resources, particularly people researching a field for the first time.
- *Simpler subject arrangement* – TNW has moved away from the Universal Decimal Classification (UDC) and adopted its own straightforward three-level scheme of subject parts, subject groupings and subject fields.
- *Navigation by topic* – TNW's new TOPIC INDEX helps you to find your way quickly from a subject heading or an alternative sought term to the right place in the main sequence.
- *New resource categorization* – TNW has replaced the 40 or so 'form headings' used in the old Walford with a new simpler set of 13 resource categories.
- *Expansion of resource types* – TNW includes the full spectrum of resources now available to the internet user, with thousands of organizational

websites and portals complementing its coverage of traditional reference tools.

- *Introductory essays* – TNW also helps the Social Sciences newcomer by offering short narrative introductions, highlighting key features of each major subject area.
- *Improved visual layout* – TNW's new typographical design and use of the resource title as the lead term for each entry makes the volume easy to scan and quick to use.

The new information universe

The world wide web has revolutionized the world of reference. The number of host computers accessible via the internet has grown at an astonishing rate over the last ten years. The leading search engine, Google, has stopped advertising the number of pages it searches; but it is several billion. The proportion of that total that might be considered as 'reference resources' is debatable, but it must run into millions.

The later editions of the old *Walford* naturally recognized the gathering momentum of electronic information services and included a separate Online and Database Services Index in each volume, which covered both standalone CD-ROM and networked online services. It is now evident that the defining development of the electronic era was not the shift from print to digital resources, but the move to a digital format that is also networked – via the internet and the web. Five aspects of this revolution are significant for reference services.

1 *Networked versions of traditional reference resources*
This area has evolved from the abstracting and indexing services offered by online hosts using proprietary search systems to electronic versions of other resources – such as data compilations, dictionaries, directories and encyclopedias – provided by aggregators with web-based interfaces. It also includes networked versions of library online public access catalogues (OPACs).

It is now increasingly rare to find a print-based reference resource that does not also have a web-based presence. CD-ROM and (especially) microform versions have been virtually eclipsed by web-based products. Many libraries now subscribe only to the networked version, which provides comprehensive access to their primary user group, but may have unfortunate consequences for other users for whom access to resources is either restricted or denied.

2 *Network availability of digital primary resources*
Following on from the networked versions of full-text secondary resources, such as encyclopedias, most of the primary journal literature in the Social Scences is now available online, via an aggregator or direct from

the publisher. Here again the trend is towards electronic-only access, controlled by licensing agreements which restrict access to members of the community, institution or corporation.

The *non-substitutability* of primary literature makes this a more serious concern than in the case of secondary resources, for which acceptable substitutes are often available. However, the 'open access movement' is starting to change this situation by encouraging scholarly authors to make their research papers and data publicly available through discipline-based or institutional repositories. This movement is now gaining high-level support within academic and official bodies, but it will take time for it to have full effect.

Web access is also being extended from 'born digital' to digitized 'legacy' artefacts, as a result of various local, national and international government-sponsored programmes. Such work encompasses a broad range of informational and other artefacts and the resulting resources frequently serve as an acceptable substitute for the 'real thing', which was formerly only accessible by visiting the relevant library, archive, museum, gallery, garden, laboratory, etc.

3 *Search engines, directories and resource discovery tools*
The creation of web search engines (such as Google) and research directories (such as Yahoo!) outside the traditional scholarly and scientific community is one of the most significant developments associated with the web. The success of such ventures is evident from the fact that large numbers of users – including students, academics and librarians – turn first to a tool like Google when seeking publicly available information.

Many other players have also tried to tame the web, producing both generic and domain-specific services, with the distinctions between 'engines', 'directories' and other tools becoming increasingly blurred. There have been numerous initiatives of this type in the academic world, with efforts at individual, institutional and national levels to develop 'subject gateways' and other resource discovery tools. These range from simple lists of web-page links to standardized descriptions of internet resources, but many of these services have proved unsustainable over time.

4 *Convergence and development of the information industry*
The Google Scholar search engine and Google's digitization agreements with major research libraries are examples of the blurring of boundaries between the commercial and academic worlds. Within the information industry sector, established stakeholders are changing and expanding their roles and competing with new entrants to the field as other players develop their roles as information providers.

Traditional online hosts are now competing with booksellers, news agencies, broadcasting networks and software developers, as well as with subscription agents, document supply centres, information brokers and digital reference services. Many public sector and other non-profit organizations are also taking on significant roles as information providers through their websites. Linking technologies and partnerships enable users to move seamlessly from one resource to another, while portal and task environments offer a range of personalized services and facilities for online transactions.

5 *Dynamic resources and collaborative content creation*
Current awareness services have similarly been transformed by new technologies, which offer the Social Science information user various options for keeping up-to-date with literature and developments in the field. Automatic e-mail alerting of journal content pages is well established and has now been supplemented by the use of RSS feeds for new web-page content from organizational and personal websites, including feeds from specialist weblogs.

Dynamic resources are becoming the norm, with content continually updated as new information enters the public domain. People have moved beyond e-mail discussion lists to new forms of online communities, using technologies such as chat rooms, instant messaging and wiki software, which allows open access for users to create and edit content on the web. The classic example here is Wikipedia, described as 'the free-content encyclopedia that anyone can edit'.

TNW helps you to negotiate the challenges of this new world in several ways:

- by identifying specific items on topics likely to be of interest
- by showing how the different subjects relate to one another
- by covering the full spectrum of print and digital resources
- by offering a pragmatic framework to structure your search.

Selection and description of resources
Selection policy
In line with our aim of helping the newcomer, we have concentrated our selection of resources on items suitable for entry to the field. These items are typically at the tertiary education level and are the kinds of resources likely to be found and used in academic and large public libraries.

The resources included aim to give international coverage, especially for organizations. The publications listed are predominantly from the UK and USA and primarily in the English language.

Our policy is to include only those resources likely

to be maintained in the medium to long term. We have generally excluded personally maintained websites, but where such resources have been included, we have generally marked them as 'personal interest sites' in the annotation.

Resource descriptions

We have based our description of resources on the current edition of the *Anglo-American Cataloguing Rules*. To aid the rapid scanning of entries, we have made the title the lead element for all descriptions.

Where an item has a particular area focus that is not obvious from its title, we have added a two- or three-letter geographical indicator. The codes cover Europe, the G8 countries, Australia and China.

Where possible, we have given indicative prices for resources, generally in the currency of the country where the publisher has its headquarters.

For practical reasons, we have often shortened URLs, which should reduce the impact of changed locators and broken links. This may require you to navigate to the specific item listed, but may also reveal additional items of interest in the process.

Resource annotations

Our annotations are intended to help you decide whether a particular resource will meet your needs. We have concentrated on providing factual information about the content and scope of resources and on highlighting any notable or unusual features. If there is a good description of the resource available from its producer, we have incorporated that in the annotation, enclosing it in single quotation marks ('...').

We have tried to make the book interesting to read by varying the style of annotation and allowing the editors to choose their own approach. The provision of in-depth reviews is beyond our scope, but we often quote from such reviews, where they usefully reinforce or extend our comments.

Associated resources

For a significant proportion of the main entries, we have appended related or associated resources, which have full descriptions and index entries, but usually shorter annotations. This practice has enabled us to include a larger number of resources in the volume than would otherwise have been possible. Examples of resources of this kind include:

- subsidiary organizations or units of an organization
- advocacy bodies associated with an organization's work
- additional resources produced by the same organization
- similar resources produced by another organization

- resources offering alternative treatments of a subject.

Organization and arrangement of entries

Generic social science resources
The first section of the book covers generic social science resources.

Tools for information professionals
This is complemented by a smaller section at the end of the sequence devoted to Tools for Information Professionals; resources more likely to be used by such professionals on users' behalfs, than directly by the users themselves.

Subject groupings
The main body of the work is divided into five parts covering 13 major subject sections:

PSYCHOLOGY, SOCIOLOGY & SOCIAL WORK
   Psychology
   Sociology
   Social Work & Welfare
POLITICS, GOVERNMENT & LAW
   Politics
   Government
   Law
FINANCE, INDUSTRY & BUSINESS
   Finance, Accountancy & Taxation
   Industries & Utilities
   Business & Management
EDUCATION & SPORT
   Education & Learning
   Sport
MEDIA & INFORMATION
   Media & Communications
   Information & Library Sciences

Subject fields
The subject sections are in turn organized into more than one hundred Subject Fields. Resources generic to a subject section are placed at the start of the section, before the first subject field heading. In some sections the Subject Fields are themselves further divided into Subject Subfields. The full list of subject fields and subfields is shown on the Contents pages.

The distribution of resources over the different levels of the hierarchy varies from subject to subject, reflecting the nature of the discipline and the judgement of the editors on the most useful balance.

Cross references
In order to maximize the number of resources included we have not duplicated resources between sections, but we have provided cross-references for resources that are relevant to more than one subject field or grouping.

Introductory essays
Each subject section is introduced by a short essay highlighting key points about the areas covered, including connections with other subjects in the volume.

Resource categories
All the resources listed in the different sections of the volume have been assigned to one of thirteen Resource Categories, which are shown in Figure 1 and listed below, with examples of the types included. These new categories replace the 'form headings' used in the old *Walford*.

Within each section, part, grouping or field, the categories are always arranged in the same order:

[1] INTRODUCTIONS TO THE SUBJECT.
Includes histories of the subject, academic course books, non-specialist overviews, alternative viewpoints.

[2] DICTIONARIES, THESAURI, CLASSIFICATIONS
Includes abbreviations and acronyms, glossaries, quotations, taxonomies and ontologies.

[3] LAWS, STANDARDS, CODES
Includes intellectual property, nomenclatures, laws, codes and theories.

[4] OFFICIAL & QUASI-OFFICIAL BODIES
Includes government departments, international agencies, quasi-official government organizations, research councils.

[5] RESEARCH CENTRES & INSTITUTES
Includes international centres of excellence, academic institutes, research foundations, commercially endowed non-profits.

[6] ASSOCIATIONS & SOCIETIES
Includes academies, scholarly societies, trade associations, advocacy and support bodies.

[7] LIBRARIES, ARCHIVES & MUSEUMS
Includes national libraries, national archives, museums, special collections.

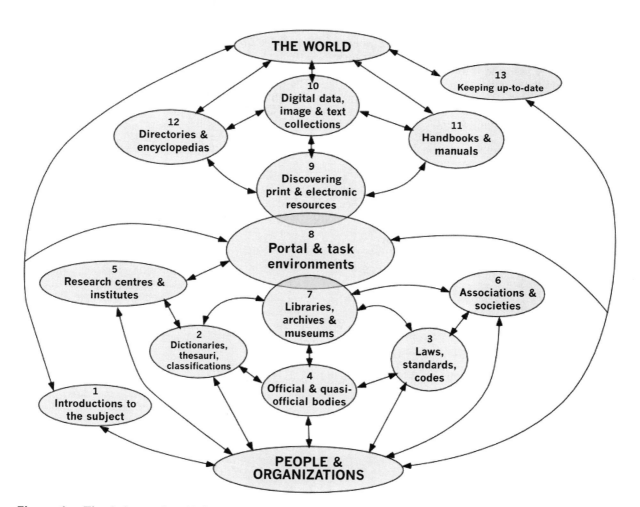

Figure 1   The Information Universe

[8] PORTAL & TASK ENVIRONMENTS
Includes aggregator/host services, e-type offerings (e-government, e-learning, e-social science, etc), one-stop shops, virtual reference services.

[9] DISCOVERING PRINT & ELECTRONIC RESOURCES
Includes abstracts and indexes, catalogues and bibliographies, finding tools, resource discovery services.

[10] DIGITAL DATA, IMAGE & TEXT COLLECTIONS
Includes social science data banks, photograph sets, primary journal and book collections, statistical series.

[11] DIRECTORIES & ENCYCLOPEDIAS
Includes biographies, almanacs, chronologies, maps and gazetteers.

[12] HANDBOOKS & MANUALS
Includes advanced textbooks, edited collections, field guides, technical compendia.

[13] KEEPING UP-TO-DATE
Includes annual reviews, professional and trade magazines, current awareness services, discussion groups.

The categories are not mutually exclusive, so where a resource could be placed in more than one category, we have usually assigned it to the category that comes first in the sequence. The distribution of resources across the different categories naturally varies from subject to subject.

Indexes

The volume concludes with two indexes, offering access to the main sequence of entries by topic, resource title or author.

Topic Index
The Topic Index lists in a single alphabetical sequence all the terms used as subject headings for the subject groupings, fields and subfields, together with alternative terms for those headings, as well as terms at a more detailed level than the subject fields. This index shows you where commonly sought terms are located in our subject structure and helps you to navigate to the right part of the main sequence.

Title/Author Index
The Title/Author Index lists the authors and titles for all resources listed, covering both main entries and associated resources. For organizations, it includes cross-references for commonly-used abbreviations and acronyms, in addition to cross-references linking parent and subordinate bodies. This index enables you to locate resource descriptions quickly when you already know the title or author.

Disclaimer

The inclusion of a resource in TNW in no way implies the publisher's and contributors' endorsement of the views contained within it.

SOCIAL SCIENCES

Social Sciences

The *Concise Oxford Dictionary* (COD) defines 'social science' as 'the scientific study of human society and social relationships'. In *The New Walford*, Volume 1, covering Science, Technology, Medicine, there was some involvement with the nature of scientific study, with what doing science entails. However, that focus was small, compared to here. There has from its 19th-century foundation been intensive discussion on the extent to which the social sciences should or can use classic positivist scientific methodology to try to establish its truths (whatever we might mean by 'truths'). Many have sought to make social science – or 'social research', an important phrase, or just 'sociology' (cf. that subject area treated later in this volume) – more of a 'humanistic' enterprise: focused on engagement and understanding, and not *per se* intent upon avoiding subjectivity and bias. However, that has just been the core epistemological debate, in recent decades enhanced with movements given labels such as 'critical stances',

'postmodernism', 'realism', 'standpoints', and so on. Thus there is a strong emphasis on methodology in this section, especially on statistical methodology.

We have needed to decide the range of subject disciplines to be treated in this volume. The second definition of 'social science' given in the COD is: 'A subject within this field, such as economics or politics'. In planning the volume, we had originally intended to include coverage of 'Economics', and also of 'Human Geography'. But eventually we decided that we could more rewardingly treat those two subjects, along with 'History', 'Archaeology', 'Anthropology' and the arts and humanities more generally, using a predominantly country lens: all of a piece in a future volume of *The New Walford*.

Finally, we have cited here a few resources which cover a wider range of subject areas than those we might consider to fall within 'The Social Sciences': but many fewer than in Volume 1 – and see also the section 'Tools for Information Professionals' at the end of this volume.

e-social science • forecasting • history of social sciences • human sciences • law & society • philosophy of the social sciences • qualitative research • quantitative social science • social & economic research • social data & statistics • social measurement • social research • social science methodology • social science theories • social surveys • social theorists • statistical methodology • systematic reviews

Introductions to the subject

1 The Blackwell guide to the philosophy of the social sciences
S.P. Turner and P.A. Roth, eds   Blackwell, 2003, 382pp. £21.99. ISBN 9780631215387.
www.blackwellreference.com/public [FEE-BASED]
'The structure of this anthology reflects the editors' views of the change in the underlying problematic governing philosophy of social science. The issues are no longer organized around the familiar topics borrowed from philosophy of science: what is a law, what is an explanation, what are the ontological units (e.g. holism v. individualism), which sciences are primary (reductionism), what is the structure of theories and so forth. Rather, we now find a field organized around a poorly bounded collection of cross-cutting debates and issues ... Many topics compete in the struggle to unify understanding of how social science *does* function as well as how it *ought* to ...'
13 excellent state-of-the-art essays organized into three Parts: I. Pasts; II. Programs; III. Problematics. Substantial bibliography.

2 Continental philosophy of social science
Y. Sherratt   Cambridge University Press, 2006, 241pp. £14.99. ISBN 9780521670982.
Provides a rewarding counterpoint to the predominant Anglo-American philosophy of social science. Particularly good at contextualizing and contrasting the two approaches,

stressing that continental philosophy of social science is 'a distinguished and autonomous strand of thought in its own right. Continental schools have their own canon of thinkers, pose their own questions, set their own agendas and have a rich, deep history stemming back to Ancient Greece, Rome and early Christendom. In fact, it is this connection to its Ancient past, let us say its *humanism*, that defines the continental tradition'.

3 The elements of social scientific thinking
K.R. Hoover and T. Donovan   8th edn, Thomson/Wadsworth, 2004, 223pp. $34.95. ISBN 9780534614119.
Good, short, 'uncomplicated' introduction. Each chapter has a helpful preview and ends with a list of concepts introduced. There is a good section on 'measuring variables and relationships'.

4 Great expectations – the social sciences in Great Britain
Commission on the Social Sciences   Transaction Publishers, 2004, 166pp. £21.95. ISBN 0765808498.
Valuable overview ranging – in Section A – from 'What are the social sciences and what are they for?' through 'Social sciences and the outside world (aka society)' to 'The future of the social sciences'. Section B provides extensive data on 'The nature, scale and financial support of the social sciences in Britain'. Good short bibiliography.

5 How to build social science theories
P.J. Shoemaker, J.W. Tankard and D.L. Lasorsa   Sage Publications, 2004, 222pp. £27. ISBN 9780761926672.
'Many of the social sciences may be held back by a lack of attention to theory building. Much research has shown an overemphasis on collection of empirical data without a clear sense of theoretical purpose. One of the easiest ways many researchers could improve their research would be through increased attention to theory building ...'
Engaging, detailed text, clearly organized and written.

6   Is rational choice theory all of social science?
M.I. Lichbach   University of Michigan Press, 2003, 315pp. $29.95.
ISBN 9780472068197.
In-depth but approachable and balanced analysis written
from the perspective of a rational choice theorist who aims
to answer the question 'by exploring three perspectives on
foils in the social sciences: *competitors* evaluate alternative
research traditions, *pragmatists* do normal science in their
own tradition and *synthesizers* develop a monopolistic center
encompassing all traditions; and three types of social
theorists: *rationalists* explain interests, *culturalists* understand
identities and *structuralists* typologize institutions'.

7   Key concepts in social research
G. Payne and J. Payne   Sage Publications, 2004, 248pp. £18.99.
ISBN 9780761965435.
Designed specifically to provide a first introduction for
students. This basic text covers terminology relating to the
key methods of social research used by social scientists.
Examples range from sampling to qualitative and quantitative
research methods. Each concept has a clear, accessible
definition, highlighting related concepts and offering
quotations from major texts. Suggestions for further reading
are provided.

**8   Knowledge and the social sciences: theory,
method, practice**
D. Goldblatt, ed.   2nd edn, Routledge, 2004, 162pp. £17.99. ISBN
9780415329767.
Takes as its point of departure the claims that all forms of
knowledge, the social sciences included, must be seen and
understood in their social context. Argues that the social
sciences both describe and transform their object of study,
though rarely in ways that social scientists intend. Introduces
students to the key epistemological and philosophical terms
and issues essential for further study in the social sciences.

9   The Norton history of the human sciences
R. Smith   Norton, 1997, 1036pp. $29.95. ISBN 9780393317336.
Well written, easily approached, comprehensive. Appendix
has extensive Bibliographic Essay whose purpose is 'a
practical one, to provide access to what, with necessarily
incomplete knowledge, are the best discussions of the topics
in this book. By "best", I mean texts that are readable,
scholarly, historical and which "say something significant".'
Originally published as The Fontana history of the human sciences,
Fontana, 1997.

■ **The Cambridge history of science: 7. The modern
social sciences** T.M. Porter and D. Ross, eds   Cambridge University
Press, 2003. £100. ISBN 9780521594424. Collection of essays providing 'a
history of the concepts, practices, institutions, and ideologies of social
sciences (including behavioural and economic sciences) since the
eighteenth century'.

**10   A realist philosophy of social science: explanation
and understanding**
P.T. Manicas   Cambridge University Press, 2006, 225pp. £14.99.
ISBN 9780521678582.
A major contribution to current debate: 'This introduction to
the philosophy of social science provides an original
conception of the task and nature of social inquiry. Peter
Manicas discusses the role of causality seen in the physical
sciences and offers a reassessment of the problem of
explanation from a realist perspective. He argues that the
fundamental goal of theory in both the natural and social

sciences is not, contrary to widespread opinion, prediction
and control, or the explanation of events (including
behaviour). Instead, theory aims to provide an understanding
of the processes which, together, produce the contingent
outcomes of experience.'

**11   Social science: philosophical and methodological
foundations**
G. Delanty   2nd edn, Open University Press, 2005, 197pp. £17.99.
ISBN 9780335217212.
Good, accessible introduction: 'What is social science? Does
social scientific knowledge differ from other kinds of
knowledge, such as the natural sciences and common sense?
What is the relation between method and knowledge? ...' and
so on.

**12   Unthinking social science: the limits of
nineteenth-century paradigms**
I. Wallerstein   Temple University Press, 2001, 286pp. $20.95. ISBN
9781566398992.
'I introduced this volume ten years ago with the question
"Why unthink?". My answer was that the presumptions of
nineteenth-century social science, "once considered
liberating of the spirit, serve today as the central intellectual
barrier to useful analysis of the social world". We now have
reached the twenty-first century and the barrier is still there,
if under siege. The resistance to change is profound ...'
'Wallerstein is always readable, often persuasive and occasionally
profound. He is a genuine scholar, with far fewer affectations than
academics of his distinction usually acquire, and he never
patronizes us ... [B]y applying world-systems theory so broadly, to
so many topics, these essays add considerably to its power.' (*The
British Journal of Sociology*)

Dictionaries, thesauri, classifications

13   Dictionary of the social sciences
C. Calhoun, ed.   Oxford University Press, 2002, 582pp. £49. ISBN
9780195123715.
'Faced with the many sources of diversity and even
contradiction in usage, we have developed a set of guidelines
for the *Dictionary*. First, we have faced the situation that there
is no clear and standard definition of the *social sciences* ...
Our approach was to cover all or some academic fields and
some interdisciplinary fields and only parts of others where
these seemed to fit unambiguously into the social sciences.
Here, we have stressed the first word in *social* science,
emphasizing coverage of those fields that most clearly focus
on social phenomena and relations ...'
Well laid-out single A–Z sequence of some 1800 entries.
Very useful 40-page historical bibliography.

■ **A dictionary of the social sciences** J. Gould and W.L. Kolb,
eds; United Nations Educational, Scientific & Cultural Organization
Tavistock Publications, 1964, 761pp. Definitely still worth consulting: clear
expository style; excellent definitions of social science terminology.

■ **A new dictionary of the social sciences** G.D. Mitchell, ed.
Transaction, 2006, 252pp. $29.95. ISBN 9780202308784. Revises and
expands the *Dictionary of Sociology* published in 1968. Designed for
beginners – especially in giving quite long entries for such key words as
authority, consensus, phenomenology, role, social stratification,
structuralism, and so on. The contributors are all scholars working in
universities, predominantly in the UK and USA.

14 **New keywords: a revised vocabulary of culture and society**
T. Bennett, L. Grossberg and M. Morris, eds   Blackwell, 2005, 427pp. £16.99. ISBN 9780631225690.
Valuable compilation, conceived as updating the Raymond Williams classic volume *Keywords: a vocabulary of culture and society*. The volume revises many terms from Williams's original list; adds discussion of new keywords; and deletes those of Williams's keywords 'felt not to have sustained their importance'. About 150 entries; extensive bibliography.

15 **The Sage dictionary of qualitative inquiry**
T.A. Schwandt   3rd edn, Sage Publications, 2007, 376pp. £34.99. ISBN 9781412909273.
Useful dictionary which is intended to guide students to the key concepts and terms associated with the history, purpose, theories and methods of qualitative research. It includes coverage of competing theoretical perspectives on the value and methods of qualitative inquiry. A reader's guide provides tips on successful use of the text.

16 **The Sage dictionary of social research methods**
V. Jupp   Sage Publications, 2006, 384pp. £19.99. ISBN 9780761962984.
Provides definitions of all the main methods and techniques relating to sociological and cultural research. Each entry contains a brief definition followed by a discussion of the distinctive features of the term, its historical background, key writers and associated concepts. This is followed by an evaluation of any controversies associated with it and a bibliography of key readings.
■ **Research methods** P. McNeill and S. Chapman   3rd edn, Routledge, 2005, 192pp. £14.99. ISBN 9780415340762. A well regarded textbook designed for use by A-Level and undergraduate students. It provides a good introduction to the main concepts, theories and methods of modern sociological research. Separate chapters cover social surveys; ethnographic and comparative methods and secondary data.

17 **The Sage dictionary of statistics: a practical resource for students in the social sciences**
D. Cramer and D. Howitt   Sage Publications, 2004, 188pp. £20.99. ISBN 9780761941385.
'This is a practical and concise dictionary that serves the everyday uses of statistics across the whole range of social science disciplines. It offers basic and straightforward definitions of key concepts, followed by more detailed step-by-step explanations of situating specific methods and techniques. It also contains lists of related concepts to help the user to draw connections across various fields and increase their overall understanding of a specific technique. A list of key readings helps to reinforce the aim of the *Dictionary* as an invaluable learning resource.'
'The authors make excellent use of illustrative examples' (*Reference Reviews*)
■ **Dictionary of statistics and methodology: a nontechnical guide for the social sciences** W.P. Vogt   3rd edn, Sage Publications, 2005, 376pp. £21.95. ISBN 9780761988557. 'The book aims to provide anyone interested in learning statistics with the sourcebook of simple definitions and explanations of statistical and statistics-related concepts. The majority of terms offer additional references to use if more information is needed on a particular topic. Additionally, many terms are accompanied by graphical material to aid understanding'.
■ **Statistics for the social sciences** R.M. Sirkin   3rd edn, Sage Publications, 2006, 610pp. £31.99. ISBN 9781412905466. Latest edition of bestseller textbook. 'The previous editions of this book were popular with

instructors because they helped build students' confidence and ability in doing statistical analysis, by slowly moving from concepts that require little computational work to those that require more'.
■ **Statistics glossary** V.J. Easton and J.H. McColl, comps   1997. www.stats.gla.ac.uk/steps/glossary/index.html. Good facility, easily navigated.

Laws, standards, codes

18 **The Blackwell companion to law and society**
A. Sarat, ed.   Blackwell, 2004, 688pp. £110. ISBN 9780631228967. www.blackwellreference.com/public [FEE-BASED]
'(A)n authoritative study of the relationship between law and social interaction.' Six parts: I. Perspectives on the history and significance of law and society research; II. The cultural life of law; III. Institutions and actors; IV. Domains of policy; V. How does law matter?; VI. Studying globalization: past, present, future.

Official & quasi-official bodies

19 **Directgov** [UK]
Central Office of Information
www.direct.gov.uk
'Public services all in one place ... (P)rovides information from across UK government departments on topics ranging from travel safety and parental leave to special educational needs and local NHS services. The site also brings together an increasing number of online government services to make your life easier ... (and) ... also gives you access to government directories, as well as links to relevant third parties who can offer additional trusted advice and support.'
■ **Office of Public Sector Information** www.opsi.gov.uk. 'Operating from within the National Archives, the Office of Public Sector Information (OPSI) is at the heart of information policy, setting standards, delivering access and encouraging the re-use of public sector information. OPSI provides a wide range of services to the public, information industry, government and the wider public sector relating to finding, using, sharing and trading information ... Operating from within OPSI, Her Majesty's Stationery Office (HMSO) continues to exist and fulfil its core activities including responsibility for the publication of legislation and the management of Crown copyright'.
■ **Policy Hub** www.policyhub.gov.uk. 'This site aims to promote strategic thinking and improve policy making and delivery across government. It endeavours to provide users with access to a range of perspectives on policy matters ...'.
■ **TSO Online Bookshop** www.tsoshop.co.uk. 'Privatised from HMSO (now OPSI) in 1996, we have a 200-year inheritance of secure, no-fail delivery to HM Government and Parliament and are the largest publisher in the UK by volume, publishing over 15,000 titles a year. In January 2007 TSO was acquired by Williams Lea, the leading global corporate information solutions provider ...'.
■ **UKGovTalk** www.govtalk.gov.uk. 'The purpose of this site is to enable the Public Sector, Industry and other interested participants to work together to develop and agree policies and standards for e-government. This is achieved through the GovTalk consultation processes'.

20 **Economic & Social Research Council** [UK]
www.esrc.ac.uk
'(T)he UK's leading research funding and training agency addressing economic and social concerns. We aim to provide high quality research on issues of importance to business, the public sector and government.'

Their splendid site has a very good section 'What is social science?' with the sub-sections: Achievements of social science; How social science affects our lives; Social science in numbers; What social scientists do. This is accessed from the 'General Public' window; other windows are 'Academic', 'Public Sector', 'Third Sector', 'Press & Media' and 'Business'. The *Social Sciences Repository* 'records the output of ESRC investments in the forms of Journal Articles, Conference Papers, Technical Reports, ePrints and Books'.

- **NSF: Directorate for Social, Behavioral & Economic Sciences** www.nsf.gov/funding/research_edu_community.jsp. NSF Directorate supporting the Foundation's prime science and engineering focus.
- **Research Councils UK** www.rcuk.ac.uk. Strategic partnership set up by the seven UK Research Councils whose mission is 'to optimise the ways that Research Councils work together to deliver their goals, to enhance the overall performance and impact of UK research, training and knowledge transfer and to be recognised by academia, business and government for excellence in research sponsorship'.
- **Social Sciences & Humanities Research Council of Canada** www.sshrc-crsh.gc.ca. Arm's-length federal agency that promotes and supports university-based research and training in the social sciences and humanities.

21 Europa: Gateway to the European Union
European Union
http://europa.eu

The home page has a section 'What the European Union does by Subject' with entries for 'Audiovisual and Media', 'Budget', 'Competition', 'Consumers', 'Culture' and so on. Clicking on, for instance, 'Information Society', leads to a page organized into: Key sites; Documentation; Summaries of legislation; Legal texts; Need more help? We can then move, for example, to the section on 'Copyright and related rights in the information society' or the 'Committee on Culture and Education' within the European Parliament.

An excellent entreé to a inevitably highly complex arena.

- **Council of Europe/Conseil de l'Europe** www.coe.int. 'Founded in 1949, the Council of Europe seeks to develop throughout Europe common and democratic principles based on the European Convention on Human Rights and other reference texts on the protection of individuals'.
- **Socio-economic Sciences and Humanities** http://ec.europa.eu/research/social-sciences. Gateway to EU research within the social sciences and humanities. Good quarterly *Newsletter*, plus useful links to comparable work elsewhere, both inside and outside the EU.

22 GAO: Accountability Integrity Reliability [USA]
Government Accountability Office
www.gao.gov

Independent, non-partisan agency that works for Congress. Very well structured website, easy to use, good search facility providing access to a remarkable range and depth of content.

- **Great Britain. National Audit Office** www.nao.org.uk. '(S)crutinises public spending on behalf of Parliament. We are totally independent of Government ... We audit the accounts of all central government departments and agencies, as well as a wide range of other public bodies, and report to Parliament on the economy, efficiency and effectiveness with which they have used public money. Our work saves the taxpayer millions of pounds every year'.

23 Government Social Research [UK]
www.gsr.gov.uk

'Social research is scientific enquiry which measures, describes, explains and predicts changes in social and economic structures, attitudes, values and behaviours and the factors which motivate and constrain individuals and groups in society. In government, this relates to policy development, implementation and delivery and to the estimation of policy impacts and outcomes. Good quality social research helps government to make better policies and deliver better services ... Working across 20 government departments, agencies and devolved administrations means that GSR members work in a wide variety of subject and policy areas.'

Very useful gateway; there is an especially good set of 'Resources', covering Better Policy Making; Centres of Excellence; Databases; GSR Staff Directory; Publications; Websites.

24 Higher Education Funding Council for England
www.hefce.ac.uk

'Promotes and funds high-quality, cost-effective teaching and research in universities and colleges in England.' (There are also the Higher Education Funding Council for Wales and the Scottish Funding Council.) Excellent source of information on work in and relating to English universities and colleges, including full data on the Research Assessment Exercise for 2001 (pending the release of data from RAE 2008).

- **HERO** www.hero.ac.uk. '(T)he official gateway to universities, colleges and research organisations in the UK'. Very useful sections on: Studying; Research; Business; Inside HE. Good news facility.
- **Higher Education Academy** www.heacademy.ac.uk. 'The Academy's mission is to help institutions, discipline groups and all staff to provide the best possible learning experience for their students.' Notable for its range of Subject Centres, including several in the social sciences.
- **JISCmail** www.jiscmail.ac.uk. Mission is 'to facilitate knowledge sharing within the UK centered academic community, using e-mail and the web, through the provision, support and development of specialist mailing list based services, enabling the delivery of high quality and relevant content'.

Organisation for Economic Co-operation & Development
See entry no. 3053

25 United Nations
www.un.org

Easily accessible from the home page of this pleasant site – naturally among much else – are: the UN System Sites (which include the 'Official Web Locator for the UN System', the 'UN Information Centres', the 'UN System Pathfinder' – links to major publications and internet resources of the UN system and the 'Depository Libraries'); Publications, Stamps and Databases; the file of Recent Additions; and the Daily Briefing.

Well worth spending time browsing around.

- **Oxford handbook on the United Nations** T.G. Weiss and S. Daws, eds Oxford University Press, 2007, 838pp. £85. ISBN 9780199279517. A more major and reflective work than Alger's *The United Nations system* (q.v.). An edited handbook of 40 chapters – but with its last chapter ('Widening participation') being by Alger himself, and with a Foreword by Ban Ki-moon.
- **UNBIS Thesaurus** http://unhq-appspub-01.un.org/LIB/DHLUNBISThesaurus.nsf. Online version based on the 4th edn (2001) in all the UN's official languages: Arabic, Chinese, English, French, Russian, Spanish. 'It is multidisciplinary in scope, reflecting the Organization's wide-ranging concerns. The terms included are meant to reflect accurately, clearly, concisely and with a sufficient degree of specificity, matters of importance and interest to the United Nations.' Part of

the United Nations Bibliographic Information System from the Dag Hammarskjöld Library.

- **Union of International Associations** www.uia.be. '(A) nonprofit clearing house for information on over 60,000 international organizations and constituencies, has been a pioneer in the provision of information on international organizations and their global challenges since its foundation in 1907. There are some very useful databases available for you on paper, online and on CD-ROM'.
- **The United Nations system: a reference handbook** C.F. **Alger** ABC-CLIO, 2006, 375pp. $55. ISBN 9781851098057. Extensive, clearly laid-out, comprehensive. The chapters 'Facts and data', 'Directory of organizations, associations and agencies', and 'Selected print and nonprint resources' are especially valuable. Good index. A mine of useful information.

26 United Nations Educational, Scientific & Cultural Organization

www.unesco.org

Portal site for the specialized United Nations agency set up 'to contribute to peace and security by promoting collaboration among nations through education, science, culture and communication in order to further universal respect for justice, the rule of law and human rights and fundamental freedoms'. Clearly laid-out, with the Themes 'Education', 'Social and Human Sciences', 'Culture and Communication' and 'Information' being of special interest here. There is also a set of Special Themes 'reflecting a transdisciplinary approach or focus on the Organization's current priorities or news related subjects'.

- **Management of Social Transformations Programme: MOST** www.unesco.org/shs/most. '(P)rimary purpose is to transfer relevant Social Sciences research findings and data to decision-makers and other stakeholders. MOST focuses on building efficient bridges between research, policy and practice. The programme promotes a culture of evidence-based policy-making – nationally, regionally and internationally. As the only UNESCO programme that fosters and promotes social science research, it is placed in a pivotal position in the overall promotion of UNESCO's goals.'
- **UNESCO Social & Human Sciences Documentation Centre** www.unesco.org/shs/shsdc. '(P)romotes international cooperation in social sciences by exchange of information and supports the social and human sciences information and documentation programmes of UNESCO by: Serving as a Clearing House for relevant UNESCO documents as well as an Information Centre for specialists at headquarters and in the field, to governmental and non governmental organizations, to Member States, and to training, research and documentation centres; Maintaining computerized and online databases on the Sector's major themes; Providing online resources in social and human sciences.'
- **UNESCO Thesaurus** http://databases.unesco.org/thesaurus. 7000 English/Russian terms (8600 French/Spanish) covering education, culture, natural sciences, social and human sciences, communication and information.

27 USA.gov

United States. General Services Administration

www.usa.gov

'The US government's official web portal'. The major section of the 'For Citizens' lens has 'Government Information by Topic' with Benefits and grants, Consumer guides, Defense and international, etc. – each heading being then sub-categorized. There are also lenses 'For Businesses and nonprofits', 'For government employees' and 'For visitors to the US'. Many other routes are provided in this well organized site.

- **GPO Access United States. Government Printing Office**. www.gpo.gov. '(A) service of the US Government Printing Office that provides free

electronic access to a wealth of important information products produced by the Federal Government. The information provided on this site is the official, published version and the information retrieved from GPO.' Note also the US Government Bookstore at http://bookstore.gpo.gov.

Research centres & institutes

28 Cathie Marsh Centre for Census & Survey Research [UK]

www.ccsr.ac.uk

An inter-disciplinary research centre based in the Faculty of Social Science and Law at the University of Manchester. Key areas of concern include research methods; issues of confidentiality and privacy relating to the collection of social research data; the analysis of social statistics; population forecasting; employment; elections and political parties. Its website provides information on the aims of the centre; its teaching courses and research. It also offers free online access to many of its working papers and newsletters. These include materials relating to the analysis of anonymized samples from the UK census.

29 Center for Spatially Integrated Social Science [USA]

www.csiss.org

'The CSISS Mission recognizes the growing significance of space, spatiality, location and place in social science research. It seeks to develop unrestricted access to tools and perspectives that will advance the spatial analytic capabilities of researchers throughout the social sciences.' Wide-ranging site organized under: Core resources; Learning resources; Spatial resources; Spatial tools; Search engines; CSISS events; and Spatial literature – the last 'currently containing over 17,000 bibliographical references that feature applications of Spatial Analysis techniques in the Social Sciences. The database is updated at least once a year'.

30 Central Archive for Empirical Social Research [GER]

www.gesis.org/en/za

Based at the University of Cologne in Germany, this organization archives primary material (data, questionnaires, code plans) and results of empirical studies in order to prepare them for secondary analyses and to make them available to scholars and the public. Its website is an excellent starting point for tracing information about European social, economic and political surveys. Its online catalogue enables researchers to browse; find information and in a small but growing number of cases directly download datasets. A wide range of subject areas is covered, including European Values Surveys; Eurostat materials; and electoral studies. The site also maintains an impressive directory of links to other data organizations in Europe.

The Archive and the Information Centre referenced below are two elements within GESIS – German Social Science Infrastructure Services.

- **International Social Survey Programme** www.issp.org. 'The ISSP is a continuing annual programme of cross-national collaboration on surveys covering topics important for social science research. It brings together pre-existing social science projects and coordinates research goals, thereby adding a cross-national, cross-cultural perspective to the individual national studies.' Useful list of members and their addresses; also an ISSP bibliography. The ISSP archive is the Zentralarchiv für Empirische Sozialforschung at the University of Cologne, Germany.
- **Social Science Information Centre** www.gesis.org/en/iz. '(C)ollects and disseminates information on the current state of research

and literature in the social sciences in the German-speaking countries as well as on the social science research in Eastern Europe'.

31   Centre for Research Methods in the Social Sciences [UK]
http://remiss.politics.ox.ac.uk
Specialist research institute based within the Department of Politics and International Relations, University of Oxford. It specializes in the development and teaching of rigorous methods of social research, focusing in particular on quantitative methods such as statistical analysis. Its website provides insight into the purpose of the centre and its current research. It includes information on research methods courses and conferences in the UK.
- **Harvard-MIT Data Center** www.hmdc.harvard.edu. Manages technology platforms for the Institute for Quantitative Social Science at Harvard on informatics and data sharing, statistical computing, and information technology.

32   ESDS Qualidata [UK]
www.esds.ac.uk/qualidata
Unit of the UK's Economic and Social Data Service, based at the University of Essex, which is a good exemplar and specializes in the collection and digitization of data from qualitative research studies. Its website provides access to a catalogue of its collections plus information about access and training. It is also making available online some of its data. Examples include '100 Families' (a collection of interviews conducted between 1985 and 1988 which gathered data on social mobility and changing family roles) and 'The Edwardians' (over 400 interviews on British family life and work before 1918).

33   Informatics Collaboratory of the Social Sciences [UK]
www.shef.ac.uk/icoss
The first large-scale dedicated facility for social science research in the UK, opened in November 2004. Its key themes are: Health and social Care; Criminology; Urban and regional lanning; Social exclusion and spatial inequalities; Computational data analysis methods.

34   Institute for Social & Economic Research [UK]
www.iser.essex.ac.uk
Within this leading Institute based at the University of Essex there are the ESRC UK Longitudinal Studies Centre and the ESRC Research Centre on Micro-Social Change. It is initially somewhat difficult to find one's way around the extensive site: best to start with the site map of the 'Whole Site' accessible from the site map of ISER. Note particularly the Hilary Doughty Research Library, which 'provides a gateway to specialist resources at ISER supporting the research activities of both the ESRC Research Centre on Micro-Social Change and the ESRC UK Longitudinal Studies Centre as well as the European Centre for Analysis in the Social Sciences and other postgraduate student programmes.'

35   Institute for Social & Economic Research & Policy [USA]
www.iserp.columbia.edu
Leading institute within Columbia University. Houses large range of specialized centres, including Center for the Study of Wealth and Inequality; Center on Political Economy and Comparative Institutional Analysis; and Paul F Lazarsfeld Center for the Social Sciences – the oldest of the ISERP centres.

36   Inter-university Consortium for Political & Social Research [USA]
www.icpsr.umich.edu
Established in 1962 and based within the Institute for Social Research at the University of Michigan. It maintains and provides access to a vast archive of social science data for research and instruction and offers training in quantitative methods to facilitate effective data use.
- **Data Documentation Initiative** www.icpsr.umich.edu/DDI. '(A)n international effort to establish a standard for technical documentation describing social science data.' A membership-based Alliance is developing the DDI specification, which is written in XML.
- **Institute for Social Research** www.isr.umich.edu. A leading American research centre. Its website provides access to press releases, information and papers from some of its influential projects. Examples include longitudinal research on health, income and ageing among the American public from the 1940s to the current day.

Max-Planck-Institut für Gesellschaftsforschung (Max Planck Institute for the Study of Societies)
See entry no. 502

37   National Centre for Research Methods [UK]
www.ncrm.ac.uk
A national network of specialist research institutes which are funded by the UK Economic and Social Research Council and coordinated by the University of Southampton. There are six units, each focusing on a different type of research: e.g. 'Developing Statistical Modelling in the Social Sciences' is at Lancaster University and the University of Warwick. The website provides free access to their newsletters, conference papers and research reports, all of which contain many examples of innovative practice.
- **Economic and Social Data Service** www.esds.ac.uk. '(N)ational data service providing access and support for an extensive range of key economic and social data, both quantitative and qualitative, spanning many disciplines and themes. ESDS provides an integrated service offering enhanced support for the secondary use of data across the research, learning and teaching communities … The Data Catalogue provides access to over 5000 computer-readable datasets for research and teaching purposes for many different disciplines.' Well organized website with access to extensive series of user guides.
- **National Centre for e-Social Science** www.ncess.ac.uk. Funded to 'investigate how innovative and powerful computer-based infrastructure and tools developed over the past five years under the UK e-Science programme can benefit the social science research community. This infrastructure is commonly known as the "Grid" …'.
- **ReDReSS Lancaster University and Science & Technology Facilities Council**. http://redress.lancs.ac.uk. Project whose main aim is 'to raise awareness and accelerate the development of a new kind of computing and data infrastructure to support the increasingly national and global collaborations emerging in many areas of social science'.

38   National Centre for Social Research [UK]
www.natcen.ac.uk
The largest independent social research institute in Britain. 'We design, carry out and analyse research studies in the fields of social and public policy – including extensive research among members of the public.' Simple yet very effective website provides access to the wide range of their work. There is an especially useful section 'How we do our research' with sub-sections: Qualitative research; Quantitative

research; Survey methods unit; CREST (Centre for Research into Elections & Social Trends).

- **European Social Survey** www.europeansocialsurvey.org. '(A)n academically-driven social survey designed to chart and explain the interaction between Europe's changing institutions and the attitudes, beliefs and behaviour patterns of its diverse populations. Now moving into its fourth round, the survey covers over 30 nations and employs the most rigorous methodologies'.
- **European Social Survey Education Net** http://essedunet.nsd.uib.no/opencms.war/opencms/ess/en. An internet-based training programme developed by the Norwegian Social Sciences Data Services. It comprises online modules which aim to teach the use of empirical data to undergraduate students using examples drawn from the real-life European Social Survey. The hands-on examples and exercises are designed to guide the users through the research process; from a theoretical problem to the interpretation of statistical results.

39 Odum Institute for Research in Social Science [USA]
www.irss.unc.edu
'Founded in 1924, the H.W. Odum Institute for Research in Social Science is the nation's oldest multidisciplinary social science university institute. Indeed, we are the oldest institute or center at the nation's first public university, UNC-Chapel Hill. The mission of the Odum Institute parallels that of the University as a whole – teaching, research and service – but the Institute's focus is on the social sciences.'

40 Roper Center for Public Opinion Research [USA]
www.ropercenter.uconn.edu
A famous library of public opinion data which is based at the University of Connecticut. Its holdings include US social, cultural and political survey results and questionnaires for over 65 years. Its website offers advice on using and interpreting social survey data for students and teachers; it also provides summaries of its holdings and recent survey results. Access to the full data and codebooks requires a subscription.

- **iPOLL** www.ropercenter.uconn.edu/data_access/ipoll/ipoll.html. Daily updated subscription database from the Center, providing access to American social and political survey data and questions from 1935 onwards. It includes presidential approval ratings and national election polls. Price on demand from the publisher's website.
- **Public Opinion European Commission.** http://ec.europa.eu/public_opinion/index_en.htm. 'Since 1973, the European Commission has been monitoring the evolution of public opinion in the Member States, thus helping the preparation of texts, decision-making and the evaluation of its work. Our surveys and studies address major topics concerning European citizenship: enlargement, social situation, health, culture, information technology, environment, the Euro, defence, etc.

41 Social Market Foundation [UK]
www.smf.co.uk
'(A)n independent think-tank, exploring ideas that link the state and the market to create a more just, free and prosperous society … Steering an independent course between political parties and conflicting ideologies, the SMF has been an influential voice in many recent debates. Our current work reflects a commitment to understanding how individuals, society and the state can work together to achieve the common goal of creating a just and free society.'

42 Social Science Research Council [USA]
www.ssrc.org
'The Social Science Research Council leads innovation, builds interdisciplinary and international networks and focuses

research on important public issues. Independent and not-for-profit, the SSRC is guided by the belief that justice, prosperity and democracy all require better understanding of complex social, cultural, economic and political processes. We work with practitioners, policymakers and academic researchers in all the social sciences, related professions and the humanities and natural sciences. With partners around the world, we mobilize existing knowledge for new problems, link research to practice and policy, strengthen individual and institutional capacities for learning and enhance public access to information. We bring necessary knowledge to public action.'

Highly rewarding site – very well structured.

43 Survey Research Center [USA]
http://srcweb.berkeley.edu
Specialist research centre located at the University of California, Berkeley, which concentrates on developing innovative empirical research methods. Its website provides information on its work on urban ethnography and census analysis and dissemination. It includes information about ongoing teaching and research programmes. Free access to some of its working papers is provided.

44 Tavistock Institute [UK]
www.tavinstitute.org
'We do research, consultancy, evaluation and professional development work to support change and learning. We also produce publications … We are interested in inter-organizational relations, the emergence of the knowledge society and problems of organization, particularly in the delivery of public policy … We like to work creatively with people involved in innovative activities, working across boundaries, or in difficult situations. In our work we combine research and analytical skills with practical help in devising solutions and in following through to implementation … We come from a variety of disciplines, including sociology, social psychology, economics, anthropology, policy science and management.'

Associations & societies

45 Academy of Social Sciences [UK]
www.the-academy.org.uk
The Academy was launched in November 1999. It is composed of academicians and learned societies in the social sciences. It organized production of the report 'Great expectations: the social sciences in Britain' (q.v.). Newsletters and bulletins are also available on the website. The website offers a clear description of this and the organization's structure and its other activities, e.g. the conferences and other events that it organizes and its contributions to relevant consultations.

- **Academy of the Social Sciences in Australia** www.assa.edu.au. Founded 1971, and 'an autonomous, non-governmental organisation, devoted to the advancement of knowledge and research in the various social sciences'.

46 Association for Qualitative Research
www.latrobe.edu.au/aqr
An international association which aims to promote the theory, practice and use of qualitative research. Its website provides information on membership, training and events. It also offers free access to *Qualitative Research Journal*, an

electronic journal which contains refereed articles on all aspects of qualitative research.

47 Association for the Teaching of the Social Sciences [UK]

www.le.ac.uk/se/centres/ATSS/atss.html
Lively site, perhaps most notable here for its section 'Good sites for sociologists on the internet', along with links to other resources aimed primarily at the secondary educational sector.

48 Association of Research Centres in the Social Sciences [UK]

www.arciss.ac.uk
A membership organization for research centres in the UK 'committed to rigorous social science research'. Some 50 research centres, both independent and within universities, are currently members. A useful gateway.

49 British Academy

www.britac.ac.uk
'(T)he national academy for the humanities and the social sciences. It is an independent, self-governing fellowship of more than 800 scholars, elected for distinction and achievement in one or more branches of the academic disciplines that make up the humanities and social sciences.'

The site has a set of useful links to a range of external resources, but more importantly offers PORTAL, 'the British Academy's directory of online resources in the humanities and social sciences. It is designed as an entry point to available resources for those working in higher education and research'. Each of the score or so sections within PORTAL (about half social science-oriented) is a simple A–Z list of titles; but each title is then given a short but informative description. A very good resource – particularly as there is also an extensive list of 'Topics' offering alternative entry points to the database.

■ **Directory of UK subject associations and learned societies in the humanities and social sciences**
www.britac.ac.uk/links/uksahss.asp. Each entry provides full contact details alongside a summary of the nature of the body.

50 Canadian Federation for the Humanities & Social Sciences

www.fedcan.ca
'Non-profit charitable organization that represents more than 50,000 researchers in 66 learned societies and 69 universities and colleges across the country.' Rich, well laid-out website giving access to much of value; for instance, details of their projects: Task Force on New Scholars; Scholarly Associations Task Force; Research Ethics; E-Publishing.

■ **Consortium of Social Science Associations** www.cossa.org. '(A)dvocacy organization that promotes attention to and Federal funding for the social and behavioral sciences. It serves as a bridge between the academic research community and the Washington policymaking community. Its members consist of more than 100 professional associations, scientific societies, universities, and research centers and institutes'. Useful regular PDF *COSSA Washington Update*. Also links to the website of the Coalition to Protect Research, other advocacy bodies, and of course to the websites of COSSA Members.

51 International Association for Social Science Information Service & Technology

www.iassistdata.org

'(I)nternational organization of professionals working with information technology and data services to support research and teaching in the social sciences. Its 300 members work in a variety of settings, including data archives, statistical agencies, research centers, libraries, academic departments, government departments and non-profit organizations.'

Somewhat basic but effective website gives access to wide range and depth of resources held elsewhere, plus details of the organization's publications and services for members. There is a nice blog IASSIST Communiqué.

52 International Federation of Data Organizations for the Social Sciences

www.ifdo.org
The site map clearly shows the range of resources accessible via the website:
■ SocSci on the Net – Survey & data (Clearing houses and gateways; International surveys; Household panels; Election studies; General election studies; Sustainable development; Further SocSci references);
■ International networks & data archives (IFDO; CESSDA; List of member archives);
■ Data archiving & distribution (Data archive workflow; Data preparation & archiving; Durable storage; Data access & conditions);
■ Methods & data analyses;
■ Study packs & sustainable development (Eurobarometer study pack; ISSP study pack).
■ **Council of European Social Science Data Archives**
www.nsd.uib.no/Cessda. Umbrella organization for social science data archives across Europe. The CESSDA Data Portal 'provides a seamless interface to datasets from 13 social science data archives across Europe' and covered 4167 studies, September 2007.

53 International Institute of Forecasters

www.forecasters.org
Founded in 1981 and 'is dedicated to developing and furthering the generation, distribution and use of knowledge on forecasting.' Very clear website; good selective set of resources; ideal place to start exploration.
■ **Forecasting principles** J.S. Armstrong and K.C. Green, comps www.forecastingprinciples.com. '(S)ummarizes all useful knowledge about forecasting so that it can be used by researchers, practitioners, and educators. (Those who might want to challenge this are invited to submit missing information.) This knowledge is provided as principles (guidelines, prescriptions, rules, conditions, action statements, or advice about what to do in given situations).' A first-class overview of the field.
■ **SPSS** www.spss.com. Site of the leading predictive analytics software company: 'Predictive analytics helps connect data to effective action by drawing reliable conclusions about current conditions and future events'.

54 Social Research Association [UK]

www.the-sra.org.uk
The aim of the SRA is to advance the conduct, development and application of social research. Its website provides information on its aims, membership and activities. It is a key resource for tracing information on social research ethics, offering free access to full-text ethical guidelines, plus PowerPoint slides and presentations from training events covering the techniques of social research. The site also contains careers guidance and job vacancy listings.

55 Social Science History Association [USA]

www.ssha.org

'The members of the Social Science History Association share a common interest in interdisciplinary and systematic approaches to historical research ...'. The Association is perhaps most notable here for its spread of Networks; currently active are: Criminal Justice/Legal; Economics; Education; Family History/Demography; Labor; Macro-Historical Dynamics; Rural; Migration/Immigration; States & Society. The Association also publishes the quarterly *Social Science History*.

Libraries, archives, museums

56 British Library

www.bl.uk

'We hold over 13 million books, 920,000 journal and newspaper titles, 57 million patents, 3 million sound recordings and so much more. Start exploring here ...'

- **British Library Inside** www.bl.uk/services/current/inside.html. Current awareness service covering 20,000 journals giving titles and bibliographic details and abstracts for some journals. Provides access to electronically delivered articles and standard document supply. Now holds details of over 20 million articles, growing by two million new records each year, 8000 every day. The site gives useful free access to the full list of titles, searchable by keyword, and providing title and ISSN (and BL shelfmark) but no other information.
- **British Library Integrated Catalogue** http://catalogue.bl.uk. Sophisticated intuitive access to details of the 13 million items in the BL's collections. The catalogue can be used either to request documents for perusal in the reference collections or order documents for supply from the delivery collections.
- **Social Sciences and Official Publications** www.bl.uk/collections/social/social.html. Focus within the Library for providing access to social science material, law, and government documents. Helpful introductory 'Resources for research' section.

57 GBV

www.gbv.de/vgm/info

The Common Library Network of the seven Federal States of Germany, with more than 770 libraries participating. Has extensive document delivery service as well as overseeing production of various databases, such as those referenced below.

- **International Bibliography of Book Reviews** www.gbv.de/gsomenu/?id=saur&ln=en. 'Reviews are an important aspect of scholarly discussion because they help filter out which work is unimportant in the yearly flood of publications and they are thus influential in determining how a work is received. The interdisciplinary *International Bibliography of Book Reviews of Scholarly Literature in the Humanities and Social Sciences* (IBR), published since 1971, is a unique source of bibliographical information.' [Note from OCLC].
- **International Bibliography of Periodical Literature** www.gbv.de/gsomenu/?id=saur&ln=en. 'Universal index of periodical literature covering basic research from all fields of knowledge, and is particularly strong in the humanities and the social sciences. Over 11,000 periodicals are indexed by this multilingual database, now containing over 1.7 million records. It is international in scope, and indexes a significant proportion the the periodicals published on the European continent.' [Description from Columbia University Libraries].

58 Library & Archives Canada

www.collectionscanada.ca

Created from the National Library of Canada and the National Archives of Canada in 2004. Wide range of services: examples below.

- **Depository Services Program** http://dsp-psd.communication.gc.ca. '(A)n arrangement with some 680 public and academic libraries to house, catalogue and provide reference services for the federal government publications they acquire under the Program'.
- **Amicus** www.collectionscanada.ca/amicus. 'Search over 30 million full records from 1300 Canadian libraries ... Access the entire database including National Library records ... The first place for items about Canada (Canadiana).' Free of charge.
- **Canadian information by subject** www.collectionscanada.ca/caninfo. Provides links to information about Canada from internet resources around the world. The subject arrangement is in the form of a 'Subject tree', based on the structure of the Dewey Decimal Classification System.

59 Library of Congress [USA]

www.loc.gov

'The nation's oldest federal cultural institution and serves as the research arm of Congress. It is also the largest library in the world, with nearly 128 million items on approximately 530 miles of bookshelves.' The link on the Home Page entitled 'Global gateway' includes a section 'Portals to the world' which, for each of the world's countries, lists 'resources selected by Library of Congress experts'. Check 'Culture', 'Media and Communications', 'Government, Politics, Law' etc. for the country of interest.

Alternatively, approach the wealth of accessible resources via the Librarians and Archivists home page, which has sections headed: Resources (e.g. Building Digital Collections; Public Service, Reference; Standards); Services (e.g. Publications, Products; Thesauri).

- **Ask a librarian ...** www.loc.gov/rr/askalib. 'Correspondents are encouraged to use local and online resources. For those seeking further assistance from the Library of Congress, the staff will respond to their reference and information needs to the extent possible.'
- **Library of Congress Authorities** http://authorities.loc.gov. Free service: 'Search and browse approximately: 265,000 subject authority records; 5.3 million name authority records (ca. 3.8 million personal, 900,000 corporate, 120,000 meeting, and 90,000 geographic names); 350,000 series and uniform title authority records; 340,000 name/title authority records'.
- **Library of Congress Classification** www.loc.gov/catdir/cpso/lcco. Letters and titles of the main classes of the LC Classification. Complete text of the classification schedules in printed volumes may be purchased from the Cataloging Distribution Service. Online access to complete text via Classification Web.
- **Library of Congress Online Catalog** http://catalog.loc.gov. Great resource – but can sometimes be difficult to get connection: 'Our peak usage is typically Tuesdays, Wednesdays, and Thursdays between 10:00am and 2:00pm (US Eastern Time)'.
- **Library of Congress subject headings** 30th edn2007. http://www.loc.gov/cds/lcsh.html. Over 280,000 total headings and references. 'The only subject headings list accepted as the world wide standard. LCSH is the most comprehensive list of subject headings in print in the world. It's the one tool no librarian should be without.'
- **Nations of the World** www.loc.gov/law/guide/nations.html. A service of the Law Library of Congress giving good lists of links for each country of the world.

60 Mass Observation Archive

www.massobs.org.uk

A specialist social research archive housed at the University of Sussex. It contains materials from the original Mass Observation social research organization (1937 to early

1950s) and newer material collected continuously since 1981. These provide a fascinating insight into the daily lives of British citizens. The website offers information on the history and contents of the archive and the mass observation method of research. It includes news about the ongoing research.

61 National Archives [UK]
www.nationalarchives.gov.uk
'The National Archives, which covers England, Wales and the United Kingdom, was formed in April 2003 by bringing together the Public Record Office and the Historical Manuscripts Commission. It is responsible for looking after the records of central government and the courts of law and making sure everyone can look at them. The collection is one of the largest in the world and spans an unbroken period from the 11th century to the present day.'
- **National Digital Archive of Datasets** http://ndad.ulcc.ac.uk. Preserves and provides online access to archived digital data and documents from UK central government departments.

62 National Archives & Records Administration [USA]
www.archives.gov
'Independent Federal agency that preserves our nation's history and defines us as a people by overseeing the management of all Federal records.' A good place to start is the web-accessible version of the *Guide to Federal Records in the National Archives of the United States* whereby 'comprehensive coverage of NARA's holdings of federal records, i.e., records that originated in the executive, judicial and legislative branches of the federal government, is provided – at a very high level'. It is also well worth checking out the services of the NARA Archives Library Information Center (ALIC).

Portal & task environments

63 H-Net: Humanities and Social Sciences Online
www.h-net.org
'H-Net is an international interdisciplinary organization of scholars and teachers dedicated to developing the enormous educational potential of the internet and the World Wide Web. Our edited lists and websites publish peer reviewed essays, multimedia materials and discussion for colleagues and the interested public.'

Excellent website, very clearly laid out and responsive: major focus on the historical aspects of the humanities and social sciences. Perhaps most valuable for its large number of Discussion Networks, which 'function as electronic networks, linking professors, teachers and students in an egalitarian exchange of ideas and materials. Every aspect of academic life – research, teaching, controversies new and old – is open for discussion; decorum is maintained by H-Net's dedicated editors.' But much else of value accessible via the site.

64 LexisNexis
http://global.lexisnexis.com/uk
The major portal providing 'customers access to 5 billion searchable documents from more than 32,000 legal, news and business sources. Corporations and legal professionals can also manage, organize and integrate their work processes using our unique set of solutions.'

65 Social Science Research Network
www.ssrn.com
'(A) worldwide collaborative of over 800 leading scholars that is devoted to the rapid worldwide dissemination of social science research. It is composed of a number of specialized research networks in each of the social sciences. Each of SSRN's networks encourages the early distribution of research results to and distributing submitted abstracts and by soliciting abstracts of top quality research papers around the world. The Networks encourage readers to communicate directly with other subscribers concerning their own and others' research. Through our e-mail abstracting journals we currently reach over 80,000 people in approximately 70 different countries ...

'SSRN supports the Open Access movement by providing free submissions to and downloads from the SSRN eLibrary ... No fee is charged for the submission of abstracts and papers for inclusion in the SSRN eLibrary and publication in e-mail journals. Authors are encouraged to submit all their research papers, including older papers.'

At end September 2007, the Network provided access to '161,900 scholarly working papers and forthcoming papers and an Electronic Paper Collection currently containing over 128,900 downloadable full-text documents'.

66 Society and Science
A. Roberts
www.mdx.ac.uk/www/study/SSHhome.HTM
A very interesting and extensive – if for some no doubt too lively – personal interest site. Divided into: Social science history timeline; Social science dictionary; People and ideas; Lectures; and Books. Very good use of hyperlinking and thus highly browsable.

67 StatLib: Data, Software and News from the Statistics Community
Carnegie Mellon University
http://lib.stat.cmu.edu
From the University's Department of Statistics and 'a system for distributing statistical software, datasets and information by electronic mail, FTP and WWW'.

68 WebSM: WebSurveyMethodology
www.websm.org
Excellent facility which originated in 1998 at the University of Ljubljana, with a similar project existing also at ZUMA, Germany. Supported 2003–2005 by the EU Fifth Framework programme. The site is 'dedicated to the methodological issues of web surveys, but it also covers the broader area of interaction between modern technologies and survey data collection'. Access to extensive sets of resources under the headings: Bibliography; Services; Community.

Discovering print & electronic resources

69 AI-GEOSTATS
European Commission. Joint Research Centre
www.ai-geostats.org
Carefully organized web resource for geostatistics and spatial statistics. Large section on Software categorized as: Points; Geostatistics; Lattices; Landscapes; Spherical; Codes; Utilities; GIS. But also covers documents, papers, books, conferences, courses, jobs, events and links.

■ **Go-Geo!** www.gogeo.ac.uk. '(A)n online resource discovery tool which allows for the identification and retrieval of records describing the content, quality, condition and other characteristics of geospatial data that exist within UK tertiary education and beyond. The portal supports geospatial searching by interactive map, grid co-ordinates and place name, as well as the more traditional topic or keyword forms of searching. The portal is a key component of the UK academic Spatial Data Infrastructure.

70 Alternative Press Index
Alternative Press Center
www.altpress.org
The Index itself is 'a biannual subject index to over 300 alternative, radical and left periodicals, newspapers and magazines. Librarians consider the API to be the most comprehensive and up-to-date guide to alternative sources of information available today'. But the site also provides access to over 400 websites providing 'Alternative viewpoints on the internet'.

71 Applied Social Sciences Index and Abstracts
ProQuest.
www.csa.com/factsheets/assia-set-c.php [FEE-BASED]
Database covering health, social services, economics, politics, criminal justice, race relations and education in 16 countries, including the UK and the USA. Provides a comprehensive source of social science and health information for the practical and academic professional.

72 Canadian Social Research Links
G. Séguin, comp.
www.canadiansocialresearch.net
Valuable, intensive personal-interest site: 'I launched the Canadian Social Research Links website on November 13, 1997. I receive no funding from any source whatsoever for this work; the biases you find are mine and mine alone.' Naturally, concentrates on Canadian developments; but much here of value more generally.

73 Current Index to Statistics
American Statistical Association and Institute of Mathematical Statistics
www.statindex.org
Covers the entire contents of over 160 'core journals', in most cases from 1975 (or first issue if later) to the current end year and pre-1975 coverage for some; selected articles with statistical content since 1975 from about 1200 additional journals (cumulatively) in related fields; about 11,000 books in statistics published since 1975.
■ **Statistics sources** 31st edn, Gale, 2007. $630. ISBN 9780787688653. A–Z dictionary covering 20,000 specific subjects, and incorporating almost 100,000 citations from more than 2,000 sources. Gale also market the *World directory of non-official statistical sources*.

74 Doing a literature review: releasing the social science research imagination
C. Hart   Sage Publications, 1998, 194pp. Published in association with The Open University., £19.99. ISBN 9780761959755.
Clear, thoughtful review: well worth perusing despite the examples now being dated. Organized: The literature review in research; Reviewing and the research imagination; Classifying and reading research; Implementation analysis; Organizing and expressing ideas; Mapping and analyzing ideas; Writing the review. (The author has subsequently published: *Doing a literature search: a comprehensive guide for the social sciences* (Sage, 2001); *Doing your masters dissertation* (Sage, 2004).)

75 Information sources in the social sciences
D. Fisher, S.P. Price and T. Hanstock, eds   K.G. Saur, 2002, 511pp. £121. ISBN 3598244398.
Excellent overview. 10 chapters: General social science information sources; Anthropology; Sociology; Psychology; Criminology; Education; Political science; Economics; Human services; Human geography. Each chapter covers and comments on the full gamut of types of resource: e.g. annuals; bibliographies; dictionaries; directories; encyclopaedias; guides and handbooks; websites; journals; abstracts, indexes and databases; official publications; statistics; research in progress; organizations. Full index of titles covered.

76 International bibliography of the social sciences
London School of Economics & Political Science
www.lse.ac.uk/collections/IBSS [FEE-BASED]
Now covers over 2,500,000 journal article, review, book and book chapter records. But its subject coverage principally focuses on anthropology, economics, politics, sociology, European studies, policy studies and social policy. The Bibliography is reproduced annually by the publishers Routledge in four volumes.

77 Intute: social sciences
www.intute.ac.uk/socialsciences
A free online service providing access to web resources specifically chosen for the education and research communities. The service has been created by bringing together two strands of the former Resource Discovery Network (RDN): Altis and SOSIG. Every resource is evaluated, categorized and annotated by subject specialists based at UK universities.
■ **Internet for Social Research Methods** L. Corti, comp.; Joint Information Systems Committee   www.vts.intute.ac.uk. One of a national series of tutorials written by qualified tutors, lecturers and librarians from across the UK. It is part of the Intute: Virtual Training Suite, funded by JISC. A nice service, whose resources are categorized as bibliographic databases; online journals; online texts; academic research resources; professional associations and societies; governmental and non-governmental organizations; research and data sources; software for social research; discussion lists and blogs; resources for learning; and resources for teaching.
■ **Internet for Social Statistics** R. Rice, comp.; Joint Information Systems Committee   Another of the very useful Intute series of tutorials written by qualified tutors, lecturers and librarians from across the UK. Here the resources are categorized as professional societies; non-governmental organizations (NGOs); national statistical organizations; other government agencies; data services; other key academic data services; electronic journals and repositories; commercial sites; learning and teaching resources; and blogs and e-mail discussion lists.

78 ISI Web of Knowledge
Thomson.
http://isiwebofknowledge.com [FEE-BASED]
'ISI Web of Knowledge is a comprehensive research platform, which means it brings together many different types of content for searching. Journal articles, patents, websites, conference proceedings, Open Access material – all can be accessed through one interface, using a variety of powerful search and analysis tools.

'Web of Science can be found within ISI Web of Knowledge. This resource offers access to journal articles in the sciences, social sciences and arts and humanities. Web of Science contains over 100 years of valuable research, fully indexed and cross-searchable.'

- **In-Cites** http://in-cites.com/research. Based on Essential Science Indicators – a resource that enables researchers to conduct ongoing, quantitative analyses of research performance and track trends in science – and providing a frequently fascinating 'behind-the-scenes look at the scientists, journals, institutions, nations, and papers selected'.
- **Journal Performance Indicators** http://scientific.thomson.com/products/jpi [FEE-BASED]. Rankings of over 10,000 of the world's most cited journals, including *Citation Impact Statistics*: average citations per paper for all papers and for cited papers published in each journal.
- **Social Sciences Citation Index** http://scientific.thomson.com/products/ssci [FEE-BASED]. '(A)ccess to current and retrospective bibliographic information, author abstracts, and cited references found in over 1,700 of the world's leading scholarly social sciences journals covering more than 50 disciplines. They also cover individually selected, relevant items from approximately 3,300 of the world's leading science and technology journals'.

79   Online information services in the social sciences
N. Jacobs and L. Huxley, eds   Chandos, 2004, 254pp. £39. ISBN 1843340690.
Four sections: 1. Case studies, describing how information is used in the health, government, academic, trades union, media and other sectors, with particular attention to online information practices; 2. Drawing the lessons from the case studies; 3. The major issues facing service providers, including selection, metadata, usability, accessibility, management and building user skills; 4. The future, covering both technological developments such as the semantic web and portals and organizational issues such as the changing role of the information professional.

80   PAIS International
ProQuest.
www.csa.com/factsheets/pais-set-c.php [FEE-BASED]
Formerly the Public Affairs Information Service. Now covers over half a million 'journal articles, books, government documents, statistical directories, grey literature, research reports, conference reports, publications of international agencies, microfiche, internet material and more. Newspapers and newsletters are not indexed'. Good 'List of Subject Headings' with 24 broad topics and 306 subtopics.
- **Australian Public Affairs Information Service National Library of Australia**. www.nla.gov.au/apais [FEE-BASED]. Now covers 'over 360,000 records, with about 12,000 new articles being indexed annually'.

81   Reader's guide to the social sciences
J. Michie   Routledge, 2001. 2 v., £250. ISBN 9781579580919.
'The aim of the *Reader's guide to the social sciences* is to do exactly what its title promises – to guide the reader towards the key texts on specific topics. The individual entries present and critically review the literature on a range of topics from the social sciences. In almost all cases the references will themselves cite a huge number of additional references, so what is provided here will serve as a useful springboard for any literature search. This is not, then, an encyclopedia ...'
About 1200 entries, most being useful introductions to the relevant subject.

82   Scopus
Elsevier.
www.scopus.com
Launched late 2004 with 13,000 journals, 4000 publishers and 5 years of backfiles. 'We are aiming for the broadest content possible, with more journals than ISI and more types of document – conference proceedings, books, series and reference works.' In late 2007 marketed as 'the largest abstract and citation database. It covers:
15,000 peer-reviewed journals from more than 4000 international publishers, including coverage of over 1000 Open Access journals, 500 conference proceedings, over 600 trade publications, over 125 book series.
30 million records, of which 15 million include references going back to 1996; 15 million pre-1996 records go back as far as 1900.
Scopus also covers 275 million quality web sources, including 21 million patents. Web sources are searched via Scirus and include author home pages, university sites and resources such as the preprint servers CogPrints and ArXiv.org, and OAI compliant resources.
The website also responds to some 'Misconceptions about Scopus content', one of which is stated as: 'There is not much social sciences content in Scopus'. The response is: 'Actually Scopus includes all of the social sciences titles in Thomson Scientific Social Sciences Citation Index®, as well as an additional few hundred titles'.

83   Social science reference sources: a practical guide
T-C. Li   3rd edn, Greenwood Press, 2000, 528pp. $157.95. ISBN 9780313304835.
'(P)rovides entries for roughly 1600 reference sources in the social sciences, including anthropology, business, economics, education, geography, history, law, political science, psychology and sociology.'

84   The social sciences: a cross-disciplinary guide to selected sources
N.L. Herron, ed.   3rd edn, Libraries Unlimited, 2002, 494pp. $60. ISBN 9781563088827.
Well laid out volume, giving often quite detailed descriptions of some 1500 sources. Part 1 covers 'General literature of the social sciences'; Part 2 'Literature of the established disciplines of the social sciences (political science; economics; business; history; law and justice; anthropology; sociology); Part 3 'Those disciplines with a social origin or that have acquired a social aspect' (education; psychology); Part 4 'Those disciplines with recognized social implications (geography; communication).
The entries in each of these 12 chapters are generally arranged by form of literature (handbooks; dictionaries and encyclopedias; indexes and abstracts: and so on), but with some variations. However, at the start of each chapter there is also a helpful and usually quite extensive essay defining the discipline and its history, methods of working and so on. A fine work.

85   Social Sciences Full Text
H W Wilson.
www.hwwilson.com/Databases/socsci.htm [FEE-BASED]
Leading tool indexing 625 periodicals, 400 peer-reviewed; full text of 215 journals back to 1995. Covers 'the latest concepts, trends, opinions, theories and methods from both applied and theoretical aspects of the social sciences'.

Website gives access to other relevant services available on WilsonWeb.

86   **WWW Virtual Library social sciences**
www.dialogical.net/socialsciences
Although many of the parts of the site have not been maintained, and thus have links which are broken, it can still be worth consulting for its very wide and detailed coverage as and when it is felt that might be worthwhile.

Digital data, image & text collections

87   **Mass Observation online**
Andrew Matthew Digital. £26,500 one off price.
www.amdigital.co.uk
This database provides online access to the original manuscripts and documents created and collected by the Mass Observation organization, based at the University of Sussex. It includes digitized versions of over 2000 file reports from 1937 to 1972, plus surveys, books, photographs and diaries relating to the project. These offer fascinating insight into British daily life during this period as well as the method of mass observation.

88   **National Statistics** [UK]
Office for National Statistics
www.statistics.gov.uk
The main site of the ONS, which 'is the government department responsible for collecting and publishing official statistics about the UK's society and economy'.
- ■ **The National Statistics Socio-Economic Classification: User manual Office for National Statistics**Palgrave Macmillan, 2005, 104pp. £50. ISBN 1403996474. Used to help compile UK statistics. There is a companion volume with the subtitle *Origins, development and use*.
- ■ **Australian Bureau of Statistics** www.abs.gov.au. Australia's official statistical organization. The 'Themes' heading leads to pages labelled: Economy; Environment and energy; Industry; People; Regional — and thence to more specialized subjects.
- ■ **Eurostat** http://ec.europa.eu/eurostat. Website of the Statistical Office of the European Union providing links to statistical information about the Member States. 'Themes' include: General and regional statistics; Economy and finance; Population and social conditions; Industry, trade and services; Agriculture and fisheries.
- ■ **FedStats** www.fedstats.gov. Gateway to statistics from over 100 US Federal agencies. The Topics A to Z has entries, for instance, for banking; children; criminal jJustice; education; international affairs; social welfare.
- ■ **Statistics Canada** www.statcan.ca. The site of Canada's central statistics agency. Very well laid out with excellent site map. The Daily – a free e-mailed bulletin – can be customized just to include 'hyperlinks to articles and product release announcements only on the subject(s) you have selected – and only on the days they appear in The Daily'.
- ■ **United Nations, Statistics Division** http://unstats.un.org. Gateway to the full range of statistics produced by the Division including the generic *Statistical Yearbook* as well as in specialized fields such as energy, environment, industry, trade. Links to other international statistics and to national offices. Includes a very useful guide Information on National Statistical Systems.

89   **NationMaster.com**
www.nationmaster.com
Fascinating, very well constructed site, 'a massive central data source and a handy way to graphically compare nations. NationMaster is a vast compilation of data from such sources as the CIA World Factbook, UN and OECD. Using the form above, you can generate maps and graphs on all kinds of statistics with ease'.

90   **Question Bank**
http://qb.soc.surrey.ac.uk
This website provides free access to a set of resources designed to teach students and researchers about professional social survey data collection, social measurement using surveys and survey questionnaire design. It is currently funded by the UK Economic and Social Research Council (ESRC). Contents include an excellent online collection of questions from real-life British social surveys, including the British Crime Survey from 2000 onwards; British Social Attitudes survey from 1999 onwards; and the Census of Population from 1991 onwards. Also available are resources for teachers, including exercises, PowerPoint slides and papers covering the techniques of social survey design.

Directories & encyclopedias

91   **The A–Z of social research: a dictionary of key social science research concepts**
R.L. Miller and J.D. Brewer, eds   Sage Publications, 2003, 345pp. £21.99. ISBN 9780761971337.
'*The A–Z of Social Research* is a "research methods" textbook with a difference. Rather than a normal text, this book can be thought of as an encyclopedia of social research. The *A–Z* is a collection of entries covering the whole expanse of social science research methods and issues, from qualitative research techniques to statistical testing and from the practicalities of using the internet to the philosophy of social research.'
   About 150 entries. Excellent.
- ■ **Key concepts in social research G. Payne and J. Payne**   Sage Publications, 2004, 248pp. £18.99. ISBN 9780761965435. Designed specifically to provide a first introduction for students. This basic text covers terminology relating to the key methods of social research used by social scientists. Examples range from sampling to qualitative and quantitative research methods. Each concept has a clear, accessible definition, highlighting related concepts and offering quotations from major texts. Suggestions for further reading are provided.

92   **Encyclopedia of law and society: American and global perspectives**
D. Clark   Sage Publications, 2007, 1808pp. 3 v., £190. ISBN 9780761923879.
A major three-volume set providing cross-disciplinary coverage of the interrelationship between law and society. Over 700 entries cover the sociology of law; law and economics; politics and law; criminology and psychology and law; and law and society activities in specific regions and countries. Materials include references from a large number of geographical areas, including North America, Australia, Europe, Africa and Asia and coverage of the key concepts, theories and research methods.

93   **Encyclopedia of measurement and statistics**
N.J. Salkind, ed.   Sage Publications, 2007. 2 v, £195. ISBN 9781412916110.
Major work 'specifically written to appeal to undergraduate students as well as practitioners, researchers and consumers of information' and whose key features are summarized to include:

- coverage of every major facet of these two different, but highly integrated disciplines with reference to mean, mode and median; reliability, validity, significance and correlation without overwhelming the informed reader;
- cross-disciplinary coverage, with contributions from and applications to the fields of: psychology; education; sociology; human development; political science; business and management; and public health;
- cross-referenced terms, a list of further readings and Website URLs after each entry, as well as an extensive set of appendices and an annotated list of organizations relevant to measurement and statistics.

- **Statistics for the social sciences R.M. Sirkin** 3rd edn, Sage Publications, 2005, 632pp. £31.99. ISBN 9781412905466. Well established introductory handbook.

94   **Encyclopedia of social measurement**
K. Kempf-Leonard, ed. Elsevier, 2005. 3 v., £600. ISBN 9780124438903.
Wide-ranging multi-disciplinary set of contributions: 'Covering all core social science disciplines, the 300+ articles of the *Encyclopedia of social measurement* not only present a comprehensive summary of observational frameworks and mathematical models, but also offer tools, background information, qualitative methods and guidelines for structuring the research process'.

95   **Encyclopedia of statistical sciences**
S. Kotz [et al.], eds 2nd edn, Wiley, 2006, 9686pp. 16 v., £2,595. ISBN 9780471150442.
http://eu.wiley.com/WileyCDA [DESCRIPTION]
Elegant work written by over 600 world-class experts, but with each entry self-contained and designed to be understood by readers with little statistical background.
'... a well-prepared and needed replacement for the first edition of a standard work ... most major academic libraries should purchase it ...' (*Choice*)

96   **International encyclopedia of the social and behavioral sciences**
N.J. Smelser and P.B. Baites, eds Elsevier, 2001. 26 v, £6,240. ISBN 9780080430768.
www.sciencedirect.com/science/referenceworks [COMPANION]
Now the major work in the field: a marvellous achievement.
'(T)here are three sets of justifications for a new encyclopedia. The first is the passage of time. Two other encyclopedias covering similar ranges of subject matter appeared in the twentieth century.

If we invoke the logic of "one-encyclopedia-every-one-third-century", a new, beginning-of-century publication seems indicated.

The second justification has to do with quality control of knowledge. New modes of publication such as the internet – with its tremendous increase in the quantity of publicly available information – are badly in need of better control of the quality of knowledge produced ...

The third and main motive for a new encyclopedia, however, must be a scientific one. Has there been a sufficient growth of knowledge and new directions of research to justify it? On this score neither we nor any of our advisers nor the publishers have ever expressed doubt: the answer is strong and positive.'

Well worth reading for those new to the field is the section 'The intellectual architecture of the encyclopedia' in the Introduction; also the entry within the body of the work entitled 'Encyclopedias, handbooks and dictionaries'.

- **Encyclopedia of the social sciences E.R.A. Seligman, ed.** Macmillan, 1930–35. 15 v.
- **International encyclopedia of the social sciences D.L. Sills, ed.** Macmillan/Free Press, 1968. www.galegroup.com [DESCRIPTION]. 17 v. [Biographical supplement: V. 18]. Via the website, access details of the announced 2nd edn of the Encyclopedia planned to be released November 2007, published by Macmillan Reference USA and distributed by Gale.

97   **Public opinion and polling around the world: a historical encyclopedia**
J. Geer, ed. ABC-CLIO, 2004, 848pp. 2 v., £128.50. ISBN 9781576079119.
Useful two-volume set which reviews the historical development of public opinion polls and polling worldwide. Contains entries relating to concepts, methodology and the use of polls in individual elections. Also offers brief biographies of some key pollsters such as MORI and Gallup.

98   **The Sage encyclopedia of social science research methods**
M.S. Lewis-Beck, A. Bryman and T.F. Liao Sage Publications, 2004. 3 v., £275. ISBN 0761923632.
Excellent work. At the outset, an A–Z listing of titles of all the (approximately 1000) entries followed by a Reader's Guide, classifying the entries under 34 broad headings (Analysis of variance; Association and correlation; Basic qualitative research; Basic statistics; Causal modeling; and so on). The entries include both brief definitions of key terms and longer discursive essays discussing the nature, history and practical application of the method. Coverage of qualitative and quantitative data techniques is provided.

'These volumes comprise an encyclopedia of social science research methods, the first of its kind. Uniqueness explains, at least partly, why we undertook the project. It has never been done before ...'

99   **The social science encyclopedia**
A. Kuper and J. Kuper, eds 3rd edn, Routledge, 2004. 2 v, £120. ISBN 0415320968.
Intended for 'a sophisticated but not necessarily specialist readership, including social scientists, students, journalists, managers, planners and administrators and indeed all those with a serious interest in contemporary academic thinking about the individual in society.'

Approximately 600 entries, each of which has references/further reading. Useful introductory Entries listed by discipline and subject covering 20 disciplines.

Tests and measures in the social sciences: tests available in compilation volumes
H. Hough, comp. See entry no. 275

Handbooks & manuals

100   **Action research**
E.T. Stringer 3rd edn, Sage Publications, 2007, 279pp. Foreword by Egon G. Guba, £24.99. ISBN 9781412952231.
First-rate handbook to action research. 'Unlike traditional experimental/scientific research that looks for generalizable explanations that might be applied to all contexts, action

research focuses on specific situations and localized solutions'. Especially valuable are two appendixes:

A. Case examples of formal reports

B. Action research web sites; about 50 sites, each with an informative annotation and categorized as General; Education; Community development and organizations; Disabilities; Health; Project management and evaluation; Women's issues; Youth.

101 Approaches to social research
R.A. Singleton and B.C. Straits   4th edn, Oxford University Press, 2005, 622pp. $83.50. ISBN 9780195147940.

'Of all the courses we teach, none is more important than research methods. Methodology is the heart of the social sciences; more than anything else, it is what distingishes social science from journalism and social commentary, from the humanities and natural sciences. Understanding social research methods, therefore should give you a better sense of sociology and related disciplines and of exactly what it is that social scientists do.'

Well produced, comprehensive text with – after two introductory chapters – 15 chapters in three Parts: I. Research design; II. Methods of data collection; III. Data processing, analysis and interpretation.

■ **Introduction to social research: quantitative and qualitative approaches K.F. Punch**   2nd edn, Sage Publications, 2005, 352pp. £21.99. ISBN 9780761944171. A useful introduction to the key methods of sociological research. The author describes the stages in research design, collection of data, and analysis in quantitative and qualitative projects. Other chapters deal with the practice and theory of mixed research methods and the ethics of research.

■ **Research methods knowledge base W.M.K. Trochim** www.socialresearchmethods.net/kb. '©comprehensive web-based textbook that addresses all of the topics in a typical introductory undergraduate or graduate course in social research methods.' Site is one element of an excellent facility for introducing and teaching students applied social research and includes tutorials on statistics and concept mapping.

102 Biographical research methods
R. Miller, ed.   Sage Publications, 2005. 4 v., £525. ISBN 9781412902298.

Elegant edited collection of readings in the series Sage Benchmarks in Social Research Methods. Four parts (which roughly map on to the four volumes): Time and biographical research; The construction of biographical meaning; Contexts; Disputes and concerns in biographical research.

■ **Comparative methods in the social sciences A. Sica, ed.** Sage Publications, 2006. £525. ISBN 9781412911443. 'This four-volume set brings together 77 articles and book chapters from key sources, spanning the history of comparative analysis in the social sciences, from ancient to modern works. The selections cover not only explanations of how to carry out comparative analysis in a reliable and creative way, but also exhaustively explore the fields of sociology, political science, anthropology and education.'

■ **Historical methods in the social sciences J.A. Hall and J.M. Bryant, eds** Sage Publications, 2005. £525. ISBN 9781412903707. 'By republishing many of the most seminal contributions in the field of historical social science, this four-volume set draws together some of the most illuminating reflections on historical-sociological research practices presently available, and should thus serve as an indispensable scholarly source for all those engaged in this interdisciplinary enterprise.'

The Blackwell companion to major classical social theorists
G. Ritzer, ed.   See entry no. 571

103 Case study research
M. David, ed.   Sage Publications, 2006, 1664pp. 4 v., £525. ISBN 9781412903837.

Part of the Sage Benchmarks in Social Research Methods series, this four-volume set brings together a comprehensive collection of articles covering the theory, method and controversies of case study research. Volume 1 covers early influential examples of case study research drawing from its applications in a wide range of social science subjects, including sociology, political science, policy and public administration studies. The succeeding volumes discuss methodology, usage and applications.

■ **Fieldwork C. Pole** Sage Publications, 2004. £525. ISBN 9781412900300. Another useful four-volume set within the Benchmarks in Social Research Methods series. Offers a comprehensive guide to all aspects of fieldwork research. Volume 1 covers the history and definition of fieldwork; volume 2 the fieldwork experience (including coverage of historical and contemporary methods); volume 3 the ethics and politics of fieldwork; volume 4 the analysis and outcomes of research.

104 A companion to qualitative research
U. Flick, E. von Kardorff and I. Steinke, eds   Sage Publications, 2004, 352pp. £26.99. ISBN 9780761973751.

Accessible, comprehensive guide to the theory and methodology of qualitative research. Includes chapters on its epistemological background, case studies of historical and contemporary practitioners and guides to styles of research. The latter includes discussion of up-to-date methods such as the use of the internet and practical issues relating to ethics and social research. The final section contains an extensive set of annotated references which can be used to guide further research. These include key books, journals and internet sites.

105 Essentials of research methods: a guide to social science research
J.M. Ruane   Blackwell, 2004, 256pp. £17.99. ISBN 9780631230496.

'(A) concise and accessible introduction to research methods in the social sciences. Written by an expert of research methods teaching, this book takes extraordinary care to focus the reader on experiences in his or her everyday life as a way of understanding and performing research methods.'

■ **A handbook for social science field research: essays & bibliographic sources on research design and methods E. Perecman and S.R. Curran, eds** Sage Publications, 2006, 280pp. £27. ISBN 9781412916813. '(P)rovides both novice and experienced researcher with valuable insights into a key list of critical texts pertaining to a wide array of social science methods useful when doing fieldwork.'

106 The European tradition of qualitative research
R. Boudon, M. Cherkaoui and P. Dem, eds   Sage Publications, 2003. 4 v., £525. ISBN 9780761974383.

A comprehensive four-volume set of scholarly essays which trace the history, evolution and current use of qualitative methods by social scientists in Europe. Topics covered include selection of the method of research; different ways of analysing data; ethical issues; and usage, advantages and challenges faced by all the key qualitative research methods. Textual analysis, non-textual analysis, interviews, questionnaires, field observations, case study methods, *verstehen* methods are all compared and contrasted.

107 Feminist research in theory and practice: feminist controversies
G. Letherby [et al.]   Open University Press, 2003, 224pp. £18.99. ISBN 9780335200283.
Offers the researcher an accessible guide to feminist method and methodology. It includes summaries of key theoretical debates, addressing the way in which politics can shape the process of research and knowledge production. It also contains practical case studies which outline different feminist research methods and provides suggestions for further reading.

108 The good research guide: for small-scale social research projects
M. Denscombe   3rd edn, Open University Press, 2007, 360pp. £18.99. ISBN 9780335220229.
Splendid text, very clearly written and presented. 15 chapters in three Parts: I. Strategies for social research; II. Methods of social research; III. Analysis. Each chapter ends with a useful checklist of key points to bear in mind: e.g. Checklist for internet research; Checklist for the use of books and other documents.

109 Interpreting qualitative data: methods for analysing talk, text and interaction
D. Silverman   3rd edn, Sage Publications, 2006, 428pp. £22.99. ISBN 9781412922456.
Aimed at 'the kind of practical skills needed to carry out a small piece of qualitative research ... I envisage this reshaped text as a companion volume to the second edition of my recent book *Doing qualitative research*. (In this book, I argue that doing qualitative research is always a theoretically driven undertaking. This means that "practical skills" are not the whole of the story, particularly if such skills are (wrongly) seen as sets of arbitary "recipes". Second, I have long argued that most dichotomies or polarities in social science are highly dangerous. At best, they are pedagogic devices for students to obtain a first grasp on a difficult field – they help us to learn the jargon. At worst, they are excuses for not thinking, which assemble groups of researchers into "armed camps", unwilling to learn from one another ...)
'That book is a guide to the business of conducting a research project at the graduate level. This book is more introductory ...'
■ **Doing qualitative research: a practical handbook** D. Silverman   2nd edn, Sage Publications, 2005, 395pp. £24.99. ISBN 9781412901970. Designed specifically for PhD students, this handy book offers guidance at all stages of the research process. Individual sections cover selecting a topic; writing a research proposal; data analysis; writing up and surviving an oral examination. Each chapter contains practical advice and checklists. Also provided is a glossary of research method terms.
■ **Qualitative research methods for the social sciences** B. Berg   6th edn, Pearson, 2006, 400pp. £39.99. ISBN 9780205503742. 'This text shows inexperienced researchers how to design, collect, and analyze data and then present their results to the scientific community. Also, this text stresses the importance of ethics in research and taking the time to properly design and think through any research endeavor'.

110 Organizing and managing your research: a practical guide for postgraduates
R. Phelps, K. Fisher and A. Ellis   Sage Publications, 2007, 290pp. £19.99. ISBN 9781412920643.
Good, clear and up to date, with four central chapters on: Communicating and networking electronically; Effective literature searching; Strategic web searching; and Managing and organizing your literature.
■ **Effective writing: a guide for social science students** P.P. Ng   Chinese University Press, 2003, 452pp. $20. ISBN 9789629961169. Particularly useful for readers whose native language is not English.

111 Philosophical foundations of social research methods
M. Williams, ed.   Sage Publications, 2006. Sage Benchmarks in Social Research Methods series. 4 v., £525. ISBN 9781412903820.
Reader with 77 chapters in four volumes: I. Social research as science or art; II. Philosophical issues in research strategies; III. Social reality and social context of social research; IV. New strategies in social research. 'The present volumes are about the philosophy of social research, rather than the philosophy of social science more broadly. The former is a narrower field than the latter and while philosophy of social science may be concerned with the philosophy underlying methodological issues, its remit encompasses social theoretical or political/moral issues about the nature of human society and our knowledge of it. Here we are only concerned with the philosophical issues underlying empirical social research ...'
■ **Philosophy and methodology of the social sciences** M.J. Smith   Sage Publications, 2005. £525. ISBN 9780761947370. 4 v. 'This four-volume set covers the traditional literature on the philosophy of the social sciences, and the contemporary philosophical and methodological debates developing at the heart of the disciplinary and interdisciplinary groups in the social sciences. It addresses the needs of researchers and academics who are grappling with the relationship between questions of knowledge construction and the problems of social scientific method.'

112 Qualitative research: theory, method and practice
D. Silverman, ed.   2nd edn, Sage Publications, 2004, 336pp. £23.99. ISBN 9780761949343.
Provides a solid introduction to a variety of methodological approaches to qualitative sociological research. Covers traditional methods as well as newer developments such as the use of visual and internet data and focus groups. Each chapter concludes with a annotated list of recommended further reading.
■ **Essential guide to qualitative methods in organizational research** C. Cassell and G. Symon, eds   Sage Publications, 2004, 388pp. £28.99. ISBN 9780761948889. 30 chapters providing very good overviews of all aspects of working within organizations. Useful bibliographies accompany each article.

113 Real world research: a resource for social scientists and practitioner-researchers
C. Robson   2nd edn, Blackwell, 2002, 599pp. £25.99. ISBN 9780631213055.
www.blackwellpublishing.com/robson [COMPANION]
A superb book, organized as Ways of using the book; Part I Before you start; Part II Designing the enquiry; Part III Tactics – the methods of data collection; Part IV Dealing with the data; Afterword; Appendix A Writing a project proposal; Appendix B The roles of practitioner-researchers, researchers and consultants in real world research; Glossary.
'This handbook will be very useful as an overview of various strategies, methods and research designs in social research, combining quantitative and qualitative research in a critical realist paradigm ... Robson's great strengths are his writing style, overall breadth of coverage and organization – huge elements needed for any book to be judged a success. This is an expert who does not intimidate or pontificate to the reader.' (*Forum: Qualitative Sozialforschung*)

114 **Research questions**
R. Andrews   Continuum, 2003, 112pp. Continuum Research Methods series, £11.99. ISBN 9780826464767.
A very good short text, within the Continuum Research Methods series. Other titles in the series include *Action research*; *Ethics in research*; *Evaluation methods in research*; *Research and gender*; *Using focus groups in research*.

115 **Researching society and culture**
C. Seale, ed.   2nd edn, Sage Publications, 2004, 544pp. £24.99. ISBN 9780761941972.
www.rscbook.co.uk [COMPANION]
Excellent edited collection of 34 chapters organized into three parts: Research contexts; Doing research; Case studies. Each chapter has a short 'Further reading' and most have a selection of 'Web pointers' (whose links are all accessible from the companion website).

116 **The Sage handbook of quantitative methodology for the social sciences**
D. Kaplan, ed.   Sage Publications, 2004, 528pp. £85. ISBN 9780761923596.
'(T)he definitive reference for teachers, students and researchers of quantitative methods in the social sciences, as it provides a comprehensive overview of the major techniques used in the field. The contributors, top methodologists and researchers, have written about their areas of expertise in ways that convey the utility of their respective techniques, but, where appropriate, they also offer a fair critique of these techniques. Relevance to real-world problems in the social sciences is an essential ingredient of each chapter and makes this an invaluable resource.'
■ **Quantitative social science** J. Scott and Y. Xie, eds   Sage Publications, 2005. £525. ISBN 9781412907408. This valuable four-volume set brings together a large number of previously published articles discussing the methodology of a range of different quantitative research methods and their applicability to the social sciences. They include discussion of both classic and cutting-edge numerical and statistical data analysis techniques.

117 **The Sage handbook of social science methodology**
W. Outhwaite and S.P. Turner   Sage Publications, 2007, 640pp. £85. ISBN 9781412901192.
'This is a jewel among methods Handbooks, bringing together a formidable collection of international contributors to comment on every aspect of the various central issues, complications and controversies in the core methodological traditions. It is designed to meet the needs of those disciplinary and nondisciplinary problem-oriented social inquirers for a comprehensive overview of the methodological literature.'

118 **Social research methods**
A. Bryman   2nd edn, Oxford University Press, 2004, 608pp. £28.99. ISBN 9780199264469.
www.oup.com/uk/orc [COMPANION]
Valuable text, especially as 'it attends to issues relating to fundamental concerns about what doing social research entails'. These include the applicability of the natural science model of the research process to the study of society; the types (if any) of the assumptions researchers make of the nature of social reality; the sorts of research findings that are legitimate and acceptable; ethical considerations concerning 'what we do to people during our investigations'.

■ **Social research methods: quantitative and qualitative approaches** W.L. Neuman   6th edn, Allyn & Bacon, 2006, 600pp. $100.20. ISBN 9780205457939. 'This highly regarded text presents a comprehensive and balanced introduction to both qualitative and quantitative approaches to social research, emphasizing the benefits of combining various approaches.'

119 **Systematic reviews in the social sciences: a practical guide**
M. Petticrew and H. Roberts   Blackwell, 2006, 336pp. £31.99. ISBN 9781405121101.
Outstanding guide to the notion of 'systematic reviews' and aimed especially at social science researchers: 'In the book we use the term "systematic review" to cover both those reviews that include a statistical summary of the included studies (a meta-analysis) and those that don't. While we use the phrase systematic "literature" reviews, not all evidence which may be useful for a review will of course appear in the published "literature" … we do not assume that only "published" literature can be reviewed'.
'This book can be read either as a "story" about systematic reviews: what they are, why they are important and what they tell us, or it can be read as a practical guide …'

120 **Ways of knowing: competing methodologies and methods in social and political research**
J.W. Moses and T.L. Knutsen   Palgrave Macmillan, 2007, 330pp. $35.95. ISBN 0230516653.
'This major new textbook on methodology in social and political science focuses centrally on the debate between positivist and constructivist approaches. It introduces in a lively and accessible way a range of key issues – from the nature of knowledge to the strengths and weaknesses of the main research methods – showing how methodological pluralism can be combined with intellectual rigor.'

121 **Writing for social scientists: how to start and finish your thesis, book, or article**
H.S. Becker   2nd edn, University of Chicago Press, 2007, 208pp. $12. ISBN 9780226041322.
'In this new edition, Becker takes account of major changes in the computer tools available to writers today and also substantially expands his analysis of how academic institutions create problems for them. As competition in academia grows increasingly heated, *Writing for Social Scientists* will provide solace to a new generation of frazzled, would-be writers.'
■ **Tricks of the trade: how to think about your research while you're doing it** H.S. Becker   University of Chicago Press, 1997, 239pp. $14. ISBN 9780226041247. Classic text covering four broad areas of social science: the creation of 'imagery' to guide research; methods of 'sampling' to generate maximum variety in the data; the development of 'concepts' to organize findings; the use of 'logical' methods to explore systematically the implications of what is found.

122 **Writing research papers in the social sciences**
J.D. Lester and J.D. Lester, Jr   Pearson/Longman, 2006, 400pp. £20.99. ISBN 9780321267634.
Detailed but easily approached manual tailored to social science needs and applications.

Keeping up to date

123 **Annual review of law and social science**
Annual Reviews, 2006. $175.00 [2006]. ISBN 0824341023.
http://arjournals.annualreviews.org/loi/lawsocsci [DESCRIPTION]
Relatively new series, the 2006 volume being the second.
Article titles include 'In the winter of our discontent: law,
anti-law and social science'; 'Governmentality'; 'Networking
goes international: an update'.

124 **The Economist**
1843–, weekly. ISSN 00130613.
www.economist.com
The leading weekly with excellent coverage of developments
in world affairs, including business, finance and economics,
science and technology, books and arts.

125 **Forum Qualitative Sozialforschung (Forum:
Qualitative Social Research)**
1999–, 3 p.a. ISSN 14385627.
www.qualitative-research.net/fqs/fqs-eng.htm
A free online academic journal covering all aspects of the
theory, practice, techniques and ethics of qualitative research
which was established in 1999 and is currently funded by the
Deutsche Forschungsgemeinschaft. Articles are published in
English, French or German triannually. Each issue contains
peer-reviewed research articles; reviews, conference listings
and debates. FQS is an open-access journal, so all articles
are available for free.

126 **Intute: social sciences blog**
**Joint Information Systems Committee and London School of
Economics & Political Science**
www.intute.ac.uk/socialsciences
Useful, well presented blog from the Editors of the Intute
social sciences service and librarians at the London School
of Economics. The site includes some useful podcasting
links.

127 **New Statesman**
1913–, weekly. ISSN 13647431.
www.newstatesman.com
'On 10 June 1988, as the magazine celebrated its 75th
anniversary, *New Statesman* merged with *New Society*, a
magazine covering the field of the social sciences, to form
the *New Statesman and Society*. (The suffix was dropped in
1996). However, despite the merger generally being seen as
a takeover by the *New Statesman*, the first two editors of the
combined magazine, Stuart Weir and Steve Platt, both came
from the editorial team of *New Society*. Another title, *Marxism
Today*, was acquired in December 1991 ...'

openDemocracy
See entry no. 1297

128 **Philosophy of the Social Sciences**
Sage Publications, 1971, qtrly. $122. ISSN 00483931.
www.sagepub.com/journals.nav
'For more than three decades *Philosophy of the Social Sciences*
has served as the international, interdisciplinary forum for
current research, theory and debate on the philosophical
foundations of the social sciences.'

129 **Prospect**
Prospect Publishing, 1995–, monthly. ISSN 13595024.

www.prospect-magazine.co.uk
'Prospect was launched in October 1995 by its present
editor David Goodhart, a senior correspondent for the
Financial Times, and chairman Derek Coombs. The aim was
to launch a monthly that was "more readable than the
Economist, more relevant than the *Spectator*, more romantic
than the *New Statesman*", as Sir Jeremy Isaacs subsequently
described *Prospect* ... *Prospect* has acquired a reputation as
the most intelligent magazine of current affairs and cultural
debate in Britain ...'

130 **Qualitative Report**
Nova Southeastern University, 1990–, qtrly. Free. ISSN 10520147.
www.nova.edu/ssss/QR
A free online journal dedicated to writing and discussion of
and about qualitative and critical inquiry which has been
published quarterly since 1990. It serves as a forum for
researchers, scholars, practitioners to publish research
essays and reviews on theories and methods of qualitative
research. The journal home page also maintains an excellent
directory of qualitative research resources, including links to
online syllabi, organizations, news services and research
projects.

131 **Social Research Update**
University of Surrey 1993–, qtrly. Print copies of the journal can be
supplied free of charge to UK-based researchers on request to the
publisher. ISSN 13607898.
www.soc.surrey.ac.uk/sru
Published online by the University's Department of Sociology
since March 1993. Offers regular updates on developments
in social research methods. Issues focus on a single theme
or method, succinctly summarizing recent developments and
debates. Many volumes cover issues relating to the
practicalities and ethics of the use of new information
technologies by social researchers. Examples include
exploiting freely available software for research, tools for
digital audio recording in qualitative research and the ethics
of internet research.

132 **Society**
Springer, 1962–, monthly. ISSN 01472011.
www.springer.com
'Springer has acquired twenty-nine journals from Transaction
Publishers, which is a major independent publisher of social
scientific books, periodicals and serials, especially in political
science, history, sociology, anthropology and psychology. The
titles include the flagship journal *Society*, which has been at
the forefront of contemporary thought in the social sciences
for 45 years.'

133 **SocietyGuardian**
Guardian News & Media.
http://society.guardian.co.uk
Of the UK national newspapers, *The Guardian* provides the
most intensive coverage of social developments.

134 **Sociological methodology**
American Sociological Association, 1969–, annual. £96. ISSN
00811750.
www.asanet.org
Annual publication of the Association. Contains scholarly
essays which discuss and evaluate the latest advances in
social research methods. This includes coverage of all

aspects of empirical research design and qualitative and quantitative data analysis. Available in print or online.

135   **Theory, Culture and Society**
Sage Publications, 1982–, 8 p.a. ISSN 02632764.
www.sagepub.net/tcs [DESCRIPTION]
One of a considerable number of 'social science' journals published by Sage, but notable for its recently promoted New Encylopaedia Project: 'The TCS special issue 'Problematizing Global Knowledge' (volume 23 (2–3) March-May 2007) is our first venture in "encyclopaedic explorations" which outlines our concern to begin to rethink knowledge under the impact of globalization and digitalization. The issue features 152 entries and supplements on a range of topics gathered under the headings: metaconcepts, metanarratives and meta-sites and institutions. Specific topics covered include clusters on classification, language, time, space, the body, science, aesthetics, culture, technology, networks, media, life, globalization, civilization, religion, modernity, the university, the public sphere ...

'Further volumes of the NEP are currently being developed and will appear in *Theory, Culture and Society* and the New Encyclopaedia Project Book Series. The first set of clusters now in preparation are: Megacities, Media, Food, Religion, Money. Others on Consumer Culture, America, the Body/Health, Public, will follow.'

PSYCHOLOGY, SOCIOLOGY & SOCIAL WORK

Psychology

Psychology is a broad subject, which, although generally considered as a social science, also has elements of biological sciences, medicine and health. There are also pure and applied aspects.

The sequence is intended to be as logical as is possible. The general section is followed by historical and theoretical aspects and psychoanalysis, progresses to methods and testing, and then proceeds through from biological processes to higher processes, developmental and social aspects, followed by the mostly more applied aspects of the subject.

It was thought to be useful to bring together all assessment resources in 'Psychological testing and assessment' rather than scattering them throughout the following subjects. On the other hand, volumes relating to specific areas of research methods were considered to be of more use within their specific subject section.

There is some overlap between 'Biological psychology' and 'Cognitive psychology and cognitive science' so the more biological resources such as cognitive neuroscience have been placed in the earlier section, whilst the comparatively new area of cognitive science, which combines cognitive psychology, psychobiology, anthropology, psycholinguistics and computer science, has been placed with cognitive psychology for convenience.

It should be noted that animal behaviour is primarily included in *The New Walford* Volume 1 so is not dealt with comprehensively here.

Sport psychology is included in the Sport section of this volume.

'Abnormal & clinical psychology' is used here to cover a wide variety of resources including psychiatry, psychotherapy, counselling and mental health.

applied psychology • behaviour • behavioural science • ethics • mind

Introductions to the subject

136 Atkinson and Hilgard's Introduction to psychology
E.E. Smith [et al.]   14th edn, Wadsworth, 2003, 768pp. $142.95. ISBN 9780155050693.
Updated edition of Atkinson and Hilgard's classic text. Covers all areas of psychology with extensive references. An excellent starting point. Further resources and web links can be found on a companion website.

137 Psychology: an international perspective
M.W. Eysenck   Psychology Press, 2004, 993pp. £24.95. ISBN 9781841693613.
An excellent introduction, including examples of research worldwide, particularly from the UK, Germany, Scandinavia, Holland, Australia and Canada in addition to the usual US coverage. Emphasizes the importance of the cross-cultural approach.

138 Psychology: the science of mind and behaviour
R. Gross   5th edn, Hodder & Stoughton, 2005, 1020pp. £26.99. ISBN 9780340900987.
Comprehensive volume, covering most areas of psychology. Up to date and includes recent studies. Suitable for a wide student readership from beginners to undergraduates.

Dictionaries, thesauri, classifications

139 APA dictionary of psychology
G.R. VandenBos, ed.   American Psychological Association, 2006, 1008pp. $49.95. ISBN 9781591473800.
Approximately 25,000 brief entries covering all areas of psychology, with many cross-references to related subjects. Also includes concise entries for psychologists, societies and organizations, psychological tests and psychotherapies, which are also listed in four appendices.

140 A dictionary of psychology
A.M. Colman   2nd edn, Oxford University Press, 2006, 880pp. £10.99. ISBN 9780198610359.
Concise entries covering psychology, psychoanalysis, psychiatry, the neurosciences and statistics. Cross-referenced and with many illustrations. Includes a comprehensive list of phobias and a list of abbreviations and symbols referring the reader to the main entry.

141 The dictionary of psychology
R.J. Corsini   Brunner-Routledge, 2002, 1156pp. £35. ISBN 9781583913284.
Includes approximately 30,000 brief entries. Comprehensive coverage of all areas of psychology and related areas of sociology and anthropology. Extensively cross-referenced and illustrated with diagrams where helpful. Appendices include DSM-IV terms, systems of treatment, measuring instruments and biographies.

142 Dictionary of psychology and psychiatry (Wörterbuch der Psychologie und Psychiatrie)
R. Haas   2nd edn, Hogrefe, 2003, 1112pp. 2 v, $169. ISBN 9780889373020.
Extensive coverage of psychology and psychiatry, including terminology from the DSM-IV and ICD-10 and newer areas such as cognitive neuroscience and computer-based assessment. Also includes lists of abbreviations.
V. 1 English–German (Englisch–Deutsch). V. 2 German–English (Deutsch–Englisch).

143 Eponyms in psychology: a dictionary and biographical sourcebook
L. Zusne   Greenwood Press, 1987, 339pp. $121.95. ISBN 9780313257506.
Unique dictionary defining terms or phrases which incorporate the name of an individual. The term is defined followed by references to where it was first used and biographical information about the person after whom it is named. Coverage is broad, including eponyms from related areas such as education, linguistics and artificial intelligence.

144   Wiley's English–Spanish Spanish–English dictionary of psychology and psychiatry (Diccionario de psicología y psiquiatría inglés–español español–inglés de Wiley)
S.M. Kaplan, comp.   Wiley, 1997, 594pp. $42.95. ISBN 9780471192848.
Consists of a total of over 60,000 entries covering all areas of psychology and psychiatry. Straightforward and easy to use: the equivalent word or phrase is given directly. There are no cross-references.

Laws, standards, codes

145   Code of ethics and conduct [UK]
British Psychological Society   2006.
www.bps.org.uk/the-society/the-society_home.cfm
New code of professional ethics, applicable from 31 March 2006. Click on the link 'Ethics, Rules, Charter, Code of Conduct'. Also links to the 'Guidelines for psychologists working with animals'.

146   Ethical principles of psychologists and code of conduct [USA]
American Psychological Association   2002.
www.apa.org/ethics/code2002.html
This version of the APA ethics code was effective from 1 June 2003. The APA also produces 'Guidelines for the ethical conduct in the care and use of animals':
www.apa.org/science/anguide.html.

Associations & societies

147   American Psychological Association
www.apa.org
Based in Washington, DC, the American Psychological Association (APA) is a scientific and professional organization that represents psychology in the USA. The website links to information for psychologists, students and the public. One can access the latest news in psychology, find information about the Association's publications and electronic products, link to the websites of the divisions of the APA, including their newsletters, the APA's ethics code, psychological testing, the APA archives and 'find a psychologist'.
'… an outstanding source of information about psychology and psychological resources on the Internet' (*Choice* July/August 2006)

148   Association for Psychological Science [USA]
www.psychologicalscience.org
The APS was founded in 1988 for the advancement of scientific psychology in the USA. The website has links to US and international psychological societies and related organizations, US government agencies and other sites of interest. There is information about APS journals and the free online news magazine, the *Observer*.

149   Australian Psychological Society
www.psychology.org.au
The largest professional association for psychologists in Australia, with the aim of advancing psychology as a discipline and a profession. The website has news, links to organizations, mental health resources, careers and 'find a

psychologist'. Some resources are available for members only.

150   British Psychological Society
www.bps.org.uk
Founded in 1901, the BPS is the representative body for all areas of psychology in the UK. The website has information about psychology, the Society's sections and divisions, the directory of chartered psychologists, ethical principles, testing centre, working party reports, consultation documents, abstracts of Society conference proceedings, research digest and *Psychologist* journal.
■ **Directory and register of chartered psychologists**
www.bps.org.uk/e-services/find-a-psychologist/directory.cfm. The directory enables one to search for a psychologist within a particular geographical area of the UK. Using the register, it is possible to check whether a named individual is a chartered psychologist. This section of the website also includes a directory of expert witnesses.

151   Canadian Psychological Association
www.cpa.ca
The Canadian Psychological Association (CPA) was established in 1939 and covers all aspects of psychology in Canada. The website is available in both French and English and includes information about psychology in Canadian universities, the CPA archives and archival material relating to the history of Canadian psychology, the code of ethics, publications, current events and news and the sections of the CPA.

152   European Federation of Psychologists' Associations
www.efpa.be
A federation of national psychology associations in Europe founded in 1981. There are now 32 member associations. It provides a forum for European cooperation in a wide range of fields of academic training, psychology practice and research. Links to the individual associations. The *European Psychologist* is the official journal of the organization.

153   International Association of Applied Psychology
www.iaapsy.org
Founded in 1920, the IAAP has members in 80 countries. The Association has 16 divisions in various areas of applied psychology. The website provides an online directory of applied psychologists, online newsletters, ethical principles and the home pages of divisions.

154   International Union of Psychological Science
www.am.org/iupsys
Aims to promote all aspects of psychology as a science and as a profession. The website includes items of news and documents and links to psychological organizations. The *International Journal of Psychology* is published under the auspices of the organization.
■ **Psychology: IUPsyS Global Resource D. Wedding and M.J. Stevens, eds**   2007 edn, Psychology Press. £25. ISBN 978184169675. CD-ROM. Free with a subscription to the *International Journal of Psychology*. Contains information about psychology world-wide, including a directory of international psychological associations, a directory of major institutions for research and training, a bibliography of world and regional psychology, a history of psychology section.

155 New Zealand Psychological Society
www.psychology.org.nz
Professional association for psychologists in New Zealand. The site provides information about psychology in New Zealand, sub-groups of the society, the ethics code, 'find a psychologist', job vacancies and links to other psychological organizations.

156 Psychological Society of Ireland
www.psihq.ie
Learned and professional body for psychology in Ireland. The website includes information about psychology in Ireland, links to university departments and psychological organizations, conference abstracts and 'find a psychologist'.

157 Psychonomic Society
www.psychonomic.org
The Society aims to promote the communication of scientific research in psychology and allied sciences and for this purpose publishes six journals: *Behavior Research Methods*; *Cognitive, Affective, & Behavioral Neuroscience*; *Learning & Behavior*; *Memory & Cognition*; *Perception & Psychophysics* and *Psychonomic Bulletin & Review*. Members of the Psychonomic Society must be doctoral level with additional published research. The website includes the Psychonomic Society Archive of Norms, Stimuli and Data.

Libraries, archives, museums

158 University of London, Senate House Library
www.shl.lon.ac.uk
Major psychology collection at the University of London, including the library holdings of the British Psychological Society. Most areas of psychology are covered in depth and special subjects include hypnosis and parapsychology. There is a collection of psychological tests and historical material is held.

Portal & task environments

159 AmoebaWeb
www.vanguard.edu/faculty/ddegelman/amoebaweb
An excellent website maintained by Douglas Degelman at Vanguard University of Southern California. Includes over 2000 links to psychological resources, including full-text journals, psychological research scales and subject-related links for most areas of psychology.

160 Athabasca University psychology resources
Athabasca University
http://psych.athabascau.ca/html/aupr/psycres.shtml
An excellent collection of links from the Centre for Psychology at Athabasca University in Canada. The 'academic content' links cover most areas of psychology such as history of psychology and sport psychology. Each section has an extensive listing of useful links. For example, the history of psychology resources include links to websites about key psychologists. There are also links to psychology departments in Canada, organizations, journals and resources for psychology students and those carrying out psychology research.

161 Encyclopedia of psychology
www.psychology.org
A very interesting site, with almost 2000 links divided into eight categories, including organizations with links to numerous associations and research institutes, nearly 100 historical links to people and the history of psychology, including some lesser-known people, links to specific topics, journals, theories and research methods. The search facility is very useful.

162 Higher Education Academy: Psychology Network
[UK]
www.psychology.heacademy.ac.uk
Supports the teaching and learning of psychology across the UK. Publishes an online newsletter, has an online database of resources and publishes online reviews of recommended psychology books. Also has links to resources such as the Association of Heads of Psychology Departments, resources for psychology practicals and JISCMail psychology mailing lists.

163 Intute: social sciences: psychology
www.intute.ac.uk/socialsciences/psychology
Free service providing access to psychology internet resources. Covers a wide range of psychological topics and includes entries for portals, journals, societies, centres, university departments, mailing lists, blogs and papers. All sites have been selected and evaluated by subject specialists. An excellent resource.

164 Psych Web
www.psywww.com
Information for students and teachers of psychology such as APA style resources, psychology departments worldwide, scholarly resources.

165 PsychNet-UK
www.psychnet-uk.com
Site developed for mental health professionals who want to know more about the psychological sciences. Includes links to resources for personality psychology, experimental design, psychopharmacology, addiction and drugs, psychological research and disorder information sheets. There is also a set of links to psychological societies and associations.

166 Psychology World Wide Web Virtual Library
www.dialogical.net/psychology/index.html
A useful site, part of the World Wide Web Virtual Library. Covers a range of topics, including information about academic psychology departments, professional societies and information about psychology journals. All sites are evaluated before being included.

167 Psychology/Psychiatry Committee web links
Association of College & Research Libraries: Psychology/Psychiatry Committee
www.ala.org/ala/acrlbucket/ebss2/psych/psychweblinks.htm
An excellent list of web links for librarians, covering a range of useful topics, including acquisitions, assessment, databases, journals, gateways, professional associations, writing resources and style guides. Selected by members of the Psychology/Psychiatry Committee as being the 'best of the best'.

■ **Core journals in psychology** 2007.
www.ilstu.edu/~brstoff/ebss/psycjournals107.htm. A listing of the most

important psychology journals found in academic libraries: arranged by subject and alphabetically, each title links to the publisher's website.

168 **PsychScholar**
http://psych.hanover.edu/Krantz
A useful source of information and resources from Hanover College, Indiana: there are links to societies, departments and psychological institutes in Europe and worldwide, links to tutorials and links to online journals. Also includes useful information about different areas of psychology.

Discovering print & electronic resources

169 **PsycCRITIQUES**
American Psychological Association
www.apa.org/psyccritiques [DESCRIPTION]
A database of book reviews in psychology, replacing the print journal, *Contemporary Psychology: APA review of books* from 2005. Approximately 18–20 reviews, mostly current, are added each week, including the review of a popular film from a psychological point of view. Includes reviews from *Contemporary Psychology* from 1956 to 2004.

170 **PsycEXTRA**
American Psychological Association
www.apa.org/psycextra/ [DESCRIPTION]
A database of grey literature. Coverage includes newsletters, magazines, newspapers, technical and annual reports, government reports, consumer brochures. There is no overlap with PsycINFO. It includes abstracts and many full-text records. The majority of the records cover material from the USA.

171 **PsycINFO**
American Psychological Association
www.apa.org/psycinfo [DESCRIPTION]
A database of abstracts to the psychological literature from the 1800s to the present. Includes journals, books and book chapters and dissertations. Broad coverage; includes related areas: social, business, neuroscience, management, medicine and social work. Records are indexed using the 'Thesaurus of psychological index terms'.
   PsycINFO Direct: Non-subscribers can search PsycINFO Direct for $11.95 for a 24 hour period:
www.apa.org/psycinfo/products/pidirect.html
■ **Thesaurus of psychological index terms** L. A. Gallagher
   11th edn, American Psychological Association, 2007, 452pp. $90. ISBN 9781591479260. Over 8,200 terms used for indexing PsycINFO and other APA databases.

Digital data, image & text collections

172 **Cogprints**
http://cogprints.org
An electronic archive for self-archiving papers in all areas of psychology and related areas of philosophy, neuroscience, linguistics, computer science and biology. The majority of papers are from the last 10 to 12 years, but there are some dating back to the 1950s.

173 **PsycARTICLES**
American Psychological Association
www.apa.org/psycarticles [DESCRIPTION]

A database of full-text articles from journals published by the American Psychological Association, the APA Educational Publishing Foundation, the Canadian Psychological Association and Hogrefe Publishing Group. Records for APA journals date back to Volume 1 of each journal.
   PsycARTICLES Direct: Non-subscribers can search PsycARTICLES Direct free of charge and view abstracts of journal articles from 1894 and selected APA book chapters. Users are charged $11.95 for each full-text record viewed, printed or downloaded:
http://psycinfo.apa.org/psycarticles/direct.

174 **PsycBOOKS**
American Psychological Association
www.apa.org/psycbooks [DESCRIPTION]
A full-text database of books. Includes 644 books published by the American Psychological Association (APA), including the *APA encyclopedia of psychology* and 495 classic psychology titles. There is an embargo of approximately 18 months before newly published titles are included.

175 **Psychology and behavioral sciences collection**
EBSCO Publishing.
www.epnet.com/thisTopic.php?marketID=1&topicID=127 [DESCRIPTION]
A subset of Academic Search Premier; coverage includes emotional and behavioural characteristics, psychiatry and psychology, mental processes, anthropology and observational and experimental methods. Provides access to over 500 full-text journals; dates available vary and many have a publisher's embargo on recent issues.

Directories & encyclopedias

176 **Biographical dictionary of psychology**
N. Sheehy, A.J. Chapman and W.A. Conroy, eds   Routledge, 2002, 704pp. £24.99. ISBN 9780415285612.
Provides biographical information for about 500 people who have made a significant contribution to psychology worldwide from the 1850s to 1990s, including those still alive today. Each entry gives dates of birth and death, nationality, professional interests, education, appointments, principal publications and further reading. There are also four indexes to facilitate use: names, interests (including APA subject divisions), key terms (concepts) and institutions.
Originally published in 1997.

Biographical dictionary of psychology
L. Zusne, ed.   See entry no. 212

177 **The Corsini encyclopedia of psychology and behavioral science**
W.E. Craighead and C.B. Nemeroff, eds   3rd edn, Wiley, 2002, 1952pp. 4 v, $400. ISBN 9780471244004.
Scholarly and substantially updated edition of *Corsini's encyclopedia of psychology* (2nd edn, 1994). Entries are of varying lengths, some substantial. Useful for the biographies of psychologists, including living and some lesser-known figures. Longer articles are signed and many include references.

178 Encyclopaedic dictionary of psychology
G. Davey, ed. Hodder Arnold, 2005, 484pp. £35. ISBN 9780340812389.

Useful introductory volume, arranged in eight sections: conceptual and historical issues, biological psychology, cognitive psychology, developmental psychology, social psychology, personality and individual differences, abnormal, clinical and health psychology and research methods and statistics. Within each section entries are arranged alphabetically, but the index will refer the user to the relevant page. Entries range from brief definitions to longer explanations accompanied by references and illustrations. Cross-referenced throughout.

179 Encyclopedia of applied psychology
C. Spielberger, ed. Academic Press, 2004, 2688pp. 3 v, $875. ISBN 9780126574104.

Sponsored by the International Association of Applied Psychology, this volume has 300 articles covering applications in all areas of psychology, including cross-cultural psychology, advertising and marketing, gender etc., in addition to the usual applied areas. Provides clear definitions of the topic, a brief review of the theoretical basis and major areas of application.

'An excellent general guide to applied psychology' (*Choice* March 2005)

180 Encyclopedia of psychology
A.E. Kazdin, ed. American Psychological Association, 2000, 4128pp. 8 v, $750. ISBN 9781557981875.

An excellent work covering all areas of psychology and related subjects. Entries are written by experts, cross-referenced and include useful bibliographies. Includes biographical entries, articles about psychology in various countries and entries for major psychological instruments.

'Impressive and authoritative' (*Choice* November 2000)

181 The Oxford companion to the mind
R.L. Gregory, ed. 2nd edn, Oxford University Press, 2004, 1004pp. £40. ISBN 9780198662242.

Over 300 contributors have provided 900 articles covering a range of topics relating to the mind, such as the brain, consciousness, depression, facial expression, social psychology and extrasensory perception. Includes biographical entries for psychologists, philosophers, neurologists and scientists. A substantial index refers the reader to relevant articles which refer to a concept.

182 Psychology departments in Britain and Ireland
www.psychology.bangor.ac.uk/undergraduate/faq_links/psych_dep.php?catid=&subid=2517

From the University of Bangor in Wales, UK, an alphabetical listing by city of all departments offering degree-level courses in psychology. Also links to PsychScholar's links to psychology departments worldwide.

183 PsycLine: your guide to psychology and social science journals on the web
www.psycline.org

A useful resource maintained by Armin Günther at the University of Augsburg in Germany. Links to the websites of over 2000 psychology and social science journals. It is possible to search by keyword, subject or alphabetically.

Handbooks & manuals

184 Handbook of international psychology
M.J. Stevens and D. Wedding, eds Brunner-Routledge, 2004, 557pp. £75. ISBN 9780415946124.

Provides an overview of psychology in 27 countries throughout the world. The entries are written by experts within the country and include information about education and training, the scope of psychological practice and future developments. Useful for the inclusion of non-western perspectives.

185 Handbook of psychology
I.B. Weiner [et al.], ed. Wiley, 2004, 7995pp. 12 v, $1260. ISBN 9780471666752.

These volumes provide a good overview of the main areas of psychology. Each volume has its own editor and can be purchased separately ($99.95–$105.00).
- **1. History of psychology** ISBN 9780471666646.
- **2. Research methods in psychology** ISBN 9780471666653.
- **3. Biological psychology** ISBN 9780471666660.
- **4. Experimental psychology** ISBN 9780471666677.
- **5. Personality and social psychology** ISBN 9780471666684.
- **6. Developmental psychology** ISBN 978047166661.
- **7. Educational psychology** ISBN 9780471666707.
- **8. Clinical psychology** ISBN 9780471666714.
- **9. Health psychology** ISBN 9780471666721.
- **10. Assessment psychology** ISBN 9780471666738.
- **11. Forensic psychology** ISBN 9780471619208.
- **12. Industrial and organizational psychology** ISBN 9780471666745.

186 International handbook of psychology
K. Pawlik and M.R. Rosenzweig, eds Sage Publications, 2000, 629pp. £85. ISBN 9780761953296.

Published as part of the International Union of Psychological Science's programme to promote knowledge of psychology and disseminate it widely. Scholarly chapters, written by an international team of eminent contributors, provide an overview of all the main areas of scientific and applied psychology, including cross-disciplinary aspects and international psychology.

Keeping up to date

187 Annual review of psychology
Annual Reviews, 2007. V.58, $75. ISBN 9780824302580 ISSN 00664308.
www.annualreviews.org [DESCRIPTION]

Volume 58 in this excellent series reviews a range of topics, including cognitive neuroscience, animal cognition, culture and mental health, personality disorders, self and identity and many more. Abstracts are freely available online, while subscribers can access the full-text.

188 APS Observer [USA]
Association for Psychological Science monthly.
www.psychologicalscience.org/observer

Psychology news from the Association for Psychological Science.

189 The BPS research digest
British Psychological Society, fortnightly.
www.researchdigest.org.uk
A useful review of recent research, primarily aimed at students, delivered free to subscribers by e-mail every two weeks.

190 Monitor on Psychology [USA]
American Psychological Association 11 p.a.
www.apa.org/monitor
Magazine of the American Psychological Association. Includes news, articles, letters and information about the divisions of the Association.

191 The Psychologist [UK]
British Psychological Society, 1988–, monthly. £50.00 p.a. ISSN 09528229.
www.thepsychologist.org.uk
The official publication of the British Psychological Society (BPS). Publishes articles which give a broad overview of a particular area. Also included are items of news about psychology in the UK, a students' page, book reviews, letters, interviews and occasional articles about psychology in other countries. The journal is sent free to members of the BPS and issues over six months old are freely available to all online.

192 Psychology in the news [USA]
American Psychological Association
www.psycport.com
From the American Psychological Association. Links to current psychology articles and press releases in the US media.

193 Psychology mailing lists
http://wjh-www.harvard.edu/soc-sci/psy/psy-maillist.html
Not a comprehensive list, but links to a range of psychology mailing lists.

History & Theories of Psychology

Gestalt psychology • history of psychology • philosophical psychology • psychological theories • psychologists • theoretical psychology

Introductions to the subject

194 History and systems of psychology
J.F. Brennan 6th edn, Prentice Hall, 2003, 368pp. £45.99. ISBN 9780130481191.
Considers the history of psychology in the context of the intellectual development of western civilization. The first part of the book covers from the Greek philosophers to the emergence of empirical psychology in the 1870s and the second part looks at the major movements that developed during the 20th century.

195 A history of modern psychology
D.P. Schultz and S.E. Schultz 8th edn, Thomson/Wadsworth, 2004, 534pp. $113.95. ISBN 9780534557751.
Coverage is from the late 19th century. The volume is organized by schools of thought and includes biographical

information on key theorists. There are also discussions on contemporary developments such as cognitive neuroscience and evolutionary psychology. Each chapter refers the reader to useful websites and the publisher has a companion site which includes supplementary information (www.thomsonedu.com).

196 History of modern psychology
C.J. Goodwin 2nd international edn, Wiley, 2005, 498pp. £33.95. ISBN 9780471658191.
Good introductory volume for students, covering from Descartes through Wundt and German psychology, American pioneers and on to the post-war period. Clearly laid out with summaries, study questions, original source excerpts and references for further reading. Also includes a glossary.

197 A history of psychology in autobiography
G. Lindzey and W.M. Runyon, eds American Psychological Association, 2007, 408pp. V. IX, $89.95. ISBN 9781591477969.
In this series, eminent psychologists report how their research interests developed alongside aspects of their personal circumstances. This latest volume contains accounts by nine leading researchers, including Aronson, Bandura and Neisser. An appendix lists the contents of volumes I to VIII.
Previous volumes, 1930–1989: various editors and publishers.

198 An introduction to the history of psychology
B.R. Hergenhahn 5th edn, Thomson/Wadsworth, 2005, 687pp. $131.95. ISBN 9780534554019.
Provides a comprehensive overview of all schools of psychology from the early Greek philosophers to the present. An appendix lists significant individuals and events in chronological order. The companion site has activities and links to websites (www.thomsonedu.com).

199 Key thinkers in psychology
R. Harré Sage Publications, 2005, 287pp. £19.99. ISBN 9781412903455.
The author has selected about 40 psychologists from the 20th century that he considers to have made the most impact on psychology. No women are included. The volume is organized by schools of thought such as behaviourists, biopsychologists and social psychologists. For each person, biographical information is given, information about his contribution to psychology and references for further reading. A very readable book.

200 Three psychologies: perspectives from Freud, Skinner and Rogers
R.D. Nye 6th edn, Brooks/Cole, 2000, 181pp. $35.95. ISBN 9780534368456.
Presents an overview of the ideas of these three theorists, with comparisons, contrasts and criticisms. An epilogue deals with rational emotive behaviour therapy. A useful volume.

Dictionaries, thesauri, classifications

201 Elsevier's dictionary of psychological theories
J.E. Roeckelein, comp. Elsevier, 2006, 679pp. €130. ISBN 9780444517500.
Alphabetical arrangement of approximately 2000 entries covering a wide range of psychological theories. Each entry

has cross-references and is followed by a list of references. Appendices cover illusions, humour and imagery and the volume concludes with a selected bibliography.

Associations & societies

202 International Society for Theoretical Psychology
www.psych.ucalgary.ca/ISTP
'The International Society for Theoretical Psychology (ISTP) is an international forum for theoretical, meta-theoretical and philosophical discussions in psychology, with a focus on contemporary psychological debates.' *Theory and Psychology* is the organization's journal. The website includes news and information about conferences and links to societies and historical sites of interest.

Libraries, archives, museums

203 The archives of the history of American psychology
www3.uakron.edu/ahap
Established in 1965 at the University of Akron, Ohio, to promote research in the history of psychology. The materials are not available online; the site is intended to document what is available within the archive. The manuscript collection includes the papers of over 740 psychologists. The archives also contain instruments and apparatuses, films, photographs, audio and video tapes, books and tests. The Mental Health History Database provides a searchable subject-based index to AHAP manuscript collections that contain materials related to mental health.

204 Museum of the History of Psychological Instrumentation
http://chss.montclair.edu/psychology/museum/museum.html
From Montclair State University in New Jersey, this is an online cyber-museum of early psychological laboratory research apparatus which includes illustrations of each piece of apparatus. The website also includes the Museum of the History of Reaction Time Research.

Portal & task environments

205 History and philosophy of psychology web resources
www.psych.yorku.ca/orgs/resource
Site maintained by Christopher D. Green at York University, Toronto, Ontario. Links to dozens of useful sites: professional societies and university programmes, sites about specific individuals, archives and collections and online books and journals. An excellent collection of links to web resources.

206 History of psychology web site
http://elvers.stjoe.udayton.edu/history/welcome.htm
Gateway to over 1000 web resources, including people (listed by birthdate and alphabetically), psychology department histories, virtual museums, photographic collections of psychologists, organizations, etc.

207 Today in the history of psychology [USA]
American Psychological Association
www.cwu.edu/~warren/today.html

A collection of dates and brief descriptions of over 3100 events in the history of psychology; this resource is an expanded version of the book by W.R. Street: *A chronology of noteworthy events in American psychology* (APA, 1994). This book is no longer in print but the online version includes hundreds of more recent entries.

Discovering print & electronic resources

208 F.C. Bartlett archive
www-bartlett.sps.cam.ac.uk/index.html
Selected full-text documents written by the British psychologist Sir Frederick Bartlett (1886–1969). The website includes a biography, the documents arranged by subject and date, a complete bibliography, photographs and links to external resources.

Digital data, image & text collections

209 Classics in the history of psychology
http://psychclassics.yorku.ca
Produced by Christopher D. Green of York University, Toronto, this useful site provides access to important historical full-text resources in the public domain. Includes 25 books and about 200 articles and chapters. The resources can be browsed by author or topic. Includes works by psychologists such as Freud, Skinner, Watson, Thorndike, Titchener and many others. Pages load instantly and it is possible to click on a footnote number and go directly to the reference.

210 Gestalt archive
International Society for Gestalt Psychology & its Applications
www.gestalttheory.net/archive
Full text Gestalt psychology articles from the International Society for Gestalt Psychology and its Applications. Includes articles from 1924 to 2004.

211 History and theory of psychology eprint archive
http://htpprints.yorku.ca
Has the goal of promoting the rapid dissemination of new work in the field, but in June 2007 only included e-prints from 1979 to 2005. Searching can be carried out by subject or year and there are simple and advanced search options.

Directories & encyclopedias

212 Biographical dictionary of psychology
L. Zusne, ed. Greenwood Press, 1984, 563pp. $139.95. ISBN 9780313240270.
An alphabetical listing of 600 eminent deceased psychologists. Entries include their contributions, place and date of birth and death, positions held and a selective list of resources for further biographical information. Includes a chronological listing by date of birth and a ranking of the relative eminence of the psychologists.

213 Eminent contributors to psychology
R.I. Watson, ed. Springer Publishing, 1974–76. 2 v, o/p.
Volume 1 lists major primary references for over 500 individuals who lived between 1600 and 1967. Volume 2 lists over 50,000 selected secondary references. The names of

those included were selected by an international panel of leading psychologists and include some key figures from related areas of philosophy and science such as Descartes, Kant and Newton.

V.1. A bibliography of primary references 1974, 470pp ISBN 0826114504

- V.2. A bibliography of secondary references 1976, 1158pp ISBN 0826117805.

214   Portraits of pioneers in psychology
American Psychological Association, 1991–2006. 6 v.
An excellent series presenting aspects of the lives and work of key figures in the history of psychology, prepared by leading scholars.

- V.1. ISBN 9780805811360, o/p (edited by G.A. Kimble, M. Wertheimer and C.L. White)
- V.2. ISBN 9781557983459, $29.95 (edited by G.A. Kimble, C.A. Boneau, M. Wertheimer)
- V.3. ISBN 9781557984791, $29.95 (edited by G.A. Kimble, M. Wertheimer)
- V.4. ISBN 9781557987136, $29.95 (edited by G.A. Kimble, M. Wertheimer)
- V.5. ISBN 9781591470175, $29.95 (edited by G.A. Kimble, M. Wertheimer)
- V.6. ISBN 9781591474173, $79.95 (edited by D.A. Dewsbury, L.T. Benjamin, M. Wertheimer)
- **Index to portraits of pioneers in psychology, vols 1–4**
  www.cwu.edu/~warren/pioneerindex.htm. A useful online index for tracing individual pioneers from the first four volumes.

Psychoanalysis

Freud • Jung

Introductions to the subject

215   The American Psychiatric Publishing textbook of psychoanalysis
E.S. Person, A.M. Cooper and G.O. Gabbard, eds   American Psychiatric Publishing, 2005, 602pp. $115. ISBN 9781585621521.
A scholarly and comprehensive reference volume, covering theoretical psychoanalysis, treatment, research, history and relation to other fields. Includes a useful glossary of psychoanalytic terms.

216   Cambridge companion to Freud
J. Neu, ed.   Cambridge University Press, 1992, 356pp. £21.99. ISBN 9780521377799.
Covers the major topics of Freud's thought such as dreams and the unconscious. Consists of specially commissioned essays which approach Freud from philosophical, historical, psychoanalytical, anthropological and sociological perspectives.

217   Cambridge companion to Jung
P. Young-Eisendrath and T. Dawson, eds   Cambridge University Press, 1997, 332pp. £15.99. ISBN 9780521478892.
Designed to be a critical introduction to Jung's work. The book commences with a chronology of Jung's life and work. Essays by renowned contributors present Jung's ideas and how they have influenced psychotherapy as well as other areas such as literature and religion. Includes a glossary of terms and references for further reading.

218   Freud and the post-Freudians
J.A.C. Brown   new edn, Free Association Books, 2004, 228pp. £18.95. ISBN 9781853437687.
Classic work, explains the basic concepts of Freudian theory and reviews the theories of the early schismatics Jung, Adler, Rank and Stekel. The British schools are also reviewed, including Rivers, Klein and Fairbairn and whole chapters are dedicated to Karen Horney, Erich Fromm and Harry Stack Sullivan.
Originally published in 1961

219   Introducing psychoanalysis: essential themes and topics
S. Budd and R. Rusbridger, eds   Routledge, 2005, 265pp. £18.99. ISBN 9781583918883.
Based on lectures given at the British Psychoanalytic Society. Provides an explanation of psychoanalysis and covers a variety of concepts such as symbolism and dreams and the Oedipus complex.

220   Psychoanalytic theory: an introduction
A. Elliott   2nd edn, Palgrave, 2002, 196pp. £19.99. ISBN 9780333919125.
A good overview of psychoanalytic theory and its social science applications. Coverage includes Freudian theory, American ego-psychology and self-psychology, British object–relations theory, French Lacanian theory, Kleinian theory and feminist and postmodern psychoanalysis. Includes useful suggestions for further reading.

Dictionaries, thesauri, classifications

221   A critical dictionary of psychoanalysis
C. Rycroft   2nd edn, Penguin, 1995, 214pp. £9.99. ISBN 9780140513103.
The volume places greater emphasis on terms used in Freudian psychoanalysis as opposed to other schools. Gives clear definitions and is extensively cross-referenced.

222   International dictionary of psychoanalysis (Dictionnaire international de la psychanalyse)
A. de Mijolla, ed.   Macmillan Reference, 2005, 1600pp. 3 v, $415. ISBN 9780028659244.
Encyclopaedic volume covering all branches of psychoanalysis. Entries include theoretical and clinical concepts, biographies of psychoanalysts worldwide, institutions and individual works. They are signed and many have bibliographies. Volume 1 includes a thematic outline and chronology.
Enhanced version of the 2002 French edition.

223   The language of psychoanalysis (Vocabulaire de la psychoanalyse)
J. Laplanche and J.-B. Pontalis   new edn, Karnac Books, 1988, 525pp. £29.99. ISBN 9780946439492.
Each entry consists of a definition followed by a longer explanation of the concept with references to the standard edition of Freud's works. The German, Spanish, French, Italian and Portuguese equivalents of each term are given.
Originally published by Hogarth Press, 1973; original French version published in 1967.

Associations & societies

224 American Psychoanalytic Association
www.apsa.org
The American Psychoanalytic Association (APsaA), was founded in 1911. APsaA, as a professional organization for psychoanalysts, focuses on education, research and membership development. The website includes links to organizations, a membership directory and the quarterly publication, the *American Psychoanalyst*.

225 British Psychoanalytical Society
www.psychoanalysis.org.uk
Originally established in 1913 as the London Psychoanalytical Society and renamed in 1919. The Society aims to develop its position 'as the leading centre of excellence in the UK in the provision of psychoanalytic training, education, publication and clinical practice and to develop a professional organization for the furthering of psychoanalysis through diversity and debate.'
 ■ **Institute of Psychoanalysis** Founded in 1924 to administer the activities of the British Psychoanalytical Association: training, publishing, public lectures.

226 International Psychoanalytical Association
www.ipa.org.uk
The IPA is the world's primary accrediting and regulatory body for psychoanalysis. The website links to constituent organizations throughout the world. Also has information about events, books and an electronic newsletter.

227 New York Freudian Society
http://nyfreudian.org
The New York Freudian Society and Psychoanalytic Training Institute were founded in 1959 to provide training and a collegial community for psychoanalysts from many disciplines. The website includes the abstracts of the standard edition of the works of Sigmund Freud.

Libraries, archives, museums

228 British Psychoanalytical Society Library
www.psychoanalysis.org.uk/library.htm
The library holds nearly 22,000 volumes from the mid–19th century to the present. Includes an extensive and valuable collection of works published in the UK, related foreign materials, donations of the private collections of many leading psychoanalysts, notably Ernest Jones, James Strachey and Donald Winnicott, roughly 1600 catalogued monographs and nearly 300 serial titles – 50 of which are active. It also houses unpublished material associated with the British Psychoanalytical Society.
 ■ **British Psychoanalytical Society Archives**
www.psychoanalysis.org.uk/archives.htm. Contains an important collection on the history of psychoanalysis, including the papers of a number of noted psychoanalysts which include manuscripts, correspondence, diaries and personal/biographical material.

229 Freud Museum, London
www.freud.org.uk
The Freud Museum in Hampstead, London, was the home of Sigmund Freud and his family when they escaped from the Nazi annexation of Austria in 1938. It remained the family home until Anna Freud, the youngest daughter, died in 1982.

The centrepiece of the museum is Freud's library and study, preserved just as it was during his lifetime. The website has information about the collections, about Freud and his writings, links to useful websites and the programme of events at the Museum.

230 Sigmund Freud archives
www.freudarchives.org
An independent organization founded in 1951. 'It is dedicated to collecting, conserving, collating and making available for scholarly use all of Sigmund Freud's psychoanalytic and personal papers, his correspondence, photos, records, memorabilia, etc.' The documents are preserved in the Freud Collection at the Library of Congress.

Discovering print & electronic resources

231 Psychoanalytic Electronic Publishing (PEP)
www.p-e-p.org
The free PEP Psychoanalytic Literature Search allows users to search the psychoanalytic literature in English from 1920 to 2006 and view abstracts. Subscribers can access the full-text archive (1886–2003), which includes both books and journals, including the complete psychological works of Sigmund Freud.

Directories & encyclopedias

232 Edinburgh international encyclopedia of psychoanalysis
R.M. Skelton, ed. Edinburgh University Press, 2006, 518pp. £115. ISBN 9780748612659.
Broad coverage, including entries for many psychoanalysts and other thinkers, the development of psychoanalysis in other countries throughout the world and topics such as art and anthropology where they relate to psychoanalysis. Most entries include references for further reading.

233 Freud encyclopedia: theory, therapy and culture
E. Erwin, ed. Routledge, 2002, 641pp. £150. ISBN 9780415936774.
Substantial articles on Freud and his influence in areas such as art and literature. Also includes articles about individuals whom Freud knew personally such as Carl Jung, Sandor Ferenczi and Melanie Klein. Includes critiques of Freudian theories.

Handbooks & manuals

234 The concordance to the standard edition of the complete psychological works of Sigmund Freud
S.A. Guttman, R.L. Jones and S.M. Parrish, eds G.K. Hall, 1980, 5950pp. 6 v, o/p. ISBN 081618383X.
Alphabetical listing of all words in the standard edition of Freud's works with the context and reference to the volumes and pages where they occur. Approximately 100 words, such as 'the', found frequently in the English language were omitted.

235 The handbook of Jungian psychology: theory, practice and applications
R.K. Papadopoulos, ed.   Routledge, 2006, 394pp. £19.99. ISBN 9781583911480.
Arranged in three parts: theory, psychotherapy and applications. Each chapter clearly introduces the topic, such as psychological types or dreams, considers later developments and concludes with a useful bibliography. Renowned contributors.

Research Methods in Psychology

behavioural research • experimental psychology • methodology • psychological research • qualitative methods • statistical methods

Introductions to the subject

236 Experimental methodology
L.B. Christensen   10th international edn, Pearson/Allyn & Bacon, 2006, 528pp. £38.99. ISBN 9780205504671.
Detailed coverage of experimental research, but the volume also includes a chapter on non-experimental approaches. Each chapter concludes with a summary, a list of the key terms and concepts, related internet sites, a practice test and exercises.

237 Introduction to research methods in psychology
D. Howitt and D. Cramer   Pearson/Prentice Hall, 2005, 372pp. £27.99. ISBN 9780131399846.
Covers both quantitative and qualitative methods. Can be used alone or with the two companion volumes.
■ **Introduction to SPSS in psychology: with supplements for releases 10, 11, 12 and 13** D. Howitt and D. Cramer   3rd edn, Pearson/Prentice Hall, 2005, 237pp. £25.99. ISBN 9780131399860. Clearly explained with screenshots of each step.
■ **Introduction to statistics in psychology** 3rd edn, Pearson/Prentice Hall, 2005, 516pp. £26.99. ISBN 9780131399853. Covers a wide range of statistical techniques from descriptive statistics through to advanced techniques such as multiple regression. Clearly laid out with step-by-step explanations.

238 Methods in behavioral research
P.C. Cozby   9th international edn, McGraw-Hill Higher Education, 2006, 410pp. £34.99. ISBN 9780071106436.
Includes information about starting research, ethics, observational methods, experiments, surveys, understanding research results, statistics and writing research reports. Each chapter includes study terms and questions.
■ **Methods in behavioral research**
http://methods.fullerton.edu/noframesindex.html [COMPANION]. Useful web-links for each chapter in the 8th edition.

239 Qualitative research in psychology: expanding perspectives in methodology and design
P.M. Camic, J.E. Rhodes and L. Yardley   American Psychological Association, 2003, 315pp. $49.95. ISBN 9781557989796.
The volume commences with chapters on epistemological issues and continues with chapters on specific qualitative methods, including discourse analysis, narrative psychology, video methods, participatory action research and ethnographic methods.

240 Research methods and statistics in psychology
H. Coolican   4th edn, Hodder & Stoughton, 2004, 711pp. £21.99. ISBN 9780340812587.
An excellent introduction to all key areas. Covers experiments, observation, interview methods, questionnaires, qualitative methods, statistical analysis, ethical issues and report writing. Clear and comprehensive.

241 Research methods in psychology
G.M. Breakwell [et al.]   3rd edn, Sage Publications, 2006, 524pp. £22.99. ISBN 9781412911283.
Very good introduction covering both quantitative and qualitative research methods and covers the research process from research design through to data analysis. Gives useful suggestions for further reading.

Dictionaries, thesauri, classifications

242 A dictionary of statistics for psychologists
B.S. Everitt and T. Wykes   Arnold, 1999, 188pp. £15.99. ISBN 9780340719985.
Provides definitions for over 1500 statistical terms used in psychology. Useful for students. Gives clear explanations, numerical examples and graphical material.

Associations & societies

243 Experimental Psychology Society
www.eps.ac.uk
Established in 1946, the EPS aims to further scientific enquiry in psychology. The society holds regular meetings, symposia and workshops and the *Quarterly Journal of Experimental Psychology* is published on behalf of the society.

Portal & task environments

244 Internet psychologist
A. Trapp, comp.
www.vts.intute.ac.uk/he/tutorial/psychologist
A free interactive online tutorial from the Intute virtual training suite to guide the user towards useful websites and online information skills for psychology.

Directories & encyclopedias

245 Encyclopedia of statistics in behavioral science
B.S. Everitt and D.C. Howell, eds   Wiley, 2005, 2352pp. 4 v, $1755. ISBN 9780470860809.
Expensive. Covers statistical methods in all areas of behavioural science, including neuroscience, behavioural genetics and cognitive science. Covers statistical methods such as factor analysis, structural equation modelling, multivariate methods, nonparametric methods etc. Also covers the design of experiments and surveys. Articles are written by an international team of expert contributors, arranged alphabetically with references and extensive cross-references.

Handbooks & manuals

246   Handbook of research methods in experimental psychology
S.F. Davis, ed.   Blackwell, 2005, 507pp. £25.99. ISBN 9781405132800.
Three parts cover historical roots, research designs and issues such as ethics and cross-cultural research and research in selected areas: comparative psychology, animals, sensation and perception, taste, olfaction, physiological psychology, memory, cognition, motivation, audition and psychophysics.
Originally published in 2003.

247   Library use: handbook for psychology
J.G. Reed and P.M. Baxter   3rd edn, American Psychological Association, 2003, 170pp. $16.95. ISBN 9781557989925.
Guides users through the research process from defining the topic through using library catalogues and online databases and locating US government documents and finding tests and measurements.

248   The psychologist's companion: a guide to scientific writing for students and researchers
R.J. Sternberg   4th edn, Cambridge University Press, 2003, 301pp. £19.99. ISBN 9780521528061.
Covers key topics for students and researchers: steps in writing papers, APA guidelines, data presentation, submitting the paper to a journal, etc. Appendices include a sample psychology paper and writing for British and European journals.

249   The psychology research handbook: a guide for graduate students and research assistants
F.T.L. Leong and J.T. Austin, eds   2nd edn, Sage Publications, 2005, 528pp. $57.95. ISBN 9780761930228.
An edited collection of 33 chapters outlining the research process from the planning stage through data collection and analysis to writing the report. Comprehensive and detailed, with additional chapters on special topics such as cross-cultural research.

250   Publication manual of the American Psychological Association
American Psychological Association   5th edn, American Psychological Association, 2001, 467pp. $27.95. ISBN 9781557987907.
The style manual for publishing papers in the majority of psychology journals. Gives detailed guidance on all aspects of presenting an article, such as how to cite references, including electronic sources, construct tables and present case studies.

251   Statistical methods for psychology
D.C. Howell   6th international edn, Thomson/Wadsworth, 2006, 760pp. £34.99. ISBN 9780495093619.
Advanced coverage, including statistics and probability, correlation and regression, analysis of variance and a range of statistical tests used in psychological research. Each chapter includes key terms and exercises.

252   Stevens' handbook of experimental psychology
H. Pashler, ed.   3rd edn, Wiley, 2004, 3288pp. 4 v, $450. ISBN 9780471650201.
The classic work in experimental psychology. Comprehensive

coverage, including recent research in areas such as neuroscience.
- V.1. Sensation and perception ISBN 9780471650140
- V.2. Memory and cognitive processes ISBN 9780471650157
- V.3. Learning, motivation and emotion ISBN 9780471650164
- V.4. Methodology in experimental psychology ISBN 9780471650171

Volumes also available separately: $105.50 each. Revised edition of 'Handbook of experimental psychology', edited by S. S. Stevens; first published in 1951. This edition first published in 2002.

Psychological Testing & Assessment

assessment at work • assessment of children • attitude measures • behavioural assessment • clinical measures • family measures • gender measures • health measures • mental measures • neuropsychological testing • personality assessment • psychiatric assessment

Introductions to the subject

253   Psychological testing: an introduction
G. Domino and M.L. Domino   2nd edn, Cambridge University Press, 2006, 640pp. £45. ISBN 9780521861816.
Sections cover basic issues such as test construction and reliability and validity; dimensions such as personality, cognition, attitudes and psychopathology; applications, including special children, the elderly and cross-cultural aspects; testing in schools, occupational and clinical and forensic settings; and other factors such as faking and the role of computers. A useful introductory text.

254   Psychological testing and assessment
L.R. Aiken and G. Groth-Marnat   12th edn, Pearson/Allyn & Bacon, 2006, 535pp. £72.99. ISBN 9780205457427.
This latest edition covers ethical and professional matters, test design, intelligence testing, neuropsychological assessment, ability testing, vocational testing, attitude testing, assessment of personality, observations and interviews, checklists and rating scales and projective techniques. Appendices cover statistical concerns, major test suppliers in the USA, websites of relevant organizations and a glossary of terms.

255   Psychological testing and assessment: an introduction to tests and measures
R.J. Cohen and M.E. Swerdlik   6th edn, McGraw-Hill, 2005, 654pp. £37.99. ISBN 9780071112604.
A comprehensive introduction to all aspects of testing and assessment. Includes historical, cultural and ethical aspects, statistical basis, intelligence, educational, personality, clinical and counselling and neuropsychological testing, career assessment and the assessment of people with disabilities. The index doubles up as a glossary.

Dictionaries, thesauri, classifications

256   Dictionary of psychological testing, assessment and treatment
I. Stuart-Hamilton   2nd edn, Jessica Kingsley, 2007. £15.99. ISBN 9781843104940.
Over 3000 definitions on statistical procedures, psychometric and other tests, categories of mental illness, mental disabilities, brain damage, etc.

Laws, standards, codes

257   The standards for educational and psychological testing [USA]
American Educational Research Association, American Psychological Association and National Council on Measurement in Education   rev. edn, American Educational Research Association, 1999, 194pp. $49.95. ISBN 9780935302257.
The purpose is to provide criteria for the evaluation of tests, testing practices and the effects of test use. Sections cover test construction, fairness in testing and testing applications. Issues covered include testing individuals with disabilities or from different linguistic backgrounds.

Associations & societies

258   International Test Commission
www.intestcom.org
'An association of national psychological associations, test commissions, publishers and other organizations committed to promoting effective testing and assessment policies and to the proper development, evaluation and uses of educational and psychological instruments.' The *International Journal of Testing* is the commission's official journal. Back copies of the ITC newsletter, *Testing International*, are available online. The site also has guidelines on adapting tests, test use and computer-based and internet testing.

Portal & task environments

259   Assessment psychology
www.assessmentpsychology.com
Links to many resources related to psychological assessment: test publishers, personality, intelligence, disability issues, professional associations and standards and codes. There are links to scales in the public domain, information about books and software and links to major resources such as the ETS test collection and Buros test reviews online.

Discovering print & electronic resources

260   ETS test collection
www.ets.org
'The Test Collection at ETS is a library of more than 25,000 tests and other measurement devices that makes information on standardized tests and research instruments available to researchers, graduate students and teachers. Collected from the early 1900s to the present, the Test Collection at ETS is the largest such compilation in the world. The tests in this collection were acquired from a variety of US publishers and individual test authors. Foreign tests are also included in the collection, including some from Canada, Great Britain and Australia.' To search the collection, click on 'Site Map' at the bottom of the page and then scroll down to 'Test Link'.

261   Health and Psychosocial Instruments (HaPI)
Behavioral Measurement Database Services (BMDS).
www.ovid.com/site/catalog/DataBase/866.pdf [DESCRIPTION]
Features material on unpublished tests, scales and questionnaires. Includes citations to the actual tests which can be ordered through the BMDS Instrument Delivery Service, citations to journal articles which contain information about specific tests and a catalogue of commercial test publishers and their instruments. The instruments are for use in the disciplines of medicine, psychology, social work, occupational therapy, physical therapy and speech and hearing therapy. Coverage is from 1985 onwards.

Directories & encyclopedias

262   Buros Institute of Mental Measures
www.unl.edu/buros
A very useful site for finding information about published tests. The 'Test reviews online' section can be searched free of charge alphabetically, by keyword or by category. Provides information about the publisher and in which volume of the *Mental measurements yearbook* a review can be found. It is possible to purchase some reviews online for $15.00.

263   Commissioned reviews of 250 psychological tests
J. Maltby, C.A. Lewis and A. Hill, eds   Edwin Mellen Press, 2000. 2 v, $129.95 each.
Gives an overview of 250 psychological tests developed during the 1990s. Covers health psychology, social psychology, personality and individual differences, developmental, occupational, educational and cognitive psychology. Each entry describes the test and provides information about its reliability and validity, where it is located and an evaluation.
- V. 1 ISBN 9780773474529
- V. 2 ISBN 9780773474543

264   A compendium of neuropsychological tests: administration, norms and commentary
E. Strauss, E.M.S. Sherman and O. Spreen   3rd edn, Oxford University Press, 2006, 1216pp. £60. ISBN 9780195159578.
Provides a comprehensive review of major neuropsychological assessment tools. Includes tests of general cognitive functioning, achievement, executive functions, attention, memory, language, visual perception, somatosensory function, olfactory function and body orientation, motor function, mood, personality and adaptive functions. Gives detailed information about each scale covered: purpose, source, administration, scoring, demographic effects, normative data, reliability and validity and a substantial list of references. Sample items are included for some.

265   Dictionary of behavioral assessment techniques
M. Hersen and A.S. Bellack, eds   Pergamon Press, 1988, 590pp. £35. ISBN 9780080319759.
An A–Z listing of about 300 measures covering a wide range

of psychological problems. Each entry includes a description and information about the scale's purpose and development, psychometric characteristics and clinical use. The 'Sources of Entries' section gives the address or journal reference for obtaining each test.

266   Directory of unpublished experimental mental measures
B.A. Goldman [et al.], eds   American Psychological Association, 1995–2007. 9 v. (published in 6 v.), $49.95 each.
Lists non-commercial tests and scales which have been developed or used in a number of psychology journals between 1970 and 2005. References to the journals are given, but the scale is not always reproduced in the article. The most recent volume has cumulative author and subject indexes.
- V.1–3: ISBN 9781557983367
- V.4–5: ISBN 9781557983510
- V.6: ISBN 9781557982896
- V.7: ISBN 9781557984494
- V.8: ISBN 9781557989512
- V.9: ISBN 9781433801372

V.1–4 originally published separately by Human Sciences Press, 1974–1985

- **Title index for the Directory of unpublished experimental mental measures: Volumes 1–7 M. Jamison** Association of College and Research Libraries, 2001, 112pp. $17.50. ISBN 9780838981740.

267   Encyclopedia of psychological assessment
R. Fernández-Ballesteros, ed.   Sage Publications, 2003, 1190pp. 2 v, £395. ISBN 9780761954941.
Alphabetical arrangement of 235 articles. Each entry includes an overview of the concept, a section on relevant measures, references and a list of related entries. A 'Reader's guide' groups the entries into nine categories such as methodology, personality, intelligence, clinical and health, educational, work, neurophysiopsychological and environmental assessment.

268   The experience of work: a compendium and review of 249 measures and their use
J.D. Cook [et al.]   Academic Press, 1981, 335pp. o/p. ISBN 0121870502.
Although over 25 years old, this volume continues to be useful as it includes information about 249 work-related scales, many of which are reproduced in full. Areas covered include work satisfaction, job perceptions, job involvement and motivation and leadership. An index of scales and sub-scales facilitates finding relevant measures.

269   Gender roles: a handbook of tests and measures
C.A. Beere   Greenwood Press, 1990, 575pp. $132.95. ISBN 9780313262784.
Describes measures relating to gender roles and attitudes, including adults' and children's gender roles, gender stereotypes, marital roles, parental roles, employee roles and multiple roles. Each measure is described, with information about its development and from where it can be obtained. Includes references to research in which the scale has been used. There are author, title, variable and scale user indexes.

270   Measures for psychological assessment: a guide to 3000 original sources and their applications
K.-T. Chun, S. Cobb and J.R.P. French   Survey Research Center, Institute for Social Research, 1975, 664pp. o/p. ISBN 0879441682.
Entries in this volume are the result of searching 26 measurement-related psychology journals from 1960 to 1970. Consists of two major sections: Primary References lists approximately 3000 references to journal articles in which the measures were first described; the Application section provides information about instances in which the measures have been used. There are also author and descriptor indexes.

271   The mental measurements yearbook
R.A. Spies and B.S. Plake, eds   16th edn, Buros Institute of Mental Measurements, 2005, 1280pp. $195. ISBN 9780910674584.
Comprehensive directory of commercially available English-language standardized tests. Alphabetical arrangement by title, each entry providing descriptive and availability information and usually one or more reviews. Volumes are published every two years and are not cumulative. Volumes 9–16 are also available online by subscription. An index of the tests reviewed in all the *Mental measurements yearbooks* is available at the Buros Institute of Mental Measurements website: www.unl.edu/buros/ (see separate entry).

272   Psychiatric instruments and rating scales: a select bibliography
Royal College of Psychiatrists   2nd edn, Royal College of Psychiatrists, 1994, 109pp. Occasional paper OP23, o/p.
A list of psychiatric scales grouped by type of disorder such as affective disorders, eating disorders, neuroses, personality disorders etc. Reference is given to where each scale can be located. Includes author and keyword indexes and an alphabetical list of scales and their acronyms.

273   Test critiques
D.J. Keyser, ed.   Pro-ed, 2005, 615pp. V. XI, $95. ISBN 9780890799260 ISSN 15539121.
After a break of 11 years, volume XI in this series reviews 43 widely used psychological tests such as the Beck Depression Inventory-II and the Coopersmith Self-Esteem Inventory. For each scale, detailed information is provided, including its uses and practical applications, guidelines for administration and scoring, reliability and validity, a critique and references for further reading. There is an index of test titles in all 11 volumes of the series, an index of test publishers, index of test authors and reviewers and a subject index.
V.I–X: 1984–1994: edited by D.J. Keyser and R.C. Sweetland.

274   Tests: a comprehensive reference for assessment in psychology, education and business
T. Maddox, ed.   5th edn, Pro-Ed, 2003, 581pp. $80. ISBN 9780890799086.
Contains information on over 3000 tests in psychology, education and business. Within each area tests are grouped by subject such as intelligence or neuropsychology. Each test is concisely described with information about its purpose, cost and availability but not evaluated. Includes indexes of publishers with web addresses, authors and test titles.

275   Tests and measures in the social sciences: tests available in compilation volumes
H. Hough, comp.
http://libraries.uta.edu/helen/test&meas/testmainframe.htm
An outstanding resource, compiled by Helen Hough, Health Sciences Librarian at the University of Texas, of some 10,800 tests and measures which can be found in 121 volumes. Coverage includes psychiatric measures, health scales, measures for nursing, alcoholism and marketing scales.

276   Tests in print, VII: an index to tests, test reviews, and the literature on specific tests
L.L. Murphy, R.A. Spies and B.S. Plake, eds   Buros Institute of Mental Measurements, 2006, 1196pp. $325. ISBN 9780910674591.
Lists all commercially published tests in print at the time of publication in A–Z order. Descriptive listings include information on each test's purpose, target population, scoring and pricing. There are indexes of publishers, acronyms, subjects and out-of-print tests. Also refers to reviews in the *Mental measurements yearbooks*.

Handbooks & manuals

277   Comprehensive handbook of psychological assessment
M. Hersen [et al.], eds   Wiley, 2003, 2400pp. 4 v, $700. ISBN 9780471416104.
This set provides thorough coverage of tests and measures available in the four areas covered by the volumes. Issues covered include psychometrics, clinical applications, ethical issues and use with special populations.
Volumes also available separately: $175.00 each.
- **1. Intellectual and neuropsychological assessment** ISBN 9780471416111.
- **2. Personality assessment** ISBN 9780471416128.
- **3. Behavioral assessment** ISBN 9780471416135.
- **4. Industrial and organizational assessment** ISBN 9780471416142.

278   Handbook of family measurement techniques
B.F. Perlmutter, J. Touliatos and G.W. Holden, eds   Sage Publications, 2001, 1264pp. 3 v, $578. ISBN 9780803972506.
Volumes 1 and 2 contain abstracts of instruments in areas such as family relations, parent–child relations and family adjustment, while volume 3 contains 168 of these scales reproduced in full with scoring instructions. Subject, author and title indexes facilitate finding relevant scales.

279   Handbook of psychiatric measures
American Psychiatric Association: Task Force for the Handbook of Psychiatric Measures   American Psychiatric Association, 2000, 820pp. $175. ISBN 9780890424155.
A compendium of rating scales, tests and measures for use with patients with mental illnesses. Includes the full range of psychiatric measures, including scales for children and adolescents, mood disorders, personality disorders and eating disorders etc. A description is given of each test with information about its clinical utility, psychometric properties and references for further reading.
The accompanying CD-ROM contains the full text of the handbook and 108 of the measures in full.

280   Handbook of psychological and educational assessment of children
C.R. Reynolds and R.W. Kamphaus, eds   2nd edn, Guilford Press, 2003. 2 v, $135.
Two-volume handbook providing excellent coverage of the assessment of children and adolescents in diverse areas. 'Intelligence, aptitude and achievement' covers the assessment of intelligence and learning styles, academic skills, ethical issues and special topics. 'Personality, behavior and context' deals with projective techniques, interviewing and observational methods, specific syndromes, objective methods, assessing adaptive skills and the family context.
Intelligence, aptitude, and achievement: 718pp, $85.00. ISBN 9781572308831
- Personality, behavior, and context: 539pp, $75.00. ISBN 9781572308848

281   Handbook of psychological assessment
G. Groth-Marnat   4th edn, Wiley, 2003, 824pp. $110. ISBN 9780471419792.
Provides a step-by-step guide to carrying out a psychological assessment, from the initial assessment interview to the psychological report. The volume reviews some of the most frequently used assessment instruments such as the Minnesota multiphasic personality inventory and the California psychological inventory. The Rorschach and Thematic Apperception Test are also included. A very useful handbook.

282   Measures for clinical practice and research
K. Corcoran and J. Fischer   4th edn, Oxford University Press, 2007, 1640pp. 2 v, £60. ISBN 9780195314908.
An excellent resource: these two volumes contain hundreds of scales in full with information for each about its purpose, a description, norms, scoring, reliability, validity, the primary reference and availability for use. Separate sections cover couples, families, children and adults and the arrangement within each section is alphabetical. Scales are also listed under the type of problem area, which includes areas such as anger and hostility, coping, eating problems, loss of control, stress, etc.
- V. 1. Couples, families and children: £29.99. ISBN 9780195181906
- V. 2. Adults: £35.99. ISBN 978019518193

283   Measures of personality and social psychological attitudes
J.P. Robinson, P.R. Shaver and L.S. Wrightsman, eds   Academic Press, 1991, 765pp. £57.95. ISBN 9780125902441.
Provides a guide to some of the most useful social measures in areas such as subjective well-being, self-esteem, social anxiety and shyness, depression and loneliness, locus of control, sex roles and values. A description of each scale is given with information about reliability and validity and where the scale can be found. In some cases the whole questionnaire is reproduced in the volume.

284   Measuring health: a guide to rating scales and questionnaires
I. McDowell   3rd edn, Oxford University Press, 2006, 748pp. £43. ISBN 9780195165678.
Provides detailed information about over 100 health measures in the areas of physical disability, social adjustment, psychological well-being, anxiety, depression,

mental status, pain and quality of life. Some complete scales are included.

285   Sourcebook of adult assessment strategies
N.S. Schutte and J.M. Malouff   Plenum Press, 1995, 482pp. £80.50. ISBN 9780306450297.
Presents a selection of scales used to assess mental disorders in areas such as delirium and dementia, schizophrenia, substance, mood, anxiety, eating and sleep disorders. For each measure the full questionnaire is included with information about the purpose and use, administration and scoring, reliability and validity and related references.

Biological Psychology

animal behaviour • behavioural biology • biopsychology • brain • cognition • cognitive neuroscience • evolutionary psychology • neuropsychology • neuroscience • perception • physiological psychology • psychopharmacology • sensation

Introductions to the subject

286   Biological psychology: an introduction to behavioral, cognitive and clinical neuroscience
M.R. Rosenzweig, S.M. Breedlove and N.V. Watson   5th edn, Sinauer Associates, 2007, 622pp. $114.95. ISBN 9780878937059.
www.biopsychology.com/5e/lbp5e/home/home.html [COMPANION]
Updated edition of popular student text providing broad coverage of biological aspects of behaviour. Sections cover biological foundations of behaviour, evolution and the development of the nervous system, perception and action, regulation and behaviour, emotions and mental disorders and cognitive neuroscience. Includes numerous illustrations, figures and tables, chapter outlines and summaries and references.
Forthcoming edition: publisher's information.

287   Biopsychology
J.P.J. Pinel   6th edn, Pearson/Allyn & Bacon, 2006, 576pp. $117.60. ISBN 9780205426515.
Good introductory coverage of biological aspects of behaviour, including disorders. Four key themes running through the volume are cognitive neuroscience, thinking critically, clinical implications and the evolutionary perspective.

288   Fundamentals of human neuropsychology
B. Kolb   5th edn, Worth Publishers, 2003, 823pp. $83.40. ISBN 9780716753001.
Thorough coverage of the brain and its relation to behaviour. Sections cover the background to the brain and nervous system, cortical organization, cortical functions, higher functions and plasticity and disorders. Clearly laid out with numerous diagrams and illustrations. Includes a glossary and 'snapshots' which illustrate the text with brief examples from journals.

289   Perspectives on animal behavior
J. Goodenough, B. McGuire and R.A. Wallace   2nd edn, Wiley, 2000, 556pp. $118.95. ISBN 9780471295020.
In three parts: Approaches to the study of animal behaviour, including learning, physiological aspects and behaviour

development; Behaviour of individual surviving in environment, including biological clocks, orientation and sexual selection; and Behaviour of groups, covering cooperation and altruism and communication. Clearly laid out volume with photographs, diagrams and tables.

290   Physiology of behaviour
N.R. Carlson   9th edn, Pearson/Allyn & Bacon, 2006, 752pp. £37.99. ISBN 9780205496921.
http://wps.ablongman.com/ab_physiopsych_studysite_1 [COMPANION]
Good student text covering biology and behaviour. In addition to sections on the nervous system, the volume has chapters on movement, sleep, human reproduction, communication and psychological and neurological disorders. Additional information is available on the companion website.

291   The student's guide to cognitive neuroscience
J. Ward   Psychology Press, 2006, 403pp. £19.95. ISBN 9781841695358.
Introduces the brain and neural structure and function and explains how their methods and procedures can throw light on the neural basis of cognition in areas such as vision, memory, language, numeracy and social and emotional behaviour.

Dictionaries, thesauri, classifications

292   Blackwell dictionary of neuropsychology
J.G. Beaumont, P.M. Kenealy and M.J.C. Rogers, eds   Blackwell, 1999, 816pp. £35. ISBN 9780631214359.
More an encyclopaedia than a dictionary, this volume has extended entries written by an international team of experts covering the whole field of neuropsychology. Some articles include diagrams and many are followed by bibliographies for further reading. Arranged alphabetically with many cross-references.
Originally published in 1996.

293   A dictionary of animal behaviour
D. McFarland   Oxford University Press, 2006, 222pp. £10.99. ISBN 9780198607212.
Covers all aspects of animal behaviour and related ethological and physiological aspects. Illustrated with explanatory diagrams and includes an index of common and Latin animal names.

294   Dictionary of biological psychology
P. Winn, ed.   Routledge, 2001, 857pp. £150. ISBN 9780415136068.
Detailed entries explaining terms across a broad area, including neuroscience, abnormal psychology, biology, psychopharmacology and animal behaviour. The entries are written by experts and many are signed. There are extensive cross-references and some entries include references to further reading.

Official & quasi-official bodies

295   Medical Research Council, MRC Cognition & Brain Sciences Unit
www.mrc-cbu.cam.ac.uk/
The Unit researches fundamental human mental processes such as memory, attention, emotion and communication. Core strengths are theory development, neuropsychology and

more clinically-oriented, interdisciplinary research. The website contains information about the work of the research groups and links to internet sites, including university departments, research institutes and organizations and sites for specific disorders such as schizophrenia.

Research centres & institutes

296 Institute of Cognitive Neuroscience
www.icn.ucl.ac.uk
An interdisciplinary research institute at University College London. 'It studies how mental processes relate to the human brain, in health and disease, for adults and children.' The website has interesting information about research areas such as computational modelling, cross-cultural factors, neuropsychology and psychophysics. There are links to affiliated institutions and press releases.

297 Max Planck Institute for Human Cognitive & Brain Sciences (Max Planck Institut für Kognitions- und Neurowissenchaften)
www.cbs.mpg.de/MPI_Base/NEU
Established in 2004 by a merger between the former Max Planck Institute of Cognitive NeuroScience at Leipzig and the Max Planck Institute for Psychological Research at Munich. Based in Leipzig, the new Institute at present consists of four departments: Neuropsychology, Cognitive neurology, Cognition and action and Neurophysics. A fifth one will be set up in the near future. Research at the Institute addresses human cognitive and cerebral processes, with particular emphasis given to action, language and music.

Associations & societies

298 B.F. Skinner Foundation
www.bfskinner.org
The Foundation was established in 1989 to publish works in the analysis of behaviour. Since then it has extended its operations. The website includes a brief biography of Skinner written by his daughter, a brief survey of operant behaviour and the Foundation's newsletter *Operants*. Registration enables access to the archival section of the site.

299 International Neuropsychological Society
www.the-ins.org
Worldwide organization committed to communication relating to brain-behaviour relationships. The Society's International Liaison Committee (www.ilc-ins.org) publishes the Society's newsletter, links to regional societies worldwide and links to information about journals.

300 Society for Neuroscience
http://web.sfn.org
Formed in 1969, the Society is an organization of scientists and physicians who study the brain and nervous system. Publishes the *Journal of Neuroscience*. The website has information about neuroscience, news items, online articles, historical information, including online classic papers and links to resources. The site also links to the Neuroscience database gateway: http://ndg.sfn.org.

Portal & task environments

301 Neuropsychology central
www.neuropsychologycentral.com
An information resource for human neuropsychology. Links to assessment, forensic and geriatric resources, organizations, journal information, treatment and rehabilitation.

302 Neurosciences on the internet
www.neuroguide.com
A searchable and browsable index of neuroscience resources available on the internet. Includes neurobiology, neurology, neurosurgery, psychiatry, psychology and cognitive science. Maintained by Neil A. Busis at the Division of Neurology at UPMC Shadyside Medical Centre, Pittsburgh, USA. Includes lists of journals with full-text, journals with abstracts and journals with tables of contents. Also includes centres and laboratories worldwide and organizations.

Digital data, image & text collections

303 BBS Prints Archives
www.bbsonline.org
The journal, *Behavioral and Brain Sciences*, publishes interdisciplinary articles in psychology, neuroscience, behavioural biology, cognitive science, artificial intelligence, linguistics and philosophy. The archives contain drafts of articles. The old archive, which requires no registration, covers 1993–2000. To search or browse the current archive free registration is required. The journal is published by Cambridge University Press.

Handbooks & manuals

304 Blackwell handbook of sensation and perception
B. Goldstein, ed. Blackwell, 2004, 788pp. £26.99. ISBN 9780631206842.
Provides scholarly overviews of a wide range of topics in vision, hearing, touch, taste and smell. Includes areas such as the perception of music and art and the development of perceptual systems.
Originally published in 2001 as Blackwell handbook of perception.

305 The cognitive neurosciences
M.S. Gazzaniga [et al.] 3rd edn, MIT Press, 2004, 1399pp. $150. ISBN 9780262072540.
Completely up-dated edition of this outstanding resource which 'continues to chart new directions in the biologic underpinnings of complex cognition'. Sections cover: Evolution and development, Plasticity, Sensory systems, Motor systems, Attention, Memory, Language, Higher cognitive functions, Emotion and social neuroscience, Consciousness and Perspectives and new directions. A worldwide team of specialist contributors.

306 The handbook of cognitive neuropsychology: what deficits reveal about the human mind
B. Rapp, ed. Psychology Press, 2001, 652pp. £22.50. ISBN 9781841690445.
Provides a comprehensive review of the study of deficits in cognition. Covers object recognition, face perception, attention, consciousness, language, memory, time and

action. Expert contributors. Includes a glossary, including neuroanatomical terms and basic brain structure diagrams.

307 **The handbook of evolutionary psychology**
D.M. Buss, ed. Wiley, 2005, 1053pp. £60. ISBN 9780471264033.
In seven parts: Foundations; Survival; Mating; Parenting and kinship; Group living; Evolutionizing traditional disciplines of psychology; Applications to other disciplines. A scholarly volume by expert contributors. Each chapter has extensive references.

Cognitive Psychology & Cognitive Science

applied cognitive psychology • cognition • consciousness • language • memory • memory disorders • perception • thinking & reasoning

Introductions to the subject

308 **Cognitive psychology**
R.L. Solso and O.H. Maclin 7th edn, Pearson/Allyn & Bacon, 2005, 623pp. $111.60. ISBN 9780205410309.
Covers all the main areas of cognitive psychology, including consciousness, cognitive neuroscience and artificial intelligence. Each chapter has a section focusing on the cognitive neuroscience perspective and many have a section on cognition in everyday life. Chapters end with a summary, list of keywords and references.

309 **Cognitive psychology: a student's handbook**
M.W. Eysenck 5th edn, Psychology Press, 2005, 646pp. £27.50. ISBN 9781841693590.
Covers the traditional topics of cognition while including new approaches such as cognitive neuroscience, research on consciousness, cognitive modelling and cognitive neuropsychology. Each chapter includes useful references for further reading.

310 **Cognitive psychology and its implications**
J.R. Anderson 6th edn, Worth Publishers, 2005, 534pp. $59. ISBN 9780716701101.
Covers the key areas of cognition, including cognitive neuroscience and individual differences. The text is accompanied by many tables and figures and the volume includes a glossary of terms.

311 **Foundations of perception**
G. Mather Psychology Press, 2006, 394pp. £24.95. ISBN 9780863778353.
A good introduction to all aspects of sensation and perception. Includes vision, hearing, touch, balance, taste and smell and individual differences. Includes chapter summaries and end-of-chapter tutorials for the study of supplementary material. Clearly laid out with diagrams, tables and illustrations.

312 **An introduction to applied cognitive psychology**
A. Esgate and D. Groome Psychology Press, 2005, 351pp. £16.95. ISBN 9781841693187.
Deals with the application of cognitive psychology to real-life settings such as improving learning effectiveness, improving

the effectiveness of air-traffic controllers and belief in the paranormal.

313 **An introduction to cognitive psychology: processes and disorders**
D. Groome [et al.] 2nd edn, Psychology Press, 2006, 476pp. £16.95. ISBN 9781841695440.
Covers the key areas of cognitive psychology: perception, attention, memory, thinking and language, with chapters on both normal functioning and disorders such as visual agnosia, prosopagnosia and amnesia.

314 **The psychology of language: from data to theory**
T.A. Harley 2nd edn, Psychology Press, 2001, 528pp. £22.50. ISBN 9780863778674.
Provides comprehensive coverage of all areas of psycholinguistics: adult and child language, speech production and comprehension, reading, bilingualism, language and memory.

Dictionaries, thesauri, classifications

315 **Blackwell dictionary of cognitive psychology**
M.W. Eysenck [et al.] Blackwell, 1990, 390pp. £22.99. ISBN 9780631192572.
Alphabetical arrangement of approximately 140 entries covering the key areas of cognitive psychology. Many entries have references for further reading.

316 **Dictionary of cognitive science: neuroscience, psychology, artificial intelligence, linguistics and philosophy (Vocabulaire de sciences cognitives: neurosciences, psychologie, intelligence artificielle, linguistique et philosophie)**
O. Houdé [et al.], eds Psychology Press, 2003, 463pp. £105. ISBN 9781579582517.
Alphabetical arrangement, with each entry broken down into up to five sections depending on which of the constituent areas of cognitive science are applicable. Useful bibliographies are appended to many entries. The dictionary is cross-referenced throughout.
Originally published as Vocabulaire de sciences cognitives: neurosciences, psychologie, intelligence artificielle, linguistique et philosophie: *Presses Universitaires de France, 1998*

Associations & societies

317 **European Society for Cognitive Psychology**
www.escop.org
Society of over 500 members, aiming to further research in cognitive psychology. The Society's official journal is the *European Journal of Cognitive Psychology*. The website has information about the Society's conferences and summer schools and also has the online newsletter. There are a few links to European societies.

Digital data, image & text collections

318 **Online papers on consciousness**
http://consc.net/online.html
Parts 1 and 2 are concerned with philosophical aspects of consciousness, but part 3 includes papers on topics such as

unconscious perception, implicit learning and memory, visual consciousness, attention and consciousness and consciousness in the history of psychology.

Directories & encyclopedias

319 **Encyclopedia of cognitive science**
L. Nadel, ed.   Nature Publishing Group, 2003. 4 v, £675. ISBN 9780333792612.
This comprehensive encyclopedia covers the full range of cognitive science: psychology, philosophy, linguistics, computer science, neuroscience and information processing. The alphabetically arranged volumes include biographies, illustrations, cross-references and indexes. The articles are written at several levels to be suitable for all users.
'...an excellent and stimulating synthesis of a very broad field' (*The Psychologist* January 2004)

320 **Learning and memory**
J.H. Byrne   2nd edn, Macmillan Reference, 2002, 650pp. $177. ISBN 9780028656199.
Overviews all areas of learning and memory. New entries to this edition include autobiographical memory, collective memory, declarative memory, déjà vu and schizophrenia and memory. 212 articles, including 30 biographical entries.
Revised edition of the Encyclopedia of Learning and memory, 1992

321 **The MIT encyclopedia of the cognitive sciences**
R.A. Wilson and F.C. Keil, eds   MIT Press, 1999, 1096pp. $78. ISBN 9780262731447.
The volume begins with introductory essays in the main disciplines of cognitive science: philosophy, psychology, neurosciences, computational intelligence, linguistics and language and culture, cognition and evolution. This is followed by the main body of entries arranged in alphabetical order. The articles are written by experts and include references and further readings.

Handbooks & manuals

322 **Cambridge handbook of thinking and reasoning**
K.J. Holyoak and R.G. Morrison, eds   Cambridge University Press, 2005, 858pp. £35. ISBN 9780521531016.
Sections cover human concepts, reasoning, judgement and decision making, problem solving, constraints on human thought, developmental and cultural aspects and thinking in practice. Chapters are written by experts in cognitive psychology, cognitive science and cognitive neuroscience. Provides scholarly overviews of these areas.

323 **The handbook of cognition**
K. Lamberts and R.L. Goldstone, eds   Sage Publications, 2005, 475pp. $140. ISBN 9780761972778.
Presents a thorough overview of current research in all areas of cognitive psychology. The volume is in six parts: Perception, attention and action; Learning and memory; Language; Reasoning and decision making; Cognitive neuropsychology; and Modelling cognition. Intended for advanced students.

324 **The handbook of memory disorders**
A.D. Baddeley, M.D. Kopelman and B.A. Wison, eds   2nd edn, Wiley, 2002, 865pp. £125. ISBN 9780471498193.

Comprehensive volume by an international team of leading memory researchers. Sections cover the theoretical background such as neurobiological foundations; varieties of memory disorder, including amnesia, neuropsychological impairments and schizophrenia; development and memory, covering from childhood to old age; and assessment and management of memory problems. Each chapter is accompanied by an extensive list of references.

325 **The Oxford handbook of memory**
E. Tulving and F.I.M. Craik, eds   Oxford University Press, 2005, 700pp. £26.99. ISBN 9780195182002.
Comprehensive coverage, including experimental research, memory in everyday life, memory and ageing, neural aspects and theories. 60 renowned contributors. A useful resource.
Originally published in 2000.

Keeping up to date

326 **Trends in cognitive sciences**
Elsevier, 1997–. €188.00 p.a. ISSN 13646613.
'Brings together research in psychology, artificial intelligence, linguistics, philosophy, computer science, anthropology, physiology and neuroscience ... provides an instant overview of current thinking for scientists, students and teachers who want to keep up with the latest developments in cognitive sciences.' Individual topics covered include animal cognition, attention, cognitive development, consciousness, emotion, intelligence, language, memory, sleep, social cognition etc.

Developmental Psychology

adolescent psychology • adult development • ageing • child development • cognitive development • developmental science • lifespan development • moral development • social development

Introductions to the subject

327 **Child development**
L.E. Berk   7th edn, Pearson/Allyn & Bacon, 2006, 784pp. $120. ISBN 9780205509942.
Good coverage of topics: history, research strategies, biological foundations, infancy, cognitive development, intelligence, language development, emotional development, the self, moral development, sex differences, the family and peers. Mainly North American perspective.

328 **Comparing theories of child development**
R.M. Thomas   6th edn, Thomson/Wadsworth, 2005, 576pp. $109.95. ISBN 9780534607173.
www.thomsonedu.com [COMPANION]
Clearly discusses a range of theories, including those of Piaget, Vygotsky, Erikson and Kohlberg, social learning and information processing. The theories are also compared and connections between them pointed out. The companion website links to websites of relevance to each chapter.

329 **The development of children**
M. Cole, S.R. Cole and C. Lightfoot   5th edn, Worth Publishers, 2005, 693pp. $74.20. ISBN 9780716755555.
Updated edition of this renowned text. Covers from before birth to adolescence. Includes cultural and neuroscience

aspects. Illustrated throughout and with many boxes of additional information on topics such as young children as witnesses and obesity.

330   Development through the lifespan
L.E. Berk   4th international edn, Allyn & Bacon, 2006, 816pp. £38.99. ISBN 9780205494842.
http://wps.ablongman.com/ab_berk_lifespan_4 [COMPANION]
Basic but informative text covering from prenatal development through to the end of life. Includes many illustrations, tables, a glossary and numerous references. The companion website includes further resources and links to websites.

331   Developmental psychology: a student's handbook
M. Harris and G. Butterworth   Psychology Press, 2002, 383pp. £17.50. ISBN 9781841691923.
The volume starts by placing developmental psychology in its historical context and then covers the development of the child from conception through to adolescence, looking at cognitive, social and linguistic development at each stage. A useful book for undergraduates with little prior knowledge of the field.

332   Introduction to developmental psychology
A. Slater and G. Bremner, eds   Blackwell, 2003, 583pp. £23.99. ISBN 9780631213963.
A good introduction covering theories and issues, infancy, childhood, adolescence and practical issues such as disorders of development. Includes sections on cognitive, social and emotional development, among others.

333   The psychology of ageing: an introduction
I. Stuart-Hamilton   4th edn, Jessica Kingsley, 2006, 336pp. £19.99. ISBN 9781843104261.
Comprehensive coverage: includes intelligence, memory, language, personality and lifestyle, mental illness and a useful glossary of technical terms.

334   Understanding children's development
P.K. Smith, H. Cowie and M. Blades   4th edn, Blackwell, 2003, 693pp. £24.99. ISBN 9780631228233.
Introduces all aspects of child development. A good student text with discussion points, recommended readings and examples.

Associations & societies

335   European Society for Developmental Psychology
www.esdp.info/Home.83.0.html
'Founded in 1994, aiming to support the interests of developmental psychologists working in Europe.' The European Journal of Developmental Psychology is published on behalf of the society. The website has links to organizations and resources.

336   Jean Piaget Society
www.piaget.org
Created as an information resource for members of the Society, the site includes a brief biography of Piaget, internet links to topics such as genetic epistemology, Vygotsky, associations and societies and references to books and articles about Piaget.

337   Society for Research in Child Development
www.srcd.org
'The Society is a multidisciplinary, not-for-profit, professional association with a membership of approximately 5500 researchers, practitioners and human development professionals from over 50 countries. The purposes of the Society are to promote multidisciplinary research in the field of human development, to foster the exchange of information among scientists and other professionals of various disciplines and to encourage applications of research findings.' Journals published include Child Development and Monographs of the Society for Child Development. The website links to 'Ethical standards for research with children'.

Libraries, archives, museums

338   Les archives Jean Piaget (The Jean Piaget archives)
www.unige.ch/piaget/
Created in 1974 at the University of Geneva. Aims to collect all the writings of Jean Piaget as well as the papers and books inspired by him. The Archives provides a reading room as well as the assistance of several psychologists and a librarian to advise users. The website includes a bibliography of Piaget's works.

Directories & encyclopedias

339   Cambridge encyclopedia of child development
B. Hopkins, ed.   Cambridge University Press, 2005, 684pp. £80. ISBN 9780521651172.
www.cambridge.org/hopkins [COMPANION]
Covers all aspects of child development. Thematically arranged with chapters covering, for example, theories, methods, prenatal development, infancy and childhood, special topics such as attention, handedness, intelligence and sex differences and also problems such as autism and dyslexia. An appendix has biographical sketches of 12 leading figures in child development. Also includes a glossary of terms, an extensive bibliography and comprehensive subject and author indexes.

340   Encyclopedia of applied developmental science
C.B. Fisher and R.M. Lerner, eds   Sage Publications, 2004, 1360pp. 2 v, £432. ISBN 9780761928201.
Interdisciplinary volume of interest to a broad audience. Topics covered include child and adult development, ecology of human development, developmental disorders, families, schools and culture and diversity. A reader's guide organizes the entries into 30 content categories to help the reader locate similar topics. A–Z arrangement of entries.

341   Encyclopedia of human development
N.J. Salkind, ed.   Sage Publications, 2006, 1616pp. 3 v, $495. ISBN 9781412904759.
'Covers topics as diverse as adolescence, cognitive development, education, family, gender differences, identity, longitudinal research, personality development, prenatal development, temperament and more.' Covers the whole of the lifespan. Contributors are experts in the fields of psychology, education, human development and family studies and gerontology.

Handbooks & manuals

342 **Blackwell handbook of adolescence**
G.R. Adams and M.D. Berzonsky, eds   Blackwell, 2005, 648pp.
£27.99. ISBN 9781405133029.
Comprehensive and scholarly coverage of a wide range of topics: biological processes, social processes and personal relationships, cognitive, moral and emotional development, development of the self-concept and problem behaviours such as eating disorders, substance use and depression. Each chapter includes key readings and references.
Originally published in 2003.

343 **Blackwell handbook of childhood cognitive development**
U. Goswami, ed.   Blackwell, 2004, 761pp. £29.99. ISBN 9780631218418.
Arranged in five parts covering infancy, early childhood, childhood, atypical cognitive development and models of cognitive development. Scholarly contributors. A good overview.
Originally published in 2002

344 **Blackwell handbook of childhood social development**
P.K. Smith and C.H. Hart, eds   Blackwell, 2004, 665pp. £25.99. ISBN 9780631217534.
A good introduction covering historical aspects, influences on development such as the family and peers, social skills, play, moral reasoning, aggression and bullying and special needs.
Originally published in 2002

345 **Blackwell handbook of early childhood development**
K. McCartney and D. Phillips, eds   Blackwell, 2005, 678pp. £85. ISBN 9781405120739.
Presents a comprehensive overview of research in child development from age two to seven, covering biological, cognitive, language, social and emotional development. Also considers applications such as poverty and starting school.
Paperback edition forthcoming: 2007, £27.99. ISBN 9781405176613

346 **Blackwell handbook of infant development**
G. Bremner and A. Fogel, eds   Blackwell, 2004, 780pp. £25.99. ISBN 9780631212355.
An excellent and scholarly overview. Four sections covering perception and cognition; social, emotional and communicative development; risk factors in development; and contexts and policy issues. International contributors.
Originally published in 2001

347 **Child psychology: a handbook of contemporary issues**
L. Balter and C.S. Tamis-LeMonda, eds   2nd edn, Psychology Press, 2006, 679pp. £60. ISBN 9781841694153.
The volume is in five parts: infancy, preschool years, childhood, adolescence and ecological influences. Issues covered include early language development, peer relationships, transition into adolescence, family environment, etc. A scholarly resource.

348 **Handbook of adolescent psychology**
R.M. Lerner and L. Steinberg, eds   2nd edn, Wiley, 2004, 863pp. $100. ISBN 9780471209485.
Concerned with all aspects of development during adolescence. The volume is in three main parts: part 1 deals with the foundations of the developmental science of adolescence (puberty, cognitive and brain development, gender, etc.); part 2 looks at social relationships and contexts in adolescence; and part 3 is about adolescent challenges, choice and positive youth development (which includes conduct disorder, substance use and developmental disabilities).

349 **Handbook of adult development**
J. Demick and C. Andreoletti, eds   Springer, 2003, 627pp. £90. ISBN 9780306467585.
Overviews the major areas of adult development: part 1 covers introductory theory and method, including learning and developmental change; part 2 covers biocognitive development issues such as memory changes, wisdom and moral development; while part 3 deals with social development aspects such as attachment and parenthood.

350 **Handbook of child psychology**
W. Damon and R.M. Lerner, eds   6th edn, Wiley, 2006, 4416pp. 4 v, $740. ISBN 9780471272878.
Scholarly volume covering the whole field of child development.
- V.1. Theoretical models of human development ISBN 9780471272885
- V.2. Cognition, perception and language ISBN 9780471272892
- V.3. Social, emotional and personality development ISBN 9780471272908
- V.4. Child psychology in practice ISBN 9780471272915

Volumes also available separately: $185.00 each.

351 **Handbook of developmental psychology**
J. Valsiner and K.J. Connolly   Sage Publications, 2002, 682pp. $130. ISBN 9780761962311.
Comprehensive overview of human development covering the whole lifespan from the prenatal stage to old age. Also includes methodological approaches, both quantitative and qualitative. Chapters are written by an international team of leading developmental psychologists.

352 **Handbook of moral development**
M. Killen and J.G. Smetana, eds   Lawrence Erlbaum Associates, 2006, 790pp. $75. ISBN 9780805861723.
Comprehensive and scholarly. Commences with the structural-developmental approach of Piaget and Kohlberg, followed by sections on aspects such as social domain theory, conscience and internalization, empathy and moral education.

353 **Handbook of research methods in developmental science**
D.M. Teti, ed.   Blackwell, 2006, 565pp. £29.99. ISBN 9781405153959.
Volume in five parts: developmental designs; general issues in developmental measurement; developmental intervention; analytic issues and methods in developmental psychology; new directions in developmental research. The volume is primarily concerned with research methods with children.
First published in 2005

354   Handbook of the psychology of aging
J.E. Birren and K.W. Schaie, eds   6th edn, Elsevier Academic Press, 2006, 564pp. £37.99. ISBN 9780121012656.
Provides a good overview of recent research on the psychology of ageing. The volume is in four parts covering concepts, theory and methods; biological and social influences; behavioural processes; and complex behavioural concepts. These sections include a wide range of topics, including cognitive neuroscience, memory, attitudes towards ageing, personality, wisdom and many more.

355   The science of reading: a handbook
M. Snowling and C. Hulme, eds   Blackwell, 2007, 661pp. £24.99. ISBN 9781405168113.
Broad overview of research in learning to read: word recognition processes, learning to read and spell, reading comprehension, reading in different languages, disorders of reading and spelling, biological bases of reading and teaching reading. Includes a glossary of terms and an extensive list of references.
Originally published in 2005.

Keeping up to date

356   Advances in child development and behavior
Academic Press, 2007, 370pp. No. 35, £57.99. ISBN 9780120097357 ISSN 00652407.
Provides scholarly reviews and articles covering recent advances in research and new points of view. Volume 35 includes articles on episodic and autobiographical memory, working memory and emotional security. The series gives a useful overview of new developments.

Personality & Individual Differences

creativity • intelligence • personality

Introductions to the subject

357   Introduction to personality and intelligence
N. Haslam   Sage Publications, 2007, 336pp. £19.99. ISBN 9780761960584.
A clear basic introduction covering personality, traits, biological, psychoanalytic and cognitive approaches, personality change, assessment and mental disorder as well as a section on intelligence. Has chapter summaries and suggestions for further reading.

358   IQ and human intelligence
N.J. Mackintosh   Oxford University Press, 1998, 419pp. £36.99. ISBN 9780198523673.
Provides an overview of the main areas, 'including the modern development of IQ tests, the heritability of intelligence, theories of intelligence, environmental effects on IQ, factor analysis, relationship of cognitive psychology to measuring IQ and intelligence in the social context.' Scholarly and clear.

359   Personality: theory and research
D. Cervone and L.A. Pervin   10th edn, Wiley, 2007, 645pp. £37.95. ISBN 9780471742418.

Introduces the main approaches to personality: Freudian, Carl Rogers, the trait theories of Allport, Eysenck and Cattell, the five-factor model, biological bases, behaviourism, Kelly's personal construct theory, social-cognitive theory, contextual aspects and assessment.

360   Personality and individual differences
T. Chamorro-Premuzic   BPS Blackwell, 2007, 195pp. £19.99. ISBN 9781405130080.
An excellent new introduction for students, including personality, intelligence, creativity, psychopathology, behaviour genetics, mood and motivation, leadership and vocational interests. The volume is clearly laid out with diagrams, tables and illustrations, key terms, chapter outlines, key readings and a glossary.

361   Perspectives on personality
C.S. Carver and M.F. Scheier   5th international edn, Pearson/Allyn & Bacon, 2004, 639pp. £76.99. ISBN 9780205375769.
Comprehensive coverage of theories of personality, with discussions of relevant research. Includes information about the five-factor model, biological processes, attachment patterns and self-actualization models.

Associations & societies

362   European Association of Personality Psychology
www.eapp.org
The association aims to promote and develop empirical and theoretical personality psychology within Europe and exchange information throughout the world. The official journal is the *European Journal of Personality*. The association runs workshops, conferences and summer schools and publishes scholarly books.

363   International Society for the Study of Individual Differences
http://issid.org
'The aim of the Society is to foster research on individual differences in temperament, intelligence, attitudes and abilities …. The Society produces scientific papers and organizes scientific meetings to discuss and exchange information and ideas relevant to the measurement, structure, dynamics and biological bases of individual differences.' The official journal of the Society is *Personality and Individual Difference*. The website has links to laboratories conducting personality research and to psychological associations.

Portal & task environments

364   Great ideas in personality
www.personalityresearch.org
Links to many useful sites and resources: journals, societies, articles, researchers and online personality tests. Some sections are more up-to-date than others. Broad coverage of personality, including attachment, evolutionary theory and psychoanalysis.

365   Human intelligence
www.indiana.edu/~intell/index.shtml
Includes numerous biographical profiles of influential individuals in the history of intelligence, from Plato through

to Sternberg, including a useful interactive map of these persons in relation to time. Also includes articles on controversies in intelligence such as the Bell Curve and Mozart effect. The section on teaching resources is limited to four syllabi.

366 **The Personality project**
www.personality-project.org
Useful site: includes recommended readings, academic pages, including information about journals, researchers and labs, non-academic pages, organizations and information for students such as US departments of psychology with personality programmes. Some pages have been updated in 2006, others are older but dates when pages were last amended are given.

367 **Personality theories**
http://webspace.ship.edu/cgboer/perscontents.html
An 'electronic textbook' compiled by Dr C. George Boeree of Shippensburg University. The site consists primarily of overviews of about 22 individual theorists, including psychoanalysts such as Freud, Jung and Adler; and others such as Piaget, Skinner, Maslow and Carl Rogers.

Handbooks & manuals

368 **Handbook of creativity**
R.J. Sternberg, ed.   Cambridge University Press, 1999, 502pp. £29.99. ISBN 9780521576048.
Experts have written chapters on a wide range of issues in creativity, including psychometric approaches, experimental studies, cases studies, biological bases, development of creativity, personality, intelligence, motivation and more. Provides good coverage and suitable for a wide readership.

369 **Handbook of intelligence**
R.J. Sternberg   Cambridge University Press, 2000, 677pp. £38. ISBN 9780521596480.
Covers the whole field of intelligence. Includes the nature of intelligence and its measurement, development of intelligence, group differences, biological aspects, information processing, types of intelligence, testing and societal aspects. In addition to human intelligence, there are chapters on animal intelligence and artificial intelligence.

370 **Handbook of understanding and measuring intelligence**
O. Wilhelm and R.W. Engle, eds   Sage Publications, 2004, 552pp. $125. ISBN 9780761928874.
Provides an overview of recent research in intelligence in the fields of methods and cognition. Chapters cover topics such as mental speed, working memory, behavioural genetics, group differences, the g factor, etc. from theoretical and assessment points of view.

Social Psychology
attitudes • cross-cultural psychology • emotions • experimental social psychology • personal relationships • self & identity • women & gender

Introductions to the subject

371 **Cross-cultural psychology: research and applications**
J.W. Berry [et al.]   2nd edn, Cambridge University Press, 2002, 588pp. £27.99. ISBN 9780521646178.
Provides a comprehensive overview of cross-cultural psychology. The volume is in three parts: Similarities and differences in behaviour across cultures considers topics such as personality, cognition, language, etc.; Pursuing relationships between behaviour and culture includes methodological concerns and theoretical issues; and Applying research findings across cultures has chapters on organizations and work and health behaviour. Each chapter includes an outline, summary, key terms and references.

372 **Introduction to social psychology: a European perspective**
W. Hewstone and W. Stroebe, eds   3rd edn, Blackwell, 2001, 752pp. £26.99. ISBN 9780631204374.
Each chapter is authored by a European expert, but the coverage is international. The volume is clearly laid out and makes a good introduction for students. Each chapter has discussion points and references for further reading. Includes the usual range of social-psychological topics with an extra section on health psychology from a social-psychological perspective and social psychology in organizations. Includes a useful glossary.

373 **The social animal**
E. Aronson   9th edn, Worth Publishers, 2003, 431pp. $40.90. ISBN 9780716757153.
Brief introduction to social psychology aimed at students. Covers important research and real-life examples in conformity, mass communication, social cognition, self-justification, human aggression, prejudice and interpersonal sensitivity.
■ **Readings about the social animal E. Aronson, ed.**   9th edn, Worth Publishers, 2004, 532pp. $23.70. ISBN 9780716759669. A collection of classic and contemporary readings to illustrate the main themes of *The social animal*.

374 **Social psychology**
R.A. Baron, D. Byrne and N.R. Branscombe   11th international edn, Pearson/Allyn & Bacon, 2006, 688pp. £40.99. ISBN 9780205450695.
Covers all the main aspects of social psychology. This latest edition has been fully updated to cover new themes, including the interplay between social cognition and social behaviour, social neuroscience, the role of non-conscious processes in social behaviour and the growing attention to social diversity. Includes chapter summaries, key points and references.

375 **Social psychology**
D.G. Myers   8th edn, McGraw-Hill, 2005, 796pp. £33.99. ISBN 9780072977516.
A good basic introduction for students. Divided into four parts covering social thinking, social influence, social

relations and applications. Includes examples of current research. Clearly laid out with illustrations and diagrams, a glossary and comprehensive list of references.

376   Social psychology
M.A. Hogg and G.M. Vaughan   4th edn, Pearson/Prentice Hall, 2005, 770pp. £33.99. ISBN 9781405821551.
An excellent up-to-date introduction, written from a European perspective while including mainstream American social psychology coverage. The volume covers all key topics and is clearly laid out, with coloured illustrations and diagrams. Each chapter begins with key terms and points to be covered and ends with a summary and further reading. A glossary defines key terms.

Dictionaries, thesauri, classifications

377   Dictionary of multicultural psychology: issues, terms and concepts
L.E. Hall   Sage Publications, 2004, 177pp. $37.95. ISBN 9780761928232.
Alphabetical listing of terms and concepts. Each entry consists of a paragraph with references for follow-up reading.

Associations & societies

378   European Association of Experimental Social Psychology
www.eaesp.org
Aims to promote excellence in European social psychology. Associated with the *European Journal of Social Psychology*, the *European Review of Social Psychology*, the *European Bulletin of Social Psychology* and the book series Monographs in European Social Psychology. The website includes information about the Association's activities and links to other societies.

379   International Association for Cross-Cultural Psychology
www.iaccp.org
'The International Association for Cross-Cultural Psychology (IACCP) was founded in 1972 and has a membership of over 800 persons in more than 65 countries. The aims of the Association are to facilitate communication among persons interested in a diverse range of issues involving the intersection of culture and psychology.' The Association holds an international congress every two years and publishes selected papers in a book.

380   International Society for Self & Identity
www.psych.neu.edu/ISSI
An interdisciplinary scholarly association of social and behavioural scientists dedicated to promoting the scientific study of the self. The website has information about what a self is, abstracts of unpublished papers which can be requested or accessed online, links to societies and research resources: online thematic bibliographies and texts.

381   Society for Personality & Social Psychology
www.spsp.org
Organization of personality and social psychologists with membership worldwide. Publishes the journals *Personality and Social Psychology Bulletin, Personality and Social*

Psychology Review and the newsletter *Dialogue*. The website has a students' corner which includes a newsletter, information about teaching and careers resources. There are also links to general resources, including organizations and journals.

382   Society for the Psychological Study of Social Issues
www.spssi.org
'An international group of over 3500 psychologists, allied scientists, students and others who share a common interest in research on the psychological aspects of important social issues. The Society is also Division 14 of the American Psychological Association. The *Journal of Social Issues* is published on behalf of the society and the SPSSI Newsletter is freely available online. The website also has a student page and there are links to social psychology syllabi.

383   Society of Experimental Social Psychology
www.sesp.org
Scientific organization dedicated to the advancement of social psychology with 700 members throughout the world. The society's official journal is the *Journal of Experimental Social Psychology*.

Portal & task environments

384   Social psychology network
www.socialpsychology.org
Maintained by Scott Plous at Wesleyan University, links to over 14,000 psychology resources. Includes links grouped into topics such as social influence and prosocial behaviour, research groups, professional journals and textbooks. In addition, there are links to other areas of psychology such as clinical psychology and history of psychology. An excellent site for psychology generally.

Digital data, image & text collections

385   Online readings in psychology and culture
www.ac.wwu.edu/~culture/readings.htm
From the Center for Cross-Cultural Research at Western Washington University, a compilation of readings on cross-cultural topics, including measuring personality, mental illness and counselling.

Directories & encyclopedias

386   Encyclopedia of multicultural psychology
Y. Jackson, ed.   Sage Publications, 2006, 535pp. $175. ISBN 9781412909488.
Alphabetical arrangement covering entries on racial and ethnic psychology not only from the social-psychological perspective but also from cognitive, environmental, cross-cultural and clinical psychology points of view.

Handbooks & manuals

387 Cambridge handbook of personal relationships
A.L. Vangelisti and D. Perlman, eds   Cambridge University Press,
2006, 891pp. £38. ISBN 9780521533591.
Covers a range of topics, including theoretical and
methodological foundations, relationships across the
lifespan, individual differences, cognition and emotion,
interactive processes, threats to and maintenance of
relationships. Scholarly contributors not just from psychology
but also from sociology, family studies and communication.

388 The handbook of attitudes
D. Albarracín, B.T. Johnson and M.P. Zanna, eds   Lawrence Erlbaum
Associates, 2005, 826pp. $59.95. ISBN 9780805844931.
Scholarly contributors review a range of topics in the areas
of measurement, attitudes and behaviour, beliefs and
attitudes, affect, attitude formation and change and research
in the 21st century.

389 Handbook of emotions
M. Lewis and J.M. Haviland-Jones, eds   2nd edn, Guilford Press,
2004, 736pp. $46. ISBN 9781593850296.
Covers all areas of human emotion: biological,
developmental, social and personality, cognition, health and
also deals with some individual emotions. Contributions by
leading researchers in this area.
Originally published in 2000.

390 Handbook of self and identity
M.R. Leary and J.P. Tangney, eds   Guilford Press, 2005, 703pp. $40.
ISBN 9781593852375.
Volume organized along the lines of five overlapping areas:
content, structure and organization of the self; agency,
regulation and control, which includes self-awareness and
self-efficacy; evaluation, motivation and emotion;
interpersonal aspects of the self, including cultural models;
and phylogenetic and ontological development, including
disturbances in personality disorders. Provides a useful
overview of this growing area.
Originally published in 2003.

391 The handbook of social psychology
D.T. Gilbert, S.T. Fiske and L. Gardner, eds   4th edn, Oxford
University Press, 1998, 1984pp. 2 v, £112.50. ISBN 9780195213768.
First published in 1954, this has since then been the classic
handbook of social psychology. This latest updated edition
has contributions by experts from all areas of the field and
includes new topics such as emotions, self, stigma, memory
and evolution.

392 Handbook of the psychology of women and gender
R.K. Unger, ed.   Wiley, 2004, 556pp. $95. ISBN 9780471653578.
Broad coverage of the topic, including developmental issues,
social roles, gender and health and gender in relation to
aspects such as power.
Originally published in 2001

393 Sage handbook of methods in social psychology
C. Sansone, C.C. Morf and A.T. Panter, eds   Sage Publications, 2004,
528pp. $110. ISBN 9780761925354.
Provides an overview of basic and applied research in social
psychology. Five main sections: introduction, fundamental
issues, design and analysis, interdisciplinary approaches and
applications.

394 The Sage handbook of social psychology
M.A. Hogg and J. Cooper, eds   Sage Publications, 2003, 525pp. £85.
ISBN 9780761966364.
Scholarly resource providing an excellent reference for the
whole field. Five sections cover history and nature of social
psychology, individual processes, interpersonal processes,
processes within groups and intergroup processes and
society. 23 chapters from an international team of experts.
'This volume is everything one would want from a one-volume
handbook of social psychology' (*Choice* April 2004)

Keeping up to date

395 Advances in experimental social psychology
M.P. Zanna, ed.   Academic Press, 2007, 440pp. V. 39, £48.99. ISBN
9780120152391.
Presents scholarly new research, theory and practice in
social psychology. Volume 39 includes contributions on
culture and personal experience and multiple social
categorization. The contents of previous volumes are listed.

396 European Review of Social Psychology
Psychology Press, 2007. V. 18, £123. ISSN 1479277X.
Published under the auspices of the European Association of
Experimental Social Psychology, this is an e-first journal.
Each article is published online shortly after it has been
accepted and a printed volume is produced the following
spring.
V.17. 2007, £65.00 ISBN 9781841698274

Abnormal & Clinical Psychology

**abnormal psychology • autism • behavioural disorders •
clinical psychology • counselling • eating disorders •
mental health • positive psychology • psychiatry •
psychopathology • psychotherapy • research methods**

Introductions to the subject

**397 Abnormal and clinical psychology: an introductory
textbook**
P. Bennett   2nd edn, Open University Press, 2006, 508pp. £26.99.
ISBN 9780335219438.
The first section deals with the background to mental health
problems, while the second section looks at individual
disorders such as schizophrenia, depression and phobias.
Chapters deal with the aetiology and treatment of conditions
which are considered from psychological, social and
biological perspectives. An excellent introductory text.

398 Abnormal psychology
A.M. Kring [et al.]   10th edn, Wiley, 2006, 667pp. $122.95. ISBN
9780471692386.
Updated version of Davison and Neale's excellent student
text covering etiology, descriptions and treatments for
psychopathological disorders, including anxiety, mood,
personality and eating disorders, schizophrenia, stress,
disorders of childhood etc. Clearly laid out with 'clinical case
boxes', 'focus on discovery boxes' and summaries. Includes a
glossary and DSM-IV-TR table.
Previous editions by G.C. Davison and J.M. Neale

399   Introduction to the psychotherapies
S. Bloch, ed.   4th edn, Oxford University Press, 2006, 443pp.
£24.95. ISBN 9780198520924.
Revised edition of successful text, outlining the major
approaches to psychotherapy and has chapters dealing with
specific client groups such as children, the elderly or the
family. The volume outlines the historical background and
ethical aspects.

400   Oxford textbook of psychotherapy
G.O. Gabbard, J.S. Beck and J. Holmes, eds   Oxford University Press,
2005, 534pp. £39.95. ISBN 9780198520641.
An excellent volume, with sections on the major types of
psychotherapy, therapy of specific disorders, psychotherapy
across the life cycle, with specific populations, including
medical patients, gender issues, sexual orientation and
cross-cultural issues and special topics such as ethics.

Dictionaries, thesauri, classifications

401   Campbell's psychiatric dictionary
R.J. Campbell   8th edn, Oxford University Press, 2004, 725pp. £42.
ISBN 9780195152210.
Alphabetical arrangement, with mostly brief entries covering
all areas of psychiatry: includes material on neuroscience,
cognitive psychology, neurodegenerative diseases, DSM-IV-
TR, psychopharmacology, psychoanalysis, psychotherapies,
etc.

402   Dictionary of counselling
C. Feltham and W. Dryden   2nd edn, Whurr, 2004, 267pp. £24.99.
ISBN 9781861563828.
Brief entries defining the key terms and concepts used by
counsellors.

Laws, standards, codes

**403   Diagnostic and statistical manual of mental
disorders: DSM-IV-TR**
American Psychiatric Association   4th edn text rev., 2000, 992pp.
$89. ISBN 9780890423349.
The most widely used diagnostic tool, used worldwide to
diagnose mental illnesses. Each disorder is accompanied by
the diagnostic criteria and descriptive details, including
information such as the prevalence and differential diagnosis.

**404   The ICD-10 classification of mental and
behavioural disorders: clinical descriptions and
diagnostic guidelines**
World Health Organization   WHO, 1992, 362pp. CHF 50. ISBN
9789241544221.
'Provides clinical descriptions, diagnostic guidelines and
codes for all mental and behavioural disorders commonly
encountered in clinical psychiatry. The book was developed
from chapter V of the Tenth Revision of the International
Statistical Classification of Diseases and Related Health
Problems (ICD-10).'
- ICD-10 Online: www.who.int/classifications/icd/en/ 2007
  version: an outline of the classification.

Mental Health Act manual
R. Jones   See entry no. 1188

Official & quasi-official bodies

National Institute for Mental Health in England
See entry no. 1192

405   National Institute of Mental Health [USA]
www.nimh.nih.gov
A government agency for research on mental and behavioural
disorders. The website provides information on a range of
psychological disorders with factsheets and booklets that can
be downloaded and some of which are also available in
Spanish. Also news items are available.

406   United Kingdom Council for Psychotherapy
www.psychotherapy.org.uk
'The UKCP exists to promote and maintain the profession of
psychotherapy and the highest standards in the practice of
psychotherapy throughout the United Kingdom, for the
benefit of the public.' The website includes information for
the public, practitioners, professionals and news. The site
hosts the UKCP register of psychotherapists.

Research centres & institutes

407   Institute of Psychiatry [UK]
www.iop.kcl.ac.uk/iopweb
The Institute of Psychiatry was opened in 1923 and provides
postgraduate education and carries out research in
psychiatry, psychology and allied disciplines, including basic
and clinical neurosciences. In 1997 the Institute became
part of King's College, London. The website includes
information about the specialist academic departments and
also mental health information.

408   National Center for Posttraumatic Stress Disorder
[USA]
www.ncptsd.va.gov/index.html
The National Center for PTSD, although primarily for US
veterans, is an excellent resource for anyone wanting
information on posttraumatic stress. There are sections of
the site for veterans and their families, health and mental
health care providers and researchers. The site has
factsheets, information on assessment measures, links to
web resources such as organizations and a link to the
PILOTS database. A very useful site for information in this
area.
- **PILOTS Database** www.ncptsd.va.gov//publications/pilots/index.html.
  A free searchable index to the world's literature on traumatic stress.

Associations & societies

409   American Psychiatric Association
www.psych.org
'The American Psychiatric Association is an organization of
psychiatrists working together to ensure humane care and
effective treatment for all persons with mental disorders,
including mental retardation and substance-related
disorders.' Over 35,000 US and international members. The
website includes information for both members and the
general public.

410 British Association for Counselling & Psychotherapy
www.bacp.co.uk
Founded in 1977 as the British Association for Counselling, the name was changed to include psychotherapy in 2000 in order to reflect the fact that it represented psychotherapy also. The website has information about the association and its activities, 'find-a-therapist' section and links to organizations both in the UK and abroad.

411 Mental Health Foundation [UK]
www.mentalhealth.org.uk
'Founded in 1949, the Mental Health Foundation is a leading UK charity that provides information, carries out research, campaigns and works to improve services for anyone affected by mental health problems.' The Foundation produces a range of publications, including reports, briefings and information booklets, many of which can be downloaded free of charge from the website.

412 Mind [UK]
www.mind.org.uk/index.htm
The leading mental health charity in England and Wales, Mind works to create a better life for everyone with experience of mental distress by advancing the views, needs and ambitions of people with mental health problems; challenging discrimination and promoting inclusion; influencing policy; and encouraging the development of quality services. The website has factsheets and booklets covering a wide range of mental disorders and other useful information and links to relevant organizations.

413 Royal College of Psychiatrists [UK]
www.rcpsych.ac.uk
The professional and educational body for psychiatrists in the UK and Republic of Ireland. Publishes books, reports and educational material for professionals and the general public. Publishes the journals *British Journal of Psychiatry*, *Psychiatric Bulletin* and *Advances in Psychiatric Treatment*: abstracts are available to all and some articles are available in full. The section of the website for 'mental health information' includes leaflets about a variety of disorders. Web links are available to many organizations. The College has a members' library and the website links to 'Key resources for psychiatric libraries'.

Libraries, archives, museums

414 Institute of Psychiatry, Library
www.iop.kcl.ac.uk/departments/?locator=12
The library is the largest psychiatric library in Western Europe, holding 3000 print journal titles, 550 of which are current subscriptions. The website links to numerous mental health resources and organizations.

415 Tavistock & Portman Centre Library [UK]
www.tavi-port.org/library.html
The library in London was set up in 1946 and covers psychotherapy, psychoanalysis, family therapy, psychiatry, clinical psychology, educational psychology, social work and the study of organizations. Although the library is primarily for members of the Tavistock Centre, as a national mental health resource, external users can use the library for a fee. The website has links to relevant websites in areas such as psychology, psychotherapy and psychoanalysis.

Portal & task environments

416 Internet mental health
www.mentalhealth.com
A free encyclopedia of mental health information created by a Canadian psychiatrist, Dr Phillip Long. The site is intended for professionals, patients, families and students and provides information about the commonest mental disorders. There is a glossary, index, search facility, magazine and internet links.

Discovering print & electronic resources

417 Autism Data
National Autistic Society
www.autism.org.uk/autismdata
Autism Data is a database of published material on autism and Asperger syndrome. It contains over 17,000 published research papers, books, articles, videos and other materials, including all the items in the National Autistic Society Information Centre Library, as well as articles on autism published in other journals. Abstracts are available for each entry. The database is freely available to all.

418 PubMed
www.ncbi.nlm.nih.gov/sites/entrez
Developed by the National Center for Biotechnology Information (NCBI) at the National Library of Medicine (NLM). Provides free access to bibliographic information for records from MEDLINE: citations and abstracts in the fields of medicine, nursing, dentistry, veterinary medicine, health care systems and preclinical sciences.

Digital data, image & text collections

419 Primary sources in counseling and psychology
Alexander Street Press.
http://alexanderstreet.com/products/psyc.htm [DESCRIPTION]
A new resource consisting of transcripts of actual psychotherapy sessions, primary first-person narrative accounts and handbooks and reference works. When complete there will be over 2000 hours of psychotherapy sessions, 40,000 pages of narratives and over 25,000 pages of reference works from Sage. There will be 40 topical subject areas, such as eating disorders and depression.

Directories & encyclopedias

420 Encyclopedia of psychotherapy
M. Hersen and W. Sledge, eds Academic Press, 2002, 1942pp. 2 v, £305. ISBN 9780123430106.
Alphabetical arrangement of over 200 topics. 'The Encyclopedia covers the major psychotherapies currently in practice as well as the classical approaches that laid the foundation for the various contemporary treatment approaches. In addition, the Encyclopedia identifies the scientific studies conducted on the efficacy of the therapies and review the theoretical basis of each therapy.'

Handbooks & manuals

421   Adult psychopathology and diagnosis
M. Hersen, S.M. Turner and D.C. Beidel, eds   5th edn, Wiley, 2007, 744pp. $105. ISBN 9780471745846.
Provides up-to-date comprehensive coverage of major psychological disorders. Covers specific disorders such as mood, eating or anxiety disorders. Introduces the principles of DSM-IV-TR diagnosis and the case-study approach demonstrates how diagnoses are made. Also covers etiology.

422   Bergin and Garfield's handbook of psychotherapy and behavior change
M.J. Lambert, ed.   5th edn, Wiley, 2004, 864pp. $179.95. ISBN 9780471377559.
Includes historical, ethical and conceptual foundations, efficacy of psychotherapy, major approaches to psychotherapy and research on special groups or settings. Comprehensive coverage.
Updated edition of Handbook of psychotherapy and behavior change, *edited by A.E. Bergin and S.L. Garfield.*

423   Comprehensive handbook of personality and psychopathology
M. Hersen and J.C. Thomas, eds   Wiley, 2006, 1565pp. 3 v, $645. ISBN 9780471479451.
Scholarly volumes covering the major theories of personality and the impact that personality has on functioning and the major classifications of psychological disorders in adults and children as well as the main treatments.
Volumes available separately ($200.00–$215.00)
- **1. Personality and everyday functioning** ISBN 9780471488378.
- **2. Adult psychopathology** ISBN 9780471488385.
- **3. Child psychopathology** ISBN 9780471488392.

424   Developmental psychopathology
D. Cicchetti and D.J. Cohen, eds   2nd edn, Wiley, 2006, 2700pp. 3 v, $645. ISBN 9780471237358.
Contributors are an international team of experts. Concerned more with the processes that lead to psychopathology than the disorders themselves. Chapters cover some psychiatric disorders such as autism, but there is considerable emphasis on factors such as the developing brain, peer relationships and attachment and stress.
Volumes also available separately: $215.00 each.
- **1. Theory and method** ISBN 9780471237365.
- **2. Developmental neuroscience** ISBN 9780471237372.
- **3. Risk, disorder and adaptation** ISBN 9780471237372.

425   Handbook of counseling psychology
S.D. Brown and R.W. Lent, eds   3rd edn, Wiley, 2000, 865pp. £75. ISBN 9780471254584.
Reviews key areas in counselling psychology: professional and scientific issues, career development and interventions. Authoritative chapters by leading psychologists in this area.

426   Handbook of eating disorders and obesity
J.K. Thompson, ed.   Wiley, 2003, 796pp. $90. ISBN 9780471230731.
Provides a good international coverage of *anorexia nervosa, bulimia nervosa,* binge eating disorder, obesity and body image disturbances. Coverage includes etiology, assessment and diagnosis and treatment.

427   Handbook of positive psychology
C.R. Snyder and S.J. Lopez, eds   Oxford University Press, 2005, 847pp. £29.99. ISBN 9780195182798.
Includes various approaches to positive psychology such as emotion-focused, cognitive-focused, interpersonal and biological approaches and covers positive concepts such as resilience, optimism, compassion, empathy and altruism. Also deals with special populations and settings: children, elderly, multicultural aspects and work. Each chapter has a comprehensive list of references.
Originally published in 2002.

428   Handbook of research methods in clinical psychology
M.C. Roberts and S.S. Ilardi, eds   Blackwell, 2005, 466pp. £24.99. ISBN 9781405132794.
Covers methods in psychopathology, assessment and therapy with both child and adult populations. Individual topics of research include vignettes which outline examples from the journal literature.
Originally published in 2003.

Keeping up to date

429   Annual review of clinical psychology
Annual Reviews, 2007. V.3, $75. ISBN 9780824339036 ISSN 15485943.
www.annualreviews.org [DESCRIPTION]
The third volume in this series gives overviews of a range of topics such as evidence-based assessment and depression in mothers. Abstracts are freely available online, while subscribers can access the full-text.

430   Clinical Psychology Review
Elsevier, 1981–, 8 p.a. $276. ISSN 02727358.
Scholarly reviews on issues such as psychopathology, psychotherapy, behaviour therapy, behavioural medicine, community mental health, assessment and child development.

Health Psychology

clinical health psychology • stress

Introductions to the subject

431   Foundations of health psychology
H.S. Friedman and R.C. Silver, eds   Oxford University Press, 2007, 416pp. £49. ISBN 9780195139594.
Examines health psychology from a theoretical, conceptual and psychological perspective. Sections cover history and methods, core concepts such as psychoneuroimmunology, personality, disease and self healing and applications such as adjustment to chronic disease and ageing and health.

432   Health psychology: a textbook
J. Ogden   4th edn, Open University Press, 2007, 528pp. £26.99. ISBN 9780335222636.
An excellent introduction. Topics covered include health beliefs, doctor–patient communication, eating behaviours, smoking and alcohol, health screening, stress, pain, cancer, HIV and heart disease. Includes a glossary of terms.

433 **Health psychology: theory, research and practice**
D.F. Marks [et al.]   2nd edn, Sage Publications, 2005, 485pp.
£24.99. ISBN 9781412903370.
Good coverage. The volume has four sections covering
context such as social inequalities and culture, health
behaviour and experience, including eating, drinking,
smoking and exercise, illness experience and health
promotion. Chapters include summaries, key terms and
ideas for future research.

434 **An introduction to health psychology**
V. Morrison and P. Bennett   Pearson/Prentice Hall, 2006, 619pp.
£27.99. ISBN 9780130994080.
Covers all the main areas of health psychology such as
smoking, exercise, stress etc. and also covers topics such as
social inequalities, cross-cultural aspects and lifespan
influences. User-friendly layout with chapter outlines,
'spotlight' boxes and key terms highlighted in the text.

Associations & societies

435 **European Health Psychology Society**
www.ehps.net
Founded in 1986, the EHPS is 'a professional organization
formed to promote empirical and theoretical research in and
applications of health psychology within Europe'. *Psychology
and Health* and *Health Psychology Review* are official journals
of the society. The newsletter, *European Health Psychologist*,
can be downloaded from the website. The site also has links
to health psychology events in Europe and a membership
directory.

Directories & encyclopedias

436 **Encyclopedia of health and behavior**
N.B. Anderson, ed.   Sage Publications, 2004, 1016pp. 2 v, $395.
ISBN 9780761923602.
'This two-volume set includes over 200 entries on topics
covering all aspects of health and behavior. In addition, the
Encyclopedia of Health and Behavior includes a
comprehensive set of additional resources with both entries
on selected organizations and an appendix with a detailed
annotated listing of such organizations as well as Websites
of interest.'

437 **Encyclopedia of health psychology**
A.J. Christensen, R. Martin and J. Morrison, eds   Kluwer, 2004,
351pp. £158. ISBN 9780306483363.
Over 200 entries, the encyclopaedia is suitable for
practitioners, students and lay persons. Provides a good
overview of health issues throughout the lifespan.

438 **Encyclopedia of stress**
G. Fink, ed.   2nd edn, Academic Press, 2007, 3000pp. 4 v, £685.
ISBN 9780120885039.
Up-dated edition covering all aspects of stress with
contributions from authors worldwide. Entries range from
molecular and biological aspects to stress in real-life such as
terrorism, war and stress at work. Very comprehensive
coverage.

Handbooks & manuals

439 **Cambridge handbook of psychology, health and
medicine**
A. Baum [et al.], eds   2nd edn, Cambridge University Press, 2007,
1062pp. £65. ISBN 9780521605106.
Completely revised and updated edition. In two parts: part I
covers psychological aspects of health and illness,
assessments, interventions and health-care practice. Part II
covers medical matters listed in alphabetical order. New
topics include diet and health, ethnicity and health, clinical
interviewing, mood assessment, communicating risk,
medical interviewing, diagnostic procedures, organ donation,
IVF, MMR, HRT, sleep disorders, skin disorders, depression
and anxiety disorders.
Forthcoming edition: entry based on publisher's information

440 **Handbook of clinical health psychology**
T.J. Boll [et al.], eds   American Psychological Association,
2002–2004. 3 v, $69.95 each.
'Topics in Volume 1 explore the role of behavior and
psychology in a wide range of medical disorders and use the
ICD-9 diagnostic classification as a basis. Volume 2
examines how behavior affects the development, progression
and treatment of specific medical disorders. Volume 3
examines the models and theories that psychologists use to
provide heuristic paradigms for health psychology.'
- V.1. Medical disorders and behavioral applications ISBN
  9781557989093
- V.2. Disorders of behavior and health ISBN
  9781591470915
- V.3. Models and perspectives in health psychology ISBN
  9781591471066

441 **Handbook of health psychology**
A. Baum, T.A. Revenson and J.E. Singer, eds   Lawrence Erlbaum
Associates, 2001, 981pp. $250. ISBN 9780805814958.
Excellent synopses of issues. Three sections: Basic
processes, including pain, personality and self-efficacy;
Crosscutting issues such as stress and ageing; and the Study
of disease such as cancer and AIDS/HIV. 51 chapters, with
substantial references, each written by a key researcher in
the field.

442 **Sage handbook of health psychology**
S. Sutton, A. Baum and M. Johnston, eds   Sage Publications, 2004,
448pp. £75. ISBN 9780761968498.
Comprehensive in-depth coverage of health psychology from
an international group of contributors. Covers a wide range
of perspectives, including lifespan, gender and cross-cultural
aspects, epidemiology, biological mechanisms of health and
illness and health-related cognitions. Also covers research
methods, assessment and professional issues.

Industrial & Organizational Psychology

business psychology • industrial psychology • organizational psychology • personnel selection • psychology of work

Introductions to the subject

443   Business psychology and organisational behaviour: a student's handbook
E. McKenna   4th edn, Psychology Press, 2006, 798pp. £24.95. ISBN 9781841693927.
Sections cover the individual, the group, the organization and management and organizational issues. Recent developments in areas such as cross-cultural issues, ethics and psychological testing and emotional intelligence are included. Special features include chapter summaries, guides to relevant readings and a glossary of key terms.

444   Industrial and organizational psychology: research and practice
P.E. Spector   4th edn, Wiley, 2005, 447pp. $101.95. ISBN 9780471690993.
Good coverage, including core topics and new developments. The volume is in five parts: introduction; assessment of jobs, performance and people; selecting and training employees; the individual and the organization; and the social context of work. Clearly explained.

445   Psychology applied to work: an introduction to industrial and organizational psychology
P.M. Muchinsky   8th edn, Thomson/Wadsworth, 2006, 572pp. $139.95. ISBN 9780534607814.
http://psychology.wadsworth.com/muchinsky8e [COMPANION]
A good introduction. Chapters cover key areas, including historical background, research methods, job criteria and predictors, personnel decisions, organizational change, teams, motivation, leadership and unions. Includes chapter outlines and summaries. Further resources and web links can be found on the companion site.

446   The psychology of behaviour at work: the individual in the organization
A. Furnham   2nd edn, Psychology Press, 2005, 720pp. £24.95. ISBN 9781841695044.
Comprehensive coverage of work and organizational behaviour, including vocational choice, personality, attitudes, motivation, stress, groups, leadership and decision-making. Historical issues and issues for the future are also included. An excellent introduction.

Associations & societies

447   European Association of Work & Organizational Psychology
www.eawop.com
Supports the development and application of work and organizational psychology in Europe and promotes cooperation between scientists and professionals. The website has an online newsletter and links to societies, congresses, journals, publishers, universities and other links.

448   Society for Industrial & Organizational Psychology
[USA]
www.siop.org
Division 14 of the American Psychological Association. 'The Society's mission is to enhance human well-being and performance in organizational and work settings by promoting the science, practice and teaching of industrial-organizational psychology.' The website includes links to other organizations, the quarterly newsletter *The Industrial-Organizational Psychologist* and a searchable international directory.

Directories & encyclopedias

449   Encyclopedia of industrial and organizational psychology
S.G. Rogelberg, ed.   Sage Publications, 2006, 1200pp. 2 v, $375. ISBN 9781412924702.
350 substantial entries providing broad and topical coverage of the field. Entries have references for further reading and there is cross-referencing between topics.

Handbooks & manuals

Blackwell handbook of personnel selection
A. Evers, N. Anderson and O. Smit-Voskuijl, eds   See entry no. 4373

450   Handbook of industrial, work and organizational psychology
N. Anderson [et al.], eds   Sage Publications, 2001, 1056pp. 2 v., $275. ISBN 9780761973706.
Comprehensive coverage. Each chapter provides an overview of the field and description of future trends. The volumes consist of 41 chapters written by experts across the world.
- V.1. Personnel psychology ISBN 9780761964889
- V.2. Organizational psychology ISBN 9780761964896.
$150.00 each.

451   Handbook of research methods in industrial and organizational psychology
S.G. Rogelberg, ed.   Blackwell, 2002, 520pp. £25.99. ISBN 9781405127004.
The volume is in four parts: Foundations covers topics such as history, ethics, reliability and validity and qualitative methods; Data collection includes surveys, computational modelling, qualitative data and cross-cultural research; Data investigation has chapters on item analysis, longitudinal modelling, etc.; and Concluding thoughts. Overall, provides comprehensive treatment of techniques and methods.

Keeping up to date

452   International review of industrial and organizational psychology
G. Hodgkinson and J.K. Ford, eds   Wiley, 2007, 324pp. V. 22, $175. ISBN 9780470031988 ISSN 08861528.
This series provides authoritative reviews of current topics and new developments written by experts in the field. Volume 22 provides overviews of developments in areas such as work–family conflict and cultural variations in job performance. Each chapter includes a useful bibliography. Includes a contents listing of all previous volumes.

Educational Psychology

educational psychology • school psychology

Introductions to the subject

453 Educational psychology: developing learners
J.E. Ormrod 6th edn, Pearson/Prentice Hall, 2007, 744pp. $116.
ISBN 9780136127024.
Organized in three main parts: Development and Diversity covers cognitive and linguistic development, development of the self and group and individual differences; Learning and Motivation includes behaviourist and social-cognitive views of learning; and Classroom Strategies deals with the learning environment, assessment and achievement. A good student text, clearly laid out with tables, figures and illustrations.

454 Educational psychology: theory and practice
R.E. Slavin 8th edn, Pearson/Allyn & Bacon, 2006, 692pp. $116.
ISBN 9780205493838.
A comprehensive text covering a wide range of topics, including cognitive and language development, personality, social and emotional development, individual differences, culture and diversity, views of learning – behavioural, cognitive, social-cognitive and constructionist, complex cognitive processes, motivation, cooperative learning, learning environments and testing and assessment. Clearly laid out with illustrations and tables and key terms listed in the margins.

Associations & societies

455 Association of Educational Psychologists [UK]
www.aep.org.uk
The professional association and trade union for educational psychologists in the UK. The journal *Educational Psychology in Practice* is published on behalf of the association.

456 International School Psychology Association
www.ispaweb.org
Founded in 1982 to promote worldwide cooperation among school and educational psychologists. The website includes documents such as the code of ethics and international guidelines for the preparation of school psychologists, links to articles and reports and many external links to organizations and resources.

457 National Association of School Psychologists [USA]
www.nasponline.org
'The National Association of School Psychologists represents and supports school psychology through leadership to enhance the mental health and educational competence of all children.' The website includes various professional standards documents and resources for members and one can download a variety of brochures, handouts and factsheets dealing with topics such as autism, bullies and victims and child mental health. There are also links to an extensive range of external resources.

Portal & task environments

458 Ed Psyc Central
http://edpsyccentral.org
Aims to provide resources for teaching and learning across the lifespan. Links to a variety of resources in educational and school psychology and related areas: organizations, regulations and ethics, articles, topic-related resources.

459 Educational psychology interactive
http://chiron.valdosta.edu/whuitt/index.html
Maintained by Dr William Huitt at Valdosta State University in the USA, this site has links to various topics in educational psychology such as intelligence and learning styles, links to internet resources and links to full-text readings: online research papers, journals and reports which are sub-divided under headings. The site also has a search facility.

460 School psychology resources online
www.schoolpsychology.net
Maintained by Sandra Steingart at the Office of Psychological Services in Baltimore. Includes a wealth of resources in areas such as learning disabilities, ADHD, functional behavioural assessment, autism, adolescence, parenting, psychological assessment, special education, mental retardation and mental health. Aimed at psychologists, parents and educators.

Discovering print & electronic resources

461 ERIC: Education Resources Information Center
www.eric.ed.gov
Provides free access to more than 1.2 million bibliographic records of journal articles and non-journal literature indexed from 1966 to the present. ERIC is sponsored by the US Department of Education, Institute of Education Sciences (IES).

Directories & encyclopedias

462 Encyclopedia of school psychology
T.S. Watson and C.H. Skinner, eds Kluwer Academic/Plenum, 2004, 392pp. $275. ISBN 9780306484803.
A useful encyclopedia, intended for both professionals and non-professionals. Alphabetical arrangement, covering a wide range of entries: includes learning disabilities and specific disorders, assessment tools used in schools, biographical profiles of key figures. Entries have bibliographies and added readings and are cross-referenced. Complements the volume edited by S.W. Lee.

463 Encyclopedia of school psychology
S.W. Lee, ed. Sage Publications, 2005, 688pp. $150. ISBN 9780761930808.
Approximately 250 entries, many substantial, covering child development, school learning, motivation, intelligence testing, learning disabilities, ethical issues, among others. There is a list of all entries at the front and the reader's guide lists relevant entries in particular subject areas.

Handbooks & manuals

464   Handbook of educational psychology
P.A. Alexander and P.H. Winne, eds   2nd edn, Lawrence Erlbaum Associates, 2006, 1075pp. $89.95. ISBN 9780805859713.
Sponsored by Division 15 of the American Psychological Association. Broad coverage which includes scholarly reviews of areas such as development and individual differences, cognition and cognitive processes, motivation and societal and cultural perspectives.

465   The handbook of international school psychology
S.R. Jimerson, T.D. Oakland and P.T. Farrell, eds   Sage Publications, 2006, 568pp. $125. ISBN 9781412926690.
Provides an international overview of school psychology. Authors from over 40 countries worldwide address the context of school psychology; its origin, history and current status; its infrastructure; the preparation of school psychologists; their roles, functions and responsibilities; and current issues impacting the field. Includes many references.

466   Handbook of school neuropsychology
R.C. D'Amato, E. Fletcher-Janzen and C.R. Reynolds, eds   Wiley, 2005, 984pp. $100. ISBN 9780471465508.
The volume is arranged in five sections: Foundations of school neuropsychological practice; Development, structure and functioning of the brain; Neuropsychological assessment for intervention; Understanding and serving learners with diseases and disorders and from special populations; and Neuropsychological interventions in schools. Appendices cover neuropsychological evaluations and there is an appendix of neuropsychology organizations and websites.

Teaching and learning: lessons from psychology
R. Fox   See entry no. 4514

Forensic Psychology

confessions • criminal psychology • eyewitness testimony • false memory • hypnosis • interrogations • legal psychology

Introductions to the subject

467   Forensic psychology
L.S. Wrightsman and S.M. Fulero   2nd edn, Thomson/Wadsworth, 2004, 454pp. £35.99. ISBN 9780534632250.
Organized in three parts: Forensic psychology and forensic psychologists; Clinical forensic psychology; and Social, cognitive and experimental forensic psychology. Ideal student text: every chapter includes an outline, summary, key terms and suggestions for further reading.

468   Introduction to forensic and criminal psychology
D. Howitt   2nd edn, Pearson/Prentice Hall, 2006, 456pp. £32.99. ISBN 9780131297586.
Provides a clear introduction, covering a wide range of topics: social context of crime, juvenile offenders, violent offenders, sexual offenders, police psychology, eyewitness testimony, offender profiling, false confessions, children as witnesses, mental illness and crime, juries, assessment of risk and more.

469   Introduction to forensic psychology: issues and controversies in crime and justice
B.A. Arrigo   2nd edn, Elsevier, 2005, 600pp. £37.95. ISBN 9780120643516.
Divided into four sections: Criminal forensics, Civil forensics, Policing and law enforcement and Corrections and prison practices. Includes case illustrations and literature reviews.

Research centres & institutes

470   Eyewitness Identification Research Laboratory. University of Texas
http://eyewitness.utep.edu
Established in 1992, the Eyewitness Identification Research Laboratory in the Psychology Department at the University of Texas at El Paso (UTEP) focuses on research in eyewitness memory, eyewitness identification, expert testimony and many aspects of face recognition. The website includes bibliographies, recent publications and links.

■ **Investigative Interviewing Research Laboratory. University of Texas** http://iilab.utep.edu/index.htm. Research carried out at the laboratory examines the social and cognitive psychological processes that underlie the interviewing of individuals in forensic settings. The main areas of research are eyewitness memory, the detection of deception, and interrogations and confessions. The website includes bibliographies of research articles in these areas.

Associations & societies

471   American College of Forensic Psychology
www.forensicpsychology.org
Founded in 1983, the College holds an annual symposium and publishes the *American Journal of Forensic Psychology*. The website has the Attorney's Directory of Forensic Psychologists Online, information about new books and also information about tapes and journal articles.

472   American Psychology–Law Society
www.ap-ls.org
'The American Psychology-Law Society, Division 41 of the American Psychological Association, is an interdisciplinary organization devoted to scholarship, practice and public service in psychology and law. [Its] goals include advancing the contributions of psychology to the understanding of law and legal institutions through basic and applied research'. The website has links to professional organizations and bibliographies on eyewitness research, false memory and jury research.

Handbooks & manuals

473   Forensic psychology: emerging topics and expanding roles
A.M. Goldstein, ed.   Wiley, 2006, 838pp. $150. ISBN 9780471714071.
Comprehensive volume covering the full range of topics: assessment, ethical issues, civil forensic psychology, criminal forensic psychology, experts in the courtroom, forensic psychological consultation, special populations and special topics. The chapters are contributed by 49 experts.

474 **The handbook of eyewitness psychology**
Psychology Press, 2006–07. 2 v.
Surveys research and legal opinions from international
experts on the accuracy and limitations of eyewitnesses as a
source of evidence for the courts. The volumes review factors
influencing witnesses of all ages – children, adults and the
elderly. Includes topics such as the use of hypnosis, false
and recovered memories, the impact of stress,
conversational memory, alibi evidence, witness credibility,
memory for faces, earwitness testimony, line-up
identification, the effects of delay on identification and
expert testimony. The impact of witness testimony in court is
considered and each volume concludes with a legal
commentary chapter.
- 1. **Memory for events** M.P. Toglia [et al.], eds   Psychology Press,
  2006, 720pp. £65. ISBN 9780805851519.
- 2. **Memory for people** R.C.L. Lindsay [et al.], eds   Psychology
  Press, 2007, 740pp. £65. ISBN 9780805851526.

475 **The handbook of forensic psychology**
I.B. Weiner and A.K. Hess, eds   3rd edn, Wiley, 2005, 912pp. $100.
ISBN 9780471692324.
Aimed at practitioners. The volume is arranged in seven
parts: Context of forensic psychology; Applying psychology
to civil proceedings; Applying psychology to criminal
proceedings; Special applications (e.g. polygraph testing and
hypnosis); Communicating expert opinions (writing forensic
reports and serving as an expert witness); Intervening with
offenders; and Professional issues.

476 **Handbook of forensic psychology: resource for
mental health and legal professionals**
W.T. O'Donohue and E.R. Levensky, eds   Elsevier Academic Press,
2004, 1064pp. £100. ISBN 9780125241960.
An excellent resource covering both law for psychologists and
psychology for lawyers. Other topics covered include ethical
issues, report writing, psychological assessment, eyewitness
testimony, recovered memory, polygraphs and juror selection.

477 **Handbook of psychology in legal contexts**
D. Carson and R. Bull, eds   2nd edn, Wiley, 2003, 670pp. £105.
ISBN 9780471498742.
Edited by a psychologist and a lawyer, this authoritative
volume looks at elements such as psychological assessments
for the courts and decision-making by judges and juries, with
contributions from the UK, Europe and North America.

478 **The psychology of interrogations and confessions:
a handbook**
G.H. Gudjonsson   Wiley, 2003, 684pp. £41.99. ISBN
9780470844618.
The book is divided into four sections: Interrogations and
confessions, Legal and psychological aspects, British Court
of Appeal cases and Foreign cases of disputed confessions.
The volume is aimed at practitioners, including psychologists
and psychiatrists, involved with investigative interviewing.

Keeping up to date

479 **Forensic Update** [UK]
British Psychological Society
www.bps.org.uk/dfp/publications/update.cfm
Regular newsletter published by the Division of Forensic
Psychology of the British Psychological Society.

Parapsychology

anomalous experience • out-of-the-body experiences •
paranormal phenomena • poltergeists • precognition •
psychic phenomena • psychical research • psychokinesis •
reincarnation • telepathy

Introductions to the subject

480 **An introduction to parapsychology**
H.J. Irwin   4th edn, McFarland & Company, 2004, 312pp. $35. ISBN
9780786418336.
Provides an overview and critical evaluation of paranormal
phenomena, including extrasensory perception, near-death
and out-of-the-body experiences, poltergeists and
reincarnation. Each chapter includes key terms and concepts
and study questions. Also evaluates the scientific status of
parapsychology.

481 **Parapsychology**
R. Wiseman and C. Watt, eds   Ashgate, 2005, 501pp. £110. ISBN
9780754624509.
A collection of articles covering a wide range of paranormal
phenomena: near-death experiences, hauntings, mediumship,
distant healing, extra-sensory perception.

482 **Parapsychology: research on exceptional
experiences**
J. Henry   Routledge, 2004, 208pp. £15.95. ISBN 9780415213608.
A good introduction to parapsychological methods and
phenomena. Contributors from the USA and UK outline
research in topics such as coincidence, telepathy,
precognition, psychokinesis, healing, apparitions,
reincarnation and out-of-the-body experiences. Possible
explanations are discussed. Each chapter includes
suggestions for further reading and a glossary of terms.

483 **Varieties of anomalous experience: examining the
scientific evidence**
E. Cardeña, S.J. Lynn and S. Krippmer, eds   American Psychological
Association, 2000, 476pp. $39.95. ISBN 9781557986252.
Reviews research in uncommon experiences, including out-of-
body, alien abduction, past-life, near-death and anomalous
healing experiences. Also deals with hallucinations,
synesthesia and lucid dreaming. Scholarly volume which
covers methodological issues, psychopathology and cultural
differences.

Research centres & institutes

484 **Koestler Parapsychology Unit** [UK]
http://moebius.psy.ed.ac.uk
The unit is part of the psychology department at the
University of Edinburgh in Scotland and aims to investigate
'the scientific study of the capacity attributed to some
individuals to interact with their environment by means other
than the recognized sensorimotor channels'. The website
includes links to societies and associations, research centres
and general links.

485 **Rhine Research Center**
www.rhine.org
An institute for the study of consciousness at Durham, North

Carolina, USA. The website includes news, a glossary of terms, information about books and readings and information about recent parapsychological research carried out at the Center.

Associations & societies

486   American Society for Psychical Research
www.aspr.com
The society was founded in 1885 to study the scientific investigation of psychic or paranormal phenomena. Based in New York, it has an extensive library and archives which contain numerous rare books and manuscripts dating from the 18th century. Members receive the quarterly journal and newsletter.

487   Parapsychological Association
www.parapsych.org
An international organization of scientists and scholars engaged in the study of psychic experiences. Links to online experiments, surveys and questionnaires, journals and publications and associations and research laboratories.

488   Parapsychology Foundation
www.parapsychology.org
A not-for-profit foundation based in New York, which provides

a worldwide forum supporting the scientific investigation of psychic phenomena. It publishes pamphlets, monographs, conference proceedings and the *International Journal of Parapsychology* and also maintains the Eileen J. Garrett Library which has over 12,000 volumes and 100 periodicals on parapsychology and related topics.

489   Society for Psychical Research [UK]
www.spr.ac.uk
Founded in 1882 by a group of scholars to investigate paranormal phenomena scientifically. Today the Society promotes research in this area by publishing scholarly reports and organizing events such as the programme of monthly lectures. There is a library with online catalogue and links to other parapsychological associations.

Digital data, image & text collections

490   Charles T. Tart homepage and consciousness library online
www.paradigm-sys.com/index.cfm
Archive containing reprints of published journal articles of the parapsychologist Charles T. Tart. The site also includes links to organizations, recommended readings and The Archives of Scientists' Transcendent Experiences (TASTE), an online journal.

Sociology

The Sociology section includes materials relating to classical and contemporary sociological theory; key figures in sociology and the sociological study of different aspects of social life worldwide. The latter encompasses a wide range of specialist sub-fields ranging from health and illness to education, work and new media. While this might seem to overlap with other sectons in this volume, in particular the Social Welfare section; which also has coverage of different age-groups, race-relations and communities; the emphasis in this section is on those resources which are primarily concerned with the application of sociological theories and research methods. The Social Welfare chapter contains those resources where the main focus is upon policy-making and the direct practical applications.

You will also find that a large number of the items evaluated in the general Social Science section are of relevance to the study of Sociology. This is because of the inter-related nature of the social science disciplines. In particular, many of the important databases described in the tracing books and journal articles sub-section provide a very good coverage of social issues which would be an invaluable background in starting sociological research.

Within the space allotted, it has not been possible to individually list every sociology resource available, however, it is hoped that the most important resources have been included and from these you will be able to explore further. Resources have been selected for their importance and quality of coverage, with the aim of offering a range of materials covering important work from different areas of the world and the main specialist sub-fields of the discipline.

The Sociology chapter is divided by subject area and within each area by resource type. Resources which cover the full range of the discipline are described in the first general section. The categories of resources listed include key organizations, introductory textbooks, dictionaries; encyclopedias and online digital libraries. If you are new to the subject area you will find that the 'introductions' resource type lists a range of widely available student textbooks and popular works. Also useful is the Portal sub-section, as the websites listed there have been chosen for their depth and range of resources. Most provide up to date directories of academic Internet resources as well as maintaining online tutorials, discussion forums and news services. Within the Associations section you will find listed the key national and international organizations of the discipline. These are a good starting point for research as many maintain large websites where you will find directories of links to many local organisations; small specialist projects and journals which space has not permitted me to list in full here. Many also have newsletters which are often one of the best sources of information on recent publications and forthcoming events. Finally don't forget to explore the resources in the general Social Sciences chapter as many provide excellent sociological coverage.

Introductions to the subject

491 A guide to writing sociology papers
Sociology Writing Group   Worth Publishers, 2001, 208pp. £16.99. ISBN 9781572599512.
A useful introductory tool for sociology students and lecturers. It provides a step-by-step guide to the writing and research process. It includes sections on note taking; preparing and writing different types of assignment; citation styles and avoiding plagiarism. Handy tips and examples are offered throughout. Bibliographical references for further reading are provided.

492 An introduction to sociology: feminist perspectives
P. Abbot, C. Wallace and M. Tyler   3rd edn, Routledge, 2005, 448pp. £20.99. ISBN 9780415312592.
Accessible introduction to feminist theory. Students will find the end of chapter summaries, glossaries of key terms and suggestions for further reading useful. Topics covered are wide-ranging and up to date. They include patriarchy, body politic, post-colonial feminism and post-modernity and feminism.

493 Sociology
A. Giddens   5th edn, Polity Press, 2006, 1094pp. £22.99. ISBN 9780745633787.
www.polity.co.uk/giddens
An excellent accessible introduction to the difficult theories and debates within sociology by leading theorist Anthony Giddens. It combines a thorough grounding in the history of sociology and its classical theories with a discussion of contemporary social change and the impact of globalization upon social life. The text is particularly useful for students as each chapter contains summary and revision points, questions for further reading and web links. The associated website offers supporting materials for students and lecturers. These include online quizzes, assignment guides and a glossary of sociological terms.

494 Sociology: themes and perspectives
M. Haralambos and M. Holborn   6th edn, Collins Educational, 2004, 1024pp. £28.99. ISBN 9780007154470.
www.haralambosholborn.com
Well established textbook for A-level students and introductory undergraduate courses. Provides a solid coverage of classical theory and methods with new chapters on emerging contemporary fields such as health, social exclusion and gender issues. Each chapter highlights key concepts and offers definitions. The associated website enables students to access online quizzes and revision guides. There is also a lecturers' section with suggested classroom activities.

■ **Sociology themes and perspectives: AS and A level student handbook M. Holborn and P. Langley**   6th edn, Collins, 2005, 240pp. £11.99. ISBN 007179472. Associated guide based on the chapter headings of the textbook, but designed specifically in relation to the requirements of British exam boards. Offers revision tips, definition of terms and model examination questions and answers.

495 Sociology matters
R. Schaefer   McGraw-Hill Higher Education, 2007, 384pp. £15. ISBN 9780073528113.
A concise introduction to the basics of sociology which is intended to answer the question of why sociology matters today. Main focus is on North America with chapters on the social system; inequality and social institutions. The approach highlights and explains key concepts.

Dictionaries, thesauri, classifications

496 The Blackwell dictionary of sociology: a user's guide to its terms
A.G. Johnson   2nd edn, Blackwell Publishing, 2000, 432pp. £17.99. ISBN 9780631216810.
A useful single-volume dictionary which aims to demystify the specialized jargon of sociology. It benefits from having a single author, which gives a continuity of voice to the entries. Entries are succinct, most offer one or two suggestions for further reading. There is a separate section of brief biographical notes which summarizes and lists the major works of key sociologists.

497 The Cambridge dictionary of sociology
B.S. Turner   Cambridge University Press, 2006, 708pp. £24.99. ISBN 9780521540469.
Authored by leading experts, this single-volume work offers an international perspective on the discipline of sociology, exploring both the American and European approaches and perspectives. It combines a thorough grounding in classical sociological theory with treatment of emerging areas such as globalization, genetics and cultural change. Entries cover the main sociological theories, schools of thought, key sociologists and current areas of debate. Many contain references for further reading.

498 A critical dictionary of sociology
R. Boudon and F. Bourricaud   Routledge, 1989, 452pp. Translated from the second edition of the French version by Peter Hamilton., £85. ISBN 9780415017459.
A unique reference work in which French scholars Boudon and Bourricaud present their own opinions on key concepts, theories and figures of classical and contemporary sociology. Entries offer readable and sometimes contentious arguments from a non-Marxist viewpoint plus bibliographies of further readings. A work to inspire thinking and debate among academic readers.

499 A dictionary of sociology
J. Scott and G. Marshall, eds   3rd edn, Oxford University Press, 2005, 736pp. £10.99. ISBN 9780198609872.
Authoritative work, containing over 2800 entries covering sociology and related fields such as psychology, economics and philosophy. The main emphasis is on a thorough coverage of concepts, theories and methods. Individual biographies are excluded except where they have given rise to particular schools of thought and living authors are generally omitted. Includes selected web-links and references for further reading.

500 The Penguin dictionary of sociology
N. Abercrombie, S. Hill and B.S. Turner   5th edn, Penguin books, 2006, 496pp. £9.99. ISBN 9780141013756.
Provides coverage of classical sociological theory, while keeping abreast of the most recent trends such as the emerging areas of globalization, popular culture and the media. Includes entries for individual writers, schools of thought and technical terms. Many entries offer suggestions for further reading.

Research centres & institutes

501 International Institute of Sociology
www.tau.ac.il/~iisoc/index.html
Created in Paris in 1893 by René Worms. Among its members and associates were prominent scholars such as: Gustave Le Bon, Karl Mannheim, Georg Simmel, Ferdinand Toennies, Thorstein Veblen and Max Weber. It remains influential in organizing world congresses of sociology. The website provides basic information on the history, aims and recent activities of the IIS.

502 Max-Planck-Institut für Gesellschaftsforschung (Max Planck Institute for the Study of Societies)
[GER]
www.mpi-fg-koeln.mpg.de/index_en.asp
Well structured website providing a detailed overview of the activities of the Institute, which is devoted to basic research in the social sciences. It concentrates on the governance of advanced industrial societies in the face of internationalization and economic globalization, in particular on the changing roles and capacities of states and other corporate actors under conditions of international interdependence and supranational integration. In the analytical perspective of an actor-centred institutionalism, projects at the Institute assess multi-level and multi-actor processes of decision making, negotiation and coordination and apply theory modules of evolutionary dynamics as well as political economy. Details are given of current research projects and programmes; a complete index of the Institute's publications; and a guide to the various organizational units of the Institute.

Associations & societies

503 American Sociological Association
www.asanet.org
The most important professional association serving sociologists in the USA. Its website is an excellent starting point for finding out about sociological education, funding and research in the USA and North America. It provides information on its main specialist research groups and journal publications. These cover all areas of the discipline, including sociological theory; methodology and the teaching of sociology. Some papers may be read online free of charge. The site also contains a specialist section of news and advice for students.

504 Asia-Pacific Sociological Association
www.asiapacificsociology.org
Non-profit organization which aims to establish a network of sociological associations, sociology departments and individual sociologists in the Asia-Pacific region. Website is a good source of information on research and events relating to sociology in Australia, New Zealand and South and South-East Asia. It includes conference information and articles from its journal.

505 Asociación Latinoamericana de Sociología (Latin American Sociology Association)
www2.udec.cl/~alas/

LASA is a professional association promoting the teaching and research of sociology in Latin America. Its website is a key resource for tracing information on South American Spanish-language sociological research. It includes recent newsletters and details about conferences, research projects and publications.

506 Association for Applied & Clinical Sociology
www.appliedsoc.org

Professional association which focuses on the practical application and practice of sociology. Its website provides information on membership, current events and conferences. It also includes details about its key publication *Applied Social Science*. A good starting point for tracing information about the current use of sociology by therapists, counsellors and consultants.

507 Association for Humanist Sociology
www.altrue.net/site/humanist/

Grouping of sociologists who aim to use sociology in an applied setting to promote social justice, peace and equality. Website provides information on membership, conferences and publications. These include tables of contents from its key journal *Humanity & Society*.

508 Association Internationale des Sociologues de Langue Française
www.univ-tlse2.fr/aislf/spip/index.php

International association which seeks to promote scholarship and cooperation among French-speaking sociologists worldwide. Its website is an excellent starting point for tracing information about Francophone sociology organizations, events and ongoing research. This includes coverage of initiatives in French-speaking African nations which may be difficult to trace elsewhere. Information is provided about its key publication *SociologieS*. This includes access to online articles and book reviews.

509 Association of Black Sociologists
www.blacksociologists.org

US-based professional organization which seeks to support sociologists of African descent. This includes enhancing the employment opportunities and knowledge of sociology among black people and ensuring that the discipline of sociology is able to study effectively problems of race and the experiences of black communities. Website provides information on conferences, recent publications and employment opportunities.

510 Australian Sociological Society
www.tasa.org.au/home/index.php

The main professional association serving sociologists in Australia. Its website provides a good starting point for tracing information on the current state of the discipline in this region of the world. It includes details of forthcoming academic conferences; educational courses; jobs; recent publications and tables of contents from its key journal titles which include *Journal of Sociology* and *Health Sociology Review*.

511 British Sociological Association
www.britsoc.co.uk

The main professional association supporting the promotion of sociology in the UK. Its website provides guidance to students on studying sociology; including lists of courses, jobs and sources of funding. Researchers will find comprehensive calendars of forthcoming events; discussion forums and details of the BSA's many special-interest research groups. Also available are tables of contents from its key journal publications which include *Sociology*; *Work, Employment and Society* and *Cultural Sociology*.

512 Deutsche Gesellschaft für Soziologie (German Sociological Society)
www.soziologie.de

Professional organization supporting sociology scholars in Germany. Its website provides information on its activities and publications. It includes details about conferences, specialist research groups and ongoing research. It is a good source of information about recent publications in German.

513 European Consortium for Sociological Research
www.tilburguniversity.nl/faculties/fsw/ecsr

Professional organization which seeks to promote sociological research in Europe by encouraging cooperation between European research centres. Membership is open to research institutes and university departments in all European countries. Its website provides information on its annual conferences and graduate student workshops. It also offers access to its newsletter and tables of contents from its journal *European Sociological Review*.

514 European Sociological Association
www.valt.helsinki.fi/esa

Academic association which seeks to promote the teaching and research of sociology in European nations. Its website provides information on the aims of the organization, its membership and forthcoming events. It includes free access to its newsletter *European Sociologist* and tables of contents from *European Societies*, the official ESA journal. These are a good starting point for tracing information on new sociology research projects.

515 European Sociology Students' Association
www.essa-sociology.org

Originally founded in 2001 as the South East Europe Sociology Students' Association, this organization seeks to promote communication between sociology students in European nations. Membership remains particularly strong in the area of South-Eastern Europe (Bulgaria, Croatia, Moldova, Romania, Serbia and Slovenia). The website offers information on the aims of the organization and its activities. It includes details about student conferences, postgraduate study and funding opportunities within the EU.

516 Heads of Departments of Sociology Council
www.soc.surrey.ac.uk/HODS

Professional body which represents departments of sociology in the universities of England, Northern Ireland, Scotland and Wales. Its website is an excellent starting point for finding information on the current organization and funding of sociology teaching and research in the UK higher education sector. It includes discussion of UK government policy and responses to new legislation and guidelines.

517   International Sociological Association
www.ucm.es/info/isa/
ISA is a key professional body for sociologists. Founded in
1949 it is a member of the International Social Science
Council and a non-governmental organization in formal
associate relations with UNESCO. Its website provides
information on its aims, history, publications and events. It
also includes tables of contents from its key journals
International Sociology and *Current Sociology*. Other features of
the site include calendars of sociology conferences
worldwide, details of funding and research opportunities for
sociologists and information about research groups and
committees supported by ISA. The latter are useful starting
points for tracing the latest research in specialist sub-fields
of sociology.

518   International Visual Sociology Association
www.visualsociology.org
The IVSA is a professional association which promotes the
use of visual images and data in sociology teaching and
research. Its website is an excellent source of information on
current trends, with listing of recent and forthcoming
conferences, links to visual sociology courses and online
syllabi. Some research papers may be accessed in full-text.
Also available are recent tables of contents from the journal
Visual Studies.

519   Sociologists Without Borders
www.sociologistswithoutborders.org/index.html
A professional network of sociologists founded in 2001 with
the aim of using sociology to combat social injustices
worldwide. It is particularly concerned with supporting the
rights of minority and indigenous populations. Its website
provides information on the aims and activities of the group.
It includes details about its journal *Societies Without Borders*,
which is a rich source of information about sociology, social
engagement and activist movements worldwide.

**520   Subject Network for Sociology, Anthropology &
Politics**
www.c-sap.bham.ac.uk
C-SAP is a specialist network of the UK Higher Education
Academy which aims to support the teaching and learning of
sociology, anthropology and politics within UK universities
and higher education colleges. It is a particularly good
source of information on recent teaching trends, including
the use of e-learning and ICT technology. Its website offers
free access to online teaching guides, a database of records
describing websites which have been catalogued for
relevance to learning and teaching in the social sciences, and
information on professional development courses for
lecturers.

Portal & task environments

521   Sociological tour of cyberspace
www.trinity.edu/~mkearl/index.html
Created by Professor Michael C. Kearl of Trinity University,
this site is good for introducing students to the use of the
internet for sociological research and study. It offers a tour of
important websites, with handy annotations on their content.
Sections include online guides to writing research papers,
sociological theory websites, sociological research methods
and data sources.

522   Sociology central
www.sociology.org.uk/
Introductory guide to sociological study created by Chris
Livesey and intended for A-level and further education
students and their teachers. It offers clear and concise
explanations of sociological terms, revision notes and online
learning packages for students, plus links to recommended
sociology websites. Lecturers may benefit from the online
lesson plans and useful directory of software applications for
developing internet-based learning programmes.

523   Sociology in Switzerland
http://socio.ch
Maintained by the University of Zurich, Sociology Institute,
this website is extremely useful for tracing information about
recent and ongoing sociological research in Switzerland and
Western Europe as a whole. In particular, its coverage of
German-language resources is very good. It links to
calendars of events, press releases from leading universities
and research organizations, and full-text electronic sociology
journals.

524   SocioSite
www.sociosite.net/about.php
Based at the Sociological Institute of the University of
Amsterdam, this site contains a comprehensive directory of
links to internet resources for sociology. Of particular value
is the detailed section on famous sociologists which links to
full-text writings by all the key figures in the discipline,
including Marx, Weber and Durkheim. There are also links to
the home pages of contemporary theorists. Other features
include directories of blogs, online journals, datasets and
research institutions.

525   WWW Virtual Library sociology
http://socserv2.mcmaster.ca/w3virtsoclib/
Part of the famous WWW Virtual Library, this site is
maintained by a representative of the Department of
Sociology, McMaster University, Canada. It is a useful
starting point for finding links to websites relevant to
teaching and research in sociology. It includes a section on
sociological theory and theorists where you can find online
versions of texts by famous sociologists. Other categories in
the directory include online course materials, research
centres, university departments and news services. Some
brief annotations on content are provided.

Discovering print & electronic resources

**526   The combined retrospective index set to journals
in sociology 1895–1974**
E. Farber   Carrollton Press, 1978. 6 v., o/p. ISBN 0840801947.
Six-volume set which provides references to approximately
400,000 sociology journal articles published during the
period 1895–1974. Useful for historical research as it
includes some older materials not covered by electronic
databases. Indexes 531 journals mainly published in the USA
and UK. Entries are arranged in broad subject categories.
There are author and keyword indexes.

527   SocINDEX
EBSCO Publishing. On demand.
www.epnet.com/thisTopic.php?topicID=138&marketID=1
High-quality index to sociological research. Covers more than

700 key sociological titles, with references to some dating back as far as 1895. Also indexes hundreds of other titles from related subject fields (including criminology; social psychology; politics and ethnic and racial studies) as well as conference papers and books. An additional feature is profiles of the most cited authors. It is possible to purchase a full-text version of the database containing full-text articles from several hundred journal titles plus selected books and papers.

528   Sociological Abstracts
Cambridge Scientific Abstracts, 1952–, monthly. ISSN 02732173.
Leading database for tracing articles covering all fields of sociology. It provides abstracts of journal articles and book reviews from over 1800 serial publications, plus references to many books, book chapters, dissertations and conference papers. Available in print or online. Coverage is from 1952 to the present.

Digital data, image & text collections

529   Anovasofie
www.anovasofie.net/
A research project funded by the European Union 2004–6 which sought to find information about the history of sociology in different European nations. Its archived website provides free access to a virtual library for the history of European sociology. This contains historical profiles for over 20 EU nations, providing facts about the historical development of sociological teaching and research in the region and examples of key research. Many of these make fascinating reading, including snippets such as the title of the first sociology book published in a particular country. The site enables cross comparison of developments in different nations. Although the original project ended in 2006 there are plans for more materials to be added.

The global site: critical gateway to world politics, society and culture
See entry no. 1270

530   Sociology: a Sage full-text collection
Sage Publications. On demand.
www.sagefulltext.com
An electronic journal subscription database which contains the full text of over 30 key titles covering all aspects of sociology and inter-related areas of the social sciences. Topics covered include gender studies, race relations and popular culture. Many of the titles offer all issues from volume one onwards online.

Directories & encyclopedias

531   The Blackwell encyclopedia of sociology
G. Ritzer, ed.   Blackwell Publishing, 2006, 6384pp. 11 v., £995. ISBN 9781405124331.
www.sociologyencyclopedia.com
Major reference work available in print or online. Contains over 1800 entries covering all aspects of sociological theory. This includes definitions of classical terms as well as coverage of contemporary theory and introductions to sociological research and traditions from non-western

regions. Also contains a timeline of key developments; lexicon and bibliography.

532   Encyclopedia of sociology
E. Borgatta, ed.   2nd edn, Macmillan Reference, 2000, 3481pp. 4 v., $756.25. ISBN 9780028648538.
Useful four-volume set, containing 370 entries arranged into 17 broad categories. These cover the organizations, theories and areas of debate of classical and contemporary sociology. There is an emphasis on North American sociology, with separate entries for key American sociological associations and authors. Each essay provides a bibliography for further reading.

533   The handbook of 21st century sociology
C.D. Bryant   Sage Publications, 2007, 1344pp. 2 v., £269. ISBN 9781412916080.
A comprehensive two-volume encyclopedia which contains essays on the history, present state and future development of the discipline, focusing specifically on examples drawn from North America, Europe and Singapore. Volume 1 traces the main phases in the historical development of the discipline and considers the development of theory and research in traditional fields such as education and politics. Volume 2 concentrates on specialist and inter-disciplinary sub-fields. It includes coverage of the main concepts and state of research in emerging areas such as popular culture and the sociology of music.

534   International encyclopedia of sociology
F.N. Magill, ed.   Fitzroy Dearborn Publishing, 1996, 1800pp. 2 v., £175. ISBN 9781884964541.
Over 300 entries intended to introduce the new student and non-specialist to the key themes, concepts and sub-fields of sociology. It provides a glossary of terms plus annotated bibliographies which offer guidance in further research.

Handbooks & manuals

535   ASA style guide
American Sociological Association   3rd edn, American Sociological Association, 2007, 48pp. £5.
Originally designed by the American Sociological Association (ASA) to help authors prepare manuscripts in the correct format for publication in its journals and monographs. However, it may also be usefully consulted by students and researchers seeking to improve the presentation of their writing. It contains the authoritative guide to the ASA style plus guidance on citing and referencing and the mechanics of manuscript preparation and submission. A list of reference sources on style and writing is also provided.

536   Companion for undergraduate dissertations: sociology, anthropology, politics, social policy, social work and criminology
www.socscidiss.bham.ac.uk
This site provides free access to a survival guide published by the Higher Education Academy's Centre for Sociology, Anthropology and Politics, the Centre for Social Work and Policy and Sheffield Hallam University. It provides useful tips on literature-searching skills and preparing a dissertation at undergraduate level. It also includes chapters for lecturers on supporting students and detecting plagiarism.

537 The Sage handbook of sociology
C. Calhoun [et al.]   Sage Publications, 2005. £130. ISBN 9780761968214.
Authoritative survey of recent developments in sociology written by a board of international experts. Includes coverage of modern sociological theory and method, key debates and emerging sub-disciplines. Chapters include the impact of science and technology on society, immigration, ethnicity and changing notions of citizenship. Contains a substantial bibliography of references to guide further reading.

538 Sociology: a guide to reference and information sources
S. Aby, J. Nalen and L. Fielding   3rd edn, Libraries Unlimited, 2006, 273pp. £44.99. ISBN 9781563089473.
A useful guide to approximately 600 English-language resources published between 1997 and 2004. It is sub-divided into general social science reference works, general sociology sources and materials relating to 23 sub-fields of sociology. Each section contains information on key handbooks, encyclopedias and online resources. Helpful annotations on price and content are provided.

Keeping up to date

539 Canadian Journal of Sociology Online
Department of Sociology, Trenty University.
www.cjsonline.ca
Well established electronic journal which offers timely articles, reviews and information on employment and events. These cover all aspects of sociological theory and practice. The website includes a substantial database of book reviews. It is possible to sign up to receive e-mail notifications of new content.

540 Contemporary Sociology: a journal of reviews
American Sociological Association, bi-monthly. £96. ISSN 00943061.
www.jstor.org/journals/00943061.html
Bi-monthly journal of the American Sociological Association which publishes reviews and discussion of recent publications. Typical issues include more than a dozen long review essays, often based around a thematic topic area and over 100 short reviews of important monographs. All sub-fields of sociology and related sociological research are covered. Each issue also contains an extensive listing of other new publications received. Subscribers may access *Contemporary Sociology* in print or online.

541 Contributions to Indian sociology
P. Calvert   Sage Publications, 1966–, 3 p.a. £42. ISSN 00699667.
www.sagepub.com/
Continuously published for over 40 years, this title contains scholarly articles and book reviews covering all aspects of sociology in India. It includes many examples of recent research by Asian scholars and reviews of texts published in India. The title is available in print or online.

542 Electronic Journal of Sociology
EJS. ISSN 11983655.
www.sociology.org
A long-established electronic journal which has been publishing scholarly articles and reviews covering all fields of sociology and sociological theory since 1994. They include many examples of recent research. Papers are subject to a process of peer review.

543 Sociological Research On-line
1996–, qtrly. £120. ISSN 13607804.
www.socresonline.org.uk/home.html
A well established British electronic journal which has published scholarly articles and book reviews covering all areas of cutting-edge theoretical, empirical and methodological sociological research since 1996. Tables of contents can be browsed on the website and a small selection of articles viewed free of charge. Access to the full archive of articles requires a subscription.

Sociological Theory & Methodology

black sociologists • Durkheim, Emile • historical sociology • Marcuse, Herbert • political sociology • social theory • sociologists • Weber, Max • women in sociology

Sociologists

Introductions to the subject

544 Routledge key sociologists series
This series, published by Routledge, is highly recommended for introducing students to the work of major sociological writers from the 19th and 20th centuries. Each volume sets the theorist in his social context, reviews his most important writings and concepts and examines his legacy to sociology.
- **Auguste Comte M. Gane**   Routledge, 2006, 176pp. £13.99. ISBN 9780415385428.
- **Emile Durkheim K. Thompson**   Routledge, 1982, 184pp. £16.99. ISBN 9780415285315.
- **Erving Goffman G. Smith, ed.**   Routledge, 2006, 160pp. £60. ISBN 9780415355902.
- **The Frankfurt School and its critics T. Bottomore**   Routledge, 2002, 96pp. £65. ISBN 9780415285384.

545 Sociological lives and ideas: an introduction to the classical theorists
F. Pampel   2nd edn, Worth, 2007, 255pp. £19.99. ISBN 9780716779155.
Designed to introduce students to the 'classic founding fathers of sociology'; this accessible textbook brings to life the theories of Karl Marx, Emile Durkheim, Max Weber, Georg Simmel, George H. Mead and W.E.B. DuBois by placing them in the context of their personal histories and the social context of their time.

Dictionaries, thesauri, classifications

546 Key quotations in sociology
K. Thompson   Routledge, 1996, 224pp. £18.99. ISBN 9780415057615.
A handy compilation of several hundred key quotations from the classic founding fathers of sociology and leading contemporary figures. The volume has listings by sociologist and sociological topic for ease of use.

547   Women in sociology: a bio-bibliographical sourcebook
M.J. Deegan, ed.   Greenwood Press, 1991, 300pp. £63. ISBN 9780313260858.
Collection of essays on over 50 women important to the founding history of sociology during the period 1840–1990. Includes coverage of theorists from North America and Europe, including many figures marginalized by other sources. Each entry contains a biography of the subject, discussion of key themes and critiques, plus a bibliography of key works and secondary sources.

Portal & task environments

548   C Wright Mills home page: a page for undergraduates
www.faculty.rsu.edu/~felwell/Theorists/Mills/index.htm
This site is one of a number of pages maintained by Frank W. Elwell, professor at Rogers State University, Oklahoma (USA) in order to support undergraduate students. The C. Wright Mills section is a compilation of substantial excerpts from Wright Mills' own writings, plus a biblography of his major works and links to related websites. Users need to register to access the full-text material.

549   Dead sociologists' society
www2.pfeiffer.edu/~lridener/DSS/DEADSOC.HTML
An excellent free site which is intended to introduce students to classical sociological theory and theorists. It is maintained by Pfeiffer University. The site includes a Dead Sociologist Index which contains biographies, discussions of concepts and links to original writings of 17 'founding fathers' of Sociology, ranging from Karl Marx to Emile Durkheim and George Herbert Mead. Much of the text is taken from *Masters of Sociological Thought: Ideas in Historical and Social Context* (2nd edn) by Lewis A. Coser. Fort Worth, Texas: Harcourt Brace Jovanovich, 1977. ISBN 0-15-555130-2 and other standard textbooks. A directory of key sociological websites is also provided.

550   Pierre Bourdieu: sociologue énervant
www.pages-bourdieu.fr.st
A French-language site created by *Le Magazine de 'l'Homme Moderne* which provides free access to many original texts of leading French sociologist Pierre Bourdieu. They include articles and interviews from the 1970s to 2003. The site also contains a collection of links to internet resources relating to the work of Bourdieu.

551   Verstehen: Max Weber's homepage
www.faculty.rsu.edu/~felwell/Theorists/Weber/Whome.htm
A site created by Frank Elwell, a professor at Rogers State University, Oklahoma (USA), to support undergraduate sociology students learning about the life and work of Max Weber. It includes a glossary of terms; quotations from his key writings; bibliographies of further readings, lecture notes and PowerPoint presentations.

Discovering print & electronic resources

552   Hans-Georg Gadamer: a bibliography
J. Nordquist, ed.   Reference & Research Services, 1998, 72pp. o/p. ISBN 9781892068019.

One of the social science bibliographies from the useful collection compiled by Nordquist, which has been published since the 1970s. Each has a specialist focus, directing the specialist straight to a selection of the most useful publications covering the subject area. The citations are arranged by type of publication (including journal articles and books); then followed by subject and author indexes. The emphasis is on English-language materials. Topics coverd include sociology; feminist theory; political theory and social policy.

■ **Paul Ricoeur: a bibliography J. Nordquist, ed.**   Reference & Research Services, 1999, 72pp. o/p. ISBN 9781892068057.
■ **Sexual harassment: a bibliography** Reference and Research Services, 2002, 68pp. £10. ISBN 9781892068330.

Digital data, image & text collections

553   Ann Oakley homepage
1100pp.
www.annoakley.co.uk/
The official home page of renown sociologist Ann Oakley, author of *The Sociology of Housework* and *Housewife*. It provides free access to a biography, plus quotations and extracts from many of her famous publications on feminism, motherhood and the sociology of gender and work from the 1970s until the present day.

554   Durkheim pages
www.emiledurkheim.com/
This website provides a biography of the great sociologist plus a complete online version of his 'De la division du travail social' (The Division of Labour in Society), in its original French-language form. It also includes a bibliography and a directory of other Durkheim web resources.

555   Erik Ohlin Wright homepage
www.ssc.wisc.edu/~wright/
The official home page of the leading sociologist, who is currently based in the Department of Sociology, University of Wisconsin-Madison. In addition to providing a biography and bibliography of the writings of Professor Olin Wright, it also offers free access to many of his recent articles, papers and interviews, including some unpublished manuscripts relating to his key works on class and social stratification.

556   Georg Simmel online
http://socio.ch/sim/index_sim.htm
An online archive of material relating to the life and work of Georg Simmel which is maintained by the Soziologisches Institut der Universität Zürich. It includes a biography, a bibliography of his writings and free access to online papers and articles. The latter include English-language translations of his key work 'The Stranger' and articles on the philosophy of value. Some materials are offered in German only.

557   Habermas forum
www.habermasforum.dk
The Habermas forum was started in 2001 by a group of professors from Denmark and Norway interested in sharing ideas and resources about the work of philosopher and sociologist Jurgen Habermas. It contains a biography of Habermas plus free access to online versions of many of his political and sociological writings from the 1950s to the current day. These include books, articles and speeches on

political philosophy, the sociology of knowledge and the state of modern European society. Other features of the site include a Habermas bibliography and reviews and articles about his work.

558 Herbert Marcuse (1898–1979)
www.marcuse.org/herbert/
An official site maintained by members of the Marcuse family. It includes information about the life, work and contribution of this leading sociologist. It offers access to some full-text publications; plus bibliographies of works by and about Marcuse and information on associated conferences and events.

559 Howard Beckers homepage
http://home.earthlink.net/%7Ehsbecker/
Official website of sociologist Howard S. Becker author of the monograph *Outsiders: Studies in the Sociology of Deviance* (1963), which developed the influential 'labelling theory'. His home page contains a bibliographic listing of his main works plus many recent full-text papers, book chapters and articles which may be downloaded free of charge. These include examples of important research on the sociology of art and music as well as recent work on sociological theory.

560 Social theory
Alexander Press. On demand.
www.alexanderstreetpress.com
A major subscription service marketed by Alexander Press, it aims to provide searchable access to full-text books and articles by key social thinkers from the 19th and 20th Centuries. Examples include classic works by Max Weber, Karl Marx, George Herbert Mead, Auguste Comte; Georg Hegel, Herbert Spencer, Antonio Gramsci, Mary Wollstonecraft, Alexis de Tocqueville and Emile Durkheim as well as more recent contemporary writings from Michel Foucault, Anthony Giddens and Theodor Adorno. Prcing details are avaiable from the publisher's website.

Handbooks & manuals

561 Cambridge companions to philosophy
www.cambridge.org/
A major series of handbooks published by Cambridge University Press. Although labelled as philosophy, the series includes volumes covering the theory and contribution of important sociologists and political thinkers. The main emphasis is on the work of major writers from the 19th and 20th centuries. Each book contains a collection of scholarly essays, which guide students to the key aspects of theory. They also discuss recent developments in the interpretation of their work. Sample chapters can be read online from the publisher's website.
- **The Cambridge companion to Durkheim** J.C. Alexander Cambridge University Press, 2005, 442pp. £17.99. ISBN 9780521001519.
- **The Cambridge companion to Marx** T. Carver, ed. Cambridge University Press, 1992, 373pp. £19.99. ISBN 9780521366946.
- **The Cambridge companion to Tocqueville** C. Welch, ed. Cambridge University Press, 2006, 460pp. £17.99. ISBN 9780521549967.

562 Sage masters in modern thought series
Sage Publications.
A major series of multi-volume sets covering influential thinkers of the 20th century. Each title covers a single

theorist; gathering together in 3 or 4 volumes a collection of some of the best published assessments and responses to his/her work. Each set includes a survey of the work of the individual, placing it in its social and historical context; discussion of his/her key concepts and theories and their impact on the development of the social sciences. Over 15 titles have currently been published.
- **Harold Garfinkel** M. Lynch and W. Sharrock Sage Publications, 2003, 1664pp. £525. ISBN 9780761974598. 4 v.
- **Manuel Castells** F. Webster and B. Dimitriou, eds Sage Publications, 2003, 1248pp. £425. ISBN 9780761940432. 4 v.

Sociological Theory

Introductions to the subject

563 Classical sociological theory
G. Ritzer 4th edn, McGraw-Hill, 2004, 544pp. £32.99. ISBN 9780071225786.
www.mhhe.com/ritzer
Provides an overview of the main classical sociological theories and schools of thought, setting them in historical context and enabling comparisons. Includes biographical sketches of principal theorists such as Marx, Durkheim and Weber and lists of key readings. Associated website includes study guides and questions for students.

564 Key concepts in critical social theory
N. Crossley Sage Publications, 2005, 336pp. £19.99. ISBN 9780761970606.
Designed specifically to provide a first introduction to difficult texts and terminology. Main focus is on sociology, though reference is also made to terminology from other social science areas such as psychology. Each concept has a clear, accessible definition, highlighting related concepts and offering quotations from key texts. Suggestions for further reading are provided.

Associations & societies

565 International Association of Labour History Institutions
An international network of labour history institutions whose members include leading research centres, archives and museums. Its website is an excellent starting point for finding information on events, publications and websites relating to all aspects of labour history, socialism and communism worldwide. It maintains extensive indexes of digital library collections relating to the political history of the 'left', gender history and trade union history. These include excellent coverage of non-English-language resources which are often omitted elsewhere.
- **IAHL serials** http://serials.ialhi.org/search.asp. Free access to a searchable database of tables of contents from over 130 leading journals covering labour and political history from the 1970s to the present day. Titles are taken from the holdings of IALHI members and include many European language newspapers and journals (in French, German, Italian and Russian) with an emphasis on socialist, communist and political left titles as well as academic publications. Key topics covered include: trade unions, Marxism, communism and anarchism. It is possible to sign up for alerts when new materials are added.

566 Social Theory Research Network
www.kuleuven.ac.be/socialtheoryeurope
A sub-group of the European Sociological Association which specializes in researching all aspects of social theory, including consideration of developing theoretical concepts and the relationship between theory and empirical research. Its website provides information on its research activities and events. It includes a listing of all its annual conference papers from 1999 onwards. Some of these may be downloaded from the website free of charge.

567 Society for the Study of Symbolic Interaction
www.espach.salford.ac.uk/sssi/index.html
A professional organization of scholars interested in qualitative research, focusing in particular on methods associated with theories of symbolic interactionism. Its website provides information on the aims and recent activities of the society. It includes details of conferences, plus tables of contents from its journal *Symbolic Interaction* and a directory of websites related to symbolic interactionism.

Digital data, image & text collections

568 Classiques des sciences sociales
http://classiques.uqac.ca/
A really wonderful site maintained by l'Université du Québec à Chicoutimi with the support of le Ville de Saguenay. It provides free access to an online library of over 2000 French-language books and texts covering all areas of the social sciences. They include French-language translations of classic sociological texts from such authors as Marx, Comte and Durkheim, examples of contemporary social theory and works on social research methodology.

Marxists Internet archive
See entry no. 1318

Directories & encyclopedias

569 Encyclopedia of social theory
A. Harrington, B.L. Marshall and H. Muller, eds   Routledge, 2006, 760pp. £130. ISBN 9780415290463.
Contains over 500 original entries covering the theory, debates and ideas central to the development of social theory from the 19th century to the present. The main emphasis is on traditions relating to Europe and North America. Coverage is cross-disciplinary, including references to sociology, psychoanalysis, post-colonial studies and feminism. Over 100 biographical entries are provided, although coverage of schools of thought is generally more detailed.

570 The Greenwood encyclopedia of world popular culture
G.C. Hoppenstand   Greenwood, 2007, 402pp. 6 v., £395. ISBN 9780313332555.
An extensive six-volume set covering a wide range of issues relating to popular culture worldwide. Each volume covers a specific region of the world, offering a broad introductory essay followed by longer entries on specific topics such as fashion, food, media, sports and recreation. Chapters include useful bibliographies of organizations, journals and websites to aid further research.

Handbooks & manuals

571 The Blackwell companion to major classical social theorists
G. Ritzer, ed.   Blackwell Publishing, 2003, 448pp. £20.99. ISBN 9781405105941.
Authoritative guide to the theory, key writings and social context of twelve major figures from the history of sociology. Each essay has been written by an established expert and is approximately 20–30 pages in length, including a full bibliography and suggested further readings. An introductory essay outlines several approaches to the study of the history of sociology. Featured theorists include Auguste Comte, Emile Durkheim, Max Weber and Talcott Parsons.

572 The Blackwell companion to major contemporary social theorists
G. Ritzer, ed.   Blackwell Publishing, 2003, 384pp. £22.99. ISBN 9781405105958.
A useful accompaniment to the *Blackwell guide to major classical social theorists*, this volume concentrates on the theory, key writings and social context of twelve major figures from contemporary sociology. These include the most important modern theorists from the 20th and 21st centuries, such as Harold Garfinkel, Erving Goffman and Anthony Giddens. Each essay has been written by an established expert and is approximately 20–30 pages in length, including a full bibliography and suggested further readings. An introductory essay provides an overview of the development of contemporary sociological theory.

573 The Blackwell companion to political sociology
K. Nash and A. Scott, eds   Blackwell Publishing, 2001, 496pp. £22.99. ISBN 9781405122658.
A collection of 38 original essays from leading international scholars. Each entry discusses the main concepts, theories and recent research. Topics are wide-ranging, including coverage of traditional themes, such as Marxism, alongside emerging areas such as feminism, post-modernism and political identity in a globalized world. References for further reading are provided.

574 Central currents in sociological theory
R. Boudon and M. Cherkaoui, eds   Sage Publications, 1998, 3328pp. 8 v., £990. ISBN 9780761962991.
Divided into two 4-volume sets, this scholarly collection of articles provides a comprehensive guide to the development of social theory from 1700 to the present which is suitable for use by researchers and advanced level students. It includes coverage of the key concepts, schools of thought and individual theorists. Each set is arranged around eight core themes: social action and basic processes of interaction; social institutions; social structure; social representations; social change; theoretical orientations; problems in the philosophy of social sciences; sociology's reflections upon itself and its relations with other social sciences.
- **Contemporary sociological theory 1920–2000** Sage Publications, 1999. £525. ISBN 0761962425.
- **Roots of sociological theory 1700–1920** Sage Publications, 2000. £525. ISBN 0761962417.

575 **Handbook of historical sociology**
G. Delanty and E.F. Isin, eds   Sage Publications, 2003, 417pp. £75.
ISBN 9780761971733.
A solid introduction to the historical development of
sociology. It comprises 26 original articles arranged into
three sub-sections: foundations, approaches and themes. The
first section contains reviews of the contributions to the
discipline of key sociologists (such as Marx, Weber, Parsons,
Foucault and Hobsbawm). The second section considers the
interrelationship between the development of sociology and
related fields such as historical geography, cultural studies
and subaltern studies. The final part contains 13 essays on
key areas of sociological research. These are wide-ranging in
scope, including coverage of traditional areas such as class
and nationalism as well as more recent areas such as urban
sociology and gender studies.

576 **The handbook of political sociology: states, civil
societies, and globalization**
T. Janoski [et al.], eds   Cambridge University Press, 2005, 838pp.
£30. ISBN 9780521526203.
A scholarly survey of the field sub-divided into several
thematic sections. Key topics include political sociology
theory and concepts; the formation, structure and transitions
of the state; civil society and the processes of political
action; state policy and the impact of globalization upon
politics. Each section contains several long essays with
extensive bibliographies to guide further reading.

Social Structure, Organization & Control

class • criminology • social control • social inequality •
social mobility • social structure • working-class studies

Social Structure

Introductions to the subject

577 **The inequality reader: contemporary and
foundational readings in race, class and gender**
S. Szelenyi and D.B. Grusky   Westview, 2006, 640pp. £27.99. ISBN
9780813343457.
A good starting point for students seeking an introduction to
examples of contemporary and classic research on social
inequality today. It includes coverage of social class, social
stratification and racial and sexual inequalities from a range
of methodological and theoretical perspectives.

Research centres & institutes

578 **CAMSIS: social interaction and stratification scale**
www.camsis.stir.ac.uk
A research project involving the construction and
dissemination of a model of social stratification called the
CAMSIS (Cambridge Social Interaction and Stratification)
scale. It provides a distinctive measure of social stratification
which is grounded in actual social behaviour. The website
provides access to information about the aims and progress
of the project, including working papers, reports and data.

These include useful contemporary discussion of how social
stratification and class should be measured.

579 **Center for Working-Class Studies**
www.as.ysu.edu/~cwcs/
A specialist research body based at Youngstown University,
Ohio. It was the first American centre to focus specifically on
the study of working-class life and culture. Its website
provides information on its aims and research. It includes
access to newsletters and details of ongoing research. Also
provided is a directory of useful resources, including a
bibliography of further readings and listing of related
websites. These focus on American working-class history and
trade union and labour history.

580 **Centre for Longitudinal Studies**
www.cls.ioe.ac.uk
An ESRC (Economic and Social Science Research Council)
Resource Centre based at the Institution of Education,
University of London. It is internationally renowned for
conducting three key surveys: the 1958 National Child
Development Study, the 1970 British Cohort Study and the
Millennium Cohort Study. These long-term studies monitor
the lives of a large number of British individuals from birth
into adulthood, analysing such factors as health,
income, educational attainment, employment and family life.
They therefore offer fascinating insight into the changing
nature of British social life, patterns of inequality and
change during the 20th and 21st centuries. The website
provides details on the aims, methodology and results of the
surveys. It includes free access to many examples of related
statistical datasets and research papers.

581 **Centre for Research on Inequalities & the Life
Course**
www.yale.edu/ciqle/
Based at Yale University, this specialist research centre is
renowned for its empirical work on inequalities of social
class, generation and gender across the contemporary life
cycle. Its website provides information on its aims, history
and activities. It includes information about its famous
German Life History Study (GLHS) which comprises more
than 12,500 quantified life histories of East and West
German women and men born between 1890 and 1971. It is
possible to search the online Ciqle Literature Database to
find references to articles, reports and statistical data
relating to its surveys. Many papers and reports may be
downloaded in full-text.

582 **Centre for Research on Socio-Cultural Change**
www.cresc.man.ac.uk
A major research centre funded by the UK Economic and
Social Research Council (ESRC) incorporating staff from the
University of Manchester and Open University. It is one of
the first specialist centres to examine cultural change and its
economic, political and social consequences. Key themes
include recent transformations in cultural values and politics;
the changing cultural economy; transformations in media
and culture. Its website provides information on cutting-edge
research in this area. It includes free access to working
papers and project reports.

583   ChangeQual: the economic change, unequal life-chances and quality of life research network
www.nuff.ox.ac.uk/projects/ChangeQual/index.asp
A major European research programme funded by the DG Research 5th Framework Programme, which is coordinated by Nuffield College, Oxford. It investigates a number of themes relating to social and economic inequality in EU nations. Key topics include the nature and consequences of changing work patterns; income inequality, poverty and lifestyle deprivation; changes in family life; comparative analysis of inter-generational wealth transference; social integration and social cohesion. Project information and full-text data and conference papers can be accessed online from the website.

584   Economic & Social Research Council, Research Centre on Micro-Social Change
www.iser.essex.ac.uk/misoc/
An interdisciplinary research centre based at the University of Essex which specializes in studying social change in the UK. Key themes include the changing nature of work roles; the family; social behaviour, beliefs and values; social stratification; and poverty. Its website provides free access to information and results from its ongoing research projects on these themes.

ESDS Qualidata
See entry no. 32

585   Havens Center for the Study of Social Structure & Social Change
www.havenscenter.org
A specialist research centre housed in the Sociology Department at the University of Wisconsin-Madison. It is the home of the 'Real Utopias' project, which discusses radical alternatives to social organization. The website has details of current research projects. It also maintains an archive of papers and lectures from visiting scholars and staff.

586   Institute for Research on World Systems
http://irows.ucr.edu
Based at the University of California, Riverside. This is a key body for interdisciplinary research into long-term large-scale social change and its ecological, geographical and political causes and effects. Its website provides information on current research into the processes of social change and globalization. It includes free access to working papers and tables of contents from the *Journal of World-systems Research*.

587   Institute for the Study of Social Change
http://issc.berkeley.edu
A specialist research unit based at the University of California, Berkeley which studies how processes of social change construct and reform categories of race, ethnicity, class and gender. Its website offers information on research projects relating to these themes. Some examples of recent research papers may be downloaded.

588   Social Issues Research Centre
www.sirc.org
An independent, non-profit, UK-based organization which conducts research on social and lifestyle issues. These cover a broad range of issues, including the changing nature of British social life and attitudes. Many reports are commissioned by consumer product companies and trace changing trends in expenditure and lifestyle choice. A few recent examples which give a flavour of the range of topics studied include Jubilee Women – Fiftysomething Women – lifestyle and attitudes now and fifty years ago; The Noughties – The Decade of Diversity. Full-text materials can be downloaded from the website.

Digital data, image & text collections

589   European Socio-economic Classification (ESeC)
www.irc.essex.ac.uk/esec
A research project undertaken by a consortium of European institutions 2004–6. It designed a classification system of socio-economic positions which could be applied in cross-cultural research studies. The archived website provides discussion of the difficulties of meaningfully classifying social and economic groups. It includes online versions of the scheme and associated research documents.

590   Family Resources Survey
Great Britain. Department for Work & Pensions   United Kingdom. Department for Work & Pensions, annual. Published online.
www.dwp.gov.uk/asd/frs/
This official survey collects information on the incomes and circumstances of private households in the UK. It has been running since October 1992. Its website provides information on the aims, methodology and results. It includes full-text annual reports from 1998 onwards. These offer insight into changing trends in household size, family income, assets and savings.

Directories & encyclopedias

591   Class in America: an encyclopedia
R.A. Weir   Greenwood, 2007, 1088pp. 3 v., £170. ISBN 9780313337192.
The first encyclopedia to focus specifically on the history and current state of class in America. This three-volume set contains over 500 short essays on social theorists, concepts, organizations and welfare programmes. It includes materials examining the intersection between class, gender and ethnicity.

Handbooks & manuals

592   The Blackwell companion to social inequalities
M. Romero and E. Margolis, eds   Blackwell Publishing, 2005, 592pp. £85. ISBN 9780631231547.
Authored by leading scholars, this single volume contains a collection of essays which survey the present scope of the discipline and its emerging areas of debate. Topics covered include racial, social and class inequalities; social exclusion in contemporary society; policy responses to social inequality; the media and technology as a site of both repression and resistance; and methodological concerns in researching social inequality.

593   The Blackwell companion to social movements
D.A. Snow, S.A. Soule and H. Kriesi   Blackwell Publishing, 2003, 776pp. £99.99. ISBN 9780631226697.
A collection of original essays by leading international scholars. Includes coverage of ethnic, social, political,

religious, economic and protest movements. Sub-divided into five main sections: the context and conditions of social movements; the field of action and dynamics; social psychological dimensions; the consequences and outcomes of movements; and finally several essays which survey several major movements. Each essay discusses the major theoretical debates and contemporary field of research.

594   British social attitudes
23rd edn, Sage Publications, 2007, annual, 272pp. £45. ISBN 9781412934329.
www.natcen.ac.uk/natcen/pages/or_socialattitudes.htm
Annual survey carried out by Britain's largest independent social research organization, the National Centre for Social Research (NatCen). Provides a fascinating insight into the social attitudes and political and economic life of Britain's population. Each volume contains essays which interpret the findings from the most recent survey and draw historical comparisons with those of earlier years. Individual surveys focus on different social, economic and political issues. Appendixes provide information on the methodology of the survey.

595   Social mobility in Europe
R. Breen, ed.   Oxford University Press, 2004, 468pp. £75. ISBN 9780199258451.
A comprehensive study of trends in intergenerational social mobility in 11 European nations between 1970 and 2000. The handbook comprises 15 essays, with detailed supporting data tables, which analyse and compare the different class structures. It includes materials from Western and Eastern European nations.

596   Social stratification
D. Inglis and J. Bone, eds   Routledge, 2006, 2240pp. 4 v., £695. ISBN 9780415361330.
This four-volume set brings together a comprehensive collection of articles covering all aspects of the study of social stratification. They include examples of classic scholarship on class, caste, ethnicity and social inequality as well as more recent research on globalization and the emergence of new forms of social exclusion.

597   Social stratification, class, race and gender in sociological perspective
D.B. Grusky   Westview, 2000, 928pp. £28.50.
A comprehensive collection of articles covering a wide range of fields of social stratification. Includes examples of classic sociological studies of class and social structure as well as more recent analyses of economic, racial and gender inequality. Topics covered include forms and sources of stratification; the structure of contemporary stratification; the consequences of stratification and its future. The volume includes a sample study plan for students.

Keeping up to date

598   Continuity and change: a journal of social structure, law and demography in past societies
Cambridge University Press, 1985–, 3 p.a. £45. ISSN 02684160.
http://journals.cambridge.org
A leading academic journal which focuses on the historical sociology of continuity and change in the social structure of past societies worldwide. Each issue contains examples of

cutting-edge research articles and recent book reviews. Available online or in print.

599   Research in social movements, conflicts and change
JAI Press, 1997–, irregular. £60.
A leading series established in 1977 by Louis Kriesberg of Syracuse University's Maxwell School of Citizenship and Public Affairs. It publishes examples of recent academic research covering social movements, conflict resolution and social and political change. Each volume focuses on a specific issue and can be purchased separately. Recent examples include coverage of identity and empowerment issues in social movements and political oppression of selected social groups.

600   Research in Social Stratification and Mobility
Elsevier, qtrly. Prior to 2006 this title was published by JAI Press approximately annually. Each title was published as a separate monograph volume., €73. ISSN 02765624.
www.elsevier.com
The official journal of the Social Stratification Research Group of the International Sociological Association. It provides access to cutting-edge research articles and book reviews covering the latest research projects on all aspects of social stratification, social class and social inequalities worldwide. It includes abstracts from conference papers presented at International Sociological Association conferences. Available online or in print.

Social Control

Introductions to the subject

601   The Oxford handbook of criminological theory
M. Maguire [et al.], ed.   4th edn, Oxford University Press, 2007, 1220pp. £36.99. ISBN 9780199205431.
www.oup.com/uk/orc/bin/9780199205431/
Well regarded textbook which provides students with a comprehensive grounding in recent criminological theory, research, policy issues and debates. It includes coverage of sociological theories of crime; the social construction of crime and crime control; and policy reactions to crime. The associated website provides online support materials, including quizzes; essay advice and suggested web-links.

602   Student handbook of criminology and criminal justice
J. Muncie and D. Wilson   Routledge Cavendish, 2004, 328pp. £21.95. ISBN 9781859418413.
Designed specifically for undergraduates, this text offers an excellent grounding in contemporary criminological theory, with a key emphasis on the British experience. Chapters cover the main theories and concepts; the political dimensions of criminal justice and the structure and operation of the agencies of the criminal justice system. Student-friendly features include definitions of key terms, suggested seminar questions and lists of further readings.

603   Understanding deviance
D. Downes and P. Rock   5th edn, Oxford University Press, 2007, 450pp. £23.99. ISBN 9780199278282.
Excellent guide to criminological theory. Provides a

chronology of the main schools of thought in Europe and North America, presenting their main theories, criticisms and concepts and placing them in their historical contexts. Includes coverage of recent themes such as social exclusion, feminist criminology and radical criminology. A bibliography of further reading is provided.

Dictionaries, thesauri, classifications

604   The Sage dictionary of criminology
E. McLaughlin and J. Muncie, eds   2nd edn, Sage Publications, 2005, 504pp. £21.99. ISBN 9781412910866.
Provides a solid introduction to key concepts and debates within criminological theory. Includes coverage of important contemporary policy issues such as anti-social behaviour, sex crime and virtual criminology. Each entry is clearly laid out, containing a definition of the term, discussion of its distinctive features, examination of any controversies in interpretation and a list of key readings for further research.

Official & quasi-official bodies

605   Scandinavian Research Council for Criminology
www.nsfk.org
Established in 1962 by the Ministries of Justice in Denmark, Finland, Iceland, Norway and Sweden with the aim of advising the governments on criminological issues, this organization offers a wealth of information on current criminological research in Scandinavian nations on its site. It includes detailed information on research projects and recent and forthcoming conferences. Also accessible is the Bibliography of Nordic Criminology. This searchable database provides references to books, articles, chapters, reports and other research material covering all aspects of criminology, including many examples of materials in Scandinavian languages not widely indexed elsewhere.

Research centres & institutes

606   Australian Institute of Criminology
www.aic.gov.au
Australia's pre-eminent national crime and criminal justice research agency. It acts to conduct research into all aspects of crime and criminological theory for the Australian government. Its website provides detailed information on its recent and ongoing research on the nature, causes and punishment of crime in Australia. It includes free access to statistics, policy papers and full-text research reports dating from the late 1990s to the present. Key themes include crime in indigenous communities, juvenile delinquency and national policing and crime prevention initiatives.

607   Center for Study & Prevention of Violence
www.colorado.edu/cspv/infohouse/databases.html
A specialist research programme based at the Institute of Behavioral Science (IBS) at the University of Colorado at Boulder which attempts to understand and prevent violence in modern society.This includes coverage of adult violence, sexual abuse and domestic violence, and juvenile delinquency. The main emphasis is on North America, though other areas of the world are also covered. Its website provides free access to a number of valuable databases.

These include VioLit, a seachable index of abstracts of articles; books and other literature relating to juvenile violence; VioSource, a database listing teaching materials and resources relating to the understanding and prevention of violence; and VioPro, a listing of American-based violence prevention, intervention and treatment programmes.

608   Centre for Crime & Justice Studies
www.kcl.ac.uk/depsta/rel/ccjs/
An independent charity, based at King's College London, which is concerned with the study of all aspects of crime and the British criminal justice system. Its website provides information on its aims and current activities. It includes access to some full-text speeches and articles. Also accessible are tables of contents and some selected papers from its key publications, *The British Journal of Criminology* and *Criminal Justice Matters*.
▪ **CrimeInfo.com** www.crimeinfo.org.uk. An information website maintained by CCJS in order to provide the general public with the real facts about crime in Britain today. Key features include: statistics about crime rates; dictionaries of terms; online fact sheets on the operation of the criminal justice system; quizzes and monthly discussion topics.

609   Centre for Crime & Justice Studies, Harm & Society
www.crimeandsociety.org.uk
A social policy think-tank based at the Centre for Crime & Justice Studies at King's College London. It was created in 2003 as the Crime & Society Foundation and has since established a strong reputation for new research on the role and current operation of the British criminal justice system. In 2007 it changed its name to Harm & Society and widened its remit to incorporate wider research into the nature and impact of risk-taking behaviours in British society. The website provides free access to many of its monographs, research reports and conference papers. It also regularly includes commentary and analysis on current events. Areas of concern include crime and punishment, youth justice and anti-social behaviour.

610   Centre for Criminological Research
www.crim.ox.ac.uk
This research centre is housed in the Faculty of Law of the University of Oxford. It is recognized as one of the UK's most prominent criminological departments conducting research into a wide range of fields covering the historical, empirical and sociological study of crime and criminal justice systems worldwide. This includes coverage of sentencing and punishment; public opinion and crime policy; victims of crime and rehabilitation. Its website provides details of its aims, courses, research projects and publications.

611   International Institute for the Sociology of Law
www.iisj.es/home.asp
Founded in 1988 by the International Sociological Association's Research Committee on the Sociology of Law and the Basque Government. It offers leading training courses in socio-legal studies. Its website provides information on the aims of the Institute, its scholarship and courses. It includes listings of forthcoming conferences and access to some of its online working papers.

612   Pathways Into and Out of Crime
www.pcrrd.group.shef.ac.uk
A major research project funded by the UK Economic and

Social Research Council (ESRC) 2003–6 which explored how children and young people who are identified as being 'at risk' of being future offenders negotiate pathways into and out of crime. Five key groups were studied: children with emotional/behavioural difficulties; members of urban black and Asian cultures; substance abusers; poor families; and families with a parent in prison.The website provides free access to information about the project, plus archived research reports and conference papers.

Associations & societies

613 American Society of Criminology
www.asc41.com/
A leading professional organization which aims to promote the scholarly study of criminology. It is wide-ranging in focus, including coverage of all aspects of the prevention, control and treatment of crime and delinquency. Its website provides details on its aims, membership and activities. It includes contents pages and some selected research articles from its leading scholarly journals: *Criminology: An Interdisciplinary Journal*; *Criminology & Public Policy*; *The Criminologist*.

614 British Society of Criminology
www.britsoccrim.org
The leading British criminological society supporting teaching and research about crime, criminal behaviour and the criminal justice system in the UK. Its website provides information about its aims, membership and recent events. It includes free access to proceedings from some of its annual conferences, book reviews and news about ongoing criminological research.

615 European Society of Criminology
www.esc-eurocrim.org
An academic society which acts as a forum for European research, teaching and/or practice in the field of criminology. Its website provides information on recent research programmes, publications and events. It includes newsletters; tables of contents from its journal *The European Journal of Criminology*; and some abstracts and presentations from recent conferences. All areas of criminology are covered, including juvenile justice and delinquency and examples of research being conducted in Eastern Europe.

616 Hate Crimes Research Network
www.hatecrime.net
A useful website for those seeking information about recent academic study on hate crime. Maintained by a network of researchers based at Portland State University; it includes coverage of the motivation and responses to racially motivated crime, religious crime and homophobia, with a particular emphasis on North America. In addition to providing information about ongoing research in Portland, it also provides listings and reviews of recent publications, conferences and news stories plus links to academic discussion forums.

617 World Society of Victimology
www.worldsocietyofvictimology.org
A non-governmental organization with Special Category consultive status with the Economic and Social Council (ECOSOC) of the United Nations and the Council of Europe which brings together researchers, victims and practitioners to advance the study of the nature and extent of victimization, its causes and remedies. It includes coverage of victims of crime, wars and violence. The website provides information on the aims and activities of the association. It includes forthcoming conference lists and newsletters. These offer insight into recent research on victims.

Portal & task environments

618 Crimetheory.com
www.crimetheory.com
This site is designed and maintained by Bruce Hoffman of the Department of Sociology at the University of Washington. It is intended as a 'one-stop' educational resource for teachers and students of theoretical criminology. It includes access to full-text classic texts; timelines of key events; glossaries of criminological terms; and brief biographies of principal theorists.

Discovering print & electronic resources

619 Criminal Justice Abstracts
Sage Publications, 1968–, qtrly. ISSN 01469177.
www.sagepub.com
Prepared in cooperation with the Don M. Gottfredson Library of Criminal Justice at Rutgers University Law Library, this key source indexes and summarizes key journal articles, book chapters, monographs, dissertations and unpublished research reports. All areas of criminology and criminal justice are covered, including crime and delinquency; criminal law; policing and delinquency. Coverage is international in scope. Available in print or electronically via a number of database services. Prices differ for individual or corporate subscribers. Details can be obtained from the publisher's website.

620 National Criminal Justice Reference Service Abstracts database [USA]
National Criminal Justice Abstracts Service   National Criminal Justice Reference Service. Available free of charge from website. Also offered via a number of commercial systems such as databases offered by CSA and EBSCO publishing.
www.ncjrs.gov/library.html
This database is compiled by the National Criminal Justice Reference Service. It provides references and abstracts of more 190,000 publications relating to all aspects of criminal justice and criminal justice policy published from 1970 to the present. These include US Federal, State and local government reports; books; research reports; journal articles; and some unpublished research papers. Topics covered include all aspects of the causes of crime, criminology and punishment of offenders. Materials have a North American bias.

Directories & encyclopedias

621 Encyclopedia of criminology
R.A. Wright and M. Miller, eds   Fitzroy Dearborn Publishing, 2005, 2000pp. 3 v., £245. ISBN 9781579584658.
A useful three-volume set, containing over 500 scholarly essays. Materials are sub-divided into a number of key themes, including criminal behaviour, the justice system,

criminal law, theories of the causes of crime and prominent practitioners. A variety of cross-disciplinary viewpoints are presented, although the main emphasis remains on contributions from North America and Europe. Suggestions for further reading and related website lists are offered.

Encyclopedia of law and society: American and global perspectives
D. Clark   See entry no. 92

Handbooks & manuals

622   The Blackwell companion to criminology
C. Sumner and W. Chambliss   Blackwell Publishing, 2003, 544pp. £149.95. ISBN 9780631220923.
26 original essays which focus on a wide-ranging collection of topics covering both classical and contemporary criminology from a global perspective. Includes entries on the relationship between theories of gender, race and crime; modern genocide; juvenile delinquency and punishment. Each essay surveys key theories, concepts and recent research.

Keeping up to date

623   Journal of criminal justice and popular culture
University of Albany, 1993–, 3 p.a.
www.albany.edu/scj/jcjpc
An open-access scholarly e-journal published since 1993 by the University at Albany School of Criminal Justice. It offers free access to articles and book reviews covering all aspects of crime, criminal justice and popular culture. The complete archive of articles can be viewed online.

Sociology of Population, Family & Gender

ageing • childhood • families • feminism • gay & lesbian culture • gender • kinship • sexuality • sociology of age-related groups • sociology of the family • women in society

Sociology of Age-related Groups

Introductions to the subject

624   Introduction to childhood studies
M. Kehily   Open University Press, 2004, 216pp. £19.99. ISBN 0335212670.
A key textbook which provides an interdisciplinary introduction to the social study of childhood. It includes coverage of historical, socio-cultural and policy perspectives. Topics include historical representations of childhood; childhood and sexuality; the sociology of childhood and the the changing nature of children's relationships with the electronic media.

Research centres & institutes

625   Bronfenbrenner Life Course Center
www.human.cornell.edu/che/BLCC/Research/index.cfm
A multi-disciplinary research centre based at Cornell University. It specializes in life-course research, focusing on change and stability in human life cycles across generations; and in different social, historical and geographical contexts. Its website provides information on its current research plus free access to examples of full-text research papers and reports. These cover a wide range of topics, including career and work pathways; the impact of poverty on development and aging; social networks, social integration and social support throughout the life cycle.

626   Centre for Research on Ageing & Gender
www.soc.surrey.ac.uk/crag
A research centre based in the Department of Sociology, University of Surrey, which is well known for its cutting-edge research into the relationship between gender and aging. Areas of concern are wide-ranging and cross-disciplinary, including coverage of how health, psychology and socio-economic position effect men and women's different experiences of growing old. Its website provides information on recent and ongoing research programmes. It also lists conferences and other events.

627   English Longitudinal Study of Ageing
www.ifs.org.uk/elsa/index.php
This research project is being conducted by a number of UK research bodies, including the Institute for Fiscal Studies and University College London. It is the first large-scale study to examine the interrelationship between the economic, social, psychological and health elements of the ageing process. Its website provides information about the aims, methodology and ongoing results of the survey. It includes free access to some online reports and papers.

628   ESA Research Network on Ageing in Europe
www.ageing-in-europe.de/
A specialist research group of the European Sociological Association which aims to act as a forum for international collaboration on research into ageing. Its website hosts the Ageing mailing list where information about conferences, publications and new research projects is regularly posted. It also provides free access to a selection of its conference papers from 2001 onwards. A wide range of topics is covered, including health and quality of life, intergenerational relationships, ageing societies and social welfare and the employment of older people.

629   Oxford Institute of Ageing
www.ageing.ox.ac.uk
A specialist research centre which studies the impact of ageing at the global, national and individual levels. Key themes of interest include the demography of ageing; changing family life and relationships; the impact of an ageing population on employment and the labour market; and health, social policy and ageing. Its website provides information on its research programmes and conferences. It offers free access to many of its working papers from 2002 onwards.

630　Sheffield Institute for Studies on Ageing
www.shef.ac.uk/sisa
An interdisciplinary research centre based at the University of Sheffield, whose main focus of interest is in issues relating to the health and quality of life of older people. Its website provides information about its recent events and ongoing research projects. Some examples of recent lectures and papers may be downloaded.

Associations & societies

631　Policy Research Institute on Ageing & Ethnicity
www.priae.org
A charitable institution which is the leading body working in the field of ageing and ethnicity in the UK and Europe. Its website provides information on the latest conferences, research and support programmes. This includes coverage of policy, research, information and practice on black and minority ethnic elders, their income, health and quality of life. It is possible to download some policy papers and reports from the website.

632　Sociology of Youth and Generation Research Network
www.valt.helsinki.fi/esa/youth.htm
A research network of the European Sociological Association which aims to encourage cross-European collaboration on the teaching and research of adolescence and youth studies, inter-generational relations and the sociology of childhood. Its website provides information about the aims and recent activities of the group, its recent conferences and discussion list.

Digital data, image & text collections

633　Survey of health, ageing and retirement in Europe
www.share-project.org
Coordinated centrally at the Mannheim Research Institute for the Economics of Aging, the Survey of Health, Ageing and Retirement in Europe (SHARE) is a multidisciplinary and cross-national database of microdata on health, socio-economic status and social and family networks of individuals aged 50 or over. Data has been collected from over 11 European nations since 2004. It constitutes a rich source of information and cross-cultural comparison on the health and well-being of this age group. Some datasets and associated code books and research papers can be downloaded free of charge from the website. Some registration required.

Directories & encyclopedias

634　Contemporary youth culture: an international encyclopedia
S.R. Steinberg, P. Parmar and B. Richard, eds　Greenwood, 2006, 650pp. 2 v., £115. ISBN 9780313327162.
A wide-ranging collection of essays written by experts covering all aspects of youth culture in the post-1945 period. It includes an introductory essay which sets youth culture in its historical context and a timeline of key events. Other essays cover youth subculture; the betrayal and use of media by adolescents; and politics and youth activism. The encyclopedia includes examples of poetry, lyrics and writings written by young people which enable them to express their viewpoint on the issues raised.

635　Encyclopedia of relationships across the lifespan
J. Turner　Greenwood, 1996, 512pp. £80. ISBN 9780313295768.
A useful single-volume cross-disciplinary work which highlights key themes and theories relating to human interaction and development between different genders, generations and across different cultures. Each entry provides a list of bibliographic references for further reading. An appendix lists professional organizations and key journals.

636　International encyclopedia of adolescence
J.J. Arnett　Routledge, 2006, 1312pp. 2 v., £215. ISBN 9780415966672.
An excellent two-volume work which contains essays on the socio-cultural lives of young people around the world. It enables cross-cultural comparisons of the historical development of teenage subcultures in individual nations; plus discussion of the contemporary lives, beliefs, generational struggles and evolving identities of adolescents in western and non-western societies.

Keeping up to date

637　Youth-Study@jiscmail.ac.uk
www.jiscmail.ac.uk/lists/YOUTH-STUDY.html
A UK-based academic mailing list. Many of the participants are members of the British Sociological Association Youth Study specialist interest group. It contains regular postings on new publications, research projects and conferences. The website offers free access to a searchable archive of all messages posted since 2003.

Sociology of the Family

Research centres & institutes

638　Centre for Research on Families & Relationships
www.crfr.ac.uk
A consortium of Scottish research centres based at the University of Edinburgh which provides high-quality research on family relationships with a particular focus on the Scottish experience. Its website contains information on its ongoing research programmes. It includes free access to the full text of many of its research briefings published since 2001. Topics covered by these include family life in Scotland; the changing roles of teenagers and grandparents; and the experiences of familes of drug users.

639　Families and Social Capital ESRC research group
www.lsbu.ac.uk/families
A network of social research projects funded by the UK Economic and Social Research Council (ESRC). A key area of concern is whether changing forms of family life have led to the development of new forms of social relationships. Strands of research are examining the impact of ethnicity; changing work and employment roles; and alterations in family structure and roles. The website provides information about the aims of the programme and its constituent

projects. It includes free access to examples of cutting-edge research reports.

640 Newcastle Centre for Family Studies
www.ncl.ac.uk/ncfs/index/
A specialist research unit based at the University of Newcastle upon Tyne. Key areas of research focus on aspects of the divorce process; juvenile justice; communication in families; children with parents in prison; and preventative programmes for children at risk of offending or anti-social behaviour. Examples of recent research papers can be read online.

Portal & task environments

641 Kinship and social organization: an interactive tutorial
www.umanitoba.ca/faculties/arts/anthropology/kintitle.html
A hypertext online tutorial created by Brian Schwimmer of the University of Manitoba to provide a detailed introduction to kinship, descent systems and social structure. Although originally designed for anthropologists, it offers useful insight into different systems worldwide. Six ethnographic case studies are used to illustrate the principles: the Akan of West Africa, the Igbo of Nigeria, Turkish peasant villagers, the Yanomamo of the Amazon, the Dani of New Guinea and the ancient Hebrews.

Discovering print & electronic resources

642 Sage family studies abstracts
Sage Publications, 1979–, qtrly. £135. ISSN 01640283.
www.sagepub.co.uk
Contains abstracts of recent journal articles, books and papers relating to new research, theory and policy on all aspects of the family and family life. Wide-ranging coverage includes family economics; gender roles; sexuality and theories; and methods in family research. Available online or in paper. Prices differ for individual or corporate subscribers.

Directories & encyclopedias

643 International encyclopedia of marriage and family
J. Ponzetti, ed. 2nd edn, Macmillan Reference, 2003, 2000pp. 4 v., £280. ISBN 9780028656724.
Useful four-volume work which surveys the patterns and variations in modern family life from a global perspective. Includes coverage of examples from nations of Africa,; Asia, the Pacific, Europe, the Middle East, the Americas and the Caribbean. Many articles are written by scholars from these regions. Coverage is broad, including articles on related issues of abortion, gay and lesbian parenting and domestic violence. Many entries contain suggestions for further reading.

Handbooks & manuals

644 The Blackwell companion to the sociology of families
J. Scott, J. Treas and M. Richards, eds Blackwell Publishing, 2004, 624pp. £90. ISBN 9780631221586.

Authoritative volume of original scholarly essays. Covers a wide range of new research on the changing nature of modern family life. Main emphasis is on the family in Europe and North America. Includes coverage of gay, lesbian and immigrant groups, plus discussion of the impact of globalization and technological change. Extensive bibliographic references are provided.

645 Handbook of marriage and the family
M.B. Sussman, S.K. Steinmetz and G.W. Peterson, eds 2nd edn, Kluwer Academic, 1999, 838pp. £88.50. ISBN 9780306457548.
A useful collection of essays from established scholars on the nature of the family and its role in society. Includes coverage of the past, present and future role of the family as well as examining diversity in modern family life, gender roles and the family and social policy. Also provided are some entries on methodologies for studying the family.

646 Handbook of world families
B.N. Adams and J. Trost Sage Publications, 2004, 704pp. £85. ISBN 9780761927631.
Provides a survey of families in 25 nations worldwide, setting them in the context of the wider social-economic and religious order of the individual state. Each entry includes a demographic and historic description profile of the country plus discussion on gender and age-related roles, child rearing practices and stresses on the family.

647 Sourcebook of family theory and research
V.L. Bengtson [et al.], eds Sage Publications, 2004, 648pp. £96. ISBN 9780761930655.
www.ncfr.org
This textbook is sponsored by the National Council on Family Relations. It aims to provide students and social workers with a solid grounding in family relations theory and research methods. It emphasizes the value of multi-methods approaches in family research by integrating theory development with the development of research methods. The National Council on Family Relations website offers access to some supporting materials, including a 'who's who' of family researchers and other interactive materials.

Sociology of Gender & Sexuality

Introductions to the subject

648 A concise glossary of feminist theory
S. Andermahr, T. Lovell and C. Wolkowitz Arnold, 1997, 256pp. £10.99. ISBN 9780340596630.
Useful introduction to over 300 theoretical concepts and theories associated with feminism in the post-1968 second wave period. Entries include definitions of key terms, discussion of their origins and any contentious issues associated with them. Wide-ranging coverage of fields, including semiotics, psychoanalysis, structuralism, post-structuralism and deconstruction.

649 Issues in feminism: an introduction to women's studies
S. Ruth 5th edn, Mayfield, 2001. £30.99. ISBN 9780767416443.
A best-selling student textbook which contains 65 reprints of famous articles discussing a wide range of theories and concepts relating to feminist theory. Includes examples of

classic and contemporary writings covering feminism, gender and women's studies. Each article is prefaced with an introduction which explains its importance and sets it in its historical and theoretical context.

650 The sociology of gender: an introduction to theory and research
A. Wharton   Blackwell Publishing, 2004, 280pp. £18.99. ISBN 9781405101257.

A useful textbook offering a concise overview of contemporary gender theory and research. It includes coverage of such themes as gender and work, gender and institutions, and the creation of a gendered identity. Works from major theorists are discussed and summarized.

Dictionaries, thesauri, classifications

651 Biographical dictionary of British feminists
O. Banks, ed.   Prentice-Hall, 1990, 224pp. o/p. ISBN 9780745001128.

Specialist collection of two volumes which conveys the variety and complexity of British feminism in the period 1800–1945. It includes many entries for figures missing from the Dictionary of National Biography (DNB). Entries are arranged alphabetically under name, but it is possible to use the subject index to trace members of the same political organization or movement. They typically provide rich descriptive detail about the life and work of the individual. Each contains a listing of key biographical sources, including references to the DNB where applicable.
- Harvester Wheatsheaf, 1990. ISBN 0745001122.
- **1. 1800–1930 O. Banks**   Longman, 1985, 256pp. o/p. ISBN 9780710801326.
- **2. 1930–1945** Prentice-Hall, 1990, 224pp. o/p. ISBN 9780745001128.

652 Biographical dictionary of women's movements and feminisms: central, eastern and south eastern Europe, 19th and 20th centuries
F. de Haan, K. Daskalova and A. Loutfi, eds   Central European University, 2006, 678pp. £45. ISBN 9637326391.

Excellent source containing biographical portraits of feminists and women's rights movements from 22 nations of Eastern and Central Europe. This includes coverage of the former Communist nations of Europe as well as Turkey, Albania and Greece. Many articles are written by scholars of the same country and highlight lesser-known figures. Emphasis is on historical figures; living writers are excluded.

653 Historical dictionary of feminism
J. K. Boles and D.L. Hoeveler   2nd edn, Scarecrow Press, 2004, 488pp. £61. ISBN 9780810849464.

Useful guide to the key persons, organizations, theories and court cases important to the history of feminist thought and the feminist movement. Main emphasis is on the USA and Europe, though there is also coverage of other areas of the world. Includes an introductory essay and chronology of key events. A bibliography of references is also provided.

Research centres & institutes

654 Feminist Majority Foundation
www.feminist.org

American organization founded in 1987 to campaign for the

legal, social and political equality of women. Its website provides information on its aims and campaigns. It is a useful source of information on the women's rights and feminist movement in the USA, providing access to news headlines; reports of recent court cases; calendars of events and full-text documents. Topics covered include women's health and reproductive rights, women's activism and women and work. The website has a large section of information on feminist research which contains links to key organizations, courses and feminist journals.

655 National Council for Research on Women
www.ncrw.org

A network of more than 100 leading US research, advocacy and policy institutes covering all aspects of research and practice relating to women's lives. Its website maintains an excellent clearinghouse of online papers, reports and factsheets from its member institutes. Other features include conference listings and a useful directory of key American research centres and experts in women's studies.

656 Safra project
www.safraproject.org

A UK-based research organization which specializes in studies and advocacy projects by and about lesbian, bisexual and transgender Muslim women. Its website is a useful source of information on issues relating to Islam and sexuality. It includes access to its research reports plus news about other projects, events and publications in this area. The main emphasis is on the UK, although there is some coverage of international issues.

Associations & societies

Fawcett Society
See entry no. 1935

657 International Association for the Study of Sexuality, Culture & Society
www.iasscs.org

IASSCS was founded in 1997. It seeks to promote the academic study of sexuality, focusing on its social, cultural and political aspects. This includes coverage of issues relating to gay, lesbian and transgender studies. Its website provides information on membership and activities. It includes details of forthcoming conferences and the contents pages of its key journal publications: *Culture Health and Sexuality* and *Sexuality Research and Social Policy*.

658 Society for the Scientific Study of Sexuality
www.sexscience.org

A US-based professional society dedicated to the academic and scientific study of all forms of human sexuality and sexual relations. This includes coverage of psychology, sociology, biology and sexual therapy. Its website offers free access to information about grants and courses in North America, directories of academic websites, and tables of contents from key academic journals, including the *Annual Review of Sex Research*, *Journal of Sex Research* and *Sexual Science*.

659 Sociologists for Women in Society
www.socwomen.org/

An international organization of social scientists,

practitioners and researchers who aim to work together to improve the position of women within sociology and society in general. The SWS website is a useful source of information about discrimination against women in the sociological profession and academia in general, and the efforts of activists to campaign against this. It includes free access to its newsletters; bibliographies of recommended books, journals and films; and information on forthcoming conferences and events.

Libraries, archives, museums

660 Glasgow Women's Library
www.womenslibrary.org.uk
A library run for and by women which is located in Glasgow, Scotland. Its collections include a large lesbian archive. The website includes information about library holdings and access. It includes an online timeline of key events in British lesbian history which is illustrated with digitized examples of its clippings of magazines, journals, newspaper articles, badges and ephemera.

661 Lesbian Herstory Archives
www.lesbianherstoryarchives.org
The oldest and largest lesbian archive worldwide, based in New York. Its website provides information on the history, holdings and activities of the archive. It also includes useful listings of new lesbian books.

662 National Women's Library
www.londonmet.ac.uk/thewomenslibrary
The largest dedicated collection of library and archive materials relating to women's history in the UK. It was originally known as the Fawcett Library and now forms part of London Metropolitan University. Holdings cover a wide variety of topics, including women's rights; the suffragette movement; sexuality; and women's family and working lives. The emphasis is primarily on women in Britain, but some international material is held. Its website provides information on the history, function and current activities of the Library. It includes online access to the Library catalogue.

Portal & task environments

663 Feminist theory website
www.cddc.vt.edu/feminism/enin.html
An excellent resource hosted by the Center for Digital Discourse and Culture at Virginia Tech University which provides students and the general reader with free access to information; explanations and links to websites relating to fields of feminist theory; different national manifestations of feminism and individual feminist writers.

664 Second wave and beyond
http://scholar.alexanderstreet.com/display/WASM/
An electronic portal launched in 2006 which aims to create an online scholarly community where researchers, activists and students can consider issues relating to feminist theories and social activism. It is peer reviewed by an academic board and currently provides access to online discussion forums; collections of oral histories of the women's movement; online reading lists; book reviews and other

writings. The main emphasis is on the experiences of American women since the 1960s.

665 Women: a gateway to Library of Congress resources for the study of women's history and culture in the United States
http://rs6.loc.gov/ammem/awhhtml/
An excellent guide to research resources held by the Library of Congress. It is based on a printed guide to the collections which has been redesigned for online use with added free access to some digitized content. Topics covered are broad, encompassing all aspects of the economic, social and political history of American women from earliest times. Advice on how to trace specific types of material (books, journal articles, archives, photographs and audio-materials) using the Library catalogues is offered. In many cases it saves time by providing direct links to the relevant online catalogues and databases. A growing number of the original primary source materials mentioned can now be accessed free of charge online. These include interesting examples of 19th-century suffragette photographs and diaries and letters from early women's rights campaigners.

666 Women and social movements in the United States, 1775–1940
http://womhist.binghamton.edu
An online resource centre for students of American women's social, economic and political history. It is maintained by an editorial board and comprises learning modules in the form of document projects, each of which is organized around a specific question about a single social movement, using examples drawn from approximately 15–20 primary resource documents. These include archival materials from women's reform organizations such as the Women's Trade Union League, the National Association of Colored Women, the National Consumers' League, the National Woman's Party and the Women's International League for Peace and Freedom. At the present time approximately 25% of the materials are offered on open access. The remaining percentage require a subscription with Alexander Street Press.

667 Women and society: an internet reference project on the world wide web
www.womenandsociety.buffalo.edu/mainpage.htm
A website for finding academic resources for women's studies. It links to internet resources organized under a number of headings, including bibliographies, filmographies, journals and associations. It also has an unpublished papers repository and course syllabi repository. The site is run by researchers at the University of Buffalo, State University of New York.

668 Women's studies database
www.mith2.umd.edu/WomensStudies
A well regarded website maintained by the University of Maryland which offers a comprehensive directory of links to internet resources covering all aspects of the academic study of women's social, economic and political lives. It includes links to books, papers, organizations and journals. Other features nclude a collection of online reading lists on different subject areas and course syllabi. The main emphasis is on English-language materials.

669   Women's studies librarian
www.library.wisc.edu/libraries/WomensStudies/
Maintained by the University of Wisconsin Library, this site offers an excellent starting point for beginning research on women's studies. It provides free access to a database of core books; WAVE (a women's studies video and audio visual listing); online research tutorials and numerous subject-based bibliographies. Also provided are directories of links to the websites of recommended journals and women's studies organizations worldwide.

670   WSSLINKS
http://libr.org/wss/wsslinks/index.html
Developed and maintained by the Women's Studies Section of the Association of College & Research Libraries, the purpose of WSSLINKS is to provide a directory of links to recommended websites covering all aspects of women's studies. It includes sections for health, history and politics. Each listing is sub-divided into resource type (including journals, organizations and research institutes). Annotations on content are provided. The main emphasis is on English-language materials.

Discovering print & electronic resources

671   Gender inn
www.uni-koeln.de/phil-fak/englisch/datenbank/e_index.htm
A searchable bibliographic database maintained by the University of Cologne which provides free access to over 8000 records relating to monographs and book chapters covering all aspects of gender studies and feminist literary criticism. Main coverage is of English-language books published in Britain and North America from 1985 onwards. Abstracts of content are provided.

672   Gender Studies Database
National Information Services Corporation. Annual subscription.
www.nisc.com/
This service consists of Men's Studies database and Women's Studies International. The latter is a well regarded resource which combines a number of long-standing bibliographic services, including Women's Studies Abstracts and Women's Studies Bibliographic Database. Together they comprise a rich source of information for locating references to journal articles, book chapters, unpublished papers, government/legal publications and reports about all aspects of gender studies. Details about online and CD-ROM pricing can be obtained from the publisher's website.

673   GENESIS: developing access to women's history sources in the British isles
www.genesis.ac.uk
The Genesis website was developed from funding from the Research Support Libraries Programme (RSLP) and is currently maintained by the staff of the Women's Library at London Metropolitan University. It enables researchers to quickly locate important materials relevant to all aspects of women's studies held in UK libraries, archives and museums. These include books, journals and archival papers relating to women's social and political history, feminism and the struggle for women's rights. Each entry provides a description of the collection and details about how to access it. The website also contains an extensive directory of women's studies websites.

674   LGBT Life with full text
EBSCO Publishing. On request.
www.epnet.com/titleLists/qt-complete.pdf
Formerly known as GLBT Life, this subscription database indexes and abstracts over 130 core journals and over 290 key books and reference works relating to all aspects of lesbian, gay, bisexual and transsexual issues. They include popular and scholarly titles covering all aspects of LGBT history, psychology, politics and culture. The database also contains the full text of a number of key journals, including *The Advocate, Gay Parent Magazine, Girlfriends, GLQ: A Journal of Lesbian & Gay Studies, James White Review, ISNA News, Ladder* and *Lesbian Tide*. These include examples of historical significant activists newspapers from the USA. A glossary of LGBT terms is also provided.

675   Men's bibliography: a comprehensive bibliography of writing on men, masculinities, gender, and sexualities
M. Flood   15th edn, 2006. ISBN 0646180886.
http://mensbiblio.xyonline.net/
A comprehensive and up-to-date bibliography of writing on men, masculinities, gender and sexualities which has been maintained and regularly updated by Michael Flood since 1992. It is available free of charge online. It lists over 16,000 books and articles which are sub-divided into over 30 subject categories. These include useful textbooks for beginners; men and feminism; research methods; and men's movements.

676   Studies on Women and Gender Abstracts
Taylor & Francis, 1995–, bi-monthly. £613. ISSN 1467596X.
Contains citations and abstracts for journal articles, books and conference proceedings on women's studies published since 1995. Wide-ranging and international in coverage. Includes materials relating to both theoretical and empirical research. Topics covered range from female culture to the social psychology of women; gender and sexuality; social policy; health; and media treatment of women worldwide. Prices differ for individual and institutional subscribers.

677   Women's Studies International
National Information Services Corporation, 1972–, qtrly. On demand.
www.nisc.com
A subscription database which contains the contents of several key bibliographic sources. These include Women Studies Abstracts; MEDLINE Subset on Women; New Books on Women & Feminism. Together they constitute a rich source of references to books, articles and papers covering all aspects of women's lives and feminist theory from approximately the 1970s onwards. They are particularly strong in indexing materials from the English-language feminist press. Further details on content and price can be found on the publisher website.

Digital data, image & text collections

678   Andrea Dworkin website
www.nostatusquo.com/ACLU/dworkin
This site is maintained by supporters to act as a memorial to the life and work of leading feminist Andrea Dworkin (1946–2005). In addition to biographical information, it also offers free access to an online library of her writings, articles, speeches and interviews. These include important

examples of her work on feminism, women's rights, sex abuse and pornography, with copyright information.

679   Contemporary Women's Issues: health and human rights
Gale, 1992–, weekly. On demand.
www.oclc.org
A subscription database which offers access to information on women in over 150 nations worldwide. A wide range of topics is covered, including health, employment, education and human rights. There is also substantial coverage of women's rights and gay and lesbian issues. Over 2000 journals and research reports are indexed. These include examples of publications from academic organizations, government bodies, intergovernmental organizations and charities. An increasing amount of the titles also offer full-text articles. Price on demand from the publisher's website.

Directories & encyclopedias

680   Completely queer: the gay and lesbian encyclopedia
S. Hogan [et al.]   Henry Holt, 1998, 704pp. £16.99. ISBN 9780805060317.
Contains entries on the history, issues, concepts and subculture of gay and lesbian life in the 20th century. Biographies of key gay and lesbian civil rights figures are provided and there are entries on the history of the struggle for equality in individual nations worldwide. Also contains a chronology of key events and a list of further readings.

681   Encyclopedia of feminist theories
L. Code, ed.   Routledge, 2000, 560pp. £26.99. ISBN 9780415308854.
Single-volume encyclopedia providing cross-disciplinary coverage of second wave feminist theory of the English-speaking world, covering the period approximately 1960–2000. Includes useful mini-biographies of key feminists which locate their thinking within the wider context of theoretical debate and offer references to further reading. An introductory essay provides an overview of the historical development of feminist theory.

682   Encyclopedia of women social reformers
H. Rappaport   ABC-CLIO, 2001, 800pp. £128.50. ISBN 9781576071014.
A comprehensive guide to the lives of key women activists from the 18th century to the 1970s. Coverage is international in scope, including examples of women's rights campaigners, suffragists, feminists and Third World political campaigners. Only women involved in peaceful lobbying are included. Therefore some examples of female revolutionaries are omitted. Each entry offers a biographical essay with references for further reading. The volumes contain detailed indexes by cause, country and name.

683   Glbtq: an encyclopedia of gay, lesbian, bisexual, transgender and queer culture
www.glbtq.com
glbtq.com provides free access to the world's largest online encyclopedia of gay, lesbian, bisexual and transgender history and culture. It comprises several thousand entries reviewed by an editorial board of academic scholars. These cover a wide range of areas, including the arts, literature and

social sciences. Individual entries cover key concepts, words, organizations and individuals. Bibliographies of further reading are provided. The site also supports online discussion forums where GLBT communities exchange news and experiences.

684   Men and masculinities: a social, cultural, and historical encyclopedia
M. Kimmel and A. Aronson   ABC-CLIO, 2003, 800pp. 2 v., £157. ISBN 9781576077740.
A valuable work which directs the focus on understanding the complexity of the origins, structures and social processes of masculinity, manhood and male behaviour in the contemporary world. Cross-disciplinary in focus, it encompasses materials from historical, psychological, sociological and biological perspectives. Topics covered include male identity, homophobia, sexual violence and pornography.

685   Routledge international encyclopedia of queer culture
D. Gerstner, ed.   Routledge, 2006, 784pp. £125. ISBN 9780415306515.
A wide-ranging work covering all aspects of gay, lesbian, bi-sexual, transgender and queer life and culture in the post-1945 period from an international and cross-disciplinary perspective. Key themes covered include education, health, homophobia and politics. Many articles offer references to internet sites and lists for further reading. An appendix lists useful archival resources and institutions.

686   Routledge international encyclopedia of women: global women's issues and knowledge
D. Spender and C. Kramarae, eds   Routledge, 2001, 1800pp. 4 v., £420. ISBN 9780415920889.
A comprehensive four-volume set containing over 900 articles written by specialists on all aspects of women's history, life and culture worldwide. It includes coverage of feminist philosophy and politics and the women's rights struggle as well as articles on women and the arts, literature and culture. Many entries provide case studies of the experiences of women from different societies around the world, enabling cross-cultural comparison. Each entry offers a bibliography of further reading.

687   The women's movement today: an encyclopedia of third-wave feminism
L.L. Heywood, ed.   Greenwood Press, 2005, 992pp. 2 v., £115. ISBN 9780313331336.
Useful two-volume set which provides a readable introduction to the most recent 'third wave feminism', dating from approximately 1990 to the present. An introductory essay provides an overview of its emergence, chronology and key themes. This is followed by over 200 entries from scholars and activists, highlighting the key concepts, theories, issues and individuals. Coverage is multidisciplinary, ranging from politics, motherhood and technology to girl power and popular culture. The main emphasis is on the women's movement in the USA. Most of the essays provide suggestions for further reading.

688   Women's studies encyclopedia
H. Tierney, ed.   Greenwood Press, 1999, 1640pp. 3 v., £235. ISBN 9780313296208.
Accessible encyclopedia designed to introduce the general

reader to a range of information on the history and contemporary concerns of women's studies. Brings together in one set articles on aspects of history, philosophy, culture and feminist thought. The main emphasis is on the experience of women in North America. Bibliographies of further reading are provided for many of the entries.

Handbooks & manuals

689 A companion to gender studies
P. Essed, D.T. Goldberg and A. Kobayashi, eds   Blackwell, 2005, 576pp. £90. ISBN 0631221093.
A wide-ranging interdisciplinary work which contains 40 essays from specialists in all areas of gender studies. The text is sub-divided into thematic areas which include discussion of the interrelationship between gender, race and class; concepts of masculinity and feminity; gender, space and identity. Each essay offers discussion and insight into recent theories and research.

690 Gay and lesbian issues: a reference handbook
C. Stewart   ABC-CLIO, 2003, 300pp. £31.50. ISBN 9781851093724.
Provides an overview of the historical development of the gay rights movement from the 1800s to the present. Entries are provided for key people, organizations, events and court cases. There are also some essays discussing continuing controversies such as gay marriage and the employment of gay and lesbian individuals in the military.

691 Handbook of language and gender
J. Holmes and M. Meyerhoff, eds   Blackwell, 2003, 776pp. £27.99. ISBN 9780631225034.
A collection of articles written by specialists that examine the ways in which men and women structure and manage their gender identities through speech. Wide-ranging in scope, it includes contributions from linguistics, psychology, anthropology and sociology. Keys areas covered include the history and theoretical background to the study of language and gender; the negotiation of gender identity; institutional discourse; gender and language stereotypes; and the importance of place and time upon gender and language.

692 Handbook of lesbian and gay studies
S. Seidman and D. Richardson, eds   Sage Publications, 2002, 464pp. £85. ISBN 9780761965114.
A collection of essays offering an excellent overview of sociological viewpoints on gay and lesbian studies. The book is sub-divided into 4 sections: history and theory; identity and community; institutions; and politics. Each section contains a number of essays by established scholars which pinpoint the key theories and sociological debates. Suggestions for further reading are provided.

693 Handbook of the new sexuality studies
S. Seidman, N. Fischer and C. Meeks   Routledge, 2006, 512pp. £95. ISBN 9780415386487.
An accessible introduction to recent sociological work on human sexuality worldwide. Over 50 short essays explore the social construction of of sexuality and the relationship between sex and power. Key topics and themes include sex as a social fact; the body; sexual identities; sexual commerce; sexual cultures; sexual politics; and regulation.

694 Handbook of the sociology of gender
J.S. Chafetz   Kluwer Academic/Plenum Publishers, 1999, 644pp. £116. ISBN 9780306459788.
A collection of scholarly essays. Sub-divided into 4 sections: basic issues (containing discussion of gender and feminist theory); macro-level institutions (international development, migration and gender) micro-level processes (socialization, identity and the development of gender roles) and gender and social institutions. Extensive bibliographies are provided.

695 Information sources in women's studies and feminism
H. Olson, ed.   K.G. Saur Verlag, 2002, 200pp. £108. ISBN 9783598244407.
Useful volume which highlights the complexity and politics of finding information on women's studies as well as offering guidance on the major sources. Includes separate chapters on researching information about diversity, lesbian studies and indigenous women.

696 St James Press gay and lesbian almanac
N. Schlager, ed.   St James Press, 1998, 800pp. £63. ISBN 9781558623583.
Provides a useful overview of gay and lesbian history, culture and community in the USA. Cross-disciplinary coverage includes chapters on gay and lesbian health, economics, marriage and politics. Also contains over 100 biographies of key campaigners, a section on historical documents (which reprints important gay rights manifestos, legislation and court cases) and the local and regional history of gay rights in the USA. Each chapter includes a list of accompanying books, journal articles and internet sites for further research.

Keeping up to date

697 H-women discussion network
www.h-net.org/~women/
A valuable online forum covering all aspects of the academic study of women, with a particular focus on the economic, social and political history of women worldwide. It forms part of the H-Net Humanities & Social Sciences OnLine network hosted by the University of Michigan and is fully moderated. Key features include book reviews; conference and job postings; online bibliographies; women's studies syllabi; and e-mail discussion groups.

Sociology of Race & Ethnicity

African-American studies • diaspora • ethnicity • multiculturalism • race relations

Introductions to the subject

698 Theories of race and racism: a reader
L. Back and J. Solomos   Routledge, 1999, 672pp. £22.99. ISBN 9780415156721.
Useful textbook, offering students an overview of the historical development of theories of race and racism. It is sub-divided into six sections which cover the origins of theories of race; sociology and theories of race; racism and anti-semitism; colonialism; feminism; and theories of race and racial identity and diversity in the modern world. A helpful bibliography of further readings is provided.

Dictionaries, thesauri, classifications

699 Dictionary of race and ethnic relations
E. Cashmore 4th edn, Routledge, 1996, 432pp. £19.99. ISBN 9780415138222.
A collection of short essays which define and analyse major concepts, theories, movements and individuals relevant to the academic study of race, race relations and ethnicity. Includes coverage of emerging areas such as post-colonialism, black feminism and hybridity. Lists of further readings are provided.

700 Dictionary of race, ethnicity and culture
G. Bolaffi [et al.], eds Sage Publications, 2002, 356pp. £19.99. ISBN 9780761969006.
Useful dictionary containing information on the definition, history, background and usage of approximately 200 key terms covering race, ethnicity and culture. Coverage is interdisciplinary, including concepts from sociology, anthropology, law and psychology. However, the main emphasis is on European and North American terminology.

Research centres & institutes

701 Centre for Research in Ethnic Relations
www.warwick.ac.uk/fac/soc/CRER_RC
The major academic body in the UK for the research and teaching of race, migration and ethnic relations, based at the University of Warwick. Its website provides information on the aims of the centre, its research, conferences and publications. It is possible to search the library catalogue of the institute online. Key areas include political participation, cultural identity, refugees, ethnic mobilization and nationalism.

702 Centre for Research on Nationalism, Ethnicity & Multiculturalism
www.surrey.ac.uk/Arts/CRONEM
CRONEM is a leading UK-based research unit based at the Universities of Surrey and Roehampton. It is particularly concerned with studying the interrelationship between nation, ethnicity, multiculturalism, citizenship and migration. Its website provides free access to reports and presentations from its ongoing work. Many of these examine sociological, psychological and economic issues relating to life in contemporary multi-cultural Britain.

703 Centre for the Study of Ethnicity & Citizenship
www.bristol.ac.uk/sociology/ethnicitycitizenship
Based at the Sociology Department of the University of Bristol, this specialist interdisciplinary research body has two key areas of interest: ethnicity and state structures and ethnicity and socio-economic structures. The latter includes coverage of racism; ethnic stratification and social mobility; and citizenship and multiculturalism in British society. Its website contains details about current research programmes and events. It offers some free acess to online articles and papers produced by staff members.

European Research Centre on Migration & Ethnic Relations
See entry no. 1546

Associations & societies

704 Association for the Study of Ethnicity & Nationalism
www.lse.ac.uk/collections/ASEN
An international and multidisciplinary network of scholars interested in ethnicity and nationalism which was founded at the London School of Economics in 1990. Publishes two key journals: *Nations and Nationalism* and *Studies in Ethnicity and Nationalism*. Its website is a good starting point for tracing information on current conferences and scholarship in this field. It includes the option of signing up to a research mailing list for regular updates on new developments.

Discovering print & electronic resources

705 Ethnic NewsWatch
ProQuest, 1990–. On demand.
www.proquest.com/
An online subscription database which indexes articles in over 250 newspapers, magazines and journals of the North American ethnic and minority press. These include many Latino, Arab-American and Jewish-American publications overlooked by other mainstream databases. Approximately 25% of titles indexed are Spanish language. The contents provide a useful insight into ethnic minority viewpoints on social issues, race relations and culture which complements the coverage offered by other databases.

706 Sage race relations abstracts
Sage Publications, qtrly. £71. ISSN 03079201.
A useful resource for tracing abstracts of recent research articles and scholarly publications covering all aspects of race relations, ethnicity and the sociology of race. Over 300 key titles are indexed. Coverage is broad, encompassing materials relating to racial theories; the social context of race; and the economic, political, legal and social position of different racial groups in modern society. Available in print or online.

Digital data, image & text collections

707 Oxford African American Studies Center
Oxford University Press.
www.oxfordaasc.com/public
An award-winning online resource centre maintained by Oxford University Press which provides subscribers with access to a wealth of full-text reference materials relating to African-American and Africana studies. There is substantial content relating to the African-American culture, social groups and political and social history, including detailed coverage of race relations and the struggle for equality. Full-text content includes key encyclopedias and reference works (*Encyclopedia of African American History 1619–1895*; *Black women in America*; *Africana*; and the *African American national biography*), full-text documents, maps, images and timelines. There is also a well organized teacher resource section. Price on request from the publisher's website.

Directories & encyclopedias

708 Encyclopedia of diasporas: immigrant and refugee cultures around the world
M. Ember, C.R. Ember and I. Skoggard Kluwer Academic, 2004, 1274pp. 2 v., £300. ISBN 9780306483219.
A key interdisciplinary work which considers the history, nature and impact of immigration on immigrants and the communities in which they settle. In addition to a survey of the reasons why migration occurs, discussion of the processes of assimilation and adaptation, the volumes also cover the impact upon the communities left behind. It also contains portraits of 60 key diaspora communities worldwide. These offer insight into the history of the group, its identity, rituals, subculture and struggle.

709 Encyclopedia of race and ethnic studies
E. Cashmore Routledge, 2004, 512pp. £100. ISBN 9780415286749.
This single-volume work is based on and complements the author's dictionary of race and ethnic relations. It contains cross-disciplinary scholarly essays on key concepts and theories derived from a variety of social science disciplines, including post-colonial studies, psychoanalysis and sociology. Some entries cover individuals, organizations and events but these are given secondary importance to the focus on specialist theoretical concepts.

710 Encyclopedia of race and racism
Macmillan Reference USA, 2007, 1500pp. 3 v., £150. ISBN 9780028660202.
Major multi-volume set which will be published at the end of 2007. It covers the anthropological, sociological, historical, economic and scientific theories of race and racism in the modern era. Over 400 articles include definitions of terms, biographies of civil rights leaders and contentious issues relating to racism. Also offers a glossary and some full-text primary source documents, including legislation.

The encyclopedia of the Indian diaspora
B. Lal, ed. See entry no. 1561

Handbooks & manuals

711 A companion to racial and ethnic studies
D.T. Goldberg and J. Solomos Blackwell Publishing, 2002, 624pp. £95. ISBN 9780631206163.
A collection of scholarly essays covering contemporary theoretical issues and debates relating to race, racism and ethnicity. A critical introduction provides an overview of the main themes and controversies. Selected essays then consider key areas such as history, political economy, theory, space and culture.

712 The early sociology of race and ethnicity
K. Thompson, ed. Routledge, 2005, 3064pp. 4 v., £695. ISBN 9780415337809.
This comprehensive four-volume collection reprints key texts offering differing perspectives on the sociology of race. It is of particular value for those seeking an introduction to the historical development of theories of race during the 20th century, including examples of early racial theories, as well as the emergence of work from black sociologists.

713 Encyclopedia of black studies
M.A. Asante and M. Karenga, eds Sage Publications, 2004, 565pp. £85. ISBN 9780761927624.
A useful resource which brings together in a single volume over 250 entries covering black and African studies. These cover the key themes, concepts, figures and terminology of the field. The Afrocentric focus means that the articles are able to offer an African focus on theories of race and the social situation of black races and black societies, with a primary emphasis on African Americans. An introductory essay provides an overview of black studies. Typical entries contain suggestions for further reading. An appendix contains an extensive bibliography; lists of black studies programmes at American universities and major black studies journals.

The Sage handbook of nations and nationalism
G. Delanty and K. Kumar See entry no. 1327

Keeping up to date

714 Ethnicities
Sage Publications, 1999–, qtrly. £55. ISSN 14687968.
A quarterly academic journal which publishes articles and reviews covering the interdisciplinary study of ethnicity, nationalism, identity and minority rights. International in scope, it includes access to reviews of the latest international research relevant to the politics and sociology of race. Available in print or online.

Sociology of the Environment
environmental sociology • rural sociology • urban sociology

Introductions to the subject

715 Environmental sociology
J. Hannigan 2nd edn, Routledge, 2006, 208pp. £19.99. ISBN 9780415355131.
A useful textbook which offers insight into contemporary approaches to environmental sociology, focusing on the major themes and perspectives in an even-handed way. Includes coverage of such topical issues as the social construction of environmental problems; the environmental justice movement and the role of the media in communicating information about the environment. It also includes a useful case study on the escalating global conflict over freshwater resources.

716 Key concepts in urban studies
M. Gottdiener and L. Budd Sage Publications, 2005, 240pp. £18.99. ISBN 9780761940982.
Designed specifically to provide a first introduction for students. This text clarifies difficult terminology relating to urban studies, urban sociology and urban geography. Each of the 40 short essays contains a clear, jargon-free definition of the term, highlighting related concepts and offering quotations from major texts which illustrate its usage.

717   Urban theory: a critical assessment
J.R. Short   Palgrave Macmillan, 2006, 272pp. £18.99. ISBN 9781403906595.
A useful introduction for students which summarizes the historical development of urban theory and its modern applications. It includes chapters which discuss different interpretations of the city and social change. Topics covered include the immigrant city; the gendered city; globalization and the city; and modern city planning.

Research centres & institutes

718   Centre for Neighbourhood Research (CNR) Archive
www.neighbourhoodcentre.org.uk
The ESRC Centre for Neighbourhood Research (CNR) received funding as part of the ESRC Evidence Network from 2001–2006. It was instrumental in conducting research into the social, economic and political importance of neighbourhoods and the relationship between social policy and context. Although the programme has now ended, its website continues to house an important archive of its working papers. It also provides free access to the Neighbourhood Question Bank (NQB), a searchable database of neighbourhood-related questions that have been asked in major British national and subnational social surveys from 1990 to 2006.

719   European Institute for Urban Affairs
www.livjm.ac.uk/eiua/
A specialist consultant research body based at Liverpool John Moores University. Its website provides information on current work areas. It includes free access to some recent research papers covering topics relating to urban regeneration, community cohesion and development in the UK.

720   Laboratoire de Sociologie Urbaine (LaSUR)
http://lasur.epfl.ch/index_en.html
A leading research institute based in Switzerland. It uses quantitative and qualitative research methods to study transformations in the contemporary city worldwide. Its website provides free access to news about its recent projects, conferences and publications. It is possible to access some working papers online. The site also offers some links to other French-language urban research institutes.

721   National Institute of Urban Affairs
www.niua.org
A leading American institute involved in research, training and information dissemination about all aspects of urban development and management.

722   Urban Institute
www.urban.org
An independent US-based social policy and research institute which specializes in the study of urban affairs and policy, with a particular focus on the USA. Its website provides free access to papers reports and social survey data from its projects many of which analyse existing US government policy initiatives. It also includes a research methods section with descriptions of commonly used urban research tools and glossaries of terms. Topics covered include metropolitan area housing and community policy and development; health care in the city; and economic policy and the social welfare of urban dwellers.

Associations & societies

723   Community web
American Sociological Association: Community & Urban Sociology Section
www.commurb.org
The website of a specialist sub-section of the American Sociological Association which specializes in the teaching and research of urban and community sociology. It provides details on the history of the organization and its recent activities. It includes tables of contents from its journal *City and Community*, which publishes research and reviews on the social aspects of city life. It also offers collections of course syllabi; directories of useful internet sites and recent book reviews.

724   European Society for Rural Sociology
www.esrs.hu
The leading European professional association for social scientists engaged in the study of rural society. Includes coverage of agriculture; rural development and change; rural identity and heritage; equality and inequality in rural society; nature and environmentalism. Its website highlights recent research; conferences and publications. It also includes reports from conferences and links to tables of contents from its journal *Sociologia Ruralis*.

725   International Network for Urban Research and Action
www.inura.org
An international network of people involved in action and research about cities. Membership includes academics and citizen activists. The INURA website provides access to newsletters; conference and publications listings. These contain information on initiatives relating to urban renewal, housing, employment and life in the city. They include examples from grassroots pressure groups.

726   International Rural Sociology Association
www.irsa-world.org
Formed in 1964, IRSA is an international consortium of regional and continental societies in rural sociology. Its objective is to promote the study of rural sociology and further the application of social research to the improvement of the quality of life for rural populations. Its website is a key source of information on activities, publications, training and research in this field. It includes access to full-text conference papers from recent world congresses. There are also useful directories of links to regional rural sociology associations worldwide. These offer the possibility of tracing information on the existence and activities of non-western sociologists.

Discovering print & electronic resources

727   URBADOC
Urbandata Association, qtrly updates. On demand.
www.urbadoc.com
A subscription database which provides references to over 70,000 articles and reports covering urban and regional

policy in Europe. It is composed of a number of leading indexes: ORLIS (Deutsches Institut für Urbanistik, Germany); Urbamet, Pascal and Francis (Association Urbamet and INIST, France) ; Urbaterr (Centro de Información y Documentación Científica, Spain) and Acompline und Urbaline (Greater London Authority, UK). Materials indexed cover issues relating to urban sociology, local government policy and city life in general. The database is currently updated quarterly.

Directories & encyclopedias

728   Encyclopedia of the city
R. Caves, ed.   Routledge, 2005, 608pp. £140. ISBN 9780415252256.
A useful interdisciplinary source of information for students of urban studies. It contains over 500 brief articles covering key topics and concepts relating to urban sociology; town planning; the culture of the city, economics and architecture. The main emphasis is on the contemporary western world. Suggestions for further readings are provided.

Handbooks & manuals

729   Handbook of rural studies
P.J. Cloke, T. Marsden and P. Mooney   Sage Publications, 2005, 368pp. £85. ISBN 9780761973324.
A comprehensive overview of the current state of theory and research. It is divided into three main sections, covering approaches to rural studies; rural research; and key theoretical coordinates and the new rural relations. Of particular value is its attention on how recent developments in political economy and cultural studies have led to new thinking in the sociological research of rural life, nature and rural social exclusion.

Sociology of Economics & Work

economic & productions systems • economic sociology • leisure • sport

Economic & Production Systems

Introductions to the subject

730   Economic sociology: an introduction
J. Hass   Routledge, 2006, 272pp. £22.99. ISBN 9780415392228.
A useful text designed to introduce students to the complexity of the sociological study of economic systems in an approachable way. It includes coverage of the historical evolution of economic systems and their current manifestations worldwide. Other features include case studies, a glossary of terms and chapter notes summarizing key points.

731   The new economic sociology: a reader
F. Dobbin, ed.   Princeton University Press, 2004, 565pp. £58. ISBN 9780691049052.
A useful volume which represents 20 classic articles which

are essential reading for students. These are arranged into four sections: economic institutions; networks; power; and cognition. An introductory essay provides background on the history and areas of interest of economic sociology.

Research centres & institutes

732   Center for the Study of Economy & Society
www.economyandsociety.org/
Based at Cornell University, this centre is the leading research organization of its kind. It covers a wide range of aspects relating to the sociological study of the economy. This includes economic sociology; network analysis; organizational behaviour; and political economy. Its website provides information on its purpose, conferences and research activities. It includes free access to its full-text working papers from 2000 onwards. These include many examples of cutting-edge research.

733   Cultures of Consumption research programme
www.consume.bbk.ac.uk
A leading British research programme co-funded by the Economic and Social Research Council (ESRC) and the Arts and Humanities Research Council (AHRC) which is conducting research into the changing nature of consumption in a globalized world. This includes coverage of transnational consumption, changing patterns of consumerism in the contemporary world; social status, lifestyle and consumption. The site includes news from the projects, plus free access to some associated research reports and conference papers.

734   Social studies of finance: an ESRC professorial fellowship project
www.sociology.ed.ac.uk/finance/
This site was originally created as part of a professorial scholarship accorded to Donald MacKenzie by the UK Economic and Social Research Council (ESRC). It provides information on British research, conferences and events relating to social studies of finance and the economy. This includes coverage of the application of sociological, anthropological and sociological methods to studies of the economy. The website has up-to-date listings of events, researchers and projects. It also provides free access to a collection of online working papers.

735   University of Pennsylvania, Economic Sociology & Organisational Studies Faculty
http://pesos.wharton.upenn.edu
A world-class centre for the teaching and research of all aspects of economic and organizational sociology which is based in the Management Department of the Wharton School and the Department of Sociology of the University of Pennsylvania. Its website offers information on current research activities. It includes newsletters containing details of recent working papers and listings of events.

Associations & societies

736   Society for the Advancement of Socio-Economics
www.sase.org
An international society which promotes the study of the relationship between economics, society, polity and culture.

Its website provides valuable information on recent events and ongoing research. It offers free access to examples of recent research papers, conference reports and tables of contents from the journal *Socio-Economic Review*. Typical topics covered include socio-economic theory; globalization and work; gender and employment; markets and institutions.

Portal & task environments

737   **Economic sociology: the European website**
http://econsoc.mpifg.de
This site is maintained by Researchers and staff of the Max-Planck Institute for the Studies of Societies in Cologne. It is an excellent starting point for keeping up to date with the latest research in Europe. It includes free access to recent and archived issues of the *Economic Sociology* newsletter which contains research articles and listings of the latest research projects, PhD titles and publications. Other features of the site include collections of links to online syllabi and a bibliography of key texts and articles relating to all sub-fields of economic sociology.

738   **Social Studies of Finance Network**
www.ssfn.org
An international network, headed by staff at the London School of Economics and Political Science, which aims to promote interdisciplinary scientific research on contemporary finance and financial markets. Its website serves to alert academic researchers to forthcoming events and conferences. It also offers online bibliographies of key readings, links to important research journals and mailing lists.

Directories & encyclopedias

739   **International encyclopedia of economic sociology**
J. Beckert and M. Zafirovski, eds   Routledge, 2006, 773pp. £120. ISBN 9780415286732.
Valuable wide-ranging source, containing essays on over 250 topics relating to the impact of social, political and cultural factors on economic behaviour. Includes coverage of classical theory as well as modern phenomena such as technology and globalization. Each entry contains a list of references for further reading.

Handbooks & manuals

740   **The handbook of economic sociology**
N.J. Smelser and R. Swedberg, eds   2nd edn, Princeton University Press, 2005, 748pp. £33.95. ISBN 9780691121260.
Useful introduction to economic sociology. 30 chapters cover all aspects of economic systems, institutions and behaviour. Combines historical and comparative coverage with essays on recent concerns such as globalization and the transition from socialism of the former communist nations of Eastern Europe. Bibliographies of further readings are provided.

741   **New developments in economic sociology**
R. Swedberg, ed.   Edward Elgar, 2005, 1248pp. 2 v., £295. ISBN 9781843765240.
A useful two-volume set which would be of value to the academic researcher. It reprints 42 articles originally

published in the period 1989–2003. They include discussion of the latest research on the classic writings of Weber, Schumpeter and Polyanyi relating to work, economics and the firm as well examples of new research on entrepreneurship and global finance.

Sociology of Work, Leisure & Sport

Introductions to the subject

742   **The sociology of work**
K. Grint   3rd edn, Polity Press, 2005, 400pp. £18.99. ISBN 9780745632506.
A useful introduction for students to classical and contemporary theories of work organization. Includes coverage of the impact of globalization. The text also offers a glossary of terms and a bibliography to guide further reading. Key websites are highlighted.

743   **Sport and society: history, power and culture**
G. Scambler   Open University Press, 2005, 224pp. £21.99. ISBN 9780335210701.
A useful introduction to sociological theories of sport. The text is divided into several parts. The first section traces the historical development of organized sports from earliest times and their contribution to societies and cultures in the western world. The second part presents concise summaries of the major sociological theories and schools of thought and seeks to develop a theory for understanding the changing role of sport in a globalized society. The final section focuses on individual themes such as violence in sport, sporting celebrities and representations of sport in the media.

Sports in society: issues and controversies
J. Coakley   See entry no. 4750

Research centres & institutes

744   **Centre for the Sociology of Sport**
www.le.ac.uk/so/css/
Based in the Sociology Department at the University of Leicester, this specialist research centre combines the resources of the Sir Norman Chester Centre for Football Research and the Centre for the Study of Sport and Society, University of Leicester. It has a strong focus on football, plus research on 'a wide range of sports and sporting issues, including, especially, work on rugby, cricket and field sports'. Football coverage includes fans, football hooliganism and the social importance of the game. The website provides information on teaching and research programmes. It also offers free access to some of its fan surveys and working papers. Downloadable factsheets and summaries of fan surveys.

745   **Football Research Organisation UK**
www.footballhooligans.org.uk/
An online research centre founded by scholar Robin Mansell, which discusses issues relating to the academic study of football in the UK. This includes coverage of the nature and causes of football hooliganism, gender and football, the media and coverage of football and racism in football. The

website provides access to lecture notes, book lists and examples of research papers.

746   LEST: Laboratoire d'Economie et de Sociologie du Travail
www.lest.cnrs.fr
A leading French-language research institute based in Centre national de la recherche scientifique. Since 1969 it has been conducting leading research on the nature and evolution of work and working life. Its website provides information on current and historical projects. Many examples of full-text publications (the majority in French) can be downloaded free of charge from the website.

University of Pennsylvania, Economic Sociology & Organisational Studies Faculty
See entry no. 735

747   University of the Witwatersrand, Sociology of Work Unit
L.L. Heywood, ed.   Greenwood Press, 2005, 700pp. £115. ISBN 9780313331336.
www.sociologyworkunit.org/
A leading African research institute based at the University of the Witwatersrand, Johannesburg. Research centres on several key themes: changing livelihoods in Southern Africa, the restructing of work, comparative labour movements and work in a globalized world. It is possible to access project descriptions and online research reports from the website. These offer insight into recent theories on work from African sociologists.

748   Working Lives Research Institute
www.workinglives.org/
A research centre based at London Metropolitan University which investigates the changing nature of work. It is particularly interested in studying the relationship of race, gender, sexuality and disability to working lives in Britain and Europe and is strongly committed to supporting the work of social justice movements and trade unions. Its website provides access to information about its ongoing research.

Associations & societies

749   British Sociological Association Sport Study Group
www.britsoc.co.uk/specialisms/123
A specialist sub-group of the British Sociological Association which was established in 1995 to promote the research and teaching of the sociology of sport in the UK. Its website provides information on its recent and forthcoming conferences and events.

750   International Sociology of Sport Association
www.issa.otago.ac.nz
Professional association which seeks to promote research into the study of sport and society. Its website is an excellent starting point for tracing information about the latest sociology of sport research and events. It includes lists of recent and forthcoming conferences and tables of contents from its quarterly journal *The International Review for the Sociology of Sport*. There is also a useful directory of links to the websites of some national and regional sociology of sport associations and sports-related academic journals.

North American Society for the Sociology of Sport
See entry no. 4757

Keeping up to date

751   Journal of Sport and Social Issues
Sage Publications, 1976–, qtrly. £55. ISSN 01937235.
www.sagepub.co.uk
The official journal of Northeastern University's Center for the Study of Sport in Society. It publishes examples of the latest research, book reviews and analysis covering a wide range of issues relating to the social impact of sport. Recent themed sections have included social issues in sport management, youth sport and sport subcultures. Tables of contents may be viewed free of charge on the publisher's website, access to the full-text requires a subscription. Available in print or online.

752   Research in Sociology of Organizations series
JAI Press, 1982–, annual. ISSN 0733558X.
www.elsevier.com
A series of research annuals published by JAI Press since approximately 1982. Coverage is broad, encompassing all aspects of the theory, methodology and practical applications of the sociological study of work, organizations and employment. Each volume contains a collection of scholarly essays which summarize the current state of research on a particular topic. Recent subjects covered include social structure and organizations, legitimacy processes in organizations and the sociology of entrepreneurship.
- **M. Lounsbury and M. Ventresca**   Elsevier, 2002. ISBN 0762308729.
- **S. Bacharach, S.M. Gabbay and R. Leenders**   JAI Press, 2001, 300pp. £61.95. ISBN 9780762307708.
- **S. Bacharach and E.J. Lawler, eds**   JAI Press, 2000, 354pp. £60.95. ISBN 9780762306329.

753   Research in the Sociology of Work: a research annual
Elsievier, 1981–, annual. £60. ISSN 02772833.
www.sociology.ohio-state.edu/work/
An edited volume of research essays published annually. Each volume focuses on one specific area relating to the sociology of work, organizational theory and industrial sociology. Recent issues have addressed themes, including globalization, work and the family, employment restructuring, trade unions and worker training.

754   Sociologie du Travail
Elsevier, 1959–, qtrly. €110. ISSN 00380296.
http://france.elsevier.com/
A leading French-language periodical published since 1959 for the Association pour le Développement de la Sociologie du Travail. It covers all aspects of the theory and research relating to the sociology of work. It is a useful starting point for tracing information on new French language publications and research. The journal may be purchased in paper or electronic formats. Tables of contents and abstracts can be viewed free of charge on the publisher's website.

Sociology of Culture, Communication & the Media

communication studies • communication technology •
internet • media • new media • science & technology

Communication Studies

Introductions to the subject

755   **Cultural theory: the key concepts**
A. Edgar and P. Sedgwick, eds   Routledge, 2002, 528pp. £14.99.
ISBN 9780415284264.
Intended to provide a first introduction to difficult
terminology, this text contains brief essays on over 350 key
terms from modern cultural theory. Topics covered include
feminism, post-modernism, semiotics and sociological
concepts of culture. Each concept is clearly defined in
accessible language, highlighting related terms and offering
quotations from key texts. Some suggestions for further
reading are provided.

756   **Cultural theory and popular culture**
J. Storey   4th edn, Prentice Hall, 2006, 191pp. £24.99. ISBN
9780131970687.
Popular textbook which provides an accessible introduction
to the main theories and concepts of cultural studies.
Includes coverage of popular culture, Marxism, feminism,
post-modernism and psychoanalysis. Includes a list of
further readings and useful journals on cultural theory and
popular culture.

757   **Doing research in cultural studies: an introduction
to classical and new methodological approaches**
P. Saukko   Sage Publications, 2003, 256pp. £20.99. ISBN
9780761965053.
A useful guide to the methodology of research in cultural
studies. It provides an overview of the history of social
research in this field and introduces the importance of the
social, political and economic context. Detailed guidance is
offered on choosing research methods, conducting qualitative
research and interpreting the results.

Dictionaries, thesauri, classifications

758   **The Sage dictionary of cultural studies**
C. Barker   Sage Publications, 2004, 256pp. £19.99. ISBN
9780761973416.
Particularly suitable as an introduction for students, this
dictionary contains over 200 entries on the key concepts,
theories and ideas that have influenced cultural studies.
Cross-references are provided to related terms and some
entries contain brief lists of recommended further reading.
An introductory essay defines and provides an overview of
cultural studies.

Research centres & institutes

759   **Center for Cultural Sociology**
http://research.yale.edu/ccs/
Specialist research unit based at Yale University which
focuses on the cross-disciplinary study of how culture
informs and structures social life. This includes coverage of
the impact of globalization. Its website provides information
about its ongoing research and teaching programme. It offers
some free access to working papers written by its staff.

Associations & societies

760   **Culture web**
www.ibiblio.org/culture
The official website of the American Sociological Association
Section on the Sociology of Culture. It provides information
on recent research, conferences and events relating to a wide
range of cultural fields, including political culture, the
relationship between culture, gender and ethnicity, and the
symbolic construction of identity and culture.

Discovering print & electronic resources

761   **Communication Abstracts**
Sage Publications, 1977–, 6 p.a. £166. ISSN 01622811.
www.csa.com
Provides abstracts of articles, reports and publications from
a wide range of international publications. These include over
160 journal titles covering all aspects of communication
studies as well as associated areas of public opinion, film
and media studies, risk communication and the role of new
technology in human communications. Available in print or
online. Prices differ for individual or corporate subscribers.
Details can be obtained from the publisher's website.

Digital data, image & text collections

762   **www.theory.org.uk**
www.theory.org.uk/
This award-winning website created by the School of Media,
Arts and Design, University of Westminster, focuses on
media and cultural studies in an innovative and fun way. It
offers free access to reviews, essays and resources on
cultural critics such as Theodor Adorno, Antonio Gramsci,
Michel Foucault, Anthony Giddons and Judith Butler and on
topics such as identity, media studies, gender studies and
queer theory. It is renowned for its 'trading cards', which
contain summaries of the theories of key writers on online
playing cards!

Directories & encyclopedias

763   **Culture: critical concepts in sociology**
C. Jenks, ed.   Routledge, 2002, 1668pp. 4 v., £625. ISBN
9780415226905.
A collection of scholarly essays covering all aspects of the
history, culture and different meanings and interpretations of
culture by philosophers, critical aesthetics, anthropologists,
sociologists and literary theorists. An introductory essay
guides the reader through the complexity of the subject area,

subsequent essays cover a large number of themes, including culture, social structure and civilization, culture, idealism and belief, culture and materialism, culture and stratification, cultural reproduction, subcultures, visual culture and urban culture.

International encyclopedia of propaganda
R. Colt   See entry no. 1392

Propaganda and mass persuasion: a historical encyclopedia, 1500 to the present
N. Cull, D. Culbert and D. Welch   See entry no. 1393

764   **St James encyclopedia of popular culture**
T. Pendergast and S. Pendergast, eds   St James Press, 2000, 3250pp. 5 v., £425.25. ISBN 9781558624009.
An enormous five-volume set containing over 2500 articles of varying lengths, covering a wide range of areas of contemporary popular culture. They include entries for television and media studies, advertising and film. There are some summaries of influential individual TV programmes, books and films. The main emphasis is on American popular culture. An introductory essay provides background on the history and significance of popular culture.

Handbooks & manuals

765   **The Blackwell companion to the sociology of culture**
N.W. Hanrahan and M.D. Jacobs   Blackwell Publishing, 2004, 520pp. £90. ISBN 9780631231745.
A collection of 28 original essays written by leading scholars. The book is wide-ranging in focus, covering the seven main themes of problems of theory and method, cultural systems, everyday life and the construction of meaning, identity and difference, collective memory and amnesia, the culture of institutions and the culture of citizenship. Each essay discusses the major theories, concepts and debates, offering suggestions for further reading.

Keeping up to date

766   **H-PCAACA** [USA]
www.h-net.org/~pcaaca
A scholarly discussion forum which forms part of the H-NET Humanities online initiative and is affiliated with the Popular Culture Association and the American Culture Association. The site includes reports on the latest initiatives of each of these organizations. It also includes regular postings on new publications, research initiatives, jobs and forthcoming conferences covering all aspects of the scholarly study of popular culture. The main emphasis is on American popular culture.

767   **Post Modern Culture Online Journal**
Johns Hopkins University Press, 1990–, 3 p.a. Price on demand. ISSN 10531920.
www3.iath.virginia.edu/pmc
A leading electronic journal of interdisciplinary thought on contemporary cultures which has published the work of such noted critics as Kathy Acker, Charles Bernstein, Bruce Robbins, Bell Hooks and Susan Howe. Each issues contains scholarly articles, essays and reviews. The website provides free access to tables of contents, access to the full-text requires a subscription.

Sociology of the Media

Digital data, image & text collections

768   **Communication and Mass Media Complete**
EBSCO Publishing. On request.
www.epnet.com
An excellent subscription database which provides an index to articles from over 400 key journal titles in subject areas relating to media and communications, including references to some titles from as far back as 1915. It incorporates the contents of CommSearch (formerly produced by the National Communication Association) and Mass Media Articles Index (formerly produced by Pennsylvania State University). Also accessible are full-text articles from over 200 of the journals. The database also contains a thesaurus of communication terms. Prices on request from the publisher's website.

Communications Technology & New Media

Research centres & institutes

769   **ESRC e-Society Programme**
www.york.ac.uk/res/e-society
A major research programme funded by the UK Economic and Social research Council (ESRC) 2002–7 to investigate the impact of digital technologies, and in particular the growth of the internet, on society. It comprises 28 projects covering six related areas of research: children and the e-society, cities and neighbourhood change, health services in an e-society, privacy, identity and trust in an e-society, socio-political divisions and change, work, consumption and business. The website provides access to a large number of research reports, articles and presentations from the projects.

770   **EU kids go online**
www.eukidsonline.net
A major research programme funded by the EC Safer internet plus Programme. During 2006–2009 it is comparing and evaluating how young people use the internet in 18 European Union states. A particular focus of interest is the social, cultural and regulatory influences affecting both risks and children's and parents' responses to them. The website provides free access to information about the project. It includes literature reviews, research papers, and links to the websites of other projects examining children's use of the internet.

771   **Pew internet and American life project**
www.pewinternet.org
This influential American research project regularly features in press stories about the growth and social impact of the internet. It is part of the Pew Research Center for the People & the Press and focuses on research relating to the impact of the internet on family and community life, working practices,

education, health care systems and civic and political life. Its website provides free access to a vast collection of topical social surveys and research reports relating to the American population. These are of great value in tracing recent and emerging trends in internet use and attitudes.

772   POLIS
www.lse.ac.uk/collections/polis/
A major research body established as a joint initiative by the London School of Economics (LSE) and London College of Communication. It aims to act as a forum for discussion among journalists and academics about the role and impact of the media on modern society. There is substantial coverage of the ethics of journalism and online media. The website provides free access to working papers, podcasts of events and blogs maintained by staff. These offer insight into ongoing research.

773   USC Annenberg Center for the Digital Future
www.digitalcenter.org
A leading institute based at the University of Southern California, Annenberg. For over 25 years it has been researching issues relating to media communications technology and policy. Its website provides information on its mission and activities. It includes access to full-text papers and research reports from its projects. These include materials relating to its Digital Futures Project which is analysing the impact and future social potential of the internet and an archive of reports from its television violence monitoring programme which operated during the late 1990s.

774   World Internet Project
www.worldinternetproject.net/
A major international collaborative project which is investigating the social, economic and political impacts of the internet worldwide. Its website provides information on the aims and findings of the project. It includes access to the latest research findings and reports from over 30 leading national research bodies and institutions which are participating.

Associations & societies

775   OURMedia/NUESTROSMedios
www.ourmedianet.org/
A global network of academics, activists, practitioners and policy experts who aim to promote the development of stronger citizen- and community-led media. This includes substantial coverage of online and technological media as well as radio and other traditional formats. Its website is a good place for locating news stories from activists, as well as listings of academic conferences, publications and events. There are links to the websites of members.

776   Society for Social Studies of Science
www.4sonline.org
A long-established scholarly society concerned with promoting social studies of science and technology. Its website provides information on recent conferences, publications and events relating to this subject area. It includes tables of contents from its academic journal *Science, Technology and Human Values* and a resource bank

for teachers containing a selection of useful course syllabi and listings of relevant audiovisual materials and journals.

777   Sociology of Science and Technology Research Network
http://sstnet.iscte.pt
A specialist research network of the European Sociological Association (ESA) which seeks to promote the development, discussion and dissemination of research on all social aspects of science and technology. This includes coverage of such topical issues as the regulation of science and technology in a globalized world, the impact and risks of biotechnology and the 'technologization' of society. Its website is an excellent starting point for tracing information on European research in this field. It includes listings of conferences and forthcoming events, plus abstracts and some full-text papers from past conferences.

Digital data, image & text collections

778   OxIS: Oxford Internet Surveys
www.oii.ox.ac.uk/microsites/oxis/
OxIS is a research project of the Oxford internet Institute, University of Oxford. It comprises a series of social surveys on the use of the internet and its impact on life in the UK. This encompasses a wide range of topics, including digital exclusion, the regulation of the internet, security and risk and the rise of online social networking. The website provides free access to a fascinating collection of online datasets, research and methodological reports published since 2002.

Directories & encyclopedias

779   Encyclopedia of new media: an essential reference to communication and technology
S. Jones, ed.   Sage Publications, 2003, 544pp. £85. ISBN 9780761923824.
More than 250 entries covering the key terms, theories and social issues relating to the development of digital communication technologies and human-computer interaction. It includes coverage of the history, technology, economics and global impact of the information revolution. Some biographical entries on key individuals are also offered. A bibliography of selected further readings is provided.

Handbooks & manuals

780   Handbook of new media: student edition
L.A. Lievrouw and S. Livingstone   2nd edn, Sage Publications, 2005, 496pp. £24.99. ISBN 9781412918732.
Aimed at advanced undergraduates and postgraduates, this collection of 22 original essays provides a scholarly overview of the current state of research. A wide range of aspects of new media are covered, including the new information infrastructure, social impact of the internet, globalization and the development of worldwide media, emerging media markets and the governance and regulation of new media technology.

The Oxford handbook of information and communication technologies
R. Mansell [et al.]   See entry no. 5408

Keeping up to date

781   Convergence: the international journal of research into new media technologies
Sage Publications, 1995–, qtrly. £60. ISSN 13548565.
www.sagepub.co.uk
An international refereed academic journal originally established by staff at the University of Luton in 1995. It is renowned for publishing timely research on a wide range of social, political and creative issues relating to the development of the media technologies. This includes substantial coverage of the social impact of the internet, online journalism and gender and technology. Tables of contents and abstracts can be viewed free of charge from the publishers website. Access to full-text articles in print or hard copy reqires a subscription.

Sociology of Religion

church-going • new age movements • religion

Introductions to the subject

782   An Introduction to the sociology of religion: classical and contemporary perspectives
I. Furseth and P. Repstad   Ashgate, 2006, 272pp. £16.99. ISBN 9780754656586.
A useful introduction to classical and contemporary theories of the sociology of religion. Includes coverage of the interaction between religion, gender and ethnicity. Other topics covered include the role of religion in the public sphere and the interrelationship between religions, conflict and violence.

Research centres & institutes

783   Center for Studies on New Religions
www.cesnur.org
International network of scholars and associations working in the field of new religious movements, minority religions and cults. Although it was originally established by members of the Catholic church, it is currently independent of any denomination. Its members seek to promote the academic study of religion and disseminate accurate information about problems associated with some of the new age movements. The website offers news on the nature and extent of new religions worldwide. It includes discussion of controversies concerning allegations of 'brain washing'. Other features include its library catalogue, lists of new publications and details about recent and forthcoming conferences.

784   Hartford Institute for Religion Research [USA]
http://hirr.hartsem.edu
The website of this leading US research institute has a very useful section on the sociology of religion containing links to key websites and a directory of sociologists working in the field. It also maintains an excellent database of articles and books relating to all aspects of the sociological study of

religion, with a particular emphasis on North American research. Many of the entries may be accessed free of charge online.

785   Pew Forum on Religion & Public Life
http://pewforum.org
A specialist project of the Pew Research Center which seeks to understand the intersection between religion, public policy and politics. Its website is a good starting point for tracing news, surveys and research. Key topics covered include the role of religion in contemporary American politics and government policy, religion and world affairs, plus discussion of controversial issues surrounding bioethics, gay marriage and religion and schooling. Its website provides free access to its surveys and full-text research reports.

786   Religion and Society Research Programme
www.ahrc.ac.uk/apply/research/sfi/ahrcsi/religion_society.asp
This major research programme was launched by the Arts and Humanities Research Council and the Economic and Science Research Council in 2007. It is the first UK research programme to foster cross-collaborative work between the arts, humanities and social sciences in order to understand the interrelationships between religion and society. Key themes include religion, identity and community, religion, violence and conflict, texts, spaces and rituals, religion, politics and the state, religion and the media, education and socialization, rituals, texts and identity. The website provides access to information on the progress of the programme and its constitutent projects. It includes full-text working papers and reports.

Associations & societies

787   Association for the Sociology of Religion
www.sociologyofreligion.com
Originally founded in 1938 as the American Catholic Sociological Society, this long-established scholarly association seeks to promote the study of the theoretical, historical and comparative study of religion. Its website offers information on training courses, conferences and publications relevant to the sociology of religion. It also offers details about its quarterly review The Sociology of Religion which contains examples of recent research.

788   British Sociological Association, Sociology of Religion Study Group
www.socrel.org.uk
A large specialist sub-group of the British Sociological Association (BSA) which seeks to promote the profile of the sociology of religion within sociology. Its website is a good starting point for tracing recent and ongoing research covering all areas of the intersection between religion, sociology and popular culture. It includes abstracts of papers from recent conferences and study days, lists of forthcoming events and recent publications. Links are provided to its online discussion forum.

789   International Society for the Sociology of Religion
www.sisr.org
Originally founded in 1948 as the Conférence Internationale de Sociologie Religieuse (International Conference for Religious Sociology), this scholarly society seeks to promote research into all aspects of the sociological study of religion.

Its website provides information on its history, conferences and publications. Also accessible are recent issues of its newsletter which contains notes about the latest research projects.

790 Society for the Scientific Study of Religion
www.sssrweb.org/
Originally founded in 1942 to promote and communicate scientific research on religious institutions, the website of this leading academic body continues to offer news, publications and conference listings about recent academic research relating to religion. This includes materials relating to the sociological, psychological and anthropological study of established and 'new wave religions' and religious cults worldwide.

Digital data, image & text collections

791 Association of Religion Data Archives
www.thearda.com/
The Association of Religion Data Archives (ARDA) strives to democratize access to the best data on religion. Founded as the American Religion Data Archive in 1997 it is currently housed in the Social Science Research Institute at the Pennsylvania State University. Its website provides free access to over 400 datasets. These provide insight into trends in churchgoing, congregation sizes and attitudes towards religion and religious beliefs, mainly in the USA but also in Europe. The site also includes national profiles of religion and religious beliefs for other nations worldwide.

Directories & encyclopedias

792 The encyclopedia of politics and religion
R. Wuthnow, ed. Routledge, 1998, 800pp. £260. ISBN 9780415187404.
An important contribution to the study of the interrelationship between politics, sociology, religion and international history. Over 200 articles trace the way in which major religions throughout history have affected social attitudes and influenced public policy. Entries cover religious movements, key individuals and events.

Handbooks & manuals

793 The Blackwell companion to sociology of religion
R.K. Fenn, ed. Blackwell Publishing, 2003, 512pp. £24.99. ISBN 9780631212416.
Collection of original essays covering all aspects of the sociological study of religion. Clearly divided into 3 sections: classical and contemporary theory, recent trends in the relation of religion to society and a discussion of the boundaries between sociology and other closely related disciplines, such as theology and social anthropology. References for further reading are provided.

Keeping up to date

794 Social Compass: revue internationale de sociologie de la religion (International review of sociology of religion)
Sage Publishing, 1953–, qtrly. £42. ISSN 00377686.
www.sagepub.com
Well established scholarly journal published in association with International Federation of Institutes for Social and Socio-Religious Research (FERES). Includes research articles and book reviews on themes relating to the sociological study of religion. Recent topics covered by themed issues include religion, culture and identity and religion and the state. Issues frequently contain selected papers from FERES conferences. Available in print or online.

Sociology of Education

educational inequality • educational sociology • social organization of schools

Research centres & institutes

795 Center for Social Organization of Schools
http://web.jhu.edu/csos
A specialist research centre based at John Hopkins University which is concerned with examining how changes in the social organization of schools can promote greater academic success among students. All age ranges are covered, from primary schooling to college. The main emphasis is on the American school system. The website provides information on the aims of the centre and its ongoing projects. It includes many examples of ongoing practical classroom and community projects.

796 Centre for Educational Sociology
www.ces.ed.ac.uk
A multi-disciplinary research centre based within the Department of Education and Society at the University of Edinburgh which is noted for its long-established research on educational policy, youth transitions, training and the youth labour market. The main emphasis is on the British experience, with a particular focus on young people in Scotland. Its website contains news from recent conferences and examples of ongoing research. It includes the full text of all CES policy briefs and many working papers from approximately 2004 onwards.

797 Research Unit for the Sociology of Education (RUSE)
http://vanha.soc.utu.fi/RUSE/
Based at the University of Turku, Finland, this specialist research unit focuses on studying the interrelationship between education and work. Key research areas include higher education, adult education, educational policy and comparisons of educational systems. Its website is an excellent starting point for tracing information on Scandinavian publications and research projects. It includes details of RUSE intiatives, plus English-language summaries of RUSE dissertations and working papers.

Associations & societies

798 American Sociological Association, Sociology of Education Section
www2.asanet.org/soe
A specialist association of American sociologists whose website provides access to newsletters containing up-to-date information on courses, events, publications and research projects. It also maintains a bibliography of key books, articles and papers about the sociology of education.

799 Sociology of Education Association
www.lmri.ucsb.edu/resources/sea/
Informal American-based association which seeks to advance scholarship in the field of the sociological study of education. Its website provides information on the aims of the association, its history and activities. It includes details of its annual conferences.

Discovering print & electronic resources

800 Sociology of Education Abstracts
Routledge, 1965–, qtrly. £310. ISSN 00380415.
www.tandf.co.uk
Essential source which has indexed key journal articles covering all aspects of the sociological study of education since 1965. Includes coverage of theoretical, methodological and policy research. Since 2005 the print annual has been issued annually; more regular updates are available via Educational Research Abstracts Online (ERA), which also contains an archive of back issues. Information on institutional and individual subscription rates can be obtained from the publisher's website.

Directories & encyclopedias

801 Education and sociology: an encyclopedia
D. Levinson, P.W. Cookson and A.R. Sadovnik, eds Garland Science, 2000, 700pp. £140. ISBN 9780815316152.
Single-volume work which highlights the key themes and controversies in the sociology of education. Coverage encompasses national and international perspectives. It also includes entries on emerging policy areas such as education and inequality, education and gender, race and educational attainment.

802 International encyclopedia of the sociology of education
L.J. Saha, ed. Pergamon, 1997, 930pp. £144. ISBN 9780080429908.
A useful collection of scholarly articles which introduce the reader to all aspects of the sociological study of education. They include coverage of educational processes and structures plus the key theories and methodology of educational sociology. Detailed bibliographies of further readings are provided.

Handbooks & manuals

803 The early sociology of education
K. Thompson, ed. Routledge, 2006, 3200pp. 7 v., £695. ISBN 9780415345279.

A comprehensive collection of reprinted 'classic articles' which trace the historical development of educational sociology from its origins in the 1920s to the 1950s. Key emphasis is on developments in the USA and Europe. Arranged into 7 thematic volume s; topics covered include principles of educational sociology, the social system of the high school, changing concepts of the relationship between school and society, and teaching practice and educational sociology.

804 The international handbook on the sociology of education: an international assessment of new research and theory
C.A. Torres and A. Antikainen, eds Rowman & Littlefield, 2003, 384pp. £21.99. ISBN 9780742517707.
A comprehensive survey of recent research covering all aspects of the sociology of education. The 18 chapters are arranged into several thematic areas: theory and methodology, sociology of education in international contexts and critical issues in sociology of education. The second section provides good coverage of examples of international research, including materials from the non-western world.

805 Sociology of education: a critical reader
A.R. Sadovnik Routledge, 2007, 552pp. £21.99. ISBN 9780415954969.
A useful collection of reprinted articles chosen by noted sociologist Alan Sadovnik which cover both classic and contemporary approaches to the sociological study of education. A wide range of areas relating to education, schooling and society are covered.

806 Sociology of education: major themes
S. Ball, ed. Routledge, 2000, 2416pp. 4 v., £695. ISBN 9780415198127.
This comprehensive set contains reprints of 100 papers important to the development of the sociology of education from the 1950s to the 1970s. The volumes are organized into four themes: theories and methods, inequalities and oppressions, institutions and processes, and politics and policies, offering researchers a wide-ranging survey of the historical evolution of the discipline.

Keeping up to date

807 International Studies in Sociology of Education
Routledge, 1991–, 3 p.a. £57. ISSN 09620214.
A well regarded journal which has published scholarly articles on topics related to the sociology of education since 1991. Coverage is international in scope with examples of materials relating to up to date research projects worldwide. Each issue focuses on a specific theme. Recent examples include social inequalities and education and the impact of globalization upon education. Available in print or online.

808 Research in the Sociology of Education
JAI Press, annual. £60. ISSN 14793539.
Published annually, this series contains scholarly essays and reviews of the latest research relating to the sociological study of education and schooling. Each volume concentrates on a different thematic issue. Recent examples have included:children's lives and schooling across societies and schools and the reproduction of social inequalities.

809   Sociology of Education
American Sociological Association, qtrly. On demand. ISSN 00380407. www.asanet.org

A long-established academic journal which has been publishing the latest research articles for over 75 years. All aspects of the sociological study of education are covered. This includes materials on a range of different age groups plus studies of the individual, institutional and social contexts of learning. The journal is available in print or online. Price details can be obtained from the publisher's website.

Sociology of Health & Illness
healthcare delivery • healthcare sociology • medical sociology

Introductions to the subject

810   Key concepts in medical sociology
J. Gabe, M. Bury and M. Elston   Sage Publications, 2004, 280pp. £18.99. ISBN 9780761974420.

Designed specifically to provide a first introduction to difficult texts and terminology. Contains 50 short essays organized into 5 key areas: the social patterning of health, including health inequalities and the social causation of health, the experience and meaning of illness, the knowledge of and practice about health, health work, and health care organization and policy.

811   The sociology of health and illness
S. Nettleton   2nd edn, Polity Press, 2006, 352pp. £16.99. ISBN 9780745628288.

A useful introduction to key contemporary debates within the field. Covers a diversity of subjects, including the social construction of medical knowledge, the sociology of the body and medical ethics concerning contemporary issues such as stem cell research. It also attempts to explore issues relating to changes in health care policy in the UK. Annotated lists of further reading are provided.

812   Sociology of health and illness: critical perspectives
P. Conrad, ed.   7th edn, Worth, 2005, 569pp. £34.99. ISBN 9781572599215.

Long-established student textbook containing 49 essays covering a wide range of issues relating to the sociological study of health, illness and healthcare. Topics covered include the social and cultural meanings of disease, the politics of healthcare and health economics. It includes some comparative studies of health care systems from North America and the UK.

813   A sociology of mental health and illness
A. Rogers and D. Pilgrim   3rd edn, Open University Press, 2005, 296pp. £23.99. ISBN 9780335215836.

The latest edition of this well regarded textbook is designed to provide a solid introduction to students of major theories of the sociology of health and mental illness. It includes coverage of stigma, the mental health profession, psychiatry and legal control and the intersection between mental health gender, age and ethnicity.

Dictionaries, thesauri, classifications

814   Dictionary of medical sociology
W.C. Cockerham and F.J. Ritchey   Greenwood Press, 1997, 130pp. £56.99. ISBN 9780313292699.

A collection of concise definitions of terms relating to all aspects of medical sociology. Each entry contains a brief discussion of the theoretical and practical applications of the term, plus information on key works in which it appears. An introductory essay provides an overview of the historical development of medical sociology.

Associations & societies

815   American Sociological Association, Medical Sociology Section
http://dept.kent.edu/sociology/asamedsoc/

One of the largest specialist sub-groupings of the American Sociological Association, uniting students, researchers and practitioners interested in all aspects of the sociological study of health and illness. Its website is a useful source of information on its recent events. It includes access to recent issues of its newsletter which contains information on conferences, publications, research projects and grant funding in North America. Directories of links to other key resources are provided.

816   British Sociological Association, Medical Sociology Study Group
www.britsoc.co.uk/specialisms/52.htm

A large specialist grouping of the British Sociological Association comprising academic scholars, researchers and students interested in all aspects of the teaching and research of the sociology of health and illness. Its website is an excellent starting point for tracing news about recent British publications, research projects and events. It includes online archives of its newsletter plus links to tables of contents from medical sociology journals.

817   European Society of Health & Medical Sociology
www.eshms.org

Professional organization which seeks to promote the study of health and society and medical sociology in European universities. This includes coverage of issues relating to health inequalities, health reform and health care services. Its website provides information on the aims and activities of the organization. It includes news about medical sociology conferences and research projects.

818   Foundation for the Sociology of Health & Illness
www.shifoundation.org.uk

A UK-based charity which seeks to promote high quality teaching and research in medical sociology. Its website provides information about its aims and activities. It includes details about research grants and awards, plus details about its academic journal *The Sociology of Health and Illness*.

Directories & encyclopedias

819 Medical sociology: major themes in health and social welfare
G. Scambler, ed.   Routledge, 2005, 1592pp. 4 v., £650. ISBN 9780415317795.
A multi-volume set which reprints articles and essays important to the historical development of medical sociology and its current research concerns. International in scope, they include coverage of social theories of health care and health systems worldwide. The first volume contains a useful introductory essay which provides background on the development of the sociological study of health and illness.

Handbooks & manuals

820 The Blackwell companion to medical sociology
W.C. Cockerham   Blackwell Publishing, 2004, 536pp. £24.99. ISBN 9781405122665.
A compendium of 26 original essays, which offer a wide scholarly coverage of the subject. Includes a very useful section which focuses on regional perspectives on the discipline, containing contributions from practitioners from Asia, Africa and Eastern Europe. Other topics covered include the sociology of the body and sociological analyses of modern health care systems. References for further reading are provided.

Keeping up to date

821 Health Sociology Review
eContent Management Pty Ltd, 1991–, 5 p.a. £80. ISSN 18340806.
http://hsr.e-contentmanagement.com/
An international scholarly journal published in association with The Australian Sociological Association (TASA). It publishes research articles and book reviews covering the policy, promotion and practice of health care from a sociological perspective. Currently approximately five issues are published per annum. Some focus on special issues. Topics recently covered include health inequalities, health policy and death and dying. Abstracts can be viewed free of charge from the website. Full text (in print or online) is for subscribers only.

822 Research in the Sociology of Health Care
Elsevier, 2006, annual. V.24, £60. ISBN 9780762313204.
www.sciencedirect.com/science/bookseries/02754959
This useful yearbook series offers scholarly articles on recent research relating to the sociological study of health and illness. Each volume focuses on a themed issue. Topics covered recently have included: social inequality and health care, technology in health care delivery and patient and provider views of health services.

823 Social Science and Medicine
Elsevier, 1978–, 24 p.a. €337. ISSN 02779536.
www.elsevier.com
An international, peer reviewed journal, published by Elsevier, which provides coverage of health, health policy and health care systems from a social sciences perspective. This includes substantial coverage of the sociology of health, health psychology and economics. it is a rich source of information on recent research and publications. Special topics covered in the last few years include the ethnography of hospitals, patient organizations and health inequalities.

Social Work & Social Welfare

The *Collins internet-linked dictionary of social work* defines social work as: 'The paid professional activity that aims to assist people in overcoming serious difficulties in their lives by providing care, protection or counselling through social support, advocacy and community work'.

At the heart of social work practice are service users. The first part of this section lists references to general resources on social work practice and the ethics, methods and evidence that underpin it, together with key organizations in the field. The second half of the section is devoted to specific groups of service users and areas of service provision, again with a focus on practice. It has content on:

- alcohol and drug misuse
- black and minority ethnic people (including refugees and asylum seekers)
- children, young people and families (including looked after children, adoption, foster care, and young offenders)
- disabilities (including physical and learning disabilities)
- mental health
- older people (including dementia, mental health, and residential care).

care • community care • ethics of social work • social services • social work & the law • social workers

Introductions to the subject

824 Clinical social work practice: an integrated approach
M.G. Cooper and J.G. Lesser   2nd edn, Allyn & Bacon, 2004, 256pp. $83.60. ISBN 9780205408115.
Aimed at advanced clinical practitioners and students. Looks at how to integrate theory and practice on multiple levels. Clinical examples are viewed through the lenses of specific theoretical models and models of intervention are discussed for individual, family or group situations.

825 Community care
N. Thompson and S. Thompson   Russell House, 2005, 112pp. ISBN 1903855586.
Provides an introductory overview of the theory base underpinning community care practice, laying the foundations for future learning and development and building on that foundation by exploring a range of practice issues.

826 Counselling skills in social work practice
J. Seden   2nd edn, Open University, 2005, 192pp. £17.05. ISBN 0335216498.
A practical no-nonsense guide to the application of counselling skills to social work practice. It is written from the author's first-hand experience of working in the field and teaching counselling skills to social work students. Contains useful hints and tips for trainees and busy practitioners and is illustrated throughout with examples of good practice.

827 Effective practice in health and social care: a partnership approach
R. Carnwell and J. Buchanan   Open University Press, 2005, 288pp. ISBN 0335214371.
Looks at partnership in human services between different professional groups delivering health and social care to a broad range of service users. Each chapter focuses on how the challenges of partnership work can be overcome and this is supported by examples from practice and research.

828 Essential theory for social work practice
C. Beckett   Sage Publications, 2006, 240pp. £17.40. ISBN 9781412908740.
Takes a realistic and honest approach to the realities of everyday practice. Part 1 establishes what social workers do and the tools they need; Part 2 considers how to assess, handle and support change in others; Part 3 explores the wide range of roles that social workers must fulfil; and Part 4 strengthens these links between theory and practice. Also includes exercises, case examples, chapter summaries and practice notes.

829 Evidence-based social work: a guide for the perplexed
T. Newman [et al.]   Russell House, 2005, 160pp. £15.50. ISBN 1903855551.
This book advises practitioners on how to formulate practice questions and find information which can answer these questions and to appraise the information for trustworthiness and relevance and build this process into practice on a regular basis.

830 Foundations of evidence-based social work practice
A.R. Roberts and K.R. Yeager, eds   Oxford University Press USA, 2006, 464pp. $69.96. ISBN 9780195305944.
Concise introduction aimed at undergraduate and postgraduate students.

831 Introduction to social work
W.O. Farley, L.L. Smith and S.W. Boyle   10th edn, Allyn & Bacon, 2005, 456pp. $80. ISBN 9780205442157.
Classic introductory text, now in its 10th edition, to social work theories and methods.

832 Introduction to social work and social welfare: critical thinking perspectives
K.K. Kirst-Ashman   2nd edn, Wadsworth, 2006, 560pp. $92.95. ISBN 9780495002444.
Introductory text that aims to enable students to grasp the essence and spirit of generalist social work and the issues in social welfare that social workers address every day. Intended to give students contemplating a career in social work a solid introduction to the profession and to ensure that they begin thinking critically at the start of their studies.

833 Introduction to social work and social welfare: empowering people
C. Zastrow   9th edn, Wadsworth, 2007, 672pp. $197.90. ISBN 9780495095101.
This book provides an in-depth overview of social work as a profession, its relationship to social welfare issues in society and the role of social work and the social worker to assess and intervene with individuals, families, groups and organizations, while at the same time empowering service users.

834 The many faces of social work clients
A.T. Morales and B.W. Sheafor   Allyn & Bacon, 2001, 284pp. $58.60. ISBN 9780205342532.
A brief introduction to social work with a range of service users, including children, older adults, women, disabled persons and members of minority racial and ethnic groups. For social workers and social work students.

835 Modern social work theory
M. Payne   3rd rev. edn, Palgrave Macmillan, 2005, 320pp. £21.99. ISBN 9781403918369.
Offers a comprehensive review of the major groupings of theories within social work, the ideas from which they come, the debates they have spawned and the advantages and problems of their implementation in practice.

836 New Zealand social work: context and practice
M. Connolly, ed.   OUP Australia & New Zealand, 2001, 394pp. £28.99. ISBN 9780195584318.
A comprehensive examination of social work theory and practice in New Zealand. Aimed at undergraduate and postgraduate students of social work, law and sociology and social work practitioners.

837 Psychoanalytic theory for social work practice: thinking under fire
M. Bowers, ed.   Routledge, 2005, 204pp. £18.99. ISBN 041533800X.
Written by practising social workers and social work educators, this text analyses psychoanalytic and psychosocial approaches to social work and relates them to current practices and values.

838 Service user and carer participation in social work
J. Warren   Learning Matters, 2007, 160pp. £15.20. ISBN 9781844450749.
This essential text examines the principal elements of service user involvement and participation across both adult and children's services, drawing together information from research, service users, carers and practitioners across both groups. Aimed at students and practioners, it includes case studies and activities and encourages reflection and the application of this knowledge to practice situations.

839 Social work: fields of practice
M. Alston   2nd edn, OUP Australia & New Zealand, 2005, 368pp. £20.99. ISBN 9780195550474.
A comprehensive text providing a broad overview of social work practice in Australia.

840 Social work and social welfare: an introduction
R. Ambrosino [et al.]   5th edn, Wadsworth, 2004, 560pp. $82.41. ISBN 9780534621773.
Covers the history, values and economic, political and cultural factors that affect social work and social welfare. Aims to give students a broad understanding of the profession of social work itself, with extensive coverage of the social work profession, a brief history of its origin, a discussion of various theoretical principles and applications of these principles to common social problems.

841 Social work in Canada: an introduction
S. Hick   2nd edn, Thompson Educational, 2005, 408pp. CDN$ 56.67. ISBN 9781550771572.
A good introduction to the history and practice of social work in Canada.

842 Social work macro practice
F.E. Netting, P.M. Kettner and S.L. McMurtry   3rd edn, Allyn & Bacon, 2003, 432pp. £84.80. ISBN 9780205380695.
This text focuses on work with organizations and communities, including planned change approaches and implementation. It is distinguished by its unique practice model that shows students how to use communities and organizations to help clients and a strong emphasis is placed on the iterative nature of planned change and the necessity of preparing oneself for conflict in any change effort.

843 Social work practice: an introduction
4th edn, Palgrave Macmillan, 2006, 322pp. ISBN 0333559096.
Discusses a wide range of theories of intervention in social work practice. Uses case material, research evidence and suggestions for further reading to encourage readers to reflect on complex issues in their own practice context.

844 Social work, social welfare and American society
P.R. Popple and L. Leighninger   Allyn & Bacon, 2005, 720pp. $87.50. ISBN 9780205487622.
This book discusses the values, ethics and knowledge needed by social workers. It also provides a political perspective on social welfare, with definitions of liberal, conservative and radical positions, to help readers better appreciate the political context of social welfare programmes. It covers diversity issues and how these affect society at all levels.

845 The task-centred book
P. Marsh and M. Doel   Routledge, 2005, 191pp. £16.99. ISBN 041533456X.
Teaches the necessary practical skills for task-centred social work by setting the approach in the context of the major concerns of modern social work and by linking it to its research basis.

846 Understanding social work: preparing for practice
N. Thompson   2nd edn, Palgrave Macmillan, 2005, 200pp. £17.09. ISBN 1403942021.
Textbook presenting an introduction to the nature of social work; its legal and policy base; the knowledge, skills and

values involved; and the challenges and pitfalls practitioners face.

847 What social workers do [USA]
M. Gibelman 2nd edn, National Association of Social Workers, 2005, 465pp. $49.99. ISBN 0871013649.
An introduction to social work, this text offers an overview of the profession in the USA and offers practical information about the current status of a range of service areas and the types of jobs available. Uses case studies and vignettes throughout.

Dictionaries, thesauri, classifications

848 Collins dictionary of social work
M. Thomas and J. Pierson, comps 2nd edn, Collins, 2006, 624pp. £9.07. ISBN 9780007214785.
Gives concise and comprehensible explanations in jargon-free language of the most important social work terms and is designed particularly for students in further and higher education.

849 Department of Health thesaurus of health and social care terms (the DH-Data thesaurus): managing in health and social care
P. Defriez, ed.; Great Britain. Department of Health 3rd edn, Stationery Office, 2002. Volume 1: alphabetical section, volume 2: hierarchical section, orphan terms, Bliss classmarks. ISBN 0113225601.
Constructed in accordance with IS 2788, this thesaurus includes coverage of health services, health administration and equipment, human biology, preventive and clinical medicine, drugs and the safety of medicines, medical supplies, pathology, nursing, social services and social work. It is the only publication of its kind in the UK.

850 Social Care Online taxonomy [UK]
Social Care Institute for Excellence rev.edn, Social Care Institute for Excellence, 2006.
www.scie-socialcareonline.org.uk/help/files/AlphaTopics180806.pdf
Social Care Online is the UK's most extensive database of social care information. An extensive taxonomy of social care has been developed to aid searching. In addition to the alphabetical topic tree, a hierarchical topic tree is also available on the database.

851 The social work dictionary
National Association of Social Workers 5th edn, National Association of Social Workers, 2003, 529pp. $54.99. ISBN 087101355X.
This key resource for social workers in the USA contains terms and definitions evaluated and edited by an expert editorial review board.

Laws, standards, codes

852 AASW code of ethics
Australian Association of Social Workers 2nd edn, Australian Association of Social Workers, 2002, 36pp.
www.aasw.asn.au/about/ethics.htm
Code setting the standard for ethical practice for social workers in Australia. Available online as a PDF.

853 Care standards legislation handbook [UK]
D. Pearl 3rd edn, Jordan, 2005, 424pp. ISBN 184661015X.
Provides details of all the most important statutes and Statutory Instruments that will be needed by those who are involved in the new regulatory system, established by the Care Standards Act 2000, for care services in England and Wales, including the regulation of childminding and day care provision for young children.

854 Code of conduct
New Zealand. Social Workers Registration Board Social Workers Registration Board (New Zealand), 2005, 10pp.
www.swrb.org.nz/codeofconduct.html
■ **Codes of conduct guidelines** 2005, 15pp.
www.swrb.org.nz/Documents/Code-of-Conduct_Guidelines.pdf.

855 Code of ethics
Canadian Association of Social Workers 2005.
www.casw-acts.ca/
Available in print and online.

856 Code of ethics for social work
British Association of Social Workers British Association of Social Workers, 2003.
http://basw.co.uk/articles.php?articleId=2
The primary objective of the Association's Code of Ethics is to express the values and principles which are integral to social work and to give guidance on ethical practice. The Code is binding on all members and the Association also hopes that it will commend itself to all social workers practising in the UK and to all employers of social workers.

857 Code of ethics of the National Association of Social Workers [USA]
National Association of Social Workers rev. edn, National Association of Social Workers, 1999.
www.socialworkers.org/pubs/code/code.asp
The National Association of Social Workers is the professional body for social workers in the USA. The core values detailed by the organization are based on: service; social justice; dignity and worth of the person; importance of human relationships; integrity; and competence.

858 Essential law for social work practice in Canada
C. Regehr and K. Kanani Oxford University Press, 2006, 220pp. CDN$ 59.95. ISBN 9780195422085.
Comprehensive legal information guide that social workers can use as they interact with the Canadian federal and provincial legal system.

859 Ethics and values in social work
S. Banks 3rd rev. edn, Palgrave Macmillan, 2006, 256pp. £17.99. ISBN 9781403994202.
A useful starting point for understanding the principles around the contruction of values and the dangers of having oppressive values. The use of examples will help students or practising social workers to focus their thinking around ethical practice.

860 Law notes series [USA]
National Association of Social Workers
www.socialworkers.org/ldf/lawnotes/default.asp
The Law notes series provides information to social workers about legal topics of concern to the social work profession in the USA. The notes address a wide range of legal topics.

861 The role of law in social work practice and administration [USA]
T.J. Stein   Columbia University Press, 2004, 467pp. $73.04. ISBN 9780231126489.
Practical and comprehensive book that addresses the relationship between social work and law and helps social workers develop the knowledge necessary to practise in a legal environment. The author focuses on how the law affects the day-to-day practice of social work; the creation, administration and operation of social service agencies; and the ways in which social workers and attorneys collaborate to serve the public.

862 Rules for social care workers and their managers [UK]
General Social Care Council   2003.
Easy-read version of a document aimed at standardizing and improving conduct and procedures for social care workers throughout the country.
  ■ **Rules for social care workers and their managers**
  General Social Care Council General Social Care Council, 2003.
  www.gscc.org.uk/NR/rdonlyres/F0073FAF-2D49-4B62-AE70-F2A87591DE0F/0/CodesofPracticepictorial.pdf.

863 Social care and the law: an NVQ related reference guide for direct staff [UK]
S. Maclean and I. Maclean   10th edn, Kirwin Maclean Associates, 2005, 112pp. ISBN 1903575346.
Concise publication giving details about the laws and policies that are relevant to social care for adults in England and Wales. Focuses on information that staff are expected to know. Areas covered include the legislative process; anti-oppressive practice; rights of service users and carers; confidentiality; health and safety; protecting vulnerable adults; community care; and standards.

864 Social work values and ethics
F.G. Reamer   3rd edn, Columbia University Press, 2006, 240pp. $29. ISBN 9780231137898.
An invaluable tool for the experienced professional and the social work student, this book provides clear guidelines for exploring and resolving the ethical issues. It includes analysis of forms of malpractice and professional misconduct in both direct and indirect practice.

865 Your induction to work in adult social care: the Skills for Care common induction standards presented for social care workers new to their post [UK]
L. Tarpey   Skills for Care, 2006, 38pp.
Written to help social care workers who are new in their post in adult care in England to complete the Common Induction Standards. This will help them to deliver high quality care to the people who use the service in which they work.

Official & quasi-official bodies

866 Australia. Department of Families, Community Services & Indigenous Affairs
www.facsia.gov.au
FaCSIA is responsible for social policies and support affecting Australian society and the living standards of all Australians, including families and children, young people, people with disabilities, carers, older people, homeless people, black and minority ethnic people and Aboriginal and Torres Strait Islander people.

867 Care Council for Wales
www.ccwales.org.uk/DesktopDefault.aspx?tabid=169
Regulatory body responsible for the social care profession in Wales. The organization agrees codes of practice which apply to social care workers and employers; maintains a register of social care workers to improve public protection; ascertains training needs and promotes training; and regulates social work qualifying and post-qualifying training.

868 Commission for Social Care Inspection [UK]
www.csci.org.uk/
Responsible for registering, inspecting and reporting on social care services in England.

869 General Social Care Council [UK]
www.gscc.org.uk/Home/
The workforce regulator and guardian of standards for the social care workforce in England, the GSCC is responsible for the codes of practice, Social Care Register and social work education and training.

870 Great Britain. Department of Health
www.dh.gov.uk/Home/fs/en
The government department responsible for the NHS and for adult social care. Its work includes setting national standards, shaping the direction of the NHS and social care services and promoting healthier living.

871 National Assembly for Wales
www.wales.gov.uk/organipo/index.htm
The Assembly is a devolved body that decides on its priorities and allocates the funds made available to it by the UK government. Powers devolved to the Assembly include health, social care, education, economic development, planning and culture. Within its powers, the Assembly develops policy and passes legislation affecting the people of Wales.

872 New Zealand. Social Workers Registration Board
www.swrb.org.nz/
The Board is responsible for establishing the criteria for registration of New Zealand and overseas qualified social workers, developing a code of conduct, establishing the policies and procedures for complaints and discipline and setting up the registration database. It promotes high standards of practice and professional conduct and makes recommendations to government relating to the regulation of the social work profession.

873 Northern Ireland Social Care Council
www.nisc.info/intro.htm
Established to raise standards in the Northern Ireland social care workforce, the organization sets standards, maintains a register of the social care workforce and deals with education and training.

874 Northern Ireland. Department of Health, Social Services & Public Safety
www.dhsspsni.gov.uk/
The Department's work includes administering the business of health and personal social services and public health in Northern Ireland.

875 Scottish Executive
www.scotland.gov.uk/Home
The devolved government for Scotland, the Executive is responsible for most of the issues of day-to-day concern to the people of Scotland, including health, social care, education, justice, rural affairs and transport.

876 Scottish Social Services Council
www.sssc.uk.com/Homepage.htm
Responsible for registering people who work in social care in Scotland and regulating their education and training.

877 Service Canada
www.servicecanada.gc.ca/en/home.shtml
Designed to help people find social welfare services provided by the Canadian government, this site contains information and links to information on disabilities, social security benefits, family and children's services, older people and much more.

878 Social Care Institute for Excellence [UK]
www.scie.org.uk/
SCIE's aim is to improve the experience of people who use social care by developing and promoting knowledge about good practice in the sector. Using knowledge gathered from diverse sources and a broad range of people and organizations, the organization provides a wider range of free resources supporting those working in social care.

879 Social Services Improvements Agency (Wales)
www.allwalesunit.gov.uk/index.cfm?articleid=19
The SSIA supports local authorities in Wales to increase the pace of improvement and excellence within social services.

880 United States. Department of Health & Human Services
www.hhs.gov/
The US government's principal agency for protecting the health of all Americans and providing essential human services, the department is responsible for a wide range of programmes, including research, disease prevention, food and drug safety, Medicare, child abuse prevention, substance misuse treatment and prevention and services for older people.

Research centres & institutes

881 Center for the Study of Social Work Practice [USA]
www.columbia.edu/cu/csswp/index.html
The Center is the only endowed research organization focused solely on the development and dissemination of social work practice knowledge in the USA. The Center's researchers are drawn from the partnerships and collaborations between the faculty and staff of the two sponsoring institutions – Columbia University School of Social Work and the Jewish Board of Family and Children's Services.

ChangeQual: the economic change, unequal life-chances and quality of life research network
See entry no. 583

882 Joseph Rowntree Foundation [UK]
www.jrf.org.uk/

One of the largest social policy research and development charities in the UK, spending about £10 million a year on a research and development programme that seeks to better understand the causes of social difficulties and explore ways of overcoming them.
- **Findings** Joseph Rowntree Foundation. www.jrf.org.uk/knowledge/findings. Findings are four-page summaries from research projects carried out by the Foundation. They are available free online and in hard copy.

883 Nuffield Foundation [UK]
www.nuffieldfoundation.org/
Well known charitable trust founded to advance 'social well-being' through research and practical experiment. The Foundation aims to achieve this by supporting work which will bring about improvements in society and which is founded on careful reflection and informed by objective and reliable evidence.

884 Personal Social Services Research Unit [UK]
www.pssru.ac.uk/
PSSRU aims to conduct long-term research to help shape the development of social and health care systems, in the UK and internationally, while also responding to more immediate research needs.

885 Social Policy Research Unit [UK]
www.york.ac.uk/inst/spru/
Research organization that aims to reflect and communicate, the experiences and views of the users and beneficiaries of services and policy interventions; engage in research that encompasses the multidisciplinary nature of service provision; and to ensure that its projects are influential in bringing about change.

Associations & societies

886 Aotearoa New Zealand Association of Social Workers
www.anzasw.org.nz/
The professional body for socal workers in New Zealand.

887 Association of Directors of Social Services [UK]
www.adss.org.uk/
Represents all the Directors of Adults Social Services (DASS) in England, Wales and Northern Ireland.

888 Association of Directors of Social Work [UK]
www.adsw.org.uk/
The ADSW is a constituted group of senior social workers working in Scottish local government who aim to promote social welfare and social inclusion and the interests of those who use their services.

889 Australian Association of Social Workers
www.aasw.asn.au/
Formed in 1946, the AASW is the professional representative body of social workers in Australia. It has a code of ethics which contains a set of principles agreed to by all members. These principles guide all social work practice.

890 British Association of Social Workers
www.basw.co.uk/
BASW is the largest association representing social work and

social workers in the UK. It publishes a range of journals and has a publishing programme of practical, evidence-based publications.

891   Canadian Association of Social Workers
www.casw-acts.ca/
A federation of nine provincial and one territorial social work organizations, CASW provides a national leadership role in strengthening and advancing the social work profession in Canada.

892   International Federation of Social Workers
www.ifsw.org/intro.html
The federation aims to promote social work as a profession through international cooperation, especially regarding professional values, standards, ethics, human rights, recognition, training and working conditions. It provides a forum for discussion and the exchange of ideas and experience through meetings, study visits, research projects, exchanges, publications and other methods of communication.

893   National Association of Social Workers [USA]
www.socialworkers.org/
NASW is the professional body for social workers in the USA.
■ **NASW news** National Association of Social Workers, 10 p.a. ISSN 00276022. www.socialworkers.org/pubs/news/default.asp. Available online and in hard copy, this newsletter is NASW's primary means of communication with its members. It contains information about association activities, developments in professional practice, and new policy initiatives.

894   Social Services Research Group [UK]
www.ssrg.org.uk/
An independent network of individuals who provide a range of research information, planning and evaluation in social care and health services. SSRG members are drawn from a wide range of professional groups and organizations sharing a common interest in the work of the caring services.

Libraries, archives, museums

895   King's Fund Information & Library Service [UK]
www.kingsfund.org.uk/Library
The King's Fund library offers a unique source for information on health and social care policy, freely available to managers and leaders in health and social care and anyone else working or interested in these areas.

896   University of the West of England, Faculty of Health & Social Care Library
www.uwe.ac.uk/library/
Based at the University's Glenside Campus, the library is freely available to all those working in health and social care.

Portal & task environments

897   care KNOWLEDGE [UK]
OLM Group
www.careknowledge.com/ck/application_store/portal/index.cfm
Part of the OLM group, CareKnowledge organizes and presents social care knowledge in a user-friendly format. It has exclusive licensed and commissioned content aimed at the busy practitioner and manager. The data is charged for.

898   Internet for Health and Social Care [UK]
Intute.
www.vts.intute.ac.uk/tutorial/health
One of the free internet tutorials provided by the Intute Virtual Training Suite, this interactive tool is designed to help students and practitioners learn how to retrieve and evaluate information from the web.

899   Intsocwork mailing list
JISCmail.
www.jiscmail.ac.uk/lists/intsocwork.html
A discussion list aimed at those who have an interest in international or comparative social work.

900   Irish social care gateway
Irish Association of Social Care Educators
http://staffweb.itsligo.ie/gateway/
Online gateway for information for social care practitioners, students, academics and those interested in care issues who are based in Ireland.

901   Social Work Access Network
University of South Carolina: School of Social Work
http://cosw.sc.edu/swan/
This website contains resources, links to associations and additional and general social work information. A useful source of general social work information.

902   Social work portal
National Association of Social Workers
www.socialworkers.org/swportal/
Online search tool designed to help students, educators, journalists, policy makers and professionals quickly find web content on a wide range of social work and social care issues.

903   Social Work World [USA]
E.R. Mitchell
http://pages.prodigy.net/volksware/socialworkworld/index.htm
A website aimed at social work and social care workers in the USA. Features include a blog and a wide range resources and links.

904   SOCIAL-WORK-SWAP mailing list [UK]
JISCmail.
www.jiscmail.ac.uk/lists/social-work-swap.html
A discussion list for social work academics, students and practitioners in the UK to discuss topics of shared interest. To join, follow the instructions given on the web page for the list.

Discovering print & electronic resources

905   Campbell Library of systematic reviews in social sciences
www.campbellcollaboration.org/
The international Campbell Collaboration (C2) is a non-profit organization that aims to help people make well informed decisions about the effects of interventions in the social, behavioural and educational arenas by preparing, maintaining and disseminating systematic reviews of studies of interventions. C2 builds summaries and electronic brochures of reviews and reports of trials for policy makers, practitioners, researchers and the public.

906 **Laing & Buisson** [UK]
www.laingbuisson.co.uk/
Laing & Buisson, an independent company, provides data, statistics, analysis and market intelligence on the UK health, community care and childcare sectors. Information is provided via a range of media, including market reports, business newsletters, conferences and directories in hard copy and electronic format. Publications can be expensive.

907 **reSearchWeb: supporting social work excellence in Scotland**
Social Care Institute for Excellence for the Scottish Office.
www.researchweb.org.uk/
reSearchWeb is funded by the Scottish Executive as a tool for the informed social work professional in Scotland. It provides a sound knowledge base on social work and social care practice and policy, with information and research that is up to date, concise but thorough and selected with practice in mind.

908 **Social Care and Social Work Careers information website** [UK]
Great Britain. Department of Health.
www.socialworkandcare.co.uk/
Essential resource for all those interested in a career in social care or social work in the UK.

909 **Social Care Online**
Social Care Institute for Excellence.
www.scie-socialcareonline.org.uk/
Social Care Online is the UK's most extensive database of social care information. Containing books, research briefings, reports, government documents, journal articles and websites, it is updated daily. Access is free.

910 **Social Policy and Practice** [UK]
Ovid.
www.ovid.com/site/index.jsp
Contains abstracted references from four UK databases: AgeInfo, Social Care Online, Acompline and Planex. Coverage includes public health, social care, homelessness and housing, crime and law and order, families, children and older people and public and social policy. Subscription required.

Digital data, image & text collections

911 **Concord Media**
www.concordvideo.co.uk/cp1home.html
Distributes DVDs and videos on a wide range of topics relevant to social care, including addiction, social welfare, counselling, mental health, children and health. The only UK organization devoted to this. The items are for sale or hire.

Directories & encyclopedias

912 **The Blackwell encyclopaedia of social work**
M. Davies, ed. Blackwell, 2000, 432pp. £19.79. ISBN 0631214518.
Draws together material from some of the key authors in social work to create an essential reference tool.

913 **Complete A–Z health and social care handbook** [UK]
J. Richards 2nd edn, Hodder & Arnold, 2003, 304pp. £10.44. ISBN 9780415258609.
User-friendly sourcebook aimed at students at all levels, this A–Z can serve as a companion to study and as a revision aid.

914 **Directions: a guide to key documents in health and social care** [UK]
L. Crecy 4th edn, Stationery Office, 2005, 194pp. £18.50. ISBN 0117034762.
Guide to more than 200 key reports and pieces of legislation published on health and social care subjects since 1986. Coverage includes primary and community care; older people; children and young people; mental health; disabilities; education; ethical issues and human rights. Each entry has an abstract.

915 **Social services yearbook 2007** [UK]
Pearson Education, 2007, annual, 880pp. £128.25. ISBN 0131984519.
The most comprehensive directory of UK social services and social care organizations, covering central and local government, the voluntary sector, arm's-length bodies and criminal justice organizations. A key reference source.

916 **Social workers' desk reference** [USA]
A.R. Roberts and G.J. Greene, eds Oxford University Press USA, 2002, 944pp. $92.34. ISBN 9780195142112.
A compendium of assessment protocols, step-by-step treatment plans, clinical wisdom and the latest evidence-based practices, this volume provides clinical social work practitioners with a comprehensive resource for virtually all aspects of their practice with clients.

917 **Voluntary agencies directory** [UK]
National Council for Voluntary Organisations 25th edn, National Council for Voluntary Organisations, 2006, annual, 521pp. £33.24. ISBN 9780719916632.
In its 25th edition, this is the established guide to the voluntary sector in the UK, listing over 2000 organizations throughout the country. Contact details, web addresses and concise descriptions of each organization's aims and objectives are included in each entry.

Handbooks & manuals

918 **Day centres handbook: a good practice guide** [UK]
T. Bradley, C. Cooper and R. Sycamore Homeless Link, 2004, 347pp. ISBN 0904951976.
This handbook is a result of a collaborative effort with day centres across the country. It can be used as a mini-course in understanding the main issues specific to day centres, as a resource for training purposes and as a tool for generating new ideas and assessing current practice.

919 **Evidence-based practice manual: research and outcome measures in health and human services** [USA]
A. Roberts and K.R. Yeager, eds Oxford University Press, 2004, 1050pp. £54. ISBN 9780195165005.
Aimed at medical, public health, psychology, social work, criminal justice and public policy practitioners, researchers and professors in the USA and Canada, this is the only

interdisciplinary volume available for locating and applying evidence-based assessment measures, treatment plans and interventions. Includes practice guidelines and exemplars of evidence-based practice and practice-based research.

920   The handbook of direct social work practice
P. Allen-Meares and C.D. Garvin, eds   Sage Publications, 2007, 752pp. $128.75. ISBN 9780761914990.
This handbook contains extensive coverage of all major topics relevant to clinical social work. It discusses the contexts of social work practice, multicultural and diversity issues, research, as well as assessment and measurement. An excellent primary text for administration courses in MSW programmes, BSW programmes and doctoral programmes and also useful for practitioners as a reference text.

921   Managing at the front line: a handbook for managers in social care agencies
T. Scragg   Pavilion, 2001, 191pp. ISBN 1841960640.
A source of information, ideas and real-life examples to help newly appointed managers get to grips with the key aspects of managing at the front line of services. Also useful to experienced managers wishing to improve performance in aspects of their existing role.

922   Managing in health and social care: essential checklists for frontline staff
W. Bryans   Radcliffe Medical Press, 2004, 104pp. ISBN 1857758560.
Short guide to managing resources in health and social care, especially how to ensure the back room supports the front line effectively. Includes sections on procurement, fund-raising, handling service users' monies and managing budgets.

923   Open hearts, open minds: a social inclusion self-assessment handbook; for staff working with the public and those who support them
S. Magne and A. McTiernan   Exeter Community Initiatives, 2004, 118pp.
A self-assessment handbook for front-line staff to help them be more effective in their work with socially excluded groups. The handbook has been produced by the LINKS Project and designed for easy use by a range of voluntary and community groups, as well as statutory organizations.

924   Social care practice handbook
Leonard Cheshire and Social Care Association   Leonard Cheshire, 2000, 254pp.
This resource covers all aspects of working with service users in health care, social care, home care, day care and short-term residential and day-care settings, including the fundamentals, such as respecting clients' rights and effective communication. Includes a code of ethics and policy on equal opportunities.

925   Social work career development: a handbook for job hunting and career planning [USA]
C.N. Doelling   2nd edn, National Association of Social Workers, 2005, 252pp. $50.99. ISBN 0871013630.
Comprehensive handbook on career management and job hunting for social workers. Includes self-assessment exercises, writing CVs and tips on choosing courses. Aimed at students, practitioners, managers and social work educators.

926   Social work skills: a practice handbook
P. Trevithick   2nd edn, Open University Press, 2005, 340pp. £15.99. ISBN 0335214991.
A clearly written and accessible text providing a detailed description of over fifty social work skills, with case examples of their creative use in practice.

927   Supervision in the helping professions: an individual, group and organizational approach
P. Hawkins and R. Shohet   2nd edn, Open University Press, 2000, 245pp. £20.89. ISBN 9781843101949.
A practical text, this book deals with all aspects of supervision and provides a meaningful blueprint for how useful and effective supervision can be. Contains models for supervising in individual, group, team and organizational settings.

928   Understanding care, welfare and community: a reader
W.R. Bytheway, ed.   Routledge, 2001, 368pp. £17.09. ISBN 9780415258609.
Care, welfare and community are three key concepts in contemporary social policy. This reader covers a wide range of topics associated with them and relevant to the delivery of care and support to adults.

Keeping up to date

929   Australian Social Work
Australian Association of Social Workers   Routledge, qtrly. Online 14470. ISSN 0312407X.
An international peer-reviewed journal reflecting current thinking and trends in social work and promoting the development of practice, policy and education. Publishes original research, theoretical papers, critical reviews that build on existing knowledge and includes reviews of relevant professional literature, commentary and analysis of social policies and encourages debate.

930   British Journal of Social Work
Oxford University Press, 8 p.a. £342.15. ISSN 00453102.
http://bjsw.oxfordjournals.org/
Published for the British Association of Social Workers, this is the leading academic social work journal in the UK. It covers every aspect of social work, with papers reporting research, discussing practice and examining principles and theories. Access to articles is via Athens password, pay-per-article, or printed copy.

931   Canadian Social Work
Canadian Association of Social Workers, annual.
The official journal of the Canadian Association of Social Workers, this publication provides a national forum in which Canadian social workers can share practice knowledge, research and skills and debate contemporary social work concerns.

932   Care and Health [UK]
www.careandhealth.com/Pages/Default.aspx
Care and Health is an online journal offering up-to-date social care news. E-mail alerts, blogs, webcasts and conference news are also available.

933 Community Care [UK]
Reed Business Information, weekly. ISSN 03075508.
www.communitycare.co.uk/home/default.aspx
Weekly journal that combines practical articles with news. Essential title for keeping up to date with what is happening in social care. Available free to those studying or working in social care.

934 Health and Social Care in the Community
Blackwell Publishing, bi-monthly. ISSN 09660410.
www.blackwellpublishing.com/
International journal with a multidisciplinary approach recognizing the common ground between health and social care in the community. The journal publishes original research papers; topical review articles; policy and practice evaluations; book reviews and special issues. Available in print and online.

935 Information for practice: news and new scholarship from around the world
G. Holden
www.nyu.edu/socialwork/ip/
Links to news and information from recognized resources worldwide. A useful resource for keeping up to date with what is happening in social work and social care globally.

936 Journal of Social Work Practice
Taylor & Francis, 3 p.a. ISSN 02650533.
Available online and in print, this journal publishes high-quality refereed articles devoted to the exploration and analysis of practice in social welfare and allied health professions from psychodynamic and systemic perspectives. This includes counselling, social care planning, education and training, research, institutional life, management and organization or policy making.

937 Practice
Taylor & Francis, qtrly. £73.50. ISSN 09503153.
www.tandf.co.uk/journals/titles/09503153.asp
Published for the British Association of Social Workers. Contains up-to-date information on social work and practice development for practitioners, managers, educators, students and policy makers. Also available online.

938 Professional Social Work [UK]
British Association of Social Workers, monthly. ISSN 13523112.
www.basw.co.uk/
Monthly magazine containing articles, news and information for members of the British Association of Social Workers.

939 Social Service Review
University of Chicago Press, qtrly. ISSN 00377961.
Each issue of *Social Service Review* brings 200 pages of research that is committed to examining and evaluating social welfare policy and practice. It provides multidisciplinary and multicultural analyses of current policies and past practices to help readers see critical problems in their broader contexts and to consider long-range solutions.

940 Social Work [USA]
National Association of Social Workers, qtrly. ISSN 00378046.
This American journal is widely read by practitioners, faculty and students. It is the official journal of the National Association of Social Workers and is dedicated to improving practice and advancing knowledge in social work and social welfare.

941 Social Work Abstracts
National Association of Social Workers, qtrly. ISSN 10705317.
NASW's abstracting service is a good starting point for literature searches in social work and social welfare. It reviews over 400 US and international journals and publishes approximately 450 abstracts in each issue.

942 Social Work Research
National Association of Social Workers, qtrly. ISBN 10705309.
Available in print and online, this journal includes analytic reviews of research, theoretical articles pertaining to social work research, evaluation studies and diverse research studies that contribute to knowledge about social work issues and problems.

Social Work Education & Training

care skills • social work & the law • training for social work

Introductions to the subject

943 Direct social work practice: theory and skills [USA]
D.H. Hepworth [et al.] 7th edn, Wadsworth, 2005, 656pp. $93.88. ISBN 9780534644581.
Textbook aimed at social work students in their foundation year. It provides an overview of the helping professions, underscored by the values and ethics of the profession, followed by clearly presented theories, skills development, case examples and classroom exercises.

944 Effective practice learning in social work [UK]
J. Parker Learning Matters, 2004, 131pp. £12.60. ISBN 1844450155.
Provides an introduction and guide to the practice learning process, which is a key part of the new social work degree programme.

945 The social work practicum: a guide and workbook for students [USA]
C.L. Garthwaite 4th edn, Allyn & Bacon, 2006, 272pp. $56. ISBN 9780205501793.
Offers a workbook format designed to facilitate the integration of social work theory and practice during a student's field practicum. It exposes students to the many facets of working in the field, including social policy, the agency and community contexts of practice, cultural diversity and the evaluation of practice. It also discusses legal and ethical issues.

Laws, standards, codes

946 Law for social workers [UK]
H. Brayne and H. Carr 9th edn, Oxford University Press, 2005, 814pp. £22.79. ISBN 0199275513.
A leading text in its field, providing students with practical information to help the understand the legal framework in which social workers act.

947 Post-qualifying framework for social work education and training [UK]
General Social Care Council   General Social Care Council, 2005, 2005pp.
The GSCC's revised post-qualifying framework for social work education and training.

948 Using the law in social work: transforming social work practice [UK]
R. Johns   Learning Matters, 2005, 161pp. £12.60. ISBN 1844450309.
Practical text providing students with an understanding of the legal framework within which social workers must work.

Official & quasi-official bodies

949 Council on Social Work Education [USA]
www.cswe.org/
The Council is the sole accrediting agency for social work education in the USA. It is a non-profit national association representing over 3000 individual members as well as graduate and undergraduate programmes of professional social work education.

950 Skills for Care [UK]
www.topssengland.net/
Skills for Care aims to support employers in improving standards of adult care provision through training and development, workforce planning and workforce intelligence. The organization promotes engagement in workforce development by networks of statutory and independent sector employers in all aspects of social care, alongside representatives of service users, informal carers, staff associations and education and training providers.

Portal & task environments

951 Internet Social Worker
www.vts.intute.ac.uk/he/tutorial/social-worker
One of the free internet tutorials provided by the Intute Virtual Training Suite, this interactive tool is designed to help students and practitioners learn how to retrieve and evaluate information from the web.

Discovering print & electronic resources

952 Leading practice: a development programme for first line managers [UK]
Social Care Institute for Excellence   Social Care Institute for Excellence, 2006. Available on CD-ROM and online.
www.scie.org.uk/publications/leadingpractice/index.asp
The programme is divided into 12 sessions and consists of activities and discussion, as well as reading suggestions. Available on CD-ROM and online.

Directories & encyclopedias

953 Compass 2006: the complete guide to careers in social work and social care [UK]
Compass Career Opportunities   COMPASS Career Opportunities, 2005, annual, 189pp. ISBN 00953659062.

Training and employment guide for the social care workforce across the UK. People who want a career in the sector, who are looking for a new job, or who need information about continuing professional development, can use it as a careers companion.

Handbooks & manuals

954 Critical thinking and analysis: a guide to enhancing reflection, learning, and writing for post qualifying social work programmes [UK]
K. Brown and L. Rutter   Bournemouth University, 2004, 51pp.
Offers students a way into applying critical thinking to their studies and their future practice.

955 The social work skills workbook [USA]
B.R. Cournoyer   5th edn, Brooks Cole, 2007, 480pp. $69.95. ISBN 9780495319467.
This workbook/textbook enables students to rehearse and practise core skills needed for contemporary social work practice. It includes case examples and situations that clearly illustrate essential skills. It also contains summaries and skill-building exercises.

956 The social work student's research handbook [USA]
D.M. Steinberg   Haworth, 2004, 171pp. $39.95. ISBN 9780789014801.
A clear and comprehensive handbook, aimed at students but also useful for practitioners.

Keeping up to date

957 Canadian Social Work Review
Canadian Association of Schools of Social Work, 2 p.a. ISSN 0820909X.
A bilingual publication, this journal provides a forum for students and educators to critically examining current and historical social work practice in Canada. The review reflects the cultural and regional diversity of Canada.

958 Journal of Social Work Education [USA]
Council on Social Work Education, 1964–, 3 p.a. ISSN 10437797.
www.cswe.org/
A refereed professional journal concerned with education in social work and social welfare, this journal aims to serve as a forum for creative exchange on trends, innovations and problems relevant to social work education at the undergraduate, master's and postgraduate levels. Available online and in print.

959 Social Work Education
Taylor & Francis, 8 p.a. ISSN 02615479.
Available in print and online, this journal contains articles of a critical and reflective nature concerned with the theory and practice of social care and social work education at all levels. It presents a forum for international debate on important issues and provides an opportunity for the expression of new ideas and proposals on the structure and content of social care and social work education, training and development.

Social Service Users

addiction • adoption • ageing • alcoholism • Asperger syndrome • autism • black & minority ethnic people • care homes • care of older people • child welfare • children, young people & families • cultural sensitivity • dementia care • disabilities • drug abuse • elder abuse • ethnic minorities • family social work • fostering • gerontological social work • hearing loss • homelessness • juvenile justice • learning disabilities • mental health • mentally disordered offenders • race equality in social services • refugees • rehabilitation • retirement • sight loss • substance abuse • youth work

Alcohol & Drug Misuse

Introductions to the subject

960   Drug treatment: what works?
P. Bean and T. Nemitz   Routledge, 2004, 249pp. £80. ISBN 0415268168.
Survey of the latest treatments for drug misusers. Also looks at: which treatments work with what sorts of abusers; what are the key indicators of likely success; does coercion work or must treatment be freely entered into; and is drug testing an essential backup for successful treatment?

961   Preventing harmful substance use: the evidence base for policy and practice
T. Stockwell, P.J. Gruenewald and J.W. Toumbourou, eds   Wiley, 2005, 476pp. ISBN 0470092289.
Offers advice on the prevention of problematic drug and alcohol use. Chapters discuss patterns of risk and related harms, interventions for children and young people, community interventions, the evidence base for prevention, the regulatory background to prevention and future directions for prevention policy research.

962   Social work with drug and substance misusers
A. Goodman   Learning Matters, 2007, 139pp. £15.20. ISBN 9781844450589.
Written for social work students, this comprehensive book covers all aspects of working with drug and substance misusers. It looks at the history and changes in policy on substance misuse and highlights the differences between working with young and adult substance misusers.

963   Substance use disorders
N.R. Lessa and W.F. Scanlon   Wiley, 2006, 312pp. £14.51. ISBN 0471689912.
Guides the reader through a continuum of care from assessment to intervention to long-term care, while looking at the latest undertanding of the science of chemical addiction. Also offers advice on the prevention.

964   Treating drug misuse problems: evidence of effectiveness
M. Gossop   National Treatment Agency for Substance Misuse, 2006, 47pp.
www.nta.nhs.uk/
A literature review of international research on drug treatment effectiveness. Examines evidence for effectiveness in drug treatment programmes, using a variety of quantitative and qualitative methodologies.

Dictionaries, thesauri, classifications

965   Alcohol addiction: a medical dictionary, bibliography, and annotated research guide to internet references
Icon Group International, 2004, 284pp. £38.95.
This 3-in-1 reference book contains a complete medical dictionary, bibliography and extensive list of internet resources. A useful one-stop shop for information on drug misuse.

Official & quasi-official bodies

966   National Treatment Agency for Substance Misuse [UK]
www.nta.nhs.uk/
The NTA is a special health authority, created by the government in 2001 to improve the availability, capacity and effectiveness of treatment for drug misuse in England.

967   United States. Office of National Drug Control Policy
www.whitehousedrugpolicy.gov/
The principal purpose of ONDCP is to establish policies, priorities and objectives for the drug control programme in the USA. The goals of the programme are to reduce illicit drug use, manufacturing and trafficking, drug-related crime and violence and drug-related health consequences.

Research centres & institutes

968   Alcohol & Drugs Research Programme [UK]
www.cph.org.uk/research_substancemisuse.asp
The Centre has an international reputation for its development of substance-use intelligence systems, evaluation and original research. In addition to projects related to both legal and illegal drug use, it also incorporates innovative work in relation to smoking and alcohol.

969   Institute of Psychiatry at the Maudsley, National Addiction Centre [UK]
www.iop.kcl.ac.uk/iopweb/departments/home/default.aspx?locator=346
The Centre includes the research and teaching activities of the Addiction Research Unit and the treatment and policy contributions of colleagues within the Addictions Division of the South London and Maudsley NHS Trust. It aims to improve understanding of addiction to drugs, alcohol and tobacco and to develop effective preventative and treatment interventions.

Associations & societies

970   Alcohol Concern [UK]
www.alcoholconcern.org.uk/servlets/home
The national agency on alcohol misuse in the UK. Aims to reduce the incidence and cost of alcohol-related harm and to increase the range and quality of services available to people

with alcohol-related problems. Provides information and encourages debate on the wide range of public policy issues affected by alcohol, including public health, housing, children and families, crime and licensing. Also supports specialist and non-specialist service providers.

971   Alcoholics Anonymous
www.alcoholics-anonymous.org/
Independent, self-funding network of men and women who want to recover from and help others to recover from, alcoholism.

972   DrugScope [UK]
www.drugscope.org.uk/
The UK's leading independent centre of expertise on drugs. Aims to inform policy development and reduce drug-related risk. Provides quality drug information, promotes effective responses to drug taking, undertakes research and advises policy makers.

Libraries, archives, museums

973   Alcohol Concern, Library [UK]
www.alcoholconcern.org.uk/servlets/home
The library, based in London, is open to members (free of charge) and non-members (charges apply). A telephone enquiry service is also available. It holds the most comprehensive collection of books and journals on alcohol-related issues in the UK. The library database is freely available on the internet.

974   DrugScope, Information & Library Service [UK]
www.drugscope.org.uk/
The information and library service is open to members (free) and non-members (charges apply). It contains a range of material on drug misuse and related issues covering four decades.

Discovering print & electronic resources

975   Addiction Search
www.addictionsearch.com/
This website is a gateway to quality-controlled, research-based addiction information for practitioners and researchers. It offers links to information about addictive substances, prevention and treatment studies, statistics, harm-reduction programmes, special populations and organizations concerned with addictive behaviour. It also includes a daily news update and featured websites, resources and research questions.

976   Alcohol Concern database
Alcohol Concern.
www.alcoholconcern.org.uk/servlets/home
The organization holds the most comprehensive collection of books and journals on alcohol-related issues in the UK. The extensive library database may be searched for free online.

977   DrugData database
DrugScope.
www.drugscope.org.uk/
This is a searchable database of over 100,000 records of

drugs literature in the English language. Available free on the web.

Directories & encyclopedias

978   Drug problems: where to get help
DrugScope   UK edn, DrugScope, 2005, 400pp. £35. ISBN 1904319394.
A comprehensive directory of drug treatment services across the whole of the UK, including prison drug services. The only directory of its kind and an essential for treatment services, GPs, social work departments, probation offices, advice and help centres and libraries.

979   Druglink guide to drugs 2006 [UK]
DrugScope, 2006, 90pp. £8.50. ISBN 1904319165.
Gives basic information on all the most widely used licit and illicit drugs and other background information on drug use. Ideal for professional development training, staff drug-awareness courses and general interest readers.

980   drugsearch [UK]
www.drugscope.org.uk/druginfo/drugsearch/home2.asp
A comprehensive, free, easy-to-use online encyclopaedia of drugs and their history, effects and the law, with a UK focus.

Handbooks & manuals

981   Alcohol, other drugs and addictions: a professional development manual for social work and the human services
A.E. Barsky   Wadsworth, 2005, 384pp. $47.95. ISBN 9780534641252.
Designed to prepare students for the realities of working with services users affected by addictions, this text provides the tools needed to competently translate addictions theory into practice. It offers a thorough examination of a range of models and perspectives for helping and it encourages critical thinking to best match approaches with clients and situations. Includes cases, exercises, role-plays and questions that encourage comprehension of concepts and application to practice.

982   Chemical dependency: a systems approach
C.A. McNeece and D.M. DiNitto   3rd edn, Allyn & Bacon, 2003, 464pp. $80.60. ISBN 9780205342754.
Classic text on substance misuse, taking a comphrehensive look at dependency and covering the most recent issues in the areas of epidemiology, etiology, substance abuse policy and treatment.

983   Parents who misuse drugs and alcohol: effective interventions in social work and child protection
D. Forrester   Wiley, 2007, 256pp. £15.99. ISBN 0470871512.
Practical text aimed at students and social workers.

984   Substance abuse: information for school counselors, social workers, therapists and counselors [USA]
G.L. Fisher and T.C. Harrison   3rd edn, Allyn & Bacon, 2004, 384pp. $83.20. ISBN 9780205403363.
This text presents balanced coverage of various treatment models as well as objective discussions dealing with

controversies in this field. Topics covered include pharmacology, assessment and diagnosis, treatment, recovery, prevention, children, families and other addictions.

985   Understanding drug issues: a photocopiable resource workbook [UK]
D. Emmett and G. Nice   2nd edn, Jessica Kingsley, 2005, 140pp. £33.25. ISBN 1843103508.
Designed for work with groups of young people, this resource features informative and balanced material on the key issues involved, including facts and fiction about drugs, peer pressure, social consequences of drug use, buying drugs, dangers involved in using, pros and cons of drug use, legal implications and effects of drugs on health.

986   Understanding street drugs: a handbook of substance misuse for parents, teachers and other professionals [UK]
D. Emmett and G. Nice   Jessica Kingsley, 2005, 336pp. £13.50. ISBN 1843103516.
Essential reference text. Provides a comprehensive overview of the key facts and core issues surrounding substance misuse. Useful for teachers, social workers, youth workers, residential home managers, policy makers and parents.

987   Working with substance misusers: a guide to theory and practice
M. Petersen   Routledge, 2002, 392pp. £18.39. ISBN 0415235685.
Handbook aimed at professionals working in the field of substance use for the first time. Each chapter highlights the appropriate evidence base, encourages students to reflect critically on what they have read and to consider the implications for practice.

Keeping up to date

988   The American Journal of Drug and Alcohol Abuse
Taylor & Francis, qtrly. ISSN 00952990.
http://taylorandfrancis.metapress.com/content/1097-9891/
Available online and in print, this multidisciplinary journal is essential reading for researchers and practitioners in a range of disciplines, including social work.

989   Daily Dose [UK]
Wired.
www.dailydose.net/index.htm
Informative online newsletter containing articles on drug and alcohol misuse gathered from the web. All articles are linked to the original.

990   DrugLink
DrugScope, bi-monthly. ISBN 03054349.
www.drugscope.org.uk/druglink/default.asp
Bi-monthly magazine aimed at UK professionals interested in drugs and drug-related topics. Includes the latest news, feature articles, interviews, factsheets, reviews and listings.

991   Straight Talk [UK]
Alcohol Concern, qtrly. £25.
www.alcoholconcern.org.uk/servlets/home
Includes information, news, articles on policy issues and details of events.

Disabilities

Introductions to the subject

992   Contemporary learning disability practice
M. Jules and M. Bollard   Quay Books, 2003, 338pp. ISBN 1856422135.
Identifies existing and emerging areas of learning-disability nursing practice. Contains chapters on court diversion; dual diagnosis; challenging behaviour; primary healthcare assessment and intervention; reflective practice and clinical supervision; cultural diversity; sensory impairment and children. Looks at different domains of practice and at the emerging evidence base.

993   Disability policy and practice: applying the social model
C. Barnes and G. Mercer, eds   Disability Press, 2004, 216pp. £16.50. ISBN 0952845091.
Aimed at academics, researchers, professionals, disabled people and lay audiences with an interest in disability issues and the ongoing struggle for a more equitable and just society.

994   Quality enhancement in developmental disabilities: challenges and opportunities in a changing world
V.J. Bradley and M.H. Kimmich   Paul H. Brookes, 2003, 340pp. $34.95. ISBN 9781557666260.
This book aims to understand the changed expectations of people with disabilities and their families in the USA. It examines the roles of Medicaid and the Centers for Medicare and Medicaid Services; addresses health and safety issues, including investigation of abuse, neglect and death; advises on the design of databases that track outcomes and target areas for service improvement; shows how to manage staffing challenges such as recruitment, retention and professional development.

995   Social work with disabled people
M. Oliver and B. Sapey   3rd edn, Palgrave Macmillan, 2006, 218pp. £17.99. ISBN 1403918384.
Introduction to social work with disabled people. Includes chapters on old and new directions in social work with disability; thinking about disability; the causes of impairment and the creation of disability; disability in the family; living with disabilities; the legal and social context of disability; and professional and organizational issues.

996   Working with people with learning disabilities: theory and practice
D. Thomas and H. Woods   Jessica Kingsley, 2003, 288pp. £16.10. ISBN 1853029734.
Brings together the relevant theory for social workers, nurses, teachers and others working with people with learning disabilities. Using jargon-free explanations and case examples, provides the theoretical understanding needed to inform good practice and help to improve quality of life for service users.

Dictionaries, thesauri, classifications

997 Dictionary of developmental disabilities terminology
P.J. Accardo and B.Y. Whitman, eds   2nd edn, Paul H. Brooks, 2002, 451pp. £18.80. ISBN 155766594X.
Aimed at professionals, parents and carers. Defines technical terms in non-technical language and covers areas such as pediatrics, anatomy, genetics, orthopaedics, neurology, pathology, pharmacology, physiology, psychiatry, psychology, education, social work, family therapy and law.

Laws, standards, codes

998 Americans with Disabilities Act
www.usdoj.gov/crt/ada/adahom1.htm
Part of the US Department of Justice website, these pages contain comprehensive information on the Act.

999 Disabled children and the law: research and good practice [UK]
J. Read, L. Clements and D. Ruebain   2nd edn, Jessica Kingsley, 2006, 304pp. £18.88. ISBN 1843102803.
Accessible guide to the laws affecting disabled children and adolescents, designed to help professionals and families to understand the legislation and apply it confidently and creatively to improve the quality of life of children with disabilities.

1000 Get in on the act: the Disability Discrimination Act 2005 explained [UK]
Local Government Association   Local Government Association, 2006, 27pp.
Brief guide explaining the key provisions of the Disability Discrimination Act 2005.

1001 Mental capacity: the new law [UK]
G. Ashton, ed.   Jordan, 2006, 411pp. £37.05. ISBN 0853089760.
Provides a commentary on both law and procedure, highlighting areas of potential difficulty and offering practical guidance on the challenges that the legislation poses. Includes the full text of the Act.

Official & quasi-official bodies

1002 Disability Rights Commission [UK]
www.drc-gb.org/
The DRC is an independent body established in April 2000 by Act of Parliament to stop discrimination and promote equality of opportunity for disabled people. The website contains a comprehensive range of resources and useful links.

1003 Great Britain. Office for Disability Issues
www.officefordisability.gov.uk/
The Office for Disability Issues is the focal point within government to coordinate disability policy across all departments. The website is a key resource for information on the UK government's policies for disabled people.

1004 National Council on Disability [USA]
www.ncd.gov/
The NCD is an independent federal agency making recommendations to the President and Congress to enhance the quality of life for all Americans with disabilities and their families. The website is a key resource for information on policies, programmes, practices and procedures that affect all disabled people.

1005 National Development Team [UK]
www.ndt.org.uk/
The NDT is an independent, not-for-profit organization that works to improve policies, services and opportunities for people who have learning disabilities or mental health problems.

Research centres & institutes

1006 British Institute of Learning Disabilities
www.bild.org.uk/
The BILD website is an essential tool for all those interested in learning disabilities. It includes a knowledge bank, publications, news and much more.
  ■ **BILD Current Awareness Service** British Institute of Learning Disabilities, monthly. www.bild.org.uk. Available in print and online, this bibliographic resource is designed to keep readers up to date with the latest publications and articles on learning disabilities.

1007 Center on Disability Studies [USA]
www.cds.hawaii.edu/
The Center is a University of Hawaii Board of Regents-recognized organization, focusing on the development and conduct of interdisciplinary education/training, research, demonstration and evaluation and university and community service. The website includes information about the Center's activities, links, news and resources.

1008 Centre for Disability Studies
www.leeds.ac.uk/disability-studies/
CDS is an interdisciplinary centre for teaching and research in the field of disability studies at the University of Leeds (England). The website contains information on research, teaching, publications, resources, events, as well as links and news.

1009 Centre of Applied Disability Studies
www.sheffield.ac.uk/applieddisabilitystudies/
The Centre promotes high quality disability research, applied and interdisciplinary in nature, in order to improve the lives of disabled people. Based at the University of Sheffield, COADS disseminates its work through research, publications, seminar series, newsletters and this website in wider pursuit of its aims.

1010 Strathclyde Centre for Disability Research
www.gla.ac.uk/centres/disabilityresearch/index.htm
The Centre's remit is to provide an academic base for research and teaching in social aspects of disability. Work in the Centre is currently research on the education, training, employment, health and legal needs of disabled people. The website contains information on research, publications and useful links.

1011 Tizard Centre
www.kent.ac.uk/tizard/
The Centre is one of the leading UK academic groups working in learning disability and community care. It

provides teaching through short courses, certificate, diploma and degree programmes at the University of Kent and elsewhere. It also maintains an extensive programme of research and consultancy, nationally and internationally.

1012   Waisman Center [USA]
www.waisman.wisc.edu/
The Center is dedicated to the advancement of knowledge about human development, developmental disabilities and neurodegenerative diseases throughout the lifespan. The website contains a wide range of useful information.

1013   Welsh Centre for Learning Disabilities
www.cardiff.ac.uk/medicine/psychological_medicine/research/welsh_centre_learning_disabilities/index.htm
A multi-disciplinary academic section of the Department of Psychological Medicine at Cardiff University. Established in 1975, it brings together a range of expertise in clinical practice, research, teaching and service development associated with many aspects of the lives of people with learning disabilities. It undertakes policy-related research for the Department of Health and the National Assembly for Wales. The Centre's applied tradition is reflected in the emphasis given in its research to the analysis of service structures and processes and how they impact on the well-being of people with learning disabilities at home, in the workplace and in the community.

1014   World Institute on Disability
www.wid.org/
WID is a non-profit research, public policy and advocacy centre dedicated to promoting the civil rights and full societal inclusion of people with disabilities. It focuses on four areas: employment and economic development; accessible health care and personal assistance services; inclusive technology design; and international disability and development. Over half of the Board of Directors and staff are people with disabilities. The website contains a wide range of information and resources.

Associations & societies

1015   Change [UK]
www.changepeople.co.uk/
An organization run by and for people with learning disabilities, it has pioneered the production of tools to make information easier to understand. The website is an essential source for people with learning disabilities, carers and professionals.

1016   Foundation for Assistive Technology [UK]
www.fastuk.org/
The voluntary organization FAST's vision is a society where disabled and older people are able to easily get hold of assistive technology (AT) at a reasonable cost, which is a pleasure to use and employs state-of-the-art design and materials. The website contains information on research carried out by FAST, services it provides, training courses and publications.

1017   Learning Disabilities Association of America
www.ldaamerica.us/
LDA is a non-profit volunteer organization advocating for individuals with learning disabilities. The membership,

composed of individuals with learning disabilities, family members and concerned professionals, advocates for the almost three million students of school age with learning disabilities and for adults affected with learning disabilities. The website contains information, a bookstore, resources and much more.

1018   MENCAP [UK]
www.mencap.org.uk/
Mencap is the UK's leading learning disability charity working with people with a learning disability and their families and carers. The website offers a wide range of information for people with learning disabilities, their carers and professionals.

1019   National Autistic Society [UK]
www.nas.org.uk/
The Society exists to champion the rights and interests of all people with autism and to ensure that they and their families receive quality services appropriate to their needs. The website includes information about autism and Asperger syndrome, the NAS and its services and activities.

1020   National Organization on Disability [USA]
www.nod.org/
The mission of NOD is to expand the participation and contribution of America's 54 million men, women and children with disabilities in all aspects of life. By raising disability awareness through programmes and information, the organization works toward closing the participation gaps. The comprehensive website includes information on community involvement, economic participation and access to independence.

1021   RADAR [UK]
www.radar.org.uk/radarwebsite/
RADAR's mission is to enable disabled people and disability organizations to initiate, develop and encourage change and campaign for a fully inclusive society. The website contains a wide range of resources, including news, publications, parliamentary information and much more.

1022   RNID [UK]
www.rnid.org.uk/
The RNID is the UK's leading charity working for change for the nation's 9 million deaf and hard-of-hearing people via campaigning and lobbying, raising awareness of deafness and hearing loss, providing services and social, medical and technical research.

1023   Royal National Institute of Blind People [UK]
www.rnib.org.uk/
The RNIB is the UK's leading charity offering information, support and advice to over 2 million people with sight problems. Doing pioneering work that helps anyone with a sight problems, not just with braille and Talking Books, but with imaginative and practical solutions to everyday challenges, the organization fights for equal rights for people with sight problems, funds pioneering research and runs innovative projects.

1024   Turning Point [UK]
www.turning-point.co.uk/
A social care organization working with individuals and their communities across England and Wales in the areas of drug

and alcohol misuse, mental health and learning disabilities. Staff have particular expertise in working with people who have complex needs and are facing multiple social challenges.

Libraries, archives, museums

1025 British Institute of Learning Disabilities, Information & Resource Service
www.bild.org.uk
BILD works with the government and other organisations to improve the lives of people with learning disabilities. It conducts research, trains staff, family carers and people with a learning disability and provides members with information on learning disabilities.

1026 National Autistic Society, Information Centre [UK]
www.nas.org.uk/
London based reference library covering all aspects of Autism, including Asperger Syndrome.

1027 Royal National Institute of Blind People, Library
[UK]
www.rnib.org.uk
The RNIB library offers a wide range of services to blind, partially sighted and sighted people. For information on how to access the library telephone www.rnib.org.uk.

Portal & task environments

1028 Americans with Disabilities Act Hot Links and Document Center
United States. Department of Labor: Office of Disability Employment Policy
www.jan.wvu.edu/links/adalinks.htm
Part of the website of the Office of Disability Employment Policy, this portal contains a comprehensive set of links to documents, websites and other information on the Americans with Disabilities Act.

Discovering print & electronic resources

1029 Autism Data
National Autistic Society.
www.autism.org.uk/autismdata
A unique bibliographic research tool aimed at anyone researching autism and Asperger syndrome. Freely available for all to access on the web.

1030 BILD Database
British Institute of Learning Disabilities
www.bild.org.uk/05casonline.htm
This is a searchable database containing references to over 40,000 journal articles, books and pieces of research covering all aspects of learning disabilities. Updated monthly and available online via subscription.

1031 Cornucopia of Disability Information (CODI)
http://codi.buffalo.edu/
The information on this site addresses local (Buffalo and Western New York), state, national and international audiences. It is a resource for consumers and professionals,

containing an internet directory of disability information and a repository of electronic documents. Subjects covered include ageing, assistive technology, children, communication, hearing, mobility and vision.

1032 Database of International Rehabilitation Research
School of Public Health & Health Professions
http://cirrie.buffalo.edu/search/index.php
Contains over 27,000 citations of international rehabilitation research published between 1990 and the present. Entries include an abstract.

1033 Women with DisAbilities
National Women's Health Information Center
www.4woman.gov/wwd/
A useful one-stop shop for disability information. Aimed at service users, carers and professionals, the site includes information and information sources on types of illness and disability; abuse; ageing; caregiving; clinical trials; living with a disability; black and minority ethnic people; disabled children; sexuality; and substance misuse.

Digital data, image & text collections

1034 Change Picture Bank [UK]
Change   Change. £64.00 single user.
www.changepeople.co.uk/
Available in CD-ROM and hard copy, this resource contains 500 high- and low-resolution pictures covering various everyday subjects. The pictures are designed to make information for people with learning disabilities more effective and accessible. The pictures can be copied and pasted into printed documents, used on websites or on flyers and posters. A single copy of the CD costs £64.00. Networking prices increase with number of users.

1035 The road ahead: information for young people with learning difficulties, their families and supporters at transition
Social Care Institute for Excellence   Social Care Institute for Excellence, 2004.
www.scie.org.uk/publications/tra/index.asp
This project explores the nature of the information needed by young people with learning disabilities, their parents and supporters at transition to adulthood. The website contains a full and an easy-read version of the report.

Directories & encyclopedias

1036 Development and disability
V. Lewis   2nd rev. edn, Blackwell, 2002, 464pp. £21.99. ISBN 0631192743.
A comprehensive and up-to-date sourcebook on a wide range of disabilities. The author reviews the research and goes on to examine the effects on physical, emotional and psychological child development. Finally, the practical and theoretical implications of the experimental findings are examined. Includes over 1100 references.

1037 The encyclopedia of autism spectrum disorders
C. Turkington and R. Anan   Eurospan, 2007, 336pp. £45.95. ISBN 9780816063994.
A reference guide to autism, including types of autism,

causes, treatments, residential care, organizations, research institutes and more.

1038 The encyclopedia of learning disabilities
C. Turkington and J.R. Harris   Europspan, 2006, 320pp. £45.95. ISBN 9780816063994.
Contains over 650 entries covering the range of learning disabilities, diagnosis and treatment. Also includes entries on adaptive skills and assistive technology.

1039 Understanding learning disabilities: the sourcebook for causes, disorders and treatments
C. Turkington and J.R. Harris   Facts on File, 2003, 320pp. £13.95. ISBN 9780816051816.
This sourcebook offers broad, comprehensive information and facts on learning disabilities, focusing on the terminology of the field and presents key topics in a chapter-by-chapter format. An extensive section of A–Z entries follows, covering psychological and medical terms, pharmacology, therapies, types of learning disabilities, their causes, their effects and their treatments.

Handbooks & manuals

1040 Clinical governance in mental health and learning disability services: a practical guide
A. James, A. Worrall and T. Kendall, eds   Gaskell, 2005, 375pp. £35. ISBN 1904671128.
Practical handbook describing the foundations and the key elements of clinical governance as they apply to mental health and learning disability services. Key topics include service user involvement; clinical audit; clinical risk management; evidence-based practice; information management; staffing; and education and training.

1041 Disability rights handbook: a guide to benefits and services for all disabled people, their families, carers and advisers [UK]
I. Greaves   31st edn, Disability Alliance, 2006, annual, 288pp. £19. ISBN 1903335302.
Essential and comprehensive guide to the UK social security system. Gives information, advice and guidance on completing forms.

1042 Handbook of disability studies
G.L. Albrecht, K.D. Seelman and M. Bury, eds   Sage Publications, 2003, 864pp. $67.95. ISBN 978076192874.
Drawing on the insights of disability scholars around the world and the creative advice of an international editorial board, the book engages the reader in the critical issues and debates framing disability studies and places them in a historical and cultural context.

1043 Handbook of learning disabilities
H.L. Swanson, K.R. Harris and S. Graham, eds   Guilford Press, 2003, 587pp. $79.05. ISBN 9781572308510.
This sourcebook offers an authoritative summary and analysis of core issues related to theory and practice in the learning disabilities field. Aimed at advanced students and practitioners.

1044 Hearing and sight loss: a handbook for professional carers
S.J. Butler   Age Concern, 2004, 317pp. £9.89. ISBN 0862423597.

Handbook offering comprehensive guidance on causes and symptoms; emotional responses to hearing and sight loss; communication; rehabilitation; legislation and guidance; and benefits and registration.

1045 Paying for care handbook: a guide to services, charges and welfare benefits for adults in need of care in the community or in care homes [UK]
H. Winfield [et al.]   5th edn, Child Poverty Action Group, 2005, 492pp. £17.57. ISBN 9781901698817.
Comprehensive and detailed, this regularly updated manual deals with the legal, financial and other issues related receiving care, whether at home or in a nursing/care home. Includes information on social security benefits, social care, housing and charges.

Keeping up to date

1046 Journal of Applied Research in Intellectual Disabilities
Blackwell, qtrly. ISSN 13602322.
Available online and in print, this journal is an international, peer-reviewed journal which draws together findings derived from original applied research in intellectual disabilities. It is an important forum for the dissemination of ideas to promote valued lifestyles for people with intellectual disabilities.

1047 Journal of Social Work in Disability and Rehabilitation
Haworth Press, 4 per volume. ISSN 1536710X.
This journal presents and explores issues related to disabilities and social policy, social work practice, research and theory.

1048 RADAR Bulletin [UK]
Royal Association for Disability & Rehabilitation. ISSN 0954237X.
Provides up-to-date information on issues connected to disability. Covers Parliament, social security, community care, housing, education and training, employment, mobility, new aids and equipment, discrimination act news, holidays, access and sport and leisure.

1049 Rehab Network [UK]
National Vocational Rehabilitation Association, qtrly. ISSN 02680548. www.city.ac.uk/sonm/rrc/
A quarterly journal concerned with vocational rehabilitation, employment and rehabilitation issues.

1050 Viewpoint [UK]
Mencap, 6 p.a. ISSN 13586076. www.mencap.org.uk/
Magazine featuring all the news, campaigns and best practice from the world of learning disability. An audio version of the magazine is available on CD, available free to people who have a learning disability.

Older People

Introductions to the subject

1051 Community care for an aging society: issues, policies, and services
C.B. Cox   Springer, 2005, 191pp. £21.91. ISBN 9780826128041.
Examines the many factors contributing to needs for care in the community among older people, as well as the ways in which impairments are defined and responded to by both the individual and society. Looks at both practice and policy issues.

1052 Evaluating mental health services for older people
J. Finch   Radcliffe, 2004, 224pp. £29.95. ISBN 9781857756104.
Provides a comprehensive account of the current developments in mental health services for older people and describes a robust model for evaluating health and social care to improve these services. Draws on international experience from the UK, Europe, the USA, Canada and Australia.

1053 Gerontological social work: a task-centered approach [USA]
M.J. Naleppa and W.J. Reid   Columbia University Press, 2003, 448pp. $66. ISBN 9780231115865.
In-depth coverage of specific client problems, such as physical or mental health, care-giving, home and personal safety, senior living and long-term care arrangements. A series of task planners offers a menu of possible actions that can resolve or alleviate a designated problem. Rating scales, schedules and other forms assist the practitioner and client in the intervention process. An appendix classified by topic lists hundreds of websites related to work with the elderly.

1054 Social work with elders: a biopsychosocial approach to assessment and intervention
K. McInnis-Dittrich   2nd edn, Allyn & Bacon, 2004, 416pp. $81. ISBN 9780205408153.
Aimed at students, this text grounds practice in theory. It looks at traditional and nontraditional interventions with older people, recognizing the heterogenity of the ageing population. Examines topics such as human behaviour in the social environment, spirituality, designing interventions and gender, race, ethnicity, sexuality and sexual orientation.

1055 Social work with older people: transforming social work practice
K. Crawford and J. Walker   Learning Matters, 2004, 276pp. £14.25. ISBN 1844450171.
Designed to help students develop a distinctive focus on social work practice in the context of working with older people, this book will enable readers to develop the knowledge, skills and values that will enable them to promote and protect the individual and collective well-being of the older people with whom they work. Contains activities and case studies throughout.

Laws, standards, codes

1056 Care homes for older people: national minimum standards and the Care Homes Regulations 2001 [UK]
Great Britain. Department of Health   3rd edn, Stationery Office, 2003, 91pp. £13.50. ISBN 9780113226078.
www.dh.gov.uk/assetRoot/04/05/40/07/04054007.pdf
This document contains a statement of national minimum standards published by the Secretary of State under section 23(1) of the Care Standards Act 2000. The standards are grouped under the following key topics: choice of home; health and personal care; daily life and social activities; complaints and protection; environment; staffing, management and administration.

1057 National service framework for older people [UK]
Great Britain. Department of Health   2001, 194pp.
www.dh.gov.uk/assetRoot/04/07/12/83/04071283.pdf
Key policy document detailing a 10-year programme of action on services for older people, aiming to support independence, promote good health, provide specialized services for key conditions and instigate culture change so that older people and their carers are always treated with respect, dignity and fairness. Also aims to ensure consistent services across the country and reduce variations in standards and service levels.
- **National service framework for older people: executive summary** 35pp. www.dh.gov.uk/assetRoot/04/05/82/95/04058295.pdf.
- **National service framework for older people in Wales** Welsh Assembly Government 2006, 237pp. www.wales.nhs.uk/sites3/documents/439/NSFforOlderPeopleInWalesEnglish.pdf.
- **National service framework for older people in Wales: executive summary** 58pp. www.wales.nhs.uk/sites3/documents/439/ExecSumEnglish.pdf.

Official & quasi-official bodies

1058 United States. Department of Health & Human Services, Administration on Aging
www.aoa.dhhs.gov/
This government website contains a wide range of information for and on older people in the USA, including news, a resource centre, an eldercare locatory and much more.

Research centres & institutes

1059 Centre for Policy on Ageing [UK]
www.cpa.org.uk/index.html
The CPA aims to influence policy, publish research, provide information and encourage good practice in all areas of work with older people.

English Longitudinal Study of Ageing
See entry no. 627

ESA Research Network on Ageing in Europe
See entry no. 628

1060   Gerontological Society of America
www.geron.org/
Established in 1945, the Society's declared mission is 'to promote the conduct of multi and interdisciplinary research in ageing by expanding the quantity of and improving the quality of gerontological research and by increasing its funding resources; and to disseminate gerontological research knowledge to researchers, to practitioners and to decision and opinion makers'.

Oxford Institute of Ageing
See entry no. 629

1061   Polisher Research Institute [USA]
www.abramsoncenter.org/PRI/
The Institute provides national leadership in improving the quality of life of older persons through the study of social and behavioural aspects of ageing. It publishes and supports research and runs a library of gerontological information.

Sheffield Institute for Studies on Ageing
See entry no. 630

Associations & societies

1062   Action on Elder Abuse [UK]
www.elderabuse.org.uk/
This organization works to protect and prevent the abuse of, vulnerable older adults in the UK and Ireland. It runs conferences and training and provides a wide range of resources on its website.

1063   Age Concern [UK]
www.ageconcern.org.uk/
Age Concern supports all people over 50 in the UK by providing essential services such as day care and information and practical publications. The organization also campaigns on issues like age discrimination and pensions and works to influence public opinion and government policy.

1064   Alzheimer's Society [UK]
www.alzheimers.org.uk/
The Society is the UK's leading care and research charity for people with dementia, their families and carers

1065   American Society on Aging
www.asaging.org/index.cfm
This is a professional body for all those working with and interested in issues around older people. The Society runs courses, produces publications and training resources and enables the exchange of knowledge and experience.

1066   National Center on Elder Abuse
www.elderabusecenter.org/
This is an internationally recognized organization which aims to educate people about elder abuse, neglect and exploitation. It provides information on elder abuse to members of the public, health and other professionals and also offers technical assistance and training. Much of this information can be found on the website.

Policy Research Institute on Ageing & Ethnicity
See entry no. 631

1067   Relatives & Residents Association [UK]
www.relres.org/
The association provides support and information via a helpline; carries out project work that focuses on specific issues (publishing practical, evidence-based publications); influences policy and practice; and works with local relatives and residents' groups in care homes.

Libraries, archives, museums

1068   Centre for Policy on Ageing, Library & Information Service [UK]
www.cpa.org.uk/index.html
The Library and Information Service is a unique resource for all people working or researching in the field of older age. For full details of CPA's information resources, contact the Head of Information.

Portal & task environments

1069   AgeSource Worldwide
American Association of Retired People
www.aarp.org/research/agesource/
This website identifies and provides links to over 300 major or unique libraries, clearinghouses, databases, directories, bibliographies and web metasites around the world that focus on ageing or closely allied subjects. Some 30 countries are represented.

Discovering print & electronic resources

1070   AgeInfo
Centre for Policy on Ageing
www.cpa.org.uk/ageinfo/ageinfo2.html
An information service about old age and ageing provided by the Library and Information Service of the Centre for Policy on Ageing, this bibliographic database is available via subscription on the web and on CD-ROM.

1071   AgeLine
American Association of Retired People
www.aarp.org/research/ageline/
This database abstracts the literature of social gerontology as well as ageing-related research from psychology, sociology, social work, economics, public policy and the health sciences. Aimed at professionals in ageing services, health, business, law and mental health. Access to the content is free.

1072   Clearinghouse on Abuse and Neglect of the Elderly (CANE)
National Center on Elder Abuse
www.elderabusecenter.org/default.cfm?p=cane.cfm
Located at the University of Delaware, this is an extensive archive of published research, training resources, government documents and other sources on elder abuse. Databases of a range of resources are freely available on the CANE website.

1073 **Health and retirement study: a longitudinal study of health, retirement, and aging sponsored by the National Institute on Aging** [USA]
http://hrsonline.isr.umich.edu/
This study surveys more than 22,000 Americans over the age of 50 every two years. It paints an emerging portrait of an ageing America's physical and mental health, insurance coverage, financial status, family support systems, labour market status and retirement planning.

1074 **SCIE practice guide: assessing the mental health needs of older people**
Social Care Institute for Excellence   rev. edn, Social Care Institute for Excellence, 2003.
www.scie.org.uk/publications/practiceguides/practiceguide02/
Describes some of the specific mental health problems that older people may experience and looks at key research and policy findings; ideas from practice and practice examples; and details of relevant legislation, guidance and standards. Aimed at front-line social work practitioners working with older people in non-specialist settings and who may have limited knowledge and experience of mental health issues.

Digital data, image & text collections

Survey of health, ageing and retirement in Europe
See entry no. 633

Handbooks & manuals

1075 **The care assistant's handbook** [UK]
H. Howard   Age Concern, 2000, 152pp. ISBN 0862422884.
Manual designed to help care assistants working in residential and nursing homes. Topics include communication skills; encouraging independence; valuing individuality and difference; promoting choice and self-esteem; recognizing rights and responsibilities; what to do when things go wrong; and maintaining a balance between safety and risk.

1076 **Clear voices: a good practice guide to involving older people and carers in strategic planning and service development**
J. Scott, R. Bhaduri and C. Sutcliffe   University of Manchester. Personal Social Services Research Unit, 2004, 50pp. ISBN 0906107997.
Represents a synthesis of best practice on the involvement of older people and carers in the strategic planning processes which inform the provision of health and social care. Derived from the views of older people and carers on the practicalities of involvement, research findings and relevant literature.

1077 **Gerontological practice for the twenty-first century: a social work perspective**
V.E. Richardson and A.S. Barusch   Columbia University Press, 2005, 491pp. $75. ISBN 9780231107488.
The authors address a wide range of issues affecting older adults, including depression, substance abuse and dementia as well as various life transitions of retirement and end-of-life care. Themes and concepts underlying this practice text are multiculturalism, empowerment and social justice. They

present an integrated practice model incorporating macro and micro levels of intervention.

1078 **Gerontological social work practice: issues, challenges, and potential**
E.O. Cox, E.S. Kelchner and R.K. Chapin, eds   Haworth Press, 2002, 204pp. $30. ISBN 9780789019400.
Presents an essential overview of the role, status and potential of gerontological social work in ageing societies around the world. Drawing on the expertise of leaders in the field, it identifies key policy and practice issues and suggests directions for the future.

1079 **A handbook of dementia care** [UK]
C. Cantley   Open University Press, 2001, 400pp. £22. ISBN 0335203833.
Handbook providing a multidisciplinary and critical guide to what we know about dementia and dementia care.

1080 **Handbook of social work in health and aging**
B. Berkman, ed.   Oxford University Press USA, 2006, 1168pp. $72.35. ISBN 9780195173727.
Authoritative, wide-ranging handbook integrating the fields of health care, ageing and social work by compiling the most current thinking on these subjects in a single volume.

1081 **Mental disorders in older adults**
S.H. Zarit and J.M. Zarit   2nd edn, Guilford Press, 2006, 468pp. £31.35. ISBN 9781572309463.
Provides foundational knowledge and skills for mental health practice with older adults and their caregivers. Draws on research and clinical expertise to comprehensively address normal ageing processes, frequently encountered clinical problems and effective approaches to evaluation, psychotherapy, family support and consultation in institutional settings.

1082 **Working with older people and their families: key issues in policy and practice**
M. Nolan, S. Davies and G. Grant, eds   Open University Press, 2001, 224pp. £19.78. ISBN 9780335205608.
Combines extensive reviews of specialist literatures with new empirical data in an attempt at a synthesis of themes about making a reality of 'person-centred' care. Includes the views of older people themselves.

Keeping up to date

1083 **Age Concern Information Bulletin** [UK]
Age Concern, monthly.
Monthly digest of news and reviews concerning issues that affect older people.

1084 **Aging Today**
American Society on Aging, bi-monthly.
www.agingtoday.org/at/at-281/toc.cfm
This bi-monthly newspaper covers developments in public policy, research, practice, media and programming in the field of ageing. Available online and in print format.

1085 **The Gerontologist**
Gerontological Society of America, 6 p.a. ISSN 00169013.
This journal provides a multidisciplinary perspective on human ageing through the publication of research and

analysis in gerontology, including social policy, programme development and service delivery. It reflects and informs the broad community of disciplines and professions involved in understanding the ageing process and providing service to older people.

1086 Journal of Dementia Care
Hawker, 6 p.a. ISSN 13518372.
www.careinfo.org/dementiacare/
Essential reading for all those working with people with dementia.

1087 Journal of Gerontological Social Work
Haworth Press, 8 p.a. ISSN 01634372.
Available electronically and in hard copy, this peer-reviewed journal contains articles on social work practice, theory, administration and consultation in the field of ageing. Aimed at all those working with older people, including social workes and health and mental health professionals.

1088 Working with Older People
Pavilion, qtrly. ISSN 13663666.
www.pavpub.com/pavpub/journals/
Aims to address the key challenges facing managers, social workers, residential care staff, day centre staff and community nurses who work with older people, as well as older people themselves, their families and carers.

Black & Minority Ethnic People

Introductions to the subject

1089 Anti-discriminatory practice
N. Thompson   4th edn, Palgrave Macmillan, 2006, 208pp. £17.99. ISBN 1403921601.
Fourth edition of a classic textbook that offers support, guidance and insight on a complex subject and is an ideal starting point or refresher for students, practitioners and managers alike.

1090 Cultural sensitivity in social and health care
R. Moore and I. MacLean   2nd edn, Kirwin Maclean Associates, 2005, 90pp. £10. ISBN 1903575281.
Outlines principles of cultural diversity in social and health care in Britain, including different ethnic and religious groups.

1091 Mental health, race and culture
S. Fernando   2nd edn, Palgrave Macmillan, 2002, 255pp. ISBN 9780333960264.
This book presents a critical account of western psychiatry and psychology seen from a cross-cultural perspective that addresses ways in which ideas about 'race' and racism continue to influence theory and practice in the field. Presents imaginative and constructive ways in which theory and practice may be restructured to take on board wisdom and technologies from all cultural traditions.

1092 Multicultural social work practice
D.W. Sue   Wiley, 2005, 384pp. $60. ISBN 9780471662525.
This comprehensive yet practical text offers students definitive guidance on culturally sensitive social work practice. It highlights the sociopolitical and social justice

aspects of effective practice and examines how social work theories, concepts and practices are often rooted in and reflective of the values of the dominant society.

1093 Our diverse society: race and ethnicity: implications for 21st Century American society
D.W. Engstrom and L.M. Piedra   National Association of Social Workers, 2006, 242pp. $44.99. ISBN 187101372X.
Practical text aimed at policy makers, social workers and students. Designed to aid understanding of current and future issues around diversity, it features chapters on demographic change; how language, religion and education transmit and transform cultural beliefs; inequalities in American organizations; disparties in health and social care services; and practice models for working with diversity.

1094 Promoting equality: challenging discrimination and oppression
A. Mullender and N. Thompson   2nd rev.edn, Palgrave Macmillan, 2004, 288pp. £16.18. ISBN 9780333993538.
Presents a clear and accessible analysis of the complexities of discrimination and oppression and the challenges of making equality practice a reality. Critical of the orthodoxies and over-simplications of political correctness, the authors offer theory combined with practice examples. Useful for students and practitioners.

1095 Religion and spirituality
B. Moss   Russell House, 2005, 108pp. ISBN 1903855578.
Starting with a celebration of diversity and the need to treat others with dignity and respect, especially when views differ widely, this book builds on the increasing recognition of people's religious and spiritual needs and explains why the issues should be taken seriously. Presents information in a way that readers can apply to their professional and personal situations.

1096 Social work practice with immigrants and refugees
[USA]
P.R. Balgopal   Columbia University Press, 2000, 288pp. $27.50. ISBN 9780231108577.
This book looks at the role of social workers serving new immigrants and refugees in the USA.

Dictionaries, thesauri, classifications

Dictionary of race, ethnicity and culture
G. Bolaffi [et al.], eds   See entry no. 700

1097 Penguin dictionary of religions
J.R. Hinnells, ed.   Penguin, 1997, 800pp. ISBN 0140512616.
Authoritative guide to every aspect of religion, past and present. Examines ancient doctrines and modern beliefs, small sects and popular movements. Draws on the expertise of over 60 contributors worldwide and is an essential reference source for both academic study and general readers.

Official & quasi-official bodies

1098 Commission for Racial Equality [UK]
www.cre.gov.uk/
Set up under the 1976 Race Relations Act, the CRE The CRE

has three main duties: to work towards the elimination of racial discrimination and promote equality of opportunity; to encourage good relations between people from different racial and ethnic backgrounds; and to monitor the way the Race Relations Act is working and recommend ways in which it can be improved.

1099 OneScotland
Scottish Executive.
www.onescotland.com/
One Scotland, the Scottish Executive's anti-racism campaign, is designed to tackle racism in that country. It aims to raise awareness of racist attitudes and highlight their negative impact, to make Scotland 'no place for racism'.

1100 United States Congress on Civil Rights
www.usccr.gov/
The government body dealing with all aspects of discrimination and civil rights in the USA.

Research centres & institutes

Centre for Research in Ethnic Relations
See entry no. 701

European Research Centre on Migration & Ethnic Relations
See entry no. 1546

1101 Race Equality Foundation [UK]
www.reu.org.uk/
The Foundation promotes race equality in social support (what families and friends do for each other) and social care (what 'workers' do for people who need support). It does this by exploring what is known about discrimination and disadvantage, by developing interventions that will overcome barriers and promote equality and by disseminating good practice through training, conferences and written material.

1102 Refugee Council [UK]
www.refugeecouncil.org.uk/
The largest organization in the UK working with asylum seekers and refugees. It gives advice and support to asylum seekers and refugees to help them rebuild their lives; works with refugee community organizations; offers training and employment courses to asylum seekers and refugees; campaigns for refugees' voices to be heard in the UK and abroad and produces authoritative information on refugee issues worldwide, including reports, statistics and analysis.

1103 Runnymede Trust [UK]
www.runnymedetrust.org/
A voluntary organization, the Trust's mandate is to promote a successful multi-ethnic Britain. The organization acts as a bridge builder between various minority ethnic communities and policy makers, stimulates debate and suggests forward-looking strategies in areas of public policy such as education, the criminal justice system, employment and citizenship.

Associations & societies

Association for the Study of Ethnicity & Nationalism
See entry no. 704

1104 Institute of Race Relations [UK]
www.irr.org.uk/
An anti-racist think-tank, the IRR concentrates on responding to the needs of black people and making direct analyses of institutionalized racism in Britain and the rest of Europe. It seeks to reflect the experiences of those who suffer racial oppression and draws its perspectives from the most vulnerable in society. Publishes research and the journal *Race and Class*.

Libraries, archives, museums

1105 Runnymede Trust Collection at Middlesex University [UK]
www.mdx.ac.uk/runnymede
The collection is an archive of documents that have been critical in the fight for racial equality in Britain since the 1960s. The Runnymede Trust – a UK organization that promotes ethnic and cultural diversity – has donated this significant collection to the Centre for Racial Equality Studies at Middlesex University.

Discovering print & electronic resources

1106 Ageing and ethnicity
AEWEB
www.aeweb.org
Gives worldwide information on issues related to minority ethnic older people. AEWEB invites people from minority ethnic backgrounds, researchers and policy makers to make contributions to the website, which contains news, downloads, links, forums, polls and much more.

Ethnic NewsWatch
See entry no. 705

Sage Race Relations Abstracts
See entry no. 706

Directories & encyclopedias

Encyclopedia of race and ethnic studies
E. Cashmore   See entry no. 709

Encyclopedia of race and racism
See entry no. 710

The encyclopedia of the Indian diaspora
B. Lal, ed.   See entry no. 1561

Handbooks & manuals

1107   The best of times: the worst of times: embedding race equality in social services
Association of Directors of Social Services   Association of Directors of Social Services, 2006, 68pp. ISBN 1854424008.
www.adss.org.uk/committee/inclusivity/besttimesworst.pdf
Available as a PDF and in hard copy, this document promotes inclusivity as being at the heart of social work practice.

1108   Collaborative programs in indigenous communities: from fieldwork to practice
B. Harrison   AltaMira Press, 2001, 264pp. £19.91. ISBN 9780759100619.
A valuable reference source for developing collaborative programmes between indigenous groups and outside experts, including those in social work and social care. Focuses on programmes with Maori communities in New Zealand and Alaskan native communities in the USA. Uses case studies throughout.

A companion to racial and ethnic studies
D.T. Goldberg and J. Solomos   See entry no. 711

1109   Culturally competent practice with immigrants and refugee children and families
R. Fong, ed.   Guilford Press, 2003, 320pp. $39. ISBN 9781572309319.
Brings together chapters by experienced practitioners, providing essential knowledge about contemporary immigrant and refugee populations and offering an up-to-date framework for culturally competent practice.

Encyclopedia of black studies
M.A. Asante and M. Karenga, eds   See entry no. 713

1110   Multicultural social work in Canada: working with diverse ethno-racial communities
A. Al-Krenawi and J.R. Graham   Oxford University Press, 2002, 408pp. CDN$ 45.50. ISBN 9780195415308.
Comprehensive text focusing on Canada's multi-ethnic society. Major themes include differential processes in seeking help and the importance of taking into account a community's history or an individual's age, gender, acculturation or socio-economic status when developing strategies for social work in multicultural settings.

1111   Social work practice and people of color: a process stage approach
D. Lum   3rd edn, Wadsworth, 2003, 360pp. £45.10. ISBN 9780534509897.
Offers a practical and well defined five-stage model of social work practice with culturally diverse communities. While the book specifically looks at practice with persons of colour (African-American, Asian-American, Latino and First Nations people), it is intended to be relevant for culturally and ethnically sensitive practice with any individual or population.

1112   Social work practice with refugee and immigrant youth in the United States
M. Delgado, K. Jones and M. Rohani   Allyn & Bacon, 2004, 304pp. $56. ISBN 9780205398836.
This book puts the newcomer experience into context and provides a guide for social workers developing interventions using a youth development paradigm. Uses case studies and examples throughout.

Keeping up to date

1113   Catalyst Magazine [UK]
Commission for Racial Equality, bi-monthly.
www.cre.gov.uk/publs/catalyst.html
An essential magazine for staying up to date with the latest thinking on race, integration and citizenship. Available in print and online.

1114   Diverse Minds Magazine
Mind.
www.mind.org.uk/
Covers news and issues around mental health services for black and minority ethnic communities.

Ethnicities
See entry no. 714

1115   International Journal on Multicultural Societies
UNESCO. ISSN 18174574.
http://portal.unesco.org/shs/en/ev.php-URL_ID=2547&URL_DO=DO_TOPIC&URL_SECTION=201.html
Scholarly and professional journal, published by UNESCO. Provides a platform for international, interdisciplinary and policy-related social science research in the fields of migration, multiculturalism and minority rights.

1116   Journal of Ethnic and Cultural Diversity in Social Work
Haworth Press, qtrly. ISSN 15313204.
This journal is dedicated to the examination of multicultural social issues as they relate to social work policy, research, theory and practice.

1117   Runnymede Bulletin [UK]
Runnymede Trust, qtrly. ISSN 1476363X.
www.runnymedetrust.org/
Presents news and analysis of key race relations issues in the UK.

1118   The Voice [UK]
GV Media Group, weekly. £0.85.
www.voice-online.co.uk/
Newspaper aimed at the UK's black community. Online version also available.

Children, Young People & Families

Introductions to the subject

1119   American juvenile justice
F.E. Zimring   Oxford University Press USA, 2005, 264pp. $42.31. ISBN 9780195181166.
A definitive volume for courses on the criminology and policy analysis of adolescence. The focus is on the principles and policy of a separate and distinct system of juvenile justice.

1120 Child neglect: practice issues for health and social care
J. Taylor and B. Daniel   Jessica Kingsley, 2005, 352pp. £19.95. ISBN 9781843101604.
With a joint health and social work focus, this interdisciplinary book is an essential resource for practitioners, academics and policy makers working towards integrated and collaborative childcare services.

1121 Children, families and communities: contexts and consequences
J. Bowes, ed.   2nd edn, OUP Australia & New Zealand, 2004, 310pp. £21.99. ISBN 9780195517354.
Examines the influences that affect a child's development, including the effects of disability; ethnicity; gender; family; school; neighbourhood, including rural, urban and remote communities; and state interventions and policies. Includes chapters on child protection and out of home care; child care and Australian social policy; and state intervention.

1122 Family support as reflective practice
P. Dolan, J. Canavan and J. Pinkerton   Jessica Kingsley, 2006, 304pp. £19.99. ISBN 9781843103202.
Family support is an increasingly important strategic approach to provision of services for children and families. This resource is aimed at all professionals working in this field.

1123 Fostering now: messages from research
I. Sinclair   Jessica Kingsley, 2005, 174pp. £16.64. ISBN 9781843103622.
Essential reading for social workers, policy makers, academics and foster carers, this text draws together research evidence and highlights the main implications for practice.

1124 An introduction to family social work
D. Collins, C. Jordan and H. Coleman   2nd edn, Wadsworth, 2006, 416pp. $54.25. ISBN 9780495092247.
Intended for students who will work with families, but who will not necessarily undertake advanced training in family therapy, this text takes a pragmatic and practical approach and provides beginning students with the foundational knowledge and skills they need for family social work.

1125 The involvement of children and young people in promoting change and enhancing the quality of social care
C. Danso [et al.]   National Children's Bureau, 2003, 29pp.
Summarizes current knowledge about the involvement of children and young people in social care and the extent to which this has brought about change and improved the quality of the services that they receive. Based on a literature review.

1126 Promoting family wellness and preventing child maltreatment: fundamentals for thinking and action
I. Prilleltensky, G. Nelson and L. Peirson   University of Toronto Press, 2001, 528pp. CDN$ 20.79. ISBN 9780802083838.
Relevant to all those involved in child welfare, as well as students and researchers. Also readable and clear enough to be of interest to the general reader. Sets out a systematic framework within which to understand, develop and implement community service systems and programmes

that promote family wellness and prevent child maltreatment.

1127 What works in probation and youth justice: developing evidence-based practice
R. Burnett and C. Roberts, eds   Willan, 2004, 267pp. £20. ISBN 184392059X.
Reviews developments in evidence-based practice within both probation and youth justice, bringing together the findings of research projects commissioned by the Home Office, the National Probation Directorate and the Youth Justice Board.

1128 Youth justice and social work [UK]
P. Dugmore, S. Angus and J. Pickford   Learning Matters, 2006, 208pp. £10.56. ISBN 184445066X.
Practical text structured around the National Occupational Standards, the values and ethics underpinning social work practice and the GSCC Code of Practice for social workers. Ideal for students studying criminology and criminal justice who wish to develop an understanding of social work practice in the youth justice context and for social work students with an interest in youth work.

Laws, standards, codes

1129 Adoption: the modern procedure [UK]
H. Swindells and C. Heaton   Family Law, 2006, 763pp. £47.50. ISBN 0853089698.
Provides an accessible and detailed examination of the procedural regime governing applications under the Adoption and Children Act 2002 that came into force on 30 December 2005. All relevant legislation etc. is contained in appendices at the end.

1130 Children: the modern law [UK]
A. Bainham   3rd edn, Family Law, 2005, 811pp. £28.50. ISBN 0853089396.
Covers every aspect of the law relating to children, including adoption; sexual offences; human rights; and child support.

1131 Family law: the essentials [USA]
W.P. Statsky   2nd edn, Thomson Delmar, 2003, 384pp. $65.07. ISBN 9781401848279.
The 'essentials' version of a larger text. Aimed at students, this book provides an introduction to family law and practice, covering such topics as premarital agreements, annulment, spousal support, child custody and more. Includes new material on civil unions, domestic partnership, domestic violence, covenant marriage and adoption by gays and lesbians.

Official & quasi-official bodies

1132 Children's Commissioner for England
www.childrenscommissioner.org/
The Commissioner looks after the interests and acts as the voice of children and young people by exposing issues informed by children and young people themselves; provoking and facilitating discussion and debate; influencing the public, parents, carers and politicians through effective advocacy, particularly through the media; informing and scrutinizing government policy; and holding organizations to

account. Focuses in particular on the needs of the most vulnerable children.

1133 Children's Commissioner for Wales
www.childcom.org.uk/english/index.html
The Commissioner represents children and young people in Wales, with the remit to ensure that they are safe from harm and abuse; get the opportunities and services they need and deserve; are respected and valued; have a voice and are able to play as full a part as possible in decisions that affect them; know about their rights and the UN Convention on the Rights of the Child.

Great Britain. Department for Children, Schools & Families
See entry no. 4428

1134 Northern Ireland. Commissioner for Children & Young People
www.niccy.org/
The Commissioner's principal aim is to safeguard and promote the rights and best interests of children and young people in Northern Ireland.

1135 Scotland's Commissioner for Children & Young People
www.sccyp.org.uk/
The Commissioner is responsible for ensuring that the UN Convention on the Rights of the Child is adhered to in Scotland.

1136 United States. Department of Health & Human Services, Administration for Children & Families
www.acf.dhhs.gov/
The ACF is a federal agency funding state, territory, local and tribal organizations to provide family assistance (welfare), child support, childcare, Head Start, child welfare and other programmes relating to children and families. Actual services are provided by state, county, city and tribal governments and public and private local agencies. ACF assists these organizations through funding, policy direction and information services.

Research centres & institutes

1137 Child Trends [USA]
www.childtrends.org/
A non-profit, non-partisan research organization dedicated to improving the lives of children by conducting and disseminating research to improve the decisions, programmes and policies that affect children and their families. The organization collects and analyses data; conducts, synthesizes and disseminates research; designs and evaluates programmes; and develops and tests promising approaches to research in the field.

1138 Children & Families Research Unit [UK]
www.dmu.ac.uk/faculties/hls/research/cfru/index.jsp
An applied research and policy think-tank which undertakes, promotes, publishes and disseminates quality research, evaluation and policy projects about a range of children and families issues.

1139 Family & Child Well-Being Research Network [USA]
www.rcgd.isr.umich.edu/nihnetwork/about/index.htm
A multidisciplinary organization drawing together researchers representing a wide range of skills, experience and knowledge in child and family-related research, including sociology, medicine, economics, public health, psychology and statistics.

1140 Institute of Child Care Research
www.qub.ac.uk/research-centres/InstituteofChildCareResearch/
The Institute aims to play a key role in influencing the development of childcare policy and practice in Northern Ireland. It has three major objectives: to identify and conduct original research into childcare needs and services through using and developing a mix of research methods and varied forms of dissemination; to offer training and consultation on undertaking and applying childcare research; and to provide postgraduate research supervision.

1141 Jordan Institute for Families [USA]
University of North Carolina at Chapel Hill: School of Social Work
http://ssw.unc.edu/jif/
The Institute is the research, training and technical assistance arm of the School of Social Work at the University of North Carolina at Chapel Hill. Addressing family issues across the lifespan, the organization brings together experts, including families themselves, to develop and test policies and practices that strengthen families and engage communities. Runs programmes and projects, does research and has a publishing programme.

Social Issues Research Centre
See entry no. 588

Associations & societies

1142 Barnardo's
www.barnardos.org.uk/
Voluntary organization providing direct support to more than 110,000 vulnerable children, young people and their families via running 383 projects at home, school and in the local community. Also does research and publishes reports.

1143 British Association for Adoption & Fostering
www.baaf.org.uk/
BAAF campaigns, produces publications, newsletters and a journal, provides advice, does consultancy and runs training courses and conferences.

1144 Child Poverty Action Group [UK]
www.cpag.org.uk/
CPAG aims are to raise awareness of the causes, extent, nature and impact of poverty and strategies for its eradication and prevention; bring about positive policy changes for families with children in poverty; and enable those eligible for income maintenance to have access to their full entitlement. Produces a wide range of publications, provides training and advice, lobbies and mounts legal test cases.

1145 Child Welfare League of America
www.cwla.org/
CWLA is an association of nearly 800 public and private nonprofit agencies that assist more than 3.5 million abused

and neglected children and their families each year with a range of services. Produces publications, runs programmes, conferences and training sessions and does research.

1146   Children's Society
www.childrenssociety.org.uk/
The Society runs projects for children, young people and their families, including work with runaways, the juvenile justice system, disabled children, young carers, traveller children and children whose parents are substance misusers. The organization also campaigns to influence policy, does research and produces publications.

1147   Family Rights Group
www.frg.org.uk/index.asp
The FRG provides advice and support for families whose children are involved with social services and develops and promotes services that help secure the best possible futures for children and families. The organization also runs events, does training and consultancy, runs projects and produces publications and policy documents.

1148   Family Welfare Association [UK]
www.fwa.org.uk/
A registered charity, the FWA provides a range of services to children and families, including home-based support; financial help in the form of grants; educational grants; and community-based mental health services.

1149   National Children's Bureau
www.ncb.org.uk
NCB is a charitable organization that acts as an umbrella body for organizations working with children and young people in England and Northern Ireland. A multi-agency network, the organization aims to share knowledge, resources and services and to provide an influential and authoritative voice for children and young people.

1150   National Society for the Prevention of Cruelty to Children
www.nspcc.org.uk/
The NSPCC aims to protect children from cruelty, support vulnerable families, campaign for changes to the law and raise awareness about abuse.

1151   NCH the Children's Charity
www.nch.org.uk/
NCH runs more than 500 projects for some of the UK's most vulnerable and excluded children and young people and their families, supporting over 160,000 people at children's centres throughout the UK. It also promotes social justice by lobbying and campaigning for change.

Sociology of Youth and Generation Research Network
See entry no. 632

Libraries, archives, museums

1152   National Children's Bureau, Library [UK]
www.ncb.org.uk
The NCB library publishes a range of professionally recognized titles in various formats, including the database ChildData; ChildData abstracts; ChildStats; and Highlights. It

also does customized literature searches, provides an enquiry service and is open to the public by appointment.

1153   National Society for the Prevention of Cruelty to Children, Library [UK]
www.nspcc.org.uk
The NSPCC Library provides a reference resource and enquiry service for practitioners, researchers, policy-makers, trainers and other child care professionals looking for up-to-date information about child protection and child abuse.

1154   National Youth Agency [UK]
www.nya.org.uk/
The NYA Library contains resources on youth work in the statutory and voluntary youth service and the major issues affecting the lives of young people in a social welfare, education and government policy context. The library is open to researchers by appointment and the catalogue is available online.

Portal & task environments

1155   Children, youth and family consortium [USA]
University of Minnesota
www.cyfc.umn.edu/welcome.html
This is an online gateway to a wide range of information and resources about children and families. It aims to connect research, teaching, policy and community practice by sharing knowledge freely.

1156   United States. Department of Health & Human Services, Child Welfare Information Gateway
www.childwelfare.gov/
The Gateway provides access to information and resources to help protect children and strengthen families. It contains a range of freely available resources, including statistics, an adoption register and databases.

Discovering print & electronic resources

1157   ChildData
National Children's Bureau.
www.childdata.org.uk/
The catalogue of the library of the National Children's Bureau, this database comprehensively covers policy, legislation, practice and research on children and young people. A subscription is required. Also available via Athens password.

1158   NSPCC Inform
National Society for the Prevention of Cruelty to Children.
www.nspcc.org.uk/
A free online resource covering child protection in the UK, this website includes information for children, parents, professionals and all those interested in the welfare of children.

1159   ORB Children's database (Northern Ireland)
Northern Ireland. Office of the First Minister & Deputy First Minister.
www.ark.ac.uk/orb/child.html
The purpose of ORB children's research database, is to provide the central source in Northern Ireland for research on all aspects of children's lives. The framework for the search

categories is based on the UN Convention on the Rights of the Child. The database is freely available to all.

1160 PAVNET [USA]
www.pavnet.org/
PAVNET (Partnerships Against Violence Network) is a 'virtual library' of information about violence and youth-at-risk, representing data from seven different Federal agencies in the USA.

Digital data, image & text collections

1161 Barnardo's Photo Archive
www.barnardos.org.uk
Dating back to 1874, this picture archive contains 500,000 images and 300 films of the visual history of Barnardo's children's homes. The archive handles enquiries from former residents, the media, publishers, researchers and others. For enquiries telephone 020 8498 7345.

1162 ChildStats.gov [USA]
United States. Federal Interagency Forum on Child & Family Statistics
www.childstats.gov/
Website offering easy access to statistics and reports on children and families in the USA, including population and family characteristics, economic security, health, behaviour and social environment and education. The site is maintained by a working group of Federal Agencies that collects, analyses and reports on data relating to children and families.

1163 National Data Analysis System [USA]
Child Welfare League of America
http://ndas.cwla.org/
Comprehensive, free-to-access website offering a wide range of statistical and other information on children and child welfare in the USA. One of the main aims of the site is to illustrate the wide variation in the ways that states collect information about child welfare issues and to help with organizing comparative data.

Directories & encyclopedias

Encyclopedia of relationships across the lifespan
J. Turner   See entry no. 635

1164 Hallmark directory of criminal justice [UK]
www.hallmarkdirectory.com/
Online resource containing details of organizations involved in criminal justice, from police stations through the CPS offices and the courts to prisons and establishments for young offenders and youth offender teams. Also includes organizations offering support to prisoners and their families and lists of solicitors franchised by the Legal Aid Board for criminal defence work.

1165 A world of prevention
Texas Youth Commission
www.tyc.state.tx.us/prevention/
An online searchable directory of resources focusing on the prevention of child and adolescent problems and the promotion of youth development in families, schools and

communities. Subjects covered include child abuse and neglect; juvenile justice; substance misuse; young people; mental health; and community development.

Handbooks & manuals

1166 Handbook of preventive interventions for children and adolescents
L.A. Rapp-Paglicci, C.N. Dulmus and J.S. Wodarski   Wiley, 2004, 484pp. £23.75. ISBN 047127433X.
Covers the various types of prevention interventions available for children and adolescents encountering emotional, health and social problems. Uses a primary prevention model. Each chapter offers an introductory summary, discusses trends; incidence; risk factors; interventions available on a universal, selective and targeted level; and concludes with future directions

1167 Handbook of youth and justice [USA]
S.O. White, ed.   Springer, 2006, 448pp. $101.85. ISBN 9780306463396.
This handbook provides a comprehensive, cross-disciplinary perspective on youth behaviour and the justice system. Leading authorities from sociology, political science, criminology, psychology, law, social work and communication analyse the connections between children and youth (in their various social situations) and the law, including the making and enforcement of legal and social policies, the role of children's rights and the operation of the legal system.

1168 The leaving care handbook: helping and supporting care leavers
A. Wheal, ed.   Russell House, 2005, 243pp. £28.45. ISBN 1903855675.
Comprehensive and practical handbook.

1169 Parent participation: improving services for children and families
D. Braun, comp.   Parentline Plus, 2005, 42pp. £5.
An accessible and easy-to-use 12-step toolkit from the Parent Policy Alliance (Family Rights Group, Family Welfare Association and Parentline Plus) which details the principles and practicalities of involving parents.

1170 A practitioner's tool for child protection and the assessment of parents
J. Fowler   Jessica Kingsley, 2003, 160pp. £17.05. ISBN 9781843100508.
This is a practical tool for the assessment of children and their families, designed to enable professionals to make decisions about child protection issues. It provides detailed checklists for collecting and interpreting information for assessment and discusses assessment of attachment, alcohol and drug use and parenting skills.

1171 Promoting the emotional well-being of children and adolescents and preventing their mental ill health: a handbook
K. Dwivedi and P. Brinley Harper, eds   Jessica Kingsley, 2004, 288pp. £18. ISBN 184310153X.
Provides overviews of the key psychological processes affecting mental health and emphasizes throughout the importance of early intervention and prevention. Section authors come from a range of professional backgrounds.

1172 Protecting children: working together to keep children safe

H. Flynn and B. Starns Heinemann Educational, 2004, 252pp. £14.24. ISBN 0435456792.

Written by authors who work in a child protection unit. Offers clear and up-to-date information on the latest legislation and guidelines in child protection. Aimed at students on Level 3 and 4 childcare courses, primary teachers, classroom assistants and playworkers.

1173 Social work with children and their families

C.G. Petr Oxford University Press USA, 2003, 352pp. $55. ISBN 9780195157550.

Integrating policy and practice, this text takes pragmatic view of services for children and families. Aimed at students and practitioners.

Keeping up to date

1174 Adoption and Fostering

British Association for Adoption & Fostering, qtrly. ISSN 03085759. www.baaf.org.uk/

This journal includes contributions from social workers, social work managers, carers, medical practitioners, lawyers and researchers. Aims to provide an inter-disciplinary, all-round perspective on new developments in practice, policy, law and research, both in the UK and overseas

1175 Child Welfare

Child Welfare League of America, 6 p.a. ISSN 00094021.

This scholarly journal covers child welfare issues, including homelessless, abuse and disabilities. It links the latest findings in child welfare and related research with the best practice, policy and programme development.

1176 Children Now

National Children's Bureau, 47 p.a. ISSN 0591017X.

Contains news and articles on current issues in the area of children's services.

1177 Childright [UK]

Children's Legal Centre, 10 p.a. ISSN 02651459.

Bulletin explaining and commenting on law and policy affecting children and young people in England and Wales.

1178 Families in Society

Alliance for Children & Families, 6 p.a. ISSN 10443894.

This core social work journal is aimed at social workers and related professionals in direct practice, management, supervision, education, research and policy and planning.

1179 Journal of Child and Family Studies

Kluwer Academic, 6 p.a. ISSN 10621024.

Available online and in print, this journal provides a forum for topical issues pertaining to the mental well-being of children, adolescents and their families. Topics covered include applied research, programme evaluation, service delivery and policy issues on areas such as emotional or behavioural disorders; child abuse and neglect; respite care; foster care; mental health care financing; homelessness; family stress; AIDS; and substance abuse.

1180 Young People Now

Haymarket Professional Publications, 47 p.a. £75.

Covers the latest news and information on every aspect of working with young people aged 11 to 25.

1181 Youth Justice [UK]

Russell House, 3 p.a. Published by Russell House on behalf of the National Association for Youth Justice. ISSN 14732254. www.russellhouse.co.uk/Pages/journals.html

Provides a major forum for discussion, dissemination and analysis. Its primary focus is on children and young people, their rights and welfare and their relation to crime.

Youth-Study@jiscmail.ac.uk
See entry no. 637

Mental Health & Social Work

Introductions to the subject

1182 The dilemma of Federal mental health policy: radical reform or incremental change? [USA]

G.N. Grob and H.H. Goldman Rutgers, 2007, 226pp. $38.21. ISBN 9780813539584.

This is an essential text on mental health policy in the USA. The authors trace how an ever-changing coalition of mental health experts, patients' rights activists and politicians envisioned a community-based system of psychiatric services, and go on to show how policies shifted emphasis from radical reform to incremental change. Many have benefited from this shift, but many are left without the care they require.

1183 Introducing mental health: a practical guide

C. Kinsella and C. Kinsella Jessica Kingsley, 2006, 158pp. £18.99. ISBN 1843102609.

An easy-to-read, jargon-free introduction to mental health written for qualified and non-qualified practitioners, housing workers, support workers, probation officers, prison health care officers, student nurses and anyone coming into contact with mental health issues.

1184 Social work and mental health

M. Golightley 2nd edn, Learning Matters, 2004, 161pp. £12. ISBN 1844450686.

Written primarily for student social workers on the new degree programme. Provides a thorough grounding in the key issues in mental health and highlights the skills and values necessary for contemporary practice.

1185 Social work in mental health: an evidence-based approach

B.A. Thyer and J.S. Wodarski, eds Wiley, 2007, 624pp. $75. ISBN 9780471693048.

A comprehensive and contemporary guide to the delivery of evidence-based care. Covering a wide spectrum of mental health disorders, the editors bring together noted experts to provide the most current, empirically supported techniques in the assessment, diagnosis and treatment of disorders as classified by the DSM-IV-TR.

Laws, standards, codes

1186 **The approved social worker's guide to mental health law** [UK]
R. Brown   Learning Matters, 2006, 180pp. £19. ISBN 9781844450626.
An invaluable text for students and practitioners, this book brings together key elements of mental health legislation, Code of Practice, Memorandum, Government Circulars and relevant case law and policy. Written in an accessible style and supported by exercises, case studies and checklists, the book provides a clear guide to the law relevant to the practice of an Approved Social Worker, as well as anticipating any changes which could come with the proposed new UK mental health legislation.

1187 **Law and mental health: a case-based approach** [USA]
R.G. Meyer and C.M. Weaver   Guilford Press, 2005, 394pp. $42.75. ISBN 9781593852214.
This text presents classic and contemporary legal cases that have set important precedents related to psychological and mental health issues in criminal and civil proceedings; the role of practitioners as expert witnesses and forensic consultants; and legal concerns in general clinical practice. It also provides a solid introduction to foundational issues in the field. Forensic and clinical professionals and undergraduate and graduate students will all find it useful.

1188 **Mental Health Act manual** [UK]
R. Jones   9th edn, Sweet & Maxwell, 2005, 893pp. £93. ISBN 0421945109.
The 'bible' of the Mental Health Act, this text is often cited in courts and tribunals and is the essential guide for mental health social workers and anyone implementing or advising on this area of law. Brings together the Mental Health Act 1983, the Code of Practice and related subordinate legislation. It also includes relevant extracts from the Human Rights Act 1988.

1189 **Mental health law: a practical guide** [UK]
B.K. Puri [et al.]   Hodder Arnold, 2005, 264pp. ISBN 0340885033.
An introductory text, aimed at students and trainees embarking on mental health nursing, psychiatry, clinical psychology or mental health social work, but with sufficient detail to carry readers through to the complex issues that will continue to face them during their years of practice. Also serves as a well referenced handbook.

1190 **National service framework for mental health** [UK]
Great Britain. Department of Health   Great Britain. Department of Health, 1999, 153pp.
www.dh.gov.uk/assetRoot/04/07/72/09/04077209.pdf
Key piece of government policy, covering the mental health needs of adults up to 65. Sets out national standards and a series of national milestones to assure progress, with performance indicators to support effective performance management. An organizational framework for providing integrated services and for commissioning services across the spectrum is also included.

Official & quasi-official bodies

1191 **National Institute for Mental Health** [USA]
www.nimh.nih.gov/
The NIMH is the lead Federal agency for research on mental and behavioural disorders in the USA. Its mission is to reduce the burden of mental illness and behavioural disorders through research on mind, brain and behaviour.

1192 **National Institute for Mental Health in England**
www.nimhe.org.uk/
NIMHE aims is to improve the quality of life of people of all ages who experience mental distress, placing service users and carers at the heart of its work. The organization works outside the NHS and runs national programmes as well as local development centres. It produces publications and takes a lead in connecting mental health research, development, delivery, monitoring and review.

Research centres & institutes

1193 **Sainsbury Centre for Mental Health** [UK]
www.scmh.org.uk/
The Centre works to improve the quality of life for people with mental health problems. It carries out research, policy work and analysis to improve practice and influence policy in mental health as well as public services.

1194 **UK Mental Health Research Network**
www.ukmhrn.info/dnn/
A Department of Health-funded network designed to provide a research infrastructure. The network supports large-scale research which will help to raise the standard of mental health and social care research throughout Britain. It also acts as a central point of information and reference, connecting service users and carers to researchers and mental health professionals.

1195 **University of Bath, Mental Health Research and Development Unit** [UK]
www.bath.ac.uk/mhrdu/intro.htm
The MHRDU undertakes research, evaluation and development in all areas of mental health, producing work which integrates qualitative and quantitative methods of research and analysis; provides a holistic picture of the phenomena being studied; and contributes to making a difference to those experiencing and working with mental health problems.

Associations & societies

1196 **Mental Health America**
www.nmha.org/
Mental Health America (formerly known as the National Mental Health Association) is the USA's leading non-profit organization dedicated to helping all people live mentally healthier lives. The website contains well organized and easy-to-find information, FAQ's and the latest news.

Mental Health Foundation
See entry no. 411

Mind
See entry no. 412

1197 National Alliance for Research on Schizophrenia & Depression [USA]
www.narsad.org/
NARSAD supports research with a scientific basis into mental health problems.

1198 National Alliance on Mental Illness [USA]
www.nami.org/
NAMI is the largest grassroots mental health organization in the USA, dedicated to improving the lives of persons living with serious mental illness and of their families. It achieves its mission via support, education, advocacy and research for people living with mental illness.

Libraries, archives, museums

1199 Mental Health Specialist Library [UK]
National Library for Health.
www.library.nhs.uk/mentalhealth/
The Mental Health Specialist Library aims to meet the information needs of health care professionals who work in the field of mental health. It is also freely available to the general public, although some visitors may find NHS Direct Online a more appropriate website for their needs.

Portal & task environments

Internet mental health
See entry no. 416

1200 Web4Health [EUR]
http://web4health.info/en/
A pan-European site, written by a team of experts appointed by the Commission of the European Communities, aiming to give good and useful free medical advice, help and self-help in the areas of mental health, psychology, personality disorders, relationships, stress, anxiety, depression, emotional abuse, substance abuse and sexual abuse. Available in German, English, Greek, Italian, Finnish and Swedish versions.

Discovering print & electronic resources

1201 Cochrane Library
Cochrane Collabroation.
www.cochrane.org/
The Cochrane Collaboration is an international non-profit and independent organization producing and disseminating systematic reviews of healthcare (including mental health care) interventions and promoting the search for evidence in the form of clinical trials and other studies of interventions.

1202 The insider's guide to mental health resources online
J.M. Grohol   Guilford Press, 2004, 306pp. $21.95. ISBN 1572302291.
Jargon-free guide to the latest online mental health resources, this manual is a valuable resource for a wide range of mental health professionals.

Directories & encyclopedias

1203 The complete mental health directory 2006 [USA]
R. Gottlieb, ed.   5th edn, Sedgwick Press, 2006, 707pp. $165. ISBN 1592371248.
Source book covering the field of behavioural health, with detailed, comprehensive and critical information aimed at people with mental health problems, their family and support network and paraprofessionals and professionals in the field.

Handbooks & manuals

1204 A handbook for the study of mental health: social contexts, theories and systems
A.V. Horwitz and T.L. Sheid, eds   Cambridge University Press, 1999, 694pp. £23. ISBN 0521567637.
Offers a comprehensive presentation of the sociology of mental health and illness. Aimed at students and professionals in the fields of sociology, social work, human relations, human services and psychology.

1205 Multi-agency partnership working and the delivery of services to mentally disordered offenders: key principles and practices
D. Browne   NACRO, 2005, 32pp. £5. ISBN 085069208.
Short text mapping out the policy framework, examining the elements of successful partnership and setting out the main protocols that underpin them in order to both inform policy makers and assist practitioners in collaborating when working with offenders with mental health problems.

Keeping up to date

1206 Journal of Mental Health
Informa Healthcare, 6 p.a. ISSN 09638237.
www.tandf.co.uk/journals/titles/09638237.html
Provides a forum for the latest ideas and evidence in the field of mental health, covering both the UK and the broader international field. Available in print and online.

1207 Mental Health Review
Pavilion, qtrly. ISSN 13619322.
www.pavpub.com/pavpub/home/index.asp
Provides current thinking and information for managers and practitioners working in the mental health field. Each issue contains a comprehensive framework feature addressing a subject of contemporary significance for mental health practice, as well as a variety of articles and case studies exploring and analysing topical issues in mental health.

1208 Mental Health Today
Pavilion, monthly. ISSN 14745186.
www.pavpub.com/pavpub/
Useful title for keeping up to date with developments in policy and practice in the mental health field. It also showcases the diversity of evidence-based best practice in the statutory, voluntary and independent sectors across the UK.

1209   Open Mind
Mind, bi-monthly. ISSN 0265511X.
www.mind.org.uk/Information/OM.htm
Provides mental health professionals, service users and carers with stimulating coverage of the widest range of mental health issues.

1210   Social Work in Mental Health
Haworth Press, qtrly. ISSN 15332985.
www.haworthpressinc.com/
The focus of this journal is on research, policy and practice in the field of mental health care services. Available in print and online.

1211   Young Minds Magazine
Young Minds, 6 p.a. ISSN 13619403.
www.youngminds.org.uk/magazine/
Aimed at those working with children and young people with mental health problems, including mental health professionals, social workers and teachers. Read it to keep up to date with issues in child and adolescent mental health, from the latest research to innovative practice.

POLITICS, GOVERNMENT & LAW

Politics

For the purposes of this volume, the section on politics concentrates mainly on resources relating to political theory and policy-making. It therefore provides coverage of a range of political ideologies and systems, as well as encompassing parliaments, political parties and movements worldwide. Resources relating to government, that is the actual machinery and bodies which carry out the executive functions at state, regional and local levels can be found in the separate Government section.

You will notice that a substantial part of the Politics section covers the field of International Relations. This focuses mainly upon IR theory and the practice of foreign policy and diplomacy. It also includes references to the topical themes of terrorism and international conflict.

In addition, you will find that a large number of resources listed in the general Social Sciences chapter are also relevant to politics. In particular, those which relate to international organizations such as the EU and United Nations are particularly useful, as the work of these bodies covers the full range of social science subject areas.

Within the constraints of space imposed by a single volume one cannot hope to provide an exhaustive coverage of all the politics resources available, especially as they are continuously growing. However, I hope that it will guide you to a range of the key resources from which you will be able to explore further.

Each subsection of the Politics section is subdivided by resource type. These include key organisations, introductory textbooks, dictionaries; encyclopedias and online digital libraries. Resources have been selected for their importance and quality of coverage, with the aim of offering a range covering important work from different areas of the world and the main specialist subfields of the discipline. Within the Associations categories you will find listed the key national and international organizations of the discipline. These are a good starting point for research as many maintain large websites where you will find directories of links to many local organizations; small specialist projects and journals which space has not permitted me to list here. Many also have newsletters which are often one of the best sources of information on recent publications and forthcoming events. You might also find it useful to browse the Portal categories, as the websites listed there have been chosen for their depth and range of resources. Most provide up to date directories of academic internet resources as well as providing online tutorials, discussion forums and news services.

Handbooks & manuals

Companion for undergraduate dissertations: sociology, anthropology, politics, social policy, social work and criminology
See entry no. 536

Political Science

comparative politics • political analysis • political biography • political quotations • political research • political scientists • political vocabulary

Introductions to the subject

1212 British politics today
D. Kavanagh and B. Jones   7th edn, Manchester University Press, 2003, 256pp. £8.99. ISBN 9780719065095.
Popular student textbook which provides an accessible introduction to changes in British politics since 1945. It includes coverage of evolving trends in organization, attitudes and political behaviour. Chapters cover key topics such as the changing social and political context of British life, the growth of the media, reform of the House of Commons and House of Lords, political devolution and relations with the European Union.

1213 Comparative government and politics: an introduction
R. Hague and M. Harrop   7th edn, Palgrave Macmillan, 2007, 355pp. £23.99. ISBN 9781403913159.
The latest edition of this well established text offers a sound introduction to all aspects of comparative politics. Coverage is international in scope and includes discussion of the role of the state in the 21st-century globalized era. Student-friendly features include case studies, charts, tables and debate boxes highlighting key questions.

1214 Comparative politics: approaches and issues
H.J. Wiarda   Rowman & Littlefield Publishers, 2006, 304pp. £19.99. ISBN 9780742530362.
An excellent introduction to the subject area which is especially useful for student use. It begins with an introduction to the field of comparative politics and proceeds to discussion of recent and future areas of research. A 'hot topics' section highlights recent areas of concern, including civil society, environmental politics and political development.

1215 Doing research in political science: an introduction to comparative methods and statistics
P. Pennings, H. Keman and J. Kleinnijenhuis   2nd edn, Sage Publications, 2006, 352pp. £24.99. ISBN 9781412903776.
Useful text for students beginning research in political science. Offers a clear guide to the main theories and methodologies. Includes coverage of both qualitative and quantitative political analysis. Topics covered include basic descriptive and inferential statistical methods and advanced multivarate methods. Each chapter contains practice exercises, summary questions and lists of further readings.

1216 Government in America: people, politics and policy
G. Edwards   7th edn, Longman, 2006. £42.99. ISBN 9790321434296.
www.longmanparticipate.com
The latest edition of this well regarded student textbook aims to provide a solid introduction to the US political

system and public policy. Chapters cover the constitution, the main political institutions, parties and patterns of political behaviour. Also covered are public policy outputs and the interaction between state and local government. The study edition includes a free login to a supporting website where students may participate in online quizzes, discussion forums and other interactive activities.

1217   Politics on the internet: a student guide
S. Buckler and D. Dolowitz   Routledge, 2005, 192pp. £12.99. ISBN 9780415267717.
Clearly written introductory guide to using the internet for political science research. Strong coverage of internet research techniques, including how to avoid plagiarism and evaluating internet resources. An appendix guides the reader to the most useful political sites online.

1218   Research methods in politics: political analysis
P. Burnham [et al.], eds   Palgrave Macmillan, 2004, 304pp. £19.99. ISBN 9780333962541.
A comprehensive introduction to the main methods of political science research. Individual chapters discuss the strengths and weaknesses of different approaches and highlight real case studies. Topics covered include qualitative and quantitive research methods, internet research and ethics in political science research. Suggestions for further reading are provided.

1219   We the people: an introduction to American politics
T. Patterson, ed.   6th edn, W.W. Norton, 2006, 770pp. £12.99. ISBN 9780072955682.
www.nortonebooks.com/
A well established textbook which provides a basic introduction to American government and politics, emphasizing its importance to everyday life. It includes coverage of the political system and institutions as well as the US role in world affairs. Each chapter contains study guidelines, highlighted key terms and self-help quizzes. The text is also offered as an e-book with associated online interactive learning activities. Details on pricing can be obtained from the publisher's website.

Dictionaries, thesauri, classifications

1220   The American political dictionary
J. Plano and M. Greenberg, eds   11th edn, Thomson Learning, 2001, 768pp. £23.99. ISBN 9780155068674.
Serves as a dictionary and study guide to the American political system. Fourteen chapters cover the most important ideas, parties and political concepts. They include coverage of the American constitution, legislative process, foreign policy and operation of federal, state and local government. Each entry provides a definition of the term and its current and historical significance.

1221   The Blackwell dictionary of political science: a user's guide to its terms
F. Bealey   Blackwell Publishing, 1999, 392pp. £23.99. ISBN 9780631206958.
A readable guide to over 1000 key concepts and terms relating to all aspects of classical and contemporary political science. Benefits from having a single author, which gives it a lively uniformity of tone that is especially suitable for

students and those new to the field. Includes a short section of biographies of political theorists and a subject index which enables quick identification of all the pages where particular terms appear.

1222   Dictionary of British politics
B. Jones   Manchester University Press, 2004, 416pp. £9.99. ISBN 9780719049583.
A useful introduction to British politics in the post 1945 period. It is sub-divided into sections for politics (political events and institutions) and people (biographical entries). Coverage of political concepts is limited except where they relate specifically to British institutions. Entries offer brief facts. There is a bibliography of references for further reading.

1223   Dictionary of modern politics
D. Robertson   4th edn, Europa Publications, 2006, 450pp. £120. ISBN 9781857433333.
Of particular value to students and those new to the field, this dictionary offers a concise guide to complex political theories. It contains over 600 entries relating to political science and international relations thinkers, theories and terminology. The significance of classical philosophers such as Aristotle, Aquinas and John Stuart Mill is introduced and related to modern political thinking. Fully revised in 2005 to cover topical subjects used in the media such as 'Third way', 'Thatcherism' and 'EU constitution'.

1224   A dictionary of political biography: who's who in twentieth-century world politics
D. Kavanagh   Oxford University Press, 2003, 538pp. £8.99. ISBN 9780192800350.
Compiled by an international team of specialists, this book contains over 1000 biographical essays on key political figures of the 20th century. They include coverage of heads of state, monarchs and dictators worldwide. Each entry provides facts on the background, career and achievements of the individual. Some critically appraisal of their impact is offered.

1225   Dictionary of the modern politics of Southeast Asia
M. Leifer   Routledge, 2000, 328pp. £22.99. ISBN 9780415238762.
Over 200 entries provide a panoramic overview of the key people, places and events which have shaped the current history and politics of the nations of South-East Asia in the post-1945 period. Easy to use, in an A–Z format with efficient cross-referencing between entries.

1226   Dictionary of the politics of the People's Republic of China
C. Mackerras, D. McMillen and A. Watson   Routledge, 1998, 288pp. £22.99. ISBN 9780415250672.
Intended for students and non-specialists, this useful work contains approximately 140 essays on key events, figures and movements central to the development of the Chinese political system in the period 1949–1997. Nine introductory essays provide background information on major Chinese political events, the economy, people and culture. Other entries include coverage of the Chinese Communist Party, key party members and policies such as the 'Great Leap Forward' and 'Cultural Revolution'.

1227 Hatchet jobs and hardball: the Oxford dictionary of American political slang
G. Barrett, ed. Oxford University Press, 2004, 320pp. £14.99. ISBN 9780195176858.
An entertaining collection of definitions of more than 600 American slang terms, ranging from the familiar 'gerrymander' to the less known and colourful. Each entry contains a definition and historical background with examples of usage.

1228 Keywords in Australian politics
R. Smith, I. Cook and A. Vromen Cambridge University Press, 2006, 238pp. £19.99.
A key reference for those seeking to understand contemporary Australian government and politics. Contains over 100 entries for theoretical and popular terms. Each entry includes a clear definition plus information on any current debates over its meaning.

1229 Oxford dictionary of political quotations
A. Jay, ed. 3rd edn, Oxford University Press, 2005, 560pp. £18.99. ISBN 9780192806161.
Contains more than 4500 incisive, witty and memorable political quotations from politicians and world leaders worldwide from the earliest time to the current day. Each entry provides information on the origin of the quotation, who said it, when and the political context. There are useful indexes of epitaphs, slogans, famous last words, newspaper headlines and misquotations.

1230 A political and economic dictionary of Africa
L. Zeilig and D. Seddon Europa Publications, 2005, 536pp. £120. ISBN 9781857432138.
One of the useful series of political and economic dictionaries published by Routledge. Each volume contains concise profiles of the politics, history and economy of each constituent nation, as well as entries on key political figures, movements and organizations.
- **A political and economic dictionary of Central and South-Eastern Europe** Routledge, 2007, 400pp. £120. ISBN 9781857433593.
- **A political and economic dictionary of East Asia** J. Hoare and S. Pares Routledge, 2005, 336pp. £120. ISBN 9781857432589.
- **A political and economic dictionary of Eastern Europe** 2nd edn., Routledge, 2007, 500pp. £120. ISBN 9781857433340. Coverage of over 22 nations in Central and Eastern Europe, the trans-Caucasus and Russian Federation. Includes material on Chechnya.
- **A political and economic dictionary of Latin America** P. Calvert Routledge, 2004, 336pp. £120.
- **A political and economic dictionary of South Asia** S. Mitra Routledge, 2006, 464pp. £120. ISBN 9781857432107. Entries include coverage of Hindu–Muslim relations and territorial disputes involving Kashmir, India and Pakistan.
- **A political and economic dictionary of South-East Asia** A.H. Tan Routledge, 2004, 344pp. £120. ISBN 9781857432268.
- **A political and economic dictionary of the Middle East** D. Seddon Routledge, 2004, 624pp. £120. ISBN 9781857432121. Includes coverage of territorial disputes and the Arab–Israeli conflict.
- **A political and economic dictionary of Western Europe** C. Annesley Routledge, 2005, 344pp. £120. ISBN 9781857432145. Includes coverage of the changing political landscape of Western Europe and its relations with the European Union.

1231 The politics book: lexicon of interesting political facts Abu Ghraib to Zippergate
N. Comfort Politicos Publishing, 2005, 400pp. £30. ISBN 9781842751381.
The successor to the popular *Brewer's politics*, this collection of political words and terminology is fascinating to dip into. It includes definitions and background information on the origins of words, concepts, political slang, individuals and organizations which regularly appear in the British and North American media. Thorough coverage of information relating to 'New Labour' and the British Labour Party.

1232 Respectfully quoted: a dictionary of quotations requested from the Congressional Research Service
S. Platt, ed. Library of Congress, 1989. ISBN 0844405388. www.bartleby.com/73
Free access (via the Bartleby.com website) to a searchable version of this well respected collection of American political quotations. It contains over 2000 famous quotations made by leading US politicians, presidents and public figures throughout history. There are subject, author and keyword indexes. Individual entries give full quotations, attributions and links to biographical information, some of which is freely accessible online.

1233 The Routledge dictionary of politics
D. Robertson 3rd edn, Routledge, 2003, 528pp. £9.99. ISBN 9780415323772.
Designed with students in mind, this dictionary offers 500 concise definitions of terms relating to modern politics. They include coverage of the basics of political theory, political ideology and political institutions.

Research centres & institutes

1234 ARK: Northern Ireland Social and Political Archive
www.ark.ac.uk/
ARK is a joint project of Queen's University Belfast and the University of Ulster which was established in 2000 and aims to create a social and political archive of information about Northern Ireland. This includes extensive coverage of the Northern Ireland conflict. Its website provides free access to a wealth of information, including surveys, qualitative research, quantitative statistical data and social commentary. A teacher's section provides information on classroom topics and online tutorials. Although these are directly linked to the Northern Ireland curriculum, they could easily be adapted for application elsewhere. Key services offered by ARK include:
- **CAIN: Conflict Archive on the Internet** http://cain.ulst.ac.uk/. An encyclopaedic resource on 'the Troubles' in Northern Ireland. Offering free access to full-text documents, photographs and research materials.
- **Northern Ireland elections** www.ark.ac.uk/elections/. This section includes information about elections in Northern Ireland since 1885, with detailed breakdowns of election results by constituency.
- **Northern Ireland Life and Times Survey** www.ark.ac.uk/nilt/. An annual survey monitoring the attitudes of people in Northern Ireland on a wide range of social and political issues. It is possible to look at the questionnaires and their results online.
- **ORB: online research bank** www.ark.ac.uk/orb/. Offers bibliographies and summaries of research about the lives of adults and children in Northern Ireland. Consists of two databases: the ORB Social Policy Database covers research carried out in Northern Ireland since 1990

and the ORB Children's Research Database concentrates on research carried out with children and young people since 2000.

1235 Centre for Democratic Institutions
www.cdi.anu.edu.au
Created by the Australian government to support emerging democracies in South-East Asia and the South Pacific, with a particular focus on Indonesia, East Timor, Papua New Guinea, Solomon Islands, Vanuatu and Fiji. Website contains useful information on ongoing research on the political systems and leadership of these nations. It also provides free access to full-text working papers and reports.

1236 Democratic Audit
www.democraticaudit.com
Non-governmental organization, attached to the Human Rights Centre, University of Essex. Specializes in conducting research into the state of democratic and political freedom in the UK and worldwide. Selected research reports can be read online. Topics covered include assessments of the conduct of UK general elections and audits of the electoral system.

1237 Institut d'Études Politiques de Paris
www.sciences-po.fr
Often referred to as Sciences-Po, this is one of the most important French institutions for the study of politics and international relations. It supports a large number of specialist research centres, including CERI (Centre d'Études et de Recherches Internationales), CEVIPOF (Centre d'Étude de la vie Politique Française), OIP (Observatoire Interrégional du Politique). Many of these provide free access to their working papers and research reports via the website. They are useful starting points for tracing information on current French political research.
■ **TUISP: Travaux universitaires inédits de science politique** http://tuisp.online.fr. This lists unpublished dissertations and theses registered for higher degrees at French universities. Updates are usually annual. An online database covers the years from 1994 onwards. More recent texts can be viewed in full text online.

1238 John F. Kennedy School of Government
www.ksg.harvard.edu
Based at Harvard University, this is one of the world's most famous centres of politics teaching and research. It supports a number of specialist research centres covering all aspects of political science, international relations and public administration. Of key interest is the Institute of Politics, whose website contains a searchable video archive of its political debates and discussions from the 1970s until the present day. Key topics include American politics, US elections and political leadership. The main website contains a large online database of its working papers.
■ **Institute of Politics** www.iop.harvard.edu [30/06/2006].

Roper Center for Public Opinion Research
See entry no. 40

1239 University of Essex, Department of Government
www.essex.ac.uk/government/
One of the highest-rated UK universities in national assessments of politics teaching and research. Its website provides information on its acclaimed summer school programme plus details of ongoing teaching and research

programmes. Recently published titles in its working papers series may be downloaded free of charge.

1240 Unlock Democracy
www.unlockdemocracy.org.uk
Unlock Democracy is a campaign of two UK-based political think-tanks, Charter88 and the New Politics Network, which was formally launched at the end of 2006. Its aim is to raise questions about legitimacy, accountability and representation in British politics. The website provides access to press releases, discussion forums and online papers. These are a useful source of information on current debates about British political funding and parliamentary and constitutional reform.

Associations & societies

1241 American Academy of Political & Social Science
www.aapss.org/
A scholarly society, originally established in 1889, which seeks to strengthen the social sciences and their usefulness to society. In particular it focuses on the interrelationship between politics and public policy. Its website provides information about the history of the academy, its membership and activities. It includes tables of contents and a small selection of free articles from its major publication, the *Annals*, plus information about conferences. All aspects of politics and public policy are covered.
■ **Academy blog** http://blog.aapss.org. A useful source of information, commentary and debate on current political issues which was created by the Academy during 2006.

1242 American Political Science Association
www.apsanet.org/
The main professional body for politics in the USA. It supports many special interest groups that conduct cutting-edge research. Its website provides information on political science education, courses, employment and conferences in North America. It is possible to view abstracts and tables of contents from its key journals *American Political Science Review*, *Perspectives on Politics* and *PS: Political Science and Politics*, online free of charge. There is also a large teaching and learning section which contains online syllabi, lesson plans and articles discussing the development of political science methods.

1243 European Consortium for Political Research
www.essex.ac.uk/ECPR/
Scholarly association which seeks to encourage the research and teaching of all aspects of political science. Membership is institutional, rather than individual. Its website provides information on its key conferences and working groups. It also includes tables of contents from ECPR publications such as *European Political Science* and the *European Journal of International Relations* and a growing archive of online papers and presentations from its conferences. The latter are a useful source of information on cutting-edge academic research and projects.
■ **ECPR Graduate Network**
www.essex.ac.uk/ecpr/graduates/index.asp. Specialist forum of the ECPR which supports the needs of graduate students. Its website offers a networking contacts database; information on student events; grants and funding.

1244   **European Political Science Network: EpsNet**
www.epsnet.org/
An association which aims to promote cooperation in the teaching of political science in European nations. Its website is particularly useful for tracing information about recent trends in the university teaching of politics. It includes recent press releases plus access to full-text conference papers from 2003 onwards. Coverage of trends in Eastern and Central Europe is especially good.

1245   **International Association for Political Science Students**
www.iapss.org/
Organization for political science students worldwide. Supports regular academic conferences, research working groups and publishes the journal *Politikon – IAPSS Journal of Political Science*. Its website provides information on forthcoming events plus free access to its newsletters and articles from the journal.

1246   **International Political Science Association**
www.ipsa.ca/
The foremost international scholarly organization for political scientists. Its website provides information on the aims of the organization, its history, membership and activities. It is an excellent starting point for keeping up to date with the latest professional developments and research as it contains, conference lists, tables of contents from its quarterly journal *International Political Science Review* and news from its many specialist research committees. There is also a useful directory of national political science associations worldwide.
   ■ **IPSA Portal: top 300 sites in political science**
   http://ipsaportal.unina.it/home.html [12/06/2006]. A gateway to political science resources on the internet which is maintained by the International Political Science Association. It has selected the top 300 political science sites for students, lecturers and researchers. They are arranged in categories which include data sets, internet, e-learning tutorials, political science institutions, and e-government sites. All resources are described by subject specialists and classified according to accessibility and usability.

1247   **Political Studies Association** [UK]
www.psa.ac.uk
The main professional body in its field in the UK. Its website is an excellent starting point for locating information about forthcoming conferences and events, undergraduate and postgraduate politics courses and ongoing research. Particularly useful is the PSA conference proceedings database which contains the full text of most of the papers delivered at PSA annual conferences since 1994. It is also possible to view the contents pages of its key publications *Political Studies*, *Political Studies Review* and the *British Journal of Politics and International Relations*. The gateway to internet sites contains an extensive collection of links to politics departments and political science associations worldwide.

Subject Network for Sociology, Anthropology & Politics
See entry no. 520

Libraries, archives, museums

1248   **Bodleian Library, Modern Political Papers Section. Department of Special Collections & Western Manuscripts**
www.bodley.ox.ac.uk/dept/scwmss/modpol/index.html
One of the largest specialist archives of political papers and manuscripts in the UK. Over 400 collections are currently available, including the papers of British prime ministers Benjamin Disraeli and Clement Attlee. It also holds the official archive of the British Conservative Party. The website provides a searchable database of guides to the collection plus information about how to access it. Future plans include some digitization, but at present the site contains mainly finding aids and catalogues only.

1249   **Welsh Political Archive**
www.llgc.org.uk/lc/awg_s_awg.htm
Coordinates the collection of materials relating to the political history of Wales. This includes records and papers of political parties, politicians, campaigns and pressure groups, leaflets, pamphlets, ephemera, posters, photographs and tapes of radio and television programmes. It has particularly strong collections of materials relating to political devolution in Wales. The website provides information on access to Welsh political archives, plus searchable catalogues and finding aids. It also contains some digitized collections of political ephemera, including documents relating to the creation of the National Assembly for Wales.

Portal & task environments

1250   **C-Span classroom**
www.c-spanclassroom.org/
C-SPAN is a public service created by National Cable Satellite Corporation. This website is designed for use by teachers. It offers free access to educational resources relating to American politics, government and citizenship. These include overviews of the American political system, plus clips of TV programmes and suggested lesson plans. Key topics covered are American elections, the function and operation of the US presidency. Registration is required to receive enhanced benefits and access some areas of the website.

1251   **ePolitix.com** [UK]
www.epolitix.com/EN
Excellent portal aiming 'to improve communication between parliamentarians, constituents and organizations. We do this in an impartial manner, publishing balanced reports and providing information without taking sides in the political debate. Working closely with parliamentarians across the political spectrum, we offer a range of opportunities for MPs and peers to explain their work. And we help the public and other organizations to engage in the political debate and shape the way that policies develop.'

1252   **Erik Herron's guide to politics in East Central Europe and Eurasia**
http://web.ku.edu/~herron/
Erik Herron is Director of the Center for Russian, East European and Eurasian Studies and Associate Professor of Political Science at the University of Kansas. His guide highlights key political internet sites for nations of Eastern

and Central Europe and Eurasia. These include links to
central government websites, official ministries, key media
agencies, political parties and think-tanks.

1253 International Knowledge Network of Women in Politics: iKNOW Politics

www.iknowpolitics.org

A joint project of the United Nations Development
Programme (UNDP), the United Nations Development Fund
for Women (UNIFEM), the National Democratic Institute for
International Affairs (NDI), the Inter-Parliamentary Union
(IPU) and the International Institute for Democracy and
Electoral Assistance (IDEA). It aims to create a website where
researchers, students and other practitioners interested in
advancing women in politics can get free access to
information and share experiences. The website contains
news on conferences and forthcoming events, fact files on
women's political involvement in specific countries worldwide
and online discussion forums. It also contains a large online
library of full-text reports, papers and handbooks. These
include advocacy and campaign materials, information on
political quotas and statistics on women's political
participation.

1254 Keele guides to Internet resources

www.keele.ac.uk/depts/por/

An excellent starting point for tracing political science
websites. Created by members of the School of Politics,
International Relations & Philosophy, Keele University, it
covers all aspects of politics and international relations. Each
list contains links to key websites. Directories are often
created to cover topical events such as British general
elections and specific world conflicts. There is also an index
of political blogs.

1255 LANIC: Latin American Network Information Center

http://lanic.utexas.edu/

LANIC is affiliated with the Lozano Long Institute of Latin
American Studies (LLILAS) at the University of Texas at
Austin. Its aim is to provide access to internet-based
information to, from, or on Latin America. Its website is an
essential source of information for all researchers of Latin
American government and politics. It includes free access to
news headlines, directories of high quality internet links and
digitized full-text collections. It is possible to trace
information by geographical region or theme.

- **Archive of web sites of political parties and elections in Latin America (APPELA)** www.archive-
  it.org/collections/archive_of_political_parties_and_elections. A database of
  over 100 archived Latin American websites relating to presidential and
  parliamentary elections that took place in South American nations during
  2005. They have been selected by the University of Texas LANIC and
  archived by the Archive-It subscription service created by the Internet
  Archive. They include sites from the main political parties and smaller
  parties. Also accessible are government websites, blogs and discussion
  forums. They provide a fascinating record of political developments at this
  time. Countries covered include Mexico, Peru, Ecuador, Bolivia and
  Argentina.

- **Castro speech database**
  www1.lanic.utexas.edu/la/cb/cuba/castro.html. Contains the full-text of
  English translations of a large number of speeches, interviews and press
  conferences made by Fidel Castro from 1950 to the present day. All data is
  based upon the records of the Foreign Broadcast Information Service, the
  US agency responsible for monitoring broadcast and print media worldwide.

- **LANIC electoral observatory**
  http://lanic.utexas.edu/info/newsroom/elections/. Access to news about
  recent and forthcoming parliamentary and presidential elections in South
  American and Latin American nations. Each entry includes links to recent
  election results and relevant websites for further research. These include
  official government departments, political parties and newspapers.

- **Latin American Open Archives Portal**
  http://lanic.utexas.edu/project/laoap/. Aims to provide free access (via the
  Open Archives Initiative) to grey literature social science publications
  published by non-governmental organizations, research institutes and
  charities based in Latin America/South America. These include statistical
  publications, pre-prints, conference papers, reports and other 'hard to
  locate' literature, much of which will be Spanish-language.

- **Latin American Periodicals Tables of Contents:
  LAPTOC** http://lanic.utexas.edu/larrp/laptoc.html. Free access to tables
  of contents from over 950 journals, primarily in the humanities and social
  sciences, published in Latin America.

- **Mexican presidential messages**
  http://lanic.utexas.edu/project/arl/pm/sample2/mexican/index.html. This
  website contains over 51,000 scanned images of 20th-century Mexican
  presidential messages. They include Los Presidentes de Mexico ante la
  Nacion (1821–1966) and the text of speeches and addresses made by
  Gustavo Diaz Ordaz, Luis Echeverria, Jose Lopez Portillo, Miguel de la
  Madrid Hurtado and Carlos Salinas de Gortari.

1256 Richard Kimber's political science resources

www.psr.keele.ac.uk

Created by Richard Kimber and hosted by Keele University.
This is a well established guide to the most important
websites relevant to the study of government and politics. It
includes political parties, political theory and political
journals. Of particular value is the section on UK general
elections. This contains lists of results for all elections from
1832 to the present. Transcripts of party election broadcasts
and the full text of election campaign manifestos from the
main UK political parties are also accessible.

1257 ViFaPol: virtuelle Fachbibliothek Politikwissenschaft

www.vifapol.de/

A gateway to academic internet resources for politics and
peace studies which is maintained by Hamburg State and
University Library. These include organizations, research
institutes and individual journals and papers. It is an
excellent site for tracing German-language materials,
although there is also strong coverage of English-language
resources. Full descriptions of content are provided.

1258 Working paper sites of political science

http://workingpapers.org/

Online library of links to websites containing politics working
papers. These include individual home pages and university
departments worldwide. The sites are useful sources of
information on cutting-edge political research. Indexes may
be browsed by political science sub-field. Topics covered
include American politics, political communication, political
theory and public administration. Some annotation on
content is provided.

Discovering print & electronic resources

1259 bopcris: British official publications collaborative reader information service
www.bopcris.ac.uk/
A free searchable database of references to over 38,000 British government documents published between 1688 and 1995 which is based on the holdings of the University of Southampton Library in association with a number of other UK academic research libraries. All areas of UK government social, economic and foreign policy are covered. There is extensive coverage of parliamentary publications and reports. In most cases the full text is not online. However there are links to other complementary services such as the 18th century Parliamentary papers project where some online access is available.

1260 The combined retrospective index set to journals in political science 1886–1974
Carrollton Press, 1978. 8 v., o/p.
Eight-volume set which provides references to journal articles covering politics, international law and public administration published during the period 1895–1974. Useful for historical research as it includes some older materials not covered by electronic databases. Indexes over 500 journals mainly published in the USA and UK. Entries are arranged in broad subject categories. There are author and keyword indexes.

1261 International Political Science Abstracts
International Political Science Association/ Sage Publications, 1951–, bi-monthly. £80. ISSN 00208345.
www.ipsa.ca/en/publications/abstracts.asp
Leading database produced by the International Political Science Association since 1951. It provides authoritative abstracts of political science articles published in scholarly journals and yearbooks worldwide. Main areas of classification are political science – method and theory, political thinkers and ideas, governmental and administrative institutions, political process – public opinion, attitudes, parties, forces, groups and elections, international relations, national and area studies. Available online or in print. Reduced rate subscriptions are available for members of the International Political Science Association.

1262 Law and politics book review
www.bsos.umd.edu/gvpt/lpbr
An electronic publication of the the Law and Courts Section of the American Political Science Association which provides reviews of in print and out of print monographs readily available in college and university libraries. The service commenced in 1981 and is currently updated monthly. All back issues can be searched via the website. Users may register to receive new editions via e-mail. Typical review essays are between 2500 and 5000 words in length, offering critical commentary on mongraphs from all areas of political science and the legal process.

1263 Neue Politische Literatur
Peter Lang, 1956–, 3 p.a. Produced by Institut für Geschichte der Technischen Universität Darmstadt, £33. ISSN 00283320.
www.ifs.tu-darmstadt.de/index.php?id=1134&L=2
A German-language subscription service which indexes and abstracts political science literature. It has been produced by Institut für Geschichte der Technischen Universität, Darmstadt, since 1956. It contains recent book reviews and critical essays on new research covering all areas of political theory, international relations and contemporary history. There is extensive coverage of research and publications from the German-speaking nations of Europe. Available in print or online. Some contents pages and reviews can be read free of charge on the website. Full access is for subscribers only.

1264 Political ReviewNet
www.politicalreviewnet.com/
Provides free access to book reviews which have appeared in politics and international relations journals issued by Blackwell Publishing. These include leading titles such as *Political Studies Review, Nations and Nationalism, Journal of Common Market Studies* and *International Affairs*. Reviews include student textbooks and academic monographs. The database of reviews may be searched by author or title.

1265 Worldwide Political Science Abstracts
Cambridge Scientific Abstracts, 1975–, monthly. On request.
www.csa.com
Indexes and provides abstracts of over 1500 key political science journal titles. Over 60% of these are published outside the USA. Also includes coverage of related areas of international relations, public administration and international law. The online database provides access to records from 1975 onwards. These include materials taken from the merged backfiles of *Political Science Abstracts*, published by IFI/Plenum 1975–2000, and *ABC POL SCI*, published by ABC-CLIO, 1984–2000. Citation searching is offered for recent records. Subscription rates are available on request.

Digital data, image & text collections

1266 18th century official parliamentary publications portal 1688–1834
www.parl18c.soton.ac.uk
This website provides free access to a wealth of UK official publications for staff and students of UK academic institutions. It contains a large collection of 18th-century British parliamentary publications, including parliamentary proceedings, reports, acts, bills and registers that have been compiled from the collections of the University of Southampton, University of Cambridge and the British Library. It draws together in one place and complements materials from House of Commons Parliamentary papers, 1801–1900 service; the EPPI: Enhanced British Parliamentary Papers on Ireland 1822–1922 service; and BOPCRIS (a finding aid to British official publications 1688–1995). There is currently no access for the general public; however this policy may be revised in future.

1267 American political prints 1766–1876
http://loc.harpweek.com/default.asp
Free access to a collection of several hundred digitized images of American political prints, etchings and cartoons published in *Harper's Weekly* between 1766 and 1876. They cover a wide range of issues which would be invaluable to political historians and researchers of the history of American political communication, including elections, political parties and the movement for the abolition of slavery. There are also many examples of political satire and caricature. Each entry contains annotations on content.

1268 Cyberdata F.E.D.E.R.E.S
http://cyberdata.federes.org
An excellent French-language politics resource maintained by a research network of universities, think-tanks and political science research institutes of South-East Europe. Partners include Institut d'Études Politiques de Toulouse, Sciences Po Bordeaux and Université de Montpellier. It provides free access to a searchable database of recent articles, papers and information about ongoing research projects. A wide range of topics is covered, including international security, political economy, European identity, political devolution, federalism and regional government

1269 EPPI: Enhanced parliamentary papers on Ireland 1801–1922
http://eppi.ac.uk/
An ongoing project to digitize and make available free of charge over 13,000 British parliamentary papers relating to Ireland, 1801–1922, which are held by the Ford Collection of British Official Publications at the University of Southampton. These include legislation, census reports, Royal Commission reports, parliamentary debates and committee papers. The site includes a comprehensive searchable database of Parliamentary Papers relating to Ireland 1801–1922, providing an invaluable source of coverage of Anglo–Irish relations and Irish political history during this period.

1270 The global site: critical gateway to world politics, society and culture
www.theglobalsite.ac.uk/
Maintained by Professor Martin Shaw of Sussex University, this site is well known for providing free access to academic resources covering international relations, globalization and world affairs. These include reprints of classic texts from theorists such as Habermas and original writings from contemporary political writers and academics. A key area of concern is the interrelationship between political, economic and cultural power. The site also includes book reviews and some obituaries.

1271 Government and politics archived web sites: UK web archiving consortium
www.webarchive.org.uk/subject/4.html
The UK Web Archive Consortium is composed of several major UK institutions, including the British Library and National Archives, who have joined together to share the costs and expertise in archiving websites. This section of their website contains a growing collection of archived UK government and political organization websites. All materials date from 2004 onwards. They include regular snapshots of the websites of the main political parties, which would enable researchers to trace their evolving use as a political communication tool. There are also collections of materials relating to specific events such as parliamentary elections, international summits and the July 2005 London terrorist attacks.

1272 History and politics out loud: a searchable archive of politically significant speeches
www.hpol.org/
Maintained and funded by the National Endowment for the Humanities with Michigan State University this site provides free access to an archive of key speeches from 19th- and 20th-century American political history. You can listen to speeches from Martin Luther King and selections from the Nixon Watergate tapes online. Transcripts are also available.

1273 MINERVA: Mapping the Internet electronic research virtual archive
http://lcweb2.loc.gov/cocoon/minerva/html/minerva-home.html
A project of the Library of Congress which is aiming to archive key internet resources for future generations. Collections currently available include the September 11 2001 web archive, US elections 2004 and the Iraq War. Each collection contains archived documents, news and commentary from leading US news services, academic institutions and other organizations, enabling researchers to consult contemporary reaction and commentary on major world events. Future collections are in progress. The website also contains technical and legal information about the process of web archiving.

1274 Political database of the Americas
http://pdba.georgetown.edu/
A joint project of Georgetown University and the Secretariat for Political Affairs of the Organization of American States. Its purpose is to offer a quick-reference database of facts on all aspects of the political systems of individual nations within the Caribbean, Latin and South America areas. Coverage is detailed and comprehensive, including information on national electoral systems and laws, election results, lists of political parties and links to data on the structure of the executive, legislature and judiciary of each of the individual nations.

1275 Political science network
Social Science Research Network (SSRN). On demand.
www.ssrn.com/psn
PSN is part of the Social Science Research Network (SSRN), a leading US-based organization that aims to facilitate the distribution of scholarly information related to the social sciences. It offers access to an online collection of journal articles, working papers, conference and job listings covering all areas of political science. Users may search the database free of charge and download some abstracts and selected open-access full-text materials; however, many full-text articles are reserved for subscribers only. Details of suubscription rates and services are provided on the publisher's website.

1276 PROL: political research online pre print server
www.politicalscience.org/
This site is maintained by a consortium of American political science organizations led by the American Political Science Association. It provides free access to working papers, conference documents and pre-publication materials from leading researchers and academics. These cover all areas of politics and public administration and include many examples of the latest research in progress. The site may be searched by keyword or author.

Directories & encyclopedias

1277 American political scientists: a dictionary
G. Hutter and C. Lockhart   2nd edn, Greenwood Press, 2002, 400pp. £58. ISBN 9780313278495.
A collection of over 190 biographical profiles of political scientists who have contributed to the intellectual

development of American politics from the 19th century to the present. Each entry contains a biographical sketch and a list of selected works. The volume also contains detailed indexes of political scientists by institution and sub-field. Plus a select biography of selected further readings on the state of American political theory.

1278 **Encyclopedia of government and politics**
M. Hawkesworth and M. Kogan, eds 2nd edn, Routledge, 2003, 1408pp. 2 v., £220. ISBN 9780415276221.
Two-volume encyclopedia containing analytical essays by critically acclaimed authors. Encompasses a wide range of political and government topics at the international, national and local levels. This includes coverage of contemporary and classical political theory, political systems and institutions and policy making. The second volume includes surveys of major contemporary issues in world politics, including the politics of cyberspace, international security after the Cold War and the impact of globalization.

The encyclopedia of politics and religion
R. Wuthnow, ed. See entry no. 792

1279 **Political handbook of Asia 2007**
Congressional Quarterly CQ Press, 2007, 882pp. £69. ISBN 9780872894976.
An authoritative source providing factual information about government and politics in Asia. It contains individual country political profiles, plus details of international organizations working in the region. An introductory essay provides an overview of recent international security and political trends in the region as a whole.

1280 **Twentieth century British political facts 1900–2000**
D. Butler and G. Butler Palgrave Macmillan, 2006, 604pp. £33.99. ISBN 9780333772225.
Comprehensive collection of facts about the people, events and institutions of British politics during the 20th century. Includes chronologies of key events, details of all general elections, lists of all major office holders and biographical notes on political leaders.

Handbooks & manuals

1281 **British political opinion, 1937–2000: the Gallup polls**
A. King and R.J. Wybrow, eds Politicos Publishing, 2001, 367pp. o/p. ISBN 9781902301884.
Valuable collection of 63 years' worth of data from Gallup opinion polls conducted among the British population between 1937 and 2000. Offers a fascinating insight into changing British social and political attitudes. The book is sub-divided into chapters ranging from levels of support for the main political parties and individual prime ministers to attitudes towards the monarchy, Europe and taxation levels.

1282 **Developments in British politics 8**
P. Dunleavy [et al.] Palgrave Macmillan, 2006, 400pp. £19.99. ISBN 9781403948434.
Latest volume in a long-established series which provides periodic overviews of key themes and developments in British politics. Contains scholarly essays on the latest research relating to the British parliament, political parties,

elections, political devolution and security in the post 9/11 world. Lists of further reading are offered.

1283 **European political facts of the twentieth century**
C. Cook and J. Paxton 5th edn, Palgrave Macmillan, 2001, 496pp. £68. ISBN 9780333792032.
Using a broad definition of Europe to encompass the region from the Atlantic to the Urals, provides access to basic facts and figures about European politics in the period 1900–1999. Includes election results, details about national parliaments and elected political parties. Contains useful coverage of the fall of communism, including a chapter on the names and composition of the new countries of Europe.

1284 **A new handbook of political science**
R. Goodin [et al.] Oxford University Press, 1998, 864pp. £31. ISBN 9780198294719.
Well regarded scholarly survey of all aspects of the discipline. Includes essays from 42 academic experts on the history and development of the study of political science, political institutions and political behaviour, comparative politics, international relations and political theory.

1285 **The Oxford companion to politics of the world**
J. Krieger [et al.], eds 2nd edn, Oxford University Press, 2001, 1050pp. £46. ISBN 9780195117394.
Intended to meet the needs of students, members of the public and professional journalists, this single volume contains over 700 articles of lengths ranging from short factual definitions to longer interpretative essays. It is arranged into ten broad thematic categories: nations, biographies, concepts, conventions, treaties and developments in international law, domestic political, economic and social issues, forms of government and institutions, historical events, international issues and international organizations. The section on historical events provides discussion of key events such as the Gulf War and the Chernobyl nuclear accident. Extensive cross-referencing guides readers to related articles within the volume.

1286 **The Oxford companion to twentieth-century British politics**
J. Ramsden, ed. Oxford University Press, 2005, 764pp. £17.99. ISBN 9780198610366.
Scholarly work which encompasses the ideas, institutions, events and places that played a key role in shaping British politics during the 20th century. Over 3000 articles and essays are provided, including discussion of every British prime minister during the period and the relationship between British politics and international events such as the development of Europe, NATO and Anglo-American relations. The book also contains a list of office holders, results of general elections and dates of ministries.

1287 **The Oxford handbook of contextual political analysis**
C. Tilly and R.E. Goodin Oxford University Press, 2006, 888pp. £85. ISBN 9780199270439.
First publication in the Oxford Handbooks in Political Science series, which aims to offer an authoritative and critical overview of the current state of the discipline. Contains a series of thought-provoking essays by leading experts which focus on political methodology, analysing how and why context matters to political science. Reference is made to the context of time, space, culture, history and discipline.

Further volumes in this series are planned to cover other areas of political methodology, political theory and political institutions.

1288 Party government in 48 democracies (1945–1998): composition, duration, personnel
J. Woldendorp, H. Keman and I. Budge   Kluwer Academic Publishers, 2000, 580pp. £162. ISBN 0792367278.
A useful handbook containing complete data on 48 Western parliamentary democracies 1945–1998. It include lists of government members, heads of state, length of government and reason for termination. Also included are background facts about individual countries' electoral systems, political systems and laws.

1289 Political chronologies of the world
Routledge, 2001, 2048pp. 6 v., £600. ISBN 9781857431193.
A 6 volume set of chronologies covering all regions of the world. Each volume contains individual country profiles with notes on key political events such as elections, political system changes, revolutions and constitutional reforms. Coverage is from ancient times until 2000, although there is a stronger emphasis on recent events. Reference is made to national and international social and economic changes which have influenced political developments.
- **A political chronology of Africa** Routledge, 2001, 512pp. £100. ISBN 9781857431162.
- **A political chronology of Central, South and East Asia** Routledge, 2001, 320pp. £100. ISBN 9781857431148.
- **A political chronology of Europe** Routledge, 2001, 384pp. £100. ISBN 9781857431131.
- **A political chronology of south-east Asia and oceania** Routledge, 2001, 248pp. £100. ISBN 9781857431179.
- **A political chronology of the Americas** Routledge, 2001, 288pp. £100. ISBN 9781857431186.
- **A political chronology of the Middle East** Routledge, 2001, 296pp. £100. ISBN 9781857431148.

1290 Political data handbook: OECD countries
J. Lane, D. McKay and K. Newton   2nd edn, Oxford University Press, 1996, 366pp. £57.50. ISBN 9780198280538.
Useful starting point for tracing basic statistical facts about OECD nations. The first section contains tables of comparative data for 24 nations covering the period 1950–1985. These enable comparisons to be made about trends in political, government and economic change. The second section contains facts about individual nations. These include election results, lists of prime ministers and details about the electoral system. Contact addresses for further information are provided.

1291 Vital statistics on American politics
H.W. Stanley and R.G. Niemi, eds   2005–6 edn, CQ Press, 400pp. Details about pricing for the online version can be obtained from the publisher's website, £45. ISBN 9781568029764.
www.cqpress.com
A rich source of statistical information about a wide range of aspects of American politics and government. It is now available in print or as a searchable online version. Topics covered include the results of all presidential, congressional and gubernatorial elections from 1788 onwards, facts and figures about US political parties, election campaign finance, public opinion ratings, the media, US government and foreign, military, social and economic policy.

Keeping up to date

1292 Annual reviews: political science
Annual Reviews, 2006, annual. Available in print or online, £93. ISBN 0824333098 ISSN 10942939.
http://arjournals.annualreviews.org/loi/polisci
One of the highly regarded Annual Reviews series which synthesises and critically reviews the latest primary research literature in a wide range of science and social science subject areas. Each year distinguished researchers select the most important topics of research in their discipline, guiding readers quickly to the key ideas and articles and highlighting emerging areas of research. The politics series is available in print or online.

1293 BBC news – politics
http://news.bbc.co.uk/1/hi/uk_politics/default.stm
Provides free access to continuously updated news headlines, plus audio and video clips from BBC news programmes. It is possible to sign up to receive RSS news feeds. Other useful features of the site include in-depth reports on key issues such as elections and political crises. These offer useful introductions to the topic, containing background information, timelines of events and analysis from political commentators.

1294 CNN Inside Politics
http://edition.cnn.com/ALLPOLITICS/
Free access to the latest political news from American broadcaster CNN. It includes the headlines plus political analysis, cartoons and audio and multimedia files of key speeches and events. The emphasis is on US political events, including coverage of elections and American foreign policy. Some archived special reports on historic elections and other key events may be accessed.

1295 Guardian Unlimited Politics
http://politics.guardian.co.uk/
Free access to the latest political news stories, cartoons, opinion polls, comment and analysis from the *Guardian* newspaper. Main emphasis is on British politics. Recent news stories can be viewed free of charge, access to most of the older materials requires a subscription. An interesting feature of the site is the 'Aristotle' database, which offers factual information about individual MPs. This includes a brief biography, map of constituency, summary of political career plus links to other websites where more detailed information on current political activities can be found.

1296 Info4local
www.info4local.gov.uk
Excellent government news website and e-mail alerting service maintained by a number of UK government departments. Although it was originally designed to provide local authority officials with updates on central government activities, it can also be successfully used by students and researchers, offering daily updates on new projects, speeches and reports. The service does not currently include all government departments; however, most major policy areas are covered and the number of bodies is growing. Users may sign up to receive updates by e-mail. These include useful summaries of content and links to full-text documents online.

1297 openDemocracy
www.opendemocracy.net/
openDemocracy.net is an online global magazine of politics and culture. It provides free access to articles, debate and discussion about current affairs. The intention is to offer members of the public the opportunity to engage with major intellectual figures. Key topics include globalization, democracy and power and ongoing conflicts worldwide. Subscribers pay to receive e-mail news updates and contribute to the discussion forums.

'(T)he leading independent website on global current affairs – free to read, free to participate, free to the world … offering stimulating, critical analysis, promoting dialogue and debate on issues of global importance and linking citizens from around the world. openDemocracy is committed to human rights and democracy. We aim to ensure that marginalized views and voices are heard. We believe facilitating argument and understanding across geographical boundaries is vital to preventing injustice.'

Political Theory

conservatism • democracy • fascism • ideologies • Marxism • nationalism • socialism

Introductions to the subject

1298 Cambridge texts in the history of political thought
www.cambridge.org/
A well regarded student textbook series published by Cambridge University Press. Currently over 100 titles have been issued, each covering key political philosophers and writers such as Thomas More and Plato. Many offer translations of classic political treatises from the original Greek and Latin. Each volume contains an introductory essay, chronology and biographical notes on the author, a selection of full-text classic writings and references for further reading. A full listing of titles can be obtained from the publishers website. Examples include:
- **More: Utopia G.M. Logan, ed.**   2nd edn, Cambridge University Press, 2002, 180pp. £7.99. ISBN 9780521525404.
- **Nietzsche: On the genealogy of morality and other writings K. Ansell-Pearson, ed.**   2nd edn, Cambridge University Press, 2006, 242pp. £7.99. ISBN 9780521871235.

Dictionaries, thesauri, classifications

1299 Biographical dictionary of neo-Marxism
R.A. Gorman, ed.   Greenwood, 1986, 463pp. £64. ISBN 9780313235139.
Contains an introductory essay on the definition and historical development of neo-Marxian theory plus 205 biographies of key members of neo-Marxist movements and parties worldwide. This includes a thorough coverage of the Frankfurt School. Each essay is followed by a list of the main primary and secondary works relating to the individual. An appendix enables individuals to be located by geographical region. A useful companion to the *Biographical dictionary of Marxism* (q.v.).

1300 A dictionary of Marxist thought
T. Bottomore, ed.   2nd edn, Blackwell Publishing, 1991, 672pp. £25.99. ISBN 9780631180821.

Regarded as a standard reference work on Marxian concepts, this volume is an ideal introduction to Marxism and the individuals and schools of thought which have shaped its development. It includes biographies of key figures, definitions of theoretical terms and summaries of key Marxist texts. Each entry offers suggestions for further reading. The volume also contains an extensive bibliography of the writings of Marx and Engels.

1301 The Palgrave Macmillan dictionary of political thought
R. Scruton   3rd edn, Palgrave Macmillan, 2007, 760pp. £9.99. ISBN 9781403989529.
Latest edition of this dictionary which is acclaimed for its concise definitions of the principal ideas, concepts and theories of modern political science. Contains particularly good discussion of key arguments and summaries of the work of major political theorists.

1302 The Routledge dictionary of twentieth century political thinkers
R. Benewick and P. Green, eds   Routledge, 1997, 296pp. £24.99. ISBN 9780415096232.
A key source for exploring the ideas and backgrounds of influential political thinkers of the 20th century. It contains entries on 170 individuals from the Western and non-Western worlds. These include such famous persons as Derrida, Chomsky and Berlin. Individual entries contain biographical details, summaries of key theories, bibliographic listings and suggestions for further reading.

Research centres & institutes

1303 CentreForum
www.centreforum.org.uk
An independent liberal think-tank which seeks to develop policy to tackle Britain's social and economic problems. Its website provides information on its aims, activities and publications. It provides free access to many of its recent pamphlets covering social policy and British politics. It also supports the Freethink discussion forum, which contains up-to-date discussion of topical issues from a liberal perspective.

Associations & societies

1304 Barry Amiel & Norman Melburn Trust
www.amielandmelburn.org.uk
A charitable trust founded in 1980 to advance public education on the philosophy and practice of Marxism, history of socialism and the working-class movement. Its website hosts an extremely useful free archive of socialist articles and papers. These include materials from the *Universities and Left Review* 1957–1959, *New Reasoner* 1957–1959 and *Marxism Today* 1980–1991. Also accessible are transcripts of annual lectures, reading guides for students and information about forthcoming conferences and events.

1305 Compass
www.compassonline.org.uk
A leading pressure group of the democratic left which was established in 2003 to campaign for reform in the UK Labour

Party and socialist movement. Its website is an excellent starting point for tracing current debate about future labour party policy and political ideology. It offers free access to up-to-date political discussion plus the full text of many of its pamphlets and other publications.

1306 ECPR Standing Group on Extremism and Democracy
http://webhost.ua.ac.be/extremismanddemocracy
A specialist sub-group of the European Consortium for Political Research which specializes in academic research on all aspects of political extremism. This includes coverage of the political parties and movements of the far right and left, the psychology of extremism and the connection between religious extremism, terrorism and political violence. The website provides information on the purpose of the group, its membership and activities. It includes free access to an archive of its electronic newsletter. This contains useful book reviews plus short articles on extremism and politics.

1307 Fabian Society
www.fabian-society.org.uk
Founded in 1884 by Beatrice and Sidney Webb, George Bernard Shaw and H.G. Wells, this organization continues to play an influential role in UK left-of-centre politics. It is affiliated to the British Labour Party but maintains editorial independence. It also supports an active youth organization called the Young Fabians. Its website provides access to information on the Fabian Society history, purpose and current activities. The latter include public lectures, publications and conferences. The site also contains discussion forums which regularly contain debate on the future direction of the British Labour Party and modern socialism.

1308 International Society for Individual Liberty
www.isil.org
International Society for Individual Liberty is an international network of libertarian organizations. Its website provides information on libertarian movements and activities worldwide. It includes recent newsletters, full-text pamphlets about the political philosophy of libertarianism plus free access to Free-Market.Net's *Freedom News Daily*, produced in cooperation with *Rational Review News Digest*, which summarizes key news stories worldwide from a libertarian perspective. Key topics include free markets and individual liberty.

1309 Youth for International Socialism
www.newyouth.com
An international organization which seeks to promote Marxism to young adults worldwide. Its website contains some useful resources for learning about Marxist political theory. They include basic study guides for students, glossaries of Marxist terminology and links to classic texts online. Other features of the site include news stories, calendars of events and links to organizations across the globe.

Libraries, archives, museums

1310 Kate Sharpley Library
www.katesharpleylibrary.net/
The Kate Sharpley Library is named after a First World War

anarchist and anti-war activist. It is based in London and specializes in the collection of materials relating to the history of the anarchist movement. This includes coverage of revolutionary anarchism, the Spanish Civil War and syndicalist workers' movements worldwide. Its website provides access to information on the history, collection and current activities of the library. It includes access to archived issues of its bulletin and a collection of online pamphlets and documents.

1311 Marx Memorial Library
www.marxlibrary.net
Specialist subscription library based in London which holds an excellent collection of books, journals, pamphlets and grey literature relating to all aspects of Marxist political philosophy, socialist history, working-class movements, labour movements, communist party and trade union history from the 1840s to the present. Its specialist archival collections include the John Williamson Collection of materials relating to all aspects of the US left and labour movement from the 1920s onwards, the Spanish Civil War International Brigade Archive, Klugmann Collection of pamphlets dating from the 1640s English Civil War and a complete collection of the *Daily Worker/ Morning Star* newspaper from 1930 to the present. Its website provides information on the history, aims and holdings of the library. It includes access to its online catalogue, plus a searchable database of books reviews taken from the *Marx Memorial Bulletin*.

1312 Wiener Library
www.wienerlibrary.co.uk
The Wiener Library is based in London. Its collections contain extensive holdings of materials relating to all aspects of the history, causes and impact of the Jewish Holocaust. These include periodicals, documents, pamphlets and books relating to fascism and the rise of the Nazi Party in 1930s Germany. German-language materials produced by right-wing organizations are available. Also held are materials relating to contemporary anti-semitism, holocaust denial and right-wing political activity in Europe. Its website provides information on the history and access policies of the Library. It also contains the library catalogue and online phograph archive. The latter includes many images of Nazi propaganda posters and political cartoons.

Portal & task environments

1313 In defence of Marxism
www.marxist.com/
Created by the International Marxist Tendency, this site operates to defend Marxism as a tool for current labour movements. Its main value is in offering free access to up to date information about communist activities worldwide. This includes news headlines and analysis of current events from a Marxist standpoint, online pamphlets and papers, audio and video clips from intellectuals and calendars of events.

1314 Marxist.Net
www.marxist.net/
This site is maintained by the Committee for a Workers' International (CWI), a socialist campaign organization with branches worldwide. It is therefore a good starting point for tracing information about current Marxist-Socialist thinking

and activities. Examples of recent pamphlets and papers can be viewed free of charge online. There are also links to full-text versions of classic works by famous theorists such as Marx, Engels, Lenin and Trotsky.

1315   The Nationalism project
www.nationalismproject.org
Created by Eric G.E. Zuelow, an Assistant Professor of European and World History at West Liberty State College, this site is well known for its excellent collection of materials related to the scholarly study of all aspects of nationalism. It includes an introductory section entitled 'What is Nationalism?' which is particularly relevant to students new to the field, as well as more advanced bibliographies of further readings, book reviews and abstracts and a growing collection of online articles and essays. Also provided is a directory of links to nationalism-related websites.

Discovering print & electronic resources

1316   English socialist periodicals 1880–1900: a reference source
D. Mutch   Ashgate, 2005, 450pp. £55. ISBN 9780754652052.
A specialist work which indexes by subject the contents of 39 key journals published by English socialists in the period 1880–1900. A clear introductory essay discusses the problem of defining socialism and considers how the socialist political message was conveyed to periodical and magazine readers. There is also a location list for tracing the full-text paper copies in British libraries. The subject categories include manifestos, cartoons and literature.

Hans-Georg Gadamer: a bibliography
J. Nordquist, ed.   See entry no. 552

Digital data, image & text collections

1317   Hannah Arendt Papers at the Library of Congress
http://memory.loc.gov/ammem/arendthtml/arendthome.html
This website provides information regarding the collected papers of the political philosopher Hannah Arendt (1906–1975), which are held at the Library of Congress in Washington. The entire collection, including Arendt's correspondence, speeches and lectures, as well as material related to her famous coverage of the trial of Adolf Eichmann, has been digitized (making up about 75,000 digital images) and can currently be viewed online at three locations: the Library of Congress, the New School University in New York City and the Hannah Arendt Center at the University of Oldenburg, Germany. A biography, timeline and selected documents, including her comments on the political philosophy of Kant, can be viewed free of charge via the internet.

1318   Marxists Internet archive
www.marxists.org/
An excellent resource which every politics student should know about. It provides free access to a wealth of contemporary and historical Marxist writings. The site is subdivided into several main sections: Marxist writers, Marxist history and Marxist reference sources. The Marxist writers section contains online archives of full-text articles, books and pamphlets from all the key classical and

contemporary figures. These range from Karl Marx to C.L.R. James. They include examples of writings in all the major European languages. The reference source section includes biographies of theorists, glossaries of terms and an encyclopedia of Marxist terminology and history.

1319   Online library of liberty
http://oll.libertyfund.org
A site maintained by the Liberty Fund which provides free access to a collection of over 1000 full-text classic (out of copyright) books and essays. All titles selected are deemed by the fund to have contributed to the understanding of conservative political philosophy, free-market politics and ideology. Topics covered include political theory, political philosophy, religion and economics. They include the complete works of many political theorists such as Plato, Tacitus, James Harrington, John Locke, Machiavelli, Montesquieu, Thomas Jefferson, Thomas Paine and Alexander Hamilton. The site also contains some teacher's guides.

1320   Stanford encyclopedia of philosophy
E. Zalta [et al.], ed.   Metaphysics Research Lab. Center for the Study of Language & Communication. Stanford University. ISSN 10955053.
http://plato.stanford.edu
Excellent free encyclopedia maintained by an international editorial board. Offers extensive coverage of political philosophy. This includes articles for political ideas, theories and concepts plus biographies of key writers. Individual essays contain useful cross-references, bibliographies of further reading and links to key web resources.

Directories & encyclopedias

1321   American conservatism: an encyclopedia
B. Frohnen, J. Beer and J.O. Nelson, eds   Intercollegiate Studies Institute, 2006, 1000pp. £28. ISBN 9781932236439.
Informative volume which provides a detailed history of the intellectual tradition of American conservatism in the post-1945 period. Contains over 600 articles on the key individuals, organizations, places and concepts which have shaped its development. It has particularly useful biographical entries on conservative philosophers, thinkers and leading Republican Party members. These include George W. Bush and Ronald Reagan. Suggestions for further reading are provided.

1322   The encyclopedia of democracy
S. M. Lipset, ed.   Routledge, 1995, 1840pp. 4 v., o/p. ISBN 9780415124263.
Detailed four-volume set containing over 400 articles on the main concepts, documents, individuals, events and movements relating to the political theory of democracy and its historical application worldwide. Includes a useful appendix of 20 primary source documents which offer important insight into how democracy has been understood and applied at different points in history. These range from the Declaration of the Rights of Man (1789) to the Universal Declaration of Human Rights and the text of selected national constitutions.

1323 Encyclopedia of democratic thought
P.B. Clarke and J. Foweraker   Routledge, 2001, 768pp. £220. ISBN 9780415193962.
Contains a collection of scholarly essays covering over 180 key topics, concepts, theories and ideas important for the understanding of the history, contemporary nature and future study of democracy worldwide. The volume is global in scope, including coverage of classic concerns as well as those relating to the emergence of new democracies. Emphasis is on theoretic concepts rather than biographies of key theorists. Suggestions for further reading are provided.

1324 Encyclopedia of nationalism
A.J. Moty, ed.   Academic Press, 2001. 2 v., $215. ISBN 9780122272325.
Useful two-volume set. Volume 1 focuses on the fundamental themes of nationalism, containing historical overviews of the history of nationalism in specific geographic regions and discussion of how social science disciplines have dealt with the question of nationalism. Volume 2 contains articles on key leaders, movements and concepts of nationalism. A glossary of terms and suggestions for further reading is also provided.

Handbooks & manuals

Cambridge companions to philosophy
See entry no. 561

1325 Handbook of political theory
G. Gaus and C. Kukathas, eds   Sage Publications, 2004, 544pp. £75. ISBN 9780761967873.
A valuable collection of scholarly essays covering a wide range of areas relating to political theory and philosophy. These include a discussion of the nature of scholarship in political theory, a survey of the history of political thought and analysis of the modern state. Each essay is approximately 20–30 pages in length, including lists of references for further reading.

1326 The Routledge companion to fascism and the far right
P. Davies and D. Lynch   Routledge, 2002, 448pp. £16.99. ISBN 9780415214957.
An excellent manual for those beginning academic research on the main political ideologies, movements and individuals associated with the political right. It offers an introductory section containing a history and chronology of key events followed by a collection of essays discussing the historical evolution and content of fascist political ideology and its practice in specific governments worldwide. The final section contains a glossary of key terms, guides to further reading and advice on research resources.

1327 The Sage handbook of nations and nationalism
G. Delanty and K. Kumar   Sage Publications, 2006, 560pp. £85. ISBN 9781412901017.
A useful collection of scholarly essays presenting a range of different voices on the theory and manifestations of nationalism worldwide. It is subdivided into three sections. The first presents classical and modern theories of nations and nationalism. The second section explores key themes, including ethnicity and nationalism, nation building and nationalism and international culture. The final section

explores the nature and role of nationalism in the globalized world.

Keeping up to date

1328 Liberator Magazine
Liberator Publications, 7/8 p.a. Some issues available online free of charge., £23.
www.liberator.org.uk/default.asp
British political magazine which has been published since 1970 by a collective. It is issued approximately 7–8 times per year and contains substantial coverage of the activities and policy of the British Liberal Democrat Party. Each issue contains news, book reviews, short articles, examples of political humour and commentary about British politics from a Liberal viewpoint. Articles from back issues of the journal may be accessed free of charge from the website. Current material is restricted to subscribers only.

1329 The Morning Star
Peoples Press Printing Society, Daily.
www.morningstaronline.co.uk
The Morning Star was founded in 1930 as the *Daily Worker* and remains the only English-language socialist daily newspaper in the world. Its website provides free access to the latest headlines. Access to most of the full-text articles, features and back issues requires a subscription. All aspects of British and world news is covered from a Marxist perspective. There is a particular emphasis on political, trade union and labour movement news.

1330 National Review
National Review, 1955–, Fortnightly. $60.
www.nationalreview.com
A magazine of political opinion which has significantly influenced American conservatism since the 1950s. Each issue contains articles, opinion pieces, political cartoons and reviews. It includes significant discussion of American republican politics and foreign policy. Available in print or online. The website also offers free access to blogs and some online commentary not contained within the print version.

1331 Political theory daily review
www.politicaltheory.info/
A great site for keeping up to date with political theory and philosophy research. Updated every day to provide summaries and links to the latest political news, book reviews, online articles and reports. These cover an extensive range of subject areas, methodologies and political viewpoints. The editor of the site is Alfredo Perez, a PhD student in political science at the New School for Social Research.

1332 The Salisbury Review
Salisbury Review, 1982–, qtrly. £20.
www.salisburyreview.co.uk
Published since 1982, this quarterly journal contains books and reviews which discuss contemporary conservative philosophy and policy. It is associated with the Salisbury Group of British Conservatives but retains editorial independence. Articles offer a conservative viewpoint on politics, philosophy and the arts. Its website is regularly updated to contain some online articles and opinion pieces, including some online only materials.

1333 World Socialist web site
www.wsws.org
Maintained by the International Committee of the Fourth International, this website provides up to date analysis and commentary on major world events from a revolutionary socialist perspective. It includes details of workers' struggles, trade union activity and left-wing political activity worldwide.

Political Systems

British Commonwealth • British Empire • colonial government • decolonization • democracy • monarchy • political parties • regime change • revolutionary movements • separatist movements • stateless nations

Introductions to the subject

1334 Models of democracy
D. Held   3rd edn, Polity Press, 2006, 338pp. £16.99. ISBN 9780745631479.
www.polity.co.uk/
Excellent student textbook offering an overview of accounts of democracy from ancient Greece to the modern day. The latest edition includes discussion of the development and possible impact of the latest forms of 'deliberative' or citizen-created democracies. The publisher maintains a companion website offering supporting study guides and web-links.

1335 The political system of the European Union
S. Hix   2nd edn, Palgrave Macmillan, 2005, 496pp. £22.99. ISBN 9780333961827.
Well-regarded student textbook offering an excellent introduction to the function, evolution and current operation of the political system of the European Union. Part 1 explains the executive, legislative and judicial systems of the EU, Part 2 the role of public opinions, parties and elections and Part 3 the policy and decision making process. It includes coverage of up-to-date issues such as the reform of the EU, economic and monetary union and EU foreign policy.

Research centres & institutes

1336 ARENA
www.arena.uio.no
ARENA is an interdisciplinary research centre based at the University of Oslo which specializes in the study of the dynamics of the changing political order in Europe. Key topics include the governance of the European Union, democracy and citizenship within Europe and European political integration. Its website provides information about ongoing research, conferences and publications. It includes free access to its well regarded ARENA working paper series from 1994 to the present.

1337 Freedom House
www.freedomhouse.org
Non-profit organization which seeks to promote democracy worldwide. Famous for its regular surveys of democratic and political freedoms. Many of these can be accessed free of charge from its website. Key titles are the annual *Freedom in the World* report which documents the state of democracy, political and civil liberties in several hundred individual

nations worldwide, the *Press Freedom* report and the annual *Nations in Transit* report which documents progress in democratization of over 20 former Communist nations from Eastern and Central Europe and Eurasia.

1338 Institute of Commonwealth Studies
http://commonwealth.sas.ac.uk
The only postgraduate research institute in the UK which specializes in cross-disciplinary studies of the history, politics and economics of the Commonwealth and former British colonies. Its website provides information on its current research teaching programmes. It includes information on its substantial library and archive holdings.
■ **Commonwealth and Latin American political archives**
http://polarch.sas.ac.uk. Site created jointly by the Institute of Commonwealth Studies (ICS) and the Institute for the Study of the Americas (ISA) to provide information about their holdings of political ephemera from Commonwealth and Latin American nations. These include books, pamphlets and posters from political parties and independence movements. Some examples have been digitized and can be viewed online.
■ **Theses in progress in Commonwealth studies** , annual.
http://commonwealth.sas.ac.uk/tip.htm [29/06/2006]. An annual listing of MPhil and PhD research being carried out at UK universities. Free access to the online version from 2003. Includes coverage of all areas of the social sciences relating to the British Empire, the Commonwealth and their member nations.

Associations & societies

International Institute for Democracy & Electoral Assistance
See entry no. 1436

1339 Transparency International
www.transparency.org/
A global civil-society organization which seeks to fight political and economic corruption worldwide. It produces a number of key measurement tools, including the Corruption Perceptions Index, the Bribe Payers Index, the Global Corruption Barometer and National Integrity System Country Studies. These contain comparisons of actual and perceived levels of political and economic transparency for over a 100 nations worldwide, enabling users to begin to analyse the state of democracy in the region. Reports from 2003 onwards may be downloaded from the website.

Portal & task environments

1340 European Integration history index
http://vlib.iue.it/hist-eur-integration/Index.html
This is a joint project of the European University Institutes Library, the Historical Archives of the European Union and the Centre Virtuel de la Connaissance sur l'Europe. It provides a very useful directory of links to internet resources relating to the history of European economic, political and social integration in the post-1950 period. These include the full text of all the main treaties in the development of the EEC, EC and European Union. Also offered are links to news services, legislation, e-mail discussion lists and online learning packages. Other sections relate to the relationship between the EU and specific European nations, EU economics and EU enlargement. All resources have short descriptions of content.

Digital data, image & text collections

1341 Archive of European integration
http://aei.pitt.edu/
An electronic archive of materials relating to the development of the European Union and European integration which is maintained by the University of Pittsburgh. It is particularly useful for students seeking to trace information about the historical development of European institutions from the 1950s to the present. It offers separate searchable indexes of official EU materials and documents produced by non-EU bodies. The types of material available from the EU include legislation, green papers, white papers and reports from official summits. The non-official collection includes a searchable database of full-text research and working papers from leading European research institutes.

1342 EUROGOV: European Governance Papers
Connex, irregular. ISSN 18136826.
www.connex-network.org/eurogov
A peer-reviewed open-access electronic journal which is produced jointly by Connex and NewGov. It aims to publish academic articles and reviews covering all aspects of European and EU governance. Topics covered include democracy, multilevel layers of government in Europe, political participation in the EU and European Union politics. Users may sign up to receive e-mail alerts when new papers are added to the site. Materials are available from No 1, 2005 onwards.

1343 Failed states index
www.fundforpeace.org/web/
Compiled annually since 2005 by The Fund for Peace and *Foreign Policy* magazine. It uses a collection of social, economic, political and military indicators to rank over 60 states worldwide in order of their vulnerability to internal conflict, political crisis and state collapse. The website provides free access to maps, country studies and risk analyses taken from all the indexes produced since 2005. Information on the methodology used to compile the Index is also provided.

Directories & encyclopedias

1344 Encyclopedia of governance
M. Bevir, ed. Sage Publications, 2006, 1232pp. £185. ISBN 9781412905794.
A useful collection of over 500 entries covering a wide range of issues, concepts and events surrounding governance in the period between the 1950s and 1970s. A key emphasis is on the changing nature and role of the state in recent times. Issues explored include the increasing transfer of powers from national governments to the private sector and the rise of new types of regional and international relationships.

1345 World encyclopedia of political systems and parties
N. Schlager, J. Weisblatt and O. Perez, eds 4th edn, Facts on File, 2006, 1664pp. 3 v., £187.50. ISBN 9780816059539.
Provides in-depth information about contemporary systems of government worldwide. The entries are arranged alphabetically by nation. Each essay contains information on the structures and powers of central and local government and the legislature, the electoral system and the main political parties. Entries for political parties include summaries of history, policy and political funding.

Keeping up to date

1346 Journal of Imperial and Commonwealth History
Routledge, 1970–, qtrly. £62. ISSN 03086534.
www.tandf.co.uk
A leading academic journal which publishes articles and book reviews covering the latest research relating to the history of the British Empire, imperialism, colonialism, the rise of nationalism and decolonization. It can be purchased in print or online. The website offers free access to tables of contents, sample articles and content alerts

Types of Political System or Government

Introductions to the subject

1347 Democracy: a very short introduction
B. Crick Oxford University Press, 2002, 144pp. £6.99. ISBN 9780192802507.
Designed as a basic introduction for the general reader, this book offers a brief introduction to the concept and practice of democracy throughout history from Ancient Greece and Rome to the present. It highlights changing concepts and developments of democracy over time.

1348 Democracy: concepts in the social sciences
A. Arblaster 3rd edn, Open University Press, 2002, 144pp. £17.99. ISBN 9780335209699.
An excellent introduction to the theory and practice of democracy for students. The author considers the meaning of democracy, its historical application and controversies and discusses the state of democracy in contemporary societies worldwide. He includes consideration of the impact of globalization upon democracy.

1349 Empire: a very short introduction
S. Howe Oxford University Press, 2002, 160pp. £6.99. ISBN 9780192802231.
A readable introduction to the history and concept of empire. Includes definitions of key political terms such as empire, colonialism and imperialism, an overview of specific empires throughout history and a topical discussion of whether the recent foreign policy of the USA and the expansion of multinational companies associated with globalization could be regarded as a modern-day empire.

1350 European democracies
J. Steiner and M. Crepaz 5th edn, Longman, 2006, 480pp. £31.99. ISBN 9780321077738.
A useful textbook which surveys the historical development of democracy in European nations. An introductory essay compares and contrasts the evolution of democratic government in North America and Europe, subsequent chapters then address key themes relating to Europe. These include coverage of the development of national and supranational political institutions, the end of the Cold War and post-communist transitions and the role of ethnic nationalism in politics.

Dictionaries, thesauri, classifications

1351   **Dictionary of the British Empire and Commonwealth**
A. Palmer   John Murray, 1996, 384pp. o/p. ISBN 9780719556500.
Provides factual coverage of the key persons, events, treaties and institutions of the British Empire. Emphasis is on Britain's overseas territories rather than the British mainland. It includes coverage of the history of the transition from the Empire to the Commonwealth and outline histories of the member states of the Empire and Commonwealth during the 20th century.

Official & quasi-official bodies

1352   **British Monarchy**
www.royal.gov.uk/
Official website of the British royal family. In addition to photographs, lists of diary engagements and biographies of the Queen and other leading members, researchers may also access transcripts (and some selected audio files) of all HM Queen Elizabeth II's Christmas broadcasts from 1952 onwards, detailed annual reports on the financial expenditure of the royal household and official press releases. There is a link to the official website of the Prince of Wales.

1353   **Commonwealth Secretariat**
www.thecommonwealth.org/
The main organizational agency of the Commonwealth. Its website provides free access to detailed information about the history, membership, structure and current activities of the Commonwealth. This includes a collection of communiques, statements, documents and webcasts from key Commonwealth events and summits. These are a good source of information on recent political, social and economic development activities in Commonwealth countries from Asia and Africa. They include election observation reports and documents relating to work in the fields of health, gender equality, development and human rights.

Research centres & institutes

1354   **Federal Trust** [UK]
www.fedtrust.co.uk
A long-established think-tank which was originally founded in 1945 by Sir William Beveridge and currently studies the interactions between regional, national, European and global levels of government. Its website offers information about ongoing research and free access to some briefing papers. Many of these focus on UK–EU relations. Other topics covered include global governance and British political devolution.

Associations & societies

1355   **Alliance for Democracy & Reform in Asia**
www.asiademocracy.org/index.php
A network of researchers, policy makers and pro-democracy activists who seek to monitor and promote democratic government in Asian nations. Its website provides information on the aims of the organization, plus access to press releases and reports from its conferences and committees.

Of particular value is the Asia Democracy Index which critically analyses and compares the state of democracy in 16 Asian nations. Also useful are reports on the conduct of presidential and parliamentary elections, many of which have been prepared by Asian scholars.

1356   **Federal Union**
www.federalunion.org.uk
UK-based organization which was founded in 1938 to campaign for federalism in the UK, Europe and the world. Its website provides information on the history, membership and activities of the group. It includes access to its press releases and some full-text papers. Topics covered include federal government in Europe and the future development of the European Union. The EU section includes a glossary of EU jargon and a collection of quotations from politicians about the EU.

1357   **French Colonial History Society**
www.frenchcolonial.org/
An academic association which seeks to promote the scholarly study of French colonial history, French migration and the history of individual French colonies. Its website provides information on its aims and activities. It includes newsletters, conference listings and details about its journal publications. It also offers a useful collection of links to internet resources relating to French colonialism.

Libraries, archives, museums

1358   **British Empire & Commonwealth Museum**
www.empiremuseum.co.uk
Based in Bristol, this award-winning museum was the first in the UK to focus on the social, political and economic history of the British Empire and Commonwealth throughout its history. Its website provides information on visiting the museum and its archives. It also offers maps and timelines of the history of the Empire.
   ■ **Images of Empire** www.imagesofempire.com. The museum's online database of images. These include fascinating photographs and film clips which bring to life the social, political and domestic life of the Empire and its citizens. The database can be searched by keyword and images viewed online. Information on copyright and reproduction fees are displayed on the website.

1359   **Open Society Archives**
www.osa.ceu.hu
A specialist collection of archives and research materials housed at the Central European University relating to the study of communism, the Cold War and human rights in Central and Eastern Europe. Its website provides information on the scope of its collections. It also includes useful news updates on material recently released from archives of the former communist nations and a growing collection of online exhibitis. The latter include an excellent digital library of declassified documents, images and teaching materials relating to the 1956 Hungarian Uprising.

Digital data, image & text collections

1360 Empire online
Andrew Mathew Digital. £15,400 one-off cost.
www.amdigital.co.uk
Empire Online is a digital archive of materials covering the history and concept of empires from 1492 to the late 20th century. It is sub-divided into thematic collections which include cultural contact 1492–1969, religion and empire, literature and empire and race, class, imperialism and colonialism, c. 1607–2007. The latter includes detailed coverage of US foreign policy in the modern world. Each section contains full-text materials, including government documents, oral history accounts, photographs and maps.

1361 Royal Commonwealth Society Photograph Collection
www.lib.cam.ac.uk/rcs_photo_project/homepage.html
The Royal Commonwealth Society Photograph Collection contains over 70,000 images from all over the world relating to the history of the British Empire and Commonwealth between 1850 and 1980. Its website, which is hosted by Cambridge University Library, provides free access to a detailed catalogue of the collection and background information on its scope and history. It also offers free access to an online gallery of over 600 digitized photographs. These include fascinating examples of royal tours of the colonies and images of daily life, education and work in the British Empire.

1362 Russian archives online
www.russianarchives.com/rao/index.html
An enormous library of online images, film clips and audio files of materials relating to the political, social and economic history of Russia and the nations of the former Soviet Union. It includes access to materials taken from leading institutions such as the Russian State Document and Photograph Archive at Krasnogorsk, the Russian State Archive of Scientific and Technical Documents in Moscow, the Hoover Institution, Stanford University Russian Collection, the Russian-American Center at the University of San Francisco and the Russian information agency Novosti. All areas of the arts, social and physical sciences are covered, including collections of political propaganda material from the Russian Communist Party. The site also hosts some online tutorials covering Russian political history.

Directories & encyclopedias

1363 Colonialism: an international, social, cultural, and political encyclopedia
M.E. Page and P. Sonnenburg, eds ABC-CLIO, 2003, 1200pp. 3 v., £180. ISBN 1576073351.
Comprehensive three-volume work which provides coverage of the history, politics, economics, geography and culture of colonialism from earliest times. Focuses on the perspective of both the colonizer and the colonized. Includes entries for key figures, institutions, concepts, events and treaties. Each volume contains useful chronologies, plus extensive illustrations and maps. Many important key documents, treaties and speeches are also reprinted.

1364 Encyclopedia of Western colonialism since 1450
T. Benjamin, ed. Thomson Gale, 2007, 1315pp. 3 v., £200. ISBN 0028658434.
Useful three-volume set which can be used to provide students with a historical perspective on the spread of western religions, ideas and world values throughout the world during the period of 1450 to the late 20th century. It contains over 400 brief articles, many with maps and illustrations, plus suggestions for further reading. Coverage includes the empires of Britain and Spain. Volume 3 contains a glossary of key terms and 62 pages of full-text primary source documents, including key treaties and legislation.

1365 Encyclopedia of world political systems
J.D. Derbyshire and I. Derbyshire Sharpe Reference, 2000, 930pp. 2 v. Previously published as *Political systems of the world*, £138.95. ISBN 0765680254.
A useful resource for comparing political systems worldwide. Volume 1 provides an introduction to understanding and comparing the different elements of political systems. It includes coverage of the executive, legislature, electoral system and constitution. Volume 2 contains detailed coverage and cross comparison of individual systems. Over 200 maps of data are provided.

Handbooks & manuals

1366 The Oxford history of the British Empire
Oxford University Press.
A major scholarly series providing a detailed history of the British Empire from the 17th century to 1999. It includes coverage of the economic, social, demographic, cultural and intellectual history of British imperialism and its impact worldwide. Published separately in five chronologically arranged volumes. Each volume contains substantial maps, tables, chronologies of key events and bibliographies of further reading.
- **1. Origins of empire N.P. Canny, ed.** Oxford University Press, 2001, 553pp. £14.99. ISBN 9780199246762.
- **2. The eighteenth century E.P. Marshall, ed.** Oxford University Press, 1998, 662pp. £25. ISBN 9780199246779.
- **3. The nineteenth century A. Porter, ed.** Oxford University Press, 1999, 800pp. £21. ISBN 9780199246786.
- **4. The twentieth century J.M. Brown, ed.** Oxford University Press, 1999, 800pp. £19. ISBN 9780199246793.
- **5. Historiography R. Winks, ed.** Oxford University Press, 1999, 260pp. £63. ISBN 9780198205661. This final volume considers how opinions have changed over time about the nature, role, and value of imperialism.

Keeping up to date

1367 H-Empire
www.h-net.org/~empire
An academic mailing list which forms part of the H-Net: Humanities and Social Sciences Online service at Michigan State University. It provides a forum for scholars researching the origin, development and decline of empires worldwide, both historically and in the modern world. Messages are regularly used to advertise new publications, jobs, grant opportunities and conferences. It is possible to view an archive of all messages from 2006 to date.

1368 Publius: journal of federalism
Oxford University Press, qtrly. £149. ISSN 17477107.
http://publius.oxfordjournals.org
A leading international journal devoted to federalism. It is
published quarterly and regularly contains articles, research
reports and book reviews relating to federal political systems
worldwide.This includes detailed coverage of devolution and
the American federal system. The website offers tables of
contents, selected free samples and the ability to sign up for
e-mail tables of contents alerts. Full-text articles are for
subscribers only. The title can also be purchased in print
format.

Regime Change

Official & quasi-official bodies

1369 United Nations and decolonization
www.un.org/Depts/dpi/decolonization/main.htm
This site provides an outline history of the dismantling of the
former colonial empires and the paths towards political
independence from 1945 to the present. It also includes a
list of countries which remain colonies and details of current
UN activities to assist them. It offers access to full-text
resolutions and documents in favour of decolonization which
have been produced by the United Nations. They include
materials published by the Special Committee on
Decolonization and the International Trustee system.

Research centres & institutes

1370 Centre for the Study of Public Policy
www.abdn.ac.uk/cspp/
The CSPP, based at the University of Aberdeen, specializes in
comparative public policy research. Since 1991 it has been
conducting a unique programme of survey research in 15
post-communist countries in Central and Eastern Europe and
the former Soviet Union which track the nature and impact of
political and economic change since the fall of communism.
Countries covered include Russia, Belarus, UKraine, Moldova,
Estonia, Latvia, Lithuania, Bulgaria, Czech Republic, Slovakia,
Hungary, Poland, Romania, Slovenia, Croatia, Serbia, East
Germany. The surveys include New Russia Barometer, New
Europe Barometer, New Baltic Barometer and New
Democracies Barometer. Topics covered include public policy,
political opinion polls, elections and democratization and
development. It is possible to access some results and
papers relating to the surveys online. Other materials may be
purchased.

1371 Crisis States Research Centre
www.crisisstates.com
A specialist research unit based at the London School of
Economics and Political Science. It aims to investigate the
process of state crisis, collapse, survival and reconstruction.
A key theme is the politics of conflict management and
democratic reform in non-western nations of Asia, Africa and
Latin America. The website provides free access to project
information, plus full-text working papers and research
reports.

**1372 Institute for the Study of Conflict, Ideology &
Policy**
www.bu.edu/iscip
ISCIP is based at Boston University. It focuses on the study
of Russia and the post-Soviet nations of Europe and the
Caucasus, concentrating specifically on destabilizing
economic, political and ethnic factors affecting economic and
political transition. Its website provides information on its
aims and current research. It includes free access to the
ISCIP Analyst which offers regular surveys of domestic
foreign policy and security issues in the region and articles
and book reviews from the journal *Perspective*.

**1373 Stanford University comparative democratization
project**
http://democracy.stanford.edu/
The website of a research project based at Stanford
University (USA) which studied the transition from
authoritarian regimes to democracies worldwide The site
contains seminar papers and syllabi from leading democracy
scholars.

Associations & societies

1374 Unrepresented Nations & Peoples Organisation
www.unpo.org
An international organization established in 1991 to act as a
forum for indigenous peoples, minority groups and occupied
nations not represented in the principal international
organizations such as the United Nations. Its website
provides a list of members and the full text of its recent
press releases and communiques. It also includes the text of
some of its reports these are useful sources of information
on the activities of independence, secession and ethnic
group movements worldwide. They include details of any
repression and human rights abuses made against the
groups.

Digital data, image & text collections

1375 Bertelsmann Transformation Index
www.bertelsmann-transformation-index.de
A global ranking which analyses the state of democratization
and transformation towards a market-based economy in over
119 nations worldwide. Data is prepared by the Bertelsmann
Stiftung and Center for Applied Policy Research (Munich) and
covers the period 2003 to the present. The website provides
free access to the country reports and rankings. It also
contains an interactive atlas of the results, which users may
download. Detailed information on the methodology used to
compile the reports is provided.

Directories & encyclopedias

1376 Encyclopedia of modern separatist movements
C. Hewitt and T. Cheetham   ABC-CLIO, 2001, 300pp. £14.99. ISBN
9781851093496.
Single-volume work covering ethnic separatist movements
worldwide. An introductory essay defines the nature, extent,
causes and outcomes of ethnic separatism in the modern
world. It also includes essays on specific nations, key
organizations and political leaders. Entries on related topics

such as nationalism and ethnic cleansing are provided. Contains numerous illustrations and maps.

1377 The encyclopedia of political revolutions
J.A. Goldstone   Fitzroy Dearborn, 1998, 580pp. £110. ISBN 9781579581220.
More than 300 entries which cover revolutions worldwide from AD 1500 to the present. The wide-ranging coverage also includes civil rights movements, independence and secessionist movements and women's rights struggles. Entries include reviews of individual movements, plus essays on how and why revolutions occur and the influence they have on history.

1378 Encyclopedia of the stateless nations: ethnic and national groups around the world
Greenwood Press, 2002, 2432pp. £270. ISBN 9780313316173.
Useful guide to over 300 nationalist and separatist groups worldwide who are currently making an impact on world politics. Includes coverage of many groups in former communist regions of Eastern Europe and Eurasia who regularly appear in world news. Each entry provides a background history of the name, aims and objectives of the national group. Maps and national flags are provided. There is also a select bibliography of further reading.

1379 Revolutionary movements in world history: from 1750 to the present
J.V. DeFronzo, ed.   ABC-CLIO, 2006, 923pp. 3 v., £175. ISBN 9781851097937.
A three-volume set which provides coverage of 79 revolutions from the American War of Independence and French revolutions in 1789 to the present. Entries provide background information on the causes, events, personalities and outcome of each revolution plus lists of references for further reading. The presence of numerous maps, photographs and illustrations make this work particularly suitable for students and the general reader.

Handbooks & manuals

1380 Elections and parties in new European democracies
R. Rose and N. Munro   CQ Press, 2003, 336pp. £62. ISBN 9781568028088.
A detailed study of transitions in electoral politics in the post-communist nations of Eastern Europe from 1989 to 2002. It includes 12 detailed country summaries covering Bulgaria, Czechoslovakia, Czech Republic, Slovakia, Estonia, Hungary, Latvia, Lithuania, Poland, Romania, Russia and Slovenia. Also offered is a collection of scholarly essays examining the general trends, and the impact of such factors as electoral laws and electoral systems on the election results and state of democracy in general.

1381 Handbook of political change in Eastern Europe.
S. Berglund, J. Ekman and F.H. Aarebrot   2nd edn, Edward Elgar Publishing, 2004, 656pp. £95. ISBN 9781840648546.
A useful collection of 12 long essays which survey the transition to and consolidation of democracy in post-communist Europe. The first three chapters examine the historical background to the changes. These are followed by 9 country surveys covering Estonia, Latvia, Lithuania, Poland, the Czech and Slovak Republics, Hungary, Slovenia, Romania

and Bulgaria. Each of these contains solid statistical data and graphs on the nature and extent of political change.

Keeping up to date

1382 Transitions Online
Transitions Online. Electronic journal. Continuously updated., $41. ISSN 12141615.
www.tol.cz/
Transitions Online publishes independent news stories, analysis and articles on the post-communist nations of Central Europe and the Balkans, Eastern Europe, Russia and the Caucasus, South-Eastern Europe and Central Asia. It regularly contains examples of articles from journalists based in these regions. The website provides free access to some articles, others are offered to subscribers only. Topics covered by the politics section include elections, analysis of post-communist political transitions plus assessments of human rights and civil liberties in the area. It is possible to sign up to receive RSS news feeds of the latest headlines.

Political Communication

e-government • political advertising • political blogging • political journalism • political rhetoric • propaganda

Introductions to the subject

1383 Current issues in political marketing
W.W. Wymer and J. Lees-Marshment, eds   Haworth Press, 2006, 347pp. £42.50. ISBN 9780789024374.
This text uses the latest insights from academic research and management theory to consider how marketing tools and concepts can be successfully transferred to politics. It examines the advantages, ethics and problems associated with political marketing. Issues covered include market identification, party branding and overcoming voter disengagement. Practical tips and case studies are provided.

1384 An introduction to political communication
B. McNair   4th edn, Routledge, 2007, 222pp. £16.99. ISBN 9780415410694.
The latest edition of this popular textbook provides a readable introduction to how political organizations use the media to communicate their message. It includes coverage of political advertising and marketing, the use of the internet and the ethics of political communication. Recent case studies such as the UK 2005 election and the 2004 American presidential election are provided.

Research centres & institutes

1385 Annenberg Public Policy Center
www.annenbergpublicpolicycenter.org
Based at the University of Pennsylvania, this is a specialist research centre which conducts research in the areas of political communication, information and society and the media. Its website provides information on its purpose and current projects. It includes free access to papers and reports prepared by the project groups. Key topics covered by these are analyses of American presidential discourse and

the study of US political advertising during election campaigns.

■ **Factcheck.org** www.factcheck.org [12/07/2006]. Annenberg Factcheck.org is a well known intiative of the centre which conducts research into the type and accuracy of claims made by presidential candidates in speeches, broadcasts and interviews.

1386   Centre for European Political Communications
http://ics.leeds.ac.uk/eurpolcom/index.cfm
EurPolCom is a major European research centre based at the University of Leeds. It has an interdisciplinary approach focusing on all aspects of political communication in a European context. This includes discussion of the political communication of European integration and the Single European Currency (Euro). Its website offers information on ongoing projects, including access to the full text of its important working paper series.

1387   Joan Shorenstein Center on the Press, Politics & Public
www.ksg.harvard.edu/presspol/index.htm
Based at Harvard University, this research centre is renowned for its study of the practical and theoretical intersection between the press, politics and public policy. Its website is one of the best places for finding academic research on political journalism, political advertising and the use of the media during election campaigns. Another recent area of interest is the media and the 'war on terrorism'. Many full-text research reports and papers can be downloaded free of charge. Most materials concentrate on American politics.

1388   Political Communication Center
www.ou.edu/pccenter/
Based at the University of Oklahoma, this institute conducts research into political communication, focusing specifically on American political advertising and broadcasting. Its website provides information on the purpose and current activities of the Center. It includes details about the holdings of the Julian P. Kanter Political Commercial Archive, which has copies of US radio party political broadcasts from 1936 onwards and TV adverts from 1956 to date.

1389   Stanford University, Political Communication Lab
http://pcl.stanford.edu/
Housed within the Institute for Communication Research at Stanford University, PCL conducts research into American political behaviour and public opinion using online and traditional methods. It is particularly noted for its research into the use of the media during election campaigns. Papers and reports covering federal and presidential elections from 2000 onwards can be accessed free of charge from its website. Other key areas include analysis of political advertising and examinations of the nature and impact of the use of the internet upon political communication.

Associations & societies

1390   Political Cartoon Society
www.politicalcartoon.co.uk/
British association which seeks to promote the study of cartoons as a source of political and social history. Its website provides information on its London Cartoon Gallery, plus recent exhibitions and events. Also provided is a brief

history of cartoons and biographies of important cartoonists from the 19th century to the present.

Portal & task environments

1391   Rhetorica network
http://rhetorica.net/
Maintained by Dr Andrew R. Cline of Missouri State University, this site offers comment and analysis of political rhetoric, political journalism and spin. The main emphasis is on examples from the USA. It includes full-text scholarly articles from the *Rhetorica Press-Politics Journal*, links to media websites and commentary on current news events. Students may also benefit from consulting the online rhetoric primer, which contains a brief history of rhetoric, introduction to the main canons and useful advice on research techniques

Directories & encyclopedias

1392   International encyclopedia of propaganda
R. Colt   Fitzroy Dearborn Publishers, 1999, 1000pp. £150. ISBN 9781579580230.
Wide-ranging volume containing over 500 entries on the history, politics, culture and sociological aspects of propaganda worldwide. Entries include notable theorists, organizations and political systems that have utilized propaganda. It includes coverage of the use of political posters and art forms as a source of propaganda. Emphasis on 19th and 20th century.

1393   Propaganda and mass persuasion: a historical encyclopedia, 1500 to the present
N. Cull, D. Culbert and D. Welch   ABC-CLIO, 2003, 450pp. £59.50. ISBN 9781576078204.
A readable introduction to the history and methods of propaganda worldwide from 1500 to the present. Comprises 250 entries on different methods of persuasion, political movements, individuals and specific films and publicity campaigns. Includes timely discussion of political communication and the 'war on terrorism'. A useful introductory essay provides background on the history and evolution of propaganda. Bibliographies of further references are provided.

Types of Communication

Introductions to the subject

1394   Iain Dale's guide to political blogging in the UK: a guide to problems and literature
I. Dale   Politicos Publishing, 2006, 32pp. £10. ISBN 1904734189.
www.iaindale.com
Iain Dale is a well known right-of-centre UK political commentator. His guide includes handy tips on maintaining a blog as well as his top 100 rankings of British political blogs. These are subdivided into lists of Labour Party, Conservative Party and non-aligned blogs. The guide can also be downloaded from his website.

Official & quasi-official bodies

1395 Great Britain. E-Government Unit
www.cabinetoffice.gov.uk/e-government/
Based within the UK Cabinet office, this is the body responsible for formulating British government IT strategy. It is therefore a key resource for locating copies of current UK government press releases, guidelines, policy documents and research reports relating to all aspects of the practice and implementation of e-government. This includes technical specifications and research, information security documents, materials relating to accessibility issues and examples of ongoing electronic government initiatives.

1396 World Bank's e-government website
www.worldbank.org/egov
This site is maintained by the World Bank's Information Solutions Group. It provides free access to an online library of materials relating to World Bank e-government programmes worldwide. Materials accessible include webcasts, online statistics, policy documents and research reports. These cover issues relating to electronic services, e-procurement, information security and ICT technology. They are a particularly rich source of information on the development and use of electronic government in developing nations.

Research centres & institutes

1397 Center for Technology in Government
www.ctg.albany.edu
Based at the University of Albany, New York, this specialist research centre works with the US government to develop and manage technology issues in the public sector, including the implementation of the electronic delivery of government services. Its website provides information on the work of the Center, its purpose and current activities. It includes access to the full text of its recent reports on technical issues, security and policy relating to e-government in the USA.

1398 Center of Excellence for Electronic Government
www.electronic-government.ch
This research centre is based at the Universität St Gallen. It conducts research into all aspects of the electronic delivery of government services, including access, infrastructure and information security in Europe. Its website provides information on the purpose and work of the centre. It includes access to the full text of a growing collection of its newsletters, working papers and reports. It also includes an impressive collection of links to e-government sites and documents available elsewhere on the internet.

Government on the web
See entry no. 2045

1399 Institute for Politics, Democracy & the Internet
www.ipdi.org/
A specialist centre based at George Washington University, it is well known for its research into the use of the internet and new communication technologies as a means to enhance democracy. The website provides access to news about recent projects and full-text papers and reports. The latter include studies on the use of mobile technology, political blogs and the web as a source of political communication in the USA. There are also free materials which offer tips for politicians on how to use the new technology to communicate with the electorate.

1400 Politech Institute: European Center of Political Technologies
www.politech-institute.org/
An international association and research body based in Brussels. It aims to act as a forum for news, research and training about the use of ICT in enhancing democracy and governance in Europe. This covers a wide range of research areas, including e-government, e-participation and e-democracy. Its website is a good source of information about current projects and events in this field. It also provides free access to articles from its journal *The European Review of Political Technologies*.

Portal & task environments

1401 Asia Pacific e-government portal
http://egovaspac.apdip.net
An online library of materials relating to electronic government development in nations of the Asia-Pacific region. It is maintained by a number of leading intergovernmental organizations, including the e-ASEAN Task Force and the Foundation for IT Education and Development (FIT-ED) and offers free access to case studies, documents, papers and reports. It is possible to browse the site or view materials relating to specific nations. Coverage includes technical and social issues associated with information technology.

1402 Government Exchange (GovXchange)
www.govx.org.uk
A portal of information on e-government initiatives which is maintained by SIAG (Socitm Information Age Group), in partnership with eGov Monitor. It offers free access to news stories, discussion and a library of full-text documents, legislation and reports covering all aspects of electronic government. This includes the technical, social and legal issues involved in the practical implementation of electronic public services. Main emphasis is on British examples.

1403 Political Advertising Resource Center
www.umdparc.org
The Political Advertising Resource Center (PARC) is a project of the Center for Political Communication and Civic Leadership at the University of Maryland which specializes in the analysis of the role of political adverts in US politics. Its website contains a wealth of useful information on this subject, including a history of the use of advertising, summaries of recent trends and information on its regulation. Also accessible is a database of examples of political adverts. This includes video clips from presidential, federal and mid-term election campaign commercials since 1994, with accompanying papers analysing their themes and impact.

Digital data, image & text collections

1404 The living room candidate: presidential election campaign commercials 1952–2004
http://livingroomcandidate.movingimage.us/index.php
Fascinating site created by the American Museum of the Moving Image in association with the Political Communication Center of the University of Oklahoma. It provides free access to over 180 examples of political adverts produced during presidential election campaigns from 1952 to 2004. Each advert contains a transcript and summary of the themes addressed. Examples from 2004 include websites and webcasts created by presidential candidates. The site also contains a teacher's resource centre with suggested lesson plans and classroom activities.

1405 United Nations egovernment readiness knowledge base
www.unpan.org/egovkb/
Created by the Division for Public Administration and Development Management (DPADM) of the United Nations Department of Economic and Social Affairs (UNDESA) this site provides researchers with free access to statistical data and selected reports about the state of e-government readiness and delivery worldwide. The primary source of the data is the United Nations Global E-Readiness Reports and Survey. It is possible to consult country profiles and build comparative graphs and charts of data. Topics covered include web access, e-participation and e-government services. Dates of coverage are displayed on the site.

Handbooks & manuals

1406 The Sage handbook of political advertising
C. Holtz-Bacha and L.L. Kaid, eds   Sage Publications, 2006, 492pp. £75. ISBN 9781412917957.
Collection of scholarly essays which examine the differences and similarities of political advertising in nations worldwide. Includes coverage of Europe, North America, Asia, Africa and Australia. Entries for individual nations contain summaries of political advertising history, regulation, structure and recent research. Examples are taken from recent election campaigns.

Keeping up to date

1407 DoWire: Democracies online newswire
www.dowire.org/
A free blog and e-mail announcements service which is invaluable for all students and researchers of online politics, e-government and internet activism. Maintained since 1998 by e-democracy expert Steven Clift, it provides regular updates on news stories with links to online reports, conference announcements and key projects. The website supports many e-mail discussion groups as well as maintaining an archive of resources, including links to online books, articles, webcasts and wikis about all aspects of e-democracy.

1408 E-Government bulletin
Headstar, 1997–. Free.
www.headstar.com/egb/
The first free e-mail newsletter to be published in the UK focusing entirely on the use of the internet and digital technologies by UK central and local government and other public service bodies. It is an excellent starting point for the latest news on e-government events, projects, services and technology. Each newsletter includes useful summaries and links to related websites. The website has a searchable archive of issues, plus online debates, blogs and conference features.

Elections
campaign finance • election law • electoral reform • parliamentary constituencies • proportional representation • referendums • voting technology

Introductions to the subject

1409 Congressional elections: campaigning at home and in Washington
P.S. Herrnson   4th edn, CQ press, 2003, 308pp. £22. ISBN 9781568028262.
A useful textbook for starting research on US elections and election campaign finance. It provides a clear explanation of each of the key stages of the campaign, the main players and regulations. Helpful features include the detailed charts and statistics on the changing patterns of congressional elections and the case studies of examples from the 2002 elections. Discussion of recent steps to reform election campaigns and political finance is provided.

1410 Politico's guide to election practice and law
S. Child   Politico's Publishing, 2001, 379pp. £40. ISBN 9781902301815.
Introductory guide to the legislation governing contemporary British electoral practice. Includes coverage of the selection of candidates, parliamentary elections, local government elections, European elections and elections in Wales, Scotland and Northern Ireland. Clear language and succinct explanations make it a particularly useful starting point for students and novices.

Dictionaries, thesauri, classifications

1411 Spanish language glossary of election terms
United States. Election Assistance Commission   2007, 73pp. www.eac.gov/research_reports_glossary.htm
This useful glossary of English terms was compiled in 2007 by the US Election Assistance Commission (q.v.). It translates from English to Spanish 1843 terms and phrases used in the administration of elections in the USA. These include terms used in state and local elections, ballot papers and election campaigns.

Laws, standards, codes

1412 US Electoral College
www.archives.gov/federal-register/electoral-college
Official site of the National Archives and Records Administration (NARA), which provides information about the American electoral college. It includes an explanation of its operation, with extracts from the relevant procedural guides and provisions of the US constitution and electoral laws. Also

provided is statistical data on elections by state for every American presidential election since 1789 and a collection of online lesson plans for teachers.

Official & quasi-official bodies

1413 EU Election observation and assistance
http://ec.europa.eu/comm/external_relations/human_rights/eu_electi on_ass_observ/index.htm
An official website of the European Union which provides information on the work of the EU in observing and monitoring elections. It contains information on codes of conduct and the methodology of international election observation missions as well as free access to an archive of all EU election observation reports from 2000 to the present. These contain detailed examination of the conduct of specific parliamentary and presidential election campaigns, analysing the legislative and organizational frameworks as well as offering insight into the state of democracy in the nation concerned. While the main focus of interest is on European countries, examples of reports from other areas of the world can also be found on the website.

1414 Federal Election Commission
www.fec.gov/
A body created by the US government which is responsible for administering and enforcing American election campaign finance regulations. Its website provides free access to full-text US electoral laws, including policy statements, advisory opinions and examples of key court cases from the 1970s onwards. It also hosts substantial databases of campaign finance reports and data. These enable users to find out who receives political donations and where they come from. It is possible to download all financial disclosure reports filed by House, Senate and Presidential campaigns since 1993.

1415 Great Britain. Boundary Committee for England
www.boundarycommittee.org.uk
A non-departmental public body which advises on and conducts regular reviews of the parliamentary boundaries in England. Its website contains useful information on the current English electoral constituencies, as well as providing free access to news headlines and consultation reports relating to ongoing boundary reviews.

1416 Great Britain. Electoral Commission
www.electoralcommission.gov.uk/
An independent body, accountable to the UK parliament, which is responsible for regulating elections and promoting voter awareness. Its website is a key resource for tracing news, legislation and full-text research documents relating to all aspects of electoral administration. The section on elections includes all UK general and local election results from 2001 onwards, plus reports on voter registration, election turnout and absentee voting. Another key feature is the online research registers. These provide official listings of UK political parties, annual accounts of political parties, information on donations made to political parties and election campaign expenditure by British political parties from approximately 2001 onwards.

1417 Great Britain. Local Government Boundary Commission for Scotland
www.bcomm-scotland.gov.uk

Official site of the organization responsible for the review of parliamentary constituency boundaries and local government structure and boundaries in Scotland. Provides free access to maps of current official Scottish Parliament regions and constituencies. Site also includes text of documents relating to the Commission, including its code of practice, biographies of the Commissioners, the text of relevant legislation and reviews currently in progress and publications.

1418 Office for Democratic Institutions & Human Rights
[EUR]
www.osce.org/odihr-elections/
The Office for Democratic Institutions & Human Rights (ODIHR) of the OSCE (Organization for Security & Cooperation in Europe) is Europe's leading agency in the field of election observation. Its website provides free access to its handbooks and guidelines relating to election administration and monitoring procedures. It also offers an extremely valuable collection of its country reports. These include assessments of the conduct and outcome of parliamentary and presidential elections in OSCE nations and some other non-OSCE areas, from approximately 1995 onwards. They are particularly useful sources of information on elections in the post-communist nations of Eastern Europe.

1419 United Nations, Electoral Assistance Division
www.un.org/Depts/dpa/ead/eadhome.htm
Part of the United Nations Department of Political Affairs. It provides assistance to nations to facilitate the organization of democratic elections. Its website provides information on its mandate and activities. It includes access to all its reports and resolutions from 1991 to the present. Also available is a directory of election experts, information on training courses and recent election news.

1420 United States. Election Assistance Commission
www.eac.gov
Established by the Help America Vote Act 2002, the EAC acts as a national clearinghouse to provide the public with information on all aspects of the administration of federal elections in the USA. Its website includes a wealth of background information about American elections. This includes press releases and news, explanations of the electoral system and voter registration procedures. Also accessible are historical datasets of election results and voter turnout levels from the 1960s to the present, full-text electoral laws and a collection of online reports, standards and regulations relating to the conduct of elections and the use of electronic voting in American elections.

1421 United States. Federal Election Committee
www.fec.gov
The Federal Election Committee (FEC) was created by the US government in 1975 as an independent regulatory body with responsibility for enforcing electoral law, disclosing campaign finance information to the public and administering the public funding of presidential elections. Its website contains detailed information about these three aspects of its role. It includes a guide to current US electoral law and proposals from the FEC about how the electoral and campaign finance laws could be reformed. Also available is detailed statistical information on campaign finance. This includes financial information about the parties, FEC audit reports of the most

recent presidential election campaigns and FEC disclosure reports filed by individual committees and campaigns. Additional features of the site are: statistics on voter registration and turnout for general elections since 1960 a directory of current election officials and access to a searchable database of advisory opinions from the mid-1970s onwards.

Research centres & institutes

1422   AEI-Brookings election reform project
www.electionreformproject.org
A joint initiative of the Brookings Institution and the American Enterprise Institute for Public Policy launched in 2006 with the aim of highlighting recent research relating to all aspects of US elections. Its website provides information about the aims of the project, its activities and events. It also acts as a clearing house, giving free access to full-text articles, papers and reports from leading US research bodies and think-tanks. Topics covered include voting technology, electoral fraud, election administration and absentee voting.

1423   Caltech-MIT voting technology project
www.vote.caltech.edu
Specialist research centre which was established to prevent a recurrence of the vote-counting problems in the 2000 American presidential election. Its website provides access to information on recent research relating to election management and integrity in the USA. It includes news stories, datasets and full-text working papers and reports. These analyse voting technology, the reliability of electronic voting systems and the risk of electoral fraud in the USA.

1424   Campaign Finance Institute
www.cfinst.org
A non-profit research institute, affiliated with George Washington University, which specializes in the study of issues relating to the economics and financing of American elections. Its website hosts a campaign finance disclosure clearing house which offers free access to full-text papers, research reports, legislation and statistics about money and American Senate, House and presidential elections from approximately 2004 to the present.

1425   Center for Responsive Politics
www.opensecrets.org/
A non-profit research group that specializes in the study of the role money plays in US elections. Its website is one of the best places for finding news reports and data about political donations and election campaign funding in the USA. It includes free access to data relating to sources of money in presidential and congressional election campaigns from 2000 onwards, lists and background on leading political donors and access to relevant codes and regulations.
- **Capital Eye** www.capitaleye.org/. The free regular newsletter maintained by the Center provides news and essays for the general public on issues relating to the role of money in the American political system. It is possible to access all issues from 2002 onwards.

1426   Centre d'Études et de Documentation sur la Démocratie Directe
http://c2d.unige.ch
C2D is a research and documentation centre on direct

democracy which is based in the Department of Constitutional Law at the University of Geneva. It conducts research on 'direct democracy'. This is defined to include coverage of national referendums and popular votes worldwide. Its website is one of the best places for locating material on historical, current and future referendums. It contains a database of referendum results from 1791 to the present, a bibliography of references to relevant journal articles and reports and an extensive library of online research papers. There is also a useful calendar of forthcoming referendums.

1427   Centre for Research into Elections & Social Trends
www.crest.ox.ac.uk/
Founded in 1994, the Centre for Research into Elections and Social Trends (CREST) is an Economic & Social Research Council Research Centre currently based jointly at the Department of Sociology, University of Oxford, and the National Centre for Social Research. It is renowned for its ongoing research into British elections. This includes coverage of local and mayoral elections and elections to the Scottish Parliament and National Assembly for Wales. Key themes of research include understanding voting intentions and trends, comparing British attitudes with other nations and the measurement of voting behaviour. The website provides free access to working papers, surveys and data produced by the centre. These include materials relating to the British Election Panel surveys from 1992 to the present.

1428   Electoral Institute of South Africa
www.eisa.org.za
A non-profit organization which aims to strengthen democracy in African nations. Its website is a rich source of information about the elections and political systems in nations of Southern Africa. It includes country profiles, archives of election results and reports on the observation of elections and the state of democracy from the mid-1990s onwards. Key countries covered are: South Africa, Angola, Botswana, Burundi, Democratic Republic of the Congo, Lesotho, Madagascar, Malawi, Mauritius, Mozambique, Namibia, Seychelles, Swaziland, Tanzania, Zambia and Zimbabwe.

1429   European election studies
www.europeanelectionstudies.net
A network of researchers who have been studying electoral participation and voting behaviour in European Parliament elections since 1979. It is possible to access information and research papers relating to their findings. These include materials relating to election manifestos. Data on voting in EU parliament elections since 2004 can also been downloaded from the website.

1430   International Foundation for Election Systems
www.ifes.org/
A private non-profit organization which was established in 1987 to support electoral and democratic institutions in developing countries. Its website is an excellent starting point for finding information about parliamentary and presidential elections worldwide. It includes extensive news headlines, background information on countries and online monitoring reports. Key features include:
- **Election guide** www.electionguide.org/ [24/06/2006]. Up-to-date news and listings of national level parliamentary and presidential elections worldwide. Entries on individual countries include basic social and

economic data taken from the Cambridge FactFinder, previous election results and facts about the electoral system. Users may sign up to receive e-mail notifications of forthcoming elections.

- **Money and politics net** www.moneyandpolitics.net/ [24/06/2006]. A special project which aims to promote transparency in elections worldwide. In addition to campaign news, the site also offers free access to databases which trace issues relating to political donations and political funding in nations worldwide.

1431   National Democratic Institute for International Affairs
www.ndi.org/
An American non-profit organization which works to strengthen democratic development worldwide. Its website provides information on its aims and recent activities, including democratic and civic education programmes and election observation missions. It maintains a particularly useful feature called Access Democracy which aims to provide democratic activists with a collection of free online resources. These include several hundred country fact files (containing recent accessments of democracy, news headlines and election monitoring reports), plus training handbooks and case studies.

Associations & societies

1432   Asian Network for Free Elections
www.anfrel.org
A network of civil society organizations which was founded in 1997 to promote democracy and free elections in Asian nations. Its website provides information on the aims of the organization, its membership and recent activities. It includes press releases about recent and forthcoming Asian parliamentary and presidential elections, plus access to a growing collection of full-text election monitoring reports. Other useful features include summaries of the constitutions, electoral laws and election codes of individual nations. Countries covered include Bangladesh, Cambodia, India, Indonesia, Japan, Nepal, Pakistan, Philippines, South Korea, Sri Lanka and Thailand.

1433   Association of Central & Eastern European Election Officials
www.aceeeo.org/
Professional association which aims to support the work of electoral officials in nations of Eastern and Central Europe and to promote democracy in this region. Its website is particularly useful for tracing information on elections and electoral system development in the post-communist nations of Europe. It includes election results, details of democratization projects and some full-text election observation reports. These cover the period since 1991.

1434   Common Cause
www.commoncause.org
An independent organization which was founded in 1970 to give citizens a voice in US politics. It is well regarded for its work on electoral reform, ethics and accountability in American government. It is possible to view a library of many of its recent reports online. These include coverage of topical subjects such as money in politics and electoral redistricting. The site also contains blogs which can be used to gain insight into the latest news stories and research.

1435   Electoral Reform Society
www.electoral-reform.org.uk
Originally founded in 1884 as the Proportional Representation Society, the ERS is one of the oldest organizations in the UK concerned with the study of electoral systems. It actively seeks to promote the Single Transferable Vote (STV) system. Its website provides information on its aims, campaigns and electoral system research. It includes access to recent news bulletins, online pamphlets and reports. These include materials relating to its campaigns to reform the British electoral system and coverage of recent election campaigns in England, Scotland, Wales and Northern Ireland.

1436   International Institute for Democracy & Electoral Assistance
www.idea.int/
An intergovernmental organization which seeks to promote the growth of democratic culture and to support electoral processes worldwide. Its website is an invaluable source of background information on political systems and elections worldwide. It provides free access to press releases, reports, statistics and facts about the key themes of democracy, political parties and women in politics.

- **Voter turnout** www.idea.int/vt/index.cfm. A searchable database of statistics for voter turnout in 171 states worldwide from 1945 onwards. It enables analysis of trends over time and between different geographical regions. Topics covered include: the effect of compulsory versus voluntary voting, the impact of the type of electoral system and the type of social, economic and political factors which encourage and discourage political involvement.
- **Women in politics** www.idea.int/gender/ [24/06/2006]. News, reports and data on women's political participation worldwide. It includes statistics on voter turnout by gender, women's political participation and details about quota systems.

1437   McDougall Trust
www.mcdougall.org.uk
UK-based charity established in 1948 to further the study of politics, functions of government, elections and electoral systems. It maintains the Lakeman Library for Electoral Studies, one of the world's most extensive collections of material on electoral issues. It also houses the archives of the Electoral Reform Society (q.v.). Its website provides information on the aims of the Trust, its organization, history and activities. Users may access tables of contents and full-text articles from its journal *Voting Matters* from 1994 onwards. Topics covered include discussion of single transferable voting systems and electronic voting.

1438   Proportional Representation Society of Australia
www.cs.mu.oz.au/~lee/prsa/
A society which supports the introduction of proportional voting in Australia. Its website provides information on its aims and campaigns. It provides free access to a good collection of news stories, online articles and reports about the history and use of PR in Australia and New Zealand. There are also directories of links to related organizations. These complement materials available on websites based in Europe and the USA.

Portal & task environments

1439   ACE electoral knowledge network
http://ace.at.org/
Launched in 2006 by a consortium of seven organizations, including UNDP, IDEA, the Instituto Federal Electoral, IFES, Democracy at Large, Elections Canada, EISA and the United Nations Department of Economic and Social Affairs. It provides free access to key resources on all aspects of election administration. These include an elections calendar, an encyclopedia of articles on election management, comparative data on elections and electoral systems in individual nations worldwide and an electronic library of electoral materials containing sample ballot papers. The site also supports discussion forums for electoral officials.

1440   Observatorio electoral Latin America (Latin American electoral observatory)
www.observatorioelectoral.org/
An excellent resource for tracing Spanish-language information about parliamentary and presidential elections in Latin American countries. In addition to current news headlines, it also offers country profiles containing details of the electoral system and recent election results. Many of the profiles contain historical datasets of election results that can be downloaded and academic papers offering analysis.

1441   Proportional representation library
www.mtholyoke.edu/acad/polit/damy/prlib.htm
An excellent online library of resources relating to proportional representation which is maintained by Professor Douglas J. Amy, Department of Politics, Mount Holyoke College. It provides free access to a collection of online introductory readings and articles, a bibliography of relevant textbooks and articles and a directory of links to the websites of relevant organizations, research bodies and campaigns worldwide.

Digital data, image & text collections

1442   American National Election Studies
www.electionstudies.org/
American National Election Studies is an organization that conducts national surveys of the American electorate. Its website contains a data centre where users may download files, surveys, questionnaires and associated documentation from 1948 onwards. Topics covered include election trends, voter turnout levels, and political participation among the American electorate. The site also contains numerous research papers which analyse the results and provide information about the methodology used to obtain them.

1443   Angus Reid Global Monitor
www.angus-reid.com/
A free database containing thousands of public opinion polls and surveys. They include voting intentions, approval ratings for governments and political leaders and reactions to world events. Materials are international in coverage, many date back to the mid-1990s. Some information on poll methodologies is provided. It is possible to use the site to trace the existence and results of polls conducted by foreign newspapers and other agencies during parliamentary and presidential elections worldwide.

1444   Australian government and politics database
http://elections.uwa.edu.au
Maintained by researchers at the University of Western Australia, this comprehensive database provides free access to a wealth of facts and figures about Australian politics from 1890 to the present. It includes results of all state assembly (lower house) general elections since 1890. Also accessible is data about individual political parties, governments and state legislatures. An additional feature is a useful glossary of Australian political terms.

1445   British Election Studies information system
www.besis.org/
A website maintained by the Centre for Comparative European Survey Data. It aims to make information, reports and data from the British Election Studies Survey accessible in a user-friendly way. As such its content complements the more in-depth materials provided by the main British Election Studies website at the University of Essex. It currently contains social survey and statistical data from 1966 to 2005. This includes full election results, results by political party and information on voter turnout levels. Access to the full data requires registration.

1446   British Election Study at the University of Essex
www.essex.ac.uk/BES/
The British Election Study (BES) has taken place at every general election since 1964. Its purpose is to understand why people vote and how and why they vote the way they do. It covers several main subject areas: political preferences and values, economic perceptions, social attitudes, dispositions to engage in different forms of political activity, and individual and household socio-demographic characteristics. Its official website at the University of Essex offers detailed scholarly information on the methodology, aims and outputs of the study. It includes press releases and full-text research papers. Links are provided to the website of the UK Data Archive, where researchers may register to gain access to the online datasets from 1963 onwards. Eligibility for this is displayed on the website. Undergraduates and the public may also find it useful to consult the complementary British Election Studies Information System (BESIS) website, which provides a clear introduction to the survey.

1447   Canadian election study
www.ces-eec.umontreal.ca/
A research project undertaken by Toronto, McGill and Montreal Universities. It conducts regular large scale surveys into the attitudes of Canadian voters. The website provides background documentation on the purpose of the survey and its methodology. It includes large-scale datasets which can be downloaded in SPSS format, research papers and copies of the questionnaires issued since 1997.

1448   David Leip's atlas of US presidential elections
http://uselectionatlas.org
This site is maintained by enthusiast David Leip from data supplied by US official electoral agencies. It provides access to all national results for candidates in US presidential elections from 1789 to the present. Maps and charts of voter turnout, total votes for candidates, states and parties are available from 1932 onwards. In addition, state election results with county level maps are offered from 1960. The site has a larger, more comprehensive set of data for presidential elections since 2000.

1449   Election results archive
http://cdp.binghamton.edu/era/index.html
This site is maintained by the Center on Democratic
Performance, Binghamton University. It provides free access
to a collection of national parliamentary and presidential
election results from over 134 countries worldwide dating
from 1974 to the present. Information on the compilation of
the data is provided on the website.

1450   General Election 2005 internet sites
www.webarchive.org.uk/col/c8100.html
The UK Web Archiving Consortium is composed of six
leading British research institutions – the British Library,
National Archives, Wellcome Library, JISC, the National
Library of Scotland and National Library of Wales – that are
seeking to archive important British websites for posterity.
Their website provides access to technical information about
the project and a searchable catalogue of archived websites.
There is a special collection of materials relating to the 2005
UK general election. These include examples of the websites
of the main political parties, pressure groups and political
commentators which have been captured on a number of
specific dates during the election campaign. They offer a
fascinating insight into the development of ideas and
political communication techniques during the election.

1451   HarpWeek presidential elections 1860–1912
http://elections.harpweek.com/
Free access to a fascinating collection of digitized political
cartoons relating to American presidential election
campaigns 1860–1912 which were originally published in
Harpers Weekly, *Vanity Fair*, *Frank Leslie's Weekly* and *Puck*.
They include many examples of political satire and
caricature. Annotations are provided which set each of the
cartoons in their historical context and explain the key
political issues at stake in each of the elections.

1452   Lijphart elections archive
http://dodgson.ucsd.edu/lij/
The Lijphart Elections archive is based at the University of
California, San Diego. It is a famous research collection of
district level historical election results for over 350 national
legislative elections in 26 nations worldwide. It covers
election results up to 2003. The catalogue of holdings also
provides references to key printed resources for tracing
electoral data on individual nations.

1453   New Zealand election study
www.nzes.org/
Based at the University of Waikato, New Zealand this major
research study analyses political behaviour in New Zealand.
The main areas of study include voting choices, political
opinions and social and demographic factors relating to
voting. Users may download NZES data files, research
publications and reports published since 1990. These are of
particular value in examining the impact of the change to a
proportional representation voting system.The site also
provides free access to data, election results and voter
turnout levels for all New Zealand parliamentary elections
from 1905 onwards.

1454   Ordnance Survey election maps
www.election-maps.co.uk/
Maintained by the Ordnance Survey mapping agency, this
site provides free access to official maps of current electoral

boundaries in Great Britain and Northern Ireland. They are
particularly useful for students and teachers, offering the
facility to view the maps in different scales or to see the
overlap between the various administrative and electoral
districts. A collection of suggested lesson plans is also
provided.

1455   Psephos Adam Carr's election archive
http://psephos.adam-carr.net/
Extensive online archive of historical election results
maintained by enthusiast Dr Adam Carr. It contains entries
for over 160 nations worldwide, offering election results and
statistics for national, presidential and local elections.
Particularly detailed is the collection of Australian election
results, which has Federal elections statistics from 1901 and
state and territory statistics from 1990. Also accessible are
geographical maps of election results for individual nations.

Directories & encyclopedias

1456   American presidential campaigns and elections
W.J. Shade, B.C. Campbell and C.R. Coenen, eds   Sharpe Reference,
2003, 1250pp. 3 v., £273. ISBN 0765680424.
Collection of 62 long essays, providing comprehensive
coverage of all US presidential elections from 1789 to 2000.
Individual entries include full election results, discussion of
the candidates, issues, campaigns and historical context. The
encyclopedia also contains entries relating to the electoral
system, electoral laws and the electorate. Other features
include chronologies of key events, maps of election results
and reprints of key primary source documents, including
speeches, election posters and campaign materials.

1457   British electoral facts: 1832–1999
C. Rallings [et al.]   6th edn, Ashgate, 2000, 336pp. £80. ISBN
9781840140538.
Single volume which contains facts and figures on all aspects
of British general elections, by-elections, European
Parliament elections, local government elections,
referendums and public opinion polls. In addition to listing
all the main election results, it also contains useful chapters
on electoral irregularities, the accuracy of public opinion
polls in predicting election results and a fun election trivia
section which will satisfy all quiz addicts.

1458   Encyclopaedia of European elections
Y. Déloye and M. Bruter, eds   Palgrave Macmillan, 2007, 552pp.
£100. ISBN 1403994846.
Over 140 articles covering the history, evolution, social,
political and economic aspects of European elections. It
includes entries for every political party in the European
parliament and discussion of the impact of the elections on
national politics in individual nations. Two introductory
essays provide background on the geography of European
electoral politics.

1459   International encyclopedia of elections
R. Rose, ed.   Palgrave Macmillan, 2000, 500pp. £130. ISBN
9780333927458.
Provides an accessible survey of concepts related to all
forms of elections worldwide. It includes coverage of
European Parliament elections, national parliamentary
elections, local elections, presidential elections and
referendums. Definitions are also provided for technical

terms relating to electoral systems and voting. An appendix provides information on elections in specific nations.

Handbooks & manuals

1460 America at the polls: a handbook of American presidential election statistics
A.V. McGillivray, R.M. Scammon and R. Cook, comps   CQ Press, 2005, 2288pp. 2 v., £185. ISBN 1568029780.
A invaluable source of American election statistics. The volumes can be purchased separately or as a set. Together they provide comprehensive data, tables and graphs offering easily understandable state-by-state results from presidential elections between 1920 and 2000. Also included are electoral college votes and data from presidential primaries.
- **1. Harding to Eisenhower: 1920–1956** R. Scammon   CQ Press, 1994, 937pp. £117. ISBN 9781568020587.
- **2. John F. kennedy to George W. Bush: 1960–2000** R. Cook [et al.]   CQ Press, 2001, 1097pp. £141. ISBN 9781568026046.

1461 Britain votes 2005
P. Norris and C. Wlezien, eds   Oxford University Press, 2005, 251pp. £16.99. ISBN 9780198569404.
Fourth volume in a well regarded series which has been published by Oxford University Press following every British general election since 2005. Written by experts, it contains a collection of scholarly essays on how and why the Labour Party won the 2005 election. These include detailed surveys of the election campaigns, opinion polls and media coverage. Also provided is an in-depth analysis of the results which includes discussion of the electoral system, economic voting and race and gender issues.

1462 British general election manifestos 1959–1987
F.W.S. Craig, ed.   3rd edn, Methuen Publishing, 1990, 544pp. £66.50. ISBN 9780900178344.
Third edition of a key series which reprints in full the election manifestos of the British Conservative, Liberal and Labour parties during the period 1900–1987. Separate manifestos issued by these parties to cover Scotland and Wales are listed but not reproduced. Each volume within the series covers a slightly different date range.
- **British general election manifestos 1900–1974** 2nd edn, Macmillan, 1975. o/p.
- **British general election manifestos, 1918–66** Methuen, 1970. o/p. ISBN 9780900178030.

1463 Congressional Quarterly's guide to US elections
J.L. Moore, J.P. Preimesberger and D.R. Tarr   5th edn, CQ Press, 2005, 1101pp. 2 v., £185. ISBN 9781568020818.
Detailed coverage of US presidential, congressional and gubernatorial elections. Explains the historical origins and evolution of American elections, offering details on the operation of the Electoral College and the performance of the main political parties. Also contains election maps, statistical results and chronologies of key events and legislation.

1464 Elections in Africa: a data handbook
D. Nohlen, B. Thibaut and M. Krennerich, eds   Oxford University Press, 1999, 1000pp. £107.50. ISBN 9780198296454.
Extremely detailed collection, giving the dates and results of all national elections, referendums and coups d'état in African states from independence until 1999. Individual

entries contain a brief history of the nation's political system, main political parties and electoral administration.

1465 Elections in Asia and the Pacific: a data handbook
D. Nohlen, F. Grotz and C. Hartmann, eds   Oxford University Press, 2001, 876pp. 2 v., £93.50. ISBN 9780199249596.
Provides detailed statistical information on all direct national elections and referendums in 61 states of Asia and the Pacific from independence to 1999. Each entry contains a historical overview of the political history, main political parties and evolution of the electoral system. An introductory essay compares the conduct of elections and electoral administration across the different nations of the region.

1466 Elections in the Americas: data handbook
D. Nohlen, ed.   Oxford University Press, 2005, 768pp. 2 v., £88. ISBN 9780199283576.
Authoritative two-volume set which contains the results of all elections and referenda in 35 nations of the Americas from the introduction of suffrage to 2005. It also includes an introductory essay on the comparative evolution of electoral systems in the region and individual country surveys which trace the historical development of the electoral system and electoral laws in specific nations. A useful index of party name abbreviations is provided.

1467 Elections in Western Europe since 1815: electoral results by constituencies
D. Caramani   Macmillan Reference, 2000, 800pp. £350. ISBN 0333771117.
Provides election results to constituency level for 18 Western European nations during the period 1815–1999. Sections on individual nations also include information on electoral law, developments in the electoral system and political party mergers and name changes. Introductory essays on the historical development of elections in Europe are also provided. Accompanying CD-ROM of data.

1468 Handbook of electoral system choice
J.M. Colomer, ed.   Palgrave Macmillan, 2004, 555pp. £79. ISBN 9781403904546.
A collection of essays which discuss the theory and practice of electoral reform in relation to the impact of electoral system choice upon democratization. It includes information on different types of electoral system, discussion of the main theoretical concepts and issues relating to them, plus case studies which review their performance in specific nations worldwide.

1469 The international almanac of electoral history
T. Mackie and R. Rose   3rd edn, Palgrave Macmillan, 1990, 511pp. £85. ISBN 9780333452790.
An authoritative compilation of electoral statistics from 25 industrialized nations: Australia 1901–1989, Austria 1919–1989, Belgium 1847–1989, Canada 1878–1989, Denmark 1901–1989, Finland 1907–1989, France 1910–1989, Germany 1871–1989, Greece 1928–1989, Iceland 1916–1989, Ireland 1918–1989, Israel 1949–1989, Italy 1895–1989, Japan 1890–1989, Luxembourg 1918–1989, Malta 1921–1989, Netherlands 1888–1989, New Zealand 1890–1989, Norway 1882–1989, Portugal 1975–1989, Spain 1931–1989, Sweden 1887–1989, Switzerland 1896–1989, UK 1885–1989 and USA

1828–1989. Each chapter gives a comprehensive listing of political parties, with data on their results in every election.

1470 Lobbying, government relations and campaign finance worldwide: navigating the laws, regulations and practices of national regimes
T. Grant Oceana, 2005, 654pp. £90. ISBN 9780379215373.
An expert guide to understanding the laws and regulations governing political activity in 30 of the major industrialized nations worldwide. The nations chosen are all members of the OECD and include USA, Australia, France and Germany. Individual country summaries highlight key areas of knowledge required by management consultants and lobbyists when operating in these countries. There is some brief comparison of the different regimes.

1471 Local elections in Britain: a statistical digest
C. Rallings and M. Thrasher, eds 2nd edn, Local Government Chronicle Elections Centre, University of Plymouth, 2003, 624pp. £125. ISBN 9780948858345.
www.plymouth.ac.uk/pages/view.asp?page=5855
Comprehensive guide to 20th-century local election results produced by staff of the LGC Local Elections Centre at the University of Plymouth. Contains ward-by-ward results for each local constituency, plus analysis of council composition, local political parties and the number of women councillors. An introductory essay analyses trends in the statistics. Additional information such as online election maps and examples of more recent research can be found on the LGC website.

1472 Media guide to the new parliamentary constituencies
C. Rallings and M. Thrasher 5th edn, Local Government Chronicle Elections Centre, 2007, 352pp. £30. ISBN 0948858451.
A well regarded guide to parliamentary constituencies which is compiled by staff of the Local Government Chronicle Elections Centre at the University of Plymouth. It is heavily used by the media to interpret the political impact of periodical reviews of the Parliamentary Boundary Commissions for England, Wales and Northern Ireland. It offers constituency-by-constituency data on changes to the electorate in the latest review. This includes detailed statistical tables on the precise composition of the new constituencies in terms of local authority wards and divisions, target lists for the main parties by rank order of swing to win, seats ranked by turnout/notional turnout at the 2005 general election. There is also a grid enabling readers to project the distribution of seats in a new House of Commons under different scenarios.

1473 A statistical history of the American electorate 1788–1999
J.G. Rusk CQ Press, 2001, 708pp. £42. ISBN 9781568023649.
Covers over 200 years of American election history, providing access to detailed statistical data and analysis of who voted and why. Includes discussion of voter turnout levels, the impact of changing electoral laws and the accuracy of election data. Materials relate to presidential, House, Senate and gubernatorial voting.

Keeping up to date

1474 UK Polling Report
http://ukpollingreport.co.uk
A free news service which summarizes and discusses recent UK political polls. It is produced in association with YouGov and covers voting intention polls conducted by YouGov, MORI, Populus and ICM. The website also offers a comprehensive listing of political blogs where further comment and discussion of polls may be easily found. While the emphasis is on recent polls, some archived materials, covering political trends from the 1980s to the present, may also be found.

International Relations

colonization • diaspora • diplomacy • European Union • foreign policy • global politics • human trafficking • international boundaries • international organizations • League of Nations • migration • refugees • theories & systems • United Nations

Introductions to the subject

1475 The globalization of world politics: an introduction to international relations
J. Baylis and S. Smith, eds 3rd edn, Oxford University Press, 2005, 848pp. £26.99. ISBN 9780199271184.
Recommended textbook which provides a readable introduction to modern international relations. Includes discussion of key concepts and theories, plus an overview of the historical development of international society since 1900. Includes chapters on the international political economy, security and terrorism in the post-Cold War world and the rise of the United Nations.

1476 International relations: a concise companion
D. Weigall Arnold, 2002, 256pp. £13.99. ISBN 9780340763339.
Designed to introduce students to the basic theories and historical context of international relations. Comprises 1500 entries covering key events, movements, concepts and organizations in the history of international relations from 1789 to 2002. Biographies are not included. Contains useful bibliographies to direct further reading.

1477 International relations theory: a critical introduction
C. Weber 2nd edn, Routledge, 2004, 208pp. £19.99. ISBN 9780415342087.
Easily accessible student guide to key theories. Explains and analyses the main areas of realism and neo-realism, idealism and neo-idealism, liberalism, constructivism, postmodernism, gender and globalization using examples of popular films to illustrate key points. Other useful features include boxed key concepts and guides to further reading.

Research centres & institutes

1478 Carnegie Council for Ethics in International Affairs
www.carnegiecouncil.org
A leading organization and think-tank providing discussions of ethics in international affairs. Its website provides information on its aims, activities, research and publications. It includes free access to a large library of transcripts of

events, audio and video interviews and discussions, and selected full-text articles from its academic journal *Ethics and International Affairs*. Key topics covered include ethics and warfare, religion in politics and global justice.

1479 Carnegie Endowment for International Peace

www.carnegieendowment.org/

Established in 1910, the Carnegie Endowment is recognized as one of the most important independent research and public policy centres covering all aspects of international relations and US foreign policy. Its website provides access to information about its research programmes and conferences. Topics covered by these include the US role in world affairs, terrorism and international security, non-proliferation, democracy and the rule of law, the position of China; and international trade and development. The website provides free access to many recently published briefing papers and reports. These frequently cover conflicts in the news such as the insurgency in Iraq and security in the post 9/11 world.

- **Central Asian voices** www.centralasianvoices.org. A specialist project of the Carnegie Foundation which provides provides free access to discussion and analysis about the five Central Asian republics of Kazakhstan, Kyrgyzstan, Tajikistan, Turkmenistan and Uzbekistan. This covers the economic; social and political development of the region. It includes news stories; full text articles; blogs and links to online documents. These cover the viewpoints of governments, journalists and scholars. There is also a useful directory of recommended websites for each nation.

1480 Centre d'Études et de Recherches Internationales

www.ceri-sciences-po.org

Founded in 1952 within the Fondation Nationale des Sciences Politiques, this is France's foremost centre for research on the international political system. Topics of interest include globalization, regional integration, the European Union, new forms of conflict, democratization, migration, nationalism and other political identities. Its website provides free access to information about current research projects and the full text of most *Etudes de CERI* from 1995 onwards, *Cahiers de CERI* from the mid-1990s to date and Russia papers from 2006 onwards.

1481 Chatham House

www.chathamhouse.org.uk/

One of the world's most famous international affairs think-tanks. Originally established in 1920 as the Royal Institute for International Affairs, its work on international security, the environment and development and international economics is regularly quoted in the press. Its website is worth checking regularly, as in addition to tables of contents from its journal *International Affairs* it often provides free access to selected briefing papers, articles and transcripts from conferences. Many of these focus on topical world events. Recent examples include the Gulf war, Islam and politics and UK–US transatlantic relations.

1482 Weatherhead Center for International Affairs

www.wcfia.harvard.edu

A leading research institute based at Harvard University. Its website provides information on teaching and research programmes covering all aspects of American foreign policy and international affairs. It is possible to download hundreds of examples of cutting-edge articles and working papers published since the late 1990s.

1483 Whitney & Betty MacMillan Center for International & Area Studies

www.yale.edu/macmillan

A major interdisciplinary research institute based at Yale University. Research covers all aspects of international affairs, international security and migration. Its website provides free access to an extensive collection of online working papers dating from the mid-1990s onwards. It is also possible to access an archive of audio and visual materials, including lectures and conferences hosted by the Center.

Associations & societies

1484 British International Studies Association

www.bisa.ac.uk

The main professional organization for scholars and practitioners of international relations in the UK. Its website provides a rich source of information on current scholarship, teaching programmes and research. It includes access to recent issues of its newsletter and tables of contents from its key publication *Review of International Studies* as well as the full text of some papers from recent annual conferences. These provide insight into the current state of IR scholarship.

- **Studying international relations** www.internationalstudies.ac.uk [24/06/2006]. Useful directory of undergraduate courses currently on offer at UK universities and colleges. Includes contact addresses, direct links to websites and helpful annotation on content and specialisms.

1485 European Information Network on International Relations

www.einiras.org

An association of European research institutions that work in the fields of documentation and information relating to international relations and world affairs. Its website provides information on the aims of the organization, its membership, events and conferences. It includes details of recent papers, some of which may be downloaded. A key theme is the availability of IR information online.

- **EINIRAS database network** http://einiras.coe.int/ [13/06/2006]. One of the key projects is the creation of this database which ultimately seeks to enable cross-searching of important international relations and politics bibliographic resources to enable researchers to quickly locate relevant book titles, articles and links to full-text working papers. It currently includes over 300,000 resources from several leading databases, including *The Royal Institute of International Affairs Journal*; articles of the database World Affairs Online of the Fachinformationsverbund Internationale Beziehungen und Länderkunde; Stockholm International Peace Research Institute; and journal articles of the CERES database of the Council of Europe.

1486 International Studies Association

www.isanet.org

Founded in 1959, the ISA is one of the largest and most respected organizations supporting the study and teaching of international affairs worldwide. Its website provides extensive information on its aims, history and activities. It includes a large collection of online conference papers from its annual conventions, plus listings of forthcoming events from many of its regional sections and specialist sub-groups. These include interesting examples of cutting-edge research. The site also contains tables of contents from the ISA's key journal publications *International Studies Quarterly*,

International Studies Review, International Studies Perspectives, Foreign Policy Analysis and *International Political Sociology*.

Portal & task environments

1487 CHOIKE: a portal on southern civil liberties
www.choike.org
This website is maintained by Instituto del Tercer Mundo, Uruguay. It provides access to press releases, commentary and full-text papers produced by non-governmental organizations and social movements from the Southern hemisphere (Africa, Asia and Latin America). These present a 'southern perspective' on world issues which is often a useful alternative to those offered by Western European and North American governments. Key topics are: civil liberties, human rights, globalization, international and regional trade, sustainable development and environmental policy. The site also includes a comprehensive directory of NGOs concerned with all aspects of civil society in the southern hemisphere.

1488 IGLOO portal
www.theigloo.org/
This site is maintained by the Centre for International Governance Innovation (CIGI), Canada. It aims to provide students and researchers with an online network for the exchange of information about all aspects of international relations. It includes links to blogs, online communities and an excellent library of internet resources. The latter contains links to a wealth of resources, including country profiles, news resources and research papers. A wide range of topics is covered, including international security, peacekeeping, international trade and globalization.

1489 WWW Virtual Library international affairs resources
www2.etown.edu/vl/
Part of the excellent WWW Virtual Library, this site offers a directory of over 2000 links to key internet resources covering all aspects of international relations. It can be browsed by geographical region or theme. Topics covered are wide-ranging in scope, including international human rights, regional security and American foreign policy. Sites include international organizations, research bodies, online journals and news media. Annotations on content are provided. The main emphasis is on English-language resources.

Digital data, image & text collections

1490 Columbia international affairs online: CIAO
Columbia University Press. Online database. USD $295 for individuals. Institutional rate calculated by number of full time students., $295.
www.ciaonet.org/
A highly regarded subscription database which contains a large number of full-text international relations journals, working papers and conference reports dating from 1991 to the present. These include publications from leading American and some British universities, NGOs and think-tanks. The database also contains original case studies written by leading international affairs experts and course packs of background readings particularly suitable for history and political science classes.

Directories & encyclopedias

1491 Encyclopedia of international relations and global politics
M. Griffiths   Routledge, 2005, 936pp. £110. ISBN 9780415311601.
A scholarly reference work providing coverage of developments in international relations theory since the ending of the Cold War, the rise of globalization and emergence of new forms of international terrorism. It contains over 50 long essays of more than 5000 words on core topics as well as other shorter entries. Topics covered draw upon recent developments in political theory, diplomacy, international security and international political economy. Each entry offers a short bibliography to guide further reading.

1492 The Greenwood encyclopedia of international relations
C.J. Nolan   Greenwood Press, 2002, 2000pp. 4 v., £270. ISBN 9780313307430.
Four-volume set containing over 6000 entries on the people, ideas and events that have shaped international relations. Primary concentration is on the history of the rise of the Great Powers and the key wars, and social and economic relations which have formed them.

1493 Twentieth century international relations
M. Cox, ed.   Sage Publications, 2006, 3328pp. 8 v., £900. ISBN 9781412910187.
A major eight-volume set of encyclopedias which provide comprehensive coverage of the key factors influencing the development of international relations in the 20th century. Contains over 80 thematically organized articles. Volumes 1–4 cover the breakdown of world peace in 1914, the emergence of the USA as a world power, the Cold War and the collapse of the Soviet Union. Volumes 5–8 explore the impact of the fall of communism in 1989. They also consider the effects of the 9/11 terrorist attacks on the future conduct of international relations.

1494 Who's who in international affairs
J. Johnson, comp.   5th edn, Routledge, 2006, 912pp. £320. ISBN 9781857433616.
A valuable source of basic biographical information on over 6000 persons associated with international affairs. These include politicians, government leaders, key diplomats, civil servants and heads of international organizations. Typical entries contain date of birth, details of education, qualifications, list of selected publications and contact address. There is a separate diplomatic representation index, listing names and contact addresses for ambassadors of 170 nations.

Handbooks & manuals

1495 International boundaries: a geopolitical atlas
E.W. Anderson   Stationery Office Books, 2003, 955pp. £60. ISBN 9780117026551.
Atlas of the international land and maritime boundaries of every currently recognized nation updated to 2003. Entries for individual countries include lists of major treaties and agreements relating to boundaries and critical assessments of current and future national border security and stability.

Keeping up to date

1496 **Le Monde Diplomatique**
Le Monde Diplomatique, monthly. £19.
http://mondediplo.com/
A leading monthly publication which focuses on international relations and political issues worldwide. It is particularly useful for providing Francophone perspectives on world events. Its website provides free access to some articles, access to the full-text and archive is for subscribers only. Subscriptions can be in print or online. The journal can be supplied in French, English and other European language versions.

1497 **Michael Moore**
www.michaelmoore.com
Official website of the famous American film-maker and social critic. It is a useful starting point for tracing examples of criticism of American foreign policy. Includes free access to a selection of his recent writings and teacher's guides to some of his famous films such as *Fahrenheit 9/11* and *Bowling for Columbine*. Also provided is a useful directory of links to the websites of social activist and protest movement groups.

1498 **NASPIR: network of activist scholars of politics and international relations**
http://groups.yahoo.com/group/naspir/
A network of scholars and researchers who support social justice and non-violent action against oppression. Their discussion forum is an excellent starting point for tracing information on radical politics and political activism. It regularly highlights new websites, conferences and publications. Topics covered have included criticism of the war in Iraq, anarchism, social movements and civil disobedience. It is possible to view all messages since 2003 on the website. Message posting requires registration.

1499 **YaleGlobal Online**
Yale Center for the Study of Globalization, 2002–.
http://yaleglobal.yale.edu/
An electronic journal published by the Yale Center for the Study of Globalization. It focuses on all aspects of the process and impact of globalization worldwide. This includes coverage of the changing nature of international relations, the international political economy, the impact on society and culture and issues relating to international security and terrorism. The site provides free access to all articles published since 2002. It also includes a growing collection of book reviews, video clips and multimedia files of academic lectures.

International Relations Theories & Systems

Dictionaries, thesauri, classifications

1500 **The Penguin dictionary of international relations**
G. Evans and J. Newnham   Penguin Books, 1998, 640pp. £10.99.
ISBN 9780140513974.
A valuable reference source for students providing definitions of the major concepts, theories and specialized terminology of international relations. Entries include citations to the individuals and works that introduced and popularized the terms. An extensive bibliography can be used to guide further reading.

Research centres & institutes

1501 **Centre for the Study of Global Governance**
www.lse.ac.uk/Depts/global/
A leading research centre based at the London School of Economics. It conducts interdisciplinary research into a wide range of areas relating to global governance. Key themes include global security, global civil society and the impact of globalization. Its website offers access to full-text working papers, research reports and public lectures. It is also possible to download free of charge all copies of the *Global Civil Society* yearbook from 2001 onwards. These contain examples of the latest research on civil society concepts, events and issues. They also contain annually updated chronologies of key civil society events.

1502 **Norwegian Institute for International Affairs**
www.nupi.no
A specialist body which conducts research into topics relating to international relations, politics and economics, with a focus on areas of central relevance to Norwegian foreign policy. Its website provides information about current research programmes and free access to recent NUPI working papers and research reports. These include strong coverage of Russian politics, international security in the Persian Gulf and European security.

Digital data, image & text collections

1503 **Chomsky.Info: official Noam Chomsky website**
www.chomsky.info
Official website of leading social scientist and political writer Noam Chomsky. It provides free access to a large selection of book excerpts, audio and video interviews, letters, journal and newspaper articles and an official blog. These cover a wide range of political and philosophical topics, including discussion of globalization, anarchism, American foreign policy, rogue states and contemporary political power. Also offered are materials relating to the conflicts in Iraq, Lebanon and the Middle East, plus some articles about Chomsky from other authors.

Handbooks & manuals

1504 **Global governance: critical concepts in political science**
T. Sinclair, ed.   Routledge, 2004, 1944pp. 4 v., £710. ISBN 9780415276610.
A useful four-volume set which reprints a collection of key essays and articles which debate the history, nature and current state of global governance. They include materials relating to the emergence and role of all the key supranational bodies and international organizations such as the United Nations and World Bank.

1505   Theories of international relations
S. Chan and C. Moore, eds   Sage Publications, 2007, 1644pp. 4 v.,
£475. ISBN 9781412920094.
A major four-volume set which brings together 80 classical
and contemporary essays influential to the development of
international relations theory. Volume 1 contains examples of
realist theory, volume 2 traces the development of pluralist
approaches, volume 3 covers structuralist approaches and
volume 4 focuses on reflexive approaches to international
relations, including constructivism, feminism,
postmodernism and critical geopolitics.

Diplomacy

Introductions to the subject

1506   Diplomacy: theory and practice
G.R. Berridge   3rd edn, Palgrave Macmillan, 2005, 272pp. £16.99.
ISBN 9781403993113.
www.grberridge.co.uk
Well-regarded textbook covering all aspects of diplomatic
theory and practice. Includes coverage of the role of the
ministry of foreign affairs, theories and skills of international
negotiation and the use of modern telecommunications
technology by diplomats. The author's personal website also
provides free access to supporting materials, including
updates to this text and notes on his other research projects.

Dictionaries, thesauri, classifications

1507   A dictionary of diplomacy
G.R. Berridge and A. James   2nd edn, Palgrave Macmillan, 2003,
312pp. £19.99. ISBN 9781403915368.
www.grberridge.co.uk
A useful introduction to the specialized terminology of
diplomacy. Also includes entries on legal terms, major world
events, international organizations and important diplomatic
figures.

Research centres & institutes

1508   Institute for the Study of Diplomacy
http://isd.georgetown.edu
ISD is part of Georgetown University's Edmund A. Walsh
School of Foreign Service. Its main focus is on studying the
foreign policy process, concentrating on how American
foreign policy decisions are made and implemented by US
diplomats. Its website provides information on its aims and
recent activities. It offers free access to a collection of online
working papers, transcripts and case studies.

Portal & task environments

1509   DiploFoundation
www.diplomacy.edu
Malta-based foundation which seeks to promote the use of
information technology in diplomacy. Its website provides
information on diplomacy conferences, postgraduate training
courses and publications. It also includes examples of web
portals which it has developed: these include online learning

tools such as dictionaries, documents and case studies
covering a wide range of areas of diplomatic practice.

1510   US diplomacy
www.usdiplomacy.org
A website maintained by the Association for Diplomatic
Studies and Training which aims to provide students and
researchers with information about the history, purpose and
current operation of American foreign policy and diplomacy.
It includes introductory essays on the work of the US
Department of State, ethics and theories of international
relations and international laws and treaties of diplomacy.
Also accessible are full-text documents, some video clips,
glossaries of acronyms, bibliographies of further readings
and links to related websites about diplomacy and
diplomats.

Digital data, image & text collections

1511   Frontline diplomacy: the foreign affairs oral history
collection of the Association for Diplomatic
Studies and Training
http://memory.loc.gov/ammem/collections/diplomacy
This site forms part of the Library of Congress American
Memory collection. It offers free access to a collection of
over 1000 transcripts of oral history interviews with leading
American diplomats covering the period from the late 1940s
to the 1990s. They offer insight into the private lives and
opinions of the officials as well as American foreign policy
during the period. Many of key international crises and wars
are covered, including the Korean War, Vietnam War, Cuban
Missile Crisis and Arab–Israeli conflict.

Directories & encyclopedias

1512   Corps diplomatique accrédité aupres des
Communautés européennes et representations
aupres de la Commission (Vade-mecum for the
use of the diplomatic corps)
2005, Office des publications officielles des Communautés
européennes, 1968–, 286pp. £7.50. ISSN 05912156.
An official listing of diplomatic and consular services
accredited to the European Union, including diplomatic
missions and representations to the EU. Includes names of
individual diplomats and contact addresses. Published in
French on a semi-annual basis by the European Commission.

1513   The Diplomatic Service list
41st edn, Stationery Office, 1966–, annual, 3331pp. £30. ISBN
9780115917844 ISSN 0419174.
Annual publication which contains organizational charts of
the British Foreign and Commonwealth Office and lists the
staff of British diplomatic and consular posts. This includes
coverage of home departments, British representation
overseas, chronological lists of Secretaries of State,
Ministers of State, Permanent Under-Secretaries and
Ambassadors, High Commissioners, Permanent
Representatives to international organizations and Governors
and Commanders-in-Chief of Overseas Territories. Also
provided are biographical notes on key members of the
British diplomatic service.

1514   The London diplomatic list
Stationery Office Books, 2005, annual. £11. ISBN 9780115917837.
www.fco.gov.uk/servlet/Front?pagename=OpenMarket/Xcelerate/Sho
wPage&c=Page&cid=1007029396086
An alphabetical listing of all the representatives of foreign states and Commonwealth countries based in London which is compiled annually by the Foreign and Commonwealth Office. It includes the names and contact addresses of all foreign embassies, ambassadors and key diplomats. A version of the list can also be consulted free of charge on the Foreign and Commonwealth Office website. This also includes some information on foreign embassies in the UK which are located outside London.

Handbooks & manuals

1515   Diplomatic handbook
R.G. Feltham   8th rev. edn, Martinus Nijhoff Publishers, 2004, 188pp. £70. ISBN 9789004141421.
A comprehensive guide to the theories, procedures and current practice of international diplomacy, of value to both students and practitioners. It includes coverage of the organization and functions of diplomatic missions and foreign ministries and the role of diplomacy in specific international organizations such as the United Nations and NATO. Other areas covered include diplomatic immunity, privileges and international law. Also provided is a useful glossary of key diplomatic terms.

1516   Historical dictionaries of US diplomacy series
J. Woronoff, ed.   Scarecrow Press.
www.scarecrowpress.com/series/
This important series, published by Scarecrow Press, provides coverage of the key theories, persons and programmes in American diplomatic and foreign policy history. It includes two different categories of books: chronologies (covering specific date ranges) and geographical overviews. Individual volumes contain a chronology, introductory essay, bibliography and A–Z dictionary style entries on persons, places, events, legislation and treaties. Examples include:
- **Historical dictionary of United States–China Relations** R. Sutter   Scarecrow Press, 2006, 288pp. £43. ISBN 9780810855021.
- **Historical dictionary of US diplomacy from the Civil War to World War 1** Kenneth J. Blume   Scarecrow Press, 2005, 512pp. £56. ISBN 9780810853775.

1517   Satow's guide to diplomatic practice
Sir E. Satow, Lord Gore-Booth and D. Pakenham   5th rev. edn, Longman, 1979, 576pp. £92.99. ISBN 0582501091.
A classic text on diplomacy which is still well regarded and consulted in foreign offices and diplomatic missions worldwide. While a little old fashioned in comparison to the other manuals and textbooks in this section, it contains advice on the conduct of diplomacy and the qualities of good diplomatic negotiation.

Keeping up to date

1518   Diplomacy Monitor
http://diplomacymonitor.com/
A great site maintained by the St Thomas University School of Law. It provides free real-time tracking of internet-published diplomacy documents worldwide. This includes materials from major international organizations, such as the United Nations and European Union, and national governments. Materials covered include press releases, communiqués, speeches, statements, papers and reports. It is particularly useful for quickly tracing recent statements on ongoing diplomatic crises.

1519   H-Diplo
www.h-net.org/~diplo
Moderated discussion list with an international editorial board which forms part of the H-Net discussion network for the Humanities and Social Sciences based at Michigan State University. It is concerned with issues relating to all aspects of diplomatic, foreign policy and international history. The site provides access to recent and archived messages and a useful collection of reviews of books, journal articles and conferences.

Foreign Policy

Official & quasi-official bodies

1520   Great Britain. Foreign & Commonwealth Office
www.fco.gov/
The British government department responsible for regulating British overseas relations and foreign affairs, and for concluding treaties involving the UK. Its website is the key source of information on British foreign policy and diplomacy. Describes the work of the department and provides free access to government press releases, speeches and policy documents covering relations with nations worldwide. Other features of the site include lists of contact addresses for UK diplomatic missions (embassies, high commissions and consulates) and travel advice for British nationals abroad.
    Full-text access to documents used in the UK treaty practice and procedures; a free treaty enquiry service (the staff of which have access to a database of 14,000 records relating to treaties since 1987 and print registers back to 1835), details of publication and presentation to Parliament and lists of treaties and status information for certain subjects or territorial areas. Important site for checking UK treaty practice and involvement.

1521   Great Britain. House of Commons. Foreign Affairs Committee
www.parliament.uk/parliamentary_committees/foreign_affairs_committee.cfm
A select committee of the UK House of Commons which analyses British foreign policy and overseas relations. Its website contains a list of current members of the Committee and links to the full text of press releases, minutes of hearings and committee reports from 1997 onwards. These include important examples of critical assessments of UK diplomacy and military deployments overseas. It also contains the annual human rights reports produced by the Committee, which provide an overview of practices worldwide.

1522   United States. Department of State
www.state.gov
The principal US government department responsible for

overseeing and implementing American foreign policy. It provides comprehensive information about the role, remit, history and current activities of the organization. This includes biographical information about past and current Secretaries of State, full-text press releases, policy documents, online speeches and reports from the department. These offer invaluable insight into all aspects of American foreign relations, including coverage of ongoing crises and conflicts. In addition, the website provides free access to a number of US Department of State publications which are of value to wider international relations issues. These include its country reports, summarizing the history and current economic and political situation within over 100 nations worldwide. Also available are a number of annual reports which can be accessed in full-text from approximately 1999 onwards. These include country reports on terrorism, country reports on human rights practices, trafficking reports, reports on US activities at the UN and the international religious freedom reports.

Research centres & institutes

1523 Foreign Policy Centre
http://fpc.org.uk/
A leading UK-based foreign policy think-tank, launched under the patronage of Tony Blair. Its website provides free access to online commentary and reports. Key topics of interest include British foreign policy, globalization, the world order after 9/11 and development and democracy.

1524 Foreign Policy in Focus
www.fpif.org
A joint project of the Interhemispheric Resource Center (IRC) and the Institute for Policy Studies (IPS). It aims to promote citizen-focused American foreign policy. Its website provides information on the purpose and current activities of the body. It includes access to the full text of its special reports and commentary on current international affairs issues. Recent topics covered include the war in Iraq and globalization.

MIT Center for International Studies
See entry no. 1659

Associations & societies

1525 Council on Foreign Relations
www.cfr.org/
A leading American think-tank which has been promoting research into foreign policy and America's role in world affairs since its founding in 1921. Its website is an excellent starting point for tracing non-partisan research and commentary on current world events. It offers free access to research papers, event transcripts and podcasts covering key political and security events. Recent examples include terrorism, the Iraq war and US foreign policy. Each section also offers background primers on the issues, reference maps and links to related United Nations resolutions and media commentary.

1526 Foreign Policy Association
www.fpa.org/
A non-profit association which exists to provide members of

the American public with independent information about world events and American foreign policy. Its website is an excellent starting point for beginning research. It contains a free resource library of materials including maps, audio and video files of speeches and events, online articles and analysis. These introduce the user to the topic and discuss and current controversies. It is possible to trace materials by geographical area or topic. Topics covered are wide-ranging and topical, including such issues as climate change, migration, human rights and war crimes.

1527 FORNET: Network of research and teaching on European foreign policy
www.fornet.info
A useful website for finding information about institutions specializing in the research and teaching of European foreign policy. This includes coverage of both the foreign policy of the EU and of individual European nations. Its website includes details about relevant conferences, events and research. Some full-text materials can be downloaded.

1528 Society for Historians of American Foreign Relations
www.shafr.org
The website of this association is an important starting point for finding information about conferences, publications and research on American diplomatic and foreign policy history. It contains newsletters from the Society and tables of contents from its leading academic journal *Diplomatic History*. Also since 2006 its annual listing of foreign policy doctoral dissertations submitted to North American universities has been accessible online.

Portal & task environments

1529 Deutsche Aussenpolitik: your gateway to German foreign policy
www.deutsche-aussenpolitik.de
An excellent portal of German foreign policy resources maintained by Trier university with funding from the ASKO EUROPA-FOUNDATION and the German Foreign Office. It offers free access to bibliographies of recent literature on German foreign policy, full-text working paper series from German universities and research institutes, online theses and a useful directory of links to key internet sites. The latter includes well written dossiers on specific aspects of international security and foreign policy. Recent examples include the German presidency of the EU 2007 and the future of NATO.

1530 Foreign Policy
www.foreignpolicy.com
An excellent site maintained by the editors of leading US journal *Foreign Policy*. It provides access to their blog which offers relevant commentary on world politics and economics, plus links to some web exclusive articles and scholarly materials from the journal Foreign Policy. The latter have included excellent resources such as the Index of Failed States and the Index of terrorism. Access to the full text of all articles from *Foreign Policy* is for subscribers only.

1531 Observatory on Italian foreign policy
www.foreignpolicy.it
Excellent resource maintained by the Department of Politics,

Institutions, History of the University of Bologna and the Diplomatic Institute of the Italian Ministry for Foreign Affairs. Provides free access and links to a wide range of resources relating to all aspects of Italian foreign policy and diplomacy, including Italian commentary on recent world events. These include working papers, a searchable database of abstracts of unpublished theses, and official publications such as government documents. Most materials date from 1980 onwards, with more extensive coverage post 2000. Information is in English or Italian.

Discovering print & electronic resources

1532   American foreign relations since 1600: a guide to the literature
R. Beisner, ed.   2nd edn, ABC-CLIO, 2003, 800pp. 2 v., £177.50. ISBN 1576070808.
Excellent two-volume set which indexes nearly 20,000 journal articles, essays, books and major websites covering all aspects of American international relations and foreign policy. Arranged chronologically, with separate sections on relations with individual nations and an introductory section which recommends general sources for tracing materials on the history of US foreign policy. Each entry has a helpful annotation on content.

Digital data, image & text collections

1533   Confidence in US foreign policy Index
www.publicagenda.org/foreignpolicy/index.cfm
A joint project of Public Agenda and *Foreign Affairs* journal, which aims to provide insight into the US public's opinion of American foreign policy. The index covers more than 25 issues through more than 80 different survey questions. These enable users to trace trends in levels of confidence. Topics include attitudes towards American involvement in particular conflicts worldwide, levels of fear about terrorism and perceptions of America's involvement in world affairs. It is possible to access explanations of the methodology used, sample questions, data and some full-text reports from the website.

1534   Country indicators for foreign policy
www.carleton.ca/cifp/
An ongoing study undertaken by the Department of Foreign Affairs and International Trade and the Norman Paterson School of International Affairs, Carleton University, Ontario, Canada which aims to collect social, economic and political data on nations worldwide. Currently, datasets include measures of conflict, governance and political instability, militarization, religious and ethnic diversity, economic performance and international relations for over 190 nations from 1985 onwards. These include risk assessments on security and terrorist threats from specific nations. Users may also access research papers and information on the methodology of the survey from the website.

1535   Digital National Security Archive
Proquest, 1945–. Price on request.
www.proquest.co.uk/products_pq/descriptions/dnsa.shtml
A subscription database supplied by the National Security Archive and ProQuest. It provides access to a collection of over 400,000 declassified documents of importance to

American foreign and military policy since 1945. Materials are subdivided into over 25 different topics. Key titles include the Berlin Crisis 1958–1962, the Iran-Contra Affair, US policy in the Vietnam War and terrorism and US policy. Each collection contains examples of full-text presidential memos, papers, directives and other secret documents. Also provided are chronologies, glossaries and bibliographies which set the materials in context.

1536   Documents on Irish foreign policy
www.difp.ie
A project of the Royal Irish Academy, the Department of Foreign Affairs and the National Archives of Ireland which aims to provide free online access to important government documents relating to Irish foreign policy and diplomacy from 1919 onwards. There are currently several hundred documents available covering the period 1919–1939, with more being added on a continuous basis. Items include letters, papers and memorandums from such key figures as Michael Collins, Eamon de Valera and David Lloyd-George. Topics include the creation of the Irish Free State, Anglo-Irish agreements in the early 20th century, relations between Britain and Ireland and the Northern Ireland troubles

1537   Foreign Relations of the United States
US Government Printing Office, 1861–.
www.state.gov/r/pa/ho/frus/c1716.htm
The Foreign Relations of the United States series is the official historical documentary record of major US foreign policy decisions that have been declassified and edited for publication. The series started in 1861 and is currently produced by the State Department's Office of the Historian. It is possible to access online free of charge volumes published since the Truman administration in 1945. These currently cover all major US foreign policy decisions, including the Korean War, Cuban Missile Crisis and Vietnam War, until the mid-1970s. Each typically contains documents from the Departments of State and Defense, National Security Council, CIA and Agency for International Development, as well as the private papers of individuals involved in formulating US foreign policy. Information on the release of more recent material is displayed on the website.

1538   Foreign Relations of the United States 1861–1960 digital collection
http://digicoll.library.wisc.edu/FRUS/
This site is a special project of the University of Wisconsin-Madison Libraries in collaboration with the University of Illinois at Chicago Libraries. It aims to make freely accessible a searchable full-text version of several hundred volumes from the FRUS from 1861 to 1960.

1539   National Security Archive
www.gwu.edu/~nsarchiv/
An independent research institute based in George Washington University, Washington DC. whose purpose is to collect and publish declassified government documents. Its website provides free access to an enormous collection of online papers and reports. These cover all the major US government foreign policy decisions and military operations from the 1950s to the present. They include the September 11 2001 terrorist attacks, the Cuban Missile Crisis and the Iran-Contra Scandal 1991. Many reveal hitherto 'hidden and secret policies'.

1540 Program on International Policy Attitudes (PIPA)
www.pipa.org

PIPA is a joint programme of the Center on Policy Attitudes (COPA) and the Center for International and Security Studies at Maryland (CISSM), School of Public Affairs, University of Maryland. It studies public opinion on international issues. This includes extensive research on attitudes towards international security crises and wars. The website provides free access to data from many recent research polls and reports.

- **Americans and the world** www.americans-world.org. Source of comprehensive information on US public opinion on international issues. Includes analysis of recent polls and research articles.
- **World public opinion.org** www.worldpublicopinion.org. Focuses on international policy research enabling users to trace materials relating to public attitudes worldwide. Includes coverage of topical issues such as the environment, globalization and development. Also includes examples which monitor citizens' attitudes towards other nations.

Directories & encyclopedias

1541 Blue guide to the archives of member states' foreign ministries and European Union institutions
www.consilium.europa.eu/cms3_fo/showPage.asp?id=717&lang=en
&mode=g

A free online guide prepared jointly by the Group of Archivists of the Ministries of Foreign Affairs of the Member States and the Institutions of the European Union which offers basic information the content, location and availability of the archives of the key institutions of the European Union and the Ministries of Foreign Affairs of its Member States. It is particularly suitable for use by researchers seeking to locate the most important archive collections in a particular region.

1542 Encyclopedia of American foreign policy
G. Hastedt   Facts on File Inc., 2004, 550pp. £52.50. ISBN 9780816046423.

A useful starting point for beginning research on the history of American foreign policy. Contains several hundred A–Z entries on key events, personalities, policies and organizations which have influenced US foreign relations from the American Revolution to the present.

Handbooks & manuals

1543 Chronological history of US foreign relations
L.H. Brune   2nd edn, Routledge, 2002, 1488pp. 3 v., £295. ISBN 9780415939140.

Comprehensive work containing summaries of all key events in American diplomatic and foreign policy history from the arrival of settlers in Jamestown in 1607 to the inauguration of President George W. Bush in 2001. Arranged chronologically with references for further reading. Also contains useful biographical information on all US Secretaries of State from 1781 to 2001.

International Migration & Colonization

Official & quasi-official bodies

1544 International Organization for Migration
www.iom.int/

The key intergovernmental organization in the field of international migration. Its terms of reference include coverage of international migration, human trafficking, illegal immigration and the health and welfare of migrants. Its website contains a wealth of information, includings its recent press releases, statistics and the full text of many of its recent reports.

- **International migration** Blackwell Publishing, qtrly. on demand from publisher. ISSN 00207985. An academic peer-reviewed journal published on behalf of the IOM. Contains scholarly articles discussing economic, social, political and legal issues relating to international migration worldwide.
- **World migration reports** IOM, irregular. £40. ISSN 15615502. www.iom.int. A regular series, updated approximately every two years, providing a global overview of the nature, extent, trends and challenges of migration. Chapters from volumes published since 2000 can be accessed freely from the IOM publications website.

1545 United Nations High Commissioner for Refugees
www.unhcr.org

The official refugee agency of the United Nations. Its website provides free access to an enormous collection of UN materials relating to refugees worldwide. These include coverage of refugee law, social policy, health and economics. Users may access UN treaties, resolutions, statistics, maps and audio and multimedia coverage of UN work in ongoing crisis regions. The large statistics database includes graphs and tables from its regular publications many of which can be downloaded from the website free of charge: examples include *Quarterly Refugee Trends* from 2002 onwards, *Asylum claims in industrialized countries* from 2002 onwards. It is also possible to read articles from *Refugees* magazine, *New issues in Refugee research* working papers and recent sections from the *UNHCR Global Annual Reports* online.

- **International Thesaurus of Refugee Terminology** www.refugeethesaurus.org. A service supported by the UNHCR which provides researchers and Librarians with a specialized vocabulary for describing terms relating to all aspects of refugee studies.
- **Refworld** www.unhcr.org/cgi-bin/texis/vtx/refworld/rwmain. A free database maintained by UNHCR which provides handy facts and figures about refugees and international migration. It includes country profiles, maps, statistics and full-text national and international legislation.

Research centres & institutes

1546 European Research Centre on Migration & Ethnic Relations
www.ercomer.eu

ERCOMER is a specialist institution situated within the Faculty of Social Sciences, Utrecht University, the Netherlands, which conducts and promotes comparative research in international migration and ethnic relations within a European context. Its key themes are migration, immigrants in host societies, and host societies' responses to immigrants and ethnic minority groups. This includes coverage of multiculturalism, ethnic conflict, racism and nationalism. In addition to providing access to many of its project reports, working papers and other publications from approximately 2000 onwards, the ERCOMER website is also well known for its virtual library of information on migration. This comprises an extensive collection of links to online papers, reports, organizational and project pages and legislation.

1547 Refugee Studies Centre, Queen Elizabeth House
www.rsc.ox.ac.uk
Established in 1982 as part of Queen Elizabeth House, the University of Oxford's Centre for Development Studies, the Centre 'has since won an international reputation as the leading multidisciplinary centre for research and teaching on the causes and consequences of forced migration'. Its website provides free access to a large range of online resources relating to its research. These include Forced Migration working papers, full-text journal articles from Forced Migration Online and teaching materials. The latter include an online training module developed to train aid workers about the psycological and social impact of becoming a refugee. Includes access to summaries of its research, lists of courses and seminars, publications, access to the two library catalogues containing details of the 45,000 items in stock and brief list of web links to associated organizations.

1548 Scalabrini Migration Center
www.smc.org.ph
A non-profit organization based in the Philippines which specializes in the study of human migration and refugee movements from and within Asia. Its website is a rich source of information about the political, social, economic, legal and psychological causes and impacts of migration and forced migration in the Asia-Pacific region. In addition to full-text access to its own recent research reports, the website also offers research news from other leading Asian organizations, statistics, maps and a useful directory of key non-governmental bodies.

1549 Sussex Centre for Migration Research
www.sussex.ac.uk/migration/index.php
A research and teaching centre based at the University of Sussex which specializes in the study of international migration and the policies that affect migrants. Its website provides information on its ongoing research, including reports from its specialist work on issues relating to migration, globalization, development and poverty. Also accessible are the full text of all its influential Sussex Migration working papers published since 2000 and tables of contents from its academic periodical *The Journal of Ethnic and Migration Studies*.

Associations & societies

1550 International Migration, Integration & Social Cohesion
www.imiscoe.org
A multidisciplinary research programme comprising researchers from over 20 key European universities. Its website includes an online library that contains full-text papers of IMISCOE members dating back to at least 2002. Also accessible is a searchable database of experts. Topics covered include the causes, nature and impact of immigration and migration.

1551 International Society for the Study of Forced Migration
www.iasfm.org
An international association of scholars and practitioners who work in the field of forced migration studies. This includes coverage of the causes, extent and impact of displacement upon refugees and host communities. The website provides information on the aims of the organization, its forthcoming conferences and ongoing research.

1552 Norwegian Refugee Council
www.nrc.no/engindex.htm
A leading independent non-governmental organization which seeks to promote the welfare of refugees worldwide. Its website provides information on its aims and projects. One of its major achievement is the establishment of the Internal Displacement Monitoring Centre (IDMC) in Geneva, which is the leading international body monitoring conflict-induced internal displacement worldwide.
- **Internal Displacement Monitoring Centre** www.internal-displacement.org/. The website provides free access to a database offering up-to-date information and analysis on internal displacement in over 50 countries worldwide. These include reports and statistics on victims of civil wars and ethnic conflicts. Materials include the economic, social and health impact of forced migrations.

Libraries, archives, museums

1553 British Library of Development Studies
A specialist research library based at the Institute of Development Studies, Brighton. It has one of Europe's largest collections covering all aspects of economic and social change in developing countries. This includes substantial holdings of books, journal, government and international organization reports relating to international migration, refugees and forced migration. Its website provides information on how to visit the library, as well as an excellent selection of subject-related research guides which highlight key texts, journals and reference resources. Its online library catalogue offers a useful starting point for tracing references as it includes selected indexing of articles from over 100 key titles.

1554 Centre d'Information et d'Études sur les Migrations Internationales (Centre for the Study of International Migration)
www.ciemi.org
Independent resource centre for documentation on migration which is based in Paris. Its purpose is to provide information for researchers and the general public on the effect of international migration on the social and cultural basis of nations. Its website provides access to the library catalogue, which is a useful source of information on French-language publications and reviews covering this subject area.

Portal & task environments

1555 December 18 Net
www.december18.net/web/general/start.php
December 18 is an online organization named after the International Day of Solidarity with Migrants, initiated in 1997 by Asian migrant organizations. Its website is run by

volunteers and aims to act as a single starting point for tracing information about migrants and international migration. It is particularly good at providing access to news, campaign and new publication alerts from NGOs and human rights organizations worldwide. Other features of the site include access to national and international legislation, glossaries of terms, online statistics, data and maps plus directories of links to migration related websites. Coverage includes human trafficking, migrant labour and the economic, social and legal aspects of migration.

1556 Forced migration online
www.forcedmigration.org
An excellent online library of resources maintained by a small team based at the Refugee Studies Centre in Oxford. It directs users to academic internet resources covering all aspects of forced migration worldwide. These include key journals, online working papers and multimedia resources. Other features of the website include directories of international migration organizations and thematic and country guides.

1557 History of international migration
www.let.leidenuniv.nl/history/migration
Maintained by researchers at the University of Leiden, this site aims to provide information and access to internet resources relevant to all aspects of the history of international migration and refugee flows from earliest times to the current day. It is divided into chronological time periods, each of which contains an overview of trends in international migration, an analysis of its causes, social, political and economic consequences and reactions. Links are provided to related websites.

1558 Human trafficking search
http://humantraffickingsearch.net/Default.aspx
A specialist web portal maintained by the National MultiCultural Institute. It offers students and researchers the ability to quickly search for internet resources (including organizations, reports, images, data and maps) on a wide range of topics relating to human trafficking. These include child labour, forced migration, trafficking in women and children and sexual slavery. The site highlights news stories and recent video resources on the issues.

1559 Migration information source
www.migrationinformation.org/
A project of the Migration Policy Institute, which is an independent think-tank based in Washington, DC. It provides free access to a wealth of data relating to migration, immigration, refugees and asylum seekers worldwide. This includes recent news stories, statistical data compiled from major international organizations, country fact files, glossaries of terms and links to key internet resources. It is an excellent starting point for researchers beginning work in this field.

Digital data, image & text collections

1560 International migration (MN series)
Great Britain. Office for National Statistics   Office for National Statistics (ONS), annual. £25. ISSN 0140900X.
www.statistics.gov.uk/STATBASE/Product.asp?vlnk=507
The MN series presents statistics on flows of international

migrants to and from the UK and England and Wales for the last 10 years. The time series data contain estimates of Total International Migration (TIM) derived from the International Passenger Survey (IPS), plus estimates of flows between the UK and the Irish Republic, and Home Office data. The statistics may be downloaded free from the website of the Office of National Statistics (ONS) or purchased in print format. Information on the methodology used to compile the results is provided.

Directories & encyclopedias

Encyclopedia of diasporas: immigrant and refugee cultures around the world
M. Ember, C.R. Ember and I. Skoggard   See entry no. 708

1561 The encyclopedia of the Indian diaspora
B. Lal, ed.   University of Hawaii Press, 2007, 416pp. £35. ISBN 9780824831462.
Key work examining the history of Indian migration from earliest times to the modern age of globalization. Includes academic articles covering the history, reasons for emigration, the experiences of immigrants in over 40 nations worldwide and their impact upon the host nations. The volume contains many photographs, tables and maps which chart the progress of South Asian migration and aspects of Asian culture. Other features include glossaries of Muslim and Hindu terms and extensive bibliographies to guide further reading.

Keeping up to date

1562 Forced Migration Review
Refugee Studies Centre, University of Oxford, 1998–, qtrly. Prior to 1990 it was published as Refugee Participation Network, Free.
www.fmreview.org
Forced Migration Review (FMR) is a free electronic journal published quarterly in English, Arabic, Spanish and French. It publishes practice-based articles on issues relating to refugees and international forced migration. These include refugee experiences and reviews of specific projects and programmes by aid workers. The website provides free access to all back issues.

1563 International migration outlook
OECD Publishing, 2006, annual, 328pp. Previous title *Trends in international migration*. First edition of new title in 2006. Also available as an e-book. Tables of contents and introduction free on website., £54. ISBN 926403627X.
www.oecd.org/about/0,2337,en_2649_33931_1_1_1_1_37415,00.html
This yearbook analyses recent trends in migration movements and policies in all OECD member countries. It includes succinct country surveys, and detailed analysis of international migration statistics. A particular focus is on flows of migrant labour. Policies in regulating migration are also reviewed. Available in print or online.

International Organizations

Introductions to the subject

1564 Basic facts about the United Nations
United Nations, 2004, 349pp. ISBN 9211009367.
Official introduction to the structure and role of the United Nations. It includes useful explanations, charts and maps of the main UN institutions and their roles. This includes coverage of peacekeeping; humanitarian; economic and social development roles. Appendices include UN membership lists 1945–2000; list of peacekeeping missions; and the contact addresses of official UN information centres. Users should consult the main UN website for more recent changes.

1565 The European Union: a guide through the EC/EU maze
S. Budd, A. Jones and A. Roney, eds   6th rev. edn, Kogan Page, 1998, 208pp. £14.99. ISBN 0749421177.
Introductory textbook intended to provide a broad understanding of the EU and guide users to sources of more detailed information. Although the rapid pace of change in Europe means that this edition cannot provide coverage of recent developments, it still offers a handy background on the historical origins, aims and evolution of the EU and its predecessors. It includes sections on key institutions and policy programmes. Suggestions for further research are provided.

1566 European Union information: a guide to official sources
P. Overy   European Information Association, 2006, 161pp. €45. ISBN 1905106092.
Written by a specialist in European Union information, this guide explains how the EU works focusing on the role of specific institutions and how policy and legislation are made. There is particularly strong coverage of the European legal system and European treaties. Advice on the content of offical EU websites and EU databases is provided.

1567 European Union information on the internet
G. Hudson   5th edn, European Information Association, 2006. £5.50. ISBN 9781905106141.
The latest edition of this handy self-help guide written by information specialists who are members of the European Information Association. It takes the form of laminated cards which can be used by library staff and the general public to quickly locate and use the most important European Union websites.

1568 Government and politics of the European Union
N. Nugent   6th edn, Palgrave Macmillan, 2006, 584pp. £20.99. ISBN 9780230000025.
Well-established textbook which provides a thorough grounding in the history, evolution, powers and policy process of the EU and its main institutions. The latest edition includes coverage of the Treaty of Nice, reform of the Common Agricultural Policy and economic and monetary union. Useful appendices include a chronology of key events in European Union history and a bibliography of further readings with links to major websites.

1569 An insider's guide to the UN
L. Fasulo   Yale University Press, 2005, 272pp. £8.99. ISBN 9780300107623.
Fascinating first-hand account of the inner workings of the United Nations by a former news correspondent. Includes coverage of the UN Security Council, General Assembly and the roles of the UN Secretary General and ambassadors. Each chapter contains an overview of the role of the body and personal recollections from leading US diplomats and UN officials on the politics of the system. Offers an interesting contrast with official encyclopedias of the organization.

Terminology, codes & standards

1570 Eurojargon: a dictionary of European Union acronyms, abbreviations and terminology
E.B. Davies, comp.   7th edn, European Information Association, 2004, 344pp. £50. ISBN 9780948272936.
A wide-ranging detailed guide which explains clearly the meanings and origins of more than 3000 acronyms, abbreviations and concepts in common use across the European Union, including many examples which appear regularly in the press but are often misunderstood. Covers of EU projects, agencies and programmes.

Dictionaries, thesauri, classifications

1571 A dictionary of the European Union
D. Phinnemore and L. McGowan   3rd edn, Routledge, 2006, 464pp. £130. ISBN 9781857433739.
Provides a concise overview of the historical development and current operation of the EU. Includes entries on EU terminology, acronyms, institutions, policies and treaties. The most recent edition contains entries on EU expansion, including profiles of the 10 nations which achieved full European Union membership in May 2004.

1572 Historical dictionaries of international organizations series
J. Woronoff, ed.   Scarecrow Press.
www.scarecrowpress.com
Key series published by Scarecrow Press. Over 18 volumes have currently been issued, covering the history of individual organizations (European Union, IMF and United Nations), organizations in specific geographic areas and those working in particular fields (such as peacekeeping and refugee aid). Each volume contains a chronology of key events, listing of acronyms and entries on the key events, persons and policies. Bibliographies of further readings are provided. A full listing of volumes in the series can be obtained from the publisher's website.
- **Historical dictionary of international organizations M. Schechter**   1998, 368pp. £56. ISBN 9780810834798.
- **Historical dictionary of international organizations in sub-Saharan Africa T. Mays and M.W. DeLancey**   2002, 408pp. £103. ISBN 9780810842571.
- **Historical dictionary of the European Union J. Roy and A. Kanner**   2006, 296pp. £49. ISBN 9780810853140.
- **Historical dictionary of the United Nations J. Fomerand**   2007, 704pp. £103. ISBN 9780810854949.

1573 IATE: interactive terminology for Europe
Translation Centre for the Bodies of the European Union in Luxembourg.
http://iate.europa.eu/iatediff/
An official EU-funded site which provides free access to an online database of EU terminology. This enables rapid checking of EU acronyms, terms and abbreviations. These cover all aspects of EU policy, including legal terminology and politics. The site may be searched in all the EU recognized languages.

1574 International organizations: a dictionary and directory
G. Schiavone 6th edn, Palgrave Macmillan, 2005, 352pp. £95. ISBN 9781403942647.
More than 200 entries on international political, economic, social and cultural organizations. Includes coverage of intergovernmental and non-governmental bodies. Useful introductory essay on the origins and development of multilateral organizations. Also includes membership tables, a glossary of terms and index of acronyms. Typical entries include the history, objectives, key activities, publications and website address of the organization.

1575 International organizations and groups – abbreviations
www.cia.gov/library/publications/the-world-factbook/appendix/appendix-a.html
This useful listing of abbreviations of key international organizations and groups is an appendix of the *CIA world factbook*. Updated annually, it provides a quick online checklist of the acronyms, membership and activities of current intergovernmental organizations. Range is limited to key organizations only. More in-depth and wider coverage is offered by the *Yearbook of international organizations* (q.v.).

Laws, standards, codes

1576 The United Nations system and its predecesors
F. Knipping [et al.], eds Oxford University Press, 2003, 1600pp. 2 v., £215. ISBN 9780198265962.
Useful source for tracing the origins, historical development and functions of the United Nations system. Reprints all the major official documents (charters, statutes and other legal instruments) from UN history. Volume 2 provides in-depth coverage of the League of Nations, examining its role, operation and tracing the roots of UN development from its eventual collapse.

Official & quasi-official bodies

1577 Reform at the UN
www.un.org/reform/
This an official website of the United Nations which provides free access to all recent press releases, speeches by the Secretary General, resolutions, summits and reports relating to the topical issue of UN reform. It includes coverage of the Secretary-General's High-level Panel on Threats, Challenges and Change and a useful chronology enabling students to trace the stages and key reports in recent UN economic, political and organizational reforms.

Research centres & institutes

1578 Bruges Group
www.brugesgroup.com
Independent UK-based political think-tank which was founded in 1989 to promote the idea of a less centralized European Union. Its website is a key place for finding information about events, research and publications which oppose greater EU integration. It includes free access to many of its articles and surveys, which contain critical commentary on the development of Britain's relationship with the EU, the European Constitution and European monetary and social integration.

1579 Fondation Robert Schuman
www.robert-schuman.eu
A leading French think-tank which aims to promote research into the progress made by the European Union. This includes coverage of the positive aspects of EU integration and political and monetary union. Its website provides free access to information on research projects and some of its publications and reports. Another feature of its website is the European elections calendar, which highlights and provides brief commentary on recent and forthcoming elections in EU nations.

1580 Global Policy Forum
www.globalpolicy.org
Based in New York, this organization seeks to monitor and promote democratic reform in the United Nations. Its website offers information on its role and activities. It includes free access to reports that critically analyse the UN. These include materials on United Nations finance, the UN Security Council and the role of the UN in international justice.

1581 Ralph Bunche Institute for International Studies
http://web.gc.cuny.edu/RalphBuncheInstitute
Originally concerned with the study of the United Nations but since 2001 has also encompassed a wider study of international relations and the international order. Its website provides information on its aims, research and publications. Key areas of work include the Inter-University Consortium on Security and Humanitarian Action (IUCSHA), the United Nations Intellectual History Project, Program on States and Security, the European Union Studies Center and the International Commission on Intervention and State Sovereignty.
■ **United Nations Intellectual History Project**
www.unhistory.org [12/07/2006].

1582 United Nations University
www.unu.edu
An educational organization which acts as bridge between the United Nations and the international academic community and as a think-tank for research on the United Nations system. Its website provides information on training courses and current research projects. It includes open access to some online learning modules, webcasts of lectures and full-text research and working papers. A wide range of issues are covered, including international environmental collaboration, peacebuilding and nationbuilding.

Associations & societies

1583   Academic Council on United Nations
www.acuns.org/
International institution created in 1987 to stimulate teaching and research in global governance and the role of the United Nations system in international relations. The website provides information on the aims of the organization and its ongoing research. It includes transcripts from its annual John Holmes memorial lectures, plus abstracts from its leading journal *Global Governance* and examples of international relations syllabi. ACUNS members may view other full-text documents online.

1584   European Community Studies Association
www.ecsanet.org
An international network of over 50 national associations of professors and researchers working in the field of European integration. Its website provides a rich source of information on teaching and learning about EU enlargement, expansion and integration. It contains information on forthcoming events, a searchable database of scholars and an online archive of papers and reports from ECSA conferences. The latter cover the period from approximately 2000 onwards. In addition to information about ongoing research on the EU, they also include some interesting materials relating to the teaching of EU studies. These include updates on courses and the the use of online learning in education.

1585   European Union Studies Association
www.eustudies.org
Leading international scholarly and professional association concerned with all aspects of the teaching and research of the European Union. Key areas of interest include EU enlargement and integration, European Union law, EU public policy and the political economy of the EU. Its website provides information on its aims, membership, training and conferences. It also provides free access to all issues of *EUSA Review*, which contains articles and book reviews. There is a separate section on teaching the EU, with examples of syllabi and lists of recommended textbooks.

1586   European Union, Databases User Group
www.eudug.eu
An organization supporting users of European Union electronic databases. Its website is a useful resource for librarians and information workers, as well as members of the public who wish to find out more about commercial and EU-produced databases and online resources covering the European Union. It contains news updates and lists of recommended databases and websites. All aspects of EU policy are covered, including legal and political subject areas.

1587   International Progress Organization
www.i-p-o.org/
A non-governmental organization that has consultative status with the Economic and Social Council of the United Nations and is associated with the United Nations Department of Public Information. It encourages the study of international democracy and United Nations reform. Its website provides free access to its recent press releases and research papers, many of which analyse the performance of the UN. Links are provided to other organizations concerned with United Nations reform.

1588   TEAM: The European Alliance of EU-Critical Movements
www.teameurope.info
TEAM (formerly The European Anti-Maastricht Alliance) is an organization of over 50 national groups from countries across Europe who are critical of the European Union and the concept of greater EU integration. Its website is an excellent starting point for tracing information about the existence and activities of EU-critical and Euro-sceptic movements. It includes details about events, publications and campaigns. In the past these have include opposition to the European constitution, the single European currency and EU expansion.

1589   Union of International Associations
www.uia.org/
An independent non-governmental organization founded in 1907 which aims to facilitate the evolution of a worldwide network of non-profit organizations. It plays a significant role in publishing information about the legal status, role, organization and membership of international organizations worldwide. Its website contains information on the purpose of the organization and a list of its members. It offers a useful listing of international organizations (with links to their websites), a calendar of international conferences and events and details about UIA publications. Selected tables of contents and articles from its scholarly journal *Transnational Associations* can be viewed online. Other products, such as the *Yearbook of international organizations*, are available online to subscribers only.

1590   United Nations Association of the USA
www.unausa.org/
An independent non-profit organization dedicated to enhancing US participation in the United Nations system. Its website includes news, factsheets and information about American activities at the UN. These cover all aspects of economic, social and human rights policy. Members of the association can also access databases of educational materials

1591   World Federation of United Nations Associations
An independent, non-governmental organization with consultative status at the Economic and Social Council (ECOSOC) of the UN. It is composed of a global network of United Nations Associations, the aim of which is to promote research, information and education about the goals of the Charter of the United Nations and the work of the United Nations system. Its website provides information about the history, purpose, membership and recent activities of the organization. It includes access to press releases and full-text policy papers. Topics covered by these include the future of the UN and United Nations reform. It also hosts a useful directory of national UN research organizations and associations worldwide.

Libraries, archives, museums

1592   Dag Hammarskjöld Library
www.un.org/Depts/dhl/
The official library of the UN. Its website is an invaluable starting point for those beginning research on all aspects of the history, function and recent activities of the UN and all agencies within the UN system. It offers free access to a wide

range of bibliographic indexes and training guides which are invaluable in helping researchers navigate through the often confusing maze of UN materials. Key features of the site include its bibliographic database UNBISNet, a chronological listing of key UN milestones, directory of UN depository centres worldwide, glossaries of UN terms and research guides for tracing UN materials. Also provided are quick links to the full text of the most widely requested UN treaties, charters and reports.

- **UN Pulse** www.un.org/Depts/dhl/unpulse/ [05/07/2006]. A blog-based service developed by the library that can be used to alert students/ researchers to a selection of the most important recently released UN reports, publications and documents.
- **UN-I-QUE (United Nations Info Quest)** http://lib-unique.un.org/lib/unique.nsf [05/07/2006]. A database which provides information on document numbers for UN materials from 1946 onwards, including annual reports from United Nations committees and commissions, UN monograph series, journals published by the United Nations and reports of conferences. Its main use is to quickly verify the symbols and dates of documents. Abstracts of content are not provided.

1593 List of depository libraries receiving United Nations material (Liste des bibliothèques dépositaires recevant les documents et publications de l'Organisation des Nations Unies; Lista de bibliotecas depositarias que reciben documentos y publicaciones de las Naciones Unidas)
United Nations, 2001, 72pp. o/p.
www.un.org/depts/dhl/deplib/
A useful directory of libraries which have been designated as official UN depositories and therefore contain substantial holdings of United Nations documents and other materials. Coverage is worldwide. Entries provide details on extent, language and dates of the materials deposited. The paper version should be viewed in conjunction with an online version maintained by United Nations Dag Hammarskjöld Library, which offers regular updates, plus news and more background information about the depository library system.

Portal & task environments

1594 Europe in the UK
www.europe.org.uk
A portal of information maintained by the European Commission Representation in the UK. It provides British citizens with news about all aspects of the European Union, free access to the latest EU documents and reports online and a directory of EU contacts in the UK. The latter includes a listing of local European Documentation Centres and libraries where further advice on researching EU matters may be sought. Other features of the site include discussion forums, information on travel in Europe and a calendar of EU events.

1595 European navigator
www.ena.lu
An excellent collection of resources relating to the history of the European Union which has been compiled for use by teachers, students and researchers by the Centre Virtuel de la Connaissance sur l'Europe. It provides access to a wealth of different types of material, including treaties, papers, cartoons, photographs and multimedia clips. These are arranged chronologically or by subject. Topics covered

include the origins of European cooperation in the post-war period, the Common Market, EU enlargement and integration, the single European market and single European surrency (euro). The documents include French- and German-language materials. Other features of the site include a glossary, thesaurus and selected bibliography of further readings.

1596 United Nations scholars workstation
www.library.yale.edu/un/index.html
An online research guide to tracing materials published by the UN which is maintained by Yale University. It includes two sections: a collection of easy-to-use indexes to the UN, arranged by resource type, subject, organization and geographic area, and a series of guides to researching particular types of UN materials in print and via the internet.

Discovering print & electronic resources

1597 The complete reference guide to United Nations sales publications 1946–1978
Unifo Publishers, 1978. 2 v., o/p. ISBN 0891110119.
Useful resource for tracing information about the existence and details of publications sold by the United Nations between 1946 and 1978. Volume 1 comprises a catalogue with document numbers; volume 2 contains indexes by keyword and title. For information on more recent publications you should consult the annual UN publications catalogue and website.

1598 ECLAS: database of the European Commission Central Library
http://europa.eu.int/eclas/
ECLAS is the online catalogue of the European Commission Central Library and a network of smaller specialized libraries and documentation centres. It consists of over 240,000 catalogue records relating to all aspects of European political, economic and cultural affairs, with over 7000 new additions made annually. It is possible to use the catalogue to trace references to the EU's official publications, commercial, academic and government reports, and selected periodical articles. There are some links to internet resources.

1599 European integration current contents
http://centers.law.nyu.edu/jmtoc/index.cfm
Provides free access to the tables of contents of over 100 journals relevant to the study of European Union law, human rights, politics, history and economics. It covers those titles taken by the European University Institute (EUI) and NYU School of Law. The database is fully searchable by author or subject keyword and it is possible to browse issues by journal. Some abstracts are provided. The majority of the material dates back to 1998. It includes some non-English-language journals. Regular updates are made fortnightly or monthly.

1600 Index to proceedings of the General Assembly
Dag Hammarskjöld Library, 1950/1–, Sessional. 2 v.
Printed bibliographic guide to the proceedings and documentation of the United Nations General Assembly. Two volumes are prepared for each session. Volume 1 contains lists of documents (giving details of their document symbols and summary of content), lists of resolutions adopted and

voting charts. The second volume is a useful index to speeches given to the General Assembly. These are indexed by speaker, country and subject content. Information on the most recent UN speeches and publications can be found on the main UN website.

1601 The Stationery Office agency catalogue
2005 edn, The Stationery Office, 2006, annual, 195pp. £8.50. ISBN 9780115008122.
Annual listing of publications from British, European and international organizations compiled by The Stationery Office (TSO). While it is restricted to those agencies for which the TSO is an agency, coverage is broad, encompassing all main EU: United Nations, World Trade Organization and World Bank institutions and it can be used as a quick starting point for checking the existence and bibliographic details of major monograph and serial publications in the last calendar year. Abstracts are not provided.

1602 UN System pathfinder
www.un.org/Depts/dhl/pathfind/frame/start.htm
The purpose of this official online guide is to enable students and members of the public to quickly identify the major print publications of the United Nations and its constituent organizations. It is arranged by theme. All aspects of UN work are covered, including international security and peacekeeping, economic and social development, the environment, disarmament, international law and human rights. Each section lists the key UN publications,such as yearbooks, handbooks, guides, bibliographies, reports and periodical publications. The main emphasis is on print resources, although some links to online versions of reference sources are provided. Electronic-only databases are generally excluded.

1603 UNBISNET: UN bibliographic information system
http://unbisnet.un.org
An excellent free bibliographic database maintained by the UN Dag Hammarskjöld Library. It contains the catalogue of all UN documents and publications indexed by the Library and the Library of the UN Office at Geneva. These include resolutions, treaties and documents from the General Assembly, Security Council and Economic and Social Council. The site also has an index to all voting records from the General Assembly from 1983 and the Security Council from 1946 onwards and an index to speeches made in the Security Council and the Economic and Social Council from 1983 and the Trusteeship Council from 1982.

1604 United Nations Documents Index
Dag Hammarskjöld Library, 1998–, qtrly. Preceded by UNDOC 1979–1996. ISSN 10207090.
The United Nations Documents Index and its predecessor UNDOC are global indexes of all UN documents indexed by the Dag Hammarskjöld Library and the UN Library in Geneva since 1979. They provide broad subject indexes to an extensive catalogue of documents issued worldwide by numerous UN organs and subsidiary bodies. These include materials from General Assembly and Security Council.
■ **UNBISnet** http://unbisnet.un.org/. The free online version. It also offers several additional features: the catalogue of the non-UN collections of the Dag Hammarskjold Library and the UN Library in Geneva; detailed voting records of resolutions adopted by the General Assembly (38th session onwards) and the Security Council (since 1946); and citations to speeches

made in the General Assembly, Security Council and Economic and Social Council from 1983 onwards.

1605 United Nations publications catalogue
United Nations Publications, 1986–, irregular.
The official publication sales list of the United Nations and its main institutional bodies. Each volume lists materials in print at the time of publication. Historical volumes are useful for checking correct bibliographic details. Researchers may find it useful to use this in conjunction with other UN indexes such as UNBIS. It is also advisable to check the main United Nations website where there is a publications section with an online catalogue listing more recent publications. The main UN website also highlights many press releases and 'grey literature' documents that may be excluded from this series.

1606 The United Nations system: international bibliography (Das System der Vereinten Nationen: internationale Bibliographie)
K.G.Saur, 1976–1991. 7 v., o/p.
A comprehensive seven-volume set, of value to scholars of the history of the United Nations. Includes references to academic materials covering the main bodies of the UN and its policies. Strong coverage of European-language materials

Digital data, image & text collections

1607 ArchiDok
http://archidok.uni-mannheim.de/en/
A long-term project of German and Austrian European Documentation Centres (EDZ) which seeks to electronically archive and make available free on the internet full-text European Union documents and reports covering all policy areas. It includes a large number of materials from the main EU institutions from 2000 onwards. Titles may be browsed or searched by keyword.

1608 European research papers archive
http://eiop.or.at/erpa
An essential website for all serious researchers. Provides free access to a searchable database of full-text academic working papers from leading university and research institutes. These include the MZES (Mannheim Centre for European Social Research), Harvard Jean Monnet Working Papers Series, materials from the Max Planck Institute for the Study of Societies, ARENA (Advanced Research on the Europeanization of the Nation-State), European Integration online Papers (EIoP). The papers cover all aspects of the history, economics, politics and governance of the European Union. Most have been published since 1997.

1609 League of Nations documents
www.yale.edu/lawweb/avalon/league/league.htm
This site is maintained as part of the Avalon Project of Yale University. It offers access to the full text of a number of primary source documents relating to the work of the League of Nations, the predecessor to the United Nations. These include the Covenant of the League of Nations and the Treaty of Locarno 1925.

1610 League of Nations Photo Archive
www.indiana.edu/~league/
A digitized collection of photographs from the Archive of the League of Nations made available on the internet via the

University of Indiana website. They cover the period 1919–1946 and include photographs of world leaders, prime ministers and foreign secretaries of the time. Also accessible are images of League of Nations conferences, commissions and assemblies. The site includes background information on the role and work of the League of Nations, organizational charts of its structure and links to other digitization projects.

Directories & encyclopedias

Corps diplomatique accredité aupres des Communautés européennes et representations aupres de la Commission (Vade-mecum for the use of the diplomatic corps)
See entry no. 1512

1611 The directory of EU information sources
15th edn, Routledge, 2006, 576pp. £240. ISBN 1857433319 ISSN 10256733.
Well-established and wide-ranging directory of information sources covering all aspects of EU activity. It includes entries on each individual EU institution; contact addresses of key EU officials; information on EU publications; and lists of the main EU websites. Also provided is information on EU grants and funding programmes; lists of law firms specializing in EU affairs; key university departments and courses; and European Union trade and commercial organizations.

1612 Directory of United Nations information sources
5th edn, United Nations, 1994, 587pp. £34. ISBN 9789211006810.
Authoritative source compiled by the Advisory Committee for the Coordination of Information Systems. Provides a simple-to-use annotated guide to the key information services (depository libraries and UN information centres); online databases and software relating to the United Nations. This includes coverage of official UN publications and commercial resources. While the lack of recent updates means that it cannot provide coverage of the most up-to-date online resources and websites, the listing of information sources can still be used as a good starting point for tracing libraries with specialist UN collections worldwide.

1613 Encyclopedia of the European Union
D. Dinan Palgrave Macmillan, 2000, 576pp. £22.99. ISBN 9780333921050.
Authoritative single-volume work containing over 700 essays on the history and development of the European Union during the 20th century. Includes long essays on key figures, events and treaties. A particular strength are the detailed appendices, which include a chronology of EU institutional change 1958–1999, tables of membership of EU institutions and a chronology of European Parliament political party groupings.

1614 Encyclopedia of the Inter-America system
G.P. Atkins Greenwood Press, 1997, 592pp. £90. ISBN 9780313286001.
A sound introductory guide to the complexities of the inter-American system (comprising the Organization of American States, Inter-American Development Bank and Inter-American Treaty of Reciprocal Assistance Regime) from 1889 to 1997. Over 250 entries cover the main concepts, treaties, individuals and policies, making clear the relationship of

these organizations with other international bodies. Also provided is a chronology of key dates and a list of the changing membership.

1615 Encyclopedia of the United Nations and international agreements
E.J. Osmanczyk, ed. 3rd edn, Routledge, 2003, 2880pp. 4 v., £375. ISBN 9780415939201.
A useful source of background information on the history, function and operation of the United Nations. Contains over 6000 entries which vary from long essays to brief definitions of terms. These cover institutions within the UN system, technical terms in international diplomacy, themes such as peacekeeping and human rights; and individual countries. Many offer references for further reading. Key UN treaties, protocols and statutes are reprinted in full. Biographical entries are not included. References to websites are limited.

1616 EU whoiswho: the official directory of the European Union
Office for Official Publications of the European Communities, annual. €5. ISSN 16803698.
http://europa.eu/whoiswho
An official directory, updated weekly on the web and providing free access to up-to-date contact addresses and organizational charts for EU institutions, bodies and agencies. It is possible to search the database by person, department or position. Entries contain basic job titles, phone numbers and addresses. Printed versions are produced annually.

1617 Europa directory of international organizations
8th edn, Routledge, 2006, annual, 744pp. £210. ISBN 9781857433791.
Provides facts and contact addresses on over 1700 international organizations worldwide. Individual entries contain details of activities, key publications, lists of leading officials and contact addresses. The volume also includes introductory articles on the role of international organizations in the modern world and a chronology of key events in their historical evolution. The full text of some key charters and documents is provided.

1618 European Union encyclopedia and directory 2007
7th edn, Routledge, 2006, 700pp. £365. ISBN 9781857433807.
Useful quick reference source which combines encyclopedia-type articles about the EU with an extensive directory of facts, figures and contact addresses. Key features include an A–Z section of definitions, acronyms and articles on each member state, details and contact addresses for all major EU institutions, plus MEPs, political interest and lobbying groups, and a statistical section covering economics, population, health and social life in Europe.

1619 Eurosource
Dod's Parliamentary Communications, 2005–, annual. 2 v., £190. ISBN 0905702565.
www.eurosource.eu.com
Annual directory which was first issued in 2005 and combines *Dod's European Companion* and *Le Trombinoscope*. Provides comprehensive coverage of the institutions, activities and leading figures of the EU. Introductory essay on the year in Europe, followed by detailed facts about the current composition, organization and activities of all the main EU institutions and agencies. Includes biographies of

key EU personnel and details about MEPs. Available in print or online.

1620 Guide to the Archives of Intergovernmental Organizations
www.unesco.org/archives/guide/index.html
Basic online guide produced by UNESCO in association with the International Council on Archives. It provides information on the official archive holdings of around 80 major intergovernmental organizations, including bodies of the United Nations and the European Union. Typical entries include a brief administrative history of the body, overview of the archives held and information on how to access them. Many of the entries are offered in French only.

Handbooks & manuals

1621 Annuaire des organisations internationales (Yearbook of international organizations)
Société de l'Annuaire des Organisations Internationales, Geneva, 1948–1965. Succeeded by *Yearbook of international organizations* (ISSN 00843814).
The predecessor to the *Yearbook of international organizations*, this publication constitutes a valuable resource for historians of international affairs. The volumes contain comprehensive listings of the names, purposes and activities of international intergovernmental and non-governmental organizations during this time period. There are also lists of contemporary abbreviations.

1622 A chronology of international organizations
Europa Publications   Europa Publications, 2007, 320pp. £110. ISBN 9781857432084.
A useful volume which draws together in one place chronologies of key dates and events in the history and evolution of all the major modern international and intergovernmental organizations. It includes separate listings for the United Nations, NATO, African Union, IMF and the European Union. An introductory essay provides general historical background on the development and role of international organizations.

1623 Chronology of the United Nations 1945–2005
K.P. Sauvant and L.J. Muller   Oceana, 2007–, 500pp. £50. ISBN 9780195323146.
A quick reference source intended to complement the *Annual review of United Nations affairs*, which will be updated every five years. It contains a chronology of key UN events and policy developments from 1945 to 2000. Entries include specific sections on key UN areas such as peacekeeping and human rights. A useful glossary of UN abbreviations and acronyms is provided.

1624 European companion 2002–3
Stationery Office, 2002, annual, 808pp. £170. ISBN 9780117027664.
Official British government guide to current EU institutions, policies and personnel. Includes detailed descriptions of the main institutions and the legislative process. Particularly good coverage of key EU political figures. Includes biographies, photographs, contact addresses, e-mail and website details for important politicians and senior civil servants.

1625 European yearbook (Annuaire Européen)
Council of Europe/Conseil de l'Europe   2005 edn, Brill, 1955–, annual. €300. ISSN 01676717.
Published annually since 1953, this publication provides an overview of the main activities and publications of 19 European supranational organizations (including EU agencies, the European Parliament and European Council), as well as the the Organization for Economic Co-operation and Development (OECD). Each volume contains a detailed survey of the history, structure and recent activities of each organization, plus membership charts and document lists.

1626 The guide to EU information sources on the internet
3rd edn, Routledge, 2005, 500pp. £362. ISBN 9781857432824.
Clearly laid-out guide which includes entries for over 2000 websites from official EU institutions and providers of information about the EU. Arranged thematically by categories which echo the names of the Directorate Generals of the European Commission. These include coverage of key themes such as EU enlargement, agriculture, justice and home affairs and trade. Entries include website addresses and keyword annotations on content.

1627 International information: documents, publications and electronic information of international organizations
P.I. Hajnal   2nd edn, Greenwood Press, 2001, 450pp. £86. ISBN 9781563088087.
Provides information on recent trends in the publication and dissemination of information by the main international organizations. Detailed entries are provided for the IMF, World Bank, European Union, United Nations and OECD. Each entry contains bibliographic details and annotations on content of all the main journal and monograph series. References are provided to print, electronic and internet publications. Guidance on the correct citation forms is also offered.

1628 Lobbying in the European Union
4th edn, Routledge, 2005, 448pp. £95. ISBN 9781857433364.
Useful guide for individuals and groups on how to lobby the EU. It provides background information on the structure of the EU decision-making process and tips on the most opportune time for lobbying. Also provided is a directory of diplomatic representations in Brussels and a listing of contact addresses of organizations, NGOs and trade unions currently involved in lobbying.

1629 The Oxford handbook on the United Nations
T. Weiss and S. Daws, eds   Oxford University Press, 2007, 838pp. £85. ISBN 9780199279517.
A major collection of scholarly essays on the history, role, current composition and future direction of the United Nations. It includes a section on the relationship of the UN with other international and regional organizations and materials on the topical issue of future UN reform. Other areas covered include the role of the UN with regard to human rights, international peacekeeping and development. Detailed bibliographic references are provided. Appendices include the full text of the Charter of the United Nations and the Universal Declaration of Human Rights.

1630 United Nations handbook
A. Ramsey   New Zealand. Ministry of Foreign Affairs, 1961–, annual. €16. ISSN 01101951.
An excellent source of quick information, particularly recommended for students and members of the public, which has been published annually by the New Zealand Ministry of Foreign Affairs since 1961. It provides a listing of all UN bodies and agencies, with clear and concise information on their roles, interrelationships and subsidiaries. Each volume also contains an overview of recent UN events, policies and activities.

1631 The United Nations system: a reference handbook
C. F. Alger   ABC-CLIO, 2006, 266pp. £55. ISBN 9781851098057.
A readable guide to the history and current operation of the United Nations which is suitable for use by the general reader. It includes reprints of key documents such as the UN Charter and the Universal Declaration of Human Rights, a chronology of events and discussion of the current controversies surrounding the desire for UN reform.

1632 Yearbook of international organizations
43rd edn, 2006/7, Union of International Associations & K.G. Saur, 1967–, irregular. Former title *Annuaire des organisations internationales*. 5 v., €1648. ISSN 00843814.
Published since 1910, this multi-volume resource work is recognized as a key resource in tracing information about international governmental and non-governmental organizations worldwide. Alphabetical and subject indexes make it easy to trace the existence of organizations. Typical entries provide profiles, histories, contact addresses and information on key publications. Volume 4 includes a bibliography of studies of international non-profit and intergovernmental organizations. Volume 5 provides detailed statistical tables on the number, types and activities of international organizations.

1633 Yearbook of the United Nations
Office of Public Information, United Nations, 1947–, annual. £114. ISSN 00828521.
http://unp.un.org/
A key publication of of the United Nations offering a comprehensive, one-volume account of all activities and publications in the calendar year, including coverage of the actions of all agencies of the UN. Volume 58 covering activities in 2004 was released in October 2006. An online/CD-ROM version containing the collected editions of yearbooks from 1946 onwards is also available. This offers enhanced keyword searching facilities.

Keeping up to date

1634 Annual review of United Nations affairs 2004/5
Oceana Publications, 1961–, annual. 4 v., £210. ISBN 0379123932.
www.oceanalaw.com/main_product_details.asp?ID=321
A commercial series which provides an annual review of UN activity. Each volume reprints key documents, agendas and resolutions from the principal United Nations organs, including the General Assembly, the Security Council, the Economic and Social Council (ECOSOC), the International Court of Justice, the Trusteeship Council and the United Nations Secretariat. It also contains essays on a topical issue such as a specific UN conference or area of work. In 2004/5 the topic chosen was development, security and reform.

Other areas covered have included human rights and UN reform.

1635 EUPolitix.Com
www.eupolitix.com/EN
Free EU news service, covers the latest developments in the European Union, European Parliament and European Commission. Site also offers some political interviews with key EU figures and policy briefings which contain introductory explanations of key areas of European policy. Emphasis is on current news stories.

1636 European access
Chadwyck-Healey, 1980–, bi-monthly. ISSN 02647362.
A useful current awareness source. Typical issues contain chronologies of key EU events, plus brief essays commenting on recent policies, treaties and EU regulations. Also maintains excellent bibliographic listings and reviews of recently published works about all aspects of EU social, economic and legal policy.

1637 International Geneva yearbook 2005–6: organization and activities of international institutions in Geneva
19th edn, Nijhoff, 1998–, annual, 648pp. £33. ISBN 9789210001540.
An excellent source of information on the recent activities of international organizations based in Geneva. This includes coverage of all the main United Nations bodies as well as many other international bodies and non-governmental organizations based there. It includes an overview of the year's main activities and publications as well as up-to-date contact addresses and names for each body. The yearbook also contains a number of essays written by experts which interpret recent economic, political and legal issues being discussed by the IGOs.

1638 Recent publications on the European Union received by the library
European Commission, 1994–, monthly. ISSN 1024011X.
A regularly monthly publication which lists new additions to the Central European Commission Library. These include listings of official EU publications, periodicals and legislation as well as other commercial publications about the EU and are therefore useful for tracing the existence of recent documents and books. Annual accumulations are published.

1639 UN Chronicle
United Nations Office of Public Information, 1975–, qtrly. Free. ISSN 02517329.
www.un.org/Pubs/chronicle/
A quarterly magazine published by the United Nations Department of Public Information to provide news to the public about current UN activities. It covers a wide range of topics covering all aspects of United Nations responsibility, including health, economic development, human rights, United Nations reform and peacekeeping operations. Each issue contains articles on current UN activities in the field, plus interviews with leading UN personnel. The full text of many articles published since 1997 can be accessed free of charge.

International Security & Conflict Resolution

air warfare • Arab–Israeli conflict • arms trade • civil wars • Cold War • current international conflicts & wars • disarmament • global conflict • international boundaries • military terminology • naval warfare • North Atlantic Treaty Organization • peace studies • peacekeeping • terrorism • war • weapons control • weapons of mass destruction

Introductions to the subject

1640   A history of warfare
J. Keegan   Hutchinson, 1993. ISBN 0091745276.

Classic work of military history which analyses three landmark battles – Agincourt, Waterloo and The Somme – from the perspective of the battlefield. The author uses his assessment to convey the reality of war for those involved. From there he speculates on future war.

Official & quasi-official bodies

1641   Common Foreign and Security Policy
http://ec.europa.eu/external_relations/cfsp/intro/index.htm

The Common Foreign and Security Policy, or CFSP, was established as the second of the three pillars of the European Union in the Maastricht Treaty of 1992. This official website, maintained by the European Commissioner for External Relations provides detailed background information on its history, implementation and recent activities. These cover conflict prevention, peacekeeping, disarmament and non-proliferation and sanctions. It is possible to access press releases, resolutions, treaties and other full-text EU documents relating to it.

1642   Regional Security System
www.rss.org.bb

An international organization which seeks to promote regional security in the Caribbean. Member nations include Barbados, Antigua, Dominica, Granada and St Lucia. Alongside the coordination of disaster aid, it also provides training for joint land and maritime operations and anti–terrorism intelligence gathering and sharing. The website provides basic information on its role, membership and activities.

United Nations. Department of Disarmament Affairs
See entry no. 1770.

Research centres & institutes

1643   Belfer Center for Science & International Affairs
http://bcsia.ksg.harvard.edu

A specialist centre of the John F. Kennedy School of Government which has a unique focus on the intersection between international relations, environmental issues and science and technology policy. It aims to use insights from scientists, social scientists and diplomats to provide solutions to world problems. Its website provides information

on its cutting-edge research and free access to a collection of its articles, papers and reports. Of particular interest is the international security programme which focuses upon perceived threats to US and international security. Recent analyses have covered diplomacy, terrorism and perceived threats from Iran, Iraq and Afghanistan. Users may view a cumulative index and recent tables of contents from its leading journal *International Security*.

1644   Berlin Information Center for Transatlantic Security
www.bits.de

A leading research centre which analyses military, security and arms control issues in Europe. Its website provides provides access to a wealth of full-text materials. These include the NATO Russia Archive of official documents relating to relations between the Russian Federation and NATO in the post-Cold War period, the CESD Archive – a collection of government and international treaties relating to the Common European Security and Defence Policy of the European Union – and EURA, an archive of papers relating to relations between Russia and the EU since 1996.

1645   British American Security Council
www.basicint.org

A non-governmental research and advocacy organization which focuses on global security issues. Key areas of concern are nuclear policies, weapons of mass destruction monitoring, military strategy and disarmament. The website provides free access to a very useful collection of online reports and newsletters produced since approximately 2000. These have recently include the Iran Update and the Afghanistan Update, which have provided news round-ups of security issues relating to nuclear weapons programmes in these regions.

1646   Brunel Centre for Intelligence & Security Studies
www.brunel.ac.uk/about/acad/sssl/ssslresearch/centres/bciss

Britain's first academic research and policy centre on intelligence and security studies, based at Brunel University. Its website offers details of current research projects, publications listings and contact details. Examples of recent work include European counter-terrorist intelligence, the role of intelligence in the war against terrorism, and intelligence and the decision to go to war in Iraq.

1647   Centre de Documentation et de Recherche sur la Paix et les Conflits
www.obsarm.org

A leading independent French research institute which specializes in issues relating to defence and international security, with a particular focus on the arms trade, armaments industry and French nuclear policy. The website is a good starting point for information on recent French-language research. It provides information on the activities of L'Observatoire des Armes Nucléaires Françaises and l'Observatoire des Transferts d'Armements. There is some free access to papers and summaries of reports, including statistics on arms sales, weapons transfers and the French defence budget. The site also contains a series of dossiers relating to current world conflicts. These offer summaries and links to key websites and online reports.

1648 Centre for Strategic & International Studies
www.csis.org

An independent US-based foreign policy think-tank which conducts research into defence and security policy, global security and regional transformations. Its website provides free access to event transcripts, briefing papers and full-text research reports from its ongoing programmes. These include coverage of many topical issues such as international terrorism, American homeland security, trade and economics. Also accessible are timely full-text reports on current conflict situations. Recent examples include Iraq, Iran, the Middle-East and Russia.

1649 Cold War international history project
http://wilsoncenter.org/index.cfm?topic_id=1409&fuseaction=topics.home

Based at the Woodrow Wilson International Center for Scholars, this programme is renowned for its research on the history of the Cold War. Its particular strength is in tracing and disseminating information from the former communist nations. It provides free access to a virtual library of declassified documents, images and working papers covering all aspects of the Cold War from the 1940s to the 1990s. Topics covered include the Cuban missile crisis of 1963, the Soviet invasion of Afghanistan in 1981 and the Hungarian uprising of 1956.

■ **Cold War files** www.coldwarfiles.org. A special educational site which teaches students how to interpret Cold War history using primary source documents. It includes multimedia files of key speeches, biographies of political leaders and suggestions for classroom activities.

1650 Cold War Studies Centre
www.lse.ac.uk/collections/CWSC

Based at the London School of Economics (LSE), this specialist centre is renowned for its research into the key political, social, intellectual, economic and military aspects of the Cold War. It includes coverage of both their historical origins and contemporary repercussions. Reference is also made to manifestations of the Cold War in non-European regions such as Southern Africa and Latin America. The website offers information on ongoing teaching and research programmes. It also provides free access to some working papers and tables of contents from recent publications, including its journal *Cold War History*.

1651 European Union, Institute for Security Studies
www.iss-eu.org

An autonomous research body created in 2001 to conduct research relating to major security and defence issues relevant to the future development of the European Union. A particular area of interest is the Common Foreign and Security Policy (CFSP). The website provides background information on the purpose and development of the CFS. It also includes free access to all issues of its flagship publication the *Chaillot Papers*. These are written by international experts and contain cutting-edge research on European security and defence issues.

1652 George C. Marshall European Center for Security Studies
www.marshallcenter.org

A research centre supported by the American and German governments which focuses on security issues in Europe. Its website provides information about the aims of the Center and access to the full text of a growing number of its publications, including Marshall Center papers and conference reports. Topics covered include civil-military relations, Russian foreign policy, globalization and international security, terrorism, international law and security, national defence and international security in Europe.

1653 Harvard project on Cold War history
www.fas.harvard.edu/~hpcws

Based at Harvard University, the project specializes in the study of declassified documents from the American government and governments of the Soviet Union and former Eastern Bloc nations. The website provides information on the aims of the project and its current activities. It includes tables of contents from its journal *Cold War Studies*, as well as some online exhibits of declassified documents and photographs. Topics covered by these currently include the history of the nuclear weapons race. The site also offers an impressive directory of links to Cold War history internet resources.

1654 Institute for Defense & Disarmament Studies
www.idds.org

An independent US-based research institution which seeks to promote arms control and disarmament. It is renowned for its studies of global military and arms control policies. The website also offers news stories, full-text papers, treaties and directories of links to related sites covering all areas of conventional weapons, nuclear weapons, weapons of mass destruction and disarmament.

■ **Arms Control Reporter** IDDS, 1982–, 11 p.a. £100. A monthly newsletter which offers a useful chronology of recent arms control talks and negotiations. A good starting point for checking the current state of play regarding individual non-proliferation treaties, covering both conventional and nuclear arms. Available in print or online. Price on request.

■ **IDDS world arms database** IDD. On demand. Statistical data on global arms holdings, production and trade for independent nations from 1972 onwards (in 2007 coverage extended to to 2004, with projections to 2015). Some data offered free of charge on the website. Payment required for full access.

1655 Institute for Security Studies
www.iss.co.za/

A leading African human security research institution. Its website provides free access to a wealth of information about regional security and conflict in Africa, with a particular focus on the region of sub-Saharan Africa. Of particular value are the fact files and situation reports on individual African nations and free access to all articles from its quarterly journal *The African Security Review*. Also available for downloading are ISS conference papers, reports and articles. Topics covered include the African security sector, conflict analysis, terrorism in Africa and corruption and governance.

1656 Institute on Global Conflict & Cooperation
http://igcc.ucsd.edu

A specialist research unit of the University of California. Its research covers issues relating to a wide range of topics involving security, environmental and economic policies. Its website provides information on its aims and current activities. It offers free access to a large number of its policy papers, briefings and reports published since approximately 1983. A key number cover issues relating to arms control, security and non-proliferation worldwide.

1657 International Boundaries Research Unit

www.dur.ac.uk/ibru

A specialist research and consultancy unit based at Durham University which is recognized for its expertise in land and sea territorial and boundary issues. Its website provides free access to a searchable archive of international boundary news, which contains over 10,000 reports from a wide range of news sources published from 1991 to March 2001, plus a directory of links to related e-mail discussion lists and websites.

1658 Jamestown Foundation

www.jamestown.org

An independent research institute which specializes in the analysis of political and economic trends. It is particularly recognized for its work on international security and the nations of Eurasia, including Russia, the former Soviet Union and China. Its website provides free access to recent research reports. These include its flagship publications *Chechnya Weekly* and *Eurasia Daily Monitor*. Back files and the latest updates are accessible.

1659 MIT Center for International Studies

http://web.mit.edu/cis/

A specialist research body based at Massachusetts Institute of Technology which supports cross-disciplinary research into a wide range of areas of international relations, including security, technology policy and globalization. The website offers free access to many online papers and reports.This includes the Foreign Policy Index – an annual audit of of US foreign policy by subject area. Also accessible is the full text of MIT International, an e-journal published since 2007. It aims to contain academic articles on international political, economic, social and technological issues offering innovative solutions to world problems.

1660 New security challenges

A major research programme funded by the UK Economic and Social Research Council (ESRC) from 2003 to 2007 supporting over 40 projects covering the area of new security challenges in the post-Cold War and post-9/11 world. Topics include gender and security, legal, organizational and regime limitations on force, economic determinants of security, new technology, weapons,media and psychological dimensions of security and human security. The main website provides information on the projects with links to their individual web pages and sites where many examples of cutting-edge research papers may be found.

1661 Norwegian Initiative on Small Arms Transfers

www.nisat.org

A joint project of the Norwegian Red Cross, Norwegian Church Aid, International Peace Research Institute Oslo and the Norwegian Institute of International Affairs which aims to block the spread of small arms worldwide. Small arms are defined to include all guns, rifles, pistols and grenades capable of being fired by a single person. The website provides information on the aims of the project, its publications and current programmes. It also provides free access to a number of detailed statistical databases. These include the world's only online global database of small arms transfers, which has information on the arms trade between some 250 states and territories over the period 1962 onwards. Also available is an archive of documents relating to black-market arms transfers and extensive links to other small arms document and data sources.

1662 Nuclear Threat Initiative

www.nti.org

A public charity founded in 1991 by philanthropist Ted Turner, it seeks to work to reduce the security threats from nuclear, chemical and biological weapons. Its website is an excellent starting point for tracing up-to-date news, facts and figures about events and holdings of these weapons worldwide. It includes the Global Security Newswire, which provides free daily news on nuclear, biological and chemical weapons terrorism and related issues. Also excellent are the country profiles, which contain overviews of the weapons programmes and controversies surrounding specific nations. They include materials for recent topical regions such as Iran and North Korea. The site also offers a teacher's section with educational modules to teach children about the issues surrounding weapons of mass destruction.

1663 RAND Corporation

www.rand.org

A leading American non-profit research and public policy institution which is famous for its high-quality research work. A wide range of social policy research areas are covered and free access is offered via the website to a large number of press releases, research papers and reports published in recent years. The International Affairs section covers security and current conflicts worldwide Other key specialist areas include the RAND Project AIR FORCE, sponsored by the US Air Force, RAND Arroyo Center, sponsored by the US Army, and RAND National Defense Research Institute, sponsored by the Office of the Secretary of Defense.

1664 Small arms survey

www.smallarmssurvey.org

An independent research project located at the Graduate Institute of International Studies in Geneva. Its website provides access to detailed information and research on small arms worldwide. This includes statistics on weapons stockpiles, arms exports and sales, case studies of disarmament in individual nations, and full-text reports on the use of guns and other light weapons in conflicts such as the civil war in Sudan. Users may download the full text of chapters from its annual *Small Arms Survey* from 2001 onwards.

■ **Small arms survey 2007: guns and the city** Small Arms SurveyCambridge University Press, 2007, annual, 368pp. £17.99. ISBN 9780521706544.

1665 Strategic Asia

http://strategicasia.nbr.org

A programme of the National Bureau of Asian research which assesses the strategic environment in the Asia-Pacific in terms of such factors as politics, the security environment and international trade. The website provides free access to its database, which contains a range of strategic military, political and economic indicators and resources for 37 countries in the Asia-Pacific region, including China, India, Japan, Afghanistan, Russia and Indonesia. The website also provides free access to all its annual yearbooks from 2000 onwards. These contain statistical facts and figures and analytical essays on strategic issues.

1666   Washington Institute for Near East Policy
www.washingtoninstitute.org
A leading think-tank on US policy towards the Middle East.
Its website provides information on the history, aims and
current activities of the body. It provides free access to
recent press releases, full-text articles and commentary on
current foreign policy. Topics covered include Islamic and
Arab politics, terrorism, oil and energy economics in the Gulf,
military and security policy, and US diplomatic relations.

Associations & societies

1667   Federation of American Scientists
www.fas.org
An association of American scientists, originally founded in
1945, who seek to engage in education and research
projects relating to a wide range of international security
issues. Key projects include arms sales monitoring, chemical
and biological weapons control, strategic security and
ballistic missile defence. The website offers free access to
some particularly useful factsheets and case studies which
clearly explain scientific terms relating to military hardware
and weapons of mass destruction. It also contains briefing
papers, news updates and reports on issues relating to
threats from WMD and efforts at disarmament. These
include special sections on current 'hot spots' such as Iran,
Iraq and North Korea.

Portal & task environments

1668   International relations and security network
www.isn.ethz.ch/
An excellent electronic clearing house for resources in the
field of international relations and security studies
maintained by the Center for Security Studies and Conflict
Research at the ETH Zurich. Key features include a
conference and events listing, access to news updates and
analysis covering all areas of international security, online
educational tutorials on international security and
disarmament issues and a comprehensive directory of
internet links.

Digital data, image & text collections

1669   CIA Freedom of Information reading room [USA]
www.foia.cia.gov/
The CIA (Central Intelligence Agency) Freedom of Information
reading room provides free access to a large collection of US
government documents which have been declassified and
released to the public under the Freedom of Information Act.
They include materials relating to the 20th-century and 21st-
century intelligence services, offering an in-depth insight into
the workings of US foreign diplomacy. The site is divided into
a number of key country and policy collections. These
include:

- **CAESAR, POLO, and ESAU Papers: Cold War era CIA
  analysis of Soviet and Chinese policy and decision
  making, 1953–1973** www.foia.cia.gov/cpe.asp. Over 11,000 pages
  of American intelligence analysis. The sections relating to Russia include
  analysis of Stalin, Khrushchev and Brezhnev; Soviet foreign policy; the
  Cuban missile crisis; communist and politburo activities; and Russian
  military and foreign policy from an American perspective. The Chinese

collection includes analysis of Mao Tse Tung; Chinese communist party
policies; the Cultural Revolution; the Great Leap Forward; and Sino-Soviet
relations.
- **Vietnam collection** www.foia.cia.gov/nic_vietnam_collection.asp.
  over 170 full-text declassified US government intelligence documents
  relating to Vietnam from 1948 to 1978. They include extensive coverage of
  US assessments of communism and the Vietnam War.

1670   Praeger security international
Greenwood Press. £1250.
www.greenwood.com/psi/
An online subscription database providing access to the full
text of over 500 books, encyclopedias, bibliographies and
chronologies relating to international security, foreign policy,
defence and military science. They include substantial
materials on American foreign affairs, security and military
strategy. Also available are news alerts relating to current
security crises worldwide. Details about pricing structures
are available from the publisher's website.

**1671   Zürcher Beitrage (Zurich contributions to security
policy and conflict research)**
Center for Security Studies (CSS), ETH Zürich, Infrequent. Free. ISSN
14233894.
www.css.ethz.ch/publications/publications/ZB
This series of occasional papers is published by the Center
for Security Studies (CSS) of the ETH Zürich (Swiss Federal
Institute of Technology). It provides scholarly discussion of a
wide range of issues issues relating to contemporary and
historical international security policy and conflict research
with a special focus on European security. Recent titles have
covered NATO, EU security, contemporary terrorism and the
Cold War. The series is published in English, German and
French. The full text of all volumes from no. 34, 1994,
onwards can be downloaded free from the website.

Directories & encyclopedias

**1672   North Atlantic Treaty Organisation: an
encyclopedia of international security**
C.T. Cobane, ed.   ABC-CLIO, 2007, 1111pp. 2 v., £124.50. ISBN
9781851098132.
The first comprehensive reference work to focus exclusively
on NATO. The two volumes contain approximately 650
alphabetically organized entries covering the history,
organization and recent activities of NATO. They also include
information on key individuals, events, operational forces and
treaties.

**1673   Weapons of mass destruction: an encyclopedia of
worldwide policy, technology, and history**
E.A. Croddy, J.J. Wirtz and J.A. Larsen, eds   ABC-CLIO, 2004, 111pp.
2 v., £165. ISBN 9781851094905.
A specialist two-volume encyclopedia covering issues relating
to chemical, biological and nuclear weapons. Contains over
500 entries arranged alphabetically covering issues related to
the history, technology, policy and controversy surrounding
WMD. A useful introduction for students of international
relations as it demystifies the scientific and military jargon
which often surrounds this new technology and offers
background on the history of its development and potential
risks in the modern security environment.

Handbooks & manuals

1674 Deadly arsenals: nuclear, biological, and chemical threats
J. Cirincione, J. Wolfsthal and M. Rajkumar   2nd edn, Carnegie Endowment for International Peace, 2005, 490pp. £17.99. ISBN 9780870032165.
Provides a comprehensive assessment of current global weapons proliferation threats, with a critical assessment of the effectiveness of international efforts at arms control and disarmament. Includes detailed maps, tables and and charts covering nuclear and non-nuclear weapons of mass destruction. These include statistics on stockpiles by individual nations and trading. Also provided are case studies of recent developments in Iraq, Iran and North Korea.

Nuclear weapons and nonproliferation: a reference handbook
S. Diehl and J. Moltz   See entry no. 1827

Keeping up to date

1675 Annual report to Congress: military power of the People's Republic of China
www.dod.mil/pubs/china.html
Free access to all US Department of Defense annual reports from 2002 to date. Each report contains statistical data on Chinese defence budgets, nuclear and conventional weapon expenditure and capabilities, plus discussion of Chinese military strategy and potential security threats to the USA and western world.

1676 Bulletin of the Atomic Scientists
Bulletin of the Atomic Scientists, bi-monthly. £20. ISSN 00963402.
www.thebulletin.org
A not-for-profit organization which has worked since 1945 to provide the public with scientifically sound information about nuclear weapons and to seek to reduce defence reliance on nuclear technology by promoting disarmament and alternative policy solutions. The website provides free access to some news stories and articles from the magazine and other news wires; other full-text materials are for subscribers only. It includes information on the famous Doomsday clock, which represents the risk of nuclear warfare in terms of a clock ticking towards midnight. In general it represents a useful source of information for members of the public seeking clear explanations of current nuclear technology issues.

1677 East Asia Strategic Review 2007
National Institute for Defense Studies   Japan Times, Ltd., 1977–, annual. Published in English and Japanese, £28. ISBN 978478901262.
www.nids.go.jp/english/index.html
An annual publication of the National Institute for Defense Studies (NIDS), a policy research arm of the Ministry of Defense (MOD), Japan. It offers a timely review of security policy and events in the Asian region in the previous calendar year. Each volume typically contains general essays on trends, assessments of US policy from an Asian perspective and individual country studies which provide an overview of current defence and foreign policy, military organization and structure and key events. Nations covered include Korea,

China, Russia, Japan, Indonesia. Volumes can be purchased in hard copy or downloaded from the website.

1678 European Security
Routledge, 1991–, qtrly. £60. ISSN 09662839.
A well regarded, peer-reviewed quarterly journal which provides a forum for the discussion of a wide range of issues relating to security in Europe. Particular areas of interest include the impact of EU enlargement upon security, NATO enlargement, transatlantic and European armaments cooperation, national defence policies of EU nations and the EU common foreign and security policy. Each issue contains articles and book reviews. Tables of contents and abstracts may be viewed free of charge online. Access to the full-text is for subscribers only. Available in print or online.

Current International Conflicts & Wars

Introductions to the subject

1679 Big wars and small wars: the British Army and the lessons of war in the 20th century [UK]
H. Strachan   Routledge, 2006, 186pp. £70. ISBN 0415361966.
The book investigates how the modern British Army has learned lessons from each successive war which might be applied to the next conflict. In the 20th century war has varied from full-scale war, 'small wars' and conflicts to counter-insurgency operations and peace support. This book argues that the Army's current doctrine remains to prepare for major war and in so doing also develop the capability to manage smaller conflicts. This excellent volume includes analysis from experts in the field, including Hew Strachan, Edward Spiers, David French, Paul Cornish, Daniel Marston, David Benest, Simon Ball and Colin McInnes.

1680 Conflict after Cold War: arguments on causes of war and peace
R.K. Betts, ed.   Longman, 2007, 672pp. £41.99. ISBN 9780205583522.
A carefully selected collection of essays which would be useful for introducing students to classic and contemporary discussion of the nature and causes of war. Includes thorough coverage of conflict and international security in the post-September 11 world, setting recent terrorism and political violence in its historical, economic and social contexts.

1681 An introduction to the causes of war: patterns of interstate conflict from World War I to Iraq
G. Cashman, ed.   Rowman & Littlefield Publishers, 2007, 400pp. £15.99. ISBN 9780742555105.
An excellent textbook which uses detailed case studies to introduce students to theoretical concepts and issues relating to the causes, nature and consequences of recent warfare. Conflicts covered include World War I, World War II, the Six Day War, the Indo–Pakistani War of 1971, the Iran–Iraq War and the Iraq War of 2003.

1682 Strategy in the contemporary world: an introduction to strategic studies
J. Baylis [et al.], eds   2nd edn, Oxford University Press, 2006, 416pp. £24.99. ISBN 9780199289783.
Useful textbook offering a solid introduction to theories and

concepts of warfare and its contemporary manifestations in the post 9/11 environment. It includes substantial coverage of topical issues relating to terrorism and weapons of mass destruction. Other chapters cover the situation in Iran, Iraq and Afghanistan, US homeland security and nuclear weapons in the 21st century.

1683 War, peace and international relations: an introduction to strategic history
C.S. Gray   Routledge, 2007, 320pp. £21.99. ISBN 9780415386395.
A useful student introduction to the history of war and peace over the last two centuries. The 14 essays set current trends in their historical context and include predictions up to 2025. Consider the causes, consequences and impact of wars.

Dictionaries, thesauri, classifications

1684 Dictionary of military terms
R. Bowyer   3rd edn, A. & C. Black, 2007, 265pp. £9.99. ISBN 9780713687354.
A useful background resource offering over 6000 up-to-date definitions of terms commonly used by the British and American forces in current peacekeeping and military operations. These include commands, tactics, weapons, logistics and strategy. Appendices include lists of military ranks, orders and symbols.

1685 Historical dictionaries of war, revolution and civil unrest series
J. Woronoff, ed.   Scarecrow Press, ongoing.
An excellent ongoing series of guides published by Scarecrow Press. They cover conflicts from ancient times to the modern day, as well as themes relating to military science and arms control. Each volume typically contains entries for key figures, events, organizations and dates. These would be particularly suitable for introducing students and members of the public to the main facts and figures. Also provided are bibliographies to guide further research. Recent examples include:
- **Historical dictionary of the Arab–Israeli conflict** P. **Kumaraswamy**   Scarecrow Press, 2006, 424pp. £66. ISBN 9780810853430.
- **Historical dictionary of the Northern Ireland conflict** G. **Gillespie**   Scarecrow Press, 2007, 320pp. £56. ISBN 9780810855830.

Official & quasi-official bodies

1686 British Army
www.army.mod.uk [16/05/2007]
The key internet resource for information about the current British Army. For the researcher it provides information on army organization, deployments and history, with links to the current regimental and corps microsites. It includes photographs, press releases and full-text reports from current operations and deployments. Also provided are sections on careers information and links to the main veterans' organizations.
- **Soldier Magazine** Soldier Magazine, 1945–, monthly. £23. www.soldiermagazine.co.uk. An official magazine of the British Army which has been published monthly since 1945. It offers news and popular articles about events, operations and British Army life. It includes letters pages which provide insight into the issues currently concerning serving personnel.

A selection of classic articles from its archives can be obtained free of charge from the website.

1687 DefenseLink: official web site for the Department of Defense [USA]
United States. Department of Defense
www.defenselink.mil
The main portal to official websites maintained by the US Department of Defense. The large website offers free access to information about the history, organizational structure and current activities of the DoD. This includes coverage of the Army, Navy, Air Force and Marine Corps. It offers free access to recent press releases, statistics, photographs, video films and clips, annual reports and other full-text documents. This includes coverage of ongoing military campaigns and operations. The site has a full directory of links to all the websites of US military DoD bodies and agencies.
- **American forces press service** www.defenselink.mil/home/news_products.html. The main gateway to official news services offered by branches of the US Department of Defense. They include press release services, TV and radio programmes and *Stars and Stripes*, the official newspaper of the DoD. The main focus is upon reporting what senior defense leaders are saying on all aspects of military life. Many of the materials are updated daily.
- **Annual defense report: Annual reports to the President and Congress** US Government Printing Office, annual. www.dod.mil/execsec/adr_intro.html. The full text of all annual reports from the Department of Defense from 2003 to date can be searched and downloaded from the website. These offer overviews of the American defence budget, recent military operations, statistics on service personnel.
- **BosniaLink** www.dtic.mil/bosnia. Official Department of Defense information system about US military activities in the Balkans. Includes press releases, maps, deployment relating to current stabilization activities and earlier involvement in the Balkans conflict.
- **Defense almanac** Department of Defense, infrequent. Free. www.defenselink.mil/pubs/almanac. A reference handbook to the US military which is regularly updated by the DoD. It provides rapid access to organizational charts, facts and figures about the role and operation of the military.
- **Department of Defense dictionary of military and associated terms** Department of Defense, 766pp. www.dtic.mil/doctrine/jel/new_pubs/jp1_02.pdf. Provides free access to the latest version of the authorized US military dictionary. It contains definitions of key military and DoD terms and acronyms. Date of last revision is provided on the website.
- **Department of Defense personnel and procurement statistics** http://siadapp.dmdc.osd.mil. Free access to the main DoD statistical series. These include military casualty statistics from recent and historic conflicts from the Korean War to the present. Also available are data on current service strengths and civilian employment from approximately 2000 onwards.
- **GulfLink** www.gulflink.osd.mil. Website of the Special Assistant for Gulf War Illnesses. Provides free access to official US government press releases, statistics and reports relating to the events of the Gulf War 1990–1 and subsequent health problems experienced by veterans. Includes consumer information on support for ex-servicemen and women.
- **Joint Chiefs of Staff** www.jcs.mil. The Joint Chiefs of Staff consist of the Chairman, the Vice Chairman, the Chief of Staff of the Army, the Chief of Naval Operations, the Chief of Staff of the Air Force, and the Commandant of the Marine Corps. The official website provides free access to recent press releases, strategy documents relating to current military deployments and transcripts of speeches from leading service personnel. The site also contains a large electronic library of online resources relating to American military doctrine. These include full text issues of the *Joint Force Quarterly* from 1993 onwards. This professional journal contains articles on issues

relating to joint doctrine, integrated operations, contingency planning and military operations.

■ **Measuring stability and security in Iraq**
www.defenselink.mil/home/features/Iraq_Reports/index.html. Free access to reports made to the US Congress since 2005 detailing the security situation in Iraq in the aftermath of the Gulf War and progress towards achieving political and economic stability in the region.

■ **Pentagon channel** www.pentagonchannel.mil. An official online news channel from the American military. It provides free access to Department of Defense news briefings, military news and interviews with top service personnel. It includes regular updates from current conflict zones. Users should note that the purpose of the site is to promote the work of the US military.

1688   French Foreign Legion (Légion étrangère)
www.legion-etrangere.com
Official website of the celebrated elite fighting force, originally established in 1831. It provides information on its history, role and current activities. It includes video clips, press releases photographs and news from some of its current deployments. Some information is offered in French only.

1689   Great Britain. House of Commons, Defence Select Committee
www.parliament.uk/parliamentary_committees/defence_committee.cfm
A select committee of the UK House of Commons which analyses British defence and military policy. Its website contains a list of current members of the Committee and links to the full text of press releases, minutes of hearings and Committee reports from 1997 onwards. These include important examples of critical assessments of the economic and human costs of UK military deployments overseas in such areas as Iraq and Afghanistan. Other areas covered include defence procurement; British arms and weapons exports and the work of the Ministry of Defence.

1690   Great Britain. Ministry of Defence
www.mod.uk
A key source of information about the history and current practice of British defence policy. It contains a very useful section for researchers which provides free access to recent MoD press releases, blog, the official YouTube channel, defence White Papers, legislation, regulations and other full-text documents. Materials cover the army, navy and air force. Themes covered include military strategy, expenditure; on-going operations and conflicts. The latter currently includes special sections on operations in Iraq and Afghanistan. A directory of links to all UK government defence agencies is provided.

■ **Defence image database.** www.defenceimagedatabase.mod.uk. Free access to a database containing thousands of digital images supplied by official Army, Royal Navy, RAF and MoD photographers. Includes photographs of staff, key personnel and images from recent combat zones such as Iraq and Afghanistan. Copyright information is supplied on the website.

■ **Defence Analytical Services Agency** www.dasa.mod.uk. A specialist body which provides free access to a large collection of UK defence statistics, many dating from the late 1990s onwards. Key series available from its website include the annual Defence statistics; Armed forces personnel statistics; Armed forces suicide reports; Deaths, medical discharges and casualty statistics for the British armed forces; and Gulf War veterans and war pensions statistics.

1691   International Atomic Energy Agency
www.iaea.org
An independent international organization associated with the United Nations which acts to develop nuclear safety standards and monitor that states comply with their commitments, under the Nuclear Non-Proliferation Treaty and other non-proliferation agreements, to use nuclear material and facilities only for peaceful purposes. Its website is particularly useful for politics students seeking information on international crises associated with the development of nuclear weapons by specific nations. For instance, in recent years, it has maintained extremely useful micro-sites on IAEA missions in Iraq, Iran and North Korea which contain press releases, statistical data and full-text reports on nuclear capacities and potential security risks.

1692   NATO (North Atlantic Treaty Organisation)
www.nato.int [24/08/2007]
Official website of the leading intergovernmental security organization, offering extensive information on the purpose, history and recent activities of NATO. It includes an online library containing basic treaties and texts, including the North Atlantic Treaty. Also accessible are press releases from 1993 onwards; transcripts and videocasts of speeches from the mid-1990s onwards; and collections of papers and resolutions from ministerial summits. These include comprehensive coverage of recent NATO operations in conflict zones such as Kosovo and Afghanistan. There is a collection of educational materials and quizzes for children.

■ **NATO handbook** NATO, 2006, Infrequent, 405pp. Free. www.nato.int/docu/handbook/2006/hb-en-2006.pdf. A detailed reference text covering all aspects of the North Atlantic Treaty Organization. Provides official facts on the structure, role, history and current operations of NATO. Includes useful structure charts and abbreviation lists. Updated periodically. All issues since 2000 accessible online.

■ **NATO review** NATO, qtrly. Free. www.nato.int/docu/review.htm. Flagship journal covering current policy issues and operations. Articles provide insight into the changing nature of the NATO alliance and do not necessarily represent the official opinion or policy of member governments or NATO. All issues from 1991 onwards may be accessed free of charge from the website.

1693   Office of the Special Representative of the Secretary-General for Children & Armed Conflict
www.un.org/children/conflict/english/home6.html
A special representative of the United Nations who works to promote and protect the rights of all children affected by war worldwide. The website offers free access to all associated United Nations press releases, resolutions, treaties, country case files and other reports. Key areas of concern include child soldiers, girls and war, refugees and sexual violence against children in war zones.

1694   Organization for Security & Co-operation in Europe
www.osce.org
The OSCE is the world's largest regional security organization. Its website provides free access to detailed official information about its history, current role and recent activities. It includes an online documents library containing full-text annual reports, resolutions, treaties and ministerial summits from its origins in 1975 to the present. Users can also sign up to receive alerts about the latest additions. Other features of the website include free access to webcasts of recent events, events calendars and factsheets. Topics covered by its politico-military section include counter-

terrorism in Europe, policing arms control, border security military reform and conflict prevention.

1695 Royal Air Force [UK]

www.raf.mod.uk

This is the official website of the British air force. It provides free access to information about the history, organizational structure and current activities of the RAF. This includes free access to press releases, online videoclips, photographs and strategy documents. The site also includes detailed information on current deployments, including facts, figures, maps and images. Other features of the site include careers information and a directory of air force-related organizations which is useful for tracing associated government agencies and veterans' support groups.

- **Air Power Review** RAF, 1997–, 2 p.a. free online. www.raf.mod.uk. Official flagship journal of the RAF. Contains scholarly articles covering military strategy, weapons and operations from a British perspective. Contributors include serving personnel. Each issue contains a book reviews section. All issues published since 2000 can be downloaded free of charge from the website.
- **RAF News** RAF, 24 p.a. £16.50. www.rafnews.co.uk. Official newsletter which offers news, views and topical articles on RAF and military aviation developments for a general audience. Some news headlines available free of charge on the website. Full access in print or online for subscribers only.

1696 Royal Navy

www.royal-navy.mod.uk

Website providing official information about British naval forces. It includes press releases, photographs and video clips, operational maps and other information about current deployments in Afghanistan and the Gulf. Also provided are sub-sections on recruitment to the Navy; facts about British naval history and the role of specific naval sections such as the Royal Marines, Fleet Air Arm and submarine division.

1697 UN Iraq: web portal for UN Agencies working in Iraq

www.uniraq.org

The main access point for information about United Nations activities in and relating to Iraq. In addition to current news stories and press releases, it also provides free access to the full text of all related United Nations documents, UN Security Council resolutions, materials from the UN Assistance Mission for Iraq (UNAMI), plus background statistics and maps of the region, transcripts of speeches, photographs and UN radio reports.

1698 United Nations Security Council

www.un.org/Docs/sc/

An invaluable source of information for those interested in the work of the UN in international security and conflict resolution. The official website provides free access to a wealth of information about the role, membership and activities of the Security Council. It is possible to use the website to consult the latest press releases and live webcasts of the most recent debates. Also accessible are searchable databases of voting reports and an index of all resolutions taken by the Council from 1946 onwards. Links are provided to the websites of UN peacekeeping missions.

1699 United States. Senate, Committee on Armed Services

http://armed-services.senate.gov

An official body of the US Senate which studies and reviews

all matters relating to the defence policy of the USA. This includes critical commentary on the administration of armed forces pay, promotions and pensions, military budgets and the conduct of recent US military operations in regions such as Iraq. The website provides free access to recent press releases and selected committee hearings and reports.

Research centres & institutes

1700 Advanced Research & Assessment Group [UK]

www.defac.ac.uk/colleges/csrc

This is the specialist research unit of the Defence Academy of the United Kingdom, which is the UK defence establishment's main higher educational institution and training unit. It conducts analyses on issues relating to operational strategy, defence and security policy of the British armed forces. Its website offers free access to news and full-text publications from its centres. It includes regional studies, analytical papers and materials relating to security and organizational reform.

1701 Center for Contemporary Conflict [USA]

www.ccc.nps.navy.mil/about.asp

A specialist unit based at the Naval Postgraduate School, Department of National Security Affairs, which analyses current and emerging issues in international security. Particular topics of concern include weapons of mass destruction, nuclear weapons, terrorism and security threats. The website provides information on current research and free access to some full-text articles and papers published by CCC. It includes all issues of its free monthly e-journal Strategic Insights from 2002 onwards. This contains timely essays and commentary on issues relating to weapons, ongoing conflicts and security. It frequently offers links to full-text Naval School postgraduate theses on these issues.

Centre de Documentation et de Recherche sur la Paix et les Conflits
See entry no. 1647

1702 Centre for Defence & International Security Studies

www.cdiss.org [17/05/2007]

A long-established specialist research centre; originally based within Lancaster University, it now operates as an independent think-tank. Key areas of concern include European security; missile threats and responses; nuclear proliferation; terrorism and counter-insurgency; space policy; aviation and maritime security; defence procurement; and Central Asian security. Its website provides information on current research areas and activities. It offers free access to a large number of its research papers that have been published since 1980.

1703 Children & Armed Conflict Unit

www.essex.ac.uk/armedcon

A joint project of the Children's Legal Centre and the Human Rights Centre at the University of Essex which analyses information on the impact of war on children. This includes substantial coverage of issues relating to child soldiers. Its website provides free access to news stories about children and war and a large number of full-text publications. These include studies conducted by the centre (and other international aid agencies) in specific war zones containing reports, statistics and eye-witness accounts of the hardship suffered.

1704   Heidelberger Institut für Internationale Konfliktforschung (Heidelberg Institute of International Conflict Research)
www.hiik.de

A non-profit German body which specializes in documenting wars and conflicts that have taken place worldwide in the post 1945 period. Its website provides free access to data and online reports. These include the Cosmio database, which contains statistical data on conflicts since 1945. Also the full text of all issues of the *Conflict Barometer* since 1997. This yearbook traces trends in the escalation and settlement of wars, civil wars and political conflicts during the previous calendar year. It is a good starting point for basic facts and figures.

1705   Households in conflict network
www.hicn.org

An international network of researchers who conduct econometric and micro-economic analysis of the causes and impact of violent conflict on individual households. Its website provides access to information about the aims of the network, recent activities and research projects. Also accessible are some full-text working papers and datasets. Topics covered include the relationship between civil wars, wars and household poverty, the economic impact of terrorism and the human impact of conflicts. Reference is made to current crisis situations, including the genocide in Rwanda, war in the Congo, and the civil war in Sudan (Darfur region).

1706   INCORE: international conflict research
www.incore.ulst.ac.uk

A joint project of the United Nations University and the University of Ulster. Although its original focus was on the Northern Ireland conflict, it now works more widely on inter-disciplinary themes relating to the research and teaching of peace, conflict and reconciliation issues worldwide. Its website offers a wealth of useful materials for the academic researcher, including full-text papers, reports and web directories.

■ **The conflict data service** www.incore.ulst.ac.uk/services/cds. Maintains a large number of country and thematic bibliographies These highlight valuable web sources of maps, documents, reports and news services for the subject area chosen. Examples of recent thematic topics include UN peacekeeping, gender and conflict, and the media and conflicts. Also available is a digital library of peace agreements.

■ **The Ethnic Conflict Research Digest** www.incore.ulst.ac.uk/services/ecrd. A valuable current awareness tool for researchers and students which publishes book reviews of recent publications relating to ethnic conflict. The full database of articles from 1994 onwards can be searched by keyword and read free of charge via the website.

Institute for Security Studies
See entry no. 1655

1707   Institute for War & Peace Reporting
www.iwpr.net

An independent UK-based organization which seeks to inform the international debate on conflict by supporting the independent media in regions in transition. Its website contains a number of really useful regional newsletters and

reports. These regularly contain materials from grassroots journalists in conflict and war zones offering local insight into the situation. They also report instances of oppression, civil rights and human rights abuses. Current newsletters cover Iran, Iran, Afghanistan, the Caucasus, the Balkans, Africa and Central Asia. New areas are constantly being developed. Recent and archived issues can be viewed free of charge via the website or users may receive materials via e-mail. Some projects also provide free access to radio and/or podcasts via the website.

1708   International Crisis Group
www.crisisgroup.org/

An independent non-governmental organization which specializes in analysing conflicts and crisis situations. It is renowned for its use of fieldwork to produce analytical reports containing practical recommendations targeted at key international decision-takers. Its website is one of the best places for locating press releases, summaries and research reports on international security situations, wars and conflicts worldwide. It also publishes *CrisisWatch*, a monthly bulletin containing concise summaries of significant conflicts and potential conflicts worldwide.

1709   King's College London, Department for War Studies
www.kcl.ac.uk/schools/sspp/ws

Based at Kings College, London, this academic research unit is highly regarded for its quality of teaching and research which covers a wide range of areas relating to international security, conflict, military strategy and war. Its website provides information on its remit, courses and research. It includes lists of recent staff publications.

1710   National Defense University
www.ndu.edu

A leading centre for military education in the USA which is administered under the direction of the Chairman, Joint Chiefs of Staff. Its mission is to provide information, training and research to aid current American military and security policy. The website provides access to press releases, full-text reports and project outcomes from its many specialist units. These include the Center for the Study of Weapons of Mass Destruction, the Center for Technology and National Security, the Policy Institute for National Strategic Studies and the Center for the Study of Chinese Military Affairs. They offer specialist discussion of current and future US military strategy.

1711   Oxford Leverhulme programme on the changing character of war
http://ccw.politics.ox.ac.uk

A major five-year programme (2003–8) funded by the Leverhulme Trust to investigate the changing nature of modern warfare. Located in the University of Oxford Centre for International Studies in the Department of Politics and International Relations in cooperation with the Faculty of Modern History and the Oxford Uehiro Centre for Practical Ethics in the Faculty of Philosophy. Key areas of research include the morality of war, detention and torture, law and war, security and war armed forces and the state, non-state actors and the UN and war. The site provides free access to press releases and synposese of the research plus some papers and reports.

1712 **Project on Defense Alternatives**
www.comw.org/pda
An initiative of the Commonwealth Institute, Cambridge, Massachusetts. Its purpose is to promote the adoption of alternative military strategies for the post-Cold War era, focusing in particular on the demilitarization of international relations. Its website provides free access to a large number of policy papers, reports and briefings from its ongoing projects. These include materials relating to Chinese military power, the revolution in military affairs, alternative security and defense strategies, and current conflicts such as Afghanistan and Iraq. Many of the resources are critical of current US defence and foreign policy.

RAND Corporation
See entry no. 1663

1713 **Royal United Services Institute**
www.rusi.org
Founded in 1831, RUSI is the oldest defence and international affairs institute in the world, conducting and disseminating research covering a wide range of issues relating to international security, military sciences and homeland security and resilience. Its website provides information on its research, conferences and publications. Some materials are offered in full-text online. These include scholarly analysis of recent current issues such as the conflict in Iraq and terrorism.

- **HSR Monitor: homeland security and resilence monitor** RUSI, 2001–, 10 p.a. £180. www.rusi.org/publication/monitor. A key publication on technical, military and practical issues relating to British homeland security. Includes coverage of risk from natural and man-made disasters, with extensive coverage of issues relating to terrorism in the post-9/11 world. Free RSS feeds and tables of contents from the website. Full article access for subscribers only.
- **RUSI Journal** RUSI, 1857–, bi-monthly. £120. www.rusi.org/publication/journal. The flagship publication containing scholarly articles and book reviews on military and defence matters. Includes extensive coverage of military operations and tactics in ongoing conflicts such as Iraq and Afghanistan. Free RSS feeds, tables of contents and abstracts of articles from the website. Full-text access for subscribers only.
- **Whitehall papers** RUSI, Infrequent. £40. ISSN 02681307. Well-regarded series of occasional papers. Each volume contains detailed scholarly analysis of international security, defence and military issues. Recent examples include the insurgency in Iraq, private defence companies and the use of private finance in defence acquistions.

1714 **Stockholm International Peace Research Institute**
www.sipri.org
An independent research foundation created by the Swedish government in 1966. Its website is a key place for locating high-quality research on issues relating to peace, disarmament and conflict resolution. It offers free access to a large number of full-text databases and research reports. Important examples include the Multilateral Peace Operations Database (which contains information on all UN and non-UN peace operations from 2000 to present); data on military expenditure (covering approximately 165 countries for the period since 1988); and data on arms production (annual statistics on the top 100 arms manufacturers, listing sales figures and numbers of employees).

- **SIPRI arms transfers database** http://armstrade.sipri.org. Free access to a searchable online database containing information on international transfers of seven types of conventional weapon from 1950 to the most recent full calendar year.
- **SIPRI yearbook 2007: armaments, disarmament and international security** Oxford University Press, 2007, annual, 752pp. £85. ISBN 9780199230211. The leading annual survey of recent trends in conflicts and security, disarmament and military spending. Each issue contains chronologies of events in the past calendar year.
- **FIRST: facts on international relations and security trends** http://first.sipri.org. A joint project of the International Relations and Security Network (ISN) and SIPRI. Designed to provide journalists and members of the public with quick access to key facts on major issues relating to international relations and security, using data drawn from a number of leading research bodies. At present 38 categories are offered, including arms production and trade, military expenditure, armed forces and conventional weapons holding, nuclear weapons and resumés of major conflicts. It includes statistical data, chronologies and basic background facts.

1715 **Strategic Studies Institute of the US Army War College**
www.strategicstudiesinstitute.army.mil
SSI is the US Army's institute for geostrategic and national security research and analysis. It aims to publish materials which bridge the gap between military science research and policy. Its website provides free access to a large collection of its books, papers and reports published since approximately 1993. Key topics covered include the global war on terrorism, homeland security, military leadership, strategy and policy. It also offers extensive regional studies on issues facing different regions of the world, including current flashpoints such as Central Asia and Caucasus and the Middle East.

Associations & societies

1716 **International Committee of the Red Cross**
www.icrc.org
One of the most important humanitarian organizations working to protect the victims of war worldwide. Its website is a useful source of information on current wars and conflicts. It includes maps, photographs, online films and reports from current humanitarian missions. These offer insight into the impact of specific conflicts on civilians. The site also includes special sections on the impact of war on women, prisoners of war and the role of aid agencies in conflict zones.

The section on international humanitarian law includes the link 'international humanitarian law', giving access to the texts of treaties and the National Implementation Database, containing national laws and case law on the implementation of humanitarian law, accessible by State and keyword.

1717 **Peace, war and social conflict**
This is a special-interest section of the American Sociological Association which focuses specifically on issues relating to military sociology, causes and dynamics of war, gender and war, and sociological studies of conflict. Its website is a useful starting point for tracing recent resources relating to this field. It includes tables of contents from leading peace studies and conflict resolution journals, curriculum guides for teaching the sociology of peace and war and links to related e-mail discussion lists.

1718 Royal British Legion
www.britishlegion.org.uk

A charity which promotes the welfare of veterans of the British armed forces. Its website provides information on its purpose and current campaigns. Its includes information on the annual Poppy Appeal and Remembrance Day commemoration. It also regularly contains critical commentary on UK government policy with regard to war pensions, war widows and the health and welfare of veterans from current and historic conflicts.

1719 Watchlist on Children & Armed Conflict
www.watchlist.org

An American based non-governmetal organization which works to ensure that the security and rights of children in armed conflicts around the world are protected. Its website provides free access to its recent press releases and full-text country reports. These contain information on the use of child soldiers in specific conflicts and the impact of wars upon the well-being and human rights of children. Reports are generally available from about 2000 onwards. Recent countries covered have included Iraq, Nepal, Sudan, Angola, Democratic Republic of the Congo and Zimbabwe.

Libraries, archives, museums

1720 Imperial War Museum
www.iwm.org.uk

An incomparable museum collection covering all aspects of 20th- and 21st-century conflict involving Britain and the Commonwealth. It is also a major national art gallery, a national records archive and a research centre for current and historical military resources.Its website provides information on its scope and collection. This includes tourist information as well as online access to its catalogues of its books, sound archives and photographic collections for researchers.

- Imperial War collections online www.iwmcollections.org.uk. This section of the website provides free access to a growing database of digitized images of over 30,000 artefacts held by the museum. They include fascinating documents, photographs, audio extracts and papers which provide insight into major 20th- and 21st-century conflicts including the First and Second World Wars, Falklands War, Korean War and Gulf Wars. Many examples provide insight into the human experience of conflict by individual soldiers, prisoners of war and civilians on the home front.

1721 Perry-Castañeda Library map collection
www.lib.utexas.edu/maps/afghanistan.html

A specialist map collection based in the Library services at the University of Texas at Austin. Its website provides free access to a large collection of its open-source geographical and political maps, including satellite images and materials compiled by the CIA. It regularly creates collections relating to nations involved in security crises, wars and conflicts. Recent examples include Afghanistan, Iran and Iraq. Each section provides access to recent and historical maps. Details about dates, sources and scale are available online.

Portal & task environments

1722 AERADE (Aerospace and defence internet gateway)
Cranfield University

http://aerade.cranfield.ac.uk [15/05/2007]

Aerade is an internet gateway managed by Cranfield University which provides access to high-quality internet resources relating to aerospace and defence. It contains links to bibliographies, data, full-text articles, documents and journals The defence subset includes coverage of resources relating to current international conflicts and crises from a miltary angle. Each resource has an annotated description of content written by a subject expert. Other features of the service include current conference and jobs listings.

1723 Britain's small wars: the history of British military conflicts from 1945
www.britains-smallwars.com

This site is maintained by military enthusiasts James Paul and Martin Spirit. It provides a history of British warfare from 1945 onwards. Conflicts covered include Indian independence and partition, Malaya, the Korean War, the Suez Canal crisis, the Northern Ireland troubles, the Falklands War, the Gulf War and conflict in Iraq. Each section provides a chronology of the conflict, containing historical details of significant battles, weapons used, information on military leaders and casualties. The majority of the descriptions are written by British ex-servicemen. Numerous links are provided to related sites.

1724 Ethics of war, peace and terrorism multimedia resources
http://ethics.sandiego.edu/Applied/Military/index.asp

A useful directory of links to academic web resources related to the philosophy of war, military ethics and just war theory which is maintained by Lawrence M. Hinman, a professor of philosophy and Director of the Values Institute at the University of San Diego. They include classic online texts, articles, military ethics case studies and some online documentaries. Most resources are free.

1725 Human security gateway
www.humansecuritygateway.info/

A joint project of the Human Security Centre (HSC) and the Canadian Consortium on Human Security (CCHS University of British Columbia) which provides researchers with a free, searchable database of links to information about wars, civil wars and security crises worldwide. These include the latest news stories plus links to recent reports, statistics and papers from research bodies, think-tanks and humanitarian agencies. Each item is fully catalogued with a description of content. Examples include the Darfur crisis, war in Iraq and the war again terrorism. It is possible to browse the site by nation or human security topic. Topics covered include international law, refugees and displaced persons and international conflict.

1726 MERIA: Middle East review of international affairs
http://meria.idc.ac.il/

MERIA is a project maintained by GLORIA (Global Research in International Affairs) of the IDC (Interdisciplinary Research Center, Israel). It provides free access to all articles from *MERIA Journal*, a quarterly scholarly publication on the Middle East, from 1997 to date. These cover all aspects of the economic, political and social life of Middle Eastern nations, including substantial coverage of the Arab–Israeli conflict and American policy towards the Middle East. Additional features of the website include tables of contents from academic journals covering the Middle-East, guides to researching the Middle East, book listings and directories of recommended internet resources.

1727 MERLN: Military education and research library network
http://merln.ndu.edu

A free website maintained by a consortium of leading US military education and research libraries, including the by the National Defense University Library, which provides free access to an extensive range of online services. These include links to worldwide military library catalogues, full-text lectures, electronic collections of papers and reports and online theses and dissertations. All areas of military science, strategic and international relations are covered.

Discovering print & electronic resources

1728 Air University Library's index to military periodicals
Air University Library, 1989–, continuous. Free.
www.dtic.mil/dtic/aulimp

An excellent free online index to important articles, news items and editorials from English-language military and aeronautical periodicals which is produced by staff of the Air University Library. It covers the most important US army, navy and air force periodicals as well as key scholarly titles from leading US and UK research institutes, from approximately 1989 to the present. The main emphasis is on military strategy, weapons and tactics. There are numerous articles on recent and ongoing conflicts in the Gulf and Afghanistan. Some annotations on content are provided.

1729 Lancaster index
Military Policy Research Ltd, 1980–, weekly. £37.50.
www.mpr.co.uk/scripts/sweb.dll/li_home [24/08/2007]

A leading index to military, defence and security affairs journal articles and monographs, its contents based largely on the holdings of Lancaster University Library. Topics covered include defence policy and military strategy in recent conflicts and wars. It also encompasses military history; the armed services and defence technology. Materials are indexed from approximately the mid-1980s onwards. Updates are made weekly. Non-subscribers may search recent articles free of charge and obtain bibliographic references. Access to older materials and abstracts of the articles referenced is for subscribers only.

1730 Military policy awareness links (MiPALs)
http://merln.ndu.edu/index.cfm?type=page&pageID=3

An excellent current awareness service maintained by the National Defense University. Each MiPAL provides links to key US policy statements on an individual country or general security related topic, plus commentary from think-tanks, non-governmental sources and scholarly journals. Some references are to subscription only resources, but these are clearly indicated. General topics include terrorism, weapons of mass destruction and US homeland security. Also covered are international security 'hotspots' such as China, Iran, India–Pakistan, Iraq and Afghanistan. The main emphasis is on current news; however, materials which are more than one year old can generally be accessed in the archive area of the website.

1731 Muir S. Fairchild Research Information Center bibliographies
www.maxwell.af.mil/au/aul/bibs/bib97.htm

Free access to a collection of several hundred bibliographies compiled since 1990 by staff at the Muir S. Fairchild Research Information Center, Air University USA. These cover a wide range of military-related topics, including all major conflicts of the 20th and 21st centuries, weapons and warfare strategies. Each bibliography provides an excellent starting point for beginning research, offering a handy list of recently published key books, journals and documents. They also have links to important websites and online documents. The emphasis is on references to US published materials. Recent examples include bibliographies on the conflict in Afghanistan and US options towards the nuclear programme in Iran.

1732 Shrivenham index
Cranfield University
http://naca.central.cranfield.ac.uk/si/ [24/08/2007]

A free index to defence journal literature produced from holdings of journals at two of the UK's leading defence libraries: the Defence Academy of the United Kingdom and Defence College of Management and Technology, Cranfield University. Includes coverage of recent conflicts and security crises such as Iran, Iraq and the Gulf War. The main emphasis is on military strategy, defence policy and weapons. Records include full bibliographic references and abstracts, links are provided to full-text web versions where available. Continuously updated.

1733 Staff College Automated Military Periodicals Index (SCAMPI)
www.dtic.mil/dtic/scampi

A specialized index to journal articles and reports maintained by the US Joint Forces Staff College Library. It provides free access to references to materials covering all areas of military and naval science, from approximately 1996 onwards. This includes strong coverage of US military operations in international crisis situations such as Iran, Afghanistan and the Gulf War, as well as American defence and security policies. The main emphasis is on the military, rather than political, aspects of the conflicts. Abstracts are not currently provided.

1734 US Army War College Library bibliographies
http://carlisle-www.army.mil/library/library_pubs.htm

The US Army War College Library is the main library of the American army's senior educational institution. Its website provides free access to its large collection of online bibliographies, which is regularly added to and updated. Currently subdivided into two main series, thematic bibliographies and periodical articles for current awareness (PACs). The former cover a wide range of military affairs issues ranging from women in the military, to the military profession, multilateral operations and homeland security highlighting key books, journal articles and internet resources. PACS are monthly current awareness listings of important journal articles covering military science and international relations which are based on titles from the holdings of the library. They are arranged by geographic region and topic. Themes covered include military strategy, weapons, insurgency and articles relating to specific topics such as Iraq, Iran and Gulf conflicts. Materials generally focus on a US military perspective. Free access to issues from 2007 onwards via the website.

Digital data, image & text collections

1735 **Armed conflict database**

International Institute for Strategic Studies, continuous updates. £450. www.iiss.org/publications/armed-conflict-database

A subscription service maintained by the the International Institute for Strategic Studies (IISS) which provides data on recent and ongoing conflicts and wars worldwide. Each entry includes historical background, information on military and human security issues, statistics on weapons casualties, plus links to related reports such as United Nations resolutions. Information on subscription rates is provided on the website.

1736 **Bitter lemons: Palestinian-Israeli crossfire**

www.bitterlemons.org/index.html

A website which is renowned for its balanced discussion of a range of issues relating to the Arab–Israeli conflict. It is edited by Ghassan Khatib, a Palestinian lecturer based at Birzeit University, and Yossi Alpher, the Israeli director of Political Security Doman. It takes a non-partisan viewpoint and regularly presents articles from both Israeli and Palestinian viewpoints. Issues are usually released weekly, each one focusing on a specific topic, offering discussion from a range of Israeli and Palestinian perspectives. All archived issues from 2001 onwards may be viewed free of charge online. Users may also sign up to receive e-mail versions of the articles. The site also links to the full text of key peace agreements and treaties relating to the conflict.

1737 **CAIN: conflict and politics in Northern Ireland (1968 to the present)**

http://cain.ulst.ac.uk/bibdbs/newlinks.html

An unmissable site maintained by the University of Ulster, providing free access to a wealth of information covering all aspects of the history of the Northern Ireland 'troubles' and peace process from 1968 to the present. It offers chronologies of key events, plus collections of photographs, full-text articles, books and government reports covering a wide range of political themes, including the background to the conflict, elections and political parties, religious discrimination and contemporary Northern Ireland society. Materials represent the full spectrum of political and religious viewpoints. They include materials published by the main political and religious organizations, as well as respected research bodies. Just a few highlights of the site are:

■ **CAIN bibliography of the Northern Ireland Conflict**
http://cain.ulst.ac.uk/bibdbs/cainbib.htm. References to over 8,000 books (and some journal articles) written about all aspects of the conflict from 1968 onwards. Includes links to many online items. Date of last update given on the website.

■ **Directory of wall murals in Northern Ireland**
http://cain.ulst.ac.uk/mccormick/index.html. A comprehensive listing of hundreds of murals which have existed in Northern Ireland from 1996 to the current day. Entries include authorship, location, status and where possible photographs of the images.

■ **Northern Ireland political ephemera collection of Peter Moloney** http://cain.ulst.ac.uk/moloney/index.html. A searchable database of items collected by Peter Moloney, it includes almost 400 images of political badges, pamphlets, posters and stickers.

■ **Sutton index of deaths from the conflict in Ireland**
http://cain.ulst.ac.uk/sutton/index.html. Information on the deaths that have resulted from the conflict in Ireland between 14 July 1969 and 31 December 2001. Compiled by Malcolm Sutton.

1738 **Combined Arms Research Library digital collections**

www.cgsc.army.mil/carl/contentdm/home.htm

A digital library of military science resources maintained by the Combined Arms Research Library (CARL). It provides free access to a large number of online full-text collections. These currently include Second World War operational plans, School of Advanced Military Studies Monographs, Master of Military Art and Science theses, Stability Operations and Support Operation reports. A full range of military history, strategy and policy topics are covered, including logistics, tactics and involvement in specific conflicts such as the Korean war, Vietnam War and Afghanistan. Materials generally provide an American military perspective on events.

1739 **Correlates of war project**

www.correlatesofwar.org

An academic study of the history of warfare, started in 1963 at the University of Michigan by political scientist J. David Singer, which is famous for its collection of quantitative statistical data on international relations. Many of its datasets can be downloaded from the website free of charge and used with proper citation These include materials on inter-, extra- and intra-state war from 1816 onwards, formal alliances and diplomatic exchanges between states 1816–, territorial changes 1816–, and membership of intergovernmental organizations from 1816 onwards. The site also includes information on the history and methodology of the project as well as examples of other projects and publications where the data has been used.

1740 **Donovan Research Library digitized monograph collection**

www.infantry.army.mil/monographs

The Donovan research library is located at the US Army Infantry school. It is in the process of digitizing a collection of over 10,000 student papers. These include dissertations, research reports, oral history accounts of battles, wartime diaries and other texts, most completed from 1900 to the present. They provide an American viewpoint on all major 20th- and 21st-century conflicts, including World War I, World War II, the Korean War, the Vietnam War and the Gulf wars.

1741 **Iraq and the war on terror: a collection of Frontline's reporting from 9/11 to the present day**

www.pbs.org/wgbh/pages/frontline/terror

This site provides free online access to a large collection of documentary films from the PBS Frontline series. They cover a wide range of issues relating to American foreign policy and the war against terrorism in the aftermath of the September 11 2001 terrorist attacks. Key topics are the Gulf War, the fall of Saddam Hussein, and subsequent violence in post-Gulf War Iraq. Each documentary has its own home page. Many contain online images, transcripts, timelines of key events and lists of teacher resources. Dates of the programmes, copyright and technical information are provided.

1742 Jane's Information Group
Jane's. ISSN 02653818.
www.janes.com
Major commercial database supplier which specializes in providing access to electronic databases and intelligence services covering defence, security, transport, public safety and law enforcement. Subscribers may access full-text e-journals, reference works, papers and reports. Major collections include intelligence centres for defence equipment and technology; defence forecasts; the defence industry and markets; military and security assessments; terrorism and insurgency. A few examples of these are listed below. Full lists of titles and prices are available from the publisher's website. Bespoke collections can also be created for clients. Non-subscribers can obtain free access to recent headlines.

- **Country risk daily report** Janes Information Group, daily. £310. www.janes.com. Daily news updates, highlighting key trends and emerging issues in international security. Each newsletters contains an average of five short pieces covering weapons, political crises and other potential sources of international instability.
- **Defence equipment library** Janes Information Group, continuous. £20,300. www.janes.com. Full-text collection of journals, intelligence services and news products covering air, land and sea defence equipment and weapons.
- **Defence magazines library** Janes Information Group, continuous updates. £5,570. www.janes.com. Groups together a collection of full-text security and defence news products providing up-to-date coverage of current trends and issues worldwide.
- **Islamic affairs analyst** Janes Information Group, continuous. £725. An English-language newsletter analysing recent political, economic and social developments in the Islamic world. Six-year online archive provided for subscribers.
- **Sentinel country risk assessments** Janes information Group, daily. £1,100. www.janes.com. A collection of in-depth data and analysis on specific countries and regions of the world. Each contains political fact files and offers daily updates on state stability, procurement and international relations. The reports are supplied in collections covering specific regions of the world. At present there are over 18 different geographical regions available.
- **World armies** Janes Information Group. £1,345. www.janes.com. Detailed data and analysis on national armies worldide. Topics covered include facts on army organization; economic statistics; details of equipment in service; and assessments of recent operations and deployments.

1743 John Pilger.com
www.johnpilger.com
Official website of the renowned investigative journalist. Provides free access to information about his life, career and the full text of a large selection of articles published since 1999. These include critical commentary on globalization, democracy and conflicts worldwide. There are significant collections of materials on human rights and conflict in Palestine, Iraq, Vietnam, Burma and East Timor.

1744 Middle East 1916 to the present: a documentary record
www.yale.edu/lawweb/avalon/mideast/mideast.htm
Part of the Avalon Project based at Yale University, which aims to make important historical documents freely available on the internet. It comprises a full-text collection of all the key international agreements relating to Palestine from 1916 onwards. Examples include the 1917 Balfour Declaration, 1978 Camp David Accords, 1979 Israeli–Egyptian Treaty, the 1993 Israel–Palestine Liberation Organization (PLO) agreement and recent Road Map peace materials. Also available are the texts of relevant UN Security Council Resolutions. Material is arranged chronologically.

1745 Question of Palestine
www.un.org/Depts/dpa/qpal
An excellent site maintained by the United Nations Division for Palestinian Rights. It offers free access to news, maps, statistics, treaties and other full-text UN documents covering all aspects of the history and current developments in the Arab–Israeli conflict and Middle East peace process from approximately 1946 onwards. This includes coverage of the Road Map peace plan. Some information on current programmes of non-governmental organizations, such as charities, working in the Middle East is also offered.

- **UNISPAL: United Nations information system on the question of Palestine** http://unispal.un.org/unispal.nsf. Direct links to key United Nations institution documents covering Palestine published from 1946 onwards. They include General Assembly resolutions, Security Council documents and resolutions and peace treaties.

1746 Saddam Hussein sourcebook: declassified secrets from US-Iraq relations
www.gwu.edu/~nsarchiv/special/iraq/index.htm
A dossier of declassified US government documents relating to Saddam Hussein and Iraq collected by the National Security Archive, George Washington University. They include letters, reports and photographs relating to American foreign policy towards Iraq, Operation Desert Storm, the Gulf War and the hunt for weapons of mass destruction. Background commentary has been added by the Archive.

Directories & encyclopedias

1747 Air warfare: an international encyclopedia
W.J. Boyne, ed. ABC-CLIO, 2002, 771pp. £118.50. ISBN 9781576073452.
A useful starting point for those seeking facts, figures and discussion on the history of war in the air from the First World War to 2001. Includes articles written by historians and combatants on key battles, tactics, and aircraft and other weapons. Although the main value of this work is its coverage of military history in the air, it also offers some essays on the use of aerial warfare in recent conflicts and its future possibilities.

1748 Conflict in Afghanistan: an encyclopedia
F. Clements ABC-CLIO, 2003, 377pp. £54.50. ISBN 9781851094028.
A good source of information on the historical background to the current conflict in Afghanistan. Alphabetically arranged entries on key events, personalities and organizations from 1747 to the beginning of the 21st century. It includes coverage of the role of Western nations in the region, the origins and impact of Al-Qaeda and the 'war on terrorism'.

1749 Encyclopedia of conflicts since World War II
J. Ciment, ed. 2nd edn, M.E. Sharpe, 2006, 1488pp. 4 v., £320. ISBN 9780765680051.
Contains descriptions and analyses of more than 170 significant post-World War II conflicts worldwide, many of which are omitted by other reference works. Includes coverage of religious and ethnic conflicts, coups and

terrorism. Also contains useful entries on key organizations, alliances and peace treaties, plus maps and glossaries of terms.

1750   Encyclopedia of religion and war
G. Palmer-Fernandez, ed.   Routledge, 2004, 512pp. V. 5 of Routledge's series of Religion and Society encyclopedias, £150. ISBN 9780415942461.
A key scholarly work offering over 140 essays covering five main topics: the role of war in the development and spread of major religions, the role of religion in major wars from earliest times to the present, the history of the religious wars in Europe (1559–1715), the relationship between theology and war (including discussion of such concepts as holy war, jihad and just war), and scholarly surveys of religious-based conflicts and wars in the contemporary world (including Bosnia, Cyprus, Cote d'Ivoire, India, Indonesia, Kashmir, Kosovo, Kurdistan, Northern Ireland, Philippines, Chechnya, Sri Lanka and Sudan). Each essay contains reprints of selected primary source documents and suggestions for further reading.

1751   Ground warfare: an international encyclopedia
S. Sandler and H. Shelton, eds   ABC-CLIO, 2002, 1067pp. 3 v., £188.50. ISBN 9781576073445.
A useful three-volume work covering ground warfare and armies from earliest time to the present. Includes entries for key military leaders, battles and individual conflicts. Includes historical background on recent arenas such as Chechnya and the Arab–Israeli conflict. Also offers numerous essays on military related topics such as tactics, weapons, psychological warfare and women and war.

1752   Naval warfare: an international encyclopedia
S. Tucker, ed.   ABC-CLIO, 2002, 1231pp. 3 v., £188.50. ISBN 9781576072196.
A useful three-volume resource for those seeking information on naval history and tactics from earliest times to the beginning of the 21st century. Contains over 1500 essays on strategy, tactics, weapons, individual navies and key battles. Provides historical background on recent activities such as operations in the Persian Gulf.

Handbooks & manuals

1753   Handbook of war studies II
M. Midlarsky, ed.   University of Michigan Press, 2000, 592pp. £19.99. ISBN 9780472067244.
A collection of scholarly articles on issues relating to recent research on the causes and nature of international warfare and political violence. Topics covered include ethnic and interstate conflict, game theory, terrorism and democratic peace theory. This volume updates the earlier *Handbook of war studies*, University of Michigan Press, 1989, ISBN 9780472082247.

1754   Peace and conflict 2008
J.J. Hewitt, J. Wilkenfeld and T. Gurr   Paradigm Publishing, 2007, biennial, 144pp. £12.99. ISBN 9781594514012.
www.cidcm.umd.edu/pc
A biennial publication of the Center for International Development and Conflict Management, University of Maryland, which tracks trends in global conflict, democratization and instability of states. The 2008 edition

includes analysis of trends in global conflict from 1946 to 2005, a global survey of all international terror events since 1970 and a detailed peace and conflict instability ledger which ranks states on future risks.The companion website offers free access to an executive summary of the report and some supporting graphs and tables.

1755   Regional guide to international conflict and management from 1945 to 2003
J. Bercovitch and J. Fretter   CQ Press, 2004, 400pp. £60. ISBN 9781568028255.
This useful handbook summarizes the causes, nature, management and outcome of 343 international conflicts and wars which took place between 1945 and 2003. It is divided into six geographical regions. Each section contains an introductory essay on the internal and external influences on conflict in the region, the interrelationship between conflicts and their general characteristics. It then lists the specific conflicts in chronological order. Maps are provided.

1756   The Routledge atlas of the Arab–Israeli conflict
M. Gilbert   8th edn, Routledge, 2005, 200pp. £15.99. ISBN 9780415359009.
The latest edition of this well regarded source contains 165 maps which illustrate the historical origins and development of the Arab–Israeli conflict from ancient times to 2005. Also includes text and quotations which set the materials in context.

1757   Warfare and armed conflicts: a statistical reference to casualty and other figures, 1500–1999
M. Clodfelter   2nd edn, McFarland & Company, 2000, 856pp. o/p. ISBN 9780786412044.
A useful chronology of the human cost of war which covers the period 1500–1999. Entries provide the names and dates of the conflict, some background on the causes and strategies, plus facts and figures on civilian and military casualties.

Keeping up to date

1758   Africa Confidential
Africa Confidential, 1960–, fortnightly. £608.
www.africa-confidential.com
A well regarded fortnightly newsletter which provides updates, commentary and analysis on significant political, economic and security developments in African nations. It includes the latest news on current wars and conflicts, in many cases using reports from local journalists. Some headlines are offered free of charge. Access to the full-text articles is for subscribers only. Available in print or online.

1759   Central Asia–Caucasus Analyst
Johns Hopkins University, 2000–, fortnightly. Free.
www.cacianalyst.org
A free fortnightly English-language journal covering current political and economic issues facing the region of Central Asia. It is published by the Central Asia-Caucasus Institute & Silk Road Studies Program, a Joint Transatlantic Research and Policy Center, affiliated with Johns Hopkins University-SAIS and Uppsala University. The website offers free access to news headlines, field reports and strategic assessments of security and ethnic group conflict in the region. It includes

scholarly analysis of Chechnya, Eurasia, the Caucasus, Afghanistan, India–Pakistan relations, the Nagorno-Karabakh conflict and China. Archived editions of the journal from 2000 to date can be downloaded.

1760   Civil Wars
Routledge, 1998–, qtrly. £54. ISSN 13698249.
www.tandf.co.uk
A leading scholarly journal containing articles and reviews on a wide range of issues relating to current and historic civil wars worldwide. It includes coverage of the causes, conduct and endings of civil wars; plus discussion of the relationship between ethnic conflict and civil war and the intractability of violence. Materials on the American, Spanish and Chinese Civil Wars are regularly published. Available in print or online. Full details from the publisher's website.

1761   EurasiaNet.org
www.eurasianet.org
An excellent free website maintained by the Central Eurasia Project of the Open Society Institute. It provides up-to-date information and analysis about political, economic, environmental and social developments in the countries of Central Asia and the Caucasus. This covers recent conflict 'hotspots' in Russia, Afghanistan and Central Asia. Users may sign up to receive daily news wires or consult the individual country files. The latter include some basic facts and figures about the current political and economic situation of the nation, plus directories of links to suggested readings and key research and monitoring organization websites.

1762   The Middle East strategic balance 2005–6
Sussex Academic, 2002–, annual. Succeeds *Middle East military balance*, 1983–2002, £29.50. ISBN 9781845191429.
An annual publication of the Jaffee Center for Strategic Studies which provides free access to authoritative statistics on current strategic developments and arms capabilities in the the Middle East. The regions include the Eastern Mediterranean (including Egypt, Israel, Jordan, Lebanon, Syria and Turkey), the Gulf (including Bahrain, Iran, Iraq, Kuwait, Oman, Qatar, Saudi Arabia and UAE), North Africa and other countries (including Algeria, Egypt, Libya, Morocco and Tunisia, Sudan and Yemen.) Each section includes detailed figures, charts and maps. Topics covered are military acquistions and sales, holdings of particular land, air and sea weapons and economic expenditure on defence and arms. Also provided are glossaries of military-related terms.

1763   Power and Interest News Report
www.pinr.com
A free independent service that provides analysis of conflicts and security crises worldwide. Its contributors include leading political analysts and academics. The site provides free access to reports and news from 2002 to date. Users may sign up to receive e-mail notifications of new reports. Topics covered include US foreign policy, world politics, nuclear politics and wars.

1764   Small Wars and Insurgencies
Routledge, 1981–, qtrly. Incorporating *Low Intensity Conflict and Law Enforcement*, £71. ISSN 09592318.
www.tandf.co.uk
A scholarly, peer-reviewed title publishing new research on

the historical, political, social, economic and psychological aspects of insurgency, counter-insurgency, limited war, peacekeeping operations and the use of force in circumstances short of large-scale international warfare. It includes reviews of new books in the subject field. Tables of contents can be viewed free online from the website. Access to the full-text requires a subscription. Available in print or electronic formats.

Peacekeeping, Peace Studies & Disarmament

Introductions to the subject

1765   Understanding peacekeeping
P. Williams, A. Griffith and S. Bellamy   Polity Press, 2003, 344pp. £17.99. ISBN 9780745630588.
An excellent introduction to the theory, practice and politics of contemporary peacekeeping. Divided into four parts: Concepts and issues related to peacekeeping; The historical development of peacekeeping from 1945 onwards; Different types of peacekeeping operations; and The future role of peacekeeping in the changing world security environment. The chapters emphasise the connection between modern peacekeepers and the wider processes of global politics, the growing impact of non-state actors and the major challenges facing peacekeepers in the future.

Dictionaries, thesauri, classifications

1766   Historical dictionary of arms control and disarmament
J.A. Larsen and J. Smith   Scarecrow Press, 2005, 424pp. £66. ISBN 9780810850606.
Offers a solid introduction to the history and evolution of arms control and disarmament, covering both conventional and nuclear weapons. Includes entries on key dates, treaties and organizations. Also provides a bibliography to guide further research.

Official & quasi-official bodies

1767   E-Mine: the electronic mine action service
www.mineaction.org
The official website of the United Nations Mine Action Service (UNMAS), which devises, implements and monitors UN programmes relating to land mines and demining worldwide. It offers free access to a wealth of online UN documents. These include reports on individual programmes, statistics, treaties, resolutions, standards on mine clearance, reports on the situation from individual countries.

1768   NGO Committee on Disarmament, Peace & Security
http://disarm.igc.org
A major body which facilitates the participation of NGOs in formal disarmament meetings at the UN and informs them about the state of play regarding disarmament and non-proliferation treaties. Its remit covers all forms of conventional and nuclear weapons. The website includes

directories of links to key websites about arms control, factsheets and country files which provide clear explanations of the issues at stake. It also offers free access to all issues of its newsletter *Disarmament Times* from 2000 onwards. This contains articles and news updates on a wide range of non-proliferation issues.

1769 Organisation for the Prohibition of Chemical Weapons
www.opcw.org

An independent international organization based in the Netherlands whose website is a key resource for detailed information about the the International Convention on Chemical Weapons. It includes the full text of the convention, lists of its signatories, factsheets about its contents and implementation, plus detailed legal advice on compliance and implementation. The site also maintains a calendar of events and conferences relating to the treaty.

1770 United Nations. Department of Disarmament Affairs
http://disarmament2.un.org

The official disarmament section of the United Nations. Its remit covers all aspects of disarmament, including conventional weapons, landmines, weapons of mass destruction and nuclear weapons. In addition to the latest press releases and links to all relevant UN committees and conferences, its website also contains an extensive electronic library of full-text materials, including UN resolutions, treaties, reports and other documents from the late 1990s onwards. It also offers free access to all editions of the *UN Disarmament Yearbook*, which contains official news reports and facts and figures on arms and disarmament initiatives worldwide.

■ **UN register of conventional arms**

http://disarmament.un.org/cab/register.html. A free database of country data on holdings and transfers of conventional arms, covering the period from 1992 to the present day. It records data on seven main categories of conventional weapons: battle tanks, armoured combat vehicles, large-calibre artillery systems, combat aircraft, attack helicopters, warships (including submarines), missiles and missile-launchers. Date of last update is recorded on the website.

1771 United Nations. Department of Peacekeeping Operations
www.un.org/Depts/dpko/dpko/

The official United Nations website which provides free access to a wealth of information on the role of the UN in international peacekeeping, its history, current operations and future. It includes free access to press releases; statistics; official documents and links to the websites of all past and current peacekeeping missions. These pages offer detailed reports on the remit, deployment, financing and work of the individual forces under international law. Also accessible via the website are all issues of the *Year in Review* from 2001 onwards. This is the flagship annual report of the organization which offers a useful summary of details and statistical facts on recent UN peacekeeping activities.

1772 United Nations. Peacekeeping Best Practices Section
http://pbpu.unlb.org/pbps/pages/public/Home.aspx

A unit of the United Nations which is responsible for gathering information on best practices in effective peacekeeping. Its website provides access to a wealth of useful full-text materials, including official press releases and an online library of publications. The latter include discussion papers and reports which consider methods in peacekeeping and lessons learnt from specific UN missions.

■ **Handbook on United Nations multidimensional peacekeeping operations** United Nations.Peacekeeping Best Practices Section, 2003, 213pp. Free. http://pbpu.unlb.org/Pbps/library/Handbook%20on%20UN%20PKOs.pdf. An introductory guide to the different aspects of complex UN peacekeeping missions. It provides background information on the roles and how they fit together. Regularly updated on the website.

1773 US Army Peacekeeping & Stability Operations Institute

A specialist research unit based within the Center for Strategic Leadership at the US Army War College in Carlisle, Pa. It provides research, training and education to support current US peacekeeping operations. Its website provides free access to many of its recent policy and research documents. Key topics covered by these include the doctrine of US peacekeeping missions and stregic issues relating to civil–military integration and the establishment of security and rule-of-law reform by peacekeeping operations in former war zones.

Research centres & institutes

1774 Acronym Institute
www.acronym.org.uk

A leading UK-based institute which conducts research and disseminates information about all aspects of conventional, nuclear and chemical weapons disarmament. Its website provides free access to a large online collection of publications. These include all issues of its monthly newsletter *Disarmament Diplomacy* from 1996 onwards which contains articles and news updates on the work of the United Nations Conference on Disarmament and ongoing arms negotiations. Also available are compilations of recent official documents and statements on arms control, nuclear non-proliferation and disarmament and online versions of the ACRONYM reports. Key areas covered by the latter include the nuclear weapons policy of the UK, the Comprehensive Test Ban Treaty and nuclear non-proliferation issues.

1775 Bonn International Centre for Conversion
www.bicc.de

An independent non-profit organization which is committed to promoting a shift in financial and economic resources away from defence and military uses towards alternative civilian roles. Its website provides a wealth of statistical information on recent conflicts, defence budgets and arms expenditure worldwide. It includes free access to working papers, datasets and treaties relating to these issues. There are particularly detailed sections on small arms. Some information is offered in German only.

■ **Training and education on small arms** www.tresa-online.org. A special project developing training modules to educate children and adults about small arms. They include technical information about types of small weapons, introductions to major arms control treaties and agreements, and lesson plans designed for trainers to reuse in the classroom. Many of the modules can be accessed free of charge from the website.

1776   Bradford University, Department of Peace Studies

www.brad.ac.uk/acad/peace

The largest dedicated peace studies research project in the world. Its website provides information on its current teaching programmes and research. This includes free access to reports published recently by many of its specialist research centres, including the Bradford Disarmament Research Centre, the Centre for Conflict Resolution and the Africa Centre for Peace and Conflict Studies.

1777   Center on International Cooperation

www.cic.nyu.edu

An independent research institute based at New York University which is renowned for its work on improving international responses to humanitarian crises and global security threats through applied research. Key areas of concern involve post-conflict peacebuilding, global peace operations and UN reform. Its website provides free access to some of its publications. These include global datasets on peacekeeping missions, briefing papers and summaries of its annual report on global peace operations which examines major current UN and non-UN peacekeeping missions worldwide. Other features of the site include policy papers and reports on its many projects associated with post-conflict reconstructions of specific regions. Recent examples include Afghanistan.

■ **Annual review of global peace operations 2007** Center on International Cooperation Lynne Rienner Publishers, 2007, annual, 390pp. £15.95. ISBN 9781588265098. The latest volume of this yearbook which analyses all UN and non-UN peacekeeping missions in operation during the calendar year. It includes illustrative maps and charts, as well as background information on aims and remits. Includes an introductory essay on the role of peacekeeping in the modern world.

1778   Geneva International Centre for Humanitarian Demining

www.gichd.ch

A research foundation which provides information on anti-personnel landmines and demining issues. Its website is one of the best starting points for tracing factual information about technical issues relating to landmines and their impact worldwide. It offers free access to news about mines and demining initiatives, technical reports on demining, full-text conventions and international treaties, plus other academic articles and discussions of the impact of mines in specific conflicts.

1779   Harvard Sussex Program

A joint research programme of Harvard University and the University of Sussex which is concerned with issues relating to biological and chemical weapons. This includes extensive coverage of disarmament initiatives. Its website provides information on ongoing research plus the full text of the *CBW Conventions Bulletin* from issue 20, June 1993 onwards. This contains news on chemical and biological arms issues worldwide, including updates on the stages of ratification of international treaties. In most cases there are links to full-text versions of the treaties online.

Institute for Defense & Disarmament Studies

See entry no. 1654

Institute on Global Conflict & Cooperation

See entry no. 1656

1780   International Peace Academy

www.ipacademy.org

An independent institution which aims to promote the peaceful resolution of conflicts worldwide. Its website provides information on its purpose, activities and publications. It includes access to the full text of many of its policy reports published from 1992 to date. These include the Coping with Crisis working paper series, which covers specific conflicts worldwide and issues relating to disarmament.

1781   Joan B. Kroc Institute for International Peace Studies

http://kroc.nd.edu

A specialist research and teaching unit based at the University of Notre Dame. It concentrates on the religious and ethnic dimensions of conflict and peacebuilding. The website provides access to numerous full-text publications dating from the late 1990s to the present. These include its biannual review *Peace Colloquy*, plus occasional papers, policy papers and event transcripts. Many of these provide insight into individual conflicts such as the Arab–Israeli dispute, Palestine, the Iraq War and Kashmir.

1782   Mine Action Information Centre

www.hdic.jmu.edu

A key research institute based at James Madison University which conducts research on the technical, social and economic effects of the use of landmines. Its website provides free access to many of its own project and research reports as well as all articles from the *Journal of Humanitarian Demining* from issue 1, 1997 onwards. In addition it also maintains a number of important databases. These include The Global Mine Action Registry, which lists organizations involved in landmine work, a database of demining incidents and victims, a glossary of abbreviations and the ORDATA (ordnance identification system), which provides technical information on the identification and features of particular types of landmines.

1783   Nobel Peace Prize

http://nobelprize.org/nobel_prizes/peace

Official website of the major peace prize. In addition to a full listing of prize-winners from 1901 onwards and information about the selection process, the website also includes a useful collection of interviews with award-winners and some online articles which discuss the history of the prize, the contribution of famous winners and the controversies associated with some choices.

1784   Program in Arms Control, Disarmament and International Security: (ACDIS)

www.acdis.uiuc.edu

A major teaching and research unit of the University of Illinois at Urbana-Champaign. Its website provides information on the aims of the centre, its publication and research projects. It includes access to the full text of all its occasional papers from 1994 to date. These cover a wide range of topics such as arms control, nuclear non-proliferation and energy security worldwide.

Project on Defense Alternatives

See entry no. 1712

1785 Public International Law & Policy Group

www.publicinternationallaw.org/areas/peacebuilding/index.html

An American non-profit organization specializing in international law issues. One of its key areas of concern covers peacebuilding in relation to international law. This includes offering legal advice to mediators, states and sub-state entities during armed conflicts and assistance with drafting peace agreements and post-conflict constitutions. The website provides free access to its Peace Agreement Drafters' Handbook, which is designed to serve as a practical guide for diplomats and lawyers involved in the negotiation and drafting of peace treaties. Also available are peace negotiation simulations and case studies covering specific recent international conflicts such as the Balkans and Iraq. Finally users may want to consult or sign up for e-mail versions of the regular *Peace Negotiations Watch* newsletter, which summarizes current developments in ongoing conflicts worldwide. Issues from approximately 2002 onwards may be viewed online.

1786 Saferworld

A UK-based independent non-governmental organization which seeks to prevent armed conflict worldwide. Its website provides information on current campaigns. These cover the arms trade, peacekeeping and conflict prevention. It is possible to access recent press releases and full-text reports from approximately 2000 onwards. These include surveys of the world arms trade, strategies for arms control in Europe, Asia and Africa, and reports of work in peace building and post-conflict reconstruction.

Stockholm International Peace Research Institute
See entry no. 1714

1787 United States Institute of Peace

www.usip.org

An independent institution established and funded by the American Congress which aims to promote the peaceful resolution of conflicts worldwide. Its website provides free access to its extensive online library of books, articles, event transcripts and webcasts. Many of these analyse the causes, nature and impact of specific ongoing conflict situations. Recently they have included collections of materials on the Gulf War and Iraq. It is possible to sign up to receive regular e-mail updates of new additions.

- **Peace agreements digital collection**
www.usip.org/library/pa.html. Part of the Margarita S. Studemeister Digital Library in International Conflict Management, provides free access to a large collection of full-text peace agreements and treaties ending inter-and intra-state conflicts worldwide since 1989.

1788 Verification, Research, Training & Information Centre

An independent research organization which is concerned with the verification and monitoring of international agreements relating to arms control and disarmament, the environment and peace. Its website provides free access to news stories, full-text reports and data relating to these areas. It includes a useful online directory of verification organizations, factsheets about weapons of mass destruction, and a database of information relating to the weapons inspections conducted in Iraq by the United Nations Monitoring, Verification and Inspection Commission (UNMOVIC) during 2002–3. Other features of the site include free access to VERTICS newletters (*Trust and Verify* and

Verification Matters) and other occasional papers. These discuss specific nuclear regimes and the theory and practice of arms control and verification.

- **Verification yearbook** T. Findlay, ed. VERTIC, 1991–2004, 263pp. ISSN 14773759. www.vertic.org/publications.asp. Flagship publication, published between 1991 and 2004 (currently suspended) which offered a good overview of trends in negotiation and compliance of treaties and agreements relating to a wide range of issues covering arms control, the environment and peacekeeping. Each volume contains a number of scholarly essays discussing specific agreements and conflict situations. The 2004 yearbook included materials relating to Libya and Iraq. Articles from issues from 2001 to 2004 can be downloaded from the website. These may be used for historical background.

Associations & societies

1789 Abolition 2000: global network to eliminate nuclear weapons

www.abolition2000.org

An association of over 2000 non-governmental organizations worldwide campaigning against all forms of nuclear warfare, weapons and testing The website details the objectives of the body and the activities of its member organizations. It is a good starting point for tracing the existence and activities of anti-nuclear campaign groups in different countries. It includes online press releases, campaign materials, articles and reports from approximately 1996 onwards.

1790 Bertrand Russell Peace Foundation

Launched in 1963 to continue the work of Bertrand Russell in promoting peace and social justice worldwide. Its website provides information on its aims, history and activities. It includes an index and access to the selected text of the Spokesman papers. Topics covered by these include nuclear disarmament, arms control and peace movements. Many materials present a socialist perspective on the issues.

- **Spokesman Journal** Spokesman books, 1981–, qtrly. £20. www.spokesmanbooks.com/Spokesman/The_Spokesman.htm. The leading quarterly publication of the Bertrand Russell Peace Foundation. Each issue contains a collection of essays and timely comment on war, peace and social justice. It includes the Peace Dossier (formerly The London Bulletin) and an extensive book review section. Recent issues have covered war crimes, genocide and the conflict in Iraq.

1791 Campaign Against the Arms Trade

www.caat.org.uk

A UK-based coalition of activist groups which are committed to ending the international arms trade. Its website provides useful information on current British grassroots campaigns and protest movements. Also available is background information on UK involvement in the arms trade, current British policy on export licences for military exports and human rights issues relating to the sale of weapons by UK companies. Users may download press releases, pamphlets and campaign materials from the website.

1792 Campaign for Nuclear Disarmament

www.cnduk.org

Britain's leading anti-nuclear weapons protest group. Its website provides information on the aims, history and recent campaigns of CND. It offers free access to calendars of events, campaign leaflets and full-text policy papers and reports. These cover topics relating to nuclear weapons,

British defence and security policy and nuclear disarmament in general.

1793 Conciliation Resources
www.c-r.org/accord/index.shtml

A UK-based charity which seeks to support people working at local, national and international levels to develop effective solutions to social, economic and political problems related to violent conflicts. Its website provides information on its aims, history and current activities. It includes recent newsletters, project reports and access to recent issues of its well regarded journal *Accord: an international review of peace initiatives*. This provides reviews of conflicts and peace building initiatives in specific countries of the world. Each issue includes full-texts and summaries of peace agreements, profiles of the main individuals and organizations involved, a glossary of important terms, maps, a chronology of the conflict and peace process, and guidance for further reading. Recent examples have covered areas, including Sudan, Northern Ireland and Sierra Leone. Other features of the website include a peace agreements index and educational resource materials for teachers.

1794 Council for a Livable World
www.clw.org

An American organization founded in 1962 by eminent nuclear physicist Leo Szilard and other scientists to oppose nuclear arms. It continues to provide Congress with scientific information about the dangers of nuclear, chemical and biological weapons. Its website provides free access to technical facts and briefings about weapons of mass destruction. It also includes fact files on the situation in specific countries such as Iran, Iraq and North Korea. These sections include facts details about the weapons, plus summaries of recent congressional activity. Other features of the site include calendars and newsletters about US national security and disarmament legislative activity.

1795 European Network Against Arms Trade
www.antenna.nl/enaat

A network of European-based activist groups and individuals. Its website provides access to information about grassroots campaigns calling for the end to arms exports and disarmament. It also includes the full text of annual arms export reports from the European Union and many individual EU member nations from 2000 onwards. These offer facts and figures about the extent, nature and changing trends in arms sales in recent years.

1796 Hague Appeal for Peace

An international network of organizations and individuals dedicated to the abolition of war, non-violence and peace, which was founded in 1999. It specializes in coordinating and developing peace education materials for children and young people. Its website provides free access to many of these, including online teaching manuals, lesson plans and syllabi. It also includes news from recent campaigns.

1797 International Action Network Small Arms
www.iansa.org

A global network of civil society organizations who campaign against the misuse of small arms and light weapons. Its website provides information on the aims of the organization, its projects, campaigns and current activities. It includes access to many online documents from its members, including newsletters, press releases, full-text papers and reports. These relate to all aspects of small arms worldwide, including women and gun violence, child soldiers, disarmament and the arms trade.

1798 International Association of Peacekeeping Training Centres
www.iaptc.org

An international organization which aims to encourage communication and cooperation between peacekeeping training and educational organizations worldwide. Its website provides basic information on its membership and activities. It includes minutes and reports from all annual conferences since 2003. These offer assessments and commentary on the current effectiveness and future needs of peacekeeping training.

1799 International Campaign to Ban Landmines
www.icbl.org

A global network of more than 1400 non-governmental organizations and groups campaigning against anti-personnel landmines. Its website is a rich source of resources about landmines and demining activities. It includes an extensive online library of photographic images (both of landmines and injuries caused by them), statistical data and country files on landmine stockpiles, and research reports on their use in specific conflicts.

■ **Index on landmines** www.icbl.org/index. The ICBL guide to landmine research resources on the internet and in printed form. Includes links to key websites and listings of major audiovisual materials.

1800 International Peace Bureau
www.ipb.org/web/index.php

An international network of over 260 organizations who are involved in peace studies, disarmament and peace education. Recent key campaigns include disarmament for development and women and disarmament. Its website contains a very useful calendar of peace-related events, plus an online directory of its members. The latter enables rapid identification of grassroots organizations worldwide, providing contact addresses and links to websites.

1801 International Peace Museums Network
www.museumsforpeace.org

A professional organization created in 1992 to support the management and staff of peace and anti-war museums worldwide. Its website 'Museums for Peace' includes a useful directory of peace museums in different countries with links to their websites. These would be useful for tracing information about recent peace and anti-war exhibitions and educational activities.

1802 International Peace Research Association
http://soc.kuleuven.be/pol/ipra/index.html

A scholarly association which was founded in 1964 to support the needs of scholars and teachers of peace studies worldwide. Its website provides information on its aims, activities and membership. It includes news from the Asia-Pacific Peace Research Association (APPRA), Africa Peace Research and Education Association (AFPREA), European Peace Research Association (EUPRA), Latin American Peace Research Association (CLAIP) and Peace and Justice Association (North America), plus information on its specialist working groups and commissions. These cover a variety of cutting-edge research areas relating to peace, including non-violence, women and war, and peace education. Other features of the site include tables of contents from its key academic publications, the *International Journal of Peace Studies* and the *Journal of Peace Education* and some online conference papers.

1803   Network for Peace
www.networkforpeace.org.uk

A major grouping of UK-based peace organizations. It was set up to continue the work of the National Peace Council. Members include nuclear disarmament campaigners, antiwar protestors, religious organizations and small grassroots peace groups. Its website maintains a good listing of UK peace organizations and a calendar of forthcoming events. A separate section provides information on the Peace Education Network, with a listing of key courses and calendars of events.

1804   Nuclear Age Peace Foundation
www.wagingpeace.org

A major non-profit organization which acts as a designated consultant to the United Nations Economic and Social Council. It comprises a worldwide network of individuals and groups committed to peace and nuclear disarmament. Its website provides information on its aims, membership and activities. It includes free access to articles, briefings and reports published since the mid-1990s. These cover international arms control intiatives, nuclear non-proliferation and peace education.

1805   Peace & Justice Studies Association
www.peacejusticestudies.org

A non-profit organization that was formed in 2001 as a result of a merger of the Consortium on Peace Research, Education and Development (COPRED) and the Peace Studies Association (PSA). It serves as a professional association for scholars in the field of peace and conflict resolution studies, aiming to forge alliances between teachers, students, activists and other peace practitioners in order to explore alternatives to violence. Its website includes free access to its newsletter *The Peace Chronicle* from 2001 onwards. This is issued 3 times per annum and regularly contains book reviews, articles and a news section on teaching peace studies.

■ **Global directory of peace studies and conflict resolution programs** 7th edn., Peace and Justice Studies Association and the International Peace Research Association Foundation, 2007. £30. ISBN 0977997901. http://peacejusticestudies.org/globaldirectory. Annotated entries on over 450 peace studies and conflict resolution courses. Also includes a listing of key journals in the field.

1806   Peace Pledge Union
www.ppu.org.uk

The oldest secular pacifist movement in the UK. Its website provides information on the aims of the organization and its current campaigns, including the work of the Peace Research and Education Trust. The latter maintains a Learn Peace section on the website which offers free access to factsheets, educational materials and suggested lesson plans for teachers.

1807   Peace Science Society
http://pss.la.psu.edu

An international scholarly society for individuals concerned

with developing theory and methods for the study of peace. Its website provides information on aims, membership and activities. It includes details of peace research with which it is associated as well as lists of forthcoming conferences and events. Also available are details about its journals, *PSS(I): conflict management and peace science* and the *Journal of Conflict Resolution*.

1808   Peace Women: women's international league for peace and freedom
www.wilpf.int.ch

An international non-governmental organization of women which has been campaigning since 1915 to bring together women of different political views and backgrounds to work for a permanent end to war. Its website provides access to information on its aims, history and recent activities. It is a useful source of news on women's anti-war and human rights movements worldwide. It also includes full-text reports on the hardships and physical and sexual abuse suffered by women during specific wars and conflicts.

■ **Reaching critical will: reaching for a critical mass of political will for nuclear disarmament** www.reachingcriticalwill.org. An excellent current awareness source maintained by the League. It offers free access to a wealth of resources about the current state of play regarding recent international nuclear disarmament initiatives. It includes news stories, conference listings, full text treaties and bibliographies of further readings, making it easy for NGOs and members of the public to keep up to date with progress.

1809   Quaker United Nations Office

This is one of the largest religious groups campaigning for peace and worldwide disarmament. Its website provides information, on its aims and work at the UN. It includes free access to press releases, annual reports and briefing papers. Topics covered include non-violence, conscientious objection to military service, child soldiers and conflict resolution.

1810   Soldiers of Peace International
www.fname.info/aisp/eng/index.php

A professional organization of civilians and soldiers who have been involved in United Nations peacekeeping since 1948. The website is a good source of information on their current activities in peacekeeping missions and mine-clearing operations. It also has some news about Blue Helmets veterans.

1811   War Resisters International
www.wri-irg.org

A network of pacifist and anti-war organizations which was founded in 1921 to promote non-violence. Its website provides information on the history of the organization and its current anti-war and peace campaigns. It also provides free access to its detailed worldwide surveys on military conscription and conscientious objection to military service as well as articles from newsletters on the state of the arms trade, women and resistance to war and news from peace movements worldwide.

Libraries, archives, museums

1812   Hiroshima Peace Museum
www.pcf.city.hiroshima.jp

A leading peace museum based at the site of the dropping of the first atomic bomb in August 1945. In addition to visitor information about the exhibition and peace memorial park, its website also serves as a centre for peace education and the promotion of nuclear disarmament. It includes a special online exhibition of photographs and eye-witness accounts relating to the horrific impact of the nuclear bomb on the people of Hiroshima. There are also transcripts of peace declarations and speeches made at the city's annual peace memorial ceremony from 1997 onwards, educational materials for teaching children about peace and links to nuclear disarmament organizations.

Portal & task environments

1813 BeyondIntractability.org: a free knowledge base on more constructive approaches to destructive conflict
An excellent educational website maintained by the University of Colorado Conflict Research Consortium which provides free access to a large collection of resources relating to all aspects of conflict resolution. Its core is a knowledge base of essays, articles and educational materials relating to over 400 topics. These include conflict stages, causes of intractable conflict, de-escalation strategies, principles of justice and fairness, suicide bombers, war crimes and ceasefires. Students may read essays and articles, listen to audiofiles, try online courses and follow up the online links and list of further readings.

1814 Opérations de paix
www.operationspaix.net
A useful directory of information about worldwide peacekeeping missions which is maintained by a network of Francophone research organizations led by the University of Montreal. It provides particularly strong coverage of missions in French-speaking nations of Africa and the work of Francophone organizations. It includes chronologies of missions, biographies of key figures, a glossary of key terms, full-text UN and other major peace document, and some online research documents from Francophone institutes. All information is in French.

1815 Partnership for effective peacekeeping
www.effectivepeacekeeping.org
A non-partisan policy working group that brings together humanitarian, human rights, peace and security and academic organizations in support of greater peacebuilding. Its website acts as a clearing house of information on effective peacekeeping as well as reviewing the work of the UN and other missions. It includes conference and training course listings, directories of peace institutes, recommended readings, plus links to full-text reports and policy papers from PEP. Topics covered include United Nations reform, US government peacebuilding projects, and gender and peace initiatives.

1816 Peace operations monitor: civilian monitoring of complex peace operations
www.pom.peacebuild.ca
A project of the Peace Operations Working Group (POWG) of the Canadian Peacebuilding Coordinating Committee (CPCC). It aims to provide an independent source of information about current United Nations and other non-UN peacekeeping missions and forces worldwide. Each country entry includes details about the mandate of the mission, its

deployment and links to news and full-text reports analysing it from a variety of perspectives. At present its coverage is restricted to a limited number of regions (mainly Afghanistan, Sudan and Haiti), although there are plans to broaden this.

1817 START web site: strategic arms reductions Problems, events, analysis
www.armscontrol.ru/start/default.htm
This website is maintained by the Center for Arms Control, Energy and Environmental Studies of the Moscow Institute of Physics and Technology (MIPT). Its purpose is to monitor and facilitate discussion on arms control and disarmament issues, with a particular emphasis on analysing differences in approach between Russian and American strategies. It is a particularly good starting point for tracing official documents, articles and reports discussing Russian and American policies and US–Russian agreements. Also provided are news updates, papers and reports on weapons of mass destruction issues, arms control and nuclear disarmament discussions. There are extensive directories of links to Russian-language resources which may be difficult to locate elsewhere.

1818 United Nations peacekeeping documentation research guide
www.un.org/Depts/dhl/resguide/specpk.htm
An excellent introductory guide prepared by the United Nations Dag Hammarskjöld Library. It provides an overview of the type of documents produced by the United Nations about its peacekeeping role and advice on how to find them. This covers the main legal, administrative and technical publications and reports, with links to free online versions where available. It also describes the basic indexes which can be used to find particular types of material issued by the UN and its main bodies.

Discovering print & electronic resources

1819 Peace research abstracts
Sage Publications, bi-monthly. Published in association with the Peace Research Institute – Dundas. Also available in online format at a higher subscription rate., £135. ISSN 00313599.
www.sagepub.com/journalsProdDesc.nav?prodId=Journal200745
Continuously published for over 40 years. Each issue contains over 400 abstracts of journal articles, book chapters, reports, government publications and theses covering the full range of topics relating to international relations, international conflicts, military policy and conflict resolution worldwide.

Digital data, image & text collections

1820 Global peace index
www.visionofhumanity.com/index.php
An online data source launched in 2007 by the Economist Intelligence Unit in association with a large number of international research institutes. It ranks over 160 nations worldwide in terms of their levels of 'peacefulness' and absence of violence. This enables comparative analysis of factors that contribute to the outbreak of war in certain areas of the world. The website provides free access to datasets and associated reports.

Directories & encyclopedias

1821 AFB Peace Research Index
www.priub.org/
A useful online index to more than 300 institutions involved in peace and conflict research and peace education worldwide which is maintained by Arbeitsstelle Friedensforschung Bonn (AFB)/Peace Research Information Unit Bonn (PRIUB). Typical entries include information on fields of expertise, plus contact addresses and links to the website where available.

1822 Encyclopedia of international peacekeeping operations
O. Ramsbotham and T. Woodhouse, eds ABC-CLIO, 1999, 300pp. £52.95. ISBN 9780874368925.
A major reference work covering the history of peacekeeping from approximately 1947 to 1999. Although it does not offer coverage of the most recent events, it includes useful factual profiles for historic UN and non-UN missions, biographical information on major figures and entries for key treaties, events and issues. Some essays discuss critical concepts such as major debates about the nature of peacekeeping and the role of peacekeeping with regard to human rights.

1823 Historical dictionary of multinational peacekeeping
T. Mays Scarecrow Press, 2003, 384pp. £55. ISBN 9780810848740.
A valuable source for all scholars of international relations, tracing the history of all major peacekeeping missions from the League of Nations in the 1920s to UN and non-UN operations in the early 21st century. Includes a detailed chronology of missions, examples of international treaties and conventions, a comprehensive acronym list and an extensive 55-page bibliography to guide further research.

1824 Peace institutes database
http://databases.unesco.org/peace
A free, searchable online database of over 600 peace research institutes and training colleges from over 90 nations which is maintained by UNESCO. Each entry gives the names, contact address and website address of the organization. It also provides some background on size of the institution and its main areas of specialization and lists key publications and journals. Although updates are infrequent, the breadth of coverage means that it offers a useful starting point for tracing the existence of relevant bodies. The date of the last update can be checked from the website.

Handbooks & manuals

1825 The Blue Helmets: review of United Nations peacekeeping
3rd edn, United Nations, 1996, 808pp. £23. ISBN 9789211006117.
The most recent edition of the official history of United Nations peacekeeping. Contains background information, facts, figures and maps of all 41 UN peacekeeping missions from 1948 to early 1996. Lists all key acronyms.

1826 Handbook of peace and conflict studies
C. Webel and J. Galtung Routledge, 2007, 424pp. £100. ISBN 9780415396653.
A collection of scholarly essays from international

contributors which is divided into four main sections: Understanding and transforming conflict; Creating peace; Supporting peace; and interdisciplinary studies of peace. Key concepts are discussed and reviewed and bibliographies of further reading provided.

1827 Nuclear weapons and nonproliferation: a reference handbook
S. Diehl and J. Moltz 2nd edn, ABC-CLIO, 2007, 335pp. £40. ISBN 9781598840711.
An authoritative guide to key events, policies, treaties and issues in nuclear disarmament from 1945 onwards. It includes coverage of American and international attitudes towards nuclear weapons and efforts to prevent their proliferation. Recent controversial issues such as the search for weapons of mass destruction in Iraq and the nuclear weapons programmes in Iran and North Korea are covered. Also provided are 21 biographical sketches of leading figures involved with nuclear weapons technology.

Keeping up to date

1828 H-Peace
www.h-net.org/~peace
An academic mailing list associated with the Peace History Society, which is concerned with issues relating to historical and contemporary peace concerns, disarmament and reconciliation. It offers regular postings on jobs, grants, conferences and events. There are also links to recent book reviews, research projects, online syllabi and tables of contents from leading peace studies and peacekeeping-related journals. Instructions on signing up are available on the website. Archives of recent messsages may be viewed by non-members.

1829 International peacekeeping
Routledge, 1993–, 5 p.a. from 2008. Originally published quarterly prior to 2008, £82. ISSN 13533312.
www.tandf.co.uk
A major forum for cross-disciplinary debate on the history, practice and policy of international peacekeeping. It includes coverage of peacekeeping with regard to issues of international politics, military affairs, international law and development studies. Recent special issues have included Afghanistan in transition; Peacekeeping and human rights; and Security sector reconstruction. There is coverage of UN and non-UN peacekeeping forces. Available in print or online. Full details from the publisher's website.

1830 International peacekeeping: the yearbook of international peace operations
H. Langholtz, B. Kondoch and A. Wells Brill, 1996–, annual. Price includes accompanying CD-ROM, £314. ISSN 1380748X.
www.internationalpeacekeeping.org
A scholarly yearbook which contains both a documentary record of events relating to war, conflict resolution, diplomacy, international law, international security, humanitarian relief and terrorism in the previous year, as well as a collection of analytical essays by leading academics. Coverage include UN and non-UN missions worldwide. The main emphasis is on policy and legal issues. A key feature is the reprints of selected 'basic documents', such as Security Council Resolutions and Reports of the UN Secretary-General, which are supplied on CD-ROM.

1831 Journal of Peace Research
Sage in association with International Peace Research Institute, Oslo, bi-monthly. £66. ISSN 00223433.
www.sagepub.co.uk
A highly regarded academic journal which has been published for over 40 years. It is interdisciplinary in nature, covering all aspects of the study of war, violence and peace studies from empirical, theoretical and policy-related perspectives. Each issue contains examples of articles on cutting-edge research, plus reviews and notes on recently published books. Tables of contents may be viewed free of charge on the publisher's website. Available in print or online to subscribers.

1832 Peace and Conflict Monitor
University for Peace, monthly. Free.
www.monitor.upeace.org/index.cfm
A free monthly publication of the University for Peace, a treaty organization of the United Nations. Each issue contains news round-ups, articles, special reports and online diaries on current issues relating to peacekeeping, peace movements and violent conflicts worldwide. Topics covered include women and war, international security, peace studies and peace research. It is possible to sign up to receive e-mail updates. An archive of back issues can be read free of charge on the website.

1833 Peace News
Peace News, 1936–, 10 p.a. £12.
www.peacenews.info
A small UK-based activist magazine which has been published since 1936. It seeks to promote pacifism and non-violence. Each issue contain news, reviews and brief articles which highlight global peace movement news, forthcoming and recent anti-war protests. Many include personal accounts from peace campaigners. Most of the issues from 1995 onwards can be accessed free of charge from the website. However, subscribers are also able to access more in-depth materials.

Terrorism

Introductions to the subject

1834 Terrorism and counterterrorism: understanding the new security environment: readings and interpretations
R. Howard and R. Sawyer, eds   McGraw-Hill Publishing Co., 2007, 576pp. £31.99. ISBN 9780072873016.
An excellent collection of introductory essays from leading political scientists, government officials and US service personnel which explore a wide range of issues relating to terrorism and counter-terrorism in the post-9/11 world. They include analysis of the philosophical, political and religious roots of terrorist activities, as well as discussion of recent incidents. Additional features include a chronology of terrorist incidents, plus listings and profiles of key terrorist groups.

1835 The terrorism reader
D. Whittaker   3rd edn, Routledge, 2007, 352pp. £21.99. ISBN 9780415422468.
A good introduction for students to the academic study of contemporary terrorism. It contains essays on a wide range of aspects, including the psychological, sociological, legal and ethical issues. A key feature is the up-to-date case studies on recent terrorist events and activities. These include materials on the London 2005 bombing, George W. Bush's war against terrorism, the IRA and UFF in Northern Ireland and the Shining Path in Peru.

Dictionaries, thesauri, classifications

1836 Dictionary of terrorism
J.R. Thackrah   2nd edn, Routledge, 2003, 288pp. £26.99. ISBN 978041529821.
A useful source of information for students and policy makers requiring definitions and descriptions relating to terrorism and political violence. Contains entries for a wide range of areas, including the history of terrorism, major terrorist groups, legal conventions, the psychology of terrorism and specific incidents (such as September 11 2001, the Oklahoma bombing and the Bali bombing). Each entry contains a select bibliography to guide further research.

1837 Historical dictionary of terrorism
S. Anderson and S. Sloan   2nd edn, Scarecrow Press, 2002, 588pp. £74. ISBN 9780810841017.
Useful source for providing background information on the historical origins of modern terrorism. Contains entries on important groups, organizations and incidents from the earliest times to the beginning of the 21st century. Includes some coverage of recent fundamentalist groups and terrorism in the post 9/11 environment.

Official & quasi-official bodies

1838 Combating Terrorism Center
www.ctc.usma.edu
A specialist research and study centre based at the US Military Academy West Point. Its website provides information on its courses and research relating to terrorism studies and US homeland security. It includes some full-text analysis briefs and papers by Center members. These offer insight into the current thinking of the American military establishment. Topics covered include US foreign policy, homeland security, the war against terrorism and the relationship between Islam, Al-Qaeda and terrorist activity.

1839 Counter-Terrorism Task Force
www.apecsec.org.sg/content/apec/apec_groups/som_special_task_g roups/count
A special body of APEC (Asia-Pacific Economic Cooperation) which is committed to fighting terrorism in the Asia-Pacific region and worldwide. Its website provides a useful starting point for information on terrorism and counter-terrorism information about Asia-Pacific nations. It provides free access to press releases, papers, reports and multilateral treaties from approximately 2002 onwards. Topics covered by these include nuclear security, terrorist financing in the Asia-Pacific region and counter-terrorist agreements.

1840 Defend America: US Department of Defense news about the war on terrorism

www.defendamerica.mil

An important website for those seeking information from the US government on its policy and current operations in the global war against terrorism. It draws together press releases, reports, statistics, images and video footage from all branches of the US military, plus documents from the relevant American government departments. The site currently includes specialist subsections on Afghanistan and Iraq. Users should note that it is used to promote and support the role of US forces and therefore does not usually contain materials critical of American involvement in these regions. The substantial directories of links to other 'war on terrorism related resources' can serve as a useful starting point for researchers.

1841 Inter-American Committee Against Terrorism

www.cicte.oas.org

An agency of the Organization of American States which promotes the exchange of information to prevent terrorism in OAS nations. It is an excellent starting point for keeping up to date with information about terrorism and counter-terrorism in Central, South and Latin America. The website contains press releases, resolutions and full-text documents from approximately 2001 onwards.

1842 National Counterterrorism Center

www.nctc.gov

The main organization in the US government responsible for integrating and analysing all intelligence pertaining to terrorism and counter-terrorism. Its website includes mission statements, press releases, speeches and full-text reports. These cover American intelligence and counter-terrorism policies and strategies. Also available is the Counterterrorism Calendar, which provides factual information on terrorist organizations and technical information on terrorist weapons.

■ **Worldwide incidents tracking system** http://wits.nctc.gov. The NCTC's database of terrorist incidents. It covers attacks worldwide from 2004 to the present. Incidents are defined widely to include examples of bombings, hoaxes, kidnapping and assassination. Individual entries provide summaries of events, information on targets and suspects and statistics of casualties and damage.

1843 National Security Australia

www.nationalsecurity.gov.au

Official website of the Australian government, overseeing all aspects of national security, civil defence and counter-terrorism. The website provides access to Australian government press releases, public information campaign booklets, transcripts of press conferences and full-text legislation and policy documents. Some of the materials cover terrorism in the Asia-Pacific region in general and there are useful links to other websites relating to counter-terrorism in this region.

1844 UK Resilience

www.ukresilience.info/index.shtm

A public information service of the British government which was established in September 2000 as part of the Civil Contingencies Secretariat. It aims to act as a central information point for all official news about disasters, emergencies and crises in the UK. This includes coverage of the risk of terrorism and responses to specific incidents.

Users may access from the website up-to-date press releases, guidelines and other documents relating to emergency preparedness, response and civil contingencies.

1845 UN action against terrorism

www.un.org/terrorism

An official website of the United Nations which gathers together a wealth of documents and reports relating to UN counter terrorist measures made in the wake of the September 11 2001 attacks. It includes access to recent press releases, Security Council resolutions, reports from the Secretary General, General Assembly and Economic and Social Council, documents from the Security Council Terrorism Committee and full-text treaties, declarations and conventions. All aspects of counter-terrorism are covered, including nuclear terrorism, the war against terrorism, the relationship between Islamic fundamentalism and terrorism and discussion of specific groups such as Al-Qaeda.

1846 United States. House of Representatives, Committee on Homeland Security

http://homeland.house.gov

An official body of the American government, created in the aftermath of September 11 2001, whose remit covers the oversight of US homeland security. This encompasses a wide range of issues relating to counter-terrorism, security and emergency preparedness. The website provides information on the history, role, membership and activities of the committee. It includes free access to press releases, full-text statements, reports, transcripts and audiofiles of hearings in which the effectiveness and future direction of US homeland security is discussed. It also offers a useful collection of links to other related websites containing homeland security legislation and documents.

Research centres & institutes

1847 Centre for the Study of Terrorism & Political Violence

www.st-andrews.ac.uk/academic/intrel/research/cstpv

Europe's oldest specialist research unit on terrorism, based at the University of St Andrews . It focuses on the study of the roots of political violence and acts as a forum for the exchange of information about its causes, nature and measures to allieviate it. The website provides information on the work of the Centre, including access to a growing collection of full-text articles and reports from its many research projects. Topics covered by these include the psychology of terrorism, international counter-terrorism measures, prevention and causes of domestic terrorism in the UK,and victims of terrorism and other forms of political violence such as ethnic conflicts and civil wars. The site also maintains impressive directories of links to other relevant print and web resources.

1848 Combating Terrorism Center at West Point

www.ctc.usma.edu

A research, education and policy institute based at the USA's leading military academy. Its key areas of concern are homeland security, counter-terrorism and weapons of mass destruction. The website provides free access to some of its project papers and reports. Recent examples include visual motifs in Jihadi internet propaganda, US foreign policy and the relationship between Islam, Al-Qaeda and terrorist activity.

1849 CREATE: National Center for Risk and Economic Analysis of Terrorism Events
www.usc.edu/dept/create
A specialist research institution based at the University of Southern California which is funded by the US Department of Homeland Security. It analyses the economics of terrorism, developing models to understand the risks and vulnerabilities from terrorist activities. Its website provides information on its remit and current activities. It includes free access to some of its research reports, articles and economic models.

1850 International Center for the Study of Terrorism
www.icst.psu.edu/default.html
A multi-disciplinary research consortium of leading universities and other educational institutions which is headed by Pennsylvania State University. Its areas of research cover all aspects of terrorism, including the motivations of terrorists, composition of terrorist groups, reactions to terrorism by society, communicating risk and counter-terrorism measures. Substantial coverage of US homeland security and the links between Islamic fundamentalism and terrorism. Its website includes free access to details about ongoing projects and some full-text papers and reports.

1851 National Consortium for the Study of Terrorism & Responses to Terror [USA]
www.start.umd.edu
A US Department of Homeland Security Center of Excellence based at the University of Maryland. It researches and provides guidance on how to reduce the risk of terrorist threats in the USA. The website offers free access to press releases, full-text research reports and data. Topics covered include counter-terrorism, societal responses to terrorism and the composition and membership of terrorist groups.
- **Global terrorism database** www.start.umd.edu/data/gtd. Offers free information on over 80,000 terrorist incidents worldwide from 1970 (in 2007 it was updated until 2004). Entries include date, location, weapons, casualties and perpetrator.

1852 National Memorial Institute for the Prevention of Terrorism
www.mipt.org
A charitable organization which seeks to provide the American public with information about terrorist groups and how to prevent terrorist attacks. Its website provides free access to a terrorism information centre which lists forthcoming events (mainly in the USA), conferences and courses.
- **Terrorism knowledge bank** www.tkb.org. A comprehensive free database of global terrorism incidents and organizations from the 1960s to the current day. It contains group profiles, statistical datasets, case studies and bibliographies of further reading for terrorist attacks and bombings.

Royal United Services Institute
See entry no. 1713

Associations & societies

1853 Citizens Against Terror
http://citizensagainstterror.net

A worldwide alliance of citizens' organizations that are working to develop civil society responses to terrorism and counter-terrorism. It is a useful source of information on the work of local grassroots groups, including those supporting victims of the 2005 London bombings and other attacks worldwide. It links to their websites many of which host discussion forums, blogs and picture exchanges expressing defiance towards terrorism.

1854 International Association for Counterterrorism & Security Professionals
www.iacsp.com
An international organization for professionals working in the field. Its website offers information about the aims of the organization and its current and forthcoming activities. It includes some press releases, message boards and details about its online courses and publications such as *Counter Terrorism & Security – the magazine for Law Enforcement, Government and Military*. Material focuses on the needs and role of the counter-terrorism professional.

Portal & task environments

1855 South Asia terrorism portal
www.satp.org
Maintained by the Institute for Conflict Management, India, this website is a key resource for students of the international relations of South Asia. It aims to provide access to data, commentary and analysis on current sectarian violence, wars and terrorism in South Asia. The principal countries covered are India, Pakistan, Bangladesh, Sri Lanka, Bhutan and Nepal. It includes coverage of the Kashmr conflict. The site offers weekly updates on security and terrorism in South Asia, links to full-text government reports, statements and legislation from South Asian nations and bibliographies of articles and books for further reading.

Discovering print & electronic resources

1856 Teaching terror: a guide to resources to support the study of terrorism and counter-terrorism
www.teachingterror.net
This site is maintained by Dr James Forest, Director of Terrorism Studies at the US Military Academy. It aims to provide teachers and lecturers with a guide to resources for introducing students to the academic study of terrorism and counter-terrorism policy. It includes directories of useful websites relating to US homeland security and cyber-terrorism, plus lists of recommended textbooks, films and examples of course syllabi from American universities.

1857 Terrorism bibliography 2007
www.au.af.mil/au/aul/bibs/terror07.htm
The latest edition of this extremely useful guide, compiled annually by staff at the Fairchild Research Information Center, Air University and offered free on the internet. It provides an extremely useful listing of recent academic articles, monographs and research papers about all aspects of international terrorism and security. Topics covered are wide-ranging, including terrorist financing, the psychology of terrorism, regional surveys and discussion of the connection between radical Islam and terrorist activity. The main emphasis is on US published material. Links are provided to

key terrorist-related websites and all earlier editions of the bibliography from approximately 2002 onwards.

Digital data, image & text collections

1858   **After Sept 11: perspectives from the social sciences**
www.ssrc.org/sept11
A thought-provoking collection of essays compiled by the Social Science Research Council. They focus on the impact of the September 11 2001 terrorist attacks on international relations and world affairs. Contributors include such famous social scientists as David Held, Charles Tilly and Immanuel Wallerstein. They include coverage of the psychology of terrorism, the relationship between Islam and politics and the impact of the attacks on world events and American foreign policy. The site also offers a useful teacher's guide with lesson plans based on the materials.

1859   **International Security and counter-terrorism reference center**
EBSCO, continuous updates. On demand from publisher.
www.epnet.com
A subscription database which provides access to a digital library of materials relating to all aspects of contemporary terrorism, international security and counter-terrorist policy. These include full-text journal articles, reports, books, statistics, legislation, news feeds and blogs. Information on subscription fees and full title lists are provided via the publisher's website.

1860   **Jane's terrorism and insurgency centre**
Jane's information Group, continuous. £7,725.
http://jtic.janes.com
A full-text library of resources relating to terrorist activity worldwide which is maintained by leading defence and international security database supplier Janes Information Group. It includes daily news updates; country and terrorist group profiles, case studies of specific incidents and expert analysis of trends. Other features include images and detailed statistical data on terrorist finance. A full list of titles include in the package and pricing details is provided on the publisher's website.

1861   **RAND Voices of Jihad database**
www.rand.org/research_areas/terrorism/database
This website is maintained by the RAND Corporation (q.v.). It provides free access to a searchable database of interviews, statements and publications from Jihad-related leaders and organizations, including sympathisers of Al-Qaeda. Each entry includes a summary of content, authorship, transcript and link to the original source website. The database is of value to researchers seeking insight into the motivations, strategies and organization of Johad related terrorist groups. The site also includes links to other full-text terrorist-related publications by RAND.

1862   **September 11 collection**
www.archive.org/details/iraq_911
A collection of video footage, documentaries and films relating to the September 11 2001 terrorist attacks compiled by Internet Archive users. They include footage of the original events plus subsequent academic and popular discussions of the causes and consequences.

1863   **The September 11 digital archive**
http://911digitalarchive.org
A project of the American Social History Project, City University of New York and the University of New York Centre for History and New Media, George Mason University, which is creating an electronic archive of materials relating to the September 11 2001 terrorist attacks against the World Trade Center. There is a special focus on the archiving of e-mail messages, photographic images and oral accounts from eye-witnesses, many of which are under-represented in 'official' histories of events.

1864   **The September 11 sourcebooks**
www.gwu.edu/~nsarchiv/NSAEBB/sept11
A major digital library of documents relating to the September 11 terrorist attacks created and maintained by the National Security Archive, George Washington University. Its main strength is in publishing declassified security documents from the American government. These include the complete air–ground transcripts of the hijacked 9/11 flight recordings as well as numerous White House memos and briefings relating to the 'war against terrorism'. Material is being continuously added to the site. Current volumes available include materials relating to US intelligence on the Taliban, US counter-terrorism policy and the hunt for Osama Bin Laden.

1865   **The September 11 web archive**
http://september11.archive.org
A joint project of the Library of Congress, Pew internet and American Life Project and WebArchivist.com. It consists of over 30,000 websites archived from September 11 2001 to December 1 2001.These include materials from national newspapers, governments, business, religious organizations, charities and individual home pages, constituting a rich source of information on the initial reporting and reaction to events. Key websites were archived several times during this period, enabling researchers to easily track the evolution of reaction.

Directories & encyclopedias

1866   **Encyclopedia of terrorism**
H. Kushner, ed.   Sage Publications, 2003, 600pp. £75. ISBN 9780761924081.
A major scholarly work offering more than 300 in-depth articles on the biographical, historical and geographical aspects of terrorism. Includes detailed entries on individual figures, groups and incidents. Excellent coverage of events relating to September 11, Saddam Hassam and Al-Qaeda. Also provided are valuable appendices that list key government organization and terrorist organizations and useful sources of further readings.

1867   **Encyclopedia of terrorism**
C.C. Combs and M. Slann, eds   2nd edn, Facts on File, 2007, 496pp. £60.95. ISBN 9780816062775.
A useful introduction for the general reader or student which contains over 350 A–Z entries on events, people and organizations, and places playing key roles in terrorism from 1945 to the present. It includes entries on 9/11, Al Qaeda and Osama Bin Laden, offering some historical background on recent events. Also provided is a chronology of key terrorist incidents from 1945 to 2006.

1868 Encyclopedia of world terrorism: 1996–2002
F.G. Shanty, R. Picquet and J. Lalla, eds   M.E. Sharpe, 2003,
1200pp. 2 v. ISBN 9781563248078.
Extremely useful two-volume set examining in detail terrorist
activity worldwide from the mid-1990s to 2002. Essays
include detailed coverage attack on 9/11, the war on
terrorism, Afghanistan, Iraq and violence in the Middle East.
There are also biographical entries on key individuals,
terrorist groups and organizations, plus a chronology of
terrorist related events. The second volume contains an
extremely useful collection of reprinted primary source
documents relating to terrorism from ancient to modern
times. These include United Nations conventions and
protocols, as well as extracts from historical manuscripts
ranging from *The Sicarii: terrorism in Roman-occupied Judea:
Josephus's account of the Sicarii* (ca. AD 75) to Roger
Casement's *Report on the Congo* (1904).

Keeping up to date

1869 The African Terrorism Bulletin
Institute for Security Studies, 2004–, qtrly. Free.
www.issafrica.org/Pubs/Newsletters/newsletterindex.html
A quarterly newsletter produced by the Organized Crime and
Corruption Programme of the Institute for Security Studies
(ISS), South Africa, which provides a balanced analysis of
recent news on terrorist activities and counter-terrorist
activities within African nations. In addition to the
summaries, it also includes links to the full text of relevant
international treaties and documents, plus articles in African
newspapers covering the stories. Users register to receive the
Bulletin via e-mail. An archive of most issues from Vol. 1,
2004 onwards is available on the website.

1870 Country reports on terrorism
Office of the Coordinator for Counterterrorism, 2004–, annual.
Previous title *Global patterns of terrorism*, free.
www.state.gov/s/ct/rls/crt
An annual report produced by the Office of the Coordinator
for Counterterrorism, US Department of State, which surveys
global trends in terrorism in the preceding calendar year.
Each report includes detailed statistical data and analysis on
a wide range of topics, including profiles of terrorist groups,
activities in individual nations, the funding of terrorists and
developments in international treaties, conventions and
protocols. Copies of all reports from 2004 onwards may be
viewed online free of charge. All copies of the predecessor
publication from 1995 to 2004 can also be accessed.

1871 Studies in Conflict and Terrorism
Taylor & Francis, 1977–, qtrly. £237. ISSN 1057610X.
www.ingentaconnect.com
A well established scholarly journal which publishes the
latest research on the nature, origins and implications of
conflict in the 21st-century world. It includes essays, analysis
and book reviews of issues relating to present-day terrorism
and insurgency. Tables of contents, abstracts and free RSS
alerting feeds can be obtained from the publisher's website.
Access to the full-text is for subscribers only. Available in
print or online.

1872 Terrorism and Political Violence
Routledge, 1988–, qtrly. £66. ISSN 09546553.
www.tandf.co.uk

Major peer-reviewed scholarly journal. Publishes articles,
reviews and symposia on all aspects of the study of the
political meaning of terrorist activity. This includes regular
discussion of such topical issues as the relationship between
religion and terrorism, political parties and terrorism and
technology and terrorism, as well as detailed studies of the
history and current activities of individual terrorist groups
and organizations. Available in print or online. Full pricing
details are available on the publisher's website.

1873 Terrorism Monitor
www.jamestown.org/terrorism/AboutTM.php
A free weekly online journal published by US organization the
Jamestown Foundation. It provides timely analysis of
terrorist organizations and incidents worldwide. Topics
covered include the relationship between radical Islam,
fundamentalism and terrorism, the war on terror and recent
intelligences relating to Al-Qaeda and Osama Bin Laden. Its
website provides access to all issues from 2003 to date.

Parliaments

**devolution • European Parliament • members of
parliament • national parliaments • regional parliaments •
transnational parliamentary bodies • women in politics**

Transnational Parliamentary Bodies

Official & quasi-official bodies

1874 Assemblée Parlementaire de la Francophonie
http://apf.francophonie.org
International organization which encourages cooperation
between parliamentarians from French-speaking parliaments
worldwide. Its website provides free access to materials
about its membership and activities. It includes full-text
agendas, minutes of meetings, webcasts and reports. These
are a rich source of general information on French-speaking
parliaments worldwide. They include coverage of
organizations and democratic development in French-
speaking Africa which may be difficult to trace elsewhere.

1875 Baltic Assembly
www.baltasam.org
An international organization which promotes cooperation
between the national parliaments of the Baltic states of the
Republic of Estonia, the Republic of Latvia and the Republic
of Lithuania. Its website is an important source of
information on political developments in this region. It
includes access to press releases, annual reports and other
full-text documents.

1876 European Parliament
www.europarl.europa.eu/
The official website provides access to information about the
role, membership and activities of the Parliament. It includes
live webcasts, press releases and extensive full-text
documents. These include agendas, reports, resolutions,
debates and committee minutes covering all aspects of its
work. Many of these date from 1999 to the present. Also
available is information on current membership of the
parliament and the work of MEPs, plus information and
results from European Parliament elections.

1877   **European Parliament UK office**
www.europarl.org.uk
The European Parliament's office in the UK exists to provide the public with basic information about the role and function of the European Parliament and its relations with the UK. It is a good starting point for tracing easy to understand factsheets and guides to the operation and recent activities of the Parliament. Its website also includes recent news headlines and lists of current British MEPs, with contact addresses.

1878   **OSCE Parliamentary Assembly**
www.oscepa.org
International body composed of the member parliaments of OSCE (q.v.) participating states. The website provides information on the aims and activities of the body. It includes the full text of its rules and regulations, minutes of proceedings, resolutions and committee reports. The latter include examples of election observation monitoring reports, details of interparliamentary activity in the OSCE area and commentary on recent security issues. Past examples have included reports on the Balkans war and the situation in Nagorno-Karabakh.

1879   **Parlamento Andino (Andean Parliament)**
www.parlamentoandino.org
The Andean Parliament is the parliamentary body of the Andean community. Members include Bolivia, Peru, Colombia, Ecuador and Venezuela. Its website provides information on the aims of the body, its membership and interparliamentary activity. This offers insight into cooperative political activity in South America. It includes access to full-text resolutions, press releases and reports. Information is in Spanish.

1880   **Parlamento CentroAmericano (Parliament of Central America)**
www.parlacen.org.gt
An international body created in 1986 by members of national parliaments from nations of Central America, including El Salvador, Honduras, Guatemala, Nicaragua and Costa Rica. Its purpose is to create a forum for the exchange of information on parliamentary democracy. Its website offers information on the purpose and operation of the parliament including a list of its members, a description of the structure of the parliament and news on current projects. General political news from Central America is also provided. All information is offered in Spanish only.

1881   **Parlamento Latinoamericano (Latin American Parliament)**
www.parlatino.org/
A regional organization comprising national parliaments from countries of Latin America. Its purpose is to defend democracy in the area and encourage integration and cooperation. Its website contains information on the purpose and activities of the Parliament. It includes a history of the organization, newsletters and details about recent and forthcoming conferences. The site is also a useful source of information about parliamentary activity in South America in general, offering news and links to the websites of the individual member states.

1882   **Parliamentary Union of the OIC Member States**
www.puoicm.org

Transnational body which aims to promote cooperation among the national parliaments of member nations of the Organization of the Islamic Conference. Its website provides access to basic information on the aims of the body, its membership and recent activities. It includes reports from its conferences and some information about its members. It is a useful starting point for tracing information about parliaments and parliamentary reform in Islamic nations.

1883   **Union Parlementaire Africaine (African Parliamentary Union)**
www.uafparl.org
An international organization which was established in 1976 to promote cooperation among African national parliaments. Its website provides basic information on the purpose of the body, its membership and activities. It includes access to some full-text statutes and resolutions. These include statements concerning terrorism and conflict in Africa. Information is offered in English or French.

Associations & societies

1884   **Asia Pacific Parliamentary Forum**
www.appf.org.pe
A professional forum for parliamentarians from national parliaments of nations of the Asia-Pacific region. Its website provides information on its history, role and activities. It also includes a directory of contact addresses and links to the websites of the national parliaments of its member states.

1885   **Commonwealth Parliamentary Association**
www.cpahq.org
An association of the national, provincial, state and territorial parliaments and legislatures of the countries of the Commonwealth which seeks to promote democracy and good governance. Its website contains press releases, programme reports and other full-text documents from the CPA. These include observations of individual elections in Commonwealth nations and programmes to promote female participation in politics. It is also a good starting point for tracing information on the parliamentary systems of individual Commonwealth nations as it contains a useful directory of contact postal and web addresses.

1886   **Conference of the Speakers of European Union Parliaments**
www.eu-speakers.org
A professional forum where speakers of the national parliaments of individual EU member states and the European Parliament meet to exchange information and ideas. The website provides information on the aims of the organization, its membership and activities. It includes press releases, details about past and forthcoming conferences, plus the full text of presidency conclusions from 2000 onwards. There is strong coverage of themes relating to national and international parliamentary procedure.

1887   **European Parliament Research Group**
www.lse.ac.uk/collections/EPRG/
A specialist postgraduate research group founded in 1998 which acts as a forum for some of the leading scholars of the European Parliament from Europe and North America. Its website provides information on recent events and research projects. It includes some working papers and

datasets which may be downloaded free of charge. Topics covered include the role and voting patterns of MEPS in the European Parliament.

1888 Inter-Parliamentary Forum of the Americas
www.e-fipa.org
An international network composed of representatives of the national parliaments of members of the Organization of American States (OAS). The website provides information on the aims of the group, its membership and activities. It provides free access to a 'virtual library' of recent press releases, resolutions, documents and reports. Topics covered by these include economic and political relations between the nations of North, South and Central America, international security and terrorism, the development of democracy and women's political participation.

Digital data, image & text collections

1889 IPEX: interparliamentary EU information exchange
www.ipex.eu
IPEX is designed to support the electronic exchange of EU-related information between national parliaments. Researchers will find it invaluable for tracing both the text of recent EU proposals and documents and information about the stage of scrutiny of specific EU regulations and proposals in national parliaments of individual member states. It is possible to search for a specific document and find information on the stage of parliamentary scrutiny which it has reached.

Handbooks & manuals

1890 Times guide to the European Parliament 1994
R. Morgan, ed.   The Times, 1994, 270pp. o/p. ISBN 072300708X.
The *Times Guide* is issued after every European Parliament election. It provides access to a comprehensive collection of background information about the role, operation and membership of the Parliament as well as a complete listing of the election results.

National Parliaments

Introductions to the subject

1891 The Congress of the United States: a student companion
D.A. Ritchie   3rd edn, Oxford University Press USA, 2006, 272pp. £30. ISBN 9780195309249.
A concise and readable introduction to the powers and operation of the American Congress. Topics covered include the powers of Congress, relations with the presidency and other branches of American government, the structure and function of Congressional agencies, key Congressional publications and the election process.

1892 How parliament works
R. Rogers and R. Walters   6th edn, Longman, 2006, 490pp. £19.99. ISBN 9781405832557.
Clear guide to the daily workings of the UK Parliament. Includes coverage of both the House of Commons and the House of Lords, plus analysis of pressures on the system, recent constitutional changes and how it might work in the future. There is a separate chapter on the law-making process and a handy glossary of parliamentary terms.

Laws, standards, codes

1893 Erskine May's treatise on the law, privileges, proceedings and usage of parliament
W. Mackay [et al.], eds   23rd edn, Butterworths Law, 2004, 1138pp. £210. ISBN 9780406970947.
Published for over 150 years. This is an authoritative and detailed guide to the regulations covering the powers and jurisdiction of the British parliament. Includes coverage of membership of both Houses, conduct of proceedings, law making and financial procedure.

Official & quasi-official bodies

1894 Great Britain. Parliament
www.parliament.uk/
The official website of the British Parliament provides free access to up-to-date information on the role, membership and activities of the House of Commons and House of Lords. In addition to the latest audio and TV webcasts of parliamentary activity it is also possible to consult daily updates of *Hansard* (the official written record of parliamentary debates) from 1995 onwards. Other useful features of the website include the Parliamentary Select Committee pages where you will find press releases, meeting transcripts and reports containing critical discussion of all aspects of UK government policy and legislation. An often overlooked but invaluable section of the website is the Commons Library research papers. These provide concise independent summaries of all proposed legislation, plus overviews of recent policy programmes and international events. They are particularly useful for students and members of the public requiring a quick introduction to background information. All papers issued since 1996 may be downloaded free of charge.
- **Hansard** www.parliament.uk/hansard/hansard.cfm [29/06/2006].
- **Parliamentary committees**
  www.parliament.uk/parliamentary_committees/parliamentary_committees16.cfm [29/06/2006].

1895 Inter-Parliamentary Union
www.ipu.org/
An international organization of parliaments of sovereign states which acts to promote parliamentary democracy worldwide. Its website is an excellent starting point for tracing facts about national parliamentary and legislative bodies worldwide. It offers free access to news headlines, directories of national parliament websites and a number of free databases.
- **Parline** www.ipu.org/parline-e/parlinesearch.asp [19/06/2006].
  Provides information on national parliaments worldwide. Entries give general information on the parliamentary chamber, the electoral system and results from the most recent election.
- **Parlit: bibliographic references parliamentary law and practice** www.ipu.org/parlit-e/parlitsearch.asp [19/06/2006].
  Searchable database of bibliographic references to books and articles relevant to the study of parliamentary law and practice. This is regularly

updated. References are available for over 30,000 journal articles taken from 160 titles and 7,000 books published since 1992.

- **Women in politics bibliographic database** www.ipu.org/bdf-e/BDFsearch.asp [19/06/2006]. Developed in association with the United Nations Development Programme. It provides bibliographic references to books, reports and journal articles on all aspects of women's participation in political life worldwide. Includes materials published since 1948.

1896 United States. House of Representatives

www.house.gov

The official website provides free access to comprehensive information on the history, role, membership and legislative activity of the US lower chamber. It includes webcasts from the House, press releases and access to the latest news. There are detailed listings of committee memberships and organizational structure charts. A large educational section offers factsheets and quizzes on the role of Congress. There is also a substantial collection of materials on the legislative activity of the House, including factsheets on how laws are made, vote call databases from 1990 onwards and indexes to current information about the current status of bills passing through Congress.

1897 United States. Senate

www.senate.gov

The official website provides free access to detailed historical and current information about the American upper chamber. It should be used in conjunction with the House of Representatives website. It includes floor schedules, daily digests of activity, proceedings and webcasts of the latest action. There is online access to the *Congressional Record* (the verbatim account of the remarks made by Senators and Representatives on the floor of the Senate and the House of Representatives) from 1990 onwards. Organizational information includes factsheets, lists of senators and committees. There is also a substantial section of information on legislation, including tracking of recent and current bills and explanations of the legislative process.

Research centres & institutes

1898 Dirksen Congressional Center

www.dirksencenter.org/

A well regarded independent institution which seeks to promote better understanding of the US Congress among American citizens. In addition to offering information about its aims and training courses, the website of the organization is also a good starting point for tracing introductory guides to the workings of the US parliamentary system. It includes a directory of links to key American government websites and a section for teachers containing suggested lesson plans and other online learning resources.

- **CongressLink** www.congresslink.org. An educational site created by the Dirksen Congressional Center to offer students and teachers introductory information on the US Congress. It covers the history of Congress, its operation and membership and how laws are made. The site contains essays, lesson plans and access to full text documents. The latter include key historical documents and legislation. There is also information on current news stories.

1899 Hansard Society

www.hansardsociety.org.uk/

A UK-based body which acts as a forum to encourage public debate about the future of parliamentary democracy. It funds the Hansard Scholars Programme to encourage international academic exchanges. Its website provides information on the purpose, research activities, events and publications of the society. Areas covered include the reform of parliament, development of electronic government, women in public life and electoral system reform. It is possible to access many full-text papers and research reports free of charge from the website.

Associations & societies

1900 Association of Secretaries General of Parliaments

www.asgp.info

A consultative body of the Interparliamentary Union which is composed of holders of office and secretaries general of national parliaments worldwide. It aims to promote interparliamentary consultation on issues such as parliamentary procedures, laws and working methods. Its website provides information on its aims, membership and activities. It includes access to a collection of its full-text press releases, documents and papers. These include coverage of such issues as the use of e-government services by parliaments worldwide, discussion of parliamentary privilege, procedures and ethics. There are also some useful summaries and reports on the workings of parliamentary systems of individual nations.

1901 ECPR Standing Group on Parliaments

www.essex.ac.uk/ecpr/standinggroups/parliaments/

A specialist research group of the European Consortium of Political Research (ECPR) which focuses on academic research into the function and operation of parliamentary bodies. Its main areas of interest include parliaments in European nations and the US Congress. Its website is a useful starting point for locating news about recent research projects, conferences and publications in this field. It provides free access to some recent examples of working papers from its members.

1902 International Commission for the History of Representative & Parliamentary Institutions

www.univie.ac.at/ichrpi

The International Commission for the History of Representative and Parliamentary Institutions (ICHRPI) is an international association which seeks to advance research into the history of parliaments worldwide. Its website provides information on its function, membership and activities. It includes details about is conferences and contents pages from all issues of its journal *Parliaments, Estates and Representation* from 1981 to the present. These provide insight into the political history and developments of parliaments in specific nations.

Discovering print & electronic resources

1903 Parliamentary Data [UK]

Great Britain. House of Commons, daily. Previously known as Polis: Parliamentary Online Indexing Service, Free.
www.polis.parliament.uk

A free, searchable index updated daily by the the staff of the Library of the House of Commons. It provides references to the proceedings and publications of the House of Commons and the House of Lords and includes the text of all Early Day

Motions from 1997 onwards. It is possible to search by date, subject keyword, type of document or member of parliament.

Digital data, image & text collections

1904 Annals of Congress (1789–1824)
http://memory.loc.gov/ammem/amlaw/lwac.html
This site is part of the American Memory Project of the Library of Congress. It provides free access to debates and proceedings in the US Congress from 1789 to 1824. They offer fascinating insight into the operation, personalities and business of the chamber. Background information on the compilation of the source and its content is provided.

1905 British history online
www.british-history.ac.uk
A digital library of full-text documents about British people, places and business from the medieval period which is maintained by the Institute of Historical Research and the History of Parliament Trust. It provides free access to a large collection of documents, reports and maps of value to economic, political, legal and religious historians. Highlights of the parliamentary history collection include The official record of proceedings in the House of Lords (1509–1717, 1832–4), records of debates from the House of Commons (1667–94) and The Journals of all the Parliaments during the reign of Queen Elizabeth (1559–1601). Also accessible are examples of diaries kept by individual MPs during this period, including Roger Whitley's Diary 1684–1697 and the parliamentary diary of Thomas Burton, MP for Westmorland (1653–59).

1906 The history of Parliament
Cambridge University Press, 1998. CD-ROM. Price is for a single user. Network use can be supplied at higher cost, £550. ISBN 9780521629072.
www.histparl.ac.uk/
A major scholarly project which aims to publish a history of the members, constituencies and activities of the Parliament of England and the UK from earliest times. Volumes currently released cover the House of Commons from 1386 to 1832 and the House of Lords from 1660 to 1832. Each book contains biographies of members, detailed summaries of constituencies and discussion of parliamentary procedures and activities. The revised text of all seven of the sets of the History of Parliament published up to 1998: 1386–1421, 1509–1558, 1558–1603, 1660–1690, 1715–1754, 1754–1790 and 1790–1820 can also be purchased in CD-ROM format. The website of the project lists forthcoming volumes. It is also useful for tracing information about other parliamentary history digitization projects.

1907 House of Commons Parliamentary Papers, 1801–1900
Chadwyck-Healey. Price on request.
www.proquest.co.uk/
This full-text subscription service is an unequalled source of information on 19th-century British parliamentary and legal history. As the working documents of government, the parliamentary papers cover all areas of social, economic and political foreign policy, providing insight into the workings of parliament at this time. They include discussion of Royal Commissions; committee reports and background on the passing of specific legislation. They also offer a fascinating insight into the characters of key politicians and social reformers. The database is fully searchable by subject keyword.

1908 Journal of the House of Representatives of the United States 1789–1873
http://memory.loc.gov/ammem/amlaw/lwhj.html
This site is part of the American Memory Project of the Library of Congress which aims to make publicly available the full text of key documents in American history. The journal contains minutes of the matters considered by the House of Representatives, its votes and actions. Background information is available on its content and it is searchable by keyword.

1909 VoteWorld: international legislative roll-call web site
http://ucdata.berkeley.edu:7101/new_web/VoteWorld/voteworld/
A project of the Institute of Governmental Studies at University of California, Berkeley, with the additional support of the Institute for European Studies. It aims to provide free access to statistical datasets of roll-call voting from legislative bodies around the world. Of particular interest are the electoral results of the United States House of Representatives and Senate from 1789 to the present and datasets relating to the European Parliament and United Nations Assembly. The project is also developing associated course materials for undergraduate and college classes. These include online animations of the US Congress.

Directories & encyclopedias

1910 Dod's parliamentary companion 2007 [UK]
Vacher Dod Publishing, 2007, annual, 1248pp. £230. ISBN 0905702662 ISSN 00707007.
www.dodonline.co.uk
Published annually since 1832. Contains facts, figures and contact addresses for the current British parliament and government departments. It includes full listings of ministers, biographies of members of the House of Commons and House of Lords, listings of all by-election results since the last general election and contact addresses for government and public offices and devolved parliamentary assemblies. Introductory essays provide an overview of the main parliamentary and legislative activity in the past year. Also available online.

1911 Vacher's Quarterly [UK]
Dod's Parliamentary Publications, qtrly. Available online or in print. Subscription details on request. Continues *Vacher's parliamentary companion*. ISSN 09580328.
A long-established pocket handbook which provides regularly updated contact details for all individuals and key political bodies within the political arena in both the UK and Europe. This includes listings of MPs, ministers and membership of UK government select committees and back-bench organizations. Available in print or online. Complements the *Dod's parliamentary companion* series.

1912 World encyclopedia of parliaments and legislatures
G.T. Kurian, eds   Fitzroy Dearborn Publishers, 1998, 916pp. £250. ISBN 9781579581213.

Produced under the auspices of the Research Committee of Legislative Specialists, International Political Science Association and the Commonwealth Parliamentary Society, this volume provides coverage of 193 national legislatures worldwide. Typical entries include an overview of the history, operation and legislative and other functions of the parliament, plus recent election results and details on members' rights and immunities. However, due to the age of the publication, details of websites are not included.

Handbooks & manuals

1913 Dod's handbook of House of Commons procedure 2006 [UK]
P. Evans   Dod's Parliamentary Communications, 2006, annual, 280pp. £52. ISBN 9780905702636.

Useful for finding information about how the British House of Commons works. Includes sections on the organization and operation of parliament and the rules and procedures for making legislation. Most recent edition includes information on the impact of devolution and the Human Rights Act. Numerous tables and diagrams illustrate the points made in the text. A glossary of parliamentary terms is provided.

1914 Dod's handbook of House of Lords procedure [UK]
P. Evans   2nd edn, Dod's Parliamentary Communications, 2006, 250pp. £45. ISBN 9780905702643.

Companion volume to *Dod's handbook of House of Commons procedure* (q.v.), offering an accessible guide to understanding the current role, organization and day-to-day operation of the British House of Lords. Illustrated with tables to highlight key points. It includes coverage of recent constitutional changes and the judicial role of the House. Also contains a glossary of terms.

1915 The Times guide to the House of Commons 2005 [UK]
Times, 2005, annual, 384pp. £50. ISBN 9780007211821.

The *Times guide to the House of Commons* has been published to cover every general election and new membership of the House of Commons since 1929. Contains an authoritative listing of MPs and members of the government. This includes information about individual constituencies. Coverage of elections includes by-election and general election results in the last calendar year, the full text of the manifestos of the main political parties and essays analysing the campaigns.

Regional & Devolved Parliaments

Official & quasi-official bodies

1916 Great Britain. Ministry of Justice: devolution
www.justice.gov.uk/whatwedo/devolution.htm

The Ministry of Justice is responsible for the management of relations between the British government and the devolved administrations in Scotland, Wales and Northern Ireland. This section of its website provides access to official

government information on devolution. It includes a history of the process and access to full-text legislation, ministerial guidance and British government reports. Also provided are links to the official websites of the main devolved administrations and government funded research programmes on devolution. Note that before May 2007 responsibility for this function was held by the Department for Constitutional Affairs (DCA) and some archived materials from this period may also be accessed.

1917 National Assembly for Wales
www.wales.gov.uk

The official website provides information on the role, structure, membership and activities of the National Assembly. It includes free access to parliamentary proceedings, biographies of current members and minutes, papers and reports from the Assembly and all its sub-committees. Materials date from 1999 onwards, proceedings are updated daily.

1918 Northern Ireland Assembly
www.niassembly.gov.uk

The official website of the Assembly provides information on the history of the Assembly, its function, membership and operation. It includes details of its relationship to the Northern Ireland peace agreement and suspension between 2003 and 2007. It is possible to access rules and regulations, lists of members and proceedings online.

1919 Scottish Parliament
www.scottish.parliament

The official website provides detailed information on the operation and business of the Scottish Parliament. Information is provided on the history of the Parliament, the buildings, how the Parliament works, news, contacts details, publications and the MSPs. There is also extensive current information on parliamentary business. This includes the parliamentary timetable, the business bulletin, the official reports for the parliamentary year, reports of the parliamentary committees, parliamentary questions and the full text of bills progressing through the Parliament.

Research centres & institutes

1920 Constitution Unit
www.ucl.ac.uk/constitution-unit/

Based in University College London, this research unit is recognized as one of the leading sources of research on constitutional reform in the UK. Since 1995 it has engaged in a wide programme of research covering political devolution, freedom of information, church–state relations and the reform of the House of Lords. Its website provides free access to examples of its research reports and papers. The section on devolution is particularly detailed, containing papers on devolution in Scotland, Wales, Northern Ireland and the English regions. It includes devolution monitoring reports which measure developments in devolution policy and its impact on institutions in Scotland and Wales from 1999 onwards.

1921 Devolution and Constitutional Change
www.devolution.ac.uk/

A major research programme funded by the UK's Economic and Social Research Council (ESCRC) between 2000 and

2006. It supported over 35 projects examining the implications of political devolution in Scotland, Wales and Northern Ireland for the UK state, society and economy. Its website provides a record of the main findings of the project. It also contains a large archive of working papers from the individual research areas. Key themes included the governance and operation of the new political institutions, with detailed analysis of the aims, establishment and operation of the Scottish Parliament, National Assembly for Wales and Northern Ireland Assembly.

1922   Institute of Governance, Scotland
www.institute-of-governance.org/
A specialist research institute based at the University of Edinburgh which focuses on current social and political issues in Scotland. This includes coverage of constitutional issues relating to Scottish devolution. It provides consultancy and research on constitutional change to the Scottish Parliament, the Scottish Executive and a range of other organizations. The website provides information on the aims of the Institute, staff and current projects. It includes news updates from the Scottish Parliament and Executive as well as free access to a large collection of articles published in the journal *Scottish Affairs* from 1999 to date. Topics covered include Scottish identity, the Gaelic language, Scottish nationalism, independence for Scotland, elections in Scotland and devolution.
    Site appears not to have been updated since October 2006.

1923   Institute of Welsh Affairs
www.iwa.org.uk/
An independent think-tank founded in 1987 which seeks to influence a wide range of areas of public policy in Wales. Interests include political devolution in Wales and Welsh culture and identity. Its website provides information on its aims and activities. It includes free access to a series of quarterly reports monitoring the aims and performance of the National Assembly for Wales from 1999 onwards. Also accessible are other working papers, articles and online debate about Welsh politics.

1924   Institute of Welsh Politics
www.aber.ac.uk/interpol/IWP
The Institute of Welsh Politics is based at the University of Aberystwyth and specializes in research on devolution in Wales, the study of the Welsh electorate, political parties in Wales and the relationship between Wales and the European Union. Its website provides information on current research and forthcoming activities. It includes a list of recent publications on issues related to Welsh politics and details of the content of its journal *Contemporary Wales*.

Portal & task environments

1925   DevWeb: the Internet guide to UK devolution
www.devolution.info
A comprehensive guide to internet sites and resources relating to UK devolution which is maintained by Jason Thomas Williams. Offers coverage of devolution in Scotland, Wales, Northern Ireland and the English regions. Coverage of elected mayors is also provided. Each section offers an overview of key dates, legislation, elections and links to

important online papers, reports, campaign groups and government departments.

Digital data, image & text collections

1926   Aspect: Access to Scottish Parliamentary Election Candidate Materials
http://gdl.cdlr.strath.ac.uk/aspect/
Fascinating digital archive of ephemera relating to elections to the Scottish Parliament created and maintained by the University of Strathclyde. It currently contains materials from the 1999 and 2003 elections. These include leaflets, flyers, posters and newsletters produced by the Scottish Office, candidates and political parties. Other features of the site include election statistics, a history of political devolution in Scotland and a bibliography of further readings.

1927   Campaign!: a century of political and social campaigning in Wales
www.llgc.org.uk/ymgyrchu/index-e.htm
A digital library of documents and images relating to Welsh political history and social campaigning during the 20th century, assembled from materials held by the National Library of Wales. They include photographs, posters, pamphlets and political ephemera. Topics covered include voting and suffrage, political devolution and the campaign for a Welsh Parliament/Assembly. Also accessible are materials relating to Welsh social history and the Welsh language. The site includes some teacher's notes on the materials and bibliographies of further reading.

1928   Stormont papers
http://stormontpapers.ahds.ac.uk
A project organized by the Centre for Data Digitization and Analysis at Queen's University Belfast and made available by the Arts and Humanities Data Service (Executive) at King's College London. It provides free access to an electronic library of full-text government reports relating to Northern Ireland during the period from 7 June 1921 to 28 March 1972. They include over 92,000 printed pages from minutes of the Stormont Parliament, the devolved parliamentary body of Northern Ireland. These provide a rich source of information on the government of the region. They include coverage of the social, economic and foreign policy of Northern Ireland and relations between the British and Irish governments at this time.

Directories & encyclopedias

1929   Dod's Scottish companion
Dod's Parliamentary Communications, 2006, annual, 650pp. £125. ISBN 9780905702629.
Annual publication which offers facts, figures and contact addresses for the current Scottish Parliament. It includes full listings of government ministers, biographies of members of the Scottish Parliament, constituency profiles, listings of all by-election results since the last general election and contact addresses for government and public offices. Introductory essays provide an overview of political devolution in Scotland, plus the main parliamentary and legislative activity in the past year

Handbooks & manuals

1930 The history of the Scottish Parliament
K.M. Brown, ed. Edinburgh University Press. 3 v.
www.st-andrews.ac.uk/~scotparl/
A major scholarly three-volume work comprising essays from
25 renowned scholars on the historical evolution of the
Scottish parliament from the 13th century to 1707. Volumes
1 and 2 examine the history of parliament under the
medieval and early modern monarchs. Volume 3 will discuss
broad themes relating to the relationship between religion
and politics in Scotland, the struggle for Scottish
independence and the legislative procedures and roles of the
parliament.
- **1. Parliament and politics in Scotland, 1235–1560**
  2004, 240pp. £55. ISBN 9780748614851.
- **2. Parliament and politics in Scotland, 1567 to 1707**
  2005, 356pp. £50. ISBN 9780748614950.
- **3. The Scottish Parliament: a thematic history** 2008. £50.
  ISBN 9780748614868. Volume currently in progress.

Members of Parliament

Official & quasi-official bodies

**1931 Great Britain. Committee on Standards in Public
Life**
www.public-standards.gov.uk
An non-departmental public body which is concerned with
standards of conduct of UK public office holders. It also
considers issues relating to political ethics and the funding of
British political parties. The website provides free access to
the full text of all its reports published since 1994. These
focus on general recommendations for improving political
integrity, whereas the work of the House of Commons Public
Standards and Privileges Select Committee often examines
cases relating to specific individuals.

**1932 Great Britain. House of Commons, Committee on
Standards & Privileges**
A select committee of the House of Commons which handles
issues relating to political ethics, parliamentary privilege and
the conduct of MPs. Its website contains a list of current
members of the Committee and links to the full text of press
releases and committee reports from 1997 onwards. These
include investigations into allegations of corruption and
abuse of privilege made against individual MPs.

**1933 United States. House of Representatives, Office of
the Clerk**
http://clerk.house.gov/
The Clerk of the House is a leading official of the US
Congress whose reponsibilites include maintaining accurate
membership information and the custody of non-current
records of the House. In addition to providing free access to
current ethics codes, membership lists and contact
addresses, its website is also a rich source of information on
American parliamentary history. It contains profiles,
membership, leadership and legislative information for all
congresses since 1789. This includes statistics on numbers
of members, lists of office holders and committee members.
Also available are online biographical profiles of

approximately 12,000 representatives, delegates, resident
commissioners and senators who have served since 1789.
- **Women in Congress** http://womenincongress.house.gov/
  [12/07/2006]. This website, based on the book *Women in Congress
  1917–2006*, contains biographical profiles of former women members of
  Congress, links to information about current members, essays, photographs
  and articles about the history and current state of women's political
  participation in the USA.

Research centres & institutes

1934 Centre for the Advancement of Women in Politics
www.qub.ac.uk/cawp/observatory.html
Based in the School of Politics and International Studies at
Queen's University Belfast. Conducts specialist research into
women's contribution to politics, government and public life
in the UK and Ireland. The website is noted for its
observatory on women's political participation, containing
up-to-date data for these countries. This includes lists of all
current and previous female public office holders, such as
MPs, judges and councillors, from approximately 1979 to the
present.

Associations & societies

1935 Fawcett Society
www.fawcettsociety.org.uk/
The Fawcett Society has a long history of campaigning for
equality between women and men in the UK on pay,
pensions, justice and politics. Its website provides
information on its history and current campaigns. Its website
provides free access to facts and figures about sexual
inequality in the UK, plus a large collection of its campaign
materials and research reports. Key areas covered include
the under-representation of women in British politics,
discrimination against ethnic minority women in the UK and
women's employment.

Portal & task environments

ePolitix.com
See entry no. 1251

Directories & encyclopedias

**1936 Biographical directory of the United States
Congress**
http://bioguide.congress.gov
This website offers free access to the official biographical
directory of the US Congress from 1774 to the present. It is
possible to search the database by name, position or political
party. Typical entries include key dates, photographs,
positions held, bibliography of key writings and sources of
archival information.

**1937 Black members of the United States Congress
with biographies: 1789–2004**
M. Amer Nova Science, 2007. £32. ISBN 1594547459.
A useful specialist guide to the history of black
representation in the American Congress. It includes an
alphabetical listing of all black members from 1789 to 2004

with biographical information and full listings of committee assignments and offices held during their period of tenure. The volume includes tables of data on black members and an introductory essay which sets the figures in their historical context.

1938 Congresspedia: the citizen's encyclopedia on Congress
www.sourcewatch.org/index.php?title=Congresspedia
An interesting project of the Sunlight Foundation and the Center for Media & Democracy which aims to build an online encyclopedia of articles about the US Congress, its senators, representatives and committees similar in form to Wikipedia, by using collaboration with US citizens. Quality of content is overseen by an academic editorial board. Entries on members of Congress typically contain biographical information, details of voting patterns, political funding and committee membership.

1939 CQ's politics in America 2006: the 109th Congress
J. Koszczuk and A. Stern　CQ Press, 2006, annual, 1224pp. £58. ISBN 9781933116105.
Well regarded directory which provides authoritative information on members of the United States Congress and their districts. It Includes individual biographies, election results and committee memberships plus assessments of personality and political agendas. State and district information includes detailed electoral district maps, historic demographic data and maps of voting trends. Available in print or online.

1940 Dod's constituency guide 2006
3rd edn, Vacher Dod Publishing, 2002–, annual, 1250pp. 2 v., £160. ISBN 9780905702599.
www.dodonline.co.uk
Detailed guide to every UK parliamentary constituency. Heavily illustrated with useful maps of electoral districts and charts of recent election results. Each entry includes a brief electoral history, current socio-economic profile of the constituency, details about the MP and contact addresses.

1941 From suffrage to the Senate: an encyclopedia of American women in politics
S. O'Dea Schenken　Grey House Publishing, 2006, 832pp. 2 v., £120. ISBN 1592371175.
A useful resource which gathers together in one place factual information about key figures from American women's political history. It includes biographies for every female US representative, senator and cabinet member(prior to 2006), plus entries for political journalists, pollsters, campaigners and key organizations. Bibliographical references follow each entry. An appendix provides a chronological history of key events and legislation.

1942 Parliamentary profiles 2001–2005 [UK]
A. Roth　Parliamentary Profiles, 2005, 1200pp. 4 v. Each volume covers a different section of the alphabet (A-D; E-K; L-R; S-Z) and is available separately (£40)., £150. ISBN 0900582480.
www.rothprofiles.demon.co.uk/profiles.html [DESCRIPTION]
Comprehensive collection of profiles of all British MPs elected in 2001. Earlier editions also available covering MPs elected in 1997 and the 1980s. Famous for its informal tone. Entries include biographic and constituency details as well as caricatures, excerpts from daily newspapers (including

tabloids) about key moments in their careers and often witty discussions of their appearance, character and political beliefs.

Keeping up to date

1943 Theyworkforyou [UK]
www.theyworkforyou.com/
Famous site maintained by an independent charity to enable members of the public to easily access information about British MPs. Entries on individual MPs include biographical and constituency facts, voting records, sources of renumeration and access to recent parliamentary speeches and written questions. Other features of the site include a glossary of parliamentary terms and parliamentary news headlines. Coverage includes the House of Commons and Northern Ireland Assembly.

Political Parties

communist parties • conservative parties • fascist parties • liberal parties • national political parties • party conventions • socialist parties • types of political party

National Political Parties

Dictionaries, thesauri, classifications

1944 Dictionary of Labour quotations [UK]
S. Thomson, ed.　Politicos, 1999, 196pp. £18. ISBN 1902301161.
Interesting collection of over 2000 political quotations from leading British socialists and members of the Labour Party. Entries range from Keir Hardie to Karl Marx and Tony Blair. They include both serious and amusing quotations from speeches, articles and papers. Materials generally date from the 20th century.

Research centres & institutes

1945 Revolts.co.uk [UK]
www.revolts.co.uk
Website of a really interesting research project established by Philip Cowley and Mark Stuart of Nottingham University. It provides independent academic analysis of MPs and peers voting patterns in the House of Commons and House of Lords. A particular focus of interest is rebellions and revolts by backbench MPs against the Labour government. It is possible to read full-text research papers, polls and reports online. Many relate to topical British politics news stories. Examples include dissension relating to the decision to go to war in Iraq and British defence policy.

Associations & societies

1946 Conservative Party [UK]
www.Conservative-party.org.uk/
Offical website of Britain's largest centre-right political party. Provides free access to the latest news stories, speeches, policy documents, manifestos and broadcasts. This includes links to the websites of special interest groups, local party

headquarters and topical campaign websites. There is a separate section for Conservative Party conference information where you can view videoclips of speeches from recent events. The emphasis is on current rather than historical policy.

1947 Democratic Party [USA]
www.democrats.org
The official website of the major American political party provides information on the history and current political policies of the party. It includes full-text policy statements and manifestos as well as audio and video clips from recent election campaigns and party conferences. The site includes links to working committees, local grassroots groups and political blogs by Democrats. These can be useful sources of information on the latest policy developments.

1948 Labour Party [UK]
www.labour.org.uk/
Official website of the British Labour Party. Provides free access to press releases, speeches, political conference webcasts, party policy statements and manifestos. Also a useful starting point for tracing the websites and addresses of local Labour Party Associations and MPs. Emphasis is on current rather than historical policy.

1949 Liberal Democrats [UK]
www.libdems.org.uk/
Official website of the British Liberal Democrat Party. Provides information on the aims, membership and recent activities of the party. Includes a listing of all MPs, with contact addresses and links to constituency information. Also accessible are recent party press releases, speeches, policy documents, election broadcasts and manifestos. Links are provided to the websites of Liberal Democrat special interest groups, associations and journal publications. Emphasis is on current rather than historical information.

1950 Republican National Committee [USA]
www.rnc.org
The official website of one of the USA's two leading political parties is a rich source of information on its history, policy and activities. It is possible to read recent policy documents, election manifestos and blogs from key members. You can also keep up to date with the latest news by viewing webcasts, party campaign videos and political interviews. Links are provided to a large number of other Republican websites, including state parties, grassroots organizations and Republican interest groups.

1951 Unión de Partidos Latinoamericanos (Union of Latin American Political Parties)
www.upla.net
An international association of political parties from Latin and South American nations who seek to promote democracy in the region. Its website provides information on the aims of the organization, its membership and recent activities. It is a good starting point for tracing news and links to political parties in the region. Most information is offered in Spanish only.

Directories & encyclopedias

1952 Encyclopedia of British and Irish political organizations: parties, groups, and movements of the twentieth century
P. Barberis, J. McHugh and M. Tyldesley   Continuum, 2000, 576pp. £50. ISBN 9780826458148.
Wide-ranging work which includes coverage of the main political parties, think-tanks and civil society campaign groups active in Britain and Ireland during the period 1900–1998. Each entry provides a summary of the history, objectives and main activities of the group. It also lists key publications. Longer essays are provided for the main political parties and the politics of Wales, Scotland and Northern Ireland. These are useful starting points for gaining an understanding of movements for political devolution in these regions.

1953 The Greenwood historical encyclopedia of the world's political parties
Greenwood Press, 1982–.
This series provides coverage of historic political parties from all areas of the world. The volumes are organized by continent or region and within each volume political groups are described alphabetically by country. Typical entries contain information on the evolution and leadership of the party, its political beliefs and key events in its history.
- **Political parties of Asia and the Pacific: 1. Afghanistan–Korea** H. Fukui, ed.   1985. £105. ISBN 9780313251436.
- **Political parties of Asia and the Pacific: 2. Laos–Western Samoa** 1985. £105. ISBN 9780313251443.
- **Political parties of the Americas** R.J. Alexander, eds   1982, 1274pp. £160. ISBN 9780313214745.
- **Political parties of the Middle East and North Africa** F. Tachau, ed.   1994, 744pp. £160. ISBN 9780313266492.

1954 Historical dictionary of United States political parties
H.J. Bass   Scarecrow Press, 2000, 448pp. £63. ISBN 9780810837362.
Contains concise entries on all US political parties and their leaders. It also includes biographical entries for all American presidents and vice-presidents, chronologies of key events, lists of key office-holders, a glossary of party acronyms and information on election results for each of the main parties.

1955 Political parties of the world
B. Szajkowski   6th edn, John Harper Publishing, 2005, 650pp. £95. ISBN 9780954381141.
A compendium of information on over 10,000 political parties worldwide. The encyclopedia is arranged alphabetically by country. Each entry includes a brief political history of the nation, entries on the history, policy and leadership of the main national political parties and data on recent election results. There are indexes of international and pan-European party organizations.

Handbooks & manuals

1956 Handbook of party politics
W.J. Crotty and R.S. Katz, eds   Sage Publications, 2006, 550pp. £85. ISBN 9780761943143.
A useful collection of essays which map the state of

scholarship about political parties worldwide. It includes coverage of definitions of the political party, the functions of the party, party organization, the relationship between the party and the state and the future development of the party in the information age. References to further readings are provided.

1957 The history of British political parties
D. Boothroyd   Methuen, 2001, 300pp. £25. ISBN 1902301595.
Factual information on more than 250 political parties that have contested parliamentary elections from 1832 to 2000. Each entry provides information on policy, plus full electoral results and contact addresses for active parties. Entries for the main political parties are fuller.

1958 National party conventions 1831–2000 [USA]
Congressional Quarterly   CQ Press, 2000, 325pp. £22. ISBN 9781568029825.
Provides a grounding on the history, purpose and functioning of every US party convention for nomination, from 1831 to 2000. Chronological entries provide facts and figures about individual conventions. These include exerpts from key speeches, information on key convention ballots and votes. There are also separate appendices offering historical profiles of the main political parties and biographies of the major presidential and vice-presidential candidates from 1789 to 2000.

1959 Political parties of Eastern Europe: a guide to politics in the post-communist era
J. Bugajski   M.E. Sharpe, 1997, 900pp. £157.50. ISBN 9781563246760.
Useful resource for understanding the history of post-communist political development in Eastern Europe. Includes entries on 18 nations. Each contains a historical overview of post-1990 political developments, election results, listing of political parties with information on their role and policies. Volume also contains an index to Eastern European political party abbreviations. Regions of the Russian Federation not classified within Europe are excluded.

Keeping up to date

1960 18 Doughty Street Talk TV [UK]
www.18doughtystreet.com
18 Doughty Street was launched in 2006. It is Britain's first internet-only politics news channel. It aims to offer alternative political interviews and academic debates to counter what it regards as the 'dumbing down' of mainstream political broadcasting. Many contributors, such as Iain Dale, are associated with the British Conservative Party. It is possible to watch programmes online or view the archive. The site also supports discussion forums and political blogs.

Types of Political Party

Dictionaries, thesauri, classifications

1961 Biographical dictionary of Marxism
R.A. Gorman, ed.   Greenwood, 1986, 388pp. o/p. ISBN 9780155068674.

www.blackwellpublishing.com
Contains over 210 biographical essays on Marxist philosophers and activists worldwide. It encompasses only philosophers defined as orthodox or materialist Marxists, exponents of non-traditional Marxist theory are covered in the companion volume the *Biographical dictionary of neo-Marxism* (q.v.). An introductory essay defines and analyses Marxian materialism. Entries list biographical dates and provide bibliographies of key works. There is extensive coverage of individuals from Africa, Asia and Latin America.

1962 A biographical dictionary of modern European radicals and socialists
D. Nicholls and P. Marsh, eds   Prentice Hall, 1988, 500pp. £122.95. ISBN 9780710810458.
Wide-ranging work which encompasses individuals who have campaigned for social, economic and political change of institutions within Europe. Includes coverage of all the main liberal and socialist reformers of the 19th and 20th centuries. Each entry offers a biographical sketch and list of key biographies for further reading.
▪ 1. 1780–1815

1963 Biographical dictionary of the extreme right since 1890
P. Rees, comp.   Harvester Wheatsheaf, 1990, 418pp. o/p. ISBN 0710810199.
Useful collection of biographies of key figures from fascist, radical right and authoritarian right movements and parties worldwide. Includes many figures excluded from dictionaries of national biographies. Bibliographies of further reading are provided.

1964 Dictionary of Conservative quotations [UK]
I. Dale   Methuen Publishing, 1999, 256pp. £18. ISBN 9781902301150.
Contains more than 2000 key quotations from important figures in the history of the British Conservative Party and the development of conservative political theory and thought. Includes extensive materials from Conservative prime ministers such as Margaret Thatcher and Winston Churchill as well as key conservative thinkers such as Edmund Burke and Roger Scruton.

1965 Dictionary of Liberal biography [UK]
D. Brack, ed.   Politicos, 1998, 413pp. £35. ISBN 9781902301099.
Over 200 biographical essays of individuals who have made a major contribution to the development of British Liberalism. Includes entries for 19th-century Liberal prime ministers, Liberal Party leaders and politicians and liberal thinkers such as Bentham and Keynes.

Research centres & institutes

1966 Bow Group [UK]
www.thebowgroup.org
One of the oldest centre-right political think-tanks in the UK. Its main purpose is to develop ideas and stimulate debate within the British Conservative Party. Its website provides information on its aims and activities. It includes free access to recent working papers and all issues of its quarterly journal *Crossbow* from 2001 onwards. These are a useful source of information on developing areas of Conservative policy.

1967 Rosa Luxemburg Foundation

www.rosalux.de

A German-based political education foundation which maintains close links with the German Left Party (Die Linkspartei.PDS). One of its specialisms is the study of political parties in Europe. There is an emphasis on left-wing and socialist parties but other political theories are also covered. Its website provides information on its library and archive holdings, plus details of conferences and ongoing research.

Associations & societies

1968 African Liberal Network

www.africaliberalnetwork.org/

An association of liberal political parties from over 15 African nations who seek to promote democratic development in Africa. Its website is a useful source of information on the state of democracy and the development of liberal parties in individual African nations as it includes news updates from members and a directory of links to their websites.

1969 Conservative History Group [UK]

www.conservativehistory.org.uk

An association which promotes the study of the history of the British Conservative Party and conservative politics in Britain. Its website provides information on its aims, membership and events. It includes free access to past issues of its journal *Conservative History*. This typically contains useful articles and reviews discussing the work of Conservative prime ministers such as Margaret Thatcher and Sir Edward Heath. Other features include a list of recommended websites for beginning research on conservative political history.

1970 Council of Asian Liberals & Democrats

www.cald.org/

An association of liberal and social democrat political parties based in Asia. Its website provides information on the purpose of the group, its membership, conferences and events. It is possible to use the website to locate the home pages of liberal parties in individual Asian countries, as well as news of recent liberal activities.

1971 Global Greens

www.globalgreens.info

An international network of green parties, ecological and conservation movements founded in 2001. Its website provides information on its history, aims and current activities. It is a good source of information on green politics worldwide as it maintains calendars of events and directories of national and regional green parties.

1972 International Democrat Union

www.idu.org/

An international association of over 70 Conservative, Christian Democrat, centre and centre-right political parties. Its website provides information on the purpose of the organization and a a directory of its members with links to their internet sites where available. It is a good place for tracing information about the existence and recent activities of right of centre political parties worldwide.

1973 International Network of Liberal Women

www.inlw.org

An international association which seeks to expand the participation of women in liberal politics at local, national and international level, worldwide. Its website provides information on the aims of the association, its membership and campaigns. It includes the full text of recent press releases and reports. These provide insight into the participation of women in liberal parties worldwide.

1974 International Young Democrat Union

www.iydu.org

A global alliance of centre-right political youth organizations from over 50 nations worldwide who share a common belief in conservative politics and free market policies. Its website provides information on the aims of the organization, its membership and activities. It is a good starting point for tracing key centre-right groups in different nations worldwide, providing a useful directory of URLs and contact addresses.

1975 Liberal Democrat History Group [UK]

www.liberalhistory.org.uk

An association which encourages research into the history of the British Liberal Democrat, SDP and Liberal Parties. In addition to information on recent events, it also includes a history of the Liberal Party, tables of contents and selected articles from its journal the *Journal of Liberal Democrat History* from 1993 onwards. Other features of the site include advice on researching British liberalism, listings of recent PhD theses and online access to a collection of audiofiles of famous speeches from Liberal party leaders and prime ministers. These include examples from Lloyd-George and Asquith.

1976 Liberal International

www.liberal-international.org/

The world federation of liberal political parties. Its website is an excellent starting point for finding out about the current activities of national liberal parties worldwide. In addition to newsletters, resolutions and documents from the central executive, it also maintains an excellent directory of member parties, which contains contact addresses and website details.

1977 Libertarian International Organization

www.libertarian-international.org/

A network which seeks to promote and coordinate the activities of libertarian and anarchist political parties, organizations and movements. Its website provides information on libertarian political philosophy. Its also contains news, calendars of events and links to the websites of libertarian organizations worldwide.

1978 Socialist International

www.socialistinternational.org

An international organization of social democratic, socialist and labour parties whose membership currently includes over 160 political parties and movements worldwide. Its website provides information on the aims of the organization, its history and activities. It includes details of international socialist conferences, ongoing political campaigns and the work of its research committees, offering insight into current socialist thinking and concerns.

Libraries, archives, museums

1979 People's History Museum
http://82.71.77.169/index.html
A national centre which aims to collect and preserve materials relating to the lives of working people in the UK. It supports the Labour History Archive and research centre, which contains historical documents from the British Labour Party and the Communist Party of Great Britain, plus workers' organizations, trades unions and women's social and political organizations. The website provides information on the archive holdings and access. Images of some objects from the collections can be viewed online.

Portal & task environments

1980 International Socialist Tendency
www.istendency.net
An international network of revolutionary socialist organizations. Its website is a good starting point for finding news stories, reports and links to the websites of communist and revolutionary workers' groups worldwide.

Discovering print & electronic resources

1981 Communist International (Comintern) Archives Project
www.loc.gov/rr/european/comintern/comintern-home.html
This website provides free access to an electronically searchable index to the Archives, prepared by the International Committee for the Computerization of the Comintern Archive (Incomka) Project. The website includes details on the transliteration of the collection and guides to searching.

Digital data, image & text collections

1982 Comintern electronic archives
IDC Publishers. €5000.
www.comintern-online.com
The Communist International (Comintern), also known as the Third International, was an international communist organization founded in 1919 by Lenin and the Russian Communist Party. Its archives are in the custody of the Russian State Archives for Social and Political History (RGASPI) in Moscow. It is a rich source of information on the political history of the Soviet Union, international communism, Cold War history and the Russian Communist party during the 20th century. The electronic archives consist of of a free online inventory to the complete Comintern Archives and a subscription-based service to 1.2 million digital images of the most frequently used documents. These are divided into a number of subseries, including the commissions, the secretariats and departments that operated under the Executive Committee of the Communist International (ECCI). Information on transliteration is provided.

1983 Communist Party biographical project [UK]
http://les1.man.ac.uk/cpgb/index.htm
A project funded by the Economic and Social Research Council (ESRC) and conducted by researchers led by the University of Manchester. It surveyed the activities and opinions of British Communist Party members from 1920 to 1991. Its archived website includes information about the aims and findings of the project. It contains its database of biographical information about approximately 3000 Communist Party members. Individual entries include dates of birth, occupation, political positions held, lists of publications and qualitative information on political beliefs.

1984 Margaret Thatcher Foundation [UK]
www.margaretthatcher.org
Essential reading for students of British Conservative Party history and conservative political thought. This website provides free access to hundreds of online documents from Margaret Thatcher's personal and public archives, a searchable database of every public statement made by her from 1945 to 1990 and a selection of key statements made after that date, plus audio and multimedia files of key speeches. Bibliographies of important books and writings are also offered.

Directories & encyclopedias

1985 Dictionary of Labour biography [UK]
G. Rosen, ed.   Methuen Publishing, 2001, 450pp. o/p. ISBN 9781902301181.
Useful single-volume work which contains biographical essays on all 20th-century Labour cabinet ministers as well as TUC general secretaries and trade union leaders. Many of the entries are written by Labour Party colleagues, offering personal insight into the achievements of the individuals described. Lists of key biographies for further reading are provided.

1986 Encyclopedia of politics: the left and the right
R.P. Carlisle, ed.   Sage Publications, 2005, 1100pp. 2 v., £145. ISBN 9781412904094.
Two-volume set containing over 450 articles on individuals, movements and parties of the political left and right worldwide. Main emphasis is on the modern world. Volume on the right includes coverage of such modern phenomena as fascism and ethnic cleansing. A full bibliography is provided.

1987 World fascism: A historical encyclopedia
C.P. Blamires   ABC-CLIO, 2006, 577pp. £128.50. ISBN 9781576079409.
This single volume contains 500 entries on the key personalities, concepts and movements associated with fascism throughout history. It provides coverage of lesser-known Hindu extremist movements as well as the best-known manifestations in 20th-century Germany and Italy. Difficult concepts such as the appeal of Nazism, the relationship between fascism and racism, homophobia and militarism are discussed. Also analysed are the reasons for the increasing popularity of neo-Nazi and other far-right movements in the contemporary world.

Handbooks & manuals

The Routledge companion to fascism and the far right
P. Davies and D. Lynch   See entry no. 1326

Keeping up to date

Labour Left Briefing [UK]
Labour Left Briefing, 8 p.a. £15.
www.labourleftbriefing.org.uk
Labour Left Briefing is a publication which acts as a forum for
socialist ideas within the UK Labour Party and trade union
movement. The print version is published approximately
eight times per year. Its website contains a selection of
articles and reviews from the journal, plus news feeds of the
latest headlines from labour parties and the labour
movement worldwide. Typical issues covered are trade union
activity, critical analysis of the direction and policy of the
British Labour Party and discussion of the international
labour movement.

Liberator Magazine
See entry no. 1328

Government

Government and politics are frequently linked in the literature. To tease them apart for this volume has not been an easy matter. We have fallen back on a distribution loosely based on the traditional concept of the separation of powers: judiciary, parliament and executive.

Broadly speaking law-making and the judiciary will be found under the main subject Law; policy-making will be found under Politics and the machinery set up to carry out agreed policy will be found here under Government.
In the main, the focus here is on the cabinet, the civil service and local government administration. A wealth of government and official publications is listed under Social Sciences, since their subject matter transcends all the subjects included in this volume and frequently even into the sciences and humanities.

The subject of government is divided simply into national and sub-national units: on the one hand central government and on the other state, regional or local government. Both categories are further subdivided by country.

The range of countries covered under central government is wider than for state, regional and local. It was a pragmatic decision based on an estimate of the large number of sources which would be eligible for inclusion at the local level in large nations. So, while Australia, Canada, Ireland, New Zealand and the USA are included under central government, they are excluded from state, regional and local government.

Information sources relating to the UK are allocated according to the countries covered. Those which feature only one of England or Wales or Scotland or Northern Ireland are placed under the specific country heading. Those which cover more than one country but not the whole of the UK are included under United Kingdom (subordinate jurisdictions). The heading UK includes only those sources focusing on all constituent countries. Sources for Guernsey, Jersey, Ireland and the Isle of Man are dealt with separately.

The majority of entries in government fall under a limited number of resource categories: official bodies, research centres, associations (especially at the local government level), sources to assist in discovering print and electronic resources, directories and yearbooks. The reason: the work of the executive is practical and essentially administrative; it produces only a limited literature about itself and introductions to the work of the executive are far less common than those of its partners: the judiciary and parliament.

Portal & task environments

C-Span classroom
See entry no. 1250

Digital data, image & text collections

House of Commons Parliamentary Papers, 1801–1900
See entry no. 1907

Keeping up to date

Info4local
See entry no. 1296

Central Institutions

Australia • Canada • European Union • Guernsey • Ireland • Isle of Man • Jersey • New Zealand • Northern Ireland • Scotland • UK subordinate jurisdictions • United Kingdom • United States • Wales

Introductions to the subject

1989 Cabinets in Western Europe
J. Blondel and F. Muller-Rommel, eds   2nd edn, St Martin's Press, 1997, 256pp. ISBN 0333683447.
Thirteen chapters, each one devoted to a different European country and its cabinet system. Standard sub-headings permit comparisons to be drawn on the origins, structure, composition and activities of cabinets. Extensive bibliography.

Discovering print & electronic resources

1990 Foreign government resources on the web
www.lib.umich.edu/govdocs/foreign.html
Comprehensive links with brief descriptions to government and semi-official organizations across the world, excluding the USA. Includes links to official documents and handbooks such as constitutions, official reports and statistics, budgets and legal databases. Compiled and maintained by University of Michigan International Documents Librarian.

1991 Governments on the WWW
www.gksoft.com/govt/en/
Comprehensive set of links to government institutions providing information on the web, including parliaments, ministries, law courts, representation in foreign countries but not educational, cultural, medical and business organizations, parliamentary groups or individual politicians. Links organized in two sets: geographically and by type of institution. No annotations to links.

1992 Sage public administration abstracts
Sage Publications, 1974–, qtrly. ISSN 00946958.
Carries about 1200 abstracts each year covering among its range of topics administrative structures and organization, national government and public services, drawn from books and journals. Author and subject indexes and annual current source list. Available in electronic form through several commercial providers, including EBSCO.

Directories & encyclopedias

1993 Agencies and public bodies directory
www.civilservice.gov.uk/other/agencies/public_bodies/index.asp
Access to the *Public Bodies Directory 1998* onwards
containing details of public bodies sponsored by the UK
government, accounting for over 850 organizations, such as
non-departmental public bodies, public corporations, NHS
bodies and public broadcasters. Directory displayed in same
image as paper version. Entries arranged by 'parent'
government department. Simple index of names of
organizations. Search facilities available.

**1994 Chiefs of state and cabinet members of foreign
governments**
Central Intelligence Agency
www.cia.gov/cia/publications/chiefs/index.html
Simple alphabetical listing of countries with details of chief
of state and cabinet members, updated weekly. Compiled
and maintained by the CIA. Note the website is secure and
the address must be preceded by https://.

1995 Government gazettes online
www.lib.umich.edu/govdocs/gazettes/
Simple alphabetical listing by country of official government
gazettes available on the web, with details of URL, language,
charges, dates covered, how searched, format and brief
description of contents. As well as gazettes, details of some
other official, especially legal, documents included in
additional entries. Compiled and maintained by the
University of Michigan Library Service.

1996 Heads of state and government
J.V. Da Graca   2nd edn rev., Macmillan, 2000, 1222pp. ISBN
0333782775.
Set out alphabetically by country, it lists monarchs,
presidents, heads of state and their dates of office. For
federated nations also includes information on individual
states. Second edition also includes information for
international organizations. Lists compiled from a variety of
secondary sources as well as correspondence with libraries,
archives and government offices. Index by name to more
than 20,000 individuals listed.

1997 International directory of government
4th edn, Routledge, 2006, 800pp. £340. ISBN 1857432762.
Worldwide coverage. Each chapter a) outlines the system of
government and legislature of a particular country, b) lists
government ministries, departments and key personnel and
c) lists under subject headings nationalized industries,
government agencies and other organizations. In total lists
over 16,500 ministries, departments, agencies and
corporations.

**1998 The international encyclopedia of public policy
and administration**
J.M. Shafritz, ed.   Westview Press, 1997, 2750pp. £379.50. ISBN
0813399777.
4-volume set, containing 900 articles, in alphabetical order
by topic, written by 462 contributors; maintains it is 'the first
truly comprehensive public affairs reference'. Each entry –
some run over 3000 words long – includes a bibliography of
key books and journal articles for further reading. Not only
an American perspective but also entries relevant to Europe
and the Middle East (e.g. Islamic administrative tradition).
Comprehensive subject index in volume 4.

1999 Official directory of the European Union 2006–07
Office for Official Publications of the European Community, 2006,
annual, 436pp. €50. ISSN 16803968.
http://europa.eu/whoiswho
Bulk of the directory provides name and contact information
for senior staff in the Community institutions, bodies and
agencies. Preceded by 11-page introduction to the
institutions of the European Union and addresses of
institutions, lists of buildings with street plans. Can search
web version by organization, person's name and carry out
hierarchical search. Updated weekly.

Handbooks & manuals

**2000 Journal of Government Information: an
international review of policy, issues and
resources**
Elsevier, 1973–, bi-monthly. Formerly known as Government
Publications Review (1973–1982). Also available in electronic format
1995–. ISSN 13520237.
Publishes reports, analyses and discussion of government
information policy and practice, including international and
inter-governmental organizations. Reviews reference works
and electronic sources. Final issue each year devoted to
notable information sources of the year from government
information agencies in Canada, Great Britain, Australia, New
Zealand and the USA as well as countries in Africa, Asia,
Europe and Latin America. Also available by subscriber-only
electronic access.

**2001 The organization of governments: a comparative
analysis of government structures**
J. Blondel   Sage Publications, 1982, 242pp. ISBN 0803997779.
Thematic discussion covering the notion of government,
development of modern government, structure, political
composition, patterns of policymaking, management and
departmental ministries, boundaries of government and
administration. Brief bibliography and basic index.
Pioneering work but now rather dated and of use mainly to
the historian of government.

**2002 The statesman's yearbook: the politics, cultures
and economies of the world**
B. Turner, ed.   142nd rev. edn, Palgrave Macmillan, 2005, annual.
£95. ISBN 1403914826 ISSN 00814601.
First published in 1864 and annually since, entries for every
country in the world describing, among other matters,
constitution and government, recent election results, names
of members of the current administration and their
positions. Every entry includes short list of references for
further reading. Reliable reference work on economy, politics,
government and social facts. Also available online as
SYBWorld, with intuitive map-based interface.

Australia

Introductions to the subject

2003 Australian mandarins: perceptions of the role of departmental secretaries
R. Hyslop   Australian Government Publications Service, 1993, 179pp. ISBN 0644245972.
Discusses the role of 'permanent head', now 'departmental secretary', within the Australian Public Service. Describes the functions, relationships and responsibilities to others in the structure of government. Information drawn from published commentary, writings on Australian administrative history and political science and oral interviews conducted in 1990. 10-page bibliography.

Portal & task environments

2004 Australian government online
www.australia.gov.au/
Official gateway site, maintained by Australian government Department of Finance and Administration, with links to over 800 Australian government websites as well as selected state and territory resources. Search facility covers over 5 million government web pages. Includes departmental websites, news updates and links to full-text government reports, statistics, legislation and papers. Excludes sponsored sites, e.g. political parties and personal pages of politicians.

Handbooks & manuals

2005 Annual report
Australia. Department of the Prime Minister & Cabinet   Australian Government Publications Service, annual. ISSN 01578340.
www.pmc.gov.au/annual_reports/index.cfm
Annual reports from 1997–1998 onwards, which are presented to Parliament in accordance with statutory requirements, available in html or pdf formats to download. Describe in readable style and presentation the role and work of the Department of the Prime Minister and Cabinet over the year. Also available as a printed publication.

2006 Cabinet handbook
Australia. Department of the Prime Minister & Cabinet   5th edn, Department of the Prime Minister, 2002.
www.pmc.gov.au/pdfs/cabineted5.rtf
Lays down procedures by which the cabinet system in Australian federal government operates. Chapters describe the organization of the cabinet, conventions and principles, the programme of meetings and who attends, cabinet business, consultation processes, preparation of cabinet documents, handling business, minutes and security. Although intended as an internal manual of guidance and procedures, provides unique insight into operation of government.

Canada

Portal & task environments

2007 Government of Canada
http://canada.gc.ca/
Official portal to Canadian government on the web. Includes under Departments and Agencies link comprehensive alphabetical listing of links to primary websites of departments, agencies and Crown corporations.

2008 Government on-line serving Canadians in a digital world
www.gol-ged.gc.ca/pub/serv-can/serv-can00_e.asp
Official website set up to fulfil Prime Minister's commitment to electronic access for Canadian citizens to federal information and services. Begun in 1999, the site reports on progress of government departments in developing e-services for citizens.

Digital data, image & text collections

2009 Cabinet decisions: Canada
www.collectionscanada.ca/archivianet/index_e.html
Database maintained by National Archive of Canada indexing over 1 million descriptions of files and documents created by departments and agencies of the Federal Government. One part includes cabinet documents from 1944 to 1974. Site is in the process of being upgraded, with phased introduction of more powerful search software.

Directories & encyclopedias

2010 Guide to Canadian ministries since Confederation
Public Archives of Canada   Government of Canada, irregular. Originally published 1983, supplement covering 3 March 1980–15 January 1993, published 1993. Also 2001 edition. Available electronically at URL below. ISSN 1711330X.
www.pco-bcp.gc.ca/default.asp?Language=E&Page=Publications&doc=min/intro_e.htm
Details dates of government ministries, names, dates of holding office and cabinet positions of ministers from 1 July 1867 to the present. Previously published in print correct to 1982, now up to date on web. Maintained by National Archive of Canada.

2011 Organization of the government of Canada
Canada. Treasury Board and Canadian Government Publishing Centre   Queen's Printer, 1958–, irregular. ISSN 04746325.
Divided into legislative, judicial and executive sections, providing a brief historical background and structure of departments, with roles and responsibilities of constituent sections. Names of chief civil servants with contact details. Organizational chart for each department described. Basic index of titles of organizations. No subject index.

Handbooks & manuals

2012 Accountable government: a guide for ministers (Pour un gouvernement responsible)
Government of Canada, 2006–, annual. ISSN 17177596.
www.pm.gc.ca/eng/media.asp?id=687
Frequently revised manual (available in printed and web formats) setting out the core principles regarding the role and responsibilities of the Prime Minister, Ministers and Secretaries of State in Canada's government. Also includes information on the duties and responsibilities of Parliamentary Secretaries. Sets out responsibilities, relations with the Prime Minister, cabinet and Parliament, portfolios, standards of conduct expected. Annexes set out the role of the Canadian executive, cabinet decision-making processes and procedures, ethical guidelines.
Versions published in 2003 and 2004 under title: Governing responsibly: a guide for Ministers and Ministers of State

2013 Info source: sources of federal employee information (Info source. Sources de renseignements sur les employés fédéraux)
Administrative Policy Branch, Treasury Board Secretariat, Government of Canada, 1990/91–, annual. ISSN 11848103.
One chapter for each federal government department or agency, providing information on the background, responsibilities, legislation, organization, the information it holds in both published and unpublished, internal form. Full details of contacts provided. Produced to assist Canadian citizens exercise their rights under the Access to Information Act and the Privacy Act.

European Union

Associations & societies

European Union, Databases User Group
See entry no. 1586

Guernsey

Introductions to the subject

2014 The government and law of Guernsey
D. Ogier   States of Guernsey, 2005, 152pp. ISBN 0954977505.
Historical description of the institutions of the Island's law and government. Eleven-page bibliography of some interest. No index.

2015 An island assembly: the development of the States of Guernsey, 1700–1949
R. Hocart   Guernsey Museum & Art Gallery, 1988, 149pp. £21. ISBN 1871560012.
Chronological history, including chapters on the government of Guernsey in the 18th century, reforms between 1803 and 1845, constitutional affairs 1844–1870, the development of parish power 1871–1904, reforms of the early 20th century, relations with the UK and the further reform of the States after 1945. Well researched in original and manuscript sources. Fills a major gap in studies of the historical development of government in Guernsey.

Portal & task environments

2016 States of Guernsey Government
www.gov.gg/ccm/portal/
Official website of the legislative and governing body for the islands of Guernsey, Alderney, Sark, Herm, Jethou, Brecqhou and Lihou. Mainly provides general information to the public on the economy, population and tourism, local government with only a selection of legislation under link 'Government'. Links to and descriptions of all the departments of government. Recent press releases and the full text of a selection of government publications. Site search facility.

Ireland

Portal & task environments

2017 Bettergov.ie
www.bettergov.ie/index.asp
Official site maintained by the Department of the Taoiseach, dedicated to modernizing the Irish Public Service. Includes descriptions of the framework and structures for reform, the thematic areas, including better regulation, financial and human resource management and the information society. Lists of publications, many available in full-text. Site search facility.

2018 Government of Ireland website
www.gov.ie/
Official gateway to the Government of Ireland. Within the list: Find information, a search engine which will search across all government department web pages. Under link 'Government Departments', lists with links to the primary departmental websites.

2019 Reach: connecting people and public services
www.reach.ie/
Official Irish government initiative to provide a single portal for citizens to connect with government – a one-stop government public service point, bringing together access to online application forms and information on government services. Only a limited number of services available so far, though the Death Event Publication Service (a single point for informing 28 government agencies of a death) has won an award.

Directories & encyclopedias

2020 Eolaire an stáit (State directory)
Department of Public Service, Dublin, 1977–.
Directory organized by government department with key contact names, addresses and phone numbers. No descriptive information on responsibilities or roles.

Handbooks & manuals

2021 Administration yearbook 2007
2007 edn, Institute of Public Administration, Dublin, 1967–, 640pp. €75. ISBN 1904541488.
Comprises three sections: directory containing name, contact details, organization description and names of key personnel

for comprehensive range of official, state, commercial, media, religious, trade and professional and social, cultural and political organizations of interest to business people. Also, diary and finally a yearbook with statistical and research data on Ireland.

Isle of Man

Portal & task environments

2022 Isle of Man Government
www.gov.im/
Official site of the Isle of Man Government. Under 'Government' link, list of departments and agencies with links to primary departmental sites with key documents available in full-text. Alternatively, a site search facility.

Jersey

Portal & task environments

2023 States of Jersey
www.gov.je
Official site of the States of Jersey, the government for the island. Under 'Government departments', list of departments with descriptions of responsibilities and further links to full text of key publications. Site search facility.

New Zealand

Official & quasi-official bodies

2024 New Zealand. Department of the Prime Minister & Cabinet
www.dpmc.govt.nz/
Official site, including list of ministers with their responsibilities, information about cabinet committees, link to the full text of the Cabinet Manual (q.v.), a record of the constitutional conventions, procedures and rules of cabinet and central executive government.

Portal & task environments

2025 New Zealand Government
www.govt.nz/
Official gateway to New Zealand government of the web. Under link 'A–Z of Government', listing of central government departments and agencies and local authorities with links to primary websites for each and details of other contact information. Also site search facility.

Directories & encyclopedias

2026 Directory of official information 2003–2005
2003 edn, Ministry of Justice, 1987–, biennial. ISBN 478201842 ISSN 0112207X.
www.justice.gov.nz/pubs/reports/2003/DO-03-05/index.html

Each department and organ of government is listed with functions, responsibilities and structure described, records and manuals held, descriptions of any advisory committees or statutory officers and their contact details. Prepared to assist individuals and organizations to know what official information is available and how to gain access to it in fulfilment of provisions in the Official Information Act 1982.

2027 The government directory 2007
Communicate New Zealand, 1987–. NZ$ 416.25 (web), NZ$ 140.00 (print).
www.nzgovtdirectory.com/
Directory containing full listings for all government, parliament and state sector organizations, including ministers, cabinet committees and select committees, senior departmental civil servants, government agencies, state-owned businesses, the judiciary and diplomatic service. Web version is a subscriber-only service updated daily throughout the year.

Handbooks & manuals

2028 The cabinet manual 2001
www.dpmc.gov.nz/cabinet/manual/index.html
Full text of the authoritative guide to central government decision-making and a primary source of information about constitutional and administrative principles and procedures in New Zealand. Chapters include the Governor-General and Executive Council, Ministers of the Crown, cabinet decision making and official information. Appendices include cabinet directions on the conduct of Crown legal business. Web version has links to other relevant guidance. Also available in print format.

Northern Ireland

Official & quasi-official bodies

2029 Northern Ireland Executive
www.nics.gov.uk/index.htm
Gateway to the government of Northern Ireland. A–Z list button leads to list of official organizations and links to them, while under separate link 'Government Departments', list of links to primary sites of each. Site search facility.

2030 Northern Ireland Office
www.nio.gov.uk/
Official site of the government department assisting the Secretary of State for Northern Ireland in his responsibilities for the government and administration of the province. Information on roles and responsibilities, with access to press releases and full text of a selection of official publications. Site search facility.

2031 Northern Ireland Ombudsman
www.ni-ombudsman.org.uk/
Official site for the organization dealing with complaints from people who believe they have suffered injustice as a result of maladministration by government departments and public bodies in Northern Ireland. Includes complaints relating to medical services. Apart from information on how to complain, who to complain about and complaint forms, also

includes list of publications available in full-text on the site. Site map but no site search facility.

2032 Northern Ireland. Office of the First Minister & Deputy First Minister
www.ofmdfmni.gov.uk/index.htm
Official site for the key department in devolved Northern Ireland government. Information on its role and responsibilities and relationship with the Secretary of State for Northern Ireland and the British government. Access to the full text of a selection of official publications. Site search facility.

Portal & task environments

2033 OnlineNI
www.onlineni.gov.uk/
Gateway listing of over 4500 websites all based in Northern Ireland, carrying information about the public services available in the province. Includes cross-site search facility, directory or organizations, free e-mail service to contact government departments, online appointment booking service with departments and text of press releases. Created and maintained by the Delivery and Information Division of the Department of Finance and Personnel. Part of the vision for e-government in the province.

Directories & encyclopedias

2034 The directory of Northern Ireland government
I. Carlton, comp.   Carlton Publishing & Printing Ltd, 2006, 350pp. £215. ISBN 1901581950.
Lists of contact information for Northern Ireland MPs, UK government ministers by department, the Northern Ireland Office, Northern Ireland and EU institutions (including MEPs), Northern Ireland Executive agencies, public bodies, local authorities and Northern Ireland Assembly members and officers and the Northern Ireland Executive. Includes biographical information for members of the Northern Ireland Assembly. No descriptive information on roles and responsibilities of departments.

Scotland

Official & quasi-official bodies

2035 Scotland Office
www.scotlandoffice.gov.uk/
Official site of the government department responsible for representing Scotland's interests at Westminster and acting as guardian to the Devolution Settlement (the Scotland Act 1998). Includes lists of publications on Scottish government and policy back to 1999, with the access to the full text of many. Site search facility.

2036 Scottish Executive
www.scotland.gov.uk/
Formerly the Scottish Office, the official website of the body responsible for devolved government in Scotland. Includes lists and biographies of Scotland's ministers, details of cabinet-related information, including the text of the guide to

collective decision-making and the Ministerial code, access to lists of publications and links to the full-text, lists of consultation and associated publications.

Links under the keyword 'Justice' lead to key facts and descriptions of the bodies responsible for the administration of criminal justice and civil law, provision of legal aid and liaison with the legal profession. Attractive and clear presentation of information both for the general public and, through links to research bodies, publications of value to the academic. Site search facility.

2037 Scottish Public Services Ombudsman
www.scottishombudsman.org.uk/
Official site of the body which deals with complaints from people who believe they have suffered injustice as a result of maladministration by the Scottish Parliament, Scottish administration, health service and local authorities, but not the Scottish Executive or any police authority in connection with the investigation or prevention of crime. Apart from dealing with how to complain, includes text of its reports of investigations and statistics. Site search facility.

Research centres & institutes

Institute of Governance, Scotland
See entry no. 1922

Directories & encyclopedias

2038 The directory of Scottish government
Carlton Publishing & Printing, 1999–, annual. ISSN 14654776.
Lists contact information for, among others, the Scottish Parliament, including MSPs by constituency and by region, Scottish cabinet and ministries, Scottish Parliament officers and staff, committees of the Scottish Parliament, Scottish Executive, Crown Office and Procurator Fiscal Service, Executive Agencies, public bodies, health bodies, Scottish local authorities, Scottish MPs in the UK Parliament, Scottish committees at Westminster, the Scotland Office, Scottish MEPs. Comprehensive and attractively presented.

2039 Scottish public bodies directory
www.scotland.gov.uk/Topics/Government/public-bodies/directory/
Alphabetical listing of Scottish official organizations which carry out responsibilities independently of ministers and government departments. List has links to pages giving contact details (including e-mail and website addresses), names of chief officers, numbers of staff, budget etc.

United Kingdom

Introductions to the subject

2040 New public administration in Britain
J. Greenwood, R. Pyper and D.J. Wilson   3rd edn, Routledge, 2002, 304pp. ISBN 0415236800.
12 chapters discuss context of British public administration, the Whitehall 'universe', cabinet and the Prime Minister's Office, ministers, local government, quangos, devolved government, privatization and accountability. Presentation of information in boxed key facts and annotated guides to

further reading. Extensive bibliography. Entirely revised text in third edition reflecting dramatic changes which the public sector has undergone in 1990s.

Official & quasi-official bodies

2041 Better Regulation Executive
www.cabinetoffice.gov.uk/REGULATION/
Agency of the Cabinet Office working to reduce administrative red tape in British government departments and public bodies. Includes access to press releases, codes of practice, full-text regulations and reports. Site search facility.

2042 Great Britain. Cabinet Office
www.cabinetoffice.gov.uk/
Official site for the government department with the responsibility of making government work better. Functions include supporting the Prime Minister, the cabinet and strengthening the civil service. Includes lists of publications available in full-text on the site, including guidelines, codes and standards.

2043 Great Britain. Ministry of Justice: devolution
www.justice.gov.uk/whatwedo/devolution.htm
Official site of the government department responsible for the overall management of relations between the UK government and the devolved administrations in Scotland, Wales and Northern Ireland. Includes history and background to devolution, full text of Devolution Guidance Notes setting out advice to the devolved administrations, Memorandum of Understanding, links to relevant Acts and links to the devolved administrations. Clearly laid out and easy to navigate.

2044 Parliamentary & Health Service Ombudsman
www.ombudsman.org.uk/
Official site of the body appointed to carry out independent investigations into complaints by members of the public against UK government departments and the NHS in England. Details role, structure, governance, policies, practices and publications, including reports of selected investigations. Also details on how to make a complaint to he ombudsman for investigation. Site search facility.

Research centres & institutes

Constitution Unit
See entry no. 1920

2045 Government on the web
www.governmentontheweb.org/
Site run jointly by the LSE Public Policy Group (London School of Economics and Political Science), the Oxford Internet Institute (University of Oxford) and the School of Public Policy (University College London) to improve knowledge and understanding of e-government and the impact of web-based technologies on government. Includes access to full text of research papers, conference contributions and articles. Unfortunately indications that parts of the site have not been updated since 2005.

Portal & task environments

2046 Consultation index: UK government public consultation
www.cabinetoffice.gov.uk/regulation/consultation/government/
Official gateway to UK government websites involved in open government and consultation with the electorate. Also links to pages discussing regulatory reform in the UK and Europe. Site search facility.

2047 Directgov
www.direct.gov.uk
Official gateway to UK government. Link 'Directories', then 'A–Z of central government', lists central government departments, executive agencies and non-departmental public bodies, also local authorities. Entries include brief description of responsibilities and contact details. Other parts of site include official forms and publications. Site search facility.

2048 Policy hub
www.policyhub.gov.uk/
Aims to promote strategic thinking and improve policy making and delivery across government. Provides access to initiatives, projects and tools that support better policy making and delivery, guidance on the use of research and evidence in the evaluation of policy and links to a wide range of resources and tools available on the web in the UK and around the world. Developed by the Strategy Unit of the Cabinet Office. Site search facility.

Discovering print & electronic resources

2049 Organisation of central government departments: a history 1964–1992
www.nuff.ox.ac.uk/Politics/whitehall/
Database set up with the aim of mapping changes in the structure of central government and departmental responsibilities. Allows users to access raw materials of the research project: details of government ministers, departmental responsibilities, functional descriptions, structure of departments and details of movements of functions between departments. Database is easy to search but appears not to be kept up to date in terms of web links to organizations and new biographical material about persons featured.

Directories & encyclopedias

2050 Civil Service statistics
HMSO, 1970–, annual.
Includes general commentary on trends and patterns in civil service staffing, tables showing numbers of civil servants, where they work and how organized. Notes on definitions and sources and a selected bibliography.

2051 Councils, committees and boards including government agencies and authorities
13th edn, CBD Research Ltd, 2004, 527pp. £163. ISBN 0900246952.
Compiled from questionnaires sent to all organizations listed, provides contact information, details of establishment, membership, terms of reference, objects and/or mission statement, geographical area of competence,

details of activities and publications. Local government and other purely local bodies excluded. A fundamental tool for tracing national and regional bodies in any part of the UK.

2052 Dod's civil service companion
E. Gunn, ed.   1st edn, Vacher Dod Publishing Ltd, 2002, 1219pp. ISBN 0905702344.
Comprehensive history and guide to civil service, including the cabinet and devolved assemblies. Detailed listings within each department, including biographical details on many staff and photographs of some top civil servants. Also essays on momentum of modernization, appendices of text of lectures on ethics and guidelines, role of special advisors (including code of conduct), general election guidance.

2053 The guide to the executive agencies
G. Brace and I. Carlton   12th rev. edn, Carlton Publishing & Printing Ltd, 2007, 350pp. £225. ISBN 1905332033 ISSN 13606689.
Directory with contact details plus guide to responsibilities and role of executive agencies. Listed alphabetically under the Secretary of State to whom they are responsible. Includes, among others, the Central Science Laboratory, Civil Service College, Defence Procurement Agency, Court Service, Companies House and Patent Office.

2054 Officials of the Secretaries of State, 1660–1782
J.C. Sainty, comp.   University of London, Institute of Historical Research, 1973, 119pp. Spine title: Office-holders: Secretaries of State, 1660–1782. ISBN 0485171422.
Meticulously researched listing of the officials who served in the offices of the Secretaries of State. Four parts: introduction to the various offices of state, list of appointments, chronological list of officials and finally, alphabetical list of officials. Invaluable tool for historians of government.

2055 Public bodies directory
2006, 352pp.
www.civilservice.gov.uk/other/agencies/public_bodies/index.asp
Access to annual volumes from 1998 onwards of the directory, in pdf format. Lists by parent government department those organizations working at 'arm's length' from government. Since 2002 has excluded the public bodies set up under devolution arrangements with Scotland, Wales and Northern Ireland. Each entry provides contact details, regulatory responsibilities, a wide range of staffing and financial statistics. Also consolidated tables of statistics from an analysis of all returns. Simple index by name of public body.

2056 Treasury officials, 1660–1870
J.C. Sainty, comp.   Athlone Press [for the] University of London, Institute of Historical Research, 1972, 161pp. Spine title: Office-holders: Treasury 1669–1870. ISBN 0485171414.
Meticulously researched listing of the officials who served in the Treasury. Four parts: introduction to the development of the Treasury, list of appointments, chronological list of officials and finally, alphabetical list of officials. Invaluable tool for historians of one of the key offices of government.

2057 The Whitehall companion
2004 edn, TSO, 1992–2004, 887pp. Appears to have ceased publication. ISBN 0117027707.
Guide to who runs central government, how they work and what they do. Listing of all UK government departments,

devolved administrations, executive agencies, other public authorities, with contact information, providing job hierarchy and responsibilities, with brief biographical details and photographs of senior civil servants. List of abbreviations, name index to staff featured and subject index.

Handbooks & manuals

2058 The Civil Service year book 2006
45th edn, HMSO, 1974–, annual, 779pp. Also available electronically. ISBN 10011430193X.
Comprehensive list of ministers giving details of holders and responsibilities, details of all central and devolved administrations, contact details, responsibilities of staff, diagrams setting out structure of larger departments, details of all Executive Agencies, non-departmental public bodes for Northern Ireland, Scotland and Wales. Clearly presented listings with contacts for freedom of information requests, indexes to individual officers featured, departments and subjects.

2059 Trade union and employee involvement in public service reform
L. Horner and S. Bevan   2004.
www.pm.gov.uk/files/pdf/Main%20Report.pdf
Government report of a study to identify innovative practice of employers working closely with trade unions and employees to improve and reshape public service. Also available in pdf format.

United States

Terminology, codes & standards

2060 Abbreviations and acronyms of the US Government
www.ulib.iupui.edu/subjectareas/gov/docs_abbrev.html
Alphabetical listing, without any dynamic search facility, of abbreviations and acronyms used by American government. Includes government departments, agencies and committees. When possible, links go directly to the official website of the organization concerned. List compiled and maintained by the Government Documents Librarian of Indiana University.

Dictionaries, thesauri, classifications

2061 The Dorsey dictionary of American government and politics
J.M. Shafritz   Dorsey Press, 1988, 661pp. $34.95. ISBN 0256056390.
Over 4000 entries on the national, state and local government and politics. Many entries over 100 words long and include lists of further reading and/or tables of statistics or even photographs. Includes entries on the significance of Supreme Court cases, biographies of key people, laws, political slang, scholarly journals and professional associations. Team of more than 25 contributed material. Appendices include text of the US constitution, guides to federal documents, statistical information on

American government and table of US presidents, elections and congresses.

Portal & task environments

2062 FirstGov.Gov
www.usa.gov/
Official gateway to the US government on the web. Links to searches by organization name for agencies, federal, state, local and tribal governments. Links from index entries to home pages of organizations. Site search facility.

2063 Official federal government websites of the executive branch
www.loc.gov/rr/news/fedgov.html
Alphabetical listing of US federal government websites for the executive branch only, with links to their respective home pages. Prepared by the Library of Congress.

Discovering print & electronic resources

2064 Cyber cemetery of US government web sites
http://govinfo.library.unt.edu/
Web archive of sites and publications of defunct US government agencies and commissions. List of links may be searched or browsed by branch of government, date of expiration or name. Site created and maintained by a partnership between the University of North Texas Libraries and the US Government Printing Office.

Digital data, image & text collections

2065 Public papers of the Presidents of the United States
www.gpoaccess.gov/pubpapers/search.html
Official record published by the Office of the Federal Register of US Presidents' public writings, addresses and remarks, back to 1991. Documents arranged in 'books' and in chronological order. Search facility over individual 'books' of material.

Directories & encyclopedias

2066 Biographical directory of the United States executive branch, 1774–1989
R. Sobel, ed.   2nd revisd edn, Greenwood Press, 1990, 567pp. $95. ISBN 0313265933.
Alphabetical listing of more than 650 people who served in cabinets of the American presidents. Each biography of about 300 words includes significant dates in the subject's life, family and other personal information, service in cabinet and political life before and after. Each entry has short bibliographical references to primary and secondary sources consulted in the preparation of the entry. Additional tables give names for cabinet of each presidential administration, heads of state and cabinet officials, analyses of military service, education, place of birth and marital information.

2067 Encyclopedia of federal agencies and commissions
K.T. Hill and G.N. Hill   Facts on File Inc, 2004, 504pp. ISBN 0816048436.
Encyclopedic guide to the history, functions and responsibilities of federal government agencies and courts. 17 chapters, each on a different group of departments or agencies, including the executive and legislative arms of government. Each entry concludes with contact details. Appendix reprints the US constitution. Bibliography of just 12 titles. Comprehensive subject index.

2068 Federal yellow book
Leadership Directories, 1976–, qtrly. $450.00 p.a. ISSN 01456202.
Contact details for over 44,000 individuals within the executive branch of the US government, located within the Washington DC metropolitan area. Departmental structures provided. Biographical information for selection of federal leaders. Subject, organization and name indexes.

2069 A historical guide to the US government
G.T. Kurian and J.P. Harahan, eds   Oxford University Press, 1998, 741pp. ISBN 0195102304.
Encyclopedic entries describe the history of the various departments and agencies of the US government; many entries of several thousand words' length and conclude with extensive bibliographies to additional books and articles. Extensive cross-referencing. Comprehensive subject index. Appendix reproduces 26 basic documents of public administration in the US: Acts, Executive Orders from 1789 to 1993.

2070 Washington information directory
Congressional Quarterly Inc, 1975–, annual. ISSN 08878064.
20 chapters, each covering a broad topic such as education, health or transportation. Contact information provided in three categories: agencies, congress and non-profit organizations. Each entry includes brief summary of responsibilities, name of organization, address, phone number, name of director or main information contact. Name and extensive subject indexes. Larger bodies have organizational charts. Ready-reference lists near back detail government websites, state officials and US embassies abroad.

Handbooks & manuals

2071 The United States government manual
Office of the Federal Register, National Archives & Records Service, 1973–, annual. ISSN 00921904.
www.gpoaccess.gov/gmanual/index.html
Official handbook of the federal government providing comprehensive information on agencies of the legislative, judicial and executive branches. Also includes quasi-official agencies, international organizations in which the US participates. Boards, commissions and committees. Lists principal officials, summary statement of agency's purpose and role in federal government, brief history of agency, description of programmes and activities. Structure diagrams for larger agencies. Published as a special edition of the Federal Register. Available on web with free quick-search facility by organization name or browseable full-text version. Archived versions 1995–96 onwards available on

web. 1950 to 1972/1973 entitled *United States government organization manual.*

Keeping up to date

2072 Congressional Quarterly: weekly report
Congressional Quarterly, 1976–, weekly. ISSN 0196612X.
Weekly series of articles of non-partisan reporting on and analysis of congressional actions, presidential activities, policy debates and other news and developments in Washington. Also available as a subscriber-only e-journal, *CQ Weekly*. *CQ guide to current American government* (semi-annual, 1996–) is a collection of articles from *CQ weekly*.

Wales

Official & quasi-official bodies

2073 Great Britain. Wales Office
www.walesoffice.gov.uk/
Official site of the Secretary of State at Westminster responsible for devolved government to Wales and representing Wales' interests in the cabinet and parliament. Provides biography of Secretary of State, list of senior personnel, history of the post, links to full text of reports and speeches and links to a small selection of legislation. Site search facility.

2074 Public Services Ombudsman for Wales
www.ombudsman-wales.org.uk/
Official site of the organization to which people submit a complaint of alleged maladministration by the Government of Wales, local government, the emergency services, environment, health, social services, housing, education and training. Includes advice on how to complain, guidance to public bodies, summaries and the full text of reports of investigations and other publications.

2075 Welsh Assembly Government
http://new.wales.gov.uk/
Official site for the executive arm of the National Assembly for Wales. Includes news, description of the work of the WAG organized by topics, lists of publications, consultations in progress, full text of legislation (including draft versions) made by the National Assembly for Wales. Site search facility.

Research centres & institutes

2076 Welsh Governance Centre
www.cf.ac.uk/euros/welsh-governance/
University research centre for investigations into legal and political matters surrounding the Welsh Assembly and the devolution of powers. Includes lists of publications and descriptions of research but site appears not to have been updated since March 2005.

Discovering print & electronic resources

2077 Wales on the web
www.cymruarywe.org/cayw/index/en/352/429

Alphabetical listing of websites, created and maintained by the National Library of Wales, with brief descriptions and links to home pages of organization involved in public administration within Wales, including those associated with the National Assembly and academic research.

Directories & encyclopedias

2078 The directory of Welsh government
I. Carlton   Carlton Publishing & Printing Ltd, 2006, 300pp. £215. ISBN 1901581985.
Lists contact information for, among others, the National Assembly for Wales, members, the Presiding Officer and Assembly staff, the Assembly cabinet and secretariat, First Minister's office, Assembly members' offices, executive agencies, public bodies, health boards and trusts, university, higher and further education, local authorities, tourist information centres, Welsh MPs and committees at Westminster, Welsh MEPs. Comprehensive and attractively presented.

Handbooks & manuals

2079 The Wales yearbook 2006: annual reference book of public affairs in Wales
D. Balsom, ed.   Francis Balsom Associates, 2005, annual, 748pp. ISBN 1901862631.
In-depth compendium, including page-long political biographies of Welsh Assembly members, MPs, MEPs. Includes individual election results. Biographies and responsibilities of Welsh Assembly ministers, register of interests, Wales in Westminster, Wales in Europe, contact information for business and finance organizations and top companies in Wales, media, national organizations in Wales, higher education, armed forces, health, legal, local government. Indexes of organizations.

State, Regional & Local Institutions

England • Ireland • local government • Northern Ireland • Scotland • UK subordinate jurisdictions • United Kingdom • Wales

Research centres & institutes

Institute of Governance, Scotland
See entry no. 1922

Institute of Welsh Politics
See entry no. 1924

Associations & societies

2080 United cities and local governments
www.cities-localgovernments.org/uclg/index.asp
Represents and defends the interests of local governments across the world. Promotes democracy and cooperation. Over 120 nations and 1000 cities are members. Site includes details of programme of work, relations with the

United Nations. Associated site: www.cities-localgovernments.org/gold/ has web links on a wide range of local government issues. United Cities appears to be associated with the International Union of Local Authorities (IULA), whose website home page appears to be the only page that is working.

Discovering print & electronic resources

2081 Oultwood LG web index
Free map and lists, by region and county, of links to local government websites in each area.
- **1. England** www.oultwood.com/localgov/countries/england.php.
- **2. Irish Republic** www.oultwood.com/localgov/countries/eire.php.
- **3. Northern Ireland** www.oultwood.com/localgov/countries/northernireland.php.
- **4. Scotland** www.oultwood.com/localgov/countries/scotland.php.
- **5. Wales** www.oultwood.com/localgov/countries/wales.php.

URBADOC
See entry no. 727

Digital data, image & text collections

Campaign!: a century of political and social campaigning in Wales
See entry no. 1927

Directories & encyclopedias

2082 European municipal directory (Annuaire des communes et régions d'Europe; Das europäische Kommunal- und Regionalregister)
Newmedia Publishing, annual. ISSN 09627820.
Arranged in two sections: for each of 27 European nations, an introduction in English to the organizations and powers of local government, followed by lists, including over 14,000 regional and local authorities, with contact details, names of chief officers. Second, for larger authorities, contact details in greater detail covering more than 20 areas of responsibility such as planning, environment and housing. Index by name of authority only for larger organizations.

Handbooks & manuals

2083 International handbook of local and regional government: contemporary analysis of advanced democracies
A. Norton Edward Elgar, 1994, 559pp. ISBN 1852780053.
Major systematic and comparative study of the differences in local and regional government between six European countries, including Britain, plus the USA, Canada and Japan. Each country has a chapter with information set out to standard subheadings. Compiled from published literature, official documents, newspaper reports and contact with politicians and officials. Extensive bibliography.

England

Official & quasi-official bodies

2084 Central & Local Government Information Partnership
www.clip.gov.uk/
Partnership between central and local government in England to aid both bodies to work together more effectively and develop an infrastructure for joint policy development, delivery and monitoring of services. Site provides details of events, publications (with links to the full-text) and details of the body's operation.

2085 Great Britain. Department for Communities & Local Government
www.communities.gov.uk/index.asp?id=1133514
Official site of the central government department responsible for national policy on local government in England. Includes links to consultation and discussion documents open for comment at present time, discussion forum on which members can leave comments, links to the full text of research statistics and publications. Site search facility available.

2086 Local Government Commission for England
www.lgce.gov.uk/
Official site of the organization responsible for the review of local government structure and boundaries in England, which reports back, with recommendations for change, to the Electoral Commission. Site includes text of documents relating to its procedures, minutes of its meetings, an alphabetical glossary of terms relating to local administration. Site search facility.

Associations & societies

2087 Society of County Treasurers
www.sctnet.org.uk/
Official site of the body comprising county council chief financial officers within England. Acts as a forum for discussion of financial management of local government, personnel and other matters relating to local government in general and County Councils in particular. Free access to 'jargon buster', a glossary of terms used in local government finance. List of links to other websites of members of Society and other, major local government associations. Part of site available to members only.

2088 Society of Local Authority Chief Executives & Senior Managers
www.solace.org.uk/
Official site for the representative body for senior strategic managers working in the public sector, the majority of its members working in local government. Has associated organizations for Northern Ireland, Scotland and Wales. Promotes public sector excellence and provides professional development. Provides access to the full text of its annual reports. Some parts of site under reconstruction or not currently available.

Portal & task environments

2089 Info4local
www.info4local.gov.uk/
Gateway site devised by central government to assist local authorities with a quick and easy way to find and link to relevant information on the websites of central government, agencies and public bodies. Information displayed by region or subject and gives details of latest consultations, publications, new web links and general news. Update daily. Site search facility.

Directories & encyclopedias

2090 Directory of English regional government 2004
Carlton Publishing & Printing Ltd, 2003, 350pp. ISSN 14713586.
Divides England (excluding London) into 8 regions and within each provides contact details for the regional development agencies, regional chambers or assemblies, government regional offices and regional cultural consortia. Includes information on MPs, MEPs, local authorities and health bodies for each region. No name index.

Handbooks & manuals

2091 Guide to the local administrative units of England
F.A. Youngs   Cambridge University Press, 1995, 939pp. £30. ISBN 0521551536.
Arranged by county and within each, by parish, provides information on the creation and abolition of parishes, existence of parish registers, changes to boundaries, civil, parliamentary and ecclesiastical organization within each parish. A mine of information for the historian of administration.

Ireland

Introductions to the subject

2092 Local government in Ireland: inside out
M. Callanan and J.F. Keogan   Institute of Public Administration, 2003, 610pp. £40. ISBN 1902448936.
29 chapters written by more than 20 different contributors describing the background, operation and structure of local government in Ireland, the operation of a variety of service departments, chapters on human resources, local government finance, regional authorities and comparisons with local government in Northern Ireland. Extensive appendices, a bibliography of 30 pages and subject index. Comprehensive treatment.

Northern Ireland

Introductions to the subject

2093 The local government system in Northern Ireland
D. Birrell and A. Hayes   Institute of Public Administration, 1999, 167pp. ISBN 1902448251.
Introductory chapter covers the development of local government prior to the reorganization of 1972, the remainder focus on post-1972. Describes functions, partnerships, finance, local government and central government bodies, politics in local government, councillors, grievances against local councils and the future of local government in the province. Useful list of references and subject index. Fills a gap in a field with a limited literature.

Associations & societies

2094 Northern Ireland Local Government Association
www.nilga.org/home.asp
Official site of the body representing the local government sector and providing a forum for debate. Provides text of its corporate documents and publications and short list of links to associated websites.

2095 Society of Local Authority Chief Executives & Senior Managers, Northern Ireland
www.solaceni.org.uk/
Official site of the Northern Ireland branch of the representative body for senior strategic managers working in the public sector, the majority of its members working in local government. Has associated organizations for England, Scotland and Wales. Promotes public sector excellence and provides professional development. Provides access to the full text of materials relating to the Local Government Task Force for the reform of local government in the province. Parts of site available to members only.

Handbooks & manuals

2096 Northern Ireland local government handbook 2004/05
M. McKernan, ed.   BMF Publishing, 2004, 269pp. ISBN 0954628411.
The first comprehensive reference guide to all aspects of the subject, each chapter commencing with a review and description, followed by contact details. Covers the role of Northern Ireland Government, functions of local authorities, how authorities operate, profiles of each local authority, the local government associations and representative groups, major issues facing local government. Simple subject index. Whole publication attractively produced and presented.

Scotland

Official & quasi-official bodies

Great Britain. Local Government Boundary Commission for Scotland
See entry no. 1417

2097 Standards Commission For Scotland
www.standardscommissionscotland.org.uk/
Official site for the body responsible for promoting and enforcing high ethical standards in Scottish public life. Legal library online includes text of various codes of practice and guidance for councillors and local authorities. Investigations link provides summaries of completed investigations.

Comprehensive links to government, local authority and public body websites.

Associations & societies

2098 Convention of Scottish Local Authorities
www.cosla.gov.uk/
Official site of the body representing Scottish local government and acting as the employers' association on behalf of all Scottish councils. Includes details of its work, links to all Scottish council websites and many other relevant organizations, press releases and the text of a few of its publications (site under reconstruction).

2099 Society of Local Authority Chief Executives & Senior Managers, Scottish Branch
www.solacescotland.org.uk/
Official site for the representative body for senior strategic managers working in the public sector, the majority of its members working in local government. Has associated organizations for England, Northern Ireland and Wales. Promotes public sector excellence and provides professional development. Provides access to the full text of its own operational documents. Some parts of site available to members only.

Directories & encyclopedias

2100 Whitaker's Scottish almanack: Scotland in one volume
4th edn, A. & C. Black, 2003, annual, 500pp. £24.99. ISBN 0713667583.
Guide and listing with chapters on Scottish government, public services, legal profession, media, culture, environment, religious bodies, societies and institutions. Descriptive essays covering history, role and responsibilities of major organizations, followed by contact details. Combines who's who with what's what in Scotland. A unique reference work.

Handbooks & manuals

2101 Scotland's yearbook
William Culross & Son, 1996–.
Directory listing in four sections covering offices and staffs of Scottish government departments, the development corporations and unitary council officials, Scottish Health Service, including boards, hospitals and health centres and clinics. National and local authority associations. No descriptive information on roles and responsibilities. Incorporates the county and municipal yearbook for Scotland and Scotland's regions.

United Kingdom

Research centres & institutes

Constitution Unit
See entry no. 1920

2102 Institute of Local Government Studies
www.inlogov.bham.ac.uk
Official site of the foremost academic research organization into public policy and management in the local government sector. Site includes access to descriptions of ongoing research, list of publications, staff biographies, events and studying at INLOGOV.

2103 Local Government Information Unit
www.lgiu.gov.uk/
Official site of an independent research and information organization representing the interests of local authorities by providing practical independent advice, resources and training. List of publications with summaries, list of policy briefings (full-text available only to members of LGIU), biographies of staff, calendar of events. Site search facility.

2104 New Local Government Network
www.nlgn.org.uk/
Official site of an independent, non-profit-making 'think-tank' whose aim is to make local government more relevant to local people. Site includes press releases, summaries of articles, summaries of publications on, for example, local political leadership, modernizing public services and details of current research. Site search facility.

Associations & societies

2105 Local Authorities Research & Intelligence Association
www.laria.gov.uk
Official site of body set up in 1974 to promote the role and practice of research within local government and provide a support network for those conducting or commissioning research. Includes details of news and events organized by the Association, list of consultations with local government being conducted by central and devolved government, list of publications and web links to relevant sites.

Portal & task environments

2106 local.gov.uk
www.local.gov.uk/
Gateway site devised by the combined local authority association in the UK, providing news and information for local authorities. Includes news pages, lists of events and publications. Site search facility.

Discovering print & electronic resources

2107 UK250.co.uk
www.localgovernmentwebsites.co.uk/
Simple alphabetical listing of a selection of local authorities in the UK with links to their home pages.

Directories & encyclopedias

2108 The municipal year book
Hemming Information Services, 1973–, annual. Formerly: Municipal year book and public utilities directory. ISSN 03055906.
Lists local authorities in the UK with comprehensive contact

information for chief officers of all departments, members of council, political composition, committee chairs and brief topographical description of the local area. Published in two volumes and available on CD-ROM. Long-established and well respected.

2109 **Shaw's local government directory 2006/07**
Shaw & Sons, 2006, 432pp. £37.50. ISBN 0721917100.
Provides contact information for all local authorities in the UK, with information relating old authorities to new ones. Gazetteer of parishes, town and community councils shows the authority within which each falls. Also lists of parish councils, parish meetings and town councils in each local authority area.

Keeping up to date

2110 **LGC.net**
www.lgcnet.com/
Site run by the leading weekly journal on local government issues. Site includes free directory with over 15,000 contact names in over 600 organizations across local government, police, fire and transport sectors. Some more sophisticated applications, such as creating mail lists, available only to subscribers.

United Kingdom – Subordinate Jurisdictions

Associations & societies

2111 **Local Government Association**
www.lga.gov.uk/About.asp?lsection=456
Official site of the body set up in 1997 to promote the interests of the approximately 500 local authorities in England and Wales. Site provides details of its campaigns, events and meetings, lobbying, press releases, lists of publications with links to the full text of some, comprehensive list of links to websites connected with the interests of the Association. Site search facility.

2112 **National Association of Local Councils**
www.nalc.gov.uk/
Official site of the body representing 10,000 parish and town councils in England and community councils in Wales. Provides links to the full text of its policy documents, a news service, list of publications and list of web links to member bodies.

2113 **National Association of Local Councils Wales**
www.nalc.gov.uk/
Official site of the body representing the 10,000 community, parish and town councils in England and Wales. Includes details of news, conferences, events, publications and web links to member associations (but restricted to those in England).

Directories & encyclopedias

2114 **The directory of local authorities**
Thomson/Sweet & Maxwell, 2005, 305pp. ISBN 0421913908.
First published in 1961, part 1 provides names and addresses of local authorities with names and contact details for a selection of the chief officers. List arranged according to type of local authority and then alphabetically. Part 2 lists names in alphabetical order of most towns, parishes, villages and other named places in England, Wales and Scotland, with references into part 1 to identify the local authority in which they are situated. Parts 3 to 5 are a range of other lists of, for example, county courts, government departments, health authorities and utilities. Comprehensive and clearly presented information.

Wales

Research centres & institutes

2115 **Centre For Local & Regional Government Research**
www.clrgr.cf.ac.uk
Centre for academic research into local government policy and management. Carries out commissioned and grant-aided research into modernization of local government, best value policies, changing roles of officials and councillors, public-private partnerships. Site includes lists of staff, descriptions of work and research, links to text of publications. Parts of site up to date, others (e.g. publications) show nothing since 2002.

Associations & societies

2116 **Society of Local Authority Chief Executives & Senior Managers, Welsh Branch**
www.solacewales.org.uk/
Official site for the representative body for senior strategic managers working in the public sector, the majority of its members working in local government. Has associated organizations for England, Northern Ireland and Scotland. Promotes public sector excellence and provides professional development. Provides access to the full text of its responses to consultations by government on local government in Wales.

2117 **Welsh Local Government Association**
www.wlga.gov.uk/
Official site of the body representing the interests of local authorities in Wales. Provides details of history and structure of local government in Wales, links to its publications, some available in full-text, news and events. Site search facility.

Law

Law and legal information are quite different in form and content from any other subject, for six reasons.

First, law is tied to territory. Parliaments or legislatures, the bodies responsible for making or amending laws, have their own 'sphere of influence' or jurisdiction, limited to a particular geographical area. In contrast, in many subjects, even in the social sciences, the basics do not vary according to country.

Second, each jurisdiction has adopted a particular system of law. There are several families of legal systems. Although a number of countries may have adopted the same legal system, it is likely that in details, as well as some basics, they will be employed differently.

Third, law is in a constant state of change in every jurisdiction. New laws are enacted, courts interpret them and settle disputes and in common law jurisdictions at least, the decisions of the superior courts make varying degrees of change to the body of law.

Fourth, not only do lawyers need to keep abreast of the most recent changes to the law but they also require access to legal information from earliest times, to study change and development and to contextualize. This is particularly true of academic lawyers.

Fifth, law has developed a number of specialist print and electronic sources: statutes, law reports, and full-text databases containing them both.

Sixth, finding legal information is not just about uncovering sources which describe or comment on the law, but also about locating the law itself.

Given all these factors, the selection of material had to be pragmatic so as to avoid unbalancing the contents of this social science volume. Even so, Law is one of the largest sections of the volume.

First, as to jurisdiction, it was decided to focus on the British Isles and a selection of other countries which have closely followed the common law system developed in England. Thus the list includes England, Wales, Scotland, Northern Ireland and two other categories: 'United Kingdom, subordinate jurisdictions' for information sources which apply to more than one of the constituent parts of the UK, and finally, 'United Kingdom', for those information sources which apply to all the constituent countries. Sections on Ireland, the Isle of Man, Guernsey and Jersey complete the British Isles; additionally Australia, Canada, New Zealand and the USA are included. Three of these additional countries have federal and state legal systems; it has been practical to focus only on the federal system.

Second, weaknesses identified in earlier editions of *Walford* have been addressed by creating a more balanced view of the whole body of law and improving coverage of topics such as jurisprudence (the study of the principles of law), comparative law (the study of the differences, similarities and interrelationships of different systems of law), sources about the different systems of law themselves and the growing and increasingly important body of international law.

Third, the historical range of material required by lawyers is acknowledged but the major accent is on resources to assist investigation of contemporary law.

Fourth, the resource category Law, Standards & Codes has been used for publications containing the law itself and thus much more frequently than by other subjects in this volume. However, it is not possible to list every source relevant to every jurisdiction covered (in England and Wales, for example, over 60 different series of law reports are published currently, each containing decisions of the courts on different areas of law and of value to both academic and practising lawyers). Selection for inclusion here has been based on general sources of law – specialist sources have been omitted. Users of *The New Walford* seeking specialist sources are directed to the range of finding tools listed under the resource category 'Discovering print & electronic resources' for assistance.

Fifth, the two resource categories 'Research centres & institutes' and 'Libraries, archives & museums' have been populated sparingly. Almost every university with a law faculty will boast a group of researchers and a specialist library. Only the leading, national centres, institutes and law libraries have been included.

I acknowledge gratefully the assistance of Petal Kinder, Court Librarian, High Court of Australia and Alan Edwards, Law Librarian, University of Otago, Dunedin, New Zealand with the identification of some entries for Australia and New Zealand.

Terminology, codes & standards

2118 Bieber's dictionary of legal abbreviations: a reference guide for attorneys, legal secretaries, paralegals and law students
M.M. Prince, comp. 5th edn, Hein, 2001. $55. ISBN 1575884089.
Two parts: alphabetical list of abbreviations followed by publication title list, allowing a search from abbreviation to title and vice-versa. Predominantly, though not exclusively, US coverage of publications, legal phrases and law acronyms. Additional entries restricted to common law jurisdictions.

2119 Cardiff index to legal abbreviations
www.legalabbrevs.cardiff.ac.uk/

Award-winning searchable index to over 17,000 abbreviations used to describe over 10,000 publications (mainly law reports and journals) drawn from over 290 jurisdictions across the world. Searches can be carried out from abbreviation to title and vice-versa. Links through the International Standard Serial Number (ISSN) in many entries to the catalogues of more than 25 university libraries based in the UK and New Zealand.

2120 Index to legal citations and abbreviations
D. Raistrick, ed. 2nd rev. edn, Bowker, 1993, 400pp. £87. ISBN 185739061X.
Alphabetical list of more than 25,000 abbreviations for publications, personalities within the legal system and acronyms for organizations drawn mainly from the UK,

Ireland, the Commonwealth and USA, but also European countries, Africa, Asia and South America. A classic work still of great value but obviously lacking the explosion in abbreviations resulting from conventional and web publishing since the early 1990s.

2121 Noble's revised international guide to the law reports
S. Noble, comp.   2nd edn, Nicol Island Publishing, 2002, 567pp. ISBN 0969946767.
Alphabetical list of abbreviations of law reports drawn only from common and civil law jurisdictions. Each entry provides details of the original tile of the publication, jurisdiction, years of cases reported and number of volumes published. Also lists of free websites carrying case law.

Dictionaries, thesauri, classifications

2122 Moys classification and thesaurus for legal materials
E.M. Moys   4th edn, K.G. Saur, 2001, 552pp. $174. ISBN 3598115024.
Two-part work: the only subject classification specifically designed for use in law libraries and used across the world; second part is an index–thesaurus to the terms employed in the classification. Classification designed for use in a library already using either the Dewey Decimal System or the Library of Congress classification for the rest of its books. A new edition is under consideration.

Laws, standards, codes

2123 Constitutions of dependencies and territories
P. Raworth, ed.   Oceana Publications, 1975–. $995. ISBN 0379002787.
Seven-volume looseleaf work, updated about eight times a year, providing English-language translations of the constitutions of the 170 dependencies and territories of 40 nations. Each entry also includes the text of related constitutional documents and a brief commentary placing recent constitutional changes in historical context. Unique and highly regarded. Also available as a subscriber-only online database: Constitutions of dependencies and territories online.

2124 Constitutions of the countries of the world
R. Grote, R. Wolfrum and G. Flanz, eds   Oceana Publications, 1971–. $2,495. ISBN 0379004674.
Twenty-volume looseleaf work, updated about nine times a year containing English translations and scholarly commentary on 187 constitutions across the world. The set is arranged alphabetically by country with separate booklets for the text of the constitution, scholarly commentary and related constitutional documents. Unique and highly regarded. Also available as a subscriber-only online database: Constitutions of the countries of the world online.

Associations & societies

2125 International Association of Law Libraries
www.iall.org
Worldwide organization founded in 1959 with members in

more than 50 countries on five continents. Members are individuals and organizations concerned with the acquisition and use of legal information issued by sources other than their own jurisdictions. Site includes details of the organization itself, publications and events, especially the annual course on international law librarianship held on a different continent each year, focusing on the legal system, information provision and legal education of that area. Site search facility.

Portal & task environments

2126 GLIN guide to law online
www.loc.gov/law/guide/nations.html
Global Legal Information Network developed by the US Library of Congress is a free, annotated compendium of links to internet law resources across the world. Links are to the full text of laws, regulations and court decisions, along with links to guides and commentaries on the law and how to find it. Links are arranged under the general headings of international, national and the USA. Although there is no site search facility indexes to the huge number of links are provided. An invaluable resource.

2127 The world law guide
www.lexadin.nl/wlg/
Portal site claiming to have over 30,000 web links to legislation, court cases, courts, law firms, organizations and articles on the law. Maintained by Lexadin, a Netherlands-based legal technology service. No annotations and no information about the selection of sites (although pages suggest anyone can add a site to the lists) as there are some important omissions relating to the UK. Quality control not as rigorous as for GLIN (q.v.).

Discovering print & electronic resources

2128 Bibliography of Commonwealth law reports
W. Breem and S. Phillips, eds   Mansell, 1991, 332pp. 7 page correction slip issued separately, £40. ISBN 978-0720120233.
Aims to record all published law reports issued by Commonwealth jurisdictions, whether primary (e.g. Canada) or subordinate (Punjab), that may be cited by lawyers for professional purposes. The Commonwealth is clearly defined in the introduction and excludes all the reports of the former British North American colonies. Entries arranged by primary then subordinate jurisdiction and finally alphabetically by title, with a second sequence listing reports on particular subjects. Descriptive not evaluative entries. Title and subject indexes. Invaluable for tracing obscure of defunct series.

2129 A bibliography of eighteenth century legal literature: a subject and author catalogue of law treatises and all law related literature held in the main legal collections in England
J.N. Adams and G. Averley   Avero (Eighteenth-Century) Publications, 1982. £220. ISBN 0907977014.
Developed out of a database of over 20,000 entries and classified according to a home-grown scheme based on the Dewey Decimal Classification. Covers the widest possible range of materials, including law reports, textbooks, legislative publications, materials on the major legal issues of the period, library sale catalogues, biographical materials,

popular materials such as poems, plays and satires on the law and the legal profession. Covers English and Scots law, the law of Ireland, France, Canada and America. Classified sequence is in printed form, the author sequence on microfiche. Location of materials in libraries across the British Isles noted for each entry.

2130 A bibliography of nineteenth century legal literature: a subject and author catalogue of law treatises and all law related literature held in the legal collections of the Inns of Court in England, the British copyright libraries, Harvard University Library, and the Library of Congress
J.N. Adams and M.J. Davies   Avero Publications, 1992. Published in 3 v. The ISBN of the first volume only is given here, £1200. ISBN 0907977421.

Covers the period 1801 to 1870 and is a continuation of the bibliography of 18th-century legal literature project (q.v.). Coverage in terms of materials and jurisdictions is similar but now includes more from Ireland and America which have a bearing on English law. Author sequence in three bound volumes, subject catalogue on microfiche.

The set is also known as BINELL: a bibliography of nineteenth-century legal literature and published by Chadwyck-Healey in 1997 as a computer laser optical disc.

2131 The common law abroad. Constitutional and legal legacy of the British Empire: an annotated bibliography of titles relating to the colonial dependencies of Great Britain held by twelve great law libraries
J. Dupont, ed.   Fred B. Rothman Publications, 2001, 1228pp. £150. ISBN 837731259.

Arranged by 173 jurisdiction of the British Empire, lists the legal and constitutional publications of the colonial era up to independence. Focuses on primary legal materials (legislation and case law) but excludes official gazettes, current treatises and materials relating to the British Isles and the USA. Lists compiled from painstaking research undertaken in the 12 major academic law libraries in the UK and USA. Each entry details holdings and the shelf mark at each library. The list for each jurisdiction is preceded by notes on the background and history of the jurisdiction. The full text of all the publications listed is being digitized at present and the whole collection will be available to purchase after 2010.

2132 Foreign law: current sources of codes and basic legislation in jurisdictions of the world
T.H. Reynolds and A.A. Flores   Fred B.Rothman Publications, 1989–. Looseleaf currently in 3 v. Accompanied by CD-ROM. $1425; with CD-ROM, $2400; CD-ROM alone $1950. ISBN 0837701406.

Eight looseleaf binders containing booklets arranged geographically across the world. Volume 1 covers the Western hemisphere, Volume 2 Europe, Volume 3 Africa, Asia and Australasia. Each country or regional organization booklet carries an introduction to the legal system followed by lists under standard subject headings by type of the major law publications and also a separate subject listing. A major and valuable reference work for the researcher.

2133 Index to legal periodicals
H. W. Wilson, 1908–, monthly. ISSN 00194077.
Indexes over 800 English language legal periodicals published in the USA, Canada, Great Britain, Australia and New Zealand. Also indexes yearbooks, annual reviews and book reviews. Articles must be at least 2 pages long to qualify. Articles indexed under subject and author, books under subject, author and title. Annual and triennial cumulations. Also available as a subscriber-only web database. An invaluable research work.

Law and politics book review
See entry no. 1262

2134 Law books in print
Glanville Publishers, 1957–, triennial. ISSN 10949119.
Listing of law books published in the English language throughout the world and in print as at 31 December 1990. Comprehensive coverage of all types of legal publication, plus inter-disciplinary materials with a law-related content. Indexes: author/title, subject, series, publisher. Supplemented by *Law books published*.

2135 Researching the legal web: a guide to legal resources on the internet
N. Holmes and D. Venables   2nd edn, Butterworths, 1999, 219pp. £45. ISBN 0406921806.
Critical review of law websites by two of the leading experts in the UK. Covers the definition of the legal web and then chapters on different law sources in turn. Books about the web date very quickly but the general descriptions rather than the details still hold reasonably well.

Digital data, image & text collections

2136 HeinOnline
www.heinonline.org
Unique, digital image archive collection of over 1200 law periodicals published in the USA and Britain, reproduced in original page format and in full-text. Coverage is from each journal's earliest issues, usually to within a year or two of the present. Also full text of a range of historic law monographs and wealth of US legal materials.

Launched in 2000, HeinOnline is a fast-expanding, subscriber-access-only library of past issues of law journals and books, presented as exact page images of the original and fully searchable. The journal and book coverage is aimed at the academic market. Unlike some databases, HeinOnline attempts to provide comprehensive historic coverage from the first issues of a title. Much of the material is not available in electronic form elsewhere. Subscriber-only access.

Directories & encyclopedias

Encyclopedia of law and society: American and global perspectives
D. Clark   See entry no. 92

2137 International encyclopedia of laws
R. Blanpain, ed.   Kluwer Law International.
Looseleaf encyclopedia currently comprising 21 distinct reference works. Each unit is an encyclopedia on a major field of law, with scholarly monographs describing how each of about 60 national legal systems governs the relevant field. Over 1200 contributors. Each monograph has a uniform structure and includes a detailed historical background,

introduction to the legal framework and in-depth analysis of relevant legislation, complete with its own subject index. Copious references to legislation and cases; many entries include a select bibliography of further books and articles. When complete the encyclopedia will comprise approximately 50 national monographs, each of about 200–250 pages.

2138 World law school directory
A.M. Beaird   3rd edn, William S. Hein, 2003, 511pp. $110. ISBN 0837738296.
Arranged by country and then alphabetically by the name of law school; provides contact information, including web addresses and list of degrees offered. Compiled from questionnaire returns and, where no response, other information to hand. Index of school names.

Handbooks & manuals

2139 Where to publish law in Great Britain and Ireland
D. Summers   Aestival Press, 1998, 246pp. £30. ISBN 0953251608.
Two parts: first, outlines steps an author needs to take when aiming for publication; second is a directory of British and Irish law publishers with contact details, company organization and structure, markets served, author assistance provided, remuneration, marketing and competitive strengths. Appendices of useful addresses, glossary of terms and lists of websites. Written by a former director of Butterworths, one of the leading law publishing houses. While details in the directory may be dated, part 1 still has timeless practical advice.

Jurisprudence

legal theory

Discovering print & electronic resources

2140 Cultbase (current legal theory)
www.cirfid.unibo.it/cult/
Free searchable database of over 19,000 references drawn from those which have appeared in the journal *Current Legal Theory* (q.v.). Many entries include abstracts. Coverage includes books, articles and contributions to anthologies in the areas of jurisprudence, philosophy of law and legal theory, published in all major languages. Choice of search available: simple text searches or advanced, selecting first form of publication and then searching on any one of a number of fields: author, title, year of publication, keywords and abstract. Anyone can submit an abstract for consideration for inclusion in the database.

Keeping up to date

2141 Current Legal Theory: international journal for documentation on legal theory (bibliography – abstracts – reviews)
Acco: Centrum voor Grondslagenonderzoek van het Recht, 1983–, 2 p.a. ISSN 07721668.
Combines articles of critical legal bibliography with lists of recent articles on legal theory and legal philosophy drawn from a wide range of journals published across the world.

Some articles listed also bear abstracts. Entire publication is in English. The publication is supplemented by the Cultbase database (q.v.).

Comparative Law

common law of Europe • comparative law • international law • transnational law

Introductions to the subject

2142 Comparative law
P. Norman
www.nyulawglobal.org/globalex/
Comprehensive research guide compiled in 2006 by the senior reference librarian at the Institute of Advanced Legal Studies, University of London. Discusses the nature of comparative law, harmonization of law, print and web sources, organizations and research institutes, research guides etc. A thorough and reliable work.

2143 Introduction to foreign legal systems
R.A. Danner and M.-L.H. Bernal   Oceana Publications, 1994, 423pp. £76. ISBN 0379213508.
21 chapters, starting with a comparison of different legal systems, followed by descriptions of the research sources for a selection of civil law, Asian and African countries. Finally, chapters on foreign law collection building, the Library of Congress classification and databases. Written before developments in web technology but the chapters on individual countries still provide good basic information.

Dictionaries, thesauri, classifications

2144 Dictionary of international and comparative law
J.R. Fox, ed.   3rd edn, Oceana Publications, 2003, 369pp. £60. ISBN 0379215012.
Carries over 2100 brief descriptions and definitions but entries also have the unique advantage of references to books, journal articles and yearbooks on international and comparative law where the terms have been described in greater detail.

Official & quasi-official bodies

International Institute for the Unification of Private Law
See entry no. 2387

Research centres & institutes

2145 British Institute of International & Comparative Law
www.biicl.org/
Official site of the organization founded in 1895 to advance the understanding of international and comparative law; to promote the rule of law in international affairs; and to promote their application through research, publications and events. *Bulletin of International Legal Developments* (q.v.), a current awareness bulletin, is one of its best-known

publications. Details of all these, plus vacancy lists and news, are provided. Attractive layout. Site search facility.

2146 **Centre for Comparative & Foreign Law Studies**
http://w3.uniroma1.it/idc/centro/centre.htm
Engages in research, organizes lectures and seminars and publishes monographs in the field of international uniform law. Has set up and is updating UNILEX, a database of international case law and bibliography on the United Nations Convention on Contacts for the International Sale of Goods 1980 and the UNIDROIT Principles of International Commercial Contracts. Printed versions of UNILEX are available from Transnational Publishers Inc, Ardsley, New York.

2147 **IUE commune casebooks for the common law of Europe**
www.law.kuleuven.ac.be/casebook/
Joint research project of the faculties of law of the University of Maastricht and the Katholieke Universiteit Leuven, to create a collection of casebooks covering each of the main fields of law and containing legislative and case law materials for the national and supra-national jurisdictions in Europe. Casebooks for tort and contract law already published and the former has been cited twice by the House of Lords in decisions. Site provides access to contents pages and links to full text of some materials mentioned. Site also provides details of the continuing research project.

2148 **Swiss Institute of Comparative Law**
http://isdc.ch/en/default.asp
Offers legal advice and assistance through a team of lawyers and law librarians based across the world, in areas of national legal systems, international private and public law and the law of the European Union. Will take legal questions from individuals, private clients, lawyers, courts, government agencies. Provides legal opinions and comparative studies. Catalogue of the library of over 300,000 titles in approximately 60 languages is available online. Also offers research and training opportunities for young lawyers.

Associations & societies

2149 **American Society of Comparative Law**
www.comparativelaw.org/
Formed in 1951 as a non-profit organization to promote the comparative study of law, the understanding of foreign legal systems through research, study and publication. Site includes details of the *American Journal of Comparative Law*, including searchable index, details of members' research interests, research funding, programme of conferences and other events, and web links to international, foreign and comparative law websites across the world.

Portal & task environments

2150 **European and comparative law**
http://civil.udg.es/epclp/
Under buttons 'general' and 'countries', web links to legal resources on websites across the world on international law, European law, European private law, uniform law and international private law. Under button 'search' links to a wide variety of legal indexes and search engines. Site is

created and maintained by the Research Group on European Private Law at the University of Girona in Spain. Unfortunately use of site is hampered by advertising pop-ups.

Discovering print & electronic resources

2151 **Multinational statutes compared: a research guide to statutes by subject**
J.S. Schultz   William S. Hein, 2003, 112pp. $35. ISBN 1575886626.
Aid to finding and constructing comparisons between statutes of different countries of the world. Main part is a listing with descriptions, arranged under broad subject headings, of current publications containing statutes on a particular topic. Valuable as a first step in deciding which source to use. Unfortunately, does not note when a source is available electronically.

Directories & encyclopedias

2152 **International encyclopedia of comparative law**
J.C.B. Mohr.
Series of softback booklets (later republished in 17 hardback volume s), created by a large panel of experts. Volume 1 provides a series of reports on the legal system of every country in the world. Volume 2 compares the various legal systems and the remaining volumes are subject-based descriptions of the comparative laws of, for example, torts, labour law and property. Acknowledged as a key source. New booklets published at intervals to update the subject section.

2153 **Modern legal systems cyclopedia**
K.R. Redden and L.L. Schlueter, eds   William S. Hein, 1983–.
20 looseleaf volumes, plus a looseleaf index volume, containing descriptions arranged under standard subject headings of the legal systems of individual countries. Each country entry is the equivalent of a small book in length. Extensive bibliography of materials referred to and further reading. At the back of the final volume is the World Law School Directory (q.v.).

Handbooks & manuals

2154 **Germain's transnational law research: a guide for attorneys**
C.M. Germain   Transnational Juris Publications, 1991–. looseleaf, $125. ISBN 0929179315.
Compendium of descriptions of research sources written in non-technical language but from a US perspective. Covers, in three parts, foreign and international law: first, procedural and practical issues; second, chapters on individual topics from air and space law to the World Trade Organization; and third, chapters on 17 individual European countries (with a relatively superficial touch for the UK). Standard headings cover guides to the law, electronic sources, subject sources, dictionaries and research bibliographies. Compiled by the Law Librarian of Cornell Law School.

Keeping up to date

2155 Bulletin of international legal developments
British Institute of International & Comparative Law, 1966–,
fortnightly. ISSN 17538491.
Summarizes the international legal news from across the
world. Each summary concludes with a web address where
further information or the original documents can be found.
Prepared by a widely respected organization. A key source.
Unfortunately not available electronically.

**2156 Digest of legal activities of international
organizations and other institutions**
International Institute for the Unification of Private Law   Oceana
Publications Inc., 1974–. ISBN 0379005255.
Summaries of the progress in the work of a wide range of
international organizations researching and reporting on
topics of interest to comparative lawyers are arranged under
general subject headings. Each entry notes the terms of
reference, summary of the topic, state of work and lists
publications produced.

2157 Uniform law review (Revue de droit uniform)
Guiffre Editore, 1973–, qtrly. ISSN 11243694.
Reports on the work of UNIDROIT (International Institute for
the Unification of Private Law) but also includes articles on
legal harmonization and integration worldwide. Current
awareness sections on case law, lists of new publications and
book reviews, research and training, implementation of new
conventions. In English and French except for articles usually
published in only one language.

Systems of Law

African law • canon law • Chinese law • civil law •
common law • Indian (Hindu) law • Japanese law • Jewish
law • Madh'habs law • Muslim law • religious legal
systems • Roman law • Romano-Germanic law • Shari'ah
law • socialist law • world legal systems

Introductions to the subject

2158 Major legal systems in the world today
R. David and J.E.C. Brierley   3rd edn rev., Stevens & Sons, 1985,
650pp. o/p. ISBN 0420473408.
Discusses the idea of a family of laws and defines the legal
families in the world. Then, each part discusses the Romano-
Germanic, socialist, common law, Muslim, Indian (Hindu),
Chinese, Japanese and African families. Extensive
bibliography. Generally acknowledged as a classic in the
literature of comparative legal study.

Directories & encyclopedias

**2159 Legal systems of the world: a political, social, and
cultural encyclopedia**
H.M. Kritzer, ed.   ABC-CLIO, 2002. ISBN 1576072312.
Country-by-country description using standard subject
headings of the structure and operational history of the
legislature and judicial systems of every country in the
world, every state in the union and every province. Created
by a team of 350 legal scholars, with nearly 400 entries in
non-technical language. Includes transnational bodies such

as the World Trade Organization. Many maps and diagrams.
Bibliography at the end of each entry.

Civil Law

Introductions to the subject

**2160 An introduction to Roman legal and constitutional
history**
W. Kunkel   2nd rev.edn, Oxford University Press, 1973, 236pp. ISBN
0198253176.
Covers the Roman state and Roman law but focuses
especially on Roman private law. Chronological presentation
in three parts: early, middle and late periods of the Empire,
including the Justinian codifications. Translated from the
original German edition. Extensive bibliographical appendix.

Laws, standards, codes

2161 Roman law library
A. Koptev and Y. Lassard, comps
http://web.upmf-grenoble.fr/Haiti/Cours/Ak/
Collection of Roman laws compiled by Alexandre Koptev at
the University of Grenoble. Laws are in full-text in Latin, with
French and English translations. What's new? link to latest
additions. Extensive bibliography on Roman law. Resources
link to extensive library of web links of value to Roman
lawyers. Clean, unfussy and attractive presentation of
valuable material.

Research centres & institutes

**2162 Max-Planck-Institut fur Europäische
Rechtsgeschichte**
www.mpier.uni-frankfurt.de/
Founded in 1964, the Max-Planck Institute for European
Legal History is a major centre conducting research into
areas, including Roman law, European legal and
contemporary law. Site includes lists of publications, access
to the library catalogue, a digital library of civil and
procedural law for Germany, Austria and Switzerland and a
short list of web links to partner institutions in Germany and
the rest of Europe and the US. Most of the site is in German
but small Union flags indicate access to text of pages in
English.

Portal & task environments

2163 Project Volterra
www.ucl.ac.uk/history/volterra/index.htm
Research project based in the History Department of
University College London, since 1995. Aims to promote the
study of Roman legislation and has created an online
searchable database on Imperial pronouncements in Latin
from the late second to mid-fifth centuries. Latest phase of
project is to produce history, with supporting database and
resources – see under link to Project Volterra II.

2164 Roman law homepage
www.jura.uni-sb.de/Rechtsgeschichte/Ius.Romanum/english.html
Site compiled and maintained at the University of
Saarbrücken by Thomas Rüfner, includes access to the Ius
Romanum mailing list and links to Roman law and legal
history resources both on the site and through links to sites
across the world. Texts are mainly in Latin (even the
annotations to some of the web link pages!) and the entire
site can be read in Latin, English, German or Italian.

2165 Roman law resources
http://iuscivile.com/
Site created and maintained by Ernest Metzger, University of
Glasgow, providing a wide range of resources for the study of
Roman law: lists of abbreviations, bibliographies, booksellers
specializing in Roman law titles, CD-ROMs on antiquity,
discussion forum, lists of events, portals, teaching materials
etc. Aims to be a one-stop shop for information and
materials on Roman law and appears to succeed in that.

Discovering print & electronic resources

2166 Index to foreign legal periodicals
American Association of Law Libraries, 1960–. ISSN 0019400X.
Indexes selected legal periodicals dealing with international
law, comparative law and the municipal law of countries
other than the USA, the British Isles and British
Commonwealth whose systems have a common law basis.
Excludes articles less than 4 pages in length and short book
reviews. Contents arranged by subject and sub-divided,
where appropriate, by country. Geographical, book review
and author indexes. Essential source for research in foreign
and comparative law.

**2167 L'année philologique: bibliographie critique et
analique de l'antiquité greco-latine**
Les Belles Lettres, 1924–. ISBN 00096697.
www.annee-philologique.com/
Index in the field of classics, with over 600,000 bibliographic
records, regularly indexing 1500 periodicals, which includes
some references to Roman law articles ands book reviews.
Published in paper and internet forms by the Société
Internationale de Bibliographie Classique. The internet
version is subscriber-only and covers the period 1949–2004.
Earlier volumes are being digitized and added steadily.

Directories & encyclopedias

2168 Encyclopedic dictionary of Roman law
A. Berger   Law Book Exchange Ltd, 2002. $110. ISBN 1584771429.
Aims to explain technical Roman terms, translate and
elucidate Latin words which have a specific connotation when
used in a juristic context or in connection with a legal
institution and provides a brief picture of Roman legal
institutions and sources as a first introduction to them. Many
entries conclude with a bibliography of further sources and
appendices include a general bibliography of additional
sources, mainly in English. Also English-Latin glossary.

Common Law

Discovering print & electronic resources

2169 Index to common law festschriften
http://magic.lbr.auckland.ac.nz/festschrift/
Free index to collections of essays written by several authors
to honour a distinguished jurist or mark a significant legal
event. Database includes about 270 common law
festschriften plus over 1000 entries for English-language
contributions to predominantly foreign-language, non-
common law publications across Europe. Site hosted and
maintained by the University of Auckland Library, under
editorial direction of Professor Michael Taggart. Simple and
advanced searches available, including by keyword, author,
title and editor of festschrift. A unique resource.

Religious Legal Systems

Introductions to the subject

**2170 An introduction to the history and sources of
Jewish law**
N.S. Hecht [et al.], comps   Clarendon Press, 1996, 484pp. £77.50.
ISBN 0198262264.
16 chapters, each written by a different author and covering
a different epoch of the Jewish law from biblical times to the
present. Each chapter written to a standard set of headings,
with a historical introduction, judicial background and legal
practice of the period, description of sources of law,
principal authorities of the period, examples of substantive
law and a bibliography.

**2171 Religious legal systems: a brief guide to research
and its role in comparative law**
M.J. Raisch
www.nuylawglobal.org/globalex/Religious_Legal_Systems.htm
Comprehensive research guide written in 2006 by the
Librarian for International and Foreign Law at the John Wolff
International and Comparative Library of the Georgetown
Law Centre. Provides an introduction to religious systems,
followed by chapters on Islamic, Jewish, Catholic, Hindu,
Buddhist and Confucian law and legal theory. Each chapter
set to a common format with sections on essential facts and
basic sources in both print and electronic format. Thorough
and authoritative.

**2172 The Sunnah: practice and law (Shari'ah and
Madh'habs)**
www.uga.edu/islam/shariah.html
Guide to Islamic law created by Dr Alan Godlas, Department
of Religion, University of Georgia (US). Annotated
description, with links to other online resources, on Islamic
practice, including the Five Pillars of Islam, the law and
schools of law or jurisprudence.

Laws, standards, codes

2173 **The canons of the Church of England**
5th edn, Church House Publishing, 1993, 188pp. ISBN 0715137522.
Looseleaf reprint of the law relating to the operation of the
Church of England, covering, among other matters, divine
service, ministers of the church, lay officers, ecclesiastical
courts and the synods on the church.

2174 **Church of England Measures**
www.opsi.gov.uk/uk-church-measures/index.htm
Official site carrying the full text of Measures of the General
Synod of the Church of England passed by Parliament since
1988 and displayed in their original form – note that no
subsequent amendments or information about repeals or
revocations are incorporated within the text. Measures
passed prior to 1988 are not available electronically.
  ■ **Factsheet L10** www.parliament.uk/documents/upload/l10.pdf. Text of
  factsheet produced by the House of Commons Information Office describing
  how the measures are made and the background to the procedures. Covers
  the preparation of measures by the ecclesiastical authorities and
  Parliamentary scrutiny.

2175 **The code of canon law: a text and commentary**
J.A. Coriden, J.T. Green and D.E. Heintschel, eds   Paulist Press,
1985, 1152pp. ISBN 0809128373.
Commentary on the code of canon law as promulgated in
1983 as a result of the Second Vatican Council. Code is
reproduced canon by canon with extensive commentary and
bibliographical references at the end of each 'book'.
Concordance between 1917 and 1983 versions. Subject
index. Has been described as a monumental achievement in
reviews given on the back cover of the paperback edition.

2176 **Meaning of the glorious Koran**
M.M. Pickthall   Oswal Printers & Publishers, 1999, 464pp. £3.50.
ISBN 8173450722.
Translation of the Quran into English by an Englishman who
was a Muslim. Includes brief commentary and annotation,
respecting the meaning and nature of the Quran.

2177 **New commentary on the code of canon law**
J.P. Beal, J.A. Coriden and T.J. Green, eds   Paulist Press International,
2000, 1952pp. £81. ISBN 0809105020.
Reports text of the code of canon law based on the
principles of the Second Vatican Council of 1983, with
scholarly commentary to each canon. Three essays on
theology and canon law, canonical overview 1983–1999 and
an overview of the Code of Canons of the Eastern Churches
introduce the volume. Comprehensive, over 90-page subject
index. Considered a landmark publication.

Research centres & institutes

2178 **School of Oriental & African Studies, Centre of
Islamic & Middle Eastern Law**
www.soas.ac.uk/centres/
Established in 1990, the Centre based at the School of
Oriental and African Studies, University of London, aims to
promote study and understanding of Islamic law and Middle
Eastern law, foster links, provide services to subscribing
members and raise funds to support these aims. Apart from
lists of events and publications, site includes extensive
library of internet links to primary sources and commentary
on Islamic and Middle Eastern law materials in general.

Associations & societies

2179 **Canon Law Society of Great Britain & Ireland**
www.clsgbi.org
Official site of the Society, which aims to foster and promote
the study of and interest in the canon law of the Roman
Catholic Church. Apart from information about the Society
itself, lists publications, including access to a list of articles
which have appeared in Canon Law Abstracts (q.v.) since
2000. Also Canon Law Links leads to a brief list of links to
the full text of documents and to canon law societies abroad.

2180 **Ecclesiastical Law Society**
www.ecclawsoc.org.uk/
Established in 1987 to promote the study of ecclesiastical
and canon law, particularly in the Church of England and
those churches in communion with it. Site includes aims,
news, events, contents list from its newsletter and journal,
summaries of decisions in ecclesiastical cases heard in the
courts and extensive indexes in pdf format to the
ecclesiastical law collection held at the Middle Temple
Library, London.

2181 **Muslim Lawyers Guild**
www.muslim-lawyers.net/
Official site of the guild run by IZ Medien, Germany. Service
for lawyers specializing in Muslim law and those looking for
legal advice on Islamic countries. Site includes news, a
'journal' which includes links to the full text of various
Islamic law sources, commentaries and articles and a 'find a
lawyer' list of lawyers and firms signed up as members of
the service.

Portal & task environments

2182 **Religion law**
www.religionlaw.co.uk/
Site compiled and maintained by Neil Addison, a barrister
based in the north-west of England. Provides information
and links relating to religion and law, covering religious
criminal offences, religious discrimination, text of
international law, links to the full text of UK official reports
and articles and comprehensive library of links to legal and
religious organizations across the world.

Discovering print & electronic resources

2183 **Canon Law Abstracts**
Canon Law Society of Great Britain, 1959–, 2 p.a. £18. ISSN
00085650.
Indexes a wide range of UK and overseas periodicals
carrying articles and book reviews on the canon law of the
Roman Catholic Church. A list of entries which appeared in
issues from 2000 onwards is on the Society's website (q.v.).

2184 **Canon law literature**
www.ulrichrhode.de/kanon/zeit_e.html
List of web links, without annotations and bibliography of
current and defunct canon law periodicals compiled by

Ulrich Rhode, Rector of the Sankt Georgen Graduate School of Philosophy and Theology, Germany.

2185 Index Islamicus: A bibliography of publications on Islam and the Muslim world since 1906
C.H. Bleaney   7th edn, Brill, 2005. €1650. ISSN 03069524.
Lists articles, books of readings and monographs on all aspects of Islamic world. Maintains the Index is a virtually complete record of works in English published in the USA, the UK and for German works; less complete outside these nations. An entire section given over to law. Original index covered 1906 to 1955, supplemented by bound volumes and now available on CD-ROM.

2186 Islamic law bibliography: revised and updated list of secondary sources
J. Makdisi and M. Makdisi, comps
Printed in 1995, 87 *Law Library Journal* 69–191, this is a revision and update of part of a bibliography published in *Law Library Journal* in 1986 (1986, 78 *LLJ* 103–189). Original listed, without annotations, primary sources of Islamic law published in Arabic and secondary sources of Islamic law published in English or French. Original also included introduction by compiler to Islamic law sources. Primary sources listed according to school of Islamic law followed by secondary listed by subject. Revision of 1995 covers only secondary sources but taken together the two lists are a scholarly work, including nearly 2000 references to secondary sources alone.

Digital data, image & text collections

2187 Al-Islam.org: digital Islamic library
www.al-islam.org/
Created and maintained by the Ahlul Bayt Digital Islamic Project, a non-profit making organization, it aims to digitize for the internet quality Islamic resources related to the history, law, practice and society of Islam. Apart from information on the project itself, the 'Library' includes more than 4300 digitized items, searchable by a Google search engine. Law items include books, lectures, articles, lists of websites.

Directories & encyclopedias

2188 Canon law
www.newadvent.org/cathen/09056a.htm
Full text of an article on canon law, written by A. Boudinhon and transcribed by David K. deWolf, published in the *Catholic encyclopedia* and made available on the New Advent site. Discusses sources, divisions, historical development, codifications and the principal canonists. Embedded links to other parts of the Encyclopedia.

2189 Encyclopedia of Islam
P.J. Bearman [et al.], eds   E.J. Brill, 1960–2005. ISBN 9004081143.
Published in 12 volumes and generally considered to be the standard reference work; includes entries on Islamic law. Began as the work of a single author but over the 50 years of compilation and publication has become the work of many hands. Available on CD-ROM and on the web. Publication of a third edition is due to start in 2007, available in print and online.

2190 Law and justice
www.fordham.edu/halsall/med/schacht.html
Free-to-view extract from chapter 4 of the *Cambridge encyclopedia of Islam* dealing with the history and early development of Islamic law and justice. Written by Joseph Schacht and available on Paul Halsall's website at Fordham University, New York.

2191 New Catholic encyclopedia
2nd rev.edn, Gale, 2003, 2000pp. $1595. ISBN 0787676942.
Multivolume reference work on Roman Catholic history and belief edited by the Catholic University of America; includes entries on Catholic canon law.

Socialist Law

Dictionaries, thesauri, classifications

2192 Mongolian–English–Russian dictionary of legal terms and concepts
W.E. Butler and A.J. Nathanson   Kluwer, 1982, 718pp. £246.25. ISBN 9024726778.
Contains nearly 11,000 words and phrases found in the Mongolian legal system, with basic English and Russian translations. Section 1 has Mongolian terms in alphabetical order with English and Russian equivalents and a reference number. Section 2 has Russian terms in alphabetical order and section 3 English words compiled on the same principles as sections 1 and 2. Covers not only legal terminology but also branches of the social sciences, military affairs, medicine and some natural sciences. Of value to lawyers engaged in commercial and legal practice and international affairs.

Laws, standards, codes

2193 Law in Eastern Europe
W. Simons and F.J.M. Feldbrugge, eds   Martinus Nijhoff, 1958–. ISSN 0075823X.
Series of more than 50 monographs published in cooperation with the Institute of East European Law and Russian Studies of Leiden University, the University of Trento and Graz and the European Academy of Bolzano. Each volume discusses a different aspect of law and reproduces in English the full text of the laws themselves.

Discovering print & electronic resources

2194 Official publications of the Soviet Union and Eastern Europe, 1945–80: a select bibliography
G. Walker   Continuum International Publishing Group – Mansell, 1982, 624pp. £95. ISBN 0720116414.
One chapter for each country: Albania, Bulgaria, Czechoslovakia, German Democratic Republic, Hungary, Yugoslavia, Poland, Romania, USSR and international organizations. Each chapter is to a standard structure, beginning with a narrative introduction to the government of the country and the organization of official publishing. Then follow sections of interest to lawyers on law, codes, the judicial system. Entries include constitutional documents,

treaties, legislation, regulations etc. A work of great scholarship and still of value to legal historians.

2195 The Soviet legal system: the law in the 1980s
J.N. Hazard, W.E. Butler and P.B. Maggs, comps   Oceana, 1984. ISBN 0379201410.
Translation into English, with commentary by the authors, of key Soviet documents produced between 1977 and 1983 on legal measures to reform the Soviet system. Includes policy documents, judicial decisions, procuratorial reports, political and academic explanations relating to the application of statutes and codes. Intended to support an introductory course in Soviet law.
- **Basic documents of the Soviet legal system** Reproduces legal documents from earlier decades.

Directories & encyclopedias

2196 Encyclopaedia of Soviet law
F.J.M. Feldbrugge, W.B. Simons and G.P. van den Berg, eds   2nd edn, Brill, 1985, 964pp. £328. ISBN 9024730759.
Contributions selected and compiled by a panel of over 50 distinguished lawyers, political scientists and researchers. Entries, which are all attributed to individuals, frequently exceed 2000 words. Extensive cross-references. Select bibliography runs to 50 pages and lists the most important statutory enactments of the Soviet government, the USSR and RSFSR (Russian Soviet Federative Socialist Republic). Up to date to 1 January 1984.

Public International Law

aviation law • criminal law • environmental law • European Community law • European Court of Justice • fisheries law • human rights law • international courts & tribunals • law of war & peace • laws concerning individuals • laws of common areas • laws of international organizations • laws of international relations • laws of international relations • League of Nations • maritime law • military law • money laundering • multilateral treaties • Red Cross • refugees • space law • terrorism • treaties • United Nations • war crimes

Introductions to the subject

2197 ASIL guide to electronic resources for international law
www.asil.org/resource/home.htm
Free web guide, revised at six-monthly intervals, evaluating, organizing and explaining electronic resources for international law. Far more than a set of links, the guide covers other electronic formats, makes comparisons with print sources. Probably the most comprehensive and up-to-date set of discussions of research strategies and analyses of resources across the whole field of public and private international law. Also available in book form but published in 2003.

2198 Columbia Law School – Arthur W. Diamond Library research guides
www.law.columbia.edu/library/Research_Guides
Series of international law research guides compiled by library staff of the Diamond Law Library, Columbia Law

School, New York. Intended for users of the library, these are in fact comprehensive, descriptive essays on key websites and the wide range of print material held by one of the major university law libraries with collections in international law in the USA. Guides are frequently updated and authoritative.

2199 George Washington Journal of International Law and Economics: guide to international legal research
Butterworths Legal Publishers, 1989–, 400pp. ISBN 0880633409.
Arranged by type of legal source and subdivided by type of publication, entries frequently include extended annotations covering both the content and value of each source. Extensive coverage but, since originally published as two issues of a US law journal, there is a US bias to the sources included.

2200 Guide to foreign and international legal databases
www.law.nyu.edu/library/foreign_intl/
Research guide to websites for international law, including useful annotations of varying length for each resource. Apart from law topics, it includes sections on foreign and international law search engines, citing electronic information, dictionaries, evaluating resources. Site search facility. Site compiled and maintained by Mirela Roznovschi, Reference/Foreign and international Law Librarian, New York University School of Law Library.

2201 International law guides – GlobaLex
www.nyulawglobal.org/globalex/
Range of nearly 20 research guides on various aspects of international law, each written by a librarian expert in the field. Each guide provides an introduction to the law, the organizations, the primary and secondary law materials. Extensive web links included, along with references to paper materials. A well respected and frequently updated series of research guides.

2202 Introduction to international and foreign legal research
M. Hoffman, comp.
www.law.berkeley.edu/library/dynamic/guide.php?guide=international_foreign/introduction
Research guide prepared in 2004 by the International and Foreign Law Librarian, University of California, Berkeley, Law Library. Covers both electronic and print sources of research guides and bibliographies, abbreviations and acronyms, international and foreign law terms and phrases, information about foreign legal systems, international organizations, journal indexes, citing materials, current awareness and useful websites. Although primarily designed for users of the Berkeley Law Library this is a thorough web research guide written by an acknowledged expert in the field.

2203 Public international law: a guide to information sources
Mansell, 1991, 331pp. ISBN 0720120829.
Divided into two parts: part 1 covers a typology of sources and resources followed by a bibliography of public inter-national law sources arranged by form of publication. Part 2 is a select subject bibliography arranged by topic. Entries are descriptive rather than critically evaluative. Detailed subject index. Even though it pre-dates the internet era this monumental work of scholarship is still of great value.

Dictionaries, thesauri, classifications

Dictionary of international and comparative law
J.R. Fox, ed.   See entry no. 2144

2204 English–French–Spanish–Russian manual of the terminology of public international law (law of peace) and international organizations
I. Paenson, comp.   Kluwer, 1983, 846pp. ISBN 9065440526.
Commentary on the history, nature, sources and content of international law, with parallel text in four languages. Supported by contents, detailed subject index and brief bibliography, all in parallel text. A unique publication.

2205 Parry and Grant encyclopaedic dictionary of international law
J.P. Grant and J.C. Baker, comps   2nd edn, Oceana Publications, 2003, 641pp. £95. ISBN 0379214490.
Concise definitions of terms, people, concepts, doctrines, cases, treaties and statutes, followed by more details discussions providing contextual information. Copious references to further research. An essential and indispensable international legal reference work.

Laws, standards, codes

2206 International legal materials
American Society of International Law, 1962–, monthly. ISSN 00207829.
www.asil.org/asilex.htm
Reproduces the text of documents across the whole range of public international law (resolutions, treaties, legislation, case law, speeches). Prides itself on reproducing official versions, though where they are not available in English, an unofficial translation is used. Some documents preceded by an introductory note on their history and significance. Available in electronic format through LexisNexis and Westlaw subscriber-only services (q.v.) and index from 1990 onwards is available free on the American Society of International Law website. Fundamental publication for the international law collection.
Contents list with summaries from Volume 36 (1997) onwards available at free web site: www.asil.org/resources/ilm.html.

2207 LexisNexis
www.lexisnexis.com
Full-text, subscriber-only database containing a wide range of materials, including *Treaties and agreements from international legal materials* (q.v.), cases and journal articles.

Research centres & institutes

2208 Hague Academy of International Law
www.hagueacademy.nl
Founded in 1923 with support from a Carnegie Endowment. Hosts a summer school with sessions on public and private international law. Papers are published in the language delivered, in *Recueil des cours de l'Academie de droit international*, commonly referred to as Hague Receuil.

2209 Max-Planck-Institut für ausländisches öffentliches Recht und Völkerrecht (Max Planck Institute for Comparative Public Law and International Law)
www.mpil.de/ww/en/pub/news.cfm
Official site of one of the foremost research bodies in Western Europe, founded in 1924 and now based in Heidelberg. Site details research programme, publications and access to the library catalogue of well over 300,000 monographs and 4000 serials from across the world. These holdings provide the basis for the preparation of the indexing service: Public International Law (q.v.).

Associations & societies

2210 American Society of International Law
www.asil.org/
Official site of the non-profit society set up in 1906 to foster the study of international law and promote the establishment and maintenance of international relations on the basis of law and justice – the foremost research organization in the subject area in the USA. Site includes details of the organization, its events and publications, including access to the free database: EISIL (Electronic Information System for International Law) (q.v.).

2211 International Law Association
www.ila-hq.org/
Official site of an international non-governmental organization founded in 1873, with members worldwide, to advance and clarify private, public and comparative law and propose solutions for the unification of these areas of law. Extensive list of publications, conference and seminar proceedings.

Libraries, archives, museums

Institute of Advanced Legal Studies
See entry no. 2781

2212 Peace Palace, Library
www.ppl.nl/
Based in The Hague, it has over 800,000 volumes, with 5000 titles added every year, and maintains it is one of the world's largest collections in the field of international law, public and private law and foreign national law. Web catalogue available to search. Extensive collection of e-resources available to search within the Library, which is open to members of the public presenting a valid ID.

Portal & task environments

2213 Electronic information system for international law
www.eisil.org/
Free portal of links to the full text of authoritative versions of primary and other international legal materials scattered across the web. Each entry includes a link to explanatory information about the particular document, including where it is printed conventionally. Links arranged by topic but advanced and cross-database searching available. A fundamental web resource for international lawyers.

2214 Foreign and international law resources: an annotated guide to web sites around the world
www.law.harvard.edu/library/services/research/gudes/international/web_resources
Portal site with thousands of links but a minimum of annotation about each site. Compiled by staff of Harvard Law School Library, probably the foremost university law library in the USA.

2215 Foreign and international law web
www.washlaw.edu/forint/forintmain.html
Portal site with thousands of links but a minimum of annotation about each site. Compiled by staff of Washburn University School of Law Library.

2216 Worldlii: international
www.worldlii.org/catalog/2500.html
Portal site with thousands of links and brief annotation about each site. Compiled by staff of the World Legal Information Institute, a non-profit body providing free access to legal information.

Discovering print & electronic resources

2217 A bibliography on foreign and comparative law: books and articles in English
Oceana, 1955–, irregular.
Lists books and articles in English language which deal with foreign law and subjects bearing on the comparative study of law. Includes entries drawn from the US, UK, Canada, Australia and New Zealand. Includes private international law an as well as international law. Most entries for books include a sentence or two of annotation on contents. Bibliography arranged into 10, later 12, broad subject headings. Hardback volumes published 3 or 4 years after the period covered. A landmark and monumental reference work. Since 1989 continued as *Szladits' bibliography*, compiled and edited by V. Pechota (q.v.).

2218 Digest of United States practice in international law
Government Printing Office, 1973–, annual.
Continuously published with slight title changes since the 1880s, summarizes treaties, executive agreements, diplomatic memoranda, legislation and federal court decisions relating to US practice in international law during a given year.

2219 Public international law: a current bibliography of books and articles
Max-Planck-Institut für ausländisches öffentliches Recht und Völkerrecht   Springer-Verlag, 1975–, 2 p.a. ISSN 03407349.
Bibliography based on the acquisitions of the Max Planck Institute Library and indexing over 1000 journals and other collected works only. Selected case notes and book reviews included. Classified according to the library's scheme. Value lies in greater focus on public international law than *Index to Legal Periodicals* and *Index to Foreign Legal Periodicals* (q.v.). Probably the most comprehensive current bibliography available.

2220 Research of articles and decisions in public international law and European law
www.jura.uni-duesseldorf.de/rave/e/ev/ev1.htm
Free database of references to articles and court decisions on public international law arranged under subject headings with web links to the full text of a small number. Entries arranged under subject headings, with subject and alphabetical indexes. Created by the Law Department of the University of Düsseldorf but parts of the database have not been updated since 2000.

2221 Szladits' bibliography on foreign and comparative law
V. Pechota, ed.   Oceana Publications, 1955–, irregular. ISSN 00677329.
This landmark and monumental reference work has undergone many changes since first published. Originally edited up to 1989 by Szladits, it covered both books and articles, was restricted to civil law jurisdictions only and was arranged by subject. Its coverage was extended to common law jurisdictions (US, UK, Canada, Australia and New Zealand) early on and after 1990 it covers only books. The arrangement is now geographical but covers both public and private international law. The bibliography is updated by annual supplements. Most entries for books include only a sentence or two annotation of the contents. Hardback volumes published 3 or 4 years after the period covered.

Directories & encyclopedias

2222 Encyclopedia of public international law
R. Bernhardt, ed.   North Holland Publishing Co, 1981–1990.
Twelve-volume set, each volume containing between 45 and 180 articles written by prominent international legal scholars and specialists on areas of public international law. Each article concludes with a short bibliography of further reading. Lacks an up-dating service so its value is lessening.

Keeping up to date

2223 American Journal of International Law
American Society of International Law, 1907–, qtrly. $235. ISSN 00029300.
Official journal of the leading research organization in the USA. Apart from conventional journal articles it includes current developments section of lengthy reviews of progress in the whole field of international law, international decisions section with lengthy commentary on recent decisions of various international courts and contemporary practice of the USA which reviews government policy and decision making and work of the courts in international law. Lengthy book reviews. Contents pages of *International Legal Materials* (q.v.) reprinted at back of each issue. Available in electronic form through JSTOR archive.

2224 ASIL Newsletter
American Society of International Law, 1970–, bi-monthly.
The newsletter itself is issued to members only but extracts are available online at www.asil.org/news.htm

2225 Bulletin of International Legal Developments
British Institute of International & Comparative Law, 1966–, bi-weekly. ISSN 17538491.
Concise, comprehensive review of latest developments in international and comparative law, covering the UK, Europe and the Commonwealth. Draws on both legal and non-legal

sources. Arranged under broad organizational headings and then by country. Generally accepted as one of the leading current-awareness sources for public international law. Unfortunately not available online.

Until 2006, Bulletin of Legal Developments, *ISSN 00074969*

2226 International law in brief
www.asil.org/ilib/ilibarch.htm

Web version of current awareness bulletin carrying summaries of latest developments in international law but with the addition, over print copy, of links to relevant websites for full-text. Compiled by editorial staff of *International Legal Materials* (q.v.).

2227 Keeping current with international law developments via the web
J. Watson, comp.

www.llrx.com/features/keeping.htm

Guide compiled in 2000 covering law portals, monitoring sites, news, inter-governmental organizations, new books and articles, web tools and e-mail. Some web links are broken, but still a worthwhile guide.

Law of War & Peace

Introductions to the subject

2228 War crimes: resources and research steps
S.J. Lamar

www.nesl.edu/research/RSGUIDES/warpath.htm

Research guide prepared in 2002 by the reference librarian of the New England School of Law, Boston, USA and intended for users of the library. Covers definition of war crimes, discussion of print and electronic sources for treaties with web links to materials produced by or about war crimes tribunals.

Laws, standards, codes

2229 Documents on laws of war
A. Roberts and R. Guelff, eds   3rd edn, Oxford University Press, 2000, 765pp. ISBN 0198763905.

Reprints the major treaties and other documents, each introduced by an explanatory note and each treaty provided with details of all states signing or adhering. Introduction to the entire volume provides a historical context and explains application to states and individuals. Appendices include one listing significant websites and another provides a bibliography on the law of war. Subject index. Scholarly and a valuable introduction to the relevant materials.

2230 The laws of armed conflict: a collection of conventions, resolutions and other documents
D. Schindler and J. Toman, eds   4th edn, Nijhoff, 2004, 1493pp. ISBN 9004138188.

Reproduces the text of 115 documents comprising conventions, draft conventions and resolutions on the law of armed conflict which have been adopted since the start of the 19th century. Provides details of signatories, ratifications and accessions correct to 15 October 2002. All documents reproduced in English. Comprehensive subject index.

Associations & societies

2231 International Society for Military Law & the Law of War
www.soc-mil-law.org/

Official site of the Belgian-based non-profit organization founded in 1956 to study and spread military law and international humanitarian law. Site includes details of events and publications. Access to the Society's newsletter is restricted to members only.

Laws of International Organizations

Introductions to the subject

2232 ASIL electronic resource guide: United Nations
K. Vinoplal, comp.

www.asil.org/resource/un1.htm

Comprehensive research guide with explanatory commentary covering among other matters research approaches and methodology, UN official internet sites, UN documents and resolutions, international courts and tribunals, bibliographic sources, related associations and organizations, libraries and research centres, research guides and current developments resources. Thorough and regularly kept up to date by the American Society of International Law.

2233 ASIL guide to electronic resources for international law: international organisations
A. Burnett, comp.

www.asil.org/resource/intorg1.htm

Comprehensive research guide with explanatory commentary covering among other matters definition of an international organization, basics of research, online discussion lists and links to inter-governmental organizations. Thorough and regularly kept up to date by the American Society of International Law.

2234 European Union legal materials: an infrequent user's guide
D.E. Alford, comp.

www.nyulawglobal.org/globalex/European_Union.htm

Research guide published in 2005, with explanatory commentary on both print and electronic sources covering the official website: Europa, the principal institutions of the EU, treatises and texts, dictionaries and directories, treaties, legislation, case law, official reports, journals and research guides etc. Thorough; contents in fact belie the 'infrequent user' subtitle.

2235 Guide to researching the Council of Europe
A. Burnett, comp.

www.llrx.com/features/coe.htm

Research guide published in 2000, covering the major institutions and their main documents and subject listing of websites related to the work of the Council of Europe. Although some web links are broken the commentary is still a valuable introduction to researching the work and publications of this organization.

2236 ILO research guide
C. Bynum
http://library.lawschool.cornell.edu/International_Reources/iloguide.htm
Research guide revised in 2002, covering the history of the organization, its organization, procedures and law materials. Extensive bibliography of further reading. Although some of the embedded web links are broken the commentary is still of value.

2237 Update: researching the United Nations: finding the organization's internal resource trails
L. Tashbrook, comp.
www.nyulawglobal.org/globalex/United_Nations_Research1.htm
Research guide updated in December 2006 by the foreign international comparative law librarian at the University of Pittsburgh School of Law, Barco Law Library. Helpfully set out according to several standard research queries and by type of United Nations research tools organized by type. Entirely focused on electronic sources.

Dictionaries, thesauri, classifications

IATE: interactive terminology for Europe
See entry no. 1573

Laws, standards, codes

2238 Basic documents of African regional organisations
L.B. Sohn, ed.   Oceana, 1971–1973. $190. ISBN 0379003619.
Four-volume collection relating to Organization of African Unity, African Development Bank, organizations of French-speaking Africa and documents relating to the association of African states with the European Economic Community. Each chapter starts with a historical survey. Comprehensive bibliography. Volume 4 covers selected Asian regional organizations (for fuller collection see *Basic documents of Asian regional organizations*). Of use only for historical research.

2239 Basic documents of Asian regional organisations
M. Haas, ed.   Oceana, 1974–1985. $430. ISBN 0379001772.
Collection of documents with a historical and analytical note on the founding and structure of various organizations, followed by copies of original documents and a bibliography of other relevant sources. Of use only for historical research.

2240 Common Market law reports
Sweet & Maxwell, 1962–, weekly. ISSN 05887445; 00103284.
Contains a selection of judgments of the European Court of Justice in English and presented in the style of a British or Irish law report with a headnote (summary). Published much more quicklyr than the authoritative source, *European Court reports* (q.v.). Full text of all judgments since 1954 is available on the EUR-Lex website of the European Union (q.v.) and longer backruns are also available on both of the subscriber-only databases: LexisNexis Butterworths (q.v.) and Westlaw UK (q.v.).

2241 Council of Europe treaty series
Council of Europe, 1949–, irregular. ISSN 0070105X.
http://conventions.coe.int/Treaty/Commun/ListeTraites.asp?CM=88&CL=ENG
Official site containing the text in either HTML or Word of the treaties of the Council of Europe. Originally known, up to end of 2003, as the European Treaty Series. Text of treaties issued in English and French. Treaties also published in paper format.

2242 Encyclopedia of European Community law
Sweet & Maxwell, 1973–. ISSN 01424564.
19-volume collection in full text of, in part A: UK legislation relating to the EC, part B: text of the EC treaties and part C: significant EC legislation in force, consolidated and with some annotations. Checklists and tables for locating legislation from official reference numbers only are a valuable finding aid. Subject index, not to the highest standards, also provided. Probably the most comprehensive commercial collection available in print. Note: EU legislation is available free on the EUR-Lex website (q.v.).

2243 Encyclopedia of European Union laws
Sweet & Maxwell.
Provides the full text of the EC constitutional texts of the treaties, the institutions of the EC and 'pillars' on the European Union. Few annotations included but the subject indexing is a useful finding aid. Note: EU legislation is available free on the EUR-Lex website (q.v.).

2244 EUR-Lex
http://eur-lex.europa.eu/en/index.htm
Official site of the European Union, providing free access to the full text of European Union law. Includes treaties, international agreements, legislation in force, legislation in draft, case law and parliamentary questions. The authoritative source.

2245 European Court reports
European Court of Justice, 1953–. ISSN 10234209.
Official reports of judgments of the European Court of Justice and the Court of First Instance, including the opinions of the Advocate-General, the judgment and the decision or order of the court. Cases reported in strict chronological order and, because of the need to have the text translated into all official languages of the EC before publication, the appearance of the title is often much delayed. Full text of all judgments since 1954 is available on the EUR-Lex website of the European Union (q.v.) and longer backruns are also available on both the subscriber-only databases: LexisNexis Butterworths (q.v.) and Westlaw UK (q.v.).

2246 European Union law reporter
CCH International, 1997–. ISBN 086325215X.
Formerly known as *Common Market law reporter* and prior to that *Common Market reports*. Commercial, looseleaf encyclopedia structured around the articles of the EC treaty with some full-text legislation, editorial commentary and reports of cases published as rapidly as possible. Not the most authoritative source (see *European Court reports*) but better currency. After the year end the cases are published in a separate bound volume, *European Community cases*. Note: EU legislation and case law is available free on the EUR-Lex website (q.v.).

2247   European Union treaties: consolidated versions
Office for Official Publications of the European Communities, 2006, 331pp. ISBN 9282431908.
http://europa.eu.int/eur-lex/en/
Latest consolidated print version contains the Treaty on European Union and the Treaty establishing the European Community, correct to November 2006. Reproduces all the protocols made both by the Treaty of Athens 2003 and the Act of Accession 2003. The most up-to-date version is on the Europa website.

2248   International law reports
E. Lauterpacht, ed.   Grotius Publications, 1919–, irregular.
Previously published as *Annual digest of public international law cases* and at another time *Annual digest and reports of international law cases*. Reports in English and in full text, significant decisions on international law from across the world, including the decisions of the International Court of Justice, the European Court of Human Rights, Inter-American Court of Human Rights, but excluding the Administrative Tribunal of the United Nations and the Court of Justice of the European Communities. Also includes decisions of courts on international law issues in a range of countries. Subject arrangement of material. Not available in electronic form. One of the most important series of international law reports published.

2249   Official Journal of the European Union
Office for Official Publications of the European Union, 1954–, 6 per week. ISSN 17252555.
http://Eur-lex.europa.eu/JOIndex.do?ihmlang=en
The official newspaper or gazette of the European Communities issued from 1954 onwards and published six times a week in five series, of which two interest lawyers: L series includes the official, full text of secondary legislation; C series, Information and Notices, including the text of proposals for legislation and lists cases brought before the Court of Justice. No longer published in print but available as a CD-ROM or on the Europa website in pdf format from 1954 onwards.

2250   Pan American Union treaty series
Organization of American States, 1934–1956.
Official, full text of the multi-lateral treaties concluded among the member states. Text in both Spanish, Portuguese, French and English. Continued by *Organization of American States treaty series* (q.v.).

2251   Reports, judgments, advisory opinions and orders
Sijthoff, 1947–. ICJ.
Official print version of reports of decisions of the International Court of Justice published in English and French. The authoritative source. Associated series *Pleadings, oral arguments and documents* provides full text of the arguments of parties before the court. Also available on the official website of the International Court of Justice (q.v.).

2252   Westlaw UK
http://westlaw.co.uk
Full-text, subscriber-only database containing the text of legislation as published in the *Official Journal of the European Community* (q.v.) since 1952, case law published in the same source 1954 and treaties between members states since 1951. This material is also available in whole or in part of the official EUR-Lex website (q.v.).

2253   World Court reports
M.O. Hudson, ed.   Oceana, 1922–1942.
Four-volume collection of the 32 judgments and 27 advisory opinions and orders of the Permanent Court of International Justice from 1922 to 1942. Includes the text of the instruments which founded the Court and by which it operated. All texts are reproduced from official publications and given in English, where available. Editorial notes precede each item. More widely available and accessible than the official publications.

Official & quasi-official bodies

2254   African Union
www.africa-union.org
Official site of the body which has replaced the Organization of African Unity to accelerate the processes of integrating the continent to play its rightful role in the global economy. Site includes access documents, including the full text of treaties, conventions and protocols and the decisions and declarations made at the Assemblies of Heads of State since 1963.

2255   Council of Europe/Conseil de l'Europe
www.coe.int
Official site of the body set up in 1949 to defend human rights, develop continent-wide agreements to standardize member countries' social and legal practices and promote awareness of European identity. Under link 'Conventions' provides access to a list and the full text of all the Council of Europe's conventions, with a chart of signatures and ratifications. No links to the European Court of Human Rights, to which alleged violations of human rights within member states are brought.

2256   Court of Justice of the European Communities
http://curia.europa.eu/en/index.htm
Official site of the permanent court to which disputes over European Union law within and between member states are brought. Includes information about the Court, texts governing its procedure, search facility across all the Court's decisions since its founding, news of cases pending and press releases.

2257   European Court of Human Rights
www.echr.coe.int/ECHR/
Official site of the permanent court to which alleged violations of the European Convention on Human Rights within member states are brought. Includes information about the Court, texts governing its procedure and access to the HUDOC case-law database (q.v.) for searches across all the Court's decisions since its founding, news of cases pending and press releases. Also access to the online library catalogue of over 25,000 items collected since 1966. A key site, well presented.

2258   International Court of Justice
www.icj/home.htm
Official site of the principal judicial body of the United Nations. Also known as the World Court. Founded in 1946 to replace the Permanent Court of International Justice. Sits in The Hague, Netherlands. Site includes history, general information about the court, the statute and rules of the court, lists of the decisions of the court leading to the full

text, lists of cases pending and press releases. Although there is no site search facility it is an easy site to navigate.

International Labour Organization
See entry no. 4346

2259 Organization of American States
www.oas.org/
Official site of the body set up to strengthen democratic values and promote human rights, among other aims, between members from North, South and Central America and the Caribbean. Site includes access to parts of Secretariat dealing with law, text of OAS charter, treaties negotiated by it and links to the Inter-American Court of Human Rights (q.v.), where alleged violations of the American Convention on Human Rights are heard. Official print versions of multi-lateral treaties concluded among OAS member states are available in Spanish, Portuguese, French and English. Print publication continues *Pan American Union treaty series* (q.v.).

Research centres & institutes

2260 Project on international courts and tribunals
www.pict-pcti.org/
Established in 1997 as a joint venture between the Centre on International Cooperation of New York University and the Foundation for International Environmental Law and Development (London) and, since 2002, the Centre for International Courts and Tribunals, University College London. The project aims to encourage the international community to think systematically about the large number of international courts and tribunals set up since the late 19th century. Site includes information about the various courts, the Centre's research themes and publications and events.

Portal & task environments

2261 International agencies and information on the web
www.lib.umich.edu/govdocs/intl.html
Comprehensive portal of links to inter-governmental and non-governmental organization websites, each entry carrying a brief annotation. Lists of links include guides to international organizations, an alphabetical list, guides to international treaty websites and a list of abbreviations for IGOs. Site compiled and maintained by the staff of the Documents Centre, University of Michigan Library.

2262 JURIST EU
www.fd.unl.pt/je/index.htm
Site of the European arm of the education portal: The Legal Education Network. Site includes links to EU official websites, lists of European law schools, links to law professors with their own websites, links to law journals and articles, conference papers online and guides to sites on European law topics. Site hosted and managed in Portugal but contributors from across Europe.

Discovering print & electronic resources

2263 European information
www.library.ex.ac.uk/internet/eurostudies.html

Portal site with a comprehensive set of links, including brief annotations, aimed primarily at those studying or researching the European Union and those interested in the research sponsored by the European Community. Compiled and maintained by Patrick Overy, European Documentation Centre Librarian at the University of Exeter.

European integration current contents
See entry no. 1599

Handbooks & manuals

2264 Hague yearbook of international law
1988–, annual. ISSN 09238298.
Summarizes the work and decisions of the International Court of Justice, the Permanent Court of Arbitration, the Iran-US Claims Tribunal and other bodies.

2265 International Court of Justice yearbook
United Nations, 1946/7–, annual. ISSN 0074445X.
Contains information about the organization, its jurisdiction, activities and administration of the Court, a well as summaries of cases before the Court, a list of Court publications, including its judgments.

Keeping up to date

2266 European current law digest
One of the key current-awareness services for legal developments in the EU and the domestic laws of European countries. Focus section at beginning of each issue provides comment on recent developments, followed by a digest under subject headings of EU law and the European law in national jurisdictions. Valuable lists of regulations, directives and draft directives. Also lists of the national implementation of EU directives. Monthly digest re-published after year end in cumulated form as *European current law yearbook*.

2267 Multilateral treaties deposited with the Secretary-General: status as at [year] (Traités multilatéraux déposés auprès du Secrétaire-Général: état [année])
United Nations, Office of Legal Affairs, 1949–, annual.
Title has varied up to 1980. Arranged in topical and chronological order providing details of accessions, reservations, ratifications etc. Cumulates information given in the monthly publication *Statement of treaties and international agreements registered or filed and recorded within the Secretariat of the United Nations*.

Laws of International Relations

Introductions to the subject

2268 ASIL electronic resource guide: treaties
J. McC. Watson, comp.
www.asil.org/resource/treaty1.htm
Comprehensive research guide with explanatory commentary covering, among other matters, research approaches and methodology, treaties on the internet, other electronic media for treaties, materials about treaties. Emphasis is on

electronic rather than print sources. Thorough and regularly kept up to date by the American Society of International Law.

2269 Fundamentals of treaty research: US and Non-U.S.
L. Louis-Jacques, comp.
www2.lib.uchicago.edu/~llou/treaties.html
Research guide originally compiled in 1998 and updated in 2001 by the Foreign and International Law Librarian to University of Chicago Law School, an acknowledged expert in international legal materials. Brief annotated entries describe and link to electronic sources as well as noting a small number of paper materials. Includes all types of information, including e-mail discussion lists.

2270 Researching non-US treaties
S. Weigmann, comp.
www.llrx.com/features/non_ustreaty.htm
Research guide to treaties to which the USA is not a signatory, compiled by the reference librarian of the International Legal Studies Library at Harvard Law School and published in 2001. Covers locating and updating multilateral treaties, drafting multilateral treaties, conferences and travaux preparatoires, bi-lateral treaties outside the USA. Covers both print and electronic sources. Authoritative and well researched but probably due for an update.

2271 Researching US treaties and agreements
M. Hoffman
www.llrx.com/features/ustreaty.htm
Research guide by the international and foreign law librarian, University of California, Berkeley, Law Library, revised and updated in 2005. Discusses the nature of treaties and agreements, the treaty-making and agreement-making processes, finding the full-text, checking status, researching updating and ratification information, legislative histories and treaty interpretation, tracing treaties from popular names and collections of US treaties on the internet. Covers print as well as electronic sources. Very full descriptions and annotations – thorough and authoritative.

2272 Treaties
www.parliament.uk/documents/upload/p14.pdf
Factsheet produced by the House of Commons Information Office and revised in 2006, explaining in accessible language the role of the UK in the treaty-making process, EU treaties, other agreements, devolution and treaties and tracing treaties. Succinct.

2273 Treaties and other sources of international law
www.law-lib.utoronto.ca/resguide/rschguid.htm
Research guide compiled by staff of the Bora Laskin Library, University of Toronto, Canada, providing extensive commentary on the basic strategies for locating international and foreign law material and especially treaties. Covers public international law, private international law and foreign law in both print and electronic sources. Canadian sources are given prominence. Thorough and well researched.

2274 United Nations documentation: research guide: international law
www.un.org/Depts/dhl/resguide/specil.htm
Research guide produced by the UN Dag Hammarskjöld Library, providing extensive commentary and annotations to web sources relating to the work in international law of the UN. Thorough, authoritative and a key site for research.

Dictionaries, thesauri, classifications

2275 Treaty reference guide and glossary of terms relating to treaty actions
http://untreaty.un.org/English/guide.asp
Guide to and glossary of terms used in the UN Treaty Collection (the most extensive available) to international instruments such as treaties, agreements, conventions, charters etc. Extensive and authoritative.

Laws, standards, codes

2276 Australian treaties library
www.austlii.edu.au/au/other/dfat/
Free library of the full text of Australian treaties from 1901 onwards, lists of Australian treaties, including those not yet in force, a guide to treaty-making in Australia and a wealth of other material. Site maintained by the non-profit making Australian Legal Information Institute with funding and material provided by the Australian Department of Foreign Affairs and Trade.

2277 British and foreign state papers
Stationery Office, 1841–1976.
Includes text of treaties, statements and various diplomatic exchanges from 1814 to 1968 as well as some treaties concluded before 1814 and still in force. Each volume contains a subject index. For cumulative chronological and subject indexes use *An index of British treaties: 1101–1988* (q.v.). BFSP continued from 1970 by *United Kingdom treaty series* (q.v.).

2278 Collection of international concessions and related instruments 595 AD–1974
P. Fischer   Oceana, 1976–1988.
13-volume set of the full text of concessions made by states giving rights and functions to private persons to carry out economic activities. No annotations or commentary.

2279 Consolidated treaty series, 1648–1918
C. Parry, ed.   Oceana, 1970–1977. $11,000. ISBN 0379130009.
Reprints in 23 volumes treaties made before the League of Nations and United Nations treaty series began. Reprinted in original language with a translation into English or French where the compiler has discovered one already available. Where no translation is available a summary is provided. Details of original source provided and subsequent history of treaty. Indexes to parties and chronological index. A foundation publication for a public international law collection.

2280 Current international treaties
T. Millar and R. Ward, eds   New York University Press, 1984. £35. ISBN 0709917589.
Brings together the texts in English of the main bilateral and multilateral treaties which form the legal skeleton of international relations up to the early 1980s. Brief commentary and introduction to each group of treaties. Index of signatories and basic topic index. Owing to age,

currency of information provided would need to be verified elsewhere.

2281 European conventions and agreements (Conventions et accords Européens)
Council of Europe, 1971–.
www.conventions.coe.int
Series of volumes containing text of all treaties concluded with the Council of Europe, published in their original form with parallel English and French texts. Official text is published in separate, loose issues. Web version available.

2282 Hertslet's commercial treaties: : a collection of treaties and conventions between Great Britain and foreign powers
L. Hertslet   1827–.
31 volumes reprinting a selection of commercial treaties and related materials created between 1354 and 1910. After this date material incorporated within *British and foreign state papers* (q.v.).

2283 League of Nations treaty series, 1920–1946
League of Nations, 1920–1946. Reprinted by Oceana, 1970.
205 volumes containing the full-text in English and French of nearly 5000 treaties registered with the League of Nations between 1920 and 1946.

2284 Major international treaties: a history and guide with texts
J.A.S. Grenville   Methuen, 1987, 268pp. £40. ISBN 0416080928.
Intended for students and general readers, provides historical context for each of the major treaties from 1914 to 1973, together with extracts from the treaties themselves. Value lies in making accessible key documents of international law and placing the analysis of the text in a historical context.

2285 Treaties and other international agreements of the USA, 1776–1949
C.I. Bevans, ed.   US. Government Printing Office, 1968–1976.
Twelve volumes containing the text of more than 7000 treaties and agreements entered into by the USA between 1776 and 1949. An official compilation organized into multilateral treaties and agreements in chronological order by date of signature, then 11 volumes of bilateral treaties and other agreements grouped by country. General index in 13th volume. Also available on the subscriber-only HeinOnline internet database (q.v.).

2286 Treaty series
Stationery Office, Dublin, 1931–, irregular.
http://foreignaffairs.gov.ie/home/index.asp?id=384
Official print text of treaties to which Ireland is a party, from 1930 onwards. The web Irish Treaty Series database provides a full title listing in chronological order (with subject search facility) and links to the full text of treaties from around 1997 onwards.

2287 United Kingdom treaty series
Stationery Office, 1892–, annual.
Official text of treaties to which the UK is party since 1970. Published as a sub-series of Command Papers, official documents originating outside Parliament but presented to it.

2288 United Nations treaty collection
http://untreaty.un.org/
Largest single collection of treaties on the internet, comprising the full text of the 2200 print volumes of the United Nations treaty series (UNTS) of over 50,000 treaties. Subscriber-only access. Searchable by various fields, including names of parties, popular names, type of agreement, date of signature. Apart from the text of treaties the collection includes electronic versions of many other 'finding' and research materials such as *Status of multilateral treaties deposited with the Secretary-General* (q.v.). Pop-up blocker software has to be disabled to enter the collection of databases.

2289 United Nations treaty series
United Nations, 1946–. ISSN 03798267.
Official text in English and French translation of all treaties entered into by any of the UN member states. Delays in publication mean that the web version on the United Nations treaty collection site (q.v.) will be more current.

2290 United States treaties and other international acts
Department of State, 1952–. ISSN 00833487.
Official reproduction of the text of all treaties and other international agreements to which the USA is party. Treaties are arranged in numerical order in which they were originally published by the Department of State in pamphlet form. No annotation or commentary. Basic subject index. Series is currently running about 20 years behind with the text of treaties originally published in the 1980s now appearing. Also available on the subscriber-only HeinOnline internet database (q.v.).

Official & quasi-official bodies

Great Britain. Foreign & Commonwealth Office
See entry no. 1520

Libraries, archives, museums

2291 United Nations depository libraries
www.un.org/Depts/dhl/deplib/countries/index.html
List, arranged by country, of the UN depository libraries which receive and hold either a full range or partial collection of UN publications (as explained in the introductory note) and are freely accessible to the general public. Each entry includes a range of contact information. List also includes UN Information Centres/Information Services and UN Offices.

Discovering print & electronic resources

2292 Canadian bibliography of international law
C.L. Wiktor, ed.   University of Toronto Press, 1984, 764pp. ISBN 0802056156.
Includes 9400 entries, arranged under subject headings, published from 1755 onwards, relating to Canada and its role in the international community. Includes publications issued within or about Canada. Covers government documents, including treaties, books, articles, theses and book reviews. In two parts: first, international law (excluding private international law), the second part on international

relations, especially foreign trade, investment, communications etc. Indexes of authors and corporate names.

2293 Catalogue of treaties 1814–1918
Oceana, 1964, 716pp. Originally published 1919.
Chronological list of treaties, with information on date and place of signature, ratification, signatory powers, where the text of the treaty can be found in treaty collections, language of the text and cross-references to later treaties which affect the treaty in question. Two-part index by countries and an index of agreements of a general international character. Also available on the subscriber-only HeinOnline internet database.

Digest of United States practice in international law
See entry no. 2218

2294 Electronic information system for international law (EISIL)
www.eisil.org/
From home page, follow links to general international law/treaty collections for quality information service provided by the American Society of International Law. Includes links to a few individual treaties, links to treaty collections and research guides.

2295 Frequently-cited treaties and other international agreements
www.law.umn.edu/library/tools/pathfinders/most-cited.html
Set up to assist law-review citation checking, site sets out a list of approximately 100 of the most frequently cited treaties, with details of where they are located in print format and, where possible, a link to the free EISL treaties database of the American Society of International Law.

2296 An index of British treaties: 1101–1988
C. Parry and C. Hopkins, comps   Stationery Office Books, 1970–1992, 812pp. £85. ISBN 0115916814.
Published in four volumes, a chronological list of all treaties in which England or the UK or another country of the Commonwealth, together with more than one foreign state, has become a party. Each entry provides details of the signatory countries but, more usefully, where the text of the treaty has been published. Indexes by subject and country. A valuable part of any international law reference collection.

2297 Index to multilateral treaties: a chronological list of multi-party international agreements from the sixteenth century through 1963, with citations to their text
V. Mostecky, ed.   Harvard Law School Library Publications, 1965–1968.
Index to 3859 treaties signed by three or more international 'persons', such as states or international organizations. Arranged chronologically from 1596 to 1963, by date of signature, or by the date on which the document was open for signature, or by the date of the conference which adopted the instrument. Details for a typical entry include a brief descriptive title in English, place of signature, a list of official and unofficial sources of the full text of the treaty and the language of the text. Combined subject and geographical (regional) index provided.

2298 Locating US treaties
http://library.law.smu.edu/resguide/treat-us.htm
Annotated guide to both print and electronic sources of the text, indexes, status-checking sources and pre-ratification texts of treaties to which the USA is party. Compiled in 2005 by staff of the Underwood Law Library, Southern Methodist University, US. Although useful since it includes print sources, some internet links are to subscriber-only sites not available to public.

2299 The Ministry of Justice's database of New Zealand's multilateral agreements
www.justice.govt.nz/pubs/reports/1996/agreements/Default.htm
Official database containing lists of multilateral agreements deposited with the United Nations to which New Zealand is party, current status and reservations and a range of other materials. Lists provide references to print versions only.

2300 Multilateral treaties: index and current status
M.J. Bowman and D.J. Harris, eds   Butterworth, 1984, 516pp. £60. ISBN 0406252777.
Lists in chronological order just under 1000 of the most important multilateral treaties. Provides names of countries party to the treaty, date of signature or accession, amendment or modifications to each treaty and, most important for researchers, where the full text of the treaty is published. Subject index provided. Invaluable finding tool which badly needs updating.

2301 United States treaty index 1776–2000
I.I. Kavass, comp.   William S. Hein, 1991–. ISBN 0899417701.
Treaties and international agreements to which the USA is party are indexed chronologically, by country, by names of international organizations, by subject, by reference number and by geographical-subject combination. Provides details of ratification dates and where the text is published. Monumental work kept up to date by consolidating supplements, the latest of which issued in looseleaf form.

2302 World treaty index
P.H. Rohn   2nd edn, ABC-CLIO, 1984. $999. ISBN 0874361419.
http://db.lib.washington.edu/wti/wtdb.htm
Main section of the 5-volume print version of this work is a chronological list (by date of signature) of over 44,000 treaties made between 1920 and 1980. Each entry states where the treaty is published, the parties and the dates of accession. Main section is supplemented by a rotated keyword index and index to parties. A whole volume devoted to a statistical analysis of the data. The most complete index to treaties of the period available. A web version with some more material from the 1990s is available but the entire work badly needs updating.

Digital data, image & text collections

2303 The Avalon project at Yale Law School
www.yale.edu/lawweb/avalon/avalon.htm
Extensive project to provide web access to primary sources in law and a selection of other social science subjects. The list of document collections includes materials on international law and diplomacy as well as domestic US law. Documents are arranged by century, with links to the full-text and cross-linking within to other documents. Searching

across full text of all documents in the Avalon collection is available. A key resource.

2304 Multilaterals project
http://fletcher.tufts.edu/multilaterals.htm
Project at The Fletcher School, Tufts University, Medford, Massachusetts begun in 1992 to make available on the web the text of international multilateral conventions and other instruments. Although originally begun to improve access to environmental law material, it now embraces treaties on human rights, commerce and trade, laws of war and arms control and other areas. Includes historical as well as contemporary material. Collection includes over 350 texts from some miscellaneous pre-1900 documents to the present. Full search facility, as well as subject and chronological listings. An invaluable resource.

Directories & encyclopedias

2305 Common names of treaties and other diplomatic agreements
www.yale.edu/lawweb/avalon/treaty.htm
List of about 40 of the best-known international treaties from the late 18th century to the present under their popular names, with links to their proper names and the full-text. Part of the Avalon project based at the Yale University Law School providing the full text of thousands of treaties.

Handbooks & manuals

2306 British yearbook of international law
Oxford University Press, 1920–, annual. ISSN 00682691.
Includes a list of treaties entered into by the UK during the year in question, information on decisions of the British courts involving questions of public and private international law and decisions of the European Court of Justice and European Court of Human Rights. Also available on the subscriber-only HeinOnline internet database.

2307 List of treaty collections
United Nations, 1956.
Lists collections of treaties published in and after 1780 up to the mid-1950s. Three parts: general collections, collections by subject and finally, collections by states. Entries listed in chronological order. Basic author/title index. Thoroughly researched.

2308 Manual of collections of treaties and of collections relating to treaties
D.P. Myers   Harvard University Press, 1922, 685pp.
Bibliography of treaties up to 1914. Sections covering general collections, collections by states and finally, collections on particular legal topics. Details of treaties are not translated but left in the original language. Comprehensive index by title of treaty, subjects and personal names.

Keeping up to date

2309 Chart showing signatures and ratifications of Council of Europe conventions and agreements
Council of Europe, Directorate of Legal Affairs, 1974–, annual.

http://conventions.coe.int
An official, diagramatic representation of progress by each member state towards the signing and ratification of conventions and agreements of the Council of Europe. The web version is incorporated within information for each treaty.

2310 Status of multilateral treaties deposited with the Secretary-General
United Nations, Office of Legal Affairs, 1959–.
http://untreaty.un.org/ENGLISH/bible/englishinternetbible/bible.asp
Provides status information for the 500-plus treaties deposited with the Secretary General of the United Nations. Available in print and web format, the latter updated daily.

2311 Treaties in force: a list of treaties and other international agreements of the United States
US. Department of State   US Government Printing Office; William S. Hein & Co Inc, 1929–, annual.
www.state.gov.s/l/treaties/
Lists treaties and other international agreements to which the USA has become party and which are in the records of the Department of State as being in force as of the specified year. Part 1 includes bilateral treaties listed by country, part 2 multilateral treaties arranged under subject headings, with lists of states which are parties to the agreement. Each entry includes details of where the text is printed.

Laws of Common Areas

Introductions to the subject

2312 ASIL electronic resource guide: international environmental law
A. Burnett, comp.
www.asil.org/resource/env1.htm
Comprehensive research guide with explanatory commentary covering, among other matters, general research strategies, primary and secondary sources, essays, press releases, directories and online discussion lists. Emphasis is on English-language internet sources, but also includes some CD-ROMs and library catalogues Thorough and regularly kept up to date by the American Society of International Law.

2313 E.B. Williams Library research guides: international environmental law
www.ll.georgetown.edu/intl/guides/InternationalEnvironmentalLaw.cfm
Research guide created and maintained by staff of the Georgetown University Law Centre Library, US, initially to aid users of that library but having links, with descriptions, to treaties, statutes, regulations, international and national case law, commercial databases, books, periodicals, other research bibliographies and organizations. Attractively presented.

Laws, standards, codes

2314 International protection of the environment
B. Ruster and B. Simma   Oceana, 1975.
28 volumes, including a single volume index, reproducing the texts of treaties and documents of international organizations in chronological order, predominantly in

English or in the original language with an English summary. Each reprint concludes with references to the source where the original is printed. No commentary. Subject, chronological and keyword indexes.

2315 International protection of the environment: conservation in sustainable development
W.E. Burhenne and N.A. Robinson, eds   Oceana, 1995. ISBN 0379102951.

In nine looseleaf volumes, this forms part of the series *International protection of the environment* (q.v.) and keeps the entire set up to date. Historical compendium of the text of environmental treaties and other legal documents from 1754 to the early 1980s. Reproduces documents without annotations or commentary. Minimal indexing.

2316 Oceans and law of the sea
www.un.org/Depts/los/index.htm

Official United Nations site on which Law of the Sea resources are published, including conventions, the work of the General Assembly in this topic area, bodies established by conventions, dispute settlement etc. Includes unedited advance texts as well as approved publications. Full site search facility. Authoritative and comprehensive.

Official & quasi-official bodies

2317 Comité Maritime International
www.comitemaritime.org/

Official site of the oldest international organization working in the field of maritime law. Based in Belgium and formally established in 1897, it aims to promote the unification of maritime law. Site includes history of the organization, details of its structure and work, pdf copy of its latest yearbook and other publications, copies of maritime conventions, work in progress and a brief list of links to international and intergovernmental bodies and maritime law associations across the world. No site search facility but easy to navigate.

2318 Inter-American Commission on Human Rights
www.cidh.org/DefaultE.htm

Official site of an autonomous part of the Organization of American states responsible, with the Inter-American Court of Human Rights, for the promotion and protection of human rights. Site includes access to its publications and under link: Basic documents, to the full text of Inter-American human rights instruments.

2319 International Civil Aviation Organization, Legal Bureau
www.icao.int/

Founded in 1940s to secure international cooperation, support for uniformity in regulations and standards, procedures and organization regarding civil aviation matters. Site includes history of the organization, its activities and publications. Of particular value to lawyers is the link to its bureaux and the Legal Bureau in particular, with access to DAGMAR, the free, searchable database of international aeronautical agreements and arrangements. Also, under 'Treaties', list and current status of international air law treaties. A valuable site.

2320 International Maritime Organization
www.imo.org/index.htm

Official site of the United Nations agency established in 1959 to provide a forum for intergovernmental cooperation on maritime safety and the prevention of pollution at sea. Site includes history, purpose and membership. Under the link 'Legal', a commentary on the organization's work and committees, with links to conventions other legal documents; the link 'Information Resources' leads to free access to MO codes and many other resources. A key site.

2321 International Tribunal for the Law of the Sea
www.itlos.org/

Official site of the judicial body established by the United Nations Convention on the Law of the Sea to regulate all ocean space, its use and resources. Site provides background information about the court, its procedures, the tribunal judges, list of cases which have been heard, with links to the full text of proceedings, orders, judgments and press releases. Links to conventions and other legal materials. Under 'Documents' is a 'Select Bibliography on Settlement of Disputes concerning the Law of the Sea'. A comprehensive and attractively presented site.

2322 United Nations. Office for Outer Space Affairs
www.oosa.unvienna.org/

Official site of the body responsible for promoting international cooperation in the peaceful uses of outer space. Apart from information on the work of the body and its committees, the link 'Space law' leads to the work of its Legal Subcommittee and links to relevant legal and administrative documents (including treaties, international agreements, declarations and resolutions of the UN) on the peaceful use of space.

Research centres & institutes

2323 European Centre for Space Law
http://edms.esrin.esa.it/ecsl/

Official site of a research organization set up by the European Space Agency in 1989 to promote an understanding of the legal framework relevant to space activities. Apart from information on its work, membership and activities, the site includes access to a database of treaties and status information, the ECSL bibliography, which includes a section on the law relating to space (but up to date only to September 1999), and general and subject specific space law bibliographies, both up to date to only 2005.

2324 Foundation for International Environmental Law & Development
www.field.org.uk/

Founded in London in 1989 by a small group of international lawyers to promote international environmental law through research, teaching, publishing and advice. Value of site lies in commentary on each area of law, with links to past and current projects of the organization. Comprehensive set of links to websites of other relevant organizations.

2325 Institute of Maritime Law
www.iml.soton.ac.uk/

Official site, based at the University of Southampton, of the largest centre in the UK for the study of maritime law for teaching, research and consultancy. Site includes general information about the Institute, its staff and activities. Extensive publications list.

2326 International Institute of Air & Space Law
http://iiasl.leiden.edu/
Official site of one of the leading international academic research and teaching institutes in the world, specializing in legal and policy issues regarding aviation and space activities. Apart from information about the Institute, its activities and staff, site includes description of the extensive library and access to its catalogue. List of 'Hyperlinks' to related websites.

Associations & societies

2327 Center for International Environmental Law
www.ciel.org/
Official site of a non-profit US-based organization working to influence international law and institutions to protect the environment, promote human health and ensure a just and sustainable society. Site has details of research programmes and staff, press releases. Unfortunately parts of the site (links to associated sites and descriptions of its own research programmes) appear not to have been updated since 2003.

Portal & task environments

2328 Air transport portal of the European Commission
http://ec.europa.eu/transport/air_portal/
Part of the European Commission Directorate-General for Energy and Transport, site provides links to sections on air transport in the European Union, air safety and security, air transport and the environment and EU policy on international air transport. Commentary in each section introduces the issues and provides links to the full text of documents. Comprehensive set of links to websites of international, governmental and commercial organizations in the field. Attractively presented.

2329 Environment law
http://libwww.essex.ac.uk/LAW/environment_law.htm
Simple page of links to international environmental law resources on the web, with minimal annotations for each link. Compiled and maintained by staff of the Albert Sloman Library, University of Essex, UK.

2330 European environmental law homepage
www.eel.nl/
Comprehensive internet service compiled and maintained by staff of the T.M.C. Asser Institute, Netherlands. Includes links and full text of key environmental legislation at European and national levels, case law from international and national courts, policy documents issued by international bodies, papers and articles submitted to the site by international environmental lawyers, national pages of legislation, cases and reviews edited by appointed correspondents, events and news. Relatively easy to navigate – no site search facility.

2331 Internet guide to international fisheries law
www.intfish.net/

Created by Oceanlaw, a commercial research and consultancy service, the site maintains it is the largest collection of free information on international fisheries law and related subjects on the web. IGIFIL Treaty Database contains links to the text of over 1000 bilateral and multilateral treaties and other instruments concerned with fisheries and marine living resource management. The cases database features material previously included in the journal *International Fisheries Law and Policy Review*. Documents database has links to the full text of 12,000 resolutions, regulations, action plans and other documents of international organizations. Site well presented but unfortunately appears not to have been updated since 2005.

2332 Spacelawstation.com
www.spacelawstation.com/
Portal to a wide range of legislation, case law, resources of international organizations and national bodies, especially the US government and its space agencies. Directories of space lawyers and educational institutions. Created by Jesse Londin, a New York-based lawyer and journalist, but the site appears not to have been maintained since 2005.

Discovering print & electronic resources

2333 ENTRI: Environmental Treaties and Resource Indicators
http://sedac.ciesin.columbia.edu/entri/
Site based at Columbia University, New York, which enables users to search for treaties by date, keyword and other fields. Usefully permits searchers to discover to which treaties a particular country or organization has signed up or is party. Layout of site and search screens rather basic but results are well worth making the effort.

2334 International environmental law and policy: a comprehensive reference source
D. Hunter, J. Salzman and D. Zaelke
www.wcl.american.edu/environment/iel/
Website based at the American University, Washington College of Law, intended to be used in conjunction with the authors' textbook but provides free access to a well laid-out and comprehensive bibliography. Annex I provides links to materials helpful when first starting to research the topic, Annex II to international organizations and Annex III a chronology of international environmental agreements. Apart from the US-bias, well recommended.

2335 The law of the sea: a select bibliography
United National Office for Ocean affairs & the Law of the Sea, 1985–, annual.
Commenced following the UN Convention on the Law of the Sea (1982) and covers books and articles – divided into over 25 detailed subject categories. Compiled by the official organization responsible for the topic area. Excludes publication by inter-governmental organizations but otherwise comprehensive and valuable.

Handbooks & manuals

2336 Yearbook of international environmental law
G. Ulfstein and J. Werksman, eds   Oxford University Press, 1990–.
ISSN 09651721.
Authoritative review of internationally significant
environmental legal developments. A 'year in review' section
summarizes year-on-year trends organized by subject matter,
key countries or regions and international governmental as
well as non-governmental organizations. Each volume
includes environmental bibliography as well as topical
articles and book reviews.

Laws of Human Rights

Introductions to the subject

2337 ASIL electronic resource guide: human rights
M. Hoffman, comp.
www.asil.org/resource/humrts1.htm
Comprehensive research guide with explanatory commentary
covering, among other matters, a brief history of human
rights intervention, methodology of human rights research,
where to start, primary and secondary sources and other
relevant websites. Thorough and regularly kept up to date by
the American Society of International Law.

**2338 Guide to international refugee law resources on
the web**
E. Mason, comp.
www.llrx.com/features/refugee.htm
Research guide first published in 2000 and revised in 2005.
Covers tracing international legal instruments, lists the
international bodies with annotations and links, tracing case
law, notes the main periodicals on the topic, tracing experts
and networking, bibliographic tools and guides – mainly
focuses on electronic sources.

2339 International protection of human rights
M.J. Raisch
www.law-lib.utoronto.ca/resguide/humrtsgu.htm
Research guide created in 2004 but regularly updated,
covering United Nations treaties and procedures, UN finding
aids in print, Council of Europe and finding its aids in print,
other human rights activities and treaties. Very full and
informative commentary with appropriate balance between
paper and electronic resources – recommended.

**2340 International women's human rights and
humanitarian law**
M.J. Raisch, comp.
www.law-lib.utoronto.ca/resguide/women2.htm
Research guide created in 2004 but regularly updated,
covering women's human rights in the context of
international law research, treaties and UN instruments,
intergovernmental organizations, violence against women,
global conferences, humanitarian law, women and
development, enforcement of women's rights, the European
system, the International Labour Organization and other
resources and selected journals. Very full and informative
commentary with appropriate balance between paper and
electronic resources – recommended.

**2341 Researching indigenous peoples' rights under
international law**
S.C. Perkins
http://intelligent-internet.info/law/ipr2.html
Extensive research guide with full commentary, created
originally in 1992 and updated in 2006. Focus is mainly on
paper sources. A work of considerable research and
scholarship.

2342 Researching international human rights law
M. Hoffman, comp.
www.law.berkeley.edu/library/online/guides/international_foreign/hum
anRights/index.html
Research guide revised in 2007 by the International and
Foreign Law Librarian at University of California, Berkeley,
Law Library. Covers general sources (bibliographies,
periodical indexes), international legal instruments, their
sources and tracing their status, case law, intergovernmental
and nongovernmental organizations, foreign law. Comprises
lists with very sparse commentary but the entire work is
comprehensive in scope.

2343 UNHR treaties
A.F. Bayefski
www.bayefski.com
Site created by Prof. A.F. Bayefski of York University, Toronto,
Canada, to enhance access by making materials associated
with the treaty system available in electronic and user-
friendly form. Provides an introduction to the treaty-making
system, the reform of the system, access to the text of the
treaties and amendments, information arranged by state and
by category of document and by theme or subject matter
(but only up to date to 2003). A unique and valuable site.

2344 United Nations research guide on human rights
www.un.org/Depts/dhl/resguide/spechr.htm
Research guide created and regularly maintained by staff of
the UN Dag Hammarskjöld Library. Focus is on the UN
bodies which contribute to making and enforcing human
rights law. Very full commentary and focused entirely on
electronic sources. Authoritative.

**2345 Update to annex: human rights, country and legal
information resources on the internet**
E. Mason, comp.
www.llrx.com/features/rsd_bib2.htm
Research guide compiled by a member of staff at the
Refugee Studies Centre, University of Oxford (q.v.) and
published in 2002. Covers legal information sources, both
international and national, human rights reports, news
services, area studies, lists of experts and organizations
offering commercial research and documentation services in
human rights. Listings are entirely of electronic sources.

Laws, standards, codes

2346 Basic documents on human rights
I. Brownlie, comp.   3rd edn, Oxford, 1992, 641pp. ISBN
0198256833.
Similar to Ghandi (q.v.) but more selective, though each
instrument is preceded by a short compiler's commentary
and a bibliography of references.

2347 Blackstone's international human rights documents

P.R. Ghandi, comp.   Blackstone Press, 2000.
Probably the most comprehensive collection of documents arranged in two sections: international and regional. Former includes mainly United Nations materials, the latter drawn from Europe, America, Africa and Arab organizations. Includes all treaties and declarations of significance. Documents arranged in chronological order under each main heading. No commentary and no information on status or coming into force.

2348 European Court of Human Rights: reports of judgments and decisions

Karl Heymanns Verlag KG, 1961–.
Commenced in 1961 but has undergone changes of name and content up to 1995. The official text of the decisions of the Court.

2349 European human rights reports

Sweet & Maxwell, 1979–.
English text of the judgements of the European Court of Human Rights, with added headnotes and summaries. Unofficial but published more quickly than the official series: *European Court of Human Rights: Reports of Judgments and Decisions* (q.v.).

2350 HUDOC: human rights documentation

http://cmiskp.echr.coe.int/tkp197/search.asp?skin=hudoc-en
Official database of the case law of the European Court of Human Rights, European Commission on Human Rights and the Committee of Ministers. Includes judgments, decisions, resolutions and reports. Searchable by a variety of fields in English or French. Under 'Help' is access to a 32-page guide in pdf format. The authoritative internet source for ECHR case law.

2351 International human rights reports

IHRR, School of Law, Nottingham University, 1994–, qtrly. £195. ISSN 1351542X.
Reproduces in English the text of statements of human rights issues made by international organizations, decisions and opinions of international organizations and the text of treaties. A key source.

2352 Refugee caselaw site

www.refugeecaselaw.org/
Site based at the University of Michigan Law School which collects, indexes and publishes selected recent court decisions that interpret the legal definition of the word 'refugee'. Includes cases from the highest national courts of Australia, Canada, France, Germany, New Zealand, Switzerland, the UK and the USA. Guided and quick searches available, complete with well designed search tutorial aids.

Official & quasi-official bodies

European Court of Human Rights
See entry no. 2257

2353 Inter-American Court of Human Rights

www.corteidh.or.cr/
Official site of the autonomous judicial institution of the Organization of American States established in 1979, whose objective is the application and interpretation of the American Convention on Human Rights and other treaties. Apart from information about the Court, its procedures and officials, access to the full text of decisions from 1987 onwards, the catalogue of the Court library (in Spanish only) and links to related organizations across the internet.

2354 United Nations High Commissioner for Human Rights

www.unhcr.org/cgi-bin/texis/vtx/home
Official site of the United Nations agency founded in 1952 to lead and coordinate international action to protect refugees and resolve refugee problems worldwide. Contains information on the human rights activities of the UN. Under 'Research/evaluation' links to RefWorld, a subscriber-only refugee encyclopedia and other links to 'Legal information', with access to national and international legal instruments on refugee law. An important site with much useful information but poorly presented, making navigation and location difficult.

Research centres & institutes

2355 Institute for the Study of Genocide

www.isg-iags.org/
A joint website: the non-profit-making institute founded in 1982 in New York to promote and disseminate scholarship and policy analyses on the causes, consequences and prevention of genocide. Site provides information about the two organizations, events, access to the full text of the newsletter. Basic bibliography. Useful, but evidence that site is updated at quite long intervals.

2356 Interights: International Centre for the Legal Protection of Human Rights

www.interights.org/
Official site of a non-governmental organization established in 1982 to develop the legal protection of human rights through effective use of international rights law. One of its most valuable features is the Commonwealth and International Human Rights Database containing over 2000 summaries of significant human rights decisions from domestic Commonwealth courts and from tribunals applying international human rights law such as the African Commission on Human and Peoples' Rights, the European Court of Human Rights and many more.

2357 International humanitarian law research initiative

www.ihlresearch.org/ihl
Official site of 'a research, policy and information project dedicated to the reaffirmation and development of international humanitarian law (IHL). Founded in 2002, the project is based at the Program on Humanitarian Policy and Conflict Research (HPCR) at the Harvard School of Public Health'. E-Library link contains the full text of news, research and analysis, judicial decisions, legal instruments and more, organized by region and topic.

Refugee Studies Centre, Queen Elizabeth House
See entry no. 1547

2358 Statewatch Observatory on EU Asylum & Immigration Policy
www.statewatch.org/
Official site of a non-profit civil rights organization, Statewatch, which provides a range of free and subscription news and more substantial information services on asylum and immigration policy within the EU and its constituent countries.

Associations & societies

2359 International Commission of Jurists
www.icj.org/sommaire.php3?lang=en
Official site of a body of eminent jurists founded in 1952 and dedicated to the primacy, coherence and implementation of international law and principles that advance human rights. Details the staff, programmes and events, and provides access to a 'legal resource centre' containing a searchable database of ICJ press releases, reports and other legal documents. Also database of publications produced since 1952.

International Committee of the Red Cross
See entry no. 1716

Discovering print & electronic resources

2360 Bibliography of research on international human rights law
D. Weissbrodt and M. Hoffman, comps
www1.umn.edu/humanrts/bibliog/BIBLIO.htm
Bibliography compiled for the University of Minnesota Human Rights Library. Covers the legal instruments produced by the major organizations (UN, ILO, UNESCO etc.), tracing the status of human rights instruments, legislative status of instruments, human rights case law etc., rules of procedure of official committees, research guides, refugee law and a list of selected textbooks. Comprehensive guide to mainly paper sources – no date of compilation of bibliography but could be as long ago as late 1990s.

2361 Bibliography on terrorism, bioterrorism, the Middle East and 9-11 related issues
C. Reynolds, comp.
www.llrx.com/features/terrorbiblio.htm
Listing of books compiled by the law librarian of a major San Francisco firm of lawyers and published in November 2001. Covers terrorism, bio-terrorism, Islam, Middle East, Afghanistan, US foreign policy – in need of updating but a useful starting point.

2362 NATLEX database
www.ilo.org/dyn/natlex/natlex_browse.home
Free, searchable database of over 55,000 records, covering 170 countries, providing abstracts of national labour, social security and related human-rights legislation maintained by the International Labour Office International Labour Standards Department. Contents browsable by country and subject and advanced search across all fields available.

2363 Netherlands Institute of Human Rights Library
www.sim.law.uu.nl/
The SIM documentation site of the Utrecht School of Law

has several free databases. Library covers books, serials, ratif (details of the ratification of international and regional human rights instruments) and the text of instruments. Case law provides access to the case decisions of a selection of international committees, courts and tribunals. Although user registration required, access is free.

Digital data, image & text collections

2364 Human rights network international
www.hrni.org/EN/default.html
Collection of online human rights materials created and maintained by the University of Brussels, Belgium. Divided into four categories: theory, rights and freedoms, protections and guarantees, and special focus. The whole range of forms of publications is included: treaties, conventions, cases, resolutions, books, articles, reports etc. References to paper versions of materials also provided. Not clear how up to date site is but not many references after 2004.

2365 Online human rights archive at Yale Law School
www.yale.edu/lawweb/avalon/diana/
Project Diana, part of the Avalon digital materials project based at Yale University, contains the text of major international human rights law cases and a wide range of international conventions, protocols and other documents, mostly originating from the United Nations. Searching facility across the collection available.

Directories & encyclopedias

2366 Encyclopedia of human rights
E. Lawson   2nd edn, Taylor & Francis, 1996, 1900pp. ISBN 9781560323624.
Compilation of human rights material arranged by subject with the full text of many instruments. Extensive bibliographies arranged by both subject and country.

Handbooks & manuals

2367 A systematic guide to the caselaw of the European Court of Human Rights
P. Kempees   Martinus Nijhoff, 1996–.
Arranged according to the structure of the Convention and its protocols, provides a summary of all the significant decisions of the Court under each. Easy to use but sometimes not entirely up to date.

2368 Yearbook of international humanitarian law
T.M.C. Asser Press. ISSN 13891359.
Articles and commentaries on current developments, reports on state practice, and documents with international humanitarian law as their focus. Available in paper format and electronically as part of Cambridge Journals Online.

2369 Yearbook of the European Convention on Human Rights
Martinus Nijhoff, 1958–.
Divided into three parts: part 1 includes basic texts and resolutions of the Consultative Assembly relating to the protection of human rights; part 2 reproduces information on the work of the EU, the Court of Human Rights and the

Committee of Ministers and part 3 includes materials from national parliaments and courts.

Laws Concerning Individuals

Introductions to the subject

2370 ASIL electronic resource guide: international criminal law
G.A. Partin, comp.
www.asil.org/resource/crim1.htm
Comprehensive research guide with explanatory commentary covering, among other matters, research guides and information networks, treaties, conventions and agreements, courts and tribunals, crime prevention, prosecution and criminal justice, sources of information on specific crimes, statistical sources, information clearinghouses and other related sources. Thorough and regularly kept up to date by the American Society of International Law.

2371 A research guide to cases and materials on terrorism
A. Grossman
www.nyulawglobal.org/globalex/Terrorism.htm
Research guide published in May 2006 covering general sources of information (including a list of websites of relevant international organizations), relevant case law (mainly US but also some UK and European), online articles, organized crime, extradition, deportation and refugees etc. Compiled by a lawyer rather than a librarian, so accent is on discussion of the law rather than the quality of the source website or paper publications.

2372 Update to international criminal law: a selective resource guide
M.J. Raisch and G. Partin
www.llrx.com/features/int_crim3.htm
Research guide published in 2001 and updated in 2002, covering a brief history of international criminal law, general background sources, treaty resources, the International Criminal Court (ICC), extradition, specific crimes. crime prevention and criminal justice. Full commentary on sources and covers both paper and electronic. Dated (pre-ICC operation) but still valuable.

Laws, standards, codes

2373 Annotated leading cases on international criminal tribunals
A. Klip and G. Sluiter, eds   Intersentia, 1999–.
Reproduces in English the full text of a selection of cases heard and decided by various International Criminal Tribunals for the Former Yugoslavia. Each case is accompanied by a brief commentary.

Official & quasi-official bodies

2374 International Criminal Court
www.icc-cpi.intl
Official site of the independent, permanent court that tries persons accused of the most serious crimes of international concern, namely genocide, crimes against humanity and war crimes. Includes details of the jurisdiction, procedures and officials of the Court. 'Legal tools' leads to an array of collections of the full text of documents created for, by and about the Court, links to related internet sites. A wealth of material well presented.

2375 Preparatory commission for the International Criminal Court
www.un.org/law/icc/prepcomm/prepfra.htm
Maintained by the United Nations Office of Legal Affairs, the site contains a selection of official documents issued since the first session of the Preparatory Commission founding the Court, including, among other materials, the Court's rules of procedure and evidence, elements of crimes, relationship of the Court to the UN.

2376 United States. Department of Justice, Computer Crime & Intellectual Property Section
www.cybercrime.gov
Clearing house for news, cases, legislation and US government information on computer crime, intellectual property, electronic evidence, internet-related crime.

Research centres & institutes

2377 International Centre for Criminal Law Reform & Criminal Justice Policy
www.icclr.law.ubc.ca
Established in 1991, the Centre is a Vancouver-based independent, non-profit-making institute affiliated to the United Nations. The Centre monitors activities in economic and organized crime. Site provides details of events, programmes of research and investigation, lists of publications, including model guidelines and strategies in various areas.

2378 International money laundering information network
www.imolin.org
Developed in 1996 under the auspices of the United Nations, the Network has the goal of assisting governments, organizations and individuals in the fight against money laundering. Site provides country pages with the full text of key national legislation on money laundering, international norms and standards, a reference section, including a bibliography of books and articles on all aspects of money laundering, and lists of new publications issued by governments and international organizations. Also, extensive list of links to related websites.

Associations & societies

2379 Coalition for the International Criminal Court
www.iccnow.org/
The Coalition is a worldwide network of over 2000 non-governmental organizations advocating the founding the International Criminal Court. Site includes details about the Coalition, history and current news about the work of the Court and progress towards ratification and implementation of the statute and other instruments connected with the Court, by member states of the United Nations.

Portal & task environments

2380 International criminal justice sources
www.criminology.fsu.edu/p/cjl-world.php
Created by Cecil Greek of Florida State University, this is a comprehensive list of links to websites for criminal law, law enforcement, crime prevention and peace-making. Includes listings for individual nations (including the UK).

Discovering print & electronic resources

2381 American Society of International Law resources on terrorism
www.asil.org/terrorind.htm
The Taskforce 'seeks to provide informed and informative debate on international law related to terrorism'. Site includes access to the full text of key treaties and conventions, articles written by law professors, roundtable conferences to discuss international terrorism. Unfortunately, the site appears not to have been added to since 2003 but still provides considerable background information to debate on the law.

2382 International Criminal Court: resources in print and electronic format
L. Louis-Jacques, comp.
www2.lib.uchicago.edu/~llou/icc.html
Annotated lists of references with the minimum of commentary and arranged by type of material, covering internet resources, followed by lists of books, journal articles and other resources (over 300 in the last three categories). Created in 1998 and updated in 2003 – a good starting point but now in need of revision, since the Court is now active.

2383 United Nations crime and justice information network
www.unodc.org/unodc/uncjin.html
Established by a United Nations mandate in 1986, the Network acts as an electronic clearinghouse for criminal justice-related matters. Site includes standards, documentation and statistics in one part and an 84-page directory of international and national organizations in another.

Handbooks & manuals

2384 IBA anti-money laundering forum: the lawyer's guide to legislation and compliance
www.anti-moneylaundering.org/index.htm
Site created by the International Bar Association (IBA) to assist the network of lawyers in dealing with current and proposed anti-money laundering legislation. Clickable world map leads to lists of countries and, for each, details of the authorities to whom money laundering should be reported, summaries of national and international legislation, national guidance to lawyers, case law and more. A valuable compendium.

Private International Law

aviation law • business law • commercial arbitration • conflict resolution • intellectual property law • trademarks • world trade law

Introductions to the subject

2385 ASIL electronic resource guide: private international law
L. Tang, comp.
www.asil.org/resource/pil1.htm
Comprehensive research guide with explanatory commentary covering among other matters the definition of private international law and discussing, with copious links and annotations, the research resources available about the international organizations involved, areas of law such as international sale of goods, international commercial arbitration, regional harmonization, private international law in the USA, resources on commercial databases, other internet research guides, law interest groups and sections. Thorough and regularly kept up to date by the American Society of International Law.

Official & quasi-official bodies

2386 Hague Conference on Private International Law
www.hcch.net/index_en.php
Official site of the international organization, with a membership of over 60 countries, set up to develop multi-lateral legal instruments to unify the rules of private international law. Provides links to the full text of its conventions, proceedings, handbooks and guides, work in progress, events and staff vacancies. Information clearly presented and authoritative.

2387 International Institute for the Unification of Private Law
www.unidroit.org
Official site of an international organization set up in 1926 as an auxiliary of the League of Nations, dedicated to the harmonization of private international law. Site includes texts of UNIDROIT conventions and other documents, work in progress, details of membership, access to the organization's online catalogue and details of depository libraries. A key site, well structured and easy to use.

Research centres & institutes

British Institute of International & Comparative Law
See entry no. 2145

Conflict Resolution Law

Introductions to the subject

2388 International commercial arbitration: locating the resources – revised
J.M. Wenger
www.llrx.com/features/arbitration2.htm#Locating%20Literature
Research guide published in 2004 covering treatises and major web resources, treaties and conventions, arbitral institutions, arbitration rules, national laws, model clauses, decisions and awards, specialized arbitration, locating literature and resources, associations. Extensive commentary and annotations to both paper and electronic resources. Comprehensive.

2389 International commercial arbitration: resources in print and electronic format
L. Louis-Jacques
www.lib.uchicago.edu/~llou/intlarb.html
Research guide originally created in 1998 and updated in 2003 by the Foreign and International Law Librarian at University of Chicago Law School, D'Angelo Law Library. Covers bibliographies and research guides, major treatises, journals, journal indexes, arbitration rules, statutes and model laws, arbitration reports, legal databases, arbitration courts and organizations, internet resources. Annotations to each entry are very brief but cover both paper and electronic sources.

2390 A selective guide to online international arbitration resources
G. Miccioli
www.llrx.com/features/intarbitration.htm
Research guide published in 2004, set out as a discussion rather than a list of the laws and legal materials. No contents list, so difficult to find way around – early sub-headings are to international organizations, followed by names of law databases. Of value but could have been better presented.

Laws, standards, codes

2391 Collection of ICC arbitral awards
Kluwer Law & Taxation Publishers, 1974–.
Contains the text of awards (judgments) in either English or French, according to the language used in giving the award. Also detailed chronological and subject indexes in both English and French.

2392 International commercial arbitration
E.E. Bergsten, ed. Oceana, 1980–. $995. ISBN 0379002663.
Contains reprints of international treaties, arbitral rules and other documents, national rules and enactments of over 100 countries. No annotations and only the briefest of introductory notes to each chapter. No index.

2393 Iran–United States Claims Tribunal reports
1981–.
Series of reports containing the text of decisions, awards and other materials emanating from the tribunal set up in 1981 to return Iran to the financial position which existed before the deposition of the Shah.

2394 Reports of international arbitral awards (Recueil des sentences arbitrales)
United Nations Office of Legal Affairs, 1918–, irregular.
Official reports of awards made by the Permanent Court of Arbitration at the Hague. Published in either English or French, depending on the language used in the Court hearing.

2395 World arbitration reporter
H. Smit and V. Pechota, comp. Butterworth Legal Publishers, 1986–. ISBN 0880630965.
Reprints the text on international conventions and other instruments, national legislation and arbitral rules for about 100 countries worldwide. Standard headings are used for court decisions and arbitral materials. Some short introductions to sections dealing with the history, role and responsibilities of international and national organizations, but otherwise no commentary. Bibliographies at the end of each section. Subject index. Updated at intervals.

Official & quasi-official bodies

2396 American Arbitration Association
www.adr.org
Official site of a private, non-profit organization founded in 1926. Provides under, link 'dispute resolution services', access to its own rules and procedures and, under 'education', access to international materials and text of a selection of US federal and state arbitration materials. Not an easy site to navigate to find key materials, and no site search facility.

2397 Arbitration Institute of the Stockholm Chamber of Commerce
www.sccinstitute.com/uk/Home/
Established in 1917 the Institute was recognized by the US and USSR as a neutral centre for the resolution of east–west trade disputes. Site includes full text of its rules, model clauses and the full text of selected arbitration laws for a few countries as well as international materials. Articles and awards printed in its publication *Stockholm International Arbitration Review* (formerly *Stockholm Arbitration Report*) available.

Court of Arbitration for Sport
See entry no. 4886

International Centre for Settlement of Investment Disputes
See entry no. 2424

2398 International Chamber of Commerce
www.iccwbo.org
Official site of the independent organization founded in 1919 and concerned with promotion of trade and the harmonization of trading practice, among whose activities include business arbitration and dispute resolution (see International Court of Arbitration), business self-regulation, fighting corruption and combating commercial crime. Site includes full text of its Rules of Arbitration, model or suggested clauses for use in contracts and business

agreements, and full text of its policy statements, codes and rules made since 1992. Key site within topic area.

2399 International Court of Arbitration
www.iccwbo.org/court/
Official site of the arbitration body formed in 1923 to resolve cross-border business disputes. It is part of the International Chamber of Commerce (ICC) (q.v.). Includes information about the Court and its procedures, various alternative dispute resolution services offered by the ICC: its dispute boards, ICC Centre for Expertise and DOCDEX service. Under links to the Court part of the site is access to a searchable database of details of where extracts from ICC arbitral awards have been published in print sources.

2400 Internet Corporation for Assigned Names & Numbers
www.icann.org
Organization responsible for the management of the generic, top-level internet domain names. Amongst detail about the organization, under Resources are details of its domain-name dispute resolution procedures.

2401 London Court of International Arbitration
www.lcia-arbitration.com/
Official site of one of the oldest arbitral institutions, established in 1892. Administers commercial arbitrations worldwide. Apart from information about the organization, includes full-text versions in nine languages of the LCIA Arbitration Rules and text of model clauses. Under 'links' there is access to key treaties, arbitration laws, other resources, including research guides.

2402 Permanent Court of Arbitration
www.pca-cpa.org
Official site of the court established in 1899 to 'administer arbitration, conciliation and fact finding in disputes involving various combinations of states, private parties and intergovernmental organizations'. Includes information about the court, the full text of its founding convention, rules of procedure, model clauses, UNCITRAL model rules etc. Free online access is provided to the full text of only a handful of recent decisions and documents of pending cases. Under 'arbitration links' an extremely valuable, detailed and annotated directory of arbitration websites and information on arbitration available online. A site full of valuable resources.

2403 World Intellectual Property Organization: Arbitration and Mediation Center
www.wipo.int/amc/en/index.html
Part of the specialized agency of the United Nations, offering alternative dispute resolution for private parties involved in international commercial disputes, especially entertainment, technology and other intellectual property. Includes full text of its Arbitration Rules in four languages and recommended contract clauses. WIPO Caseload Summary provides access to case examples only, of some of the disputes handled, but not full text. Site search facility. Entire site is easy to use.

Research centres & institutes

2404 Australian Centre for International Commercial Arbitration
www.acica.org.au
Founded in 1985, the Centre was founded to support and facilitate international arbitration and promote Australia as a venue for international commercial arbitration. Site includes the Centre's arbitration clauses and arbitration rules.

2405 Commercial Arbitration & Mediation Centre for the Americas
www.adr.org/sp.asp?id=22092
Hosted by the American Arbitration Association, the Centre seeks to provide commercial parties in the Americas with a forum for the resolution of private commercial disputes and is designed to be consistent with the North American Free Trade Agreement. Site includes its arbitration rules and model clause.

2406 European Court of Arbitration
http://cour-europe-arbitrage.org
A private organization, based in Strasbourg, specializing in swift arbitrations across Europe. Site can be accessed in several languages, the English section having details of the Court's arbitration rules. Other parts of the site lead only to an e-mail address.

2407 International Institute of Conflict Prevention & Resolution
www.cpradr.org
Official site of a US member-based, non-profit organization acting as a resource for lawyers seeking arbitrators and mediators and providing details of its arbitration clauses, rules and procedures.

Portal & task environments

2408 Lovells international arbitration guide
www.lovells.com/Arbitration/
Free site, though users need to register, created by a major UK and international firm of lawyers, providing a guide to arbitration, access to a drafting engine to permit the creation of arbitration clauses which can be printed or downloaded, links to a range of relevant sites of other institutions, associations and libraries, a library of international and national laws and much more.

Discovering print & electronic resources

2409 Kluwer Arbitration Online
www.kluwerarbtration.com
Site run by a major law publisher offering free access to search the full-text or summaries of key conventions, legislation, case law (decisions and awards), commentary drawn from a range of secondary publications and the 'Milan' bibliography on arbitration. The results of all searches are lists of citations but only subscribers to the site can go on to access the full text of materials.

Directories & encyclopedias

2410 Directory of arbitration web sites and information on arbitration available online
R.E. Goodman-Everard, comp.
www.arbitration-icca.org/directory_of_arbitration_website.htm
Hosted by the International Council for Commercial Arbitration, the directory was compiled by a practising South African lawyer and last checked in 2000. Some links are broken but the comprehensive list of websites, each entry with a few words of annotation, still has some value.

Business Law

Introductions to the subject

2411 ASIL guide to electronic resources for international law: international economic law
J.M. Wenger
www.asil.org/resource/iel1.htm
Comprehensive research guide with explanatory commentary covering, among other matters, an overview of international economic law research, international financial law, regional economic integration, international development law, private international law, international business regulation, intellectual property law, locating literature, other research guides and reference materials. Thorough and regularly kept up to date by the American Society of International Law.

2412 ASIL guide to electronic resources for international law: international intellectual property law
J. Franklin
www.asil.org/resource/ip1.htm
Comprehensive research guide with explanatory commentary covering, among other matters, an overview of international intellectual property law, general search strategies, research guides and bibliographies, primary (including national legislation and cases) and secondary sources, specialist organizations' electronic newsletters and discussion lists. Thorough and regularly kept up to date by the American Society of International Law.

2413 A guide on the harmonization of international commercial law
D.E. Alford
www.nyulawglobal.org/globalex/Unification_Harmonization.htm
Research guide published in 2005 covering the supra-national organizations, treaties, 'soft law' (standards, principles and best practices), research institutes, research guides and teaching materials. While mainly focusing on electronic sources (especially web-based) also includes print materials. Thorough and well presented.

2414 Legal protection of cultural property: a selective resource guide
L. Tang
www.llrx.com/features/culturalproperty.htm
Research guide by the reference librarian of Georgetown University Law Library, USA, published in 2004 and updated in 2006. Covers primary and secondary law sources, international and regional efforts to protect cultural property, responses to Nazi looting, cultural property stolen in Iraq.

Commentary and annotations are limited but guide covers both paper and electronic sources.

2415 New horizons: resources for international competition law research
J.M. Wenger
www.llrx.com/features/newhorizons.htm#International%20Organizations
Research guide published in 2005 covering sources of information about international organizations, regional bodies, national competition authorities, commentary on national laws, other research guides, periodical literature, specialized competition journals, speeches and press releases, dictionaries and glossaries, bibliographies and commercial databases. Covers both paper and electronic sources with often full annotations to particular materials.

2416 Update to researching intellectual property law in an international context
S. Weigmann
www.llrx.com/features/iplaw2.htm
Research guide published in 2000 by the Senior Reference Librarian and Instructor at the Boston University School of Law. Covers the nature of intellectual property (IP) law, international and regional IP law regimes, non-governmental organizations, institutes and associations, secondary sources, copyright, patent and trademark law sources, foreign laws on IP(with links to individual IP laws of each country). Full commentary covering both paper and electronic sources – very thoroughly researched but due for an update.

Laws, standards, codes

2417 Canadian tax treaties
http://fin.gc.ca/treaties/treatystatus_e.html
Part of the official site of the Canadian government Department of Finance, providing lists of tax treaty negotiations (to which Canada is party) which are about to or actually taking place, notices of treaties coming into force and the status of tax treaties to which Canada is party, arranged according to country. Links to the full-texts of treaties where available.

2418 Guides to European taxation
International Bureau of Fiscal Documentation, 1963–. ISBN 9076078106.
Series of looseleaf volumes setting out under standard subject headings a discursive commentary on the law relating to taxation in more than 20 European countries. References to original documents but none reproduced. Guide produced by an authoritative team of experts.

2419 International investment laws of the world
International Centre for the Settlement of Investment Disputes
Oceana.
Arranged alphabetically by country, reproduces legislation, rules and codes on investment within each country. No annotations or commentary and no indexes.

2420 International labour law reports
Sijthoff & Noordhoff, 1978–, annual. ISBN 908602798.
Reprints labour law judgments in English made by the highest courts in 10 jurisdictions, including the UK, USA and

a number of European and Asian countries. Each report is supported by an annotated commentary by the editorial team.

2421 International regulation of finance and investment
R.J. Rabalais, ed.   Oceana, 1992–. ISBN 0379012677.
Eight-volume reprint in English translation of international investment laws and the laws of a number of countries. Very little annotation or commentary. Minimal indexing.

2422 International tax treaties of all nations
W. Diamond and D. Diamond, eds   Oceana, 1975–.
Reprints in English the text of all tax treaties between two or more nations, with a short introductory paragraph of commentary by the editors of each document. Minimal indexing.

2423 Texts of treaties administered by WIPO
www.wipo.int/treaties/en/
Part of the World Intellectual Property Organization site providing access to the full text and summaries of all the treaties administered by the Organization, together with details of contracting parties.

Official & quasi-official bodies

2424 International Centre for Settlement of Investment Disputes
www.worldbank.org/icsid/index.html
Official site of the autonomous organization, with close ties to the World Bank, created in 1966 to facilitate the settlement of investment disputes between member governments and foreign members who are nationals of other member governments. Site includes information about the organization itself, the text of its founding convention, rules of procedure for arbitration proceedings, lists of pending and concluded cases with details of where the text is published and, under online decisions and awards, free access to full text of decisions from approximately mid-1990s onwards. Also free access to full text of ICSID's many publications. Finally, listings of over 1100 bi-lateral investment treaties between members organized chronologically and by country, together with valuable introduction and extensive bibliography to the topic. An important and comprehensive site.

2425 International Federation of Reproduction Rights Organizations
www.ifrro.org/
Official site of an international organization whose members are national copyright centres and associations with the aim of fostering international copyright principles. As well as information about the organization and its publications, site includes a free, searchable database of national and international copyright legislation submitted by members with web links to the full text, where available. Overall site search facility available.

2426 World Intellectual Property Organization
www.wipo.org
Comprehensive official site of 'a specialized agency of the United Nations, dedicated to developing a balanced and accessible international intellectual property (IP) system, which rewards creativity, stimulates innovation and

contributes to economic development while safeguarding the public interest'. At left of home page resources displayed according to audience (journalists, business, students) while at top, access to particular programmes of work and resources, including texts of treaties, conventions, regulations and other documentation. A key site.

Research centres & institutes

2427 American Antitrust Institute
www.antitrustinstitute.org/
Official site of an independent, Washington-based, non-profit education, research and advocacy organization, whose aim is to increase competition. Under link 'Antitrust resources' are commentary and materials relating to the US enforcement agencies, antitrust laws, guidelines etc. Also searchable listings and directories for US government antitrust organizations.

2428 Queen Mary Intellectual Property Research Institute
www.qmipri.org/index.html
Focus for research into all aspects of intellectual property law and policy. Site includes details of the staff and research work of the Institute, access to summaries of articles in the Institute publication *Queen Mary Studies in Intellectual Property Law and Policy* and details of the specialist library collection (catalogue not available on the internet). No site search facility but information clearly and attractively presented.

Associations & societies

2429 Commercial Bar Association
www.combar.com/
Formed in July 1989 to bring together self-employed barristers who practise in the field of international and commercial law. Contents of site include lists of publications (mainly responses to consultations and speeches), searchable directory of barristers specializing in commercial law and details of how to join the commercial bar. Site search facility.

2430 International Bar Association's Global Competition Forum
www.globalcompetitionforum.org/index.htm
Official site of the international organization, with 16,000 individual members and over 190 bar associations or law societies, set up to influence the development of international law reform and shape the future of the legal profession. Links to its own papers, reports and speeches, links to clearly displayed notes on and the full text of national laws (mainly on commercial law matters) of a very large number of countries worldwide, and web links to academic, commercial, professional and governmental organizations. A comprehensive collection of materials.

Portal & task environments

2431 Electronic library on international tax law and the CISG
www.cisg.law.pace.edu/
Collection of materials relating to the United Nations

Convention on Contracts for the Sale of Goods (CISG). Created and maintained by Pace University School of Law, New York. Includes full text of the CISG, annotated article by article guides to the CISG, searchable libraries of cases on the CISG, legislative history and scholarly writing. Free to use and well maintained for currency.

Handbooks & manuals

2432 Digest of commercial laws of the world
N.S. Kinsella, comp. Oceana, 1998–, 8 p.a. Looseleaf. ISBN 0379010003.
Compilation of expert commentary written by lawyers who practise in each of the 47 jurisdictions covered. Each country entry is to a standard structure to aid comparison. Includes sample forms, original articles and the full text of the most important treaties. Updated about eight times a year.

2433 Trademarks throughout the world
A.J. Jacobs 4th edn, Clark Boardman Callaghan, 1992. ISBN 9789991049052.
Country-by-country summary of the laws and procedures relating to the definition, registration and classification of trademarks. Appendices include the text of international laws on the topic. An invaluable work of reference.

2434 Transnational contracts
L.J. Bogard, G.W. Thompson and N. Peterson, eds Oceana. ISBN 0379102005.
Six-volume looseleaf publication containing a series of monographs on the planning and execution of international sales contracts in commercial law. Within volume 1, each monograph provides commentary on the stages in the process, the other volumes reprint the text of international treaties and other documents. Regulatory issues which arise in the international movement of goods are highlighted.

Trade Law

Introductions to the subject

2435 Revised guide to international law sources on the internet
M. Hoffman
www.llrx.com/features/trade3.htm
Research guide compiled in 2002 by the then International and Foreign Law Librarian at the E.B. Williams Law Library, Georgetown Law Centre, Washington, US. Covers an introduction to trade law, research guides, bibliographies, web collections on trade and economic law, international agreements, lists of international organizations, dispute settlement sources, US government and other country guides, statistics, sources of commentary and analysis. Although it covers only electronic sources the commentary is extensive, with comprehensive coverage of topics. A key site.

2436 WTO and GATT research
J. Rehberg
www.law.nyu.edu/library/wtoguide.html
Research guide compiled in 2006 by a member of the New York University School of Law Library. Extensive listings of

and commentary on both paper and electronic sources. Recommended.

Laws, standards, codes

2437 Lex Mercatoria
http://lexmercatoria.net/
Comprehensive site started by the Law Faculty of the University of Tromsø, Norway, hosted by the Law Faculty of the University of Oslo, Norway, in fellowship with the Institute of International Commercial Law, Pace University, School of Law, White Plains, New York, USA, and associated with Cameron May, a major UK and international firm of lawyers. Contains the full text of primary and secondary materials relating to, among others, international economic law, tax and financial regulation, trade law, carriage of goods and maritime law, private commercial law, commercial arbitration, international environmental law. A key site.

2438 World trade and arbitration materials
Kluwer, 1989–. ISBN 107226583.
Reproduces the text (without commentary) of recent arbitral awards, court decisions and policy documents of the World Trade Organization (q.v.).

2439 World trade law
www.worldtradelaw.net/
Private site owned by two former international trade lawyers, Simon Lester and Kara Leitner, and based in Florida, USA. Free part of site provides access to primary materials, including GATT/WTO and NAFTA decisions in summary and a large collection of web links to other sites. Subscriber-only section provides access to full text of reports and arbitrations, plus commentary and analysis on legal developments.

2440 World Trade Organization dispute settlement reports
Cambridge University Press, 1996–.
Official text of the decisions of the World Trade Organization Panel and Appellate Body on trade disputes and arbitration awards. Publication available in English, French and Spanish editions.

Official & quasi-official bodies

2441 United Nations Commission on International Trade Law
www.uncitral.org
Established by the United Nations in 1966, UNCITRAL exists to promote harmony and unity in international trade. Its arbitration rules may be used by any public or private organization. Extensive site provides access to information about UNCITRAL, text of UN resolutions and related documents, UNCITRAL texts, arbitration documents and case law (CLOUT): Case Law on UNCITRAL Texts, selected abstracts of decisions and awards from courts in countries which have enacted the UNCITRAL Model Law. A key site.

2442 World Trade Organization
www.wto.org/
Formed in 1995, the Organization deals with the rules of trade between nations at global and near-global level.

Between 1948 and 1994 the WTO was preceded by the General Agreement on Tariffs and Trade (GATT). Site includes details of history, operation, text of official and legal texts, publications, online access to some features of the catalogue of the WTO library and the WTO documents online database. Site easy to navigate and with clear explanations.

Discovering print & electronic resources

2443 Brooklyn Law School international trade web guide
http://brkl.brooklaw.edu/screens/itrade.html
Research guide prepared in 2002 by staff of the Brooklyn Law School Library, New York. Focuses on trade law research in the Americas. Covers only electronic sources, but some full annotations to key materials.

Aviation Law

Laws, standards, codes

2444 Shawcross and Beaumont air law
J.D. McClean, ed.   LexisNexis Butterworths, 1997–. ISBN 0406945810.
Originally published in 1936 as a hardback publication, it is now a three-volume looseleaf work. Volume 1 describes the law and administration of civil aviation, carriage by air and competition law relating to aviation. Volume 2 reprints the text of multilateral and bilateral agreements and European Community materials. Volume 3 reprints UK legislation. Comprehensive subject and other indexes. The standard work.

National Jurisdictions

Australian law • Canadian law • English law • Guernsey law • Irish Republic law • Isle of Man law • Jersey law • New Zealand law • Northern Ireland law • Scottish law • UK law • UK subordinate jurisdictions • US law • Welsh law

Australia

Introductions to the subject

2445 Concise legal research
R. Watt   5th edn, Federation Press, 2004, 271pp. ISBN 1862875154.
Includes chapters on citation practice, primary sources of law for the Commonwealth of Australia, New South Wales, selected Australian jurisdictions and the UK, delegated legislation, law reports and secondary source materials, finding the law of New Zealand, Canada, India, USA, international law and the legal materials of the European Union. Latest edition updated with references to internet sources. Publication grew out of a legal research skills programme at the University of Technology, Sydney, and is intended for an undergraduate audience.

2446 Effective legal research
I. Nemes and G. Cross   2nd edn, Butterworths, 2000, 448pp. ISBN 0409317063.

Introductory guide to legal research, with worked examples, flow charts, diagrams and exercises for both paper and electronic sources. Takes a 'form of publication' approach, with chapters on citations, electronic searching, internet-based research, secondary sources, case law, legislation and a final chapter taking an international perspective, briefly discussing legal research techniques for the UK, Canada, USA, European Union and international law in general.

2447 Finding the law: a guide to Australian secondary sources of legal information
C. Fong and G. Ellis   Legal Information Press, 1990, 698pp. ISBN 9780731695904.
Arranged by subject headings, lists digest, encyclopedias, commentaries (including books and journal articles), relating to Australian law. Accent on materials published between 1970 and 1990. Includes author index. Intended for law students, practitioners and researchers. Value now limited.

2448 Legal research materials and methods
E. Campbell, L. Poh-York and J. Tooher   4th edn, LBC Information Services, 1996, 516pp. ISBN 0455214115.
Covers the structure of the Australian legal system, sources of law, UK legislation, Australian government publications and parliamentary information, international law and the law of the European Union. Focus is mainly on paper sources, since it was published early in the web revolution, and on the needs of law practitioners rather than academics.

2449 Researching and writing in law
T. Hutchinson   2nd edn, Law Book Co, 2006, 461pp. ISBN 0455222789.
In two parts: first, discussing how to formulate and write a legal research project (aimed from the level of undergraduate assignment up to Master's level) and second, checklists for locating and validating the law, covering sources for the laws of Australia (including all the states), England, Canada, USA, European Union, New Zealand and India. Fully up to date with web addresses. The checklists laid out as tables, are an unusual yet very easy to use feature, aiding the selection of appropriate sources for the research query in hand.

2450 Update to researching Australian law
www.llrx.com/features/australian3.htm
Guide providing background information on the Australian legal system, institutions and materials such as legislation, cases, treaties and commentary on the law. Also lists main law publishers and principal texts selected by the author of the site, covering broad topic areas. An authoritative and frequently updated source compiled by Nicholas Pengelley, a well respected law librarian.

Terminology, codes & standards

2451 Australian and New Zealand legal abbreviations
C. Fong and A.J. Edwards   Australian Law Librarians Group, 1995, 126pp. ISBN 0959135987.
Alphabetical list of abbreviations for Australian and New Zealand law publications and some non-Australian and New Zealand publications which regularly include Australian and New Zealand law material. Aims to supplement the *Index to legal abbreviations and citations* (q.v.) and *Bieber's dictionary of*

legal abbreviations (q.v.). Covers acronyms for organizations and personalities within the legal systems.

2452 Australian guide to legal citation
Melbourne University Law Review Association, 1998, 158pp. ISBN 0734013485.
A style guide to the way in which Australian law materials should be cited, based on best practice and clarifying existing customs. Also includes style guides to the law publications of Canada, USA, New Zealand, the UK and for international legal materials. Carries some weight as an authority, since it is prepared by one of the leading Australian law journals.

2453 Australian legal citation: a guide
C. Fong　Propect, 1998, 154pp. ISBN 1863161171.
Style guide in two parts: part 1 covers the principles of legal citation, part 2 comprises a list of Australian law reports and journals with recommended or preferred ways of citing them. Published around the same time as the *Australian guide to legal citation* (q.v.) but without the authority of that publication.

Laws, standards, codes

2454 Acts of the Parliament of the Commonwealth of Australia passed during the year
Australian Government Publishing Service, 1901–, annual. ISSN 07276311.
The official version of federal legislation, published as a consolidated set in 12 volumes covering 1901 to 1973, supplemented by annual volumes of new Acts, with reprints in pamphlet form of individual Acts which have been amended.

2455 Australasian Legal Information Institute: AustLII
http://Austlii.law.uts.edu.au/
Free public information service of legislation, treaties, decisions of courts and tribunals and, in addition, a selection of materials from other public organizations such as law reform bodies and government commissions. Contains the full text databases of most Australian legislation and court decisions. However, legislation is displayed in its un-amended form as originally passed and there are not the links to commentary on legislation and cases found in some commercial services. Operated jointly by the faculties of Law at the University of Technology, Sydney and the University of New South Wales. Funded by a wide rage of stakeholders. Winner of many website awards. Has become the model for many legal information institutes which have developed across the world.

2456 The Australian Law Journal reports
Lawbook Company, 1927–, monthly. ISSN 00049611.
Published as part of the *Australian Law Journal* and provides 'advance reports' (i.e. unapproved reports) of the decisions of the High Court, prior to their publication in *Commonwealth Law Reports* (q.v.).

2457 The Australian law reports
Butterworths, 1974–. ISSN 03100014.
Reports in full text cases decided in a wide range of federal courts with greater speed than some other publications. The

series is not authorized (that is, the judges do not check the reports before publication).

2458 ComLaw
www.comlaw.gov.au/
Public access to Bills, Acts and regulations of the Commonwealth of Australia, maintained by the Australian Attorney-General's Department in their up-to-date version (called compilations), including amendments and repeals. Includes the Federal Register of Legislative Instruments listing legislative items and subsequent amendments and repeals. ComLaw includes the former SCALEplus service (scaleplus.law.gov.au) of compilations of Acts.

2459 The Commonwealth law reports: cases determined in the High Court of Australia
Lawbook Company, 1905–, irregular. ISSN 00697133.
Authorized reports (that is reports approved by the judges before publication) of cases principally decided in the High Court of Australia.
'Probably the most widely used and important of all Australia's report series.' (Watt R, *Concise legal research*. Federation Press 1993, p61.)

2460 Commonwealth statutory rules
A consolidated set of the secondary federal legislation published in 1956, supplemented by annual volumes of new statutory rules together with tables of regulations made and amended.

2461 Federal Court reports
1984–.
The authorized reports of the Federal Court.

2462 Federal law reports
1957–.
Reports cases heard in the state courts exercising federal jurisdiction, courts of the two Territories and some other categories of court.

2463 LexisNexis
www.lexisnexis.co.uk/news_and_business/index.asp?business_home.html
Full text, subscriber-only database covering a range of law reports and law-finding tools (e.g. Butterworths Current Law, q.v.) for the federal jurisdiction of Australia.

2464 Westlaw UK
http://westlaw.co.uk
Subscriber-only database, including an Australian law library with the consolidated version of the Acts of the Commonwealth of Australia, the full text of reported and unreported decisions of the High Court of Australia and the Federal Court of Australia.

Official & quasi-official bodies

2465 Australia. Attorney-General's Department (Commonwealth)
www.ag.gov.au/
Provides expert support to the government in the maintenance and improvement of Australia's system of law, justice, national security and emergency management. Site

includes text of press releases, speeches, annual reports and statements.

2466 Australian Human Rights & Equal Opportunity Commission
www.hreoc.gov.au/index.html
National independent statutory body responsible for inquiring into alleged infringements under anti-discrimination and human rights legislation, including monitoring the enjoyment or otherwise by indigenous people of their rights under the law and sex discrimination in the workplace.

2467 Australian Law Reform Commission
http://alrc.gov.au/
National independent statutory body responsible for inquiring into areas of law reform at the request of the Attorney-General of Australia and making recommendations to government. Site provides free access to all of its reports and many other related publications.

Associations & societies

2468 Australian Bar Association
http://austbar.asn.au/
Represents the interests at federal level of barristers who are members of the state Bars. Site has links to directories of barristers in the individual states and the text of some Bar publications.

2469 Australian Law Librarians' Association
www.allg.asn.au/index.htm
Formerly the Australian Law Librarians' Group, the association aims to promote a cooperative network for Australian law libraries and librarians, to provide forums for continuing education programmes and conferences and to lobby to promote the interests of law libraries and access to legal information within the wider community. Publishes quarterly journal, *Australian Law Librarian* (not available on website). Note that the web address given here is due to change with the name change of the association.

2470 Law Council of Australia
http://lawcouncil.asn.au/
Aims to represent the legal profession at national level, to speak on behalf of its constituent bodies (the state and territory professions) on national issues affecting the legal profession and to promote the administration of justice, access to justice and general improvement of the law. Site includes press releases, publications, policies, guidelines and links to related sites.

Libraries, archives, museums

2471 National Library of Australia
www.nla.gov.au/
Major collection of legislation, cases, law and commentary on the laws of Australia and the Asia/Pacific region. Some commercial law databases are available to the public in the Reading Rooms. No links from top level pages but details of law material given at
nla.gov.au/apps/eresources/item?id=1501&laoditem=true

Portal & task environments

2472 Australian Law Online
http://australianlawonline.gov.au/accesspoint?action=menuHome
Portal website providing access to law and justice-related information and services of the Australian government and to a selection of non-government organizations. Topics are described in plain English rather than legal jargon. Site includes a search facility to aid selection of the most appropriate pages and links on the site.

2473 WebLaw
http://weblaw.edu.au/weblaw/index.phtml
Free subject gateway to quality-assessed law websites maintained cooperatively by a large number of Australian universities and government organizations, including the Commonwealth Parliamentary Library and Australian Law Reform Commission. Each subject section is arranged according to type of legal material and each source briefly described. A search facility permits searching across the entire site.

Discovering print & electronic resources

2474 The Australian digest: a digest of the reported decisions of the Australian courts and of Australian appeals to the Privy Council
3rd edn, Law Book Co, 1988–. Looseleaf.
Summarizes reported Australian cases from 1825 onwards arranged under broad subject headings. Each subject title is updated by annual supplements filed at the back and cumulated at the year end. Monthly updating achieved through the *Australian Legal Monthly Digest* (q.v.).

2475 Australian law on the internet
www.nla.gov.au/oz/law.html
Selection of Australian law website links, grouped by jurisdiction. Site compiled by staff of the National Library of Australia.

Index to legal periodicals and books
See entry no. 2904

2476 Wicks subject index to Commonwealth legislation
B.M. Wicks   Law Book Co, 1989–, annual. ISSN 10343822.
First published in 1975, the subject index is in two parts: first, Acts of the Parliament of the Commonwealth of Australia and, second, Regulations made under those Acts. Within each part the titles of new legislation are arranged under broad subject headings. Each entry is very brief, so it is important to use the lists in conjunction with the contents pages of the Acts and Regulations themselves to discover a more detailed breakdown of subjects.

2477 World law: Australia
www.worldlii.org/catalog/1.html
Comprehensive list of links to websites of Australian law and legal information, arranged by jurisdiction or subject or organization, and with search facility across all entries. Very brief annotations to each link. Part of the World Legal Information Institute service developed by the Australasian Legal Information Institute (q.v.).

Directories & encyclopedias

2478 **Australian legal directory**
Law Council of Australia, 1977–, annual. ISSN 0155297X.
Prepared from information available to the Australian Law
Council and associated bodies. It is in three parts: listing by
Australian state and town of solicitors' firms, companies,
government organizations and barristers. Second part is an
alphabetical list of the names of legal practitioners and the
third part an alphabetical directory of law firms. Value
limited since part 1 gives contact information only and there
is no index or information on areas of practice specialization.

2479 **Blackstone's Australian legal words and phrases
simplified**
J.M. Bishop   Blackstone Press, 1993, 302pp. ISBN 1875114297.
Basic dictionary to the use of legal language in Australia.
Accent is on words and phrases used in general legal
practice, especially business and commerce. Few words or
phrases for criminal law. Designed for use by legal assistants
and lay people. Appendix of diagrams of the Australian court
structure and a bibliography of other law dictionaries.

2480 **Butterworths concise Australian legal dictionary**
P. Butt, ed.   3rd edn, LexisNexis Butterworths, 2004, 526pp. ISBN
0409321230.
Contains over 8000 terms presented in their Australian
context, supported by references to the authority for the
definition in legislation and case law. Definitions drafted by
120 experts from a diverse range of legal backgrounds.
Includes Latin words and phrases, biographical entries for
significant legal historians, scholars, judges, old English
terms, international law terms, brief descriptions of
landmark decisions of the High Court of Australia. Copious
appendices, including the text of the Australian
Commonwealth constitution, preferred citations for law
reports and popular names of Australian cases. Current, 3rd
edition, is an update of *Butterworths Australian legal dictionary*.

2481 **Halsbury's laws of Australia**
Butterworths, 1991–. ISBN 0409304360.
Entirely looseleaf encyclopedia in over 30 volumes, covering
the whole law of Australia. Aims to provide a narrative
statement on all law topics for all nine Australian
jurisdictions, with copious footnotes to original legislation
and case law. Does not discuss the law but merely states the
principles. Comprehensive subject index, table of cases and
table of statutes. Entire work updated monthly. The
Australian equivalent of *Halsbury's laws of England* (q.v.). In
direct competition with the *Laws of Australia* (q.v.).

2482 **Laws of Australia**
Lawbook Company.
Entirely looseleaf encyclopedia covering the whole law of
Australia, regularly updated by supplements inserted at the
end of each subject section. In direct competition with
Halsbury's Laws of Australia (q.v.).

2483 **Lawyers.com.au**
www.lawyers.com.au/
Free-to-use directory of lawyers practising in Australia.
Searchable three different ways: alphabetically, by practice
area and postcode. Each entry contains firm profile and
contact details. Legal professionals pay an annual fee to be
listed.

Keeping up to date

2484 **Australian current law**
Butterworths. ISSN 00450405.
Aims to keep *Halsbury's laws of Australia* (q.v.) up to date but
incidentally can be used as a current awareness service.
Includes summaries of latest developments in legislation and
case law and lists of recent books and articles published.
Since 1991 published in two separate series: *Australian
current law legislation* (q.v.) and *Australian current law reporter*
(q.v.).

2485 **Australian current law legislation**
Butterworths, 1991–, monthly. ISSN 10360425.
Details recent legislation and legislative amendments for all
Australian jurisdictions. No commentary or abstracts just
one- or two-line 'alerts' for each entry. Also available as
subscriber-only CD or web service. Competes with *Australian
legal monthly digest* (q.v.).

2486 **Australian current law reporter**
Butterworths, 1991–, monthly. ISSN 10360425.
Digests the unreported (that is, as yet unpublished)
judgments of a wide range of Australian federal and
specialist courts and tribunals. Also available as subscriber-
only CD or web service. Competes with *Australian legal
monthly digest* (q.v.).

2487 **Australian Law Librarian**
Australian Law Librarians' Association, 1992–, qtrly. $A115.00
annually. ISSN 10396616.
Official, quarterly journal of the Australian Law Librarians'
Association (q.v.) containing articles and news of law
libraries, legal information and publishing.

2488 **Australian legal monthly digest**
Law Book Co, 1947–, monthly. ISSN 00040646.
Aims to keep *The Australian digest* (q.v.) up to date but
incidentally can be used as a current awareness service.
Comprises two monthly booklets, one a digest of recent
developments in the law, with summaries of latest
developments in legislation, case law, recent journal articles
and notes appearing in selected Australian and overseas
journals and other sources, such as official publications, with
full bibliographical references to the original materials.
Second booklet comprises tables and indexes. Competes
with the both *Australian current law legislation* (q.v.) and
Australian current law reporter (q.v.).

Canada

Introductions to the subject

2489 **Banks on using a law library: a Canadian guide to
legal research**
M.A. Banks and K.E.H. Foti   6th edn, Carswell, 1994, 334pp. ISBN
045955252X.
Well respected and thorough guide to the contents and use
of a Canadian law library and electronic law resources – but
pre-dates the internet. The first edition, published in 1969,
was intended for first-year law undergraduates. The addition
of a considerable amount of more detailed material now

puts it in the class of major reference work rather than student guide.

2490 Best guide to Canadian legal research
www.legalresearch.org/
Free website providing advice and guidance on strategies and techniques for researching Canadian law, lists and guides to electronic law sources, researching federal and provincial legislation effectively and links to websites on researching the laws of other jurisdictions. Site compiled by Catherine Best, a research lawyer with a major law firm and Adjunct Professor of Law at the University of British Columbia.

2491 The Canadian legal system
G.L. Gall   5th edn, Carswell, 2004, 713pp. ISBN 0459241532.
Covers the history, sources and divisions of Canadian law, constitutional structure and institutions, federalism and the role of the judiciary and the legal profession. Extensive bibliographies of books and articles at the end of each chapter. Aimed at the law student and general reader but takes a jurisprudential and philosophical, rather than practical, approach to the Canadian legal system.

2492 Legal research handbook
D.T. MacEllven [et al.]   5th edn, LexisNexis Butterworths, 2003, 506pp. ISBN 0433437693.
Originally based on lecture notes but now much supplemented, this guide focuses on Canadian legal materials but also includes chapters on English, French, European Union, American, Australian and New Zealand law. Text aims to be correct to June 2003. Viewed as the standard work, simply referred to as 'MacEllven'.

2493 Legal writing and research manual
M.J. Iosipescu and P.W. Whitehead   6th edn, LexisNexis Butterworths, 2004, 247pp. ISBN 0433442794.
Covers an introduction to the Canadian legal research, the primary and secondary sources of law, computerized legal research, legal writing, writing a brief and a factum and the general rules of citation. Appendices on the recommended methods of citing legal materials and lists of common abbreviations. Aimed at first-year law students to aid not only their research but also their writing and drafting skills, so covering some different ground to MacEllven's *Legal research handbook* (q.v.).

2494 The practical guide to Canadian legal research
R. Castel and O.K. Latchman   2nd edn, Carswell, 1996. ISBN 9780459554309.
Systematic guide to the conduct of Canadian legal research, including not only descriptions of a wide variety of legal materials but also chapters on research techniques and strategies and guidelines for writing law essays and research memoranda. Brief chapters on English and American legal research. Probably more accessible and relevant to the needs of a law student than *Banks on using a law library* (q.v.).

2495 Researching Canadian law
www.nyulawglobal.org/globalex/Canada.htm
Free-to-use, comprehensive research and resource guide for Canada describing the legal system, its literature, law schools and the legal profession, law libraries, publishers, dictionaries, directories, discussion lists and more. Written by Ted Tjaden, a lawyer-librarian at the Bora Laskin Law Library, University of Toronto, and published in 2005.

Terminology, codes & standards

2496 Canadian guide to uniform legal citation (Manuel canadien de la référence juridique)
6th edn, Thomson Carswell, 2006. ISBN 0459243942.
Bilingual style guide setting out the general rules for citation practice, covering legislation and case law for Canada, the UK, the USA, France, New Zealand, Singapore, South Africa and from electronic sources, government documents, international law and secondary sources. Includes many examples to assist interpretation. Bilingual subject index. Appendices of recommended or preferred citations to law reports and journals.

Dictionaries, thesauri, classifications

2497 Canadian law dictionary
J.A. Yogis   5th edn, Barron's Educational Series, 2003, 276pp. ISBN 0764125699.
Brief entries include short quotations or summaries from legislation or case law, with full bibliographical citations to the original publication. Focuses on Canadian usage. Appendices include extracts from key Canadian legislation, lists of common abbreviations and bibliographies of books and articles used in the compilation of the dictionary. Intended for the law student or lay person unfamiliar with basic legal terminology.

2498 The dictionary of Canadian law
D.A. Dukelow   3rd edn, Carswell, 2004, 1429pp. ISBN 045924129X.
Comprehensive dictionary to legal words and phrases based on Canadian usage, drawn from legislation and case law. Entries have brief quotations from original sources with full bibliographical references attached. Includes Latin as well as English phrases.

2499 The encyclopedia of words and phrases and legal maxims
G.D. Sanagan, ed.   3rd edn, Richard de Boo, 1979–. ISBN 0888200633.
Alphabetical listing of words and phrases extracted from Canadian judicial decisions and legislation, with summaries of the definition given by judges and legislators. Full bibliographical citations to the original publications. Under each entry definitions for each Canadian province are noted separately. Looseleaf format, updated with blue-page cumulative supplements filed at the front of each of the four volumes.

2500 A handbook of Canadian legal terminology: revised and updated
W.J. Flynn   Stoddart, 1986, 117pp. ISBN 0773751076.
Very brief (often only one line) entries for about 1200 legal terms used in the Canadian legal system. Includes Latin phrases. Intended for lay people, paralegals, business people, social workers, and students not requiring a technical explanation.

2501 Words and phrases judicially defined in Canadian courts and tribunals (Termes et locutions definés par les tribunaux canadiens)
Carswell, 1993. 8 volumes.
Compiled by a team of lawyers to identify from case law over 50,000 'considerations' of words and phrases by the

Canadian courts and tribunals. Each entry has a brief summary or quotation from an original source, with a full reference to the original publication attached. Many cross-references. Can search by jurisdiction, area of law, name of judge and level of court. Each volume kept up to date by annual, cumulative supplement published in softback.

Laws, standards, codes

2502 Annual volumes of statutes
1867–, annual.
Official, bound volumes of the Acts passed by the federal Parliament of Canada each calendar year.

2503 Canada Federal Court reports (Recueil des arrêts de la Cour fédérale du Canada)
Queen's Printer for Canada, 1971–. ISSN 03842568.
Official reports of all cases decided in the Federal Court. The text is in both English and French. The Canadian courts prefer citation to the versions of cases in this series over any other publication. Reports of the Federal Court are available on the internet from 1993 onwards.

2504 Canada Gazette (Gazette du Canada)
http://canadagazette.gc.ca/index-e.html
Official newspaper of the federal government of Canada. Amendments to the Canadian Constitution in the form of proclamations and proposed regulations are published in Part I. Subordinate legislation in the form of regulations is published in Part II. Part III contains the text of recently passed Acts of the Canadian Parliament. Available on the internet from January 1998 onwards.

2505 Canada law reports. Exchequer Court of Canada
Registrar of the Court, 1923–1971. ISSN 03842517.
Official reports of the Exchequer Court, continuing the *Reports of the Exchequer Court of Canada* (q.v.) and, in turn, continued by *Canada: Exchequer Court reports* (q.v.).

2506 Canada law reports. Supreme Court of Canada
F.A. Acland, 1923–1970. ISSN 03842509.
Official reports of the Supreme Court, continuing the *Reports of the Supreme Court of Canada* (q.v.) and, in turn, continued by *Canada: Federal Court reports* (q.v.).

2507 Canada Supreme Court reports (Recueil des arrêts de la Cour Suprême du Canada)
Registrar, Supreme Court of Canada, 1970–. ISSN 00454230.
Official reports of all cases decided in the Supreme Court. The text is in both English and French. The Canadian courts prefer citation to the versions of cases in this series over any other publication. Reports of the Supreme Court are available on the internet from 1985 onwards.

2508 Canadian legal information institute
www.canlii.org/
Free-public information service containing the full text of most Canadian federal and provincial legislation, cases and commentary. The component collections are arranged by jurisdiction but there is a cross-site search facility. It is important to check whether the text of legislation retrieved is consolidated (i.e. takes account of amendments and repeals). The case law lacks the added links to commentary provided by some of the commercial databases.

2509 Consolidated regulations of Canada
1978.
The latest consolidated set of regulations for Canada that were in force on 31 December 1977. Regulations arranged under broad subjects and with all amendments etc. included. A quarterly list published in *Canada Gazette* Part II (q.v.) indicates more recent regulations and their effect on those included in the 1978 consolidation. Although these are the official indexes and supplements, the unofficial *Canada regulations index* (q.v.) is to be preferred for ease of use and added features.

2510 Dominion law reports: a weekly series of reports of cases from all the courts of Canada
Canada Law Book, 1912–. ISSN 00125350.
Unofficial cross-Canada law reports, including cases decided in both the federal and provincial courts. The reports are in full text in English. There is duplication with other series of federal and provincial law reports. Nevertheless, they are Canada's national law reports and probably the most widely held by law libraries outside Canada.

2511 Federal trial reports
Maritime Book Co, 1986–.
Unofficial reports of cases heard in the Trial Division of the Federal Court.

2512 LexisNexis Butterworths
www.lexisnexis.com
Full-text subscriber-only database, including comprehensive coverage of current Canadian federal legislation. Associated with Quicklaw (q.v.), with access to consolidations of statutes and regulations. Also full text of a number of key law reports such as *Dominion law reports* (q.v.), *Exchequer Court cases* (q.v.) and cases of the federal and supreme courts.

2513 National reporter: a series of law reports for the publishing of judgements of the Supreme Court of Canada and the Federal Court of Canada
Maritime Law Book, 1974–. ISSN 0317641X.
Unofficial series of reports, including a wider range of federal cases than the two official series *Canada: Federal Court reports* and *Canada: Supreme Court reports*). There is considerable duplication with the official series but the *National reporter* publishes the text of decisions more rapidly and the indexing of material is better.

2514 The provincial statutes of Canada
Government Printer, 1841–.
Published as a supplement to the *Canadian Gazette* (q.v.) – the authoritative version. Available in both printed and electronic form.

2515 Quicklaw
www.lexisnexis.ca/ql/en/about/about.html
Previously known as QL or QUIC/LAW, this is the main Canadian commercial, subscriber-only, online full-text law database, including both reported and unreported cases, federal legislation, commentary and current awareness services. Cross-database and content-specific searching are available. The value-added elements include the links created between the various source materials, the ability to select how to display results and set up personal alerts to new developments.

2516 Reports of the Exchequer Court of Canada
Queen's Printer, 1891–1923. ISSN 03842533.
Usually referred to as the Exchequer Court reports, these are the official reports of cases decided by one of the federal courts. Continued by a set combining the reports of both courts under the title *Canada Law reports* (q.v.).

2517 Reports of the Supreme Court of Canada
Queen's Printer, 1878–1923. ISSN 03842495.
Usually referred to as the Supreme Court reports, these are the official reports of cases decided by one of the federal courts. Continued by a set combining the reports of both courts under the title *Canada Law reports* (q.v.).

2518 Revised statutes of Canada, 1985: prepared under the authority of the Statute Revision Act (Lois révisées du Canada, 1985: revision réalisée sous le régime de la Loi sur la révision des lois)
Queen's Printer, 1985–1993. Looseleaf.
The most recent consolidation of federal primary legislation in bound volumes and looseleaf format up to date to 31 December 1984. The text of Acts is arranged under broad subject headings based on the English title of the Act. A series of supplements contain Acts published more recently than the main volumes. Acts are printed in parallel columns in English and French.

2519 Statutory orders and regulations
Government Printer, 1947–.
Published as a supplement to the Canadian Gazette (q.v.) – the authoritative version. Available in both printed and electronic form.

2520 Westlaw International
http://westlawinternational.com
Subscriber-only database containing full text of Supreme Court, Federal Court, Exchequer Court and Quebec decisions of national importance, topic–based law reports, the full text of legislation on a range of topics and the full text of the Canadian Abridgement (q.v.).

2521 Westlaw UK
www.westlaw.co.uk
Subscriber-only database, including a Canadian library with federal, provincial and territorial statutes currently in force in Canada as well as recently enacted legislation not yet in force, an English-language version of the Consolidated Regulations of Canada, and the full text of decisions of the federal, provincial and territorial courts.

2522 WestlaweCARSWELL
www.westlawecarswell.com
Subscriber-only internet-based research service for Canadian law, comprising a number of separate value-added products. They include LawSource (Canadian cases, statutes, citators, case digests, finding tools and commentary) and a number of topic specific databases such as CriminalSource.

Official & quasi-official bodies

2523 Canada. Department of Justice
http://canada.justice.gc.ca/en/index.html
Government department responsible for ensuring an accessible, efficient and fair system of justice and providing legal services to the government, its departments and agencies. Site provides access to the full text of a departmental publications and has links to the Justice Laws website (q.v.).

2524 Justice Laws website
http://laws/justice.gc.ca/en
Official website of the Department of Justice for Canada, containing a free database of the consolidated (that is, amended and in force) Acts and regulations of Canada. Subject, title and chapter number searches available and supported by clearly presented help pages. Links also provided to a range of related Canadian legal sources on the web.

Associations & societies

2525 Canadian Bar Association
www.cba.org/CBA/Gate.asp
The professional association representing lawyers, judges, notaries, law teachers and law students across Canada. Aims include to improve the law and the administration of justice, improve access to justice, equality in the legal profession and the justice system. Site includes text of many of the Association's publications but some, including the directory of members, are available only to CBA members.

2526 Federation of Law Societies of Canada
www.flsc.ca/
The national coordinating body of the 14 law societies in Canada which have responsibility to regulate Canada's lawyers and Quebec's notaries. Includes links to the Acts, regulations and codes of conduct of all the law societies it represents.

Libraries, archives, museums

2527 University of Toronto, Bora Laskin Library
www.law-lib.utoronto.ca/
Maintains it has over 250,000 volumes, including the primary law of Canada, the USA and UK and selected other jurisdictions, and subscribes to over 700 scholarly law periodicals.

2528 York University (Canada), Law Library
http://Library.osgoode.york.ca/
The Law Library of Osgoode Hall Law School, York University maintains it 'has the largest collection of any law library in the British Commonwealth, currently approaching 500,000 volumes, which includes a unique collection of Canadian legal texts and primary sources'.

Portal & task environments

2529 Bora Laskin Law Library – legal resources
www.law-lib.utoronto.ca/resources/index.htm
Extensive, quality-controlled list of links to websites of use to the Canadian law researcher. At the time of compiling this entry the currency of information was not as good as other web gateways.

2530 Canadian legal resources
www.gahtan.com/cdnlaw/
Maintains it provides a gateway to over 1400 law websites relevant to Canadian law. Sites arranged by topic but no annotations are provided. Users may suggest sites for inclusion. Created and maintained by a Toronto law attorney, Alan M. Gahtan.

2531 LexUM
www.lexum.umontreal.ca/
Comprehensive gateway site listing, under very broad headings, annotated links to hundreds of websites containing law resources or run by law organizations, both academic and professional. Cross-site search facility is available and the entire site can be read in either English or French.

2532 World law: Canada
www.worldlii.org/catalog/213.html
Comprehensive list of links to websites of Canadian law and legal information, arranged by jurisdiction or subject or organization and with search facility across all entries. Very brief annotations to each link. Part of the World Legal Information Institute service developed by the Australasian Legal Information Institute (q.v.).

Discovering print & electronic resources

2533 Canada regulations index (Index des règlements du Canada)
Carswell, 1983–, monthly.
Unofficial but comprehensive listing of regulations included in the Consolidated Regulations of Canada, 1978 and the Canada Gazette (for both titles see above).

2534 The Canadian abridgment
3rd edn, Thomson Carswell, 2003.
The most comprehensive and widely available digest of Canadian case law, drawn from the Supreme Court, all federal and common law provincial courts, decisions of federal significance from the courts of Quebec (which has its roots in French as well as English law). The digested (summarized) cases are arranged under subject headings. The publication is kept up to date through issues of Canadian Current Law – Case Law Digests. Entire service available as a subscriber-only database, Canadian Law Online (CLO). The Canadian Abridgment also includes a case citator, tables of the judicial consideration of statutes, rules, interpretation of words and phrases and an index to legal literature. Paper version updated by softcover supplements. Available electronically as part of the WestlaweCARSWELL database (q.v.).

2535 Canadian case citations (Références jurisprudentielles Canadiennes)
Carswell, 1992–. ISSN 11926813.
National case citator in 22 volumes, providing the case name, where the case was reported (that is, published), subsequent decisions or developments in the same case and how the decision has been treated in later judicial decisions. Covers all reported decisions of the Canadian provincial and federal courts and tribunals since 1867, all unreported decisions of the Court of Appeal and the Supreme Court of Canada since 1987 and unreported (unpublished) decisions

of the superior courts since 1993. Kept up to date by annual cumulative supplements published in softback.

Current Law Index
See entry no. 2902

2536 Current statutes citations (Références législatives Canadiennes)
Thomson Canada. ISSN 11981121.
A component of The Canadian Abridgment (q.v.) providing, in 20 volumes, a national statute citator. Lists Canadian federal, provincial and territorial statutes as well as international statutes and those of foreign states which have been considered in Canadian courts and tribunals. Includes reported and unreported decisions of the Canadian Court of Appeal since 1987 and the Canadian superior courts since 1993 in which statutes have been interpreted. Amendments to statutes also noted.

2537 Index to Canadian legal literature (L'index à la documentation juridique au Canada)
Carswell, 1991–, 8 p.a.
The most comprehensive subject index for finding both textbooks (including theses, government publications, law society and bar publications and continuing education materials) and articles on Canadian law. The range of material included is extensive, from academic through to practitioner and to popular works. Both English and French language material is indexed. Issued in eight volumes with looseleaf supplements, author and subject indexes. Forms a part of The Canadian Abridgment (q.v.) but also available as a separate library edition. Bound volumes updated by annual softback supplements. Available electronically as part of the WestlaweCARSWELL database (q.v.).

2538 Index to Canadian legal periodical literature
Canadian Association of Law Libraries, 1963–, irregular. ISSN 03168891.
Indexes not only Canadian law journals only but also articles related to law in non-legal Canadian journals. In addition covers published lecture series, collections of essays and book reviews. Duplicates some of the material in Index to Canadian legal literature (q.v.) but strength is in coverage of non-legal material and book reviews.

2539 Regulations judicially considered (Réglements cités)
Thomson Canada, 2005. ISBN 0459243012.
Lists, in 6 volumes, Canadian federal, provincial, territorial and foreign regulations which have been considered by the Canadian courts and administrative tribunals. Includes reported decisions and unreported decisions from January 1997 onwards.

Directories & encyclopedias

2540 Canadian encyclopedic digest
3rd edn, Carswell, 1973–.
Commentary on all the federal laws of Canada and the provincial laws of Ontario, with copious footnotes giving references to legislation and cases. Entire publication is in looseleaf, making updating easier – yellow supplements at the front of each volume update the white-page main text. pages contain the latest changes. Comprehensive research

guide and key to the whole service. Available electronically as part of the WestlaweCARSWELL database (q.v.).

2541 Canadian law list
Canada Law Book Inc, 1951–, annual. ISSN 00848573.
www.canadianlawlist.com/
Comprehensive directory of judges, law firms, barristers, solicitors, notaries and corporate counsel. Part 1 displays 'professional cards' of law firms, giving names of partners and sometimes specialities. Part 2 listing by province and town of judges, barristers and solicitors. Part 3 is an alphabetical listing by names of individuals. Index by organization only. Poor indexing by specialization. Web version provides contact details only. Available to buy on CD-ROM or free to search on the web.

2542 Lexpert
www.lexpert.ca
Free site providing law firm news and a number of searchable directories. Of most value to professional business lawyers or those seeking employment in law firms: Canadian Legal Lexpert Directory, Lexpert/American Lawyer Guide to the leading 500 lawyers in Canada, various training and legal recruitment directories. Entries in the directories include profiles of law firms, the client base and contact details.

Keeping up to date

2543 Canadian current law: case digests
Carswell, 1996–, monthly. ISSN 12054585.
Digests the most recent and significant decisions of Canadian courts and tribunals, including the most recent unreported decisions of the Canadian appellate, superior and provincial courts, classified according to the Canadian Abridgment classification scheme. Acts as the monthly update to several units of *The Canadian Abridgment*: the case digest, consolidated table of cases and words and phrases. Text in English but some of the preliminary pages are in English and French.

2544 Canadian current law: legislation
Carswell, 1991–, 8 p.a. ISSN 1183062X.
Summarizes recent legislative activity in the Parliament of Canada and in legislatures of the provinces and territories of Canada. Notes changes with references to the *Canada Gazette* (q.v.) where new legislation is published. Essentially in English with some summaries in French. *Canadian current law legislation annual* consolidates the individual issues and acts as a permanent record.

England

Laws, standards, codes

2545 English reports
W. Green, Stevens, 1900–1930.
Most comprehensive of three sources (the others are the *Revised Reports* and the *All England law reports* reprint) for reprints of law reports of cases heard in the English courts and published between 1571 and 1865. The cases themselves date from 1220 to 1865 and are reproduced

verbatim in the original language: English, Norman-French or Latin – no translations. Only a case-name index is published with the paper set. Title also available as a two set CD-ROM and as a web version on the HeinOnline (q.v.) subscriber-only database, both mediums having the advantage of comprehensive search facilities.

2546 Measures of the General Synod of the Church of England
www.opsi.gov.uk/legislation/uk-meas.htm
Official text of legislation relating to the operation of the Church of England. Printed loose issues published initially, followed at the year end by a comprehensive set as part of Public General Acts and General Synod Measures (see under Law: National Jurisdictions: United Kingdom). Web version from 1988 onwards available free but technically the paper version is the authoritative text.

Guernsey

Introductions to the subject

2547 The constitution and administration of Sark
J.M. Beaumont   Guernsey Press, 1993, 32pp. ISBN 0952206706.
The main source for information on Sark, but now dated in view of the radical changes to the Sark constitution made in autumn 2006.

2548 Information sources in law
J. Winterton and E.M. Moys, eds   2nd edn, Bowker-Saur, 1997, 673pp. ISBN 1857390415.
Chapter by Woodman: The Isle of Man and the Channel Islands, briefly describes the legal system of the Bailiwick of Guernsey, introductory works on the legal literature and legal research, the key sources of legislation and case law, government information, directories, bibliographies, current information sources and useful addresses. Even though published before the internet revolution, still of great value because of the thoroughness of the research.

2549 Introduction to the Bailiwick of Guernsey – law developments
Babbe Le Pelley Tostevin
www.legal500.com/lfe/frames/gu_fr.htm
Brief article providing background information on the Bailiwick, outlining the court system, the sources of law, procedures of the Royal Court of Guernsey and nature of litigation in Guernsey. Prepared by staff of a Guernsey-based law firm but available free.

2550 Laws of Guernsey
G. Dawes   Hart Publishing, 2003, 789pp. ISBN 1841133965.
The first comprehensive textbook on the legal system, laws and legal institutions of the Bailiwick, which also includes Alderney and Sark. Includes chapters on planning law, family, trusts, succession, income tax, company, employment, health and safety, the civil and criminal courts and their procedure. Appendices include the text of key legislation. Extensive bibliography and subject index.

Laws, standards, codes

2551 Ordres en Conseil: Orders in Council and other matters of general interest registered on the records of the island of Guernsey
Greffier, 1803–.
The authoritative source for Orders in Council made by the Privy Council in London applying to Guernsey. Considerable delay in publication.

2552 Recueil d'Ordonnances
Official source for legislation made by the States of Guernsey.

Official & quasi-official bodies

2553 Bailiwick of Guernsey: law officers of the Crown
www.gov.gg/ccm/navigation/government/law-officers/
Official web pages explaining the functions and services of the Law Officers of the Crown in the Bailiwick. Provides contact information and lists key legislation (mainly company and commercial), with links to the full text of a selection.

2554 Sark Government
www.sark.gov.gg/
Official website of the smallest of the four major Channel Islands. As well as background historical, economic and geographical information it includes the full text of key constitutional documents, background information on the legislative body, including committee reports, minutes and agendas.

Associations & societies

2555 Guernsey Bar
www.guernseybar.com/
Official website, including a history of the Bar, directory of advocates, information about instructing a Guernsey advocate, guidance on civil and criminal litigation procedure, a dictionary of legal terms and links to summaries of cases, articles and other Guernsey legal materials.

Portal & task environments

States of Guernsey Government
See entry no. 2016

Discovering print & electronic resources

2556 A legal bibliography of the British Commonwealth of Nations
2nd edn, Sweet & Maxwell, 1957.
Volumes 1 and 2 contain listings covering publications up to 1800 and from 1801 to 1956, respectively.
'The best bibliographical source for older material.' (Woodman: 'Isle of Man and Channel Islands' in *Information sources in law* (q.v.), p. 619)

2557 World law: Guernsey
www.worldlii.org/catalog/2790.html
Comprehensive list of links to websites of Guernsey law and

legal information, arranged subject or organization and with search facility across all entries. Very brief annotations to each link. Part of the World Legal Information Institute service developed by the Australasian Legal Information Institute (q.v.).

Keeping up to date

2558 Guernsey Law Journal
H.M. Attorney General, Twice yearly.
The only legal periodical published in the Channel Islands. From the outset intended as an index and record of legal developments in Guernsey rather than an academic or practitioner journal in he conventional sense. Digest section, arranged by subject, summarizes legislation and court judgments over the previous six months. Includes full reports of the Guernsey Court of Appeal. Also longer articles of commentary on the law.
'It is the essential information source for law in the Bailiwick of Guernsey.' (Woodman: 'Isle of Man and the Channel Islands' in *Information sources in law* (q.v.))

Irish Republic

Introductions to the subject

2559 Guide to Irish law
www.nyulawglobal.org/globalex/Ireland.htm
Commentary and bibliographic resource guide compiled by Dr Darius Whelan, Lecturer in Law, University College Cork and published on the New York University Law School website in June 2005. Outlines the development of the Irish legal system, reviews print and electronic research sources and the websites of courts, the government, law firms and barristers. Also guidance on books, journals and discussion lists.

2560 How to use a law library: an introduction to legal skills
P. Thomas and J. Knowles   4th edn, Sweet & Maxwell, 2001, 294pp.
ISBN 0421744103.
Chapter by Aston, 'Irish law', includes brief note of the complex legal history of the province, followed by comprehensive discussion of legal materials and databases and websites illustrated with many sample pages. An authoritative commentary by Jennifer Aston, Consultant Librarian, Law Library, Dublin.

2561 Information sources in law
J. Winterton and E.M. Moys   2nd edn, Bowker-Saur, 1997, 673pp.
ISBN 1857390415.
Chapter by Furlong, 'Ireland', briefly describes the legal system of Ireland, introductory works on the legal literature and legal research, the key sources of legislation and case law, government information, encyclopedias, directories, bibliographies, indexing and abstracting services, dictionaries, current information sources and useful addresses. Even though published before the internet revolution, still of great value because of the thoroughness of the research.

2562 Legal publishing and legal information: small jurisdictions of the British Isles
W. Twining and J. Uglow Sweet & Maxwell, 1981, 181pp. ISBN 0421289309.
Describes the Irish legal system and attempts to extend the bibliography contained in *A legal bibliography of the British Commonwealth of Nations to 1980* (q.v.). But, according to Furlong ('Ireland' in *Information sources in law* (q.v.) p. 260), 'the best and most comprehensive bibliography' covering the period from 1950 onwards is O'Malley, *Sources of law* (q.v.).

2563 Sources of law: an introduction to legal research and writing
T. O'Malley 2nd edn, Round Hall Sweet & Maxwell, 2001, 357pp. ISBN 1858001854.
The most comprehensive guide to legal research in Ireland primarily aimed at law students. Describes the source materials of Irish law and how to use them, together with a chapter on legal writing. Extensive appendices, including a glossary of terms and a list of Irish law books published since 1950.
'An excellent subject guide to Irish legal textbooks.' (Aston in Thomas and Knowles (q.v.), p. 208)

Dictionaries, thesauri, classifications

2564 Glossary of legal terms
http://indigo.ie/~kwood/legalterms.htm
Free glossary compiled by Kieron Wood, a Dublin-based barrister. About 400 short definitions with occasional references to legislation, arranged alphabetically. Focus on the practice of law rather than its academic study. Elsewhere on the site a collection of links to Irish law web resources.

2565 Murdoch's dictionary of Irish law
H. Murdoch 4th edn, LexisNexis, 2004, 1243pp. ISBN 1854753622.
Mix of short and substantial entries with up-to-date references to relevant legislation and case law under each entry. In addition, explains Latin words and phrases. Also entries for organizations with a law remit. Appendices of law report abbreviations and lists of books on Irish law used in the compilation of the entries. Latest edition includes references to websites where further information on particular words, phrases and organizations available. Designed for law students and practising lawyers.
'Cannot be praised too highly … excellent entries on every aspect of Irish law.' (O'Malley: *Sources of law* (q.v.), p.130)

Laws, standards, codes

2566 The Acts of the Oireachtas
Stationery Office, Dublin, 1922–, annual.
Authoritative version of both public and private Acts which are first published singly and then in annual bound volumes (usually only in English) under the title *Acts of the Oireachtas as promulgated*. Also includes amendments to the constitution.

2567 British & Irish Legal Information Institute
www.bailii.org/
Free access to legislation as passed by the Irish Parliament from 1922 onwards, but no facility to check whether it is in force, has been amended or repealed. Also access to the transcripts (that is, the unedited text) of decisions of the Irish Supreme Court (1999–), Irish High Court (1996–) and the decisions of a number of regulatory bodies. Also Irish Law Reform Commission Papers and Reports (1976–). The only free searchable database of judgments for Irish law.

2568 Constitution of Ireland (Bunreacht na hÉireann)
Stationery Office, 2003, 235pp. ISBN 0755714857.
www.taoiseach.gov.ie/index.asp?docID=243
Text of the Irish Constitution together with amending acts printed in English and Irish on opposite pages. Amendments to the constitution are published in the relevant annual volume of *Acts of the Oireachtas* (q.v.).

2569 Iris Oifigiúil
Government Supplies Agency, 1922–. ISSN 03321274.
www.irisoifigiuil.ie/
The official newspaper for the government of Ireland is published on Tuesday and Friday of each week. It lists Acts promulgated, Statutory Instruments published and other Stationery Office publications, as well as containing legal notices and other official government information. The full text of the Gazette from January 2002 onwards is available in pdf format with search facilities.

2570 Irish current law statutes annotated
J. Aston [et al.], eds Round Hall Sweet & Maxwell, 1984–.
Looseleaf volumes containing the text of Acts issued as a series of releases during the year. Not the authoritative version (see *Acts of the Oireachtas*) but has the added value of extensive annotations and detailed commentary to most Acts, explaining the background, meaning and effect of the Act as a whole and individual sections. Comprehensive subject, alphabetical and chronological indexes covering the period 1984 onwards. From 1993 includes legislation and case citators (to trace amendments to legislation and where the courts have considered and interpreted particular sections of Acts and Statutory Instruments).
'Very valuable service.' (O'Malley: *Sources of law* (q.v.), p.62)

2571 Irish law reports monthly
Round Hall Press, 1981–, 14 p.a. ISSN 03323293.
Together with the *Irish reports*, the only general series of law reports: that is, not restricted to publishing cases on a particular topic or from a particular court. Well respected series publishing the full text of decisions in the Superior Courts (the High Court, Supreme Court and the Court of Criminal Appeal).

2572 Irish legal information initiative
www.ucc.ie/law/irlii/index.php
Free database created by the Law Faculty, University College Cork, to complement those on the British and Irish Legal Information Institute (BAILII) site (q.v.). Contains the full text of statutes from 2002 onwards, searchable indexes of Statutory Instruments (2002 onwards), case law (1997 onwards) linked to BAILII full-text transcripts and periodical articles (also 1997 onwards). Current work to increase comprehensive coverage of Irish case law both in terms of courts and backfiles.

2573 Irish reports: 1838–1893
Butterworth Ireland, 1838–1893.
Reprint of 270 volumes of the predecessor publications to the *Irish reports* which commenced in 1894 (q.v.).

2574 Irish reports: 1894–
Incorporated Council of Law Reporting for Ireland, 1894–. ISSN 03324702.
Principal and most authoritative source for full-text reports of cases decided in the Superior Courts (the High Court, Supreme Court and the Court of Criminal Appeal). Continues the Irish Reports 1838–1893 (q.v.).

2575 Irish Statute Book
www.irishstatutebook.ie
Free access to the full text of Acts and Statutory Instruments from 1922 onwards. The site is arranged in three sections: Acts of the Oireachtas, Statutory Instruments and a chronological list of statutes. The first two sections are arranged by date and can be viewed only alphabetically or chronologically. The text of all the materials is stated as originally passed, so care should be taken when referring to older material which may have been subsequently amended or repealed.

2576 LexisNexis
www.lexisnexis.ie
Subscriber-only database containing the full text of the Irish Reports 1950–, some other series of reported (published) judgments from 1950 to the early 1908s and selected unreported Irish decisions from 1985.

2577 Statutory instruments
Stationery Office, Dublin, 1948–, annual.
Official, full text of subordinate legislation, first published as single copies and then as annual bound volumes. Up to 1973 the text is in both English and Irish. From 1974 the text is solely in the language in which they were made, usually English.

2578 Statutory rules and orders
Stationery Office, Dublin, 1922–1947. Continued by Statutory Instruments.
Official sets of the full text of subordinate legislation in both English and Irish, collected in three series (1922–1938, 1939–1945, 1946–1947), each with its own index volume. Continued by Statutory instruments (q.v.).

2579 WestlawIE
www.westlaw.ie/
Commercial full-text database containing contents of various Round Hall Sweet & Maxwell law publications, including 12 looseleaf services of consolidated legislation, 9 journals, 5 law reports and a current-awareness service. Maintains that its 'content and coverage is unparalleled'.

Official & quasi-official bodies

2580 Courts Service of Ireland
www.courts.ie/courts.ie/library3.nsf/PageCurrentWebLookUpTopNav/Home
Official website providing background information on the history, organization and role of the courts. Includes lists of court offices with contact details. A number of practice materials are included: the full text of court rules and fee orders for the Superior Courts, Circuit and District Courts, forms and practice directions. Lists of current and future cases. Also includes a Judgments Database for the Supreme Court (2001–) and the High Court and the Court of Criminal Appeal (2004–). Finally, a glossary of terms is included.

2581 Law Reform Commission of Ireland
www.lawreform.ie/index.htm
Official site of the body set up in 1975 to review the whole body of Irish law and make recommendations for reform. Includes details of the membership of the Commission, its methods and programme of work, with summaries of law currently under review. All the Commission's reports and consultation papers are provided in full text. Also selective list of links to internet sources for Irish, international and European law.

Associations & societies

2582 Bar Council of Ireland
www.barcouncil.ie/
Official site of the Irish Bar, the regulatory body for barristers practising in Ireland. Includes background information on the Irish Bar, its role, functions and the membership of various committees. Searchable directory of barristers and guidance on instructing a barrister. Selected articles from the *Bar Review* are freely available, together with a selection of conference papers and links to other Irish law sites.

2583 Law Society of Ireland
www.lawsociety.ie
Official site for the educational, representative and regulatory body of the solicitors' profession in Ireland. Apart from material about the society, how to become a solicitor and complaints procedure, the site includes a searchable directory of Irish law firms and free client care publications.

Libraries, archives, museums

2584 Trinity College Dublin, Library
www.tcd.ie/Library/subjectguides/law/index.php
Law library is part of Ireland's largest library and serves the country's oldest law school. Since 1801 Trinity College Library has been a copyright deposit library for British and Irish publications. Very little information about the law library itself can be gleaned from the website.

Discovering print & electronic resources

2585 A bibliography of periodical literature relating to Irish law
P. O'Higgins   Northern Ireland Law Quarterly, 1966. ISBN 085389227X.
Lists around 5000 articles from over 130 journals, arranged within broad subject headings with cross-references. Subject and other indexes are provided along with lists of journals cited and their abbreviations. Supplements published in 1973 and 1983.
'Provides an excellent historical coverage.' (Aston in Thomas and Knowles (q.v.), p.208)

2586 Chronological table of the statutes
Stationery Office, Dublin, 1996.
Official cumulative lists of new statutes and pre-existing statutes affected, amended or repealed by new legislation.

Usually published some years after the materials in question were passed.

2587 Index to Irish superior court written judgments 1976–1982
J. Aston and M. Doyle, eds   Irish Association of Law Teachers, 1984.
Also known as the Red Index, it covers both reported and unreported cases and includes alphabetical and subject indexes. Continued by the Blue Index (q.v.).

2588 Index to superior court written judgments 1983–1989
J. Aston, ed.   General Council of the Bar of Ireland, 1991.
Also known as the Blue Index, it continues the Red Index (q.v.).

2589 Index to the High Court and Supreme Court written judgments
Bar Council & Law Society of Ireland, 1976–.
Also known as the Pink Pages or Pink Sheets, a subject index to the large number of unreported (unpublished) decisions of the Irish courts. Issued on average three times a year, the final issue cumulating the whole year. Recent versions also include an alphabetical list of all cases. For the series of consolidations of the Pink Pages see the relevant *Index to superior court judgments.*

2590 Index to the statutes
Stationery Office, Dublin, 1986.
A subject index to the statutes, published as a single bound volume covering 1922 to 1985 and supplemented by individual pamphlets to 1989. Of use only for historical research.

2591 Index to the Statutory Instruments
Stationery Office, Dublin, 1944–.
Official, non-cumulative index published on an occasional basis. Consists of alphabetical lists but does not provide any information on whether the instruments are in force, repealed or amended – see *Irish current law statutes annotated* for more up-to-date and better information.

2592 Index to unreported judgments of the Irish superior courts 1966–1975
J. Aston [et al.], eds   Irish Association of Law Teachers, 1990.
Also known as the Green Index, it covers unreported cases only and includes an alphabetical listing, subject index and tables of legislative materials judicially considered.

2593 Irish digests 1893–
Butterworth Ireland, 1995.
Reprints the early digests to 1993 and has been added to by new publications at irregular intervals. Provides summaries of and indexes to cases published in the *Irish reports* and *Irish Law Reports Monthly* (q.v.) and a number of law report publications covering cases decided in Ireland and Northern Ireland. Does not include unreported (unpublished) cases. Includes name and subject indexes as well as a citator listing case law and legislation followed, overruled or considered by the reports digested.

2594 Irish law site
www.irishlaw.org/
Extensive lists of links to free sites, including the guide to Irish law by Whelan (q.v.), legislation, cases and subject lists of websites. Lists of solicitors firms and barristers chambers across Ireland, with links; lists of Irish law publications with links to Amazon; links to Northern Ireland and British law websites. Site hosted by the Faculty of Law, University College Cork.

2595 Irish-Law.com
http://freepages.genealogy.rootsweb.com/~irishancestors/Law/index.html
Free site created by Sean E. Quinn, Lecturer in Law at Letterkenny Institute of Technology, County Donegal, comprising links to other Irish law websites in lists arranged by type of legal material and by subject. Also includes a section on organizations in the law (law firms, law schools and libraries), portals, gateways and directories on the internet to assist in finding the law. Finally, links to law resources in a selection of other common law countries.

2596 IRLII periodical index
www.ucc.ie/law/irlii/periodicals/periodicals.php
Free index to the contents of 17 legal journals from 1997 onwards, created as part of the Irish Legal Information Initiative (q.v.). Searchable by individual journal or by keyword.

2597 A legal bibliography of the British Commonwealth of Nations: Ireland
2nd edn, Sweet & Maxwell, 1957.
Volume 4 on Ireland is a compilation arranged by both subject and author in a single index (and therefore a little awkward to use) of Irish law books and publications up to 1956.
'The most significant bibliography of early Irish law books and publications.' (Furlong: 'Ireland', in Winterton and Moys (q.v.), p.260)

2598 Legal Island
www.legal-island.com/
Free site provided by a commercial organization involved in law training, conferencing and delivery of legal information, containing annotated links to law websites for Ireland and Northern Ireland, law firms, bar councils, government organizations, and information, e-mail lists and guidance on using the internet for legal research.

Legal journals index
See entry no. 2803

2599 World Law: Ireland
www.worldlii.org/catalog/2227.html
Comprehensive list of links to websites of Irish law and legal information, arranged by jurisdiction or subject or organization and with search facility across all entries. Very brief annotations to each link. Part of the World Legal Information Institute service developed by the Australasian Legal Information Institute (q.v.).

Directories & encyclopedias

2600 The law directory
Incorporated Law Society of Ireland, 1886–, annual.
Lists names and business addresses of all solicitors and barristers, together with details of judges and officers of the courts.

2601 The legal profession in Ireland 1789–1922
D. Hogan   Incorporated Law Society of Ireland, 1986, 176pp. ISBN 090202728X.
History of barristers and solicitors through to the partition of Ireland, providing a description of the origins of the modern Irish legal profession. Chapters cover the development of the Inns of Court, life at the Bar, foundation of the Law Society, the reform of legal education. Appendices containing statistical tables. Bibliography and subject index.

Handbooks & manuals

2602 Annual review of Irish law
Round Hall Sweet & Maxwell, 1987–. ISSN 07911084.
Arranged in chapters under broad subject headings. Traces new developments in legislation and the decisions of the courts. Outlines each statute, lists Statutory Instruments published during the year and analyses key superior court and some circuit court decisions, including unreported cases.
'The volumes provide a comprehensive overview of Irish legal developments and are helpful as annual digests and as a continuing work of reference.' (Furlong: 'Ireland', in Winterton & Moys (q.v.), p. 262)

Keeping up to date

2603 Firstlaw
www.Firstlaw.ie/
Commercial, subscriber-only current awareness service covering new legislation, case law and general articles on Irish law from January 1999 onwards.

2604 Irish current law monthly digest
Round Hall Sweet & Maxwell, 1995–, 11 p.a. ISSN 13572679.
Cumulative list of statutes with details of commencement and arranged under broad subject headings: digests of recent cases and lists of articles appearing in Irish journals and references to articles on Irish law in UK and other English language journals. The monthly parts are cumulated into an annual volume.

2605 Irish law log weekly
Round Hall Sweet & Maxwell, 1996–, 37 p.a. ISSN 13932659.
Provides summaries of all written and some *ex tempore* (oral) judgments delivered during the period covered. Also includes lists of words and phrases judicially considered and defined. Annual bound volumes additionally contain indexes to cases, statutes and constitutional provisions.

Isle of Man

Introductions to the subject

2606 Information sources in law
J. Winterton and E.M. Moys, eds   2nd edn, Bowker-Saur, 1997, 673pp. ISBN 1857390415.
Chapter by Woodman, 'The Isle of Man and the Channel Islands', briefly describes the legal system of the Isle of Man, introductory works on the legal literature and legal research, the key sources of legislation and case law, government information, directories, bibliographies, current information sources and useful addresses. Even though published before the internet revolution it is still of great value because of the thoroughness of the research.

2607 Law publishing and legal information: jurisdictions of the British Isles
W. Twining and J. Uglow   Sweet & Maxwell, 1981, 181pp. ISBN 0421289309.
Describes the legal system and practice on the Isle of Man and its legal research sources. Although rated by Woodman ('Isle of Man' in Winterton & Moys (q.v.) p. 604) as 'the best starting point for research' it is now increasingly out of date.

Laws, standards, codes

2608 Acts of Tynwald
www.gov.im/infocentre/acts/welcome.xml
Acts are published in print form individually but the most accessible source is the free site, Isle of Man Government Infocentre (q.v.), with the full text of the Acts of the Isle of Man Parliament (Tynwald) from the first Act of 2001 onwards. Acts are listed by year in chapter number order and reproduced in the form as passed; that is, there is no information whether the Act is in force, has been amended, and how, or has been repealed.

2609 Isle of Man Government: Information Centre
www.gov.im/Infocentre/acts/
Official site providing access to the text of Acts of Tynwald passed after 1 January 2001 in their original form as passed – no amendments or repeals included. Also lists of Acts arranged alphabetically and chronologically, with details of regulations made under each Act.

2610 Juta's statutes of the Isle of Man, 1999
R.M. Ford, ed.   3rd edn, Juta, 2000. ISBN 0702140600.
Complete, full text of the statutes from 1471 to 1999, kept up to date by annual supplements, the latest of which published for 2003. Published in print and CD-ROM form but has probably ceased publication.

2611 LexisNexis
http://lexis.com
Full-text, subscriber-only service containing the Isle of Man Acts of Tynwald in force as at July 2002. The database contains the Isle of Man Statutes as published by the Isle of Man Government. Statutes are organized under topic headings and then chronologically within topics.

2612 The Manx law reports
Law Reports International, 1985–. ISSN 0267534X.
The only law report publication containing the full text of cases heard in the island's High Court and the High Bailiff's Court. Covers the period 1952 onwards.

2613 The statutes of the Isle of Man
Blackhall Publishing, 2003. 8 v. ISBN 1842180649.
Text of Isle of Man legislation in force as in 2002, the final volume of the eight-volume set acts as a noter-up, to update the text to 1 January 2004. Statutes arranged under broad subject headings, such as employment, commercial law revenue. Chronological and alphabetical tables of statues in force in final volume.

Associations & societies

2614 Isle of Man Law Society
www.iomlawsociety.co.im/default.htm
Official site of the body which represents and regulates
advocates practising on the Isle of Man. Describes the
history, role and organization of the society. Searchable
directory of members according to company name, practice
area and individual member's name.

Libraries, archives, museums

2615 Isle of Man Central Reference Library, Douglas
www.douglas.gov.im/councilinfrmation.asp?ID=1025
Most important publicly accessible reference library on the
Island and has collections of government publications,
including all legislation in force. Two other libraries on the
Isle of Man have law collections (the Library of the Attorney
General's Chambers and the Isle of Man Law Society Library)
but access is restricted.

Discovering print & electronic resources

2616 A legal bibliography of the British Commonwealth of Nations
2nd edn, Sweet & Maxwell, 1957.
Volumes 1 and 2 contain listings covering publications up to
1800 and from 1801 to 1956, respectively.
'The most comprehensive older bibliography.' (Woodman: 'Isle of
Man and the Channel Islands', in Winterton & Moys (q.v.), p. 609)

2617 A list of constitutional and Privy Council judgments affecting the Isle of Man from 1523 to 1991 and a complete list of the written reasons for judgments of HM High Court of Justice of the Isle of Man and other Manx courts from 1884 to 1991
Isle of Man Government   2nd edn, Government Printer, 1992.
'A very important source of precedents' (Woodman: 'Isle of
Man', in Winterton & Moys (q.v.) p. 607) listing all cases in
manuscript and printed sources (with bibliographical details)
and covering not just decisions on the Island but also
appeals to the Privy Council in London.

2618 Manx cases: index to cases 1884–1988
D. Prater   Isle of Man Law Society.
The only index to Manx cases of the period available.

2619 Manx cases: subject index 1884–1971
D. Prater   Isle of Man Law Society.
The only subject index to Manx cases of the period available.

2620 World law: Isle of Man
www.worldlii.org/catalog/2799.html
Comprehensive list of links to websites of Manx law and
legal information, arranged by jurisdiction or subject or
organization and with search facility across all entries. Very
brief annotations to each link. Part of the World Legal
Information Institute service developed by the Australasian
Legal Information Institute (q.v.).

Keeping up to date

2621 Manx law bulletin
Attorney General's Chambers, 1983–. ISSN 02679795.
Lists Acts recently passed by Tynwald, gives details of
legislation in force and summaries of forthcoming bills (draft
legislation). Notes new UK legislation which extends to the
Isle of Man. Includes notes of recent case decisions. Also
information on developments in the Island's legal profession
as well as articles and notes on legal topics.
'The main source of current information on Manx law.'
(Woodman: 'Isle of Man', in Winterton & Moys (q.v.), p.609)

Jersey

Introductions to the subject

2622 Information sources in law
J. Winterton and E.M. Moys, eds   2nd edn, Bowker-Saur, 1997,
673pp. ISBN 1857390415.
Chapter by Woodman, 'The Isle of Man and the Channel
Islands', briefly describes the legal system of the Bailiwick of
Jersey, introductory works on the legal literature and legal
research, the key sources of legislation and case law,
government information, directories, bibliographies, current
information sources and useful addresses. Even though
published before the internet revolution, still of great value
because of the thoroughness of the research.

Laws, standards, codes

2623 Jersey law reports
A. Milner, ed.   Law Reports International, 1985–, 2 p.a. ISSN
09517936.
Full text reports of cases decided in the Jersey courts from
1985 onwards. Continues Judgments of the Royal Court of
Jersey (q.v.) and published on the authority of the Royal
Court.

2624 Jersey Legal Information Board
www.jerseylegalinfo.je/
Comprehensive, official website containing all laws in force,
Jersey Law Reports 1981–, unreported judgments 1997–
(unregistered users have access to summaries only), practice
directions and rules of the Royal Court, full text of the Jersey
Law Review 1997– and a searchable directory of Jersey law
firms and a discussion forum.

2625 Judgments of the Royal Court of Jersey and of the Court of Appeal of Jersey
States Greffe, Jersey, 1950–1988. ISSN 09517944.
Full text reports of cases decided in the Jersey courts from
1950 to 1984. Continued by Jersey law reports (q.v.).

2626 Recueil des lois de Jersey
The full and authoritative text of legislation which required
approval by the Privy Council in London from 1771 to 1960.
Published in eight volumes. The early volumes are entirely in
French. Continued in looseleaf format in English as Laws.

2627 Regulations and orders
The full and authoritative text of legislation passed by the States of Jersey which does not require approval by the Privy Council in London.

Official & quasi-official bodies

2628 Jersey Law Commission
www.lawcomm.gov.je/
Official site of the body responsible for the review and development of the law and legal system of the Island. Includes selected topic reports and consultation papers in full-text from 1998 onwards and its Annual Report from 1996 onwards.

2629 States of Jersey. Judicial Greffe
www.statesassembly.gov.je/frame.html
Official site of the government department responsible for the administrative and secretarial services in the Island's Courts and delivering information services relating to the courts to the legal profession and public. Outlines the roles of the various sections of the department with the full text of guidance notes issued by the department. Includes full text of proposed legislation (called *projets*) from 1997 onwards. Provides access to the databases of the Trademarks, Patents and Designs Registries. Staff contact details are provided.

Discovering print & electronic resources

2630 General index of legislation
Bigwood Printers, 1966–, annual.
Looseleaf publication, also referred to as 'Jersey legislation in force' (after the spine title), is a subject index to *Laws* and *Regulations and orders* (q.v.).

2631 A legal bibliography of the British Commonwealth of Nations
2nd edn, Sweet & Maxwell, 1957.
Volumes 1 and 2 contain listings covering publications up to 1800 and from 1801 to 1956, respectively.
'The best bibliographical source for older material.' (Woodman: 'Isle of Man and Channel Islands', in Winterton & Moys (q.v.), p. 619)

2632 Table des décisions de la Cour Royale de Jersey, 1885–(1978)
Bigwoods, Jersey, 1896–1980.
Digest of unreported decisions heard in the Royal Court between 1885 and 1978. The text of the decisions is in French up to the 1960s.

2633 World law: Jersey
www.worldlii.org/catalog/2791.html
Comprehensive list of links to websites of Jersey law and legal information, arranged by subject or organization and with search facility across all entries. Very brief annotations to each link. Part of the World Legal Information Institute service developed by the Australasian Legal Information Institute (q.v.).

Keeping up to date

2634 Jersey Law Review
Jersey Law Review Ltd, 1997–, 3 p.a. £120. ISSN 13669354.
Each issue carries summaries of recent cases selected from both Jersey and Guernsey, with short summaries of Jersey legislation. The only current awareness source available.

2635 JLIB News
www.jerseylegalinfo.je/publications/newsletter/default.aspx
Online newsletter of the Jersey Legal Information Board, including the full text of issues from August 1999 onwards. Provides news of developments relating the Jersey Legal Information Board, its website and the continuing conversion and display of Jersey legal materials in electronic format.

New Zealand

Introductions to the subject

2636 An introduction to New Zealand law and legal information
www.nyulawglobal.org/globalex/New_Zealand.htm
Free research guide published in August 2005 to the law and legal materials of New Zealand, written by Margaret Greville, Law Librarian at the University of Canterbury, New Zealand. Not only covers the primary sources of law (Acts and cases) but a valuable feature is the extensive listing of sources covering very specific legal topics.

2637 Introduction to the New Zealand legal system
R.D. Mulholland   10th edn, Butterworths, 2001, 516pp. ISBN 0408716339.
Covers the place of law within New Zealand society, the constitution of New Zealand, the courts and judges, legislation, court actions, judicial process, the concept of legal personality and chapters on the law relating to contract, agency, sale of goods, personal property, hire purchase, the law of property, torts, trusts, consumer, the family and ending with a chapter on the literature of New Zealand law and research. Appendices include the text of selected judgments for class study, glossaries of terms, abbreviations, a legal writing style guide and the text of the Treaty of Waitangi and the Constitution Act 1986. A popular and accessible text.

2638 Legal research and writing in New Zealand
M. Greville, S. Davidson and R. Scragg   2nd edn, LexisNexis NZ, 2004, 438pp. ISBN 0408716908.
In two parts: legal information, describing both printed and electronic sources; and part 2, on research and writing, covering writing for academic and practice, the rules of citation, good legal English and grammar. Written to support teaching and legal research and writing skills in both academic and practice environments.

2639 Maori and indigenous legal resources
www.waikato.ac.uk/library/resources/law/s_indig.shtml
Although set up only in 1990 to support the newly established School of Law, the law library specializes in collecting Maori and indigenous law generally. This site provides links to guides to the law of indigenous peoples

across the world and extensive bibliographies and other lists of materials.

Terminology, codes & standards

2640 Australian and New Zealand legal abbreviations
C. Fong and A.J. Edwards   2nd edn, Australian Law Librarians' Group, New South Wales Division, 1996, 126pp. ISBN 0959135987.
Alphabetical list of abbreviations for Australian and New Zealand law publications and some non-Australian and New Zealand publications which regularly include Australian and New Zealand law material. Aims to supplement the *Index to legal abbreviations and citations* (q.v.) and *Bieber's dictionary of legal abbreviations* (q.v.). Covers acronyms for organizations and personalities within the legal systems.

Laws, standards, codes

2641 LexisNexis
www.lexisnexis.co.uk/news_and_business/index.asp?business_home.html
The only law material relating to New Zealand included within this full-text, subscriber-only database are a number of law report series, including New Zealand Law Reports (q.v.) and New Zealand District Court Reports.

2642 The New Zealand law reports
New Zealand Council of Law Reporting, 1883–, irregular. ISSN 0110148X.
The most authoritative set of general law reports (that is, not restricted to a particular topic or court) for New Zealand.

2643 New Zealand Legal Information Institute
www.nzlii.org/
Free public information service with access to databases containing the full text of treaties, decisions of courts and tribunals and, in addition, the publications of the NZ Law Commission and a number of university law reviews. However, the case reports are in the form of transcripts, without the value-added features found in some commercial services. Operated jointly by the Faculties of Law at the University of Otago and the University of Wellington and the Australasian Legal Information Institute.

2644 New Zealand legislation
www.legislation.govt.nz/
Free public access to the current full-text versions (with amendments incorporated) of Acts of Parliament and regulations. Repealed and revoked legislation is not included. Although the site is run by the New Zealand Parliamentary Counsel Office in association with a private publisher, it states that the information is not official or authoritative. The printed paper version is the official version. The site is updated monthly. It is a temporary site and will be replaced as part of project to make all New Zealand legislation, including Bills, available to the public free of charge around mid-2007.

2645 Reprinted Statutes of New Zealand
Government Printer, 1979–.
The fourth consolidation of the statutes (incomplete?) which reprints the text of all Acts and when the set is complete details of revisions will be printed. In the meantime,

researchers may need to use the earlier edition of 1958–1961.

2646 The statutes of New Zealand
1841–. ISSN 01115626.
Annual volumes containing the Acts passed during the year – the authoritative source for the original version of an Act, but note that subsequent amendments and repeals are not inserted in the text of an Act.

Official & quasi-official bodies

2647 Courts of New Zealand
www.courtsofnz.govt.nz/
Provides information about the role, history and structure of the courts. Lists forthcoming business of the courts and brief summaries of decisions in past cases, including transcripts of hearings. Text of out-of-court speeches given by judges and annual reports of the various courts.

2648 New Zealand Law Commission
www.lawcom.govt.nz/
A central advisory body established by statute in 1985 to undertake the systematic review, reform and development of the law of New Zealand. Terms of reference, preliminary papers and reports of all its investigations are available in full text on the site.

2649 New Zealand. Ministry of Justice
www.justice.govt.nz/
Formed on 1 October 2003 from the merger of the Department of Courts with the Ministry of Justice, this site explains the work of the Ministry and the courts, with sections of information designed for the public, law professionals and the media. Comprehensive list of links to court websites.

2650 New Zealand. Parliamentary Counsel Office
www.pco.parliament.govt.nz/
Government department responsible for drafting and publishing New Zealand legislation. Provides links to free access databases containing the text of Acts and regulations (see New Zealand legislation website) and other sources.

Associations & societies

2651 Auckland District Law Society, New Zealand
www.adls.org.nz
The largest regional organization of lawyers in the country; provides continuing legal education and other services. Website includes a directory of lawyers and publications on matters of topical interest from its Public Issue Committee. ADLS Library and Research Centre is not open to the public but houses an extensive law collection. Extensive yet selective guide to websites with links to legislation and case law for New Zealand, Australia and other common law jurisdictions.

2652 New Zealand Law Librarians' Association
www.nzllg.org.nz/index.cfm
Represents law librarians, provides a focus for knowledge-sharing through conferences and other events and the LAW-IB e-mail listserv.

2653 New Zealand Law Society
www.lawyers.org.nz
Official site for the organization which regulates, represents, oversees the training and continuing legal education of lawyers in New Zealand. Sections of site for members, the public and overseas lawyers wishing to practise in NZ. Access to full text of many of the society's publications.

Libraries, archives, museums

2654 University of Auckland, Library
www.library.auckland.ac.nz/subjects/law/home.htm
The Davis law library serves New Zealand's largest law faculty and has extensive collections of New Zealand law and the laws of other common law jurisdictions.

Discovering print & electronic resources

2655 The abridgement of New Zealand case law
H.J. Wily, ed.   Butterworths, 1963–.
Digests reported (i.e. published) cases which appeared in the *New Zealand law reports* (NZLR) for the High Court, the Court of Appeal and on appeal to the Privy Council, arranged by subject. Also includes a list of words and phrases judicially considered. Updated by Permanent Supplements published after much delay. Does not cover any other series of law reports than NZLR. Duplicates material found in indexes to NZLR and on LexisNexis.

Index to legal periodicals and books
See entry no. 2904

2656 New Zealand case law digest
Brooker & Friend, 1990–.
Provides summaries of legislation and cases, including many unreported decisions. Covers the superior courts and selected tribunals.
'As the publishers note, this publication does fill a gap by covering those cases not reported and is more comprehensive in its summaries than the case digests in Butterworths current law.' (Watt: *Concise legal research* (q.v.) p. 114)

2657 Tables of New Zealand acts and statutory regulations in force
Government Printer, 1977–, annual. Title varies.
Lists all types of national and provincial legislation, with amendments to a stated date.

2658 World law: New Zealand
www.worldlii.org/catalog/242.html
Comprehensive list of links to websites of New Zealand law and legal information, arranged by subject or organization and with search facility across all entries. Very brief annotations to each link. Part of the World Legal Information Institute service developed by the Australasian Legal Information Institute (q.v.).

Digital data, image & text collections

2659 The knowledge basket
www.knowledge-basket.co.nz/gpprint/docs/welcome.html
A series of news, business, science and legal databases about New Zealand. Some parts of the service are free to access, for others there is a charge. For lawyers, free access to the full text of Bills and Supplementary Order Papers from 6 September 2004 onwards is of most interest.

Directories & encyclopedias

2660 Directory of decisions
www.waikato.ac.nz/library/resources/law/decisions/
Lists courts, tribunals, statutory authorities in New Zealand which make legal or quasi-legal decisions and reports. Provides brief information on their jurisdiction, governing legislation, administering bodies, contact details, availability of decisions, information on indexes of decisions and holdings of libraries across New Zealand. An invaluable resource.

2661 Law (year): the professions guide
Brooker & Friend & Law Corporation (NZ) Ltd, 1990–, annual.
Lists New Zealand lawyers and law firms.

2662 The laws of New Zealand
Butterworths of New Zealand, 1997–.
30 ring binders containing booklets, each on a different legal topic. Provides commentary on the statutory and case law of New Zealand arranged by subject with copious footnotes. Updated through two looseleaf binders of individual pages. Comprehensive indexes in two further looseleaf binders. The equivalent of *Halsbury's laws of England* (q.v.) but in a quite different format.

2663 LexisNexis legal A–Z
E. Knight, ed.   LexisNexis, 2002, 763pp. ISBN 0408716967.
Directory of contact information on lawyers, legal executives, patent attorneys, law librarians, courts, government departments and organizations, auctioneers, valuers, expert witnesses and legal recruitment agencies. Easy-to-use basic information.

2664 New Zealand barristers and solicitors directory
Auckland District Law Society, 2 p.a.
Lists New Zealand lawyers and law firms.

2665 New Zealand Commentary on Halsbury's Laws of England
Butterworths, 1974–.
Provides a brief but comprehensive commentary on New Zealand law. Replaced by *The laws of New Zealand* (q.v.).

2666 New Zealand register
Law Book Co, 1950–, annual.
Lists New Zealand lawyers and law firms.

Handbooks & manuals

2667 Butterworths annotations to the New Zealand statutes
Butterworths, 1982–, irregular. Looseleaf.
Provides amendments to current statutes and notes of cases reported in other Butterworths publications on sections of a statute.

Keeping up to date

2668 Butterworths current law digest
Butterworths. ISSN 14783673.

Two looseleaf binders updating the tables and indexes appearing with *LexisNexis Butterworths current law* (q.v.) and covering the whole period since its inception in 1979. Also reprints summaries of cases which have yet to transfer from *LexisNexis Butterworths current law* to *LexisNexis Butterworths current law digest*. Also includes a table of journal articles noted in the other publications since 1979. The second part of the three-part current law set of publications.

2669 LexisNexis Butterworths current law
LexisNexis NZ Ltd, 1974–. ISSN 14775611.

Booklet published fortnightly noting new bills, Acts, regulations, recent New Zealand decisions and important overseas decisions. Case name and inadequate subject indexes. Annual volume includes a list of Acts affected by newer legislation noted in the volume. The first part of the three-part current law set of publications.

2670 LexisNexis Butterworths current law digest
Butterworths, 1979–. Continues Butterworths current law. ISBN 0110070X.

Cumulation of the unreported cases of the High Court and Court of Appeal noted in *LexisNexis Butterworths current law*. Also contains useful tables of statutes and cases cited and a subject index. Published as a series of hardback volumes each covering a three-year cumulation. The third part of the three-part current law set of publications.

Northern Ireland

Introductions to the subject

2671 How to use a law library: an introduction to legal skills
P.A. Thomas and J. Knowles   4th edn, Sweet & Maxwell, 2001. ISBN 0421744103.

Chapter on Northern Ireland describes the complex constitutional background to the province, with short descriptions in a narrative style of a very wide range of publications and websites. Although aimed at the student market the detail is considerable and authoritative, written by John Knowles, the Sub-Librarian for Law and Official Publications at Queen's University, Belfast.

2672 Information sources in law
J. Winterton and E.M. Moys, eds   2nd edn, Bowker-Saur, 1997, 673pp. ISBN 1857390415.

Chapter by Woodman, 'Northern Ireland', briefly describes the legal system of the province, introductory works on the legal literature and legal research, the key sources of legislation and case law, government information, directories, bibliographies, current information sources and useful addresses. Even though published before the internet revolution it is still of great value because of the thoroughness of the research.

2673 Law publishing and legal information: small jurisdictions of the British Isles
W. Twining and J. Uglow, eds   Sweet & Maxwell, 1981, 181pp. ISBN 0421289309.

Chapter by Greer and Boyd on Northern Ireland, outlines the special features of the jurisdiction from 1920 followed by a descriptive survey of the legal literature. The select bibliography updates that given in *Legal bibliography of the British Commonwealth of Nations, Volume 4: Irish Law to 1956* (q.v.).

Laws, standards, codes

2674 Belfast Gazette
www.gazettes-online.co.uk/index.asp?webType=1

The official newspaper of the UK government relating to Northern Ireland. Includes legal notices especially relating to business and commercial law. Work in progress to digitize the whole set from 1921 onwards.

2675 British and Irish Legal Information Institute
www.bailii.org/databases/databases.htm#nie

Free, public information service, including the text of Northern Ireland Statutes from 1495– Northern Ireland Orders in Council 2001– and Statutory Rules of Northern Ireland 2001– a wide range of transcripts of the decisions of the courts of Northern Ireland and reports, discussion papers and consultation papers of the Office of Law Reform and Law Reform Advisory Committee. Note that much of the recent legislation is displayed in its unamended form. For cases there is no indication of whether they are still good law and they lack the value-added links to other legal materials provided by some of the commercial databases.

2676 LexisNexis Butterworths
www.lexisnexis.co.uk/index.htm

This international database includes only the *Northern Ireland law reports* from 1945 onwards and the *Northern Ireland judgments bulletin* from 1985 onwards.

2677 The Northern Ireland judgments bulletin
Butterworths, 1997–.

Also known as the Blue Book, it covers a wider range of courts than the Northern Ireland Law Reports and publishes the decisions more rapidly. It was formerly known as the *Northern Ireland law reports bulletin of judgments delivered in the courts of Northern Ireland* and although it started in 1971 it only became more widely available outside the province in 1985. The original publisher up to the 1990s was the Incorporated Council of Law Reporting in Northern Ireland.

2678 Northern Ireland law reports
Butterworths, 1992–, qtrly.

The principal and most authoritative law reports for the province, originally published up to 1992 by Incorporated Council of Law Reporting for Northern Ireland. Contains cases from the High Court and Appeal Courts in Northern Ireland and cases on appeal from those courts to the House of Lords.

2679 Northern Ireland legislation
www.opsi.gov.uk/legislation/northernireland/ni_legislation.htm

Official site containing the full text of Acts of the Northern Ireland Assembly, explanatory notes to these Acts and

Statutory Rules of Northern Ireland. Links to Northern Ireland Orders in Council from 1987 onwards and UK Acts and Statutory Instruments which apply exclusively or primarily to Northern Ireland. Note that the text of all materials is as originally passed and does not include subsequent amendments, repeals or revocations.

2680 Northern Ireland statutes
HMSO Belfast, 1921–, annual.
Authoritative version of Acts of the Parliament of Northern Ireland, Northern Ireland Orders in Council and Measures of the Northern Ireland Assembly. Also includes a table listing all UK Acts of Parliament which apply as a whole or in part to Northern Ireland.

2681 Northern Ireland statutory rules
HMSO, Belfast, 1922–, annual.
Authoritative text of delegated legislation made by authorities within Northern Ireland. Prior to 1974 volumes were entitled *Statutory rules and orders*. Also includes a table of all Statutory Instruments made at Westminster which extend to Northern Ireland. Available in their unamended form on the OPSI website at www.opsi.gov.uk/legislation

Statute law database
See entry no. 2767

2682 The statutes revised, Northern Ireland
2nd edn, HMSO, Belfast, 1982. ISBN 0337233640.
The main cumulation of statute law applicable to Northern Ireland. Provides the definitive text as at 31 May 1981 except for UK statutes passed at Westminster since 1920 that extend, or apply, to Northern Ireland. Comprises 13 looseleaf volumes arranged chronologically. An annual cumulative volume lists amendments, repeals etc., up to 31 December of the year covered. For legislation passed after 31 May 1981 use the *Northern Ireland statutes* (q.v.). Available in electronic form on both the official Updated Statutes of Northern Ireland and unofficial BAILII websites (q.v.).

2683 Statutory rules of Northern Ireland
www.opsi.gov.uk/legislation/northernireland/ni-srni.htm
Official site containing the full text, as originally passed, of Statutory Rules of Northern Ireland from 1991 onwards. From June 2004 the Explanatory Memorandum setting out a brief statement of the purpose of a statutory rule and providing information about its purpose is published here – these memoranda are not available in printed form. Note that the text of all the materials does not include any subsequent amendments, repeals or revocations.

2684 Updated statutes of Northern Ireland 1921 to 2004
www.opsi.gov.uk/legislation/northernireland/nisr/ni-welcome.htm
Official site containing the Acts made at Westminster from 1921 to 2004 relating to Northern Ireland amended as at 31st December 2004. It applies the *Cumulative supplement to the statutes revised* (q.v.) to the text of the *Northern Ireland statutes* (q.v.). There is no subject search facility – access is chronological only.

Official & quasi-official bodies

2685 Criminal justice system Northern Ireland
www.cjsni.gov.uk/
Official site for seven statutory agencies whose aim is 'to support the administration of justice, to promote confidence in the criminal justice system and to contribute to the reduction of crime and the fear of crime'. Explains role of each organization, links to associated bodies, provides full text of many publications, including policy documents and a glossary of terms. Site search facility provided.

2686 Law Reform Advisory Committee for Northern Ireland
www.lracni.org/advisory-committee/index.cfm
Official site of the independent body which keeps the civil law of Northern Ireland under review and makes recommendations on its reform. Provides details of current consultations and an archive of completed work and publications. Site search facility available.

2687 Northern Ireland. Courts Service
www.courtsni.gov.uk/en
Official site of the service providing administrative support to the Northern Ireland Courts, including enforcing judgments, supporting the Lord Chancellor in judicial appointments and the operation of the legal aid system. Displays a small selection of judgments and Practice Directions, departmental contact details, key publications both at policy level and procedural forms and leaflets. Strong accent on provision of educational materials for children and the public.

2688 Northern Ireland. Department of Finance & Personnel, Office of Law Reform
www.olrni.gov.uk/
Official site of the body responsible for brining forward proposals for the reform of the civil law in Northern Ireland, especially in family and property law, tort, contract and mental incapacity and decision-making. Describes current and past projects, with links to publications and the Law Reform Advisory Committee (q.v.) which the Office administers. Also details of contacts, links to associated organizations.

2689 Northern Ireland. Legal Services Commission
www.nilsc.org.uk/
Official site of the body responsible for administering the legal aid system in the Province. Searchable directory of solicitors, copies of key policy and procedural documents, information of research and public consultations in progress, links, contact details and press information.

Libraries, archives, museums

2690 Queen's University Belfast, Library
www.qub.ac.uk/directorates/InformationServices/TheLibrary/
The largest academic law library in the province, serving the oldest law school, where law has been taught for over 150 years. The Law Library is part of the main university library but the website provides no details of its strengths.

Discovering print & electronic resources

2691 Chronological table of the statutes: Northern Ireland
HMSO Belfast, every 3 years.
Covers all Northern Ireland legislation since 1310, arranged into sections: pre-Union, UK legislation in force in Northern Ireland, Acts of the Parliament of Northern Ireland, Assembly Measures and Northern Ireland Orders in Council. An authoritative source, weakened by delays in preparation and publishing.

2692 Index to Northern Ireland Cases 1921–1997
Butterworths.
Indexes cases published in a range of law reports, not just those published by Butterworths, including some English series: The Law Reports: Appeal Cases, Criminal Appeal Reports and Tax Cases. Each entry carries only catchwords (the subject index terms which appeared at the head of the full report). Also includes lists of statutes and words and phrases judicially considered.

2693 Index to the statutes: Northern Ireland
HMSO, Belfast, every 3 years.
A subject index to all Acts in force in Northern Ireland except for a few excluded categories. An authoritative source, weakened by delays in preparation and publishing.

2694 Index to the Statutory Rules: Northern Ireland
HMSO, Belfast, every 3 years.
Indexes subordinate legislation for Northern Ireland by subject. Subdivided by the statutory powers under which the Statutory Rules have been made.

2695 Index to the Statutory Rules and Orders of Northern Ireland
TSO Belfast, every 3 years.
Subject index to the delegated legislation for the province. An authoritative source, weakened by delays in preparation and publishing.

2696 Legal bibliography of the British Commonwealth of Nations
2nd edn, Sweet & Maxwell, 1957.
Volume 4: Irish law to 1956 has been described by Woodman (chapter in Winterton & Moys (q.v.) p. 568) as 'the standard older bibliography' and is arranged by both subject and author in a single index (and therefore a little awkward to use) of Irish law publications up to 1956, with the items relating to Northern Ireland indicated by '(NI)' after them. Although bibliographical details are sparse, a good starting point for historical legal research.

Legal Island
See entry no. 2598

Directories & encyclopedias

2697 Digest of Northern Ireland law
B. Dickson and D. McBride   2nd edn, SLS Publishing, 1995. ISBN 0853895864.
Each chapter of this 13-volume 'encyclopedia' is written by an expert contributor on the subject. Individual chapters can be purchased separately.

'Designed to provide reliable, practical guidance on Northern Ireland law and written in a style suitable for those without formal legal training.' (Thomas & Knowles: *How to use a law library* (q.v.), p. 188)

Keeping up to date

2698 Bulletin of Northern Ireland law
SLS Publishing/Faculty of Law, Queen's University Belfast, 1981, 10 p.a. ISSN 02606550.
Summaries of legislation, cases and other legal developments arranged under subject headings. Also available online as a subscription service.
'The principal source of current legal information.' (Woodman in Winterton & Moys (q.v.), p. 569)
'An invaluable current awareness work.' (Knowles in Thomas & Knowles (q.v.), p. 189)

Scotland

Introductions to the subject

2699 Finding the law: a handbook for Scots lawyers
J.W. Colquhoun   T. & T. Clark, 1999, 164pp. ISBN 0567005461.
11 chapters, each one describing a different form of legal material and the relevant paper and electronic sources relevant to researching Scots law. Unfortunately now becoming dated on two counts: the movement away from CD-ROM sources towards the internet and the advent of the Scottish Parliament. However, the greater depth of background information in this book may appeal to some readers over the shorter but more up to date contributions by Hart in Winterton & Moys (q.v.) and Clinch (q.v.).

2700 Information sources in law
J. Winterton and E.M. Moys, eds   2nd edn, Bowker-Saur, 1997, 673pp. ISBN 1857390415.
Chapter on Scotland by Hart briefly describes the legal system of Scotland, introductory works on the legal literature and legal research, the key sources of legislation and case law, government information, directories, bibliographies, current information sources and useful addresses. Even though published before the internet revolution it is still of great value because of the thoroughness of the research.

2701 A legal history of Scotland
D.M. Walker   W. Green, 1988–2004.
The first narrative account of the historical development of the legal institutions and system of concepts, doctrines and principles forming Scots law. Chronological presentation. Extensive bibliography of sources. Comprehensive subject index. Final volume brings account up to the end of 2000.

2702 Sources of legal information
www.rgu.ac.uk/library/howto/page.cfm?pge=27148
Created by Robert Gordon University Library, Aberdeen, this very detailed guide to the sources of law held in the library provides sufficient information to be an introduction to and advice on Scottish legal research for students. Also selection of web links to law sites across the world. Attractive presentation.

2703 Using a law library: a student's guide to legal research skills
P. Clinch   2nd edn, Blackstone Press, 2001, 358pp. ISBN 1841740292.
Chapters by Hart on Scotland describe each legal source (legislation, case law etc.) in turn, followed by descriptions of the publications and databases which either contain the original text or assist exploitation of it and finally provide answers to common legal research queries.

Dictionaries, thesauri, classifications

2704 Bell's dictionary and digest of the law of Scotland
G. Watson   8th edn, Bell & Bradfute, 1890, 1138pp.
The classic work.

2705 Dictionary of words and phrases: judicially defined, and commented on, by Scottish Supreme Courts
A.W. Dalrymple   Green, 1946.
Better known by its spine title: Scottish judicial dictionary.

2706 Glossary of legal terms
S.R. O'Rourke   4th edn, Thomson/W. Green, 2004, 136pp. ISBN 0414015363.
1500 brief definitions of basic legal words and phrases in a Scottish context. Entries do not include citation to legislation of case law. Latest edition includes terminology of Scottish devolution and the implementation of the European Convention of Human Rights. Extensive cross-references. Brief list of common legal abbreviations. Intended for students and the lay person.

2707 Glossary of Scottish and European Union legal terms and Latin phrases
S. Styles, N.R. Whitty and R.C. Lane, comps   2nd edn, LexisNexis UK, 2003, 182pp. ISBN 0406949476.
First appeared as part of the respected *Laws of Scotland* publication (q.v.). Deals with general Scottish legal terminology and Latin words and phrases which, since Roman law is an important source of Scots law, are still in frequent use. Also includes a large number of words and phrases no longer in common use.

2708 Scottish contemporary judicial dictionary of words and phrases
W.J. Stewart   W. Green/Sweet & Maxwell, 1995, 638pp. ISBN 0414010086.
Examines the English language as it has been interpreted in the Scottish courts, concentrating on words judicially considered since 1946, but including entries derived from a range of other law digests, so taking the coverage back to 1800. Entries include quotations from or summaries of cases, with full bibliographic citations. Tables of cases and statutes referred to.

2709 Trayner's Latin maxims: collected from the institutional writers on the law of Scotland and other sources
4th edn, W. Green/Sweet & Maxwell, 1993, 635pp. Reprint of the 4th edition published in 1894. ISBN 0414010612.
Provides greater detail on Latin maxims and phrases than is available in other Scottish law dictionaries.

Laws, standards, codes

2710 Acts of the Parliaments of Scotland 1424–1707
2nd edn rev., HMSO, 1966, 191pp. First published 1908.
Reprints the Acts still in force after the Statute Law Revision (Scotland) Act 1964.
'One of the most convenient sources.' (Hart in Winterton & Moys (q.v.) p. 578)

2711 Acts of the Scottish Parliament
Stationery Office.
www.opsi.gov.uk/
The official versions of ASPs appear as individual copies at first and are eventually issued by the Queen's Printer bound into annual volumes. The text of ASPs is also available on the web. Note that in all these formats the text of the Act remains in its original form and is unconsolidated: that is, it does not include subsequent amendments or repeals.

2712 British and Irish Legal Information Institute
www.bailii.org/databases.html#scot
Free access to legislation as passed by the Scottish Parliament from 1999 onwards but no facility to check whether it is in force, has been amended or repealed. Also access to the transcripts (that is, the unedited text) of decisions of the Court of Session (1998–), High Court of Justiciary (1998–) and the Sheriff Court (1997–). Also publications of the Scottish Law Reform Commission.

2713 Cases decided in the Court of Session
Bell & Bradfute, 1822–. Alternative title: Sessions Cases. Publisher varies.
Now generally referred to as Sessions Cases. The most authoritative source for the full text of decisions of the Court of Session, House of Lords and the High Court of Justiciary in three separately paginated sequences.

2714 Edinburgh Gazette
1699–.
www.gazettes-online.co.uk/index.asp?webType=2
Official newspaper of the UK Government. Published twice a week on Tuesday and Friday. Contains notices as required by law such as insolvency notices as well as government legal information. Website has searchable full-text version from 1998 onwards and a separate searchable archive from 1820–2001.

2715 LexisNexis Butterworths
www.lexisnexis.co.uk/index.htm
Commercial database, including access to the full text of the Acts of the Scottish Parliament in force and links to Statutory Instruments made under the Scotland Act 1998. In addition, the database provides access to a limited number of specialized Scottish law reports and the electronic version of *The Laws of Scotland* (q.v.).

2716 Parliament House book
W. Green, 1982–. Looseleaf. ISBN 0414006887.
Contains legislation, practice notes, solicitors' rules and guidance notes issued by government departments and public offices relating to private law and court procedure.
'An indispensable aid to the Scottish lawyer.' (Hart in Winterton & Moys (q.v.) p. 589)

2717 Scotland legislation
www.opsi.gov.uk/legislation/scotland/about.htm
Official site managed by HMSO on behalf of the Queen's
Printer for Scotland. Contains the full text of all Acts of the
Scottish Parliament (1999–), the Explanatory Notes to the
Acts and Scottish Statutory Instruments (1999–) and
accompanying Executive Notes (2005–). The Executive Notes
set out a brief statement of the purpose of the instrument
and provide information about its policy objectives and
implications. They are not available in printed form. The
legislation is as passed and no details of subsequent
amendments, repeals or revocations are given.

2718 The Scots Law Times
W. Green, 1893–, weekly during the law term. ISSN 0036908X.
Carries the full text of the decisions of a much wider
selection of courts than Session Cases as well as a
Parliamentary news section noting the introduction and
progress of Scottish Bills. Other news items include articles
on legal developments and book reviews.

2719 Scottish current law statutes, 1949–1990
Sweet & Maxwell, 1949–1991, annual.
Reprints all Acts of Parliament at Westminster but includes
materials relating only to Scotland: Acts of Adjournal and
Sederunt. Valued for the annotations and commentary which
started in 1950 in a small way, but became more extensive
as the series developed. Note that the text of every Act
remains in the form originally passed and no details of
subsequent amendments or repeals are given. From 1991
the title merged with *Current law statutes* and the Scottish
materials were no longer included until the advent of the
Scottish Parliament, when a separate section for Scotland re-
appeared.

Statute law database
See entry no. 2767

2720 Westlaw UK
http://westlaw.co.uk
This commercial legal database includes access to the full
text of the Acts and Statutory Instruments of the Scottish
Parliament in their amended form, statutes and Statutory
Instruments made at Westminster currently having effect in
Scotland and the two major Scottish law reports: *Session
cases* and *Scots Law Times*.

Official & quasi-official bodies

2721 Council on Tribunals, Scottish Committee
www.council-on-tribunals.gov.uk/scottish/scottish.htm
Official site of the government body responsible for keeping
under review the constitution and working of tribunals and
inquiries in Scotland. Provides links to biographies of its
committee members and to publications.

2722 Crown Office & Procurator Fiscal Service
www.crownoffice.gov.uk/
Official site of the body 'responsible for the prosecution of
crime in Scotland, the investigation of sudden or suspicious
deaths and the investigation of complaints against the
police'. Describes roles and responsibilities within the
Service, information for victims of crime, those called to be
witnesses in court and policy documents and guidelines. Site
search facility available.

2723 Scottish Courts Service
www.scotcourts.gov.uk/
Official site sponsored by the Scottish Courts Service, for
information on all civil and criminal courts in Scotland. Tabs
at top lead to information designed either for the general
public or professions. Apart from background information on
the history and jurisdiction of each court, location and
contact information provided. Free databases of Court of
Session and High Court of Justiciary and Sheriff Courts
judgments from 1998. Rules of court, practice notes and
guidance. Lists of daily business. A comprehensive site
attractively presented.

Scottish Executive
See entry no. 2036

2724 Scottish Law Commission
www.scotlaw.gov.uk/
Official site of the independent body responsible for
recommending reforms to improve, simplify and update the
law of Scotland. Includes details of its role, responsibilities,
membership, publications, programme of work and lists of
discussion papers and reports, some of which are available
in full-text. Site search facility included.

2725 Scottish legal aid board online
www.slab.org.uk/
Official site of the body responsible for managing the legal
aid system in Scotland. Details its role, responsibilities,
contact details, provides access to its corporate plan and
annual report, research programme and the full text of some
research publications. Site search facility available.

2726 Scottish Legal Services Ombudsman
www.slso.org.uk/
Official site of the body responsible for the investigation of
complaints about the way in which The Law Society of
Scotland or the Faculty of Advocates has handled a
complaint against a practitioner or complaints that these
bodies have acted unreasonably in refusing to investigate a
compliant about a practitioner. Describes: the role and
responsibilities of the body; making a complaint. Lists of
contacts. Site search facility available.

Associations & societies

2727 Faculty of Advocates
www.advocates.org.uk/
Official site of the body representing lawyers who have been
admitted to practise as Advocate before the courts of
Scotland. Provides details of the profession, instructing an
advocate, becoming an advocate and the Advocates Library
(q.v.). Includes full text of the Guide to Professional Conduct.

2728 Law Society of Scotland
www.lawscot.org.uk/
Official site of the governing body for Scottish solicitors.
Describes its role, information about becoming a solicitor, a
searchable directory of solicitors, using a solicitor, making a
complaint. Full-text copies of some publications, including
Professional practice rules and guidelines.

Libraries, archives, museums

2729 Faculty of Advocates, Advocates Library
www.advocates.org.uk/library/index.html
Founded in 1689, it is the working library for the Faculty of
Advocates (the lawyers who represent clients in the Scottish
courts). It has claimed copyright privilege for law
publications published in the British Isles since 1709. Its
stock is available to others via the National Library of
Scotland. Site provides access to the library catalogue and
information on using the library and contact details.

2730 Glasgow University Archive Services
www.lib.gla.ac.uk/Depts/MOPS/Offpub/scotindex.shtml
As well as holding copies of all the papers of the Scottish
Parliament and Scottish Executive published since July 1999,
the Maps and Official Publications Unit staff have created
links to the Scottish Parliament and Scottish Executive
websites making it easy to trace Acts, Bills, Scottish
Statutory Instruments and all other Scottish official
publications on the internet. Effective presentation and easy
to navigate. Elsewhere, the University Library has a leading
collection on Scots law.

2731 University of Edinburgh, Law & Europa Library
www.lib.ed.ac.uk/resbysub/law.shtml
The Law and Europa Library, a part of the large Edinburgh
University Library service, is one of the largest academic law
libraries in Scotland. Extensive collections of Scottish, UK,
international and some foreign law. The website is designed
for the use of students of the University rather than
outsiders and there is very little information describing the
extent of the collections There are links to the University
catalogue.

Portal & task environments

2732 Absolvitor
www.absolvitor.com/index.html
Free portal site created by Iain A. Nisbet, Associate Solicitor,
Govan Law Centre. Provides links to Scots law firms
searchable by location or area of specialization, links to
Scottish law schools, with advice to prospective students, a
legal library (under reconstruction when viewed), legal
humour and the profession portrayed in films. Very attractive
and accessible presentation of information.

2733 Scottish law online
www.scottishlaw.org.uk/
Created by Kevin F. Crombie, a Glasgow University law
graduat,e this portal lists hundreds of links with the focus on
Scots law and legal materials. Selection of value to both
academic and practising lawyers. However, some links are
broken or out of date and parts of the site (e.g. links to the
Scots Law Student Journal) have not been maintained since
2002. Worth a look nevertheless.

2734 University of Dundee – legal web sites library
www.dundee.ac.uk/law/Resources/index.php
Created by the University of Dundee School of Law, a list of
web links to law sites across the world of value to
academics. However, the subject headings and the site links
themselves are arranged in no particular order and the
selection of sites omits some major ones: there are no links

to the official collections of Scots legislation, for example.
Limited use.

Discovering print & electronic resources

2735 Faculty digest
W. Green, 1924–.
Digests cases decided in the Scottish supreme courts, from
1868 onwards, from a range of general law report
publications. Also includes tables of cases judicially referred
to, legislation judicially commented on and words and
phrases judicially considered.

**2736 A legal bibliography of the British Commonwealth
of Nations**
2nd edn, Sweet & Maxwell, 1957.
Volume 5: Scottish law to 1956 is arranged by both subject
and author in a single index (and therefore a little awkward
to use) of Scottish law books and publications up to 1956.
'A reliable source.' (Hart in Winterton & Moys (q.v.) p. 589)

Legal journals index
See entry no. 2803

Digital data, image & text collections

2737 Scottish law articles
www.legal500.com/devs/uk/sl/current.htm
Created by the commercial organization: Legal500, in
association with a number of law firms, provides the full text
of newsletter articles from 2002 to (currently) 2005 created
by the law firms on various Scots law topics of current
interest. Navigation of the site is not easy – need to chop
back the URL to get to earlier articles.

Directories & encyclopedias

2738 Blue Book
Law Society of Scotland, 2004, annual. ISBN 0406973822.
Official directory of the Law Society of Scotland.
Authoritative lists of advocates, solicitors and law firms and,
in addition, addresses for courts, tribunals, legal societies
and organizations, central government departments, public
offices and local government authorities, with contact details
of key personnel.

**2739 The laws of Scotland: Stair memorial
encyclopaedia**
Butterworth, 1987–. Looseleaf. ISBN 040623700X.
25 volumes provide commentary on the law of Scotland
divided alphabetically into 136 broad subject titles.
Consolidated indexes and tables supplement the indexes
within each volume. An annual cumulative supplement and
looseleaf noter-up service keep the main volumes and tables
up to date. Encyclopedia also available on the subscription-
only LexisNexis Butterworths database (q.v.).

2740 The Scottish jurists
D.M. Walker   W. Green, 1985, 492pp. £39. ISBN 0414007573.
Introductory chapter explains the concept of the 'Scottish
jurist' (a term of imprecise meaning), followed by five
chapters discussing the major jurists from earliest times to

the twentieth century. Each entry is a legal biography. Extensive bibliography given as an appendix.

2741   The Scottish law directory 2006: the directory of the Law Society of Scotland
T. & T. Clark, 1895–, annual. ISBN 1405715863.
Also known as the 'White Book', it lists advocates, solicitors and law firms, together with the addresses for courts, tribunals, legal societies and organizations, central government departments, public offices and local government authorities, with contact details of key personnel. For each firm notes the categories of work undertaken but provides no index to assist identifying firms by their work.

Handbooks & manuals

2742   Scottish current law case citator
Sweet & Maxwell, 1948–.
An alphabetical list by case name of reported decisions of the Scottish courts, detailing alternative versions of reports, information on how the decisions were viewed in later cases and cross-references to *Scottish current law yearbook* and *Current law yearbook*, where summaries of the decision will be found. An invaluable tool. Published as a separate Scottish edition in volumes covering 1948–1976, 1977–1988 and then merged as a section within [Current law case citator.

Keeping up to date

2743   Greens Weekly Digest, current Scottish case law
W. Green, 1986–, 40 p.a.
Carries summaries of the decisions of the Scottish courts arranged under subject headings.

2744   Scottish Parliament Business Bulletin
Scottish Parliament, 1999–. ISSN 14670275.
www.scottish.parliament.uk/business/businessBulletin/index.htm
Published daily on the web when the Scottish Parliament is sitting, the *Business Bulletin* details current, future and past business of the Parliament. The associated What's New? pages list in detail the business for the present day with comprehensive links to proposed legislation, committee documents and background materials.

United Kingdom

Introductions to the subject

2745   Butterworths legal research guide
G. Holborn   2nd edn, Butterworths, 2001, 423pp. ISBN 0406930236.
Popular guide to legal research – divided into two parts: a narrative text covering basic techniques, textbooks and secondary sources, legislation, case law, international materials, official publications and researching the law in a selection of jurisdictions outside England and Wales. The second part is an extensive quick reference guide (a summary of the first part) to researching common research problems. Very detailed – if there is a fault, the index at the back is of an unconventional structure and makes tracing discussion of a particular title difficult.

2746   A guide to the UK legal system
www.nyulawglobal.org/globalex/United_Kingdom.htm
Published in November 2005 by the respected then Law Librarian of the University of Kent at Canterbury. A guide to the legal system, including constitutional reform and the courts, describes primary and secondary sources of UK law, parliamentary information, legal publishers, legal profession, legal education. Fully annotated with links to web resources.

Dictionaries, thesauri, classifications

2747   Butterworths company law dictionary
E.R. Hardy Ivamy, ed.   Butterworth, 1983, 208pp. £13.50. ISBN 0406681619.
Compact dictionary on a specialized area of law, suitable for student use. Basic, lacks currency and has not been updated but is only title on this area.

2748   Dictionary of commercial law
A.H. Hudson, ed.   Butterworths, 1983, 308pp. £15. ISBN 0406681597.
Compact dictionary on a specialized area of law, suitable for student use. Basic, lacks currency and has not been updated but is only title on this area.

2749   Dictionary of employment law
N.M. Selwyn, ed.   Butterworths Law, 1985, 300pp. £21.95. ISBN 0406207909.
Compact dictionary on a specialized area of law, suitable for student use. Basic, lacks currency and has not been updated but is only title on this area.

2750   Dictionary of insurance law
E.R. Hardy Ivamy, ed.   Butterworths, 1981, 176pp. £7.50. ISBN 0406603006.
Compact dictionary on a specialized area of law, suitable for student use. Basic, lacks currency and has not been updated but is only title on this area.

2751   A dictionary of law
E.A. Martin and J. Law, eds   6th edn, Oxford University Press, 2006, 608pp. £11.99. ISBN 0192800698X.
Contains over 4300 entries providing concise explanations of legal terminology for UK, European and international law. Features web addresses in some entries, references to key cases on general points of law and guide to writing and citation.

2752   Dictionary of law
4th rev. edn, Bloomsbury Publishing plc, 2004, 336pp. £9.99. ISBN 0747566364.
Compact general law dictionary specially designed for those without a qualification in law. Aimed at surveyors, accountants, civil servants, local government officers, social workers, probation officers and business people who require some knowledge of the precise meaning and spelling of legal terms used in their work. The terms selected for inclusion focus on the modern-day practice of law and the explanations given are often lengthy.

2753   Dictionary of shipping law
E.R. Hardy Ivamy, ed.   Butterworths Law, 1984, 336pp. £15.95. ISBN 0406624003.
Compact dictionary on a specialized area of law suitable, for

student use. Basic, lacks currency and has not been updated but is only title on this area.

2754 Jowitt's dictionary of English law
J. Burke, ed.   2nd rev. edn, Sweet & Maxwell, 1977, 1942pp. o/p. ISBN 0421230908.
Two-volume, comprehensive dictionary of legal terms with full explanations and quotations from Acts and cases to aid understanding. Kept up to date by means of irregular paperback supplements.

2755 Latin words and phrases for lawyers
R.S. Vasan   Law & Business Publications (Canada) Inc, 1981, 335pp. $35. ISBN 0889290040.
Compilation of significant Latin words, phrases and maxims currently in use, as well as some of historical significance. Wherever possible entries include a note of the literary source for the word, phrase or maxim. Cross-reference section at the end of the volume lists maxims under general legal subject headings. Brief bibliography of sources.

2756 A legal thesaurus
C. Miskin, comp.   3rd edn, Legal Information Resources, 1999. £55. ISBN 1870369297.
The only alphabetical listing of legal terms designed for use in the UK; against each entry are noted broader, narrower and related terms. In an electronic form not generally available, it has been incorporated within the Westlaw UK (q.v.) suite of databases and drives the subject search function.

2757 Osborn's concise law dictionary
M. Woodley and S. Bone, eds   10th edn, Sweet & Maxwell, 2005, 499pp. £9.95. ISBN 0421900504.
Frequently revised and, including a wide range of modern-day and historical terms, this dictionary has the added bonus of a list of law reports with their common abbreviations and a table of the regnal years of the English sovereigns (which will assist in locating very old Acts). Probably the best general dictionary of law for student use.

2758 A selection of legal maxims, classified and illustrated
H. Broom   8th edn, Law Book Exchange, 2000, 993pp. $125. ISBN 158477052X.
First published in 1845 and reprinted and updated in many editions both in the UK and abroad, this classic work sets out the principles within the various branches of law, explaining their meaning with reference to extensive case and statute law and the writings of historically respected authors such as Coke and Blackstone.

2759 Stroud's judicial dictionary of words and phrases
D. Greenberg and A. Milbrook   7th rev. edn, Sweet & Maxwell, 2006. £495. ISBN 0421929707.
Provides details of the interpretations by judges of words and phrases, as well as definitions included in statutes. The 6th and 7th editions contain considerably fewer entries than the previous editions, so reference may need to be made to older editions for more obscure words first defined in very old cases. Kept up to date by annual, softback, cumulative supplements. A standard work to be found in the majority of law libraries in the UK.

2760 Words and phrases legally defined
Butterworth Law, 1998, 320pp. £295. ISBN 0406904766.
Similar to *Stroud's judicial dictionary* (q.v.) but, uniquely, provides lengthy verbatim quotations from speeches and judgments. Also has a selection of statutory definitions. Jurisdictional coverage is wider, including extensive references to Commonwealth and US material.

Laws, standards, codes

2761 Acts of the UK Parliament/Public General Acts and General Synod Measures
Statutory Publications Office, 1831–.
www.opsi.gov.uk/acts.htm
The OPSI version or Queen's Printers Copy is the official first printing of primary legislation which has successfully passed through Parliament in Westminster and received the Royal Assent. The loose, officially published, paper copy of individual Acts is the version accepted by the courts in litigation. At the year end these loose issues are bound into volumes entitled the *Public General Acts* and *General Synod Measures*. No indication of repeals or amendments is given in either the paper or the free web versions. From 1999 the website has provided, in addition, the Explanatory Note for each Bill (q.v.). Since the law is subject to constant change through amendment and repeal, caution should be exercised and checks made in other, often commercial, sources that the text provided in this version is still in force and has not been superseded by more recent legislation.

2762 British and Irish Legal Information Institute
www.bailii.org/
Provides free access to a series of case law and legislation databases obtained from a wide range of public bodies, comprising both published and unpublished sources. The site includes decisions of the higher courts for England and Wales, the decisions of a number of tribunals, decisions of the higher courts of Scotland, Northern Ireland and Ireland. In addition UK legislation from the official OPSI website is included. Apart from free access the advantage of this site is that these disparate sources are brought together in a common database format and multiple source searches can be undertaken. The disadvantage over commercial subscription sites is that a) no added value is provided in terms of links to commentary, b) the text of statutes is left in its original, unamended form and c) no details are given of whether a case is still good law.

2763 Current law statutes
Sweet & Maxwell, 1948–. Up to 1993 known as *Current law statutes annotated*.
Reproduces the text of all Pubic General Acts and, since 1992, all Private Acts. For most Acts extensive editorial material is added: commentary written by experts on the meaning and effect of the legislation and details of where in Hansard parliamentary debates on the Bill can be found. One of the most useful sources for research on UK statutes but the text of each Act remains in its unamended form.

2764 Explanatory notes to Public Acts
Statutory Publications Office.
www.opsi.gov.uk/legislation/uk-expa.htm
Since the late 1990s many Public Bills of Westminster have been accompanied by a separate document called

Explanatory Notes. Prepared by the government department sponsoring the Bill, the notes are intended for non-lawyers to help inform debate and understanding of the purpose of the legislation. The Notes are usually published at the same time as the first printing of the Bill so do not take into account any subsequent amendments or renumbering of clauses. Only if the Bill is heavily amended during its passage through Parliament are revised Notes published.

2765 Justis
www.justis.com/

Independent electronic publisher with a range of subscriber-only case law (for example, *The Law Reports*, *Weekly Law Reports*, the *Times Law Reports*) and legislation databases. Justis takes law reports and legislation from a number of other publishers and adds value by providing sophisticated searching, linking and cross-referencing between databases. The JustCite feature is a very useful citation database identifying where cases have been reported and on which databases available in the UK (both free and subscriber-only) the full text will be found.

2766 LexisNexis Butterworths
http://lexisnexis.com/uk/legal/

LexisNexis Butterworths is part of one of the world's largest subscriber-only full-text law database systems. It features the full text of Acts and Statutory Instruments made at Westminster and a database of UK case law drawn from the a wide range of published and unpublished sources. Also includes full text of a selection of practitioner texts and a newspaper database with the full text of UK national newspapers from 1990 onwards. In direct competition with Westlaw UK (q.v.).

2767 Statute law database
www.statutelaw.gov.uk

The official, consolidated version of primary legislation (Acts and Orders in Council) for the UK, including Orders in Council of the devolved legislatures in Scotland and Northern Ireland. Currently in force or in force as at any date from 1 February 1991, as well as all secondary legislation (Statutory Instruments) enacted from 1991. For a minority of items of revised legislation, the changes from 2002 to date have yet to be added – check the update status of legislation link. Some inaccuracies have been located in the text, so caution is advised. The database 'is free of charge to be viewed on screen, copied, printed out for private study and research purposes or for internal circulation with in an organization'. The database replaces the defunct printed publication *Statutes in Force*.

2768 Statutory Instruments
Stationery Office Ltd, 1890–.
www.opsi.gov.uk/stat.htm

The OPSI version of a Statutory Instrument is the official version of secondary legislation which has successfully passed through Parliament in Westminster. At the year end these loose issues are bound into volumes entitled the *Statutory Instruments 20–*. No indication of repeals or amendments is given in either the paper or the free web versions (1987 onwards only). Website provides the text of draft Statutory Instruments and, in addition, from June 2004, the Explanatory Memorandum for each instrument laid before Parliament. Since the law is subject to constant change through amendment and repeal, caution should be exercised and checks made in other, often commercial, sources that the text provided in this version is still in force and has not been overtaken by more recent legislation.

2769 Westlaw UK
http://westlaw.co.uk/

Popular subscriber-only database containing the text of legislation in force at the present time for the UK. Based on the Statute Law Database (q.v.), it includes the ability to view legislation as it stood at any time back to 1 February 1991. Additional feature is ability to view and print consolidated legislation in pdf format. Also includes over 180,000 full-text reports of cases from the UK's leading law report publications, access to the leading UK law journal indexing service (Legal Journals Index), the full text of over 35 law journals and a range of practitioner books with authoritative commentary on the law. In direct competition with LexisNexis Butterworths (q.v.).

Official & quasi-official bodies

2770 Great Britain. Ministry of Justice
www.justice.gov.uk

Official site of the government department formed in May 2007 responsible for, among many areas, the criminal justice system, the functioning of the courts and tribunals, the preparation of sentencing guidelines and the operation of the prison and probation services. Vast array of pages with links to recent and past publications.

2771 Judicial Appointments Commission
www.judicialappointments.gov.uk/

Official site of the independent body responsible for selecting candidates for judicial office on the basis of merit. Includes pages on role and remit, procedures, research, history and context of the Commission and contact information.

Research centres & institutes

2772 Research Development & Statistics Directorate
www.homeoffice.gov.uk/rds

Section of the Home Office providing background statistical series and research reports to assist policy making. Links to the key series: Statistical Bulletins, Research Studies and Development Practice Reports, both current and past publications (even a few from 1969 onwards).

2773 UK Centre for Legal Education
www.ukcle.ac.uk/

UKCLE was formed in 2000 as a successor to the National Centre for Legal Education. The aim of both organizations was to support and improve legal education in the UK in both the academic and vocational sectors. The website sets out the Centre's strategies, publications, details of its own conference and workshop programme.

Associations & societies

2774 British Maritime Law Association
www.bmla.org.uk/

Official site of the association whose aims include promoting the study and development of British maritime and mercantile law, and promoting and considering the unification of law between different nations. Details of constitution, members (with contact information), document archive of current and past papers back to 1997.

2775 Environmental Law Foundation
www.elflaw.org/
Official site of charity linking communities and individuals to legal and technical expertise to prevent damage to the environment. Lists publications but only a few are available from the website.

2776 Planning & Environment Bar Association
www.peba.info/
Association of barristers specialising in planning, environment, compulsory purchase, highways, housing, rating and other aspects of local government and administrative law. Includes directory of solicitor and barrister members and list of web links to associated associations and organizations.

2777 Society of Legal Scholars
www.legalscholars.ac.uk/text/index.cfm
Official site of the learned society for those who teach law in universities or similar institutions or are engaged in legal scholarship. Formerly known as the Society of Public Teachers of Law. Links to a limited number of its papers and publications on legal education and scholarship in the UK.

2778 United Kingdom Environmental Law Association
www.ukela.org/
Official site of the UK forum which aims to make the law work for a better environment and to improve understanding and awareness of environmental law. Includes information about the association, events, publications (including numerous responses to UK and devolved government consultations), a set of useful web links to associated organizations and press releases. No site search facility but easy to navigate.

Libraries, archives, museums

2779 Bodleian Law Library
www.ouls.ox.ac.uk/law
One of several UK law libraries with collections benefiting from the legal deposit by publishers of law books published in the British Isles. Extensive holdings covering a wide range of jurisdictions, concentrating on the UK, Commonwealth, USA, individual European countries and the European Union. UK and Irish collection has great historical depth. Site has guides by subject and jurisdiction and access to the entire Oxford University Library online catalogue.

2780 Cambridge University, Squire Law Library
http://squire.law.cam.ac.uk/index.php
One of several UK law libraries with collections benefiting from the legal deposit by publishers of law books published in the British Isles. Extensive holdings covering a wide range of jurisdictions, concentrating on the UK, with special collections of antiquarian legal history material, historical labour law and legal biographies. Also Commonwealth, North American, French, German and international and comparative law collections. Site includes guides to each collection and access to the online catalogue.

2781 Institute of Advanced Legal Studies
www.ials.sas.ac.uk
Conceived as the national academic institution, attached to the University of London, serving universities through its national legal research library. World-class collection of over 279,000 volumes, including a UK national law library and strengths in common law, civil law and Roman-Dutch law systems throughout the world and material in western European languages for all jurisdictions. Also extensive collections of international and comparative law. Site has access to online library catalogue and a number of free databases developed by the Institute.

2782 School of Oriental & African Studies, Library
www.soas.ac.uk/library/
Extensive academic law collections on the countries of Africa (excluding Romano-Dutch jurisdictions, held at the Institute of Advanced Legal Studies), Asia and the Middle East. Material in western, Asian and African languages. Especially strong on customary law, Islamic law, Bangladesh, China, India and Pakistan. Site has access to the library catalogue and guides to collections.

Portal & task environments

2783 Adviceguide
www.adviceguide.org.uk/
Created by Citizen's Advice (formerly the Citizen's Advice Bureau) the site provides independent legal advice on a wide range of topics, including benefits, housing, employment and debt, consumer and legal issues, details of other organizations which provide advice and legal information. Site includes access to factsheets summarizing the law. Site divided into jurisdictions: England, Wales, Scotland and Northern Ireland; factsheets clearly indicate to which jurisdiction information applies.

2784 Delia Venables legal resources
www.venables.co.uk/
Gateway providing annotated links to a huge number of important law websites relating to the UK and Ireland. The law, the legal profession, law students and legal information for companies and businesses are catered for. Links are also arranged by topic. The sites selected are of greater interest to the practising as opposed to the academic lawyer, complementing the other major UK law gateway, Lawlinks (q.v.).

2785 Intute: social sciences: law
www.intute.ac.uk/socialsciences/law/
Formerly known as SOSIG Law, provides searchable list of links to thousands of web resources, worldwide, of both primary and secondary law sources, which have been added to the database only after thorough evaluation. Descriptive records provided for each entry. An award-winning site edited by librarians from two major academic law libraries in the UK – Institute of Advanced Legal Studies (q.v.) and University of Bristol.

2786 Lawlinks: legal information on the internet
http://library.kent.ac.uk/library/lawlinks/default.htm
Award-winning, comprehensive gateway of links, with annotations, to UK, EU and international law resources. Covers not just the law itself but also the legal profession,

legal publishing and electronic discussion lists. Annotations provide useful commentary on the value to UK lawyers of each of the sites selected. The bias is towards sites of interest to academic as opposed to practising lawyers and complements the Delia Venables site (q.v.). A site search engine is available.

Discovering print & electronic resources

Bibliography of Commonwealth law reports
W. Breem and S. Phillips, eds   See entry no. 2128

2787 **Chronological table of local legislation 1797–1994 and chronological table of private and personal Acts 1539–1997: 1999 supplement**
Great Britain. Law Commission   Stationery Office Ltd, 2000, 124pp. £47.
Official lists in date order of Local Acts made between the end of 1994 and the end of 1999, with details of repeals, supplementing the main volumes listed below.

2788 **Chronological table of local legislation, 1797–1994**
Great Britain. Law Commission and Great Britain. Scottish Law Commission   Stationery Office Ltd, 1996, 2836pp. £180. ISBN 0110430026.
www.opsi.gov.uk/chron-tables/chron-index.htm
Official lists in date order of over 26,500 Local Acts made from 1797 up to the end of 1994, with details of repeals. The introduction explains the background to this huge project and also lists the libraries and record offices where collections of Local Acts may be found. The web version of this publication (at the time of checking) is up to date to December 2005 and is to be preferred.

2789 **Chronological table of private and personal acts**
Law Commission for England & Wales and Scottish Law Commission   Stationery Office, 1999. £75. ISBN 0110430069.
www.opsi.gov.uk/chron-tables/chron-index.htm
Official printed lists in date order of thousands of Private and Personal Acts made from 1539 up to the end of 1999, with details of repeals. The web version of this publication (at time of checking) is up to date to December 2005 and is to be preferred.

2790 **Chronological table of the statutes: 1235–1999**
Stationery Office Ltd, 2001, 2422pp. £200. ISBN 0118403842.
Lists in date order all Public General Acts passed at Westminster between 1235 and the end of 2004, Scottish Parliament 1999 to the end of 2004, Acts of the Parliament of Scotland 1424 to 1707 and Church Assembly Measures and General Synod Measures 1920 to the end of 2004. Against each entry are details of repeals and amendments. Even though the latest volume is not completely up to date, it is very useful for historical research when checking details about Acts repealed long ago.

2791 **Current awareness for legal information managers database**
http://ials.sas.ac.uk/library/caware/caware.htm
Searchable, free database of books and articles relevant to law librarians and legal information professionals, derived from the current awareness column appearing in each quarterly issue of *Legal Information Management*, the

professional journal of the British and Irish Association of Law Librarians. The database started in 2000 and includes bibliographic details only.

2792 **Current legal information**
www.sweetandmaxwell.co.uk/online/cli.html
A suite of subscriber-only databases, some of which are also embedded within the Westlaw UK database (q.v.). Includes Current Law Cases (digests of all reported cases dating back to 1947), Case Citator, Legislation Citator, LRDI (an index of legal current awareness information) and Legal and Financial Journals Index. Available as CD-ROM and on the web.

2793 **Current legal research topics database**
http://ials.sas.ac.uk/library/clrt/clrt.htm
The free database lists the research topics in law (that is, the titles of the dissertations) being pursued at the present time by postgraduate law students (M.Phil and PhD only) based in the UK. Searches may be made by subject, keywords in the title, jurisdiction, student name and university name. The database is updated annually by means of a survey of all UK law schools. The database continues the *List of current research topics* (see *Legal research in the United Kingdom*).

2794 **Devolution in the United Kingdom: a revolution in online legal research**
www.llrx.com/features/devolution.htm
Article written by a respected librarian based in the USA on the legal aspects of devolution in the UK since 1998. Outlines the process of devolution, the key legislative materials and impact on online legal research. A valuable introduction but, since published in June 2001, would benefit from updating, especially for the web links and contents of the electronic sources.

2795 **The Digest**
Butterworths, qtrly. £3,000. ISBN 0406025002.
The Digest has three main purposes: to summarize over 250,000 cases drawn from over 1000 different series of law reports covering the whole case law of England and Wales from the 16th century onwards, together with a selection of cases from the courts of Scotland, Ireland, Canada, Australia, New Zealand and other Commonwealth countries; to act as a case citator, listing subsequent citations to that case and, finally, to act as a finding tool for the correct citation of cases not included in *Current law case citator* (q.v.) by reason of date (pre-1947) or jurisdiction. The richness of the resource is unmatched but its value for up-to-the minute research is limited by the quarterly updating.

2796 **FLAG Project**
http://ials.sas.ac.uk/library/flag/flag.htm
Award-winning, freely searchable inventory or guide to the foreign, international and comparative law holdings of over 60 UK universities, the Inns of Court libraries in London and the National Archives. Searches may be made by jurisdiction, type of legal material and region of the UK. The purpose of the database is to assist users locate sources of law close to their usual base. It is neither a catalogue nor a title listing but aims to highlight where in the UK are located, for example, collections of legislation for Poland, case law for Singapore or the official publications of the World Trade Organization.

2797 Guide to law reports and statutes
4th edn, Sweet & Maxwell, 1962, 143pp. o/p.
Provides numerous tables and lists to legislation and law reports, including list of historic editions of statutes, a table of regnal years, alphabetical lists of law report publications from earliest times with their commonly used abbreviations. An invaluable reference tool when trying to trace very old statutes or old and obscure law reports.

2798 Halsbury's Statutory Instruments
rev. edn, Butterworths Law, 1986–. Published in a set of 22 volumes with looseleaf updates. £1899. ISBN 0406996172.
Summarizes many but not all Statutory Instruments of general application and includes the full text of a few. It includes only SIs made at Westminster – it excludes those made by the Welsh Assembly or extending only to Scotland. As the balance between summaries and full-text has moved rapidly in favour of summaries, the value of the publication to lawyers has decreased but the range of indexes can still be of use in tracing SIs from minimum information.

2799 Index to the local and personal Acts 1850–1995
R. Devine; Great Britain. House of Lords　Stationery Office Ltd, 1996, 2309pp. £180. ISBN 0110430034.
Six-volume index listing all Private Acts arranged in alphabetical order by title, with cross-references to personal names and places.

2800 Index to the statutes: covering the legislation to 31st December
Stationery Office Ltd, 1998, 1947pp. £235. ISBN 0337236429.
This publication provides a subject index to the defunct publication *Statutes in force*. Although no use for current research because the current and probably last edition is so out of date, it can still be of use for historical legal research. In some respects both the publications mentioned here have been overtaken by the free Statute Law Database (q.v.).

2801 Infolaw
www.infolaw.co.uk/
Web information service mainly, though not exclusively, designed for practising lawyers by Nick Holmes, a well known commentator on the UK legal web. 'Lawfinder' section provides free access to an index of probably thousands of web legal resources, including UK legislation, cases, government documents, EU materials, directories, forms and precedents, directories of solicitors and barristers and sections on overseas law. Access to the full text of some materials is restricted to subscribers. A cornucopia of links.

2802 Lawyers' law books: a practical index to literature
D. Raistrick and J. Rees, eds　3rd rev. edn, Bowker, 1997, 600pp. £81. ISBN 1857390873.
A quite detailed subject listing of encyclopedias, periodicals and textbooks, with an author index. There is no evaluation of sources. Most texts listed were published after 1980 but a few older and still useful titles are also included. The publication is unique but is becoming less and less useful as time passes.

2803 Legal journals index
Sweet & Maxwell, 1986–. Originally published in paper format now only available as a subscriber-only database.
www.sweetandmaxwell.co.uk/online/cli.html
Established in 1986 and now available only by subscription

in electronic format, this database quickly established itself as the foremost law periodical indexing service for the UK. It indexes over 500 titles published in the UK as well as a large number of English-language legal journals published in EU countries. Its subject coverage is very wide, including not only law as such but also such topics as the legal profession, education, training and information technology. It has indexed all Scottish journals since inception in 1986, and Irish legal journals since 1993. The database is available as part of Current Legal Information and Westlaw UK (q.v.).

2804 Legal online resource database
www.biall.org.uk/LORD.asp
Searchable database enabling users wishing to find in which databases and websites particular law reports, journals, newsletters, directories, etc. published in the British Isles are available in electronic form. Simple and effective to use.

2805 Legal research in the United Kingdom 1905–1984: a classified list of legal theses and dissertations successfully completed for postgraduate degrees awarded by universities and polytechnics in the United Kingdom from 1905–1984
University of London, Institute of Advanced Legal Studies, 1985, 304pp. ISBN 0901190292.
Lists arranged by subject and then chronologically of the titles of theses successfully submitted to over 40 universities and colleges in the UK. It still has value as a permanent record of legal research completed. The listing was updated until October 1988 by an annual publication, *List of current research topics*, but both have been overtaken by the Current legal research topics database (q.v.).

2806 World Law: United Kingdom
www.worldlii.org/catalog/267.html
Comprehensive list of links to websites of United Kingdom law and legal information, arranged by jurisdiction or subject or organization and with search facility across all entries. Very brief annotations to each link. Part of the World Legal Information Institute service developed by the Australasian Legal Information Institute (q.v.).

Directories & encyclopedias

2807 Chambers UK – a client's guide to the UK legal profession 2005
R. Ghosh [et al.]　Chambers & Partners. £75. ISBN 0855141158.
Annual guide to the top 1000 law firms and all barristers' chambers in the UK, with useful specialists lists indicating which firms and chambers are best known for particular areas of expertise and also regional listings. Indexes assist in finding firms or sets of chambers handling particular types of legal business.

2808 Directory of British and Irish law libraries
P. Fothergill　8th edn, Legal Library Services, 2006, 222pp. £73. ISBN 0950208167.
Lists geographically by country and then by city or town, the libraries and information units in organizations which have members of the professional association for law librarians and which responded to a postal survey questionnaire conducted on behalf of the Association. This is not a complete listing of members or organizations. Each entry provides contact details, indicators of the size and range of

stock and services, and details of whether public access is provided. Indexes by organization name, by type of organization (academic, law firm, government etc.) and subject strengths.

2809 Directory of registers and records
T.M. Aldridge 5th rev. edn, Sweet & Maxwell, 1993, 160pp. £26. ISBN 0752000012.
Contains a wealth of information on the location of and how to obtain access to a wide range of records of value in legal practice. Includes information on: birth certificates, wills, county court judgments, closed burial grounds, lotteries and Jersey companies. Although in need of updating it is certainly 'a remarkably useful work' (Holborn, G. Butterworths Legal Research Guide (q.v.) para 2.69)

2810 Oxford companion to law
D.M. Walker Clarendon Press, 1980, 1366pp. £45. ISBN 019866110X.
Contains thousands of dictionary-like entries on the principal legal institutions, courts, judges, jurists, systems of law, branches of law, legal ideas, concepts, doctrines and principles of law. Includes entries on civil law systems, so of value to Scots lawyers. However, the lack of a new edition confines its value to historical legal research.

2811 Shaw's directory of courts in the United Kingdom 2006/07
Shaw & Sons, 2006, annual, 464pp. £46.50. ISBN 07291916333 ISSN 0264312X.
Provides contact information for all courts, coroners, the Crown Prosecution Service, Procurator Fiscal Service (Scotland) and penal establishments in the UK. Maintains it is the most comprehensive reference work of its type. Well established and trusted directory.

Handbooks & manuals

2812 BIALL handbook of legal information management
L. Worley Ashgate, 2006, 288pp. £70. ISBN 9780754641827.
Chapters cover the growth of law librarianship, analyses of different types of service and users, research techniques, sourcing and organizing different types of legal information, choosing and purchasing library management systems, managing budgets, staff management, copyright and data protection issues, knowledge management and virtual learning environments. A valuable compendium to modern law librarianship.
'BIALL has brought together an unparalleled team of respected experts to provide authoritative and up-to-date best practice guidance on the key legal information issues for every type of service, focusing particularly on the balance between electronic and printed resources, free and charged services and electronic and on-site access.'

2813 Current law legislation citator
Sweet & Maxwell. Comprises the Statute Citator and the Statutory Instrument Citator.
Known originally as *Current law statute citator*, this set of volumes covering the period from 1947 onwards, is a valuable tool for discovering whether a particular Act has come into force, has been amended, has had detailed rules, orders or regulations made under it, is still in force or has been considered by the courts, and the meaning of sections

interpreted by the courts. Similar information is given about Statutory Instruments but in the *Statutory Instrument citator* which commenced in 1993. The electronic version of these citators is embedded within the Westlaw UK database (q.v.).

2814 Manual of law librarianship: the use and organization of legal literature
E.M. Moys 2nd rev. edn, Gower Publishing Ltd, 1987, 952pp. £100. ISBN 056603512X.
Pioneering bibliographical account in the English-speaking world on all aspects of law librarianship. Although parts of every section show their age, especially those on law library practice, there is still much of value in the descriptions of the basic literature of law in common law and other legal systems. The chapters on legal materials outside the common law have not been up-dated in the *BIALL handbook* (q.v.) and remain useful survey. Detailed indexes of works cited and subjects.

2815 Manual of legal citations: British Isles
University of London, Institute of Advanced Legal Studies, 1959, 94pp. ISBN 0901190098.
In two parts: British Isles and British Commonwealth. Aims to be a style guide for the citation of law materials, together with lists of preferred abbreviations for law reports. Devised by academic lawyers – the publication has had little impact in standardizing citation practice but the lists of abbreviations are still of use.

2816 Oxford standard citation of legal authorities
http://denning.law.ox.ac.uk/published/oscola.shtml
OSCOLA is a style guide and citation standard for legal writing devised by the Faculty of Law at the University of Oxford. The site is free and sets out standards for legal authors when citing materials and compiling footnotes. It is the only publicly available citation and style guide specifically designed for use by UK lawyers.

Keeping up to date

2817 Current Law Monthly Digest
Sweet & Maxwell, 1947–, monthly.
Provides brief summaries of recent Acts, Statutory Instruments and case law (both UK and EU), together with details of the authors and titles of new books and periodical articles, as well as major government publications. The arrangement is by broad subjects making it easy to scan for personal current awareness. After the year end the monthly issues are replaced by the consolidated *Current law year book*. Together, *Current Law Monthly Digest* and the *Current law year books* from 1947 onwards are a fundamental finding resource in a UK law library.

2818 Lawtel
www.lawtel.com
Subscriber-only database – essentially for current awareness. Summaries of new case law, legislation (including Bills of Parliament), government publications and articles from about 50 journals are added to the site every 24 hours. Subscribers can set up daily or weekly alerting bulletins on topics of their choice. There is a backrun of material to 1984 but no feature to indicate if cases summarized are still good law. Other databases available at extra cost provide access to

EU law, reports of cases on quantum of damages in personal injury claims, and law directories.

2819 What's new on the UK legal web?
www.binarylaw.co.uk/
Free site containing a blog by Nick Holmes, a publishing consultant specializing in UK legal information and Managing Director of infolaw (q.v.). As well as a blog on his own topics, the site has lists, with links, of UK law blogs and UK law and related feeds. Represents the unofficial side of keeping up to date with legal developments and opinions about them.

United Kingdom – Subordinate Jurisdictions

Introductions to the subject

2820 Effective legal research
J. Knowles and P.A. Thomas   Sweet & Maxwell, 2006, 187pp. ISBN 0421922702.
In essence this is a new edition of a part of the long-established and well regarded Dane & Thomas, *How to use a law library*, 4th edn Sweet & Maxwell, 2001. It concentrates on how to undertake research of the law of England and Wales, European human rights law and the law of the EU. A brief appendix covers major sources of Scots and Northern Ireland law.

2821 History of English law
W.S. Holdsworth   rev.edn, Methuen, 1956–1972. In 17 volumes.
Monumental 17-volume description of English legal history from Anglo Saxon times to the Judicature Acts of the latter part of he 19th century. Continued by others after the author's death towards the end of the project. Thoroughly researched and indispensable for the legal historian, but being replaced by the *Oxford history of the laws of England* (q.v.), which has the benefit of modern research and scholarship.

2822 Information sources in law
J. Winterton and E.M. Moys, eds   2nd edn, Bowker-Saur, 1997, 673pp. ISBN 1857390415.
Chapter on England and Wales by Clinch, Thrift, Way and Holborn briefly describes the legal system of England and Wales, introductory works on the legal literature and legal research, the key sources of legislation and case law, government information, directories, bibliographies, current information sources and useful addresses. Even though published before the internet revolution, it is still of great value because of the thoroughness of the research.

2823 Oxford history of the laws of England
Oxford University Press, 2004. Series in progress.
Detailed survey of the development of English law and its institutions from earliest times until the 20th century, drawing heavily on recent research using unpublished materials. Comprises 12 volumes, each by a different author and covering a different time period. Replacing the *History of English law* (q.v.).

2824 Using a law library: a student's guide to legal research skills
P. Clinch   2nd edn, Blackstone Press, 2001, 346pp. ISBN 1841740292.
Covers the sources and techniques of researching the law of England and Wales, Scotland, European human rights and EU law. Each chapter has a common and user-friendly structure covering a description of the source of law, a description of each publication or database which either contains the text of the original source or is an aid to exploiting it, and a section on how to answer common research queries relating to the source. Additional chapters cover finding and using a law library, keeping up to date and undertaking a piece of extended legal research effectively and efficiently.

Dictionaries, thesauri, classifications

2825 Biographical dictionary of the common law
A.W.B. Simpson   Butterworths Law, 1984, 588pp. £42.95. ISBN 040651657X.
Provides biographies of about 700 famous lawyers who achieved prominence before 1939. Focus is on English common law and England and Wales especially. Intended as a pointer where to go next for further information, so entries focus more on references to other bibliographies, articles, essays and even where portraits or photographs of personalities may be found, rather than describing lives in detail. Unique but badly in need of updating.

2826 A dictionary of legal quotations
J.S. Stebbings and C. Stebbings, comps   Croom Helm, 1987, 210pp. Published in India. ISBN 0709914032.
Lists quotations under 160 broad headings, with a keyword index to assist finding where an entry for a quote referring to two or more topics is printed. Also indexes of authors and sources.

Laws, standards, codes

2827 All England Law Reports
Butterworths, 1936–, weekly. ISSN 00025569.
Along with *The Law Reports* (q.v.) and the *Weekly Law Reports* (q.v.) one of the major series of law reports publishing the full text of a selection of cases of general as opposed to specialist legal interest. The reports are available electronically as part of the subscriber-only database: LexisNexis Butterworths (q.v.). There is considerable though not total overlap with the cases reported in the other two series. A selection of earlier cases is published in *All England law reports reprint, 1558–1935*.

2828 Halsbury's statutes of England and Wales
4th edn, Butterworths, 1985–. ISBN 0406214093.
Aims to provide up-to-date versions of all Public General Acts (with a few minor exceptions) in force in England and Wales and, in addition, copious commentary and notes. The main part of the publication consists of 50 bound volumes setting out the text of legislation, arranged under broad subject headings. Additional volumes provide details of changes affecting the main volumes, the text of recent statutes not yet printed in the main volumes and various indexes, tables and other research tools. In all this is a key publication for

the academic and practitioner law library. Also available as part of the LexisNexis Butterworths subscriber-only database (q.v.).

2829   The Law Reports

Incorporated Council of Law Reporting for England & Wales, 1865–. The most authoritative series of law reports by reason of the judges checking the text before publication. Further, they are the only series to provide skeleton arguments of counsel argued before the court. Along with the *All England Law Reports* (q.v.) and the *Weekly Law Reports* (q.v.) they publish the full text of a selection of cases of general as opposed to specialist legal interest. The reports are available electronically as part of the subscriber-only databases: LexisNexis Butterworths (q.v.), Justis (q.v.) and Westlaw UK (q.v.). There is considerable though not total overlap with the cases reported in the other two series.

2830   Weekly Law Reports

Incorporated Council of Law Reporting for England & Wales, 1953–, weekly. ISSN 00193518.

The contents of Volumes 2 and 3 of this publication provide advance publication of cases destined to appear in *The Law Reports*. Together with the *All England Law Reports* (q.v.) the *Weekly Law Reports* is one of the major series of law reports publishing the full text of a selection of cases of general as opposed to specialist legal interest. The reports are available electronically as part of the subscriber-only database: Westlaw UK (q.v.) and Justis (q.v.). There is considerable though not total overlap with the cases reported in the *All England Law Reports* (q.v.).

Official & quasi-official bodies

2831   Council on Tribunals

www.council-on-tribunals.gov.uk/

Official site of the government body responsible for keeping under review the constitution and working of tribunals and inquiries in England, Wales and Northern Ireland – there is a separate Scottish Committee. Details its standards, consultative process, links to copies of its publications, news and contacts.

2832   Criminal justice system

www.cjsonline.gov.uk

Official site providing information about the criminal justice system in England and Wales. Easy access to information for members of the public coming into contact with the system either as a victim, witness, defendant, offender or juror. Although primarily intended for public use information and links are provided for further study.

2833   Crown Prosecution Service

www.cps.gov.uk/

Official site of the government department responsible for prosecuting criminal cases investigated by the police in England and Wales. While mainly intended for the public, the section for professionals includes links to technical publications intended for prosecutors and caseworkers.

2834   Great Britain. Department for Constitutional Affairs

www.dca.gov.uk/

Official site for the government department responsible for

running the courts, improving the justice system, upholding human rights and information rights law, running elections and modernizing the constitution. Links under publications lead to large library of official papers, reports, research documents, statistics and speeches.

2835   Her Majesty's Court Service

www.hmcourts-service.gov.uk/

Official site of the government agency responsible for managing many of the courts in England and Wales. Includes a court finder database, copies of official forms, cause list (calendar of forthcoming actions to be heard) and the full text of a selection of judgments.

2836   Law Commission for England & Wales

www.lawcom.gov.uk/

Official site of the independent body responsible for keeping under review the law of England and Wales and making recommendations for its reform. Apart from information about the role of the Commission, the crucial value of the site is access to the full text of its consultation papers from 1996 onwards and its reports from 1998 onwards. Lists of all its consultation papers and reports are also available.

Associations & societies

2837   Council for Licensed Conveyancers

www.theclc.gov.uk/

Official site of the professional association for specialist property lawyers dealing with the transfer of buildings and/or land from one owner to another. Two parts to site: information for the public, including a searchable directory of members and where they practise, guide to professional conduct and complaints procedure. The professionals site covers qualifying, rules and technical information.

2838   General Council of the Bar for England & Wales

www.barcouncil.org.uk/

Official site of the professional body for barristers in England and Wales – lawyers qualified to represent clients in court. Includes information about the structure and role of the Council, how the Bar operates, an online directory of practising barristers, how to become a barrister and complaints procedures for the public.

2839   Institute of Legal Executives

www.ilex.org.uk/

Official site of the professional body of lawyers who work alongside solicitors and barristers in a technical and specialized capacity. Includes searchable directory of members, how to become a legal executive and access to the indexes (but only up to date to 2004 when searched in 2007) to the Institute's journal *The Legal Executive*.

2840   Law Society of England & Wales

www.lawsociety.org.uk/

Official site of the body which represents solicitors in England and Wales. Provides information on its role, the work of its members (including the Solicitors-Online directory of law firms and individual solicitors who have asked to be included), training to become a solicitor, complaints procedures and downloadable copies of publications in all these areas. Site search facility available.

Libraries, archives, museums

2841   Law Society of England & Wales, Library Services
www.lawsociety.org/.uk/productsandservces/libraryservices.law
Probably the most extensive law library for practising
solicitors and their staff and students following the Legal
Practice Course of training in England and Wales – it is not
open to students generally or members of the public. Its
special value to academics is its extensive collections on
legal history and the practice of law, including holdings of
directories of lawyers. The online catalogue, Catalyst, is
searchable at www.catalyst.lawsociety.org.uk/

Portal & task environments

2842   Lawbore
www.lawbore.net
Law gateway designed by staff of City University, London to
provide legal information and links for students. The site is
organized by subject, with sections of background
information on each topic with links to relevant websites,
articles and documents. Some links are available only to
students of City University. Current legal news stories feature
prominently.

Discovering print & electronic resources

2843   law-index@swarb.co.uk
www.swarb.co.uk/
Created and developed through the initiative of one solicitor,
David Swarbrick, this site provides access to lawindexpro, a
subscriber-only index of well over 110,000 cases, some with
summaries and many with cross-references to other
materials, a free judgments database of the full text of 60
judgments, 'law bytes' – free advice sheets intended for the
public – and a statutes database of extracts of well over 330
statutes, some not available freely anywhere on the web.

2844   A legal bibliography of the British Commonwealth of Nations
2nd edn, Sweet & Maxwell, 1957.
Volume 1: English law to 1800 and Volume 2: English law
1801–1954 are arranged by subject, with a separate author
index. This thoroughly researched bibliography of English law
books and publications is correct to 1954.
'The standard bibliography.' (G. Holborn *Butterworths legal
research guide* (q.v.), para 2.16)

Directories & encyclopedias

2845   Atkin's court forms
I. Foster [et al.]   Butterworths Law, 1991–. Set of 41 volumes.
£3,950. ISBN 0406083029.
Reprints court forms and procedural documents used in civil
proceedings. Provides commentary and checklists for
practice and procedure. The main work of over 50 volumes
of forms and precedents is arranged in subject groups.
These volumes are kept up to date by a looseleaf service.
Additional volumes include the text of key rules and indexes
to the set. An essential source for the litigation lawyer. Has
been available as a subscriber-only CD database but the title

is planned to be added to the LexisNexis Butterworths
database shortly (q.v.).

2846   The Bar directory 2006
Sweet & Maxwell, 2006. ISBN 0421960205.
www.legalhub.co.uk/legalhub/app/main
The official listing of barristers, produced for the General
Council of the Bar. Listing by type of work of each set of
chambers, type of work by individual barristers, chambers
by location, listings of barristers in private practice,
employed barristers (that is, not working on own behalf) and
non-practising and names of individual barristers overseas.
Also index of languages spoken. The majority of sections in
the printed directory are available free to search on the Legal
Hub website.

2847   Butterworths law directory 2005
Butterworths Law, annual. £69. ISBN 1405709855.
www.lawyerlocator.co.uk
An alternative to *Waterlow's solicitors' and barrister's directory*
(q.v.), listing for England and Wales solicitors in practice and
barristers (except non-practising). The section relating to
solicitors can be searched free on the web.

2848   Directory of solicitors and barristers
Law Society, 2006, 2200pp. £94.95. ISBN 1853285633.
www.solicitors-online.com
The official listing of solicitors regulated by the Law Society
for England and Wales, barristers regulated by the Bar
Council for England and Wales and also Fellows of the
Institute of Legal Executives and licensed conveyancers. The
list of solicitors' firms and individuals is arranged
geographically with details of the work they undertake. The
internet version is available on the Law Society website, free
to use.

2849   Encyclopedia of forms and precedents other than court forms
5th edn, Butterworths. Also available as a subscriber-only database
on LexisNexis Butterworths, £3,600.
Contains a wide range of non-litigious forms and precedents
(i.e. forms and precedents used in legal transactions outside
the courts) and is an authoritative guide to the drafting of
legal documents. Over 40 volumes provide the text of forms
and documents arranged by subject, kept up to date by a
looseleaf service with an annual consolidated index.

2850   Halsbury's laws of England
4th edn, Butterworths Law, 1991–. £5,082. ISBN 0406047766.
Over 50 volumes of commentary on the whole law of
England and Wales, written by editorial staff, linking
legislation and case law together. The arrangement of the
narrative text is by subject. No original materials are
included but the title is the best starting point for general
research – especially practitioner as opposed to academic –
of a legal topic. There are seven parts to the encyclopedia,
which is kept up to date by looseleaf supplements and a
booklet issued monthly. A key research publication found in
virtually every academic library, solicitors' firm, barristers'
chambers and many large public libraries. Also available as
part of the subscriber-only LexisNexis Butterworths database
(q.v.).

2851 The legal 500
J. Pritchard   rev. edn, Legalease, 2005, 1376pp. £120. ISBN 1903927501.
www.icclaw.com/l500/uk.htm
A who's who of law practitioners. Aims to provide evaluative guidance on the specialisms and reputations of particular firms of solicitors and barristers' chambers in England and Wales as well as information not found in other directories, such as the number of staff, recruitment of trainee solicitors and a history of the firm. The intended readership is commercial clients. Inclusion is selective and tends to concentrate on the larger firms but there is editorial comment on smaller firms. Short entries are free but longer entries are made on payment by the firm. Available on the internet, free to use, together with a range of similar directories on the website for other parts of the world.

2852 List of English law officers, King's Counsel and holders of patents of procedure
J.C. Sainty, comp.   Seldon Society, 1987. £32.
Lists holders of the offices of King's sergeant, attorney-general, solicitor general, advocate general and King's counsel from the time of the institution of the office to the time of discontinuation or 1984. Each list preceded by an introductory note giving details of the method of appointment, tenure etc. Invaluable tool for researching historical legal biography.

2853 Waterlow's solicitors' and barristers' directory 2007
Waterlow Professional Publishing, 1844–, annual. £76.95. ISBN 1857830865.
www.connectinglegal.com
Lists for England and Wales solicitors geographically by firm and alphabetically by the name of the individual solicitor. The type of work carried out by each firm is listed. Barristers' chambers, Queen's Counsel (senior barristers), judges, Benchers of the Inns, Recorders and members of the Institute of Legal Executives are also listed. The directory is also available to search free on the web – the site claims that all the Waterlow's web directories are fully updated twice a month.

Handbooks & manuals

2854 Current law case citator
An alphabetical list by case name of cases from the courts of England, Wales and Scotland reported between 1947 and the present with a) a comprehensive list of references to where the case was originally reported; b) a judicial history of each case, detailing reported appeals to a higher court; c) details of whether courts in later cases have applied, considered, approved, disapproved, followed or referred to the original decision; and d) details of where the original case s summarized in the sister publication, *Current law yearbook*. A unique, invaluable and indispensable part of a UK law library. The data contained in the citatory is embedded in the subscriber-only Westlaw UK database (q.v.) and in the Current Legal Information suite of materials.

Keeping up to date

2855 Daily Law Notes
www.lawreports.co.uk/
Official site of the Incorporated Council of Law Reporting (ICLR). ICLR was established by members of the legal profession in 1865 and the site provides free access to summaries of cases to be published in full-text in two of its flagship printed publications: Weekly Law Reports (q.v.) and Industrial Cases Reports. Access to summaries on WLR Daily and ICR Express is by lists arranged by court or date or case name – it is not searchable in any more sophisticated way. A free e-mail case summary alert service is available.

2856 Halsbury's Laws Monthly Review
Butterworths Law, monthly. Integral part of the Halsbury's Laws of England encyclopedia.
Booklet containing summaries of very recent developments in legislation and case law relating to England and Wales, arranged under the same broad subject headings as *Halsbury's laws of England and Wales* (q.v.) encyclopedia, to which it forms part of the updating service.

United States

Introductions to the subject

2857 Computer aided legal research
J.A. Long   Thomson/Delmar Learning, 2003, 233pp. ISBN 0766813339.
Covers the comparison of manual and electronic research tools and methods, an introduction to internet research, federal and state sources, subject sources, using Westlaw and Lexis, CD-ROMs and Loislaw (an internet and CD-ROM US-only research service). Attractively presented with many screenshots, tables and bullet point lists. However, electronic sources evolve fast and the publication will date quickly.

2858 Cornell legal research encyclopedia
www.lawschool.cornell.edu/library/encyclopedia/encyclopedia.html
Online resource and bibliography still under development by librarians at the Cornell Law School Library. Four parts: subject section has table of topics with web links; countries section lists a wide selection of countries, some with extensive essays on the legal sources, others links and lists of printed titles. US section has links to lists of web links and in some cases references to printed materials containing statute and case law; international law section has not been built. Presentation and content vary greatly across the site and many parts have not been updated since 2000.

2859 Finding the law
R.C. Berring and E.A. Edinger   11th edn, West Publishing Co, 1999, 393pp. ISBN 0314232168.
Covers the context of legal research, followed by individual chapters on sources of US law, legal history, constitutional law, administrative and executive publications, court rules and practice, secondary authority and research strategies. Extensive appendices reproducing a court opinion, with annotations on how to read it. Has become a classic handbook on US legal research skills.

2860 Fundamentals of legal research
R.M. Mersky and D.J. Dunn   8th edn, Foundation Press, 2002, 821pp. ISBN 158778064X.
Detailed guide to US legal research, organized by form of publication, with extensive appendices on legal abbreviations, the national reporter system etc. Over 200 illustrations in the text, many from electronic sources. Intended as a student text but almost a work of legal bibliography. A classic.

2861 A guide to the US federal legal system web-based public accessible sources
www.nyulawglobal.org/globalex/United_States.htm
Research guide describing the US federal system, its legislation, the judiciary, the executive branch and administrative law. Numerous links to web resources and some to site offering tutorials in researching federal law. Written by Gretchen Feltes, Faculty Services/Reference Librarian at New York University Law School. Originally published on the web in 2002, updated in 2005 and again in 2006.

Terminology, codes & standards

2862 The Bluebook: a uniform system of citation
18th edn, Harvard Law Review Association, 2005, 415pp. ISBN 9786000143299.
Style guide for the citation of law materials, providing examples and lists of approved abbreviations for publications. Mainly focused on the US jurisdiction and its publishing output, there are also sections for overseas jurisdictions, both common law and civil law. Devised, compiled and regularly updated by the editors of the leading US academic law journals, the Bluebook has become the recognized statement of good practice within the USA but less so outside that jurisdiction.

2863 Introduction to basic legal citation
www.law.cornell.edu/citation/
Guide to citation of contemporary US law materials for students, compiled by Peter W. Martin and placed on the prestigious Cornell Law School site. Based on the authoritative *Bluebook* (q.v.) it provides explanations and examples of the use of the Bluebook system as well as considerable background detail on the development of the principles of citation and citation manuals.

2864 Prince's Biebers dictionary of legal citations
6th edn, William S. Hein, 2001, 390pp. ISBN 1575886693.
Devised to assist the legal profession in citing legal authorities in accordance with the rules given in *The Bluebook* (q.v.). Acts as a companion to it by applying the rules to publications, abbreviations and organizational names, with the aim of encouraging uniformity in the citation of legal documents.

Dictionaries, thesauri, classifications

2865 Black's law dictionary
B.A. Garner, ed.   8th edn, West, 2004, 1810pp. £45. ISSN 03151990.
First published in 1891 and now containing over 43,000 definitions of legal terms, including Latin words and phrases, over 3000 accompanied by extensive quotations from the

legal literature to support the lexicographer's statement. Includes extensive appendices of lists of legal abbreviations, legal maxims, the text of the constitution of the USA, British regnal years and a bibliography of the sources used to compile entries in the dictionary. Generally considered to be the leading US law dictionary.

2866 Burton's legal thesaurus
W.C. Burton, comp.   3rd edn, Macmillan Library Reference USA, 1998, 1012pp. ISBN 0028653378.
Equivalent of *Roget's Thesaurus* (for literary composition) but focusing on law terms. Sets out in alphabetical order a broad selection of legal terms followed by synonyms and related words. Excludes archaic and stilted words. Includes non-legal words commonly used by the legal profession and foreign phrases. Two parts: a main entry with definition, lists of synonyms, associated concepts and foreign phrases; second index of words with synonyms. Probably a unique publication.

2867 A dictionary of modern legal usage
B.A. Garner, comp.   2nd edn, Oxford University Press, 1995, 953pp. ISBN 0195142365.
Not only a dictionary but includes illustrations on the correct use of legal terms and advice on when and when not to employ words. A legal equivalent of H. W. Fowler's *Dictionary of modern English usage*. Many quotations from original sources with detailed citations. Although an American publication with an accent on US definitions and useage, it is of use in all common law jurisdictions.

Laws, standards, codes

2868 American law reports
Lawyers Cooperative Pub. ISSN 10622446.
A system of commercially published law reports in three issues covering the Supreme Court, Federal Court and the state appellate courts. Only selected cases ('the leading decisions') are reported, followed by an often extensive annotation – the main value of the service.

2869 Code of federal regulations
US General Services Administration, National Archives & Records Service, Office of the Federal Register, 1949–, annual.
Official compilation by topic of the delegated legislation made by the US Congress, following a similar structure to the official US code for primary legislation.

2870 Constitutions of the United States: national and state
Legislative Drafting Research Fund   2nd edn, Oceana Publications, 1974–. $995. ISBN 0379001861.
In seven looseleaf volumes provides the text of the US constitution, each of the 50 state constitutions plus the constitutions of the 15 US territories. Updated about six times a year. No editorial annotations or commentary at present but starting 2007, releases will include commentary as state constitutions updated. No index. Also available as a subscriber-only online database: Constitutions of the United States: national and state online.

2871 The Federal cases: comprising cases argued and determined in the circuit and district courts of the United States from the earliest times to the beginning of the Federal reporter, arranged alphabetically by the titles of the cases and numbered consecutive
West Publishing Co, 1894–1897.
A reprint of the many series of law reports containing federal circuit and district court cases, originally published between 1789 and 1880.

2872 Federal Register
Office of the Federal Register, National Archives & Records Service, General Services Administration, 1936–, daily. ISSN 00976326.
Official publication appearing every working day, containing the text of all administrative rulings or regulations of general application issued by the executive or other independent government agencies. Also available through the HeinOnline electronic journal subscriber-only database (q.v.).

2873 The Federal reporter
West Publishing Co, 1880–1988.
Unofficial publication containing reports of cases decided in the Circuit Courts of Appeal and principal federal courts other than the Supreme Court, such as those dealing with disputes against the US government, customs, patents, military appeals and taxes.

2874 The Federal supplement
West Publishing, 1932–.
An unofficial publication containing, since 1932, the decisions of the lowest level of federal court: the District Courts.

2875 LexisNexis
http://global.lexisnexis.com/us
Full-text, subscriber-only database with comprehensive coverage of statute and case law materials for the federal jurisdiction of the USA.

2876 Supreme Court reporter
West Publishing, 1883–1990.
Commercial publication of the decisions of the Supreme Court from 1882 onwards – consequently does not cover volumes 1 to 105 included in the official *United States reports* (q.v.). Provides cross-references into other West Publications. Succeeded by *West's Supreme Court reporter* (q.v.).

2877 United States code
www.house.gov
The official compilation of the Acts of Congress in a topic arrangement. Available on the US House of Representatives website. The versions by commercial publishers (*United States code annotated* (q.v.) and *United States code service*) are to be preferred for the extensive annotations provided.

2878 United States code annotated
West Group, 1927–. $2,805. ISSN 22048097.
Although an unofficial version, more often cited in preference to the official version, *United States code* (q.v.). Extensive cross-references and annotations. Over 300 volumes updated by annual pocket parts which slip into the main volume.

2879 United States reports: Cases adjudged in the Supreme Court
US Government Printing Office, 1754–.
Official reports of cases decided by the US Supreme Court – in citation as authority the publication takes precedence above all others. But, the publication does not provide the additional, value-added features found in the commercial and unofficial reports such as *United States Supreme Court reports* (q.v.) or *Supreme Court reporter* (q.v.). The complete set of US reports is available on the subscriber-only databases LexisNexis and Westlaw but various incomplete sets are available free on the FindLaw, Cornell and Supreme Court websites (q.v. all references).

2880 United States statutes at large
1848–.
Official bound volumes of the Acts of Congress passed during each session. Slow to publish and no quick reference to later amendments. Not widely held in libraries. Although the most authoritative source to cite, for research a preferable source is the *United States code* (q.v.), which is a compilation by topic.

2881 United States Supreme Court reports
Lawyers' edn, Lawyers Co-operative Publishing Company, 1957–. ISSN 01618261.
Commercial, unofficial publication similar to the official US reports but with unique features, including summaries of the arguments placed before the court, extensive annotations and commentary to each case, cross-references to other Lawyers Cooperative publications and annual pocket parts to each volume providing citations made more recently to cases in the volume and corrections made to reports by justices after the Lawyers' Edition of the original case was published.

2882 Westlaw International
http://westlawinternational.com
Subscriber-only database containing headnotes (summaries) of over 20 million US federal and state cases, full text of cases and legislation for specific subject areas, access to electronic versions of over 700 law journals and reviews, full text of practitioner works and monographs.

2883 Westlaw UK
www.westlaw.co.uk/
Subscriber-only database with a US law library, including the *United States code annotated* (q.v.), *Code of federal regulations* (q.v.), the full text of cases from the Supreme Court, Courts of Appeal and District Courts and specialized case law.

2884 West's federal reporter
West Publishing Co, 1880–, irregular. ISSN 10483888.
Originally titled *The federal reporter*, contains reports of cases, with annotations, decided in the circuit courts of appeals and district courts of the USA and the court of appeals of the District of Columbia.

2885 West's Supreme Court reporter
West Publishing Co, 1990–. ISSN 10483802.
Commercial publication of the decisions of the Supreme Court from 1882 onwards – consequently does not cover volumes 1 to 105 included in the official *United States reports* (q.v.). Provides cross-references into other West Publications.

Official & quasi-official bodies

2886 United States. Department of Justice
www.usdoj.gov/
Official site of the Department of Justice. Describes the structure, operation and activities of the Department, its divisions and bureaux. Under 'Resources' are files of publications, including trial documents for major recent cases involving the department. Site search facility available.

2887 US Courts. Federal Judiciary
www.uscourts.gov/index.html
Official site of the US courts. Apart from explanations of the role and history of the federal courts, explains the role of the courts with background information on the federal courts. Library of publications available in seven languages. Interactive maps to aid locating courts and extensive FAQ list. Site search facility available.

Research centres & institutes

2888 American Law Institute
www.ali.org/
Official site of a non-profit making body set up in 1923 to clarify and improve the law through research and reform. Details of the governance of the Institute, its projects and publications. Its most important publications are the *Restatement of the law* (q.v.) and the codifications of law, including the Model Penal Code and the Uniform Commercial Code. These may be ordered from but not viewed on the site. Site search facility available.

Associations & societies

2889 American Bar Association
www.abanet.org/
Official site of the national body representing lawyers in the US. Extensive collection of pages of description with links a) for members about the organization, its governance and publications, b) on legal education and student resources and c) to the numerous divisions of the ABA which specialize in improving the law in specialized practice areas and making information about it more widely available. Links to the Martindale Lawyer Locator database (q.v.) to assist tracing lawyers, firms and law schools.

Libraries, archives, museums

2890 Columbia Law School Library
www.law.columbia.edu/library
One of the major law libraries of the USA, with over 1.1 million volumes and over 6800 serial subscriptions. The site includes access to the Pegasus Law Library catalogue and the full text of a series of guides on foreign and international law sources.

2891 Harvard Law School, Library
www.law.harvard.edu/library/
Founded in 1723, the library now holds more than 1.5 million books and manuscripts. The site provides access to the HOLLIS library catalogue. Extensive list of full-text guides

to researching US, international, comparative and foreign law.

2892 New York University, Law School
www.law.nyu.edu/library/
Founded in the 1830s, the library has an extensive collection of US and especially New York State materials and collections covering a selection of countries of Western and Eastern Europe, Latin America, Commonwealth and Asia. The site includes access to the JULIUS online catalogue and the full text of an extensive set of guides to domestic, foreign and international law sources.

2893 Yale Law School, Library
www.law.yale.edu/library/
One of the major law libraries of the USA, with nearly 800,00 volumes of print materials and approximately 10,000 active serial titles. The foreign and international law collection is especially strong. The site provides access to the MORRIS online catalogue and the full text of an extensive set of subject guides and lists of websites.

Portal & task environments

2894 American law source on-Line
www.lawsource.com/also/
Portal site with array of links to freely accessible websites containing US, Canadian and Mexican law. In addition links to sources of commentary of the law and practice aids available free or at a reasonable charge from governmental and non-profit providers. Structure, use and limitations of the site are clearly provided.

2895 FindLaw
www.findlaw.com/
Portal site in two parts: for the public and for the lawyer. Includes links to the full text of US legislation, case law and a news service. Online dictionary of legal terms (on the public site under the A–Z section for each subject group of links) and the Findlaw Lawyer Directory, containing a database of over 1 million US lawyers.

2896 Hieros Gamos
www.hg.org/
Vast portal of links to law websites across the world. Access to US law and through the Law for 230 countries link to overseas materials. Directories of law firms worldwide and many other predominantly US-based law professionals. Directory of law schools worldwide but information under the heading for England (which includes entries for Wales!) is at least five or six years out of date. The only entry under the UK is for Northern Ireland.

2897 Katsuey's legal gateway
www.katsuey.com/
Free gateway to thousands of substantial yet free web links of relevance to the work of US attorneys and legal professionals. Some overseas sites listed. Links arranged under about 40 general subject headings.

2898 RefLaw: the virtual law library reference desk
www.washlaw.edu/reflaw/reflaw.html
Extensive, free lists of annotated links to sites concerned with law, government and politics, mainly with a US focus.

Site maintained by the staff of Washburn University School of Law Library.

2899 United States law sources on the web
www.law.harvard.edu/library/services/research/guides/united_states/index.php
Freely accessible, extensive lists of links, some annotated, to web and printed sources on US federal law. Sources arranged under four very general headings: constitutional, legislative, executive and administrative and judicial.

2900 World law: United States of America
www.worldlii.org/catalog/268.html
Comprehensive list of links to websites of US law and legal information, arranged by jurisdiction or subject or organization and with search facility across all entries. Very brief annotations to each link. Part of the World Legal Information Institute service developed by the Australasian Legal Information Institute (q.v.).

Discovering print & electronic resources

2901 Bibliographic guide to law
G.K.Hall, 1975–, 2 p.a. Supersedes: Law book guide. ISSN 03602745.
Lists recent publications catalogued by the Library of Congress on criminology, diplomacy, forensic medicine, international arbitrations, international law, international organizations, international relations and the law of the USA (including federal, state, city and territories). Single combined author, subject and title sequence.

2902 Current Law Index
Information Access Group, 1980–, monthly. ISSN 01961780.
Index to contents of over 875 law journals published in the USA, Canada, the UK, Ireland, Australia and New Zealand. Includes academic reviews, bar association journals, specialist subject journals and selected journals covering allied disciplines, such as criminology and accountancy. Published monthly with quarterly and annual cumulations. Also available on the subscriber-only LegalTrac CD-ROM database. Titles selected for inclusion by a Committee of the American Association of Law Libraries.

2903 Fair Courts E-Lert
http://brennancenter.org/articles.asp?key=539
Searchable database of articles from newspapers and journals back to 1 January 2000 on topics related to judicial independence, appointments, controversial decisions and judicial reform. Produced by the Brennan Center of New York University Law School and freely available. Associated e-mail alert service is available free.

2904 Index to legal periodicals and books
H.W.Wilson Co, 11 p.a. ISSN 10794719.
US publication which indexes leading law periodicals published in a number of English-language countries. A valuable service, useful not only for finding material relating to USA, but also comparative writing among other common law jurisdictions, including Australia and New Zealand. Entries from 1981 onwards are available on a subscriber-only web version of the publication.

2905 Index to periodical articles related to law
Glanville, 1958–, qtrly. ISSN 00194093.

Indexes articles which do not fall within *Index to legal periodicals* (q.v.) but which are of relevance to the work of US academic lawyers. Includes substantial articles only, published in English, throughout the world. Arranged in four parts: list of subject headings, index of articles arranged by subject, list of journals indexed and author index. Five-, ten- and thirty-year cumulations. Well established and valuable.

2906 Martindale-Hubbell international law digest
LexisNexis, 2005. ISBN 151606499.
Compendium of laws of countries across the world comprising both commentary and copies of actual documents most frequently required by practising US lawyers. The US Digest section summarizes federal and state statute law under over 100 standard headings, with additional references to cases. International Digest summarizes laws of 81 countries.

Digital data, image & text collections

HeinOnline
See entry no. 2136

2907 Law Library Microform Consortium
www.llmc.com/
'A non-profit consortium of libraries devoted to providing economical access to a wide range of legal and law-related materials.' The material is generally historical backruns of law journals, treatises and statutes. The vast catalogue of material was originally for sale as microfiche but is being transferred to electronic format. The collections are mainly US-focused but there are extensive foreign and international collections.

2908 Tribal law gateway
www.narf.org/nill/triballaw/index.htm/
Online lists hosted by the National Indian Law Library, part of the National American Rights Fund (NARF), of the largest collection of print and electronic resources on tribal codes and constitutions of the sovereign tribes and Alaska Native villages in the US. The collection is still being digitized; some materials are not yet available over the web.

Directories & encyclopedias

2909 American jurisprudence: a comprehensive text statement of American case law as developed in the cases and annotations in the Annotated report system; being a rewriting of ruling case law to reflect the modern developments of the law
W.A. Estrich, ed.   Lawyers Co-operative Publishing Co. £2,756. ISSN 13504006.
Encyclopedia of American law in around 140 volumes, organized alphabetically into over 400 subjects. Updated by pocket parts which slip into the back of the main volumes. Unlike its competitor *Corpus juris secundum* (q.v.), does not attempt to cite all reported cases in its footnotes. Citations to cases are to the associated publication *American law reports* (q.v.).

2910 Corpus juris secundum: a complete restatement of the entire American law as developed by all reported cases
W. Mack and D.J. Kiser American Law Book Co, 1936–. £3011. ISSN 22023000.
Encyclopedia of American law in over 160 volumes organized alphabetically by subject. Updated by pocket parts which slip into the back of the main volumes. Unlike its competitor *American jurisprudence* (q.v.) attempts to cite all reported cases in its footnotes. Also available as a web version on the subscriber-only database run by Westlaw (q.v.).

2911 Lawyers.com
www.lawyers.com/index.php
Free, online directory of mainly US lawyers and law firms (despite the 'worldwide' tag) made available by Martindale-Hubbell. Searchable by geographical location, type of work and law firm name.

2912 Martindale-Hubbell lawyer locator
Martindale-Hubbell Law Directory Inc, 1931–, annual. ISSN 01910221.
www.martindale.com/locator/home.html
Probably the best known and most comprehensive directory of lawyers in the USA. Web version is a subscriber-only site, Martindale-Hubbell lawyer locator.

2913 The restatement in the courts
American Law Institute.
The first and still the main undertaking of the American Law Institute (q.v.). The restatement seeks to reduce uncertainty and increase clarity of the legal principles on which basic legal topics are founded. Now in their third series, these volumes restate the principles of subjects such as Agency, Contracts, Torts and Trusts. Although works of great scholarship, their aim is to be of value to judges and practising lawyers. A fundamental resource for a US law collection.

Handbooks & manuals

2914 Shepard's Citations
An elaborate system of identifying subsequent citations to a particular case. Similar in purpose to *Current law case citators in the United Kingdom* (q.v.) but operates on the case citation not the case name. A user can 'Shepardize' a case electronically on LexisNexis, the subscriber-only database (q.v.). There are similar citators for legislation and law reviews.

Keeping up to date

2915 Current publications in legal and related fields
William S. Hein, 1952–, monthly.
Intended as a current awareness listing of new and forthcoming books in English published throughout the world, except titles published in India and Pakistan. Information drawn from publishers' lists, catalogues and other alerting services, so many entries prepared without physically examining items. Where available, lists of contents and short descriptions provided. Simple listing by author – no frills. No subject or jurisdictional indexes.

2916 JURIST The Legal Education Network
http://jurist.law.pitt.edu/
Web-based legal news and research service edited by Prof. Bernard Hibbetts at the University of Pittsburgh School of Law. Produced as a public service for people learning, teaching and researching law. Material is written by expert lawyers and leading US policy makers. Concentrates on legal issues and events with jurisprudential, social and political implications rather than crimes, trials and celebrities. Accent on US content, though there is a World file section.

2917 United States code Congressional and administrative news
West Publishing Co, 1952–, monthly. ISSN 15486885.
Unofficial, commercial publication – the quickest way to find all the public laws enacted by the US Congress. Pagination matches that of the official *Statutes at large* (q.v.) but with, in addition, a range of valuable information sources to aid background research into legislation.

2918 The United States law week: a national survey of current law
Bureau of National Affairs, 1933–, weekly.
www.bna.com/products/lit/uslw.htm
Summarizes significant federal and state court and administrative cases, with links to BNAs other publications both in printed and electronic form. Also provides analyses of case decisions.

Wales

Dictionaries, thesauri, classifications

2919 Geiriadur newydd y gyfraith: Saesneg–Cymraeg (The new legal dictionary: English–Welsh)
R. Lewis Gomer, 2003, 1234pp. ISBN 1843231018.
Set in parallel columns English and Latin legal terms are translated into their Welsh equivalents. Dictionary is supplemented with translations of key, historic legislation relating to Wales, oaths and court phraseology. A work of great scholarship and highly regarded.

Laws, standards, codes

2920 Wales legislation
www.opsi.gov.uk/legislation/wales/wales_legslation.htm
Official site containing the full text of Statutory Instruments made by the National Assembly for Wales, free to use. Note that the SIs are displayed in their original form without the addition of amendments or notification of repeals.

2921 Wales legislation online
www.wales-legislation.org.uk/en/intro.html
Free site which aims to identify the functions transferred to and performed by the National Assembly for Wales, arranged under subject headings, together with an explanation of those functions retained by central government in Westminster. Two parts to site: Acts and Orders which were transferred; Statutory Instruments (SIs) made by the National Assembly for Wales, general SIs made by central government applying to Wales and commencement orders.

Site created and run by Cardiff Law School but funded by the Welsh Assembly Government.

Official & quasi-official bodies

Welsh Assembly Government
See entry no. 2075

Libraries, archives, museums

2922 Cardiff University, Law Library
www.cardiff.ac.uk/schoolsanddivisions/divisions/insrv
The largest law collection in Wales, serving one of the largest law schools in the UK. Very little Welsh law existed until the National Assembly was founded in 1999, so only a very small part of the collection relates to the law of Wales itself. An adjacent collection, the Salisbury Collection, includes historical Welsh material, including Welsh public and private Acts and medieval Welsh law texts.

Discovering print & electronic resources

2923 Acts of Parliament concerning Wales, 1714–1901
T.I. Jeffreys Jones   University of Wales Press, 1959, 343pp.
'A transcription of the long titles of those acts ... that either deal with Wales or give special regard to places or persons in Wales.' Listing by broad subject matter and then chronologically of the long titles of public and private Acts that either deal exclusively with Wales or have special regard to places or persons in Wales. Where Acts have been repealed this is noted. Detailed subject index. Section relating to private Acts is continued by *Welsh local and personal Acts 1900–1999* (q.v.).

2924 Handlist of the Acts of native Welsh rulers, 1132–1283
K.L. Maund   University of Wales Press, 1996, 165pp. ISBN 0708313337.
Description of Acts issued on behalf of the native Welsh rulers in the 12th and 13th centuries. Entries arranged geographically by ancient county. Each entry describes briefly the document, where the manuscript is deposited and where notes and commentary have been published. Index of persons and places. An essential finding tool for researchers into Welsh medieval legal history.

2925 A legal bibliography of the British Commonwealth of Nations
2nd edn, Sweet & Maxwell, 1957.
Volume 2: English law 1801–1954, is a thoroughly researched bibliography. Contains, in volume 1, a separate section on Welsh law books published up to 1800, but in volume 2 English and Welsh publications are interfiled in a single alphabetical sequence arranged by author.

2926 Welsh local and personal Acts 1900–1999
P. Keelan and A. Nash, comps   2004.
www.cardiff.ac.uk/schoolsanddivisions/divisions/insrv/libservices/scholar
Free, MS Access database listing all Welsh-related local and personal Acts, including information on repeals, correct to 1999. 700 Acts featured with details, including date, short and long titles and subject keywords. Database extends the information on private Acts given in *Acts of Parliament concerning Wales, 1714–1901* (q.v.). Searchable by subject or date or combination of the two or can display all records. Easy to use and brings together materials drawn from a number of sources. Accessed by link 'Welsh Local Acts 1900–1999' on Welsh Collections page of SCOLAR, Special Collections and Archives, Cardiff University.

FINANCE, INDUSTRY & BUSINESS

Finance, Accountancy & Taxation

Reference resources covering the fields of finance, accountancy and taxation have altered and expanded dramatically in the last decade. This is reflected by the large number of online databases and websites included in this section of the book. The currency of information can be of vital importance in this subject area, and printed information can rapidly become outdated. Authors traditionally limited to publishing relatively infrequently in books and journals can now publish immediately on their own weblogs, or contribute to wikis. The sheer number of such online resources means that guides such as *The New Walford* are increasingly important in the identification of good, high-quality sources of information.

Enabling access to detailed and accurate financial data, expensive subscription databases such as Bloomberg offer an unrivalled level of comprehensive information. However, it is also possible to get a wealth of data from freely available websites, such as Yahoo! Finance. A number of free- and subscription-based resources are highlighted. More traditional print-based resources are still of great value, and many textbooks in this field are now accompanied by companion websites. However, hard-copy directories and manuals containing financial information are now dwindling in value as more up-to-date information can invariably be found online.

In comparison to finance resources, information about accounting is more heavily weighted towards print materials. Printed accountancy resources detailed include dictionaries, journals, accounting standards and a large number of textbooks. A number of accountancy associations and institutes also publish valuable information on their websites. Taxation resources are available in abundance on the internet, ranging from personal weblogs to official government websites. A number of these have been included alongside subscription databases, books and journals.

Portal & task environments

Social Studies of Finance Network
See entry no. 738

Finance

financial terminology • history of finance • statistics

Introductions to the subject

2927 A financial history of the United States
M.G. Myers   Columbia University Press, 1970, 451pp. ISBN 0231024428.
Covers US financial history from the colonial period until the mid-1960s, examining both public and private finance. Significant periods in US history are detailed from a financial perspective, including the American Civil War, World War 1 and World War 2. A fascinating history written in a spare, uncluttered style.

2928 A financial history of Western Europe
C.P. Kindleberger   2nd edn, Oxford University Press, 1993, 544pp. £40. ISBN 0195077385.
Divided into five main parts: Money, Banking, Finance, The Interwar Period and After World War 2. Begins with the evolution of money in Western Europe, encompassing events such as the 1929 stock market crash and European economic integration. Includes a detailed glossary, chronology and histories of major European economies, including Germany and Italy. A wide-ranging, detailed study, invaluable to financial historians.

2929 The Review of Financial Studies
Oxford University Press, 1988–, 6 p.a. $55. ISSN 08939454.
www.sfs.org
Published on behalf of the Society for Financial Studies, this journal promotes new research on financial economics, balancing theoretical and empirical contributions. Recent articles have examined trends in IPOs, portfolio selection and interest rate movements.

Dictionaries, thesauri, classifications

2930 Dictionnaire de l'anglais economique, commercial et financier: Anglais/Française, Français/Anglais (Dictionary of economic, commercial and financial English: English/French, French/English)
Langues Pour Tous, 2003, 775pp. €23. ISBN 2266068822.
Useful English/French dictionary covering around 85,000 economic and financial terms. Vocabulary covers both macroeconomic and microeconomic terminology and variations between British and American terms are highlighted. Suitable for both business and financial professionals.

2931 Financial glossary
http://tradition.axone.ch/
Includes over 5000 financial terms in English, French and Italian. Terms can be viewed alphabetically or using the simple search function. The site is basic but effective.

2932 Handbook of international financial terms
P. Moles and N. Terry   Oxford University Press, 1999, 688pp. £45. ISBN 0198294816.
Aims to be the most comprehensive financial reference book, providing definitions for obscure terms such as 'Butterfly',

'Streaker' and 'Cocktail Swap', alongside more common financial expressions. Definitions are clear and supplemented with graphs, equations and examples where required. As the book was published in 1997 some entries have dated, but the vast majority are still applicable today.

2933 International dictionary of finance
G. Bannock and W.A.P. Manser   4th edn, Profile, 2003, 287pp. £25. ISBN 1861974787.
Excellent financial dictionary providing succinct and authoritative definitions of over 2000 terms. The five principal subjects covered in the book are money markets, commodity markets, securities markets, banking and insurance. Specialized financial terminology is vast and ever-increasing and the book is an invaluable tool for finance professionals and the public.

2934 Penguin international dictionary of finance
G. Bannock and W.A.P. Manser   3rd edn, Penguin, 1999, 290pp. ISBN 0140514139.
Covers five main areas: banking, commodity markets, insurance, money markets and securities markets. Also includes foreign-language terms and explanations of acronyms and abbreviations. Definitions are succinct and informative, although the book is now starting to become slightly dated.

2935 Reuters financial glossary
2nd edn, Pearson Education, 2003, 231pp. £16.99. ISBN 1903684366.
www.glossary.reuters.com
This excellent glossary is available in hard copy and online. The printed version is well presented and makes good use of diagrams and worked examples. The online version takes the form of a wiki, allowing users to edit and add entries as they wish. Both versions contain web references for key terms, although the great advantage of the online glossary is that web references can be accessed with a single click.

Research centres & institutes

2936 Center for Financial Studies
www.ifk-cfs.de
The Center for Financial Studies publishes independent research on financial markets. A regular newsletter is available via the home page, alongside a wide range of working papers on topics such as monetary policy, unemployment and inflation. The site is also available in German.

2937 Centre for the Study of Financial Innovation
www.csfi.org.uk
Independent think-tank producing research on the future of the financial services industry. The Centre also acts as a forum for financial practitioners to share ideas on financial innovation and regular events are held which are advertised on the website. Results of such events are published on the website in the form of minutes.

2938 Institute for Fiscal Studies [UK]
www.ifs.org.uk
Independent research organization aiming to promote effective economic and social policies. Regularly published reports available on the website cover topics such as

company taxation, poverty and public spending. This site also provides a detailed analysis of Budget statements made by the Chancellor of the Exchequer.

2939 Salomon Center
http://w4.stern.nyu.edu/salomon
Part of the Leonard N. Stern School of Business at New York University. The Salomon Centre publishes high-quality research in financial economics. Topics covered include financial econometrics, debt markets and corporate governance. A large selection of working papers and journal articles published by the Center are detailed on the site.

Social studies of finance: an ESRC professorial fellowship project
See entry no. 734

Associations & societies

2940 The American Finance Association
www.afajof.org
Described as 'the premier academic organization devoted to the study and promotion of knowledge about financial economics'. Website content includes news, jobs and a selection of interesting video interviews on the history of finance. A worldwide directory of finance faculty is also provided. Presentation is a little old-fashioned and would benefit from a revamp.

2941 European Finance Association
www.efa-online.org
The EFA is a professional society for academics and practitioners interested in financial management and financial theory. Content on the website is somewhat limited but includes details of financial journals and links to other international finance organizations.

2942 French Finance Association
www.affi.asso.fr
Available in French and English. Areas of the site such as discussion forums, journal articles and newsletters are restricted to members only. Latest news stories are available free of charge and a useful directory of related web links is provided.

2943 International Association of Financial Engineers
www.iafe.org
Home page of the professional society for quantitative finance professionals. The members-only section includes videos of selected IAFE events, discussion boards and an IAFE wiki. Freely available information features a variety of student resources, including a detailed list of professional development online services.

2944 Milken Institute [USA]
www.milkeninstitute.org
The Milken Institute is an independent economic think-tank aiming to improve lives and economic conditions through policy recommendations. Primary areas of research include global capital markets, financial innovation and maximizing human capital. The Institute publishes a large selection of detailed research reports and articles on these topics, which can be downloaded free of charge.

Discovering print & electronic resources

2945   A bibliography of finance
H. Edwards and R. Brealey   MIT Press, 1991, 822pp. £58.95. ISBN 0262023199.

Comprehensive bibliography covering the entire field of finance. Contains over 12,000 entries from approximately 120 periodicals. The core of the bibliography is articles written by financial economists and published in finance journals. Publication dates range from 1730 to 1989, although the majority of the bibliography details articles from the 1980s.

Digital data, image & text collections

2946   Edgar Online [USA]
www.edgar-online.com

Subscription database containing interactive business and financial information on global companies. Content available includes SEC filings, fundamental data, insider trades, institutional holdings, initial public offerings, conference calls and annual reports.

2947   Financial statistics [UK]
Stationery Office, monthly. ISSN 0015203X.
www.statistics.gov.uk

Provides key financial and monetary statistics for the UK. Includes data on public sector finances, banks and building societies, interest and exchange rates, capital issues and money supply and credit. The complete publication and additional time series data are available for download from the National Statistics website.

2948   International financial statistics
International Monetary Fund, 1948–, monthly. ISSN 00206725.
http://ifs.apdi.net/imf

Weighty monthly publication, also available online. Recognized as a standard source for statistics on all aspects on international finance. Data published covers virtually every country in the world and includes exchange rates, liquidity information, interest rates, government transactions, prices and national accounts.

■ **International financial statistics yearbook** International Monetary Fund, annual. ISSN 02507463.

2949   Mergent Online
www.mergentonline.com

Subscription database providing company accounts for over 30,000 companies globally. The strength of the database lies in the broad range of countries covered – over 100 at present – and all financial data can be downloaded into Excel. Annual reports can also be viewed in PDF format. A rather hidden but useful area of the site are industry research reports covering areas such as Telecommunications and Retailing.

Directories & encyclopedias

2950   Elsevier's dictionary of European Community company/business/financial law: in English, Danish and German
H. Bock, G. Frey and I. Bock   Elsevier, 1995, 539pp. £119. ISBN 0444817832.

Dictionary, including a number of highly specific terms used in texts related to European law, finance and business. An emphasis is placed on complex phrases and everyday abbreviations. A useful resource for business people or students translating between Danish, German or English texts.

2951   Encyclopedia of banking and finance
G.G. Munn, C.J. Woelfel and F.L. Garcia   9th edn, McGraw-Hill, 1991, 1097pp. ISBN 0077073940.

Published since 1924 and recognized as the standard authority in its field. Contains over 4000 entries comprising definitions, historical backgrounds, illustrative examples and statistical data. Many of the statistics and examples cited and now dated, but much of the content is still relevant.

Handbooks & manuals

2952   Advanced modelling in finance using Excel and VBA
M. Jackson and M. Staunton   Wiley, 2001, 263pp. £60. ISBN 0471499226.

One of very few books examining the use of VBA (Visual Basic for Applications) functions within Microsoft Excel. Examines the more complex areas of Excel macros and VBA programming. Models within the book include equities, equity options and bonds.

2953   Government finance statistics yearbook
International Monetary Fund, 1977–, annual. ISSN 02507374.

Contains detailed data on revenues, expenses, assets and liabilities of governments. Data is summarized in world tables and provided in more detail in individual country tables. The data is not supplemented by any charts or graphs, but is granular and covers an extremely broad variety of countries.

Keeping up to date

2954   Environmental finance
Fulton Publishing, 1999–, 10 p.a. ISSN 14688573.

Magazine covering the impact of environmental issues on the world of finance, claiming to be 'the only global publication dedicated to this fast-changing area'. News and analysis is provided on topics, including green investments, carbon emissions and weather-risk management. The magazine also features new environmental initiatives and changes in global environmental legislation.

2955   Financial News Online
www.efinancialnews.com

Subscription-only website, also available in print. Provides regular news updates throughout the day on the investment banking and securities industry. Detailed insight and analysis is provided and an e-mail alert facility is also available. The website is divided into four main sectors: asset management, investment banking, private equity and trading and technology. This helps to make finding news stories of interest fast and straightforward.

2956   Financial Times
Financial Times, daily. ISSN 03071766.
www.ft.com

One of the world's leading business newspapers and an

authoritative source of financial news and information. Provides detailed comment, analysis and market data. The newspaper's online presence, FT.com, claims to be 'the world's most popular audited business website' with over 2.7 million unique monthly visitors. Additional website content includes podcasts and RSS feeds.

2957   Financial World
monthly. £75 per year. ISSN 14656078.
www.financialworld.co.uk
Aimed at finance service professionals and students, this magazine provides up-to-date information on the financial services industry. The magazine also incorporates careers guidance, comments and opinions. The companion website features some freely available online exclusive content. Recent articles have covered topics, including the role of women in private banking.

2958   International Financial Services London
www.ifsl.org.uk
IFSL promotes the international activities of UK-based financial services. This excellent site is a good source of free up-to-date statistics covering areas such as hedge funds, pensions and financial market trends. The site is also a strong source of data regarding London's share of international financial markets. An extensive range of time series data is also available to be downloaded.

2959   Journal of Applied Corporate Finance
Blackwell Publishing, qtrly. £56 per year. ISSN 10781196.
Journal publishing work by academics and practitioners covering topics, including corporate strategy, risk management, capital structure and corporate governance. Articles are varied – recent submissions include 'Rail companies: prospects for privatization and consolidation', 'The case for real options made simple' and 'The limits of financial globalization'.

2960   Journal of Corporate Finance
Elsevier Science Publishers, 5 p.a. €54 per year. ISSN 09291199.
Publishes high quality research in areas, including financial structure, corporate governance, international financial management, payout policies and financial contracts. Recent popular articles include 'Ownership structure and corporate performance', 'Corporate philanthropic practices' and 'Capital structure in venture finance'.

2961   Wilmott
John Wiley, 2002–, 6 p.a. ISSN 15406962.
www.wilmott.com
Leading magazine for the quantitative finance community founded by Dr Paul Wilmott. Has an eye-catching presentation style and features new research, detailed analysis and features on latest products. The online version is similarly innovative, featuring blogs, a wiki and a wide range of downloadable audiovisual content.

2962   Yahoo! Finance
www.finance.yahoo.com
Incredibly comprehensive finance website. Includes news, videos, market data, a currency converter and personal finance guides. Major company profiles are extremely detailed and far better than those on many subscription services. A wealth of historical share price data is available to be downloaded and charted.

Financial Markets

capital markets • City of London • commodity markets • derivative, futures & options markets • financial charts • Japanese financial markets • UK companies • Wall Street

Introductions to the subject

2963   All you need to know about the City: who does what and why in London's financial markets
C. Stoakes   Four by Four Publishing, 2005, 235pp. £9.95. ISBN 0954637224.
Extremely useful guide condensing everything you need to know about the City of London into a compact, interesting text. The book does not claim to be comprehensive or definitive, but provides a handy overview of how the City functions. Includes details on the reasons why companies float on the stock exchange, the basics of investment banking and a bluffer's guide to economics. The text is ideal for anyone about to begin work in the City and feeling a little out of their depth.
Publisher is now Longtail Publishing: www.allyouneedtoknowguides.com/city.htm

2964   Arbitrage guide to financial markets
R. Dubil   John Wiley & Sons, 2004, 331pp. £55. ISBN 0470853328.
'This is an excellent introduction to the financial markets by an author with a strong academic approach and practical insights from trading experience. It equips readers to understand the fundamentals of markets, valuation and trading. I would highly recommend it to anyone looking to understand the essentials of successful trading, structuring or using the entire range of financial instruments available today.' (Varun Gosain, Principal, Constellation Capital Management, New York)

2965   Financial markets and corporate strategy
M. Grinblatt and S. Titman   2nd edn, McGraw-Hill, 2001, 880pp. £44.99. ISBN 0071123415.
Described by the authors as 'the cutting-edge textbook in corporate finance'. Primarily designed for MBA students and advanced undergraduates, the book is also of value to finance professionals. Covers topics, including debt financing, pricing derivatives and risk management. The text is reader-friendly and written in an accessible style, but the presentation of charts and graphs is disappointingly bland and colourless.

2966   First Wall Street: Chestnut Street, Philadelphia, and the birth of American finance
R.E. Wright   University of Chicago Press, 2005, 209pp. $25. ISBN 0226910261.
Story of the first stock exchange in the USA, founded in Philadelphia in 1790 and known as 'Chestnut Street'. The book examines how Philadelphia played a key role in financing the American Revolution and how the city became home to the Bank of the United States and the US Mint. An interesting read covering the largely forgotten story of Philadelphia in the birth of US finance.

2967   Guide to financial markets
M. Levinson   4th edn, Economist/Profile Books, 2005, 250pp. £20. ISBN 1861979568.
Best-selling, compact guide to financial markets. Covers areas, including foreign exchange markets, money markets, bond markets and securitization. The text is regularly

updated to ensure financial data is current. The text is clear and concise throughout – an ideal handbook for understanding global markets.

2968 International financial markets and the firm
P. Sercu and R. Uppal   Thomson, 1995, 752pp. ISBN 1850321019.
Popular textbook covering international aspects of modern financial theory. The book is aimed at undergraduate and MBA students and is divided into four parts: International Financial Markets, Exchange Rate Determination, International Risk Management and International Capital Budgeting. The book includes useful end-of-chapter summaries and exercises.

2969 Japanese financial markets
J. Ujiie, ed.   2nd edn, Woodhead, 2002, 480pp. £135. ISBN 1855735962.
A key work on one of the most important financial centres in the world, written by leading analysts from the Nomura Group. The book is divided into four main parts comprising an overview of Japanese financial markets, information on market participants, details on the markets themselves and a brief examination of the future outlook. A valuable and thorough resource.

2970 The stock exchanges of Ireland
W.A. Thomas   Francis Cairns, 1986, 273pp. £30. ISBN 0905205340.
Definitive history of Irish Stock Exchanges. Of great value to financial historians interested in this area.

Dictionaries, thesauri, classifications

2971 International dictionary of the securities industry
S. Valentine   2nd edn, Macmillan, 1989, 228pp. ISBN 0333449738.
Over 2000 terms used in the financial services industry are defined. Coverage includes terms used in US, Japanese and European stock markets. A detailed and handy dictionary, although now rather dated.

Official & quasi-official bodies

2972 City of London
www.cityoflondon.gov.uk/Corporation/business_city/research_statistics/research_publications.htm
The City of London provides local government services for the 'Square Mile', the financial and commercial heart of Britain. Their research publications page provides a number of meaty reports on key financial issues, available to download free of charge. Recent reports have included 'The importance of wholesale financial services to the EU economy', 'The competitive impact of London's financial market infrastructure' and 'Stamp duty: its impact and the benefits of its abolition'.

2973 World Federation of Exchanges
www.world-exchanges.org
Home page of the international exchange industry trade organization. Includes a list of members and affiliated members alongside a range of exchange statistics. A selection of publications can also be downloaded from the site and there is additional content in the members' area.

Associations & societies

2974 The Securities Industry and Financial Markets Association
www.sifma.org
Created as a result of a merger between the Securities Industry Association and the Bond Markets Association, SIFMA represents over 650 companies globally. The well presented site includes a good selection of market research, statistical information and surveys related to securities and financial markets. The site also includes information on regulatory issues and offers a free daily briefing service.

Portal & task environments

2975 Big Charts [USA]
http://bigcharts.marketwatch.com
Free charting website offering regularly updated financial news stories and charting options. Creating a simple chart is extremely straightforward, while the interactive charting facility is very impressive and clearer than many subscription services. The 'Big Reports' function presents a good overview of stock markets, covering the main stock movers on the US and Canadian markets.

2976 Corporate Information
www.corporateinformation.com
Subscription site which also provides some information free of charge. Brief business overviews of major companies alongside a summary of recent stock performance can be accessed without subscription. More in-depth company profiles, including a detailed analysis of sales and dividends are available at a cost. The site also produces a number of rankings and country profiles. Navigation is simple, although the site itself is a little dated in appearance.

2977 Global Financial Data
www.globalfinancialdata.com
Subscription database providing an extensive collection of long-term financial and macroeconomic data series. Over 3000 financial indicators are provided, in some cases dating back several centuries. Data can be graphed or downloaded to a spreadsheet. Although data content is strong the graphical interface is a little clunky and could be more user-friendly.

2978 Silicon Investor
http://siliconinvestor.advfn.com
Popular site featuring discussion boards covering stock, commodity and foreign exchange markets. The site also features news and market data, although the discussion boards appear to be the focus of the site and are heavily used.

2979 StockCharts.com
www.stockcharts.com
Excellent site for creating financial charts. Creating a basic chart is easy, but an array of additional features is available to customize charts as desired. The 'Chart School' feature has many articles about the analysis of stock charts and instructions on how to use the charting tools.

Digital data, image & text collections

2980 Bloomberg
www.bloomberg.com
Powerful but expensive subscription database offering
analysis and data for international financial markets.
Bloomberg offers a wide range of analytical functions,
including the ability to find background data on stocks,
bonds, market indices, currencies and commodities. The
database can also be used to create technical and
fundamental analyses including a variety of charting options.
Custom reports can also be produced. Provides extensive job
listings.

2981 Datastream
www.datastream.com
Subscription database offering current and historic financial
markets data. Datastream is particularly powerful statistical
database, containing up to 50 years of financial history – it
is therefore ideal for detailed time series requests and
custom report generation. The database contains detailed
figures covering bonds, commodities, foreign exchange and
futures markets.

2982 Euroland
www.euroland.com
Specializes in company information from a wide range of
international stock markets. Searches by sector allow stocks
from different worldwide exchanges to be compared side by
side. Some stocks also feature in-depth details, including
press release archives, profiles and company presentations.
Much information is presented in multiple languages. The
site also enables users to create their own stock portfolios
and watchlists.

2983 Ex-Dividend.com [USA]
www.ex-dividend.com
Provides dividend information for stocks on the NYSE,
NASDAQ and AMEX markets. Users can search the site for
dividend payments by date, stock symbol or company name.
A subscription service offers additional features such as
information on special dividends and the ability to create a
watchlist portfolio. The site benefits from a clear, simple
presentation and a lack of advertisements.

2984 Hoovers
www.hoovers.com
Subscription database providing company profiles, news and
financial data. Strengths include detailed company histories
and imaginatively written company profiles, often featuring
weak (but oddly entertaining) puns. However the database is
not as strong on company financial information and offers
little flexibility with regard to customization of data.

Directories & encyclopedias

2985 Global stock markets factbook
Standard & Poor's, annual. ISSN 1530678X.
Yearly publication ideal for providing a detailed insight into
the global economy. The factbook provides details on the
performances of world stock markets for the past decade,
including markets in both developed and emerging
economies. Data and charts are extremely well presented,
making good use of clear space and colour.

2986 Moodys
www.moodys.com
Registration is required for this detailed website. Content
includes ratings on over 170,000 securities, detailed
information on credit markets and credit trends and training
and teleconference options. Moody's also provide a range of
subscription databases covering a wide range of financial
data.

2987 Who's who in the City
CaritasData, 2006, 1470pp. £179. ISBN 1904964265.
Leading reference source of over 16,000 key City employees.
The directory includes details of staff at regional offices of
major city firms as well as lists of business advisors. Contact
details are provided alongside educational backgrounds, job
titles and recreational activities (including 'chocolate' and
'avoiding gardening').

Handbooks & manuals

2988 Econometrics of financial markets
J.Y. Campbell, A.W. Lo and A.C. MacKinlay   Princeton University
Press, 1997, 611pp. £45. ISBN 0691043019.
Graduate-level textbook aimed at industry professionals and
PhD and MBA students. Covers the complete field of
empirical finance. Early chapters focus on stock markets,
while later chapters cover derivative securities and fixed-
income securities. Focuses almost exclusively on the US
domestic asset markets. A detailed and accessible text.

2989 Handbook of world stock, derivative and commodity exchanges: 2005
Mondo Visione, 2005, 1015pp. ISBN 0953582353.
Exhaustive reference work detailing world exchanges. For
each exchange a brief history is provided, alongside
information regarding the structure of the exchange, market
size and trading statistics. Information on trading systems
used and settlement and clearing times is also noted. The
handbook also lists details of regulators and a glossary is
supplied.

2990 Standard & Poor's emerging stock markets review: performance, valuations and constituents
Standard & Poor's, monthly. ISSN 15339742.
Publication measuring movements of stock prices and total
returns in global emerging stock markets. The beginning of
each publication provides a brief overview of key markets.
Later sections provide detailed data on individual markets.
The publication is a useful source for identifying trends and
growth markets.

2991 Stock exchange yearbook [UK]
Waterlow, 1874–, annual. ISSN 13583514.
Provides detailed information on companies listed on the
London and Irish stock markets as well as companies listed
on the Alternative Investment Market (AIM). Details of new
issues, company name changes and deletions are supplied.
The yearbook also includes information on the Top 1000
unquoted companies.

Keeping up to date

2992 Financial market trends
Organisation for Economic Co-operation & Development, 1977–, 2 p.a. ISSN 0378651X.
Twice-yearly update on trends and prospects in the major financial markets of the OECD area and beyond. In-depth articles focus on specific issues related to financial sector development – recent articles have examined the relationship between the housing market and household debt and the causes and effects of the private equity boom. Financial sector statistics are profiled periodically, covering areas such as insurance and bank profitability.

2993 Financial markets, institutions and instruments
Blackwell Publishing, 5 p.a. ISSN 09638008.
Four of the five issues of this journal published annually are devoted to a single topic explored in depth. The special fifth issue highlights the most significant developments in money and banking, securities and corporate finance. Recent topics highlighted include the asset management industry in Asia and European banking integration.

2994 InvestorGuide.com
www.investorguide.com
Excellent source of US stock research, including charting, latest news, company profiles and stock analysis. The site is also a strong source of mutual fund information. InvestorGuide.com features a rolling news page and a 'University' section which provides detailed guides to a wide range of finance topics. A further useful feature is the business and financial glossary.

2995 Journal of Financial Markets
Elsevier, 1998–, qtrly. €52. ISSN 13864181.
Contains research on applied and theoretical issues related to securities trading and pricing. Topics covered include the role of information in securities markets, the analysis and design of trading mechanisms and optimal order placement strategies. Recent popular articles have included a survey of market microstructure and a study of liquidity supply in electronic markets.

2996 Journal of International Financial Markets, Institutions and Money
Elsevier, 5 p.a. €317 per year. ISSN 10424431.
Topics covered by this journal include foreign exchange markets, international investment banking, international monetary systems and central bank intervention. Recent popular articles include 'Does cross-ownership affect competition?' and 'Volatility and correlation in international stock markets and the role of exchange rate fluctuations'.

2997 The Kirk Report
www.thekirkreport.com
Interesting blog on the stock market written by individual investor Charles E. Kirk, who aims to help the 'little guy' investor. The site has featured in publications, including *Forbes*, *Barron's* and *Business Week*. The blog is updated on an extremely regular basis and is very well written. Presentation is crisp and clear.
'Promises more food for thought than blind recommendations, and delivers on that promise. Viewers can sign up for a free, weekly e-mail newsletter. And unlike many financial blogs, the site is ad free!!' (Carrie Lee, CNN Money http://money.cnn.com/2005/10/06/markets/financial_blogs/index.htm)

2998 Reuters
http://today.reuters.com/investing
An excellent source of market data and breaking news stories. The site is clearly presented, offering in-depth coverage of the major financial markets alongside currency, options, bonds and commodities data. The site also offers 30 tailored RSS feeds and video content. The site provides over 1.5 million analyst research reports, although this service is chargeable. Reuters also offer subscription databases, including Wealth Manager and 3000Xtra.

2999 Seeking Alpha
http://seekingalpha.com
Seeking Alpha provides stock market opinions and analysis selected from blogs, money managers and investment newsletters. The site also creates a one-page daily summary of top market and stock-related stories and adds features such as conference call transcripts and stock picks. The site focuses on analysis rather than news and is an excellent interface for keeping up to date with comment and opinion in the financial world.

3000 UK Company News
www.companynews.co.uk
Subscription website offering profiles of new issues, directories of large and small companies, press releases, news and company results. The site also offers a messenger service providing e-mail alerts covering market news. Presentation on the site is a little basic and some areas require updating.

Money Markets & Capital Markets

Introductions to the subject

3001 Equity markets in action: the fundamentals of liquidity, market structure and trading
R.A. Schwartz and R. Francioni   John Wiley & Sons, 2004, 468pp. £60. ISBN 047146922X.
Extensive, up-to-date handbook examining the nature of markets and exchanges. Contains detailed chapters on both the US and European markets. Also examines issues such as regulation, liquidity and the intricacies of trading. Accompanied by a CD with an interactive trading simulation, this book is an invaluable guide to equity markets.

3002 High finance in the euro-zone: competing in the new European capital market
W. Ingo and R.C. Smith   Financial Times Prentice Hall, 2000, 344pp. £45. ISBN 0273637371.
Slightly dated yet detailed guide to European financial markets. Includes chapters on the euro, mergers and acquisitions, privatization and corporate governance.

3003 Managing currency crises in emerging markets
M.P. Dooley and J.A. Frankel   Chicago University Press, 2003, 443pp. ISBN 0226155404.
Collection of papers from a 2001 National Bureau of Economic Research conference, published in conjunction with comments and discussion. An advanced-level text which includes papers on global interest rates, financial restructuring and the role of the IMF and World Bank.

Dictionaries, thesauri, classifications

3004 Wall Street words: an essential A–Z guide for today's investor [USA]
D. Scott 3rd edn, Clarion, 2004, 432pp. ISBN 0618176519.
Excellent dictionary featuring over 4500 entries, including financial terms and investment concepts. Definitions are concise, although some more complex terms are fleshed out with case studies or brief discussions. Also includes tips from financial experts on areas, including tax law, financial advising and accounting.

Official & quasi-official bodies

3005 Australian Securities Exchange
www.asx.com.au
Primary stock exchange in Australia, formerly the Australian Stock Exchange. The well presented website features market data, news stories and information on forthcoming events. An information box highlighting the performance of leading companies is particularly useful. The site also offers online classes covering areas such as 'analysing and selecting shares' and 'the essentials of options investing'.

3006 Euronext
www.euronext.com
The official website of the Amsterdam, Brussels, Lisbon and Paris stock exchanges. The home page provides fundamental market data alongside a rolling selection of latest company press releases. Data is also available on bonds, derivatives and currencies. The statistics centre is particularly useful, featuring a range of daily and monthly statistics.

3007 Hong Kong Stock Exchange
www.hkex.com.hk
Detailed home page covering Hong Kong exchanges. Includes breaking news, trading information and company profiles. Monthly data and statistics on securities and derivatives markets is also supplied. An annual factbook providing an overview of the Hong Kong markets can be downloaded alongside a number of useful research papers.

3008 London Stock Exchange
www.londonstockexchange.com
The London Stock Exchange website is packed full of information. Private investors researching a specific stock can access the Investor Centre which also includes links to a wide variety of guides for both first-time and experienced investors. A number of interactive tools are available for tracking or screening stocks. The 'Company Watch' report (available for a fee) provides a five year overview of a company's strengths, weaknesses and financial trends. The site also includes detailed information on the history and workings of the Exchange as well as a selection of factsheets full of statistics.

3009 NASDAQ Stock Market [USA]
www.nasdaq.com
The NASDAQ home page is bursting at the seams with stock market data. The site provides free stock quotes, as well as information on pre-market and after-hours stock trading. Other data available includes analyst recommendations, market volumes and news stories. Details on the workings of the NASDAQ itself are also available. Stock-comparison

charts can be created, allowing up to 25 stocks to be charted for an interval of up to ten years.

3010 New York Stock Exchange
www.nyse.com
The New York Stock Exchange (NYSE) is the world's largest equities exchange. The home page is virtually identical to the Euronext home page, following the merger of their respective holding companies in April 2007. As would be expected, the site includes detailed market data, listings information and a history of the exchange. The site also features regular publications such as the NYSE Magazine, an exchange blog and occasional video interviews with prominent CEOs.

3011 Tokyo Stock Exchange
www.tse.or.jp/english
English-language site of the Tokyo Stock Exchange features an in-depth history of the Exchange. More current information includes detailed market data and statistics. Basic company information is also available. The 'TSE Daily Report' can be freely downloaded from the site and provides a useful summary of market trades and volumes.

3012 Toronto Stock Exchange
www.tsx.com
Canada's leading stock exchange. The home page includes details on new stock listings, market summaries and in-depth data. The site also supplies information on the history of the exchange, monthly trading summary factsheets and profiles of stock market sectors.

Research centres & institutes

3013 Center for Research in Security Prices
www.crsp.uchicago.edu
Established in 1960, CRSP is part of the University of Chicago's Graduate School of Business. Aims to provide complete and easily usable securities data. The Center offers six databases covering stock data, indices and mutual funds. All databases are updated monthly (with the exception of the mutual funds database, which is updated quarterly).

Digital data, image & text collections

3014 Dow Jones Indexes [USA]
www.djindexes.com
Best known for providing the Dow Jones Industrial Average, the Dow Jones Indexes site showcases a wide selection of index information. The home page includes a range of historic data back to 1895, featuring annotated charts and downloadable spreadsheets. Current index information is also provided and detailed charting and analysis options are available. A variety of index-related research and data reports are listed. Multimedia content includes videos of speeches and panel discussions.

3015 Standard & Poor's
www.standardandpoors.com
Standard and Poor's home page features links to a large selection of downloadable content covering worldwide markets. Information on various S&P indices is provided in the form of useful factsheets and research documents. The

site also provides detailed information on credit ratings and disseminates a range of more general financial publications.

Directories & encyclopedias

3016 Euromoney encyclopedia of debt finance
T. Rhodes, ed.   Euromoney, 2006, 261pp. ISBN 1843742691.
Helpful guide for bankers, investors, rating agency specialists and treasury teams. The first part of the encyclopedia covers core products in debt finance, such as covered bonds, convertible bonds and private placements. The second part of the book gives examples of the use of these markets in practice. The book is written by a wide range of contributors from major companies, including Goldman Sachs, Lehman Brothers and BNP Paribas.

Keeping up to date

3017 Euromoney
Euromoney Institutional Investor, monthly. ISSN 00142433.
www.euromoney.com
Trusted source of information on activity across capital markets. Content coverage includes alternative investments, banking, debt, emerging markets, equity and structured finance. The magazine also publishes results of regular surveys covering a wide range of areas. A recent in-depth survey focused on private banking. Online facilities include an archive back to 1996, RSS news feeds and industry benchmark data.

3018 International Financing Review
Thomson Financial, weekly. ISSN 09530223.
www.ifre.com
Up-to-date source on capital markets information. The magazine provides commentary, analysis and in-depth data on developments in equity capital markets, securitization, leveraged finance and emerging markets. The accompanying subcription website features an archive covering over ten years and is easy to navigate.

3019 Journal of International Money and Finance
Elsevier, 8 p.a. €92 per year. ISSN 02615606.
Scholarly journal of theoretical and empirical research in international finance and international monetary economics. Topic coverage includes foreign exchange options, international capital markets and international fiscal policy. The most popular recent articles have focused on competition between European financial markets and the use of foreign direct investment.

Commodity Markets

Introductions to the subject

3020 Power of gold: the history of an obsession
P. Bernstein   John Wiley & Sons, 2001, 448pp. ISBN 0471003786.
Describes the myths, explorations and history surrounding the world's obsession with gold. Contains numerous interesting stories and anecdotes, alongside a comprehensive history of the power and influence gold exerts.

'…readers with an interest in history or finance will welcome Bernstein's interesting history of gold and money in the West.'
(*The Independent*, 20 October 2000)

3021 World commodities and world currency
B. Graham   McGraw-Hill, 1944, 182pp. ISBN 0070248060.
Details Graham's thoughts on the importance and growth of world commodity stabilization, stockpiling and the implications for world currencies. The text, although now over 60 years old, is a classic in its field and provides a detailed historical analysis of commodities and currencies.

Dictionaries, thesauri, classifications

3022 Dictionary of international trade: 4,071 international trade, economic, banking, legal and shipping terms
E.G. Hinkelman   World Trade Press, 1994, 279pp. ISBN 0963186485.
Claims to be the most authoritative dictionary of international trade terms. Although now slightly dated, the terms included are clearly defined. Appendices include details of international trade resources, a useful list of weights and measures, alongside global dialling codes and world currencies.

Official & quasi-official bodies

3023 London Metal Exchange
www.lme.com
The world's leading non-ferrous metals market has a snazzy website which is speedy and easy to navigate. Includes a detailed history of the LME as well as in-depth information on how trading functions. Market data from the Exchange is freely available (although registration is required). LME also provides a variety of training (both free and fee-based) and these are advertised, while training materials in a selection of languages are also available.

Portal & task environments

3024 Commodity World
www.commodityworld.com
Provides free information for commodity traders worldwide. Data available includes market commentaries, trading tips, price quotes and charts and futures and options data. Presentation is basic and much information is limited to links to external websites, but the site is a useful gateway to an extensive selection of information on commodities.

Digital data, image & text collections

3025 Commodity Trader
www.commoditytrader.net
Features a range of online data for futures trading, foreign exchange trading and stock trading. Interactive charts can be viewed for stocks and metals and a range of delayed charts are available for other commodities. The site is a good source for latest news developments. Includes the ability to filter stories by commodity.

Handbooks & manuals

3026 CRB commodity yearbook
Wiley, annual. ISSN 10762906.
Claims to be 'the single most comprehensive source of commodity and futures market information available'. Provides crucial information on over 100 domestic and international commodities, including seasonal patterns, historical data, current prices and trading patterns. A brief article on each commodity outlines recent trends and potential future prospects.

3027 Gold trading boot camp: how to master the basics and become a successful commodities investor
G.T. Weldon   Wiley, 2007, 348pp. ISBN 0471728004.
Provides an accessible guide to trading on the commodities market. Coverage includes trend identification, global trade and managing risk. The text is supplemented with detailed analyses of charts and full investment advice. Focuses on gold trading, although much of the information proffered also applies to other commodities.

3028 Industrial commodity statistics yearbook
United Nations, annual. ISSN 02577208.
Published in English and French, this annual compilation of statistics on worldwide industrial production features data split by country and geographical region. Statistics cover a ten-year period and approximately 600 commodities.

Keeping up to date

3029 Commodity market review
Food & Agriculture Organisation of the United Nations, 1995–, biennial. ISSN 1020492X.
www.fao.org
Analyses important agricultural commodity market developments. Recent articles have focused on the EU banana market, market profiles in dairy markets and global trade in rice. The Review can also be viewed by accessing the FAO website and searching for 'Commodity Market Review'.

Derivative, Futures & Options Markets

Introductions to the subject

3030 Derivatives markets
R.L. McDonald   2nd edn, Addison Wesley, 2006, 964pp. ISBN 0321311493.
Thorough yet accessible insight into derivatives markets. The book begins with an introduction to forwards and futures markets, then examines options, financial engineering and advanced pricing theory. Calculations in the book can be replicated using Excel spreadsheets on the CD-ROM which accompanies the text.

3031 Financial engineering: derivatives and risk management
K. Cuthbertson and D. Nitzsche   Wiley, 2001, 776pp. £45. ISBN 0471495840.
www.wiley.co.uk/cuthbertson [COMPANION]
Full examination of futures, options, swaps and risk management. Theoretical ideas are illustrated throughout

with real-world examples. No prior knowledge of the subject is assumed. Complex ideas are expressed with clarity but the presentation throughout is somewhat uninspired, lacking the colour and accessibility of other texts.

3032 Introduction to futures and options markets
J. Hull   3rd edn, Prentice Hall, 1998, 471pp. ISBN 0137833172.
Introduction to futures and options markets ideal for those with a limited background in mathematics – unlike many books in the field it contains no calculus. Coverage includes hedging strategies, interest-rate futures and swaps. As with all books by John Hull, the text is extremely well written and refreshingly free of jargon.

3033 Options, futures and other derivatives
J. Hull   6th edn, Prentice Hall, 2005, 789pp. £51.99. ISBN 0131499084.
Extremely popular text covering advanced topics in derivatives pricing. Each chapter is extremely well structured, beginning with learning objectives and concluding with a chapter summary, questions and problems and further reading. Content ranges from futures markets and interest rates to weather derivatives and exotic options.

3034 Paul Wilmott introduces quantitative finance
P. Wilmott   2nd edn, John Wiley, 2007. £39.99. ISBN 0470319585.
Designed specifically for university students, this guide to quantitative finance is extensive and highly accessible. Presentation is outstanding throughout, explaining complicated theories clearly, highlighting learning objectives and providing useful exercises. The guide is supported a CD-ROM containing spreadsheets and Visual Basic programs which implement techniques found in the text.

3035 Strategic investment: real options and games
H.T.J. Smit and L. Trigeorgis   Princeton University Press, 2004, 471pp. £48.95. ISBN 0691010390.
Presents a new perspective on strategic investment, aimed at both professional and academic readers. Chapters include Corporate finance and strategic planning; Corporate real options; Games and strategic decisions; Simple strategic investment gains. A complex text which requires a high level of pre-existing financial knowledge.

Official & quasi-official bodies

3036 Chicago Board of Trade
www.cbot.com
Information on the leading futures and options exchange. Available market data is extensive, including historical data, commentaries and delayed quotes. There is also a detailed history of the exchange and a useful glossary of frequently used terms. The site features 'webinars' – online interative seminars covering topics related to trading on the exchange. The Chicago Board of Trade has now merged with the Chicago Mercantile Exchange.

3037 Chicago Board Options Exchange
www.cboe.com
Home page of the first US options exchange, founded in 1973. The site is extremely detailed and features quotes, market data and news. An innovative idea is the ability to register and customize the home page to display content

relevant to user needs. The site also includes a range of excellent online tutorials.

3038 Eurex
www.eurexchange.com
Eurex is 'the world's largest derivatives exchange and the leading clearing house in Europe'. The effective and unfussy website includes detailed information on a huge range of Eurex products, such as equity and credit derivatives. Market data includes daily and monthly statistics and delayed quotes. The site is also available in German.

3039 International Securities Exchange
www.iseoptions.com
The home page of the world's largest equity options exchange features data on equity and index options as well as regulatory information. The most useful area of the site covers market data, including details on exchange volume and the most active issues. Tools available on the site include both a basic and advanced options calculator.

3040 New York Mercantile Exchange
www.nymex.com
Home page of the world's largest physical commodity futures exchange. The front page of the site includes a useful overview of major commodities such as crude oil, natural gas and gold. NYMEX regularly publishes press releases and these are archived on the site. In depth details on each market are provided and there is plenty of information on the history and operation of the Exchange itself.

Handbooks & manuals

3041 Fixed income markets and their derivatives
S.M. Sundaresan   2nd edn, Thomson South-Western, 2002, 717pp. ISBN 032400446X.
http://sundaresan.swcollege.com
Detailed textbook, including chapters focusing on topics such as emerging debt markets, yield-curve analysis and credit risk. Mathematically advanced concepts are displayed as appendices at the end of each chapter. Not the most accessible text, but extremely comprehensive.

3042 Real options and investment under uncertainty: classical readings and recent contributions
E. Schwartz and L. Trigeorgis   MIT Press, 2004, 881pp. £29.95. ISBN 0262693186.
A collection of almost 40 readings by leading thinkers on the subject of real options and capital investment under uncertainty. Includes a combination of new material and classic works. Topics covered are broad in scope, including 'A new approach to evaluating natural resource investments', 'Strategic growth options' and 'Investment in technological innovations'.

Keeping up to date

3043 Journal of Derivatives
Institutional Investor, 1998–, qtrly. $395 per year. ISSN 10741240.
Billed as the leading analytical journal on derivatives theories. Includes articles on valuation models for derivative instruments and securities, alongside tools and models for financial risk management. Recent articles include 'Pricing

and hedging of contingent credit lines' and 'Calibration risk for exotic options'.

3044 Journal of Futures Markets
John Wiley, 1981–, monthly. ISSN 02707314.
Details the latest developments in financial futures and derivatives with articles written by finance academics and professionals. Coverage is both theoretical and practical and includes financial engineering, hedging strategies, portfolio optimization, financial instruments and risk management.

Financial Institutions

Bank of England • banks & other lending institutions • charities • European Central Bank • hedge funds • investment funds • multinational banks • pension funds • trusts • venture capital companies • World Bank

Introductions to the subject

3045 Financial institutions, markets and money
D.S. Kidwell [et al.]   9th edn, Wiley, 2005, 680pp. £72.95. ISBN 0471697575.
Provides an up-to-date overview of the US financial system, covering institutions and markets, alongside an introduction to international financial markets. Primarily a student text, the book is split into five main sections: The financial system; How interest rates are determined; Financial markets; Commercial banking; and Financial institutions. An excellent learning tool for students – difficult concepts are described with clarity and the presentation is reader-friendly throughout.

3046 Major financial institutions of the world: 2005
8th edn, Graham & Whiteside, 2005. 2 v. ISBN 1860994210.
Directory covering more than 9000 global financial institutions, including banks, investment, insurance and leasing companies. Entries include company contact details, brief financial information for the past two years, number of employees and a succinct business description. Although the directory was published in 2005 much financial data extends only as far back as 2002, so the information provided, although thorough, quickly becomes dated.

Official & quasi-official bodies

3047 Bank for International Settlements
www.bis.org
International organization fostering international financial and monetary cooperation and serving as a bank for central banks. The site includes details on the history and structure of the Bank, links to central bank websites and a large research hub of downloadable articles. A range of statistics on areas, including banking, derivatives and securities can also be accessed. The site is easy to navigate and highly-recommended.

3048 Federal Reserve [USA]
www.federalreserve.gov
The Federal Reserve is the central bank of the USA, founded by Congress in 1913 to provide a stable monetary and financial system. The site is well presented, prominently displaying breaking news and recent statistical releases. A

range of consumer guides can also be downloaded, providing advice on issues such as choosing a credit card and identity theft. The Federal Reserve also provides a good selection of RSS feeds for both news and data.

3049 Financial Services Authority
www.fsa.gov.uk
The rather stern appearance of the FSA website is a little offputting, but it does contain a lot of useful information. Features details on reporting requirements for small companies and also includes the option for businesses to submit returns online. The FSA Library contains a range of consumer research and economic papers. The consumer-focused pages of the site have a more informal presentation style and include jargon-free details on key financial products such as mortgages and credit cards.

3050 House Committee on Financial Services [USA]
http://financialservices.house.gov
The website states that the Committee 'oversees all components of the nation's housing and financial services sectors, including banking, insurance, real estate, public and assisted housing and securities'. The site is an excellent source of information on latest political initiatives, featuring detailed press releases and hearing transcripts. Webcasts of hearings are also available.

3051 International Finance Corporation
www.ifc.org
The IFC website features an array of free research and publications covering subjects such as financing, sustainability and corporate governance. Some documents are translated into alternative languages in addition to English. The site is also a good source of information on financing initiatives in specific countries and includes a regularly updated news page.

3052 International Monetary Fund
www.imf.org
Includes a useful guide for 'first time visitors' which provides advice on navigating the extensive IMF site. A range of time series data can be downloaded covering IMF lending, exchange rates and other economic and financial indicators. The Country Information section includes latest IMF data on member countries. The IMF also produces a great number of publications – documents such as the regularly updated, detailed World Economic Outlook can be downloaded free of charge.

3053 Organisation for Economic Co-operation & Development
www.oecd.org
Group of now 30 countries 'best known for its publications and statistics. Its work covers economic and social issues from macroeconomics, to trade, education, development and science and innovation'.

The clearly laid-out site provides – via the Statistics Portal – access to statistical data by topic: Agriculture and fisheries; Development; Education and fraining ... Regional statistics; Social and welfare statistics; and Transport. You can browse 'By Topic', 'By Country', 'By Department'. There is a comprehensive set of online services with full-text access to a very wide range of documents. An example might be: 'Measuring and fostering the progress of societies', June

2007, Turkey (Second OECD World Forum on 'Statistics, Knowledge and Policy').

The site contains a wealth of economic and financial data. The statistics section alone is home to publications such as OECD Main Economic Indicators, providing detailed comparisons between countries on a range of key indicators, including interest rates. Annual factbooks are also available for download. The site benefits from a well thought-out navigation system which allows users to browse by country or by topics such as tax, investment and corporate governance.

3054 Royal Mint
www.royalmint.gov.uk
Stylish website of the Royal Mint, responsible for providing UK coinage. The site contains information on the history of the Royal Mint, including information on decimilization. Incredibly detailed data is also supplied – for example latest figures show there are 10,576 million one penny coins in circulation in the UK.

3055 United States. Department of the Treasury
www.ustreas.gov
Well designed website which contains a vast range of financial information. Key topics covered include currency, accounting, financial markets, taxes and technology. The Treasury Media Center includes an archive of event webcasts such as Treasury press conferences. A selection of links to tax forms is available for taxpayers, alongside resources such as interest rate statistics and quarterly financing estimates.

3056 World Bank
www.worldbank.org
Detailed website featuring plenty of downloadable content. Over 15,000 documents can be downloaded free of charge, including operational documents, research papers and most World Bank publications. The site is also a strong source of statistical data, country information and global financial trends.

Research centres & institutes

3057 Financial Institutions Center
http://fic.wharton.upenn.edu/fic
Part of the Wharton School of the University of Pennsylvania. The research focus of the Center is threefold – improving productivity and performance; managing financial risks; and assessing the competitive structures of institutions and markets. The site provides links to working papers, policy briefs and case studies.

Associations & societies

3058 APACS: the UK payments association
www.apacs.org.uk
Well presented website of the UK trade association for payments and for institutions that deliver payment services to customers. The site includes useful histories regarding payment methods such as cash, cheques and credit cards. Detailed statistics include payment trends back to 1998 and clearing data. A helpful glossary of payment terms is also provided.

3059 International Compliance Association
www.int-comp.org
The ICA has a well designed and detailed home page.
Information on ICA courses is accompanied by job listings,
events details and a clearly presented bookshop. The site
also acts as a useful gateway to other online regulatory
resources via an extremely thorough A–Z list of web links.

Handbooks & manuals

3060 Mergent bank and finance manual
Mergent FIS, 2001–, annual. 3 v. ISSN 05450152.
Published in three parts. Volume 1 covers banks, trust
companies, savings and loan associations and federal credit
agencies. Volume 2 covers insurance, finance and real estate
investment companies. Volume 3 covers unit investment
trusts. Each organization profile includes a history, overview
of the business and recent financial data.

Keeping up to date

3061 Institutional investor
Euromoney Institutional Investor, monthly. ISSN 00203580.
www.iimagazine.com
Key source of up-to-date financial information and
institutional investing financial news. The magazine regularly
profiles chief executives and publishes in-depth articles on
areas including pensions, real estate and trading. The
magazine also publishes regular rankings covering areas
such as hedge funds. The companion website is well
designed and features bi-monthly newsletters and a
searchable archive.

Banks & Other Lending Institutions

Introductions to the subject

3062 British multinational banking 1830–1990
G. Jones   Clarendon Press, 1995, 511pp. £30. ISBN 019820602X.
Traces the history of British multinational banks from their
origins in the 1830s until the 1990s. Contains useful insights
into the internal management and organization of
multinational banks as well as providing a comprehensive
historical record. The book also tabulates the long-term
financial records of a selection of major British multinational
banks.

3063 Investment banking: a tale of three cities
S. Hayes and P. Hubbard   Harvard Business School Press, 1990,
424pp. ISBN 0875842208.
Records the history of international banking, focusing on the
USA, UK and Japan. Although some of the coverage on
'current' banking is a dated, historical coverage is strong,
detailed and well written.

3064 Money and banking in the UK: a history
M. Collins   Croom Helm, 1988, 640pp. ISBN 0709907605.
Classic text tracing the history of banking in the UK from the
early 19th century. Details economic crises, changes in
legislation and many other factors which have affected the
banking industry. Each chapter is completed with a detailed

bibliography of additional sources. A key work for financial
historians.

Dictionaries, thesauri, classifications

3065 Dictionary of banking terms
T.P. Fitch   4th edn, Barron's, 2000, 529pp. £10.99. ISBN
0764112600.
Over 3000 terms related to banking are defined clearly and
concisely in a handy reference guide. Includes a list of world
currencies by country (now somewhat out-of-date, owing to
the introduction of the euro) and common banking
abbreviations and acronyms. An ideal handbook for
consumers and finance professionals alike.

3066 Dictionary of finance and banking
J. Smullen and N. Hand   3rd edn, Market House, 2005, 448pp.
£10.99. ISBN 0198607490.
Covers every aspect of finance, including commodities,
insurance, stocks and shares, M&A and international trade.
The dictionary has strong international coverage and is more
up to date than many competitors, covering topics such as
European monetary union.

**3067 Dictionary of international banking and finance
terms**
Financial World Publishing   Financial World Publishing, 2001,
360pp. £15. ISBN 0852976321.
Defines over 4000 terms in the fields of retail and wholesale
banking, from 'abatement' to 'zloty'. Includes well
established terms as well as everyday jargon, acronyms and
newly adopted financial terminology. Each definition is
extremely succinct and clear. An excellent reference book for
students and professionals.

Laws, standards, codes

3068 Banking Code Standards Board
www.bankingcode.org.uk
The Standards Board monitors compliance with and enforces
the Banking Code. The site provides details of which
organizations have signed up for the Banking Code, as well
as in-depth information on the Code itself. The home page
also provides details on how customers should approach
making a complaint about a financial institution.

Official & quasi-official bodies

3069 Bank of England
www.bankofengland.co.uk
The Bank of England site is extremely well designed and
contains a wide range of current information as well as a
history of the Bank. An interactive statistical database can
be searched for financial and monetary statistics. Regular
publications available through the site include the Inflation
Report, Financial Stability Report and Quarterly Bulletin.
There are also a large number of articles and statistics about
banknotes and currency and educational materials for
schools and colleges are provided.

3070 Bank of Japan
www.boj.or.jp/en

As is to be expected, the Bank of Japan home page contains a large selection of statistics on the Japanese financial system, including monetary policy information, survey results, working papers and other research. Regular publications such as the *Bank of Japan annual review* are archived and available to download. The site also features a 20-minute introductory video and a virtual tour of the Bank.

3071 Deutsche Bundesbank
www.bundesbank.de

Impressive website providing a range of information on the Bundesbank alongside detailed financial statistics. Time series data can be downloaded covering areas such as money market rates, debt securities and euro conversion rates. Monthly statistical reports can also be downloaded. The site also provides a detailed overview of the Bundesbank and is uniformly well presented and easy to navigate.

3072 European Central Bank
www.ecb.int

Excellent website featuring detailed information on European currencies, monetary policies and payments. Statistics available include the Bank's monthly bulletin and data on areas, including interest rates, consumer prices and exchange rates. Many areas of the site are available in a wide variety of languages, including Czech, Estonian and Slovenian. The site also includes a detailed glossary and live webcasts of press conferences.

3073 Federal Deposit Insurance Corporation [USA]
www.fdic.gov

Supervises over 5000 state chartered banks and savings banks that are not members of the Federal Reserve System. The site includes a wealth of statistics and bank data. An institution directory provides comprehensive financial and demographic data for ever FDIC-insured institution, including the most recent quarterly financial statements and details on branch locations.

3074 Federal Reserve Bank of New York
www.ny.frb.org

Attractive website containing information on one of the key regional Reserve Banks which make up the Federal Reserve System. A history of the Bank is available, alongside speeches by former presidents of the Bank. Research publications on the site are particularly strong and include statistics on household debt, interest rates and global economic indicators.

Research centres & institutes

3075 Institute of International Bankers [USA]
www.iib.org

Home page of 'the only national association devoted to representing the interests of the international banking community in the United States'. Content includes a calendar of events and details of legislative and regulatory issues. The Institute's annual global survey is particularly comprehensive and can be downloaded free of charge.

3076 Lafferty Group
www.lafferty.com

Subscription-based site offering research on global retail banking, cards and payment services. Research databases available include World Card Intelligence (WCI), which covers over 60 countries and the International Branch Banking Database (IBBD). IBBD content is extensive and includes images of bank branch exteriors and interiors, as well as branch literature.

Associations & societies

3077 American Bankers Association
www.aba.com

Content on this large website includes benchmarking and survey research, personal finance guides and a comprehensive list of financial websites. Training facilities available for a fee include telephone and webcast briefings on topics such as credit scoring and bank regulation. Most content on the site is immediately available although for many articles free registration is required.

3078 Association Française des Banques
www.afb.fr

French language only. The home page of the French Bankers' Federation includes information on the sector such as data on salaries and regular press releases. An alerting system tracking updates to the site is also provided.

3079 Association of German Banks
www.german-banks.com

Available in English and German. Includes a detailed set of statistics on the German banking industry, results of banking surveys and details on other banking markets in Central and Eastern Europe, including Slovenia, the Baltic States and the Czech Republic. A range of useful booklets covering areas such as online banking security and credit scoring can also be ordered or downloaded.

3080 British Bankers' Association
www.bba.org.uk

Home page of the leading UK banking and financial services trade association. Includes a glossary of banking terms and historic BBA LIBOR rates. A range of statistics on mortgages and consumer lending is also available. The site also features a news page and links to codes of good practice. The BBA also publishes an annual abstract of banking statistics, offering online access to over 25 years of banking data.

3081 Building Societies Association
www.bsa.org.uk

The BSA is the trade association of all UK building societies. The website is easy to navigate and includes a range of industry related publications and comprehensive statistics on the building society sector. Consumer advice and factsheets include information on building society takeovers and flotations. A detailed document outlines all historical name changes and mergers in the industry.

3082 European Banking Federation
www.fbe.be

The European Banking Federation (EBF) represents over 5000 European banks and 2.3 million employees. Annual reports and EBF publications are available through the home page. A broad selection of statistics can also be downloaded. The site is easy to navigate, although pages can be very slow to download.

3083 European Mortgage Federation
www.hypo.org/Content/Default.asp
Groups national associations and individual lenders from European member states. The site is a good source of up-to-date information – recent publications available through the site have included a factsheet on housing policy in Poland. A large range of mortgage industry data is also available, including a detailed Quarterly Review, an executive summary of which can be downloaded free of charge.

Digital data, image & text collections

3084 Bankscope
http://bankscope.bvdep.com
Subscription database containing financial information on over 27,000 world banks, including detailed accounts and ratios. Ratings reports are also supplied, alongside details of major shareholders and company subsidiaries. Annual and interim reports are also available for download.

3085 British banking: A guide to historical records
J. Orbell and A. Turton   Ashgate, 2001, 663pp. £61.99. ISBN 0754602958.
Details over 700 archive collections in record offices, university and local libraries and banks themselves. Includes an introduction outlining the historical structure and functions of British banking. Each entry contains a brief history of the institution, followed by address and holdings information. Also includes a useful bibliography of individual bank histories.

3086 National Information Center [USA]
www.ffiec.gov/nicpubweb/nicweb/NicHome.aspx
The National Information Center defines itself as 'a repository of financial data and institution characteristics collected by the Federal Reserve System'. Examples of data provided include lists of the Top 50 bank holding companies by asset size and annual peer reports on bank holding companies dating back to 2002. Detailed financial data for each company can also be downloaded.

Handbooks & manuals

3087 Bankers' almanac and year book
Thomas Skinner Directories, 1866–, 2 p.a.
A classic source which has now been published for well over 150 years. Contains details of thousands of banks worldwide – balance sheet figures are included where possible. Published in five volumes, the first two volumes contain details of banks in alphabetical sequence. Volumes 3 and 4 contain geographical listings of banks. Volume 5 contains details of liquidations, name changes and banking associations.

3088 Bankers' almanac world ranking
Thomas Skinner Directories, 1985–, annual. ISSN 02680270.
A publication which has recently benefited from a makeover, improving presentation throughout. Includes over 3000 major international banks ranked by total assets. Banks are

indexed alphabetically and ranked by country. Percentage increases or decreases in asset value over the prevous year are also provided.

3089 Building societies yearbook: official handbook of the Building Societies Association
Charterhouse Communications Group, annual. ISSN 00683566.
Published by the Building Societies Association, the official yearbook includes a complete alphabetical listing of members, including key information and balance sheets. A selection of statistics covering mortgage lending, deposits and loans are also detailed. Further information includes lists of building society branches and agencies, merger statistics and a directory of surveyors. The yearbook is accompanied by a CD-ROM.

Keeping up to date

3090 The American Banker
Thomson Financial. ISSN 00027561.
www.americanbanker.com
Well established resource for banking and financial service professionals. The mission statement of the magazine is to 'go beyond headline news, to research issues, analyse the strategies and profile the personalities that influence events'. As such, a large amount of detailed comment and analysis is published, as well as up-to-date news. The accompanying website has a sensible navigation and good links to other relevant sites.

3091 Bank of England Quarterly Bulletin
Bank of England, 1960–, qtrly. ISSN 00055166.
Provides commentary on UK monetary policy and market developments. Also includes reports and analysis on both national and international financial and economic issues. Summaries and complete issues of the Bulletin can be downloaded free of charge from the Bank of England website.

3092 The Banker
Financial Times Business Information, monthly. £289 per year. ISSN 00055395.
www.thebanker.com
The Banker publishes detailed news and comment on developments in the global banking sector. Articles cover topics, including retail banking, regulatory issues and new technology. Regular supplements are published, many of which focus on emerging economies. The magazine also publishes detailed surveys and reports – recent reports have included 'Top 100 Chinese banks' and 'Retail banking 2015'.

3093 European Card Review
6 p.a. £100 p.a. ISSN 13606069.
www.europeancardreview.com
Leading magazine covering the European payments cards business. Includes editorial coverage on payments in Western Europe as well as developments in economies in Central and Eastern Europe. Topics include regular country profiles, new vendor products and detailed statistics.

3094 Journal of Banking and Finance
Elsevier, monthly. €141 per year. ISSN 03784266.
Aimed at financial economists and policy makers, this monthly journal publishes research on financial institutions

and money and capital markets. An emphasis is placed on theoretical developments and their practical implementation. Recent popular articles have included works on worldwide corporate valuation, M&A in the European financial industry and the liquidity of bank assets.

3095   Journal of Money, Credit and Banking
Ohio State University Press, 6 p.a. $79 per year. ISSN 00222879.
Leading professional journal covering credit markets, financial regulation, portfolio management, international payments and fiscal policy. Recent articles have focused on topics, including exchange rates, US monetary policy and inflation dynamics.

3096   World bank directory
Accuity, annual. ISSN 15380920.
Comprehensive international directory of banks, arranged alphabetically by country. Within each country record, details of bank branches located within individual cities are provided. The directory also includes details of bankers associations and a listing of the Top 1000 US Banks.

3097   World banking abstracts
Blackwell, 6 p.a. ISSN 02659484.
Also available as an online subscription service. Provides details of important articles published in over 400 banking and finance publications. Abstracts are concise (75 words) and cover topics, including law and regulation, technology, pensions and financial institutions. A useful source for keeping up to date with research developments in banking.

Venture Capital Companies

Introductions to the subject

3098   Venture capital and private equity: a casebook
J. Lerner, F. Hardymon and A. Leamon   3rd edn, Wiley, 2005, 570pp. £36.95. ISBN 0471230693.
Comprehensive guide to all stages of the venture capital process, including raising funds, investing in companies and exiting investments. The presentation of the text is a little cramped and lacking in visual inspiration, but the writing itself is detailed and thorough. The text follows a case study format, using real-world examples to bring life to the complex issues discussed.

Associations & societies

3099   British Business Angels Association
www.bbaa.org.uk
Organization promoting business angel finance to fund risk capital requirements. Acts as a portal for those looking to invest and those looking for funding. Includes a number of useful guidelines as well as a range of successful case studies.

3100   British Venture Capital Association
www.bvca.co.uk
Industry body for UK private equity and venture capital firms and their advisers. The home page includes useful FAQ regarding venture capital and well presented case studies on

the industry. BVCA members have access to additional publications and research.
- **BVCA directory** British Venture Capital Association, annual.

3101   Business Partners
www.businesspartners.com
Fee-based website connecting entrepreneurs and companies with potential investors and partners. Searches can be made by a range of options, including value, location and sector. Additional content includes case studies, legal information, investor guidelines and company research.

3102   European Venture Capital Association
www.evca.com
Represents the European private equity sector, with over 1000 members. The site includes details of forthcoming events and regularly updated news coverage. Additional content includes key facts on the private equity sector and details of industry standards.
- **EVCA yearbook** EVCA, annual. Well presented guide providing an overview of the European venture capital market. Profiles on individual countries include data on funds raised, investments and macro-economic indicators.

3103   National Venture Capital Association [USA]
www.nvca.org
The home page of the NVCA includes a useful overview of the venture capital industry and links to a select number of venture capital companies. News on upcoming NVCA events is also provided.
- **National Venture Capital Association Yearbook** National Venture Capital Association, annual. Includes details on investments, portfolio company valuations, IPOs and acquisitions.

Digital data, image & text collections

3104   Capital IQ
www.capitaliq.com
Subscription database offering data on global public and private companies. Excellent source of data on venture capital companies. The database features extensive information on company boards of directors and executives. Profiles of over 100,000 companies are supplied and PDFs of annual reports can be downloaded. Capital IQ also offers a news analysis, filtering and alerting service. A database of M&A transactions from 1998 onwards is also included.

3105   VentureXpert Web
www.venturexpert.com
Subscription database covering venture funds, private firms, executives, venture-backed companies and limited partners. Also provides analytics for fund commitment disbursements, statistics and performance. Searching facilities are extensive and allow in-depth criteria to be utilized to narrow down results.

Directories & encyclopedias

3106   Asian private equity 300: the 2006 guide to private equity and venture capital in Asia
17th edn, AVCJ Group, 2005, 404pp. ISBN 9627472265.
A who's who's of the leading venture capital and private equity firms in Asia, containing over 1500 companies. Data

provided on each company includes contact details, funds managed, investment preferences and a brief company description. The guide also features a number of rankings and overviews of the Asian private equity industry.

3107   Directory of venture capital and private equity firms, domestic and international
9th edn, Grey House Publishing, 2005, 1053pp. ISBN 1592370624.
Comprehensive listing of over 3000 venture capital and private equity firms. Appoximately 40% of the firms listed are US-based. Listings include company address, phone number, website, mission statement and investment criteria. The directory has no additional features beyond the listings, but the information provided is in-depth and clear.

3108   Directory of venture capital and private equity service providers
Dow Jones, 2006, 181pp. ISBN 1893648834.
Lists almost 400 service providers for the venture capital and private equity industry. The book is divided into sections such as attorneys, software developers, accounting firms and executive recruiters. As would be expected, contact details are provided alongside a brief description of areas of practice and current specialities. Details of clients currently served by the providers are also supplied.

3109   Galante's venture capital and private equity directory
Dow Jones, annual.
Mammoth guide to the fast-changing world of venture capital and private equity. Designed primarily for finance and investment professionals, the book contains a number of ranked lists, including the 500 largest US venture capital and private equity firms. The comprehensive list of US firms includes company overviews, contact details and e-mail addresses for key personnel. Coverage of major international organizations is also supplied.

3110   Pratt's guide to private equity sources
Thomson Financial, 2006, annual. ISSN 08841616.
Long-established directory, now considered an industry benchmark. Contains over 5500 listings of global private equity firms, including details such as type of firm, geographical preferences and size of investments considered. The directory also includes numerous useful articles discussing the background of the industry, how to raise private equity and sources of financing.

3111   Report on investment activity [UK]
British Venture Capital Association, annual. ISSN 13678558.
Annual publication by the British Venture Capital Association. Includes a useful summary of UK investment activity, which breaks down venture capital investment by industry sector and by region. Statistics on sources of private equity are also provided. Extensive appendices include data on European and worldwide investment. An excellent summary of recent venture capital investment.

3112   Venture capital report directory: private equity and venture capital in the UK and Europe
Temple Cloud, 2005. 2 volumes. ISBN 0954679113.
www.vcrdirectory.co.uk
Also available online via subscription. Includes details on over 3000 venture capital investors of all descriptions. The directory is divided into two volumes: the first covering the

UK; the second focusing on Europe, Israel and South Africa. The directory benefits from a high level of detail, including lengthy profiles of key management figures, data on investment prefrences and preferred exit routes.

Keeping up to date

3113   Asian Venture Capital Journal
AVCJ Group, weekly. $995 per year. ISSN 10123334.
www.asianfn.com
Key source of information on private equity and venture capital activities in the Asia-Pacific region. The journal provides coverage of fund-raising, investments and the people behind the deals. Standard features include 'Movers and shakers', 'Asia-Silicon Valley currents' and 'Regional news'.

3114   European Venture Capital Journal
Venture Economics, 10 p.a. ISSN 09541675.
www.evcj.com
Provides news coverage, features and data on private equity deals and venture capital in the European market. The magazine has regular features, including deal of the month and company profiles. Online content includes a searchable archive back to 1999. The website also features legal and regulatory information and RSS feeds.

3115   Institutional Investor's Alpha
Institutional Investor, 6 p.a.
www.alphamagazine.com
Regular slimline magazine featuring well written articles and profiles focused on private equity and hedge funds. The subscription website features additional content, including rankings and a bi-monthly newsletter.

3116   Private Equity International
Investoraccess, monthly. ISSN 14748800.
www.privateequityinternational.com
Magazine providing information and insight for institutional investors and market practitioners on the world of private equity. Each issue features global news, detailed reports and themed articles covering areas such as liquidity, valuation or fundraising. The magazine also publishes value-added data, including survey results and league tables, such as the PEI 50, which ranks the world's 50 largest private equity firms.

3117   PrivateEquityOnline.com
www.privateequityonline.com
Subscription-based site. News stories on private equity deals are divided geographically, alongside more in-depth articles and features. Although news content is detailed and timely, the site possesses no additional features such as a search facility to screen private equity deals.

3118   Real Deals [EUR]
Caspian Publishing, 24 p.a. ISSN 14687038.
www.realdeals.eu.com
Fortnightly magazine providing news and data on European private equity. Subscription includes access to the Real Deals website featuring regularly updated private equity news and the searchable 'Done Deals' database. The magazine also publishes regular special reports on topical issues which are available both in print and online.

3119 Venture Capital: an international journal of entrepreneurial finance
Taylor & Francis, qtrly. ISSN 13691066.
Publishes research-based papers on all aspects of private equity finance, including corporate venture capital, investment patterns and economic impacts. Coverage includes established venture capital markets such as the USA as well as emerging markets. Regular special issues are devoted to a single theme, such as a recent issue on gender and entrepreneurial finance.

3120 Venture Capital Analyst: technology edition
Dow Jones, monthly. ISSN 10999302.
Publication focusing on the role of information technology in the venture capital industry. Subscribers have access to an online archive dating back to 1999. Each issue includes news and commentaries on developing technologies, profiles of entrepreneurs and companies and statistics and rankings on the venture capital industry.

Investment Funds

Introductions to the subject

3121 Absolute returns: the risk and opportunities of hedge fund investing
A. Ineichen   Wiley, 2003, 514pp. £47.50. ISBN 0471251208.
A comprehensive, practical guide to the hedge fund industry. An overview of the industry is followed by chapters examining the risks associated with hedge fund investments. The author has the ability to present complex issues in a straightforward manner, meaning the book is ideally suited for novices and experts alike.

3122 Energy and environmental hedge funds: the new investment paradigm
P. Fusaro and G.M. Vasey   Wiley, 2006, 215pp. £80. ISBN 0470821981.
Examines the rapidly growing market of energy hedge funds – over 450 existed at the time of publication, with many new funds emerging weekly. The book is 'envisioned as a road map to identify investment opportunities in these new and volatile markets'. Includes chapters on weather hedge funds, energy indexes and the future outlook for energy supply.

3123 How to invest in hedge funds: an investment professional's guide
M. Ridley   Kogan Page, 2006, 409pp. £25. ISBN 0749445769.
Nicely written starting point to gain an understanding of the world of hedge funds. The book begins by examining common misconceptions about hedge funds and includes an interesting section on the evolution of the hedge fund industry. Practical advice includes a chapter on how to select a hedge fund. The book is well presented, making good use of bullet points, diagrams and glossaries.
'Matthew Ridley's admirably clear book contains everything you wanted to know about hedge funds but were afraid to ask.'
(*Financial News*)

Research centres & institutes

3124 BNP Paribas Hedge Fund Centre
www.london.edu/hedgefunds
Research centre of London Business School examining all aspects of hedge fund investing. The Centre publishes regular newsletters and provides links to a variety of working papers and published papers on the industry.

Associations & societies

3125 Alternative Investment Management Association
www.aima.org
An excellent site. The 'Knowledge Centre' section displays high-quality research, most of which is available free of charge. A valuable 'Alternative Investment Bibliography' of books, journals and research papers is also provided. Additional information for investors and regulators is available on a members-only basis.

3126 Hedge Fund Association
www.thehfa.org
The HFA website contains information on the Association, facts about hedge funds and details on investment strategies. News content is updated regularly and a wide range of more in-depth articles on the industry can also be accessed. Hedge fund events and conferences are advertised and a message board is also available. Additional content is supplied to members.

3127 International Project Finance Association
www.ipfa.org
The IPFA website is dedicated to representing the interests of private sector companies involved in project finance and Public Private Partnerships (PPPs). News stories are regularly updated and a detailed overview of the workings of project finance is also provided. A document library includes working-group papers and a variety of international presentations.

3128 London Investment Banking Association
www.liba.org.uk
Principal UK trade association for companies active in the investment banking and securities industry. The LIBA publishes papers on areas, including accounting, corporate finance, financial crime and taxation. The site also supplies a limited amount of careers information but is generally lacking in useful content.

Portal & task environments

3129 Brill.com
www.brill.com
Basic-looking mutual funds website including profiles of mutual fund managers and extensive frequently asked questions in the 'Funds 101' section. The site also has an A–Z listing of mutual funds and a selection of features and articles on the industry.

3130 Harvard Business School, Project Finance Portal
www.hbs.edu/projfinportal
Reference guide covering project finance and public-private partnerships (PPPs). Contains over 900 links to relevant sites

alongside useful references for books, articles and case studies. A range of league tables is also published, as well as information on ratings agencies, legal issues and project finance software.

3131 The Hedge Fund Marketing Alliance
www.hedgefundmarketing.org
Designed for hedge fund professionals and financial advisors. Includes a comprehensive list of hedge fund resources, with links to many detailed documents. A useful feature for professionals is the message board, which appears to be heavily used. 'Cheat sheets' on the website provide quick reference guides to all aspects of hedge funds – however, they are only available for a fee.

Digital data, image & text collections

3132 Lipper HedgeWorld
www.hedgeworld.com
Comprehensive hedge fund website – some content is free (although registration is required) while premium members paying a fee have access to updated news stories, monthly research charts and an extensive archive. Free content includes a daily newsletter and a useful fund tracker function.

Directories & encyclopedias

3133 Mergent unit investment trust: annual payment record [USA]
Mergent FIS, annual. ISSN 10536175.
A yearly cumulative report of declared payments for unit investment trusts. The publication is solely devoted to recording payments and includes no further information.

Handbooks & manuals

3134 Handbook of hedge funds
F. Lhabitant   Wiley, 2006, 637pp. £100. ISBN 0470026634.
Intended as a comprehensive reference tool for investors and fund managers. The book includes details of the historical background of the industry, regulatory information, details of investment strategies and tips on portfolio construction. An up-to-date and detailed guide to a burgeoning industry.

3135 Investment trust companies
Cazenove & Co, monthly.
Monthly tabulated data containing profiles of investment trust companies, information on new issues and corporate activity and detailed trusts sector analysis.

3136 Mutual fund investor's guide 2004
K. Kazanjian   Portfolio, 2004, 528pp. ISBN 1591840317.
Mutual fund reference book which provides profiles on one hundred 'Powerhouse Performers' with excellent track records. Performance data is also available for more than 10,000 funds, featuring annualized returns for the previous one, three and five years. The book is comprehensive although, as with much mutual fund information, it dates fairly quickly once it has been published.

Keeping up to date

3137 Hedge Fund Center
www.hedgefundcenter.com
The Hedge Fund Center is not aligned with an investment manager or consulting firm and therefore claims to provide objective, unbiased advice. Alongside news stories the site includes detailed articles on the industry, such as the origin of hedge funds, hedging techniques and the differences between mutual funds and hedge funds. A range of statistics is also available – from useful data on the growth of the industry to the less useful information that '8% of hedge fund managers admit to wearing odd socks more than once a week'.

3138 Hedge Fund Intelligence
www.hedgefundintelligence.com
Claims to be 'the biggest provider of hedge fund news and data in the world', supplying information on over 7500 funds. Data on hedge fund indices can be viewed or downloaded free of charge. A range of databases is available on a subscription basis. The site is also a good source for job vacancies in the industry. Reports on the industry can also be viewed, with a particularly strong focus on Europe, Asia and South Africa.

3139 HedgeFundRegulation.com
www.hedgefundregulation.com
Advertised as 'the leading online community for hedge fund regulation'. Features links to hedge fund regulation news sources, as well as a range of articles on topics such as hedge fund fraud cases and forming a hedge fund. A number of links to hedge fund associations, magazines and blogs are provided.

Trusts & Charities

Terminology, codes & standards

3140 UK charity ethical investment: policy, practice and disclosure
N. Kreander, V.A. Beattie and K. McPhail   Certified Accountants Educational Trust, 2006, 124pp. ISBN 1859084311.
Research report providing a useful overview of the UK charity sector. The study examines issues of accountability, investment policies and ethical investments. Almost 200 UK charities were surveyed as part of the research and the results are presented clearly and succinctly. Details of best-practice ethical investment disclosures are provided in the appendices.

Official & quasi-official bodies

3141 Charity Commission [UK]
www.charity-commission.gov.uk
The regulator and registrar for charities in England and Wales. The site is extremely well presented and includes information on registering a charity, including links to registration application packs. The site also includes detailed data on the income of registered charities for the past decade as well as a searchable online register of charities.

Guidance for charities on issues such as campaigning and international fundraising is also provided.

Research centres & institutes

3142　American Institute of Philanthropy

www.charitywatch.org

A charity watchdog aiming to help donors make informed giving decisions. Includes an index of top-rating charities by sector, as well as a complete A–Z list of charities. A number of articles are also available, ranging from 'Tips for donating a car to charity' to 'Seven tips for reducing unwanted mail and phone appeals'.

3143　Institute of Fundraising [UK]

www.institute-of-fundraising.org.uk

Home page of the professional membership body for UK fundraisers. The site provides detailed information for both fundraisers and donors, including information on tax-effective giving and charity law. A range of publications on fundraising are also detailed and can be ordered through the site. A Frequently Asked Questions section is particularly thorough and useful.

Associations & societies

3144　Charities Aid Foundation

www.cafonline.org

Organization aiming to raise the profile of charities. Publications available on the site include 'International comparisons of charitable giving', 'Charity trends' and information on payroll donations to charity. The site is also a good source of charity news and publicizes details of regular charity workshops.

3145　Charity Navigator [USA]

www.charitynavigator.org

Leading evaluator of over 5000 American charities. The charities covered are measured in terms of how responsibly they function day to day and how well positioned they are to sustain progress over time. The site can be navigated by charity name, location or type of activity. Rankings of efficient and inefficient charities are also provided.

3146　GuideStar UK

www.guidestar.org.uk

The site is billed as 'a single, easily accessible source of detailed information about every charity and voluntary organization in the UK'. Currently contains details of over 168,000 registered UK charities, using records from the Charity Commission. The search screen is easy to navigate and the appearance of the site is clear and crisp.

3147　Independent Sector [USA]

www.independentsector.org

A leadership forum for US charities, foundations and corporate giving programmes. Research available on the website includes a selection of statistics about US charitable giving as well as a number of in-depth reports. A section on public policy covers areas, including accountability, charitable reform and estate tax.

Directories & encyclopedias

3148　Directory of grant-making trusts

Charities Aid Foundation, biennial. ISSN 00705624.

Contains details of the largest 2500 trusts and foundations in the UK which give grants to organizations – the blurb of the text boasts that collectively the trusts have over £3 billion of awards at their disposal. Entries include contact details, types of grants provided and examples of recent grants. Details of how to apply are also provided.

Handbooks & manuals

3149　Charity choice UK

17th edn, Waterlow Professional Publishing, 2005, 912pp. ISBN 1857830350.

www.charitychoice.co.uk

Details over 10,000 UK charities. Address details, brief descriptions and website links are provided. Donations can also be made using an online bequest facility. The hard copy version of *Charity choice* includes charities listed by sector, although similar searches can be replicated online, which has the benefit of being more up-to-date.

Keeping up to date

3150　Charity trends

Charities Aid Foundation, annual.

Annual analysis of charities' finances. The report includes an executive summary of the finances of the UK charity sector before exploring specific topics in depth. Areas covered include tax-efficient donations by individuals and trends in company giving. The report also includes a league table of the Top 500 fundraising charities.

Pension Funds

Introductions to the subject

3151　International pension funds and their advisers

8th edn, Aspire Publications, 2007, 1408pp. £410. ISBN 9781905366156.

Directory of pension funds across the world, containing detailed listings of 3400 major international pension funds, listed by country. The Top 100 global funds are also ranked by capital value. Each pension fund featured includes contact details, a portfolio summary, membership statistics and details of advisers. Newly covered countries include Costa Rica, Uruguay and Venezuela.

3152　Pension finance

D. Blake　John Wiley & Sons, 2006, 465pp. £34.99. ISBN 0470058439.

Cass Business School professor David Blake has produced a comprehensive grounding in the theory and practice of pension finance. Written at a time when many countries in the world with ageing populations are facing a pension finance crisis, the book contains detailed information on subjects such as corporate pension finance and pension fund management. An advanced-level text for practitioners and researchers.

3153 Pensions pocket book
NTC, 2006, annual, 256pp. £37.50. ISBN 9781905366231.
Described as 'the compact contact book for the pension fund industry', the Pensions Pocket Book condenses the contact details of advisors and employers in the sector into a handy reference guide. Details for major UK pension funds are limited to fund name, capital, number of members, contact name and telephone number.

Research centres & institutes

3154 Pension Research Council
www.pensionresearchcouncil.org
Part of the Wharton School of the University of Pennsylvania. Aims to stimulate debate on policy issues affecting pensions and other employee benefits. The site is well designed and includes links to working papers, books and news items.

3155 Pensions Institute [UK]
www.pensions-institute.org
The only UK research centre focused entirely on pensions, based at Cass Business School. A large selection of working papers can be downloaded alongside a selection of longer, independent reports.

Associations & societies

3156 National Association of Pension Funds
www.napf.co.uk
The NAPF is a leading industry body for UK pensions, with over 1300 members providing pensions to over 10 million working people. The home page includes regularly updated press releases archived from 2001. Key statistics on the pension industry are also covered, including data on state pensions and population demographics. Information on training courses and seminars held by the NAPF is also provided.

3157 Pension Benefit Guaranty Corporation [USA]
www.pbgc.gov
Federal corporation protecting the pensions of nearly 44 million Americans in over 30,000 pension plans. A great deal of consumer information on pensions is supplied, alongside a wealth of resources for financial practitioners. Relevant news stories are regularly featured and the site is also available in Spanish.

3158 Pension Protection Fund
www.ppf.gov.uk
The Pension Protection Fund website provides members of the Fund with general information on the scheme. Relevant publications can also be downloaded from the website – other useful features include a glossary and links to other pensions resources.

Directories & encyclopedias

3159 Pension funds and their advisers
AP Information Services, annual. ISSN 01406647.
Provides contact details for thousands of pension fund managers and the financial details of the pension funds they

control. Over 2500 pension funds are covered, providing addresses, phone numbers, fax numbers and website details. The book also includes a list of UK pension funds ranked by size and a history of UK pension provision.

Handbooks & manuals

3160 Restructuring retirement risks
D. Blitzstein, O.S. Mitchell and S.P. Utkus, eds Oxford University Press, 2006, 272pp. $85. ISBN 0199204659.
Produced by the Pension Research Council, this text is a timely examination of problems affecting pension funds, such as volatile capital markets and changes in population structure. The book offers guidance for policymakers and members of pension plans in order to minimize risk and create sustainable pension provision.

Keeping up to date

3161 IPE.com [EUR]
www.ipe.com
Claims to be 'Europe's premier pensions website'. Notable features of the IPE (Investment & Pensions Europe) site include a webcasts section featuring interviews, presentations and commentaries. Registration is required to access news content. A range of white papers can be freely downloaded

3162 Pension Service [UK]
www.thepensionservice.gov.uk
Contains details for pensioners as well as those planning for their retirement. Includes state pension forecasts and a wide range of guides covering all aspects of pensions. A number of claim forms can also be downloaded. The site is easy to navigate and is refreshingly free of jargon.

3163 Pension Trends
Palgrave Macmillan, annual.
www.statistics.gov.uk
Available through the UK Office for National Statistics website and in printed form. *Pension trends* provides a thorough statistical analysis surrounding pensions, drawing data from government departments and external organizations. Coverage in the latest report includes demographic factors affecting demand for pensions, state and private pension provision and developments in pension legislation. Individual chapters are updated regularly online.

Financial Management

acquisitions • buyouts • corporate insolvency • corporate restructuring • financial risk • investment appraisal • land & property finance • mergers • personal finance • portfolio investment • takeovers

Introductions to the subject

3164 Corporate finance
R. Brealey, S. Myers and F. Allen 8th edn, McGraw-Hill Irwin, 2005, 1028pp. ISBN 0071117997.
Extremely popular text describing the principles and theory of corporate finance. Coverage is very broad, including topics

such as options, debt financing, mergers and risk management. The design and structure of the book is very strong – each chapter concludes with a summary, practise questions and relevant web links. The authors also provide details of related websites at the outset of each major section of the book – a very valuable feature.

3165   Corporate finance: theory and practice
A. Damodaran   2nd edn, Wiley, 2001, 982pp. £81.50. ISBN 0471392200.
www.wiley.com/college/damodaran [COMPANION]
Comprehensive text focusing on applying complex financial theory to real firms. Principles outlined in the book are illustrated with reference to publicly traded companies such as Boeing and The Home Depot. The strength of the book lies in the concentration on putting detailed theory into practice using clear, worked-through examples.

3166   Corporate finance theory
W. Megginson   Addison-Wesley, 1997, 506pp. ISBN 0673997650.
Surveys the most important theoretical concepts in corporate finance, examining whether the theories have been supported by empirical research. The focus on theory results in a text-heavy book, which nevertheless is written in an accessible style. Recommended for those with a strong prior understanding of corporate finance.

3167   Finance for managers
Harvard Business School Press, 2003, 210pp. £11.99. ISBN 1578518768.
www.elearning.hbsp.org/businesstools
Provides the fundamentals of financial literacy, offering managers key information for financial planning, budgeting and forecasting. Coverage includes understanding financial statements, taxation issues and calculating investment values. A range of free interactive tools is available at the Harvard Business Essentials companion website.

3168   The new corporate finance: where theory meets practice
D. Chew   3rd edn, McGraw-Hill, 2001, 670pp. £42.99. ISBN 007233973X.
A collection of readings drawn from the *Journal of Applied Corporate Finance*. Topics covered include internet investment banking, measuring and hedging currency risks and Initial Public Offerings. Articles are written by prestigious authors, including Richard Brealey, Joel Stern and Roger Ibbotson.

3169   Revolution in corporate finance
J. Stern and D. Chew   4th edn, Blackwell, 2003, 631pp. £35. ISBN 1405107812.
A strong, thorough and detailed text covering core finance topics, including market efficiency, capital structure and risk management. Content is focused around seminal articles from the *Journal of Applied Corporate Finance*. Notable contributors include Aswath Damodaran of New York University detailing 'The promise of real options'.

3170   The theory of corporate finance
J. Tirole   Princeton University Press, 2006, 644pp. £35.95. ISBN 0691125562.
Jean Tirole provides a comprehensive introduction to modern corporate finance theory in this clearly presented text. The book is lengthy and encompasses a range of topics,

including takeovers, corporate governance, borrowing and investor activism.

Dictionaries, thesauri, classifications

3171   Dictionary of international investment terms
J.O.E. Clark   Financial World Publishing, 336pp. £15. ISBN 0852975775.
Summarizes terms used in global financial markets, covering stock market language, indices and regulations. The dictionary has an international focus and definitions are precise and clear.

Research centres & institutes

3172   Institute of Credit Management
www.icm.org.uk
Home page of the professional body representing the credit management sector. Presentation is a little basic but useful resources include a job search facility, details of the ICM accreditation scheme and book recommendations. A members-only section contains details on areas such as pay awards and benchmarking.

3173   Securities and Investment Institute
www.securities-institute.org.uk
The largest professional body for workers in the UK securities and investment industry, with over 30,000 members. The website includes a large amount of information on professional development in the industry, including a full training section and guidance for qualifications and exams. A members-only section of the site features podcasts by leading figures from companies such as Deutsche Bank and Allianz Global Investors.

Associations & societies

3174   Association of Corporate Treasurers
www.treasurers.org
International body for finance professionals working in treasury, risk and corporate finance. Content includes policy and technical information, including a wide range of resources in topics such as debt finance, cash flow forecasting and pension risk management. The home page also details training courses and qualifications and a monthly newsletter is also published.

3175   European Financial Management Association
www.efmaefm.org
Association founded to disseminate knowledge regarding European financial decision making. The site provides links to a number of useful sites providing data on the European economy and also provides basic details on European financial education. At the time of writing the site features a constantly scrolling news page which is ideal for speed readers but may be a little disorientating for everyone else.

3176   Financial Management Association
www.fma.org
The FMA was established in 1970, developing and disseminating knowledge concerning financial decision making. The FMA home page includes details of conferences

and meetings and information on membership options. The site also provides details on a range of financial journals, including FMA Online, the FMA e-journal. Journal content includes PowerPoint presentations and a large selection of videos.

Portal & task environments

3177   Investopedia
www.investopedia.com
This highly recommended site includes an extremely useful dictionary of investment terms for anyone who doesn't know their EBITDA from their CAGR. The dictionary also features slang terms such as a 'Bo Derek' (apparently used to describe 'a perfect stock or investment'). The site has an excellent tutorial section, which covers popular finance topics at both basic and advanced levels. News, stock data, exam preparation advice and in-depth articles are also available.

Discovering print & electronic resources

3178   Wachowicz's Web World
http://web.utk.edu/~jwachowi/wacho_world.html
The slightly bizarre presentation of this website should not detract from the strong content within. The site groups together website links by topic based on the chapter headings in the *Fundamentals of financial management* textbook. Each link has a brief review and the site is regularly updated.

Keeping up to date

3179   European Financial Management [EUR]
Blackwell Publishing, 5 p.a. ISSN 13547798.
Research for executives and academics on the financial management of European corporations and financial institutions. Areas covered include European stock markets, eurobond and eurocurrency markets and corporate restructuring. Recent articles include 'A breakdown of the value effects of international cross-listing' and 'Risk measures for hedge funds'.

3180   Financial Management (UK)
Chartered Institute of Management Accountants, monthly. ISSN 14719185.
Official magazine of the Chartered Institute of Management Accountants (CIMA). Includes articles on technical issues, student exam papers and careers alongside news and features on the accountancy industry. The magazine also regularly profiles senior management accountants as well as accountants at the beginning of their careers.

3181   Financial Management (US)
Financial Management Association, qtrly. ISSN 00463892.
Flagship journal of the Financial Management Association. Publishes in-depth research by leading academics on a wide range of financial management issues. Recent articles have included 'Penny stock IPOs', 'Value of conglomerates and capital management conditions' and 'Liquidity risk and venture capital finance'.

3182   Journal of Investment Management
qtrly. $325 per year. ISSN 15459144.
www.joim.com
Aimed at both practitioners and academics, this journal bridges the theory and practice of investment management. Special issues are regularly produced – a recent special issue focused on hedge fund analysis.

3183   Journal of Multinational Financial Management
Elsevier (North-Holland), 5 p.a. €316 per year. ISSN 1042444X.
Publishes articles dealing with the management of international enterprises. Topics covered include international mergers, political risk assessment, foreign direct investment and international tax management. Recent articles include 'Foreign direct investment and forward hedging' and 'Persistence characteristics of Latin American financial markets'.

Investment Appraisal

Introductions to the subject

3184   Investments
W.F. Sharpe, G. Alexander and J. Bailey   Prentice Hall, 1998, 962pp. ISBN 013011507X.
An undergraduate and graduate-level text designed to provide a solid theoretical framework of prominent investment concepts. The authors also illustrate the practical applications of these concepts and make good use of regular summaries and revision questions. Topics covered include fixed-income securities, portfolio analysis, securities markets and investment companies.

3185   Investments
Z. Bodie, A. Kane and A. Marcus   6th edn, Irwin, 2004, 1090pp. ISBN 007293414X.
Sixth edition of the popular textbook, intended for courses in investment analysis. The authors state that they 'make every attempt to strip away unnecessary mathematical and technical detail'. Coverage includes portfolio theory, securities, mutual funds and risk. A list of web links relevant to each chapter, on the inside front cover of the book. is an excellent starting point for further research.

3186   Irrational exuberance
R.J. Shiller   2nd edn, Princeton University Press, 2005, 304pp. £17.95. ISBN 0691123357.
Shiller's influential book explores market volatility, ranging from stock markets to the housing market. The author details a number of factors which he believes have led to stocks being overvalued, such as the rise of the internet and increased information on financial news in the media. Shiller now identifies that after the stock market bubble burst in 2000 investors moved their money into housing – another bubble potentially waiting to burst. A widely read and widely discussed work.

3187   Only three questions that count: investing by knowing what others don't
K.L. Fisher, J. Chou and L. Hoffmans   Wiley, 2007, 448pp. £18.99. ISBN 047007499X.
The only three questions that count being: What do you believe that is actually false? What can you fathom that

others find unfathomable? What the heck is my brain doing to blindside me? Fisher provides a wealth of new investment ideas and strategies for picking winning stocks. The text is informative and entertaining – although politicans may take offence at being labelled as 'blood-sucking creatures'!

3188   Project financing
P. Nevitt and F.J. Fabozzi   7th edn, Euromoney, 2001, 498pp. £110. ISBN 1855647915.
Includes numerous examples of project financing to illustrate key issues such as risk allocation, effective project structuring and the role of government. The book is well structured, taking a logical progression through the intricacies of project finance. Chapters include details on choosing a bank, types of leases and controlling risk.

3189   Project financing: asset-based financial engineering
J. Finnerty   2nd edn, John Wiley, 2007, 476pp. £65. ISBN 0471146315.
Examines the success or otherwise of project financing, using examples of well known fiascos such as Eurotunnel and Euro Disney. The book begins with a brief examination of what project financing is and why it is needed, before exploring issues such as the source of project funds and government issues. The book concludes with in-depth case studies of well known project finance initiatives.

3190   Quantitative investment analysis
R.A. DeFusco, D.W. McLeavey and J.E. Pinto   2nd edn, Wiley, 2007, 566pp. £65. ISBN 0470052201.
The authors outline the tools and techniques required to apply quantitative methods to investment appraisal. The book introduces a strong mathematical and statistical framework, covering areas such as probability distributions, sampling and hypothesis testing. Each concept is introduced using simple terminology before exploring more complex techniques and equations.
■ **Quantitative investment analysis workbook** R.A. DeFusco, D.W. McLeavey and J.E. Pinto   2nd, Wiley, 2007, 205pp. ISBN 047006918X.

3191   Stochastic dominance: investment decision making under uncertainty
H. Levy   Springer, 2006, 439pp. £77. ISBN 0387293027.
Covers three basic approaches to decision making under uncertainty: the stochastic dominance approach; the mean-variance approach; and the non-expected utility approach. Heavy on mathematics and statistics, therefore a background in these areas would be beneficial for readers.

3192   Why stock markets crash: critical events in complex financial systems
D. Sornette   Princeton University Press, 2004, 448pp. £13.50. ISBN 0691118507.
The author uses scientific theory to explain how and why stock markets crash, outlining the complex systems and critical phenomena which result in stock market plunges. Sornette contends that the seeds of stock market downfalls are sown months or even years in advance. The author examines historical precedents and uses his theory to speculate on crashes of the future. An interesting read for investors and non-investors alike.

Handbooks & manuals

3193   Equity valuation and analysis with eVal
R. Lundholm and R. Sloan   2nd edn, McGraw-Hill, 2006, 342pp. £62.99. ISBN 0073309699.
Examines the practical problem of valuing a company using real-world data. The book aims to demystify the mechanics of equity valuation and provides guidance on calculating a company's worth. Concepts are described clearly and real-world examples are used effectively to illustrate points. The text is supplied with eVal, an Excel-based program used to calculate company valuations.

3194   Mastering investment: your single-source guide to becoming a master of investment
J. Pickford, ed.   Financial Times Prentice Hall, 2002, 368pp. £35. ISBN 027365926X.
The bulk of articles in this book have been written by leading academics from global business schools. The text covers essential topics regarding the principles and practice of investment, including hedge funds, risk and investment psychology. The book is primarily concerned with professional investment and is therefore not suitable for beginners.

3195   Technical analysis of stock trends
R.D. Edwards, J. Magee and W.H.C. Bassetti   9th edn, CRC Press, 2007, 789pp. ISBN 0849337720.
Classic text first published in 1948 and now in its ninth edition. The book explores the behaviour of investors and markets and is a benchmark by which other investment methodologies are measured. New content has been added to bring the text up to date with the modern investment world.

Keeping up to date

3196   What investment
Charterhouse Communications Ltd, monthly. £33.75 per year. ISSN 0263953X.
www.whatinvestment.co.uk
The longest-established UK investment magazine offers stock market analysis, reviews of latest investment options and pension fund statistics. Additional regular content includes league tables for unit trusts covering 1, 3, 5 and 10 years performance. The accompanying website is well presented and offers a large amount of the magazine content free of charge.

Financial Risk

Introductions to the subject

3197   Credit risk: pricing, measurement and management
D. Duffie and K.J. Singleton   Princeton University Press, 2003, 396pp. £39.95. ISBN 0691090467.
Discusses alternative approaches to credit risk modelling and provides assessments regarding their relative strengths and weaknesses. An advanced-level text which combines historical evidence with institutional considerations to evaluate appropriate models.

3198 Econometrics of individual risk: credit, insurance and marketing
C. Gourieroux and J. Jasiak   Princeton University Press, 2007, 241pp. £44.95. ISBN 0691120668.
Details the often underappreciated individual risks faced by banks, insurers and marketers. The book takes a practical approach, aiming to solve the risk problems faced by businesses today. Practical problems addressed include credit scoring and profit maximizations from promotional mailshots.

3199 Economic and financial decisions under risk
L. Eeckhoudt, C. Gollier and H. Schlesinger   Princeton University Press, 2005, 234pp. £23.95. ISBN 0691122156.
Provides a concise summary of financial risk, covering a broad range of topics. The text begins with the fundamentals of risk management and risk aversion. These concepts are then applied to insurance decisions and portfolio choice. Later chapters focus on risk management and risk sharing.
'This very fine work is well suited as a textbook for students of both economics and finance.' (Francisco Gomes, London Business School)

3200 New financial order: risk in the 21st century
R.J. Shiller   Princeton University Press, 2004, 384pp. ISBN 0691120110.
www.newfinancialorder.com
The author of *Irrational exuberance* (q.v.) proposes a new risk management infrastructure to secure the wealth of nations. Shiller details potential problems created by new technologies and outlines future solutions. The companion website includes references, web links and PowerPoint slides.

3201 Quantitative risk management: concepts, techniques, and tools
A.J. McNeil, R. Frey and P. Embrechts   Princeton University Press, 2005, 538pp. £51.95. ISBN 0691122555.
A fairly advanced text suitable for undergraduates, postgraduates and finance professionals. The book provides a comprehensive analysis of modelling techniques and theoretical concepts in the field of quantitative risk analysis. Concepts covered include risk aggregation and loss distributions. As would be expected, the book is heavy with mathematical and statistical content, so readers will find a strong background in these areas advantageous.

3202 Risk intelligence: learning to manage what we don't know
D. Apgar   Harvard Business School Press, 2006, 210pp. £17.99. ISBN 1591399548.
Aims to help readers of all risk aptitudes to assess and improve their 'risk IQs'. The book is a practical guide to making decisions about non-financial risks (e.g. operating, security and strategic risks) by adapting the financial risk management framework. Chapters outline practical ways in which the reader can learn strategies to make the outcome of risks less uncertain.
'The chapter on using networks and partnerships is excellent and well worth reading' (*Financial Times* 2 August 2006)

3203 Risk management: approaches for fixed income markets
B. Golub and L. Tilman   John Wiley & Sons, 2000, 312pp. £55. ISBN 0471332119.
Examines modern fixed-income risk measurement and management. The book includes practical applications of a variety of risk management and measurement techniques. Theoretical, technical and computational issues are also covered in depth. Recommended for fixed-income portfolio managers and scholars interested in the topic.

Research centres & institutes

3204 American Academy of Actuaries
www.actuary.org
The American Academy of Actuaries represents US actuaries from all practice areas. Journal content can be downloaded alongside relevant monographs and reports. A directory of actuaries can be searched and there is extensive content covering codes of practice and professionalism.

3205 Institute of Actuaries
www.actuaries.org.uk
Detailed home page for the actuarial profession. Includes training and development schedules, a bulletin board, statistics and careers advice. Also includes a directory of UK actuaries for people looking to find an actuarial adviser.

3206 Zell Center for Risk Research
www.kellogg.northwestern.edu/research/risk/index
Part of the Kellogg School of Management. The goal of the Center is to 'promote the study and understanding of the way people perceive risk'. The site provides details of research into risk and outlines topics discussed at the regular conferences organized by the Center.

Associations & societies

3207 American Risk & Insurance Association
www.aria.org
Billed as 'the premier academic organization devoted to the study and promotion of knowledge about risk management and insurance'. The site includes a selection of useful teaching tools, a newsletter and links to related organizations.

3208 Global Association of Risk Professionals
www.garp.com
Resources available on this website for risk professionals include daily risk news, a regular newsletter and forum. The site also includes details on professional qualifications and forthcoming risk management events. A fee-based digital library allows journal articles and book chapters to be digitally downloaded.

3209 Society of Actuaries
www.soa.org
Website of the largest professional actuarial organization in the world. Includes information on exams and assessments and an up-to-date events calendar. A directory of members can also be searched. Although the site looks extremely professional it is somewhat lacking in detailed articles that can be found elsewhere on the web.

Digital data, image & text collections

3210 Risk Measurement Service
London Business School Financial Services, qtrly. ISSN 02613344.
Published by the Institute of Finance & Accounting, Risk Measurement Service is available as a quarterly publication or a monthly data feed. The publication provides risk measures and other key data for over 3000 UK shares, including all UK companies with a full listing on the London Stock Exchange, as well as all stocks on the Alternative Investment Market (AIM). Used by fund managers, brokers, researchers, analysts and other professionals.

Handbooks & manuals

3211 Credit risk modeling: theory and applications
D. Lando   Princeton University Press, 2004, 310pp. £48.95. ISBN 0691089299.
Advanced text examining numerous models devised to analyse credit risk. The author aims to deliver the basic mathematical structure of each credit risk model in turn and provides an extensive selection of further reading. Suitable for those with a strong background in financial engineering or financial mathematics.

Keeping up to date

3212 Journal of Credit Risk
Incisive Media, qtrly. £115 per year. ISSN 17446619.
www.journalofcreditrisk.com
International journal focused on 'the measurement and management of credit risk, the valuation and hedging of credit products and the promotion and greater understanding in the area of credit risk theory and practice'. Most research is of a highly technical nature and therefore not accessible for a wide audience.

3213 Journal of Risk and Insurance
Blackwell, qtrly. ISSN 00224367.
www.journalofriskandinsurance.org
Flagship journal of the American Risk and Insurance Association, claiming to be 'the most well recognized academic risk and insurance journal in the world'. Areas of specialization include insurance regulation, risk management in the public and private sectors and the economics of employee benefits.

3214 Risk
Incisive Media, monthly. ISSN 09528776.
www.risk.net
Risk covers all aspects of financial risk management and global derivatives markets. Claims to be 'the world's leading financial risk management magazine'. Regular detailed supplements cover topical industry issues such as credit risk, electronic trading or coverage of emerging markets. The magazine is informative and accessible – essential reading for this area.

3215 Risk Management and Insurance Review
Blackwell Publishing, 2 p.a. £119. ISSN 10981616.
Publishes high-quality applied research and discussion in the field of risk and insurance. A 'Perspectives' section features articles providing new insights on literature, business practice and public policy. Recent feature articles have examined topics, including motor insurance fraud and perfomance analysis of pension fund management companies.

Portfolio Investment

Introductions to the subject

3216 Becoming rich: the wealth-building secrets of the world's master investors: Buffett, Icahn, Soros
M. Tier   St Martin's Press, 2005, 358pp. ISBN 0312339860.
Reveals the investment strategies of Warren Buffett, Carl Icahn and George Soros. The authors identify that although their investment strategies may appear divergent, they all share the same mental habits and strategies, which fly in the face of traditional Wall Street thinking. An extremely accessible read written in an entertaining style.

3217 Introduction to structured finance
F.J. Fabozzi, H.A. Davis and M. Choudhry   Wiley, 2006, 385pp. £52.50. ISBN 0470045353.
Examines the key elements of structured finance, explaining concepts and principles in a clear and detailed fashion. Areas covered include securitization, interest rate derivatives, complex leasing transactions and project financing. A convenient reference guide for professionals and specialists in the field.

3218 Investment analysis and portfolio management
F.K. Reilly and K. Brown   8th edn, Thomson South-Western, 2006, 1174pp. ISBN 0324289030.
Substantial text with strong coverage of capital market theory, security analysis, portfolio theory and international investments. A new and useful feature of this edition are 'investments online' internet links which provides URLs for websites relevant to the chapter. Sample examination questions are also included.

3219 Investors and markets: portfolio choices, asset prices and investment advice
W.F. Sharpe   Princeton University Press, 2006, 221pp. £23.95. ISBN 0691128421.
Nobel Prize-winning financial economist William F. Sharpe explains his approach to asset pricing. The author has a spare style of writing, making the text snappy and easy to comprehend. The book also summarizes much of Sharpe's previous work in financial economics and provides extremely useful insights for both finance professionals and investors.

3220 New market wizards: conversations with America's top traders
J. Schwager   HarperCollins, 1994, 512pp. £9.99. ISBN 0887306675.
Extremely popular book offering an insight into the minds of successful traders. Interviews with top traders help to reveal their personal philosophies and market strategies. The text is extremely easy to read and although the book is over a decade old the advice offered is still relevant.

3221 Quantitative equity portfolio management: an active approach to portfolio construction and management
L.B. Chincarini and D. Kim   McGraw-Hill, 2006, 658pp. £42.99. ISBN 0071459391.
Offers step-by-step strategies for maximizing alpha, a key measure of portfolio performance. Accompanied by a CD-ROM which contains practical exercises using actual historical stock data. The text is heavy on mathematical detail, so a strong background in this area is advantageous.

3222 Quantitative management of bond portfolios
L. Dynkin [et al.]   Princeton University Press, 2006, 978pp. £50. ISBN 0691128316.
Heavyweight text providing detailed practical solutions and quantitative approaches to asset management. The book is written by five leading authorities from Lehman Brothers and is based on practical problems the authors have faced and the methodolgies they have implemented. Coverage includes investment styles, managing credit and mortgage portfolios, performance attribution and risk optimization.

3223 Taming risk: complete credit portfolio management
M. Fisher   Euromoney, 2005, 224pp. £145. ISBN 1843741334.
Comprehensive guide to the implementation of credit portfolio management. The book is divided into three parts: a background to the subject, techniques available to manage portfolio risk and details of practical problems facing investors. The book, although expensive, is a clearly written guide to this expanding field.

3224 Understanding asset allocation: an intuitive approach to maximizing your portfolio
V. Canto   Financial Times Prentice Hall, 2006, 314pp. £20.99. ISBN 0131876767.
The author outlines strategies for maximizing returns on investments. Over 25 years of historical performance data is provided in order to illustrate the success of the strategies described. The text is clearly presented, using numerous global stock market statistics to identify trends and patterns, such as the comparative performance of large-cap and small-cap stocks.

Portal & task environments

3225 Financial Wonder
www.financialwonder.com
Popular website offering Microsoft Excel templates which can be used for budgeting, forecasting and projections. Formulas are available free of charge and the site is very easy to navigate. A range of useful video tutorials on using the software are also provided for beginners.

3226 IBM Investor Tools
www.ibm.com/investor/tools/index.phtml
A deceptively basic-looking site which contains a couple of excellent features. Two investment guides cover 'How to read financial statements' and 'How to read annual reports' – both guides are concise and full of useful information. A section on investor tips is well thought out and a key resource list provides details of leading websites, publications and media broadcasts.

3227 JaxWorks
www.jaxworks.com
JaxWorks is the 'small business spreadsheet factory' offering a selection of free Excel workbooks and spreadsheets covering a variety of financial, accounting and sales functions. The site is mercifully free of advertising and pop-ups and includes business-plan tools and training guides for most Microsoft Office applications. It also includes a comprehensive list of acronyms and a collection of online calculators covering areas such as productivity analysis and business evaluation.

Keeping up to date

3228 Investors Chronicle [UK]
Financial Times Business Information, weekly. £3.50. ISSN 00210161. www.investorschronicle.co.uk
Investors Chronicle is an excellent source of news and tips for UK shares. The companion website (which requires registration) publishes magazine articles and tips immediately. Presentation both online and in hard copy is clear and writing is succinct.

3229 The Journal of Portfolio Management
Euromoney Institutional Investor, qtrly. $489 per year. ISSN 00954918.
Publishes analysis and practical techniques in institutional investing. Research areas include performance measurement, asset allocation, risk management, market trends and portfolio optimization. Recent articles have included 'Robust portfolio optimization', 'Analysis of the interest rate sensitivity of common stocks' and 'Does size matter?' (a historical analysis of the impact of portfolio size).

3230 Random Roger's Big Picture
http://randomroger.blogspot.com
Stock market blog covering portfolio management, options, foreign stocks and much more. Blog entries can be sorted using the indexing terms at the end of each entry. The site is well written, often using eye-catching images to bring potentially dry topics to life.

Corporate Restructuring

Introductions to the subject

3231 Cases in corporate acquisitions, buyouts, mergers and takeovers
K. Hill, ed.   Gale, 1999, 1505pp. ISBN 0787638943.
Approximately 300 entries containing details of notable corporate acquisitions, buyouts, mergers and takeovers. Each entry is restricted to around 2500 words and includes an overview, history of the companies and major players involved, in addition to a review of the outcome. A useful bibliography at the end of each entry highlights further reading.

3232 Corporate bankruptcy: tools, strategies and alternatives
G.W. Newton   Wiley, 2003, 280pp. £33.50. ISBN 0471332682.
Aims to describe the bankruptcy process, beginning with the identification of cases of financial difficulty and ending with the confirmation of a plan. Chapters include Impact of

bankruptcy filing; Recovery of property; Business valuation; and Chapter 11 reorganization. Includes useful exhibits showing examples of documents such as Voluntary Bankruptcy Petitions.

3233 Greed and corporate failure: the lessons from recent disasters
S. Hamilton and A. Micklethwait   Palgrave Macmillan, 2006, 207 pp. £25. ISBN 1403986363.

Highlights eight case histories of corporate failure. Includes companies which have entered administration or liquidation as well as those which have suffered a collapse in shareholder value. Enron is the best-known case examined, but other examples include Swissair, Marconi and WorldCom. The text succeeds in distilling complex financial collapses down to the essential facts and is very readable as a result.

3234 Mastering the merger: four critical decisions that make or break the deal
D. Harding and S. Rovit   Harvard Business School Press, 2004, 224 pp. £19.99. ISBN 1591394384.

Identifies the four crucial areas which affect the success or failure of M&A deals. The authors state that 70% of M&A deals fail and describes how the most successful deal makers have beaten the odds through due diligence. Many examples of successful and unsuccessful mergers are scattered through this enlightening text.

3235 Mergers, acquisitions and corporate restructurings
P. Gaughan   4th edn, John Wiley, 2007, 648 pp. £50. ISBN 0471705640.

The new edition of this text explains each form of restructuring works, illustrated by US and international case studies. Recent trends examined in the text include takeovers by private equity firms and defensive tactics in hostile takeovers. The book is nicely broken up with statistics and relevant examples and is an authoritative resource in the field.

3236 Takeovers, restructuring and corporate governance
J.F. Weston, M.L. Mitchell and J.H. Mulherin   4th edn, Prentice Hall, 2003, 720 pp. £47.99. ISBN 0131225537.

Undergraduate/graduate-level text on mergers and acquisitions (M&A). The book provides conceptual discussions on why mergers take place, using numerous case studies to illustrate points. Areas covered include international takeovers, financial restructuring, accounting for M&As and takeover defences. The text is highly detailed, although the general presentation is uninspired.

Associations & societies

3237 American Bankruptcy Institute
www.abiworld.org

Extensive website of the largest non-partisan organization devoted to matters related to insolvency. Online resources include news headlines, bankruptcy statistics, legislative news and opinion polls. Multimedia content includes podcasts with ABI scholars. The site also contains detailed information for anyone contemplating filing for bankruptcy.

Portal & task environments

3238 Dealogic
www.dealogic.com

Dealogic provide over 40 subscription-based products covering global capital markets and corporate finance activity. The range of products includes M&A Analytics, which offers a comprehensive view of worldwide merger and acquisition activity. Other products available include Investment Banking Analytics, Loan Analytics and the transaction and relationship management platform DealAxis.

3239 Merger Network [USA]
www.mergernetwork.com

Claims to be 'the leading online matching service for buyers and sellers of businesses'. The site is easy to navigate and registration is required. Companies for sale can be searched by industry, location and sales value. Businesses featured range from sushi bars and car washes to retail chains and apartments.

Digital data, image & text collections

3240 Bankruptcy Data [USA]
www.bankruptcydata.com

Subscription site providing access to thousands of business bankruptcy filings. The database currently lists over 400,000 bankruptcy filings. Additional content includes *Bankruptcy Week*, a newsletter summarizing recent bankruptcy events, a searchable news archive going back to 1987 and an annual yearbook.

3241 CorpfinWorldwide
www.corpfin.co.uk

Subscription database featuring company financial deals completed since 1993, updated daily. Detailed information on each transaction is available in addition to over thirty key financials. Data can be exported into spreadsheets and league tables can also be produced. The website also publishes freely available M&A Monthly Reviews, covering mergers and acquisitions and CQ Monthly Reviews, covering market and company activity.

3242 FactSet Global Filings
www.europrospectus.com

Subscription database offering 'quick, online access to hundreds and thousands of prospectuses, SEC filings and M&A documents from all over the world'. Documents are provided from banks, stock exchanges and issuers and can be downloaded in Microsoft Word or PDF format.

3243 Merger Market
www.mergermarket.com

Subscription-based site dedicated to M&A. News and analysis on latest M&A deals are updated on a daily basis and a database of European, Asian and American transactions with fully sourced financials can also be searched. The site also publishes round-ups of merger activity and produces league tables which can be tailored by individual subscribers.

3244 SDC Platinum
Thomson.
www.thomson.com/content/financial/brand_overviews/SDC_Platinum
Subscription database providing detailed information on M&A transactions and IPO data. Data goes back to 1979 for US companies and 1985 for international companies. SDC Platinum offers flexible search criteria and report output: M&A deals can be identified by criteria, including industry sector and region and reports can be produced for Word or Excel.

3245 Thomson Deals
http://mergers.thomsonib.com
Subscription database offering details of global M&A transactions data and analysis from 1977 onwards. Over 400,000 transactions are detailed, including tender offers, management buyouts and rumoured deals. The initial search screen provides an extremely useful overview of M&A activity. Search facilities are very powerful and easy to use, although training may be required to exploit them fully.

3246 Zephyr
http://zephyr.bvdep.com
Subscription database from Bureau van Dijk offering information on mergers and acquisitions, initial public offerings (IPOs) and private equity deals. The database contains details on over 500,000 transactions and up to 100,000 deals are added yearly. Deals involving European and American companies date back to 1997.

Directories & encyclopedias

3247 Bizbroker [USA]
www.bizbrokerdirectory.com
An extensive directory of over 5000 M&A professionals and business brokers, primarily focusing on the US and Canada. Brokers can be searched by state or province. A small number of brokers in Australia and South Africa are also listed.

Handbooks & manuals

3248 Global insolvency and restructuring yearbook
L. Paul   Euromoney, 2006, 140pp. ISBN 1843742284.
A regularly updated compendium of short articles exploring latest developments in corporate restructuring. Includes a directory of global insolvency and restructuring companies.

3249 Mergers: what can go wrong and how to prevent it
P. Gaughan   John Wiley, 2005, 356pp. £36.99. ISBN 0471419001.
A practical guide aimed at seeking out the best merger and acquisition targets. Includes a chapter on merger success research, which examines high-profile successes and failures, including companies such as United Airlines, General Electric and Mattel. The text is clearly written and an excellent introduction to the potential benefits (and pitfalls) of M&A.

Keeping up to date

3250 Acquisitions Monthly
IFR Publishing, monthly. ISSN 09523618.
www.aqm-e.com

Publishes comments, critical analysis and comprehensive statistics on the latest issues in acquisitions, mergers and buyouts. *Acquisitions Monthly* also publishes industry league tables alongside the latest news on each month's new M&A transactions. Regular supplements cover topics in depth – recent supplements have focused on France, Germany and management buy-outs. The companion website features a searchable archive going back to 1999.

3251 The Deal
38 p.a. $265. ISSN 15419878.
www.thedeal.com
Magazine covering M&A, private equity, venture capital, corporate restructuring and bankruptcy. The accompanying subscription website features a regularly updated blog, detailed news stories and e-mail news alerts. The site also features a useful calendar of forthcoming initial public offerings and pending mergers.

3252 Mergers and Acquisitions [USA]
SourceMedia, monthly. ISSN 00260010.
Journal focusing entirely on the M&A industry, covering topics, including acquisition pricing, strategy, valuation and taxes. Each issue also includes listings and details of the latest M&A deals. Recent articles have focused on burgeoning M&A activity in Africa and the role of private equity capital.

3253 Mergers and Acquisitions Report
SourceMedia, weekly. ISSN 10993428.
www.mareport.com
Previously called *Mergers and Acquisitions International*. This weekly magazine provides information on M&A deals, restructurings and bankruptcies. Coverage of pending and ongoing deals is provided alongside insights into industry trends and profiles of the major players involved. Quarterly rankings of M&A advisors are also published.

3254 The smartest guys in the room: the amazing rise and scandalous fall of Enron [USA]
B. McLean and P. Elkind   Penguin, 2004, 464pp. £8.99. ISBN 0141011459.
As the authors state, 'Enron is well on the way to becoming the most intensively dissected company in the history of American business'. The book is a compulsive page-turner, highlighting the greed and corruption that ultimately led to the bankruptcy of a major US corporation. Also available as a feature film – *Enron: the smartest guys in the room*.

Land & Property Finance

Introductions to the subject

3255 Beyond the bubble: how to keep the real estate market in perspective – and profit no matter what happens
M.C. Thomsett and J. Kahr   AMACOM, 2007, 229pp. $16.95. ISBN 0814474098.
Concise text examining the factors driving changes in real estate markets. The book contains advice on areas such as the best times to buy and to sell, how to anticipate real estate downturns and the impact of local and regional

influences such as pollution and crime statistics. The text is both up to date and thorough.

3256 Commercial real estate: analysis and investments
D.M. Geltner [et al.]   2nd edn, Thomson South-Western, 2007, 848pp. £51.99. ISBN 0324305486.
Lengthy and exhaustive text focusing on commercial real estate analysis, with a particular emphasis on economics. The text is scattered with relevant real-world examples and is a good starting point for research into property finance.

3257 Complete guide to investing in property
L. Hodgkinson   Kogan Page, 2006, 353pp. £11.99. ISBN 0749444932.
Compact guide to all aspects of property investment. Coverage includes developing property, the buy-to-let market, commercial property and buying property abroad. The text is written in a friendly style and is very accessible, although the book is interspersed with a large number of advertisements.

3258 How to avoid property tax
C. Bayley   7th edn, Taxcafe UK, 2005, 243pp. £24.95. ISBN 1904608264.
A detailed practical guide to a topic which has been receiving an increasing amount of media coverage in recent years. Includes advice on how to avoid capital gains tax and income tax. Coverage on inheritance tax is brief. The book is clearly written and presented and not encumbered by unnecessary illustrations.

3259 How to make money in commercial real estate: for the small investor
N. Masters   2nd edn, Wiley, 2006, 304pp. ISBN 0471752614.
Designed to help small investors create valuable real estate portfolios. The book begins by outlining the benefits of real estate compared to other forms of investment, before examining different types of real estate and their potential long-term profits. The second part of the book takes a more practical approach, exploring how to find a suitable property, negotiate an acceptable price and manage your investment. The book is a good starting block for budding property entrepreneurs.

3260 Investing in real estate
A. McLean and G.W. Eldred   5th edn, Wiley, 2005, 314pp. ISBN 0471741205.
Billed as 'the bestselling guide to real estate investing', the updated version of this text covers a variety of tactics for real estate investing, including tips on negotiating deals and spotting market trends. Chapters cover areas such as drafting a rental agreement, how to find real estate bargains and options for securing financing. A good starting point for investors in this field.

3261 Maverick real estate investing: the art of buying and selling properties like Trump, Zell, Simon and the world's greatest land owners
S. Bergsman   Wiley, 2005, 304pp. £11.99. ISBN 0471739472.
Demonstrates how to successfully buy and sell properties by following strategies set by moguls such as Donald Trump. Each chapter profiles a different high-profile investor and areas covered include the importance of location, how to use other people's money and how to make 'safe gambles'.

3262 Property finance
D. Isaac   2nd edn, Palgrave Macmillan, 2003, 260pp. £30.99. ISBN 0333987144.
Overview of property finance providing an understanding of key concepts, structures and institutions for students and practitioners. Some data used is now a little dated – for example a chapter on property lenders uses statistics from 1990 to 1995. However, the text is very well written and includes good introductory reading on areas, including equity finance, joint ventures and securitization.

3263 Real estate finance and investments
W.B. Brueggeman and J.D. Fisher   13th edn, McGraw-Hill, 2007, 688pp. £47.99. ISBN 0071259198.
www.mhhe.com/bf13e
Aims to enhance understanding of the risks and rewards involved in financing and investing in real estate. Coverage includes Real Estate Investment Trusts (REITs), mortgages and risk analysis. The book is well presented, although some may find it a little text-heavy. A new element of this edition of the text is the introduction of 'WebApp' exercises, which require readers to find relevant information on the internet.

3264 Real estate finance and investments: risks and opportunities
P. Linneman   2nd edn, Linneman Associates, 2004, 278pp. ISBN 0974451835.
Wharton School of Business professor Linneman is one of the top real estate scholars in the USA. This text combines the theory and practice of real estate finance and is less algebra-focused than similar books in the field. The book is consistently well presented and clearly written. Chapter coverage includes real estate company analysis, bankruptcy basics and exit strategies.

3265 Real estate market valuation and analysis
J. Kahr and M.C. Thomsett   Wiley, 2005, 245pp. £45. ISBN 0471655260.
In-depth examination of the core tools of estate valuation. Chapters are divided between different forms of real estate, including family homes, retail, offices and industrial properties. The book is accompanied by a CD-ROM which includes information on how demographic data such as household income and crime shape real estate valuations.

Official & quasi-official bodies

3266 Council of Mortgage Lenders
www.cml.org.uk
The CML website provides a range of useful statistics on the UK housing and mortgage markets and on payment of a subscription these can also be manipulated through an interactive database. Publications available include research articles and in-depth reports – annual publications include a yearbook and the UK Housing Review. The CML also provides a range of consumer guides on home buying and selling.

Research centres & institutes

3267 Paul Milstein Center for Real Estate
www0.gsb.columbia.edu/realestate
Part of Columbia Business School, this research institute offers a leading real estate MBA programme and publishes

regular working papers. These are made available through the site alongside supplementary material such as Powerpoint slides. The site also provides data on the annual cost of home ownership and a selection of useful web links.

3268 Samuel Zell & Robert Lurie Real Estate Center
http://realestate.wharton.upenn.edu
Part of the Wharton School of the University of Pennsylvania. Publishes a biannual *Real Estate Review*, presenting latest research and analytical findings. A large selection of research can also be downloaded; however, full-text articles are for members only.

Associations & societies

3269 American Real Estate Society
www.aresnet.org
Provides links to the five journals published by the Society: *Journal of Real Estate Research*, *Journal of Real Estate Portfolio Management*, *Journal of Real Estate Literature*, *Journal of Real Estate Practice and Education* and *Journal of Housing Research*. A video history of the society and benefits of membership is also available. Some may find the banner heading on the site featuring constantly moving US skylines a little nausea-inducing.

3270 British Property Federation
www.bpf.propertymall.com
The BPF aims to sustain and promote the interests of UK property owners. The BPF home page includes news on campaigns the organization is involved in, such as promoting sustainable housing. The site also includes research documents covering issues such as the regenerative impact of the London Olympics in 2012. Events run by the organization are also detailed on the site.

3271 Investment Property Forum [UK]
www.ipf.org.uk
Home page of the UK body aiming to 'improve the awareness, understanding and efficiency of property as an investment'. Research reports are available but can only be downloaded by members. Details of training courses are also provided but overall the site is somewhat lacking in 'meaty' information.

3272 National Association of Real Estate Investment Trusts
www.nareit.com
NAREIT represents US REITs and publicly traded real estate companies worldwide. Much content is free, although members have access to additional resources such as an online member directory and a bi-monthly magazine. A range of real estate index data is available for download, including historical market capitalizations of the REIT industry from 1971 to the present.

3273 National Council of Real Estate Investment Fiducaries
www.ncreif.com
A non-partisan collector and disseminator of real estate performance information. The flagship index produced is the NCREIF Property Index (NPI), which consists of both equity and leveraged properties. The NPI is displayed prominently on the home page. Quarterly reports on the real estate

market are also published. Some material is only accessible to subscribers.

3274 Property Council of Australia
http://propertycouncil.gravitymax.com.au
Content includes regularly updated global property news and a downloadable 'Build Your Wealth' handbook designed to provide fund managers, investors and financial planners with key information regarding the fundamentals of sound property investing. Australian content is divided by state and the magazine *Property Australia* is available to download monthly.

3275 RICS Foundation
www.rics.org
The extremely well designed website for the Royal Institution of Chartered Surveyors. A number of useful guides are available for consumers on topics such as buying and selling property and boundary disputes. The RICS also publishes regular market surveys on property and construction markets. The site features a 'find a surveyor' search, news stories and a range of in-depth features on a large range of topics related to surveying. Highly recommended.

Discovering print & electronic resources

3276 CB Richard Ellis
www.cbre.com
The home page of this leading real estate services company is unusual in that it also provides access to detailed research reports. The 'Research Centre' section of the site includes details on global market rents, property vacancies in the US and reports focusing on local property markets.

3277 Grubb & Ellis [USA]
www.grubb-ellis.com/Research
Useful research hub for the real estate market. Market research reports can be downloaded free of charge and cover the entire USA and a large number of individual cities. A range of regularly updated research articles and white papers are also available. Presentation is uniformly strong, in particular the market forecasts section, which takes the form of an interactive map complete with detailed PDFs.

3278 King Sturge
www.kingsturge.com/research
The home page of the international property consultants is a good source of publications on the international property market. Registration is required in order to download the content. Publications focus on the UK but also include European countries, particularly those in Central and Eastern Europe.

Digital data, image & text collections

3279 IPD Index
www.ipdindex.co.uk
IPD supplies independent property market indices and portfolio benchmarks. The site includes detailed information covering the property sector in a range of countries, with particularly detailed data available for the UK. Indices for derivatives are available covering the UK, France and Germany.

Handbooks & manuals

3280 Europe real estate yearbook
M. Dijkman and A. Schiller   Europe Real Estate Publishers, 2007, 788pp. £47.50. ISBN 9077997113.
Includes a selection of articles on real estate. Individual country profiles are well presented and detailed, including information on current and future major real estate projects and demographic data. A financial section lists details of the largest real estate funds in Europe. Brief profiles of the major players are also provided. An essential reference guide for the European real estate industry.

3281 Handbook of commercial real estate investing
J. McMahan   McGraw-Hill, 2006, 393pp. ISBN 007146865X.
Establishes guidelines for three major areas of commercial real estate – investment transactions, asset management and financial reporting. The text is clearly presented and makes good use of case studies such as retail land development in San Francisco. The text focuses on the USA, although many of the principles discussed have a wider application.

3282 Property investors management handbook
P. Robinson   Emerald, 2006, 137pp. £9.99. ISBN 1903909996.
Straightforward guide to the law and practice of investing in, letting and managing residential property. Areas covered include looking for a property, finding tenants, managing property and rent issues. Although the guide is brief, it deals with the fundamentals of property investment and is a good staring point for would-be landlords.

3283 The real estate investment handbook
G.T. Haight and D. Singer   John Wiley & Sons, 2005, 544pp. £47.50. ISBN 0471649228.
Billed as 'an essential tool for current and aspiring commercial real estate investors looking to develop and evaluate commercial real estate properties'. Individual chapters focus on specific real estate investment opportunities, such as apartments, undeveloped land, shopping centres and restaurants. Each chapter is supplemented by real-world examples – in the case of restaurants this involves a detailed examination of the costs of leasing property to a McDonald's franchisee. A highly practical and useful text.

Keeping up to date

3284 City Offices
www.cityoffices.net
Advertised as 'the leading site for information about the commercial property market in London and other major cities in the UK and Europe'. The website divides information by city and includes latest commercial property news and details of recently completed office developments. Information regarding available commercial property space in each city is also provided. Subscription-based premium content includes details of key developers, agents, contractors, architects and consultants in each city.

3285 Commercial Investment Real Estate [USA]
6 p.a. $45.
www.ciremagazine.com
Bi-monthly magazine covering the commercial real estate industry. Coverage includes new technologies, latest real estate transactions and best practice guidelines. The magazine is supported by a website featuring online exclusive content. Recent features include an analysis of how demographics affect market trends and resource guides covering tax issues and office properties.

3286 Estates Gazette [UK]
Estates Gazette Ltd, 1858–, weekly. ISSN 00141240.
www.egi.co.uk
A leading commercial property magazine published since 1858. Each issue features latest news on the property market, alongside details of hundreds of properties and investment opportunities. Regular regional focus features provide in-depth coverage of property developments in specific UK regions. The companion subscription website features news, research and legal information.

3287 Property Investor News
Farscape, monthly. £89 per year. ISSN 14789361.
www.property-investor-news.com
Monthly magazine offering up-to date-information on UK and international property markets. Online content includes brief weekly news stories. A 24-hour news feed is also available online, although this seems a little basic and would benefit from being more selective. News headlines such as the recently featured 'Police raid house' are unlikely to be of interest to property investors. A useful feature of the site is a list of upcoming property auctions, covering the entire UK.

3288 Property Week [UK]
Property Media, weekly. ISSN 13541471.
www.propertyweek.com
Leading news magazine for the commercial property market. Features include news, statistics and rumours in the property industry. The magazine is also a strong source of jobs in the industry and is essential for property professionals to keep in touch with national developments in the market. Regular supplements provide profiles of the property market in specific areas of the UK.

3289 Real Estate Journal [USA]
www.realestatejournal.com
Advertised as 'the Web's premier guide to buying, selling and enjoying a residential property'. Content includes advice on buying and selling such as negotiating tips and details on tax and insurance. A multimedia section includes discussion forums, podcasts, videos and calculators. The site also includes an extensive searchable directory of residential properties.

Personal Finance

Introductions to the subject

3290 Financial Times guide to investing
G. Arnold   Financial Times Prentice Hall, 2004, 410pp. £22.99. ISBN 0273663097.
Highly recommended guide to all aspects of investing. The book succeeds in demystifying the world of financial investments, containing advice on buying and selling shares as well as easy-to-understand details of other investment opportunities such as bonds, options and spread betting.

The text is succinct, jargon free and ideally suited for investment novices.

3291 Financial Times guide to using the financial pages
R. Vaitilingam   5th edn, Financial Times Prentice Hall, 2006, 314pp. £19.99. ISBN 0273705032.
Deservedly popular guide to understanding financial pages. The book is an ideal companion for beginners bemused by the reams of financial data published daily in newspapers such as the *Financial Times*. The text also includes clear and concise summaries of terms used in areas such as the futures and options markets. The latest edition has been updated to include electronic sources of financial data, but the overall focus is still firmly on print media. Highly recommended.
'An invaluable and straightforward guide' (*Business Age*)

3292 Investor's toolbox: using the right tools to fine tune your financial future
H. Harington and A. Hoar   Financial Times Prentice Hall, 2004, 254pp. £25. ISBN 0273663089.
Describes a comprehensive range of investor tools and techniques, including spread betting, short selling, covered warrants, options and futures. As with other FT Prentice Hall books the presentation throughout is clear and the text free of jargon. An excellent introduction to the many tools available for investors.

3293 Math of money: making mathematical sense of your personal finances
M.D. Davis   Copernicus, 2001, 199pp. ISBN 0387950788.
A mathematical-based approach to personal finance. Davis tackles topics such as mortgages, retirement and bonds with the effective use of mathematical formulae and calculated examples. A fascinating chapter on the psychology of investing examines the often irrational human behaviour on display among stock market investors.

3294 More than you know: finding financial wisdom in unconventional places
M.J. Mauboussin   Columbia University Press, 2006, 268pp. £18. ISBN 0231138709.
Snappily written guide outlining new approaches to understanding concepts such as investment risk and competitive strategies. The author makes interesting links between disparate ideas, asking how investors can learn from a multidisciplinary perspective. The book is a very interesting read and provides the answer to the rarely asked question: 'What does guppy mate selection tell us about stock market booms?'

3295 Personal finance
G. Callaghan, I. Fribbance and M. Higginson, eds   Wiley, 2006, 461pp. £26.99. ISBN 0470028556.
A UK-centred introductory personal finance text, published to accompany an Open University course. Case studies are effectively used to highlight the issues raised by topics such as debt, pensions and budgeting. Statistics are up to date and presentation throughout is well considered and clear.

3296 Personal finance: turning money into wealth
A.J. Keown   2nd edn, Prentice Hall, 2000, 606pp. ISBN 013026928X.
Primarily a student text, assuming little prior knowledge of the subject matter. Aims to introduce the principles and applications of personal finance. Divided into five main parts:

Financial planning; Managing your money; Protecting yourself with insurance; Managing your investments; and Retirement and estate planning. Presentation is clear and accompanied by learning checklists and self-assessment questions.

3297 Wealth: grow it, protect it, spend it and share it
S.E. Lucas   Pearson, 2007, 384pp. £9.99. ISBN 0132350114.
Key text on personal financial management. Lucas treats managing and growing wealth as a jigsaw puzzle which involves family relationships, investing, philanthropy, taxes and spending. The book contains valuable advice and is written in a user-friendly, practical style.

Portal & task environments

3298 Digital Look
www.digitallook.com
Excellent site offering advice on personal finance and stock market data. A 'financial health check' section details best-buy credit cards, savings accounts, loans and current accounts. The site also contains breaking financial news and links to real-time streaming share prices. A share portfolio tracker allows users to follow the performance of their stocks online.

3299 Interactive Investor
www.iii.co.uk
Wide-ranging site covering market data, personal finance, share dealing and betting. Market coverage is particularly strong and includes a round-up of finance stories featured in daily newspapers. Personal finance content includes online calculators, investment advice and best-buy rankings. The site also has an excellent financial glossary.

3300 Oanda
www.oanda.com
Well designed foreign exchange website. Tools range from basic currency converters to Java-based charting tools enabling the graphical display of historical currency prices. Currencies can also be ordered and purchased through the site. The site includes the 'FXTrade' feature which allows clients to trade directly in the foreign exchange market.

3301 xe.com
www.xe.com
Claims to be 'the world's most popular currency and foreign exchange site'. Offers an easy-to-use converter for all known world currencies, covering 180 currencies in over 250 geographical locations. Presentation is clear and the site is extremely user-friendly. Also includes charting options and historical rate tables.

Keeping up to date

3302 CNN Money
http://money.cnn.com
An excellent source of financial news and personal finance advice. The home page features breaking news stories and a large selection of video news items. Detailed market data is also provided and users of the site can create and track their own stock portfolios. The personal finance section includes money-saving tips, essential guides and financial calculators.

3303 Finance intelligence [UK]
Mintel Publications, irregular.
Series of market research reports produced by Mintel, focusing on the UK. Covers a wide range of consumer-based personal finance issues, accompanied by in-depth surveys and market data. Recent reports have focused on topics, including mortgages, savings accounts and stakeholder pensions.

3304 Fool.com
www.fool.com
Excellent personal finance site. The site publishes detailed advice on financial products, including mortgages, loans, credit cards and savings accounts. Coverage of stock markets is also strong and discussion boards are wide-ranging and extremely popular. The UK version is available at www.fool.co.uk.

3305 FreeMoneyFinance.com
www.freemoneyfinance.com
Financial blog with the stated aim to 'grow your net worth'. Postings cover topics such as retirement, college funding, wedding costs and debt. Links to popular postings are also available with eye-catching titles such as 'Eight secrets of financial happiness' and 'Make sure your financial advisor is not a loser'. The site is snappily written and regularly updated.

3306 LearnMoney.co.uk
www.learnmoney.co.uk
Site focusing on providing personal finance help, money-saving tips and 'how to' guides. Personal finance areas covered include mortgages, equity release and credit cards. A section on the stock market and share trading covers areas such as spread betting and traded options. Presentation is basic but the free guides provided are both clear and useful.

3307 Money Management
Financial Times Business, monthly. £71.50 per year. ISSN 00286052.
Monthly magazine covering areas, including pensions, mortgages, taxation and ethical investments. Statistics featured in each issue include details on pension funds and investment trusts, complete with a useful list of rankings. Detailed articles cover topical issues such as sub-prime mortgages. Regular topical supplements are also published in addition to the magazine.

3308 Money-zine.com [USA]
www.money-zine.com
Takes the form of an online magazine covering issues in finance, investing and careers. Includes topics such as buying a home, debt consolidation and retirement. A range of free online tools are also available, including a bond yield calculator and a mortgage cost calculator. The site could benefit from a stronger navigation and clearer design, but contains many well written articles.

Accounting

auditing • financial reporting • management accounting

Introductions to the subject

3309 Financial accounting
W.T. Harrison and C.T. Horngren   6th edn, Pearson/Prentice Hall, 2005, 720pp. £45.99. ISBN 0131499459.
www.prenhall.com/harrison
A student text focused on teaching the fundamentals of accounting. Each chapter begins with a financial statement extract from well known companies such as Apple Computer and Merrill Lynch. The presentation throughout is excellent, making good use of colour, illustrations and real-world examples. A strong and justifiably popular accounting text.

3310 Financial accounting: an introduction to concepts, methods and uses
C.P. Stickney and R.L. Weil   12th edn, Thomson South-Western, 2006, 845pp. £87.99. ISBN 0324381980.
www.thomsonedu.com/accounting/stickney [COMPANION]
Comprehensive and popular text, with coverage focused on the concepts, methods and uses of accounting. Each chapter begins with clear learning objectives and ends with a summary and self-study questions. The book is now in its 12th edition and is regularly updated to include significant changes in accounting – for example, the newest edition has an increased emphasis on ethical considerations of financial reporting.

3311 Forging accounting principles in five countries: a history and an analysis of trends
S.A. Zeff   Stripes Publishing, 1972, 332pp.
Examines the historical development of accounting principles in England, Scotland, Mexico, the USA and Canada. The text is dated, but as stated in the foreword, 'accountants cannot properly build for the future unless we understand what has happened in the past'.
'A piece of research of major importance to everyone concerned with the development of accounting principles.' (Edward Stamp)

Dictionaries, thesauri, classifications

3312 Accounting thesaurus: 500 years of accounting
R. Chambers   Oxford Pergamon, 1995, 1011pp. £97.95. ISBN 0080425739.
Covering over 500 years of accounting literature, this thesaurus compiles over 5000 quotations relating to all aspects of accountancy. Topics covered include the economic background of accounting, income calculation and dated valuation of assets and equities. The compendium draws from a vast array of literature, ranging from Shakespeare and Samuel Pepys to modern-day accounting standards. A unique, expansive work.

3313 Macmillan dictionary of accounting
R. H. Parker   2nd edn, Macmillan, 1992, 307pp. ISBN 0333455487.
Accounting dictionary which not only defines terms but sets out practices and discusses theories. A number of brief biographies of contributors to accounting literature are also provided. Extremely well written, but now rather dated.

Laws, standards, codes

3314 Applying international accounting standards
K. Alfredson [et al.]   John Wiley, 2005, 1102pp. £34.99. ISBN
0470804947.

Hefty textbook aimed at accounting students and
practitioners, examining international accounting standards
in relation to specific industries. Also includes an
introduction to the financial reporting procedures outlined in
the IFRS (International Financial Reporting Standards). Well
presented and makes good use of relevant, up-to-date case
studies to illustrate specific points.

Research centres & institutes

3315 American Institute of Certified Public Accountants
www.aicpa.org
Includes a variety of useful professional resources for
accountants, including technical help and details on peer
reviews. The AICPA also publishes a weekly news update and
a monthly newsletter. The career planning section of the site
appears particularly useful and includes competency self-
assessment tools and a range of recruitment tips.

**3316 Center for Excellence in Accounting & Security
Analysis**
www0.gsb.columbia.edu/ceasa
Part of Columbia Business School, the CEASA aims to
provide practical solutions in financial reporting and analysis.
The Center is not long established, so downloadable content
through the site is limited.

**3317 Institute of Chartered Accountants in England &
Wales**
www.icaew.co.uk
The largest professional accountancy body in Europe has an
equally extensive website. Includes resources divided by
accountancy topics such as regulation, corporate governance
and professional ethics. Also includes an online search
facility for locating a chartered accountant and a well
organized library and information service. Online library
services include a useful dictionary of accountancy
abbreviations and a range of subject resource guides. Some
services are available to ICAEW members only.

3318 Institute of Financial Accountants
www.ifa.org.uk
Includes details of the IFA examination syllabus, regularly
updated news stories and a selection of relevant web links.
Freely available content on the site is at a minimum –
membership is required in order to access additional
information.

Associations & societies

3319 American Accounting Association
http://aaahq.org
The AAA 'promotes worldwide excellence in accounting
education, research and practice' – however, the website is a
tad dated. Notable features include details of awards made
available to accountants and a comprehensive list of
accountancy resource links. The strongest areas of the site

are the detailed accountancy sections, covering subjects such
as auditing, Information systems and public interest.

3320 Association of Chartered Certified Accountants
www.accaglobal.com
The ACCA is the world's largest global professional
accounting body and benefits from a well structured home
page. A section for accountancy students offers examination
paper resources and training information. Information for
ACCA members includes professional standards and online
access to the ACCA professional magazine. The site also
offers advice to the public on how to find an accountant,
although there is no online search facility.

Discovering print & electronic resources

3321 Accountancy Direct
Butterworth.
Subscription database. Provides online reference service for
accountancy professionals, offering key printed reference
sources such as *UK accounting standards* and *Butterworths
company law handbook*. The database also contains the major
financial reporting GAAP 'toolkits', including accounting and
auditing standards. Comprehensive commentaries and
worked examples are provided.

Handbooks & manuals

3322 Accounting trends and techniques
Y. Iofe and M. Calderisi, eds   58th edn, American Institute of
Certified Public Accountants, 2004, annual, 668pp. ISBN
0870516043.
An annual survey examining the accounting aspects of the
annual reports of 600 US corporations. Significant trends in
accounting practice are highlighted, including developments
in terminology and financial statement format. Also includes
recommendations on annual report presentation.

3323 Advanced accounting
P. Fischer, W. Taylor and R. Cheng   9th edn, South-Western, 2005,
1224pp. ISBN 9780324304015.
Comprehensive and authoritative accounting text covering a
diverse range of accounting topics. Supplemented by a CD-
ROM containing step-by-step tutorials. Claims to be the only
accounting text to offer complete coverage of derivatives.

3324 Advanced accounting
D.C. Jeter and P.K. Chaney   2nd edn, John Wiley, 2004, 969pp.
£36.95. ISBN 0471451827.
Divided into four main sections: accounting for mergers and
acquisitions, accounting in the international marketplace,
partnership accounting and fund and non-profit accounting.
Each chapter is supplemented by multiple-choice questions
and exercises.

3325 Advanced accounting: concepts and practice
A.J. Pahler   8th edn, Thomson South-Western, 2003, 1091pp. £82.
ISBN 0324183437.
Comprehensive textbook aiming to bring real-world
accounting principles to a student level. The latest edition
examines the collapse of Enron Corporation in late 2001 and
discusses various aspects of Enron's accounting practices,

highlighting the broader changes to accountancy resulting from the collapse.

3326 International finance and accounting handbook

F. Choi, ed.   3rd edn, Wiley, 2003, 888pp. £95. ISBN 0471229210.

A lengthy collection of articles contributed by leading experts in finance and accountancy. The volume is divided into seven parts: Globalization of financial markets; Financial analysis; World scene of accounting and reporting practices; International accounting harmonization; Reporting issues; International transfer pricing and taxation; and International auditing. Articles include practical examples and case studies and provide extremely valuable insights for practitioners in the field.

Keeping up to date

3327 Accountancy

Institute of Chartered Accountants in England & Wales, monthly. £74.95 per year. ISSN 00014664.
www.accountancymagazine.com

Covers a wide range of issues for accountants, including technical matters, business news and careers features. Up-to-date information on regulatory and legal information is also published. Other features of the magazine include surveys of the profession, latest developments in financial reporting and a regular section examining accountants in practice.

3328 Accountancy Age

VNU Business Publications, weekly. ISSN 00014672.
www.accountancyage.com

A leading UK finance weekly for accounting and finance professionals, featuring news, in-depth articles and jobs. The companion website includes details of surveys covering topics ranging from salaries to environmental initiatives in accounting. An interesting feature of the site is 'Accountancy Age TV', which features professional interviews on latest accountancy topics.

3329 Accountants World

www.accountantsworld.com

An extremely useful resource with a wide range of content. News headlines are regularly updated and can be e-mailed direct to your inbox. Research resources and guides cover areas such as taxation, payroll and small businesses. A range of online tools and calculators are also provided. Online discussion groups are heavily used and can be used for networking or answering accountancy queries.

3330 Journal of Accounting Research

University of Chicago, 5 p.a. £79 per year. ISSN 00218456.
Journal publishing original research on accounting issues. Published as four regular issues and a conference issue containing papers from the annual research conference held at the University of Chicago. Published articles are wide-ranging – recent articles have covered topics ranging from stock price volatility and market transparency to the more populist 'Investor reaction to celebrity analysts'.

3331 Journal of International Financial Management and Accounting

Blackwell Publishing, 3 p.a. £87 per year. ISSN 09541314.
Publishes research on international aspects of financial

management and reporting, auditing, taxation and banking and financial services. Also includes latest book reviews. Recent articles have included an examination of whether investors really value corporate governance and case studies based in Korea, Hong Kong and Russia.

Management Accounting

Introductions to the subject

3332 Financial and management accounting: an introduction

P. Weetman   4th edn, Financial Times Prentice Hall, 2006. £38.99. ISBN 0273703692.
www.pearsoned.co.uk/weetman [COMPANION]

A student-level text concentrating on the use of real-world examples to illustrate financial and management accounting principles. Case studies within the book include well known UK companies such as BP, Sainsbury's and Matalan. Hypothetical 'experience-driven conversations' between two managers are scattered through the text to highlight particular issues and problems. The book is well structured and includes a useful glossary.

3333 Introduction to management accounting

C. Horngren, G. Sundem and W. Stratton   13th edn, Prentice Hall, 2004, 823pp. £51.99. ISBN 0131273078.

Best-selling text emphasizing decision making skills in management accounting. The book makes excellent use of colour diagrams and includes case studies of well known companies, including DaimlerChrysler and IBM. Coverage includes cost allocation, capital budgeting and management control systems.

3334 Management accounting

P. Weetman   Financial Times Prentice Hall, 2006, 566pp. £36.99. ISBN 0273701991.
www.pearsoned.co.uk/weetman

Text placing a strong focus on real world examples providing a solid foundation in the principles of management accounting. Content includes budget preparation and control, capital investment appraisal and performance evaluation. Detailed questions at the end of each chapter help to test understanding.

3335 Management accounting for business

C. Drury   3rd edn, Thomson Learning, 2005, 549pp. £37.99. ISBN 1844801527.

Aimed as an introductory text for undergraduate or MBA students. Covers all aspects of management accounting, including budgeting, cost assignment and capital investment decisions. The book has a strong international focus, although most of the assessment questions are set in a UK context. Drury has produced a well written, clearly presented text well suited to the target audience.

3336 Management and cost accounting

C.T. Horngren, A. Bhimani and S.M. Datar   3rd edn, Financial Times Prentice Hall, 2005, 974pp. ISSN 0273687514.
www.pearsoned.co.uk/horngren

Hefty text taking a strong European focus on contemporary issues within management and cost accounting. The book is well illustrated and includes a number of in-depth case studies and assessment material. The text successfully manages to be detailed and comprehensive without leaving the reader overwhelmed with the sheer volume of information.

Dictionaries, thesauri, classifications

3337 Management accounting official terminology
Chartered Institute of Management Accountants   2nd edn, CIMA Publishing, 2005, 156pp. £17.99. ISBN 075066827X.
A concise dictionary of management accounting terms. Somewhat confusingly the book is not laid out as a traditional dictionary but divided into chapters such as 'Financial accounts', 'Budgeting' and 'Performance measures'. Terms are then listed alphabetically within each chapter. Definitions are clear and the book makes good use of diagrams and charts.

Research centres & institutes

3338 Chartered Institute of Management Accountants
www.cimaglobal.com
Well designed website of one of the leading membership bodies for management accountants. Content includes details on CIMA professional qualifications, news and job vacancies. A strong selection of resources is available, including discussion papers, technical reports and detailed research.

Handbooks & manuals

3339 Valuation: measuring and managing the value of companies
T. Koller, M. Goedhart and D. Wessels   4th edn, Wiley, 2005, 742pp. £52.50. ISBN 0471702218.
Offers up-to-date information on valuing companies for students, academics, managers and investors. The book began life as a handbook for McKinsey consultants and consequently has a strong practical application. The book outlines fundamental principles of value creation, offers a step-by-step approach to valuing a company and applies value-creation principles to managerial problems. The text is snappily written, well presented and makes good use of real-world case studies.

Keeping up to date

3340 Advances in management accounting
Elsevier, annual. £59.99. ISSN 14747871.
Publishes lengthy articles on a wide range of topics in present-day management accounting. Relevant for both practitioners and academics. Recent articles have focused on employee motivation, managing environmental practices and measuring non-financial performance of the healthcare industry.

3341 Management Accounting Research
Chartered Institute of Management Accountants   Elsevier, qtrly. €152 per year. ISSN 10445005.
Contributions to this journal include case studies, field work, analytical modelling, scholarly papers and review articles.

Recent articles have included 'Human capital, pay structure and the use of performance measures in bonus compensation' and 'Entrepreneurial control and the construction of a relevant accounting'.

Financial Reporting

Introductions to the subject

3342 Analysis and use of financial statements
G. White, A. Sondhi and D. Fried   3rd edn, Wiley, 2003, 767pp. £39.99. ISBN 0471375942.
Aims to better the understanding of financial statements by equity and credit analysts. An extremely in-depth text, updated to include latest accounting practices. A little text-heavy compared to other books in the field, although certainly comprehensive.

3343 Business fairy tales
C. Jackson   Thomson South-Western, 2006, 281pp. £24.99. ISBN 0324305397.
Promises to expose the 'grim realities of fictitious financial reporting', examining companies such as WorldCom, Enron and Sunbeam. Each chapter is centred on a specifc company, beginning with the lessons to be learnt from the financial mismanagement in each particular case. The text is a good overview of the area, providing a broader perspective than the many texts devoted to Enron and WorldCom.
'Jackson walks the reader through the various ways unsuspecting investors can be led down the garden path through accounting tricks.' (*Barron's Magazine* 25 September 2006)

3344 Corporate financial accounting and reporting
T. Sutton   2nd edn, Financial Times Prentice Hall, 2004, 722pp. £35.99. ISBN 0273676202.
www.booksites.net/sutton [COMPANION]
Clear and thorough examination of all aspects of financial reporting. Updated to incorporate changes to International Accounting Standards, the book covers accounting requirements of both European and non-European companies. Covers topics such as accounting for pension costs and foreign operations, which do not usually appear in many introductory texts.

3345 Corporate reporting and company law
C. Villiers   Cambridge University Press, 2006, 338pp. £55. ISBN 0521837936.
Explores the disclosure requirements of companies, examining the UK regulatory framework in detail. The book is divided into three main sections: General issues, Financial reporting and Narrative reporting. A conclusion draws together the main issues in the text and makes useful recommendations on company reporting standards.

3346 Financial intelligence: a manager's guide to knowing what the numbers really mean
K. Berman and J. Knight   Harvard Business School Press, 2006, 255pp. £14.99. ISBN 1591397642.
Teaches the basics of finance, arguing that financial reporting is as much an art as a science. The authors state that not everything can be quantified, meaning that accountants always rely on estimates, assumptions and personal judgements. The book details strategies such as

'managing the balance sheet' and is an excellent learning tool for non-financial professionals.

3347 Financial statement analysis and security valuation
S.H. Penman   3rd edn, McGraw-Hill, 2006, 776pp. £44.99. ISBN 0071254323.

Outlines techniques concerned with calculating the fundamental value of a business through financial statement analysis. Each chapter concludes with a helpful list of 'key concepts' and a self-study exercise using a real-world company as a case study. A detailed and advanced-level text which requires a sound financial background.

3348 International guide to interpreting company accounts
C. Nobes   3rd edn, Informa Professional Publishing, 2001, 190pp. £595. ISBN 1902581164.

Designed to help those interpreting international financial statements, the book begins by examining the scale of accounting differences between different jurisdictions. The book also examines the effect of harmonization of accounting and places a particular focus on the details of Japanese accounting. At just 190 pages, this book is extremely expensive.

3349 Principles and practice of group accounts: a European perspective
A. Pierce and N. Brennan   Thomson Learning, 2003, 576pp. ISBN 1861529287.

Clearly presented text providing examples of the application of accounts regulations for 60 major European companies, including Diageo, Ericsson and AstraZeneca. Each chapter includes worked-through examples of group accounting practices. Topics covered include mergers, foreign subsidiaries and rights issues.

Terminology, codes & standards

3350 International financial reporting standards: a practical guide
H. van Greuning   4th edn, World Bank, 2006, 312pp. £22.95. ISBN 0821367684.

Summarizes each International Financial Reporting Standard and provides case studies stressing the practical applications of each concept. Key concepts are clearly defined and information is provided on the scope of the Standard and how it applies to presentation and disclosure. Suitable for executives, managers or financial analysts who lack a strong background in accountancy.

3351 Wiley GAAP 2005: interpretation and application of generally accepted accounting principles [USA]
B. Epstein, R. Nach and E. Black   John Wiley, 2006, 1288pp. ISBN 0471798207.

Covers developments in generally accepted accounting principles (GAAP). Each chapter focuses on a specific topic, such as investments, long-term debt and earnings per share. The text is extremely detailed and is accompanied by a CD-ROM.

Laws, standards, codes

3352 International GAAP 2005: generally accepted accounting practice under international financial reporting standards
M. Bonham [et al.]   LexisNexis, 2004, 2024pp. £96.99. ISBN 140570098X.

Written by financial reporting experts from Ernst & Young, this text helps to interpret International Financial Reporting Standards. The book includes information on the development of International GAAP (Generally Accepted Accounting Practice), followed by hundreds of pages detailing how the rules should be applied. Clear examples of good accounting practice are generously scattered through the text.

3353 UK and international GAAP: generally accepted accounting practice in the United Kingdom and under international accounting standards
A. Wilson [et al.]   7th edn, Butterworths Tolley, 2001, 2288pp. ISBN 0406945527.

Definitive text on the theory and practice of UK and international financial reporting written by experts from Ernst & Young. The book begins with over 150 pages on the development of the accounting process before examining in depth the current accounting rules, illustrated with detailed explanations and discussion. A huge guide of great practical use.

3354 Wiley IFRS 2006: interpretation and application of international financial reporting standards
B.J. Epstein and A.A. Mirza   Wiley, 2006, 1072pp. £52.50. ISBN 0471726885.

Although not 'compact' as claimed on the dust jacket, this 1072-page book is certainly comprehensive. The guide contains detailed analysis of the application of International Financial Reporting Standards (IFRS) and contains many real-world examples. The text also includes a useful comparison of IFRS and US GAAP standards.

Official & quasi-official bodies

Companies House
See entry no. 4033

Research centres & institutes

3355 Center for Financial Reporting & Management
http://groups.haas.berkeley.edu/accounting/
Part of the Haas School of Business at the University of California, Berkeley. Haas has a leading selection of faculty specializing in all aspects of accounting, including internal controls, management accounting and financial reporting.

Portal & task environments

3356 Shibui Markets
www.shibuimarkets.com/index.html
Billed as the 'leading global financial portal built on the spirit of Shibui', i.e. understanding rather than simply knowing financial information. Registration is free and the website contains hard-to-find data concerning global corporations

alongside information on foreign currencies and bonds. The global coverage of the website is impressive, although more granular data can be found on subscription databases.

3357 uk-wire.com
http://moneyextra.uk-wire.com
Claims to be 'the ultimate company announcement service'. Provides up-to-the-minute links for UK company announcements. These can be filtered by index (e.g. FTSE 100, AIM), sector, or just for a specific company. The interface is simple and easy to use, although the site is a little overrun with online adverts.

Discovering print & electronic resources

3358 CAROL – Company Annual Reports On-Line
www.carol.co.uk
Offers online access to company balance sheets, profit and loss accounts and additional financial data. Access is free of charge, although registration is required. The site is extremely easy to navigate and also includes a useful list of links for worldwide stock exchanges.

3359 SCoRe – Search Company Reports
www.score.ac.uk
SCoRe is a catalogue of printed company reports held in UK libraries. Holdings include current and historic reports. The catalogue details a number of collections, including the British Library. Access and entry requirements for each collection are provided and maps of collection locations are also displayed.

Digital data, image & text collections

3360 Amadeus
www.bvdep.com
Subscription database from Bureau van Dijk. Amadeus is a pan-European database containing financial information on almost 9 million public and private companies in 38 European countries. Ranked lists of firms can be produced using an extensive and flexible search facility. Results can easily be exported to a spreadsheet. The database offers standardized annual accounts for up to ten years.

3361 Perfect Filings
www.perfectinfo.com
Global subscription database containing over 7 million company filings. Content includes annual reports, 10-Ks, SEC filings, prospectuses and company news. The single search screen is easy to navigate and filings can be searched using over 3000 indexed classifications. An excellent source of company data.

3362 US Securities & Exchange Commission
www.sec.gov/edgar.shtml
The Securities and Exchange Commission website includes a detailed company filings system known as EDGAR (the Electronic Data Gathering, Analysis and Retrieval system). Annual reports to shareholders need not be submitted on EDGAR, though 10-K filings have to be provided. The site includes a helpful tutorial, links to the latest filings and a wide-range of document search options.

Keeping up to date

3363 Company Reporting
Company Reporting Ltd, monthly. ISSN 13557696.
www.companyreporting.com
Monitors the financial reporting practices of UK and European companies, focusing on the FTSEurofirst 300 and UK FTSE 350. Company Reporting is a useful resource for financial officers and auditors interested in keeping abreast of latest reporting standards. Member-only content is also available on the companion website, which has a rather sparse presentation.

Auditing

Introductions to the subject

3364 The audit process
I. Gray and S. Manson   3rd edn, Thomson Learning, 2004, 819pp. £39.99. ISBN 1861509465.
Introduction to the audit process, featuring sections on corporate governance, assurance services and audit regulation. The text makes good use of examples, case studies and questions. Presentation is clear although a greater use of colour would have been beneficial. A clever feature of the book is notes in the margins which summarize key points or add relevant further information.

3365 Auditing
A. Millichamp   8th edn, Continuum, 2002, 440pp. £32.99. ISBN 082645500X.
Widely used as a course text on accountancy and business courses. Provides thorough yet accessible coverage of all aspects of auditing. Topics are presented in a clear point-by-point style, followed by quick self-test questions and more complex examination questions. Students may find the 'How to pass auditing examinations' guidelines particularly helpful.

3366 Auditing and assurance services: an integrated approach
A.A. Arens, R.J. Elder and M.S. Beasley   10th edn, Prentice Hall, 2004, 791pp. £49.99. ISBN 0131457349.
Aimed as an introduction to auditing for students with no significant experience. Extremely detailed content, although text-heavy presentation can be offputting. Each of the chapters sets learning objectives at the outset and concludes with detailed discussion questions and problems. A partial annual report is included as an insert to the book in order to illustrate examples within the text.

3367 Auditing for managers: the ultimate risk management tool
K.H.S. Pickett and J.M. Pickett   John Wiley & Sons, 2005, 353pp. ISBN 0470090987.
A practical-based text, Auditing for managers is an ideal reference tool for managers conducting an audit. Written in a jargon-free style with effective use of illustrations, the book examines the importance of audits and outlines successful audit review strategies. Each section of the book ends with a brief summary of the contents of the section – this is particularly useful for those too busy to read the entire book and also acts as an aide-mémoire.

3368 Environmental auditing
H. Woolston   British Library, Science Reference & Information Service, 1993, 77pp. ISBN 0712307893.
A brief yet informative guide to environmental audit. Provides an overview of the environmental auditing process, before examining legal and practical aspects of an audit. Also included are details of further sources of information on environmental audits. The text is jargon free and a good starting point for those unfamiliar with the topic.

3369 History of auditing: the changing audit process in Britain from the nineteenth century to the present day
D. Matthews   Routledge, 2006, 184pp. £70. ISBN 041538169X.
Matthews traces the history of auditing from its Victorian beginnings to the present. Includes an in-depth analysis of nineteenth-century accounting and an examination of the impact of computing on the audit process. The book concludes by examining the role of auditors in the US collapse of Enron and Worldcom. An interesting history for both auditing professionals and economic historians.

3370 Modern auditing
G. Cosserat   2nd edn, John Wiley & Sons, 2004, 616pp. £33.99. ISBN 0470863226.
Designed to provide 'a comprehensive and integrated coverage of the latest developments in the environment and methodology of auditing'. Coverage includes professional ethics, e-commerce and auditing and audit sampling. The book includes a glossary of technical terms and a variety of multiple-choice questions to test comprehension of the text.

Terminology, codes & standards

3371 Wiley practitioner's guide to GAAS 2005: covering all SASs, SSAEs, SSARs, and interpretations
D.M. Guy, D.R. Carmichael and L.A. Lach   Wiley, 2006, 832pp. ISBN 0471798304.
Offers a clear interpretation of auditing standards, alongside advice and best practice. The text includes an exhaustive glossary. New editions are frequently published.

Laws, standards, codes

3372 Principles of auditing: an introduction to international standards on auditing
R. Hayes [et al.]   2nd edn, Financial Times Prentice Hall, 2004, 692pp. £39.99. ISBN 0273684108.
Based on International Standards on Auditing (ISAs), this text describes the development and practical use of all ISAs and other national auditing standards. Case studies featuring companies such as Enron and Xerox are used throughout the book. Each chapter concludes with a useful summary and a selection of questions, exercises and cases.

Handbooks & manuals

3373 Auditing and reporting
Croner. CCH Group, 2007.
Full text of all UK exposure drafts and accounting standards. Includes ethical standards for auditors, international standards for auditing and practice notes. Published on behalf of the Institute of Chartered Accountants in England and Wales (ICEAW).

Keeping up to date

3374 Journal of Accounting, Auditing and Finance
Greenwood Publishing, qtrly. $90 per year. ISSN 0148558X.
Publishes studies in accounting and related fields. Recent articles have included 'Audit committee financial literacy: a work in progress', 'Organizational structure and earnings management' and 'Institutional holdings and analysts' stock recommendations'.

Taxation

company taxation • personal taxation • tax law

Introductions to the subject

3375 Many unhappy returns: one man's quest to turn around the most unpopular organization in America
C. Rossotti   Harvard Business School Press, 2005, 340pp. £16.99. ISBN 1591394414.
Charles O. Rossotti describes how he transformed the Internal Revenue Service, having been appointed as IRS Commissioner in 1997. The book provides an insight into the IRS itself as well as details on successful ways to lead and implement change. The text is scattered with amusing anecdotes, such as Rossotti being asked a few months into his new job, 'How does it feel to be the most hated man in America?'

Official & quasi-official bodies

3376 Australian Taxation Office
www.ato.gov.au
Offers tailored content for individuals, businesses and non-profit organizations. Users can fill in tax returns online or use one of the many calculators covering areas such as income tax and capital gains tax. The site also provides well written guides to the many different forms of taxation.

3377 Great Britain. HM Revenue & Customs
www.hmrc.gov.uk
Everything you needed to know about the UK Revenue and Customs Service. Information on the site is divided logically into information for employers, information for businesses and information for individuals. A number of tax forms can be completed online and a large range of information sheets and brochures can be downloaded. Online tools available include a company car fuel benefit calculator and a statutory maternity pay calculator.

3378 United States. Customs & Border Protection
www.cbp.gov
Includes a history of the US Customs & Borders Service, statistics, latest news and publications. Also includes travel advice and detailed information on importing and exporting goods.

3379 United States. Internal Revenue Service
www.irs.gov

All you need to know about US taxation – covers taxation on individuals, businesses, charities and much more. The site is well organized and easy to navigate although it is easy to become overwhelmed by the huge amount of information available. Tax forms and publications are available to download – some forms are available to complete online and numerous online tax calculation tools are also available. The site includes a search facility enabling users to check that charities are registered. A large selection of resources for tax professionals may also be accessed.

Research centres & institutes

3380 Tax Foundation [USA]
www.taxfoundation.org

Formed in 1937. The Tax Foundation home page now takes the form of a blog containing the latest news on tax policy. The site is very well structured, containing articles indexed by subjects such as income taxes, tax reform and gambling taxes. The Foundation also produces a number of regular reports and an array of data on tax rates can be downloaded. Podcasts on a range of tax-related topics are also freely available. A very strong, thought-provoking site.

Associations & societies

3381 Chartered Institute of Taxation [UK]
www.tax.org.uk

The leading professional body in the UK concerned with taxation. The site includes a directory of Chartered Tax Advisers and information on professional standards. A 'Tax technical area' features news, research papers and consultation documents. Information on professional examinations can also be downloaded.

3382 Federation of Tax Administrators [USA]
www.taxadmin.org

Useful site providing information on a wide range of tax-related issues. Content includes state-by-state comparisons of tax rates and revenues, technological developments and a section devoted to motor fuel tax. A number of research reports can also be downloaded, although these are not particularly current.

Portal & task environments

3383 Tax History Project [USA]
www.taxhistory.org

Excellent site providing information on the history of US public finance. Includes an innovative 'virtual museum' outlining American tax history, which includes pictures and sound clips and manages to bring a potentially dull subject to life. Additional content includes a selection of tax-themed cartoons, detailed articles and links to a range of presidential tax returns.

Discovering print & electronic resources

3384 Tax and Accounting Sites Directory
www.taxsites.com

Deceptively basic-looking site offering a wealth of links to useful websites covering tax, accounting and payroll topics. Links are divided into broad categories such as International tax, Financial reporting and Accounting software. A few of the links provided are dated or just lead to details of books on Amazon.com, but generally this site is a very good starting point for an online trawl of accountancy or taxation resources.

3385 Tax Resources on the Web
www.taxtopics.net

A basic-looking yet highly detailed list of tax resources available online. Links are organized by subject area (e.g. divorce, property tax, retirement) – the site is regularly updated and free of advertisements. An excellent gateway to numerous online resources.

3386 Will Yancey's Home Page
www.willyancey.com

The basic presentation of this site means the focus is on the content, which is uniformly strong. Maintained by Dr Will Yancey, an accountant from Dallas, the site includes well organized links to tax, accounting, finance and law resources. The site is uncluttered by adverts and is an excellent starting point for research in the field.

Digital data, image & text collections

3387 BNA Tax Management [USA]
www.bnatax.com

Subscription site, although some information is freely available. Includes latest news on federal and state taxes and resources covering recent legislation. Subscription content includes the BNA Tax Management Library, which includes productivity tools, research, analysis and commentaries.

3388 CCH
http://tax.cchgroup.com

CCH provides subscription tax and accounting services and databases. The company also publishes research reports and produce books and journals. A particularly wide range of products is available covering sales tax for retail and manufacturing. An e-mail news alert system is available and CCH also provides detailed tax legislation coverage.

Keeping up to date

3389 LowTax.net
http://lowtax.net

The slightly messy presentation style of this site can be offputting, but it does include a wealth of content. The site is an excellent source of information on offshore and low-tax regimes worldwide. Profiles of each jurisdiction are particularly useful, featuring many sections, such as an executive summary, news coverage and tax data. A section of the site is also devoted to the growing issue of the tax implications of e-commerce.

3390 Tax Almanac [USA]
www.taxalmanac.org
Online tax research resource for tax professionals using wiki technology. Content is written by tax professionals and includes a selection of research articles and news stories. An online discussion forum is particularly heavily used. As with other wikis, caution should be used over the reliability of information that can be edited by an outside community, although as the site states, 'the breadth and depth of tax knowledge contributed by a large community adds tremendous value'.

3391 Tax Analysts [USA]
www.taxanalysts.com
Subscription site publishing information resources and in-depth taxation news. News services are available on a federal, state and international level. Special publications include The Exempt Organization Tax Review, which provides comprehensive information on non-profit organizations.

3392 Tax Policy Center [USA]
www.taxpolicycenter.org
Strongly recommended website published by the Urban Institute and the Brookings Institution. One of the most valuable sources of information on the site is the 'Tax facts database', which covers long-term data on areas, including state tax revenue, income tax rates and corporate taxation. A wide range of articles and research on tax issues are freely available. The Tax Policy Center also features a microsimulation model of the federal tax system that can estimate the impact of new tax proposals.

3393 TaxProf Blog [USA]
http://taxprof.typepad.com
Excellent blog aimed at tax academics, covering news, information and useful resources. The site features abstracts of newly published research, book reviews and details of key readings in the field. The site also provides links to latest rankings of tax programmes as well as webcasts on topical tax issues.
'The undisputed champion of tax blogging.' (*Tax Notes*)

Tax Law

Introductions to the subject

3394 Basic international taxation: volume 1
R. Rohatgi   2nd edn, Richmond Law & Tax, 2005, 467pp. ISBN 1904501575.
Comprehensive overview of the basic principles of international taxation. Includes broad summaries of domestic tax systems and analysis of model tax treaties. A glossary of taxation terms is also included. The text is supported by a second volume which covers practical guidance on international tax planning techniques.

3395 EU taxation law
L.W. Gormley   Richmond Law & Tax, 2005, 346pp. £95. ISBN 1904501559.
Extensive examination of all aspects of EU tax law, which the author recognizes is 'more complex than ever and is frankly in need of consolidation, reform and simplification'. The book is divided into five main sections: taxation on imports

and exports; VAT; excise duties; company taxation; and taxation of savings income.

3396 Tax systems and tax reforms in Europe
L. Bernardi and P. Profeta   Routledge, 2004, 305pp. £90. ISBN 0415322510.
This text features contributions from leading scholars on developments in European tax regimes. Part I of the book contains four articles providing an overview of tax systems and tax reforms in Europe. Part II details case studies of tax systems in France, Germany, Ireland, Italy, Spain, the Netherlands and the UK.

3397 Taxation
A. Melville   12th edn, Financial Times Prentice Hall, 2006, 656pp. £38.99. ISBN 0273708716.
A leading, comprehensive guide to taxation in the UK. The book is updated annually to ensure accuracy and covers both personal and business taxation. The text makes good use of worked examples and explanations and definitions provided are clear and concise. New topics covered include the taxation treatment of civil partners.

3398 Taxes and business strategy: a planning approach
M. Scholes, M. Wolfson and M. Erickson   3rd edn, Prentice Hall, 2005, 556pp. £92.99. ISBN 0131465538.
An MBA-level text covering tax planning and strategy, incorporating fundamentals of corporate finance and microeconomics. Each chapter concludes with useful summary points, discussions, questions and exercises.

3399 Zurich tax handbook
A. Foreman and G. Mowles   Pearson Education, 2006, 772pp. ISBN 0273709976.
Provides comprehensive coverage of every aspect of UK taxation. Divided into chapters covering areas such as self assessment, business finance and tax-efficient investments. The guide is detailed yet tries to avoid the use of jargon prevalent in many detailed works on tax. As such, it is an invaluable resource for professionals and private individuals.

Official & quasi-official bodies

3400 Joint Committee on Taxation [USA]
www.house.gov/jct
Surprisingly basic site which features a full list of Joint Committee on Taxation publications. Other content is scarce but includes information on the history and role of the Joint Committee.

Handbooks & manuals

3401 Tolley's Yellow Tax Handbook
LexisNexis Butterworths. Annual. 4v. £94.95. ISSN 01413856.
Key reference source containing up-to-date tax legislation, annotated with cross-references to commentary and tax cases. Legislation included covers areas such as income tax, capital gains tax, corporation tax, inheritance tax, national insurance contributions and tax credits.
Available as part of the Tolley's Taxation Service on CD-ROM. New edns of the Yellow/Orange Tax Handbooks are also updated weekly on the internet.

Keeping up to date

3402 British Tax Review
Sweet & Maxwell, 6 p.a. £383 per year. ISSN 00071870.
Provides in-depth analysis of tax law for practitioners, policy makers and academics. Articles published cover domestic, international and comparative topics across the entire field of tax law. The journal also provides case notes on relevant European court decisions and reviews on major new publications. Regular special issues focus on major tax topics.

3403 Legalbitstream [USA]
www.legalbitstream.com
Regularly updated and free database specializing in US federal income and estate tax law. The database searches an array of documents from the Supreme Court, Circuit and District Courts, the US Federal Circuit and the Tax Court. Search facilities are simple to use and uncluttered and despite the site being commercially supported there are very few intrusive adverts.

Personal Taxation

Introductions to the subject

3404 Daily Telegraph tax guide
D. Genders   Constable & Robinson, 2007, 221pp. £9.99. ISBN 1845295870.
Updated annually, this guide offers clear and helpful advice for taxpayers. The guide includes details of the latest Budget and covers areas, including VAT, inheritance tax and capital gains tax. The book is jargon-free and includes useful worked examples, tax-saving hints and advice on planning tax affairs for the the forthcoming financial year.

3405 Individual taxes: worldwide summaries
John Wiley & Sons, 1000pp. ISBN 0471740705.
Provides a comprehensive summary of individual taxes and tax rates in over 120 countries. Details covered include recent significant developments, territoriality and residence, deductions and tax credits. As with much printed material on taxation, content quickly becomes outdated, so new editions are regularly printed.

3406 Tax havens today: the benefits and pitfalls of banking and investing offshore
H. Barber   Wiley, 2007, 324pp. £22.99. ISBN 047005123X.
Detailed guide to offshore tax havens. The book highlights the benefits of investing offshore, advice on strategies needed and profiles of world tax havens. The fourth part of the book is particularly useful, highlighting a range of tax haven resources, including periodicals, books and online resources. An excellent guide for this burgeoning research topic.

3407 The UK pocket tax book
annual.
www.pwc.com/uk/eng/ins-sol/publ/pwc_uk-pocket-tax_may07.pdf
Updated annually and made available through the tax section of the PricewaterhouseCoopers website, this guide contains a summary of UK personal and corporate taxation rates. Content includes information on income tax, tax-efficient investments, corporation tax, inheritance tax and VAT. The guide is clearly presented and is a concise, up-to-date and extremely useful reference guide.

3408 The Which? guide to giving and inheriting: tax efficient ways to pass on money, property and other valuables
J. Lowe   8th edn, Which? Books, 2005, 288pp. £11.99. ISBN 1844900169.
As with all Which? guides, this book is clearly presented and offers practical, sensible advice on avoiding tax penalties. 'Could be the wisest investment you will ever make.' (*Irish Times*)

Official & quasi-official bodies

United States. Internal Revenue Service
See entry no. 3379

Portal & task environments

3409 TaxCentral [UK]
www.taxcentral.co.uk
Online tax community created in collaboration with HM Revenue & Customs. The site includes a number of useful tax calculators, including a student loan calculator, stamp duty calculator and VAT calculator. Other areas of the site provide links to tax rebate forms and offer guidance on tax self-assessment.

Handbooks & manuals

3410 Tolley's income tax [UK]
LexisNexis UK, annual. ISSN 0305893X.
Definitive work on income tax, providing comprehensive coverage of statute law, case law and HMRC practice. The book is easy to navigate as content is organized alphabetically by sections such as banks, capital allowances and property income. The guide is updated annually to ensure that new legislation is accurately covered.

Keeping up to date

3411 Tax World
www.taxworld.org
Comprehensive site covering many aspects of personal taxation, with a particularly strong focus on inheritance tax and income tax. The site is a good source of current tax information but also includes an interesting 'History of taxation' section beginning with taxes collected in ancient Egypt and Greece.

3412 Uncle Fed's Tax Board [USA]
www.unclefed.com
Comprehensive tax site containing advice on completing tax paperwork, contact details for tax professionals, latest tax news and links to documents published by the Internal Revenue Service (IRS). Useful for personal finance purposes and for research by tax professionals. The site links to all IRS tax forms and provides instructions on how they should be completed.

Company Taxation

Introductions to the subject

3413 KPMG Corporate Tax Rate Survey
http://tinyurl.com/ynv9mz
Published annually, this concise document is an excellent resource for providing an 'at a glance' comparison of worldwide corporate tax rates. Covers 86 countries from Albania to Zambia. A brief paragraph on each country details any specific information on corporate taxes.

Research centres & institutes

3414 Oxford University Centre for Business Taxation
www.sbs.ox.ac.uk/tax
Independent research centre based at the Said Business School, promoting effective policies for business taxation. The site provides access to a limited selection of working papers and reports.

3415 Tax Research Institute [UK]
http://tri.nottingham.ac.uk
Based at the University of Nottingham, the Tax Research Institute was founded in 2004 to conduct high-priority research into taxation. Reseach specialisms include tax administration, compliance issues and the economic effects of taxes and benefits. The site is well presented, although current content is noticeable by its absence.

Associations & societies

3416 American Taxation Association
http://aaahq.org/ata/index.htm
Membership of the ATA is available to those with an interest in tax education and research. The presentation of the site is somewhat basic. Content includes the *ATA Newsletter* and information on the *ATA Journal of Legal Tax Research*. At the time of writing a list of research resources on the site is under development.

Portal & task environments

3417 1040.com [USA]
www.1040.com
Excellent site offering downloads for a vast array of tax documentation. The search facility allows users to narrow searches to a particular US state or to search across forms for the entire country. In addition to the proliferation of forms, the site also provides a useful tax calendar and tax calculator.

3418 Ernst and Young Library
www.ey.com/global/content.nsf/International/Dynamic_Library
The Ernst & Young Library includes dozens of free, downloadable research reports – coverage of company taxation is strong, but there are also reports on venture capital, auditing, accounting and fraud. Recent reports have focused on tax aspects of mergers and acquisitions in Hong Kong and the impact of VAT worldwide. The reports are extremely detailed and rival the content of many reports found on expensive subscription databases.

Digital data, image & text collections

3419 Kleinrock [USA]
www.kleinrock.com
Subscription services for tax and accounting professionals. Federal tax issues are covered by Federal TaxExpert, which contains a comprehensive library of 100,000 cases and rulings. TaxExpert software is also available for the individual states of California and New York. 'Total Kleinrock Office' provides a suite of tax products available on CD, in print and online.

Handbooks & manuals

3420 Using a company to save tax
L. Hadnum   Taxcafe UK, 2007, 140pp. £24.95. ISBN 190460854X.
Concise guide explaining how, by setting up a limited company, it is possible to save money in tax and national insurance. The guide is highly practical and easy to read. Chapter 13 has the unromantic title 'Using your spouse for further tax savings'.

Keeping up to date

3421 International Tax and Public Finance
Springer, 6 p.a. ISSN 09275940.
Publishes research on theoretical and empirical aspects of tax policy, including expenditure and financial policies. The journal places an emphasis on open-economy issues such as the impact of taxation on international trade. Each issue includes a 'Policy watch' section which discusses a recent policy issue or highlights recent tax developments.

3422 Small Business Taxes and Management [USA]
www.smbiz.com
A site that looks very basic but contains a lot of useful information for small and medium-sized businesses. The site supplies information on latest tax legislation and news stories affecting small companies. A calendar of tax priorities is published alongside 'how to' guides and a large selection of useful web links.

3423 Tax Research UK Blog
www.taxresearch.org.uk/Blog
An interesting, regularly updated blog written by Richard Murphy, covering topics in tax and corporate accountability. The site has no flashy graphics or pictures, meaning the quality of the writing is of paramount importance. Thankfully, Murphy is able to write snappily and informatively on a wide selection of topics.

Industries & Utilities

The Editorial Board took the decision at the start of *The New Walford* project that resources on companies, industries and markets should be grouped in the wider context of business, economics and management rather than being scattered as entries under generic subjects. Thus, the resources in this section focus on how companies within market sectors operate and make a profit or loss, rather than the processes by which they actually manufacture, extract, produce, or create their goods (for which the relevant subjects remain the starting point).

The section is not an attempt to be comprehensive but rather provides an illustrative overview of the resources available for key market sectors within the economy. More and more of these resources are available only electronically as use of the internet transforms the collation, publication and analysis of detailed financial and organizational information from around the world. Many are compilations of external and in-house research and so come at high prices (reflecting their value to their core audience). Fortunately, such material continues to be made available to non-specialist enquirers through national libraries.

Utilities – electricity and gas, water and sewerage, and telecommunications – have been grouped together in a sub-section because the market sectors in which they operate are regulated to a greater or lesser extent by governments across the world. Here, the resources include the 'how' of such regulation alongside the 'how' of company operation. Once again, resources covering the production processes of each individual utility can be found in the relevant subject headings.

Introductions to the subject

3424 Creative economy: how people make money from ideas
J. Howkins   new edn, Penguin, 2002, 288pp. £9.99. ISBN 0140287949.
An author with deep experience of international creative industries explains why the selling of 'intellectual property' has become so important within the global economy.

3425 From Empire to Europe: the decline and revival of British industry since the Second World War
G. Owen   HarperCollins, 2000, 544pp. £8.99. ISBN 0006387500.
A former editor of the UK *Financial Times* charts the reasons for Britain's industrial decline after the Second World War.
'Qualifies as one of the most compelling works to appear in recent decades on the economic evolution of the United Kingdom since the end of the Second World War.' (*New Statesman* 13 December 1999 www.newstatesman.com/199912130053)

3426 Industry and Firm Studies
V.J. Tremblay and C.H. Tremblay   4th edn, M.E. Sharpe, 2007, 400pp. £47.17. ISBN 0765617234.
New coverage of professional sports, soft drinks, distilled spirits and cigarettes complements revised and updated chapters on airline services, retail and commercial banking, health insurance, motion pictures and brewing. The book includes firm case studies of General Motors, Microsoft, Schlitz and TiVo.

3427 Knowledge and competitive advantage: the coevolution of firms, technology, and national institution
J.P. Murmann, G. Jones and L. Galambos   Cambridge University Press, 2006, 316pp. £15.99. ISBN 0521684153.
http://professor-murmann.net [COMPANION]
Uses the development of the synthetic dye industry in Great Britain, Germany and the USA to demonstrate how differences in educational institutions and patent laws affected the growth of a new industry in the three countries.

'All International Business scholars can learn from Murmann's evolutionary models of organizational mechanisms.' (*Journal of International Business Studies* (2004) **35** p.560–3.)

3428 Leviathans: multinational corporations and the new global history
A.D. Chandler and B. Mazlish, eds   Cambridge University Press, 2005, 264pp. £15.99. ISBN 0521549930.
www.cambridge.org/catalogue/catalogue.asp?isbn=9780521549936 [DESCRIPTION]
Covers the history, development, cultural and social implications of the multinational corporation and the major role that such corporations play in globalization.
'The summaries of multinational development ... are successful' (*Business History Review* **80** p.194)

3429 Paths of innovation: technological change in 20th-century America
D.C. Mowery and N. Rosenberg   Cambridge University Press, 1999, 224pp. £15.99. ISBN 0521646537.
Demonstrates how the simultaneous emergence of new engineering and applied science disciplines in the universities, in tandem with growth in the research and development industry and scientific research, has been a primary factor in the rapid rate of technological change.

3430 Sources of industrial leadership: studies of seven industries
D.C. Mowery and R.R. Nelson   Cambridge University Press, 1999, 401pp. £21.99. ISBN 0521645204.
Describes and analyses how seven major high-tech industries evolved in the USA, Japan and Western Europe. The industries covered are machine tools, organic chemical products, pharmaceuticals, medical devices, computers, semiconductors and software.

3431 Strategy and structure: chapters in the history of the industrial enterprise
A.D. Chandler   MIT Press, 1962, 463pp. £23.95. ISBN 0262530090.
Classic text from 1962 (winner of the 1964 Thomas Newcomen Award in Business History) which, by studying US

giants such as General Motors and DuPont, explains the way industrial enterprises change.

Dictionaries, thesauri, classifications

3432 North American Industry Classification System
www.census.gov/epcd/www/naics.html
'NAICS is a unique, all-new system for classifying business establishments. It is the first economic classification system to be constructed based on a single economic concept. Economic units that use like processes to produce goods or services are grouped together. This "production-oriented" system means that statistical agencies in the United States will produce data that can be used for measuring productivity, unit labor costs and the capital intensity of production; constructing input-output relationships; and estimating employment-output relationships and other such statistics that require that inputs and outputs be used together.'

■ **Classifications: sorting things out with classifications**
Office for National Statistics. www.statistics.gov.uk. Good introduction:
'Classifications facilitate the accurate and systematic arrangement of data according to common properties so that the resulting statistics can be easily reproduced and compared over time as well as between different sources. Classification is thus an essential part of statistics, and standard classifications are key instruments of official statistics. One of the key principles of the *National Statistics Code of Practice and Protocol on Statistical Integration* is the promotion and use of common statistical frames, definitions and classifications. In the UK, three widely-used standard classifications are the: *Standard Industrial Classification (SIC)*; *Standard Occupational Classification (SOC)*; *National Statistics Socio-economic Classification (NS-SEC)*'.

Laws, standards, codes

3433 American National Standards Institute
www.ansi.org
Private non-profit organization established to coordinate the development of 'voluntary consensus standards' for products, services, processes and systems produced in the USA. Its main functions are to support development and approve national voluntary standards; establishes accreditation programmes; work with government departments and agencies on standards issues; and act as the US representative to international standards organizations. Website provides detailed information about the Institute and its activities, plus news, forthcoming events and information on the various levels of membership available. Site also contains a useful collection of internet resources, publications and documents, many of which are freely available to non-members.

■ **NSSN: a national resource for global standards**
www.nssn.org. '(S)earch engine that provides users with standards-related information from a wide range of developers, including organizations accredited by the American National Standards Institute (ANSI), other US private sector standards bodies, government agencies and international organizations ... (It) has become the world's most comprehensive search engine for standards with more than 300,000 records'.

3434 British Standards Institution
www.bsi-global.com/
Founded in 1901. The BSI's main activities include certification of management systems and products; product

testing services; the development of private, national and international standards; and providing training and information on standards and international trade. The Institute is made up of four business units, including BSI British Standards, a national standards body responsible for 'drafting, publishing and marketing standards and related information products'. The website provides information on the Institute and its various services, products and publications. The BSI also has a library available to BSI and committee members and students. It contains a dedicated reading area in which visitors can consult print and electronic collections of standards, catalogues, books and journals. Members of the public can also use of the BSI Library on a reference basis at a charge of £25 per half day.

■ **European Committee for Standardization** www.cen.eu.
'Contributes to the objectives of the European Union and European Economic Area with voluntary technical standards which promote free trade, the safety of workers and consumers, interoperability of networks, environmental protection, exploitation of research and development programmes, and public procurement.'

3435 International Organization for Standardization
www.iso.org
Founded in 1947, a federation of national standards institutes from 157 countries, responsible for producing worldwide industrial and commercial standards. The website contains a comprehensive overview of the ISO structure, standards and its products and services. The ISO's standards catalogue is also available from the website and can be searched freely. The full text of any standard may be purchased online. The ISO also produces a range of guideline documents, manuals, standards compendia, handbooks and other standards-related publications which can be purchased from the website.

■ **World Standards Services Network** www.wssn.net. '(N)etwork of publicly accessible World Wide Web servers of standards organizations around the world.'

Official & quasi-official bodies

3436 Business Europe
www.businesseurope.eu
A collective of 39 business federations from 33 EU and EEA countries which liaise with the institutions of the EU on business matters. The history and growth of the collective matches that of the EU, which makes it an invaluable resource on how business influences the workings of the EU.

Companies House
See entry no. 4033

Confederation of British Industry
See entry no. 4034

3437 Great Britain. Department of Trade & Industry
www.dti.gov.uk
UK government department responsible for policy towards business and international trade. Note that some policy documents are published only through this site.

3438 Office of the United States Trade Representative
www.ustr.gov
Founded in 1962, this US government agency has offices in

Brussels and Geneva and handles US relations with trade bodies such as the World Trade Organization.

UK Trade & Investment
See entry no. 4042

3439 **United States. Department of Commerce**
www.commerce.gov
US government department responsible for promoting economic development and technological advancement. Website is a key source on the regulation of business in America.

Research centres & institutes

3440 **Corporate Research Foundation**
www.researchfoundation.com/pages/home.asp
Research into best business practices in nine countries on three continents: UK, Switzerland, Spain, South Africa, the Netherlands, Germany, China, Belgium and Australia.

Associations & societies

3441 **US Chamber of Commerce**
www.uschamber.com
The world's largest business federation, representing more than 3 million businesses around the world. Comprehensive website has links to all manner of business concerns within America and to America's business concerns around the world.

Libraries, archives, museums

British Library, Business & IP Centre
See entry no. 3893

3442 **Business Reference Services** [USA]
www.loc.gov/rr/business
Prime source for business directories in the USA. Website has authoritative free subject guides on all aspects of researching business within America.

Portal & task environments

3443 **Business Eye Directory of Business Support Services**
Welsh Assembly Government
www.businesseye.org.uk
Commended in the 2006 ISG/Bookdata Reference Awards. A free, impartial service for businesses in Wales which gathers together sources of information from the public, private and voluntary sectors.

Discovering print & electronic resources

3444 **Business information sources: a beginner's guide**
C. O'Hare Facet Publishing, 2007, 160pp. £34.95. ISBN 9781856046039.
Written by an experienced practitioner, this short book is an easy-to-assimilate introduction to the world of printed and online business information sources.

3445 **Directory of business information sources** [USA]
R. Gottlieb, ed. Grey House Publishing Inc, 2007, 2300pp. $195. ISBN 1592371469.
www.greyhouse.com [DESCRIPTION]
Details associations, newsletters, magazines, trade shows, directories, databases and websites which focus on each of 98 industry sectors within the USA

3446 **SCoRe: The national UK catalogue of printed company reports**
www.score.ac.uk
Allows the holdings of key business libraries within the UK to be searched for current and historic printed company reports. Does not include holdings of digital versions. Useful links page to other sources of company reports around the world.

3447 **Strauss's handbook of business information** [USA]
R.W. Moss Greenwood, 2003, 480pp. £54.95. ISBN 9781563085208.
An acclaimed update to the classic 1988 handbook by Diane Wheeler Strauss. Integrates internet and online resources into a revised review of print resources.

3448 **Trade directories of the world**
Croner Publications Inc. Looseleaf updated.
www.croner.com [DESCRIPTION]
Comprehensive guide to 3000 trade, industrial and professional directories indexed by trade and profession, countries and publisher.

Digital data, image & text collections

Mintel
See entry no. 4185

Directories & encyclopedias

3449 **Applegate directory**
www.applegate.co.uk/
Information on more than 250,000 companies cross-referenced to more than 45,000 products within the UK and Irish manufacturing and technology sector.

3450 **Asia's 10,000 Largest Companies 2006**
ELC International 18th edn, ELC International, 2006, annual, 853pp. Price of CD-ROM includes a copy of the printed directory, £500+VAT. ISBN 0948058897.
www.elcinternational.com [DESCRIPTION]
Financial and contact information on the most important companies in the following countries: Hong Kong, Japan, Malaysia, Philippines, Taiwan, Indonesia, South Korea, Singapore, Thailand and China.

3451 **Britain's top employers: best examples of HR management**
Corporate Research Foundation Guardian Newspapers Ltd, 2006, 384pp. £14.99. ISBN 0852650620.
Written by business journalists, objective company summaries cover areas, including pay and benefits,

promotion and development, training, company culture, innovation, diversity, social responsibility, corporate governance and environmental record.

3452 Company Information
Kompass   annual. 50 volumes covering individual countries.
www.kompass.com
Building upon their Big Black Books of company and product information worldwide, Kompass' website gives access to this information on over 2 million companies in over 70 countries. Initial details are free; subsequent information can be bought on a 'pay-as-you-go' basis.

3453 DandB Business Registers
Dun & Bradstreet   AP Information Services Ltd, 2006, annual. 34 v.
www.apinfo.co.uk/dnb/br/ [DESCRIPTION]
Over 680,000 UK and Irish businesses covered in regional volumes of around 20,000 business. Each business has either at least five employees or a turnover in excess of £250,000.

3454 Directory of American firms operating in foreign countries
B.D. Fiorito   19th edn, Uniworld Business Publications Inc, 2007. ISBN 0836000579.
www.uniworldbp.com [DESCRIPTION]
Covers 4060 firms with over 63,000 branches in 191 countries

3455 Directory of foreign firms operating in the United States
B.D. Fiorito, ed.   13th edn, Uniworld Business Publications Inc, 2006. ISBN 0836000544.
3500 non-US companies owning nearly 10,000 businesses.

3456 Europe's 15,000 largest companies 2006
ELC International   30th edn, ELC International, 2006, 1223pp. CD-ROM of Directory also available, £275. ISBN 0948058846.
www.elcinternational.biz [DESCRIPTION]
Includes the latest member states of the European Union.

3457 Foreign companies yearbooks
Commercial Intelligence Service. 50 v.
www.businessmonitor.com [DESCRIPTION]
Corporate data on foreign companies operating in selected countries around the world.

3458 Hoover's handbook of private companies [USA]
12th edn, Hoover's Inc, 2007, annual, 586pp. $175. ISBN 1573111155.
www.hooversbooks.com [DESCRIPTION]
Covers 900 US enterprises which are not listed on the public stock markets

3459 Kelly's industrial directory
120th edn, Reed Business Information, 2006, annual, 2340pp. ISBN 0610006762 ISSN 14671220.
www.reedinfo.co.uk [DESCRIPTION]
Claims to be the leading directory for UK products and services. Has a 200 year history and currently covers 94,600 companies. Also available online for a fee as Kellysearch.

Key British enterprises
See entry no. 4084

3460 Kompass register
Kompass, 2006.
www.kompass.co.uk/ [DESCRIPTION]
Available in UK and international editions, this directory has been published for over 40 years. UK edition covers 45,000 companies. 50 international editions cover countries worldwide. A particular feature is the coverage of trade and brand names. The associated online database is free to search and returns basic information.

3461 Regional leads report
Key Note   Key Note.
www.keynote.co.uk [DESCRIPTION]
Information on over 1.4 million British companies in 71 regional volumes.

3462 Standard & Poor's register of corporations, directors and executives [USA]
78th edn, McGraw-Hill, 2006, annual. 2 v. ISSN 03613623.
Profiles over 75,000 US corporations, 350,000 of their executives, with 70,000 detailed biographies.

3463 United Kingdom's 5000 Largest Companies 2006
ELC International   ELC International, 2006. Price of CD-ROM includes a copy of printed directory, £250+VAT. ISBN 0948058900.
www.elcinternational.biz [DESCRIPTION]
The CD-ROM offers significantly more detailed data, including additional named individuals in top management, ownership information and textual descriptions of business activities.

3464 Waterlow's unquoted companies
Jordans   20th edn, CaritasData, 2007, annual.
Financial and market profiles of the 20,000 leading unquoted companies registered in Great Britain

3465 Who owns whom
AP Information Services, annual. 8 v., £1,975.
www.apinfo.co.uk [DESCRIPTION]
First published in 1958. A key source of information on the corporate structure of over 1.4 million businesses worldwide. Divided into four regional groupings: UK & Ireland, Continental Europe (including Eastern Europe & Russia), North & South America and Australasia, Asia, Middle East & Africa.

Handbooks & manuals

3466 Occupational outlook handbook [USA]
Bureau of Labor Statistics   biennial. ISSN 00829072.
www.bls.gov/oco
Key source for career information within the USA. Details required education and training for each job, potential earnings, expected job prospects, working conditions and what actually is done on the job. Revised every two years.

Keeping up to date

3467 Business Information Review
Sage Publications, qtrly. £49. ISSN 02663821.
http://bir.sagepub.com [FEE-BASED]
The only UK journal devoted to business information

provision. Reviews and evaluates sources and comments on trends within the sector and within business generally.

3468 Business Insights
www.globalbusinessinsights.com [FEE-BASED]
Business Insights is a market research database offering strategic market analysis The reports are produced in association with leading industry experts focusing on: consumer goods; energy; financial services; healthcare; telecoms; e-commerce; and human resources. Content is global in coverage with a strategic focus. A full subscription entitles full-text access to all the reports contained in the database. Non-subscribers can purchase individual reports which can then be downloaded directly from the website.
Formerly Reuters Business Insights.

3469 Business Ratio Report
Key Note, annual.
www.keynote.co.uk [DESCRIPTION]
148 reports covering UK industry by sector. Each report offers performance analysis and financial information on the major companies within the sector covered.

3470 The Information Advisor [USA]
R. Berkman, ed.   Information Today, monthly. $189.
www.informationadvisor.com [DESCRIPTION]
Founded by Robert Berkman in 1988 and still edited by him, this monthly newsletter is a key resource in discovering US business information resources. Now supported by the editor's blog and a monthly e-letter of the best business research sites.
- **Best business web sites** monthly, www.bestbizweb.com.
- **Intelligent Agent** R. Berkman   www.ia-blog.com.

3471 Marketline Business Information Center
Datamonitor
http://dbic.datamonitor.com [FEE-BASED]
High-value market research profiles of 10,000 companies, 2000 industry sectors and 50 countries. Fee-based with no free information.

Aerospace Industry (Civilian)

air transport • airlines • avionics manufacturers • low-cost airlines

Introductions to the subject

3472 Airbus Industrie: conflict and cooperation in US-EC trade relations
S. McGuire   Palgrave Macmillan, 1997, 232pp. £72. ISBN 9780333687178.
Uses the story of this European consortium and its rivalry with Boeing to explore how trade conflicts between America and Europe begin and are resolved.

3473 Aviation century
R. Dick and D. Patterson   Firefly Books.
www.fireflybooks.com [DESCRIPTION]
Five volumes covering the development and interaction of the civilian and military aviation industries during the 20th century.
- **1. The early years** R. Dick and D. Patterson   2003, 240pp. $39.95. ISBN 1550464078.

- **2. The golden age** 2004, 288pp. $39.95. ISBN 1550464094.
- **3. World War II** R. Dick and D. Patterson   2004, 352pp. $39.95. ISBN 1550464264.
- **4. Wings of change** 2005, 288pp. $39.95. ISBN 1550464280.
- **5. War and peace in the air** 2006, 352pp. $39.95. ISBN 1550464302.

3474 Come fly with us!: a global history of the airline hostess
J. Omelia and M. Waldock   Collectors Press, 2004, 160pp. £15.99. ISBN 1888054611.
Stunning visuals, many from the archives of the world's great airlines, help create a sense of the early days of flying, while the book closes with a glimpse of the future of air travel.

3475 Deep stall: the turbulent story of Boeing commercial airplanes
P.K. Lawrence and D.W. Thornton   Ashgate, 2005. £30. ISBN 0754646262.
Study of the decline and re-emergence of Boeing as a major civilian and defence aircraft manufacturer.

3476 Industrial diversification and innovation: an international study of the aerospace industry
F. Texier   Edward Elgar, 2000, 258pp. £74. ISBN 1840644524.
Comparative case study of the aerospace industry in France, Sweden and South Korea.
'Worthwhile reading for anyone interested in the history of the aircraft industry, as well as for students of innovation studies in general' (*Journal of Evolutionary Economics* **11**(3) 2001 p385–8)

3477 No frills: the truth behind the low-cost revolution in the skies
S. Calder   Virgin Books, 2002, 256pp. ISBN 185227932X.
Story of the changes in air travel due to advent of the 'low-cost' airlines.

3478 Straight and level: practical airline economics
S. Holloway   2nd edn, Ashgate, 2003, 654pp. £27.50. ISBN 0754619303.
Explains how market liberalization and deregulation continue to provide new opportunities for airline executives, making extensive use of examples of what is being done in practice. Primarily written for those in middle and senior management positions within the airline industry, for executives and companies supplying the industry such as airframe, powerplant and avionics manufacturers and for those in financial institutions; it should also be of value to students of air transport.

Official & quasi-official bodies

3479 Aviation Directorate
www.dft.gov.uk/pgr/aviation/
All aspects of the regulation of civil aviation in Britain are covered.

3480 European Civil Aviation Conference
www.ecac-ceac.org/index.php
Consists of 42 member states and deals with many facets of civil aviation matters.

3481 Federal Aviation Administration [USA]
www.faa.gov
American regulatory body with an emphasis on safety in the civilian aerospace industry.

Research centres & institutes

3482 Aerospace Manufacturing Research Centre
www.cems.uwe.ac.uk/amrc/
UK national centre of expertise for aerospace manufacturing research.

Associations & societies

3483 Aerospace Industries Association [USA]
www.aia-aerospace.org
Trade association for American commercial and military aviation manufacturers, along with their major suppliers. Useful statistics and library areas and invaluable links to the websites of member companies.

3484 Airport Operators Association
www.aoa.org.uk
Trade association for 71 British airports.

3485 British Airports Group
www.sbac.co.uk/pages/08679562.asp
The British Airports Group (BAG) is the leading representative body for UK companies involved in the overseas airport development sector. BAG's membership currently consists of over 200 companies of all sizes whose products and services are required in the strategic planning, finance, design, construction, equipping, securing, management and operation of airports and air traffic control systems.

British Business & General Aviation Association
See entry no. 3828

3486 Confederation of European Aerospace Societies
www.ceas.org/
Pan-European groups of aerospace interests. Useful links to the leading aeronautics and astronautics societies.

3487 International Air Transport Association
www.iata.org
Global trade association for the commercial airline business. Comprehensive website on all aspects of the airline business with very useful links to all member airline companies.

3488 National Business Aviation Association [USA]
www.nbaa.org
Promotes the civil aviation industry in America.

3489 Royal Aeronautical Society
www.aerosociety.com/
The UK professional forum for all engaged in the aeronautics and astronautics industries.

3490 Society of British Aerospace Companies
www.sbac.co.uk/
UK trade association for companies supplying civil air

transport, aerospace defence, homeland security and space industries.

3491 UKSpace
www.sbac.co.uk/pages/43611913.asp
Trade association of the British space industry.

Portal & task environments

Air transport portal of the European Commission
See entry no. 2328

Discovering print & electronic resources

3492 Airlines of the World
www.kls2.com/airlines/
Official and unofficial web pages of airlines worldwide.

3493 Aviation Portal (Wikipedia)
http://en.wikipedia.org/wiki/Portal:Aviation
Featured portal within Wikipedia – comprehensive coverage of airlines, airports and aircraft manufacturers

Directories & encyclopedias

3494 ABC aerospace directory
http://abc.janes.com/ [DESCRIPTION]
Authoritative and comprehensive resource covering the aerospace industry. Entries cover address, telephone, fax and electronic contact details; previous organization identities; financial and statistical information; personnel details, parent and subsidiary information; and products and services.

3495 Jane's aircraft component manufacturers
http://jacm.janes.com/ [DESCRIPTION]
Coverage of companies and organizations that provide, produce and repair components for fixed- and rotary-wing aircraft for both the civil and military markets. Comprehensive details on more than 100 aircraft currently in production.

Keeping up to date

3496 Aerospace Technology
www.aerospace-technology.com
Latest news releases, information on projects, white papers, event information and coverage of products and services.

3497 Aviation Today [USA]
www.aviationtoday.com
News and information site building upon the magazine of the same name. Useful guide to the American view of the aviation business.

3498 AviationWeek.com
www.aviationweek.com
News and information from *Aviation Week* for aerospace/defence professionals. A mixture of freely available news and subscriber content.

3499 Flight International
www.flightinternational.com
News, information and comment site built upon the
reputation and resources of the 90-year-old monthly
magazine. Particularly strong on the European marketplace.

3500 Shephard Group
www.shephard.co.uk
Niche publisher of magazines and directories on the civilian
and defence aerospace industries. Online site has news and
directory information along with specialized information
areas on the helicopter industry, the unmanned vehicle
industry and the in-flight entertainment sector.

Agriculture, Horticulture, Fishing & Forestry

agricultural machinery • agriculture • farming • fishing
industry • forestry • horticulture • timber

Introductions to the subject

3501 Agricultural Notebook
R. Soffe, ed.   20th edn, Blackwell Science Ltd, 2003. £44.99. ISBN
0632058293.
Standard work of reference first published in 1883. Divided
into four parts: crops, management, animal production and
farm Equipment. New sections in this edition: marketing
perspective on diversification; organic farming; and farming
and wildlife.

**3502 Reforming the Common Agricultural Policy:
history of a paradigm change**
I. Garzon   Palgrave Macmillan, 2006. £45. ISBN 023000184X.
Compares three successive major reforms of the Common
Agricultural Policy of the EU and demonstrates the influence
of related issues such as international trade negotiations and
budget constraints.

**3503 Seeds of change: six plants that transformed
mankind**
H. Hobhouse   2nd edn, Shoemaker & Hoard, 2006. £8.61. ISBN
1593760493.
A history of six commercial plants – sugar, tea, cotton,
potatoes, quinine and coca.

3504 Seeds of wealth
H. Hobhouse   Pan, 2004. £10.99. ISBN 0330488120.
Focuses on the economic consequences of the exploitation of
rubber, timber, tobacco and the wine grape.

**3505 Shooting the net: personal insights into the past,
present and future of the British fishing industry**
M. Charman   Silver Link Publishing Ltd, 2004, 128pp. £16.99. ISBN
185794223X.
Charts 100 years of the changing life and work of those who
man the UK trawler fleet.

3506 So you want to start a nursery
T. Avent   Timber Press, 2003, 340pp. £17.99. ISBN 0881925845.
A realistic overview of the tools and knowledge needed to
succeed in the garden nursery business in the UK.

3507 Woodland management: a practical guide
C. Starr   Crowood Press Ltd, 2005, 160pp. £16.99. ISBN
1861267894.
Comprehensive guide to the ownership and management of
UK woodlands.

Dictionaries, thesauri, classifications

Dictionary of the pulp and paper industry
M. Svaton   See entry no. 3724

Laws, standards, codes

3508 Agriculture
World Trade Organization
www.wto.org/english/tratop_e/agric_e/agric_e.htm
Access to the official documents behind and official news on,
the ongoing world agricultural trade negotiations.

Official & quasi-official bodies

3509 Agriculture & Rural Development [EUR]
http://europa.eu/pol/agr/index_en.htm
Source for policy documents on pan-European agricultural
matters.

3510 Food & Agriculture Organization
www.fao.org/
Since 1945 this agency of the United Nations has been a
neutral source of information on agriculture, forestry and
fisheries practices and nutrition.

3511 Forestry Commission
www.forestry.gov.uk/
UK government executive agency charged with the oversight
of forests and their sustainable development.

**3512 Great Britain. Department for Environment, Food
& Rural Affairs**
www.defra.gov.uk/
UK government department covering farming, food, water
and the sustainable development of the countryside.

3513 Seafish
www.seafish.org/
Since 1981 this non-departmental public body has worked
across all sectors of the UK seafood industry, bringing
together fishermen, fish processors, wholesalers, seafood
farmers, fish fryers, caterers, retailers and the import/export
trade.

3514 United States. Department of Agriculture
www.usda.gov
US government department setting policy on food,
agriculture and the exploitation and conservation of natural
resources.

Associations & societies

3515 Confederation of Forest Industries (UK) Ltd
www.confor.org.uk/
UK industry body for the forest industries and the supply of timber and timber products.

3516 Horticultural Trades Association
www.the-hta.org.uk/
Trade body for UK garden centres and other garden retail businesses, landscapers, growers and suppliers to the garden trade.

3517 National Farmers' Union
www.nfuonline.com/
UK representative body for farmers.

3518 United Kingdom Forest Products Association
www.ukfpa.co.uk/
Technical and commercial support to the UK forest products industry.

Libraries, archives, museums

3519 National Agricultural Library [USA]
www.nal.usda.gov
One of the world's largest information sources on agricultural topics, with a mass of freely available information on the website.

Portal & task environments

3520 The Wood Explorer Inc
www.woodexplorer.com/default.asp
A worldwide knowledge base for the wood, timber and forest industries, featuring commercial information on 5000 tree species.

Digital data, image & text collections

3521 FAOSTAT
Food & Agriculture Organization
http://faostat.fao.org
Multilingual site offering statistics on all aspects of agriculture and the business of agriculture for over 200 countries and 200 primary products.

Keeping up to date

3522 Agmachine.com
www.agmachine.com/
Worldwide coverage of machinery and equipment, with links to company websites and sections on news, publications, events and institutions.

3523 Farmers Weekly interactive
www.fwi.co.uk
Built around the content of the leading UK farming newspaper, this website offers updated news, product information and the latest and historical price trends for agricultural produce.

3524 Horticulture Week
www.hortweek.co.uk/
Buyers guide to UK suppliers of horticultural products and services to the horticultural industry.

3525 Timber Trades Journal
www.ttjonline.com/home.asp
News and buyer's guide for those in the timber products industry.

Automotive Industry (Civilian)

automobile industry • motor manufacturers • vehicle building

Introductions to the subject

3526 The automobile: a chronology of its antecedents, development and impact
C. McShane   Fitzroy Dearborn, 1997, 222pp. ISBN 1579580211.
Seeks to list the major events in the history of the automobile through to 1994. Useful statistical appendices.

3527 British motor industry
J. Foreman-Peck   Manchester University Press, 1995, 323pp. ISBN 071902613X.
A non-technical account of the rise and decline of the UK motor industry during the 20th century.

3528 British motor industry 1954–94: a case study in industrial decline
T.R. Whisler   Oxford University Press, 1999, 428pp. £77.50. ISBN 0198290748.
'An interesting and insightful addition to the already voluminous literature on the post-war decline of British manufacturing industry in general, and its automobile industry in particular.' (*Organization Studies* March-April 2002)

3529 The origin of competitive strength: fifty years of the auto industry in Japan and the US
A. Kawahara   Springer-Verlag Tokyo, 1998, 278pp. £54. ISBN 4431702237.
Compares Toyota Motor Corporation and General Motors and poses questions about the true nature of competitive strength in the automotive industry and among its leading corporations.

3530 Time for a model change: re-engineering the global automotive industry
G.P. Maxton and J. Wormald   Cambridge University Press, 2004, 294pp. £25. ISBN 0521837154.
The automotive industry ranks among the most significant business phenomena of the 20th century and today accounts for almost 11% of the GDP of North America, Europe and Japan and one in nine jobs. This book highlights the challenges and opportunities that exist for managers, legislators, financial institutions and potential industry entrants.

3531 World history of the automobile
E. Eckermann   updated edn, SAE International, 2001, 371pp. ISBN 076800800X.
Details the development of the automobile from its beginnings until the start of the 21st century. Some

emphasis on European developments and in particular on companies in Germany.

Official & quasi-official bodies

Great Britain. Department for Transport
See entry no. 3820

United States. Department of Transportation
See entry no. 3825

Associations & societies

3532 Japan Automobile Manufacturers Association
www.jama.org
Trade association representing 14 Japanese car, truck, bus and motorcycle manufacturers. Comprehensive website offering a wealth of information on the Japanese view of the automotive industry.

3533 Society of Motor Manufacturers & Traders
www.smmt.co.uk
Key trade body in the UK for the promotion of the motor industry.

3534 Vehicle Builders & Repairers Association Ltd
www.vbra.co.uk/default.asp
Established in 1914, the trade organization for the vehicle body building, commercial vehicle repair, tail lift repair and car body repair industry within the UK.

Libraries, archives, museums

3535 The Archive of the British Motor Industry Heritage Trust
www.heritage-motor-centre.co.uk/sectionpages/archive_index.html
[DESCRIPTION]
Contains the company archives of British Leyland and its constituent companies, Aston Martin and Lucas, along with a unique photographic record of the UK motor industry from its birth to the present.

Discovering print & electronic resources

3536 Auto Industry
Automotive Directorate
www.autoindustry.co.uk
Aims 'to provide the single, definitive point of reference on the web for the UK auto industry.' Sections on relevant sources, statistics, companies, education, regions, SMMT and a library that includes a dictionary of terms used in the trade. In addition to the dictionary, the library contains some useful articles on all aspects of the automotive industry, including company strategies, inward investment, lean manufacturing, transport and the environment. The statistics section has lists of the top vehicle manufacturers, component suppliers and UK-owned suppliers. The section on global markets has quite detailed market overviews of the motor industry in various countries around the world. The site also has a comprehensive auto industry directory

searchable by product name or service and vehicle design or company name.

Directories & encyclopedias

3537 An historical who's who of the automotive industry in Europe
J.P. Norbye   McFarland & Company, 2004, 336pp. ISBN 0786412836.
Biographical dictionary profiling inventors, designers, engineers, entrepreneurs, executives and others who shaped the European motor industry from its beginnings in the late 19th century to the present.

Keeping up to date

3538 Automotive Online
www.automotive-online.com
Sections covering world news, vehicle news and data and analysis. The news stories are current, with a weekly review and a news archive. Within data and analysis there is information on marketing and distribution, manufacturing and the supply chain, the car aftermarket, systems and e-business, finance, legislation, components and suppliers and market data. There is a very useful directory of who's who in the automotive industry. Within the section for vehicle news there are items covering road tests, new model launches and UK prices and specifications. Of particular value are the manufacturer histories which provide detailed background on the major car makers.

Chemicals & Plastics Industries

chemical industry • petrochemical companies • plastics industry

Introductions to the subject

3539 Chemical industry at the millennium: maturity, restructuring and globalization
P.H. Spitz, ed.   Chemical Heritage Foundation, 2005, 400pp. £23.60. ISBN 0941901343.
Industry experts look at the trends and market factors that have affected the chemical industry in the recent past.

Knowledge and competitive advantage: the coevolution of firms, technology, and national institution
J.P. Murmann, G. Jones and L. Galambos   See entry no. 3427

3540 Shaping the industrial century: the remarkable story of the evolution of the modern chemical and pharmaceutical industries
A.D. Chandler   Harvard University Press, 2005, 266pp. £19.95. ISBN 067401720X.
'Typically ambitious broad-brush history but with a strong and sustained thesis that one comes to associate with someone who has been justifiably annointed the dean of business history.' (http://eh.net/bookreviews/library/1172)

Associations & societies

3541 Chemical Heritage Foundation
www.chemheritage.org
Offers many tools for the researcher, the student and those who want to explore and discover how the chemical and molecular sciences have changed the world in which we live.

3542 Chemical Industries Association
www.cia.org.uk
UK trade association for the chemical industries.

3543 Society of the Plastics Industry [USA]
www.plasticsindustry.org
Since 1937 has been representing the businesses involved in the entire plastics processing chain in America, from raw material to finished products.

Discovering print & electronic resources

3544 ChemIndustry.com: Chemical Search Engine
www.chemindustry.com/
Leading comprehensive directory and search engine for chemical and related industry professionals.

Directories & encyclopedias

3545 Major chemical and petrochemical companies of the world
S. James, H. Porter and M. Scott, eds   9th edn, Graham & Whiteside, 2007. $995. ISBN 9781860994968.
Profiles of over 7000 companies, including brand names and trademarks.

Keeping up to date

3546 ICIS
www.icis.com/
Global information provider for the chemical and oil industry.

Construction & Building Industries

building industry • civil engineering • engineering construction • heating & ventilation • plant hire • tunnel construction

Introductions to the subject

3547 Construction industry of Great Britain
R.C. Harvey   2nd edn, Laxton's, 1997, 322pp. ISBN 0750636564.
A detailed picture of Britain's construction industry at the end of the 20th century. Covers how it operates, through a range of technical and management topics.

Associations & societies

3548 Construction Industry Council
www.cic.org.uk

Representative body for associations and research bodies in the UK construction industry.

3549 Engineering Construction Industry Association
www.ecia.co.uk/
Industry body for the UK engineering construction industry.

3550 Heating & Ventilating Contractors Association
www.hvca.org.uk/
Trade body for companies active in the design, installation, commissioning and maintenance of heating, ventilating, air conditioning and refrigeration (hvacr) products and equipment.

Directories & encyclopedias

3551 Civil engineering yearbook
1st edn, McMillan Scott, 2005. £25.
A useful directory for those involved in the civil engineering market.

3552 Concrete industry yearbook
McMillan Scott, 2006. £25.
In-depth articles on developments in the industry

3553 International tunnelling directory
Wilmington Media Ltd, 2006, annual. ISSN 1462425X.
Directory of over 200 products and services and more than 1100 companies operating worldwide.

3554 UKplantguide
McMillan Scott, 2005. £40.
Provides an effective 'one-stop shop' for companies with a serious interest in purchasing or hiring plant equipment. The publication is designed to aid key decision makers in their choice of plant for the construction and materials handling sectors.

Keeping up to date

3555 Construction News
1963–, weekly. ISSN 00106860.
www.cnplus [COMPANION]
Serving the UK construction industry for over 130 years, this weekly newspaper has built a supporting website for subscribers which gives access to a news archive, directory of suppliers and briefings and guides to the various sectors within the industry.

3556 Elevation: a view of the UK lift industry
www.elevation.co.uk/ [DESCRIPTION]
Trade magazine for the UK lift industry

3557 Engineering News-Record [USA]
1917–, weekly. ISSN 0013807X.
www.enr.com/
News, analysis, commentary and data for the US construction industry.

3558 Tunnels and Tunnelling International
Wilmington Group plc, monthly.
Leading UK and international monthly magazine for the tunnelling industry.

Cosmetics & Toiletries Industries

beauty industry • hairdressing • perfume manufacturers • toiletries manufacturers

Introductions to the subject

3559 Inventing beauty: a history of the innovations that have made us beautiful
T. Riordan   Broadway Books, 2004, 333pp. £9.66. ISBN 0767914511.
An American view of how the beauty and cosmetics industry developed, from the Victorian era to the present.

Official & quasi-official bodies

3560 Hairdressing & Beauty Industry Authority
www.habia.org/
UK government-approved standards-setting body for hair, beauty, nails, spa therapy, barbering and African–Caribbean hair.

Associations & societies

3561 European Cosmetic Toiletry & Perfumery Association
www.colipa.com/
European trade association representing the interests of the cosmetic, toiletry and perfumery industry, set up in 1962.

3562 Fragrance Foundation
www.fragrance.org/
Established in 1949 by six industry leaders affiliated with Elizabeth Arden, Coty, Guerlain, Helena Rubenstein, Chanel and Parfums Weil, to develop educational programmes about the importance and pleasures of fragrance for the American public. Today, The Fragrance Foundation has become an international source for historical, cultural, scientific and industry-related reference materials. The Foundation maintains one of the most extensive print and video fragrance libraries in the world. It publishes educational and sales training materials and a bi-annual *Fragrance Trends Forecast Report*. The Foundation produces videos and consumer publications, develops and mounts exhibitions and holds seminars and symposia for its members as well as for the international fragrance industry.

Directories & encyclopedias

3563 BeautyBuyer.co.uk
www.beautybuyer.co.uk/
Beauty equipment suppliers in the health, beauty and spa industries.

3564 Cosmetics and toiletries guide [USA]
Grey House Publishing, 2006, 500pp. $895. ISBN 1592371329.
Comprehensive guide to the cosmetics and toiletries industry in the USA

3565 World cosmetics and toiletries marketing directory 2005
Euromonitor International, 2005. £675. ISBN 1842643541.
www.euromonitor.com/World_Cosmetics_and_Toiletries_Marketing_D irectory_2005
Profiles the leading cosmetics and toiletries companies worldwide.

Keeping up to date

3566 cosmetics business
www.cosmeticsbusiness.com/
Leading site for cosmetics market research and analysis, cosmetic science and technology, worldwide industry news and product innovation.

3567 esprit
www.esprit-magazine.co.uk/
A business magazine for the premium side of the perfumery, cosmetics and skincare market covering the industry in the UK and Republic of Ireland. Launched in April 1988. Supported by the *Esprit beauty industry directory*, which lists 1500 beauty/grooming products and brands and approximately 1500 companies involved in manufacturing, retailing, distribution and marketing of fragrances, cosmetics, skincare and toiletry lines. Two indexes covering companies and products/brands.

3568 GCI Magazine
www.gcimagazine.com/
Business news and resources from *Global Cosmetic Industry Magazine*.

Luxury Product and Service Briefing
See entry no. 3788

Defence Industry

armaments industry • defence equipment • military vehicles • shipbuilding (naval)

Introductions to the subject

Aviation century
R. Dick and D. Patterson   See entry no. 3473

Deep stall: the turbulent story of Boeing commercial airplanes
P.K. Lawrence and D.W. Thornton   See entry no. 3475

3569 Differences between military and commercial shipbuilding: implications for the United Kingdom's Ministry of Defence
J. Birkler, D. Rushworth and J. Chiesa   Rand, 2005, 134pp. ISBN 083303670X.
An examination of the feasibility of UK shipbuilders expanding outside their domestic military contracts into the worldwide commercial or foreign military markets. Based on literature reviews and surveys and interviews of major shipyards.

3570 **Monitoring the progress of shipbuilding programmes: how can the Defence Procurement Agency more accurately monitor progress?**
M.V. Arena, J. Birkler and J.F. Schank   Rand, 2004, 84pp. £12.50. ISBN 0833036602.
Explores the reasons for and ways to anticipate schedule delays in shipbuilding programmes. Based on surveys of major US, UK and European shipbuilders and other extensive industry research.

3571 **Outsourcing and outfitting practices: implications for the Ministry of Defence shipbuilding programmes**
J.F. Schank, H. Pung and G.T. Lee   Rand, 2004, 95pp. £18.50. ISBN 0833036351.
Advises how the UK should best use modern outsourcing and outfitting practices for shipbuilding in the years to come.

3572 **The United Kingdom's nuclear submarine industrial base: Ministry of Defence roles and required technical resources**
J.F. Schank, C.R. Cook and R. Murphy   Rand, 2005. V. 2, £14.95. ISBN 0833038451.
Recommends measures and structures the UK Ministry of Defence can adopt to better manage its risks and responsibilities in the acquisition of nuclear submarines.

Official & quasi-official bodies

3573 **Defence Equipment & Support**
www.mod.uk/DefenceInternet/MicroSite/DES/
Formed in April 2007 through the merger of the Defence Procurement Agency and the Defence Logistics Organization. Equips and supports the UK armed forces in all operations. Website explains how companies are involved in this process.

3574 **Defence Procurement Agency**
www.mod.uk/DefenceInternet/MicroSite/DPA/
UK executive agency of the Ministry of Defence which purchases equipment for all of Britain's armed forces. In April 2007 became part of the MoD's Defence Equipment & Supply Agency.

Associations & societies

Aerospace Industries Association
See entry no. 3483

3575 **Defence Manufacturers Association**
www.the-dma.org.uk/
The UK's defence trade association, with over 615 members.

Society of British Aerospace Companies
See entry no. 3490

Society of Maritime Industries
See entry no. 3832

Directories & encyclopedias

Jane's aircraft component manufacturers
See entry no. 3495

3576 **Jane's international defence directory**
P. Partridge, ed.   22nd edn, Jane's Information Group, 2006, annual, 1457pp. ISBN 0710627572.
http://idd.janes.com
Authoritative resource detailing thousands of organizations and personnel in the defence industry. Features government and diplomatic agencies; associations, defence forces as well as manufacturers, distributors and sales and service companies; and company divisions and field offices.

Keeping up to date

AviationWeek.com
See entry no. 3498

3577 **Defence Management Journal**
PSCA International, qtrly. £295. ISSN 14642646.
www.defencemanagement.com [FEE-BASED]
The journal combines views from defence industry manufacturers and defence researchers with those from the armed forces 'user' community. Subjects covered include developments in logistics, military vehicles, marine, air and land equipment, educational and training resources. Supported by comprehensive 'portal'-style website.

3578 **Jane's Defence Weekly**
1984–, weekly. ISSN 02653818.
www.janes-defence-weekly.com
Award-winning publication with a reputation for breaking world exclusive news and for expert, meaningful interpretation of what we see on the ground, at sea and in the air, and in boardrooms and command centres throughout the world.

Shephard Group
See entry no. 3500

Electronics & Electrical Industries

computer manufacturing • consumer electronics • electrical engineering • software industry

Introductions to the subject

3579 **Computer: a history of the information machine**
M. Campbell-Kelly   2nd edn, Westview Press, 2004, 360pp. £24.99. ISBN 0813342643.
Traces the story of the computer from the birth of the technology to the dotcom boom.

3580 **From airline reservations to Sonic the Hedgehog: a history of the software industry**
M. Campbell-Kelly   MIT Press, 2004, 372pp. £10.95. ISBN 026253262X.
A starting point for understanding how fundamental component of computer history developed within the USA.

3581 From underdogs to tigers: the rise and growth of the software industry in Brazil, China, India, Ireland, and Israel
A. Arora and A. Gambardella, eds Oxford University Press, 2006, 326pp. £17.99. ISBN 0199205310.
Examines the reasons behind the phenomenon of software companies establishing themselves in Brazil, China, India, Ireland and Israel.

3582 Inventing the electronic century: the epic story of the consumer electronics and computer industries
A.D. Chandler Free Press, 2001, 321pp. £25. ISBN 0743215672.
Documents the rise and fall of big players in the consumer electronics and computer industries in America.

Synthetic worlds: the business and culture of online games
E. Castronova See entry no. 3613

Dictionaries, thesauri, classifications

3583 Acronym addiction
B.R. Santo IEEE Spectrum Online, 2006.
www.spectrum.ieee.org/oct06/4657
Electronics acronyms and initialisms uncovered.

3584 Comprehensive dictionary of electrical engineering
P. Laplante 2nd edn, CRC Press Inc, 2005, 840pp. £39.99. ISBN 0849330866.

Associations & societies

3585 Electrical Contractors Association
www.eca.co.uk/
Founded in 1901, the Association represents companies in all sectors of the electrical engineering industry: from plugs to power stations and from fibre optics to factories.

3586 Electronics Scotland
www.electronics-scotland.com
Independent trade association representing the electronics sector in Scotland.

3587 European Association of Electrical Contractors
www.aie-elec.org/
Pan-European association of 21 national associations covering more than 175,000 companies.

3588 European Committee of Electrical Installation Equipment Manufacturers
www.cecapi.org/
Established in 1967 to represent Associations of Manufacturers of Electrical Installation Equipment within member states of the European Union.

3589 European Electronic Component Manufacturers Association
www.eeca.org/
Represents the major companies involved in the manufacturing of electronic components within Europe.

3590 Intellect
www.intellectuk.org/
Trade association for the UK hi-tech industry, covering the information technology, telecommunications and electronics sectors.

Keeping up to date

3591 Electronicstalk
www.electronicstalk.com/
Provides information from electronics manufacturers and distributors for design, development and manufacturing engineers.

3592 ElectronicsWeekly.com
www.electronicsweekly.com
The UK's leading website for electronics professionals, being the online arm of *Electronics Weekly*, for over 40 years the leading source of information in the UK electronics industry. The site offers a daily diet of news, analysis, feature and business stories.

3593 European Electronic Markets Forecast
Reed, monthly. £360.
Market and business briefings on the European and global electronics industry.

3594 Yearbook of World Electronics Data Series
REED, 2005. 4 volumes – Book & CD-ROM, £4440.
www.rer.co.uk/publications/yearbooks/index.shtml [DESCRIPTION]
The definitive market reference to global electronics production and markets, covering 51 countries and 10 principal product groups.

Entertainment, Sport & Leisure Industries

gambling industry • leisure industry • leisure parks • music industry • sports business • television industry

Introductions to the subject

3595 All you need to know about the music business
D.S. Passman 3rd edn, Penguin, 2004, 467pp. £18.99. ISBN 0141018453.
Comprehensive guide to the legal and financial aspects of the business, such as record contracts, managers, music publishing, touring and fees. Also covers the technological advances that are reshaping the business.

3596 Business of culture: strategic perspectives on entertainment and media
J. Lampel, J. Shamsie and T.K. Lant, eds Lawrence Erlbaum, 2006, 328pp. £69.50. ISBN 0805851054.
Provides serious analysis of the cultural industries – media, entertainment, film, music and the arts – from a business perspective. A useful primer on cultural industries for students and scholars who are engaging in the study and research of this area for the first time.

3597 Business of sports
S. Rosner and K.L. Shropshire, eds   Jones & Bartlett, 2004, 776pp.
£38.99. ISBN 0763726214.
An overview of major sports business issues.

3598 Creativity and innovation in the music industry
P. Tschmuck   Springer, 2006, 281pp. £77. ISBN 1402042744.
An international history of the music industry from 1877 to
the digital music revolution offered by the internet, music
online services and MP3 technology.

3599 Economics of football
S. Dobson and J. Goddard   Cambridge University Press, 2001,
458pp. £32.50. ISBN 0521661587.
Detailed economic analysis of professional football at club
level, using a combination of economic reasoning and
statistical and econometric analysis. Based on English club
football, with a wide range of international comparisons.
Specific topics include the links between football clubs'
financial strength and competitive balance and uncertainty of
outcome; the determinants of professional footballers'
compensation; measuring the football manager's
contribution to team performance, the determinants of
managerial change and its effects on team performance;
patterns of spectator demand for attendance; predicting
match results, betting on football and the market in football
clubs' company shares.

3600 Economics of gambling
L.V. Williams, ed.   Routledge, 2003, 270pp. £80. ISBN 0415260914.
Leading experts such as David Peel, Stephen Creigh-Tyte,
Raymond Sauer and Donald Siegel cover economic themes,
including betting on the horses, over-under betting in football
games, national lotteries and lottery fatigue, demand for
gambling and the economic impact of casino gambling.

3601 Economics of recreation, leisure and tourism
J. Tribe   3rd edn, Elsevier, 2004, 445pp. £24.95. ISBN 0750661801.
Discusses themes such as how is the provision of leisure and
tourism determined and could it be provided in a different
way? What are the key opportunities and threats facing
leisure and tourism and environmental impacts? How can
economics be used to manage leisure and tourism?
Examples from Brazil, China, India and Japan, as well as
Europe, North America and Australia.

3602 Economics of sport: an international perspective
R. Sandy, P.J. Sloane and M.S. Rosentraub   Palgrave Macmillan,
2004, 368pp. £32.99. ISBN 9780333792728.
Applies the theories and techniques of economic analysis to
sport and topics related to the business of sport. Has an
international perspective, primarily the US, Canada, Europe
and Australia and contains case studies.

3603 Economics of sport and recreation
C. Gratton and P. Taylor   2nd edn, Spon Press, 2000, 244pp. £27.99.
ISBN 0419189602.
Analysis of sport's contribution to the global economy
covering sports goods industry, the economics of sports
sponsorship, the economics of major sports events, the
economics of professional team sports and the economic
relationship between sport and broadcasting.

Economics of sports broadcasting
C. Gratton and H.A. Solberg   See entry no. 3718

**3604 Entertainment industry economics: a guide for
financial analysis**
H.L. Vogel   6th edn, Cambridge University Press, 2004, 634pp. £30.
ISBN 0521836123.
Examines the business economics of the major
entertainment enterprises: movies, television and cable
programming, music, broadcasting, casino-wagering and
gambling, sports, publishing, performing arts, theme parks
and toys, mainly from an American viewpoint.

3605 European television industries
P. Iosifidis, J. Steemers and M. Wheeler   BFI, 2005, 186pp. £14.99.
ISBN 1844570592.
Reviews how European broadcasters are facing up to the
challenges of deregulation and the digital revolution.

3606 How to survive and succeed in the music industry
T. Saccone   Emerald, 2003, 143pp. £10.99. ISBN 1903909252.
Introduces how the music industry operates within the overall
business environment.

3607 Leisure industries
K. Roberts   Palgrave Macmillan, 2004, 288pp. £17.99. ISBN
140390412X.
A sociological approach to the entire field of leisure from the
point of view of leisure providers. Explores the distinctive
character and qualities of the main types of leisure, from the
'big three' of tourism, the media and hospitality, to activities
such as shopping, sport, gambling and 'events'. Contents
are: Introduction; Voluntary associations; The public sector;
Tourism; Sport: origins and development; Sport: commercial
inroads; Events; The media and popular culture; The media:
recent developments; Hospitality; Gambling; The arts;
Leisure policies.

**3608 Music – the business: the essential guide to the
law and the deals**
A. Harrison   3rd edn, Virgin Books, 2005, 304pp. £22.50. ISBN
1852272597.
UK-specific guide to contract law as applied to the music
industry.

3609 Music genres and corporate cultures
K. Negus   Routledge, 1999, 209pp. £17.09. ISBN 0415174007.
Explores the seemingly haphazard workings of the music
industry, tracing the uneasy relationship between economics
and culture; 'entertainment corporations' and the artists they
sign. Examines the contrasting strategies of major labels
such as Sony and Polygram in managing different genres,
artists and staff. Based on over 70 interviews with music
industry personnel in Britain and the USA.

3610 People's game? Football, finance and society
S. Morrow   Palgrave Macmillan, 2003, 244pp. £23.38. ISBN
033394612X.
An examination of the changing face of football, looking at
issues such as the role of the stock exchange, the viability of
the stakeholder approach and the 'new economics' of
football.

3611 Recording industry
G.P. Hull   2nd edn, Routledge, 2004, 336pp. £24.95. ISBN
0415968038.
Brief but comprehensive overview of how records are made,
marketed and sold.

Sport in the city: the role of sport in economic and social regeneration
C. Gratton and I. Henry See entry no. 4845

3612 Sports Inc: 100 years of sports business
P. Schaaf Prometheus Books, 2004, 394pp. £18.99. ISBN 159102112X.
Traces the global evolution of sports entertainment, dissects current trends and forecasts the likely evolution of sports as a major international enterprise.

3613 Synthetic worlds: the business and culture of online games
E. Castronova University of Chicago Press, 2005, 332pp. £18.50. ISBN 0226096262.
Comprehensive look at the online game industry, exploring its implications for business and culture.

Official & quasi-official bodies

3614 Great Britain. Department for Culture, Media & Sport
www.culture.gov.uk
UK government department championing the tourism, creative and leisure industries

Associations & societies

3615 Autocycle Union
www.acu.org.uk
Governing body of motorcycle sport throughout Britain. It is recognized by the Federation Internationale de Motorcyclisme (FIM) of which the ACU was a founder member in 1904.

3616 British Association of Leisure Parks, Piers & Attractions Limited
www.balppa.org/
Founded in 1936, represents the interests of owners, managers, suppliers and developers in the UK's commercial leisure parks, piers, zoos and static attractions sector.

3617 Institute of Leisure & Amenity Management
www.ilam.co.uk
Professional body for the leisure industry, representing the interests of leisure managers across all sectors and specialisms of leisure.

Discovering print & electronic resources

3618 Information sources in music
L. Foreman, ed. K.G. Saur, 2003, 444pp. ISBN 359824441X.
Includes chapters on music publishing and publishers and new music: its publication and dissemination.

Directories & encyclopedias

Encyclopedia of international sports studies
R. Bartlett, C. Gratton and C. Rolf, eds See entry no. 4638

3619 Music management bible
Music Managers Forum Sanctuary Publishing, 2003, 352pp. £14.99. ISBN 1844920259.
A guide to professional music management, with sections explaining the workings of a management contract, contract length, fees, trial periods, etc.

3620 SGB UK: Sporting Goods Business
Datateam Publishing Ltd, annual.
Detailed guide to the entire UK sports industry providing information on UK buying groups and multiples, manufacturers and distributors, brand names and their suppliers, equipment, wholesalers, independent sales agents, trade and sports associations, governing bodies and exhibition organizers.

3621 Showman's directory
Lance Publications, annual.
www.showmans-directory.co.uk
Contact information for organizers of large and small UK events, with a listing of the major events in the year ahead.

3622 Sporting goods industry: history, practices and products
R.A. Lipsey McFarland & Company, 2006, 169pp. £20.95. ISBN 0786427183.
Covers every major aspect of the sporting goods industry: the development of the industry; the industry's structure and size; manufacturers' products and market shares; channels of distribution; sports medicine and product liability; sports marketing, including licensing, endorsement and sponsorship; the use of traditional media and market research; sales trends and profitability; and e-commerce. Also provides directories of sporting goods vendors, retailers and multi-sport media and trade associations.

3623 The White Book
Ocean Media Group, annual. £90.
www.whitebook.co.uk
An essential reference tool for anyone involved in event production. The annual directory provides contacts to providers of services, equipment and entertainment used throughout the industry.

3624 World Radio TV Handbook
N. Hardyman, ed. 60th edn, WRTH Publications, 2005, annual, 704pp. £22.50. ISBN 0953586480.
www.wrth.com
A comprehensive guide to broadcasting around the globe.

Handbooks & manuals

The commercialisation of sport
T. Slack, ed. See entry no. 4916

Keeping up to date

3625 Access All Areas
Ocean Media Group, 10 p.a.
www.access-aa.co.uk/
Leading trade magazine for the events sector covering all the key events in the British calendar.

Engineering, Manufacturing, Metalworking & Woodworking

domestic appliance manufacturers • engineering industries • manufacturing • metalworking • steel industry • toolmaking • woodworking

Introductions to the subject

3626 The global restructuring of the steel industry: innovations, institutions and industrial change
A.P. D'Costa   Routledge, 1999, 248pp. £75. ISBN 0415148278.
Draws upon case studies of the steel industry in the US, Japan, South Korea, Brazil and India to explain how and why the steel industry has shifted from advanced capitalist countries to late-industrializing countries.

3627 The industrial revolutions: the metal fabrication and engineering industries
S. Pollard   Blackwell Publishing, 1994, 440pp. ISBN 0631181210.
Describes innovations in the manufacture of simple tools and screws and of more complex articles such as watches and clocks and examines the rise of the early stages of mass production engineering and the development of true mass-production of metal goods.

3628 The Posco strategy: a blueprint for world steel's future
W.T. Hogan   Lexington Books, 2001, 128pp. £52. ISBN 0739103016.
Charts the rise of South Korea's Pohang Iron and Steel Company and the impact it has had on this small country. A case study in how a non-industrialized economy can be so dramatically modernized by the development of a single industry.

3629 The rise and transformation of the UK domestic appliances industry
S. Cam, P. Fairbrother and T. Nichols   Cardiff University School of Social Sciences, 2003, 85pp. ISBN 1904815022.
www.cardiff.ac.uk/socsi/resources/wrkgpaper42.pdf
Useful overview of the changing fortunes of the British domestic-appliance manufacturing industry.

3630 Statistics in industry
R. Khattree and C.R. Rao, eds   Elsevier, 2003, 1187pp. £116.50. ISBN 0444506144.
Serves as a reference for researchers in industrial statistics/industrial engineering and a source of information for practising statisticians/industrial engineers. Covers industrial process monitoring, industrial experimentation, industrial modelling and data analysis.

Official & quasi-official bodies

3631 Com-met 2005
www.com-met2005.org.uk/
Launched in 2000, this partnership between the DTI and UK production machinery and tooling companies aims to tackle the dominance of German, American and French companies in the marketplace.

3632 Community Research & Development Information Service [EUR]
http://cordis.europa.eu/en/home.html
Information supporting European research and development (R&D) and innovation activities.

3633 EUREKA
www.eureka.be/home.do
Created as an intergovernmental initiative in 1985. Aims to enhance European competitiveness through support to businesses, research centres and universities who carry out pan-European projects to develop innovative products, processes and services.

3634 Manufacturing Advisory Service
www.mas.dti.gov.uk/
Launched in 2002 to help UK manufacturers share knowledge, improve productivity and achieve success in an increasingly competitive global economy.

Associations & societies

3635 Association for Manufacturing Excellence – UK
www.mynott.com/AME-UK/
UK Chapter of the USA-based AME.

3636 British Engineering Manufacturers' Association
www.bema.co.uk/
Founded in 1936, the Association fosters cooperation in areas of mutual concern among British engineering and manufacturing companies.

3637 British Woodworking Federation
www.bwf.org.uk/
Leading representative body for the UK woodworking industry and builders' joinery and represents leading manufacturers, distributors and installers of doors, windows, conservatories, staircases, architectural joinery, timber-frame buildings and engineered timber components.

3638 Confederation of British Metalforming
www.britishmetalforming.com/
Leading trade association for UK manufacturers of fasteners, forgings and pressings, with associate members, including suppliers of materials, equipment, consumables and services, universities (both in the UK and overseas) and research bodies.

Engineering Construction Industry Association
See entry no. 3549

3639 Engineering Employers Federation
www.eef.org.uk/UK/
Trade body representing 6000 UK manufacturing, engineering and technology-based businesses.

3640 Engineering Industries Association
www.eia.co.uk/
Promotes the engineering industry in the UK, Europe and global markets.

3641 European Committee of Domestic Equipment Manufacturers
www.ceced.org/
Pan-European association covering 24 national associations representing 22 countries.

3642 Institute of Sheet Metal Engineering
www.isme.org.uk/
A learned body with individual membership open to those employed in the sheet-metal and associated industries.

3643 Institution of Engineering & Technology
www.theiet.org/
Formed in spring 2006 by the coming together of the Institution of Electrical Engineers (IEE) and the Institution of Incorporated Engineers (IIE).

3644 Manufacturing Foundation
www.manufacturingfoundation.org.uk/
Researches into manufacturing issues and provides policy advice to national and regional government. Focused on the West Midlands of the UK.

3645 Metalforming Machinery Makers' Association
www.mmma.org.uk
Promotes the interests of companies involved in the manufacture and sale of metalforming machinery and ancillary products in the UK.

3646 UK Spring Manufacturers Association
www.uksma.org.uk/ [19/08/2006]
Provides a directory of manufacturers of spring components.

3647 UK Woodchain
www.ukwoodchain.ltd.uk/
A consortium of UK trade and professional bodies that is the standard-setting body for wood-using industry occupations.

3648 Woodworking Machinery Suppliers Association
www.wmsa.org.uk/
Represents most significant suppliers to the UK market, with around 90 companies in membership.

Directories & encyclopedias

3649 Aluminium Suppliers Directory
2006. €16.
www.alu-verlag.de/lieferverzeichnis/?language=GB
More than 5000 source references, encompassing about 800 companies in the aluminium producing and processing industry, the supply industry, metal trading and a wide variety of service industry providers.

3650 GMTA
www.gtma.co.uk
Source of suppliers in toolmaking (moulds & dies and press tools), metrology, precision machining, tooling technologies and rapid product development.

Keeping up to date

3651 The Engineering Workplace
www.engineering.co.uk/

Electronic centre of trade for UK engineering.

3652 Metal Bulletin
www.metalbulletin.com/
Comprehensive markets information and prices for the global metals and steel industries.

Environmental Industry

environmental management • environmental monitoring equipment • geoenvironmental engineering • landscape industries • waste management

Introductions to the subject

3653 Living our values
Guardian Unlimited   Guardian News & Media, 2006, annual. Free.
www.guardian.co.uk/values/socialaudit/
Fourth in an annual series whereby the social, ethical and environmental impact of the company is independently audited. Valuable in demonstrating what is involved in such an undertaking.

3654 The reporter's environmental handbook [USA]
B.M. West, M.J. Lewis and M.R. Greenberg   3rd edn, Rutgers University Press, 2003, 304pp. $24. ISBN 0813532876.
Written by American academics as a 'how-to' guide for journalists, this is a useful introduction to the complexities of the interaction between industry and the environment.

Laws, standards, codes

3655 The ISO 14000 Toolkit
$199.
www.14000-toolkit.com [FEE-BASED]
Implementation guide for the international standard on environmental management.

Associations & societies

3656 Association of Geotechnical & Geoenvironmental Specialists
www.ags.org.uk/
Non-profit trade association established to improve the profile and quality of geotechnical and geoenvironmental engineering. Membership comprises UK organizations and individuals having a common interest in the business of site investigation, geotechnics, geoenvironmental engineering, engineering geology, geochemistry, hydrogeology and other related disciplines.

3657 British Association of Landscape Industries
www.bali.co.uk
Established in 1972 to provide a voice for landscapers and raise standards throughout the industry.

3658 British Urban Regeneration Association
www.bura.org.uk
Formed in 1990 to provide a forum for the exchange of ideas, experience and information for the regeneration sector.

3659 Council of Gas Detection & Environmental Monitoring
www.cogdem.org.uk/
Represents over 40 companies from around the world involved in CO and industrial gas detection, analysis and portable environmental monitoring.

3660 Environmental Industries Commission
www.eic-uk.co.uk/
Launched in 1995. Now has over 290 member companies providing environmental technology equipment and services.

3661 Institute of Environmental Management & Assessment
www.iema.net/
UK non-profit organization dedicated to the professional development of individuals and organizations involved in environmental management auditing and assessment.

3662 UKSpill
www.ukspill.org/
Replaces BOSCA as the UK national organization representing the commercial and related interests of the UK oil spill industry.

Portal & task environments

3663 MineralsUK
www.bgs.ac.uk/mineralsUK/home.html
A wealth of information on mineral resources, mineral planning, policy and legislation, sustainable development, statistics and exploration provided by the British Geological Survey's Centre for Sustainable Mineral Development.

Directories & encyclopedias

3664 EIC guide to the UK environmental industry
McMillan Scott, 2005. £90.
www.eic-guide.co.uk/
An invaluable reference tool for sourcing environmental equipment and services, with high- quality editorial. Endorsed as the industry yearbook by the DEFRA/DTI Joint Environmental Markets Unit.

3665 EIC Land Remediation Yearbook
www.eic-yearbook.co.uk/
An essential reference source on land remediation and an invaluable tool for information on suppliers of land remediation services.

3666 Waste management yearbook
McMillan Scott, 2006, annual. £25.
Alphabetical and classified listings of companies offering products and services to the waste industry.

Extraction Industries
coal industry • gas industry • mineral extraction • mining • oil industry • petroleum production • quarrying

Introductions to the subject

3667 Age of oil: the mythology, history and future of the world's most controversial resource
L. Maugeri   Praeger, 2006, 340pp. £28.99. ISBN 0275990087.
Describes the colourful history of the industry and explains the fundamentals of oil production.

3668 Big coal: the dirty secret behind America's energy future
J. Goodell   Houghton Mifflin, 2006. $25.95. ISBN 9780618319404.
The result of three year's journalistic research, this book examines the impact that mining and using coal has had on America and China.

3669 The changing world of oil: an analysis of corporate change and adaptation
J. Davis   Ashgate, 2006, 218pp. £50. ISBN 0754641783.
Aims to help extend readers' understanding of the oil industry beyond the more conventional studies of the industry.

3670 Coal: a human history
B. Freese   Perseus, 2003, 320pp. $20. ISBN 9780738204000.
Social, industrial,and environmental history of the impact of coal from 12th-century England to the world at the start of the 21st century

3671 Color of oil: the history, the money and the politics of the world's biggest business
M. Economides and R. Oligney   Round Oak Publishing, 2000, 201pp. £18.95. ISBN 0967724805.
An in-depth look at the industry, from the wildcatters of the 1930s to the giant corporations of today.

3672 Fundamentals of natural gas: an international perspective
V. Chandra   Pennwell Books, 2006, 250pp. £37.12. ISBN 1593700881.
Detailed discussion of the entire natural gas value chain, including emerging sectors such as Liquefied Natural Gas (LNG), Gas-To-Liquid (GTL) and Coal Bed Methane (CBM), with coverage of commercialization and marketing issues and current and emerging international players.

3673 The future of global oil production: facts, figures, trends and projections, by region
R.D. Blanchard   McFarland, 2005, 311pp. £20.95. ISBN 0786423579.
Examines US capacity, along with the production futures of each of the major oil-producing regions: Western Europe, Mexico and Canada, South and Central America, Asia, the Middle East, the former Soviet Union and Africa. Heavily illustrated with charts and tables.

3674 The global oil market: risks and uncertainties
A.H. Cordesman and K.R. Al-Rodhan   Center for Strategic &
International Studies, 2006, 176pp. ISBN 089206479X.
A study of the global oil market illustrated by graphs, tables
and a risk assessment for producers and consumers.

3675 The history of the British coal industry
Commissioned by the then National Coal Board in 1975, this
is the definitive history of the industry.
■ **1. Before 1700: towards the age of coal** J. Hatcher   OUP,
  1993. £79. ISBN 9780198282822. Winner of the Wadsworth Prize for
  Business History.
■ **2. 1700–1830: the industrial revolution M.W. Flinn and D.**
  Stoker   Clarendon Press, 1984, 491pp. ISBN 9780198282839.
■ **3. 1830–1913: Victorian pre-eminence R. Church, A. Hall**
  and J. Kanefsky   Clarendon Press, 1986, 831pp. £100. ISBN
  9780198282842.
■ **4. 1914–1946: the political economy of decline B. Supple**
  Clarendon Press, 1987, 752pp. £100. ISBN 9780198282945. Written by the
  Professor of Economic History at Cambridge University.

3676 Natural gas and geopolitics: from 1970 to 2040
D.G. Victor, A.M. Jaffe and M.H. Hayes, eds   Cambridge University
Press, 2006, 534pp. £60. ISBN 0521865034.
Investigates the interplay between economic and political
factors in the development of natural gas resources and how
gas is and will be fed to consuming nations.

3677 Oil: anatomy of an industry
M. Yeomans   New Press, 2006, 272pp. £8.99. ISBN 159558028X.
Contains a brief history of petrol and analysis of the
American consumer's love affair with the car, along with a
political anatomy of the global oil industry, including its
troubled relationship with oil-rich, democracy-poor countries.

3678 The oil market in the 1990s: challenges for the
new era: essays in honor of John K. Evans
R.G. Reed, ed.   Westview Press, 1989, 214pp. ISBN 0813308194.
Festschrift by friends and admirers of John K. Evans (Royal
Dutch Shell and Hawaiian Independent Refinery). Essays
examine the impact of current problems on the structure
and place of the oil industry as it faces the 21st century.

3679 Oil titans: national oil companies in the Middle
East
V. Marcel and J.V. Mitchell   Brookings Institution, 2005, 322pp.
£11.99. ISBN 0815754736.
Tells the stories of Saudi Aramco, Kuwait Petroleum Corp.,
the National Iranian Oil Co., Sonatrach of Algeria and the
Abu Dhabi National Oil Co. and explains the complex bond
between each state and its oil company.

3680 The politics of the global oil industry: an
introduction
T. Falola and A. Genova   Praeger, 2005, 262pp. £25.99. ISBN
0275984001.
Introduces the oil industry and the countries, companies and
people who shape it, with particular reference to seven major
oil exporters – Iraq, Mexico, Nigeria, Norway, Russia, Saudi
Arabia and Venezuela.

3681 Russian oil economy
J.I. Considine and W.A. Kerr   Edward Elgar, 2002, 360pp. £79. ISBN
1840647582.
A detailed history of the development of the Russian oil

economy, with consideration of its future role and
significance in the global energy market of the 21st century.

3682 Technical progress and profits: process
improvements in petroleum refining
J. Enos   Oxford University Press, 2002, 318pp. £39.50. ISBN
0197300235.
Concentrates on technical changes, using as its basis the
main petroleum refining process fluid catalytic cracking, and
relates them to the long-term pattern of costs and profits
displayed within the industry.

Dictionaries, thesauri, classifications

3683 A dictionary for the oil and gas industry
Petroleum Extension Service   PETEX, 2005, 324pp. $55. ISBN
0886982138.
Contains over 11,000 definitions of terms used in petroleum
geology, exploration, drilling, production, pipelining,
processing, refining, accounting and marketing. Also
included are the addresses and phone numbers of industry
associations and government agencies, a list of common
abbreviations, SI units and a table of metric equivalents.

Official & quasi-official bodies

3684 Coal Authority
www.coal.gov.uk/
Government agency tasked with facilitating the exploitation of
the UK's coal resources, while providing information and
addressing liabilities for former coal extraction sites.

Associations & societies

Society of Maritime Industries
See entry no. 3832

Portal & task environments

MineralsUK
See entry no. 3663

3685 UK Oil Portal
Great Britain. Department of Trade & Industry
www.og.dti.gov.uk/portal.htm
The work of Oil and Gas Directorate includes the promotion
and regulation of the exploration and development of UK oil
and gas resources; consideration of environmental issues
and the needs of other land and sea users; the promotion of
open and competitive markets and the collection, analysis
and dissemination of data.

Directories & encyclopedias

3686 Directory of mines and quarries
British Geological Survey, 2005. £40. ISBN 0852724454.
Comprehensive information on the 2 300 active mines and
quarries in Britain, including those in Northern Ireland, the
Isle of Man and the Channel Islands. Contains a commentary

on the UK minerals industry, accompanied by statistical information.

3687 International guide to the coalfields
Tradelink Publications Ltd, 2006, 200pp. £130. ISBN 0952883589.
First published in 1948. Regarded as the 'Bible of the Industry'.

3688 International mining directory
D. Nelson, ed.   2004, 800pp. £120. ISBN 0749441658.
For over 25 years has been listing all the mining and mining equipment companies worldwide.

3689 International petroleum encyclopedia
Culinary & Hospitality Industry Publications Services, 2005, 250pp. $194.
Information on oilfields, pipelines, refineries, tanker terminals and other elements of the extraction and delivery chain.

Major chemical and petrochemical companies of the world
S. James, H. Porter and M. Scott, eds   See entry no. 3545

3690 The MCM global oil and gas directory
103rd edn, MCM Directories, 2005, annual, 448pp. ISBN 0954707508.
Provides information on the activities and financial performance of 270 major industry players along with 750 specialist oil and gas service companies and equipment suppliers. Also offers a who's who of 4000 key personnel from the international oil and gas industry, cross-referenced to the producers, service companies and associations.

3691 Pegasus Oil gas and energy directory
www.uk-oil-gas.co.uk/
Searchable directory of information on around 3000 companies within the oil and gas sectors.

3692 UK quarries and mines
McMillan Scott, 2005. £25.
Dedicated to those involved in both quarries and mines and those organizations who trade within this industry.

3693 World oil and gas review
D. Yergin; Eni   Eni, 2006, annual, 107pp. with CD ROM.
www.eni.it/wogr_2006/index.html
Produced by Eni, an Italian based oil and gas production company, as part of their 'What is Energy' information service.

Keeping up to date

ICIS
See entry no. 3546

3694 Minerals Engineering International
www.min-eng.com/index.html
'The largest source of information on mineral processing & extractive metallurgy on the net.'

3695 MQ World: A Mine of Information
www.mqworld.com [19/08/2006]

Access to information on over 10,000 operations worldwide, from exploration through to production.

3696 WorldOil.com: the oilfield information service
www.worldoil.com
Built around the content of the monthly 90-year-old *World Oil* magazine, the site offers access to articles, suppliers directory and research and statistics.

Food, Beverages & Tobacco Industries

brewing • coffee • food processing • media businesses • soft drinks • tea • tobacco industry • wines & spirits

Introductions to the subject

3697 La diva nicotina: the story of how tobacco seduced the world
I. Gately   new edn, Scribner, 2002, 416pp. £7.99. ISBN 9780743208130.
Well received history of the impact that the take-up of tobacco has had on the population of the world. Written by a smoker.

3698 Tea: addiction, exploitation and empire
R. Moxham   Constable & Robinson, 2004, 242pp. £7.99. ISBN 1841199176.
A former tea planter explains how, over four centuries of British and world history, tea was traded, grown, manufactured and marketed to satisfy the British thirst for fine tea and large profits.

3699 Uncommon grounds: the history of coffee and how it transformed the world
M. Pendergrast   new edn, Texere Publishing, 2001, 320pp. £18.99. ISBN 9781587990885.
Comprehensive and readable account of the business and social history of the market in coffee.

3700 The US brewing industry: data and economic analysis
V.J. Tremblay and C.H. Tremblay   MIT Press, 2005, 392pp. £25.95. ISBN 0262201518.
Analysis of the American brewing industry, covering its history and the laws and regulations that govern it as well as practical aspects of the business and econometric analyses of production and demand.

Official & quasi-official bodies

3701 Food Standards Agency
www.food.gov.uk
UK independent government department set up by an Act of Parliament in 2000 to protect the public's health and consumer interests in relation to food.

3702 United States. Food & Drug Administration
www.fda.gov
An agency of the US Department of Health and Human Services. Website details the work of the Agency, with links

to other organizations working in each of the specialist areas that it covers.

Associations & societies

3703   British Soft Drinks Association
www.britishsoftdrinks.com
Represents UK producers of soft drinks, including carbonated drinks, still and dilutable drinks, fruit juices and bottled waters. Membership covers around 90% of the manufacturers, factors and franchisors of Britain's soft drinks.

3704   Confederation of Food & Drink Industries of the European Union
www.ciaa.be/pages_en/homepage.asp
European body representing the food and drinks industries.

3705   Food & Drink Federation
www.fdf.org.uk
Represents the UK food and drink manufacturing industry.

igd
See entry no. 3776

3706   Wine & Spirit Trades Association
www.wsta.co.uk
Established in 1824, the 242 members represent the UK wine and spirit supply chain: producers, importers, wholesalers, bottlers, warehouse keepers, freight forwarders, brand owners, licensed retailers and consultants.

Directories & encyclopedias

3707   Major food and drink companies of the world
H. Brewin, S. James and H. Porter, eds   10th edn, Graham & Whiteside, 2007. $995. ISBN 9781860995002.
Profiles of over 9800 companies, including brand names and trademarks.

3708   Plunkett's food, beverage and tobacco industry almanac
Plunkett Research, annual. $280.
Industry analysis and research.

3709   Thomas food and beverage market place 2006
[USA]
L. Mars-Proietti   Grey House Publishing, 2005, 1000pp. £449.95. ISBN 1592370977.
www.greyhouse.com [DESCRIPTION]
3-volume buying and marketing guide for the US food and beverage industry.

3710   World drinks marketing directory
Euromonitor International, annual. £675.
www.euromonitor.com/drinksdirectory
Two-volume directory to the global drinks market. Profiles the leading drinks companies worldwide, from the major multinationals to individual country companies.

3711   World Food Marketing Directory 2005
Euromonitor International, 2005. £675. ISBN 1842643525.
www.euromonitor.com/World_Food_Marketing_Directory_2005

Two-volume directory covering all aspects of the food industry. Profiles over 1500 leading food companies worldwide, with detailed information on the top 50 food multinationals. Also included are global market share tables and key information sources to consult for further information.

Keeping up to date

3712   Food Processing Intelligence
www.fpi-international.com/index.html
Independent analyses of current trends and technological advances in the food processing industry.

3713   The Grocer
www.thegrocer.co.uk/
Launched in 1862, the weekly magazine for the UK food and drink retail sector. Readership encompasses every aspect of the industry, from retailers to growers, food processors and manufacturers.

3714   just-drinks
www.just-drinks.com
Since 1999 has been offering a global news, along with market analysis and research for both the alcoholic and soft drinks sectors.

3715   World Tobacco
www.worldtobacco.co.uk/
Based on *World Tobacco* magazine, the site contains comprehensive data and analysis on tobacco markets around the world. Includes the World Tobacco Directory: a comprehensive at-a-glance guide to the industry.

Media, Publishing & Film Industries

broadcasting • publishing

Introductions to the subject

3716   Broadcasting in the United Kingdom: a guide to information sources
B. MacDonald   2nd edn, Academi, 1994, 336pp. ISBN 0720122058.
Chronology of all the important events in the history of broadcasting in the UK since 1896. Explains the legislative and constitutional framework of British broadcasting at the date of publication, provides a guide to reference and research materials and includes a directory of archives, libraries and museums essential for research in broadcasting. Though dated, a useful introduction for researchers.

Business of culture: strategic perspectives on entertainment and media
J. Lampel, J. Shamsie and T.K. Lant, eds   See entry no. 3596

3717   Can the market deliver?: funding public service television in the digital age
T. Little and D. Helm, eds   John Libbey, 2006, 192pp. £15.71. ISBN 0861966627.
Commissioned by the BBC as a contribution to the debate

about the provision of public service television in the digital age and the BBC's public purposes and funding. The contributors include Dieter Helm of New College, Oxford, Andrew Graham, Master of Balliol College, Oxford and Gavyn Davies, former Chairman of the BBC.

3718 Economics of sports broadcasting
C. Gratton and H.A. Solberg   Routledge, 2006, 240pp. £80. ISBN 0415357799.
Covers an overview of historical and modern sports broadcasting; an introduction to the key agents in sports broadcasting, from the viewers to the sponsors; the regulations governing televised sport; questions of ownership, trade and commodity in sport; and demand, value and the future of sports broadcasting.

Entertainment industry economics: a guide for financial analysis
H.L. Vogel   See entry no. 3604

European television industries
P. Iosifidis, J. Steemers and M. Wheeler   See entry no. 3605

3719 History of independent television in Britain
Palgrave Macmillan.
Six-volume series.
- **1. Origin and foundation 1946–62** B. Sendall   Palgrave Macmillan, 1982, 440pp. £76.50. ISBN 0333309413.
- **2. Expansion and change 1958–68** Palgrave Macmillan, 1983, 446pp. £70. ISBN 0333309421.
- **3. Politics and control 1968–80** J. Potter   Palgrave Macmillan, 1989, 400pp. £75. ISBN 0333330196.
- **4. The companies and their programmes** Palgrave Macmillan, 1990, 528pp. £75. ISBN 0333455436.
- **5. ITV and IBA 1981–82 – the old relationship changes** P. Bonner and L. Aston   Palgrave Macmillan, 1998, 560pp. £65. ISBN 0333647734.
- **6. New developments in independent television 1981–92 – Channel 4, TV-am, cable and satellite** Palgrave Macmillan, 2002, 480pp. £65. ISBN 0333647742.

3720 Uncertain vision: Birt, Dyke and the reinvention of the BBC
G. Born   Secker & Warburg, 2004, 352pp. £17.99. ISBN 0436205629.
Concentrates on the Corporation during the later 1990s, the last years of the regime of the former director-general John Birt. Also addresses the new challenges of satellite and digital broadcasting.

Official & quasi-official bodies

Great Britain. Department for Culture, Media & Sport
See entry no. 3614

Directories & encyclopedias

World Radio TV Handbook
N. Hardyman, ed.   See entry no. 3624

Handbooks & manuals

Assessing media education: a resource handbook for educators and administrators
W.G. Christ, ed.   See entry no. 5077

3721 Keyguide to information sources in media ethics
B. MacDonald and M. Petheram, eds   Mansell, 1998, 384pp. £95. ISBN 0720121280.
Divided into three parts: an overview of the literature, covering the mass media in general, telecommunications, broadcasting in all its forms, cinema and video, the press, advertising, publishing and ethical issues, such as government policy and influence, legislation, codes of practice, censorship and reportage issues; an annotated bibliography; and an international directory of organizations. Detailed index.

Keeping up to date

3722 Broadcast
EMAP, weekly.
www.broadcastnow.co.uk
News and analysis from the UK broadcasting industry, supported by special reports available as premium content on the associated website.

3723 Publishers Weekly
Reed, weekly. $240.
www.publishersweekly.info
Published in America but with an international brief. Covers every aspect of book publishing in all formats. Supported by interactive website with premium content available to subscribers.

Paper & Packaging Industries

canning • packaging industry • plastic packaging • pulp & paper industries

Dictionaries, thesauri, classifications

3724 Dictionary of the pulp and paper industry
M. Svaton   Elsevier, 1992, 524pp. ISBN 0444987894.
An English, German, French, Spanish and Russian vocabulary of terms relating to pulping and papermaking technologies, cellulose and paper chemistry, properties of pulp and paper mills, pulpwood and other raw materials for pulping and operations for converting paper and board.

Associations & societies

3725 British Plastics Federation
www.bpf.co.uk
Leading trade association of the UK plastics industry. Website has a sub-sector market group on packaging, with information on training, awards, industry news, environmental issues, business support network and an ask the expert service.

3726 Can Makers
www.canmakers.co.uk/
Trade body representing the UK manufacturers of beer and carbonated soft drink cans. Website has information on the history of can-making, consumer information, drinks market information, news and links to further sources

3727 Flexible Packaging Association
www.flexpack.org/
Trade organization for flexible packaging converters and suppliers. Website has industry information, news, buyers' guide, environmental issues, achievement awards and a calendar of events.

3728 Metal Packaging Manufacturers Association
www.mpma.org.uk/
Represents the interests of companies involved in the production of light metal containers, closures and components. Website has information on statistics, news, awards, design, a member directory and a listing of useful links.

3729 Packaging & Industrial Films Association
www.pifa.co.uk/
Industry news, a buyers' guide, market information and a calendar of events.

3730 Packaging Federation
www.packagingfedn.co.uk/
Representative body of the UK packaging manufacturing industry. Members include major manufacturers from all sectors of the industry, including paper and board, plastics, metals and glass. The website has industry news, legislation, events, publications and a company directory.

Directories & encyclopedias

3731 Converter directory
Faversham House Group, 1976–, annual. ISSN 03092143.
A guide to the paper, board, film and foil converting industry with details of manufacturers and suppliers of products and equipment used in the industry.

3732 Folding carton industry manual and directory
Bruton Business Publications, 1980–, annual.
Information on industry associations, educational institutes and product and equipment suppliers. Also contains technical information such as factsheets of machine and carton board specifications.

3733 Institute of Packaging directory and Packaging Review buyers guide
Institute of Packaging. ISSN 02652773
Directory of company contacts of packaging manufacturers in the UK. Also contains research reports on the market, new technology information, new design information and case studies.
Latest edition 2003. The Institute of Packaging is now a division of IOM3 The Institute of Materials, Minerals and Mining.

3734 Packaging industry directory
CMP Information Ltd. ISSN 02699834
Source guide to products, services, trade names and brands for the packaging industry in the UK, with a who's who of the sector.

3735 Packaging machinery directory
Packaging Machinery Manufacturers Institute.
Guide to the global packaging industry, including technology and equipment available from the industry.

3736 Processing and packaging machinery directory
Processing & Packaging Machinery Association, 1994–, annual. ISSN 13560212.
Sourcebook for over 1000 processing and packaging machinery suppliers and manufacturers worldwide.

3737 Who's who in packaging
Turret RAI, 1999–, annual. ISSN 1468327X.
A listing of companies serving the packaging industry, with details of their specific area of service or specialism.

Keeping up to date

3738 Food Packaging Bulletin
Research Information, 1992–, monthly. ISSN 13550477.
Newsletter for the glass, plastic and metal packaging industry, offering information on regulations, legislation and recycling.

3739 Packaging Magazine
1998–, fortnightly. ISSN 14614200.
www.packagingmagazine.co.uk
Industry news, case studies, legislation and the latest manufacturing techniques.

3740 Packaging News
1954–, monthly. ISSN 00309133.
www.packagingnews.co.uk/
UK industry news, events, new technology, case studies and a supplier directory.

3741 Packaging Today
2004–, monthly. ISSN 17477468.
www.packagingtoday.co.uk/
Industry news, case studies, product reviews, company directory and exhibitions.

3742 Pira International Ltd
www.pira.co.uk/
Commercial consultancy business that specializes in the packaging, paper, printing and publishing industries. Website has industry news, publications to buy, contacts, information centre, training and testing service information.

3743 Plastics in Packaging
Sayers Publishing Group, 2001–, monthly. ISSN 14765241.
www.plasticsinpackaging.com/
Trade magazine covering plastics, resins and packaging machinery and products. Also has country profiles and product news. .

Pharmaceutical, Healthcare & Biotechnology Industries

biotechnology • drugs industry • healthcare industry

Introductions to the subject

3744 The biotech industry: a global, economic and financing overview
B. Bergeron and P. Chan John Wiley, 2004, 362pp. £55. ISBN 0471465615.
Written by a renowned business columnist and an entrepreneurial scientist in the biotech area. A thorough look at the current state of the biotechnology industry, including where major research is being conducted, where it's being applied and where money and intellectual capital are flowing.

3745 The business of healthcare innovation
L.R. Burns, ed. Cambridge University Press, 2005, 398pp. £24.99. ISBN 0521547687.
An analysis of business trends in the manufacturing segment of the health care industry, with a detailed overview of the pharmaceutical, biotechnology, genomics/proteomics, medical device and information technology sectors.

3746 Drug discovery: from bedside to Wall Street
T. Bartfai and G.V. Lees Elsevier Academic Press, 2006, 301pp. £19.99. ISBN 0123695333.
Tells the story of drug development by using real stories from inside the process.

3747 The economics of biotechnology
M. McKelvey and L. Orsenigo, eds Edward Elgar Publishing Ltd, 2005, 800pp. £110. ISBN 1843767767.
Covers the economics and business side of the social scientific debate about the economics of 'modern biotechnology' or 'the biotechnology industry'.

3748 From physick to pharmacology: five hundred years of British drug retailing
L. Hill Curth Ashgate, 2006, 180pp. ISBN 075463597X.
Examines the growth in the retailing of medicinal drugs from the 16th to the 21st centuries.

3749 Innovation and entrepreneurship in biotechnology, an international perspective: concepts, theories and cases
D. Hine and J. Kapeleris Edward Elgar, 2006, 259pp. ISBN 1843765845.
Explores both the theoretical and practical aspects of entrepreneurship in the biotechnology industry, focusing on the innovation processes underpinning success for new biotechnology firms (NBFs).

3750 Innovation in pharmaceutical biotechnology: comparing national systems at the sectoral level
Organisation for Economic Co-operation & Development OECD, 2006, 187pp. £31. ISBN 9264014039.
Looks at the innovation system in pharmaceutical biotechnology in eight OECD countries. This report summarizes the results of studies, providing a comparative analysis of participating countries' performance in science and innovation in biopharmaceuticals. It highlights specific characteristics of the national biopharmaceutical innovation systems.

3751 Key issues in the pharmaceutical industry
A. McIntyre John Wiley, 1999, 224pp. £100. ISBN 0471965189.
Explains how and why the modern pharmaceutical industry evolved and explores important topics such as drug promotion and regulation.

Shaping the industrial century: the remarkable story of the evolution of the modern chemical and pharmaceutical industries
A.D. Chandler See entry no. 3540

Official & quasi-official bodies

United States. Food & Drug Administration
See entry no. 3702

Directories & encyclopedias

3752 Chemist and druggist directory
2004/5 edn, CMP Information. £90. ISBN 0863825613 ISSN 02625881.
www.cmpdata.co.uk/chemist/
Published for over 135 years, provides information on the entire pharmaceutical and healthcare industries.

3753 Major pharmaceutical and biotechnology companies of the world
S. Hoernig, L. Romiti and S. Ward, eds 9th edn, Graham & Whiteside, 2007. $995. ISBN 9781860995026.
Profiles include brand names and trademark information.

Professions, Consulting & Service Industries

professions • security companies • service industries

Introductions to the subject

3754 The formation of professions: knowledge, state and strategy
R. Torstendahl and M. Burrage, eds Sage Publications, 1990, 215pp. ISBN 0803982518.
Concentrates on the formation of the professions and the relationship of this to knowledge and the state. A companion volume to *Professions in theory and history: rethinking the study of the professions.*

3755 Managing services
A. Nankervis Cambridge University Press, 2005, 362pp. £24.99. ISBN 0521606519.
Explores the strategic management of services through an Integrated Services Management Model which links operational, marketing, financial and human resource management functions within a broad and diverse collection of international, regional and local service contexts. Has a particular focus on the Asia-Pacific and Australasian regions.

3756 Managing the professional service firm
D. Maister   Free Press, 2003, 368pp. ISBN 0743231562.
Professional service firms differ from other business enterprises in two distinct ways: they provide highly customized services and they are highly personalized, involving the skills of individuals. This book explores issues ranging from marketing and business development to multinational strategies, human resources policies to profit improvement and strategic planning to effective leadership.

3757 Professional services firm bible
J. Baschab and J. Piot   Wiley, 2004, 576pp. ISBN 0471660485.
Comprehensive guide to running a professional services organization.

3758 Professionalism: the third logic
E. Freidson   Polity Press, 2001, 250pp. £16.99. ISBN 0745603319.
Discusses how historic and national variations in state policy, professional organization and forms of practice influence the strength of professionalism.

3759 Professions in theory and history: rethinking the study of the professions
M. Burrage and R. Torstendahl, eds   Sage Publications, 1990, 256pp. ISBN 0803982526.
Concentrates on the theory and historical development of professions. Companion volume to *The formation of professions: knowledge, state and strategy*.

3760 Service innovation: organizational responses to technological opportunities and market imperatives
J. Tidd and F.M. Hill, eds   Imperial College Press, 2003, 437pp. £48. ISBN 1860943675.
Brings together academic research and management practice on innovation in services and identifies a range of successful organizational responses to current technological opportunities and market imperatives.

3761 Service management: strategy and leadership in the service business
R. Normann   3rd edn, John Wiley, 2000, 254pp. £27.50. ISBN 0471494399.
Looks into the special characteristics of services and explains the conditions necessary for success in the management of service organizations.

3762 Services management: an integrated approach
B. Van Looy, P. Gemmel and R. Van Dierdonck, eds   2nd edn, Financial Times Prentice Hall, 2003, 529pp. £41.99. ISBN 027367353X.
Examines the nature of services and their fit with the management process. Discusses three central areas for any service manager: customers, employees and operations. Also addresses performance management and service strategy.

3763 Winning at service: lessons from service leaders
W. Schmidt, G. Adler and E. van Weering   John Wiley, 2003, 184pp. £24.95. ISBN 0470848235.
Interviews with four CEOs: Thomas Berglund of Securitas and J. Philip Sorensen of Group4Falck (the world's two largest security companies), Francis Mackay of Compass plc and Pierre Bellon of Sodexho Alliance (the world's two largest food service companies).

Retail, Luxury Goods, Consumer Goods, Textiles, Clothing & Footwear Industries

catering • clothing • consumer goods • fashion industry • footwear • furniture & furnishings industries • jewellery • luxury goods • mail order retailing • retailing • supermarkets • textile industry • watch & clock makers

Introductions to the subject

3764 The coffee-house
M. Ellis   Phoenix Press, 2005, 352pp. £8.99. ISBN 0753818981.
Traces the history of the coffee house from the first, opened in London in 1652, through the boom years of the 18th century and the decline during the 19th century to the revival of the 1950s and the arrival of retail chains in the 1990s.

3765 The emergence of modern retailing, 1750–1950
N. Alexander and G. Akehurst, eds   Frank Cass Publishers, 1998, 184pp. ISBN 0714644811.
Considers the emergence and development of modern retailing from a historical and management perspective.

3766 Mail order retailing in Britain: a business and social history
R. Coopey, S. O'Connell and D. Porter   Oxford University Press, 2005, 258pp. ISBN 0198296509.
Comprehensive history of the British mail order industry, showing how British general mail order industry firms such as Kay and Co., Empire Stores, Littlewoods and Grattan grew from a range of businesses as diverse as watch sales or football pools. Also draws parallels and contrasts with the mail order industry of the USA.

3767 A nation of shopkeepers: retailing in Britain 1550–2000
L. Ugolini   I B Tauris & Co Ltd, 2002, 288pp. ISBN 1860647081.
Reflects research on retail history and cultures of consumption.

3768 Retailing: an introduction
P. Brittain and R. Cox   Financial Times Prentice Hall, 2004, 320pp. ISBN 0273678191.
Comprehensive introduction to all aspects of retailing and the fundamental elements of retail management and a retail organization's activities.

3769 Trolley wars: the battle of the supermarkets
J. Bevan   Profile Books Ltd, 2006, 272pp. ISBN 1861976968.
Tells the business stories behind the battle for supremacy among the supermarket chains in Britain, focusing on the social changes that have accompanied and underpinned it.

3770 The world textile industry
J. Singleton   Routledge, 1997, 216pp. £80. ISBN 0415107679.
Explains how and why the locus of competitive advantage in textiles and apparel has moved from country to country, particularly in the period since 1945.

Associations & societies

3771 British Furniture Manufacturers
http://bfm.org.uk/
Has been representing the interests of the furniture industry for more than 50 years. Has a broad-based membership covering domestic, contract, office and kitchen manufacturers as well as a number of suppliers to the industry and retailers.

3772 British Jewellers Association
www.bja.org.uk/
UK trade association with over 600 member companies, representing manufacturers, bullion suppliers, casting houses, diamond and gem dealers, designer jewellers and silversmiths, equipment suppliers and wholesalers.

3773 British Retail Consortium
www.brc.org.uk/
Trade association representing the whole range of retailers, from the large multiples and department stores through to independents, selling a wide selection of products through centre-of-town, out-of-town, rural and virtual stores.

3774 British Textile Machinery Association
www.btma.org.uk/
British textile machinery and equipment manufacturers.

3775 British Watch & Clock Makers Guild
www.bwcmg.co.uk/
Supports those who are professionally engaged in any branch of horology and allied crafts.

3776 igd
www.igd.com/
Research organization supporting the food and grocery businesses.

3777 National Association of Goldsmiths
www.jewellers-online.org/
Supports members in all aspects of running a jewellery business.

Discovering print & electronic resources

3778 Inteletex.com: textile news and industry analysis
World Textile Publications Ltd.
www.inteletex.com/
Comprehensive site for the world textile industry, with news and features, events calendar and buyers' guides for new and used equipment.

Directories & encyclopedias

3779 Bar and restaurant
McMillan Scott, 2006. £25.
Essential reading for all tenants, leaseholders, free traders and anyone working in the licensed trade industry. Has a substantial directory section featuring manufacturers and suppliers and buyers' guide.

3780 The British jeweller yearbook
EMAP, annual.
www.britishjewelleryyearbook.com
A–Z company listings and commodity indexes.

3781 Furniture and furnishings directory
2004/5 edn, CMP Information, annual. £90. ISSN 17441153.
www.cmpdata.co.uk/furniture/
Covers the entire UK furniture, furnishings, carpet and floorcoverings industries, with information on over 11,000 companies, along with brands and trade names indexes.

3782 Retail trade international 2005
Euromonitor International, 2005. £5000. ISBN 1842643576.
www.euromonitor.com/Retail_Trade_International_2005
Comprehensive study of the global retailing industry. Analyses key trends and developments in 52 countries, ranging from the impact of internet shopping to the use of store and loyalty cards.

3783 World retail data and statistics 2006/2007
Euromonitor International, 2006. £375. ISBN 1842644289.
www.euromonitor.com/World_Retail_Data_and_Statistics_2006_2007
Contains an extensive range of retailing statistics such as retail sales, retail prices, retail outlets and comparative rankings across 52 countries.

Keeping up to date

3784 Basel Magazine
CRU Publishing, 1999–, monthly. ISSN 14654539.
Covers diamonds, watches, designers, luxury goods, market reports and trade show reviews.

3785 Fashion Monitor
www.fashionmonitor.co.uk/ [19/08/2006]
UK's leading provider of news, events and contacts information to the style and beauty industries.

The Grocer
See entry no. 3713

3786 How Britain shops
Verdict Research   1999–, annual.
www.verdict.co.uk
Independent analysis of the retail industry.

3787 just-style.com
www.just-style.com
Research store with instant access to over 1500 reports, books and research products from leading market information providers.

3788 Luxury Product and Service Briefing
Atlantic Publishing, 1995–, monthly.
News on the luxury goods industries, including fashion, beauty, fragrances, jewellery, publishing, travel, hotels and art.

3789 Retail Week
www.retail-week.com/
Business information for the retail industry.

Shipbuilding Industry (Civilian)

marine engineering • naval architecture • ship repairing

Introductions to the subject

3790 Industrial dislocation: the case of global shipbuilding
D. Todd   Routledge, 1991, 292pp. ISBN 0415042135.
A study of the decline and depression of shipbuilding in developed western countries and the rapid growth of this industry in the newly industrialized countries of the Far East.

3791 Rise and fall of British shipbuilding
A. Burton   Constable, 1994, 272pp. ISBN 0094729204.
An account of the successful development of the British shipbuilding industry and navy, followed by discussion of its disintegration and collapse through its failure to adapt and meet modern requirements.

Associations & societies

3792 Institute of Marine Engineering, Science & Technology
www.imarest.org/
International professional membership body and learned society for all marine professionals, bringing together marine engineers, scientists and technologists.

3793 International Marine Contractors Association
www.imca-int.com
International trade association representing offshore, marine and underwater engineering companies.

3794 Royal Institution of Naval Architects
www.rina.org.uk/
Professional institution whose members are involved at all levels in the design, construction, maintenance and operation of marine vessels and structures in over 90 countries.

3795 Shipbuilders & Shiprepairers Association
www.ssa.org.uk/
Represents UK companies engaged in building ships, converting them for other uses, repairing and maintaining them. The membership also includes suppliers, consultants, sub-contractors and academics.

Directories & encyclopedias

3796 Where to build and where to repair
53rd edn, seadirectory.com, 2006.
Comprehensive company profiles of more than 550 important shipyards and repair yards worldwide. The database include senior management, addresses, e-mails, websites, docking facilities and repair services

Keeping up to date

3797 ship-technology.com
www.ship-technology.com/
Supplies the latest news releases, detailed information on industry projects, white papers, event information and a thorough breakdown of products and services.

Tourism Industry

hospitality industry • travel industry

Introductions to the subject

3798 Business of tourism
J.C. Holloway and N. Taylor   7th edn, Financial Times Prentice Hall, 2006, 716pp. £32.99. ISBN 0273701614.
Examines the role of tourism in the economic development of a country and the interplay between the public and private sectors. Tourism operations within each sector – attractions, carriers, tour operating, retailing, accommodation and tourist offices – are described in detail. Takes account of the growing significance of sustainable tourism.

3799 Dark tourism: the attraction of death and disaster
M. Foley and J. Lennon   Thomson Learning, 2000, 256pp. £28.99. ISBN 9780826450647.
Examines the phenomenon of tourism to places of death and disaster, focusing on sites in Poland, Germany and USA..
■ **Dark tourism** Guardian. www.guardian.co.uk/travel/darktourism. Introduction by Professor Lennon.

Economics of recreation, leisure and tourism
J. Tribe   See entry no. 3601

3800 Global tourism
W.F. Theobald   3rd edn, Elsevier Butterworth-Heinemann, 2004, 561pp. £32.99. ISBN 0750677899.
Topics covered include the future of tourism, differences in the travel characteristics of significant travel segments, sustainability standards in the global economy, crisis management in tourist destinations, tourism and social identities, and tourism, mobility and global communities.

3801 Management of tourism
L. Pender and R. Sharpley, eds   Sage Publications, 2004, 347pp. ISBN 0761940227.
Demonstrates the scope and significance of tourism as a business.

3802 Tourism: principles and practice
D. Gilbert, A. Fyall and J. Fletcher   3rd edn, Financial Times Prentice Hall, 2004, 720pp. £34.99. ISBN 027368406X.
Introduces the fundamental principles of tourism and shows the impacts and influences of this fast-changing industry on its environment and vice versa.

3803 Tourism: principles, practices, philosophies
C.R. Goeldner and J.R.B. Ritchie   10th edn, John Wiley & Sons, 2005, 608pp. £45.95. ISBN 0471450383.
In six parts, covering an overview of the industry; how tourism is organized; travel behaviour; tourism supply, demand, policy, planning and development; research and marketing; and future prospects.

3804 Tourism management: managing for change
S. Page   2nd edn, Butterworth-Heinemann, 2006, 496pp. £24.99.
ISBN 0750682051.
http://books.elsevier.com/companions/0750682051/
Introduces key concepts such as the development of
tourism, tourism supply and demand and the future of
tourism.

**3805 Worldwide destinations: the geography of travel
and tourism**
C. Cooper and B.G. Boniface   3rd edn, Butterworth-Heinemann,
2004, 528pp. £22.99. ISBN 0750659971.
Examines the basic principles underlying the geography of
tourist demand, supply and transportation, together with a
broad survey of world tourism generating and destination
regions.

Dictionaries, thesauri, classifications

3806 Dictionary of leisure, travel and tourism
K. McAdam, H. Bateman and E. Harris   Bloomsbury Publishing,
2005, 380pp. ISBN 0747572224.
Topics covered include travel, tourism, ticketing, hotels and
staff, restaurants, kitchens, table settings, service and
cooking, along with general business, accounting and
personnel terms. Supplemented by quick-reference lists of
airline and airport codes, currencies, international dialling
codes, time zones, balance sheets and international public
holidays.

3807 Dictionary of travel and tourism
A. Beaver   2nd edn, Cabi Publishing, 2005, 384pp. ISBN
0851990207.
Provides over 7000 definitions of travel and tourism
terminology used throughout the world, highlighting the
many differences between US and European usage.
References are provided for further reading.

Official & quasi-official bodies

3808 British Tourism Development Committee
Established in 1995, it advises on matters, including the
European Union, product development, environmental,
transport and tourism issues and strategic aspects of
marketing policy.

**Great Britain. Department for Culture, Media &
Sport**
See entry no. 3614

3809 World Tourism Organization
www.world-tourism.org/
Global forum for tourism policy issues and practical source
of tourism know-how, run by an agency of the United
Nations.

Research centres & institutes

**3810 Moffat Centre for Travel & Tourism Business
Development**
www.moffatcentre.com
Established in 1998 through the endownment of the

founders of the A.T. Mays travel agent chain. Website
provides useful links to research on the UK travel and
tourism sector.

Associations & societies

3811 British Hospitality Association
www.bha.org.uk/
Has been representing the hotel, restaurant and catering
industry for 90 years.

3812 Tourism Alliance
www.tourismalliance.com/
Seeks to establish and maintain a favourable operating
environment for all businesses involved in the delivery of
tourism, particularly in England.

Keeping up to date

Luxury Product and Service Briefing
See entry no. 3788

3813 Travel trends
Office of National Statistics   Palgrave Macmillan, 2005, 201pp.
ISBN 1403993092.
Presents the main annual results from the International
Passenger Survey (IPS), which collects information from a
random sample of passengers as they enter or leave the UK
by the principal air, sea and tunnel routes. Updated annually,
Travel trends presents detailed analysis on visits overseas
residents made to the UK and on visits UK residents made
abroad. It also presents information on the long-term trends
in travel to and from the UK, over a twenty-year period and
also shorter term trends, over a five-year period. It is the key
guide to travel patterns and shows why and how people
travelled, where they stayed and how much they spent.

3814 Ukinbound
www.ukinbound.org/
Comprehensive information about UK tourism, aimed at
travel trade professionals and visitors from around the world.

Transport & Distribution Industries

air transport • distribution management • freight •
logistics • materials handling • passenger transport •
ports • railways • road haulage • shipping • warehousing

Introductions to the subject

**3815 The box: how the shipping container made the
world smaller and the world economy bigger**
M. Levinson   Princeton University Press, 2006, 387pp. ISBN
0691123241.
Tells the dramatic story of the container's creation, the
decade of struggle before it was widely adopted and the
sweeping economic consequences of the sharp fall in
transport costs that containerization brought. Published on
the fiftieth anniversary of the first container voyage, this is
the first comprehensive history of the shipping container.

3816 On different tracks: designing railway regulation in Britain and Germany
M. Lodge   Greenwood Press, 2002, 248pp. £50.99. ISBN 0275976017.
Investigates how Britain and Germany regulated their railways at three different points in time over the past century – after World War 1, after World War 2 and in the 1990s. Its central focus is the design of regulatory regimes and the impact of institutional factors on the selection of design ideas and on processes of isomorphism. By placing a comparative analysis of regulatory design in a historical context and an institutional framework, the author contributes to the current debate on the emergence of the regulatory state in the late 20th century.

3817 Shipping company strategies: global management under turbulent conditions
P. Lorange   Elsevier, 2005, 209pp. £57.99. ISBN 0080446116.
Case studies of shipping firms around the world illustrate the changing fortunes of the shipping business.

Official & quasi-official bodies

3818 Commission for Integrated Transport
www.cfit.gov.uk
UK independent body advising the government on integrated transport policy. Provides expert advice supported by independent research.

3819 Freight Best Practice
www.freightbestpractice.org.uk/
Promotes operational efficiency within freight operations in England.

3820 Great Britain. Department for Transport
www.dft.gov.uk
UK government department responsible for all transport issues.

3821 Great Britain. Maritime & Coastguard Agency
www.mcga.gov.uk
UK agency responsible for implementing the Government's maritime safety policy.

International Maritime Organization
See entry no. 2320

3822 Network Rail [UK]
www.networkrail.co.uk/
Not-for-profit company responsible for the track and signalling of Britain's railways.

3823 Office of Rail Regulation [UK]
www.rail-reg.gov.uk/
An independent statutory body responsible for access to, and the safety of, Britain's railways.

3824 Transport Office [UK]
www.transportoffice.gov.uk/
Website designed to be a 'first point of call' for all government processes and information for commercial transport businesses in the UK.

3825 United States. Department of Transportation
www.dot.gov
The Department was founded in 1967 to 'serve the United States by ensuring a fast, safe, efficient, accessible and convenient transportation system that meets our vital national interests and enhances the quality of life of the American people, today and into the future.' The website's Business Services section includes details of new regulations, online forms and a 'business opportunities' page.

Associations & societies

3826 Association of Train Operating Companies [UK]
www.atoc.org
Represents British train operating companies (TOCs) to the government, regulatory bodies, the media and other opinion formers on transport policy issues.

3827 British Air Transport Association
www.bata.uk.com
Trade association for UK-registered airlines.

3828 British Business & General Aviation Association
www.bbga.aero/
Trade body representing business and general aviation. Member companies include aircraft manufacturers, commercial and corporate aircraft operators, flying training organizations, aircraft maintenance companies and companies offering a whole range of supporting services.

3829 Chamber of Shipping
www.british-shipping.org
Trade association for UK-based ship-owners and ship managers, with 134 members and associate members representing over 793 ships, about 21 million gross tonnes, including deep-sea bulk, short-sea bulk, containers, ferry, cruise, offshore support and specialized operators.

3830 Freight Transport Association [UK]
www.fta.co.uk/
Represents the interests of companies moving goods by road, rail, sea and air.

3831 Passenger Shipping Association [UK]
www.the-psa.co.uk
Represents the leading cruise and ferry companies operating in the UK.

3832 Society of Maritime Industries
www.maritimeindustries.org/
Promotes and supports companies which build, refit and modernize warships and supply equipment and services for all types of commercial and naval platforms, ports and terminals, infrastructure and maritime security, offshore oil and gas and marine science and technology.

Directories & encyclopedias

3833 Freight industry yearbook
20th edn, McMillan Scott, 2006, annual, 140pp. £125.
Covers road transportation, shipping, rail freight and air freight.

3834 Little red book
T. Pattison, ed. 60th edn, Ian Allan, 2005, annual. £35. ISSN 00760013.
Leading directory to the road passenger transport industry. Provides detailed information on operators in Britain along with information on suppliers, societies, licensing, etc.

3835 Marine and ports review
McMillan Scott, 2006. £25.
Contains a directory of port services and suppliers, a list of European directives and changes in legislation.

3836 Materials handling yearbook and directory
McMillan Scott, 2006. £25.
Covers all aspects of the handling and storage industry, including forklift trucks, conveyors, racking and shelving and warehouse management software.

3837 Road Haulage Association yearbook
Road Haulage Association 2007–8, Ten Alps Publishing, 2007, annual. £100.
Comprehensive directory of the RHA members giving full contact details and specialisations on a regional basis.

Handbooks & manuals

Handbook of logistics and distribution management
A. Rushton, P. Croucher and P. Baker See entry no. 4282

3838 RHA haulage manual
Road Haulage Association 2006–7, Ten Alps Publishing, annual. £30.
'Whether you need to check your facts on traffic regulations or vocational driver licensing, health & safety or plating and testing, this manual has it all – written in a clear, easy-to-read style.'

Utilities

electricity generation & supply • energy supply • gas production • mobile phones • sewage industry • telecommunications • waste disposal • water industry

Introductions to the subject

3839 Energy, the state and the market: British energy policy since 1979
D. Helm Oxford University Press, 2004, 490pp. £21.99. ISBN 0199270740.
A major study of the new market approach to energy policy in Britain since 1979. It describes the miners' strike, the privatizations of the gas, electricity, nuclear generation and coal industries and looks at events such as the dash for gas, regulatory failures in setting monopoly prices and the takeovers and the consolidations of the late 1990s.

3840 The Utilities Journal
Oxera, 1998–2005, monthly. Ceased publication March 2005; replaced by *Agenda*. ISSN 14610256.
Published between 1998 and March 2005, this journal provided news, analysis and commentary on legislative, regulatory, competition, economic, financial and environmental issues in the UK and European utilities sectors. It remains a valuable resource on the developments in the sector at the time.

Laws, standards, codes

3841 Utilities Act 2000 [UK]
Stationery Office Books, 2000, 166pp. £15.55. ISBN 0105427004. www.opsi.gov.uk/acts/acts2000/ukpga_20000027_en_1
'An Act to provide for the establishment and functions of the Gas and Electricity Markets Authority and the Gas and Electricity Consumer Council; to amend the legislation regulating the gas and electricity industries; and for connected purposes.'

Keeping up to date

3842 Utilities Policy
Elsevier, qtrly. ISSN 09571787.
International journal addressing economic, environmental, institutional, legal, liberalization, management, organization, performance, planning, policy, pricing, privatization, regulation and strategic issues across the energy, water, transport and telecommunications utilities.

Electricity & Gas

Introductions to the subject

3843 Electricity before nationalisation: a study of the development of the electricity supply industry in Britain to 1948
L. Hannah Johns Hopkins University Press, 1979, 467pp. ISBN 0801821452.
Commissioned by the UK Electricity Council in 1972, this major contribution to the economic history of Britain presents a 'warts and all' view of the development of the industry based on original documents and a wide range of secondary sources.

3844 Electricity markets: investment, performance and analysis
B. Murray Wiley, 1998, 276pp. £100. ISBN 0471985074.
Aims to increase understanding of the impact of deregulation on the theory and practice of investment appraisal within the market for electricity in the UK.

3845 Electricity markets: pricing, structures and economics
C. Harris Wiley, 2006, 542pp. £60. ISBN 0470011580.
Provides a descriptive and cross-disciplinary approach to the electricity markets, allowing traders and analysts to understand the market, its policies and how they drive prices, emissions and security.

3846 Engineers, managers and politicians: the first fifteen years of nationalized electricity supply in Britain
L. Hannah Johns Hopkins Univ Press, 1982. ISBN 0801828627.
A 'masterly account' of the first years of the nationalized electricity industry in Britain which builds upon the history

presented in Professor Hannah's earlier book *Electricity before nationalisation* (q.v.).

3847 Power loss: the origins of deregulation and restructuring in the American electric utility system
R.F. Hirsh   MIT Press, 2002, 418pp. £24.95. ISBN 0262582198.
Explains how and why the radical restructuring of the American electricity generation and distribution industry took place.

3848 Reshaping European gas and electricity industries: regulation markets and business strategies
D. Finon and A. Midttun   Elsevier, 2004, 412pp. £97.50. ISBN 0080445500.
Analyses the key issues facing the European energy industry, from a regulatory, market and business perspective. Current challenges within the field are also reviewed, including competitive and environmental issues.

Official & quasi-official bodies

3849 Energywatch [UK]
www.energywatch.org.uk/index.asp
The independent 'watchdog' for consumers of gas and electricity services within the UK. The website has a full range of publications, FAQ on the two industries, and a very comprehensive contact list.

3850 Ofgem [UK]
www.ofgem.gov.uk/ofgem/index.jsp
UK regulatory body. Website explains role and hosts numerous factsheets on the gas and electricity marketplace.

Discovering print & electronic resources

3851 Guide to UK electricity services
www.electricity-guide.org.uk/
Launched in 2005, this is a simple but effective website which describes and links to the key sources of information on the electricity industry in the UK.
■ **Guide to UK gas services** www.gas-guide.org.uk/. Also launched in 2005 and performs a similar function for the gas industry.

Directories & encyclopedias

3852 Electricity information
International Energy Association   IEA/OECD, 2006, annual, 708pp. CD-ROM version available. ISBN 9264110143.
Provides a comprehensive review of historical and current market trends in the OECD electricity sector.

3853 World directory of nuclear utility management
American Nuclear Society   18th edn, American Nuclear Society, 2006, annual, 248pp. Print and CD-ROM versions, $850.
Lists key personnel at nuclear utility headquarters and nuclear plant sites, along with worldwide plant listings (arranged alphabetically by country and utility). Also contains a listing of international nuclear-related organizations, with contact information.

Keeping up to date

3854 UK Power Magazine
McMillan Scott, qtrly. £20.
Aims to keep the UK power generation and distribution industry informed of emerging technologies, imminent product launches and the diversity of ongoing power generation projects.

Telecommunications

Introductions to the subject

3855 Great telecom meltdown
F.R. Goldstein   Artech House, 2005, 191pp. £48. ISBN 1580539394.
An authoritative account of what contributed to the failure of so many telecom firms between 2000 and 2002 in the USA.

3856 Restructuring telecommunications: a study of Europe in a global context
P.J. Curwen   Macmillan, 1997, 220pp. £50. ISBN 0333722299.
Examines the changes that have been occuring in the industry in recent years, with case studies of the UK, Germany and the USA.

Official & quasi-official bodies

Ofcom
See entry no. 5193

Associations & societies

Intellect
See entry no. 3590

Directories & encyclopedias

3857 Major telecommunications companies of the world
H. Brewin, A. Gallico and L. Romiti, eds   10th edn, Graham & Whiteside, 2007. $995. ISBN 9781860994951.
Profiles of over 3500 companies worldwide, with brand name and trademark information.

Keeping up to date

3858 Comms Business
www.cbmagazine.co.uk
News and features, supported by an events and suppliers directory.

Water & Sewage

Official & quasi-official bodies

3859 Consumer Council for Water [UK]
www.ccwater.org.uk/
Represents consumers of water and sewerage services in

England and Wales. Informative website with links to all the water companies covered by the Council's work.

3860 Drinking Water Inspectorate [UK]
www.dwi.gov.uk/
Government agency regulating drinking water supplies in England and Wales.

3861 Great Britain. Department for Environment, Food & Rural Affairs
www.defra.gov.uk/environment/water/
UK government information on all aspects of water policy in England, including water supply and resources and the regulatory systems for the water environment and the water industry. Source for official documents and links to associated bodies.

3862 Ofwat [UK]
www.ofwat.gov.uk/
The economic regulator for the water and sewage industry in England and Wales. The website has a full range of publications, FAQ for both consumers and the companies, and a very comprehensive list of links to company and water-related information sites.

3863 Water Industry Commission for Scotland
www.watercommission.co.uk/
The economic regulator for the water and sewage industry in Scotland. The website explains the relationship with Scottish Water, and makes available the reports that it produces.

Associations & societies

3864 Chartered Institution of Water & Environmental Management
www.ciwem.org/
Leading professional body for engineers, scientists and others working in the water and environmental management industries. Website has useful publications and links sections.

3865 International Water Association
www.iwahq.org
Global network of water professionals whose website aims to be the 'global water reference point'. Extensive resource section.

3866 Water UK
www.water.org.uk/
Industry association for all UK water and wastewater suppliers. Website has a variety of resources which are freely accessible, along with content for Water UK members.

Discovering print & electronic resources

3867 Guide to UK water services
www.water-guide.org.uk/
Launched in August 2005, a fun and informative site on the water industry in the UK. Part of the Guides Network created by independent researchers.

Keeping up to date

3868 Water and Wastes Digest
www.wwdmag.com
Serves the water and wastewater industries, tracking the equipment, chemicals, software and wastewater treatment services being used.

Business & Management

It will come as no surprise to learn that the development of the internet has had a huge impact on the way in which we conduct business and on how we access and use information. Nowhere is this more apparent than in the provision of business information. The sheer quantity and variety of online resources, covering virtually every area of business, is staggering. This proliferation of internet-based material has had a profound effect on the more traditional print sources. Bibliographies, journals, dictionaries, encyclopaedias, directories and handbooks are increasingly becoming available in both electronic and print formats. Similarly, most of the business and trade magazines and many of the established textbooks are now supplemented by companion websites. Often these sites provide special web-only content and other resources which are freely available.

The last few years have also seen an ever-increasing number of websites using socially interactive media such as weblogs, podcasts, wikis, social networking communities and knowledge sharing forums. These new tools are having a profound effect on the ways in which we communicate. Now more than ever people have the opportunity to exchange ideas and opinions with a huge audience, connect to experts through Q&A and discussion forums and tap into the collective knowledge of organizations.

With such a large and diverse field as business and management, it was decided that the best way of finding suitable resources would be divide the subject into the different business processes or activities involved in running an organization. Within these subject fields, resources have been included to serve three distinct audiences: research and teaching materials for the academic community; practical advice and guidance for business start-ups and SMEs; and finally resources offering practitioners the opportunity of continuing their professional development. Obviously many of these resources offer useful information to all three of these target audiences. For example, trade associations and professional societies not only provide good practice and professional development opportunities but also offer online resources that would be of use to academia or those starting their own businesses. Similarly, the proliferation of websites dedicated to business start-ups and small businesses also offer an incredible range of information and services drawn from universities, government agencies, commercial enterprises and membership organizations.

The New Walford has tried to reflect these changes by substantially increasing the types of resources included under each subject area. It is hoped that this will aid the user in finding their way through the vast information landscape.

Introductions to the subject

3869 Business: the ultimate resource
2nd edn, A. & C. Black, 2006, 2064pp. £40. ISBN 9780713675092.
www.ultimatebusinessresource.com/
This impressive volume, both in size and scope, is a one-stop-shop for practical and strategic advice on all areas of current business practice. Fully cross-referenced, the volume is divided into six main sections: best practice guides – overviews of key problems and business issues; management checklists and action lists; management library – summaries of the most influential business books of all time; business thinkers and management giants – profiles of top management gurus; a business dictionary; and business information sources. Purchase also includes free monthly updates available by registering on the website.

3870 Business in context: an introduction to business and its environment
D. Needle   4th edn, Thomson Learning, 2004, 646pp. £32.99. ISBN 1861529929.
www.thomsonlearning.co.uk/ [DESCRIPTION]
Intended as an introduction to the key functions within the business environment, this thoroughly revised edition places increased emphasis on globalization, ethics and the effect of technology on business. The book also has a companion website containing an online glossary, chapter learning objectives and associated web links.

3871 Business information on the net
K. Blakeman
www.rba.co.uk/sources/index.htm
RBA Information Services was set up in 1989 by Karen Blakeman, an information professional of more than 20 years. The site provides training and advice on how to find business information on the internet. There are a range of guides and factsheets on how to perform effective searches, which can be purchased directly from the site. Blakeman has also put together a collection of freely available business-oriented resources such as business directories, statistics, market and industry research, stock market data, company- and country-specific information and day-to-day business essentials (telephone directories, exchange rates, interest rates, travel information and acronym finder). Nicely laid out and full of useful information, this site is one for your favourites.

3872 Classics in management thought
C.L. Cooper, ed.   Edward Elgar, 2000. Elgar mini series (2 v.), £325. ISBN 1858989116.
www.e-elgar.co.uk/
This book brings together some of the most influential articles in management over the past 50 years. Volume 1 covers general management theories, leadership, motivation and organizational behaviour. Volume 2 focuses on the organization, with a large part of the volume dedicated to organizational structure. This two-volume set contains a well thought out selection of articles that provide the reader with an invaluable overview of the field of management thinking.

3873 History of management thought
D.A. Wren   5th edn, Wiley, 2004, 519pp. £70.95. ISBN 0471669229.
http://eu.wiley.com/
This book presents a chronological framework of management theories by profiling eras and identifying distinct trends and movements in the field of management

thought. The author argues that by 'tracing the origin and development of modern management concepts, a more logical, coherent picture of the current state of management practice and a clearer understanding of the analytical and conceptual tools of the trade can be achieved'. The fifth edition presents new sections on technology, discussing its impact on management thought, as well as revisiting issues such as business ethics, corporate governance and corporate responsibility.

3874   Introduction to management

R. Pettinger   4th edn, Palgrave Macmillan, 2006, 696pp. £35.99. ISBN 023000038X.
www.palgrave.com/
This well respected textbook is ideal for students studying management for the first time. It presents the reader with a well written, accessible introduction to the subject. Each chapter is packed with learning aids such as case vignettes, summary boxes, key points and concepts boxes and discussion questions. Now in its fourth edition, it has been updated to include chapters on innovation, enterprise, risk management, ethics and responsibility. See publisher's website for a contents and a sample chapter.

3875   Management: concepts and practices

T. Hannagan   4th edn, Financial Times Prentice Hall, 2004, 695pp. £41.99. ISBN 0273687689.
Well structured, with an easy-to-read style, this book provides introductions to the main concepts and practices in the field of management. Each chapter starts with a list of learning outcomes, provides a summary of the main features covered and ends with a case study, a set of review questions and a useful list of references and further readings. Also contains a 'travel guide' designed to help readers in finding their way around the book. Content covers both a European and international perspective and includes topics like managerial decision making, ethical and environmental issues, leadership and globalization, as well as a new chapter on public sector management.

3876   Ultimate business library: the greatest books that made management

S. Crainer and D. Dearlove   new edn, Capstone, 2002, 324pp. £15.99. ISBN 1841120596.
Summaries of over 75 business books that have had significant impact on business thinking. Each entry provides a short introduction to the author, followed by a summary of the book. A good resource for those wishing to gain a snapshot of the most influential management thinkers and their works.

Dictionaries, thesauri, classifications

3877   Biographical dictionary of management

M. Witzel, ed.   Continuum, 2006, 1176pp. £42.90. ISBN 0826490654.
www.continuumbooks.com/
The *Biographical dictionary of management* charts the historical development of management by presenting the biographies of over 600 individuals considered to have made a significant contribution to the field of management. As well as biographical information, each entry presents an analysis of the subject's key work, writings and contributions. Taking a global approach, it covers a wide range of subjects from

countries, including the USA, UK, Canada, Australia, Japan, China, Korea, France, Germany, Italy, Poland, Czechoslovakia, India and Brazil. This two-volume dictionary is a great reference source for anyone wishing to gain an insight into the individuals who have helped to shape the history of management.

3878   Dictionary of business and management

J. Law   4th edn, Oxford University Press, 2006, 568pp. Oxford paperback reference, £10.99. ISBN 0192806483.
www.oup.com
This comprehensive dictionary covers the concepts, theories and terminology used in the fields of business strategy, marketing, taxation, accounting, operations management, investment, banking and international finance. With over 6700 terms, this impressive work also covers US business terms; financial jargon; new terminology used in 'fast-changing fields' such as current affairs, human resource management and e-commerce; social psychology as it relates to management, for example group task theory, role theory and leadership theory. The new edition also includes an appendix listing useful websites and addresses for further research. A valuable reference tool equally suitable for students on business and management-related courses or business professionals.

3879   Dictionary of business terms

J.K. Shim   Thomson, 2004, 441pp. £26.99. ISBN 0324205457.
www.thomsonedu.com/
An impressive dictionary that attempts to cover terms related to 'every functional aspect of an organization'. This general business dictionary contains nearly 3200 terms all of which include contextual examples to help aid understanding. For some of the more complex topics an analysis is also provided, along with further reading references to related web pages.

3880   London classification of business studies

London Business School Library, 2005.
www.london.edu/
The *London classification of business studies* is both a thesaurus of indexing terms covering the areas of business and management and a specialized classification scheme. The thesaurus is published in two parts. Part one contains an alphabetic listing of the classification notation, showing the hierarchical order from broad subjects down through their sub-divisions. Part two contains an alphabetical list of subject terms showing hierarchical relationships. This scheme is one of the few classification schemes and thesauri which cater specifically for business literature and resources. It is used by a number of UK and international business schools, corporate libraries and information centres. A graphical version of the scheme is freely available from the London Business School library website.

3881   Routledge dictionary of business management

D.A. Statt   3rd edn, Routledge, 2004, 168pp. £14.99. ISBN 0415328195.
www.routledge.com
David Statt presents a 'fully comprehensive resource for those wanting to know about the world of business management. Students and working professionals alike can enjoy quick and accessible definitions and the extensive cross-referencing system allows readers broader access to subject areas. This dictionary covers all the topics, issues

and terms in the field, including business economics, consumer behaviour, corporate strategy, financial management, human resource management, information technology, management accounting, marketing, organizational behaviour and work psychology.'

3882 Wiley book of business quotations
H. Ehrlich, ed. Wiley, 2000, 448pp. £15.99. ISBN 047138447X.
http://eu.wiley.com/
Presented in a quick and easy-to-use style, quotes are organized into themes covering everything from marketing to sex in the work place. The quotes are also thoroughly indexed by names and companies. With more than 5000 quotations, this comprehensive reference provides a unique look at the thoughts and views of those who have helped to shape today's business world. 'This book is an indispensable resource for business people, writers, politicians, public speakers and anyone who wants to make sense of today's business world.'

Laws, standards, codes

3883 Business guide to legal literacy: what every manager should know about the law [USA]
H. Hasl-Kelchner Jossey-Bass, 2006, 372pp. £19.99. ISBN 0787982555.
www.hasl-kelchner.com/index.shtml
The general aim of this book is to improve legal literacy in organizations. Focusing on the 'frontline manager', it uses real-life legal and business case studies to demonstrate the legal consequences of business decision making. It provides practical advice and guidance on what managers should know in order to both anticipate and deal with legal risk, identify the infrastructure necessary to support a legal literacy initiative and improve communications throughout the organization. The book has an impressive appendix which contains the ABCs of legal literacy; lessons of Sarbanes-Oxley; excerpts from the Federal organizational sentencing guidelines, 2004; and a useful bibliography.

3884 Business law [UK]
J. Rush and M. Otley Thomson Learning, 2006, 416pp. £33.99. ISBN 184480173X.
Written in a non-technical and jargon-free style, this book is primarily aimed at non-law students taking a business studies course. It focuses on seven key areas: the English legal system; contract law; tort; supply of goods and services; company law; consumer, employment; and agency law. Each area uses case study examples to help develop a better understanding of how the law is relevant to contemporary business practice. The book comes with a companion website which provides additional learning material and twice-yearly update bulletins containing details of relevant common law, statutory and constitutional developments.

Research centres & institutes

3885 Advanced Institute of Management Research [UK]
www.aimresearch.org/home.html
Based at the London Business School, AIM is a multi-council initiative of the UK's Economic and Social Research Council (ESRC) and the Engineering and Physical Sciences Research

Council (EPSRC). It commissions research and fellowships in four key areas: recasting productivity for the 21st century; sustained innovation; adapting management practices; and excellence in public service delivery. The website provides free access to a range of academic publications, working papers, case studies and executive briefings. It also contains details of the Institute's workshops, conferences and other forthcoming events.

3886 Conference Board [USA]
www.conference-board.org/ [FEE-BASED]
The Conference Board, is a non-profit, global business organization whose mission is to 'create and disseminate knowledge about management and the marketplace to help businesses strengthen their performance and better serve society'. Perhaps best known for producing a number of economic statistics, including the Consumer Confidence Index (CCI), the Board also conducts research, convenes conferences, assess trends and publishes information and analysis. Membership includes full access to the Board's research and economic data, a subscription to its monthly magazine, access to its business information service and updates on member briefings and research reports.
■ **Conference Board Review** monthly. $59. ISSN 1046090X.

3887 Erasmus Research Institute of Management
www.erim.eur.nl/
ERIM is an interfaculty research school of the Rotterdam School of Management and the Rotterdam School of Economics based at the Erasmus University. The Institute's aim is to contribute to 'research that enables organizations to assess and improve their business processes in order to perform in a profitable and responsible way'. In particular, ERIM research is directed at the management of the firm in its environment and intra- and inter-firm relations. The website contains details of forthcoming seminars and conferences, plus the research and publications of the Institute.

3888 European Business History Association
www.ebha.org/
Based at the University of Glasgow, EBHA is a 'professional body for individuals interested in the development of business and management in Europe from the earliest time to the present day'. It aims to promote research, teaching and general awareness of all aspects of European business and management history. All members receive its biannual newsletters plus a member's discount for leading journals in this field, including the *Business History Review* (produced by Harvard Business School) and *Business History*.

Associations & societies

3889 Academy of Management [USA]
www.aomonline.org/
AOM describes itself as the oldest and largest scholarly management association in the world, with members drawn from 98 nations. As well as publishing four scholarly journals, proceedings and a newsletter, the Academy's 24 divisions and special interest groups produce newsletters for their constituent members. Membership includes a subscription to all four of its journals plus a quarterly newsletter; affiliation with two divisions or interest groups of the Academy; discounted rates for the annual meeting and

job placement service. Members have access to a members-only area of AOM Online, including the highly valued electronic article retrieval service for all the Academy journals.

- **Academy of Management Journal** bi-monthly. ISSN 00014273. www.aom.pace.edu/amjnew/ [DESCRIPTION]. A well respected management research journal.
- **Academy of Management Perspectives** qtrly. ISSN 15589080. www.journals.aomonline.org/amp/ [DESCRIPTION]. Previously known as the *Academy of Management Executive*, this journal has a strong focus on the techniques, trends and issues in managing an organization.
- **Academy of Management Review** qtrly. ISSN 03637425. www.aom.pace.edu/AMR/ [DESCRIPTION]. An influential journal presenting conceptual papers that seek to advance the science and practice of management.

3890 American Management Association
www.amanet.org/ [REGISTRATION]

The American Management Association specializes in management development and executive training, providing training seminars in 18 different business and management subject areas. Individual membership ($225 a year) includes a monthly e-newsletter, the Association's own journal, *MWorld*; unlimited access to an online library containing case studies, how-to articles, best practices, book extracts and profiles of leading executives/companies. The website also provides a number of free resources (requires registration), including help sheets on management topics, e-books, journal articles, book reviews, interactive self-assessments and selected content from the members' area.

3891 British Academy of Management
www.bam.ac.uk/

A professional organization committed to the advancement of management research. The site provides details of its activities, newsletter, annual conference and special interest groups. BAM also publishes the *British Journal of Management* and the *International Journal of Management Review*. Membership of BAM is open to anyone with a direct interest in management research and includes free subscriptions to both its journals, plus membership of up to three of its special interest groups. Subsidized subscription rates available for students.

- **British Journal of Management** Blackwell Publishing, qtrly. £159. ISSN 10453172. www.blackwellpublishing.com/. The official journal of the BAM, includes articles from across the full range of business and management disciplines. See publisher's website for subscription details, a full-text link to a featured article and a list of the top 20 most popular articles in the last 12 months.

3892 European Academy of Management
www.euram-online.org

EURAM is a professional association aimed at anyone with an interest in the field of management. Its main areas of interest include general management, strategy, corporate governance, organizational theory, organizational behaviour and decision making. EURAM's aim is to 'promote critical examinations of the historical and philosophical roots of management theory and praxis'. The Association organizes an annual conference, details of which can be found on the website. It also edits a journal called the *European Management Review*. Annual membership (€100) includes free online access to the journal and free attendance at the Academy's annual conference.

- **European Management Review** Palgrave Macmillan, 3 p.a. £85. ISSN 17404754. www.palgrave-journals.com/. *European Management Review* is the exciting new forum for international management research supported by the European Academy of Management. See publisher's website for a free online issue.

Libraries, archives, museums

3893 British Library, Business & IP Centre
www.bl.uk/bipc/

The British Library Business & IP Centre boasts the most comprehensive UK collections of business and intellectual property information. Business information sources published in the UK are collected as comprehensively as possible; sources published elsewhere are taken selectively. This information is practical rather than theoretical in nature. The centre provides free access to 40 subscription databases which cover company, business and industry information and financial news. There are also a number of intellectual property databases available listing patents, trade marks and registered designs. The Centre boasts a large collection of market research reports, business and management journals and UK and overseas business directories. A fee-based research service is also available.

3894 Business Archives Council [UK]
www.businessarchivescouncil.org.uk/

The Council aims to promote the preservation of business records of historical importance, to supply advice and information on the administration and management of both archives and modern records and to encourage interest in the history of business in Britain. The Council publishes an annual journal in two separate issues, one covering technical aspects: *Business Archives: principles and practice*; the other, *Business Archives: sources and history*, covering business archives as source material for historians. There is also a freely available online quarterly newsletter containing information on exhibitions, publications, courses and Council events and services.

3895 Business Archives Council of Scotland
www.archives.gla.ac.uk/bacs/default.html

BACS was established primarily for the active preservation of Scottish business records by providing a range of services, help and advice to companies interested in records management. Topics covered include disaster management; electronic records management; freedom of information; and intellectual property. Membership is open to anyone with an interest in the surveying and preservation of business archive collections in Scotland. Annual subscription: individual £10, institution £20, corporate £50.

3896 City Business Library [UK]
www.cityoflondon.gov.uk

The City Business Library is a public reference library provided by the Corporation of London. It holds a comprehensive collection of UK and overseas directories, as well as economic data, company information and domestic market research. Business topics such as management, law, banking, insurance, statistics and investment are also well represented. The library holds 700 periodicals and takes 50 daily newspapers and provides an indexing and abstracting service. There is also a fee-based research service and free public internet access, which is bookable up to 24 hours in advance. The library's catalogue is available from their website.

3897 Glasgow University Archive Services [UK]
www.archives.gla.ac.uk/

Although the prime purpose of GUAS is to collect business records to support research and teaching in Glasgow University, the collection is open to the public and is well used by the international academic community. The types of record typically sought include board minutes and supporting papers, correspondence of major figures in business, financial, technical, production and personnel records, plans, photographs and marketing material. Indeed, its business records centre contains one of the largest dedicated collections of business records in the world. It holds records of almost every commercial and industrial activity that has been pursued in the west of Scotland in the last 200 years.

Portal & task environments

3898 BestofBiz [UK]
www.bestofbiz.com [FEE-BASED]

A management and business research portal originally set up to address the research needs of the London Business School alumni. It aims to combine the theory of management with practical guidance for people running their own business. This is a subscription service which provides access to a wealth of resources, including action and best practice lists for a range of everyday business tasks; management book reviews; an online business dictionary; business briefings and research guides; introductions to management theories; and 'Business brain' – a tool for finding web resources, articles, reports and useful organizations.

3899 Biz/Ed
www.bized.co.uk/

Biz/Ed is a free, online service for students, teachers and lecturers of business, economics, accounting, leisure and recreation and travel and tourism. The website provides an impressive array of learning materials such as worksheets, glossaries, data banks and study skills. There is a unique section called 'Virtual worlds' which provides a range of simulation exercises such as Virtual factory and Virtual economy. The Company info section provides company profiles and financials and access to *The Times 100* case studies. For educators, the site provides lesson plans and a current topics section providing academic information related to economics and business topics currently in the news.

3900 Free management library
www.managementhelp.org/

An impressive links site that provides free, online resources covering the areas of business, management and organizations. Its overall goal is to provide managers (especially those with very limited resources) with practical information about personal, professional and organizational development. Aimed at both non-profit and for-profit organizations, the library is organized into a staggering 675 different management-related categories. Each topic provides a basic introduction, practical advice, related links and access to online discussion groups and newsletters (e-zines).

Digital data, image & text collections

3901 ABI/INFORM global
ProQuest.
www.proquest.com/ [DESCRIPTION]

A well respected source of business information for more than 30 years. This database contains content from thousands of journals enabling researchers to keep track of business trends, management techniques, corporate strategies and industry-specific topics. It offers in-depth coverage from over 2770 publications, with more than 1840 available in full-text, 14,000 full-text doctoral dissertations and master's theses. It also contains information on more than 60,000 companies as well as executive profiles, reports on market conditions and in-depth global business case studies. See publisher's website for a full product guide and example searches.

3902 Business Source Complete
www.epnet.com/

This well regarded database provides bibliographic and full-text content covering the main areas of business, including marketing, management, MIS, POM, accounting, finance and economics. It contains full-text access to over 1200 scholarly journals and practitioners' publications such as the *Harvard Business Review*. Additional non-journal content includes financial data, books, monographs, major reference works, conference proceedings and case studies. It also offers access to industry and market research reports from Datamonitor, country economic reports from the Economist Intelligence Unit (EIU), Global Insight, ICON Group and CountryWatch; detailed company profiles for the world's 10,000 largest companies as well as Bernstein's white and black book series with financial information. See the website for a full list of titles contained in the database and information on how to obtain a free institutional or business trial.

3903 Wilson business full-text
www.hwwilson.com/

This database provides access to a multitude of well known business sources, from *The New York Times* and the *Wall Street Journal* to a whole range of industry, trade and scholarly journals. Coverage includes full text for over 480 business periodicals back to 1995, plus indexing and abstracting of approximately 600 industry and trade journals and related periodicals back to 1982. Other features include product reviews, interviews, biographical sketches, corporate profiles, obituaries, surveys, book reviews, reports from associations, societies, trade shows and conferences. See publisher's website for full details.

Directories & encyclopedias

3904 Capstone encyclopedia of business: the most up-to-date and accessible guide to business ever!
Capstone Publishing, 2003, 479pp. £20. ISBN 1841120537.

Contains over 1000 entries covering all areas of business and management. Organized alphabetically, includes business terms and concepts, thinkers and practitioners, organizations, brands and companies.

3905 Encyclopedia of management
M.H. Helms, ed.   5th edn, Thomson Gale, 2005, 1003pp. £169. ISBN 0787665568.
www.gale.com/
Last published in 2000, this new edition has been fully revised and updated to reflect the current trends in management. The encyclopaedia covers 303 management terms, concepts and theories. Many of the concepts included go beyond the traditional brief dictionary-style definition, providing detailed essays which include background, current applications, schools of thought and further recommend reading.
'*Encyclopedia of Management* does a fine job of explaining both the practical and theoretical aspects of current management concepts in language accessible to the layperson. It is a worthwhile addition for public, business, and undergraduate libraries.' (*Booklist* (15 June 2000))

3906 Fifty key figures in management
M. Witzel   Routledge, 2003. Routledge key guides, £15.99. ISBN 0415369789.
www.routledge.com
Presents the biographies of 50 influential people who have helped to shape the practice of management, either by their ideas, writings and teachings, or through practical examples of leadership. It covers both well known and controversial figures from the Renaissance to present day.

3907 International directory of business biographies
N. Schlager, V. Torrado-Caputo and M. Mazurkiewicz, eds   rev. edn, St James Press, 2004. 4 v., £240. ISBN 1558625542.
www.gale.com/
This four-volume set provides in-depth biographical information on more than 600 industry leaders, entrepreneurs and notable business people worldwide. Each entry emphasizes leadership and management styles, business strategies and industry impact and provides in-depth bibliographies designed to facilitate further research. Also available in e-book format.

3908 Referenceforbusiness.com [USA]
www.referenceforbusiness.com/
An extremely useful collection of online encyclopaedias which includes the *Encyclopaedia of small business*, *Encyclopaedia of American industries* and the *Encyclopaedia of management*. Other useful features on this site include company histories, which provide a good overview of each company, contact details, competitor information and further references; Leading American business, which includes a timeline of American business; Business biographies – presenting over 600 in-depth essays on industry leaders, including biographical information, career paths, achievements, leadership strategies and management styles; Business plans – online versions of the 11 volumes of the Business plans handbook containing business plans written by North American entrepreneurs and examples on how to structure, compose and write their own business plans.

3909 Thinkers 50
www.thinkers50.com/?page=2005 [COMPANION]
Produced by Suntop Media in association with the European Foundation for Management Development (EFMD), the Thinkers 50 is a survey site seeking to identify who business people, consultants, academics and MBA students consider the most influential living management thinkers of the

moment. The bi-annual survey is a good reference tool for management students or researchers wanting to know 'which thinkers and ideas are in – and which have been consigned to business history'.

3910 World directory of business information libraries
Euromonitor International, 2007, 485pp. £400. ISBN 9781842644157.
www.euromonitor.com/
This directory provides information on where to find libraries specializing in business information. Includes business schools, private companies, trade organizations and any other collections, provided public access is allowed. Features include major public collections of business and reference titles around the world, including details of opening hours and admission policies. Also provides information on electronic access services, where available. See publisher's website for further details and sample pages.

3911 World directory of business information websites
Euromonitor International, 2007, 200pp. £400. ISBN 9781842643839.
www.euromonitor.com/
This directory includes over 3900 detailed descriptions of both free and fee-based business information websites. The directory is divided into industry sectors and contains sources from 82 countries. See publisher's website for sample pages and brochure.

Handbooks & manuals

3912 Financial Times handbook of management
S. Crainer and D. Dearlove, eds   3rd edn, Financial Times Prentice Hall, 2004, 1094pp. £40. ISBN 0273675842.
An impressive volume that attempts to capture the current state of management. It opens with a review of the state of management in the 21st century, then goes on to cover the fundamental principles of management, including strategy, globalization, human resources, operations, marketing and finance, as well as information, knowledge and ethics. Each section provides summaries of key management concepts, relating them to the ideas and theories of management thinkers and practitioners. The new edition also takes on a more practical, hands-on approach to management by, including a new section on essential management skills.

3913 IEBM handbook of management thinking
M. Warner, ed.   new edn, Thomson Learning, 2000, 816pp. International encyclopedia of business and management series, £41.99. ISBN 1861526326.
www.iebm.com
This handbook brings together those theorists, researchers and practitioners, both historical and contemporary, considered to have helped shape modern business and management thinking. Organized alphabetically, each entry provides a brief introduction to the person's background, lists their major works, school of thought and then provides a summary of their major themes and contributions. Each entry concludes with a short evaluation and a list of further readings. Ideal for anyone wanting a quick overview to the main thinkers in the field of management.

Keeping up to date

3914   California management review
Haas School of Business   University of California at Berkeley, Haas School of Business, qtrly. $75. ISSN 00081256.
http://cmr.berkeley.edu/
Published quarterly by the Haas School of Business at the University of California at Berkeley, the CMR is aimed at those who study management and those who practise it. It provides details of the latest research and creative thought in three main areas: strategy and organization, global competition and competitiveness and business and public policy. CMR also focuses on contemporary developments in the global economy, strategies for innovation, strategic planning, the management of technology, corporate culture, managing human resources and business ethics.

3915   Forbes [USA]
Forbes Global, bi-weekly. ISSN 14671654.
www.forbes.com/ [COMPANION]
Well known, bi-weekly magazine covering global business stories about companies, products and financial events. Perhaps best known for its series of published lists, including the Forbes 500, an annual ranking of the top 500 American companies, Forbes Global 2000, an annual ranking of the top 2000 corporations in the world and The Rich List, the 400 richest Americans. There is an online version of the magazine which includes full text of some of the articles from the current issue and free online access to all the lists that Forbes produce.

3916   Fortune
Time Inc, bi-weekly. £24.99. ISSN 07385587.
http://money.cnn.com/magazines/fortune/ [COMPANION]
America's longest-running business magazine providing information on economic, political and social trends that affect the business environment. *Fortune* magazine is also well known for its regular researched and ranked lists, including Best companies to work for; Fortune 500, 1000 and Global 500 – lists of companies ranked by gross revenue; America's most admired companies; Best companies for minorities and the fastest growing companies. Companion website includes selected full-text articles from past and current issues, news and analysis, web-exclusive stories and specials, plus free online access to all of its lists.

3917   Management Today [UK]
Haymarket Press, monthly. £54. ISSN 00251925.
www.clickmt.com/public/home/index.cfm [COMPANION]
Published since 1966, *Management Today* is a monthly magazine aimed at managers of all levels. It contains articles and practical advice on a range of current management-related issues. Companion website features free content, including editorial, advertising, marketing, media and PR information. It also features a careers database and an events calendar.

3918   McKinsey Quarterly
McKinsey & Company, qtrly. ISSN 00475394.
www.mckinseyquarterly.com/ [COMPANION]
The *McKinsey Quarterly* is produced by the global management consulting firm McKinsey & Company. It features articles on a range of business and management issues covering the private, public and non-profit sectors. Available in print and electronically, the quarterly magazine also includes a number of special issues throughout the year that focus entirely on a specific theme. The magazine has a companion website which has featured articles from the print version plus web-exclusive content. Free registration provides readers with online access to hundreds of articles, newsletters and topical alerts. A paid subscription to the journal includes a print copy and web access to all the journals articles dating back to 1992.

Management Development
business leadership • entrepreneurship • leadership training • management education • virtual teams • women entrepreneurs

Introductions to the subject

3919   Business leadership: a Jossey-Bass reader
Jossey-Bass, 2004, 832pp. Jossey-Bass business and management series, $30. ISBN 0787973416.
www.josseybass.com/WileyCDA/
This book provides an excellent starting point for those wanting a general introduction to some of the best thinking on leadership. It presents a collection of articles from leading authorities in this field and includes topics such as vision setting, ethics, dealing with change, leadership development, corporate culture and organizational performance. The book is divided into six main sections: What makes a great manager?; Creating and shaping the work environment; Communicating, leading and motivating people; Getting the work done; Leading complex organizational processes; Sustaining the great manager. See publisher's website for full table of contents.

3920   Developing management skills
D.A. Whetten and K.S. Cameron   7th edn, Prentice Hall, 2007, 625pp. £38.94. ISBN 0131747428.
http://vig.prenhall.com/home
This textbook presents an impressive exploration of the skills necessary for effective management. The authors takes a skills-based and interactive approach, using a range of exercises and examples in an attempt to 'bridge the gap between learning management skills and applying those skills to the managing job at hand.' Divided into four main sections covering personal, interpersonal, group and specific communication skills, this text emphasizes the importance of understanding your own behaviour in order to develop professionally.

3921   Essential readings in management learning
C. Grey and E. Antonacopoulou, eds   Sage Publications, 2006, 429pp. £29.99. ISBN 1412901421.
www.sagepub.co.uk
Explores the concepts, theories and issues in management and organizational learning by bringing together a collection of articles published in the journal *Management Learning*. The articles are organized under six key headings: organizational learning and learning organizations; individual learning; critical approaches to management education and learning; pedagogical practice; globalization and management learning; beyond management learning. Although primarily aimed at MBA, Master's and PhD students, this textbook would also be an invaluable resource

for those working in human resources or management education.

'It is a valuable source book and a fine piece of scholarship containing useful ideas for current and future HRD experts. It should indeed be an essential reading for management scholars and academics. It contains perhaps the most thoughtful and provocative papers not just focusing on management learning but also reflecting on wider issues in leadership and human resource development.' (www.rphrm.curtin.edu.au/index.html)

3922 Gurus on leadership
M. Thomas   Thorogood, 2006, 164pp. £14.99. ISBN 1854183516.
www.thorogoodpublishing.co.uk/
Intended as a quick reference guide to current themes and issues on leadership, this compendium provides the reader with a concise overview of some of the concepts and approaches of key writers in the field of leadership. See publisher's website for contents, introduction and PDF sample chapter.

3923 How to be an even better manager: a complete A–Z of proven techniques and essential skills
M. Armstrong   6th edn, Kogan Page, 2006, 333pp. £11.99. ISBN 074944262X.
www.koganpage.com/
Practical guide covering 50 specific areas of management which are organized into the three key areas: managing people; managing activities and processes; managing and developing oneself. This book provides advice and guidance in a clear and accessible way with the author explaining what managers need to understand and how to put what they learn into practice.

'Those with managerial responsibilities will find this a useful guide to keep on their shelves and dip into for background material and guidance on a range of business topics.' (*Business Franchise*)

3924 Management stripped bare: what they don't teach you at business school
J. Owen   2nd edn, Kogan Page, 2006, 183pp. £8.99. ISBN 0749446676.

'This book is about business as it is – not as it should be.' Written with the premise that in the real world, managers learn by experience, the book presents an A–Z list of 130 commonly faced management challenges. Each challenge is discussed using real-case examples of both successful and unsuccessful responses. This book provides an interesting alternative to the standard management books by trying to focus on the everyday practicalities of being a manager.

3925 MBA handbook: skills for mastering management
S. Cameron   5th edn, Financial Times Prentice Hall, 2004, 414pp. £38.99. ISBN 0273684671.
www.pearsoned.co.uk/
'A vital resource and survival guide for MBA students, covering everything they need to know about choosing the right course, study skills and assessments and post-MBA job opportunities. Prepares and supports students throughout their studies.' New to this edition: coverage of video conferencing, GMAT and problem-based learning; a revised chapter on projects and dissertations – including plagiarism, internal consultancy and electronic searches; expanded coverage of issues relating to students with English as a second language; a dedicated chapter on using key mathematical techniques and applications. A companion

website is available for this textbook containing worksheets, checklists and additional materials.

Laws, standards, codes

3926 Management Standards Centre [UK]
www.management-standards.org/
'The Management Standards Centre (MSC) is the Government recognized standards setting body for the management and leadership areas.' Following an extensive research project, the Centre has created a new set of standards which 'describe the level of performance expected in employment for a range of management and leadership functions/activities'. These defined managerial competencies have been built around six key functions that the MSC believe shape effective management and leadership: managing self and personal skills; providing direction; facilitating change; working with people; using resources; achieving results. The website contains the latest edition of the National Occupational Standards (NOS) which can be freely downloaded from the site or purchased in CD-ROM format.

Research centres & institutes

3927 Centre for Women Business Leaders [UK]
www.som.cranfield.ac.uk
Based at Cranfield School of Management, 'the Centre aims first to understand the issues facing senior women managers and second the impact of organizational and personal factors on women's managerial careers'. The Centre's research themes cover such areas as leadership, mentoring and work–life balance. As well as research papers, the site offers details of short management development programmes; women as leaders workshop; advice on mentoring systems in the workplace; executive coaching and advice on how organizations can set up a women managers network, providing support and information to women managers who may be in token/minority positions.

3928 International Institute for Management Development
www.imd.ch/index.cfm?bhcp=1
A not-for-profit foundation located in Lausanne, Switzerland, IMD is a leading name in executive education. 'Every year, some 5500 executives, representing over 70 nationalities, attend more than 20 open-enrolment executive development programs (including an intensive MBA program) as well as company-specific partnership programs'. Also produces the *World competitiveness yearbook*, which ranks countries according to economic, political, financial and social criteria based on the results of a survey completed by business executives worldwide. Website contains details of the Institute's current research, books, working papers and case studies. Also gives details of its current courses and programmes.

3929 Leader to Leader Institute
www.pfdf.org/index.html
Formerly the Peter F. Drucker Foundation for Nonprofit Management, the Leader to Leader Institute is an organization dedicated to 'providing social sector leaders with essential leadership wisdom, inspiration and resources to lead for innovation and to build vibrant social sector

organizations'. The website details the Institute's books and articles, conferences, self-assessment tools, guides and action series. It also produces a quarterly journal called *Leader to Leader*, offering 'cutting-edge thinking on leadership, management and strategy written by today's top thought leaders from the private, public and social sectors'. Two articles from each issue plus the editor-in-chief's columns are available online to non-subscribers.

Associations & societies

3930 Chartered Management Institute

www.managers.org.uk/

The CMI came into being after a merger between the British Institute of Management and the Institution of Industrial Managers. It is 'a nationally accredited organization, responsible for setting standards in management and recognizing excellence through the award of professional qualifications.' The website contains details of all the Institute's training and development courses, awards and research programmes. Members benefit from online access to 'an extensive library of books and articles on management, access to full-text articles from 200 key management journals and many other business and trade publications, quick and easy retrieval of information on 100 key management topics and links to over 800 management-related websites.' The Institute also produces a bi-monthly journal, *Professional Manager*.

- **Professional Manager** CMI, bi-monthly. £21.60. ISSN 09696695. The official magazine of the CMI. Website contains selected content and book reviews from the current issue for non-subscribers.

3931 European Foundation for Management Development

www.efmd.org/html/home.asp

Based in Brussels, the EFMD is a network association specializing in the field of management development. With more than 600 member organizations from academia, business, public service and consultancy in 65 countries, it provides a 'forum for information, research, networking and debate on innovation and best practice in management development'. It is also recognized as an accreditation body for management education. Site provides details of its international seminars and conferences, current projects and publications.

3932 Group of International Professional Bodies

www.group-ims.com/default.htm

This website contains details of five professional bodies: the Institute of Management Specialists (IMS); the Institute of Manufacturing (IManf); Professional Business & Technical Management (PBTM); the Academy of Multi-Skills (AMS); and the Academy of Executives & Administrators (AEA). 'Each body provides professional status and recognition through designatory letters, the option to study for certificate and diploma courses and subscription (including free career advertising for members) to the journals. There are various levels of membership based on qualifications held, knowledge, skill and experience (KSE) and position'.

3933 National Association of Women Business Owners

[USA]

www.nawbo.org/

With membership of some 10.6 million women-owned businesses, this US-based organization provides resources, advocacy and networking opportunities specifically for women entrepreneurs. Site provides a useful list of links to relevant resources and organizations, details on how to join and information on their annual conference.

3934 National Federation of Independent Business [USA]

www.nfib.com/page/home

Founded in 1943, NFIB is a lobbying organization currently representing 600,000 small and independent businesses with the aim of influencing governmental decision making. The website contains details of the Association's publications and referral programmes, a selection of free resources which includes articles providing practical information and tips for small-business owners, plus full-text access to the Association's official magazine *MyBusiness*. Site also links to a free business advice service called SCORE (Service Corps of Retired Executives).

Libraries, archives, museums

3935 London Business School, Library

www.london.edu

The London Business School Library is a specialist academic library covering the areas of business and management. It holds a wide range of printed and electronic resources that support the learning, teaching and research activities of the school's communities. The Library is also a member of SCoRE ('Search Company Reports'), an online catalogue of printed company reports held in UK libraries, holding a large print collection of annual reports for over 9000 companies with back files for many UK companies going back to the 1960s. Members of the public can pay to visit the library on a reference-only basis. There is also a fee-based business information service for external clients. The library website details opening hours, admission policy and services. The library catalogue is available online.

Portal & task environments

3936 Better Management.com

www.bettermanagement.com/

Bettermanagement.com is a portal aimed at providing educational resources for executives. Its library contains more than 3000 articles, white papers and case studies arranged by topics, industries and world regions. Topics include business intelligence; customer relationship management; financial management; IT management; leadership; risk management, scorecard and performance management and supply chain management. The site also offers a range of free online learning resources and recommended business books and produces weekly webcasts from 'thought leaders from around the world'.

3937 Businesscases.org

www.businesscases.org/

Produced by the Limelight Publishing Company, this site provides up-to-date business case studies for teaching. Areas covered include marketing, small businesses, international business, management, business information systems, accounting, operations management, public sector management, human resources and leisure. Free summaries for each case are available but to view the full text, the cases must be purchased (usually around £10 per case) and are only available electronically. Limelight also welcomes submissions of new cases – instructions are given on the site.

3938 BusinessSchools.com
www.businessschools.com

An online directory containing links to business school websites, ratings, advice on applying for financial aid, career resources, accreditation and lots more useful information. Search by name of institution, location (worldwide coverage) and/or programme.

3939 MBA program information site
www.mbainfo.com/

Describes itself as 'the most comprehensive source of information and advice on MBA programs'. The site contains details of over 2800 MBA degree programmes from 1400 universities, business schools and management colleges in 140 countries worldwide. Divided into two main sections: the MBA database, which can be searched using a range of different criteria; and the MBA advice pages, a great reference tool for anyone thinking of studying for an MBA, covering everything from applying for a course, funding and pre-MBA programme reading to a useful jobs and careers section. Site also contains a link to an MBA blog and an MBA graduates' network.

3940 TopExecEd.com
www.topexeced.com/

A searchable website that provides details of executive MBA programmes and executive education courses worldwide. Pre-registration is required to gain full access to the site (free). Each entry provides an organizational profile, details of courses and a link to the website. Site also contains a news and articles section.

3941 Value Based Management.net
www.valuebasedmanagement.net/

'Value Based Management.net is a management portal specifically aimed at the information needs of senior executives with an interest in value creation, managing for value and valuation.' The site contains an impressive amount of content, although its presentation can be a little offputting at first glance. It offers a range of learning materials that explain management methods, models and theories covering five main subject areas: strategy – value creation; valuation – decision making; organization – change – culture; communication – marketing; leadership – management. Topics are alphabetically listed under each category; these can be further refined by choosing to view by material type which includes articles, books, magazines and related organizations. Also contains a very useful FAQ section and a hall of fame section providing profiles of industry thought leaders.

Discovering print & electronic resources

3942 Entrepreneurship research portal [USA]
Ewing Marion Kauffman Foundation
www.research.kauffman.org/

The Entrepreneurship research portal is an annotated directory of 'academic and policy-orientated research' which includes articles, working papers, conference papers, reports

and links to data sources. Content is regularly updated by the portal's hosts the Ewing Marion Kauffman Foundation in partnership with the University of Illinois at Urbana-Champaign and the Social Science Research Network (SSRN). Browse by topic, publication/source or author or use the search facility to locate material. The majority of resources are freely accessible. Free registration allows users to save documents of interest to a personal profile and receive e-mail notifications about new research and events. A fantastic reference tool for cross-disciplinary research on entrepreneurship.

3943 getAbstract
www.getabstract.com/

getAbstract is a personalized weekly abstract service that e-mails subscribers five-page, PDF summaries of the latest business books. Each summary provides a concise overview of the book's key ideas and concepts. The books are also rated by applicability, innovation and style. Subscribers can create a personal profile and receive summaries for books from 12 different subject areas (two levels of subscription are available – see website for details). Non-subscribers can view titles, a short overview about the book and the author and see the book ratings. There is also a direct link to Amazon, for those wishing to purchase titles.

3944 ManagementFirst
www.managementfirst.com/

Primarily aimed at the 'working manager', ManagementFirst is an impressive selection of resources organized into specialized sites called 'community home pages', which cover management styles; marketing; change management; strategy; human resources; knowledge management; healthcare; E-business; quality; and the public sector. Each section contains articles, business news, management theories, guru interviews, case studies and reviews. The site also contains a resource centre which provides access to material for management training and development, articles, discussion forums and book and web reviews. A monthly newsletter is available for download. This site is freely available to all Emerald subscribers, with selected content available for non-subscribers. Well worth a look.

3945 Summaries.com
http://summaries.com/index.html

This service e-mails subscribers an eight-page executive summary of a new business book every week. Different subscription plans are available – see website for outline of plans and prices.

Digital data, image & text collections

3946 European Case Clearing House
www.ecch.com/ [DESCRIPTION]

The ECCH is an 'independent, non-profit, membership based organization dedicated to promoting the case method of learning'. Its collection of management case studies and journal article reprints is the largest in the world. Anyone can search the ECCH's online database but users must register (free) if they wish to view online inspection copies or purchase material. The ECCH also offers institutional memberships – see website for full subscription details.

3947 Fifty lessons

www.50lessons.com [FEE-BASED]

Fifty Lessons is a fully indexed digital business library containing more than 500 individual lessons from over 100 high international business leaders. Search by topic, business leader or how-to-advice for lessons covering a wide range of industry sectors, job functions and business issues. Various subscription packages available – see website for more details.

Directories & encyclopedias

3948 Encyclopedia of leadership: a practical guide to popular leadership theories and techniques

M. Hiebert and B. Klatt, eds   McGraw-Hill, 2001, 479pp. £58.99. ISBN 0071363084.

This encyclopaedia is a well designed, quick reference guide to over 200 business theories, tools and techniques. Fully cross-referenced, the encyclopaedia is organized into 15 categories. Each entry provides a brief summary, with skill development worksheets for 130 of the most popular leadership theories and techniques. Many of the entries also come with evaluation questionnaires, exercises, graphics and checklists.

Handbooks & manuals

3949 Handbook of management and leadership: a guide to managing for results

M. Armstrong and T. Stephens   Kogan Page, 2005, 242pp. £27.50. ISBN 0749443448.

This handbook is intended to provide practical guidance to managers on the key skills and processes necessary for successful management and leadership. Written in an accessible and easy-to-read style, it covers key management theories and best practice. The book is aligned to the Chartered Institute of Personnel and Development (CIPD) Managing for results professional standards and covers four main areas: the practice of management; delivering change; enhancing customer relations; enabling continuous improvement. The book is packed with checklists, helpful summaries and best-practice case studies from a number of international organizations.

'Includes international case studies and is packed with information on key theories and best practice. Written in a clear readable style, it has many checklists, diagrams and summaries … useful reading for managers and students.' (*Business Executive*)

3950 Leadership manual: your complete practical guide to leadership

H. Owen, V. Hodgson and N. Gazzard   Pearson/Prentice Hall Business, 2004, 360pp. £19.99. ISBN 0273675516.

'The *Leadership Manual* deals with the real issues faced by the majority of people at work today.' Using real-life examples taken from a survey of 500 managers, the book provides its readers with a range of practical advice and ideas on how to develop their leadership skills and deal with the day-to-day challenges that leaders typically face.

'A comprehensive and practical guide which avoids the twin dangers of being either too simplistic or too theoretical.' (Tracy T. Manning, PhD, Senior Scholar, Academy of Leadership, University of Maryland)

3951 Management bible

B. Nelson and P. Economy   John Wiley, 2005, 295pp. £13.99. ISBN 0471705454.

A comprehensive collection of 'concise essentials' for anyone wanting to improve their management skills. The book offers a range of strategies and techniques on how to deal with the realities of day-to-day management tasks – from how to motivate employees, monitoring performance and work with teams, to how to take disciplinary action and terminate employment. Divided into five sections: What managers do; Key management skills; Managing projects; money management challenges; The future of management. Each section features interviews with managers and business thought leaders, case studies, worksheets and questionnaires, plus real-life Q&A from practising managers.

3952 Mastering virtual teams: strategies, tools, and techniques that succeed

D.L. Duarte and N.T. Snyder   3rd edn, Jossey-Bass, 2006, 251pp. Jossey-Bass business and management series, £29.99. ISBN 0787982806.

www.josseybass.com/

Mastering virtual teams offers a range of practical tools and advice on how to lead and participate in a virtual team. The revised and expanded 3rd edition includes a CD-ROM which contains 'useful resources that allow virtual teams to access and use the book's checklists, assessments and other practical tools quickly and easily'. Also available as an e-book, see publisher's website for details.

3953 New manager's handbook

M. Stettner   McGraw-Hill Publishing, 2006, 128pp. £8.99. ISBN 0071463321.

www.mcgraw-hill.co.uk/

Specifically aimed at anyone taking on a management role for the first time, this handbook provides practical advice on managing and motivating people. With a heavy emphasis on communication skills, the author takes 24 commonplace situations and provides examples of how these problems should be approached. Covering everything from how to give feedback to how to get feedback, this book provides 'easy-to-implement practices to help new managers succeed from day one'.

3954 Our turn! Ultimate start-up guide for female entrepreneurs [UK]

A.B. Patel, N. Royston and N. Patel   Harriman House Publishing, 2005, 300pp. £12.99. ISBN 1897597479.

www.harriman-house.com

'Produced in association with the Women in Business team at HBOS, *Our turn!* is intended to encourage women to strike out and take a different approach to business, rather than conform to the conventional strategies and styles often instigated and developed by men.' This is essentially an entrepreneurial handbook specifically aimed at women. It provides invaluable advice and guidance on setting up and running a business, covering everything from how to raise funds for a new venture to how to construct a business plan. The book comes with a useful set of appendices which includes venture capital deal components; accounting definitions; a sample press release; an alphabetical list of UK networks and a collection of opinions and advice from top business women who have managed to run successful businesses.

3955 Successful entrepreneur's guidebook: where you are now, where you want to be and how to get there [UK]
C. Barrow, R. Brown and L. Clarke　2nd edn, Kogan Page, 2006, 384pp. £19.95. ISBN 0749446927.
www.kogan-page.co.uk

This guidebook is a result of research carried out at the Cranfield School of Management. It explores the characteristics of successful enterprises and examines the types of problems that owner-managed firms are likely to encounter. The research involved analysing the accounts of over 15,000 firms in order to identify what makes a business successful. The authors then collated the types of problems that small businesses are most likely to encounter and suggest different ways of anticipating and dealing with them. Full of useful case studies and assignments, the book aims to help entrepreneurs develop both their business and themselves by answering the following three questions: where is the business now? what are its strengths and weaknesses?; where can the business go from here? This is an impressive guide to 'strategy, finance and management for entrepreneurs'.

Keeping up to date

3956 Emerald Now
www.emeraldinsight.com/i

Emerald Now is a fortnightly newsletter containing a round-up of reviews and selected articles from Emerald Publishing. The newsletter also contains interviews with management experts in the areas of marketing, quality, HR and general management. This is a useful tool for keeping up-to-date with the latest in management thinking. A full-text archive of the newsletter back to 2000 is available. Free registration is required to receive the newsletter by e-mail.

3957 Harvard Business Review
Harvard Business School Publishing, monthly. $165. ISSN 00178012.
www.harvardbusinessonline.hbsp.harvard.edu

Well respected practitioners' magazine produced by the Harvard Business School. Contains articles, case studies, tips and other material covering current management research and practice. Companion website contains both current and past issues of the magazine plus web-exclusive content. Two levels of subscription are available – a basic subscription includes the print version of the magazine plus online access to the current issue and a year's worth of back issues. The premium subscription includes the magazine, online access to the current issue, a year's worth of back issues and access to over 2000 articles from the HBR archives. Individual articles can be purchased online from the Harvard Business Online website.

Management Activities
business information systems • business planning • corporate strategy • knowledge management • management techniques • office management • project management • strategic management

Introductions to the subject

3958 Administrative office management: an introduction [USA]
Z.K. Quible　8th edn, Pearson Prentice Hall, 2004, 596pp. £43.99. ISBN 0131287338.
http://vig.prenhall.com/

Comprehensive in scope, this book offers an introduction to the areas of administrative and office management. The author attempts to show what office managers really do by exploring the full range of office management topics, covering everything from selecting, managing and motivating staff to budgetary control. Each chapter features a selection of 'action-oriented minicases' to provide practical examples of each topic under discussion. The updated edition also features a new chapter on applications software, including word processing, spreadsheets, databases, presentation software, desk-top publishing and scheduling software. This book has an easy-to-read style making it an invaluable resource for both students and practitioners alike.

3959 Business information systems: technology, development and management for the e-business
P. Bocij [et al.]　3rd edn, Financial Times Prentice Hall, 2005, 752pp. £42.99. ISBN 0273688146.
www.pearsoned.co.uk/

Primarily designed for students with no prior knowledge of information systems or IT, this book is also a useful source of information for those already working in this field. It guides the reader through the process of 'choosing, developing and managing information systems to achieve business aims'. The third edition also provides 'updated coverage of contemporary topics like security, knowledge management and new technologies'.

3960 Corporate strategy
R. Lynch　4th edn, Financial Times Prentice Hall, 2005, 830pp. £41.99. ISBN 0273701789.
www.pearsoned.co.uk/

'Its combination of readability, comprehensive coverage and up-to-date case studies clearly demonstrate exactly what strategic theory is and how it translates into practice in the real world.' The fourth edition comes with thoroughly updated references, 80 global case studies and a new chapter on government, public sector and not-for-profit strategy. The book takes a very practical approach throughout, helping the reader to understand the theory behind the practice. See publisher's website for contents and a sample chapter. Companion website for this addition includes chapter overviews and key concepts and online glossary.

3961 Gurus on managing people
S. Kermally　Thorogood, 2005, 153pp. £14.99. ISBN 1854183206.
www.thorogoodpublishing.co.uk

'A one-stop guide to the world's most important writers on managing people. Summarizes all the key concepts and the contribution of each of the leading thinkers in the field, with pro's and con's of each theory.' See publisher's website for full table of contents and a sample chapter.

3962   Introduction to knowledge management: KM in business
T.R. Groff and T.P. Jones   Butterworth-Heinemann, 2003, 183pp. £19.95. ISBN 0750677287.
www.elsevier.com/
A thorough introduction to a wide range of knowledge management tools, techniques and terminology. The authors adopt a very practical approach to the subject by focusing on real-world business examples. Each chapter concludes with discussion and review questions, plus a vocabulary review. Contents: Introducing KM; Personal KM; Capture and corroborate; Organize and secure; Analyse and collaborate; Story telling and knowledge transfer; Systems thinking; Harnessing Metcalfe's Law; 3D communication; Building-in knowledge exchange; Developing KM strategies; The ethics of KM; Metrics and the taming of wicked problems; Careers in KM.

3963   Knowledge management yearbook 2000–2001
J.W. Cortada and J.A. Woods, eds   Butterworth-Heinemann, 2000, 561pp. £80. ISBN 0750672587.
www.elsevier.com
An anthology of articles written by KM experts selected to represent the current, practical and authoritative writings of the time. 'Covering topics such as knowledge-based strategies, organizational learning, knowledge tools, techniques and processes'. It has a comprehensive reference section which contains an extensive bibliography, glossary of terms, quotes, directory of relevant web resources, KM organizations and periodicals. The yearbook is divided into five parts covering The nature of knowledge and its management; Knowledge-based strategies; Knowledge management and organization learning; Knowledge tools, techniques and processes; Knowledge reference materials.

3964   Managing teams successfully: how to work with others and come up with results
A. & C. Black, 2007, 96pp. £6.99. ISBN 0713681543.
www.acblack.com/
This book offers a concise introduction to the techniques, skills and methods needed for successful team management. Suitable for those new to the management role or for those wanting to brush up on existing skills.

3965   Project management fundamentals: key concepts and methodology
G.T. Haugan   Management Concepts, 2006, 292pp. £27.99. ISBN 156726171X.
www.managementconcepts.com/
Project management fundamentals offers a step-by-step approach on how to implement and adapt project management tools and techniques to manage projects successfully, 'no matter the size or complexity' of the project involved. The book takes the reader through the basic concepts and demonstrates how PM tools and techniques can be applied effectively. It also examines how project management methodology can be tailored to meet the individual needs of each project and organization. The book is divided into four parts: Part 1 presents an introduction and overview; Part 2 examines PM methodology; Part 3 looks at how to apply PM methodology, using different

scenarios to illustrate real-life applications; Part 4 discusses environmental and facilitating elements such as human resource management, procurement and risk management.

3966   Ultimate strategy library: the 50 most influential strategic ideas of all time
J. Middleton   Capstone, 2003, 244pp. Capstone Reference, £15.99. ISBN 1841121800.
John Middleton, founder of the Bristol Management Research Centre, has put together a collection of articles from those thinkers considered to have had the greatest impact on the subject of strategy. Middleton outlines their work and assesses their contribution and impact. Book also contains a brief history of strategy, an annotated bibliography and a glossary of strategy terms. A useful reference tool for those wishing to gain a greater understanding of the development of this subject area

3967   Writers on strategy and strategic management: the theory of strategy and the practice of strategic management at enterprise, corporate, business and functional levels
J.I. Moore   2nd edn, Penguin, 2001, 320pp. Penguin business, £14.99. ISBN 0140284443.
www.penguin.co.uk/
This is an ideal sourcebook for those wishing to gain an overview of strategic management theory and practice. In this updated edition, the author presents summary versions of some of the key thinkers in this field. Contents: Part 1, The shapers and movers; Part 2, The consultants; Part 3, The scholars and researchers; Part 4, The developers and teachers; Part 5, The incrementalists; Part 6, The analysts of decline.

Dictionaries, thesauri, classifications

3968   Dictionary of strategic management
A. Prasad   Excel Books, 2004, 344pp. £9.99. ISBN 8174463003.
Definitions of terms and concepts most commonly used in the field of strategic management.

3969   Key concepts in business practice
J. Sutherland and D. Canwell   Palgrave Macmillan, 2004, 294pp. Palgrave key concepts series, £11.99. ISBN 1403915318.
www.palgrave.com/
Another title from the Palgrave key concepts series of business glossaries. Well laid out and easy to use, contains over 500 major concepts, terms, theories and theorists. Arranged alphabetically, entries are fully cross-referenced and provide readers with further reading and website references.

Research centres & institutes

3970   Center for Information Systems Research
www.mitsloan.mit.edu/cisr/
Established at the MIT Sloan School of Management in 1974, the Center's mission is to 'develop concepts and frameworks to help executives address the IT-related challenges of leading increasingly dynamic, global and information-intensive organizations'. CISR research covers three broad areas: managing the IT resource; IT and business strategy; managing across boundaries. The site

provides abstracts of its research projects, full-text access to the CISR working paper series and details of its annual conference and sponsor forums. Also includes profiles and bibliographies of the Centre's researchers and faculty members.

3971 Information Systems Research Centre

www.som.cranfield.ac.uk/som/research/centres/isrc/

'ISRC is one of the leading academic research centres in Europe and has conducted pioneering work in many areas of IS management'. Based at Cranfield School of Management since 1993, this research centre examines a range of IT activities within the business world. Current research projects focus on topics such as business benefits from IT investments, futures for e-commerce and the organizational development of knowledge management. Details of courses and the Centre's research projects can be found on the website.

3972 Project Management Institute

www.pmi.org/

The PMI is a non-profit professional association dedicated to developing and promoting global standards in the field of project management. With over 200,000 members from 125 countries, the Institute offers a wide range of seminars, educational programmes and professional certification. In addition, Knowledgebase (PMI's online catalogue) provides abstracts of the Institute's published journal articles and conference papers. Items can be purchased via a document delivery service ($15 per article/paper for non-members). PMI also publishes a range of project management books, training tools and learning products, which can be purchased via the online bookstore. Membership benefits include a range of complementary publications, discounted document delivery and subscriptions to the three periodicals that the Institute publishes.

- **PM Network** monthly. ISSN 10408754. A professional magazine aimed at project management decision-makers, providing the latest news of techniques and best practices. Selected content from current issue is available free from the website.
- **PMI Today** monthly. A monthly newsletter for PMI members providing information on the Institute's activities, events, services and volunteer opportunities, plus technical activities in the areas of certification, research, standards, education and training.
- **Project Management Journal** qtrly. ISSN 01475363. 'A quarterly refereed journal containing advanced, state-of-the-art project management techniques, research, theories, and applications'.

3973 University of Toronto, Knowledge Management Lab

www.cs.toronto.edu/km/

Based in the Department of Computer Science at the University of Toronto, the KM Lab 'conducts both basic and applied research in support of concepts, methodologies and software tools for the management of knowledge'. Browse the website to see current research projects. The publications page is currently being updated but full-text links to related research material and web links are available via the project pages.

Associations & societies

3974 Association for Strategic Planning [USA]

www.strategyplus.org/

Founded in 1999, ASP is a not-for-profit professional association dedicated to enabling 'people and organizations to succeed through improved advancing strategic thinking, planning and action'. Membership benefits include free subscription to notable strategy journals, access to the Association's membership directory, career opportunities, annual conference, book reviews and articles of interest.

3975 Association of Project Managers [EUR]

www.apm.org.uk/

APM is Europe's largest national project management association, with over 14,500 individual and 350 corporate members throughout the UK and abroad. The Association provides qualifications and professional development schemes. It also publishes a range of resources, including the *APM body of knowledge*, a sourcebook of project management knowledge and good practice. Website contains a very useful online glossary of project management terms.

- **APM body of knowledge** 5th edn, APM, 2006, 200pp. £25.95. ISBN 1903494133. The *APM body of knowledge* provides clearly written guidance on project management knowledge and good practice. The book is divided into seven sections, each with a brief introduction, and contains 52 knowledge areas (or topics). It can be purchased from the APM website, individual members can download the *APM body of knowledge* free of charge.

3976 Institute of Administrative Management

www.instam.org/

Established in 1915, the IAM is a professional body for administrative management. It offers a range of internationally recognized professional qualifications and continuing professional development schemes. Membership also includes a free subscription to the Institute's journal, *Manager: the British journal of administrative management*. Although most of the site's content is restricted to its members, the IAM reading room, an online collection of some of the Institute's own articles and papers, is available to non-members and is well worth a look.

- **Manager: the British journal of administrative management** bi-monthly. £65. ISSN 13535188. Reports on the latest techniques and developments in the field of administrative management.

3977 International Association for Management of Technology

www.iamot.org/

IAMOT is a non-profit organization that sponsors research, projects and annual international conferences on the management of technology. Membership benefits includes a discounted registration fee for the Association's annual conference, access to all information posted on the website, the IAMOT newsletter, discounts for certain professional journals and priority status in receiving reports and publications sponsored by IAMOT. Members also get a free one-year subscription to the Association's official journal *Technovation: the international journal of technological innovation, entrepreneurship and technology management*.

- **Technovation: the international journal of technological innovation, entrepreneurship and technology management** Elsevier, monthly. ISSN 01664972. www.elsevier.com/. The international journal of technological innovation, entrepreneurship and technology management is aimed at industry practitioners, academia,

Government, financial institutions and research organizations, or anyone interested in 'technological trends and breakthroughs which will support innovation'. See publisher's website for subscription details, most downloaded articles and a free sample issue.

3978 Strategic Planning Society
www.sps.org.uk/

The Strategic Planning Society (SPS) is a London-based membership organization dedicated to fostering and promoting research and best practice in 'strategic thought and action'. The Society seeks to 'create a link between the academic and practitioner worlds of strategy by keeping strategists up-to-date with developments in strategy-related research and practice'. Membership benefits include access to online discussion groups, a document library which includes articles, white papers and research reports on strategy development, plus a free subscription to the society's publications *Long Range Planning* and *Strategy* magazine.

■ **Long Range Planning** Strategic Planning Society and European Strategic Planning Federation/Elsevier, bi-monthly. £199. ISSN 00246301. www.elsevier.com/. Jointly published with the European Strategic Planning Federation, *Long Range Planning* is described as ' the leading international journal in the field of strategic planning, featuring original articles that aim to assist senior managers, administrators, and academics involved in strategy, by focusing on concepts and techniques that professionals can apply in setting goals and developing strategies to achieve them'.

Libraries, archives, museums

3979 Drucker Archives
www.druckerarchives.net/data/index.htm

Peter F. Drucker is generally considered to be one of the most influential management and business thinkers of the 20th century. The archive, which is based at the Claremont Graduate University in California, is the most comprehensive source of information on the life and works of Professor Drucker. Maintained by the Drucker Institute, the archive is available to researchers and students both physically and electronically. The electronic archive is fully searchable, containing details and, in some cases, digital copies of the physical collection.

Portal & task environments

3980 Center for Business Planning
Business Resource Software
www.businessplans.org

Created by Business Resource Software, Inc, this web resource is packed with useful information covering every aspect of planning a business. The site provides sample business plans, plus articles on how to create typical business documents such as marketing strategies. There is a web directory containing hundreds of sites offering research materials on topics such as venture capital, new products, market analysis, competitive analysis, production management, tax problems, legal issues and financial statements. The website also offers a number of interactive services, including 'Strategy insight', which enables users to test their business ideas by answering a set of 60 questions about their product and industry. The answers are then compared against a database of proven business principles and an assessment about the user's market position,

potential for success and problems are given (registration required).

3981 Knowledge Board
www.knowledgeboard.com/

The Knowledge Board is a knowledge management portal funded by the European Commission. It describes itself as a 'self-moderating global community thinking and collaborating on subjects around (but not limited to) Knowledge Management'. Once registered (free), the site provides an impressive range of resources, including an extensive bibliography on knowledge management, online access to a range of papers and articles, a searchable directory of Knowledge Board registered members and useful web links. Registered users can also list their blogs on the site and post comments to a discussion board.

3982 Knowledge Management Resource Center
www.kmresource.com/

Knowledge Management Resource Center is a service run by the IKM Corporation. It is a comprehensive collection of knowledge management resources organized in a simple, user-friendly way. Resources are arranged into 17 categories, which include case studies; international KM; professional organizations; periodicals and related sites. KnowledgeLinks is a particularly useful category, providing links to other websites that contain related articles, essays, white papers, reports, reviews and presentations.

3983 Management Logs
www.managementlogs.com/

Management Logs consists of 34 discussion forums on management topics ranging from business ethics to risk management. The logs are open to all but to add a new topic (free) registration is required.

3984 PMFORUM
www.pmforum.org/

'The mission of the PMFORUM is to use the internet to provide an economical forum for the promotion and exchange of project management information and knowledge worldwide.' An impressive website packed with free information and resources. The online library provides access to a wealth of free material, including case studies, student papers, reports, presentations and project audit reports. There is an online glossary, a worldwide directory of PM organizations, a directory of leading sources of information on globally-accepted PM practices, applications and techniques. Users can also sign up for a free subscription to *PM World Today Newsletter*, for the latest notices, reports, news and information related to project management from around the world.

3985 Project management knowledge base
http://projectmanagement.ittoolbox.com/

The project management knowledge base is one of the specialized communities available on ITtoolbox. The idea behind the ITtoolbox websites is 'to provide an online platform that enables anyone to share and gain peer knowledge about information technology'. The PM community web pages offer an impressive selection of free information and resources. Browse by topic or content-type for industry articles, white papers, research reports, FAQ and how-to-guides. Register to join discussion groups and forums, view or create your own blog and add, edit or organize the ITtoolbox Wiki. Subscribe for a selection of e-mail updates which includes new content posted to the site, using your own choice of keywords; latest events and webcasts; job opportunities or daily e-mails showing the most-viewed KM content for that day.

3986 Themanager.org
www.themanager.org/

Themanager.org is a portal managed by RMP (Recklies Management Project GmbH), a management consultancy company based in Germany. Its main function is to 'provide relevant information for all people who take part in business life'. This portal is well organized, presenting a range of material on key management topics. Search or browse using the suggested topics and sub-topics menu to access full-text links to articles, studies, checklists, FAQ, news and other publications. Regularly updated, new content is listed on the home page. Site users can also register free for Themanager.org-newsletter which features new developments in all areas of management and lists the latest additions to the website.

Discovering print & electronic resources

3987 Business process trends
www.bptrends.com/

A good source of business process information aimed at the global business community. Website offers plenty of free resources available: articles, columns, white papers, technical briefs and product reviews. A free monthly newsletter is posted on the site. Each newsletter features an in-depth article on a relevant topic and promotes best practices in business process change. In addition, free membership includes a monthly e-mail aimed at providing up-to-the-minute analysis and opinion on current issues, trends and directions. All the past issues are archived and available on the site.

3988 HBS Working Knowledge
Harvard Business School
www.hbswk.hbs.edu/

'HBS Working Knowledge is a forum for innovation in business practice, offering readers a first look at cutting-edge thinking and the opportunity to both influence and use these concepts before they enter mainstream management practice'. HBS working knowledge is a showcase for the ideas and research of Harvard Business School faculty, including working papers, cases, course materials, journal articles, books and book chapters. Browse content by topic, industry, geography and faculty. Updated almost daily, users can subscribe to their RSS feed to get daily notifications of new content.

Digital data, image & text collections

3989 Business and management practices (BusManagement)
www.gale.com/

The Business & management practices database is a bibliographic database that concentrates on the practical aspects of business management, with particular emphasis on the processes, methods and strategies of managing a business. It seeks to provide 'real-world know-how that

focuses on how organizations make and implement decisions, develop and launch new strategies and plan for change'. With coverage of more than 1000 professional and trade journals search, 'Business & management practices is the only database that lets you search by a specific department or function within an organization'. See website for a full listing of titles, database factsheet and pricing.

Directories & encyclopedias

3990 Blackwell encyclopedia of management: management information systems
S. Nickles and G. Davis, eds   2nd edn, Blackwell Publishing, 2006, 392pp. £85. ISBN 1405100656.
www.managementencyclopedia.com/

The second edition of this encyclopedia has been updated to reflect recent developments in the use of management information systems. This edition focuses on 'new applications of information technology to organization systems, new processes enabled by the internet and new technologies applied by managers and their business implications; provides coverage of technologies that are important to organization systems, including radio frequency identification (RFID); features entries from over 90 international academics and professionals working in the field'.

3991 Blackwell encyclopedia of management: strategic management
J. McGee, ed.   2nd edn, Blackwell, 2006, 325pp. Blackwell encyclopedia of management ; v. 12, £85. ISBN 1405118288.
www.managementencyclopedia.com/

This updated edition outlines the key trends in the field of strategic management, placing a heavy emphasis on both competitive strategy and competitive advantage. It also covers: the resource-based view; recent developments around the knowledge-based view; an introduction to the 'new economy'; the economics of knowledge; the nature of network externalities.

3992 Dictionary of strategy: strategic management A–Z
C.A. Booth and L. Kelly   Sage Publications, 2004, 187pp. £23.99. ISBN 0761930728.
www.sagepub.co.uk/

The authors present over 550 strategy terms 'in a historical context showing how views have changed and evolved and inviting the reader to think more deeply about the issues raised. It offers a flexible framework for understanding terms and topics in a broader strategic management perspective. The terms and concepts reflect very recent material from magazines, academic journals and conferences to bring the reader the latest cutting-edge research and debates'. See website for sample pages.

3993 Encyclopedia of knowledge management
D.G. Schwartz, ed.   Idea, 2005, 600pp. £160. ISBN 1591405734.
www.idea-group.com/

This encyclopedia provides comprehensive coverage of 'past, present and emerging directions of knowledge management'. With 940 definitions, it contains in-depth descriptions of key terms, technologies, theories, applications and concepts in the field of knowledge management, plus over 3600 references. Print edition comes with free access to the electronic version for the life of the edition.

3994   Gurus on e-business
J. Middleton   Thorogood, 2006, 192pp. £14.99. ISBN 1854183869.
www.thorogoodpublishing.co.uk/
'This book explores the impact and significance of e-business as illustrated by the work and thinking of a number of key players in the field. Its aim is to be an accessible guide for business people who are looking to make optimal and profitable use of e-business, as well as students and others who are looking for a deeper understanding of the subject'. See website for full contents and sample pages.
'A more than useful book to help cope with the overwhelming impact of the e-world' (*Business Executive* Autumn 2006)

Handbooks & manuals

3995   Handbook of knowledge management
C.W. Holsapple, ed.   Springer. 2 v. International handbooks on information systems.
www.springer.com/
This is an authoritative two-volume reference work dealing with all aspects of knowledge management. Presents 60 chapters tackling the field of knowledge management from a wide variety of perspectives. Volume 1 contents: Foundations of knowledge management – Knowledge: a key organizational resource – Knowledge processors and processing – Influences on knowledge processing. Volume 2 contents: Technologies for knowledge management – Outcomes of knowledge management – Knowledge management in action – The knowledge management horizon. This is an excellent resource for both practitioners and researchers.
- **Vol 1. Knowledge matters** 2004, 734pp. £42.50. ISBN 3540200053.
- **Vol 2. Knowledge directions** 2004, 775pp. £42.50. ISBN 3540200193.

3996   Handbook of management techniques: a comprehensive guide to achieving managerial excellence and improved decision making
M. Armstrong   3rd rev. edn, Kogan Page, 2006, 736pp. £26.96. ISBN 0749447664.
www.kogan-page.co.uk/
'A Handbook of Management Techniques boasts over 100 systematic and analytical methods used by managers to assist in decision making and to improve efficiency and effectiveness. The techniques contained in this weighty tome (over 700 pages) cover all fields of modern management. Diagrams support the text throughout and, as always, the acclaimed author, Michael Armstrong writes in an accessible and easy-to-read style'.

3997   Mastering strategy: the complete MBA companion in strategy
Financial Times Prentice Hall, 2000, 436pp. FT mastering series, £29.99. ISBN 0273649302.
www.pearsoned.co.uk/
Mastering strategy is a collaboration of the University of Chicago, INSEAD, University of Michigan Business School, SAID Business School and the *Financial Times*'s editors. The text presents a 'rich mix of thought leadership covering all the top strategy issues, from mergers and acquisitions, risk, technology and alliances, to knowledge, governance, globalization and leadership'. With contributions from some of the world's top strategists, the book explores the subject using case studies and examples to demonstrate how some of the leading companies are tackling this area.

3998   Next generation business handbook: new strategies from tomorrow's thought leaders
S. Chowdhury, ed.   Wiley, 2004, 1344pp. £70. ISBN 0471669962.
www.wiley.com
This handbook is an impressive collection of essays on business strategy written by up-and-coming business thinkers and experts from business schools around the world. Contains 68 chapters covering the areas of leadership; strategy; customer management; entrepreneurship; people management; networked business. See publisher's website for full contents, index and sample chapter.

3999   Oxford handbook of strategy: a strategy overview and competitive strategy
D. Faulkner and A. Campbell, eds   Oxford University Press, 2006, 1031pp. Oxford handbooks in business and management, £39.99. ISBN 0199275211.
www.oup.com/
'The handbook will be of considerable value to researchers, graduate students and teachers whose interest in the subject area has advanced beyond that of the traditional textbooks and to managers and consultants who seek an authoritative, accessible and up-to-date discussion of the fundamentals of strategy. Chapters examine six key areas: approaches to strategy, strategic analysis and formulation, corporate strategy; international strategy; strategies of organizational change; and strategic flexibility and uncertainty'.

4000   Practice of making strategy: a step-by-step guide
F. Ackermann and C. Eden   Sage Publications, 2004, 265pp. £24.99. ISBN 076194494X.
www.sagepub.co.uk
A very accessible text that seeks to explain the processes and practical applications of strategic management theories. Each chapter explores a theory and suggests how this may be put into practice. Although this text is predominantly aimed at MBA students, its practical emphasis makes it an invaluable reference source for anyone concerned with translating strategic theory into management practice. Fully cross-referenced, it features a selection of case vignettes and practical advice on the methods, tools and techniques used in the process of strategy-making. The book also has a companion website which includes a student workbook and teacher's slides.

4001   Project management life cycle: a complete step-by-step methodology for initiating, planning, executing and closing a project successfully
J. Westland   Kogan Page, 2006, 237pp. CD-ROM, £35. ISBN 0749445556.
www.kogan-page.co.uk
Presents a complete methodology for the management of projects. The author provides a step-by-step guide on how to implement best practice methods in-house rather than outsourcing. He describes in detail four stages of the project lifecycle: 'initiation, planning, execution and closure' in a clear and well written way, avoiding industry jargon. The book also outlines the Method 123 Project Management methodology.
'This book covers all of the essential elements of project management and provides the tools needed to manage projects

from initiation to closure.' (Michael Cook, National President, Canadian Institute of Management)

4002 Strategic planning workbook
N. Lake   2nd edn, Kogan Page, 2006, 256pp. The Sunday Times business enterprise guide, £19.99. ISBN 9780749445096.
www.kogan-page.co.uk
An invaluable reference tool for managers, this book provides a framework for putting together and implementing a strategic plan. 'This workbook will not intimidate those who shrink in horror at the mention of strategic planning! In a clear and accessible style Neville Lake draws on a mixture of his own diagnostic tools, analytical techniques and decision making processes, guiding the reader through the four key stages involved in strategic planning: strategic thinking (insight); collecting the right data (information); making the right decisions (imperatives); making the difference (implementation)'.
'Workbook designed for busy organization managers provides tools for strategic planning.' (*Journal of Economic Literature*)

Keeping up to date

4003 Knowmap
Stanford Solutions, bi-monthly. ISSN 14991209.
www.knowmap.com/
KnowMap, the knowledge management, auditing and mapping magazine, is a web-based journal aimed at practitioners, professionals and managers involved in knowledge management. With an emphasis on the practical applications of KM, the site features book and article reviews, case studies, tools for learning, jobs and news of forthcoming events. Much of the content is available to non-subscribers, including an open articles section. There are three levels of subscription, see website for more information and details of a trial subscription.

4004 Project Manager Today [UK]
£38. ISSN 13666851.
www.pmtoday.co.uk/
'A topical mix of news, comment and case studies as well as, each month, an in-depth review of an individual piece of project management software'. Subscribers to the magazine also get access to a members-only website where they can view the current issue and search and download articles from past issues. The site includes an online encyclopaedia, a qualifications and job vacancies section and latest software reviews, which are available for download free of charge. Subscribers can also buy books at discounted prices and find contact details for professional project management associations in different countries. See website for details and a free trial subscription.

4005 Strategic Management Journal
Wiley, monthly. Comes with occasional special issues, £220. ISSN 01432095.
http://eu.wiley.com/
Covering all aspects of strategic management, SMJ is 'devoted to the improvement and further development of the theory and practice of strategic management and it is designed to appeal to both practising managers and academics'. Topics covered by this journal include 'strategic resource allocation; organization structure; leadership; entrepreneurship and organizational purpose; methods and

techniques for evaluating and understanding competitive, technological, social and political environments; planning processes; and strategic decision processes'.

4006 Strategy and Business
Booz Allen, qtrly. $48. ISSN 1083706X.
www.strategy-business.com/ [DESCRIPTION]
'*Strategy and Business* is a thought-leadership business magazine for senior business executives and the people who influence them, reaches more than 100,000 readers worldwide.' Website provides free access to content in the current issue, including case studies, interviews, scholarly research, journalistic reports and profiles (requires free registration).

The Enterprise

company names • e-commerce • family businesses • non-profit organizations • small businesses

Introductions to the subject

4007 Company director's desktop guide [UK]
D. Martin   4th edn, Thorogood, 2006, 320pp. + CD-ROM, £18.99. ISBN 1854183176.
www.thorogoodpublishing.co.uk
This book offers practical guidance on the legal roles and responsibilities of company directors. Written in an accessible format, avoiding jargon and over-technical language, this fully updated and revised edition includes new material on employee comparability and consultation, including part time employees and fixed term contract personnel; accounting for 'human assets'; the operating and financial review; and corporate social responsibility. This book comes with a CD-ROM, containing a range of Companies House forms and explanatory notes. See publisher's website for full table of contents and a sample PDF chapter.

4008 Complete e-commerce book
J. Reynolds   2nd edn, CMP, 2004, 374pp. £21.99. ISBN 1578203120.
http://books.elsevier.com/
A comprehensive handbook that provides step-by-step guidance on setting up and running a successful e-commerce site. Covers everything from selecting the right software, programming, marketing, customer care and order processing to warehousing and shipping. The expanded and updated second edition also covers more recent e-commerce issues and developments, including online auctions, peer-to-peer file sharing, web logs, search engine marketing and security considerations.

4009 Complete small business guide: a sourcebook for new and small businesses [UK]
C. Barrow   8th edn, Capstone, 2006, 463pp. £14.99. ISBN 1841126861.
http://eu.wiley.com/
Complete small business guide is a 'one-stop resource' for business information specifically aimed at the start-up or small business. It takes the user through all the stages of setting up a business from scratch, including how to create a business plan. It identifies some of the pitfalls that new businesses can typically face. It tackles the legal, financial and practical aspects of raising capital, employing and

training staff, marketing, VAT and tax requirements, new technology and starting up overseas. The book also offers sources of direct help, with an extensive list of useful addresses. 'It is a comprehensive guide to everything you need to know to start, survive and succeed in business'.

4010 Family business sourcebook [USA]
C.E. Aronoff, J.H. Astrachan and J.L. Ward, eds   3rd edn, Family Enterprise Publications, 2002, 752pp. $119. ISBN 1891652060.
www.efamilybusiness.com/
Family business sourcebook is a comprehensive reference tool for family-run businesses and the professionals that serve them. It presents a collection of articles previously published in journals such as the *Family Bbusiness Review, Harvard Business Review* and the *Nation's Business*. The articles cover topics such as succession, strategic planning, gift and estate taxes, family relations, women in family businesses and internationalization.

4011 International business environment: global and local marketplaces in a changing world
J. Morrison   2nd edn, Palgrave Macmillan, 2006, 516pp. £29.99. ISBN 1403936919.
www.palgrave.com
'The book offers a clear and accessible introduction to the key dimensions of the international business environment, including economic, political, cultural, technological and financial dimensions. The approach is genuinely international, highlighting transitional and developing economies as well as the advanced economies. Global issues, including ethical dimensions and social responsibility are emphasized, as are management implications'. This is a well structured book which sets out a list of learning objectives at the start of every chapter, provides summaries of its key points, topical case-studies, review questions, suggested further readings and a very useful feature called 'web alert' which suggests websites of interest. Sample chapter is available from the publisher's website.

4012 Nonprofit organizations: theory, management, policy
H.K. Anheier   Routledge, 2004, 450pp. £25.99. ISBN 0415314194.
www.routledge.com/
This text provides a complete overview of the non-profit and voluntary sector, including non-governmental organizations, philanthropic foundations and civil society institutions. With an international perspective, the book details the historical background to these types of organization and explores the theories, management approaches and policy analysis currently prevailing in this field. This book will enable readers to understand what a non-profit or voluntary organization is; place the sector in a historical context; understand the current size and structure of the non-profit sector; understand organizational behaviour; and demonstrate how non-profits gain funding and manage their resources.

4013 Understanding and managing public organizations
H.G. Rainey   3rd edn, Jossey-Bass, 2003, 512pp. The Jossey-Bass public administration series, £34.99. ISBN 0787965618.
www.josseybass.com/
The first edition of this title won the Best Book Award, Public Sector Division, Academy of Management, in 1992. The updated edition draws 'on a review of the most current research about government organizations and managers – and about effective and ineffective practices in government –

this important resource offers specific suggestions for managing these challenges in today's public organizations. Using illustrative, real-life vignettes and examples, the book provides expert analysis of organizational design, goals, power, effectiveness, leadership, motivation and work attitudes, decision making and more.' See publisher's website for table of contents and sample PDF excerpt.

Dictionaries, thesauri, classifications

4014 Dictionary of civil society, philanthropy and the non-profit sector
H.K. Anheier and R. List   Routledge, 2005, 306pp. £10. ISBN 1857431669.
The dictionary is intended as a one-stop resource for information on the key people, concepts and organizations involved with the not-for-profit sector (NFS). It contains nearly 300 entries covering concepts and terms such as citizenship, social capital, non-profit management, corporate responsibilities and social origins theory. It also provides regional information; profiles of key personalities and organizations involved in the third sector; information on how the sector operates e.g. Fair Trade, grassroots organizations and exit strategies.

4015 Dictionary of e-business: a definitive guide to technology and business terms
F. Botto   2nd edn, Wiley, 2002, 368pp. £60. ISBN 0470844701.
http://eu.wiley.com/
This dictionary is an excellent reference source for anyone wishing to get to grips with the terms being used in the fast-moving e-business environment. It offers detailed definitions of terms and phrases currently used in e-business and related technology and provides short articles for some of the more complex topics. This fully updated second edition contains over 350 entries covering new areas such as wireless and mobile technologies, Java, XML, security, customer relationship management, mCommerce and NETSome.
'Overall, this is a clearly set out and easy to use book ... and will be of value to anyone wanting a quick reference guide' (*Reference Reviews* July 2003)

4016 Dictionary of international business terms
J.J. Capela and S. Hartman   3rd edn, Barron's, 2004. Barron's business guides, £10.99. ISBN 0764124455.
http://barronseduc.com/
An impressive dictionary that contains approximately 5000 terms relating to international business, including international finance and marketing, foreign exchange, import/export, trade organizations and business terminology commonly used in different countries. This updated edition also reflects many of the recent trends in this area, such as trade agreements, cartels and innovations in international business. Acronyms and abbreviations are covered and appendices include international information sources and organizations.

4017 Dictionary of international business terms
J.O.E. Clark   Financial World, 2004, 368pp. £15. ISBN 0852975740.
www.financialworldpublishing.com/
One in a series of dictionaries specializing in international banking and finance published by Financial World Publishing. Suitable for those wishing to gain a broad understanding of

terms relating to areas such as business accounting, stock markets, wholesale and retail banking, taxation, law, trade finance, real estate and investment. With nearly 5000 terms, coverage also includes many economic terms and standard international terms used in both Europe and the US.

4018 E-Business glossary [CAN]
www.e-future.ca/alberta/ebusiness/efc_e-business_glossary.asp
The E-business glossary is an online resource maintained by the Alberta E-Future Centre. The Centre was set up to provide free, impartial and easy-to-understand e-business advice and information for small and medium-sized businesses, based in Alberta, Canada. Although intended for a Canadian audience, the glossary is still useful for anyone wanting a quick definition of e-business terms.

4019 English to Spanish business glossary
A.D. Miles
www.andymiles.com/
An online glossary of business terms covering financial, management and commercial vocabularies. Contains 8000 terms in both languages. This glossary is updated every two months. Users can subscribe to a free e-mail newsletter notifying them of new words added to the glossary.

4020 German business dictionary: American and German business terms for the internet age
K. Roland, ed.　Schreiber Publishing, 425pp. £21.50. ISBN 0884003108.
A comprehensive source for German business terms used in all areas of business, including banking, accounting, insurance, real-estate, import-export, taxes and business law. Also includes computer-related terminology and business terms of international organizations such as the United Nations, the World Bank and the IMF.

4021 Global business dictionary: English-French-German-Russian-Chinese-Japanese
M. Sofer　Schreiber Publishing, 2005, 458pp. £29.50. ISBN 0884003094.
This dictionary translates terms related to banking, insurance, real estate, export-import, the stock market, plus computing and internet-related terminology from English into five languages: Chinese, French, German, Japanese, Russian and includes Canadian terms that differ from the French. No pronunciation guide included.

4022 Harrap Japanese business management dictionary
H. Takamizawa and J. Coveney; McKinsey & Company　Harrap, 1999, 188pp. £9.99. ISBN 0245606629.
Presents 7000 words and phrases used in business and management. Includes terms covering topics such as corporate planning, IT and marketing. Compiled in conjunction with the international management consultants, McKinsey, this is a valuable resource for anyone doing business with Japanese companies.

4023 Italian business dictionary
M. Sofer and M. Pizarro, eds　Schreiber Publishing, 2006, 344pp. £13.21. ISBN 0884003191.
Includes words and phrases used in accounting, economics, insurance, real estate, modern banking, computing and internet-related terms. Many of the terms used are American-specific.

4024 Key concepts in international business
J. Sutherland and D. Canwell　Palgrave, 2004, 283pp. Palgrave key concepts series, £12.99. ISBN 1403915342.
www.palgrave.com/
Another glossary from the Key concepts series covering the major concepts, terms and theorists in international business. Entries are fully cross-referenced, with suggested further readings and website references. With over 500 key terms, this glossary is a 'must-have reference for anyone studying a business-related course or those simply wishing to understand what international business is all about'.

4025 Oxford business French dictionary
M. Chalmers and M. Pierquin, eds　Oxford University Press, 2002, 663pp. £14.99. ISBN 0198604831.
www.oup.co.uk/
A helpful aid to students studying a combined French and business course, or for those conducting business in the French-speaking world. Covers many core business activities including finance, management, sales and marketing and e-commerce, and also covers internet-related terms. 'Detailed treatment of all vocabulary items is provided, along with thousands of example phrases illustrating important constructions. The extensive supplementary material offers sample business correspondence, including Curriculum Vitaes; faxes, e-mails and invoices; lists of countries, nationalities, languages and currencies; and guidance on using the telephone.'

4026 Spanish business dictionary: multicultural business Spanish
M. Sofer　2nd rev.edn, Shengold Publishers, 2005, 348pp. £21.50. ISBN 0884003019.
This dictionary contains commonly used business terms throughout the Spanish-speaking world. Containing over 39,000 words and phrases covering all aspects of business, this revised edition also features hundreds of new computer and internet-related terms regularly used in business.

Laws, standards, codes

4027 ByteLawyer's online e-law centre
www.bytelawyer.com/
The ByteLawyer's online e-law centre is a site run by Harry S.K. Tan, a law professor at the Nanyang Business School, Nanyang Technological University Singapore. The website covers international news, reports and commentary on e-business law developments, as well as information on the management of e-business law issues. The Technews section of the website is updated almost daily, providing the latest news on topics such as cybercrime, virus reports, computer security, online banking and e-business law. Users can register to receive 'ByteBiz brief', a free electronic newsletter covering the latest developments in e-business, technology and the internet. The site also links to Professor Tan's personal blog 'ByteLawyer briefing', which provides commentary on the effects of new developments in technology and law on business and society.

4028 Law for the small business: an essential guide to all the legal and financial requirements [UK]
P.E. Clayton   12th edn, Kogan Page, 2007, 192pp. Sunday Times business enterprise series, £15.99. ISBN 0749449551.
www.kogan-page.co.uk/

A title from the Sunday Times business enterprise series, this book provides essential guidance on key legal issues affecting small businesses. Written by a practising solicitor who also lectures on business law, the book covers all relevant areas of current UK company law, including taxation; cash and credit; patents, copyrights and trade marks; debt collection; bankruptcy and liquidation; takeovers and mergers; and employment law. The content is well organized, with an easy-to-use style which makes it particularly useful for anyone planning to set up their own business, or indeed for those already operating one.

'An extremely useful guide to the legal minefield' (*The Guardian*)

4029 Legal500.com
www.icclaw.com/

Legal500.com is the online version of the following directories: *Legal 500*; *US Legal 500*; *European Legal 500* and the *Pacific Legal 500*. The Legal 500s are a range of directories providing information on law firms and lawyers as well as the latest commercial law developments for each region. Search by company name, location or speciality. Each entry provides contact details, firm and lawyer profiles and the firm's specialist areas of practice. The site is well laid out and easy to navigate.

4030 New legal framework for e-commerce in Europe
L. Edwards, ed.   Hart, 2005, 521pp. £35. ISBN 1841134511.
www.hartpub.co.uk/

This book presents a collection of essays drawn from both academia and practice that discuss recent legislation governing European electronic commerce. The main focus of the text is the European Electronic Commerce Directive and its effects on the UK since it came into force. The book concentrates on areas of the directive such as 'contracting online, internet service provider liability, consumer privacy, including spam and "cookies", country of origin regulation and online alternative dispute resolution (ODR)'. Other laws and directives covered include the Privacy and Electronic Communications Directive, the Distance Selling Directives, the Electronic Money Directive, the Lawful Business regulations on employee surveillance, the disability discrimination rules affecting websites and the extension of VAT to online transactions. 'Both the European framework and the rules as implemented in the UK are examined and critiqued for how well they meet the needs of business and consumers'.

Official & quasi-official bodies

4031 Advisory Commission on Electronic Commerce [USA]
www.ecommercecommission.org/

The Advisory Commission on Electronic Commerce (ACEC) was created by the US Congress to report on the critical issues surrounding electronic commerce and tax policy, including the global implications of these developments. The Commission completed its work in 2000 and although the site is no longer updated, it provides webcasts and transcripts from previous Commission meetings and has an electronic library of more than 200 documents submitted by the public concerning the work of the Commission, many of which are available full-text.

4032 Business Gateway [UK]
www.bgateway.com/

The Business Gateway is a partnership between the Scottish Enterprise, Scottish Executive and local authorities. It aims to support economic development in Scotland by providing a range of key services for those wishing to start or develop their own businesses. The site offers information and advice on all aspects of business, including finance and grants; taxes, returns and payroll; employing people; health and safety; sales and marketing and IT and e-business. A well thought out site that is easy to navigate.

4033 Companies House [UK]
www.companieshouse.gov.uk/

Companies House is an executive agency of the Department for Business, Enterprise and Regulatory Reform (BERR). It provides information on over 2 million limited companies registered in Great Britain. 'The main functions of Companies House are to incorporate and dissolve limited companies; examine and store company information delivered under the Companies Act and related legislation; and make this information available to the public'. Users can search the site freely for company information and download statutory forms free of charge. Basic information on companies, free of charge, includes date of incorporation, registered office and nature of business. There are also guidance notes freely available for download (PDF) which provide information on the formal and legal procedures for setting up and running a UK company. A subscription service is available for those who wish to regularly download company information such as annual reports and company financial information.

- **Companies House Library** The online library provides resources in the following categories: Companies House corporate information i.e. annual accounts and business plans; policy documents – both internal and external policies; guidance booklets; full listing of online forms; *Register* magazine archive – available to subscription holders only; a miscellaneous section which contains general published information not covered by the other headings.

4034 Confederation of British Industry
www.cbi.org.uk/

The CBI is a lobbying organization for UK business on both national and international issues. Working with the UK government, international legislators and policy-makers, the CBI's main aim is to help UK businesses to compete effectively. The site provides details of the organization and its work, including details of its business surveys which can be subscribed to by both member and non-members (see site for prices); news releases; abstracts and selected content from the CBI magazine *Business Voice*; and information on its policy work. Site also features an online bookshop for CBI publications, a calendar of events, details of the CBI's annual conference and links to related sites.

4035 Enterprise Directorate
www.dti.gov.uk/bbf/small-business/index.html

Formerly known as the Small Business Service, the Enterprise Directorate is the Department for Business, Enterprise and Regulatory Reform (BERR) expert policy unit on small business issues throughout Government. It provides information and support to small businesses. In addition, it provides grants to help companies develop technological innovation, this includes the Small Firms Loan Guarantee Scheme which guarantees loans for businesses that would normally be refused due to a lack of security and the Shell Technology Enterprise Programme, which assists small firms in the recruitment of skilled graduates. The agency also carry out a range of surveys and produce a number statistics such as SME statistics, business survival rates, VAT stats and surveys looking at the progress of small business in disadvantaged communities.

4036 Great Britain. Department for Business, Enterprise & Regulatory Reform
www.berr.gov.uk/
The BERR brings together the functions of the former Department of Trade and Industry. Its main aim is to 'create the conditions for business success through competitive and flexible markets that create value for businesses, consumers and employees. It drives regulatory reform and works across Government and with the regions to raise levels of UK productivity.' The website offers press releases; statistics; papers; legislation, regulation and other documents covering the following areas: trade; regional economic performance; business sectors; business relations; employment issues; energy; and innovation.

International Chamber of Commerce
See entry no. 2398

4037 International Trade Administration [USA]
www.trade.gov/index.asp
The International Trade Administration (ITA) is a division of the US Department of Commerce. Its main aim is to 'create prosperity by strengthening the competitiveness of US industry, promoting trade and investment and ensuring fair trade and compliance with trade laws and agreements'. The website of the ITA provides a wealth of information and services on US international trade policy. This is a very useful site for US industry-specific information, including the latest industry news and a range of detailed analysis and statistics. Also provides information on import, export and trade issues.

4038 Office of Government Commerce [UK]
www.ogc.gov.uk/
The OGC is an independent office of the Treasury that works with public sector organizations, advising them on how to develop efficient procurement procedures. Website features information on procurement policies and initiatives, it also provides free access to a range of procurement publications and guidance documents. There is a resource toolkit section which contains links to guides, websites, software, training and a range of other information that is designed to improve management procedures. This section also has a link to Prince2, the standard UK government method for project management developed by CCTA, part of the Office of Government Commerce.
- **Prince2** www.ogc.gov.uk/prince2/ [31/07/2006]. PRINCE2 (Projects in Controlled Environments) 'is recognized as a world-class international product and is the standard method for project management, not least because it embodies many years of good practice in project management and provides a flexible and adaptable approach to suit all projects. It is a project management method designed to provide a framework covering the wide variety of disciplines and activities required within a project.'

4039 Partnerships UK
www.partnershipsuk.org.uk
Partnerships UK (PUK) is a public-private partnership which was formed in 2000 out of HM Treasury. It is dedicated to 'support and accelerate the delivery of infrastructure renewal, high quality public services and the efficient use of public assets through better and stronger partnerships between the public and private sectors'. The website provides full details of the partnership and its activities. It also includes a fully searchable database which contains the details of over 814 projects, case studies, guidance documents and a video and image library.

4040 Scottish Enterprise
www.scottish-enterprise.com
Scottish Enterprise is an economic development agency funded by the Scottish Executive. It provides advice and support for business start-ups and existing small businesses. The website details its services and provides a wealth of information that can be freely downloaded. This includes evaluations and economic impact studies, e-business and economic research and a whole range of market sector reports, industry overviews and statistics. The site also contains information specifically aimed at new business, providing advice and guidance on every aspect of running a business. Despite the huge range of information available, the site is nicely laid out and easy to navigate.

4041 Strategis [CAN]
www.strategis.ic.gc.ca/engdoc/main.html
Strategis is a website produced by Industry Canada, a Canadian federal government department. It is an impressive site specifically designed to provide business and industry information to Canadian businesses. It contains a huge range of resources covering international trade and investment, economic analysis and research, business legislation, business support services and tools, industry information and news plus consumer information and advice. Although the site is dedicated to Canadian business needs, it does offer information and services that would be of interest to others, including company information; trade data online – a database which can provide customizable reports on Canada and US trade in goods with over 200 countries; a trademark database; monthly economic indicators; and bibliographic data on patents filed at the Canadian Intellectual Property Office. Given the vast amount of information held on this site, the site map makes it remarkably easy to navigate.

4042 UK Trade & Investment
www.uktradeinvest.gov.uk/
UK Trade & Investment is a government organization that provides support for UK companies doing business internationally and for overseas enterprises looking to set up or expand in the UK. The website is organized into two sections. For UK companies doing or wanting to do business abroad, the site offers a huge range of advice and support on market entry. There is a sector section containing an A–Z list of industry profiles, providing overviews and a whole range of related information sources and content. The country section provides country profiles and suggestions for potential business opportunities for UK businesses. For overseas companies looking to do business in the UK, the site also offers information and advice, available in a range of languages. The site has a searchable events database giving details of trade fairs, conferences and seminars. This is an

impressive website but to take full advantage of the information and resources on offer users must register (free).

4043 United States. Small Business Administration
www.sba.gov/

The US Small Business Administration (SBA) was founded in 1953 as an independent agency of the federal government. Its main function is to protect the interests of US small business enterprises. The site is wide in scope and extremely well organized. The planner section contains information and a range of how-to guides for all stages of setting up and running a small business. The tools section includes laws and regulations; free, online publications covering management questions; podcasts on a range of small business topics; related research and statistics from the Office of Economic Research; and VOICE, an online chat discussion archive that presents questions from small business owners and responses from business experts.

Research centres & institutes

4044 Center for Research in Electronic Commerce
http://cism.mccombs.utexas.edu/

Based at the University of Texas at Austin, the CREC is a research centre specializing in the fields of information systems and management, electronic commerce and the digital economy. The site provides full-text access to the Centre's research reports, articles and working papers. Also contains details of conferences and jobs in the field of electronic commerce.

4045 Centre for Business Research [UK]
www.cbr.cam.ac.uk/

The Centre for Business Research (CBR) is a multi-disciplinary research centre based at the University of Cambridge. The Centre conducts its research in two main areas: the enterprise and innovation programme – which studies the factors affecting the growth and survival of the UK's small and medium-sized enterprises (SMEs); and the corporate governance programme, which looks at the effects of corporate governance structures and regulations on the firm. The CBR produces a number of surveys on small and medium-sized enterprises which can be purchased from the site (executive summaries can be downloaded for free). Working papers are also available online from 1995. The Centre's newsletter *Top Floor*, which contains news on its latest research and conferences, is available online or users can register and receive a printed copy for free.

4046 Centre for International Business
http://web.apu.ac.uk/aibs/geru/

The Centre for International Business is based at the Ashcroft International Business School, part of Anglia Ruskin University. It specializes in research and consultancy work in the area of 'skills and knowledge development for international SMEs.' The website contains information on the Centre's activities and features full-text links to a range of its research publications.

4047 ECommerce Innovation Centre
www.ecommerce.ac.uk/

Based at Cardiff University, the eCommerce Innovation Centre is a self-funded, research and consultancy centre formed to promote and encourage a 'greater understanding of electronic commerce in international trade.' The website provides details of the Centre's past and current projects and gives free access to a collection of real-life case studies from its project work with SMEs. The eCIC also participates in and presents at a wide range of conferences throughout the UK and overseas; details of these presentations can be found on the website. The site offers an archive of press releases and related web links section.

4048 MIT Center for Digital Business
http://ebusiness.mit.edu/index.html

'The MIT Center for Digital Business is an industry funded research program at the MIT Sloan School of Management'. The Center has established a large-scale research program with corporate sponsors to investigate the latest trends and techniques in digital business. Research is currently focused in five main areas: digital marketing strategy; digital productivity; IT products and services; communication futures; and interdependence of security and the extended enterprise. Site details the Center's current research projects, seminars and conferences. Working papers and research briefs can be downloaded freely and users can subscribe to a free fortnightly e-mail newsletter.

Associations & societies

4049 Academy of International Business
www.aib.msu.edu/

Established in 1959, the AIB is an international association made up of scholars, consultants and researchers from 75 different countries around the world. Its main objective is to 'foster education and advance professional standards in the field of international business'. The website contains a careers section which provides job postings of a variety of international business related positions. The site's resource section offers a well organized set of material for both teaching and research purposes and includes a series of very useful annotated web links. The Academy also publishes the *Journal of International Business Studies* (JIBS).

■ **Journal of International Business Studies** Palgrave Macmillan, bi-monthly. £96. ISSN 00472506. www.jibs.net/ [DESCRIPTION]. 'Scope includes research on multinational and transnational business activities, strategies and managerial processes that cross national boundaries, joint ventures, strategic alliances, mergers and acquisitions interactions of such firms with their economic, political and cultural environments, as well as cross-national research involving innovation entrepreneurship, knowledge based competition, judgement and decision making, bargaining, leadership, corporate governance and new organizational forms.'

4050 European Council for Small Business & Entrepreneurship
www.ecsb.org/

'The European Council for Small Business and Entrepreneurship (ECSB) is a non-profit organization whose main objective is to advance the understanding of entrepreneurship and to improve the competitiveness of SMEs in Europe. ECSB facilitates the creation and distribution of new knowledge through research, education and the open exchange of ideas between professions and across national and cultural borders'. The council organize a number of conferences for its members, including RENT (Research in Entrepreneurship and Small Business), an annual conference jointly run with the European Institute for

Advanced Studies in Management (EIASM). Details of past and present conferences, including conference proceedings, which can be downloaded freely, can be found on the website.

4051 Federation of Small Businesses [UK]
www.fsb.org.uk/
Formed in 1974, the FSM is a lobbying group with over 200,000 members across 33 regions. It is dedicated to promoting and protecting the interests of UK small business owners and the self-employed. The website holds a substantial amount of useful information for small businesses although finding it can be rather a daunting prospect. FSB publishes its own paper-based magazine *First Voice*, which presents news and advice for small businesses. Contents and selected articles from the magazine are freely available from the website.

4052 Forum of Private Business [UK]
www.fpb.org/
Established in 1977, the Forum of Private Business is a pressure group representing 25,000 UK-based private businesses. The Forum bases its campaigns on referendums and supplementary surveys conducted among its own members. It also carries out various online surveys which are open to all. Copies of these surveys can be purchased online from the FPB shop (summary findings to some of the surveys can be freely downloaded). The FPB provides a range of services and products to help with the day-to-day running of smaller businesses, which can be purchased online.

4053 Institute for Family Business [UK]
www.ifb.org.uk/
The IFB is the UK's only independent network for family run businesses. It seeks to 'to raise the profile of issues relating to the family firm and promote a level playing field for the sector'. The Institute offers a range of educational programmes and seminars throughout the year. It also sets up networking events and conferences, carries out research and provides advocacy. Details of the Institute's current research and publications can be found on the website (some of which has been made freely available).

4054 National Council of Nonprofit Associations [USA]
www.ncna.org/
The National Council of Nonprofit Associations (NCNA) is a network of state and regional not-for-profit associations dedicated to helping 'small and midsize nonprofits: manage and lead more effectively; collaborate and exchange solutions; engage in critical policy issues affecting the sector; and achieve greater impact in their communities.' The website provides information on current issues in the sector. This includes a policy and advocacy section presenting an overview of current issues, advice on how to take action and links to related documents and publications. The resources area provides toolkits, reports and has a list of links to other organizations. There is also an events calendar and a separate members' area, which offers a state association directory.

Libraries, archives, museums

4055 Hagley Museum & Library [USA]
www.hagley.lib.de.us/

Located in Delaware, the Hagley Museum & Library houses a 'collection of manuscripts, photographs, books and pamphlets documenting the history of American business and technology'. This includes papers and company records ranging from 18th century merchants to present-day telecommunication companies. The museum and library is organized and maintained by the Center for the History of Business, Technology and Society. The library and archival collections are open to the public for research and the Library also offers an interlibrary loans service, online searching and a photocopying and photographic service. An online library catalogue, collection inventories and collection guides are available from the website.

4056 Information Centre for Entrepreneurship
www.bibl.hj.se/ice/
Based at Jönköping University, the Information Centre for Entrepreneurship (ICE) was created to support the educational and research activities of the University's business school. The collection consists of books, dissertations, working papers, conference proceedings and periodicals in the areas of entrepreneurship, innovation and small business. The collection is open to the general public and there is a fee-based document delivery service for paper copies of individual chapters in books and articles from their own journal collection. Users can search for journal articles using the Centre's database ESMELIT, available (free) from the website. Site also contains annotated links to other entrepreneurship sites.

4057 Library of Congress, Business Reference Service
www.loc.gov/rr/business/
The Business Reference Service provides advice and guidance on the business collections held by the Library of Congress. The Service is available for all library users, whether in person, by telephone, correspondence, or e-mail. There is an indirect reference service available from the website, which contains a wide range of impressive bibliographic guides and research reports prepared by the division's subject specialists. This includes a comprehensive list of internet resources on business and economics topics arranged by subject.

4058 Westminster Reference Library [UK]
www.westminster.gov.uk/libraries/findalibrary/westref.cfm
Westminster Reference Library is a public library that specializes in business information. This includes approximately 600 quick-reference sources on all aspects of economics and business, a wide range of national and international business directories, company and industry information sources, statistics, an extensive collection of UK official publications, law – including an online law information gateway to relevant websites and a substantial collection of EU material. The Library's catalogue is available from the website.

Portal & task environments

4059 Business Eye [UK]
www.businesseye.org.uk/
Business Eye is a free, impartial information service specifically aimed at Welsh businesses. It runs a number of regional centres which provide events and workshops. It also has an impressive website, packed with advice, help sheets,

links, case studies, latest news and statistics covering all the main areas of business. Topics include starting a business; finance and tax; HR and staff; office and administration; sales and marketing; IT and commerce. The site hosts a discussion forum, an events section and contains a directory of online sources of other business advice, information and financial support services. Business eye provides a free call back service: users can fill out an online enquiry form and receive a telephone answer within 2 working days. Site visitors can also register to receive a monthly e-mail newsletter providing updates on the latest business support news, events and courses, regulations and awards. Website is available in Welsh.

4060 BusinessZone [UK]
www.businesszone.co.uk/
BusinessZone is a resource portal aimed at small businesses. It provides a compendium of information and tools on a range of different subjects. It offers daily news coverage and a range of expert guides that provide advice on everything from performance indicators and Excel spreadsheets to basic accounting standards. The site contains tax and finance advice, company information and covers training and HR topics. Most services are free but pre-registration is required. A unique feature of this site is its 'Any answer' section, which contains over 5000 business questions from professionals, complete with answers (all registered users are invited to add their comments).

4061 ECommerce-guide.com
www.ecommerce-guide.com/
'The goal of ECommerce-Guide.com is to provide the single best source of independent, up-to-date information about electronic commerce'. The site offers daily news, feature articles, case studies and an e-commerce events calendar. There is a discussion forum section which hosts a number of e-commerce-focused discussion groups. Site visitors can view the threads but need to register in order to answer or post messages. The Products section of the site offers a range of product reviews of tools and software used for building e-commerce site. There is also a useful FAQ section providing advice and guidance on how to set up and run a successful e-business.

4062 Europa – Your Europe: business [EUR]
www.ec.europa.eu/youreurope/nav/en/business/index.html
The Your Europe portal is an excellent source of information from the European Commission for European citizens wishing to work or study in another EU country, or for European businesses wanting to relocate or extend their business in the EU. The information provided is divided in two areas, one covering information for citizens and the other for businesses. The Business area provides general EU-wide business information in a variety of subject areas and languages. EU-wide and country specific information pages contain a general introduction to the topic and a set of useful links and addresses to external sources of information. The Citizen section of the site contains detailed practical information on rights and opportunities in the EU, covering working, studying and living in Europe, plus advice on consumer protection. The website is nicely put together and despite the huge amount of information covered, is easy to navigate.

4063 globalEDGE
http://globaledge.msu.edu/
globalEDGE is an online directory of publicly available web resources covering the subject area of international business. Organized and maintained by the Center for International Business Education and Research at Michigan State University, the site is impressive both in size and content. Resources are organized into several areas. The 'Country insight' section contains information on the business climate, history, political structure and economic conditions for 197 countries. This includes statistical data and country-specific international business links. The 'Global resources' section is an annotated directory of international business resources covering areas such as trade law. Other features include market potential indicators, based on an indexing study conducted by MSU-CIBER; a glossary of terms and acronyms used for international business; online discussion forums and a latest news section. There is also an 'Academic' section that contains resources specifically aimed at teachers, researchers and students. Considering the amount of information that this website holds, it is surprisingly easy to navigate. This is a great source of global business news and information, making it a valuable reference tool for academics, students and professionals alike.

4064 Mind Your Own Business [USA]
www.mindyourownbiz.org/default.shtml
The Mind Your Own Business website was created by the US Small Business Administration and Junior Achievement, a not-for-profit organization whose aim is to 'inspire and prepare young people to succeed in a global economy'. It is a portal aimed at young entrepreneurs wishing to start, run or develop their own businesses. The aim is to support and promote teen entrepreneurship by providing advice and guidance on what they see as the five steps of business ownership: explore; decide; build; connect and succeed.

4065 Small Business Research Portal [UK]
www.smallbusinessportal.co.uk/index.php
The Small Business Research Portal is a list of annotated links to internet sites intended to help small business, researchers, policy makers and support agencies. The main objective of this site is to provide a 'definitive portal for small business research'. Browse or use the site's search facility to find inks, which are grouped together in 13 different categories. The website offers recent job adverts and links to other sites covering the latest news on small business and related research and policy news. The site itself is designed to be quick and easy to use, with any unnecessary graphics and other features removed to avoid slow response rates. Its simplicity of use and the fact that new items are added on a continuous basis makes it a valuable reference source.

4066 SmallBusiness.co.uk [UK]
www.smallbusiness.co.uk/
One of several business and finance websites produced by Vitesse Media plc. SmallBusiness.co.uk offers advice on how to set up and run small businesses. The site offers free online advice in the form of news articles, guides, tips and features. Content is divided into ten key areas of business decision making: start a business; small business finance; sales and marketing; legal services; starting a business abroad; franchise zone; business premises; business banking; business technology; and human resources. It also

offers a Q&A forum, which contains questions and comments on a variety of useful small business topics. Site users need to be registered in order to post or respond to any of the questions.

4067   Webpractices.com
www.webpractices.com/index.html
Webpractices.com is a private resource directory for the e-commerce community. It is a collection of resources aimed at anyone interested in planning, building and running a successful web business. The site is packed with information, offering articles, presentations, technical advice and other resources that promote good web business practices. There is a useful section that provides examples of the best and the worse websites. Material is selected by the site's editor-in-chief but anyone from the web community is invited to be an 'active contributor ' to the site.

Discovering print & electronic resources

4068   Encyclopedia of business information sources
L.D. Hall, ed.   21st edn, Gale Research Intenational, 2006, 1319pp. £247. ISBN 078768306X.
www.gale.com/
'Encyclopedia of business information sources identifies live, print and electronic sources of information listed under alphabetically arranged subjects'. Within each subject, resources are then arranged by type (directories, databases, newsletters, indexes, research centres, etc.). See publisher's website for PDF sample pages.

4069   ENTERWeb
www.enterweb.org/
An impressive annotated list of resources on enterprise development, business, finance, international trade and the economy. The main focus is on 'micro, small and medium scale enterprises, cooperatives, community economic development, both in developed and developing countries'. All of the resources on this site are reviewed individually and rated by the ENTERWeb team, from average to outstanding, 'according to content depth and value added, while also considering design, ease of navigation and speed of loading. For each category best resources are listed first'. The site has a rather busy home page which can be a bit offputting, but selecting the main menu option presents the site's material as a subject list. Resources can also be viewed by geographic location or via an alphabetical index. The site can be viewed in English or French.

Digital data, image & text collections

4070   ABI/INFORM Dateline [USA]
http://proquest.com/
ABI/INFORM Dateline is a database that specializes in local and regional business publications with 'news about local companies, plus analysis and information on local markets'. Use Dateline to 'research employment opportunities, compile data on benefits and compensation, learn about corporate strategies and other topics from a local and regional perspective'. It includes 175 publications, with more than 170 available in full text; these include major business publications, daily newspapers, wire services and area business publications. Website contains a range of product

information (PDF & Word format) plus training material on database searching.

4071   Business and Company ProFiles ASAP
www.gale.com
'Business & Company ProFiles integrates information from Business Index ASAP and the full text of PR Newswire releases with over 200,000 combined directory listings including the Graham & Whiteside international company directories.' The database includes key business, management and economic journals, national newspapers, industry publications and full-text company directory of US and international listings, including private company data. See publisher's website for list of titles, search tips and full product information.

4072   Business and Company Resource Center
www.galegroup.com/BusinessRC/
'The first of its kind, Business and Company Resource Center brings together a wide variety of global business information, enabling users to efficiently research business case studies, competitive intelligence and career and investment opportunities'. The database includes records covering company profiles, industry rankings, products and brands, company performance ratings, investment reports, industry statistics, current investment ratings, financial ratios, industry news and analysis. See publisher's website for an electronic tour of the database and information on a free trial.

4073   Center for Entrepreneurial Leadership Clearinghouse on Entrepreneurship Education
www.celcee.edu/
Created in 1996 as a joint project of the University of California, Los Angeles, and the Kauffman Center for Entrepreneurial Leadership, CELCEE is a non-profit organization that specializes in information sources related to entrepreneurship education. These resources, which include journal articles, conference proceedings, pamphlets, curriculum guides, government publications, videos, books and computer software, are then annotated and added to a free online database. The database is fully searchable and updated on a weekly basis. CELCEE publishes several digests and brief summaries (EdInfos) which provide overviews and references on current issues relating to entrepreneurship. The website also houses a collection of links to organizations dealing with entrepreneurship and entrepreneurship education.

4074   Factiva
www.il.proquest.com/
Factiva is a web-based information service that can be used for searching and monitoring global news and business information. It contains full-text global coverage from newspapers, academic journals, trade and industry magazines and websites, both same-day and archival. It also provides company profiles, financial and stock performance, company-to-industry comparative reports, market index reports, latest press releases and selected web links. See website for more details on pricing, a full product overview and search guides.

4075   Northern Light business research engine
www.nlresearch.com/
The business research engine is a website created by the

Northern Light Group, a company based in Cambridge, Massachusetts, that specializes in creating research portals. It is essentially a large database containing articles, white papers, case studies and news reports covering a wide range of industries. Refreshingly simple to use, the database can be searched by industry or by resources type. Site visitors have free access to white papers and news resources but have to subscribe to gain full access to content taken from journals and trade magazines. There are various subscription levels, including a 24-hour day pass.

Directories & encyclopedias

4076   Blackwell encyclopedia of management: international business
J.M. McNett [et al.], eds   2nd edn, Blackwell, 2006, 368pp. Blackwell encyclopedia of management V. 6, £85. ISBN 0631234934. www.managementencyclopedia.com
'Provides clear, up-to-the-minute definitions and explanations of the key concepts in the fast-changing field of international management. This revised edition covers recent developments arising from globalization, the internet, e-commerce and meta-markets. Information on new International Standards is included together with the impact of the European Union and the new geo-political areas of the Russian Federation and China.'

4077   Business organizations, agencies and publications directory
L.D. Hall, ed.   19th edn, Thomson Gale, 2006, 2033pp. £338. ISBN 0787678295.
www.gale.com/s
A comprehensive source of business information describing organizations, their products and services specially aimed at business and industry. 'Content is arranged under five broad categories: US and international organizations; Government agencies and programs; facilities and services; research and educational facilities; publications and information services'.

4078   D&B million dollar directory [USA]
Dun & Bradstreet, annual. ISSN 10934812.
www.apinfo.co.uk/
The *Million dollar directory* profiles leading US private and public companies. The directory contains easy-to-use cross-references; primary and secondary lines of business; and the names and titles of company officers and directors. Available either as a five-volume set with the first three volumes containing alphabetical listings, while the fourth and fifth are cross-referenced volumes grouped geographically by US state and Standard Industry Classification (SIC). Alternatively, there is a separate publication called the *Million dollar directory top 50,000*, which presents the leading 50,000 US businesses.

4079   D&B principal international businesses
Dun & Bradstreet, annual. ISSN 00976288.
www.apinfo.co.uk/
Aimed at anyone currently selling internationally, this annual publication provides information on the top 100,000 companies worldwide (based on a total number of employees). It covers key information on all types of businesses in more than 140 countries. Information is presented in three ways: geographically, by product classification and alphabetically.

4080   Encyclopedia of corporate names worldwide
A. Room   McFarland, 2002, 585pp. £52.50. ISBN 0786412879. www.mcfarlandpub.com/
A fascinating encyclopedia that provides the origin and etymology of more than 3500 commercial names, including both company names and the names of products and services. Geographic coverage is mainly US and UK, with some coverage of European and Japanese products.

4081   Europa: key European enterprises
Dun & Bradstreet, 2006. 4 v., £600. ISBN 1860715885. www.apinfo.co.uk/
This four-volume directory provides 'comprehensive business information for over 50,000 leading European companies'. The largest companies from each country have been selected using criteria based on annual sales and number of employees. In addition, the directory provides aggregated statistical and geographical information for each company, This includes statistical profiles of companies by country and the top 5000 companies ranked by annual sales in Europe. Volumes 1–3 present an alphabetical list of the top companies for each country. Volume 4 presents company indexes, rankings, statistics and tables.

4082   Gale encyclopedia of e-commerce
J.A. Malonis, ed.   Gale, 2002. 2 v., £216.31. ISBN 0787656607. www.gale.com/
This two-volume set examines the topics, companies, people, events and legislation relating to the world of e-commerce. Containing over 470 detailed essays, the encyclopaedia presents case studies, individual and organizational profiles of industry leaders and a chronology and timeline of key events in e-commerce development. Also covers common questions about website development, financing, advertising and other related topics. Each section finishes with source suggestions for further study and there is a subject index to organization names, personal names, industries and subject terms. See publisher's website for full table of contents, indexes and sample pages.

Gurus on e-business
J. Middleton   See entry no. 3994

4083   International directory of company histories
St James Press, irregular. ISSN 15570126.
www.gale.com/stjames/
A multi-volume series that provides detailed information on the historical development of the world's most important companies. Entries for each company provides information on 'the founders, expansions and losses, labour/management actions, NAIC codes, key dates, ticker symbol, principal subsidiaries, principal divisions, principal operating units, principal competitors and other significant milestones'. Each volume includes a cumulative index to all companies mentioned in that volume and all previous volumes in the set. Ideal for students, job candidates, business executives, historians and investors requiring 'accurate and detailed information' on the world's largest and most influential companies.

4084   Key British enterprises
Dun & Bradstreet, annual. £660.00 + p&p. ISSN 01425048. www.apinfo.co.uk [DESCRIPTION]
This four-volume directory presents information on the UK's top 54,000 companies. Volumes 1–3 contain alphabetical

listings of the companies, with Volume 4 providing cross-referenced indexes and company rankings. 'All of the companies featured in the directory have been selected on the basis of meeting at least one of the following criteria: 80 or more employees; Sales turnover in excess of £8 million; Total assets in excess of £30 million'. Companies cover a range of business activities, including agriculture, forestry & fishing; mining; construction; manufacturing; transportation; communication; public utilities; wholesale trade; retail trade; finance, insurance and real estate; business services; social services and public administration.

4085 **Small business sourcebook** [USA]
S.D. Hill, ed.   22nd edn, Thomson Gale, 2007. 2 v., $499. ISBN 0787688568.
http://gale.cengage.com/
The *Small business sourcebook* is an impressive two-volume set presenting annotated lists of information sources for those wishing to start, develop and maintain small businesses. Volume 1 provides detailed entries on more than 26,000 live and print sources of information for 340 industries of interest to small businesses, ranging from accounting to word-processing services. Volume 2 provides the same detailed information on more than 30,000 sources of information for 99 general small business topics, including management, marketing, business trends and labour relations. In addition, Volume 2 features over 10,006 state listings and over 1084 relevant US federal government agencies and branch offices. A Master Index lists all the entries of Vols. 1 and 2 in a single alphabetic sequence. This is a comprehensive guide to sources of information on all aspects of US-based small business.

Handbooks & manuals

4086 **Entrepreneur's information sourcebook: charting the path to small business success** [USA]
S.C. Awe   Libraries Unlimited, 2006, 245pp. £19.99. ISBN 1591582423.
http://lu.com/
A well put-together source of entrepreneurial resources. Provides a comprehensive list of both print and electronic resources on a wide range of entrepreneurial topics. Contents include everything from exploring the attributes of entrepreneurs to managing employees. Taking a practical, step-by-step approach. Each business process is described in detail and includes an annotated list of related and supplementary resources. There is a glossary at the end of the volume which includes related website addresses and an extensive index. 'A first (and last) stop for any small business owner or would-be entrepreneur'.

4087 **Growing business handbook: inspiration and advice from successful entrepreneurs and fast growing UK companies** [UK]
A. Jolly   9th edn, Kogan Page, 2006, 366pp. £25. ISBN 0749448075.
www.kogan-page.com
Now in its 9th edition, this handbook is a practical resource tool for expanding businesses. It presents best practice guidance from practitioners in established businesses and organizations and explores the first-hand experiences of entrepreneurs. Contents include: Growth challenges (strategy and planning); Gaining market share; Exploiting ideas (innovation, creativity and IP); Entrepreneurial skills; People

and performance; Cash flow and working capital; Property and locations; Controlling growth; Global expansion; Acquisitions and disposals; Growth capital; Enterprise risk; Business technology; and Smarter organizations.

4088 **Handbook of family business and family business consultation: a global perspective**
F.W. Kaslow, ed.   International Business Press, 2006, 464pp. £35.95. ISBN 0789027771.
www.haworthpress.com/
A detailed examination of the structure and dynamics of family-run businesses in thirteen countries (Brazil, Canada, Chile, Ireland, South Korea, Lebanon, Mexico, Saudi Arabia, Scotland, Trinidad & Tobago, Turkey, UK and the USA). The book provides a historical look at the development of family-run businesses and discusses a wide range of current topics, such as the importance of family businesses to the economy worldwide, sibling rivalry and other family conflict, the roles of non-family employees in family businesses and the impact of globalization. Tables and figures, further readings and a helpful glossary have been included to aid understanding of the more complex topics. An 'essential read for family business consultants, family business owners and Family Business Forum staff and member families, as well as professors and students in MBA programs and family business courses'.

4089 **Hoover's handbook of world business**
14th edn, Hoover's Handbooks, 2007, 407pp. $190. ISBN 1573111163.
www.hoovers.com/
A title from the Hoovers handbook series that provides in-depth information on the world's largest, fastest-growing and most influential public and private companies. This title contains over 300 profiles of influential firms from 'Canada, Europe and Japan, as well as companies from the fast-growing economies of such countries as China, India and Taiwan.' Each entry includes a company overview, history, executives, locations, products, competitors and historical financials.

4090 **International handbook of women and small business entrepreneurship**
S.L. Fielden and M.J. Davidson   Edward Elgar, 2005, 450pp. Elgar original reference series, £95. ISBN 1843760126.
www.e-elgar.co.uk/
Despite the increasing number of women entrepreneurs over the past few years, the authors argue that in terms of research, female entrepreneurship has received comparatively little attention from the academic community. This book attempts to redress this imbalance by bringing together a review of the research that has been carried out in this area. Divided into five sections: Part I concentrates on identifying the typical characteristics and personality traits of women entrepreneurs. Part II examines the constraints that can inhibit women's success and the strategies adopted to overcome these constraints. Part III looks at the experiences of women from different ethnic backgrounds trying to set up their own small business. Part IV discusses female entrepreneurship from a global perspective. The final section presents emerging themes that will have a global impact on women business owners. Also available in e-book format.

4091 Oxford handbook of international business
A.M. Rugman and T.L. Brewer, eds   Oxford University Press, 2003, 877pp. £31. ISBN 0199258414.
www.oup.com/
Brings together a collection of articles written by leading scholars in the field of international business. 'The book is split into five major sections, providing comprehensive coverage of the following areas: the history and theory of the multinational enterprise; the political and policy environment of international business; strategies of multinational enterprises; the financial areas of the multinational enterprise (marketing, finance and accounting, HRM and innovation); and business systems in Asia, South America and the transitional economies.' See publisher's website for a sample chapter (PDF).

4092 Public administration and public management: the principal-agent perspective
J-E. Lane   Routledge, 2006, 292pp. £19.99. ISBN 0415370167.
www.routledge.com/
This book presents a comprehensive analysis of the public sector and how it operates. Covers topics such as the principal–agent framework; public principals and their agents; the economic reasons of government; public organization, incentives and rationality in government; the essence of public administration: legality and the rule of law; public policy criteria: public teams and private teams; public firms; public insurance; and public management policy. 'Essential reading for those with professional and research interests in public administration and public management'.

4093 Small business handbook: the complete guide to running and growing your business [UK]
S. Parks   Pearson/Prentice Hall Business, 2006, 197pp. + CD-ROM, £18.99. ISBN 0273695312.
www.pearsoned.co.uk/
'Intended as an essential reference for anybody starting their own business'. An impressive handbook offering guidance on all aspects of running a business, everything from planning for growth, staff management, finance, finding suppliers, customer care to devising an exit strategy. The book also comes with a CD-ROM containing a range of useful templates and essential documents. Plus it features audio clips of successful entrepreneurs offering their tips and techniques for running a successful business. 'The book is endorsed by the Institute of Entrepreneurs and by a wide range of entrepreneurs who have been there and done it.'

Keeping up to date

4094 Business 2.0
Time Inc, 11 p.a. ISSN 15381730.
www.money.cnn.com/magazines/business2/ [COMPANION]
Business 2.0 was originally started to cover the rise of the 'new economy', focusing on the relationship between technology and business. Since then, the magazine has expanded to include emerging technologies, marketing, strategy and business models, trends and opportunities. One of the magazine's most popular features is its annual '101 dumbest moments in business'. Companion website, hosted by CNNMoney.com, provides content from the current and past issues plus special articles from the magazine's writers. RSS feed available for latest news and stories.

4095 BusinessWeek
McGraw-Hill. ISSN 00077135.
www.businessweek.com/ [COMPANION]
BusinessWeek was first published in 1929 and since then has become a well respected business publication. The magazine features news stories on financial markets, industries and technology. It contains company profiles, interviews with high-profile business men and women and covers developments within business and the economy at large. BusinessWeek is also famous for its annual ranking of business school MBA programmes in the USA. Subscription to the magazine comes with free access to BusinessWeek online. Non-subscribers can register for the online version of the magazine and gain free access to the magazine archive, a free newsletter and the site's forums and message boards.

4096 E-commerce times
ECT News Network, Inc.
www.ecommercetimes.com/
Launched in 1998, E-commerce times is an e-business and technology news site and an anchor publication of the ECT News Network, a US-based e-business and new technology publisher. It describes itself as a 'must-read for IT professionals and other key decision-makers'. The site links to stories and news items, with weekly archives available for keyword searching or browsing. There is a large directory of companies supplying electronic commerce products and services plus research reports on a range of e-business topics (free pre-registration required to use this service). Site also has a career section and an online forum.

4097 Family Business: the guide for family companies [USA]
Family Business Publishing Company, qtrly. ISSN 1047255X.
www.familybusinessmagazine.com/index.html [COMPANION]
First published in 1989, Family Business is a quarterly magazine aimed at owners and managers of family companies. It focuses on issues such as succession planning, estate and tax planning, business strategy and wealth preservation. The companion website to the magazine contains a searchable archive of more than 15 years of Family business articles (including those from the current issue). Non-members can download individual articles for $10 each; current Family Business subscribers get unlimited access to all articles in the library for the length of their print subscription.

4098 Fast Company
Fast Company, monthly. ISSN 10859241.
www.fastcompany.com/ [COMPANION]
A monthly magazine covering new and emerging business trends in technological innovation, digital media, change management, leadership, design and social responsibility. Companion website contains the current magazine, back issues, discussion forums and other online features such as podcasts and weblog entries from the magazine's staff. Non-subscribers can see selected articles from the current edition and have full access to archive editions. The website also provides a number of free online guides for small businesses covering a variety of different business areas such as leadership, marketing and branding, sales, customer services and innovative strategies.

4099 L'Expansion [FRA]
www.lexpansion.com/ [COMPANION]

A French business magazine that provides news articles on companies and businesses in France and worldwide. Has regular features on the French and global economy, including economic data and indicators. Also gives sales turnovers for the 100 leading French companies or sectors and carries a regular advice feature for new graduates. Website contains selected free material but most of the content is only available for subscribers. An excellent source of information for anyone wishing to learn about French business, companies and management (available only in French).

UK Company News
See entry no. 3000

Business Responsibility

business ethics • corporate governance • social accountability

Introductions to the subject

4100 Business environment
I. Worthington and C. Britton   5th edn, Financial Times Prentice Hall, 2006, 527pp. £36.99. ISBN 0273704249.

A well established textbook aimed at students taking a first course in the business environment as part of a business or finance degree. It offers a comprehensive analysis of both the internal and external factors affecting today's business environment. 'Fully updated with the most recent developments in business, the book includes material on: social responsibility and ethics in business; regional and national government; the European Union; public-private partnerships; outsourcing and transitional markets'. Every chapter provides a full case study and mini-case vignettes that use real-life companies to illustrate a range of business environment issues. Comes with companion website.

4101 Corporate responsibility code book
D. Leipziger   Greenleaf, 2003, 512pp. £50. ISBN 1874719780.
www.greenleaf-publishing.com/

A comprehensive 'how-to' guide, the *Corporate responsibility code book* is a 'guide for companies trying to understand the landscape of corporate responsibility and searching for their own, unique route towards satisfying diverse stakeholders'. Based on interviews with academics, those responsible for setting and implementing standards and other key stakeholders from around the world, the book is designed to help companies select, develop and implement their own codes of conduct. It covers a wide range of issues from human rights, labour and environmental management to corruption and corporate governance. It also provides the full text of many of the codes profiled.

'This excellent review provides more clarity and greater understanding for all interested parties about the current state of play in codes of conduct. This book will serve not only businesses but also readers interested in better grasping the current debate about codes of conduct, their effectiveness and credibility' (Dominique Bé, European Commission)

4102 Ethics and the conduct of business
J.R. Boatright   5th edn, Pearson/Prentice Hall, 2005, 451pp. £39.99. ISBN 0131947214.
www.pearsoned.co.uk/

'Comprehensive and far-reaching in scope' this text provides in-depth coverage of a wide range of business ethics issues, including ethics in the world of business; ethics in finance; ethics in corporations; and international business ethics. Each chapter includes real-life examples and cases to illustrate many of the issues. The revised and updated fifth edition includes new topics such as internet privacy, managing conflicts of interest, foreign sweatshops, hostile takeovers and fairness in financial markets and financial services. This text provides an excellent introduction to some of the 'ethical issues that corporate decision makers face in developing policies about employees, customers and the general public'.

4103 A history of corporate governance around the world: family business groups to professional managers
R.K. Morck, ed.   University of Chicago Press, 2005, 687pp. National Bureau of Economic Research conference report, £57. ISBN 0226536807.
www.press.uchicago.edu

'*A history of corporate governance around the world* provides historical studies of the patterns of corporate governance in several countries – including the large industrial economies of Canada, France, Germany, Italy, Japan, the UK and the USA; larger developing economies like China and India; and alternative models like those of the Netherlands and Sweden.'

'Still, this is a rich book that sets a solid benchmark for the comparative study of the history of CG, and its relevance to IB. It offers a welcome exploration of another way to explain why CG differs across countries by noting the relevance of history' (Pierre van der Eng in *Journal of Business Studies*)(http://aib.msu.edu/jibs/bookreviews/html/2006-07.asp [26/11/06]

4104 Principles of contemporary corporate governance
J.J. Du Plessis, J. McConvill and M. Bagaric   Cambridge University Press, 2005, 395pp. £29.99. ISBN 0521617839.
www.cambridge.org/

Presents a concise introduction to the 'key topics and emerging themes in corporate governance'. Suitable for both law and business students, as well as business practitioners, this book is written in an 'easy-to-follow' style, with thorough explanations and analysis of key corporate governance principles. The book attempts to explain the rules and principles that regulate corporate governance. Geographic focus is on Australia, but also includes the UK, US and Germany. There is a detailed examination of board and committee structures, risk management policies, auditors and audits and the duties and liabilities of directors. The book finishes off by looking at current policy issues and the impact on future developments and possible corporate governance trends. Contents: Part 1 – corporate governance: an overview; Part 2 – corporate governance in Australia; Part 3 – corporate governance in practice; Part 4 – corporate governance: an international perspective; Part 5 – corporate governance: going forward.

Laws, standards, codes

4105 Company law and corporate governance [EUR]
www.ec.europa.eu/internal_market/company/index_en.htm
Company law and corporate governance is a section on the
EU single market thematic website hosted by EUROPA.
Maintained by the Internal Market and Services Directorate
General (DG MARKT), a department of the European
Commission, the key objective of the website is to 'increase
knowledge of and support for the EU Single Market among
interested citizens, businesses, journalists and other
stakeholders by providing users with clear, up to date and
easily navigable information in at least three languages
(English, French and German)'. The site provides online
access to directives, regulations, recommendations, news
and information on financial crime, plus other related
documents.

4106 European Corporate Governance Institute
www.ecgi.org/
The ECGI is an international non-profit association that
provides 'a forum for debate and dialogue between
academics, legislators and practitioners, focusing on major
corporate governance issues and thereby promoting best
practice'. The Association's primary role is to 'undertake,
commission and disseminate research on corporate
governance' which it then distributes, along with other
relevant material, through its website. Resources freely
available include research projects, clinical papers, finance
and law working papers; a useful section providing full-text
links to codes organized by country; external links to
organizations involved with corporate governance and
information on conferences, discussions and current
transatlantic debates. This is a well organized website that is
updated regularly.

**4107 Law and ethics in global business: how to
integrate law and ethics into corporate governance
around the world**
B.L. Nelson   Routledge, 2005, 302pp. £29.99. ISBN 041537779X.
www.routledge.com/
'This book provides comprehensive and, above all, business
focused guidance on the fundamentals of business law and
how they should be integrated into ethical and effective
business decisions. It concentrates on legal principles and
thereby is able to articulate the impact of global business
law and its international applications and provides a
comprehensive overview of the legal and ethical principles
which both facilitate and regulate corporate business.'

Official & quasi-official bodies

4108 Competition Commission [UK]
www.competition-commission.org.uk
The Competition Commission is an independent public body
that was established by the Competition Act 1998, replacing
the Monopolies and Mergers Commission in 1999. The
Commission conducts in-depth inquiries into mergers,
markets and the regulation of the major regulated industries.
The website provides information about the Commission, its
current inquiries and a searchable directory of all its past
inquiries. Full-text access is freely available for most of the
Commission's output, including notices, actions and

decisions; evaluation reports; occasional papers; consultation
documents; and inquiry reports.

4109 Corporate governance
www.oecd.org/topic/0,2686,en_2649_37439_1_1_1_1_37439,00.
html
This section of the OCED website is dedicated to improving
the 'quality of governance within enterprises'. The site
contains a huge range of resources, including a range of
related publications, documents, statistics and news on
policy initiatives. It also features country-specific information
covering company law and corporate governance; corporate
responsibility; entrepreneurship at local level; institutions,
governance and development; governance and privatization of
state-owned assets; insolvency and corporate distress;
disclosure and accounting reforms and guidelines for
multinational enterprises. The OECD principles of corporate
governance can be freely downloaded in 12 different
languages. This website is an excellent starting point for
anyone wishing to get to grips with the area of corporate
governance.

4110 CSR.gov.UK
www.csr.gov.uk/
This site is a UK government gateway aimed at 'developing
corporate social responsibility' in the UK and encouraging
UK businesses to consider the economic, social and
environmental impacts of their activities. Contains
information on relevant policy and legislation, projects and
initiatives involved across the CSR agenda, links to websites
providing best practice guidelines and online access to a
range of CSR-related publications that can be freely
downloaded.

4111 EnviroWindows [EUR]
www.ewindows.eu.org
The purpose of EnviroWindows is to facilitate access to
'information on products, practices, use of natural resources
and corporate environmental performance. It helps local
authorities to communicate with concerned citizens,
professionals, policy makers and corporations'. The site is
maintained by the European Environment Agency and offers
two main services: interest groups and an information portal.
The interest groups section is intended to provide a forum for
environmental professionals to exchange resources, ideas
and information. The information portal is divided into four
separate areas, featuring a variety of related documents and
tools for download. Site also contains information on
conferences, training and jobs, with links to an environmental
news service and the opportunity to ask questions of
environmental experts around the world. Not the most
intuitive of websites but does contain a useful selection of
content.

4112 United States. Office of Government Ethics
www.usoge.gov/index.html
US Office of Government Ethics (OGE) is a small government
agency that creates and enforces ethical standards and
codes of practice for all government employees. The site
contains lists of ethics statutes and regulations, executive
orders and *Federal register* issuances that pertain to ethics.
There are also full-text links to conflict of interest laws and
ethics regulations and miscellaneous resources, such as OLC
opinions, court cases and the annual conflict of interest
prosecution survey. Another useful section on this site is an

A–Z collection of links to other government (federal, state and local) and non-government websites that contain ethics information.

Research centres & institutes

4113　Centre for Corporate Accountability [UK]
www.corporateaccountability.org
The Centre for Corporate Accountability is a charity concerned with the promotion of workers and public safety. Originally set up in 1999 as a not-for-profit organization, it received charitable status in 2004. The organization has two main functions. It carries out research into 'matters relating to law enforcement and corporate criminal accountability' and provides an advice service. The CCA is the only non-governmental organization in Britain that provides free, independent and confidential advice and assistance to anyone who has suffered as a result of a work-related injury or families suffering bereavement from a work-related death. Site contains details of its research, safety statistics, press releases, publications, a newsletter and a bibliography.

4114　European Centre for Corporate Governance
www.ljmu.ac.uk/eccg/Index.htm
Based at the Liverpool John Moores University, the ECCG seeks to be the 'leading centre in Europe for advancing knowledge and practice in corporate governance.' It assists directors and senior executives to develop their leadership skills in order to 'shape their organizations and enable them to ethically compete in a complex and dynamic global environment.' Research carried out by the Centre is focused on corporate governance and related issues, which includes risk management, corporate performance and leadership. Details of the Centre's research can be found on the website. There is also a very useful research links and contacts page.

4115　Institute for Corporate Culture Affairs
www.cca-institute.org/
Established in 2003, the Institute for Corporate Culture Affairs (ICCA), based in Frankfurt, is an independent not-for-profit organization dedicated to promoting corporate social responsibility (CSR) to leading global companies, 'ensuring its integration into their daily business and offering long-term support to secure future progress'. To this aim the Institute's main activities include knowledge dissemination, networking and primary research. The website contains details about the Institute, activities and membership benefits, which includes access to a global online directory of CSR practices being used by some of the world's leading companies. The site also provides details of the Institute's main publications.

4116　Institute for Global Ethics
www.globalethics.org/
The Institute for Global Ethics (IGE) is an independent, non-profit organization that is 'dedicated to promoting ethical action in a global context'. The Institute seeks to 'elevate awareness of ethics and provide practical tools for making ethical decisions'. The website features an interesting section called Dilemmas, a list of real-life situations highlighting an ethical problem that needs to be resolved. Other resources include full-text access to white papers, book extracts, the Institute's newsletter and magazine *Ethical Connections*.

■ **Ethics Newsline** Institute for Global Ethics, Weekly. Features news and information on ethics and current events. Free online access, with an option to receive the newsletter via e-mail.

4117　Institute of Business Ethics
www.ibe.org.uk
The Institute of Business Ethics (IBE) was established in 1986 with the aim of encouraging 'high standards of business behaviour based on ethical values'. It offers practical advice and training on ethical issues such as policy design and implementation. It undertakes research and surveys into good practice and ethical business conduct. The Institute's impressive website gives details of its services and training, forthcoming IBE events, projects and publications. There is a useful section containing annotated links to both UK and international business ethics and corporate responsibility websites. It also sets out detailed guidelines for businesses on how to develop, implement and maintain their own code of ethics, with an examples section that provides links to the home pages of companies that have their own code of ethics in place.

Associations & societies

4118　Asian Corporate Governance Association
www.acga-asia.org/
Founded in 1999, the ACGA is a non-profit membership organization dedicated to the development and improvement of corporate governance in Asian markets through research, advocacy and education. Its website provides country snapshots, regional analysis and country-specific codes and rules, articles, surveys and reports, plus annotated web links. Much of the material is freely available to non-members. Membership to the ACGA is open to corporations only, benefits include access to a 'premium content' section of the website that contains more specialized documents and presentations, complimentary copies of reports, articles and submissions that ACGA produces, plus a complimentary seat at its annual conference.

4119　Corporate Watch
www.corporatewatch.org
Corporate Watch is a small research and publishing group actively 'supporting the campaigns which are increasingly successful in forcing corporations to back down. Corporate Watch is part of the growing anti-corporate movement springing up around the world.' This is an interesting website that contains reports, briefings and articles on its key research projects; profiles of large companies, giving details of company personnel, office locations, industry areas, lobbying activities and corporate crimes; industry overviews and a detailed guide on how to research companies. The site features a free bi-monthly newsletter and archive going back to 1996. Users can register to receive the newsletter via e-mail.

4120　European Business Ethics Network – UK
www.ebenuk.org/
Established in 1994, EBEN-UK is the UK association of the European Business Ethics Network. Its main purpose is to 'provide a forum for academics and practitioners to discuss and debate issues to do with business ethics/corporate social responsibility.' The site contains the Network's online newsletter, details of its conference programme and

occasional regional workshops, book reviews, links to other websites connected to business ethics and information on how to become a member.

4121 International Corporate Governance Network
www.icgn.org/

The International Corporate Governance Network (ICGN) is a not-for-profit organization dedicated to promoting good corporate governance globally. The Network has four primary objectives: 'to provide an investor-led network for the exchange of views and information about corporate governance issues internationally; to examine corporate governance principles and practices; to develop and encourage adherence to corporate governance standards and guidelines; to generally promote good corporate governance'. See website for details of membership and the Network's annual conference.

4122 International Society of Business, Economics & Ethics
www.isbee.org/

'The International Society of Business, Economics & Ethics (ISBEE) is the first worldwide professional association to focus exclusively on the study of business, economics and ethics'. Its membership is made up of both academics and professionals who have an interest in business ethics. The website provides details of the Society's conference, publications, related documents and a useful links section to web pages of other organizations concerned with business ethics. The Society also produces an online newsletter which can be freely downloaded. Perhaps the most noteworthy feature of this website is its searchable bibliography containing more than 4000 references to articles published in the major journals on business and economic ethics over the last 20 years (up until May 2005).

4123 Social Accountability International
www.sa-intl.org/

Social Accountability International (SAI) is a 'non-governmental, international, multi-stakeholder organization dedicated to improving workplaces and communities by developing and implementing socially responsible standards'. The organization works directly with companies, non-governmental organizations, labour and trade unions promoting the SA8000 system, which is a voluntary international standard for improving working conditions. Full details of the standard and the organization's programmes can be found on the website. Site also contains ethical sourcing resources, news and events, useful links, articles and membership details.

Libraries, archives, museums

4124 Corporate Governance Library
www.corpgov.net/library/library.html

The Corporate Governance site at CorpGov.net contains an online library which has an excellent selection of material on corporate governance. The library includes an annotated bibliography, excerpts and reviews of recent books, online articles, codes and principles and other related documents, plus a very useful list of organizations and journals related to the subject area of corporate governance. An excellent starting point for those wishing to find out more about this subject area.

4125 Corporate Library [USA]
www.thecorporatelibrary.com/

The Corporate Library was founded in 1999 with the aim of providing a comprehensive collection of material on corporate governance plus executive and director compensation and company performance data. It regularly publishes reports, surveys and in-depth studies on current issues relating to corporate governance and compensation, which can be purchased directly from the website. The library offers a variety of different subscription services, including Board Analyst, a database containing information on corporate governance and compensation. Details of all its services can be found on its website.

Portal & task environments

4126 Business for Social Responsibility
www.bsr.org/

BSR is a global, non-profit organization dedicated to advancing the field of corporate social responsibility by helping 'companies of all sizes and sectors to achieve success in ways that demonstrate respect for ethical values, people, communities and the environment'. It provides information, tools, training and advisory services to promote corporate social responsibility. The website offers a large collection of online tools and guidelines for responsible business practices, most of which are freely available. Resources include a useful collection of 'Issue briefs', which are basically overviews of corporate social responsibility issues such as business ethics; governance and accountability; community investment and the environment. Site contains full details of membership benefits and services.

4127 E-businessethics.com
www.e-businessethics.com/

This site is an excellent source of information on business ethics, corporate citizenship and organizational compliance. 'The goal of this site is to create a virtual community of organizations and individuals that share best practices in the improvement of business ethics. Much of this site's content is being provided by businesses, non-profit organizations, government agencies and academics that support interactivity and accessibility of information.' Content includes case studies; recommended books; links to other websites of interest and essays on internet privacy. There is also a teaching resources section that includes PowerPoint presentations and other useful sources of teaching material.

4128 EthicsWeb
www.ethicsweb.ca/resources/business/

BusinessEthics.ca is one of the websites available from EthicsWeb.ca (a collection of ethics-related websites run by Chris MacDonald, an Associate Professor of Philosophy at Saint Mary's University in Halifax, Canada). The site contains both Canadian and international resources, including articles, case studies, books, news reports and links to other institutes and organizations. Website also links to Professor MacDonald's business ethics blog.

4129 GreenBiz
www.greenbiz.com/

Greenbiz is a web resource published by Greener World Media, Inc., who state that their main mission is to 'provide clear, concise, accurate and balanced information, resources and learning opportunities to help companies of all sizes and sectors integrate environmental responsibility into their operations in a manner that supports profitable business practices'. The site is packed with useful resources, including how-to-guides, easy-to-read subject overviews, reports and tools. It includes an extensive list of links to other useful organizations and websites. Also features latest news and developments, an event calendar, plus a jobs and careers section. Registered users receive a free subscription to a fortnightly e-newsletter. Greenbiz has also launched three additional websites: GreenerBuildings.com which provides free, web-based resources specifically aimed at providing advice and guidance on green building practices; ClimateBiz.com which contains a range of resources to help companies and sectors 'understand and address climate change in a way that aligns environmental responsibility with business success'; GreenBizLeaders.com – a site created in partnership with the US Environmental Protection Agency that contains a searchable collection of real-life examples of companies which are attempting to adopt environmentally responsible business practices. Links to these sites can be found on the main GreenBiz website.

Directories & encyclopedias

4130 Blackwell encyclopedia of management: business ethics
P.H. Werhane and R.E. Freeman, eds   2nd edn, Blackwell, 2006, 582pp. Blackwell encyclopedia of management v. 2, £85. ISBN 1405100133.
www.managementencyclopedia.com/
This updated edition includes new topics such as e-business, internet and business ethics, nanotechnology and biodiversity, corporate citizenship, the Sarbanes-Oxley Act and socially responsible investing. Many of the entries, especially those covering different countries, have been 'updated to reflect the current business climate of those countries'. Also incorporates the lessons learned from well publicized cases of financial corruption in companies such as Enron, WorldCom, Global Crossing and Tyco.

4131 Encycogov
www.encycogov.com/
Encycogov is an online encyclopaedia specializing in the field of corporate governance. In addition to providing general information on corporate governance issues, it offers in-depth information on specific topics such as decision and monitoring systems, remuneration and bankruptcy systems, ownership, creditor and capital structures and the market for corporate control. Search or browes by topic. Also contains an A–Z bibliography and list of references.

Handbooks & manuals

4132 Governance of public and non-profit organizations: what do boards do? [UK]
C. Cornforth, ed.   Routledge, 2005, 259pp. Routledge studies in the management of voluntary and non-profit organizations 6, £22.99. ISBN 0415359929.
www.routledge.com/
Presents a thorough analysis of the role and functions of governing boards within public and non-profit organizations.

An ideal reference source 'for academics and students with an interest in the governance and management of public and non-profit organizations and will also be of value to policy makers and practitioners who wish to gain a deeper understanding of how boards work and what can be done to improve their performance.'

4133 The ICCA handbook on corporate social responsibility
J. Hennigfeld, M. Pohl and N. Tolhurst, eds; Institute for Corporate Culture Affairs   John Wiley & Sons, 2006, 420pp. £45. ISBN 0470057106.
http://eu.wiley.com/
Produced by the Institute for Corporate Culture Affairs, the handbook on CSR offers practical guidance on developing and implementing corporate social responsibility within organizations. Divided into three sections, the first provides a thorough introduction to the general concept of CSR, its background and development. The second section examines the different approaches taken by organizations in their implementation and practice of CSR, providing 'first-hand insights from well known CEOs, academics and organizations' on their experience and understanding of putting CSR into practice. The final section concludes with a critical perspective on ranking and auditing tools.

4134 Research handbook on corporate legal responsibility
S. Tully, ed.   Edward Elgar, 2005, 430pp. Elgar original reference, £115. ISBN 1843768208.
www.e-elgar.co.uk/
With contributions from leading academics, practitioners and policy makers from North America, Europe and Australia, this handbook provides a detailed examination of the theory and practice of corporate legal responsibility. It presents a historical look at the development of corporate legal responsibility, discusses the current legal situation and identifies possible future developments in this area. Chapters cover a range of global issues from environmental protection and sustainable development to the rights of women and children working in the textile industry. Other topics discussed include international aspects of corporate liability and corruption; directors' duties within the UK; corporate criminal liability in the USA; corporate environmental liability within the European Union; and protecting supplier interests through English company law.

Keeping up to date

4135 Business Ethics: a European review
Blackwell Publishing, qtrly. Subscription price for individual print and online, €135. ISSN 09628770.
www.blackwellpublishing.com
'The review provides a forum for business people and academics to exchange experiences of ethical challenges, to debate perspectives on ethical issues and to generate insights and new ways of thinking about the ethical dimensions of national and global business'. Website provides details of subscription plus a free online sample of a selected issue.

4136 CRO Magazine [USA]
CRO Corp, LLC, bi-monthly.
www.thecro.com/
*CRO Magazine] is a US-based, online publication produced by
The CRO, a membership organization specifically aimed at
providing information and best practice to corporate responsibility
officers. The magazine, which incorporates* Business Ethics
Magazine, *focuses exclusively on corporate ethics and
corporate social responsibility. With a readership of over
20,000 corporate and non-profit leaders, the magazine which
is hosted on the TheCRO.com website, features the Business
Ethics 100 best corporate citizens list, the Business Ethics
Awards and exclusive CRO conference coverage. Articles,
which are arranged by topic, can be freely accessed,
including a monthly archive for each topic.*

4137 Ethical Performance
Dunstans Publishing, monthly. Annual subscription (Print & online),
£348. ISSN 14646315.
www.ethicalperformance.com
Ethical Performance is a global newsletter that specializes in
corporate social responsibility, focusing on how large
companies and investing institutions are addressing human
rights issues such as ethics in the supply chain and the
environment. The newsletter is available in print and
electronic format. Users can become 'site guests' and have
free access for a 30-day trial period.

4138 Ethikos and Corporate Conduct Quarterly
Ethikos, bi-monthly. $185. ISSN 08955026.
www.singerpubs.com/ethikos/ [COMPANION]
Now in its 19th year, *Ethikos* is a bi-monthly publication that
examines ethical and compliance issues in relation to
business. Using a 'unique case-study approach' it essentially
reports on organizations and their real-life experiences in the
area of business ethics and compliance. Articles are written
by those involved in this area, namely compliance and ethics
officers, ombudspersons and practising professionals in the
fields of law, accounting, management and government.
Selected articles from past issues and a free sample of an
entire issue are available for download from the website.
'As an educator and researcher in business ethics, I need to stay
abreast of developments and best company practices. *Ethikos* is
an excellent source of information on both.' (Lynn Sharp Paine,
John G. McLean Professor, Harvard Business School)

4139 Journal of Business Ethics
Springer Netherlands, semi-monthly. ISSN 01674544.
www.springer.com/
'Since its initiation in 1980, the editors have encouraged the
broadest possible scope. The term "business" is understood
in a wide sense to include all systems involved in the
exchange of goods and services, while "ethics" is
circumscribed as all human action aimed at securing a good
life. Systems of production, consumption, marketing,
advertising, social and economic accounting, labour
relations, public relations and organizational behaviour are
analysed from a moral viewpoint.' The journal attracts a
broad readership level that encompasses the business
community, universities, government agencies and consumer
groups. See publisher's website for full subscription details.

4140 Multinational Monitor
Corporate Accountability Research Group   Essential Information
Inc. $45. ISSN 01974637.

www.multinationalmonitor.org/ [COMPANION]
Multinational Monitor is a non-profit magazine that was
founded in 1980 by Ralph Nader, the American attorney and
political activist. It was originally set up to track corporate
activities, particularly in the Third World. Articles typically
focus on the areas of globalization, health and safety issues,
labour union representation, developing economies,
multilateral banks, privatization and the environment. The
print version of the journal is available by subscription, with
a free, full-text version available from the website, including
archive issues back to 1981.

Marketing

brands • consumer groups • consumer research •
customer relations • direct marketing • e-marketing •
internet fraud • market research • niche marketing

Introductions to the subject

4141 Customer relationship management
E. Peelen   Financial Times Prentice Hall, 2005, 433pp. £37.99. ISBN
027368177X.
www.pearsoned.co.uk/
The book provides a thorough understanding of all aspects
of customer relationship management, covering strategy,
organization, marketing and information technology. Features
include case studies, 'practitioner insight' boxes to help
illustrate CRM in a practical context and review questions at
the end of each chapter.

4142 Global marketing management
K. Lee and S. Carter   Oxford University Press, 2005, 544pp. £33.99.
ISBN 0199267529.
www.oup.com/
A good introductory text that provides up-to-date coverage of
the 'essential elements of planning and implementing a
global strategic marketing plan'. The book also covers some
of the more contemporary issues in the area of global
marketing management, such as the increasing significance
of the service sector, rapid changes in technology and the
need for more socially responsible and ethical business
practices. There is a companion website available which
features a whole range of teaching materials for lecturers,
plus a list of useful websites, web exercises and further
reading references for students.

**4143 Internet marketing: strategy, implementation and
practice**
D. Chaffey [et al.]   3rd edn, Financial Times Prentice Hall, 2006,
550pp. £39.99. ISBN 0273694057.
www.pearsoned.co.uk/
Building on the success of the first two editions, this edition
provides an in-depth guide on how organizations can best
use the internet to support their marketing activities. New
features include 'in-depth global cases illustrating best
practice and the challenges of online marketing from well
known global e-businesses, including Amazon and eBay;
updated references to the full range of digital media,
including blogging, RSS, instant messaging, podcasting,
digital TV and mobile marketing; improved four colour design
to increase clarity and ease readability; greater focus on
strategy and development, with a revised chapter on
improving e-marketing performance.' This text is a useful

source of information for practitioners wishing to update their e-marketing knowledge and skills. A companion website is available containing extra study material for students and relevant resources designed for lecturers.

4144 Key marketing skills: strategies, tools, and techniques for marketing success
P. Cheverton   2nd edn, Kogan Page, 2004. with CD-ROM, £19.95. ISBN 0749442980.
www.kogan-page.co.uk/
Presents a range of practical information and advice on how to manage the marketing process. The book takes a very hands-on approach by using real-life, good and bad examples of marketing practice. Covers everything from devising a marketing plan to implementing successful customer relationship management. This revised and updated edition now includes international case studies and planning models. There are also new sections on 'brand management, how to brief an agency and how to conduct a self-assessment health check of your current level of marketing excellence'. The accompanying CD-ROM contains a ready-to-use Directional Policy Matrix (DPM), a marketing planning template, a range of interactive exercises, case studies and a presentation pack of tools and models.

4145 Market research in practice: a guide to the basics
P. Hague, N. Hague and C.-A. Morgan   new edn, Kogan Page, 2004, 244pp. Market research in practice series, £18.99. ISBN 0749441801.
www.kogan-page.co.uk
One of the titles in the Market research practice series, published in association with the Market Research Society. Aimed at the complete novice, this is a good introductory text to the various tools and techniques used in market research. Contents cover: 'the role of market research; market research design; desk research; focus groups and in-depth interviews; sampling; questionnaire design; interviewing; self-completion questionnaires and e-surveys; data analysis and report findings.' Also outlines current data protection legislation and details the professional ethics incorporated in the MRS code of conduct.
'A nice job of explaining the whole process of research, from the initial inkling of the need to do research through reporting the results.' (*Quirk Magazine*)

4146 Marketing insights from A to Z: 80 concepts every manager needs to know
P. Kotler   Wiley, 2003, 206pp. £19.99. ISBN 0471268674.
http://eu.wiley.com/
A very readable introduction to a range of marketing concepts from the 'father of modern marketing', Philip Kotler. Aimed at the busy executive and marketing professional, the book presents 80 fundamental marketing-related concepts, including advertising; branding; competitive advantage; creativity; customer relationship management; database marketing; differentiation; positioning; segmentation; and strategy. Topics are organized alphabetically.
'This wonderful work ... Kotler has succeeded in producing a book that appeals to both the seasoned pro and the novice' (*Marketing Business* June 2003)

4147 Psychology of consumers: consumer behavior and marketing
L. Perner

www.consumerpsychologist.com/
Interesting website run by Lars Perner, Assistant Professor of Clinical Marketing at the Marshall School of Business, University of Southern California. The site provides a brief introduction to the psychology of consumer behaviour and the basics of marketing. Also covers topics such as research methods, learning and memory, social influences, attitudes, culture, motivation, perception and decision making. Ideal for anyone wanting a taster of the basic theories of this subject area.

Dictionaries, thesauri, classifications

4148 Dictionary of marketing
A. Ivanovic and P.H. Collin   3rd edn, Bloomsbury, 2003, 400pp. £9.99. ISBN 0747566216.
www.bloomsbury.com
Now in its 3rd edition, the *Dictionary of marketing* presents a comprehensive, clearly written vocabulary of marketing terms. Each entry includes phonetic pronunciation, a note on grammar and an 'encyclopaedic type commentary'. The dictionary also highlights the differences between British and American usage. Ideal for anyone studying a marketing-related course and for practitioners 'looking to understand the terms crucial to the growth and success of their business.'

4149 International dictionary of marketing: over 2000 professional terms and techniques
D.L. Yadin   Kogan Page, 2002, 441pp. £14.99. ISBN 0749435321.
www.kogan-page.co.uk/
Provides 2000 encyclopaedic marketing-related definitions. Covering terms from all areas of marketing, including marketing communications; the media; advertising; public relations; sales promotion; corporate communications; and the internet.

4150 Marketing terms.com
www.marketingterms.com/
This is a well laid-out, useful online glossary covering basic terminology relating to online marketing. Browse alphabetically or by category. As well as a definition, each entry contains general information about how the term relates to other marketing terms and gives suggestions for related websites and articles for each term.

Laws, standards, codes

4151 Marketinglaw.co.uk [EUR]
www.marketinglaw.co.uk/
A dedicated online resource for advertising and marketing law, launched in September 1999 by pan-European law firm Osborne Clarke. The site provides 'regularly updated information for brand-owners and marketing professionals, including in-depth analysis of the latest marketing and brand law issues, national and international case reports, previews of up-and-coming legislation affecting marketing, plus legal checklists and template agreements'. Registration for full site access is currently free and includes a regular e-mail update facility.

Official & quasi-official bodies

4152   econsumer.gov
www.econsumer.gov/english/index.html
econsumer.gov was set up in 2001 in response to the increasing amount of internet fraud. The project, which involves countries belonging to ICPEN (the International Consumer Protection Enforcement Network), aims to increase consumer protection and consumer confidence in e-commerce. The project has two components, a multilingual public website and a government, password-protected website. The public site provides general information about consumer protection in the participating countries, including contact information for consumer protection authorities, online shopping tips and an online complaints form. The incoming complaints are then added to a database operated by the US Federal Trade Commission and made available on the government website for investigation.

4153   Great Britain. Office of Fair Trading
www.oft.gov.uk/default.htm
The main aim of the Office of Fair Trading is to promote and protect consumer interests throughout the UK and to ensure that businesses are both fair and competitive. The website provides information about its role and activities and contains press releases, official reports and guidelines which can be accessed free of charge. The site is split into two main areas: the business information area provides information relating to businesses and markets, including details of mergers, market studies and Competition Act decisions; the consumer information area provides general advice on consumer rights on everything from buying a car to dealing with doorstep sellers.

Research centres & institutes

4154   Academy of Marketing [UK]
www.academyofmarketing.info
The Academy of Marketing (formerly the Marketing Education Group) is a learned society dedicated to serving the educational and research needs of marketing researchers, educators and professionals. It is also a market interest group of the Chartered Institute of Marketing (CIM). Website provides details of the Academy's conferences, special interest groups and its JISCmail discussion list.

4155   Academy of Marketing Science
www.ams-web.org/
Founded in 1971, AMS is an international, scholarly, professional organization dedicated to creating and disseminating marketing knowledge and best practices around the world. Website contains membership information, details of the Academy's conferences, special interest programmes and symposia, plus a job section for postings of academic jobs in marketing. The Academy also produces two journals, a quarterly newsletter, an annual membership directory and proceedings from its annual conference, *Developments in marketing science*.

■ **Academy of Marketing Science Review** Academy of Marketing Science, irregular. ISSN 15261794. www.amsreview.org/. The Review is the Academy's own free, peer-reviewed, online journal. It contains articles in the areas of marketing and consumer behaviour. All issues of the Review are available free of charge via the internet, no pre-registration or subscription required.

■ **Journal of the Academy of Marketing Science** Sage Publications, qtrly. ISSN 00920703. www.sagepub.com/. 'The *Journal of the Academy of Marketing Science* is an international journal for the study and improvement of marketing. Founded and sponsored by the Academy of Marketing Science, the journal serves as a vital link between research and practice'.

4156   Chartered Institute of Marketing [UK]
www.cim.co.uk/cim/index.cfm
The CIM was founded in 1911, receiving its Royal Charter in 1989. The organization is the largest body of marketing professionals in the world, representing over 50,000 members. Its mission is to provide support for marketing professionals by working closely with the marketing industry, government and commerce to develop marketing practice and standards. The CIM is also one of the main providers of marketing education and training. Website details information on events, membership, marketing and sales qualifications, training and career support. Also contains some useful resources, including full-text articles, case studies, market reports and profiles of the world's top companies. Some of this information is free to non-members.

4157   Marketing Science Institute
www.msi.org/
Located in Cambridge, Massachusetts, the Marketing Science Institute is a non-profit organization 'dedicated to bridging the gap between marketing science theory and business practice'. Details of the Institute's current research programmes can be found on their website, along with a conference calendar. The Institute publishes working papers, conference summaries and reports on a broad range of marketing topics, which can be purchased online. It also produces a free online newsletter called *Insights from MSI*, which features articles on key research findings and provides direction to more in-depth analysis. An archive of past issues is available from the site. Website contains the current issue of *MSI Review*, a newsletter featuring news from the 'MSI community, including interviews, highlights from recent conferences, awards, competitions and research initiatives'.

Associations & societies

4158   American Marketing Association
www.marketingpower.com/
With 38,000 members worldwide, the AMA is a non-profit organization dedicated to promoting education and career development for marketing professionals. It is a 'leading source for information, knowledge sharing and development of the marketing profession'. The AMA's website, MarketingPower.com contains a wide range of information, products and resources aimed at the marketing professionals. Non-members can register online for free and gain access to best practice articles, webcasts from thought leaders in the marketing field, an online dictionary of marketing terms and a marketing management blog. The Association also produce a number of well respected marketing journals.

■ **Marketing Research** qtrly. $110. ISSN 10408460. Articles are written by and for market research managers and practitioners. Most important of all, its content is practical and actionable. In each issue, readers find coverage of legislative and regulatory issues, demographic and social change, research methods and management tools.

- **Journal of International Marketing** qtrly. ISSN 1069031X. Every issue of JIM features research-backed analysis of the latest marketing theories, in-depth think pieces from active practitioners in international marketing, succinct executive summaries of each article, detailed coverage of market-driven innovations and methods and salient book reviews.

- **Journal of Marketing** qtrly. $130. ISSN 00222429. Established in 1936, the *Journal of Marketing* presents new ideas and theories of marketing thought and practice and reviews current trends and developments within the field of marketing. Website provides subscription details plus the table of contents and article summaries for the current issue. There is also a link to the journal's blog.

- **Journal of Marketing Research** qtrly. $130. ISSN 00222437. Published quarterly, the *Journal of Marketing Research* deals with the philosophical, conceptual and technical aspects of marketing research. JMR helps academicians and practitioners of marketing research stay current with the latest techniques, methods and applications of the marketing research function.

- **Journal of Public Policy and Marketing** semi-annually. $110. ISSN 07439156. Published every six months, this journal features articles on the marketing implications of recent public policy developments, both actual and anticipated.

4159   Association for Consumer Research
www.acrwebsite.org/

The aim of the Association for Consumer Research is to 'advance consumer research and facilitate the exchange of scholarly information among members of academia, industry and government worldwide'. To this end, ACR hosts and supports a number of conferences and publishes research publications. All ACR proceedings are available online and can be searched by author, keyword, title, or year. The Association's website is very well organized and easy to navigate, presenting resources according to audience: for consumers; for marketers; for public policy makers; for researchers; for PhD students and for the press. Each section contains annotated links to articles and related websites. Another interesting feature on the website is the *Knowledge Exchange*, a free, online discussion forum on which, anyone can post a question or initiate a topic for discussion. There is a searchable archive of prior questions and topics.

4160   Consumers' Association [UK]
www.which.co.uk/

The Consumers' Association is an independent organization that campaigns on key issues for consumers in a number of areas, including shopping rights, personal finance, food and health. The Association conducts in-depth investigations and produces reports that compare both goods and services. It is totally self-funded through the sale of the magazine *Which?* and a range of other specialized products.

- **Which?** monthly. ISSN 00434841. First launched in 1957, *Which?* magazine now tests around 2000 products a year. As well as testing a variety of consumer products, the magazine carries out surveys on consumer satisfaction covering everything from banks to the most absorbent nappies. It provides advice to consumers about their legal rights and, through undercover reporting, exposes companies that do not comply with statutory regulations. Subscription includes print copy and access to the Which? website – see site for full details.

4161   Consumers International
www.consumersinternational.org/

Consumers International (CI) is an independent, non-profit organization that supports and represents consumer groups and agencies from around the world. With a membership of over 230 organizations in 113 countries, it seeks to 'promote a fairer society through defending the rights of all consumers, especially the poor, marginalized and disadvantaged.' CI campaigns for policies which respect consumer concerns. Details of its campaigns and programmes can be found on the website, along with its publications, most of which can be freely downloaded.

4162   Direct Marketing Association [EUR]
www.dma.org.uk/content/home.asp

Founded in 1992, the DMA is Europe's largest trade association in the marketing and communications sector. The Association's main aim is to promote and protect the direct marketing industry by raising industry standards and consumer confidence. The DMA campaigns on behalf of its members against adverse legislation from government and other regulatory bodies and provides its members with up-to-the minute information, research and legal advice. The Association has produced the *DM Code of Practice* which can be purchased electronically from the site. It also provides best-practice guidelines, which are supplementary to the Code and can be freely downloaded.

4163   European Marketing Confederation
www.emc.be/activities_rss.cfm

The European Marketing Confederation (EMC) is the 'umbrella organization for marketing, sales and communication associations across Europe'. It is primarily concerned with promoting and developing marketing as a 'fundamental business process.' The EMC has four main goals: protecting its members interests; setting standards for marketing education and training across Europe; supporting the science and practice of sales, marketing and communication; providing information, studies and best practice. Website gives details of membership and ongoing projects. There is also a free, searchable database of articles and related documents, plus a calendar of events.

4164   European Society for Opinion & Marketing Research
www.esomar.org/

Based in the Netherlands, the ESOMAR is an professional association dedicated to 'promoting the value of market and opinion research'. It has a membership drawn from 100 countries, covering a wide range of industry sectors, from advertising and media agencies, universities and business schools to public institutions and government authorities. Amongst its activities, the ESOMAR manages a comprehensive programme of industry-specific and thematic conferences and produces a range of publications which can be purchased directly from the website. It also actively encourages self-regulation and has produced a code of practice, the ICC/ESOMAR international code of marketing and social research practice, which can be freely downloaded from the website. Site features a searchable, online directory of market research, marketing and advertising associations plus the ESOMAR directory of research organizations, a searchable database of over 1700 major research organizations worldwide.

4165   Institute of Sales & Marketing Management [UK]
www.ismm.co.uk/

Founded in 1966, the ISMM was set up to 'promote standards of excellence in sales and sales management and to enhance the status and profile of sales as a profession'. The Institute offers support, advice and training to sales professionals and is responsible for establishing benchmarks of professionalism in sales. Details of the ISMM activities and membership benefits can be found on the website.

- **Winning Edge** 10 p.a. ISSN 14703009. *Winning Edge* is the official magazine of the Institute. Published ten times a year, it provides news on the latest developments in the field, plus practical advice and guidance to help develop sales skills and increase motivation. Print and online editions are freely available to Institute members.

4166   Market Research Association
www.mra-net.org/

Established in 1954, the MRA is a leading association concerned with promoting excellence in the opinion and marketing research industry. With an international membership, the MRA represents companies and professionals engaged in all areas of marketing and opinion research, including end-users, full service researchers, data collectors and support service providers. The website contains the usual membership information plus details of the Association's certification programme, training and educational events. The MRA's own code of marketing research standards and other best practice guidelines can also be freely downloaded from the website. It also produces a number of publications, including the *Blue book research services directory*, *Alert!*, the Association's official magazine and Alert! blog, a forum which discusses topics raised in the newsletter.

- **Blue book research services directory** Marketing Research Association, annual. $182.90. www.bluebook.org/ [DESCRIPTION]. Published annually, the directory is a 'one-stop reference source' for consumer and opinion research services. It includes descriptions of services and facilities owned and operated by data collection and research companies, as well as, suppliers of related services throughout the USA, Canada and other countries. Volume 1 contains detailed listings arranged by geographic location. Volume 2 is arranged by the type industry and works as a cross-reference to Volume 1. Available both in print format and online.
- **Glossary of marketing research terms** Glossary contains terminology and phrases used within the opinion and marketing research field. Also attempts to show all the commonly used abbreviations and acronyms.

4167   Market Research Society
www.marketresearch.org.uk/

The MRS is a professional association representing the 'providers and users of market, social and opinion research and business intelligence'. With a global membership, the Association's main aim is to promote professional standards and confidence in the market research industry, both in the UK and internationally. MRS offers a variety of qualifications and membership grades, as well as a range of training and professional development resources to support them. The website contains membership information, forthcoming events, plus details of its conferences and publications. The codes/guidelines section contains codes of practice and guidance documents which can be freely downloaded. There is also an impressive FAQ section, covering a wide range of topics related to conducting market research. The site hosts Geodemographics Knowledge Base, a comprehensive directory of selected websites for those interested in the application of geodemographics and geo-spatial analysis.

- **International Journal of Market Research** WARC, 6 p.a. ISSN 00253618. 'The IJMR provides a forum for practitioners, academics and others to share and discuss all aspects of research: applications, methodologies, new technologies, technology transfer from related areas,

solutions, strategic and management issues'. See website for tables of contents of current and past issues.

- **Research** monthly. £130. ISSN 09696709. www.research-live.com/index.aspx?pageid=102 [COMPANION]. Monthly magazine featuring industry news and analysis, both national and international. The magazine has a companion website called research-live.com. Visitors can register for free and gain full access to the latest industry news, a searchable jobs section with an e-mail vacancy watchdog service, plus a searchable archive of published *Research* magazine features and web-exclusive articles. Also contains a listing of UK and international industry events and a careers Q&A service managed by a team of recruitment specialists.

4168   National Consumer Council [UK]
www.ncc.org.uk/

The NCC is an independent, government-funded public body set up to safeguard the interests of consumers. It provides consumer advocacy, campaigns for change and conducts research and policy analysis. The NCC funds the Consumers in Europe Group, an organization which represents the interests of UK consumers to European Union (EU) institutions. The website holds a comprehensive range of information, FAQ, events, publications and news items. Navigate by information type or by subject.

Portal & task environments

4169   CustomerThink.com
www.customerthink.com

Previously know as CRMGuru, CustomerThink.com is an online community focused on customer relationship management (CRM). The site is a repository for information on CRM containing articles, discussion, newsletters and online events. To gain full access users must register (free). Registered users can then post blogs, news and comments to the site and receive a weekly e-mail newsletter and announcements of new content added. A very useful feature of this site is its online forum, a searchable discussion forum which contains questions on CRM issues from members. Comments and suggestions are then posted by Gurus, members of the CustomerThink Panel of industry experts.

4170   eMarketer
www.emarketer.com/

eMarketer provides market research and trend analysis on internet, e-business, online marketing, media and emerging technologies. It 'aggregates and analyses information from over 2000 sources and brings it together in analyst reports and daily research articles'. Most of the material is only available to subscribers, although some of the reports and articles can be purchased by non-subscribers. eMarketer produces a free daily newsletter which looks at new e-business and internet marketing trends and contains two new articles each weekday (registration required).

4171   KnowThis.com: marketing virtual library
www.knowthis.com/

The main objective of this site is to provide unbiased, high-quality information to academics, business professionals and students in marketing and related fields such as advertising, selling and promotion. The KnowThis team review and annotate every article and report on external internet resources included on the site. The website also offers tutorials covering a variety of marketing topics; a marketing blog; a collection of freely available market research reports;

and a database of marketing stories sourced from other internet sites. The Insights section is a regular feature that provides information on a wide range of research-tested methods for improving online marketing. This research is carried out in association with MarketingExperiments.com and the full results are published in the *Marketing Experiments* journal. The range of material on this site makes it a valuable resource.

4172   Market Research Portal
www.marketresearchworld.net/
The Market Research Portal (MRP) offers online resources and research-related articles aimed at market research buyers, researchers, students and anyone with an interest in the market research industry. Set up and run by a team of consultants based in the UK, the site offers a comprehensive collection of articles; research survey findings sourced from the UK, Europe and the rest of the world; advice and guidance on the market research process, tools and techniques; a discussion forum for questions and advice; marketing research news; FAQ; a glossary; and a jobs forum.

4173   Marketer's portal
www.marketersportal.com/index.cfm
Boasting over 5000 links, this site is a directory of online resources for marketers. It links to leading commercial and brand sites by category; top media sites; sites of 'daily interest' which include headings such as travel, media news, magazines and companies/people; 'useful sites' such as marketing and market research, advertising resources and internet marketing. The site also contains a quotes section and a timeline of the history of marketing and communication, starting as far back as the 11th century.

4174   Marketingteacher.com
www.marketingteacher.com/
Marketing teacher is a learning tool for anyone teaching, studying or working in the field of marketing. It aims to provide explanations of key marketing topics in clear, jargon-free language. The site is run by a group of lecturers based in Chichester and includes free access to PowerPoint presentations and lessons complete with exercises and answers on a range of marketing topics. Users can also join MarketingCitizens, a free online community of practice and knowledge exchange. The community consists of two main areas, the knowledge exchange, which enables marketers to exchange experience, knowledge and ideas on any marketing topic, and a free blogging area.

4175   MarketingUK
www.marketinguk.co.uk/
MarketingUK is a business portal for marketing professionals with a searchable directory of services and web resources under broad categories, including associations and supplier directories; information, theory and education; CRM; market research; publications; financial and industry websites; jobs and other useful sites. Site also contains UK industry data by sector. Users can register for a free, regular e-mail newsletter with details of new web resources and surveys added to the site.

4176   net consumers
European Research into Consumer Affairs
www.net-consumers.org/erica/
net consumers is the website of the European Research into

Consumer Affairs (ERICA), a research centre co-funded by the European Commission that carries out research into consumer issues across the European Union. The home page provides advice and guidance on a range of topics (available in all the EU languages), including child safety on the internet, buying online, keeping warm and healthy eating. The research reports and various related publications can be freely downloaded from the site.

4177   SearchCRM.com
http://searchcrm.techtarget.com/
SearchCRM.com is a portal dedicated to providing free information, advice and guidance on customer relationship management (CRM). It provides daily news, expert tips, white papers, discussion forums and webcasts. Resources are arranged under seven main headings and then by type of resource: news; expert technical advice; reference and learning; and definitions. Registered users of the site can ask the 'Experts' questions related to CRM strategy and implementation and read previous questions and responses.

Discovering print & electronic resources

4178   Marketresearch.com
www.marketresearch.com/
A collection of 'more than 110,000 market research reports from over 550 leading global publishers', which can be purchased and downloaded directly from the site. Browse or search reports by topic. Each report entry has an abstract, table of contents and suggested related reports. Registered users can also search inside individual reports to see how often and in what context keywords appear.

4179   Report finder
www.the-list.co.uk/
Presents executive summaries and table of contents of market research and company reports. Search or browse the reports free of charge and purchase directly online. Covers both UK and European reports.

Digital data, image & text collections

4180   Datamonitor
www.datamonitor.com/
Datamonitor is a leading provider of online database and analysis services for key industry sectors, including consumer goods; energy and utilities; financial services; transport and logistics; technology; retailing; pharmaceutical and healthcare; and automotive industries. The market research reports provide market intelligence, analysis and forecasting and can be purchased directly from the site. Search or browse by industry sector; users can then view a brief introduction, scope of report and see its table of contents. The companies section of the website contains over 10,000 company profiles which can be freely viewed providing brief overviews of each company, contact details and website link. See site for full details of subscription services.

4181   Frost & Sullivan
www.frost.com/ [DESCRIPTION]
Frost & Sullivan are a business research and consulting firm that produce in-depth, global market research and a wide

range of technical and strategy reports covering the following industries: food and drink; healthcare; medical technology; chemicals and plastics; automation; electronics, energy systems, environmental and building technologies; and information and communication technology. These reports are available via a subscription-based online database. See website for full details of the different services offered.

4182   Global market information database (GMID)
Euromonitor International.
www.euromonitor.com/
GMID is an online database that provides business intelligence on countries, consumers and industries. It offers statistics, market reports, company profiles, plus country, market, consumer and lifestyle profiling. Covering 205 countries, the database contains a staggering amount of information, including demographic, economic and marketing statistics, analysis of political and economic indicators; historical trends and forecasts; income, expenditure and lifestyle statistics; global, regional and national market research reports; company profiles; and market size data for hundreds of consumer products. See publisher's website for more subscription details.

4183   International Business Strategies
www.internationalbusinessstrategies.com/
International Business Strategies offers 'international market research reports on more than 130 topics from more than 75 countries. Reports include market size information, market access strategies, market share, export and import information, market analysis, market trends, competition, domestic production, best sales prospects, statistical data, tariffs, regulations, distribution and business practices, end-user analysis, trade shows and contact points'. Search by country or topic, reports can be purchased directly from the site, available in PDF format for online viewing and/or download.

4184   Keynote [UK]
www.keynote.co.uk/
Keynote is a publisher of market research data covering a broad range of industries. Keynote reports can be accessed via a subscription database. Non-subscribers can view report titles alphabetically or under market sector headings. The executive summaries and table of contents for each report are also freely available. See website for subscription details and a selection of free full-text examples of their reports.

4185   Mintel [UK]
www.mintel.com [FEE-BASED]
A market research company with a global track record stretching back 35 years, Mintel produces a range of market intelligence, research and analysis reports. It covers a wide range of markets, including consumer goods, food and drink, holidays and travel, and catering and leisure, in the UK, Europe and the USA. The website contains full details of products and services. Non-subscribers can search or browse the reports, view the table of contents free of charge and purchase individual reports online. Useful press releases available without charge which give a snapshot of the findings of the paid reports.

4186   Reuters/University of Michigan Surveys of Consumers [USA]
University of Michigan: Survey Research Center

www.sca.isr.umich.edu/
The Surveys of Consumers have been conducted by the Institute for Social Research (ISR) at the University of Michigan since 1946. Carried out on a monthly basis, the surveys are intended to represent consumer attitudes and expectations about the US economy. Data from the survey is also used to produce the Index of Consumer Sentiment and the Index of Consumer Expectations. At the start of 2007, Reuters took over the distribution rights and the survey was renamed the Reuters/University of Michigan Surveys of Consumers. The pre-2007 survey output can be accessed via the University's Michigan website, free of charge. The site contains the monthly reports plus a range of related data, including a time-series archive and methodology information. For the most recent data use the web link to the Reuters site.

Directories & encyclopedias

4187   Blackwell encyclopedia of management: marketing
D. Mercer, ed.   2nd edn, Blackwell, 2006, 416pp. £85. ISBN 1405102543.
www.managementencyclopedia.com/
This new and completely revised edition has been updated to include 'cross cultural marketing, research in marketing methodologies, societal marketing and marketing strategy'. It also attempts to assess the use of information and communications technologies and their impact on marketing.

4188   Collins internet-linked dictionary of marketing
C. Doyle   new edn, Collins, 2005, 384pp. £9.99. ISBN 0007205848.
www.collins.co.uk/
An authoritative, up-to-date guide to marketing terms. Covers everything 'from 'global marketing' to 'relationship marketing', from 'b2b marketing' to '1 to 1 marketing', from 'viral marketing' to 'ideas marketing'. The Collins dictionary is the ideal guide to this all-pervasive subject.

4189   Directory of international direct and e-marketing: a country-by-country sourcebook of providers legislation and data
7th edn, Kogan Page, 2003, 976pp. £95. ISBN 0749439777.
A comprehensive directory of services and resources for marketing professionals dealing with international direct and online marketing. Divided into two parts. Part 1 contains articles highlighting direct marketing trends, including choosing the right media; the usefulness of text messages in direct marketing; web-to-mobile SMS applications; attracting the right sort of attention with e-marketing; and the history of mobile communications. Part 2 contains over 50 country profiles, providing basic demographic and economic data; language and cultural considerations; legislation and consumer protection; country DM associations; and postal services. Published in association with the Federation of European Direct Marketing (FEDMA) and the American Direct Marketing Association (DMA).

4190   Encyclopedia of consumer brands [USA]
J. Jorgensen, ed.   St James Press, 1993. 3 v., £176.40. ISBN 1558623353.
www.gale.com
A three-volume set presenting information on 600 of the most popular brands in America. Volume 1 covers consumable products, Volume 2 covers personal products and Volume 3 covers durable goods. Some entries are for

individual products while others are for brand names. Entries include brand history, current status (at time of publishing), brand logos or photos and sources for additional information.

4191 Handbook of niche marketing: principles and practice
T. Dalgic, ed.   Haworth Press, 2005, 256pp. £35.95. ISBN 078902330X.
www.haworthpress.com/
Explores the theories, strategies and real-life applications of niche marketing. The handbook presents a collection of articles from respected authorities in this field. Contents include niche marketing theory; niche verses mass marketing; choosing niche strategy; brand loyalty; customer satisfaction issues; overlap; and product-line cannibalization. It also provides practical guidelines for using niche marketing strategies in a variety of different markets. 'This well referenced guide includes extensive tables, graphs, illustrations and real-life case studies to clearly illustrate ideas and concepts'.

Handbooks & manuals

4192 AMA guide to the globe: managing the international marketing research
H. Edmunds   South Western College Publishing, 2006, 314pp. £32.99. ISBN 0324313314.
www.swlearning.com/amabookstore/ama.html
Offers comprehensive guidance on how to initiate and manage a global marketing research project. Using case study examples throughout, the book takes the reader through each stage of the process, providing 'step-by-step guidance on the basic issues and tasks involved in the global research process'. Topics covered include: handling the proposal process; choosing the appropriate methodologies; selecting vendors; dealing with the language barrier and cultural issues; coordinating the international research project; how to deal with likely problems; ethics in international research; and how to present the results.

4193 Handbook of CRM: achieving excellence in customer management
A. Payne   Butterworth-Heinemann, 2005, 438pp. £29.99. ISBN 0750664371.
http://books.elsevier.com/
An extensive overview of the field of customer relationship management. Exploring the concepts that underpin successful CRM, the handbook provides ' clear and comprehensive explanations of the key concepts in the field; vignettes and full case studies from businesses internationally; definitive references to a range of sources for further information on every aspect of CRM; templates and audit advice for assessing your own CRM needs and targets'.

4194 Handbook of marketing
B.A. Weitz and R. Wensley, eds   Sage Publications, 2006, 582pp. £29.99. ISBN 1412921201.
www.sagepub.com/
A thorough exploration of some of the major contributions to the theory of marketing. Each chapter provides an overview of scholarly research in a specific area of this field. It also provides an extensive bibliography of research and identifies and discusses areas for further research.

4195 International marketing research: opportunities and challenges in the 21st century
A. Rialp and J. Rialp, ed.   Elsevier, 2006, 444pp. Advances in International Marketing ; vol 17, £57.99. ISBN 0762313692.
www.elsevier.com/
A title which brings together a collection of essays examining issues in the field of international marketing. With contributions from scholars from all over the world, essays cover export and multinational marketing from both a theoretical and practical perspectives. 'While some authors focus on managerial issues in international marketing, others take a public policy or comparative perspective. Similarly, while some authors may confine their analyses to well established concepts or methodologies in international marketing, others have the opportunity to incorporate new and innovative perspectives.'

4196 International marketing strategy: analysis, development and implementation
I. Doole and R. Lowe   4th edn, Thomson Learning, 2004, 445pp. £34.99. ISBN 1844800253.
http://hed.thomsonlearning.co.uk
This well respected textbook is divided into three main sections: Part 1, Analysis, presents an introduction to international marketing, including the social and cultural considerations; Part 2, Strategy development, includes global and market entry strategies; Part 3, Implementation includes communication, pricing and international distribution and logistics. The book places a strong emphasis on the importance of managers building the necessary skills to work effectively in the global marketplace. This new and completely revised edition also includes additional chapters on how new technologies can help to gain and manage international business and also looks at ethical considerations in international marketing.

4197 Market research handbook: measurement, approach and practice
J. Xu   iUniverse.com, 2005, 204pp. £10.50. ISBN 0595364012.
www.iuniverse.com/bookstore/
The book presents a detailed examination of the specific measurements used by market researchers, providing definitions and using practical case studies to demonstrate method. Specifically, it details the techniques and application know-how from the professional research agencies, making this a useful reference source for both practitioners and students.

Keeping up to date

Business Insights
See entry no. 3468

4198 Marketing [UK]
Haymarket Publishing, weekly. £135 annual sub. ISSN 00253650.
www.haymarketbusinesssubs.com/home/
A weekly magazine for the UK marketing industry, containing news and analysis across marketing, media, branding, direct marketing and retail. Subscribers to the print magazine also gain access to an online version hosted on the Brand Republic website, a showcase for Haymarket publishing magazines. Online version features a weekly consumer survey of UK commercials, job vacancies in marketing, links

to useful marketing sites and stories from the current week's magazine.

4199 Marketing Experiments Journal
www.marketingexperiments.com/
A free, twice-monthly e-mail report that summarizes the results of MarketingExperiments.Com (MEC), an online marketing research laboratory dedicated to exploring successful internet marketing methods. Free subscription to the journal includes access to more than 60 research briefs covering topics such as site conversion, online marketplaces, pay-per-click strategies and e-mail marketing.

4200 Marketing Today
Peter DeLegge Consulting.
http://marketingtoday.com
A free online magazine published by Peter DeLegge Consulting. Provides articles and trend analysis on a range of marketing issues, with a heavy emphasis on online and business-to-business marketing. Articles are presented in dedicated sections, including trade shows and events; marketing law resources; search engine marketing; marketing tools; and a jobs/careers section. Users can also access a marketing blog and subscribe to a free e-newsletter.

4201 Marketing Week [UK]
Centaur Communications, weekly. £110.00 annual sub. ISSN 01419285.
www.marketingweek.co.uk/ [COMPANION]
A weekly magazine for UK marketing, advertising and media professionals. It provides the latest industry news, product launches and campaigns, reports and analyses on brand developments and marketing and marketing-related vacancies in the UK. Its companion website MarketingWeek.co.uk contains news, jobs, reviews, surveys, sector insights and career advice for marketing and marketing-related professionals. It also features a research section containing selected articles from the magazine, plus a useful directory of leading marketing suppliers. In addition, the site features e-mail services, including daily breaking news and job e-mail alerts (pre-registration required).

4202 Sales and Marketing Management
www.salesandmarketing.com/smm/index.jsp
A magazine aimed at sales and marketing practitioners, featuring industry news, trends, analysis, research and case studies. Its companion website provides free full-text articles of the current issue, the tables of contents for archive issues, book reviews, industry events and links to industry guides and contacts. Site also contains webcasts, white papers, blogs and exclusive research. Users can freely register for a range of e-newsletters.

Advertising & PR
brands • marketing campaigns • organizational communication • product placement • public relations

Introductions to the subject

4203 Brands
M. Danesi   Routledge, 2006, 160pp. Routledge introductions to media and communications series, £15.99. ISBN 0415279984.
www.routledge.com/

Presents a clearly written introduction to brands and brand identity, examining the historical development of brands and their increasing importance to today's consumer culture. The author explores how advertising campaigns can be used to create powerful brand images and sell anything from cars to nappies. The book is an excellent introduction to this topic covering the origins of brands; naming and brand image; the importance of design and logos; how to analyse brand image using semiotic theory; brands and consumer culture; advertising campaigns; global brands; and the anti-brand movement. Also contains an annotated guide to further reading, details of useful websites and a comprehensive bibliography.

4204 Everything you should know about public relations: direct answers to over 500 questions
A. Davis   Kogan Page, 2003, 280pp. £17.99. ISBN 0749439254.
www.kogan-page.co.uk
A collection of over 500 questions and answers selected to demystify the issues and processes involved in the field of public relations. The book also uses a range of real-life examples to help demonstrate and explain exactly how PR can help build businesses. This well written, easy-to-read account of PR practice is ideal for anyone wishing to gain a better understanding of PR and its capabilities.

4205 Practice of advertising
A.R. Mackay, ed.   5th edn, Elsevier Butterworth-Heinemann, 2004, 400pp. £24.95. ISBN 0750661739.
http://books.elsevier.com/
An impressive overview of the advertising industry. Contents: marketing and the place of advertising within it; how advertising works; integrated marketing communications; the advertiser; the advertising agency; media; advertising creativity; press production; TV, radio and cinema production; printing; advertising planning and budgeting; getting the best from advertising agencies and other outside suppliers; media research; consumer research; business-to-business advertising; services advertising; recruitment advertising; directory advertising; international advertising; sales promotion in marketing; advertising: self-regulation and the law; training for a career in advertising. This text is ideal for those wanting a good overall grounding in the subject.

4206 PRdisasters.com
www.prdisasters.com/
PRdisasters.com is an interesting website that provides an alternative look at the practice of public relations. The site is dedicated to demonstrating how 'not' to manage PR activities by exposing 'the real PR cock-ups; the gaffes and howlers made by spin doctors, PR consultants and the client organizations they represent.' Site also contains news, views and trends from the world of public relations and related business. A fascinating insight.

4207 PRhistory.com [USA]
www.prhistory.com/
PRhistory.com was created by Alex Breve while he was studying for his Master's degree in public relations at the Rowan University in New Jersey. Breve wanted to create an online resource dedicated to PR and its history that was accessible to both students and the general public. The website is nicely put together, providing a potted history of public relations complete with timeline (American emphasis). Site also examines various PR models as well as containing

several PR case studies, an annotated list of relevant websites and organizations plus a selection of biographies of leading figures in the development of PR.

4208   Public relations disasters: inside stories and lessons learnt
G. McCusker   Kogan Page, 2006, 328pp. £12.99. ISBN 0749445726.
www.kogan-page.co.uk/
An alternative look at the world of PR. This book is a 'how-not-to guide' presenting 79 real-life public relations disasters from around the world. A useful learning tool for anyone working in the media-related industries. Book has a companion website.
'Covers some of the biggest PR disasters in recent years and should be read by those in the field (entry level and experienced) to help avoid these types of situations.' (*New York Monthly*)

4209   Public relations in Britain: a history of professional practice in the twentieth century
J. L'Etang   Lawrence Erlbaum, 2004, 275pp. £41.95. ISBN 080583804X.
www.erlbaum.com/ME2/Default.asp
Using 'oral history interviews and extensive archival research', this book attempts to examine the links between the development of public relations in Britain during the early twentieth century and the key political, economic, social and technological developments during this period. A well written, thorough examination of the development of British PR. Contents: Preface. British public relations: definitions and debates. Propaganda, information and intelligence (1914–45). Establishing the profession (1945–60). The shape of things to come: The emergence of consultancy (1948–69). Professional dilemmas: Public relations, media and politics (1948–70). Crime and punishment: codes and regulation (1948–98). Educational developments (1948–98). Implications and conclusions. Appendices: Researching the history of British public relations: an account of methods employed. List of interviewees. Interview guide.

4210   Public relations in practice
A. Gregory, ed.   2nd edn, Kogan Page, 2003, 210pp. PR in practice series, £16.99. ISBN 0749433817.
www.kogan-page.co.uk/
A title from the PR in practice series, published in association with the Chartered Institute of Public Relations. Discusses main areas of public relations from the practitioner's point of view. International in scope, a practical guide to the necessary skills for practising PR professionals. 'Subjects covered include marketing communications; internal communication; financial public relations; government and local government relations; public relations for non-commercial organizations; business-to-business public relations; international communications; sponsorship; pressure groups; corporate social responsibility; public relations for the services sector'.

Dictionaries, thesauri, classifications

4211   Elsevier's dictionary of advertising in English, German, French and Russian
S.G. Manoilova and D.H. Konstantinova, eds   Elsevier Science, 2002, 562pp. £105. ISBN 0444506918.
www.elsevier.com/

A dictionary containing terms commonly used in the field of advertising, including the related spheres of 'marketing and market research, creativity (graphic design, text writing and concept development, photography and film-making basics), media, prepress and typography'. See publisher's website for sample pages.

Laws, standards, codes

4212   Committee of Advertising Practice [UK]
www.cap.org.uk
CAP is the advertising industry body responsible for writing and enforcing the UK advertising codes, administered by the Advertising Standards Agency. There are two committees that are responsible for the codes, CAP (Broadcast) and CAP (Non-broadcast). The latest editions of the codes are available for download from the website. There is also a searchable advice database which contains notes and guidance on particular issues covered by CAP, including information on relevant code clauses and adjunctions. CAP also provide a free professional advice service to advertisers and marketers about the Non-broadcast Code and how it applies to specific marketing communications. Other useful features on the site include Ad Alerts, which are short guides on creating advertisements for particular products; copy advice case studies and a range of advertising checklists.

4213   European Advertising Standards Alliance
www.easa-alliance.org/
Based in Brussels, the European Advertising Standards Alliance (EASA) is a non-profit organization representing the advertising industry in Europe. Its main concerns are: 'promotion and development of self-regulation in the advertising sector; support of existing advertising self-regulatory systems; management and coordination of the EASA's cross-border complaints mechanism; provision of information and research concerning advertising self-regulation'. Nicely laid out site (although some of the sections are still under construction) providing information on EASA, its activities and details of the self-regulatory organizations (SROs) that make up EASA. There is a section explaining self-regulation, with a useful FAQ and advice area, plus press releases and information on EASA publications. The site also contains a section explaining the cross-border complaints system, detailing how members of the public can make complaints about advertisements.
- **Advertising self-regulation in Europe: the blue book** 5th edn, EASA, 2005. €175. Detailed overview of self-regulation in advertising across Europe. Provides: country analyses of statutory and self-regulatory structures; overview of SROs' composition and their main activities; comprehensive tables offering a useful comparison of SRO functions and code rules; analysis of the key issues in advertising standards today, including advertising aimed at children; information about EASA and its structure and activities, including the cross-border complaints system. Also contains a glossary of terms. Can be purchased directly from the EASA website.

4214   European handbook on advertising law
Z. Yaqub and C. Lord   Cavendish, 2006, 911pp. £159.50. ISBN 1859412874.
Provides an overview of the main advertising laws and regulations of the 15 EU Member States, as well as in Switzerland and Australia. Each chapter presents a general overview of the country's advertising media and examines

the rules which govern them. Covers a range of industry sectors that include the food, alcohol, pharmaceuticals, tobacco and television industries. Also provides useful addresses and appendices that cover the country-specific directives and codes of practice regulating the advertising industry.

4215   National Advertising Division [USA]
www.nadreview.org/

Part of the Council of Better Business Bureaus, NAD is responsible for reviewing the practice of the US and Canadian advertising industry. Its main aims are to 'provide a system of voluntary self-regulation, minimize government intervention and foster public confidence in the credibility of advertising'. Website details the work of the organization and provides information on how to file a complaint. There is a searchable database of NAD case reports, which are available for download to members (individual case reports are available to the general public and media upon request). Site also contains NAD press releases to the media on honesty in advertising plus findings from inquiries regarding national advertising, which can be freely downloaded.

Official & quasi-official bodies

4216   Advertising Standards Authority [UK]
www.asa.org.uk/asa/

'The Advertising Standards Authority is the independent body set up by the advertising industry to police the rules laid down in the advertising codes'. The Broadcast and Non-broadcast advertising codes can be freely downloaded from the website. There is a searchable archive of ASA's complaints investigations and adjudications, plus research reports, case studies, briefings, statistics and details on how to make a complaint. The site offers a nicely put-together range of 'guided tours' providing information on what the ASA can offer advertisers, new media, schools and colleges, and consumers.

4217   Great Britain. Office of Communications
www.ofcom.org.uk

'Ofcom is the independent regulator and competition authority for the UK communications industries, with responsibilities across television, radio, telecommunications and wireless communications services'. Website contains a huge amount of information, including codes and policies, industry-specific guides, details about the research that is undertaken, consumer guides, and market research and statistics, all of which can be freely downloaded.

Research centres & institutes

4218   Chartered Institute of Public Relations [UK]
www.ipr.org.uk/

The Chartered Institute of Public Relations is a professional organization representing PR practitioners in the UK. With over 8000 members, the main functions of the CIPR are concerned with raising industry standards. It provides a variety of training courses and programmes; conducts research; produces policies on a range of PR issues; enforces a code of practice; and produces publications on a variety of topics (see website for details). The site also offers

a job section and a useful directory for individuals and organizations looking for a PR consultant/consultancy.

4219   Institute of Practitioners in Advertising [UK]
www.ipa.co.uk/

'The IPA is the industry body and professional institute for leading advertising, media and marketing communications agencies in the UK'. It is concerned with promoting its members' interests and developing and maintaining the standards of professional practice within the advertising industry. Much of the content on the website is for members only but non-members can register freely to gain access to a selection for resources, including best-practice guides; agency censuses dating back to 1998; selected industry statistics and rankings; a searchable directory of useful websites; and a sizeable collection of documents and presentations that can be freely downloaded.

Associations & societies

4220   Ad Council [USA]
www.adcouncil.org/

The Ad Council is a private, non-profit organization that conducts public service advertising campaigns. It commissions the help of volunteer ad agencies 'on behalf of non-profit organizations and government agencies in issue areas such as improving the quality of life for children, preventative health, education, community well being, environmental preservation and strengthening families.' Site details the Organization's current campaigns and news. Visitors to the site can sign up for a free e-mail newsletter and RSS news feed. There is also a link to Adlibbing, the council's own blog.

4221   Advertising Association [UK]
www.adassoc.org.uk/

The Advertising Association is a non-profit organization representing the interests of the UK advertising industry. Its aim is 'to promote and protect the rights, responsibilities and role of advertising in the UK'. The Association's website is a useful starting point for an overview of the industry. It contains industry news and updates, position papers on key issues affecting the advertising industry, an events diary and an annotated list of related websites. The Advertising Association produces a range of statistical publications and commissions and publishes independent research, ad hoc pamphlets, monographs and books dealing with a variety of advertising-related topics.

- **Advertising statistics yearbook** WARC, annual. £195. www.store.warc.com/ [DESCRIPTION]. Published annually, the yearbook provides complete statistical coverage of the UK's advertising and media markets, including trend analysis for newspapers and magazines, TV and radio, cinema, directories, direct mail and the internet.
- **European Advertising and Media Forecast** WARC, 18 p.a. £1,365. www.store.warc.com/. Published 18 times per year (four newsletters, two data-books and twelve monthly updates by e-mail.'Offers the most comprehensive databank on European adspend trends currently available'. Published in association with the Advertising Association and the Advertising Information Group.

4222   Advertising Research Foundation [USA]
www.thearf.org/

'Founded in 1936 by the Association of National Advertisers and the American Association of Advertising Agencies, the

ARF leads key industry learning initiatives that increase the contribution of research to better marketing, more effective advertising and profitable organic growth'. Site details the Foundation's current research projects, forthcoming events and membership benefits. Under the resource section there is a link to the Roy Morgan Info Center, a collection of free research articles and papers on a variety of industry topics hosted by Roy Morgan International. The ARF also runs a series of presentations from industry leaders that address topical issues in advertising and marketing research. These are available in the form of webcasts and can be purchased by non-members (free to members). The Foundation produces the *Journal of Advertising Research*, free to its members.

■ **Journal of Advertising Research** WARC, qtrly. £187. ISSN 14707853. 'The mission of the *Journal of Advertising Research* (JAR) is to act as the research and development vehicle for professionals in all areas of marketing including media, research, advertising and communications. The JAR provides a forum for sharing findings, applications, new technologies and methodologies, and avenues of solution. Its primary audience is the practitioner at all levels of practice'. See journal homepage for subscription details and table of contents and abstracts going back to 1993.

4223   American Advertising Federation
www.aaf.org/
The AAF is a trade association representing 50,000 professionals in the advertising industry. Based in Washington, DC, it has a national network of clubs and connects the industry with an academic base through its 210 college chapters. Its mission is to protect the rights of its members by monitoring advertising-related legislation at local, state and federal levels. It is also concerned with promoting best practice in the industry. The site details the current work of the Federation and the various membership schemes and benefits.

4224   International Association of Business Communicators
www.iabc.com/
Founded in 1970, the IABC is a professional association representing more than 14,000 business communication professionals in over 70 countries. This includes professionals working in such areas as public relations/media relations, corporate communications, public affairs, investor relations and marketing communication. The main aim of the IABC is to establish and support 'standards of quality and innovation in organizational communication'. To this end, the Association provides an accreditation programme, industry awards, an international annual conference and a range of products, services and networking opportunities for its members. The website contains full details of the Association's products, services and activities, including its official magazine *Communication World*.

■ **Communication World** IABC, bi-monthly. $150. ISSN 07447612. http://iabcstore.com/ [DESCRIPTION]. The IABC's official magazine is dedicated to communication management, covering 'the latest in communication research, global perspectives, technology, best practices and trends through in-depth reports and insightful interviews'.

4225   International Public Relations Association
www.ipra.org/
Established in 1955, the IPRA is an international association for communication professionals with a membership drawn from 96 countries. It is concerned with the promotion of

public relations on a global level, providing professional development and networking opportunities for its members worldwide. Membership benefits include access to the IPRA electronic discussion forum and to a virtual library offering a wide range of material, including conference papers; summaries of entries to its Golden World awards, IPRA gold papers providing in-depth analysis on topics such as corporate social responsibility, evaluation and globalization; and articles from FrontLine, the Association's bi-monthly online magazine.

4226   Public Relations Society of America
www.prsa.org/
With a membership made up of over 28,000 professional and student members, the PRSA claims to be the world's largest organization for public relations professionals. 'Chartered in 1947, PRSA's primary objectives are to advance the standards of the public relations profession and to provide members with professional development opportunities through continuing education programs, information exchange forums and research projects conducted on the national and local levels'. Site provides details of the organization's activities and services. Membership benefits include free access to a fully searchable database of articles and papers taken from the PRSA publications *PR Tactics* and *The Strategist*. Non-members can now search the database for free and purchase individual documents directly from the site.

4227   World Federation of Advertisers
www.wfanet.org/
The World Federation of Advertisers (WFA) is a global organization representing the interests of the advertising profession. It is a 'worldwide network of 55 National advertiser associations on five continents and over 40 of the world's top 100 marketers'. Membership benefits include access to a members-only section of the website featuring key publications, including a monthly newsletter, the WFA EU brief, which provides a weekly round-up of related EU regulatory developments; best-practice guides and model contracts; a statistics page with key data for advertisers, including current ad spend per industry sector; and free access to selected content from WARC.com (World Advertising Research Centre).

Libraries, archives, museums

4228   Advertising Icon Museum [USA]
www.advertisingiconmuseum.com/
A 'virtual' museum containing an extensive collection of advertising icons spanning a century of American history. Take a virtual tour of the museum and select an icon of interest to see a close–up image and learn about the story behind their creation and the brands that they represent. The physical version of the museum is currently under construction in Kansas City, due to open in late 2008, and will house the largest collection of three-dimensional advertising icons in the world. This is a well organized, easy-to-use website and completely addictive.

4229   Museum of Brands, Packaging & Advertising [UK]
www.museumofbrands.com
This is a fascinating museum that houses a unique collection of over 10,000 consumer goods spanning the Victorian age

right up to the present. The museum was a result of the work of historian Robert Opie, who at the age of 16 began to collect and record some of the everyday products around us, starting with a packet of Munchies. The collection now includes a huge variety of products from our daily life, including toys, comics, magazines, newspapers, technology, travel, fashion and design, as well as packaging and advertisements.

4230   Museum of Public Relations [USA]
www.prmuseum.com/

Based in New York, the Museum of Public Relations was established in 1997 to present the history and impact of the US public relations industry. The museum also has a companion website which explores 'how ideas are developed for industry, education, government and how they have been applied to successful public relations programs since the PR industry was born'. The site contains online exhibitions of the lives of some of the major pioneers in the field, presenting their careers, timelines and images, including video footage and interviews. The museum houses a reference library open for research by appointment only. A bibliography of the library's books and journal articles can be accessed from the website.

Portal & task environments

4231   Advertising Educational Foundation
www.aef.com/index.html

Created in 1983, the AEF is a non-profit, operating foundation supported by ad agencies, advertisers and media companies. It is 'the advertising industry's provider and distributor of educational content to enrich the understanding of advertising as an essential component of our economic and social system.' This valuable website is packed with a wide variety of information and resources relating to advertising. This includes teaching and learning resources, book extracts, career guidance, video interviews with industry leaders, a calendar of events, online discussion groups and a large collection of advertising articles and commentaries. Site also features the foundation's journal *Advertising and Society Review*; registration (free) is required to access journal content.

■ **Advertising and Society Review** qtrly. ISSN 15347311. http://muse.jhu.edu/journals/asr/indexb.html. Contains articles, essays, interviews and roundtable discussions on the subject of advertising and its relationship to society, culture, history and the economy. It is published quarterly in electronic form and distributed through Project Muse of The Johns Hopkins University Press. Can also be accessed via the AEF site, registration required.

4232   All about public relations
www.aboutpublicrelations.net/mbio.htm

An impressive website dedicated to providing information and resources to the PR community. Now features over 1200 links to how-to PR articles, websites and other related resources. Primary topics include marketing, crisis management, media relations and ethics. There is also a job and careers section and a handy collection of desk reference resources.

4233   PRaxis: public relations resource centre
http://praxis.massey.ac.nz/home.html

'PRaxis was launched in 2003 as a public relations and

communication resource and a meeting space for academics, students and industry practitioners.' An easy-to-navigate website featuring an annotated links section that lists useful URLs, complete with a quick-reference system using symbols to designate academic, quasi-academic, industry and commercial materials; PRaxis newsletter, which covers industry and academic issues, as well as announcing new developments on the PRaxis site; an announcements page for notices about conferences, calls for papers and related news; a discussion forum exclusively for PR educators. The website is also home to PRism, a free online journal.

■ **PRism** annual. ISSN 14484404. PRism is a free-access, online, refereed public relations and communication research journal. Contains articles, commentary and a range of book reviews and/or conference reports. Published annually, with special issues published on an ad hoc basis.

4234   Texas advertising
University of Texas at Austin: Department of Advertising
www.advertising.utexas.edu/

Texas advertising is a website specializing in advertising/public relations education and research, maintained by the Department of Advertising at the University of Texas at Austin. Site provides an extensive directory of organizations and websites. There is also a research section containing online papers written by the university's own students, as well as links to advertising-related papers that appear elsewhere on the web. Site also holds a range of bibliographies on a selection of advertising topics, biographies of advertising practitioners, information on advertising law and ethics and other useful resources.

4235   World Advertising Research Center
www.warc.com/

The World Advertising Research Center (WARC) is a leading supplier of market intelligence to the global marketing, advertising, media and research communities. 'WARC is an independent organization that works closely with trade associations, industry bodies and blue chip companies around the world, including the Advertising Research Foundation, Institute of Practitioners in Advertising, ACNielsen, ESOMAR and the US Association of National Advertisers.' WARC produces an impressive online service which includes 'over 25,000 articles, case studies, research reports and summaries, augmented with best practice papers, practical guides, daily news, e-mail bulletins and statistical data. Covers the key areas of: communications effectiveness; marketing and brand strategy; media planning and buying; market research and methods; and consumer insight and behaviour'. See website for subscription details and a 7-day free trial of their services.

■ **World advertising trends** WARC, annual. £250. ISSN 17445477. An annual publication focusing on world trends in advertising expenditure; country-by-country advertising expenditure statistics; total adspend for TV, magazine, newspaper, cinema, radio, outdoor and internet advertising; purchasing power parities (PPPs) for all major markets.

Discovering print & electronic resources

4236   New PR/wiki
www.thenewpr.com

The NewPR/wiki was started in 2004 by Constantin Basturea, a director at Converseon, a media communications agency. The wiki has three main function: firstly, it provides a collaborative tool for PR professionals and anyone else interested in the practice of public relations; secondly, it provides a free repository of PR-related resources, including articles, books, case studies, reports and surveys, blogs and other related types of material; thirdly, it provides an open space for anyone to ask questions, post their ideas, or start a project. This is an impressive site, well worth a look.

4237 PR Books [UK]
http://prbooks.pbwiki.com/
PR Books is a wiki dedicated to listing recommended PR books for students of public relations. It was set up by Richard Bailey, a lecturer in public relations at Leeds Metropolitan University. Browse titles using the A–Z subject list or see titles selected by the editor. There is a bias in favour of both UK and more recent texts. Site also contains links to other PR relevant sources (newspaper articles, weblogs, biographies etc.). Anyone can amend and add to the recommendations, but a password is required – see site for details.

Digital data, image & text collections

4238 Ad*Access [USA]
http://scriptorium.lib.duke.edu/adaccess/
Ad*Access is a pilot project funded by Duke University Endowment Library to make a selection of historical advertisements available for study and research. The site contains over 7000 images of adverts from the US and Canada 0–911 and 1955. This fascinating collection is organized by the subject areas of radio, television, transportation, beauty and hygiene and World War II. Each subject links to a brief historical overview of that topic and provides a bibliography of additional readings. There is a timeline outlining major events in the world and US between 1915–55, providing a general context for the ads in the project, nearly all of which are from US publications.

4239 adflip
www.adflip.com/
adflip.com is a searchable database of classic print advertisements from the 1940s up to the present. Search by categories such as electronics, entertainment, fashion, food, health and beauty and music. This is a subscription service but visitors to the site can search the database and see a selection of advertisements in each category for free. See site for more details and subscription packages.

4240 Brand hype
www.brandhype.org/MovieMapper/index.jsp
A fascinating website that looks at the use of product placement in films. Maintained by the Department of Communication Studies, Concordia University in Montreal, it is intended to stimulate critical debate about the use of product placement. The site contains articles, a discussion forum and a critical video about product placement, *Behind the screens*. The main feature of the website is Movie Mapper, a searchable database of product placements in films. Visitors can search by actor, film title, brand name, etc.; each hit provides basic film and character information and a detailed list of the brands that appeared in the film.

Directories & encyclopedias

4241 Advertisers annual: the blue book [UK]
Hollis, 2006, annual. £275. ISSN 00653578.
www.hollis-publishing.com/
Published annually. Contents include 3000 UK advertising agencies; 2000 top-spending major advertisers; 20,000 brands linked to client companies and the agencies they employ; and 4000 media advertising contacts (including ABC/VFD Data).
'Advertisers Annual is an all-encompassing bible of the advertising world' (Media Week)
'Immensely valuable key reference source, reliable and very easy to use' (Advertising Association)

4242 Concise encyclopedia of advertising
K. Clow and D. Baack   Haworth Press, 2005, 213pp. $29.95. ISBN 0789022117.
www.haworthpress.com/
This dictionary 'provides brief, easy-to-understand definitions and explanations of common advertising terms and covers all major concepts used in the industry'. An excellent reference tool for anyone wishing to get to grips with the terminology commonly used in this industry.

4243 Encyclopedia of major marketing campaigns [USA]
Gale Research International   2nd edn, Thomson Gale, 2006, 2000pp. 2 v. set, $330. ISBN 0787673560.
http://gale.cengage.com
Examines major marketing and advertising campaigns of the 20th century. Each campaign has a three- to five-page entry providing: an overview of the campaign; a historical context; breakdown of the target market, competition and market strategy; a review of the outcome of the campaign. Entries also come with further information for researchers, including references to competitors and an annotated list of further reading. Entries are alphabetically arranged by company name. Volumes include a general index listing product names, advertising agencies and people, plus a subject index. Also available as an e-book.

4244 Encyclopedia of public relations [USA]
R.L. Heath, ed.   Sage Publications, 2004. 2 v., £140. ISBN 0761927336.
www.sagepub.co.uk/
A two-volume encyclopedia exploring the development of the field of public relations. Contains nearly 450 entries covering the fields of communication, advertising, marketing and politics. The primary focus is on US public relations, offering a thorough introduction to practice of PR, charting its historical development and introducing the reader to some of the key figures who developed and expanded the profession. The encyclopedia also examines the theory and practice of PR and looks at some of the key challenges of the profession.

4245 Hollis Europe
Hollis, 2006, annual, 600pp. £145. ISSN 09623590.
www.hollis-publishing.com/
An annual directory containing details of over 3000 PR consultancies across 37 countries; public affairs, government relations and EU specialists; an A–Z of European sponsorship specialists; a skills index and resource register; in-house contacts in Europe's leading companies; education and research bodies; and a list of PR support services

across Europe. Some of the data from this directory is also available from Hollis-PR.com, an online database of global PR and press contacts.

4246 Hollis UK public relations annual

Hollis Publishing, annual. £145. ISSN 13649000.
www.hollis-publishing.com

Published annually, the directory provides a comprehensive list of contacts in the press and public relations industries. Also includes think-tanks and political parties, pressure and advice groups. Accompanying website contains data from the UK public relations annual and Hollis UK Press. Search by keyword or browse by type or specialism of agency. Non-subscribers have limited access to this site.

4247 Plunkett's advertising and branding industry almanac [USA]

Plunkett's Research, 2007, annual, 556pp. $279.99. ISBN 1593920814.
www.plunkettresearch.com/

Plunkett's Research is a leading provider of industry sector analysis and research. It produces a number of specialized business and industry almanacs containing market analysis, industry information, business statistics, financial histories, technology trends, corporate profiles and executive contacts. The *Advertising and branding industry almanac* provides a comprehensive industry overview, complete with company profiles and a range of statistics and trends in the areas of marketing, advertising, branding, online and media strategies and consulting.

Handbooks & manuals

4248 Advertising handbook

S. Brierley   Routledge, 2003, 320pp. Media practice series, £18.99. ISBN 0415243920.
www.routledge.com/

A comprehensive introduction to the practice of advertising. It explores the role of the advertising agency and its relationship with clients and the media. The handbook follows the development of advertising and looks at the changes that have helped to shape the profession, including the impact of new media, internet and digital technologies and the influence of industry regulations. Packed with facts, figures, statistics, acronyms, abbreviations, high-profile campaigns, profiles, illustrations, exercises, a glossary and useful website references.

4249 Global public relations handbook: theory, research and practice

K. Sriramesh and D. Vercic, eds   Lawrence Erlbaum, 2003, 564pp. LEA's communication series, £107.95. ISBN 0805839232.
www.erlbaum.com/ME2/default.asp

This handbook examines the current practice of public relations in 18 countries, including the transitional economies of Eastern Europe and Asia. Each country-specific chapter provides a thorough overview of the history, development and current status of its public relations industry. This is an informative and useful book for both academics and researchers wanting a thorough understanding of the nature of public relations around the world and for practitioners working in an increasingly global business environment.

'Overall, the book provides an excellent resource on global public relations for practitioners, students, and scholars. University libraries will find this volume to be a valuable addition to support both undergraduate and graduate curricula. Scholars will benefit from the book's precise descriptions of local activities and the important contexts that influence public relations around the world.' (*Journal of Mass Media Ethics*)

4250 Handbook of corporate communication and public relations: pure and applied

S. Oliver, ed.   Routledge, 2004, 456pp. £100. ISBN 0415334195.
www.routledge.com/

This handbook offers a thorough exploration of corporate communication. Divided into four sections, covering corporate communication at national level; corporate communication at international level; managing image, identity and reputation; the future for corporate communication theory and practice. With contributions from academics based in Europe, Asia and North America, the text uses a range of contemporary case-studies to draw out 'the most pertinent best practice outcomes and theoretically based applications'. This handbook is an ideal reference source for anyone wanting a thorough understanding of the practice of corporate communication and public relations.

4251 IABC handbook of organizational communication: a guide to internal communication, public relations, marketing and leadership

T.L. Gillis, ed.   4th edn, Jossey-Bass, 2006, 546pp. $95. ISBN 9780787980801.
www.josseybass.com/

The primary objective of this book is to provide both a theoretical and practical understanding of the communication functions of an organization. Contributions are drawn from leading experts in the field and cover corporate communication such as internal communication, public relations, marketing and communication strategy. Case studies are used throughout the text and 'new topics such as globalization and crosscultural communication, new technologies and employment patterns, corporate responsibility, research measurement and ROI and the virtual corporation' are also covered in this updated edition. The text is written for professionals working in a wide range of organizations, covering large and small, public, private and not-for-profits. See publisher's website for table of contents, index and chapter excerpt.

4252 Public relations handbook

A. Theaker   2nd edn, Routledge, 2004, 366pp. Media practice series, £70. ISBN 0415317924.
www.routledge.com/

The *Public relations handbook* provides a 'detailed introduction to the theories and practices of the public relations industry'. Covering PR at all levels, this revised edition features new case studies plus examples of campaigns from a wide range of organizations and sectors. It also looks at the impact of new technologies such as WiFi and podcasting. Other content includes interviews with PR practitioners; a new section on blogging, podcasting, WiFi and Bluetooth; specialist chapters on not-for-profit PR; up-to-date risk management research; and specialist chapters on financial public relations, business ethics and the use of online promotion.

Keeping up to date

4253 Admap
WARC, monthly. £272. ISSN 00018295.
www.admapmagazine.com/ [COMPANION]
Provides up-to-date articles and commentary on 'cutting-edge practice, important issues and new thinking worldwide about advertising and marketing communications'. See companion website for full subscription details, content list for current and past issues and a downloadable (PDF) bibliography of published articles back to 2001.

4254 Advertising Age
Crain Communications, weekly. Print $349, online only $149. ISSN 00018899.
www.adage.com/ [COMPANION]
A magazine from Crain Communications that provides news, analysis, information and data on advertising, marketing and media. The companion website provides selected online access to the weekly publication plus a range of web-only content, including articles and commentary; electronic newsletters; live events and conferences; streaming video, audio webinars, podcasts and blogs. Site visitors can register for free to receive a range of e-mail products, purchase articles or article packs and read online daily news stories for seven days after the date of publication.

4255 Campaign
Haymarket Publishing. £140. ISSN 00082309.
www.haymarketbusinesssubs.com/
A weekly magazine for the communications industry providing media news and analysis plus industry jobs. The online version is available from the Brand Republic website. To access content, users must subscribe to either the magazine or the website. See publisher's website for subscription prices.

4256 PRWeek
Haymarket Business Publications, weekly. £120. ISSN 02676087.
www.prweek.com/ [COMPANION]
A leading weekly magazine for public relations practitioners published by Haymarket. It provides news, analysis and features about the public relations industry. *PRWeek* also produces a number of benchmark reports and industry surveys, including the annual ranking of the top 150 PR consultancies and salary survey. Its companion website links to US, UK, Asian and German editions. Content on website is restricted to subscription-holders only.

Physical Distribution Management

distribution management • logistics • purchasing • supply chain

Introductions to the subject

4257 Global logistics: new directions in supply chain management
D. Waters   5th edn, Kogan Page, 2006, 464pp. £29.95. ISBN 074944813X.
www.kogan-page.co.uk
This established textbook brings together contributions from a wide range of specialists to discuss key logistics issues. The updated edition identifies 'current trends, best practices and latest thinking in global logistics'. Contents: new directions in logistics; formulating logistics strategy; agile supply chain operating environments; developing supply chain relationships; demand-flow leadership; supply chain management; information technologies for supply chain management; outsourcing; risk in the supply chain; delivering sustainability through supply chain management; performance measurement and management in the supply chain; road transport optimization; retail logistics; global sourcing and supply; developments in Western, Central and Eastern Europe and China.

4258 Manager's guide to distribution channels
L. Gorchels, E. Marien and C. West   McGraw-Hill, 2004, 225pp. £24.99. ISBN 0071428682.
www.mcgraw-hill.co.uk
The *Manager's guide to distribution channels* provides a step-by-step guide on how to increase the 'operational effectiveness and profitability' of marketing channels and distribution programs, as well as develop and maintain distribution relationships. The book is divided into three main sections: Part 1 provides an overview of the issues and decision making processes involved in the distribution channel; Part 2 defines channel and coverage requirements and examines both domestic and foreign channel design issues; Part 3 focuses on the strategies for increasing distributor sales and developing and maintaining channel relationships.

4259 Manager's step-by-step guide to outsourcing
L. Dominguez   McGraw-Hill, 2006, 288pp. £16. ISBN 0071458247.
www.mcgraw-hill.co.uk/
A very accessible and clearly laid-out guide to developing and executing an outsourcing strategy. The book provides a step-by-step look at the processes involved, covering which areas of business should be selected for outsourcing; how to select an outsourcing partner; how to develop an effective team; creating an effective transition plan; dealing with employees and stockholders; and overcoming language and cultural barriers.

4260 Managing the supply chain: the definitive guide for the business professional
D. Simchi-Levi, P. Kaminsky and E. Simchi-Levi   McGraw-Hill, 2003, 307pp. £29.99. ISBN 0071410317.
www.mcgraw-hill.co.uk/
This text provides an in-depth, practical examination of supply chain strategies and technologies and discusses how these can be used to gain an advantage in the marketplace. Global in coverage, the book contains real-life case studies and examples to demonstrate how top companies remain competitive by developing and implementing successful supply chain strategies. Includes chapters on supply chain alliances, outsourcing, procurement and supply contract, product design, information technology and customer value.

4261 Purchasing and supply chain management
K. Lysons and B. Farrington   7th edn, Prentice Hall, 2005, 709pp. £41.99. ISBN 0273694383.
www.pearsoned.co.uk/
Now in its seventh edition, this text is an excellent introduction to both supply chain management and purchasing strategy. Following the syllabus of the Chartered

Institute of Purchasing and Supply (at both foundation and professional stages), this updated edition has a strong emphasis on purchasing strategy, including public sector purchasing, e-procurement, RFID, value management and fraud. New chapters discuss supplier relationships, product innovation and supplier involvement. Additional features include cases studies, discussion questions in every chapter, a comprehensive bibliography and sample past examination questions from CIPS. The book is clearly written, with a well organized structure, making it equally suitable as a quick-reference source for practitioners.

4262 Supply chain management: in theory and practice
[EUR]
B.D. Jespersen and T. Skjott-Larsen Copenhagen Business School Press, 2005, 170pp. £14. ISBN 8763001527.
www.cbspress.dk/
Presents a thorough overview of supply chain management. 'A major part of the book is devoted to the implications of new concepts such as customer relationship management, supplier relationship management, vendor-managed inventory, efficient consumer response and collaborative planning, forecasting and replenishment. A number of cases are illustrating the theoretical discussions. It has a European perspective, both in terms of examples and themes.' Contents: Supply chain management – in theory and practice; SCM frame of reference; Strategic implications of the SCM concept; Process orientation and relationship management; Information systems as a lever for company processes; Performance measurement in supply chains; Implementation of the SCM concept; Sanistaal's SCM partnerships.

Dictionaries, thesauri, classifications

4263 Dictionary of logistics and supply chain management: English–German, German–English
J. Kiesel 14th rev.edn, Wiley-VCH, 2006, 676pp. £29.95. ISBN 3895782726.
www.wiley-vch.de/publish/en/
Revised edition contains over 13,600 terms in the areas of production, purchasing, distribution and trade. A useful reference tool for anyone involved in the logistics and supply chain process. Covers topics such as 'customer, employee, competition and process orientation, time management, innovative strength, increased productivity, high quality and the motivation and qualification of employees to overcome technical and process and cultural barriers in a global competitive environment'.

4264 Dictionary of transport and logistics
D. Lowe Kogan Page, 2002, 281pp. £35. ISBN 0749435712.
www.kogan-page.co.uk/
Endorsed by the Institute of Logistics and Transport, this dictionary contains definitions of over 3000 terms, abbreviations and acronyms in the field of transport and logistics. Both UK and EU terms are covered. An ideal reference tool that will prove valuable 'to readers from all sectors and at all levels from students and junior staff to top management'.

4265 Logistics glossary
Supply Chain & Logistics Institute
www.scl.gatech.edu/apps/glossary/

An online glossary maintained by the Supply Chain and Logistics Institute. Browse terms using the alphabetical listing.

4266 Official dictionary of purchasing and supply
H.K. Compton and D. Jessop 2nd edn, Liverpool Academic Press, 2001, 187pp. £18.99. ISBN 190350001X.
www.liverpoolacademic.com/
Includes terms and concepts used in purchasing, supply, logistics and contract negotiation. Geographic coverage: British, European and international terminology. Recommended by the Chartered Institute of Purchasing and Supply, this is a useful reference tool suitable for both practitioners and students in the purchasing and supply chain fields. This updated edition includes cross-references, acronyms and new entries on e-commerce terminology.

Laws, standards, codes

4267 Law for purchasing and supply
S. Griffiths and I. Griffiths 3rd edn, Financial Times Prentice Hall, 2002, 384pp. £42.99. ISBN 0273646796.
www.pearsoned.co.uk/
A good introduction to a complex area of law. Divided into five main sections covering the law of contract; the supply of goods and services; the law of tort; consumer protection; and related legislation, which includes outsourcing competition law, intellectual property, international trade and insurance. Each chapter introduces the topic area, explains the relevant law and gives practical examples of how the law is applied. The third edition includes additional coverage of related European law and international trade and contracts plus a revised chapter on employment law.

4268 Legal aspects for purchasing and supply chain management [UK]
I. Longdin Liverpool Academic Press, 2005, 287pp. £26.99. ISBN 1903499089.
www.liverpoolacademic.com
Provides an overview of the current legal principles relating to purchasing and supply. Starting with an outline of the basic principles of contract and commercial law, the book goes on to provide practical advice on a range of issues, including international trade and the required documentation, dispute resolution, legal aspects of tendering and outsourcing and insurance law. The book's non-technical style makes it accessible to those with no prior legal experience.

4269 Transportation, logistics and the law [USA]
W. Augello and M.K. Reynolds 2nd edn, Transportation Consumer Protection Council, 2004, 835pp. $150. ISBN 0971523215.
www.transportlawtexts.com/index.html
Covers the laws and regulations governing transportation and logistics, from and within the US. Print and a CD-ROM version of the book are available. There is also a subscription service providing updates on new court and agency decisions, legislation, regulations and other important developments in the transportation and logistics industry. See publisher's website for further details and full table of contents.

Research centres & institutes

4270 Chartered Institute of Logistics & Transport [UK]
www.ciltuk.org.uk/pages/home
The Chartered Institute of Logistics and Transport in the UK (CILT-UK) is an independent professional body for individuals associated with the logistics, supply chain and transport industries. The Institute provides a recognized qualifications programme and a range of other training and development courses. It houses one of the largest, specialist collections of logistics, supply chain and transport information in the world. Members can access a range of online resources from the website and visit the Institute's two libraries, one based in London, the other in Corby. Non-members can visit the library in Corby and use the information service for a fee – see the website for further details.

4271 Chartered Institute of Purchasing & Supply
www.cips.org/
An education and qualifications body for purchasing and supply chain professionals. The website provides details of its activities and services. The Institute's code of practice and a purchasing and supply management model can be freely downloaded from the website. A range of guides and documents addressing key issues and topics effecting the purchasing and supply chain management profession are also available and can be purchased directly from the Institute's online bookshop. Other useful features include a FAQ section, an online glossary and an annotated list of external websites.
- **Supply Management** Redactive Publishing, fortnightly. £80. ISSN 13622021. www.supplymanagement.com/ [COMPANION]. The Institute's official magazine is available free to Institute members. It features news, articles and analysis. The companion website SupplyManagement.com offers selected content from the print magazine, industry news, an archive of past articles, a searchable events diary, an e-mail news alert and a commodity price database (CIPS members and magazine subscribers only). All articles are freely available to site visitors.

Associations & societies

4272 Council of Supply Chain Management Professionals
www.cscmp.org/
Originally founded as the National Council of Physical Distribution Management (NCPDM), the Council of Supply Chain Management Professionals (CSCMP) is an association for those involved in supply chain management. CSCMP provides educational, career development and networking opportunities to its members. Website gives details of membership, the Council's annual conference and other forthcoming events. Membership benefits include free online access to the *Journal of Business Logistics* (JBL) and a range of other resources. Non-members can freely access the Council's sponsored logistics case studies going back to 1996. There is also a free downloadable supply chain and logistics glossary and a useful reading list compiled for the Council's annual conference.

4273 European Logistics Association
www.elalog.org/
The European Logistics Association is a federation made up of 30 national organizations, covering countries in Central and Western Europe. The main aim of the ELA is to 'provide a forum for cooperation for any individual or society concerned with logistics within Europe and to assist industry and commerce in Europe'. Accordingly, the Association formulates educational standards for the profession and encourages member nations to set up vocational qualifications procedures to enable the standards to be accepted on a pan-European basis. Website provides details of its activities, including information on its standards and certification programmes. The ELA conducts and publishes educational surveys in various fields of logistics which can be purchased directly from the website.
- **Supply Chain Standard** Centaur Communications, 10 p.a. £130. Official magazine of the Association, providing 'in-depth coverage of strategic supply chain management issues by Europe's leading consultants, analysts and practitioners.' Previously known as *Logistics Europe*.

4274 Institute for Supply Management
www.ism.ws/
Founded in 1915, the Institute for Supply Management (ISM) is a not-for-profit association representing supply management professionals from around the world. The Institute's main objective is to promote the profession by developing professional skills and knowledge. It provides a wide range of educational products and programs to its members, including online access to the Association's monthly magazine *Inside supply management*; access to an extensive database of information, articles and other resources; an online career centre; and subject-based discussion forums. Visitors to the site can view and freely download the Institute's international conference proceedings going back to 1994.
- **Journal of Supply Chain Management: a global review of purchasing and supply** Blackwell Publishing, qtrly. $98. ISSN 15232409. Suitable for both supply management professionals and academics. Non-subscribers can browse previously published articles going back to 1965, access a series of interviews conducted with leading supply management professionals back to 2000 and read published book reviews going back to 1998 from the ISM website.

4275 International Purchasing & Supply Education & Research Association
www.ipsera.com/index.asp?lg=
'IPSERA is a multi-disciplinary network of academics and practitioners dedicated to the development of knowledge concerning purchasing and supply management.' Site contains information about the Association, its activities and membership benefits. It also contains a database of research papers on purchasing and supply which can be freely searched by research topic, name or keyword. Retrieved documents can be viewed and downloaded by non-members for free.

4276 Supply Chain Council
www.supply-chain.org/
The Supply Chain Council is a not-for-profit trade association representing the interests of practitioners in a broad range of industry sectors, including manufacturers, services, distributors and retailers. The website is divided into public and members-only sections. The public section offers an overview of SCOR (Supply-Chain Operations Reference-model), a 'process reference model developed and endorsed by the Council as a cross-industry standard diagnostic tool for supply-chain management.' Non-members can also view a calendar of upcoming events and general information on the association.

4277 Transportation & Logistics Council

www.tlcouncil.org

Formerly known as the Transportation Consumer Protection Council (TCPC), the TLC is a not-for-profit trade association 'dedicated to serving the interests of the shipping community through education and representation in issues relating to the transportation of goods'. Site has a useful Q&A section, on which non-members can post their own questions and browse past questions and answers. The Council's publication can be purchased directly from the website. Membership benefits include *TransDigest*, a monthly newsletter containing information on recent developments in all modes of transportation.

Portal & task environments

4278 Global supply chain intelligence portal (GSCI)

www.gscintell.com/

This portal is a subscription service run by Transport Intelligence, a company specializing in research and analysis for the logistics industry. It provides access to a range of profiles, including regional and country; industry sector (consumer, high-tech, automotive, healthcare and pharmaceutical, fashion, etc.); industry segment; companies in all key logistics markets. Also contains an archive of news analysis briefs and daily updates. See publisher's website for details of content and subscription information

Directories & encyclopedias

4279 LogisticsWorld directory

www.logisticsworld.com/

LogisticsWorld is a directory offering service and contact information for companies and organizations in the transportation, logistics and supply chain industries. Also contains some useful online tools, including currency and country ISO codes, harmonized tariff schedule, NAICS and SIC codes, world time zones, FIPS country codes and other useful reference tools.

4280 Plunkett's transportation, supply chain and logistics industry almanac [USA]

Plunkett Research, 2007, annual, 696pp. $299.99. ISBN 1593920857. www.plunkettresearch.com/

A comprehensive overview of the global transportation and logistics sector. The almanac contains information on the latest trends and technology; business and industry contacts; professional organizations, industry associations and government agencies related to the industry; related internet sites and other resources; statistical tables covering both historical data and forecasts; an industry glossary and thorough indexes. The corporate profiles section includes in-depth profiles of nearly 500 leading companies from all areas of the transportation and logistics industry. The almanac comes with a CD-ROM version of the company database. Search by company, headquarters location, revenues or specific industry sectors.

Handbooks & manuals

4281 Handbook of global supply chain management

J.T. Mentzer, M.B. Myers and T.P. Stank, eds Sage Publications, 2007, 600pp. $125. ISBN 9781412918053. www.sagepub.com

Aims to provide a comprehensive understanding of the field of global logistics and supply chain management. Content is drawn from international contributors from both academia and practice. Features an examination of emerging developments in the practice of GSCM and identifies the methods and perspectives on GSCM that have 'emerged from logistics, operations, marketing, management, economics, sociology, personnel, information systems and international relations'.

4282 Handbook of logistics and distribution management

A. Rushton, P. Croucher and P. Baker 3rd edn, Kogan page, 2006, 576pp. £37.50. ISBN 0749446692. www.kogan-page.co.uk

The *Handbook of logistics and distribution management* provides an excellent introduction to the field. Divided into six sections, the book covers concepts of logistics and distribution; planning for logistics; procurement and inventory decisions; warehousing and storage; freight transport; and operational management. The latest edition includes new material on receiving and despatch, plus new technologies such as radio frequency identification (RFID), voice technology, satellite crane systems and dynamic pick systems.

Appealing to students, newly appointed managers and experienced practitioners alike, this definitive text explains the nuts and bolts of the modern logistics and distribution world in plain language. Richly illustrated throughout, the third edition of this popular handbook has been completely restructured and fully revised to include the most up-to-date information. An invaluable guide for distribution, logistics and supply-chain managers.

4283 Handbook of supply chain management

J.B. Ayers 2nd edn, Auerbach Publications, 2006, 608pp. £44.99. ISBN 0849331609. www.crcpress.com/

Describes how supply chain management has evolved over the years and explores how the techniques currently used in strategic planning and operations improvement could find new applications in managing supply chains. This second edition also introduces topics that have grown in 'visibility' since the previous edition, including drivers of supply chain change; project management approaches; globalization; and the 'lean' and Six Sigma movements and their application to SCM. The book offers a very practical analysis of each topic, using case studies to illustrate successful and not-so-successful SCM practice. Packed with helpful tips and insights, the handbook has a glossary and a large bibliography of related readings.

4284 Supply management handbook

J.L. Cavinato, A.E. Flynn and R.G. Kauffman 7th edn, McGraw-Hill, 2006, 945pp. $129.95. ISBN 0071445137. www.mhprofessional.com/

Formerly known as *The purchasing handbook*, this updated and fully revised edition explores, identifies and discusses supply chain sources and strategies. 'Topics include what key organizations are doing now to develop and implement next-generation supply methodologies; an organization's duty to and interaction with society and insights for addressing the evolving concept of social responsibility in the supply arena; a five-step best practices framework for implementing total cost of ownership in supply management; logistics considerations for the supply management professional; supply management in a risk-sensitive environment; sharpening your supply management skills.'

Keeping up to date

4285 ASCET: achieving supply chain excellence through technology
Montgomery Research Inc., annual.
www.ascet.com/welcome.asp
ASCET is one of several projects run by Montgomery Research, a company that 'publishes thought leadership initiatives that focus on the convergence of technology and business'. The ASCET project provides insights and practical guidance on supply chain management. Launched seven years ago, an annual online volume is published which examines a particular topic in the field of SCM. Users can view the content of the current and past volumes freely but pre-registration is required to view and download the papers. A print version of the volumes can be purchased directly from the site's online bookstore.

4286 Logistics Management [USA]
Reed Business information, monthly. $254. ISSN 15403890.
www.logisticsmgmt.com/ [COMPANION]
A monthly publication from Reed Business Information aimed at supply chain professionals. The magazine offers industry news and in-depth analysis on the major forms of freight transportation, plus information on products, technologies, government regulations and international logistics. LogisticsMgmt.com is a companion website to the magazine providing free access to selected content from the current and past issues, plus additional resources such as white papers, case studies and webcasts on a variety of related topics.

4287 Logistics Manager [UK]
Centaur Communications, monthly. £55. ISSN 13535595.
www.centaursubs.co.uk
A monthly magazine aimed at supply chain practitioners. It features 'in-depth case studies detailing how organizations are reducing operating costs and boosting the efficiency of their goods-to-market operations. There is extensive coverage of new distribution and other logistics contracts, industrial property developments, vehicle fleet updates, innovations and information systems technology.' See publisher's website for information on subscription packages.

4288 Purchasing Magazine [USA]
Reed Business Information, 19 p.a. ISSN 00334448.
www.purchasing.com/ [COMPANION]
Provides supply chain management and e-procurement practitioners with 'how-to-buy information to perform their jobs, including forecasts, proprietary data, strategic sourcing ideas and interpretive articles written by an experienced staff of editors. Scope is global, but primary focus is on the US and Canada. Coverage includes all products and services; special editions cover electronics and technology, metals and

the chemical process industries'. Purchasing.com is a companion website to the magazine. Users can register free to receive e-mail newsletters and can access selected premium content from the current and past issues.

4289 SupplyChainDigest newsletter [USA]
weekly.
www.manufacturing.net/scm/
SupplyChainDigest is a free, weekly, online newsletter containing information, news and commentary for supply chain and logistics professionals. It reviews hundreds of news articles, research reports, analyst opinions and other news sources. The site also provides a series of free, on-demand videocasts and webinars. Registration is required to access full content.

Operations & Technology Management

facilities management • innovation management • outsourcing • production & manufacturing management • production scheduling • quality management

Introductions to the subject

4290 Operations management
N. Slack, S. Chambers and R. Johnston   5th edn, Financial Times Prentice Hall, 2006, 728pp. £44.99. ISBN 140584700X.
www.pearsoned.co.uk/
An impressive introduction to the processes and activities associated with operations management. The book presents a well structured and practical exploration of key areas in this field. Each chapter contains examples of operations in practice to demonstrate real operational issues faced by businesses; critical commentaries to show a diversity of view points; a range of case studies; and selected further readings and useful websites. A very well thought-out and readable textbook.

4291 Operations management for competitive advantage
R.B. Chase, F.R. Jacobs and N.J. Aquilano   11th edn, McGraw-Hill Irwin, 2006, 806pp. with DVD, £41.99. ISBN 0071115528.
http://catalogs.mhhe.com/mhhe/home.do
An established textbook now in its eleventh edition, providing comprehensive coverage of the concepts, processes and methods involved in operations management. Using a variety of real-world examples, articles, illustrations, problems and case sudies this is an ideal text for students studying business-related courses and equally suitable for professionals working in this field. The text focuses on strategic and management issues as opposed to engineering or technical issues. Topics such as globalization, supply chain strategy and enterprise resource planning (ERP) are explored. Includes a DVD featuring outlines of each chapter and video clips illustrating the application of operations concepts in global companies.

4292 Purchasing principles and management
P. Baily [et al.]   9th edn, Financial Times Prentice Hall, 2004, 427pp. £43.99. ISBN 0273646893.
www.pearsoned.co.uk
Now in its ninth edition, this text provides a comprehensive overview of the purchasing function. Published in association

with the Chartered Institute of Purchasing & Supply (CIPS), it is written in a clear and easy-to-read style. The content is divided into four main sections. 'Objectives and organization' examines strategic themes and the scope of purchasing; 'Key considerations' looks at issues such as quality and price; 'Specialized aspects' covers the latest developments in technology and e-commerce; and 'Systems and control' concentrates on personnel and performance.

4293   Total facilities management
B. Atkin and A. Brooks   2nd edn, Blackwell Publishing, 2005, 238pp. £37.50. ISBN 1405127902.
www.blackwellpublishing.com/
Provides a comprehensive overview of facilities management and examines how this can affect an organization and its business objectives. Content: an introduction to facilities management; developing a strategy for facilities management; retaining services in-house vs. outsourcing; change management; human resources management implications; policy and procedures for outsourcing; policy and procedures for in-house provision; service specifications, service level agreements and performance; employment, health and safety considerations; workplace productivity; facilities management service providers; managing service provider and supplier relationships; contract management and financial control; benchmarking best practice; public-private partnerships; education, training and development; innovation, research and development. Also includes a glossary.

Dictionaries, thesauri, classifications

4294   Key concepts in operations management
J. Sutherland and D. Canwell   Palgrave Macmillan, 2004, 277pp. Palgrave Key Concepts series, £11.99. ISBN 1403915296.
www.palgrave.com/home/index.asp
A glossary from the 'Key Concepts' series. Contains nearly 600 concepts, terms, theories and theorists in the area of operations management. Entries are arranged alphabetically and are fully cross-referenced. The glossary also suggests further reading references and useful websites. Illustrations are used to help explain complex terminology. Ideal for anyone wanting to get to grips with the basic concepts and terminology used in the field.

Official & quasi-official bodies

4295   Innovation [UK]
Great Britain. Department of Trade & Industry
www.dti.gov.uk/innovation/
Innovation is a website created and maintained by the Department of Trade and Industry (DTI) that provides practical information for businesses on how they can improve their key business processes in order to compete effectively in the global environment. It seeks to 'facilitate the transfer of knowledge between the role of research and development and explain how businesses can access the practical support available for R&D and innovative projects'. The website contains a wealth of information and resources, including advice on standards and technical regulations; a section on benchmarking innovation performance which includes a self-assessment tool to benchmark your own business; an archive of annual broadcasts (1997–2005) of world-renowned

innovators sharing their thoughts on innovation; a section on leadership skills for innovation; DTI innovation policy; and a whole range of related statistics.

Research centres & institutes

4296   Center for Quality Management [USA]
www.cqm.org/
The CQM is a non-profit organization that offers educational programmes, research, advisory services and networking activities in the area of total quality management (TQM). The Center is mainly based in the USA but has chapters in Central Europe and Finland. The website provides details of the Center's research initiatives, courses, workshops and networking events. It also produces a range of manuals, videos and books which can be purchased online. Site visitors can freely access an archive of the Center's own online journal *CQM journal*, which was published from 1993–2003.

4297   CoPS Innovation Centre [UK]
www.cops.ac.uk/index.php
The CoPS Innovation Centre is a joint venture between the Science and Technology Policy Research Unit at the University of Sussex and the Centre for Research in Innovation Management at the University of Brighton. The Centre works with industry, policy makers and others in the academic community to increase understanding of 'how innovation works in complex capital goods, industrial systems, constructs and networks.' Website contains information about the centre and its work. There is a searchable database of CoPS publications, conference and working papers are freely available for download but this requires pre-registration.

4298   Exeter Centre for Strategic Processes & Operations [UK]
www.centres.ex.ac.uk/xspo/
The Exeter Centre for Strategic Processes & Operations (XSPO) is a research centre within the School of Business and Economics at the University of Exeter. It undertakes research for both the public and private sectors and has four main areas of research interest, which are: 'identifying the relationship between managing processes and customer satisfaction; developing a set of rules and guidelines for improved process design; linking value creation and process design to generate increased revenue; developing strategies for business process outsourcing'. The Centre provides a range of external courses for companies wishing to expand their process modelling and analysis capabilities. Website contains a full bibliography of its research projects, articles, conference papers and book chapters.

4299   Outsourcing Institute
www.outsourcing.com/
The OI describes itself as 'a neutral professional association dedicated solely to outsourcing'. It tailors resources and solutions to the specific needs and interests of buyers, service providers and industry influencers. To gain full access to the website users must register under one of the three categories mentioned. Each contains links to research, articles and best practice guides, plus links to networking events, services and solutions.

Associations & societies

4300　American Society for Quality
www.asq.org/

The ASQ is a professional association dedicated to advancing 'learning, quality improvement and knowledge exchange to improve business results and to create better workplaces and communities worldwide.' It offers technologies, tools and training to quality practitioners and everyday consumers. A nicely organized website packed with useful information and resources. Selecting a topic opens up a general overview from which users can then view a topic tutorial; see related books, articles and case studies; view related training and certification programmes; or see forthcoming networking events. The site also offers a searchable article abstracts database, an online glossary and a blogs section on quality-related topics. See website for subscription prices and benefits.

■ **Quality Progress** ASQ, monthly. $110. ISSN 0033524X. The ASQ's flagship publication featuring in-depth articles describing the application of innovative methods. Topics include knowledge management, process improvement and organizational behaviour. Includes an annual salary survey which is compiled and published each December.

4301　Association for Operations Management
www.apics.org/default.htm

Established in 1957, the Association is a not-for-profit global educational organization specializing in the field of operations management. The Association has a current membership of nearly 50,000 individuals from 20,000 companies representing the manufacturing, service, retail and wholesale industries. It offers a wide range of courses, programs, certification exams and educational material, details of which can be found on the website. Membership benefits include full access to the APICS website, which covers access to the APICS publications database containing articles, conference proceedings and industry information; online access to the Association's monthly trade magazine; best practice guides; discussion lists and forums; APICS Webinars – 60-minute seminars featuring an educational discussion, case studies and a Q&A session. See website for information on the various membership rates.

4302　British Quality Foundation
www.quality-foundation.co.uk/

The British Quality Foundation (BQF) is a not-for-profit organization that 'promotes business excellence' to private, public and voluntary sector organizations in the UK. The website details information on the Foundation's history and core activities, including the business excellence model that it has developed. Site also details membership benefits and the Foundation's products and publications, which can be purchased online.

4303　European Foundation for Quality Management
www.efqm.org/

Based in Brussels, the EFQM is a not-for-profit membership foundation that promotes total quality management (TQM) in Europe. The site features the EFQM model of excellence and provides details of its publications, which can be ordered online. It runs a range of training courses and workshops, as well as organizing an Excellence award scheme. Members benefit from a whole range of online resources, including benchmarking reports, tools, articles and a good practice database which contains best management practices

adopted by winners and finalists of the Foundation's award for the past five years. Non-members can register for limited access to the site, including a range of free podcasts and video interviews.

4304　European Operations Management Association
www.euroma-online.org/

EurOMA is a European-based 'network of academics and managers from around the world interested in developing operations management'. The Association organizes an annual conference and a series of workshops throughout the year. Its members receive a regular newsletter and a discounted subscription to the Association's official publication the *International Journal of Operations and Production Management*. Website details the Association's history and background, membership benefits and forthcoming events.

■ **International Journal of Operations and Production Management** Emerald, monthly. ISSN 01443577. www.emeraldinsight.com. 'The IJOPM draws together information at the forefront of the discipline, providing sound guidance for those concerned with the management of systems, whether in academic institutions, industry or consultancy. Highly respected worldwide, and associated with EurOMA, this information resource seeks to raise standards in every aspect of operations and production management.' See publisher's website for subscription details and free sample articles.

4305　European Organization for Quality
www.eoq.org/start.asp

The European Organization for Quality (EOQ) is an interdisciplinary, not-for-profit organization founded in 1956. The Brussels-based organization is made up of '34 national quality organizations in Europe, as well as institutions, companies and individuals from all over the world'. Website contains details of its activities, membership, annual conference and forthcoming events. The EOQ vision document, which sets out the background to the 'evolution of quality in Europe as it relates to other parts of the world' can be freely downloaded from the website.

4306　International Society of Six Sigma Professionals
www.isssp.com/

Officially launched in October 2001, the ISSSP is a professional society dedicated to the 'advancement of education, research and implementation of the Six Sigma methodology through resources in live, print and electronic media'. The Society boasts a global community made up of individuals, practitioners and corporate members across a wide range of industries. Membership benefits include online access to a range of resources, including the iKnow database containing archived audio-video training, articles and white papers and over 600 presentations from top conferences and industry events; webcasts and Q&As on Six Sigma awareness, project and deployment case studies, product and service demonstrations, methodologies and tools; online discussion forums; and access to the Society's official magazine. The Society runs a range of educational programmes and organizes an annual leadership conference. See website for full details of activities and membership details.

■ **iSixSigma Magazine** CTQ Media LLC, bi-monthly. $79.95. www.isixsigma-magazine.com/. The official magazine of the International Society of Six Sigma Professionals is aimed at readers of all experience levels. It offers practical advice, information on the latest methodologies and analysis of current trends, issues and news. Available in both print and electronic format.

4307 National Outsourcing Association [UK]

www.noa.co.uk

The NOA is an independent, not-for-profit trade association whose main objectives are to promote best practice, service and innovation in the application and development of outsourcing; to lobby national governments, regulators and the EU on issues affecting the collective interests of its members; and to deliver information on market developments in business outsourcing to its members. Site details membership benefits which include a free subscription to *Outsource* magazine and a members-only area of the website containing a plethora of information, including white papers, research, opinion pieces and presentations

4308 Product Development & Management Association

www.pdma.org/

Founded in 1976, the Product Development & Management Association (PDMA) is a global association representing product development and management professionals. Its mission is to 'improve the effectiveness of individuals and organizations in product development and management'. The PDMA website contains information about its activities, membership and forthcoming events, including its annual conference. It has a members-only section, which hosts an online membership directory and full-text articles from the *Journal of Product Innovation Management* (JPIM). Members gain exclusive access to the 'Body of knowledge' which contains information on all aspects of product development and management across the entire lifecycle. Non-members get free, full-text access to Visions, the PDMA's own magazine, going back to 1995. Site also contains an online glossary, the PDMA blog and a discussion forum (requiring registration).

- **Journal of Product Innovation Management** Blackwell Publishing, 6 times p.a. ISSN 07376782. Features research, theory and practice in new product and service development. See publisher's website for subscription details and content from a sample issue.

4309 Production Operations Management Society

www.poms.org/

POMS is an international organization 'representing the interests of POM professionals from around the world'. The main purpose of the Society is to improve the understanding and practice of production and operations management (POM) by disseminating information on POM and promoting the improvement of POM practice and its teaching. The website is easy to navigate, containing information about the Society, its activities, membership benefits and information on its journal the *Production and Operations Management Journal*. It also offers a selection of free resources, including full-text access to the POMS chronicle, a news and discussion magazine, a PDF version of the *Encyclopedia of operations management terms* and glossary; a comprehensive online list of OM course syllabi from leading US universities; and a range of downloadable OM tools.

- **Encyclopedia of operations management terms** A.V. Hill 2003. www.poms.org/EducationResources/omencyclopedia.pdf. An encyclopedia of OM terms in PDF format which contains definitions of terms and concepts from the field of operations management. Written by Arthur V. Hill, Professor of Operations and Management Science, Curtis L. Carlson School of Management, University of Minnesota.

Portal & task environments

4310 BPR online learning center

www.prosci.com/

The BPR online learning center is one of seven specialized portals sponsored by Prosci, a company involved in business process design and change management research. The portal offers a range of resources aimed specifically at anyone involved in business process reengineering. Resources include benchmarking studies, reengineering toolkits and templates which can be purchased online. The site features a free online tutorial series, a directory of tools and a list of consultants and vendor partners for reengineering and process improvement projects. Users can register to receive e-mail notification when new content is added.

4311 iSixSigma.com

www.isixsigma.com

iSixSigma.com is an online content provider for the Six Sigma community. It offers free information resources to 'help business professionals successfully implement quality within their organizations'. There are some excellent features on this well put-together website, including articles, tools and templates; best practice guides; a jobs section; latest news and events; blogs and discussion forums; and related organization links. Resources are organized into 'channels', which are basically eight different topic areas covering Six Sigma, Europe, financial services, software/IT, innovation, healthcare, outsourcing/offshoring and business process management. Other features include an online quality dictionary and a range of e-mail newsletters that users can freely subscribe to.

4312 Managing innovation website

www.managing-innovation.com/innovation/cda/index.php

A well organized companion website to the book *Managing innovation*, maintained by the authors Joe Tidd, John Bessant and Keith Pavitt. The site is specifically aimed at instructors and students studying innovation and technology management. It is organized into five resource types, including a very useful case studies section. Each case record contains an abstract and either a PDF link for download or a link to the relevant website or clearing house for purchase. Browse by theme, sector or geographic area. The toolbox section contains tools that can be browsed by themes associated with developing innovation management capability. There is an exercises and games section and a special teaching resources area requiring registration. The site also offers a link to a free PDF version of the *AIM innovation directory*, a guide to innovation management research in the UK.

- **Managing innovation: integrating technological, market and organizational change** J. Tidd, J. Bessant and K. Pavitt 3rd rev edn, Wiley, 2005, 600pp. £34.99. ISBN 0470093269. http://eu.wiley.com/.

4313 TOMI (Technology and operations management index)

www.sussex.ac.uk/Users/dt31/TOMI/index.html

Originally called Twigg's operations management index, TOMI is the brainchild of David Twigg, a lecturer at the University of Sussex. The main aim of the site is to provide users with a basic introduction to the area of technology and operations management, including related areas such as 'purchasing, product development, innovation management, manufacturing strategy, inventory control, logistics, quality and service operations'. As well as links to organizations and other websites, the site offers a useful reading list containing a selection of recommended books and articles, plus a links section to websites that offer podcasts about innovation. A really good starting point for anyone with wishing to develop their knowledge in this field.

Discovering print & electronic resources

4314   OMC Operations Management Center
www.mhhe.com/omc/index.html
The OM Center is sponsored by McGraw-Hill Irwin and is intended as a 'focal point' for finding operations management resources for students and academics. It offers an impressive collection of free articles and links to OM-related publications, organizations and websites. Additionally, the site contains links to textbook support pages; a list of McGraw-Hill Irwin textbooks, videos and digital solutions pages; OM software (companies, demos and downloads) and daily OM newsfeeds.

Digital data, image & text collections

4315   Best Practice Database
www3.best-in-class.com/Database
An online membership database of more than '3000 business improvement techniques for a variety of industries and functions'. It contains insights, best practices and metrics from executives in global companies. It covers six main topics: sales and marketing; human resources; business operations; customer services; internet and e-business; and knowledge management. There are various levels of subscription – see site for full details. The database can be browsed freely by main topic and individual reports can be purchased on a pay-as-you-go basis. Website also offers an RSS feed for 'Best practice of the day', plus a 'What's new' section with complimentary excerpts of research to non-members and monthly e-mail alerts on new research added to the database.

4316   Facility management reference library
E. Bas [et al.]   2nd edn, CRC Press, 2005. CD-ROM, $450. ISBN 0849395682.
www.crcpress.com
This CD-ROM contains a collection of 11 books in PDF format, covering all aspects of facilities management. Contents: Bioterrorism; Cyber terrorism; Facility manager's guide to security – protecting your assets; Handbook of facility assessment; Water quality and systems; Disaster and recovery planning; Facility manager's handbook; Indoor air quality; Lighting upgrades; Boiler operator's handbook; Pump user's handbook – life extension.

Directories & encyclopedias

4317   Blackwell encyclopedia of management: operations management
N. Slack and M.E. Lewis, eds   2nd edn, Blackwell, 2006, 376pp. Blackwell encyclopedia of management ; v.10, £85. ISBN 1405110961.

www.managementencyclopedia.com/
This encyclopedia provides concise definitions and explanations of the key concepts within the field of operations management. Fully revised and updated, it contains 256 entries, including 93 new entries, across a wide range of areas such as service, strategy, technology and innovation. All the bibliographies have also been significantly updated and extended.

4318   Encyclopedia of production and manufacturing management
P. Swamidass, ed.   Kluwer Academic, 2000, 979pp. £362. ISBN 0792386302.
www.springer.com/
Available in print and online, this encyclopaedia presents over 100 in-depth articles and more than 1000 shorter entries on the concepts, practices and techniques involved in production and manufacturing management. 'The range of topics and depth of coverage is intended to suit both student and professional audiences.'

Handbooks & manuals

4319   Facilities management handbook [UK]
F. Booty, ed.   3rd edn, Butterworth-Heinemann, 2006, 473pp. £49.99. ISBN 0750668423.
http://books.elsevier.com/
A comprehensive guide covering all aspects of facilities management. This is a well organized book packed with useful checklists and practical guidance, ideal for facilities managers and related professionals. Contents include complying with the law; health and safety; employment law; property law; finance management; risk management; outsourcing; transport; IT and communications; space design and management; access, safety and security; maintenance and repair.

4320   Handbook of production scheduling
J.W. Hermann, ed.   Springer Verlag, 2006, 318pp. International series in operations research & management science, £77. ISBN 0387331158.
www.springer.com/
The Handbook provides a practical introduction to 'real-world' production scheduling in factories and industrial settings. The main aim of this book is to help practitioners improve production scheduling in their own organization. It does this by taking a very hands-on approach to explaining the concepts and processes involved, using industry case studies to present the key techniques and tools used in production scheduling systems. The practical focus of this text makes it ideal for 'production managers, plant managers, industrial engineers, operations research practitioners, students studying operations research and industrial engineering, researchers in OR and industrial engineering'.

4321   Operations and process management: principles and practice for strategic impact
N. Slack [et al.]   Financial Times Prentice Hall, 2005, 531pp. + CD-ROM, £47.16. ISBN 0273684264.
www.pearsoned.co.uk/
This text approaches the topic from a managerial perspective, providing clear and concise coverage of the core principles and processes involved in the management of

business operations. The book is packed with examples and case studies to provide insight into the day-to-day realities of managing operations. The accompanying CD-ROM features a range of resources, including animated diagrams, checklists, a downloadable list of principles from each chapter and a video of the author giving further guidance on key concepts and questions. See publisher's website for sample chapter.

4322 Outsourcing handbook: how to implement a successful outsourcing process
M.J. Power, K.C. Desouza and C. Bonifazi   Kogan Page, 2006, 222pp. £30. ISBN 0749444304.
www.kogan-page.co.uk
The Handbook offers practical guidance and advice on the entire outsourcing process. A great reference tool, aimed at any size of business. Contents: What is outsourcing?; Ten common traps of outsourcing; How to manage outsourcing engagements successfully; The outsourcing lifecycle; Defining your needs; Types of vendors; Negotiation and contract management; Management of the relationship; Continuing, modifying, or calling it quits; The exit strategy; Repeating the process; Industry best practices; The future of outsourcing. 'A hands-on and applied approach to exploring the intricacies of commencing, managing, renewing and/or terminating outsourcing engagements.' (*Journal of Economic Literature*) 'Provides a strategy that any manager can implement.' (*European Foundation for Management Development*, Vol 50, Issue 1)

4323 Oxford handbook of innovation
J. Fagerberg, D.C. Mowery and R.R. Nelson, eds   new edn, Oxford University Press, 2006, 656pp. Oxford handbooks in business and management, £27.50. ISBN 0199286809.
www.oup.com/
The Oxford handbook of innovation provides a 'comprehensive and holistic understanding of the phenomenon of innovation'. It presents 21 articles from leading experts from a variety of different fields, each focusing on a specific aspect of innovation. The articles have been organized into four main sections: 'section one focuses on the creation of innovation, with particular focus on firms and networks; section two looks at the wider systematic setting currently influencing innovation and the role of institutions and organizations in this context; section three explores some of the diversity in the working of innovation over time and across different sectors of the economy; and section four examines the consequences of innovation on economic growth, international competitiveness and employment'. The book also includes an informative introductory essay and a guide to further reading for each chapter. See publisher's website for contents and a sample chapter.

4324 Product design and development
K. Ulrich and S. Eppinger   3rd edn, McGraw-Hill/Irwin, 2003, 366pp. £40.99. ISBN 0071232737.
www.ulrich-eppinger.net/ [COMPANION]
A clearly written textbook providing a detailed overview of production development techniques from the perspectives of marketing, design and manufacturing. Primarily developed for students on interdisciplinary courses but equally suitable for practising professionals. Divided into 16 chapters, each one presenting a different development method using a range of industrial examples and case studies to help provide a more practical understanding. The third edition contains two new chapters covering robust design and

patents and intellectual property. To supplement the text the authors have developed a companion website which contains additional references, examples and links to resources related to each chapter.

Keeping up to date

4325 Outsource Magazine [UK]
EMP Media, qtrly. £39.
www.outsourcemagazine.co.uk/ [COMPANION]
A quarterly magazine published independently but in association with the National Outsourcing Association, covering issues, trends and cases relating to outsourcing. Magazine has a companion website which contains content from the print version and exclusive web features. Non-subscribers can register (free) to access selected content from the print version.

4326 Production, Planning and Control
Taylor & Francis, 8 p.a. ISSN 09537287.
www.taylorandfrancisgroup.com/
'Brings together research papers on all aspects of production planning and control and the management of operations in all industries. The journal focuses on research that stems from an industrial need and can guide the activities of managers, consultants, software developers and researchers. It publishes accessible articles on research and industrial applications, new techniques and development trends.' See publisher's website for subscription prices, table of contents alerts and a free sample issue (site registration required).

Human Resource Management

employment law • health & safety at work • industrial relations • personnel management • wages & salaries • working conditions

Introductions to the subject

4327 Employer's handbook: an essential guide to employment law, personnel policies and procedures [UK]
B. Cushway   5th edn, Kogan page, 2007, 336pp. £40. ISBN 9780749449728.
www.kogan-page.co.uk
A comprehensive source book aimed at small and medium-sized businesses. Provides clear, practical guidance on UK employment law and best practice for managing people. 'This new edition has been fully updated to take account of the changes arising from the Employment Equality (Age) Regulations 2006, the Work and Families Act 2006, Maternity and Paternity Leave and the Paternity and Adoption Leave (amendment) Regulations 2006. There is also new information on case law decisions affecting the handling of grievances as well as updated figures relating to the national minimum wage, statutory sick pay, maternity pay and redundancy pay compensational limits for unfair dismissal'.

'A practical, jargon-free guide. Focuses on both the legal and non-legal essentials for effective people management.' (*People Management*)

4328 Human resource management in Europe: evidence of convergence?
C. Brewster, W. Mayrhofer and M.J. Morley, eds   Elsevier Butterworth-Heinemann, 2004, 486pp. £25.99. ISBN 0750647175. http://books.elsevier.com/

With the expansion of cross-border alliances and mergers in recent years, the need for a thorough understanding of human resource management in a European context has become essential. This book introduces readers to the different environments, approaches and practices that exist across Europe for managing human resources. Content is drawn from recognized authorities in the field and uses data from CRANET-E, the world's largest longitudinal and comparative HRM survey. 'An essential book for anyone interested international and comparative HRM.' See publisher's website for full contents listing and a free sample chapter.

4329 International human resource management and international assignments
M.J. Morley, N. Heraty and D.G. Collings   Palgrave MacMillan, 2006, 224pp. £55. ISBN 1403942986. www.palgrave.com/

With the increasing globalization of business, this book brings together some of the leading authorities in the field of HRM to present a more in-depth understanding of human resource management in an international context. Contents: introduction; international human resource management in global perspective; human resource management in the global village; transnational roles and transnational rewards: global integration in executive compensation; development of an efficient architecture for the inpatriation of managers; building effective expatriate–host country national relationships: the effects of human resources practices, international strategy and mode of entry; international assignments and boundaryless careers: a study of the career orientations of German and Singaporean expatriates; boundaryless global careers: the international itinerants; repatriate assets: factors impacting knowledge transfer. See publisher's website for contents and sample chapter.

4330 Introduction to human resource management: a guide to personnel in practice [UK]
D. Currie   CIPD, 2006, 316pp. Chartered Institute of Personnel & Development, £33.99. ISBN 1843981394. www.cipd.co.uk/Bookstore/

Primarily aimed at CIPD students and students on foundation degree programmes, this text 'offers a basic and practical introduction to HR and personnel issues'. Recognizing the need for a balance between academic and practical understanding, the book provides its readers with an understanding of the relevant theoretical concepts of HR and the need to develop competencies and skills in their practical application. See publisher's website for full table of contents and a sample chapter.

4331 Readings and cases in international human resource management
M.E. Mendenhall, G.R. Oddou and G.K. Stahl, eds   Routledge, 2006, 400pp. £29.99. ISBN 0415396883. www.routledge.co.uk/

A good introduction to human resource management from an international and cross-cultural perspective. The book presents a collection of readings and cases selected from prominent authors and researchers to explore human resource issues in a global context. Contents divided into nine sections: the context of international human resource management; strategy and international HRM; staffing for international operations; management development; performance appraisal and compensation; labour and employee relations; cross-cultural issues in productivity and quality; HR issues in international joint ventures; managing expatriate assignments. Book has a companion website containing additional resources and related web-links – see publisher's website for further details.

4332 Shaping your HR role: succeeding in today's organizations
W. Kahnweiler and J. Kahnweiler   Butterworth-Heinemann, 2005, 264pp. £21.99. ISBN 0750678232. http://books.elsevier.com/

Written by two experienced HR professionals, this book is ideal for anyone working in HR wishing to develop their role and skills in this area. Combining theory, practical case studies and interviews with directors of human resources from organizations from a cross-section of industries and sectors, the book presents a range of current issues and trends in this field.
'This book is worthwhile for anyone in HR but particularly so for those somewhat new to HR and those considering an HR career. I wish I had read this book twenty years ago.' (Steve Hewitt, Senior Professional in Human Resources, The Hewitt Group)

4333 Theory and practice of training
R. Buckley and J. Caple   5th edn, Kogan page, 2004, 324pp. £25. ISBN 0749441569. www.kogan-page.co.uk

Written for those just starting out in the training profession, this book presents a comprehensive introduction to the main topics in this area. 'The book is illustrated throughout with real-life examples and numerous figures and diagrams'. It examines: the role of training in organizations; proactive and reactive assessments of training needs; theoretical models of training; competence-based training; training objectives; training strategies and training methods; and validation, evaluation and assessment of training.

Dictionaries, thesauri, classifications

4334 Dictionary of human resources and personnel management
P.H. Collin and A. Ivanovic, eds   3rd edn, Bloomsbury, 2003, 400pp. £9.99. ISBN 0747566232.

With over 7000 terms covering all aspects of human resources, including recruitment and selection, appraisals, payment systems, dismissals and industrial relations. An ideal reference tool for anyone working in HR departments, recruitment consultants and employment lawyers.

4335 EMIRE database [EUR]
www.eurofound.eu.int/emire/emire.html
The EMIRE database is the online version of the *European employment and industrial relations glossaries*, which explain the national industrial relations systems of the EU member states through their terminology. Browse the alphabetical list

of terms for each country, or use the search function for specific topics. It is worth noting that the industrial relations glossaries in this database are not systematically updated and some of the information may not reflect the current situation.

4336 European industrial relations dictionary
European Foundation for the Improvement of Living & Working Conditions
www.eurofound.europa.eu/areas/industrialrelations/dictionary/index.htm
An online dictionary containing nearly 300 terms commonly used in employment and industrial relations at EU level today. Browse the alphabetically listed entries or use the search function. Each entry provides a concise definition and any relevant contextual information, with links to any relevant EU legislation and case law. The dictionary is updated annually.

4337 Human resources glossary: the complete desk reference for HR executives, managers and practitioners [USA]
W.R. Tracey   3rd edn, St Lucie Press, 2003, 824pp. £56.99. ISBN 1574443518.
Contains over 8500 entries, including information on federal laws, amendments and court decisions relating to the field of human relations; updates on new acronyms, abbreviations and other terms related to HR; and full contact details for over 350 associations and other related organizations.

4338 Key concepts in human resource management
J. Sutherland and D. Canwell   Palgrave Macmillan, 2004, 272pp. Palgrave key concepts series, £11.99. ISBN 1403915288.
www.palgrave.com/
Contains over 500 major concepts, terms, theories and theorists relating to the field of human resources – arranged alphabetically. Ideal for a quick overview of the terminology used in this field.

Laws, standards, codes

4339 A–Z of employment law: a complete reference source for managers [UK]
P. Chandler   4th edn, Kogan Page, 2003, 700pp. £49.95. ISBN 0749438894.
www.kogan-page.co.uk
A useful desktop companion, providing jargon-free advice and guidance on UK employment legislation. Contents include parental leave; unfair dismissal; disciplinary and grievance procedures; holidays and holiday pay; working time (young persons); the national minimum wage; adoption leave and pay; paternity leave and pay; new maternity rights; flexible working; fixed-term employees; part-time workers; the Tax Credits Act 2002; the Employment Act 2002. Also contains useful addresses and alternative sources of information.

4340 Emplaw [UK]
www.emplaw.co.uk
The Emplaw site was created in 1997 by an ex-City of London solicitor and co-author of the Law Society's employment law handbook. This excellent site has two levels of access. Employees, employers and professionals can have free access to more than 4500 cross-referenced fact cards detailing the basics of UK employment law (browse the

alphabetical index or use the search function). Professional users (lawyers and HR professionals) must subscribe to the site. At present, professional users can benefit from a free 30-day trial of the full subscription service. The site also offers a Find-a-Lawyer directory which can be searched by location.

4341 Health and safety handbook: a practical guide to health and safety law, management policies and procedures [UK]
J. Stranks   Kogan Page, 2006, 240pp. £38. ISBN 0749443928.
www.kogan-page.co.uk
A practical handbook providing clearly written guidance on how to comply with health and safety law and procedures for the workplace. Key areas of health and safety are covered, including principles of health and safety law; health and safety management; the working environment; engineering safety; fire prevention and protection; electrical safety; health and safety in construction operations; occupational health; personal protective equipment; human factors; hazardous substances.

4342 State by state guide to human resources law [USA]
J.F. Buckley and R.M. Green, eds   Aspen Publishers, 2006, annual. Kept up to date by midyear supplements; some guides accompanied by special supplements with distinctive titles, $229. ISBN 0735553017.
www.aspenpublishers.com/
This annually produced publication is designed as a quick-reference to the employment laws of the 50 US states and the District of Columbia. It offers concise overviews of each topical area; tables summarizing the law in each state and how it applies to specific situations; reference to court cases and state statutes with complete citations to the original source for every law and regulation discussed.

Official & quasi-official bodies

4343 Age Positive [UK]
www.agepositive.gov.uk/
Age Positive is a campaign that promotes the benefits of employing a mixed-age workforce to include both older and younger people. The campaign encourages employers to consider their recruitment, training and retention strategies and ensure that they do not discriminate against someone because of their age. The Age Positive team are part of the Department for Work and Pensions. Their website details the work that they do. It also contains case studies, good practice standards, events and news. A range of publications and factsheets can be freely downloaded from the site.

4344 Europa: health and safety at work [EUR]
www.ec.europa.eu/employment_social/health_safety/index_en.htm
The H&S@work section of the Europa website presents information on the official EU policies on health and safety. The website provides a historical background to the policies and strategies of the European Commission. There are links to a large selection of related statistics, case law and legislation, as well as information on the purpose and work of the various committees set up by the Commission.

4345 Great Britain. Health & Safety Executive
www.hse.gov.uk/
The Health & Safety Executive was set up to enforce the

health and safety regulations created by the Health & Safety Commission. The Executive's website provides details of the work that it does, including past and future campaigns. It contains a whole range of resources that would be of use to anyone wishing to find out more about occupational health and safety issues, whether it be for themselves or for their own employees. Site content includes information on legislation; a variety of publications that can be purchased directly from the site; free full-text access to research reports funded by the Executive; and a range of statistics on work-related ill-health, injuries, dangerous occurrences, enforcement and gas safety produced by HSE's Statistics Branch. The site also contains an online injury reporting form.

4346   International Labour Organization
www.ilo.org/

Founded in 1919, the International Labour Organization is a United Nations specialized agency whose main function is to promote social justice and internationally recognized human and labour rights. The website details the activities of the ILO and its various offices, departments and programmes. It also contains a staggering number of resources, including 29 different databases, access to the IOLEX database of full text of standards and fundamental principles of rights at work of over 180 conventions and over 190 recommendations, conference documents. Free access to Labordoc, the ILO publications catalogue, which includes all ILO priced and unpriced publications and thousands of references to journal articles, working papers, documents and free online publications.

- **Labour force surveys** Compiles websites which contain data from national statistical agencies, the ILO and other sources. Includes links to source websites and references to print publications available in the ILO Library.
- **CISDOC** Covers occupational health and safety, law and regulations, chemical safety data sheets, training material, journal articles, books and ILO Conventions.
- **Conditions of work and employment database** Includes comprehensive legal information from countries around the world. Covers maternity protection, minimum wages and working time.
- **e.quality@work** The ILO's information base on equal opportunities for women and men, containing guidelines and legislation on equal employment opportunities in the workplace.
- **Labordoc** www.labordoc.ilo.org/ [31/07/2006]. Labordoc contains references and full-text access to the literature on all aspects of employment, including sustainable livelihoods and the work-related aspects of economic and social development, human rights and technological change. Material includes books, articles, reports and journals available at the ILO Library in Geneva and several ILO libraries around the world.
- **Laborsta** ILO's premier database on labour statistics covering employment, unemployment, wages and related variables.

4347   United States. Office of Personnel Management
www.opm.gov/

The OPM is an independent agency of the US Government that deals with pay and conditions of US government employees. Its website provides detailed information on current salary scales, career structure, employment legislation, pension rights and labour relations in the USA. The site includes recent news releases, statistics, federal jobs listings, upcoming events, numerous human resources reports, various calculators, manuals and handbooks and a database of publications. Nicely laid-out website with resources organized by target audience: job seekers, federal

employees, retirees and families, and HR practitioners and agencies.

Research centres & institutes

4348   Academy of Human Resource Development
www.ahrd.org/

'The Academy of Human Resource Development was formed to encourage systematic study of human resource development theories, processes and practices; to disseminate information about HRD, to encourage the application of HRD research findings and to provide opportunities for social interaction among individuals with scholarly and professional interests in HRD from multiple disciplines and from across the globe.' Website details membership benefits, forthcoming events and conferences and information on the Academy's awards programme. The Academy's' conference proceedings are available online, with full-text access dating back to 1999. The Academy also produces a number of journals, details of which can be found on the website.

- **Advances in Developing Human Resources** Sage Publications, qtrly. $93. ISSN 15234223. 'Balancing theory and practice, each issue of the journal is devoted to a different topic central to the development of human resources. *Advances* has covered subjects as wide-ranging and vital as performance improvement, action learning, on-the-job training, informal learning, how HRD relates to the new global economy, leadership, and the philosophical foundations of HRD practice'.
- **Human Resource Development International** Routledge, 10 p.a. £98. ISSN 13678868. www.tandf.co.uk/j.
- **Human Resource Development Quarterly** Jossey-Bass, qtrly. $109. ISSN 10448004. www.josseybass.com/. Jointly sponsored by the Academy and the American Society for Training and Development.
- **Human Resource Development Review** Sage Publications, qtrly. $86. ISSN 15344843. www.sagepub.com [DESCRIPTION]. 'The journal provides new theoretical insights that can advance our understanding of human resource development'.

4349   Center for Advanced Human Resource Studies
www.ilr.cornell.edu/cahrs/default.html

The Center for Advanced Human Resource Studies (CAHRS) is a research centre attached to the School of Industrial and Labor Relations at Cornell University. The Center's main objective is to 'foster excellence in human resource management research, practice and education' by working directly with leading companies from around the world. Site contains the Center's current projects and details of its sponsors. There is a full-text archive of its working papers and free online access to 'hrSpectrum' a bi-monthly newsletter providing up-to-date information on CAHRS and its sponsorship activities, plus the latest developments in research, teaching and employment; archives freely available going back to 1996.

4350   European Foundation for the Improvement of Living & Working Conditions
www.eurofound.eu.int/about/index.htm

A European Union body established specifically to inform EU policy on living and working conditions in Europe. The Foundation provides information and advice in four main areas: employment and working conditions; work–life balance; industrial relations and partnerships; social cohesion. It carries out a number of regular pan-European surveys which are published on the website. The site provides an overview of each of the Foundation's areas of research and links to related publications and sources of information. The Foundation produces an online newsletter *Communiqué*, which is published 10 times a year. It contains articles on current research developments and activities, including conference reports, publication reviews and interviews with EU policymakers and researchers. The newsletter also advertises forthcoming events. Users can register to receive it by e-mail.

4351 Incomes Data Services [UK]
www.incomesdata.co.uk/
Established in 1965, the Incomes Data Services (IDS) is an industrial relations research centre which provides information on wages, salaries and conditions of employment, which it publishes through a wide variety of subscription services and publications.

- **IDS Diversity at Work** monthly. £345. ISSN 17437350. A monthly journal examining workplace diversity, equal opportunities and discrimination law.
- **IDS Employment Law Brief** 24 p.a. £495. ISSN 03089312. Features new UK and European employment laws and decisions of tribunals and the courts along with the implications for employers and employees. Comes with the Employment law handbook and supplement.
- **IDS Executive Compensation Review** monthly. £425. ISSN 13514954. Monthly briefing on the salaries and benefits of managerial and professional staff. Subscription includes in-depth research files on selected topics and access to an online salary survey directory.
- **IDS HR Studies** 24 p.a. £420. ISSN 03089339. Analysis of HR and personnel policy and practice. Subscription includes fortnightly issues that focus on a particular HR topic; and access to an online searchable database of company case studies.
- **IDS Pay Benchmark** 3 p.a. £230.05. ISSN 14741792. Information on pay and jobs, average earnings and job weight.
- **IDS Pay Report** 24 p.a. £485. ISSN 00193461. Fortnightly bulletin on pay and conditions across the UK.

4352 Work Foundation [UK]
www.theworkfoundation.com/
The Work Foundation, formerly the Industrial Society, is a not-for-profit research and consultancy organization whose main purpose is to improve the quality of working life. It offers consultancy, research and advocacy in the core areas of leadership, performance, people, public value and the future of work. Details of the Foundation's research can be found on the site, along with an extensive collection of publications and research projects which can be downloaded free of charge.

Associations & societies

4353 American Society for Training & Development
www.astd.org/
Established in 1944, the ASTD claims to be the world's largest association dedicated to workplace learning and performance professionals. Membership benefits include access to online communities enabling practitioners to access resources, articles, discuss projects and share experiences; discussion boards on a variety of related topics; access to Trainlit, a database of articles and papers on workplace learning and performance from around the world. The site also contains a number of newsletters, conference proceedings, white papers and other publications, some of which are free to non-members. Non-members can download

free online reading lists on a variety of topics covered by the Society's magazine *T+D*. Articles from the magazine can be purchased online.

- **T+D** monthly. $165. ISSN 15357740. www.astd.org/TD/ [COMPANION]. A monthly magazine available to ASTD national members and by subscription and single-copy sales. Features articles on training and development trends and current workplace topics. The magazine also has its own blog which can be accessed from the website.

4354 European Association for Personnel Management
www.eapm.org/
Founded in 1962, the EAPM is an umbrella organization representing personnel management associations and institutions from France, Germany, Sweden, Switzerland and the UK. Its main aim is to 'promote and develop knowledge of personnel issues, personnel activities and their importance to industry, commerce and both public and private sector administration'. The website provides further information on the Association's activities, including details of its biennial conference. Other features on the website include country profiles containing a brief introduction to current labour market conditions, tax and social insurance law and general trends in HR for each country. There is a 'quick survey' section which invites users to vote on a topical HR issue and view answers to the current and past questions. There are also a number of publications providing information of various aspects of labour legislation, all freely available for download.

4355 Federation of European Employers
www.fedee.com/
FedEE is an employers' association which was established with EU funding in 1989. The Federation is dedicated to providing jargon-free, expert advice and information on HR issues to companies operating internationally across Europe. It provides its members with information on employment law, pay and labour relations. Members also gain access to a whole wealth of HR resources which can be accessed via a members-only area of the website. Although most of the resources are only available to members there is a featured pages section which presents useful, concise overviews of a variety of employment issues.

4356 International Public Management Association for Human Resources [USA]
www.ipma-hr.org/
The International Public Management Association for Human Resources is an organization that represents the interests of all US public sector HR professionals. Its main objective is 'to provide human resource leadership and advocacy, professional development, information and services to enhance organizational and individual performance in the public sector'. As well as running a number of professional development courses and certification programmes, the organization provides its members with a whole range of resources, including benchmarking and best practice; discussion lists; a jobs forum; online access to the Association's quarterly journal and a weekly e-mail newsletter. The organization carries out a number of surveys and studies on a range of HR issues, some of which are available online for non-members. There is also an interactive programme of online seminars that focus on current and emerging HR issues in the pubic sector, which can be purchased directly from the website.

4357 Society for Human Resource Management [USA]
www.shrm.org/
Founded in 1948, the Society for Human Resource Management (SHRM) was set up to advance the profession by ensuring that 'HR is recognized as an essential partner in developing and executing organizational strategy'. With more than 205,000 individual members, the Society's mission is to represent the needs of HR professionals by providing educational and training opportunities and ensuring continuing professional development and best practice. The Society's website SHRM Online holds an impressive collection of resources for its members covering every area of human resources. Non-members can sign up for a free subscription to HR Week, a weekly e-newsletter presenting HR news stories, links to new content added to the website plus information about SHRM programmes and forthcoming events.

4358 World Federation of Personnel Management Associations
www.wfpma.com/
The World Federation of Personnel Management Associations (WFPMA) was founded in 1976 to 'aid the development and improve the effectiveness of professional people management all over the world'. The Federation is a global network made up of more than 70 national personnel associations representing over 400,000 people management professionals. The website provides details of the WFPMA's biennial world congress on people management. Visitors can view and download articles from current and past issues of the Association's quarterly e-newsletter WorldLink – browse content by author, country or topic. The site also details the Association's projects, including HR competencies and professional standards around the world, global labour resourcing and a survey of HR global challenges, past, present and future – all of which can be freely downloaded.

Portal & task environments

4359 Businessballs
www.businessballs.com/
An interesting website established by the Alan Chapman consultancy in 1999. The idea behind it is to provide a range of free resources and tools to facilitate 'free ethical learning and development resources for people and organizations'. The website is not searchable at present, content is listed in a long, partially alphabetized list, which is not particularly helpful. There is a strange mixture of contents, including an introduction to cockney rhyming slang and a guide to the Greek alphabet. However, it is worth persevering, as there is a great selection of useful resources here, covering brief introductions to various theories and concepts related to personality types and organizational dynamics; online team-building games and other motivational training resources; samples and templates from everything from service contracts to replying to customer complaints; and a whole range of materials for personal development.

4360 HR zone [UK]
www.hrzone.co.uk/
HR zone is an example of one of the growing numbers of dedicated online communities that have appeared on the internet over the last five years. Claiming a membership of over 20,000 UK HR professionals, HR zone provides up-to-date information, tools and resources to its community and enables HR professionals to interact, debate and share knowledge with each other. To gain full access to the resources users must register (free), and can then post questions and start discussion topics. There is a separate features section run by a panel of the site's contributors which provides advice and guidance on a range of typical HR issues and situations. This a clearly laid-out site containing a useful selection of material.

4361 HR.com
www.hr.com/
HR.com is a free website that claims to be the 'largest social network and online community of HR executives'. It provides industry-related news, articles and case studies which are organized into what it calls 'communities' (basically HR related topics). Within each of these topics there are related webcasts, blogs and discussion forums. To access the content in the 'communities' section of the website, visitors are required to register first (free). Registration also includes unlimited access to an archive of over 500 webcasts. One thing to note is that free registration comes with the obligation to subscribe to HR Promotions – direct advertising e-mails from one or more of the sites 'valued vendors'.

4362 HR-Guide
www.hr-guide.com/
Started in 1999, the HR-Guide website is a directory of links for human resources professionals and students. It provides links to related websites; free web-based computer programs for HR professionals and students; and provides guides to HR related topics. Not the best laid-out website – a search function would be very helpful – but it does contain a good selection of useful links and materials.

4363 HRM Guide
www.hrmguide.net/buscon1.html
'HRM Guide is a network of HR and other websites providing information and links to articles about human resource topics, personnel, people management and other work-related issues'. There are five HRM Guide websites that cover the geographic regions of the UK, Australia, Canada, New Zealand and the USA. These are free and do not require any form of registration or membership to use. The site caters for human resource practitioners, researchers and students. Those looking for a basic introduction to HR topics are advised to use the thematically organized HR topics section, which provides articles, case studies, review questions and further reading suggestions. Practitioners are advised to use the country-specific gateways to find current news and articles on HR practice, surveys and legislation changes.

4364 Training zone
www.trainingzone.co.uk/
Sister site to HR Zone, this site is an online network of currently 35,000 registered users. Members are encouraged to submit news and information, participate in discussions, post questions and interact with others using the service. It provides a range of resources, including learning materials such as how-to guides, articles and case studies and commercial products, including books, surveys, software and online directories. Those wishing to use the site must register (free) first, although this does not give full access to all resources, as some carry additional charges.

Discovering print & electronic resources

4365   Human Resources Abstracts
Sage Publications, qtrly. $266. ISSN 00992453.
www.sagepub.com
Aimed at the busy professional wanting to stay abreast of developments in the areas of manpower and human resource development. This quarterly journal provides abstracts and citations of articles, books and papers in the field of human resources studies, including human resources management. Sample issue available from publisher's website.

4366   International Abstracts of Human Resources
IAHR, qtrly. $125. ISSN 15428397.
www.humanresourcesabstracts.com/subscribe.php [COMPANION]
The *International Abstracts of Human Resources* (IAHR), previously known as *Personnel Management Abstracts*, was first started in 1955. In 1960 it was acquired by the University of Michigan and in January 1983 became an independent journal. Now also available as an online database containing more than 24,000 abstracts published in IAHR from 1995 to the present. Abstracts are organized into 80 different categories and can be searched by keyword, title, author and journal. A restricted trial search of the database is available from the website.

Digital data, image & text collections

4367   EIROonline (European industrial relations observatory on-line)
www.eiro.eurofound.eu.int/
European Industrial Relations Observatory (EIRO) was started in 1997 as a project of the European Foundation for the Improvement of Living and Working Conditions. The main purpose of EIRO is 'to collect, analyse and disseminate high-quality and up-to-date information on key developments in industrial relations in Europe'. This information is then added to a free online database which currently contains more than 8000 records dating from 1997 to the present. Database contents include news and feature articles; comparative studies; annual reviews; annual updates on key issues such as pay and working time; thematic and sectoral analyses; and content from the *EIRObserver* bulletin. There is also a very useful collection of industrial relations website links arranged by country and then under the categories of employers, trade unions, government and other.

4368   Labourline [EUR]
European Trade Union Institute for Research, Education & Health & Safety
www.labourline.org/
Labourline is the online catalogue of the European Trade Union Institute for Research, Education and Health and Safety (ETUI-REHS) documentation centre, a specialized institute of the European Trade Union Confederation (ETUC). Open to the general public, the documentation centre holds a unique collection of literature covering the fields of European and international industrial relations and health and safety issues. Labourline contains references to the majority of resources available and currently contains more than 42,000 bibliographic references, many of which now provide a link to the full text or website. The catalogue is fully searchable, users can also view the centre's latest

acquisitions by material type or use the 'Highlights' section, which contains up-to-date bibliographic references on selected issues such as nanotechnology, violence at work and social dialogue.

4369   Management and organization studies: a SAGE full-text collection
Sage Publications.
www.sagefulltext.com/home.aspx?id=1
Sage have produced a number of discipline-specific research databases containing material from their most popular peer-reviewed journals. The management and organization studies database includes 'the full text of 40 journals published by Sage and participating societies, encompassing over 50,500 articles and up to 60 years of backfiles'. Although this covers a broad range of management topics there is a heavy emphasis on organizational behaviour, organizational development, organizational theory, industrial psychology and human resource management. See website for information on subscription prices and how to arrange a 30-day trial.

Directories & encyclopedias

4370   Blackwell encyclopedia of management: human resource management
S. Cartwright, ed.   2nd edn, Blackwell Pub, 2005, 488pp. Blackwell encyclopedia of management V. 5, £85. ISBN 1405116978.
www.managementencyclopedia.com/ [DESCRIPTION]
The new edition of this dictionary contains over 600 entries, including terms and concepts reflecting emerging topics such as workplace bullying, emotional intelligence, the virtual organization, the balanced scorecard, generation X, human capital theory, action learning and teams, change and personal development plans.

4371   Personnel manager's yearbook [UK]
22nd edn, AP Information Services, 2006, annual. £157. ISBN 1905366043.
www.apinfo.co.uk/pmy/
This yearbook provides contact information for personnel, HR and senior business contacts in major UK and Irish companies. The latest edition includes detailed listings of over 81,000 personnel, HR and senior business contacts in over 12,400 companies; over 6500 suppliers and advisers to the personnel sector; listings of other key business contacts, including managing directors and CEOs, health and safety managers, IT managers and payroll managers/officers and finance directors. Companies must have over 100 employees or a designated HR contact to be included in the directory.

4372   Training manager's yearbook [UK]
8th edn, AP Information Services, 2007, annual. £117. ISBN 1905366051.
www.apinfo.co.uk/tmy/
The *Training manager's yearbook* provides training contacts details for UK companies. The directory includes 'detailed listings of over 12,900 training decision-makers from over 8600 major UK companies; details of major company training budgets, number of training staff and types of training undertaken (both in and out-of-house), where available; details of 4400 suppliers of products and services to the UK training sector; listings of multiple training contacts, including training directors, training managers,

training officers, training & development managers and IT training managers'. Also provides company breakdowns by geographical region and industry.

Handbooks & manuals

4373   Blackwell handbook of personnel selection
A. Evers, N. Anderson and O. Smit-Voskuijl, eds   Blackwell Publishing, 2005, 558pp. £75. ISBN 1405117028.
www.blackwellpublishing.com
The *Blackwell handbook of personnel selection* provides a critical review of the theories, concepts and professional practice in the field of selection and assessment. The book is divided into five main parts covering preparation for selection; the tools used for selection; decisions and their contexts; criterion measures; and emerging trends and assessment for change. Content is global in scope.

4374   CIPD reward management [UK]
M. Childs   CIPD, 2005. Chartered Institute of Personnel & Development (loose leaf), £305. ISBN 1843981033.
www.cipd.co.uk/RewardManagement/
A subscription service for people-management practitioners dealing with reward management covering organizations of all sizes and sectors. Includes up-to-date information on the legal framework; technical information such as tax implications and practical illustrations using case studies drawn from real-life experience. Subscription package includes a looseleaf volume with regular updates that provide information on the most recent developments in reward management, plus online access to a fully searchable companion internet resource. A 28-day free trial providing unlimited access to the online and hard-copy manual is available, see website for details.

4375   Coaching manual: the definitive guide to the process, principles and skills of personal coaching
J. Starr   Prentice Hall Business, 2002, 237pp. £16.99. ISBN 0273661930.
www.pearsoned.co.uk/
Written in a clear and easy-to-follow style. The author covers the fundamental skills of coaching by providing advice, tips, checklists and a range of activities designed to develop coaching skills.

4376   Group trainer's handbook: designing and delivering training for groups
D. Leigh   3rd edn, Kogan Page, 2006, 192pp. £27.50. ISBN 0749447443.
www.kogan-page.co.uk/
This handbook explores the latest thinking in group training methods. It examines the stages of designing and developing a successful training course and discusses the key skills needed to deliver effective group training. The book is clearly written and covers the following areas: setting objectives; delivering lesson plans; building rapport; managing delegate behaviour; using visual support; question-handling techniques; coping with stress; and giving and receiving feedback. An ideal reference source suitable for anyone involved in group training or responsible for a team's professional development.
'If you are new to training, this would be an ideal starter book for you. It covers all the key areas you'd expect, from setting objectives to the training environment.' (*Training Journal*)

'An indispensable source of practical advice and assistance for training and development, accessible to every reader, ranging from the student to the professional trainer.' (*Personnel Today*)

4377   Handbook of employee reward management and practice
M. Armstrong and T. Stephens   Kogan Page, 2005, 478pp. £27.50. ISBN 074944343X.
www.kogan-page.co.uk
Covers both theory and the practical application of reward management. Written in an accessible style the book uses checklists, diagrams and summaries to explain the key theories and best practice in employee reward. Contents include the fundamentals of reward management and its conceptual framework; establishing job values and relativities; grade and pay structures; contingent rewards; reward management for special groups; employee benefits and pensions; reward management procedures and cases.

4378   Handbook of human resource management practice
M. Armstrong   10th edn, Kogan Page, 2006, 982pp. £35. ISBN 0749446315.
www.kogan-page.co.uk
'Considers the HR function in relation to the needs of the business as a whole'. This updated edition presents in-depth coverage of managing people; performance management; HRM processes; human resource development; work and employment; rewarding people; organizational behaviour; employee relations; organization, design and development; health, safety and welfare; people resourcing; and employment and HRM services. There are also new sections covering 'human capital management, the role of the front-line manager, developing and implementing HR strategies and learning and development.'

4379   Handbook of work based learning
I. Cunningham, G. Dawes and B. Bennett   Gower, 2004, 297pp. £75. ISBN 0566085410.
www.gowerpub.com/
This handbook examines the strategies, tactics and methods for supporting work-based learning. 'The three main parts of the handbook, which focus in turn on strategies, tactics and methods, are written for both the learner and the professional developer alike. Each includes a description of the process (strategy, tactic or method), provides examples of what it looks like in action, explains the benefits and the likely limitations and provides a set of operating hints for applying the process'. Contents: Part 1 – the rationale for work-based learning; Part 2 – strategies for work-based learning and development; Part 3 – tactics for work-based learning and development; Part 4 – methods for work-based learning and development; Part 5 – conclusions and directions. See publisher's website for sample chapter and introduction (PDF).
'A splendidly upbeat book that leaves you in no doubt that informal, work-based learning must take centre stage if there is to be a quantum leap in learning productivity and effectiveness.' (*Training Journal* July 2004)

4380   Handbook of workplace diversity
A.M. Konrad, P. Prasad and J.K. Pringle, eds   Sage Publications, 2006, 551pp. £85. ISBN 0761944222.
www.sagepub.co.uk/
'The *Handbook of workforce diversity* is an indispensable

resource for students and academics of human resource management, organizational behaviour, organizational psychology and organization studies'. The book is divided into three main sections. The first examines the current theoretical perspectives on workplace diversity, discussing how and why its study follows different directions. The second section critiques both the quantitative and qualitative research methods used within the field and the third focuses on the similarities and differences between workplace groups.

4381 Pay and benefits sourcebook [UK]
Croner. Looseleaf handbook with regular updates; CD-ROM and online version also available, £525.
www.croner.co.uk/
The *Pay and benefits sourcebook* provides information on all the key components involved in a pay package such as: designing a payment system; performance-related pay; benefits; sick pay and maternity. The full subscription package consists of a looseleaf handbook with regular updates, a monthly newsletter, plus a CD-ROM version and access to an online version also containing the latest updates.

Keeping up to date

4382 Croner's reference book for employers [UK]
Croner Publications, monthly. Print looseleaf and online versions, £743.08. ISSN 00701580.
www.croner.co.uk/
A 'one-stop reference work' that provides up-to-date information on employment legislation. Covers essential issues such as recruitment; contracts of employment, employee rights; industrial relations; health and safety; termination of employment; pay and pensions; training and development; key rates and data. The full subscription package includes a handbook clearly explaining HR topics, monthly updates, a fortnightly newsletter, a range of practical guides issued 2/3 times a year plus online access and a CD-ROM version.

4383 Human Resource Management International Digest
Emerald, 7 p.a. £5119 plus VAT. ISSN 09670734.
www.emeraldinsight.com/
The digest presents the latest trends and developments in human resource management. The main aim of the journal is to help those working or studying in this field to 'gain a quick insight into the main issues affecting organizations today'. Content is drawn from over 400 international management journals and covers the following areas: developing HRM strategies; employment law, managing employees in mergers and acquisitions, recruitment policies; employee retention strategies; managing employees during times of change, promoting leadership and succession planning; employee development strategies.

4384 People Management [UK]
Personnel Publications, fortnightly. Magazine of the Chartered Institute of Personnel and Development (CIPD), £90. ISSN 13586297.
www.peoplemanagement.co.uk/ [COMPANION]
The official magazine of the CIPD covers the latest news and information on trends in human resources, from a wide range of sources and industry sectors. It also features other

areas of interest to personnel professionals, such as corporate strategy, employee relations, equal opportunities, health and safety, recruitment and selection, reward and retention, training and development and employment legislation. Companion website contains articles and features from the print publication plus special web-only content. Site visitors can access current content but must subscribe to the magazine to view archived content.

4385 Personnel Today [UK]
Reed Business Information, weekly. £71. ISSN 09595848.
www.personneltoday.com/Home/Default.aspx [COMPANION]
A weekly magazine providing the latest news, trends, analysis, benchmark data and jobs in the HR community. Accompanying website contains articles and features from the print version plus web-only content, much of which can be freely viewed. Website also features discussion forums and a range of HR guides that can be purchased online.

Decision Sciences

business decisions • business statistics • operations research

Introductions to the subject

4386 Basic business statistics: concepts and applications
D. Levine, T.C. Krehbiel and M.L. Berenson   10th edn, Pearson/Prentice Hall, 2005, 898pp. +CD-ROM, £43.99. ISBN 0131975811.
Adopting an applied approach, the authors attempt to relate the concepts and applications of statistics to the functional areas of business, such as accounting, marketing, management, economics and finance. In line with this, at the start of each chapter there is a 'Using statistics' section which demonstrates the practical application of the topic under discussion in a typical business scenario. This text also emphasizes how computer software such as Excel, Minitab and SPSS are now an integral part of statistical analysis. The accompanying CD-ROM comes with additional features, including PHStat 2, a program containing macros that enhance Excel, plus data files for Minitab, Excel SPSS and Visual Explorations.

4387 Business decision analysis: an active learning approach
G. Hackett and P. Luffrum; Open Learning Foundation   Blackwell, 1999, 618pp. + CD-ROM, £23.99. ISBN 0631201769.
www.blackwellpublishing.com/
A title from the Open Learning Foundation series offering a comprehensive introduction to quantitative analysis within the context of business decision making. The text covers some of the key topics in the field, including 'an introduction to model building for business decision analysis, linear programming, regression analysis, time-series analysis and simulation techniques'. It contains a range of activities and exercises to aid understanding of the subject. Primarily designed for undergraduate students on business studies degree courses.

4388 Decision support systems: frequently asked questions

D.J. Power   iUniverse, Inc, 2004, 252pp. £10.99. ISBN 0595339719. www.iuniverse.com/bookstore/

The book introduces the reader to the field of decision support systems (DSS) by presenting 83 frequently asked questions (with answers) about computerized decision support systems that were published in *DSS News* from 2000 through to 2004. The questions cover a broad range of topics, including what is a DSS? what kind of DSS does Mr. X need? does data modelling differ for a Data-Driven DSS? is a Data Warehouse a DSS? is tax preparation software an example of a DSS? what do I need to know about Data Warehousing/OLAP? what is a cost estimation DSS? what is a spreadsheet-based DSS? A thoughtful and well put together resource for IT specialists, students, academics and managers.

4389 Essentials of business statistics

B.L. Bowerman, R.T. O'Connell and J.B. Orris   McGraw-Hill/Irwin, 2004, 618pp. + CD-ROM. ISBN 0072827823.

A clearly written, easy-to-use textbook that covers core business statistical concepts. The use of case studies and examples helps to demonstrate the different statistical areas and their application. The authors present a 'non-calculus-based approach', covering both descriptive and inferential statistics, with an emphasis on the business application. The accompanying CD-ROM contains additional material, including MegsStat, Excel templates, data files, tutorials, web links to exercises and self-quizzes. In additions, it also features PowerPoint presentations and Visual Statistics 2.0 and other additional material.

4390 Introduction to operations research

F.S. Hillier and G.J. Lieberman   8th edn, McGraw-Hill, 2004, 1061pp. + CD-ROM, £43.99. ISBN 007123828X. http://highered.mcgraw-hill.com/sites/0073017795/information_center_view0/ [COMPANION]

Highly regarded textbook covering the basic concepts, techniques, applications and research trends in the field of operations research (OR). The eighth edition includes new chapters on 'metaheuristics, constraint programming, multi-echelon inventory models, spreadsheet modeling and more'. There is an accompanying CD-ROM featuring a special chapter on 'The art of modelling with spreadsheets'; several new or expanded sections on spreadsheet modelling; additional software options, including LINDO, LINGO, Crystal Ball Professional Edition (including OptQuest and CB Predictor modules) and Solver Table; and a glossary for every book chapter. There is a companion website offering additional material.

4391 Management science: an anthology

S. Eilon, ed.   Dartmouth, 1996. History of management thought series (3 v.), £315. ISBN 1855215160.

This is an impressive collection of influential papers in management science and operational research, providing a much-needed historical perspective on the subject. Spanning three volumes and over 1500 pages, the anthology introduces the reader to a range of specialist topics developed in the literature of management science. Volume 1 concentrates on the history and philosophy of management science. It also examines the concepts and theories involved in planning, strategy, production and inventory. Volume 2 covers distribution, finance and forecasting. Volume 3 looks

at decision theory, the public sector, techniques, methodology and industrial application.

Research centres & institutes

4392 Decision Sciences Institute

www.decisionsciences.org/

The Decision Sciences Institute (DSI) is a professional organization specializing in the application of quantitative and behavioural methods in the business environment. 'Through national, international and regional conferences, competitions and publications, the Institute provides an international forum for presenting and sharing research in the study of decision processes across disciplines.' The Institute publishes two academic journals, as well as *Decision Line*, the Institute's official news publication. Details of the Institute's activities, publications and members can be found on the website.

■ **Decision Line** DSI, 5 p.a. $20. ISSN 07326823. www.decisionsciences.org/. The official news publication of the Institute, which includes a wide range of practical and educational features, as well as information on members, regions, annual meeting events, placement activities and faculty position ads. Selected content from each issue (from 1993) is freely available from the website.

■ **Decision Sciences** Blackwell Publishing, qtrly. ISSN 00117315. www.blackwellpublishing.com/ [DESCRIPTION]. Publishes peer-reviewed, scholarly research about decision making within the boundaries of an organization, as well as decisions involving inter-firm coordination. Subscribers to *Decision Sciences* also receive a full subscription to *Decision Sciences Journal of Innovative Education*.

■ **Decision Sciences Journal of Innovative Education** Blackwell Publishing, 2 p.a. ISSN 15404609. www.blackwellpublishing.com [DESCRIPTION]. Dedicated to the publication of research relevant to teaching and learning issues in the decision sciences. A peer-reviewed journal, it focuses on both quantitative and behavioural approaches to managerial decision making.

4393 European Association for Decision Making

www2.fmg.uva.nl/eadm/home.html

The European Association for Decision Making is 'an interdisciplinary organization dedicated to the study of normative, descriptive and prescriptive theories of decision making'. Its main activities include organizing a biannual conference; publishing a newsletter; sponsoring the de Finetti Prize for promising PhD students; maintaining an electronic mailing list for EADM members; and supporting small-scale workshops. Membership is open to anyone with a relevant advanced academic degree (PhD or its equivalent) and who is active in the field of judgement and decision making. Full details of the Association's activities can be found on the website.

4394 Institute for Operations Research & the Management Sciences

www2.informs.org/

The Institute for Operations Research & the Management Sciences (INFORMS) was established in 1995 with the merger of the Operations Research Society of America (ORSA) and the Institute for Management Sciences (TIMS). It serves as a 'focal point for professionals in the field of operations research, enabling them to communicate with each other'. The Institute publishes 12 scholarly journals, a membership magazine and organizes national and international conferences. It runs a number of specialized members' groups, an educational programme and a series of awards and prizes. Details of all the Institute's activities can be found on the website. The site also contains a huge amount of information and resources. Most notably it hosts a number of searchable databases, most of which are freely available. A great resource for all levels of interest in OR.

- **Conference presentation database** A full searchable database of presentations presented at ORSA/TIMS and INFORMS meetings going back as far as 1990.
- **Presentation database** Provides links to PowerPoint slides, PDFs, and other material from conference presentations; Browser must be Java-enabled, alternatively there is a browsable list.
- **Working paper database** Provides links to current research reports. Browser must be Java-enabled to use this system. For those that cannot access the archive, there is a link to a browsable list of papers.
- **INFORMS OR/MS resource collection** www2.informs.org/Resources/. A useful collection of links to related websites and resources covering all aspects of OR and the management sciences. Includes a wide range of specialized topic and resource guides plus links to discussion and newsgroups.
- **Management Science** monthly. $233. ISSN 00251909. http://mansci.pubs.informs.org/ [DESCRIPTION]. 'The journal promotes the science of managing private and public sector enterprises through publication of theoretical, computational, and empirical research that draws on a wide range of management sub-disciplines, including accounting, business strategy, decision analysis, finance, information systems, marketing, operations management, operations research, organizational behaviour, and product/technology management'.
- **Operations Research** bi-monthly. $186. ISSN 0030364X. 'Aimed at practitioners, researchers, educators, and students alike, Operations research publishes articles that span areas of operations research. Topics include: computing and decision technologies; decision analysis; environment, energy, and natural resources; financial engineering; manufacturing, service, and supply chain operations; marketing science; military and homeland security; optimization; policy modelling and public sector OR; revenue management; simulation; stochastic models; telecommunications and networking; and transportation'.

4395 MIT Operations Research Center
www.web.mit.edu/orc/www/research/index.html
Founded in 1953 by the Massachusetts Institute of Technology (MIT), the Operations Research Center (ORC) was formed with the 'explicit objective of becoming the focus of interdepartmental and interdisciplinary activity'. To this end, the Center includes staff from a wide range of MIT departments and offers educational and research opportunities to students, including Master's and PhD courses in the field of operations research. See website for full details of current programmes and research activities. Other features include an online list of technical reports which can be purchased directly from the Center; free full-text access to the Center's working paper collection; and a useful OR links section.

4396 Rutgers Center for Operations Research
www.rutcor.rutgers.edu/
The Rutgers Center for Operations Research was established in 1982 to coordinate the OR activities of Rutgers, The State University of New Jersey, and 'to act as a focal point for the development of operations research in the state of New Jersey.' In addition to running a doctoral programme, the Centre also sponsors interdisciplinary research projects, runs conferences and colloquia on current areas of interest in OR and publishes an international technical report series which

can be downloaded freely from the website (files are in Postscript or PDF format).

Associations & societies

4397 Association of European Operational Research Societies
www.euro-online.org/
Based in Brussels, the Association of European Operational Research Societies (EURO) is a member of the International Federation of Operational Research Societies (IFORS). It is a non-profit association dedicated to the promotion of operational research throughout Europe. The EURO website contains information on the Society's history and structure, member societies, working groups and research activities. EURO also organizes a conference and mini conference series, publishes an online newsletter (requires site registration) and the *European Journal of Operational Research*, details of which can be found on the site.

- **European Journal of Operational Research** Elsevier, 24 p.a. ISSN 03772217. www.elsevier.com/. The Journal publishes 'papers that contribute to the methodology of operational research (OR) and to the practice of decision making'. Aimed at researchers and practitioners working in the area of operational research/management science.

4398 Canadian Operational Research Society
www.cors.ca
The main purpose of the Canadian Operational Research Society (CORS) is to 'advance the theory and practice of OR'. It does this in three ways: promoting the exchange of ideas by organizing a national conference and holding regular membership meetings throughout the year; running an educational program of study, the CORS diploma; publishing the *Infor Journal* and the *CORS Bulletin*, which is freely available from its website, going back to 1996. Full details of the Society, its activities and publications can be found on the website.

- **Infor Journal** University of Toronto Press, qtrly. $60. ISSN 03155986. www.utpjournals.com/. Jointly sponsored by the Canadian Information Processing Society and 'combines the theory, methodology and practice of both information systems and operational research'. Single issues may be purchased directly from the website. Subsidized subscription rate is available for students ($40).

4399 Decision Analysis Society
http://decision-analysis.society.informs.org
The Decision Analysis Society is a subdivision of INFORMS, the Institute for Operations Research and the Management Sciences. Based at the Fuqua School of Business, Duke University, the Society promotes the 'development and use of logical methods for the improvement of decision making in public and private enterprise'. DAWeb, the Society's website has a very useful and well presented collection of DS related material, including a lexicon of technical terms commonly used in decision making; annotated bibliographies and reading lists; annotated book reviews; links to decision analysis courses and syllabi; full-text access to the newsletter *Decision Analysis* going back to 1992; a full-text working paper archive; and a related links section.

4400 International Federation of Operational Research Societies
www.ifors.org/
The International Federation of Operational Research

Societies (IFORS) is an umbrella organization that is made up of national operations research societies from 45 countries covering the geographical areas of Asia Pacific, Europe, North America and South America. It currently has a membership of over 25,000. The Society's mission is to 'promote operations research as an academic discipline and a profession'. The website contains the usual information about the Society and its activities. It includes information on its publications, which include the journal *International Transactions in Operational Research*, the IAOR (*International Abstracts in Operations Research*), plus the IAOR bulletin and newsletter. The website is also home to TUTORial.

- **International Transactions in Operational Research**
  Blackwell Publishing, bi-monthly. £102. ISSN 09696016. An international focus on the practice of operational research and management science. See publisher's website for subscription details and a free sample issue.
- **TUTORial** www.tutor.ms.unimelb.edu.au/frame.html. TUTORial is an online tutorial system for operations research and management science topics. It is an initiative of the IFORS Educational Resources Committee. The main aim of this project is to develop a large library of self-contained modules, each dedicated to a specific topic. Currently the areas covered include dynamic programming, graphs and networks, integer programming, linear programming, and simulation.

4401 OR Society
www.orsoc.org.uk/
Founded over 50 years ago, the OR Society has over 30,000 members in 53 countries. It claims to be 'the world's oldest-established learned society catering to the Operational Research (OR) profession'. The Society provides training, conferences, publications and information to those working in OR. It also provides a range of free information and resources about operational research to anyone interested in this field. In fact, the website is a real gem. It offers a great introduction to the field of OR, examining the history and development of the field. There is a fascinating series of examples demonstrating how OR is involved in many of the day-to-day aspects of our lives. It has a small collection of free articles about operational research taken from the OR newsletter and *OR Insight*, plus full-text access to *Issue ExplORer*, an occasional publication which focuses on OR issues relevant to the UK business community. An invaluable reference tool catering for all levels of interest in OR.

Libraries, archives, museums

4402 Operational Research and Operational Research Society Archive [UK]
www.warwick.ac.uk/services/library/mrc/ead/335col.htm
Based at the Modern Records Centre, University of Warwick, the archive has been deposited by the Operational Research Society and various practitioners of operational research. It is a collection of material relating to the history, development and practice of operational research in Great Britain and to pioneers and practitioners in this field. The archive is partially listed and brief records can be viewed online. The Modern Records Centre uses a special classification scheme which is compatible with ISAD(G): General International Standard Archival Description (2000). The archive is freely open for research, see the Centre's website for specific access conditions.

Portal & task environments

4403 DSSResources.COM: Decision support systems resources
www.dssresources.com/
DSSResources.COM (decision support systems resources) is a web-based repository providing information and guidance to anyone interested in the use of information technologies and software to improve decision making. The target audience covers practitioners and students in information science, managers interested in management information systems (MIS) and academics in MIS and decision support systems (DSS). The website contains a huge amount of information and useful resources. There are two subscription rates which give unlimited access to the site's content. However, a lot of free material is available, including case studies, an online glossary, interviews with 'thought leaders' in the field of DSS and much more. The site also features 'Ask Dan', which is a question-and-answer section managed by the site's editor Dr Dan Power, an information systems professor and author of the book *Decision support systems: frequently asked questions*, which features some of the Q&A on the site. Well organized and well worth a look.

4404 OpsResearch.com
www.opsresearch.com/
A website offering a collection of 500 Java classes for developing operations research programs and other mathematical applications. The site also includes documentation and tutorials, plus free downloadable software. There is an OR books section, newsletter and a members' services page; however, it appears that some of these services are no longer updated.

Discovering print & electronic resources

4405 Annals of operations research
Springer, irregular. ISSN 02545330.
www.springer.com/
Available in both print and electronic format, *Annals of operations research* is a series of volumes dedicated to identifying the main trends and developments in the field of operations research. Each volume has one or more guest editors who are responsible for selecting what appears in that issue. Content will include original manuscripts, survey articles, selected and tested computer programs and conference proceedings. See publisher's website for subscription details and a selection of most-viewed articles.

4406 Annotated bibliography on decision theory and uncertainty
www1.fee.uva.nl/creed/wakker/refs/rfrncs.htm
Written by Peter P. Wakker, a professor affiliated to the Econometric Institute at the Erasmus University, Rotterdam, and the Department of Quantitative Economics at Maastricht University, the bibliography can be downloaded for free and is available in both word and PDF format.

4407 Decision Science Research Institute
www.decisionresearch.org/
Founded in 1976, the Decision Science Research Institute is an independent, non-profit research corporation 'dedicated to helping individuals, industry, government and society understand and cope with the complex and often risky

decisions of modern life'. The Institute's website is a good starting point for bibliographic references covering decision making and risk management as it contains a database of over 500 publications dating back to 1962. The database includes articles from journals such as *Risk Analysis, Science, Journal of Risk and Uncertainty, Management Science* and the *Journal of Behavioral Decision Making*, as well as books, chapters in books and reports. A complete list of publications can be downloaded in PDF format, alternatively the database can be searched by year. The site also contains information on the Institute's projects.

4408   Decision Science Resources
H. Arsham
http://home.ubalt.edu/ntsbarsh/Business-stat/Refop.htm
This is one of several web pages created by Dr Hossein Arsham, the Wright Distinguished Research Professor in Management Science and Statistics at the University of Baltimore. First launched 1995, this is a very impressive collection of online courses, tutorials, books, journal websites and links to societies and organizations in the areas related to decision sciences. It also contains a huge bibliography of articles. Regularly updated, it is an invaluable reference source for anyone interested in this subject area.

4409   IAOR online (International abstracts in operations research)
Palgrave.
www.iaor-palgrave.com/content/html/index.htm
IAOR Online is the electronic version of the journal *International Abstracts in Operations Research*. It is a searchable database of bibliographic and abstract information in the field of operations research and management science. Sourced from over 180 of the world's leading journals the database contains approximately 55,000 abstracts, from 1989 to the present. See publisher's website for subscription details and information on a free 30-day trial.

4410   Optimization and operations research sites
J.E. Mitchell
www.rpi.edu/~mitchj/sites_or.html
This website was created by Professor John E. Mitchell of the Rensselaer Polytechnic Institute in New York. It provides an impressive selection of resources, including a list of subject related conferences, past and present; test cases for various types of problems; links to resources on computational logic and integer programming; software packages; and links to relevant personal, organizational and corporate home pages. The site also links to a Bibtex database containing a bibliography of references on optimization (900K) compiled by Professor Mitchell. This includes articles, technical reports, books, proceedings, PhD theses and manuals. A searchable version is available from the site.

Directories & encyclopedias

4411   Encyclopedia of operations research and management science
S.I. Gass and C.M. Harris, eds   2nd edn, Kluwer Academic, 2001, 917pp. £334. ISBN 079237827X.
www.springer.com/u
A valuable work containing specially commissioned articles from leading figures in the field of operations research, plus

several hundred brief dictionary-type entries. The articles are intended to provide decision makers with a general introduction to each area. Full table of contents can be downloaded from the publisher's website.

4412   Who's who in the management sciences
C.L. Cooper, ed.   Edward Elgar, 2000, 484pp. £170. ISBN 1840642378.
www.e-elgar.co.uk
'A unique source of reference, including entries on 350 leading scholars in the field specializing in areas such as accounting, finance, management economics, organizational behaviour, marketing, human resource management, management information systems, operations management, business ethics, strategic management and international management.' Also available on CD-ROM.

Handbooks & manuals

4413   Blackwell handbook of judgement and decision making
D.J. Koehler and N. Harvey, eds   Blackwell, 2004, 664pp. £90. ISBN 1405107464.
www.blackwellpublishing.com/
The handbook presents a comprehensive overview of the current topics and research in the 'study of how people make evaluations, draw inferences and make decisions under conditions of uncertainty and conflict'. This well organized and clearly presented book gives an overview of both past and current research in this area, discusses the future directions and explores the applications of judgment and decision making research in a variety of different professional contexts.
'Exactly what a good handbook should be; comprehensive, representative, authoritative, authentic and well written' (Kenneth R. Hammond, University of Colorado at Boulder)

4414   Handbook of decision making
G. Morçöl, ed.   CRC Press, 2006, 664pp. Public administration and public policy series V. 123, $139.95. ISBN 1574445480.
www.crcpress.co.uk/
An invaluable text offering a thorough introduction to the theories and methods in the field of decision making, combined with a more practical understanding of how these methods are applied. The handbook is well presented, starting with an general introduction to the field, then dividing the content into three sections covering theories, context and methods. As well as discussing the mainstream methods of decision making such as cost-benefit analysis, the book also explores some of the emerging methods such as geographic information systems, Q-methodology and conflict management. There is a strong emphasis on the practical applications of these methods and a range of examples in the areas of budgeting, public administration/governance, drug trafficking and information management systems are examined.

EDUCATION & SPORT

Education & Learning

Education and learning are a central part of our lives and there is increasing reference to lifelong learning in the workplace as well as in relation to health and well-being. In the UK, the Every Child Matters agenda has had an impact on the understanding of a holistic view of childhood and learning, and this approach is reflected worldwide.

Of necessity, coverage here focuses on a relatively narrow understanding of education and learning, with an emphasis on the terminology and legal aspects of education systems and the theory of learning and teaching. The main bulk of entries have been organized primarily by age phase but it was felt useful to provide a specific overview of all aspects of inclusive education.

comparative education • history of education • learning • learning sciences • philosophy of education

Introductions to the subject

4415 American educational history: school, society, and the common good
W.H. Jeynes Sage Publications, 2007, 469pp. £45. ISBN 9781412914215.
Examines historical trends that have helped shape schools and education in the USA. There is a 'strong emphasis on recent history, most notably post-WWII issues such as the role of technology, the standards movement, affirmative action, bilingual education, undocumented immigrants, school choice'.

4416 Education in Britain: 1944 to the present
K. Jones Polity Press, 2003, 202pp. £15.99. ISBN 9780745625751.
Chapters are: 1. Post-war settlements; 2. The golden age? 3. Expansion, experiment, conflict; 4. Conservatism – triumph and failure; 5. 1997–2002: New Labour – the inheritors.

4417 Education in England, Wales and Northern Ireland: a guide to the system
G. Holt [et al.] 3rd edn, NFER, 2002, 461pp. £27.99. ISBN 9781903880388.
Provides an excellent overview of how the education system is organized in England, Wales and Northern Ireland. It is structured by phase, from pre-school to higher education, with an additional section on special education. The glossary and detailed index make this a very usable guide.

4418 Education in the United Kingdom
L. Gearon, ed. David Fulton, 2002, 246pp. £22.99. ISBN 9781853467158.
A very useful book summarizing the education systems of the UK. It provides details of changes and developments up to its publication in 2002, concentrating on structures and organization.

4419 Historical foundations of education: bridges from the ancient world to the present
J.B. Tehie Pearson Merrill Prentice Hall, 2007, 312pp. $49.33. ISBN 9780130617071.
Covers education in the Greek and Roman Empires and in the Middle Ages; rebirth of learning: Renaissance and Reformation; formation of the American education system; modern educational problems and reform movements (1930–present).

Introduction to the foundations of American education
J. Johnson [et al.] See entry no. 4492

4420 Philosophy of education
N. Noddings 2nd edn, Westview, 2007, 270pp. £14.99. ISBN 9780813343235.
'Acclaimed as the "best overview in the field" by *Teaching Philosophy* and predicted to "become the standard textbook in philosophy of education" by *Educational Theory*, this now-classic text includes an entirely new chapter on problems of school reform, examining issues of equality, accountability, standards and testing.'

4421 Philosophy of education: an anthology
R. Curren, ed. Blackwell, 2007, 582pp. £19.99. ISBN 9781405130233.
60 readings categorized as follows: Part I: The nature and aims of education (What is education?; Liberal education and the relationship between education and work; Autonomy and exit rights); Part II: Educational authority (The boundaries of educational authority; The commercialization of schooling); Part III: Educational responsibilities (Educational adequacy and equality; Diversity and non-discrimination; Impairment, disability and excellence); Part IV: Teaching and learning (Teaching; Discipline and care; Inquiry, understanding and constructivism; Critical thinking and reasoning; Grading and testing); Part V: Curriculum and the content of schooling (Moral education; Curricular controversies).

4422 Rethinking the history of American education
W.J. Reese and J.L. Rury, eds Palgrave Macmillan, 2007, 304pp. $69.95. ISBN 0230600093.
Forthcoming text described by Jonathan Zimmerman as 'the best set of essays ever published about the history of American education. If our schools and colleges are "contested terrain", their history is even more so: over the past half-century, historians have differed sharply over the scope, purpose and meaning of education. These essays provide close analyses of the scholarly debates as well as wise suggestions for future research. We can only hope that the next generation of historians follows their cue.'

Dictionaries, thesauri, classifications

4423 Dictionary of British education
P. Gordon and D. Lawton Woburn Press, 2003, 303pp. £28.99. ISBN 9780713040517.
This excellent volume provides a guide to the education

systems of the UK and includes alphabetical listings of definitions in education and training and acronyms and abbreviations as well as historical background and details of changes in the systems up to 2002.

4424 The Greenwood dictionary of education
J.W. Collins and N.P. O'Brien, eds   Greenwood, 2003, 431pp. $69.95. ISBN 9780897748605.
Well designed and well presented (and very well reviewed) work: 'Each of the definitions is 25–250 words and has been written by a knowledgeable practitioner or researcher in the field. Included are acronyms and initialisms commonly used in the field, names and descriptions of relevant organizations and important legal decisions relating to education. An extensive bibliography provides useful sources for further research.'

Laws, standards, codes

4425 OECD handbook for internationally comparative education statistics: concepts, standards, definitions and classifications
2004, 271pp. £31. ISBN 9264104100.
Aims to help facilitate more effective policy use of the comparative statistics and indicators produced by the OECD relating to the functioning and impact of education systems, covering early childhood, through formal education, to lifelong learning and training opportunities. The handbook also provides a ready reference of international standards and conventions for others to follow in the collection and assimilation of educational data.
■ **International handbook of comparative education** R. Cowen and A.M. Kazamias, eds   Springer, 2008. £346. ISBN 9781402064029. www.springer.com [DESCRIPTION]. Announced two-volume compendium.

Official & quasi-official bodies

4426 Education
www.oecd.org/education
Education gateway within OECD's website. Good sets of resources, including coverage of these broad topics: pre-school and school; higher education and adult learning; education, economy and society; human capital; research and knowledge management. Gives detailed worldwide statistics and access to websites of ministries of education.
■ **Education at a glance Organisation for Economic Co-operation & Development**, 2007. ISBN 9789264032880. OECD indicators provide quantitative, internationally comparable data allowing governments to see their education systems in the light of other countries' performances, but they are also useful to parents and others looking at the the quality of learning outcomes in schools.

4427 European Commission, Directorate for Education & Culture
http://ec.europa.eu/education/index_en.html
The major focus within the European Union on 'Education and Training', the Directorate's website's broad areas cover news, programmes and actions, policy areas and documentation. Use the site map to navigate around the density of resources accessible from here, leading to 'Recognition and transparency of qualifications', 'The

Lifelong Learning Programme 2007–2013', 'The proposed European Institute of Technology', and so on.

4428 Great Britain. Department for Children, Schools & Families
www.dcsf.gov.uk
The Department for Children, Schools & Families was one of three new government departments set up by the Prime Minister on 28 June 2007. 'In addition to its direct responsibilities, the department will lead work across Government to improve outcomes for children, including work on children's health and child poverty.'
■ **Education and skills: Wales Welsh Assembly Government**. http://new.wales.gov.uk/topics/educationandskills. The current 'Topic' gateway to this arena for Wales.
■ **Education and training: Scotland Scottish Executive**. www.scotland.gov.uk/Topics/Education. Provides information and statistics on all aspects of education and learning in Scotland.
■ **Northern Ireland. Department of Education** www.deni.gov.uk. Responsible for the central administration of all aspects of education and related services in Northern Ireland – excepting the higher and further education sector, responsibility for which is within the remit of the Department for Employment and Learning.

United Nations Educational, Scientific & Cultural Organization
See entry no. 26

4429 United States. Department of Education
www.ed.gov
'ED was created in 1980 by combining offices from several federal agencies. ED's mission is to promote student achievement and preparation for global competitiveness by fostering educational excellence and ensuring equal access. ED's 4500 employees and $71.5 billion budget are dedicated to: Establishing policies on federal financial aid for education and distributing as well as monitoring those funds; Collecting data on America's schools and disseminating research; Focusing national attention on key educational issues; Prohibiting discrimination and ensuring equal access to education.'

Research centres & institutes

4430 CILT, the National Centre for Languages [UK]
www.cilt.org.uk
'The National Centre will collect, interpret and provide information on languages and language teaching and learning; it will offer high quality professional support to those involved in language teaching and training and to the users and providers of language services. It will develop and disseminate innovation in the teaching and learning of languages and in language training. It will promote and support languages for employment and will promote languages and intercultural competence to people of all ages and in all walks of life. It will support national policies for languages and promote the language interests of the UK in the European and international context.'

4431 Institute of Education Sciences [USA]
http://ies.ed.gov
Established within the US Department of Education by the Education Sciences Reform Act of 2002. Wide-ranging site principally giving access to details of the work of the

National Center for Education Research, National Center for Education Statistics, National Center for Education Evaluation and Regional Assistance and National Center for Special Education Research.

4432 National Foundation for Educational Research [UK]
www.nfer.ac.uk

This major research organization provides research services in the UK and internationally and the website provides details and documentation of research completed and in progress. Regular updates and news are also available by e-mail.

Associations & societies

4433 Association for Science Education [UK]
www.ase.org.uk

The professional body for those involved in science education at all levels from pre-school to higher education. A rather overcrowded website includes information on membership and publications, as well as details of conferences and events, news on the National Curriculum and other resources.

4434 Association of Teachers of Mathematics [UK]
www.atm.org.uk

Aims 'to encourage the development of mathematics education such that it is more closely related to the needs of the learner'. Its excellent website provides access to a range of teacher resources, an online journal with some material available to non-members and news of conferences and events.

4435 Campaign for Learning [UK]
www.campaign-for-learning.org.uk

An independent charity, the Campaign for Learning is working for an inclusive society in which learning is understood, valued and accessible to everyone as of right. The website provides a helpful definition of learning as well as access to resources and research reports.

4436 Education International
www.ei-ie.org

Represents teachers and education workers worldwide and seeks to improve their welfare and status. The website provides links to publications and the online resource library.

4437 Geographical Association [UK]
www.geography.org.uk

Essential website for geography teachers and educators; frequently updated with news and resources.

4438 International Reading Association
www.reading.org

Major website providing information on reading and literacy: 'For 50 years, the International Reading Association has been a professional home for those who help others learn to read. Today, our network and resources reach hundreds of thousands of teachers, researchers, students, administrators, tutors, parents and others – in every part of the world.'

Libraries, archives, museums

4439 Newsam Library & Archives [UK]
www.ioe.ac.uk/is

The most comprehensive education library and archives in Europe, the website provides a portal to a range of electronic resources, many of which are freely available. The library catalogue provides links to full-text documents on the web as well as details of printed resources.

Portal & task environments

4440 AfricaEducation
http://africaeducation.org

This invaluable website provides a comprehensive portal of links to information and resources on education in Africa, including libraries, books and journals, teachers' resources, news services, conference listings and information on financial support.

4441 Becta [UK]
www.becta.org.uk

Becta is the UK government's lead partner in the strategic development and delivery of its e-strategy. Its very comprehensive website provides access to recent news, research and publications on all aspects of the use of technology in learning. Becta also works with industry to ensure the right technology is in place to improve learning and the site provides details of specifications, tools and procurement schemes.

■ **NAACE** www.naace.co.uk. 'NAACE is the professional association for those concerned with advancing education through the appropriate use of information and communications technology (ICT). The Association was established in 1984 and has become the key influential professional association for those working in ICT in education'.

4442 Education Resources Information Center: ERIC [USA]
Institute of Education Sciences and United States. Department of Education
www.eric.ed.gov

Enormous free database with links to full-text documents, covering US and international research in education: 'The world's largest digital library of education literature'.

4443 Eurydice: the information network on education in Europe
www.eurydice.org

A most important resource, Eurydice offers a range of publications on education in Europe covering such issues as key competencies, school hours, ICT and initial teacher education requirements. The website also provides access to a database of information and statistics on education systems in Europe. It is 'an institutional network for gathering, monitoring, processing and circulating reliable and readily comparable information on education systems and policies throughout Europe', now part of the EU Socrates programme.

The wide range of very useful pblications and databases offered by Eurydice is described on the website; one good example is detailed below.

■ **Thesaurus for education systems in Europe** 2006. 'TESE is a multilingual documentary language intended to make it easier to record and search for information. This thesaurus, which is concerned with the focus of action of the Eurydice Network, namely education policies and systems in Europe, takes account of the most recent developments in the educational field … It is planned that this first edition of TESE should be in 14 languages, namely Czech, Dutch, English, Estonian, Finnish, French, German, Greek, Italian, Latvian, Lithuanian, Polish, Portuguese and Spanish. It will be possible to access these language versions on this website as they become available. An online version of TESE will be made available for browsing at a later stage …'.

4444 Inspiring learning for all [UK]
Museums, Libraries & Archives Council
www.inspiringlearningforall.gov.uk
Supporting learning in museums, libraries and archives, the website provides guidance on learning and learning styles.

4445 Learning: Online learning, support and advice [UK]
BBC
www.bbc.co.uk/learning
This well designed BBC site provides a portal to a wide range of resources offered by the BBC and other organizations. Much of the material is visual or interactive, making full use of new technologies.

Discovering print & electronic resources

4446 British Education Index
www.leeds.ac.uk/bei [FEE-BASED]
The BEI office within Leeds University Library provides a number of information services relevant to the work of researchers, policy makers and practitioners in the fields of education and training. This is a key resource for UK researchers.
- ■ **British Education Internet Resource Catalogue**
  http://brs.leeds.ac.uk/~beiwww/beirc.htm. 'A freely accessible database of information about professionally evaluated and described internet sites which support educational research, policy and practice'.
- ■ **Education-Line** www.leeds.ac.uk/educol. 'A freely accessible database of the full text of conference papers, working papers and electronic literature which supports educational research, policy and practice'.

4447 Education: a guide to reference and information sources
N.P. O'Brien   2nd edn, Libraries Unlimited, 2000, 189pp. $45. ISBN 9781563086267.
Guide to the key reference and information sources in the field of education. Mostly US, UK, Canada, Australia and the Netherlands. Organized in categories and types of publication with good index.

4448 How to find out in education: a guide to information sources
C. Drinkwater and G. Price   Librarians of Institutes & Schools of Education, 2003, 65pp. £10.49. ISBN 0901922374.
This practical guide provides listings of information sources for students, researchers and librarians, both in print and online. Although published in 2003, it is an excellent starting point for essential information about the English education systems and also includes a chapter on the international perspective.

4449 Internet for education [UK]
G. Price, R. Evans and A. Welshman, comps
www.vts.intute.ac.uk/he/tutorial/education
One of a national series of tutorials written by qualified

tutors, lecturers and librarians from across the UK. Covers UK government and official sites, other organizations; full-text sources, statistics and research, communications and mailing lists, teaching materials, international education, and catalogues and bibliographies.

4450 Intute: social sciences: education
www.intute.ac.uk/socialsciences/education
'(P)rovides free access to high quality resources on the internet. It treats educational studies as a distinct field, with the educational aspects of other disciplines handled elsewhere. Each resource has been evaluated and categorized by subject specialists based at UK universities. The target audience is students, staff and researchers in higher and further education.'

Digital data, image & text collections

4451 National Center for Education Statistics [USA]
http://nces.ed.gov
Located within the US Department of Education and the Institute of Education Sciences, this is the primary federal entity for collecting and analysing data related to education. The website provides a huge range of statistics on education in the USA as well as international comparisons.

4452 Research and Statistics Gateway [UK]
www.dfes.gov.uk/rsgateway
'Following the creation of two new Departments on 28 June 2007, this site contains details of the research and statistics publications produced by the Department for Education and Skills (DfES) from 1998 to 28 June 2007 and will contain publications produced by both the Department for Children, Schools and Families (DCSF) and the Department for Innovation, Universities and Skills (DIUS) from 29 June 2007 until further notice.'

Directories & encyclopedias

4453 Dictionary of British educationists
R. Aldrich and P. Gordon   Woburn Press, 1989, 272pp. ISBN 0713040114.
This dictionary provides biographies of about 450 educationists dating from 1800 to the late 1980s.
- ■ **Biographical dictionary of North American and European educationists** P. Gordon and R. Aldrich   Woburn Press, 1997, 528pp. ISBN 0713040254. Companion volume providing pen portraits of more than 500 American, Canadian and European educationists of the 19th and 20th centuries who were no longer living in 1997.

4454 Education: the complete encyclopedia
T. Husén [et al.]   Elsevier, 1998. CD-ROM, £3590. ISBN 9780080429793.
The *International encyclopedia of education* provides descriptive information on education systems throughout the world in a simple standardized format. The 2nd edition appeared as 12 printed volumes in 1994. More detailed information on higher education is provided in the *Encyclopedia of higher education*, which came out a little earlier. Its first volume covers national systems of higher education and three further volumes contain articles on specific issues. *Education: the complete encyclopedia* includes updated versions of both these publications on one CD-ROM.

As well as being more recent, issued in 1998, it has the advantage of electronic searching capabilities.

- **Encyclopedia of higher education** B.R. Clark and G.R. Neave, **eds** Elsevier; originally published by Pergamon, 1992. £750. ISBN 9780080372518.
- **International encyclopedia of education** T. Husén and T.N. Postlethwaite, **eds** 2nd edn, Elsevier; originally published Pergamon, 1994. £2970. ISBN 9780080410463.

4455 Education Yearbook [UK]
Pearson Education, 2007, 768pp. £110.00 [2007/2008]. ISBN 9780132405461.
'(T)he UK's most comprehensive source of information on professionals in the education arena. Designed for use as a one-stop guide, the *Education Yearbook* contains details of over 19,000 education professionals, ensuring you are able to find exactly who you want to contact, both quickly and efficiently.' Covers the whole gamut of relevant organizations from 'Central government' through 'Assessment bodies, research and advisory bodies' and 'Educational visits, travel and services' to 'Education related organizations and resources'.

- **Directory of vocational and further education** Pearson Education, 2007, annual, 456pp. £95.00 [2007/2008]. ISBN 9780132405454. Comprehensive coverage of the sector in the UK. Originally published by Pitman.
- **Education authorities directory and annual** School Government Publishing, annual. ISSN 00709131 www.schoolgovernment.co.uk [DESCRIPTION]. 'Widely recognised as the standard reference source to education throughout the United Kingdom, containing names, addresses, telephone numbers and website addresses of more than 13,500 local education authorities, schools, colleges and other educational institutions in the United Kingdom. The "Yellow Bible" is fully researched in depth for each new edition.' The publishers also offer *The primary education directory* and *The special education directory*.
- **Primary education yearbook** Pearson Education, 2007, 848pp. £90.00 [2007/2008]. ISBN 9780273714811. Covering England, Scotland, Wales and Northern Ireland, this Yearbook contains detailed information for central and local government, 2200 pre-school/nurseries, 23,000 primary schools and 370 middle schools.

4456 Encyclopedia of education
J.W. Guthrie [et al.], eds 2nd edn, Macmillan Reference, 2003. 7 v., $1050. ISBN 9780028655949.
Although labelled a second edition, all the articles are new. Some 850 articles of between 1 and 20 pages. Concentrates on the USA, but with some international coverage.

4457 Encyclopedia of educational leadership and administration
F.W. English, ed. Sage Publications, 2006. 2 v., £160. ISBN 9780761930877.
600 entries, presenting 'the most recent theories, research, terms, concepts, ideas and histories on educational leadership and school administration as it is taught on PGCE courses and practised in schools and colleges today'.

Handbooks & manuals

4458 The Cambridge handbook of multimedia learning
R. Mayer, ed. Cambridge University Press, 2005, 663pp. £32. ISBN 9780521547512.
'(C)onstitutes the world's first handbook devoted to comprehensive coverage of research and theory in the field of multimedia learning. Multimedia learning is defined as learning from words (e.g. spoken or printed text) and pictures (e.g. illustrations, photos, maps, graphs, animation or video).'

4459 The Cambridge handbook of the learning sciences
R.K. Sawyer, ed. Cambridge University Press, 2006, 627pp. £27.99. ISBN 9780521607773.
'Learning sciences is an interdisciplinary field that studies teaching and learning. The sciences of learning include cognitive science, educational psychology, computer science, anthropology, sociology, neuroscience and other fields ...' The handbook's 34 contributions effectively span this extensive knowledge landscape.

4460 The handbook of blended learning: global perspectives, local designs
C.J. Bonk and C.R. Graham, eds Wiley, 2006, 585pp. £39.99. ISBN 9780787977580.
'Blended learning' is the combination of multiple approaches to learning: typically, a combination of technology-based materials and face-to-face sessions used together to deliver instruction. In this very useful summary of the state of the art, covering the full range of learning situations, there are 39 contributions structured into eight parts: 1. Introduction to blended learning; 2. Corporate blended learning models and perspectives; 3. Higher education blended learning models and perspectives; 4. For-profit and online university perspectives; 5. Cases of blended learning in higher education from around the world; 6. Multinational blended learning perspectives; 7. Workplace, on-demand and authentic learning; 8. Future trends in blended learning.

4461 The Jossey-Bass reader on educational leadership
M. Fullan, comp. Jossey-Bass, 2007, 474pp. $32. ISBN 9780787984007.
26 essays organized into six parts: I. The principles of leadership; II. Moral leadership; III. Culture and change; IV. Standards and systems; V. Diversity and leadership; VI. The future of leadership.

Educational Theory
educational research • theory of learning

Introductions to the subject

4462 Educational research: an introduction
M.D. Gall, J.P Gall and W.R. Borg 8th edn, Pearson/Allyn & Bacon, 2007, 672pp. £38.99. ISBN 9780205503452.
Described as 'the most comprehensive and widely respected text for scholars and graduate-level students who need to understand educational research in depth and conduct original research for a dissertation or thesis.'

4463 Educational research: planning, conducting, and evaluating quantitative and qualitative research
J.W. Creswell 3rd edn, Prentice Hall, 2007, 670pp. $103. ISBN 9780136135500.
Clearly laid-out text, suitable for those new to the arena: 18 chapters in three parts: I. An introduction to educational research; II. The steps in the process of research; III. Research designs.

4464 Introduction to theories of learning
B.R. Hergenhahn and M. Olson   7th edn, Pearson Education International, 2005, 506pp. £49.99. ISBN 9780131278219.
Historical approach organized primarily around the key figures in development of learning theory: Thorndike, Skinner, Hull, Pavlov, etc.

■ **Fifty modern thinkers on education: from Piaget to the present** J.A. Palmer [et al.]   Routledge, 2001, 290pp. £14.99. ISBN 9780415224093. Among those included are: Pierre Bourdieu; Elliot Eisner; Hans J. Eysenck; Michel Focault; Henry Giroux; Jurgen Habermas; Susan Isaacs; A.S. Neill; Herbert Read; Simone Weill.

4465 Multiple intelligences: new horizons
H. Gardner   Rev. edn, Basic Books, 2006, 300pp. $19.95. ISBN 9780465047680.
Developments based on the author's classic work *Frames of mind*, based on the notion that there are separate human capacities, ranging from musical intelligence to the intelligence involved in self-understanding.

4466 The Sage handbook for research in education: engaging ideas and enriching inquiry
C.F. Conrad and R.C. Serlin, eds   Sage Publications, 2006, 598pp. £85. ISBN 9781412906401.
'The Handbook is written in lively, welcoming prose and central to the handbook is an intention to encourage and help researchers place ideas at the epicenter of inquiry. In addition explicit discussion of the fundamental challenges that researchers must consciously address throughout their inquiry are identified and solutions provided to help future researchers overcome similar obstacles.'
'*The SAGE handbook for research in education* is the best research text I've come across. It's beautifully written, comprehensive and most importantly, students find it engaging. The text includes many different voices and encourages students to find their own research voice. I've planned my entire class around the chapters in the book.' (Marybeth Gasman, University of Pennsylvania)

4467 The theory and practice of learning
P. Jarvis, J. Holford and C. Griffin, eds   2nd edn, Routledge, 2003, 198pp. £26.99. ISBN 9780749438593.
'An overview of the basic theories of learning. It looks at how these have developed and demonstrates how they can be put into practice. The authors put forward their own theory as well as examining others.'

■ **The theory and practice of teaching** P. Jarvis, ed.   2nd edn, Routledge, 2006, 257pp. £23.99. ISBN 9780415365253. 'This fully updated second edition contains new material on e-moderating and its implications for teaching theory, issues surrounding discipline, and the ethical dimensions of teaching. *The theory and practice of teaching* will be of interest to anyone wanting to develop a deep understanding of the key themes and latest developments in teaching, and is an ideal companion volume to *The theory and practice of learning*.'

Dictionaries, thesauri, classifications

4468 Elearning: the key concepts
R. Mason and F. Rennie   Routledge, 2006, 158pp. £13.99. ISBN 9780415373074.
Useful guide covering, for instance, blogging, course design, plagiarism, search engines and Virtual Learning Environments. Further reading.

■ **Philosophy of education: the key concepts** J. Gingell and C. Winch   Routledge, 2008. ISBN 9780415428927. New edn announced for 2008; last edn 1999.

4469 Learning theories: A to Z
D.C. Leonard   Oryx Press, 2002, 249pp. $75. ISBN 9781573564137.
'This book is a substantive dictionary of over 500 terms relating to learning theories and environments. Definitions range from approximately 100 to 700 words and each term is identified by the primary type of learning theory to which it applies: cognitivism, constructivism, behaviorism, humanism, or organizational learning.'

4470 The new taxonomy of educational objectives
R.J. Marzano and J.S. Kendall   2nd edn, Sage Publications, 2007, 193pp. £25. ISBN 9781412936293.
'It's been more than 50 years since Benjamin Bloom published his *Taxonomy of Educational Objectives* and Bloom's taxonomy is one of the most widely known and used models in education. While still useful, Bloom's taxonomy doesn't represent the most current research on the nature of knowledge and cognition, nor does it reflect the movement to standards-based education. Marzano's taxonomy is based on three domains of knowledge (information, mental procedures and psychomotor procedures) and six levels of processing (retrieval, comprehension, analysis, knowledge utilization, metacognitive and self-system).'

Research centres & institutes

4471 Centre for the Use of Research & Evidence in Education [UK]
www.curee-paccts.com
CUREE 'supports and develops the effective use of research and evidence in education in order to improve practice and policy and to help raise standards.' The website brings together an impressive listing of research and publications from a number of organizations. The Bubble map of free resources is a particularly useful resource for students and new researchers.

4472 Evidence for Policy & Practice Information & Coordinating Centre [UK]
http://eppi.ioe.ac.uk/cms
The EPPI Centre, based in the Social Science Research Centre at the Institute of Education, University of London, focuses on developing researchers' skills as well as providing reviews on an increasing range of education topics.

4473 Harvard Graduate School of Education
www.gse.harvard.edu
Oversees a wide range of research initiatives, for example: Center on the Developing Child; Change Leadership Group; Civil Rights Project; Collaborative on Academic Careers in Higher Education; Dynamic Development Laboratory; etc.

4474 Penn Graduate School of Education [USA]
www.gse.upenn.edu
Another US-based school with a wide spectrum of research activities, including participation in the Consortium for Policy Research in Education (CPRE), a joint effort of the graduate schools of education at Penn, Harvard, Stanford, the University of Michigan and the University of Wisconsin-

Madison, which focuses on school reform, governance, policy and finance.

Associations & societies

4475 American Educational Research Association
www.aera.net
AERA is an international professional organization with the primary goal of advancing educational research and its practical application. As well as details of meetings and publications, the website provides details of annual awards for research and publications.

4476 Australian Association for Research in Education
www.aare.edu.au
AARE is an association of 'persons interested in fostering educational research in Australia'. The organization's website provides membership information, details of its journal, conferences and workshops as well as news and notices.

4477 British Educational Research Association
www.bera.ac.uk
BERA is a membership organization with a broad aim 'to sustain and promote a vital research culture in education'. Its website provides information about publications, including the highly rated *British Educational Research Journal*, and conferences. It also provides an excellent list of external links to other educational research associations.

- **British Educational Research Journal** Taylor & Francis, bi-monthly. £833. ISSN 01411926. 'The journal is interdisciplinary in approach, and includes reports of case studies, experiments and surveys, discussions of conceptual and methodological issues and of underlying assumptions in educational research, accounts of research in progress, and book reviews'.

4478 European Educational Research Association
www.eera.ac.uk
Membership of EERA is open to individual research associations in European countries and the website provides links to these.

Discovering print & electronic resources

4479 Current Education Research in the UK
National Foundation for Educational Research
www.ceruk.ac.uk
This important resource, sponsored by NFER and with support from the UK Department for Education and Skills (now the Departments for Children, Schools and Families and Innovation, Universities and Skills) and the EPPI Centre, aims to provide a complete record of ongoing educational research. The free database covers a wide range of studies, including commissioned research and PhD theses, across all phases of education from early years to adults.

Directories & encyclopedias

4480 Encyclopedia of education and human development
S.J. Farenga and D. Ness, eds   M.E. Sharpe, 2005. 3 v., $349. ISBN 9780765612687.
'(P)rovides comprehensive coverage of educational theory

and practice from the primary grades through higher education. The set integrates numerous theoretical frameworks with field-based applications from many years in educational research and features contributions from respected specialists in education, psychology, sociology, philosophy, law and medicine.' Seven sections: I. Constructs of learning; II. Philosophical, social and political issues in education; III. Levels in educational practice; IV. Physical, motor and cognitive domains; V. Educational issues concerning diverse populations; VI. People; VII. Organizations.

Handbooks & manuals

4481 Handbook of complementary methods in education research
J.L. Green [et al.], eds; American Educational Research Association
3rd edn, Lawrence Erlbaum, 2006, 865pp. £55.50. ISBN 9780805859331.
Major handbook bringing together the wide range of research methods used to study education, making the logic of enquiry for each method clear and accessible. An introductory Part I examines common philosophical, epistemological and ethical issues facing researchers from all traditions and frames ways of understanding the similarities and differences among traditions. Part II – the core of the work – presents 35 chapters on research design and analysis. Part III examines how the research carried out has evolved over time in such areas as: classroom interaction; language research; issues of race, culture and difference; policy analysis; programme evaluation; student learning; and teacher education.

- **Research methods in education** L. Cohen, L. Manion and K. Morrison   6th edn, Routledge, 2007, 638pp. £24.99. ISBN 9780415368780. www.routledge.com/textbooks/9780415368780 [COMPANION]. Well established text. Covers the whole range of methods currently employed by educational research at all stages. It is divided into five main parts: the context of educational research; planning educational research; styles of educational research; strategies for data collection and researching; and data analysis.

Handbook of educational psychology
P.A. Alexander and P.H. Winne, eds   See entry no. 464

4482 Handbook of teacher education: globalization, standards and professionalism in times of change
T. Townsend and R. Bates, eds   Springer, 2007, 756pp. £230. ISBN 9781402047725.
47 chapters in seven parts (plus an Introduction and Afterword): 1. Globalization and diversity: promise or problem? 2. Standards and accountability: what does it mean to be a good teacher and how can we make it happen? 3. Getting the brightest and making them the best; 4. Teacher induction: from neophyte to professional in three easy steps; 5. Continuous development of teachers: the challenge to change; 6. The reflective practitioner: the way forward; 7. The impact of technology: tool of the trade or the terror for teachers?

International handbook of school effectiveness and improvement
T. Townsend, ed.   See entry no. 4513

4483 The international handbook of virtual learning environments

J. Weiss, ed.   Springer, 2006. 2 v. Springer international handbooks of education series, V.14., £307. ISBN 9781402038020.

63 contributions, organized in four parts: I. Foundations of virtual learning environments; II Schooling, professional learning and knowledge management; III Out-of-school virtual learning environments; IV. Challenges for virtual learning environments.

4484 Learning theories: an educational perspective

D.H. Schunk   5th edn, Prentice Hall, 2008, 578pp. £52.99. ISBN 9780132435659.

http://vig.prenhall.com/home [DESCRIPTION]

Well established and comprehensive. Chapters are: 1. Learning: introduction, issues, historical perspectives; 2. Conditioning theories; 3. Social cognitive theory; 4. Cognitive information processing theory; 5. Cognitive learning processes; 6. Constructivist theory; 7. Cognition and instruction; 8. Development and learning; 9. Neuroscience of learning; 10. Content-area learning; 11. Motivation; 12. Next steps.

4485 The Praeger handbook of education and psychology

J.L. Kincheloe, R.A. Horn and S.R. Steinberg, eds   Praeger, 2007. 4 v., $400. ISBN 9780313331220.

'Currently, there is an information gap between scholars and practitioners in the field of educational psychology concerning recent and on going developments. At this time there is no one source that provides a broad and comprehensive presentation of these changes. This work bridges the gap by providing a much needed explication of how educational psychology can meet the needs of diverse students, families and schools.'

'This set would be a very good reference resource for many high school students ... Recommended.' (*Library Media Connection*)

4486 The Sage handbook of e-learning research

R. Andrews and C. Haythornthwaite, eds   Sage Publications, 2007, 539pp. £85. ISBN 9781412919388.

Very well reviewed text edited by UK/US authors: 'This handbook provides a state-of-the-art, in-depth account of research in the rapidly expanding field of E-learning. The first of its kind, it provides reviews of over 20 areas in E-learning research by experts in the field and provides a critical account of the best work to date. The contributors cover the basics of the discipline, as well as new theoretical perspectives. Areas of research covered by the Handbook include Contexts for researching e-learning; Theory and policy; Language and literacy; Design issues; History of the field.'

4487 The Sage handbook of research in international education

M. Hayden, J. Levy and J. Thompson, eds   Sage Publications, 2007, 501pp. £85. ISBN 9781412919715.

'This book analyses the origins, contributions and interpretations of international education. The authors identify approaches to research that will progress our knowledge and understanding of the field and extend and even redraw it, on the basis of the research evidence presented.'

'This volume is another valuable Sage contribution to the expanding literature on international education. Not all handbooks are described as essential reading but this one will be, and will become an indispensable work of reference highly recommended for education libraries (both academic and governmental) and for the bookshelves of individual researchers and all involved in international education ... the three editors and their fellow authors can take a collective pride in having given us an excellent volume which very successfully completes a chronological and theoretical journey through the issues, practices and future questions presented by international research and practice in international education' (*Journal of Research in International Education*)

Teaching and learning: lessons from psychology

R. Fox   See entry no. 4514

4488 Towards a comprehensive theory of human learning

P. Jarvis   Routledge, 2006, 218pp. £23.99. ISBN 9780415355414.

'As interest grows in theories of lifelong learning not only across society but also as an area of serious academic study, the need has arisen for a thorough and critical study of the phenomenon. This distillation of the work of renowned writer Peter Jarvis addresses this need, looking at the processes involved in human learning from birth to old age and moving the field on from previous unsystematic and mainly psychological studies. Instead, Jarvis argues that learning is existential and so its study must be complex and interdisciplinary ...'

'Jarvis is intellectually eclectic on a grand scale, and attempts to contextualise his views within existentialist philosophy, phenomenology, social anthropology, psycho-analysis, and many other schemes of thought. All of this is accomplished with great zest and verve.' (*British Journal of Educational Technology*)

Schools

elementary education • primary education • teaching skills

Introductions to the subject

4489 Classroom teaching skills

K.D. Moore   6th edn, McGraw-Hill, 2007, 369pp. £50.99. ISBN 9780073525815.

http://highered.mcgraw-hill.com/sites/0073525812 [COMPANION]

12 chapters in four parts: Part 1. Setting the stage for effective teaching; Part 2. Planning instruction; Part 3. Implementing instruction; Part 4. Assessing instruction.

4490 Introduction to early childhood education: preschool through primary grades

J.A. Brewer   6th edn, Pearson/Allyn & Bacon, 2007, 552pp. £54.99. ISBN 9780205491452.

Comprehensive and well structured introduction, based on experience in the US system.

4491 Introduction to teaching: becoming a professional

D. Kauchak and P. Eggen   3rd edn, Pearson Merrill Prentice Hall, 2008, 528pp. $100. ISBN 9780131994553.

US-based text which introduces students 'to the real world of teaching, providing education students with an honest look at the students, classrooms and schools they'll encounter. Three themes central to teaching today – professionalism, diversity and decision making – are woven through the text to give students deeper understanding of the teaching profession and to better prepare them for that profession. Two questions frame the text, 'Do I want to be a teacher?' and 'What kind of teacher do I want to become?'

4492 Introduction to the foundations of American education
J. Johnson [et al.]   13th edn, Pearson/Allyn & Bacon, 2005, 544pp. £65.98. ISBN 9780205457816.
Well established text designed to give students an overview of the historical, legal, philosophical, social and practical aspects of American education.
14th edn, 2008 announced.

Philosophy of education
N. Noddings   See entry no. 4420

4493 School: an introduction to education
E.S. Ebert and R.C. Culyer   Thomson Wadsworth, 2007, 624pp. ISBN 9780534524654.
Innovative text responding to the US INTASC (Interstate New Teacher Assessment and Support Consortium) standards, which expect teachers to be 'reflective, knowledgeable, highly skilled and creative professionals who are lifelong learners and have the ability to think critically about a multitude of issues'.

Dictionaries, thesauri, classifications

4494 Primary education: the key concepts
D. Hayes   Routledge, 2006, 208pp. £14.99. ISBN 9780415354837.
'Presenting a balance of theoretical insight and practical advice, this text is a clear and accessible guide to the key issues relating to primary education. Alphabetically arranged and fully cross-referenced to ensure ease of use, entries include both curriculum specific terms, as well as those that are more generic, such as: assessment; objectives; coping strategies; differentiation; behaviour; special needs; time management.'
■ **Secondary education: the key concepts** J. Wellington
Routledge, 2006, 193pp. £14.99. ISBN 9780415344043. Similar work whose 'important topics' are listed as including: assessment; citizenship; curriculum; e-learning; exclusion; theories of learning; work experience. The publishers have also announced: *Special educational needs: the key concepts* (Routledge, 2008).

Laws, standards, codes

4495 Qualifications & Curriculum Authority [UK]
www.qca.org.uk
QCA regulates the public examination system and is the primary resource for information about qualifications, assessment and curriculum development in England.
■ **National Curriculum online** www.nc.uk.net. The key site for teachers and parents providing full details of the national Curriculum for England.

4496 Teachers and the law [UK]
K. Insley; Institute of Education   2007, 35pp. £11.99. ISBN 085473774X.
This invaluable guide, primarily aimed at new teachers in England, provides essential information on the complex legal requirements affecting teachers and schools.

■ **Teachers and the law** USAL. Fischer, D. Schimmel and L.R. Stellman   7th edn, Pearson Allyn & Baker, 2007, 480pp. $85.80. ISBN 9780205494958. 'The only text that provides a question and answer format which addresses every aspect of school law from a teacher's perspective'.

Official & quasi-official bodies

Great Britain. Department for Children, Schools & Families
See entry no. 4428

National Institute for Literacy
See entry no. 4565

4497 Office for Standards in Education, Children's Services & Skills [UK]
www.ofsted.gov.uk
This website provides details of the school inspection process as well as access to reports carried out in schools and other education institutions.

4498 Training & Development Agency for Schools [UK]
www.tda.gov.uk
'We work with schools to develop staff and ensure that schools can recruit good-quality, well trained people. We support schools to provide extended services for parents, children and young people.'

Associations & societies

4499 Advisory Centre for Education [UK]
www.ace-ed.org.uk
Independent registered charity, which offers information about state education in England and Wales for parents of school age children. It provides advice on issues, including exclusion from school, bullying, special educational needs and school admission appeals. The site also offers a number of publications, including a quarterly magazine, *Ask ACE*, and describes seminars available to parents, governors and education professionals.

4500 Association for Citizenship Teaching [UK]
www.teachingcitizenship.org.uk
ACT is the professional subject association for those involved in citizenship education. As well as links to useful resources and its termly journal *Teaching Citizenship*, the website provides details of the association's annual conference and other staff development opportunities. Also offers a helpful news reporting service on the home page.

4501 Association of School & College Leaders [UK]
www.ascl.org.uk
ASCL is the professional association for leaders of secondary schools and colleges. The site provides news bulletins and a useful calendar of training and other events.

4502 Booktrust [UK]
www.booktrust.org.uk
'An independent national charity that encourages people of all ages and cultures to discover and enjoy reading'. Website is useful source of information on projects and prizes and other initiatives related to the UK book industry, but is

confusing to navigate and gives no information on the organization's constitution and funding.

- ■ **Bookstart** www.bookstart.co.uk. One of a number of projects run under the auspices of Booktrust. It 'aims to promote a lifelong love of books and is based on the principle that every child in the UK should enjoy and benefit from books from as early an age as possible'.

4503 General Teaching Council for England
www.gtce.org.uk

The GTC is the professional body for teaching in England. Its overall purpose is 'to help improve standards of teaching and the quality of learning in the public interest'. The excellent website includes details of professional registration, regulation and education policy; access to latest news stories and GTC's online publications, including *Research of the Month* and their magazine *Teaching*.

4504 Independent Schools Council [UK]
www.isc.co.uk

'(R)epresents 1280 independent schools educating more than 500,000 children. Our schools are accredited by the Independent Schools Inspectorate (ISI) and the Head of each ISC school is a member of one of our five Heads' Associations. ISC schools cover the entire academic range. They also cover a wide social range, with nearly a third of children receiving help with fees ...'

Well designed website with five windows onto its extensive content: Parent Zone; Teaching Zone; International Zone; Job Zone; Member Zone.

- ■ **The independent schools guide** Kogan Page for Gabbitas, annual, 576pp. £15.99 [2007–2008]. ISBN 9780749449483. This guide provides an overview of the independent sector in five geographical areas: England, N. Ireland, Scotland, Wales, and overseas. The second section of the guide provides details of individual schools.
- ■ **SchoolSearch** John Catt Educational. www.schoolsearch.co.uk. Gathering together data from a range of guides published by John Catt, this comprehensive website provides details of UK independent schools, boarding schools, London schools, preparatory schools, special needs schools, international schools and 16+ schools.

4505 National Literacy Trust [UK]
www.literacytrust.org.uk

'We have a vision of a society in which everyone has the reading, writing, speaking and listening skills that they need to fulfil their own and, ultimately, the nation's potential. To make a real difference, whole communities need to work together. We help to make this happen.'

Excellent site map, plus A–Z list of sections. The literacy news pages cover news from the media in the last four weeks. There is an extensive set of downloadable resources, a good FAQ section and a valuable links facility, divided into about 20 sections (e.g. Children's specialist bookshops; Libraries and reader development, including school libraries; Prisoners and their families; Volunteering and mentoring). There are also details of the Trust's policy, project and research involvements. An exemplary resource.

Portal & task environments

4506 Teacher Training Resource Bank [UK]
Training & Development Agency for Schools
www.ttrb.ac.uk

The TTRB is a three-year project which provides access to a research and evidence base informing teacher education.

Materials are quality-assured through a rigorous process of academic scrutiny and monitoring undertaken by a team of expert teacher educators from all over the UK. As well as the searchable resource bank, the website also provides an e-librarian service; with access to previous questions and answers, this is becoming an exceptionally useful resource for teachers and teacher educators.

4507 TeacherXpress
Logotron.
www.teacherxpress.com

'The education web all in one place for busy teachers.'

Innovative and very interesting portal: 'Software robots manage the page: One robot is responsible for checking all the links and mailing a status report each day; A second robot is responsible for taking new entries from e-mail messages and inserting them into an appropriate category on the page; A third robot is responsible for removing entries from the page, based upon a number of criteria; A fourth robot is responsible for periodically re-ordering the links within categories, according to the level of use by users.

'No human programmer can understand the code that makes these robots work – they are all the product of genetic programming. Genetic programming is an advanced, automated method for creating working software objects from a high-level logic statement of a problem ...'

Digital data, image & text collections

4508 Teachers.tv [UK]
Education Digital.
www.teachers.tv

Teachers TV is a TV channel, available through Freeview, cable, satellite and over the web, providing learning opportunities for teachers and others interested in education. Its searchable website is a useful resource in itself.

Directories & encyclopedias

Council of International Schools
See entry no. 4539

4509 Early childhood education: an international encyclopedia
R.S. New and M. Cochran, eds   Praeger, 2007. 4 v., $475. ISBN 9780313331008.

'Over three hundred entries in volumes 1, 2 and 3 cover such topics as: accountability; assessment; biculturalism; bullying; child abuse; early intervention; ethnicity; Head Start; IDEA; No Child Left Behind; Zero to three. Volume 4 covers the international structure and policies of early childhood education outside of the US via narrative chapters on industrialized and developing nations.'

'Prepared for a large, diverse audience, this distinctive encyclopedia, with its cross-cultural focus and outstanding features, will be extremely valuable to undergraduate students. Essential. Lower-/upper-level undergraduates, professionals, and general readers.' (*Choice*)

Handbooks & manuals

4510   Education: the practice and profession of teaching
R. McNergney and J. McNergney   5th edn, Pearson Allyn & Bacon, 2006, 496pp. £53.99. ISBN 9780205485581.
http://wps.ablongman.com/ab_mcnergney_practprof_5 [COMPANION]
Comprehensive US-based text which integrates the core foundations of education with case-based analysis, practical examples of technology in the classroom and personal encounters with diversity.

4511   Elementary education: a reference handbook [USA]
D.A. Harmon and T.S. Jones   ABC-CLIO, 2005, 261pp. $45. ISBN 9781576079423.
Overview of elementary education in the USA, spanning its history, foundations, curriculum models, technology, assessment and special programmes.
'Harmon and Jones ... have provided a "one-stop" experience for everyone interested in elementary education ... Large public libraries, academic libraries supporting programs in education, and even school media centers with professional development collections should be sure to buy this book.' (*American Reference Books Annual*)

4512   Extended schools manual
S. Blandford   Pearson Education, 2007, 304pp. £86.49. ISBN 9780273708797.
36 chapters in 12 sections: 1. Policy and practice; 2. The community; 3. Remodelled schools; 4. Pathfinder models; 5. Managing extended schools; 6. Planning monitoring and review; 7. Implementing policy; 8. Financial management; 9. Recruitment and selection; 10. Professional development; 11. Professional standards; 12. Extending the extended school.

Handbook of teacher education: globalization, standards and professionalism in times of change
T. Townsend and R. Bates, eds   See entry no. 4482

4513   International handbook of school effectiveness and improvement
T. Townsend, ed.   Springer, 2007. 2 v., £245.50. ISBN 9781402048050.
www.springer.com/uk/home/education [DESCRIPTION]
'The target audience for the book will be researchers and research students, people involved in the training of educational leaders, policy makers and educational leaders based in schools or school authorities'.
One of the Springer International Handbooks of Education: *see the website for details of other volumes in the series not referenced elsewhere herein.*

4514   Teaching and learning: lessons from psychology
R. Fox   Blackwell, 2005, 304pp. £19.99. ISBN 9781405114875.
Guide to child psychology and the psychology of teaching. Part I. Beginning to teach; Part II. The psychology of human learning and motivation; Part III. Extending teaching.

4515   Teaching and learning science: a handbook
K. Tobin, ed.   Praeger, 2006. 2 v., $200. ISBN 9780313335730.
Work about 'the learning of science' (rather than 'learning science'). Consists of '66 chapters written by more than 90 leading educators and scientists. The volumes are informed by cutting-edge theory and research and address numerous issues that are central to K-12 education' (in the USA).

Further & Higher Education

colleges • distance education • higher education • universities

Introductions to the subject

4516   Beyond mass higher education: building on experience
I. McNay; Society for Research into Higher Education   Open University Press, 2006, 240pp. £25.99. ISBN 9780335218578.
'This collection looks forward to the next decade of higher education and identifies strategic issues that need to be tackled at institutional and management levels. It considers how far the higher education system has adapted to respond to the requirements of a mass and universal system, rather than struggling to sustain an elite system with mass participation.'

4517   British universities: past and present
R. Anderson   Hambledon Continuum, 2006, 241pp. £40. ISBN 9781852853471.
Both a concise history of British universities and their place in society over eight centuries and an analysis of current university problems and policies as seen in the light of that history. Chapters are: 1. Serving church and state; 2. Currents of change; 3. Oxbridge reformed; 4. Effortless superiority; 5. Province and metropolis; 6. National identities; 7. Ideas of the university; 8. Interwar conservatism; 9. Postwar revolution; 10. The Robbins era; 11. State or market? 12. Past and present.

4518   The challenge to scholarship: rethinking learning, teaching and research
G. Nicholls   RoutledgeFalmer, 2005, 162pp. £80. ISBN 0415335329.
'Lively and engaging investigation that seeks to establish what it means to be a scholar and the value of scholarship. It addresses current concerns and tensions, including the scholarship of teaching and the relationship between teaching and research.'
Series: Key Issues in Higher Education.

4519   Equity and excellence in American higher education
W.G. Bowen, M.A. Kurzweil and E.M. Tobin   University of Virginia Press, 2005, 453pp. $18.95. ISBN 0813925576.
'Thomas Jefferson once stated that the foremost goal of American education must be to nurture the "natural aristocracy of talent and virtue." Although in many ways American higher education has fulfilled Jefferson's vision by achieving a widespread level of excellence, it has not achieved the objective of equity implicit in Jefferson's statement ...'
'Everyone who cares about opportunity in the United States should read this book. With careful analysis and valuable new data, the authors examine the chances for low-income Americans to attend college and offer some unexpected findings and thoughtful suggestions for reform.' (Derek Bok)

4520   Indoctrination U: the left's war against academic freedom
D. Horowitz   Encounter Books, 2007, 159pp. $21.95. ISBN 1594031908.
'In 2003, David Horowitz began a campaign to promote

intellectual diversity and a return to academic standards in American universities. To achieve these goals he devised an "Academic Bill of Rights" and created a national student movement with chapters on 160 college campuses. His efforts have inspired legislation at the federal level and in more than a dozen states, led to the passage of an "Academic Bill of Rights" by student governments from Montana to Maine and dramatically transformed the national debate on academic issues.

'In dramatic commentary, Indoctrination U. unveils the intellectual corruption of American universities by faculty activists who have turned America's classrooms into indoctrination centers for their political causes ...'

Dictionaries, thesauri, classifications

4521 Distance education: definition and glossary of terms
L.A. Schlosser and M. Simonson; Association for Educational Communications & Technology   2nd edn, Information Age Publishing, 2006, 160pp. $39.99. ISBN 1593115156.
Second edition based on AECT's original work. The definition of distance education and much of the supporting narrative offered in this edition of *Distance education* is based on *Teaching and learning at a distance: foundations of distance education* (3rd edn, Pearson Merrill Prentice Hall, 2006).

Laws, standards, codes

4522 The law of higher education
D.J. Farrington and D. Palfreyman   Oxford University Press, 2006, 638pp. £78.95. ISBN 9780199297450.
Comprehensive and practical guide to the UK law of higher education, providing extensive treatment of the complex legal framework in which universities work and the remedies which may be sought in the event of disputes.

Official & quasi-official bodies

4523 European Centre for the Development of Vocational Training
www.cedefop.europa.eu
CEDEFOP is the European Agency to promote the development of vocational education and training (VET) in the European Union. As well as news and publications, the website provides access to CEDEFOP's library catalogue with access to electronic publications from the European states on vocational education and training.

4524 Great Britain. Department for Innovation, Universities & Skills
www.dius.gov.uk
Brings together functions from the former Department of Trade and Industry, including responsibilities for science and innovation, with further and higher education and skills, previously part of the Department for Education and Skills.

Higher Education Funding Council for England
See entry no. 24

4525 International Centre for Technical & Vocational Education & Training
www.unevoc.unesco.org
UNESCO's Education website provides access to a wide range of strategic information, statistics and resources, with particular emphasis on current campaigns: Education for All; the UN Millennium Development Goals; the UN Literacy Decade 2003–2012; the UN Decade of Education for Sustainable Development 2005–2014; and the EDUCAIDS Global Initiative on Education and HIV/AIDS. A most important resource for education worldwide.

This segment of the overall site relates to TVET: 'TVET is concerned with the acquisition of knowledge and skills for the world of work. Throughout the course of history, various terms have been used to describe elements of the field that are now conceived as comprising TVET. These include Apprenticeship Training, Vocational Education, Technical Education, Technical-Vocational Education (TVE), Occupational Education (OE), Vocational Education and Training (VET), Career and Technical Education (CTE), Workforce Education (WE), Workplace Education (WE) etc. Several of these terms are commonly used in specific geographic areas'.

Research centres & institutes

4526 Education Subject Centre [UK]
http://escalate.ac.uk
ESCalate is part of the Higher Education Academy. As the Subject Centre for Education it supports developments in teacher education, education studies programmes, continuing and adult education and lifelong learning and HE studies in further education colleges. The website includes details of projects and conferences, book reviews and a regular newsletter and bulletin.

4527 European Centre for Higher Education
www.cepes.ro
'UNESCO-CEPES (the European Centre for Higher Education/Centre Européen pour l'Enseignement Supérieur) was established in September 1972 with a view to promoting cooperation in higher education among Member States of the Europe Region (the countries of Europe, North America and Israel) ... The activities of UNESCO-CEPES are focused foremost on higher education in Central and Eastern Europe.' Good range of resources on website.

4528 Higher Education Policy Institute [UK]
www.hepi.ac.uk
Established in November 2002, with the aim to ensure as far as possible that higher education policy development in the UK is informed by research and by knowledge of the experience of others. Useful range of publications.

4529 Oxford Centre for Higher Education Policy Studies [UK]
http://oxcheps.new.ox.ac.uk
Mission is: 'To improve understanding of higher education by challenging existing thinking and received wisdom in higher education policy-making; and, on the basis of a rigorous programme of applied comparative research and consultancy successfully linking theory and practice in higher education, to generate an informed debate on topical higher education issues.'

Associations & societies

4530 Global University Network for Innovation
www.guni-rmies.net

GUNI is composed of UNESCO Chairs in Higher Education, research centres, universities, networks and other institutions highly committed to innovation in higher education. More than 100 institutions from around the world are GUNI members. GUNI was set up by UNESCO, the United Nations University (UNU) and the Technical University of Catalonia (UPC) in 1999 with the aim of following up the decisions taken at the World Conference on Higher Education (WCHE) held in Paris in 1998.

4531 Higher Education Research & Development Society of Australasia
www.herdsa.org.au

The HERDSA website provides basic information about the Society and its journal and conferences.

4532 Society for Research into Higher Education [UK]
www.srhe.ac.uk

'UK-based international learned society concerned to advance understanding of higher education, especially through the insights, perspectives and knowledge offered by systematic research and scholarship. The Society aims to be the leading international society in the field, as to both the support and the dissemination of research.' Active Society offering a good range of services, some only accessible to SHRE members: Networks; Publications; Research; Links; Events.

4533 Universities & Colleges Admissions Service [UK]
www.ucas.com

'We are the organization responsible for managing applications to higher education courses in the UK. Not only do we process more than two million applications for full-time undergraduate courses every year, but we help students to find the right course. We try to make things run as smoothly as possible by providing innovative online tools which make it easier for students and HEIs to manage applications and offers.' UCAS also organizes conferences, education fairs and conventions across the UK and produces a wide range of publications.

- ■ **The big guide for entry to university and college in 2008** 2008, UCAS Media, annual, 1632pp. £31.50. ISBN 9781843610670. www.ucasmedia.com/publications-services [DESCRIPTION]. 'This Book and CD-ROM package is the only guide to contain complete entry requirements for all UK higher education courses using the UCAS tariff.' One of a wide range of publications produced under the UCAS umbrella.

Portal & task environments

4534 The observatory on borderless higher education
Association of Commonwealth Universities and Universities UK
www.obhe.ac.uk

Joint initiative of ACU and Universities UK but 'now 100% funded by subscriptions and consultancy and has over 160 institutional subscribers from more than 40 countries ... The Observatory offers a unique service: an environmental scanning facility on higher education issues ... The term "borderless education" encompasses a broad range of activities and developments which cross (or have the potential to cross) the traditional borders of higher education, be they geographical, sectoral or conceptual. So, for example, the Observatory will track developments in areas such as e-learning, growth in private and corporate education, developing markets and international collaboration.'

Directories & encyclopedias

4535 Barron's profiles of American colleges
27th edn, Barrons, annual. Includes CD-ROM, $28.99 [2007]. ISBN 0764179039.

America's definitive guide to all accredited four-year colleges and universities, this text provides comprehensive profiles of more than 1650 schools. Each school receives Barron's exclusive academic rating system, which advises students on its degree of academic competitiveness – from 'non-competitive' to 'most competitive'.

4536 British qualifications: a complete guide to educational, technical, professional and academic qualifications in Britain
37th edn, Kogan Page, 2006, 1040pp. £48. ISBN 9780749448035.

'The new edition of this highly successful and practical guide provides thorough information on all developments. Fully indexed, it includes details on all university awards and over 200 career fields, their professional and accrediting bodies, levels of membership and qualifications ... It acts as a one-stop guide for careers advisors, students and parents and will also enable human resource managers to verify the qualifications of potential employees'

4537 British vocational qualifications: a directory of vocational qualifications available in the UK
9th edn, Kogan Page, 2007, 464pp. £40. ISBN 9780749448127.

'Provide(s) up-to-date information on over 3500 vocational qualifications in the UK. Practical and easy to use, this popular reference book provides a simple guide for anyone needing advice on vocational education. Not only suitable for students, it's an excellent source of knowledge for careers advisors, human resource managers, employees and teachers'.

4538 Commonwealth universities yearbook: a directory to the universities of the Commonwealth and the handbook of their Association
Association of Commonwealth Universities   81st edn, 2007, annual. 2 v., £200. ISBN 9780851431901 ISSN 00697745.

Alphabetical sequence of Commonwealth countries with list of universities in each country. Provides a profile of each university: details of courses, statistics, library holdings, research strengths, key academics. Also includes a short introduction to the HE system for the larger countries.

4539 Council of International Schools
www.cois.org

'(N)ot-for-profit association of schools and post-secondary institutions working collaboratively for the continuous improvement of international education ... The Council of International Schools currently includes in membership over 460 accredited post-secondary higher education institutions that support international education and the goals of the Council ... Higher education members must meet at least one of the following conditions: (1) accreditation by a regional accrediting organization, (2) official recognition by the Ministry of Education (or its equivalent) in the country in which the institution is located.'

- ■ **The CIS higher education directory** J. Bingham　John Catt Educational for CIS, 2007, annual, 672pp. £40.00 [2008]. ISBN 9781904724469. Provides up-to-date information on member colleges in Australasia, Britain and Europe, Canada, Mexico, the Middle East and the USA.

4540　Encyclopedia of distributed learning
Sage Publications, 2004, 549pp. $145. ISBN 9780761924517. Includes over 275 entries, each written by a specialist in that area, giving the reader comprehensive coverage of all aspects of distributed learning, including use of group processes, self-assessment, the life line experience and developing a learning contract.

'This volume will appeal to a wide array of readers, from novices to those already working in the field. Recommended for all collections.' (*Choice*)

4541　International handbook of universities and other institutions of higher education
International Association of Universities　18th edn, Palgrave Macmillan, 2005, biennial, 3248pp. $340. ISBN 9781403906885 ISSN 00746215.

www.unesco.org/iau/onlinedatabases [COMPANION]

Lists 9000+ universities in 183 countries and provides contact details, faculties and student statistics. (The IAU itself has a very partial membership of universities in some 150 countries.) The URL provides free (but not very sophisticated) access to a World Higher Education Database, reproducing some of the content of the Handbook.

4542　World of learning
Europa, 2007, annual, 2952pp. £500.00 [2008]. ISBN 9781857434361 ISSN 00842117.

www.worldoflearning.com [COMPANION]

Listing of international organizations, followed by a an A–Z list of countries with details of their learned societies, research institutes, libraries and archives and universities. Core directory, but now also accessible online.

Handbooks & manuals

4543　Academic reading
K.T. McWhorter　6th edn, Pearson/Longman, 2007, 512pp. £36.99. ISBN 9780321471697.

Advanced-reading text that focuses on comprehension and critical thinking and providing strategies for reading in the major academic disciplines. 18 chapters in three parts: I. Fundamentals of reading strategies; II. Critical reading strategies; III. Academic reading strategies.

4544　The academic's handbook
A.L. DeNeef and C.D.W. Goodwin, eds　3rd edn, Duke University Press, 2007, 407pp. $24.95. ISBN 9780822338741.

Collection of essays for those planning or beginning an academic career.

4545　Adults in higher education: learning from experience in new Europe
R. Mark, M. Pouget and E. Thomas, eds　Peter Lang, 2006, 512pp. £49. ISBN 9783039107179.

Result of research carried out by the partners in the Adults Learning and Participating in Education (ALPINE) Project, a

project that is principally concerned with increasing the amount of adult education provided by European universities. Notable for its contributions from experienced adult education practitioners from 20 European countries, who have each determined the nature and extent of the current provision of adult higher education in their own country.

4546　Encyclopedia of distance learning
C. Howard [et al.]　Idea Group Reference, 2005. 4 v., £635. ISBN 1591405556.

'This encyclopedia offers the most comprehensive coverage of the issues, concepts, trends and technologies of distance learning. More than 450 international contributors from over 50 countries.'

- ■ **Handbook of distance education** M.G. Moore, ed.　2nd edn, Lawrence Erlbaum, 2007, 690pp. $195. ISBN 9780805858471. Leading award-winning handbook from pioneer in the field.
- ■ **International handbook of distance education** T. Evans, M. Haughey and D. Murphy　Elsevier, 2008, 796pp. £150. ISBN 9780080447179. Announced work which '(a)ims to provide a comprehensive selection of essays on topics that encompass the traditions of distance education practice built during the past century; reflect contemporary issues and practices; and pose a critical awareness of the emergent concerns of the changing field'.

4547　Facilitating reflective learning in higher education
A. Brockbank; Society for Research into Higher Education　2nd edn, Open University Press, 2007, 368pp. £29.99. ISBN 9780335220915.

Detailed text covering the principles of learning and reflection, how to facilitate learning and reflective practice and a series of exemplar case studies

4548　Handbook of online education
S. Bennett [et al.]　Continuum, 2007, 345pp. £35. ISBN 9780826472960.

Provides a range of practical, innovative ideas to promote active learning online.

Handbook of teacher education: globalization, standards and professionalism in times of change
T. Townsend and R. Bates, eds　See entry no. 4482

4549　Higher education in the Internet age: libraries creating a strategic edge
P.S. Breivik and E.G. Gee　rev.edn, Praeger, 2006, 322pp. $49.95. ISBN 9780275981945.

'Based on their 1989 award-winning book in the ACE series, *Information literacy: revolution in the library*, this new work from Breivik and Gee addresses the unique challenges of today's information-overloaded culture while responding to the significant changes that have occurred on campuses during the past fifteen years. Chief among these changes are the pervasive use of the internet, growing community engagement, distance education, the emphasis on more active learning and the assessment of student learning outcomes ...'

'Far too often, presidents, academic vice presidents and other campus leaders fail to take advantage of the contributions their campus libraries can make toward achieving institutional visions and priorities. In this age of information, libraries can and should be one of the primary strategic tools. By highlighting the extensive and successful use some campus leaders have made of library resources and personnel, the authors hope to inspire others to see their libraries strategically.' (*CAUT Bulletin*)

4550 International handbook of higher education
J.J.F. Forest and P.G. Altbach, eds   Springer, 2006. 2 v., £307. ISBN 9781402040115.
Designed to provide a central, authoritative reference source on the most essential topics of higher education. Part 1 covers 'Global themes and contemporary challenges'; Part 2 has chapters on experience in the differing regions and countries of the world.

4551 The lecturer's toolkit: a resource for developing assessment, learning and teaching
P. Race   3rd edn, Routledge, 2007, 267pp. £26.99. ISBN 9780415403825.
Topics covered include learning styles; assessment; lecturing; personal management skills; formative feedback; large and small group teaching; blended learning; resource-based and online learning; peer observation of teaching.

4552 Managing higher education in colleges
G. Parry, A. Thompson and P. Blackie   Continuum, 2006, 166pp. £22.99. ISBN 9780826488466.
UK-based text. Chapters are: Introduction; Changing contexts; Changing strategies; Alternative futures; Partnerships, frameworks and networks; Funding, fees and facilities; Management, organization and staffing; Teaching, learning and scholarship; Quality assurance, quality enhancement; Sustainability; Distinctiveness; Leadership; Afterword.

4553 New players, different game: understanding the rise of for-profit colleges and universities
W.G. Tierney and G.C. Hentschke   Johns Hopkins University Press, 2007, 216pp. $38. ISBN 9780801886577.
Detailed and rewarding comparison of for-profit and not-for-profit models of higher education to assess the strengths and weaknesses of both.

4554 Online learning and teaching in higher education
S. Bach, P. Haynes and J.L. Smith   Open University Press, 2007, 209pp. £25.99. ISBN 9780335218295.
What are the links between theory and practice in the area of online learning in higher education? What are the strengths and weaknesses of the online approach? How can online learning be used to enhance the student experience?

4555 The scholarship of teaching and learning in higher education: an evidence-based perspective
R.P. Perry and J.C. Smart, eds   Springer, 2007, 813pp. £115.50. ISBN 9781402049446.
'(B)rings together pre-eminent scholars from Australia, Canada, Europe, the Middle East and the USA to critically assess teaching and learning issues that cut across most disciplines. In addressing long-standing and newly emerging issues, the researchers examine the scientific evidence on what constitutes effective teaching in college classrooms, on the psychometric integrity of measures of teaching effectiveness and on the use of such measures for tenure, promotion and salary decisions.
'Systematically explored throughout the book is the avowed linkage between classroom teaching and motivation, learning and performance outcomes in students ...'

4556 Teaching and learning in further education
P. Huddleston and L. Unwin   3rd edn, Routledge, 2008, 240pp. £22.99. ISBN 9780415413497.

Announced new edition of a text presenting a practical guide to teaching and learning within the context of the changing FE environment, addressing the diverse nature of the curriculum and of the student body for which it is designed.

Keeping up to date

4557 The Chronicle of Higher Education [USA]
Chronicle of Higher Education, Inc., weekly. $90. ISSN 00095982.
http://chronicle.com [COMPANION]
Reliable source of news, information and jobs for college and university faculty and administration, published in three sections: news; *The Chronicle Review*, a magazine of arts and ideas; and *Careers*, which features career advice and job listings.

4558 The Times Higher Education Supplement [UK]
weekly. £54. ISSN 00493929.
www.thes.co.uk
Renowned publication for individuals working in higher education. THES 'reports and encourages debate on news, issues and intellectual developments across the whole range of academic life and reviews a wide range of books and journals.'

Lifelong Learning
adult education • continuing education

Introductions to the subject

4559 Adults learning
J. Rogers   5th edn, Open University Press, 2007, 272pp. £18.99. ISBN 9780335225354.
The classic introduction. 'How do adults really learn? How do I handle the first class or session? How can I get my material across in a way that will interest and excite people? ...'

4560 Learning for life: the foundations for lifelong learning
D.H. Hargreaves   Policy Press, 2004, 114pp. £16.99. ISBN 9781861345974.
Radical analysis challenging the myth that lifelong learning can or should be separated – in any sense – from school education.

4561 Lifelong learning and the new educational order
J. Field   2nd edn, Trentham Books, 2006, 204pp. £16.99. ISBN 9781858563466.
'Lifelong learning remains an explosive policy issue. In Britain and elsewhere, governments are actively encouraging citizens to learn and to apply their learning across their lifespan. Yet governments often seem uncertain over the best means of achieving this desirable goal. John Field's book explores the background to this sudden rise of interest among policy-makers, maps existing patterns of participation, evaluates the measures being developed to promote lifelong learning and assesses the prospects of achieving a viable learning society.'
'... an authoritative and compelling account [that] provides a broad vista in a few pages ... fluent and highly accessible.' (*Higher Education Review*)

■ **Social capital and lifelong learning** J. Field   Policy Press, 2005, 176pp. £24.99. ISBN 9781861346551. 'This book provides a fascinating account of the real nature of learning that should challenge those who fail to acknowledge the broader contexts in which people become "educated".' (*Widening Participation and Lifelong Learning*).

Laws, standards, codes

4562 Qualifications systems: bridges to lifelong learning
2007, 237pp. £32. ISBN 9789264013674.
Countries are now interested in developing broad systemic approaches to qualifications. These broad national approaches and their positive consequences are examined in this book.

Official & quasi-official bodies

4563 Learndirect [UK]
www.learndirect.co.uk
Learndirect has been developed by the University for Industry (UfI) to provide post-16 education and its website provides access to guidance and information about courses, including e-learning and training centres. Learndirect also works directly with employers to provide in-service training.

4564 Learning & Skills Council [UK]
www.lsc.gov.uk
'The Learning and Skills Council exists to make England better skilled and more competitive ... We have a single goal: to improve the skills of England's young people and adults to ensure we have a workforce of world-class standard ... The LSC is responsible for planning and funding high quality education and training for everyone in England other than those in universities ... Our vision is that by 2010, young people and adults in England have knowledge and skills matching the best in the world and are part of a truly competitive workforce.'

4565 National Institute for Literacy [USA]
www.nifl.gov
Federal Agency which 'provides leadership on literacy issues, including the improvement of reading instruction for children, youth and adults. In consultation with the US Departments of Education, Labor and Health and Human Services, the Institute serves as a national resource on current, comprehensive literacy research, practice and policy'.
■ **Literacy.org: Research and Innovation for a More Literate World** University of Pennsylvania. www.literacyonline.org. '(A) gateway to electronic resources and tools for the national and international youth and adult literacy communities. This site is jointly sponsored by the International Literacy Institute (ILI) and the National Center on Adult Literacy (NCAL) at the University of Pennsylvania Graduate School of Education'.

Research centres & institutes

4566 Centre for Research in Lifelong Learning [UK]
http://crll.gcal.ac.uk
The Centre was the first of its kind in the UK and came into existence on 1 August 1999. It was funded by a Research

Development Grant from the Scottish Higher Education Funding Council for the first three years and now is self-funding. Useful sets of resources, including an extensive links list.

4567 National Institute of Adult Continuing Education [UK]
www.niace.org.uk
The leading non-governmental organization for adult learning in England and Wales.
■ **Basic Skills Agency** www.basic-skills.co.uk. 'The Basic Skills Agency at NIACE is committed to finding, developing and disseminating good practice in literacy, language and numeracy'.

Associations & societies

4568 European Association for the Education of Adults
www.eaea.org
'EAEA is a European NGO with 120 member organizations in 41 countries working in the fields of adult learning.' Lively multilingual site; good news and events service – especially rewarding when combined with their 'Topics' facility: over 55 topics in 5 categories.

Directories & encyclopedias

4569 International encyclopedia of adult education
L.M. English   Palgrave Macmillan, 2005, 750pp. £105. ISBN 9781403917355.
'This encyclopedia has been developed by a board of 10 international scholars from Australia, Canada, UK, South Africa, USA and Switzerland. There are over 170 entries, 17 countries and 6 continents represented and there are authors from the most respected adult education departments in the world. The 110 scholars who contributed to this encyclopedia have diverse linguistic, ethnic and national perspectives and have made this encyclopedia a truly global effort.'
'... this is a really useful and user-friendly book. All entries are well structured and well written, and provide a clear introduction to a wide range of issues pertaining to the broad field of adult education.' (*Studies in the Education of Adults*)

Handbooks & manuals

4570 The adult learner: the definitive classic in adult education and human resource development
M.S. Knowles, E.F. Holton and R.A. Swanson   6th edn, Elsevier, 2005, 378pp. £27.99. ISBN 9780750678377.
'This much acclaimed text has been fully updated to incorporate the latest advances in the field. As leading authorities on adult education and training, Elwood Holton and Dick Swanson have revised this edition building on the work of the late Malcolm Knowles. Keeping to the practical format of the last edition, this book is divided into three parts. The first part contains the classic chapters that describe the roots and principles of andragogy, including a new chapter, which presents Knowles' program planning model. The second part focuses on the advancements in adult learning with each chapter fully revised updated, incorporating a major expansion of Androgogy in Practice. The last part of the book will contain an updated selection of

topical readings that advance the theory and will include the HRD style inventory developed by Dr Knowles.'

The standard work in the field of andragogy.

Adults in higher education: learning from experience in new Europe
R. Mark, M. Pouget and E. Thomas, eds   See entry no. 4545

4571 **Handbook of adult development and learning**
C. Hoare, ed.   Oxford University Press, 2006, 579pp. £48. ISBN 9780195171907.
US-originated work with 22 contributions organized into six parts: I. Foundations; II. Do development and learning fuel one another in adulthood?: four key areas; III. The self-system in adult development and learning; IV. The higher reaches of adult development and learning; V. Essential contexts for the learning, developing adult; VI. Adult development and learning, measured and applied.

4572 **The handbook of experiential learning**
M. Silverman, ed.   Jossey-Bass, 2007, 386pp. $95. ISBN 9780787982584.
Covers a broad range of experiential learning methods, including games and simulations, action learning, role-play and 'improv', story-telling, adventure activity, reflective practice, and creative play.

4573 **Lifelong learning: concepts and contexts**
P. Sutherland and J. Crowther, eds   Routledge, 2006, 247pp. £60. ISBN 9780415443050.
After an introductory overview, 20 wide-ranging chapters in three parts: I. Perspective on adult and lifelong learning; II. Institutions and issues for lifelong learning; III. Informal and community contexts for lifelong learning.

Towards a comprehensive theory of human learning
P. Jarvis   See entry no. 4488

Inclusive Education

gifted children • learning disabilities • multicultural education • special education

Introductions to the subject

4574 **Achievement and inclusion in schools**
K. Black-Hawkins, L. Florian and M. Rouse   Routledge, 2007, 161pp. £19.99. ISBN 9780415391986.
'This practical and timely text evaluates the relationship between achievement and inclusion. The authors argue that high levels of inclusion can be entirely compatible with high levels of achievement and that combining the two is essential if all children are to have the opportunity to participate fully in education.'

4575 **Deconstructing special education and constructing inclusion**
G. Thomas and A. Loxley   2nd edn, Open University Press, 2007, 184pp. £21.99. ISBN 9780335223718.
Contents: 1. Special education theory and theory talk; 2. The knowledge-roots of special education; 3. The great problem of "need": a case study in children who don't behave; 4. Thinking about learning failure, especially in reading; 5.

Modelling difference; 6. Inclusive schools in an inclusive society? Policy, politics and paradox; 7. Constructing inclusion; 8. Inclusive education for the twenty-first century: histories of help; hopes for respect.
'... a striking, thought-provoking yet lyrical account which is both uncompromising in its stance and refreshing in its intellectually sophisticated critique.' (*British Journal of Special Education*)

4576 **Inclusion**
L. Evans   David Fulton, 2007, 120pp. £9.99. ISBN 9781843124535.
Introduction to the basic principles of educational inclusion and the UK statutory requirements.

4577 **Multicultural and diversity education: a reference handbook**
P.M. Applebaum   ABC-CLIO, 2002, 191pp. $55. ISBN 9781576077474.
Somewhat dated now, but a good introductory overview, especially of the historical context.
'... accessible handbook ... succinctly covers the historical background of multicultural/diversity education and reviews contemporary trends and developments ... Highly recommended. All levels.' (*Choice*)

Associations & societies

4578 **Alliance for Inclusive Education** [UK]
www.allfie.org.uk
Allfie is a 'national network of individuals, families and groups who work together to help change our education system'. The changes they wish to bring about are based on their conviction that 'all young people need to be educated in a single mainstream education system which can support all young people to learn, play and live with each other'. The site includes a range of resources and the magazine *Inclusion Now*, as well as news of campaigns to support their beliefs.

4579 **British Dyslexia Association**
www.bdadyslexia.org.uk
The BDA describes itself as 'the voice of dyslexic people'. As well as promoting early identification and support in schools, it represents the needs of dyslexic people on leaving school, in higher education and in work. The dyslexia-friendly website provides comprehensive explanations of dyslexia as well as support and training information.

4580 **Council for Exceptional Children**
www.cec.sped.org
The largest international professional organization dedicated to improving educational outcomes for individuals with exceptionalities, students with disabilities, and/or the gifted.

4581 **Development Education Association** [UK]
www.dea.org.uk
DEA is a national network of some 250 member organizations that share a commitment to development education. The website provides clear information about Development Education and links to a wide range of resources.

4582 **Global Campaign for Education**
www.campaignforeducation.org
'(P)romotes education as a basic human right and mobilizes public pressure on governments and the international community to fulfill their promises to provide free, compulsory public basic education for all people; in particular for children, women and all disadvantaged, deprived sections of society.' The website provides resources and campaign materials to support these aims.

4583 **National Association for Special Educational Needs** [UK]
www.nasen.org.uk
'(T)he leading organization in the UK which aims to promote the education, training, advancement and development of all those with special and additional support needs. NASEN reaches a huge readership through its journals: *British Journal of Special Education*, *Support for Learning*, new online publication *Journal of Research in Special Educational Needs* and the magazine *Special*.'

4584 **Skill: National Bureau for Students with Disabilities** [UK]
www.skill.org.uk
'We are a national charity promoting opportunities for young people and adults with any kind of impairment in post-16 education, training and employment.' Well designed and presented website providing access to extensive resources.

4585 **TechDis** [UK]
www.techdis.ac.uk
TechDis 'aims to be the leading educational advisory service, working across the UK, in the fields of accessibility and inclusion'. The website provides legal information, resources and guides to enhance accessibility and focuses on specific key topics affecting the education sector, such as e-learning, m-learning and developing technologies. The site also provides FAQ and access to an enquiry service.

Portal & task environments

4586 **Inclusive Education** [UK]
www.unesco.org/education/inclusive
Wide-ranging gateway within the UNESCO Education Section, covering concepts, action areas, guidelines; Education for All flagship programme and online materials.

4587 **Young, Gifted and Talented** [UK]
Great Britain. Department for Children, Schools & Families
http://ygt.dcsf.gov.uk
Excellent engaging and colourful gateway managed by the CfBT Education Trust on behalf of the Department.
■ **CfBT Education Trust** One of the top 20 charities in the UK: 'Established 40 years ago CfBT Education Trust now has an annual turnover exceeding £100 million and employs more than 2,000 staff worldwide who support educational reform, teach, advise, research and train. Since we were founded, we have worked in more than 40 countries around the world, including the UK, managing large government contracts and providing education services as well as managing directly a growing number of schools'.

Directories & encyclopedias

4588 **Special education directory** [UK]
2007/8 edn, School Government Publishing, 2007, biennial. £70. ISBN 9780900640865.
Comprehensive listing of special schools in the UK. 'Its detailed indices by special need covering some 1400 special schools and some 3000 mainstream schools with specific special needs units make it an unrivalled reference source for parents and education professionals alike.'

Handbooks & manuals

4589 **Encyclopedia of special education: a reference for the education of children, adolescents, and adults with disabilities and other exceptional individuals**
C.R. Reynolds and E. Fletcher-Janzen, eds   3rd edn, Wiley, 2007. 3 v, $451.20. ISBN 9780471678021.
The major work in the field, an excellent and comprehensive compendium. The 3rd edition has been thoroughly updated to include the latest information about new legislation and guidelines. In addition, this comprehensive resource features school psychology, neuropsychology, reviews of new tests and curricula that have been developed since publication of the second edition in 1999, and new biographies of important figures in special education.

4590 **Exceptional lives: special education in today's schools**
A. Turnbull, H.R. Turnbull and M.L. Wehmeyer   5th edn, Pearson Merrill Prentice Hall, 2007, 528pp. $106.67. ISBN 9780131708693.
Comprehensive handbook, notable for its series of chapters devoted to understanding students with learning disabilities, communication disorders, emotional or behavioral disorders, attention-deficit/hyperactivity disorder, mental retardation, severe and multiple disabilities, autism, physical disabilities and other health impairments, traumatic brain injury, hearing loss and visual impairments, and those who are gifted and talented.

Extended schools manual
S. Blandford   See entry no. 4512

4591 **Making inclusion work**
F. Bowe   Pearson/Merrill/Prentice Hall, 2005, 656pp. $96. ISBN 9780130176035.
16 chapters in six parts: 1. Setting the stage for successful inclusion; 2. Students in the inclusive classroom with higher-incidence disorders; 3. Students in the inclusive classroom with lower-incidence disorders; 4. Teaching in the inclusive classroom; 5. Other aspects of teaching in the inclusive classroom; 6.Content-area instruction.

4592 **Managing special and inclusive education**
S. Rayner   Sage Publications, 2007, 232pp. £22.99. ISBN 9781412918893.
10 chapters in three parts: I. Understanding special education and an inclusion policy: the knowledge context?; II. Inclusive leadership, managing change and networking: the professional learning context? III. Inclusive leadership and managing change: enabling the learning professional.

4593   The Praeger handbook of special education
A.M. Bursztyn, ed.   Praeger, 2007, 199pp. $79.95. ISBN 9780313332623.

Coverage includes history of special education; special education and society; law and special education; specific disabilities; teaching methods and interventions; policies and practices; families and disability; and research in special education.

'The topics are well chosen and the narratives well written. The book would be a great primary or companion text to use in upper-level education and special education courses. Highly recommended. Upper-division undergraduates through practitioner.' (*Choice*)

4594   The RoutledgeFalmer reader in inclusive education
K. Topping and S. Maloney, eds   Routledge, 2005, 263pp. £25.99. ISBN 9780415336659.

Eighteen chapters divided into topic areas, including concepts and contexts; exclusion; gender, race, disability and social class; action in schools; post-school; promoting and managing systemic change.

4595   Teacher's guide to inclusive education: 750 strategies for success: a guide for all educators
P.A. Hammeken   Peytral Publications, 2007, 343pp. $39.95. ISBN 9781890455101.

'This award-winning best-seller will guide you through all areas of inclusive education – from implementation to working with colleagues. The publication includes hundreds of practical, teacher-tested adaptations and modifications conveniently numbered and organized by topic.'

One of a range of publications from this US-based publisher on 'inclusion'.

4596   What successful teachers do in inclusive classrooms: 60 research-based teaching strategies that help special learners succeed
S.J. McNary, N.A. Glasgow and C.D. Hicks   Corwin Press, 2005, 152pp. $25.95. ISBN 9781412906296.

Bridging the gap between theory and practice, this book focuses on extending academic research to classroom practices that address the problems faced by teachers working with special-needs students in inclusive classrooms.

Sport

There has been a tremendous explosion of interest in the subject of sport as an area of academic study. Whereas in previous editions of *Walford* the focus was on the activities themselves, now coverage includes sport and leisure management, sports science and the sport and leisure industries. There is interest in sports psychology, performance and coaching as it relates to professionals and elites, as well as health-related physical activity and recreational participation in sport. Please note that sports medicine was covered in Volume 1 of *The New Walford* and that the general topic of leisure will be covered in Volume 3.

It is impossible to include resources for all sports but the major activities are featured and links can be found from the websites of the more general sports organizations such as Sport England, UK Sport and Sport Canada.

Some sports continue to produce printed reviews of the year or yearbooks but only a small number of these have been included. More up-to-date statistics, results and rules for specific sports can generally be found from the website of the relevant sport's governing body.

Although the internet is the first port of call for many researchers these days, books can provide essential background reading and easier topic exploration. Many publishers' websites provide detailed information about titles available, some featuring excerpts, sample chapters or supporting websites.

Introductions to the subject

4597 Introduction to physical education, fitness and sport
D. Siedentop   6th edn, McGraw-Hill, 2006, 480pp. £35.99. ISBN 9780071107488.
17 chapters organized into five parts: I. Understanding the context of lifespan sport, fitness and physical education; II. Sport; III. Fitness; IV. Physical education; Putting it all together: building a national infrastructure to support physical activity and healthy lifestyles.

4598 Research methods for sports studies
C. Gratton and I. Jones   Routledge, 2003, 304pp. £28.99. ISBN 9780415268783.
Topics covered include conceptual models; qualitative research methods; choosing an appropriate research design; undertaking a literature review; key research methods such as questionnaires, interviews, content analysis and ethnographic studies; analysing data, including an introduction to SPSS, as well as guides to descriptive and inferential statistics; writing a research report; the internet as a research tool.

Dictionaries, thesauri, classifications

4599 The Sage dictionary of sports studies
D. Malcolm   Sage Publications, 2008, 304pp. £19.99. ISBN 9781412907354.
Forthcoming work, with each entry providing 'a basic definition, a guide to research themes and a clear account of the relevance of the concept in understanding sport'.

4600 Sport and physical education: the key concepts
T. Chandler, M. Cronin and W. Vamplew   2nd edn, Routledge, 2007, 266pp. £14.99. ISBN 9780415417471.
A–Z guide written specifically for students of sport studies and physical education and having wide coverage, e.g.: coaching, drug testing, hooliganism, cultural imperialism, economics, gay games, amateurism, extreme sports, exercise physiology, Olympism.

Official & quasi-official bodies

4601 Council of Europe/Conseil de l'Europe: Sport
www.coe.int/t/dg4/sport
Sport section of the CoE (Council of Europe) website contains the European Sport Charter and other reference texts. Promoting 'sport and the social and health benefits which it brings to individuals and to society', topics include sport for all, violence and anti-doping. Browse reference texts by general topic, or CoE sports policy and legal documents by year from 2002 to 2005. Available in English and French.

Department for Culture, Media and Sport
See entry no. 5050

4602 European Non-Governmental Sports Organisation
www.engso.com
Non-profit European sports organization comprising 40 national sports confederations or national Olympic committees, representing 'national sport in its broadest sense'. Policy documents and guidelines; youth section featuring multilingual guidelines; member list and summaries of annual country reports from 2001 to 2005; details of events, development group and European Union working group. Search facility but no site map.

4603 Great Britain. House of Commons, Culture, Media & Sport Committee: Reports and Publications
www.parliament.uk/parliamentary_committees/culture_media_and_sport/culture_media_and_sport_reports_and_publications.cfm
This committee examines the expenditure, administration and policy of the DCMS (Department for Culture, Media and Sport) and its associated public bodies. Links to all documents published by the Committee since 1997, including reports, oral evidence and uncorrected evidence. These are available in full-text online; more recent reports also in PDF format.

4604 United Nations Environment Programme: Sport and Environment
www.unep.org/sport_env
The Sport and Environment pages of the UNEP website feature information on its activities relating to the promotion of environmental awareness and consideration in sports,

including forums and conferences. There are also details of publications and downloadable reports, online exhibitions and video clips. The news centre includes press releases and speeches.

Associations & societies

4605 Central Council of Physical Recreation [UK]
www.ccpr.org.uk
Independent 'umbrella organization for the national governing and representative bodies of sport and recreation in the UK'. Monthly policy updates; government consultation responses; sport and recreation funding information; events. Large number of downloadable publications relevant to sports organizations. Details of members in each division, linked to websites. Equality Trainers Database. Members' area.

■ **The organisation of sport and recreation in the UK** K. Gill and M. Welch   2005. Freely available. http://yorkshiresport.org.uk/ccpr. 'The aim of this CCPR book is to provide sports administrators with information on the organisation of sport, physical recreation and exercise in the UK. It also provides a source of reference for students, the youth services, libraries and the media.'

■ **Smart Sport and Recreation** www.smart-sport.org. CCPR's 'new member support initiative', with guidelines, templates and practical examples covering child protection, corporate governance, equality, finance, human resources, marketing and risk management.

4606 General Association of International Sports Federations
www.agfisonline.com
GAISF (Association Générale des Fédérations Internationales de Sports) brings together over 100 international sports organizations to 'defend worldwide sport, become better informed and to inform' and 'to cooperate together and to coordinate their activities'. Searchable calendar of events, results listings and list of members, linked to websites. Details of publications, news and information about GAISF-related events. Members' intranet. Also in French.

4607 International Association for Sports Information
www.iasi.org
'Worldwide network of information experts, librarians, sports scientists and managers of sports libraries, information and documentation centres', founded in 1960. Information for physical educators, sport scientists and researchers. Details of publications, projects, database search guides and resources, such as bibliographies, publishers, booksellers and web directories. Conference proceedings and a manual for sports information centres. Site available in several languages.

■ **World directory of sports information centres and experts** www.directory-iasi.org. Database of sports libraries, documentation centres and sports collections with details of subject strengths of each institution and areas of sport information expertise. Set up in 2001 by IASI and the IOC (International Olympic Committee). Search by continent, country, name of institution or area of expertise.

4608 International Council of Sport Science & Physical Education
www.icsspe.org
Originally founded in Paris in 1958, the ICSSPE is concerned with 'the promotion and dissemination of results and findings in the field of sport science and their practical application in culture and educational contexts'. Free resources include anti-doping booklet, coaching bibliography by W. D. Gilbert, papers on performance and on the benefits of physical activity and the 1964 ICSPE/UNESCO declaration on sport. Information on projects, research and events.

■ **Directory of sport science** 4th edn2007. $19.95. ISSN 17293227. www.icsspe.org/portal/index.php?w=0&wert=3500&z=3&sta=0 [DESCRIPTION]. Updated to include details of 19 sport science disciplines, plus practical details of how students can study in the different fields. Formerly known as *Vade Mecum*. Available as CD-ROM.

4609 International Sport & Culture Association
www.isca-web.org
Created in 1995 as an 'alternative to the increasingly performance-based attitude of the international sports federations'. Over 130 listed member organizations (mainly non-governmental) across four continents. Information about supporting organizations and sections for young people, coaches and leaders, including policy statements. Also news, events and library with articles, newsletter and ISCA newsletter. Available in English, French and Spanish.

4610 Scottish Sports Association
www.scottishsportsassociation.org.uk
Established in 1983, the SSA represents the interests of over 70 sports governing bodies in Scotland. Details of consultations with the Scottish parliament, calendar of events, news, details of forums and link to SportScotland list of governing bodies.

4611 Sport & Recreation Information Group [UK]
www.sprig.org.uk
An organization promoting information sources relating to leisure, tourism, sport, recreation and hospitality aimed at publishers, academics, students, practitioners and professionals in libraries and information services. Details of events, publications and awards. Access to the SPRIG bulletin and to most conference presentations for members only.

■ **Archives of LIS-Sprig@jiscmail.ac.uk: leisure, tourism and sport information sources** www.jiscmail.ac.uk/lists/LIS-SPRIG.html. SPRIG e-mail discussion list, hosted by JISCmail. Archives date back to November 1999.

■ **How To Find Out Guides** www.sprig.org.uk/htfo/htfoindex.html. Online versions of the SPRIG printed guides, in the process of being updated. Topics covered include sports history, sports medicine, sports physiotherapy, leisure, sports nutrition, physical education, statistics and sport in general.

Portal & task environments

4612 Australian Institute of Sport
www.ais.org.au
Elite sports training institution with comprehensive website giving details of individual sports programmes (35 programmes in 26 sports) and facilities for athletes and coaches. Sections on clinical services, including psychology and physical therapies and sports sciences (biomechanics, physiology and nutrition). Nutrition section covers information of interest to elites, recreational athletes and the general public.

■ **AIS Applied Research Centre publications** www.ais.org.au/research/rpphome.asp. Sub-set of the NSIC (National Sport

Information Centre) Catalogue, listing over 2000 publications by AIS researchers since 1981. Publications and presentations from biomechanics, medicine, nutrition, physiology, physiotherapy and psychology. Search by department, author, sport or topic.

- **AIS sports nutrition** www.ais.org.au/nutrition. Factsheets on wide range of nutritional issues including hot topics in sports nutrition, nutrition for particular sports and dietary supplements, as well as career guidance, travel factsheets, recipe database and abstracts of nutrition research. Selected chapters from publications by AIS staff are available full-text.

4613 Australian Sports Commission
www.ausport.gov.au

'Australia's primary national sports administration and advisory agency', coordinating sport from grassroots level to elites. Extensive website: information for clubs, coaches, officials, sports scientists, sports medics, athletes, students, teachers and the public. Details of development programmes and policy issues such as disability, ethics, schools and women. Information on playing specific sports and topics in sport. Focus on Australian resources; some international material. Search by keyword or browse broad topics.

- **National Sport Information Centre** www.ausport.gov.au/nsic. 'Australia's premier information resource centre for sport and its related disciplines'. Access to image library of 25,000 images; full-text archive; databases of Australian events, courses and libraries; online catalogue and document delivery service (chargeable).
- **SportScan** www.ausport.gov.au/nsic/sportscan. Freely available, selective database of sport science, coaching and administration articles from key overseas journals published since the mid-1980s. Priced document delivery service available; users can register for free monthly e-mail updates. Browse subject headings or search by keyword, using SIRC thesaurus headings. Formerly known as Sports Journal Update.

4614 Biz/Ed: Leisure, Sport and Recreation
www.bized.co.uk/learn/leisure

Service of Thomson Learning, the educational publisher. Although aimed primarily at business and economics students, hosts a range of datasets and has learning materials section with worksheets, background information, presentations and study skills. Sport, leisure and recreation topics are suitable for BTEC and undergraduate levels (or their equivalents), unless otherwise specified.

- **At your leisure archive** www.bized.co.uk/current/leisure. Archive of topical issues, currently 2004 onwards. Includes student tasks and activitities.

4615 Hospitality, Leisure, Sport & Tourism Network [UK]
www.heacademy.ac.uk/hlst

One of 24 subject centres aiming to promote high quality learning and teaching practice in UK higher education. Features news, events, details of projects and extensive resources section, including 'Guide to current practice', 'Baseline statement', LINK newsletters, electronic journal, resources guides, case studies, research gateway and catalogue of new publications. Visual site map.

- **Catalogue of new publications**
www.heacademy.ac.uk/hlst/resources/newpublications. Books listed by author and title. Hyperlink to more information such as a general description, ISBN number, price and publisher. Useful list of publishers.
- **The Research Gateway**
www.heacademy.ac.uk/hlst/resources/researchgateway. An 'online resource to support student research project work in Hospitality, Leisure, Sport and Tourism', created by Tess Kay and Leigh Robinson from Loughborough University.

- **Resource guides** www.heacademy.ac.uk/hlst/resources/guides. 'Intended to provide a compact, but essential guide to the texts, journals, websites and other resources in specific areas that may be covered within hospitality, leisure, sport and tourism programmes.' Read on screen to use hyperlinks, or print off for reference.
- **Journal of Hospitality, Leisure, Sport and Tourism Education** 2002–, 2 p.a. Freely available. ISSN 14738376. www.heacademy.ac.uk/hlst/resources/johlste. Peer-reviewed, international e-journal of the HLST Network. JoHLSTE 'aims to promote, enhance and disseminate research, good practice and innovation in all aspects of education in the hospitality, leisure, sport and tourism subject areas'.

4616 Human Kinetics
www.humankinetics.com

More than simply a publisher's website. Details materials on all aspects of physical activity, the HK website covers books, journals, software, videos and distance education programmes; sections for students, teachers and distance learners. Ancillary materials for new higher education textbooks, online study guides, resources for teachers and online education centre. Search for products, journal titles or journal articles, plus browse by subject feature.

- **Human Kinetics journals: search journals**
www.humankinetics.com/products/journals/searchAbstracts.cfm. Useful facility to search all, selected or individual journal titles published by Human Kinetics, by article title, keyword, abstract or author. Abstracts freely available; option to purchase full-text articles for non-subscribers.
- **UKPE.HumanKinetics.com** http://ukpe.humankinetics.com. One of several HK programmes, developed in conjunction with the Youth Sport Trust. Lesson plans and tips, annotated links and suggested booklists for UK sports colleges.

4617 International Platform on Sport and Development
Swiss Academy for Development
www.sportanddev.org

Information resource centre focusing on disability, economic development, gender, social cohesion and trauma. Extensive collection of documents and easy-to-follow site map. Includes major UN and other official reports, conference proceedings, research and background reports. Search resources by keyword or type; projects by keyword, organization, target group or subject, as well as country or region.

4618 Singapore Sports Council
www.ssc.gov.sg

Details of services for Singapore residents and athletes, covering participation, excellence and industry. Information and Resources section contains advice on doping control, directory of associations and facilities, financial information relating to sports charities (institutions of a public character) and best-practice guidance.

- **SSC Sports Museum** www.sportsmuseum.ssc.gov.sg. One of a huge number of sports museum and halls of fame sites on the internet, which vary in the amount of information offered. Contains sections on history, traditional games and the Olympics, as well as visitor information, search facility and interactive games, including ping-pong.

4619 Sport & Recreation New Zealand
www.sparc.org.nz

Government body responsible for sport and recreation in New Zealand. Comprehensive website with detailed site map. Sections for academics, athletes, coaches, councils, doctors, employers, national sport organizations, parents, patients, regional sports trusts, researchers, sports clubs, students, teachers and others. Information on sport development, elite sport and research and policy, including the New Zealand Sport and Physical Activity Survey.

- **SPARC Facts 97–01** www.sparc.org.nz/research-policy/research-/sparc-facts-97-01. Gathered from the NZ Sport and Physical Activity Surveys from 1997 to 2001: analysed to provide statistics and information on participation by age, gender, demography, ethnicity and sport.
- **New Zealand Academy of Sport** www.sparc.org.nz/elite-sport. Details of the high-performance strategy, coaches, athletes and support teams.

4620 Sport & Recreation South Africa
www.srsa.gov.za

National governmental department responsible for sport and recreation in South Africa, replacing the South African Sports Commission. Website divided into sport in South Africa, the SRSA and its activities and the Sport Atlas, an A–Z listing of sports. Archives of news, features and publications. Some full-text documents, web index and search facility.

- **Knowledge Base** www.srsa.gov.za/KnowledgeBase.asp. A 'library of information on topics of common interest to the sporting fraternity' with 'basic information, website links, documents to download, and also our own experience from answering thousands of queries each year about sport in South Africa'.
- **SportLit** www.srsa.gov.za/Library.asp. 'Online database of all the documents held in the SRSA documentation centre in Pretoria, South Africa. It consists of about 20,000 entries ranging from scientific articles to popular magazines, conference material, videos, CDs and many others.' E-mail request facility; no details of charges.

4621 Sport Canada
www.pch.gc.ca/sportcanada

Part of Department of Canadian Heritage, with three divisions: Major games and hosting; Sport policy; Sport programs. Navigate by right-hand menu rather than left-hand departmental menu. Official languages corner, details of funding programmes and research. 'Key sport links', major events schedule to 2012, news and extensive collection of downloadable documents covering policy, legislation, research, participation and other topics. Also available in French.

- **Sport Lexicon** www.pch.gc.ca/progs/sc/lex/index_e.cfm. Covers 35 summer sports, individually listed in English and French. Originally compiled in 1999.

4622 Sport England
www.sportengland.org

Brand name of the English Sports Council and government body responsible for the development of community sport in England. Quite complex website aimed largely at sports clubs, students, local authorities and schools. Search or browse; extensive A to Z site index. Regional information, funding and participation. 'Resources' feature research, planning, links and downloadable reports. 'News and Media' includes information on funding priority sports.

- **Sport England: courses** www.sportengland.org/courses. Links to UK sports courses. Search by institution, subject, course type, suggested career path or location.
- **Active Places** www.activeplaces.com. Database of sports facilities in England. Search via interactive map, postcode, distance or facility type.

4623 Sport Information Resource Centre
www.sirc.ca

Canadian resource centre providing international sport-related research, covering over 62 languages and dating back to 1800. Freely available resources to download on fitness, injuries, nutrition and sport administration, as well as the SIRC conference calendar, sports jobs, publisher information, a periodical listing and SportQuest database. SIRC produces the fee-based database, SportDiscus.

- **Online resources** www.sirc.ca/online_resources. Sample articles from the SIRC Sport Library on topics including nutrition, medicine and youth sports.
- **SIRCThesaurus** 6th edn. $95.00 (online). www.sirc.ca/products/sircthesaurus [FEE-BASED]. The 'world's most comprehensive collection of controlled sport terminology. encourages users around the world to share a standard sport vocabulary'. Terms used in SportDiscus database. Available in printed form, CD-ROM or online; fees vary.
- **SportQuest** www.sirc.ca/online_resources/sportquest.cfm. Extensive database containing links to websites, which can be searched by keyword or browsed by sport, sports topic (divided into general, sport science or special interest) or non-sport-specific topic. Advanced search facility.

4624 Sport Northern Ireland
www.sportni.net

Formerly Sports Council for Northern Ireland. Aims to develop 'sport from grass-roots to elite standard'. Details of sports development activities, funding programmes and links to NI governing bodies of sports. Publications include downloadable reports, presentations and research papers. Site also features corporate plan, newsletter, *SportsZone* magazine and link to Active Places NI.

- **Sport Northern Ireland Research Library** www.sportni.net/research. Downloadable research documents, reports, studies and surveys relating to sports issues, plus archive on a wide range of topics.

4625 Sports Council for Wales
www.sports-council-wales.org.uk

Responsible for 'developing and promoting sport and active lifestyles in Wales'. Focus on workplace, communities and performance; A to Z of sports and of Welsh town facilities. Searchable publications database of downloadable factsheets, research papers, sport profiles, funding and corporate publications. Print copies on request. Downloadable catalogue of current publications, some freely available plus carriage (limit 20 items). Annotated links. Also available in Welsh.

- **Framework for the development of sport and physical activity** www.sports-council-wales.org.uk/12201.file.dld. Produced by SCW in 2005 in response to the Welsh Assembly's strategy document 'Climbing Higher'.

4626 Sportscotland
www.sportscotland.org.uk

National agency for sport in Scotland. Directory of governing bodies with associated links. Search or browse extensive resource library of largely downloadable SportScotland publications. Policy and strategy documents, careers information, news, events, sport profiles and squad profiles. Expandable site map and search facility.

- **Child protection in sport** www.childprotectioninsport.org.uk. Service of SportScotland and CHILDREN 1st to provide 'advice, training and resources to help sports organisations to keep children safe in and through sport'. Case studies, sample policy and procedures documents, downloadable newsletters, links and details of publications for download or purchase.

Discovering print & electronic resources

4627 Intute: social sciences: sport and leisure practice
www.intute.ac.uk/socialsciences/sport
Free online service providing access to the best web resources for education and research, aimed at UK higher and further education. Created by network of UK universities and partners whose subject specialists select, describe and evaluate websites in the database. Intute: Social Sciences was formed from two hubs of the former RDN (Resource Discovery Network), Altis and SOSIG.
- **Internet for Leisure, Sport and Recreation**
  www.vts.intute.ac.uk/tutorial/sport. One of over 65 free online tutorials provided by the Virtual Training Suite on a wide range of subject areas to improve internet literacy skills.

4628 Know the Game series: Sports
A. & C. Black.
www.acblack.com
A. & C. Black publishes large number of books on sport and leisure, including the established *Know the game* series covering individual activities. Title descriptions, bibliographical details plus the option to purchase online. Subject area offers related e-mail newsletter.

4629 Leisure Tourism Database
www.leisuretourism.com [FEE-BASED]
Web-based service produced by CABI Publishing providing access to leisure, recreation, tourism and hospitality research. Over 78,000 research abstracts from over 400 publications. Direct linkage to institutional full-text holdings or single-article purchase possible. Academic research, industry reports and books, reviews and news. Institutional subscription required.
- **Leisure, Recreation and Tourism Abstracts** CABI Publishing, 1976–, qtrly. £315.00 personal [2007]. ISSN 02611392. www.cabi.org/AbstractDatabases.asp?SubjectArea=&PID=5 [DESCRIPTION]. A 'printed abstracts database of internationally published research in leisure, tourism, recreation, hospitality, sport and the cultural industries'. Leisure Tourism Database is an enhanced online version of this.

4630 Routledge Sport and Leisure Studies
www.routledge.com/sport
Part of the Routledge publisher's website providing details of academic and professional texts in sport and exercise science, sport studies, leisure and recreation management, coaching, physical education and research methods. Use the left-hand menu for textbooks, series, highlights and journals or to access downloadable catalogues. Subscribe to eUpdates, free contents-alerting service. Part of the Taylor & Francis Group.

4631 Scholarly Sport Sites
www.ucalgary.ca/lib-old/ssportsite
Subject directory of 'websites which will assist the serious sports researcher, kinesiology librarian, sport information specialist, college/university student and faculty'. Covers archives, organizations, standards, events, databases, full-text material, libraries, photographs, publishers and serials. Developed by Gretchen Ghent from the University of Calgary in association with NASLIN and IASI.
- **NASLINE** 1993–, 2 p.a. Free to download. www.naslin.org/nasline.html. North American Sport Library Network newsletter. Available online 1995 onwards. Covers 'forthcoming NASLIN conferences ... full-text papers and documents available online, new sport-related websites, and a large section of bibliographic citations to recent publications including monographs, conference proceedings and new serials'.

4632 Sport and leisure research on disc [UK]
University of Sheffield
www.shef.ac.uk/library/cdfiles/sport.html [DESCRIPTION]
Database covering UK dissertations and theses at doctorate and master's level. Approximately 1000 titles covering sport- and leisure-related topics with contributions from 18 institutions. Funded initially by the English Sports Council and Sheffield University Library, now self-financing. Note that access is restricted to staff and students registered at the University. Local user guide publicly available.
- **Sport and leisure research on disc: a user guide NIS 76** www.shef.ac.uk/library/libdocs/nis76.pdf.

4633 Sport, leisure and tourism information sources: a guide for researchers
M. Scarrott Butterworth-Heinemann, 1999, 267pp. £39.99. ISBN 9780750638647.
Still-useful text with coverage of a wide range of resources: the internet; libraries; journals; bibliographies, abstracts and indexes; statistics and market research; European Union information; sport, leisure and tourism organizations.

4634 SportDiscus
EBSCO Publishing. Now an EBSCOhost Research Database.
www.sirc.ca/products/sportdiscus.cfm [FEE-BASED]
Subscription-based database provided by SIRC in Canada, covering sport, health, fitness and sports medicine, plus related disciplines. More than 700,000 references and abstracts from periodicals, books, e-journals, conference proceedings, dissertations and websites. Coverage back to 1800, including over 20,000 theses and dissertations. Institutions can link journal subscriptions to full-text articles; individual articles available via the SIRC Document Delivery Service. Free trial option.
- **A basic guide to searching SportDiscus on EBSCO** www.iasi.org/pdf/BriefEBSCOSearchGuideSPORTDiscus.pdf. Two-page guidance sheet from IASI.
- **SportDiscus with full text: database coverage list** www.epnet.com/titleLists/s4-coverage.pdf. Alphabetical list of titles covered by SportDiscus database. Also in Excel and HTML formats.

4635 Sports Publishing [USA]
www.sportspublishingllc.com
US-based publisher specializing in popular American sports. Browse or search professional American football, baseball, basketball and hockey teams, US colleges, biographies of sports personalities or popular sports.

Digital data, image & text collections

4636 HowStuffWorks: Sports
http://entertainment.howstuffworks.com/sports-channel.htm
Founded by Professor Marshall Brain in 1998. Huge collection of articles explaining 'how the world actually works' for the general public. Sport is covered as part of Entertainment. Clear explanations followed by links to related articles and websites. Growing number of video clips.

4637 Pandora, Australia's web archive: sports and recreation
http://pandora.nla.gov.au/subject/25
Archive of online materials and websites 'about Australia, ... by an Australian author on a subject of ... significance and relevance to Australia, or ... by an Australian author of recognized authority', established initially in 1996 by the National Library of Australia. Sub-sections on Olympic Games, Paralympic Games and sporting personalities, plus other sports-related material.

Directories & encyclopedias

4638 Encyclopedia of international sports studies
R. Bartlett, C. Gratton and C. Rolf, eds   Routledge, 2006, 1584pp. 3 v., £360. ISBN 9780415277136.
A–Z arrangement. Principal entries of 3000 words covering disciplinary areas, e.g. sports economics, sports history; large informational entries of 1200 words on broad topics, e.g. resistance training, diagnosis of sports injuries; medium informational entries of 600 words on more specific topics, e.g. cross-training, projectile motion; small entries of 300 words comprising entries on narrower topics and small overviews directing the reader onwards.

4639 Encyclopedia of leisure and outdoor recreation
J. Jenkins and J.J. Pigram   Routledge, 2003, 595pp. £112. ISBN 9780415252263.
A–Z arrangement with comprehensive coverage, examples of entries being: Aborigines; back-country; back-packing; barriers; camping; Canada Land Inventory (CLI); capability; dance; day trip; decentralization; decision making.

4640 Encyclopedia of world sport: from ancient times to the present
D. Levinson and K. Christensen, eds   ABC-CLIO, 1997. 3 v., $345. ISBN 9781576076606.
www.abc-clio.com [FEE-BASED]
250 entries arranged A–Z, each having from 500 to 8000 words and each with a bibliography. Good cross-referencing. 'This encyclopedia will be of great value to students and will also appeal to sports-minded leisure readers. The emphasis on the history and societal influence of athletics will keep the set from quickly becoming dated as is often the case with sports reference books that rely heavily on statistics, scores, and records' (*School Library Journal*)

4641 ESPN sports almanac: the definitive sports reference book
G. Brown and M. Morrison   Hyperion, 2007, 976pp. $12.99. ISBN 9781933060163.
'If one book could settle every heated sports argument, this would be it. From record holders to champions, auto racing to the Iditarod, ballparks, business news and Who's Who to the dearly departed athletes of the year past, the *ESPN sports almanac* serves up so much vital information at such a rapid clip: hundreds of photos, thousands of tables, countless facts and figures, plus expert analysis from ESPN's most popular personalities ...'

4642 Sports illustrated almanac
Sports Illustrated Books, 2006, annual, 864pp. $12.99. ISBN 9781933405469.
http://sportsillustrated.cnn.com [COMPANION]

A leading US-based annual with comprehensive coverage of all sports.

Handbooks & manuals

4643 Researching leisure, sport and tourism: the essential guide
J.A. Long   Sage Publications, 2007, 234pp. £19.99. ISBN 9780761944546.
'Comprehensive and informative book written especially for new and inexperienced researchers in the fields of leisure, sport and tourism, both full-time students and people in employment having to conduct their own research or make use of other people's research. Unlike generic research texts that do not "speak" to people in this field, this richly flavoured book immediately engages the reader by using subject-specific examples and explaining the central methodological issues in straightforward terms ...'

Keeping up to date

4644 BBC sport
http://news.bbc.co.uk/sport
Up-to-date news and statistics on major sports, including football, motor sport and cricket, plus disability sport and the Olympics. Links to video/audio feeds, television/radio schedules, scores and fixtures and 606, the Five Live debate section. Calendar, weather, sport editors' blog and link to Health and Fitness pages. Optional international version.
 ■ **Sport Academy** http://news.bbc.co.uk/sport1/hi/academy. Features tips, guides and information on skills and rules for participants in a range of sports.

Coaching & Performance
drugs in sport • sports physiology • training

Introductions to the subject

4645 Beginning athletics: what to teach and coach
C. Johnson   Neuff Athletic Equipment, 2004, 150pp. Illustrated by Kirsty Gunter, £19.90. ISBN 9780954684600.
Well regarded introduction.

4646 The coaching process
L. Kidman and S. Hanrahan   2nd edn, Thomson Learning Australia, 2004, 232pp. AUS$49.95. ISBN 9780864694614.
Comprehensive text, structured in six sections: I. Introduction (1. Successful coaching; 2. Developing a coaching philosophy); II. Athlete development (3. Your athletes); III. The training session (4. Managing athletes; 5. Creating a positive environment; 6. Instructional techniques; 7. Enhancing skill and technique; 8. Enhancing performance with mental skills); IV. Competition (9. Coaching during competitions); V. Factors influencing coaching (10. Parents; 11. The balancing act); VI. Continuing to develop as a coach (12. What now?).

4647 Drugs in sport
D.R. Mottram   4th edn, Routledge, 2005, 420pp. £27.99. ISBN 9780415375641.
Contents are: 1. An introduction to drugs and their use in

sport; 2. Drug use and abuse in sport; 3. Central nervous system stimulants; 4. WADA regulations in relation to drugs used in the treatment of respiratory tract disorders; 5. Androgenic anabolic steroids; 6. Peptide and glycoprotein hormones and sport; 7. Blood boosting and sport; 8. Drug treatment of inflammation in sports injuries; 9. Alcohol, anti-anxiety drugs and sport; 10. Creatine; 11. Doping control and sport; 12. Prevalence of drug misuse in sport.

4648 Dying to win: doping in sport and the development of anti-doping policy
B. Houlihan   2nd edn, 2002, 247pp. Published in France, £17.95. ISBN 9789287146854.

'Doping in the sports world is taking on dramatic proportions. Today, doping may make the difference which could win an athlete a gold medal, lucrative sponsorship and global adulation. But doping undermines the integrity of sport and is a real danger to the health of thousands of athletes. Drug abuse in sport has now become an acute international problem.'

4649 Genetically modified athletes: biomedical ethics, gene doping and sport
A. Miah   Routledge, 2004, 208pp. £26.99. ISBN 9780415298803. www.gmathletes.net [COMPANION]

15 chapters in five sections: 1. Anti-doping and performance enhancement; 2. From drugs to genes: conceptual links and differences; 3. The moral status of genetic modification in sport; 4. Re-defining ethical approaches to performance enhancement in sport; 5. Human rights and legal implications.

'Miah's book is a thought-provoking read that raises important questions about sport and society. It is a truly boundary-crossing piece of work, one within which students and scholars in a number of disciplines, from sociology and law to sports studies, will find much material to mine.' (*Times Higher Education Supplement*)

4650 In pursuit of excellence: a student guide to elite sports development
M. Hill   new edn, Routledge, 2007, 121pp. £22.99. ISBN 9780415423540.

Offers new students a comprehensive introduction to the phenomenon of the pursuit of excellence in sport.

4651 Physiology and performance
4th edn, Sports Coach UK, 2003, 166pp. £9.99. www.sportscoachuk.org [COMPANION]

An easy-to-read introduction to fitness and how the body works to achieve improved strength, speed and flexibility.

4652 Sport mechanics for coaches
G. Carr; American Sport Education Program   2nd edn, Human Kinetics, 2003, 237pp. $34. ISBN 9780736039727.

'An acute understanding of sport mechanics can mean the difference between average and elite sport performance. Without it, teachers, coaches and performers are seriously disadvantaged in selecting the best techniques to use, observing faults and identifying their causes and devising ways to make corrections. Yet many coaches and athletes have avoided studying sport mechanics because they're intimidated by the scientific terminology and mathematics traditionally associated with the subject …'

4653 Sports coaching concepts: a framework for coaches' behaviour
J. Lyle   Routledge, 2002, 343pp. £27.99. ISBN 9780415261586.

Contents: A. What is coaching about? (1. The historical setting; 2. Developing a conceptual framework; 3. Defining the coaching process; 4. The role of the coach); B. How do coaches behave? (5. Modelling the coaching process; 6. Coaching practice); C. Coaching as an interpersonal relationship (7. A question of style and philosophy; 8. A humanistic approach); D. Coaching in its social context (9. Motives and recruitment into coaching; 10. Where are the women coaches?; 11. Ethics and the sport coach); E. How do we evaluate coaching? (12. Coaching effectiveness; 13. Coach education and the future).

4654 Sports training principles
F. Dick   5th edn, A. & C. Black, 2007, 400pp. £24.99. ISBN 9780713682786.

Covers: anatomy and basic biomechanics; energy production systems; psychology, learning procedures and technical training; performance components – strength, speed, endurance and mobility; training cycles, periodization, adaptation to external loading and coaching methods.

4655 Successful coaching
R. Martens   3rd edn, Human Kinetics, 2004, 509pp. $39.95. ISBN 9780736040129.

Developing your coaching philosophy; Determining your coaching objectives; Selecting your coaching style; Coaching for character; Coaching diverse athletes; Communicating with your athletes; Motivating your athletes; Managing your athletes' behavior; Coaching the games approach way; Teaching technical skills; Teaching tactical skills; Planning for teaching; Training basics; Training for energy fitness; Training for muscular fitness; Fueling your athletes; Battling drugs; Managing your team; Managing relationships; Managing risk.

Official & quasi-official bodies

4656 English Institute of Sport
www.eis2win.co.uk

EIS fronts a nationwide network of training facilities and support services for world-class athletes in the UK. Details of UK regional centres and information on nutrition, physiotherapy, psychology, strength and conditioning, biomechanics and other aspects of sports science and medicine. Search or browse by sport or region.

- **Scottish Institute of Sport** www.sisport.com. Scottish equivalent of EIS, featuring a virtual athlete, athlete zone and series of case studies, as well as details of regional centres, services and activities.
- **Sports Institute Northern Ireland** www.sini.co.uk. Northern Irish equivalent of EIS. Sections on athletics, rugby, hockey and Gaelic football include athlete profiles and entry standards. Extensive collection of articles on Gaelic football, plus strength and conditioning, details of services and athlete tools such as planners and CV guidance.
- **Welsh Institute of Sport** www.welsh-institute-sport.co.uk. National Sports Centre for Wales, providing support for recreational athletes and those with disabilities but with a primary focus on elite athletes. Useful collection of links to Welsh sports clubs and governing bodies. Site available in English and Welsh.

4657 UK Sport
www.uksport.gov.uk

UK government agency aiming to 'work in partnership to

lead sport in the UK to world-class success'. Manages public investment in sport and distributes National Lottery funds. Encourages best practice and ethical, drug-free sport; supports major events. Sections on standards, development and investing in sport and events; news, links to national governing bodies and international federations; video lounge. Large number of full-text reports and policy documents for download. ReadSpeaker facility.

- **Major sports events: the guide**
  www.uksport.gov.uk/pages/major_sports_event_the_guide. An 'invaluable resource for those contemplating staging an event', updated in February 2005. Downloadable in sections.

4658 World Anti-Doping Agency
www.wada-ama.org

International independent organization established in 1999 to 'promote, coordinate and monitor the fight against doping in sport in all its forms'. Materials for athletes and anti-doping organizations, quiz, glossary and digital library of relevant publications. Copies of the Copenhagen Declaration on Anti-Doping in Sport from 2003 downloadable in English and Spanish. Site available in French.

- **Prohibited List** www.wada-ama.org/en/prohibitedlist.ch2. An international standard identifying 'substances and methods' prohibited within competitions, outside competitions and in particular in sports. Updated annually and first published in 1963.
- **World Anti-Doping Code** www.wada-ama.org/en/dynamic.ch2?pageCategory.id=582. WADA coordinated the development and implementation of the World Anti-Doping Code, a 'framework for harmonized anti-doping policies, rules, and regulations within sport organizations and among public authorities'.

Portal & task environments

4659 100% ME
UK Sport
www.100percentme.co.uk

Athlete-centred education programme provided by UK Sport to promote drug-free sport among UK sporting community. Details of the National Anti-Doping Programme, implementation of the Prohibited List, Therapeutic Use Exemption (TUE) and supplements in sport. Information for national governing bodies, schools and athletes. Video clips, downloadable factsheets and other documents. Anti-doping pack for purchase.

- **100% ME: it's what's inside that counts** 98pp.
  www.100percentme.co.uk/store/1130347619.853.pdf. Handy summary of information available for athletes.

4660 Coaches' Information Service
www.coachesinfo.com

Sports science information service for coaches developed in conjunction with ISBS (International Society of Biomechanics in Sport) and the University of Edinburgh. Browse by sport or general coaching topic, or search by keyword or title. Most recent and popular articles, together with latest news, highlighted. Free access to abstracts and online articles of varying lengths. Site map lists all articles and section editor biographies.

4661 National Strength & Conditioning Association [USA]
www.nsca-lift.org

US organization for science and industry professionals aiming to 'support and disseminate research-based

knowledge and its practical application to improve athlete performance and fitness'. Freely available resources include summaries of NSCA position statements; information on anabolic steroid abuse; searchable database of trainers; registry of coaches and NSCA's *Performance Training Journal*. Members' area. Training videos and podcasts.

- **Journal of Strength and Conditioning Research** 1987–, qtrly. $150 international institutions [2006]. ISSN 10648011. http://nsca.allenpress.com/nscaonline/?request=get-moreinfo&issn=1533-4287. Online ISSN 15334287. Search issues from 1987 onwards or browse available issues from left-hand menu by author or keyword. Abstracts freely available but full-text access is for subscribers or on a pay-per-view basis.
- **Strength and Conditioning Journal** 1979–, bi-monthly. $150 international institutions [2006]. ISSN 15241602. http://nsca.allenpress.com/nscaonline/?request=get-moreinfo&issn=1533-4295. Online ISSN 15334295. Search issues under its various titles from 1979 onwards or browse via left-hand menu by keyword (1999 onwards) or author. Other details as for *Journal of Strength and Conditioning Research*.

4662 Sports Coach
www.brianmac.co.uk

Website of UK athletics coach Brian Mackenzie. Articles and information for athletes and coaches on fitness training, sport science, coaching and specific sports. Browse long left-hand menu or search by keyword. A–Z topic listing. 'Library Index' groups articles under general coaching or training issues, sport-specific articles and topic-related literature reviews. Sample training programmes; newsletter. Details of Peak Performance publications.

4663 Sports Coach UK
www.sportscoachuk.org

Formerly the National Coaching Foundation, Sports Coach UK has been tasked to lead the development and implementation of the UK Coaching Framework. Details of progress so far; coaches' learning zone featuring factsheets and other resources; coach development; events, news and research section with details of projects and publications.

- **Coaching Research Database**
  www.sportscoachuk.org/research/database. Developed by Sports Coach UK, supported by the AAASP and BASES coaching iInterest groups. Details of books, journal articles, conference papers, reports and theses dating back to 1989.

Discovering print & electronic resources

4664 An annotated bibliography and analysis of coaching science
W.D. Gilbert   AAHPERD, 2002, 196pp. Free to download.
www.aahperd.org/Research/pdf_files/grantees_coaching_science.pdf

Online annotated bibliography and analysis of published research on coaching science covering English-language research published in scientific journals between 1970 and 2001. Over 1100 papers reviewed; 611 included. Details of research methodology and summary of data and coaching trends. Alphabetical list of authors; subject index subdivided into aspects of behaviour, cognition, demographics, development and assessment.

Also available from the ICSSPE website at www.icsspe.org/portal/download/pdf/bibliography.pdf

4665 Coaching Science Abstracts
1995–, 6 p.a. CD-ROM version available for purchase ($54.99 plus $10.00 outside US).
http://coachsci.sdsu.edu
Online abstracting and indexing service for sports coaches and others interested in applied sport science, promoting evidence-based research. Originate from personal files of Dr Brent S. Rushall from San Diego State University. Contain bibliographic details and link to summaries of papers. Individual issues usually based on particular theme; short introduction. Browse or use keyword search facility.

4666 Coachwise 1st4sport
www.1st4sport.com
Part of Coachwise Ltd, trading arm of Sports Coach UK. Specialist publisher and supplier with online and mail order facility selling books, videos, DVDs, coaching aids, training tools and sports-related software. Browse by individual sports or subject area; search by keyword or advanced search. Advice from sports experts and reading room with extracts from a range of books.

Digital data, image & text collections

4667 Drug Information Database
www.didglobal.com
Searchable database of UK-, Asian- or Canadian-licensed pharmaceutical and over-the-counter medicinal products prohibited, not prohibited or prohibited in particular sports by WADA. Project partners UK Sport and CCES. Glossary, search help, FAQ, useful links and advice on checking medication. Acceptance of terms and conditions required. Note no multiple location search. Also available in French.

Handbooks & manuals

4668 Better coaching: advanced coach's manual
F.S. Pyke   2nd edn, Human Kinetics, 2001, 264pp. $29. ISBN 9780736041133.
'*Better coaching* provides updated information on the sport sciences, including anatomy, physiology, psychology, biomechanics and skill acquisition, which are vital for coaches in a range of sports. It features practical guidelines to develop athletes' endurance, speed, strength, power and flexibility and also uses of a range of case studies, examples and anecdotes to de-mystify some of the more technical sports science information. Coaching tips at the end of each chapter summarize key messages from each chapter.'

4669 Drugs and doping in sport: socio-legal perspectives
J. O'Leary   Routledge, 2001, 320pp. £44.95. ISBN 9781859416624.
'*Drugs and doping in sport* brings together work from leading academics, practitioners and administrators, analyses contemporary socio-legal and political themes related to doping in sport. It provides a challenging and often controversial view of doping issues and confronts political and legal orthodoxy, supplying the reader with a unique insight into this fascinating area of academic study.'

4670 Notational analysis of sport: systems for better coaching and performance in sport
M. Hughes and I. Franks, eds   2nd edn, Routledge, 2004, 304pp. £31.99. ISBN 9780415290050.
'Notational analysis is used by coaches and sport scientists to gather objective data on the performance of athletes. Tactics, technique, individual athlete movement and work-rate can all be analysed, enabling coaches and athletes to learn more about performance and gain a competitive advantage.
'Systems for notational analysis are becoming increasingly sophisticated, reflecting the demands of coaches and scientists, as well as improvements in technology. This new edition is updated with information about the latest technology and research in notational analysis. There's also practical guidance for constructing notational systems for any sport and relating data to real-life performance and coaching.'

4671 Sports coaching cultures: from practice to theory
R.L. Jones, K. Armour and P. Potrac   Routledge, 2004, 184pp. £26.99. ISBN 9780415328524.
'Responding to the fast growing subject in academic sports departments, this groundbreaking new coaching studies text offers a view that focuses the coach as a person and the coaching practice as a complex social encounter. Unlike existing titles in the field which look at coaching as a science, this book examines the personalities, histories, relationships and individual styles of eight coaches at the top of their profession.'

4672 The successful coach: guidelines for coaching practice
P. Crisfield, P. Cabral and F. Carpenter   Sports Coach UK, 2003, 90pp. £9.99.
Chapters are: 1. The coach at work; 2. Planning coaching programmes and sessions; 3. Conducting coaching sessions; 4. Evaluating performance; 5. Your responsibilities and liabilities.

4673 Understanding sports coaching: the social, cultural and pedagogical foundations of coaching practice
T.G. Cassidy, R.L. Jones and P. Potrac   Routledge, 2004, 213pp. 2008 edn announced, £27.99. ISBN 9780415307406.
Four sections: Section 1: 1. Reflection; 2. Coaching methods; 3. Providing feedback to athletes; 4. Quality in coaching; 5. Developing a coaching philosophy. Section 2: 6. Understanding the learning process; 7. 'Developing' athletes; 8. Understanding athletes' motivation; 9. Understanding athletes' identities. Section 3: 10. Examining coaches' content knowledge; 11. Assessing athletes' understanding; 12. Coaching athletes with a disability: exploring issues of content. Section 4: 13. The discourses of sports coaching; 14. Coaching ethics; 15. Coaching holistically: why do it and how we can frame it? 16. Coaching holistically: a way forward for coach education.

Health Related Physical Activity

exercise • fitness • physical activity • sports psychology

Introductions to the subject

4674 **Concepts of physical fitness: active lifestyles for wellness**
C. Corbin [et al.]   14th edn, McGraw-Hill, 2007, 480pp. £35.99. ISBN 9780073523576.
'Provides readers with self-management skills necessary to adopt a healthy lifestyle. This well established text uses a proven conceptual format, brief concepts rather than chapters, to provide information in a useful and concise way and is organized to focus on "process" or lifestyle changes with early coverage of planning so students can apply the concepts immediately.'

4675 **Fitness and health**
B.J. Sharkey and S.E. Gaskill   6th edn, Human Kinetics, 2006, 448pp. $27.95. ISBN 9780736056144.
19 chapters in six parts: I. Physical activity, fitness and health; II. Aerobic fitness; III. Muscular fitness; IV. Activity and weight control; V. Performance; VI. Vitality and longevity.

4676 **Physical activity and health: the evidence explained**
A.E. Hardman and D.J. Stensel   Routledge, 2003, 289pp. 2008 edn announced, £29.99. ISBN 9780415270717.
In three parts. Part 1. Assessing the evidence (1. Introduction; 2. The nature of different types of evidence; 3. Physical activity, physical fitness and all-cause mortality). Part 2. Effects of exercise. Physical activity and risk of disease (4. Cardiovascular disease; 5. Risk factors for cardiovascular disease; 6. Exercise and Type II diabetes; 7. Overweight and obesity; 8. The insulin resistance syndrome; 9. Cancer; 10. Osteoporosis). Part 3. Ageing, therapeutic exercise, physical activity in public health concerns (11. Physical activity, exercise and ageing; 12. Therapeutic exercise; 13. Risks and hazards of exercise; 14. Physical activity, fitness and public health policy).

4677 **Physical activity epidemiology**
R.K. Dishman, R.A. Washburn and G.W. Heath   Human Kinetics, 2004, 467pp. $69. ISBN 9780880116053.
'This is the first textbook dedicated solely to the epidemiology of physical activity and the only complete reference written for students. It is a practical and informative resource for both students of epidemiology and established professionals. The authors provide detailed discussion of real-life examples to assist students' understanding of how physical activity epidemiology is used and applied. The book covers all the important areas, including disease mortality, risk factors, chronic diseases and cancer and immunity.'
'*Physical Activity Epidemiology* is a wide-ranging, absolutely current, and commonsense guide to health in terms of physical exercise, as viewed from population-based studies. From prelude to postlude, the book is comprehensive and detailed, yet it is pleasurable to read, to contemplate over, and to reread as a reference text.' (*American Journal of Epidemiology*)

4678 **The psychology of physical activity: determinants, well-being and interventions**
S. Biddle and N. Mutrie   2nd edn, Routledge, 2007, 448pp. £27.99. ISBN 9780415366656.
'(A) comprehensive account of our psychological knowledge about physical activity covering motivation and the psychological factors associated with activity or inactivity; the feel-good factor – the psychological outcomes of exercising, including mental health illness and clinical populations; interventions and applied practice in the psychology of physical activity; current trends and future directions in research and practice.'

4679 **Research methods in physical activity**
J.R. Thomas, J.K. Nelson and S.J. Silverman   5th edn, Human Kinetics, 2005, 455pp. $75. ISBN 9780736056205.
www.humankinetics.com/ResearchMethodsInPhysicalActivity
[COMPANION]
Well established, comprehensive textbook. 21 chapters organized into four parts: I. Overview of the research process; II. Statistical and measurement concepts in research; III. Types of research; IV. Writing the research report.

Research centres & institutes

4680 **Canadian Fitness & Lifestyle Research Institute**
www.cflri.ca/eng
'National research agency concerned with educating Canadians about the importance of leading healthy, active lifestyles', established in 1980. Extensive collection of downloadable full-text reports and documents; Progress in Prevention bulletins; Tips for Being Active; physical activity statistics. Occasional papers and reviews, information about projects and research and more specific data on Canadian provinces. Also available in French.
■ **CFLRI publications** www.cflri.ca/eng/publications. List of publications from 1981, *Canada Fitness Survey* to the latest *Annual Capacity Study* and *Physical Activity Monitor*.
■ **The research file** www.cflri.ca/eng/research_file. Series of over 130 one-page summaries of research findings in the area of physical activity, produced between 1991 and 2001, including references to further information.

4681 **Cooper Institute** [USA]
www.cooperinst.org
Research centre, founded in 1970, 'dedicated to advancing the understanding of the relationship between living habits and health and to providing leadership in implementing these concepts to enhance the physical and emotional well-being of individuals', based in Dallas, Texas. Abstracts of related research publications; summary reports; courses, manuals and other products for purchase.
■ **Active Living Partners** www.activeliving.info. Educational programme developed by Human Kinetics in partnership with The Cooper Institute, addressing 'physical inactivity and unbalanced eating, two leading causes of obesity, heart disease, and other chronic ailments'.

Associations & societies

4682 American Alliance for Health, Physical Education, Recreation & Dance
www.aahperd.org
Alliance of five US national associations, six district associations and the Research Consortium, supporting those involved in physical education, leisure, fitness, dance, health education and all specialisms involved in achieving a healthy lifestyle. Publications include the *Journal of Physical Education, Recreation and Dance* and *Research Quarterly for Exercise and Sport*. Includes the following organizations:

■ **American Association for Physical Activity & Recreation** www.aahperd.org/aapar. Created by merger of the AALR (American Asssociation for Leisure and Recreation) and AAALF (American Association for Active Lifestyles and Fitness) in 2005, AAPAR promotes 'meaningful physical activity and recreation' in the US community by supporting teachers, trainers and community leaders. Publications include eight journals, discounted for members, and freely available position papers on disabilities, aquatics, ageing and leisure education.

■ **National Association for Girls & Women in Sport** www.aahperd.org/nagws. Promotes opportunities for all girls and women in sport. Publications include the GWS gazette, *Women in Sport and Physical Activity Journal*, and downloadable articles. Research and background information on Title IX, the federal law prohibiting sex discrimination in education.

■ **National Association for Sport & Physical Education** www.aahperd.org/naspe. Largest of the five national associations in AAHPERD, NASPE is a 'non-profit professional membership association that sets the standard for practice in physical education and sport'. Details of programmes, accreditation and awards; position statements; national standards and appropriate practices for PE; catalogue of publications. Monthly teacher's tool box, survey results and link to the *Shape of the Nation Report* 2006.

4683 Association for the Study of Obesity [UK]
www.aso.org.uk
Founded in 1967 and dedicated to the understanding and treatment of obesity. Obesity Resource Information Centre includes online factsheets, details of Primary Care Trust strategies and useful links. Searchable portlet facility covering news, ASO conference papers and other website content. Some abstracts available. Membership open to professionals in the field.

4684 Australian Council for Health, Physical Education & Recreation
www.achper.org.au
ACHPER is a non-profit, national professional association for people in Australia working in health education, physical education, recreation, sport, dance, community fitness or movement sciences. Site contains details of publications, membership, conferences, branches and ACHPER activities.

4685 Canadian Association for Health, Physical Education, Recreation & Dance
www.cahperd.ca
Aims to promote healthy development of children and young people through quality school-based physical and health education. Sections on PE, health education, intramural recreation and dance, each with news, resources and guidance on promotion. Quality Daily Physical Education (QDPE) and Quality School Health (QSH) programmes. Index of journal articles, some with abstracts; full-text articles for purchase. Teaching tips for members. Also available in French.

■ **Physical and Health Education Journal** 1933–, qtrly. $70.00 (personal subscription, outside Canada). ISSN 14980940. www.cahperd.ca/eng/journal. A 'forum to highlight, analyze, discuss and share many of the leading-edge teaching techniques, hot issues, and school successes in the fields of school health and physical education'. Sample copy to view; individual articles to order from CAHPERD.

Portal & task environments

4686 American College of Sports Medicine: Public Resources
www.acsm.org/Content/NavigationMenu/ResourcesFor/GeneralPublic/ACSM_Public_Informat.htm
ACSM promotes 'public awareness and education about the benefits of physical activity for people of all ages, from all occupations'. Free resources include brochures and factsheets, current comments, information about US courses and quarterly newsletter, *Fit Society*. Brochures on selecting and using sports aids and other topics for download or by post (charges for multiple copies). Multilingual position stands. Links to ACSM fitness initiatives and other web resources.

■ **ACSM's guidelines for exercise testing and prescription** 7th edn, Lippincott Williams & Wilkins, 2005, 370pp. £19.50. ISBN 9780781745901. Summarizes recommended procedures for exercise testing and exercise prescription in healthy and diseased individuals. Written by international experts.

■ **Current comments** www.acsm.org/AM/Template.cfm?Section=Current_Comments1. Series of over 50 proactive statements on sports medicine- and exercise-related topics of general interest. Written in understandable language for the public. Topics range from Alcohol and Athletic Performance to Youth Strength Training.

4687 British Heart Foundation National Centre for Physical Activity & Health
www.bhfactive.org.uk
Based at Loughborough University, BHFNC promotes physical activity, by helping professionals 'stimulate more people to take more activity as part of everyday life'. Practical guidance for professionals plus research summaries, case studies and background information; sections on young people, older adults, the workplace and primary care. Information Centre with research, publications, useful links, reviews, key document summaries and conferences.

■ **Information Centre: references** www.bhfactive.org.uk/information-centre/references.html. Twenty regularly updated lists of references on activity-related topics, from physical activity and dog ownership to research on pedometers.

4688 Canadian Society for Exercise Physiology
www.csep.ca
Voluntary organization of professionals interested in scientific study of exercise physiology, including physical activity, fitness, health, nutrition, epidemiology and human performance. Details of conferences and CSEP certification. Study guides and CSEP journal, *Applied Physiology, Nutrition and Metabolism* (formerly *Canadian Journal of Applied Physiology*). Free access to symposium presentations and physical activity readiness questionnaires (including in pregnancy). Also available in French.

■ **Physical activity guides**
www.csep.ca/main.cfm?cid=574&nid=5138. Produced by CSEP and
Public Health Agency of Canada. Aimed at adults, children, adolescents and
older adults; downloadabie in English and French. Free hard copies to order.
Links to background and support papers.

4689 Division of Nutrition & Physical Activity [USA]
www.cdc.gov/nccdphp/dnpa/
Part of the US CDC (Centers for Disease Control and
Prevention), promoting public health. Useful A to Z topic
index or browse via sections on nutrition, physical activity
and obesity. Publications include *Morbidity and Mortality
Weekly Reports* and bibliographies of staff publications. US-
focused data and statistics; training and software tools.

■ **Nutrition resources for health professionals**
www.cdc.gov/nccdphp/dnpa/nutrition/health_professionals. Links to key
resources such as government recommendations, factsheets, press
releases and MMWRs.

■ **Physical activity resources for health professionals**
www.cdc.gov/nccdphp/dnpa/physical/health_professionals. Similar
coverage for physical activity.

4690 ExRx: Exercise Prescription on the Net
www.exrx.net
Online resource for exercise professionals, coaches and
fitness enthusiasts, with exercise and muscle directory and
links to articles on exercise-related topics, including weight
training, kinesiology, conditioning, fitness testing, diet and
nutrition, psychology, anabolic steroids and bodybuilding.
Some include bibliographies. Questions and comments;
online forum; details of books, videos and software; links to
related websites, scientific abstracts and online journals.
Site content also available on CD-ROM, priced $59.95

4691 International Fitness Association
www.ifafitness.com
Fitness information for professionals and enthusiasts. Free
online courses and tests in nutrition, senior fitness and
aerobics; fee for certification. Online aerobics videos. Full-
text online books (see below). Exercises for kickboxing,
kickboxing aerobics, sports training, step aerobics and
weight training. Health advice and articles (medical
disclaimer); information on nutrition, supplements, fitness
calculators, fitness FAQ, links and message boards.

■ **Fitness ABCs** 2nd edn. Free to download. www.ifafitness.com/book1.
Manual providing course material for FIA accreditation. Nutrition, training,
physiology, kinesiology and fitness testing, plus forms, charts and
bibliography.

■ **Stretching** 1998. Free to download. www.ifafitness.com/stretch. Guide
produced by Brad Appleton in 1998, covering physiology, flexibility,
stretching types, techniques, splits and range of motion. References.

4692 Lifestyle Information Network [CAN]
www.lin.ca
Provides 'knowledge-based forum exchanging value added
information services for the enhancement of individual and
community well-being through health, parks, recreation,
sport and culture', primarily in Canada. 'Special collections'
section links to journals, conference papers, news, mailing
lists and websites, many of interest outside Canada.

■ **National Recreation Database**
www.lin.ca/index.cfm?fuseaction=recreationdatabase.showmain. Canada's
National Recreation Database, re-badged as the Knowledge Bank. Focuses
on 'practical, proven and frequently unpublished information which is not
available from traditional sources such as libraries and bookstores'. Use

keyword or advanced search, or browse by population or topic. Most
resources freely available.

4693 National Coalition for Promoting Physical Activity
[USA]
www.ncppa.org
Group of American national organizations aiming to promote
a more physically active lifestyle within the USA. Full text of
landmark reports, statistics and research papers, plus links
to other web resources, tools to promote physical activity
(including the *State Coalition handbook*) and details of NCPPA
publications. List of members.

4694 National Heart Forum
www.heartforum.org.uk
Alliance of over 50 UK organizations 'working to reduce the
risk of coronary heart disease and related conditions'.
Sections on CHD and its risk factors; publications; policy and
campaign issues. NHF reports downloadable or hard copy for
purchase. Archive of quarterly magazine 2003 onwards.
Latest policy and research developments; archive of
government consultations and NHF responses.

4695 SafeSport
www.safesport.co.uk
Commercial site aiming to provide a 'reference point on
playing sport safely' for the public. Features, articles and
advice by professional journalists and experts, covering
general exercise advice, risk management, nutrition, avoiding
injuries and other topics. Site map of articles, newsletter and
search facility.

Discovering print & electronic resources

4696 MedlinePlus: Sports Fitness
www.nlm.nih.gov/medlineplus/sportsfitness.html
Service from US NLM (National Library of Medicine) and NIH
(National Institutes of Health). Links to full-text articles or
abstracts on health-related topics, including fitness and
exercise. All organized similarly, featuring basics (latest news
and prevention), learn more (more specific information and
nutrition), research, reference (dictionaries, directories,
statistics, organizations and publications), multimedia
tutorials and information for different age groups/genders.
Links to related sections on sports and exercise.

■ **MedlinePlus: Sports Safety**
www.nlm.nih.gov/medlineplus/sportssafety.html. Similarly laid out resource
focusing on safety aspects and featuring articles on specific sports.

Digital data, image & text collections

**4697 National Electronic Injury Surveillance System
(NEISS) On-Line** [USA]
www.cpsc.gov/library/neiss.html
US Consumer Product Safety Commission database of
emergency visits to NEISS hospitals 1991 onwards, providing
statistics of product-related injuries, including sports.
Includes age, gender, diagnosis, part of body, ethnic
background, if work-related and other variables. Drop-down
box of product codes; useful alphabetical coding manual of
products. Sample cases online. Guide for researchers.

Handbooks & manuals

4698   Active living every day
S.N. Blair [et al.]   Human Kinetics, 2001, 198pp. $29.95. ISBN 9780736037013.
www.activeliving.info [COMPANION]
'The only book that offers a 20-week, self-paced plan to help you become more physically active – without requiring vigorous exercise to see results. The concepts presented in this book can be used anytime, anywhere. You choose what form of activity you enjoy the most; from dancing to walking to yard work, it's up to you – whatever keeps you moving and off the couch ...'

4699   Fitness professional's handbook
E.T. Howley and B.D. Franks   5th edn, Human Kinetics, 2007, 568pp. $69. ISBN 9780736061780.
'Formerly titled *Health fitness instructor's handbook*, this full-color text has undergone a title change to better reflect its extensive use in the field. Reflective of updates made in the seventh edition of ACSM's *Guidelines for exercise testing and prescription*, it serves as an essential text for those seeking ACSM health/fitness instructor certification and an invaluable reference for certified fitness professionals striving to stay informed amid ongoing research advances.'

4700   Motivating people to be physically active
B.H. Marcus and L.H. Forsyth   Human Kinetics, 2003, 220pp. $35. ISBN 9780736040648.
Chapters are: 1. Description of physical activity interventions; 2. The stages of motivational readiness for change model; 3. Integrating other psychological models and theories; 4. Learning about physical activity mediators; 5. Evaluating and measuring physical activity mediators; 6. Successful physical activity interventions using the stages model; 7. Assessing physical activity patterns and physical fitness; 8. Using the stages model in individual counseling; 9. Using the stages model in group counseling programs; 10. Using the stages model in work-site programs; 11. Using the stages model in community programs.

4701   Perspectives on health and exercise
C. Riddoch and J. McKenna, eds   Palgrave Macmillan, 2002, 291pp. £21.99. ISBN 9780333787007.
Contributed essays: 'Although it is widely accepted that active people are healthier, there is still much to be understood about the relationship between health and exercise. There are many questions to be explored such as "how much?" and "what type of activity?" Also, "are there population differences?" and "what prevents people from being active?" This text considers physical activity and health from a range of perspectives, encompassing many of the traditional academic disciplines, to provide a unique overview of this developing field.'

4702   Physical activity and health
C. Bouchard, S. Blair and W. Haskell   Human Kinetics, 2007, 409pp. $69. ISBN 9780736050920.
'*Physical activity and health* is the first textbook to bring together the results of the most important studies in this rapidly changing field and offers a detailed yet concise and clear presentation of key concepts. The text provides a conceptual framework to help readers relate results from single studies or collections of studies to the overall

paradigm linking physical activity and physical fitness to health.'

4703   Physical activity and obesity
C. Bouchard   Human Kinetics, 2000, 400pp. $64. ISBN 9780880119092.
Nineteen contributed chapters organized into: Part I. The obesity epidemic; Part II. The biological and behavioral determinants of obesity; Part III. Physical activity in the prevention and treatment of obesity; Part IV. Physical activity, fitness and health in the obese state.

4704   Physical activity and psychological well-being
S. Biddle, K. Fox and S. Boutcher, eds   Routledge, 2000, 205pp. £27.99. ISBN 9780415234399.
Topics covered include anxiety and stress; depression; mood and emotion; self-perceptions and self-esteem; cognitive functioning and ageing; psychological dysfunction.

International Competitions
Commonwealth Games • Olympic Games

Introductions to the subject

4705   A brief history of the Olympic Games
D.C. Young   Blackwell Publishing, 2004, 184pp. £15.99. ISBN 9781405111300.
'Classics professor David Young, who has researched the subject for over 25 years, reveals how the ancient Olympics evolved from modest beginnings into a grand festival, attracting hundreds of highly trained athletes, tens of thousands of spectators and the finest artists and poets ...'
'An impressively comprehensive, clear and often vivid survey of the ancient Olympics ... The book is packed with carefully considered interventions in long-standing debates.' (*Journal of Hellenic Studies*)

4706   The Olympic Games: a social science perspective
K. Toohey and A.J. Veal   2nd edn, CABI Publishing, 2007, 320pp. £27.50. ISBN 9780851998091.
'This revised edition contains much new data relating to the Sydney 2000 Games and their aftermath; and preparations for Athens 2004 and Beijing 2008 Games. The book is broad-ranging and independent in its coverage and includes the use of drugs, sex testing, accusations of power abuse among members of the IOC, the Games as a stage for political protest, media-related controversies, economic costs and benefits of the Games and historical conflicts between organizers and host communities.'
'Toohey's and Veal's excellent book should be put on the reading list of every sports course in English-speaking universities' (*International Review of the Sociology of Sport* (on the 1st edn))

■ **The Olympic games: a bibliography** A.J. Veal and K. Toohey
140pp. Free to download.
www.business.uts.edu.au/olympic/downloads/olympic_bib_update2.pdf.
One of a series of bibliographies on sport and leisure topics produced by the School of Leisure, Sport and Tourism at the University of Technology Sydney, originally published in 1995. Now around 1800 entries (April 2007); frequently updated. Online Bibliography No. 2.

4707 The Olympic Games explained: a student guide to the evolution of the modern Olympic Games
V. Girginov and J. Parry   Routledge, 2005, 272pp. £22.99. ISBN 9780415346047.
A comprehensive introduction to the central themes and background of the modern Games.

Dictionaries, thesauri, classifications

4708 Historical dictionary of the Olympic movement
B. Mallon and I. Buchanan   3rd edn, Scarecrow Press, 2006, 411pp. $92. ISBN 9780810855748.
A very detailed and well structured work covering all facets of the Olympics. *The A–Z of the Olympic movement* is a reprint of this title.
'Buchanan and Mallon provide comprehensive, clearly written, and well-organized historical information about the Olympic movement. Highly recommended.' (*Choice* (on the previous edn))

Official & quasi-official bodies

4709 Commonwealth Games Federation
www.commonwealthgames.com
Responsible for direction and control of the Commonwealth Games, which originated as the British Empire Games in 1930. Clickable map of participating countries, CGF constitution, FAQ and calendar of events. Advanced search facility for athletes, results and records going back to 1930; search options such as sport, discipline, country, games location, gender and medal level. Members' area.
- **Commonwealth Games Legacy: Manchester 2002**
  www.gameslegacy.com. Archived site of the Manchester 2002 Games, including a document and report archive, the searchable Games Final Report, statistical information, image gallery and the effect on regeneration, as well as reports of the actual games.

Research centres & institutes

4710 Centre d'Estudis Olímpics
http://olympicstudies.uab.es/eng
One of several centres for Olympic studies around the world for the academic community, based at Universitat Autònoma de Barcelona (UAB). Details of projects, thematic dossiers and research topics. Full text of lectures and working papers on aspects of the Games and their administration, plus key Olympic issues. Link to UAB library catalogue. Search facility from home page only. Also available in Spanish and Catalan.
- **Olympic studies international directory**
  http://olympicstudies.uab.es/directory. Joint project with the Olympic Studies Centre at Lausanne. Contains 'detailed information on the academic activities, research or documentary collections of those institutions relating to the Olympics and those authors undertaking research on the Olympics'. Currently being updated.

Associations & societies

4711 British Olympic Association
www.olympics.org.uk
One of 205 national Olympic committees in five continents, the BOA is responsible for promoting the Olympic movement in the UK. Contains information about past and present games, as well as Team GB, the BOA, factsheets for students and teachers area. Athletes area, newsroom and 'chill zone'.

4712 Play Fair at the Olympics
www.fairolympics.org
Campaign launched in 2004 by Oxfam, Global Unions and the Clean Clothes Campaign to promote workers' rights in the sportswear industry. Includes Oxfam report on business practices in the global sportswear industry, background reports and link to PlayFair 2008.

4713 Special Olympics
www.specialolympics.org
Organization 'dedicated to empowering individuals with intellectual disabilities to become physically fit, productive and respected members of society through sports training and competition', covering 30 'Olympic-type summer and winter sports'. Research on health, attitudes and programming impact. Initiatives on leadership and young athletes. International programme locator, language guide, sections for competitors, coaches, volunteers and supporters.

4714 World Games
International World Games Association
www.worldgames-iwga.org
Founded in 1981, the IWGA administers the World Games, covering sports not currently in the Olympic Games. Details of member organizations and their websites (32 in 2007), video clips, information about sports and athletes, news, features and document library giving details of the constitution and rules. E-mail newsletter and archive of downloadable IWGA publications, *World Games Forum* and *World Games News* back to 1996.

Portal & task environments

4715 International Olympic Committee
www.olympic.org
Comprehensive website on the Olympics with profiles of athletes and sports past and present; details of summer and winter games held since 1896, plus ancient Olympics and future games. Results database, search facility and useful site map. News; background of IOC and Olympic movement; museum; education section. Link at foot of each page to all site documents, including factsheets and Olympic Charter. *Olympic Review* magazine online January 2000 onwards. Also available in French.
- **London 2012** http://main.london2012.com. Future and some past games have their own websites; this is London's main site for 2012, including publications covering the bid process and background documents on strategy and organization.
- **Multimedia gallery** www.olympic.org/uk/utilities/multimedia/gallery. Vast multimedia gallery of photographs, films and audio documents, searchable by athlete, team, sport or games date.
- **Olympic Museum Lausanne**
  www.olympic.org/uk/passion/museum. Details of temporary and permanent exhibitions, virtual tour and educational programme for secondary schools, plus visitor information.

4716 International Paralympic Committee
www.paralympic.org
Global governing body of Paralympic Movement, aiming to develop 'sport opportunities for all persons with a disability

from the beginner to elite level'. Comprehensive website featuring games history, anti-doping, classification, results, rankings and media centre. Specific summer and winter sports, including news, rules, classification and equipment. Browse or search preferable to rather unwieldy site map. Extensive FAQ. Aids for visually impaired.

- ■ **IPC Handbook**
  www.paralympic.org/release/Main_Sections_Menu/IPC/IPC_Handbook. Divided into two sections and downloadable in individual chapters, plus list of acronyms. Undergoing revision 2007.
- ■ **The Paralympian** 1999–, qrtly. Free to download.
  www.paralympic.org/release/Main_Sections_Menu/News/Newsletter. Official IPC magazine, available online or in printed form (latter by registration).
- ■ **Paralympic Games historical results database**
  www.paralympic.org/release/Main_Sections_Menu/Sports/Results/paralympics_search_form.html. A 'comprehensive collection of Paralympic Games results from 1960 to 2006. The database includes all preliminaries, heats and finals plus useful information such as scores, times, distances, etc, as well as the achievement of world and Paralympic records'. Searchable by competition, sport or event. More detailed searches by athlete or by participation and medallist report available for Paralympic Games.

Digital data, image & text collections

4717 The Ancient Olympic Games Virtual Museum
http://minbar.cs.dartmouth.edu/greecom/olympics [REGISTRATION]
Project sponsored by the Foundation of the Hellenic World and Dartmouth College in New Hampshire, USA. Includes definitions, slide show, information about Olympia, history of the ancient games and details of contests. Although users are asked to register, guests are allowed access to most sections.

4718 Olympics through time
http://sunsite.informatik.rwth-aachen.de/olympics
Established educational site produced by the Foundation of the Hellenic World. Divided into prehistory, antiquity, revival and comments. Each section has further headings and hyperlinks. Images include short descriptions. Comments section features expert interviews, user survey, bibliography and glossary.

Directories & encyclopedias

4719 The complete book of the summer Olympics: Athens 2004 edition
D. Wallenchinsky Sportclassic Books, 2004, 1152pp. $24.95. ISBN 9781894963329.
The classic text covering all aspects of the Games.
There are parallel edns for previous Summer and Winter Olympic Games.
'An indispensable addition to the shelves of both sportswriters and serious fans … an extremely meticulous piece of scholarship.' (*New York Times Book Review*)

4720 Encyclopedia of the modern Olympic movement
J.E. Findling and K.D. Pelle Greenwood Press, 2004, 602pp. $78.95. ISBN 9780313322785.
Contributors cover each of the Summer and Winter Olympics held so far, plus the forthcoming Beijing 2008.

4721 Whitaker's Olympic almanack 2004: the essential guide to the Olympic Games
S. Greenberg, ed. A. & C. Black, 2003, 304pp. £16.99. ISBN 9780713667240.
'This is the most authoritative and entertaining collection of Olympic facts, records and statistics from the ancient games right up to the present – making essential reading for Olympics enthusiasts everywhere. *Whitaker's Olympic almanack* includes profiles of every summer and winter Olympic games; summaries of Olympic history, sports, events, people and performances and medal tables by sport and year.'

Handbooks & manuals

4722 Global Olympics: historical and sociological studies of the modern games
K. Young and K. Wamsley, eds Elsevier JAI, 2005, 311pp. £59.99. ISBN 9780762311811.
'(D)raws together some of the world's leading scholars on critical issues emerging from ancient Olympic contests and over one hundred years of modern Olympic history. A wide range of expertise permits the authors to address these issues from varied perspectives, while encompassing an in-depth assessment of the current literature and debates on the Olympics.'

4723 Inside the Olympic industry: power, politics, and activism
H.J. Lenskyj SUNY Press, 2000, 216pp. $20.95. ISBN 9780791447567.
'In a startling exposé of the Olympic industry, Helen Jefferson Lenskyj goes beyond the media hype of international goodwill and spirited competition to uncover a darker side of the global Games. She reports on the pre- and post-Olympic impacts from recent host cities, bribery investigations and their outcomes, grassroots resistance movements and the role of the mass media in the controversy …'.

4724 Mega-events and modernity: Olympics and expos in the growth of global culture
M. Roche Routledge, 2000, 281pp. £26.99. ISBN 9780415157124.
Explores the social history and politics of 'mega-events' from the late 19th century to the present.

4725 Post-Olympism?: questioning sport in the twenty-first century
J. Bale and M. Christensen, eds Berg, 2004, 276pp. £15.99. ISBN 9781859737194.
15 contributors provide a wide reflective survey of the Olympic movement as it stands in the early part of this century.

Physical Education

Introductions to the subject

4726 Landmarks in the history of physical education
P.C. McIntosh Routledge, 2007, 240pp. Originally published 1957; 2nd edn 1981, £85. ISBN 9780415432627.
Examines physical education in classical Greece and Imperial

Rome during the 1st and 2nd centuries AD and in Italy and England during the Renaissance. Each of these periods witnessed remarkable developments in the practice and theory of physical education: developments which still have present-day significance. The second part of the book traces the simultaneous development of physical education in different parts of the USA and Europe from the end of the 18th century onwards.

4727 Learning to teach physical education in the secondary school: a companion to school experience
S. Capel, ed. 2nd edn, Routledge, 2004, 343pp. £22.99. ISBN 9780415336369.
Draws together background information about teaching and about physical education, basic teaching skills specifically related to PE and broader knowledge and understanding of PE issues in the wider environment.

4728 Physical education: essential issues
K. Green and K. Hardman, eds Sage Publications, 2005, 248pp. £19.99. ISBN 9780761944980.
Aimed at students of physical education and sport in schools and consists of a collection of readings, covering a variety of themes, historical and contemporary.

4729 Physical education and the study of sport
R. Davis, J. Roscoe and R. Phillips 5th edn, Elsevier Mosby, 2004, 656pp. Includes CD-ROM, £25.99. ISBN 9780723433750.
Colourful text designed particularly for A-Level courses in the UK. Contains 25 chapters organized into three parts: 1. The performer in action; 2. The performer as person; 3. The performer in a social setting.

4730 Sport and PE: a complete guide to Advanced Level study
K. Wesson [et al.] 3rd edn, Hodder & Stoughton, 2005, 848pp. £24.99. ISBN 9780340817018.
Leading text, now tailored to the needs of the different examining boards in the UK.

4731 Understanding physical education
K. Green Paul Chapman Publishing, 2007, 288pp. £22.99. ISBN 9781412921138.
Announced text focusing on the UK but incorporating a global dimension. Topics planned to be covered are: The requirements of National Curriculum Physical Education; The current 'state' of physical education; The relationship between physical education and sport; Extra-curricular physical education; Lifelong participation in sport and physical activity; Assessment and examinations in physical education; Social class, gender, ethnicity and inclusion in relation to physical education; Teacher training and continuing professional development.

Research centres & institutes

4732 Institute for Outdoor Leadership & Education [USA]
www.indiana.edu/~outdoor/IOLE.htm
'A resource for academics and practitioners in the fields of Adventure Education and Outdoor Leadership', created by graduate students and staff at Indiana University. Resources include link to *Journal of Experiential Education*, selected articles from *International Journal of Wilderness*, archived

copies of *Research Connections* and *Bradford Papers Online*. Some Indiana sites were under redevelopment in August 2007.

4733 Institute for Outdoor Learning [UK]
www.outdoor-learning.org
'Encourages outdoor learning by developing quality, safety and opportunity to experience outdoor activity provision and by supporting and enhancing the good practice of those who work in the outdoors.' Guide to outdoor learning; careers advice; professional development and information centre. Publications include *Horizons* and *Journal of Adventure Education and Outdoor Learning*.
- **The outdoor source book** www.outdoor-learning.org/providers/osb. Searchable directory of outdoor learning and training providers in the UK. Enhanced version available to purchase in printed format and/or as CD-ROM.

Associations & societies

4734 Association for Physical Education [UK]
www.afpe.org.uk
Formed 2005 by amalgamation of BAALPE (British Association of Advisers and Lecturers in Physical Education) and PEA UK (Physical Education Association of the UK). Committed to 'promoting and maintaining high standards and safe practice in all aspects and at all levels of physical education'. Includes professional development, jobs, policy documents and details of publications; some video clips. Health and safety downloads for members.

4735 International Council for Health, Physical Education, Recreation, Sport & Dance
www.ichpersd.org
Founded in Rome in 1958 by teachers and representatives from 16 countries to promote standards and disseminate knowledge; now members from over 145 countries. Sends quarterly *Journal of ICHPER-SD* to all 208 countries and self-governing territories of the world. Details of standards for use in PE, programmes, news and commission interest areas.

4736 International Society for Comparative Physical Education & Sport
www.iscpes.org
Research and educational organization, founded in 1978. Its purpose is 'to support, encourage and provide assistance to those seeking to initiate and strengthen research and teaching programs in comparative physical education and sport throughout the world'. Note that some information is encrypted for members only.

4737 National Council for School Sport [UK]
www.yst.org.uk/ncss
Umbrella body for national school sport associations, federations of local school sport associations and other UK national organizations promoting sport in schools, which aims to 'create a high quality school sport national competition framework implemented locally with opportunities for all' by 2010. List of local and national members.

Portal & task environments

4738   International Association for Physical Education in Higher Education
www.aiesep.ulg.ac.be
Association Internationale des Écoles Supérieures d'Education Physique, an international organization of universities, colleges, individuals and institutions of sport science promoting research and professional practice in sport and physical education through international cooperation. Details of conferences and seminars, publications and Cagigal lectures, some full-text.

- **AIESEP Research Data Bank** www.aiesep.ulg.ac.be/ardb.htm.
  ARDB provides summaries of research projects on sport pedagogy covering teaching, teacher education, coaching, youth sport, physical activity, comparative PE and adaptive PE.
- **Rethinking games teaching R. Thorpe, D. Bunker and L. Almond, eds** University of Technology, Loughborough, 1986, 79pp. Free to download. www.tgfu.org/articles/PHED%20RETHINKING%20GAMES.pdf. 'First TGfU resource that launched the TGfU approach into the PE community. With the permission of the Editors the whole book can be downloaded here'.
- **Teaching Games for Understanding** www.tgfu.org. Endorsed by AIESEP, the TGfU task force is a 'global representative group of institutions and individuals committed to the promotion and dissemination of scholarly inquiry and practical applications in teaching for understanding within sport coaching and physical education'. Statements on games sense, play practice, tactical games and tactical decision learning, as well as articles and other resources.

4739   Outdoor Education Research & Evaluation Center
www.wilderdom.com/research.php
Produced by Australian academic, James Neill, to 'enhance the quality and accessibility of philosophy, theory, research and evaluation about outdoor, experiential education and related programs. User-friendly summaries of the main topics are provided, along with online links to full-text articles and further information'. Includes bibliographies, conferences, theses, activities, courses, jobs and experts listing. Keyword index.

4740   The Outdoor Index
www.reviewing.co.uk/outdoor/outindex.htm
Internet resource guide for those working or researching in outdoor education and/or experiential learning, provided by Roger Greenaway. Contains links, details of books, discussion lists, workshops and articles (some full-text), many relating to reviewing and evaluating activities.

4741   PE Central [USA]
www.pecentral.org
Established US site with resources for 'teachers, parents and others who work with youngsters to guide them in the process of becoming physically active and healthy for a lifetime'. Search whole site or just lesson ideas. Covers assessment, best practice, adapted PE, pedometers, preschool and positive learning; resources for children and adolescents; professional development and research. Blog, jobs and annotated links to related sites.

Handbooks & manuals

4742   Developing the physical education curriculum: an achievement-based approach
L.E. Kelly and V.J. Melograno   Human Kinetics, 2004, 363pp. $54. ISBN 9780736041782.
www.humankinetics.com/DevelopingThePhysicalEducationCurriculum [COMPANION]
13 chapters in four parts: I. Understanding curriculum development; II. Planning the physical education curriculum; III. Implementing the physical education curriculum; IV. Evaluating and communicating the physical education curriculum.

4743   International comparisons of physical education: concepts, problems, prospects
U. Pühse and M. Gerber, eds   Meyer & Meyer Sport, 2004, 720pp. €59.95. ISBN 9781841261614.
Worldwide survey of the state of physical education in different countries contributed by experts in each area.

4744   Student learning in physical education: applying research to enhance instruction
S.J. Silverman and C.D. Ennis, eds   2nd edn, Human Kinetics, 2003, 352pp. $54. ISBN 9780736042758.
'Nationally and internationally recognized teacher educators and physical education scholars have thoroughly revised and updated this new edition for today's physical education programs. The expanded and comprehensive references, featuring more than 1000 bibliographic entries, have also been updated and provide a springboard to further research.'

Sociology & Philosophy of Sport

ethics in sport • fair play • philosophy of sport • sport sociology

Introductions to the subject

4745   Ethics in sport
W.J. Morgan   2nd rev. edn, Human Kinetics, 2007, 512pp. $54. ISBN 9780736064286.
35 chapters in five parts: I. Metaethical considerations of sport; II. Competition and fair play: considerations of winning, cheating and gamesmanship; III. The limits of being human: doping and genetic enhancement in sport; IV. Gender and sexual equality in sport; V. Select issues in the social ethics of sport: violence, exploitation, race, spectatorship and disability.

4746   Global sport: identities, societies, civilizations
J. Maguire   Polity Press, 1999, 239pp. £17.99. ISBN 9780745615325.
Still-useful overview considering conceptual and theoretical issues alongside a review of the globalization of sport and its consequences.

4747   Group dynamics in sport
A.V. Carron, H.A. Hausenblas and M. Eys   3rd edn, Fitness Information Technology, 2005, 377pp. $49. ISBN 9781885693631.
21 chapters in seven parts: 1. Introduction; 2. Group

environment; 3. Member attributes; 4. Group structure; 5. Group cohesiveness; 6. Team process; 7. Forming the group.

4748 Sport and society: a student introduction
B. Houlihan   2nd edn, Sage Publications, 2007, 552pp. £24.99. ISBN 9781412921367.
Forthcoming second edition of a well received volume which 'provides students and lecturers with a one-stop text that is comprehensive, multi-disciplinary, accessible, international and engaging'.

4749 Sport, leisure and culture in twentieth-century Britain
J. Hill   Palgrave, 2002, 241pp. £17.99. ISBN 9780333726860.
Three parts covering Commercial sport and leisure; Leisure, the home and voluntary activity; Public policy: the role of the state.

4750 Sports in society: issues and controversies
J. Coakley   9th edn, McGraw-Hill, 2007, 600pp. £41.99. ISBN 9780071104364.
'(T)he definitive text for the sport sociology course. Taking a global, issues-oriented approach to the study of the role of sport in society, this text encourages the discussion of current sports-related controversies and helps students develop critical thinking skills.'

4751 Understanding sport: an introduction to the sociological and cultural analysis of sport
J. Horne, A. Tomlinson and G. Whannel, comps   Spon, 1999, 298pp. £29.99. ISBN 9780419136408.
Designed to help students understand the context of sport and the place it has in the lives of individuals as well as in modern British society as a whole.

Research centres & institutes

4752 Canadian Centre for Ethics in Sport
www.cces.ca
CCES's purpose is 'to promote ethical conduct in all aspects of sport in Canada'. Sections on doping-free sport and fair play, plus details of other initiatives, glossary of terms and wide range of resources, including policy documents, videos, research papers and educational materials, many available to download free. Available in English and French.

Centre for the Sociology of Sport
See entry no. 744

4753 Chester Centre for Research into Sport & Society
[UK]
www.chester.ac.uk/ccrss
Established at University of Chester in 2004 (then University College Chester), focusing on sociology of sport and exercise. Features listings of publications by staff members; some available full-text. Topics include sports injuries, doping and association football.

Associations & societies

4754 British Philosophy of Sport Association
www.philosophyofsport.org.uk
Aims 'to promote and disseminate research and scholarship

in the philosophy of sport'. Teaching resources, discussion forum, events and JISC mailing list. New journal for 2007, *Sport, Ethics and Philosophy*, published by Routledge.

4755 European Fair Play Movement
www.fairplayeur.com
Established in 1994 'to promote Fair Play and Tolerance in the broadest sense (in sports and everyday life) at European level'. Bibliography of fair play references, mainly in German or French. Details of declarations, congresses and list of members. Website colour scheme can make it hard to read.

4756 International Association for the Philosophy of Sport
www.iaps.net
Founded in 1972, its main purpose is 'to stimulate, encourage and promote study, research and writing in the philosophy of sporting (and related) activity'. Resources include details of conferences, websites and doctoral theses. Full-text newsletter online 2000 onwards.
- **Journal of the Philosophy of Sport** Human Kinetics, 1974–, 2 p.a. $47.00 individual [2007]. ISSN 00948705. www.humankinetics.com/JPS. Online ISSN 1543-2939. Abstracts and tables of contents available from 1980. Full-text access for subscribers and IAPS members only.

4757 North American Society for the Sociology of Sport
www.nasss.org
Founded 'to explore sociological aspects of play, games and sport' and 'also now informed by a variety of interdisciplinary areas', including ageing, the body, disability, extreme sports, fandom, sexuality, discrimination and youth sport. Active community with blog, newsletters, bulletin board and conferences. Directory of Experts, due for update (August 2007).
- **Sociology of Sport Journal** Human Kinetics, 1984–, qtrly. $60.00 individual [2007]. ISSN 07411235. www.humankinetics.com/SSJ. Online ISSN 15432785. Official NASSS journal, free to members. 'Research articles, annotated bibliographies, research notes, book reviews, and short papers on curriculum issues.' Contents and abstracts freely available; facility for ordering individual articles online.

Portal & task environments

4758 Play the Game
www.playthegame.org
Initiative founded by three main sports organizations in Denmark with the International Federation of Journalists to provide a 'home for the homeless questions in sport' and aiming 'to strengthen the basic ethical values of sport and encourage democracy, transparency and freedom of expression in world sport'. Details of conferences, theme pages and publications.
- **Knowledge Bank**
www.playthegame.org/Knowledge%20Bank/Articles.aspx. Database of full-text articles on contemporary sports issues, plus conference presentations. Search by keyword, subject, author or year or browse by author or topic. Includes author profiles and links to related articles. Site map lists all articles, news and authors.

Digital data, image & text collections

4759 SOSOL: Sociology of Sport Online
http://physed.otago.ac.nz/sosol
Archived journal, formerly an 'international electronic forum for the dissemination of research and theory relating to the sociological examination of sport, physical education and coaching'. Hosted by the School of Physical Education, University of Otago; peer-reviewed papers freely available in full text. Archive covering 1998 to 2004 resource for researchers.

Handbooks & manuals

4760 Ethics, money and sport: this sporting Mammon
A. Walsh and R. Giulianotti   new edn, Routledge, 2007, 158pp. £22.99. ISBN 9780415333399.
'Unique in its focus on the ethical dimension of the powerful economics of today's sport, this book will be of interest, not only to those in the fields of sports studies and ethics of sport, but also to academics, researchers and students in philosophy of morality, sociology and the ethics of globalization as viewed through the ultimate globalized phenomenon of modern sport.'

4761 European cultures in sport: examining the nations and regions
J. Riordan and A. Kruger, eds   Intellect Books, 2003, 192pp. £19.95. ISBN 9781841500140.
A comparative guide to sport across Europe, in terms of its relative political and social status, its development and the ways in which it has contributed to national achievement. Covers ten major European states.

4762 Fair play in sport: a moral norm system
S. Loland, ed.   Routledge, 2002, 175pp. £26.99. ISBN 9780419260707.
'(P)resents a critical re-working of the classic ideal of fair play and explores its practical consequences for competitive sport. By linking general moral principles and practical cases, the book develops a contemporary theory of fair play.'

4763 Genetic technology and sport: ethical questions
C. Tamburrini and T. Tännsjö, eds   Routledge, 2005, 223pp. £24.99. ISBN 9780415342377.
Will the genetic design of athletes destroy sport ... or will it lead to a new and extraordinary age of athletic achievement? Exploring a new territory in sport and ethics, this edited collection contains some of the best new writing that has emerged from the debates concerning the uses of genetic technologies to improve sport performance ...'

4764 Handbook of sports studies
J. Coakley and E. Dunning, eds   Sage Publications, 2002, 608pp. £29.99. ISBN 9780761949497.
'(T)his vital handbook marks the development of sports studies as a major new discipline within the social sciences ... Key aspects of the Handbook include an inventory of the principal achievements in the field; a guide to the chief conflicts and difficulties in the theory and research process; a rallying point for researchers who are established or new to the field, which sets the agenda for future developments; a resource book for teachers who wish to establish new

curricula and develop courses and programmes in the area of sports studies.'

4765 Sports ethics: an anthology
J. Boxill, ed.   Blackwell Publishing, 2003, 351pp. £20.99. ISBN 9780631216971.
Edited collection, including 10 essays specially written for the volume. The book is organized into: Introduction – the moral significance of sport; Part I. Sport and education; Part II. Sport and sportsmanship; Part III. Sport and competition; Part IV. Sport and drugs; Part V. Sport and violence; Part VI. Sport and gender; Part VII. Sport and racial issues; Part VIII. Sport and role models.

4766 Values in sport: elitism, nationalism, gender equality and the scientific manufacturing of winners
C. Tamburrini and T. Tännsjö, eds   Spon, 2000, 246pp. £26.99. ISBN 9780419253709.
Wide-ranging collection of essays tackling some of the most difficult moral dilemmas in the field.

Sports Activities

aeronautic sports • athletics • badminton • baseball • basketball • cricket • cycling • equestrian sports • football (soccer) • football (US) • golf • gymnastics • ice hockey • motor sports • rugby • skiing • swimming • tennis • walking • yachting

Dictionaries, thesauri, classifications

4767 Wisden dictionary of cricket
M. Rundell   3rd edn, A. & C. Black, 2006, 224pp. £8.99. ISBN 0713679158.
' ... not only an A–Z guide to all things cricket, it also includes illustrations showing positions and strategy and quotations from cricket literature worldwide ...'

Laws, standards, codes

4768 The sports rules book
T. Hanlon, ed.   2nd edn, Human Kinetics, 2004, 315pp. $19.95. ISBN 9780736048804.
Useful tool for understanding the procedures, main features and guidelines for 47 sports.
'... a helpful source ... designed to aid administrators, coaches, players, and fans who want a basic idea of how various sports are played. It could also help potential officials get to know what a sport is about.' (*Referee Magazine*)

Official & quasi-official bodies

4769 Natural England: leisure
Natural England
www.naturalengland.org.uk/leisure
Formed from English Nature and parts of the Countryside Agency and Rural Development Service, Natural England promotes 'access, recreation and public well-being' as part of its work. Leisure section covers access and recreation, including walking for health, national trails and the new national outdoor recreation strategy.

Libraries, archives, museums

4770   National Sporting Library [USA]
www.nsl.org
Founded in 1954 in Middleburg, Virginia. Mission to 'preserve and to share the art, literature and culture of horse and field sports'. Over 15,000 titles on horse and field sports, including fishing, hunting, horse racing and art. Online catalogue and list of subject headings. Library includes related fiction, rare books, journals and archives. Full-text newsletter.

Portal & task environments

4771   Badminton England
www.badmintonengland.co.uk
Governing body for badminton in England. Background information about the organization and sport; laws; conditioning advice; details of national rankings, clubs and leagues; coaching; events and school section. Extensive support information, including anti-doping policy and equal opportunities. Search facility; site map featuring A to Z listing option as alternative to structural guide.

4772   British Cycling
www.britishcycling.org.uk
Governing body for competitive cyclists, formerly British Cycling Federation. Sections on types of cycling: BMX, track and road racing, disability cycling, mountain biking, cyclo-cross, speedway, cross-country and recreational cycling. Personalization facilities for members. Searchable database of results, facilities, news and clubs. UK coach listing and downloadable *Coaching Insight* articles.
- **Go-Ride** www.go-ride.org.uk. British Cycling programme for under-18s, aiming to teach cycling skills and promote the sport of cycling. Coaching activities, skills tests and talent team tests. Interactive map of UK club locations, safety tips, plus guidance on cycling gear and types of bikes. Guide to cycle racing, news and links. Facility to register for league tables. Click on the 'launch' icon to access the site.

4773   British Equestrian Federation
www.bef.co.uk
National governing body for horse sports in the UK. Comprises 16 member organizations representing: show jumping, eventing, dressage, horse driving trials, enclosure riding, vaulting, reining, disabled, riding schools and the various mounted sports. Details of programmes, news, international and national events, volunteering and research.
- **British Equestrian Federation Researching Equine Database** www.wuerd.org. Formerly the World Undergraduate Equine Research Database (WUERD), providing details of research on equine topics. Re-launching in 2007 as BEFRED.

4774   British Gymnastics
British Amateur Gymnastics Association
www.british-gymnastics.org
BAGA is the governing body for gymnastics in the UK, trading as British Gymnastics. Information on the sport and organization. Features substantial number of results, performance, technical and other documents to download, including the members' handbook. Note: there may be files in the download area despite a zero indicator.

4775   British Horse Society
www.bhs.org.uk
UK's largest equestrian charity. Information about riding clubs, safety, competitions, access, information and education. Trade directory and extensive links. Sixty leaflets to download, details of publications and search facility.
- **The BHS manual of equitation** British Horse Society 4th edn, Kenilworth Press Ltd, 2006, 144pp. £14.95. ISBN 9781872119335. One of many BHS publications.

4776   British Swimming
www.britishswimming.org
National governing body for swimming, diving, water polo, open water and synchronized swimming in UK, comprising the English, Scottish and Welsh Amateur Swimming Associations. Medical and sports science-related information, health and safety guidelines and corporate strategy documents. Section for teachers and coaches. News, health advice and spectator guides.
- **ASA handbook 2006** www.sportcentric.com/vsite/vcontent/page/custom/0,8510,5157-180816-198034-40179-266054-custom-item,00.html. Many sports organizations allow access to their official handbooks and rules. The *ASA handbook*, for example, can be downloaded in sections.

4777   Cricinfo
www.cricinfo.com
Comprehensive site claiming to be 'the world's leading cricket website'. News, results and fixtures, plus sections on women's cricket, statistics, results archive and profiles of players and grounds. International coverage – separate country pages. Explanation, glossary and history of the game. Publications include *The Wisden Cricketer* and *Cricinfo Magazine*. Wisden Almanack archive.
- **The Cricinfo guide to international cricket** S. Lynch, ed. John Wisden & Co Ltd, 2006, 256pp. £8.99. ISBN 9781905625017.
- **Wisden almanack archive** www.wisden.com. Covers 1864–2007. Search by keyword or subject; browse by year. Includes: reports and scorecards from Test and one-day internationals; essays, features and articles; authoritative accounts, Editor's Notes and obituaries.
- **Wisden cricketers' almanack** M. Engel, ed. John Wisden & Co, 2007, annual, 1664pp. £40. ISBN 9781905625024, ISSN 01429213. Classic annual printed edition. Other editions available.

4778   England & Wales Cricket Board
www.ecb.co.uk
National governing body for cricket in England and Wales, 'one single unified body responsible for the management and development of every form of cricket for men and women, including clubs, schools, juniors and youth, disabilities cricket, representative, first class and international cricket'. Accordingly, website covers all these and more; sections for supporters, statistics, regulations, technical information and broadband feeds.
- **Play-Cricket** www.play-cricket.com. ECB's 'online cricket network for all Clubs, Leagues, Cup Competitions and County Boards. It is the official source of all information and statistics on club cricket for all cricketers and supporters'. Searchable directory of cricket clubs, mainly in England and Wales.

4779   Fédération Aéronautique Internationale
www.fai.org
World air sports federation, founded in 1905. 'A non-governmental and non-profit making international organization with the basic aim of furthering aeronautical

and astronautical activities worldwide'. Links to microsites of the various FAI sports and technical commissions; news, events, records and documents centre, including downloadable *FAI sporting code*. Large number of mailing lists.

4780 Fédération Internationale de l'Automobile
www.fia.com

'Governing body of motor sport worldwide ... an independent world body concerned with a wide range of automotive, motoring and mobility issues'. Downloadable policy documents; information about and regulations of the various FIA championships, news and events, media centre and FIA archive of press releases. Microsite of motor sport history 1904 to 2004; photographic timeline, text downloadable in chapters.

■ **FIA Institute for Motor Sport Safety** www.fiainstitute.com. Aims 'to promote improvements in the safety of motor sport', managing research, training and medical control for the FIA. Research groups, working groups and research projects. Articles, multilingual training videos, details of events and conference reports. Downloadable publications include factsheets and *A Driver's Guide to Safe Motor Sport* (2005).

4781 Fédération Internationale de Natation
www.fina.org

FINA is 'the worldwide swimming sports organization', covering swimming, water polo, diving, open water, synchronized swimming and masters swimming. Website has rules and regulations for each discipline, athlete biographies, anti-doping section and events. Details of publications, records, results and rankings. Video clips and links to national federations.

4782 Fédération Internationale des Associations de Footballeurs Professionels
www.fifpro.org

FIFPro is the 'worldwide representative organization for all professional players', covering 42 national associations, as at August 2007. Provides support for players in national and international disputes and 'pursues equal rights and obligations for all players all over the world'. Members' area. Also available in Spanish.

4783 FIFA.com
Fédération Internationale de Football Association
www.fifa.com

Mission to 'develop the game, touch the world, build a better future'. Extensive website covering developing the game; social responsibility; marketing and media. Downloadable rules and regulations, statistics, factsheets and archive of technical reports relating to past tournaments such as the Olympics and World Cup. 'Classic Football' covers all aspects of the history of the game. News and features, video clips and photographs.

4784 Football Association [UK]
www.thefa.com

Official website of the FA (Football Association of England), covering football from grassroots to international level. Complex site structure, with information on the England national teams, Euro 2007, the FA Cup, FA organization and women's football and grassroots, including sections for players, parents, coaches, referees, schools and clubs and information on the leagues and facilities.

4785 Football Foundation [UK]
www.footballfoundation.org.uk

UK's largest sports charity, funded by the FA Premier League, the FA and the government. Mission is 'to improve facilities, create opportunities and build communities', working 'to increase participation in grass roots football'. Sections for the public, clubs, education, youth groups, local authorities, charities, business and partners. Advice on funding and best practice. Downloadable reports, datasheets and newsletters.

■ **Register of English football facilities** www.reff.org.uk. Project funded by Football Foundation. Searchable by postcode, town or facility name, or by pitch size or surface type. Results displayed as interactive map or list. Detailed location maps; information about amenities.

4786 International Association of Athletics Federations
www.iaaf.org

International governing body for athletics. News, results and alphabetical listing of athletes and their biographies. Video clips and podcasts; photo gallery and results from past championships. IAAF site has downloads section containing manual for IAAF federations, scoring tables and other documentation, plus background information on athletics and extensive links.

4787 International Basketball Federation
www.fiba.com

World governing body for basketball, with links to all international member federations. 'Basketball basics' include rules, regulations, fundamentals and a glossary. Experts' corner, with information on coaching, refereeing and medical issues. News, events and interactive section.

4788 International Rugby Board
www.irb.com

Founded in 1886. World governing body for rugby union, based in Dublin, Ireland. News; hall of fame; anti-doping guidance; online coaching tool (requires registration); articles; details of tournaments and rankings. Downloadable rules and regulations; link to World Cup site. Overviews of national unions with links to respective websites, such as the RFU.

4789 International Ski Federation
www.fis-ski.com

Founded in 1924, covers Alpine, freestyle, cross-country, Nordic combined, speed and grass skiing, plus snowboarding, ski jumping, telemark and masters. Athlete biographies, news, anti-doping policy, results, rules and interactive media guide. Downloadable rules and publications by discipline. Members, area. Also available in French and German.

4790 International Tennis Federation
www.itftennis.com

World governing body for tennis. Aims 'to develop the game at all levels at all ages for both able-bodied and disabled men and women'. Microsites for: juniors, men, women, seniors, wheelchair tennis, coaching, development, Olympics, Paralympics, technical aspects and anti-doping, each with their own resources. ITF section features overview, rules and searchable list of 205 member associations. Database of players.

4791 Lawn Tennis Association
www.lta.org.uk
Governing body for tennis in Great Britain. Comprehensive website covering history of the game, top-level performance, playing, spectating, tennis in the community and news. Directories section includes tournaments, links and downloadable rules, policies and resources for clubs, schools and coaches. Other LTA sites include the Blueprint for British Tennis.
- **Wimbledon** www.wimbledon.org. Official website with news and information about past and future tennis championships: Wimbledon history; event guide; virtual tour; free video clips (chargeable video on demand service); museum details. Short downloadable information sheets from Media Centre. Link to Wimbledon media archive.

4792 Motor Sports Association [UK]
www.msauk.org
'Recognized as the sole governing body of motor sport in Great Britain' by the FIA. Details of events, regional associations, directory of clubs and downloadable newsletter. Information on getting started, types of racing events and technical FAQ.

4793 Motorsport Industry Association
www.the-mia.com
UK-based trade association for the motor sport sector. Motor sport news and press releases, information about the industry and careers guidance. Activities and events; membership information and education section. Members' area.
- **Motorsport Research** www.motorsportresearch.com. MIA service providing 'facts, figures, statistics, information, publications and reports relating to the motorsport industry'. Searchable database of business and technology reports, most for purchase (MIA members' discount) but significant number free to download.

4794 The Pony Club
www.pcuk.org
'International voluntary youth organization for those interested in ponies and riding.' Searchable database of UK pony clubs and riding centres. Details of events, training and efficiency tests and the various disciplines such as show jumping, dressage, eventing and polo. Information about insurance, hats, child protection and hunting policy for parents and kids section.
- **The manual of horsemanship: the official manual of the Pony Club** B. Cooper, ed.   13th edn2006, 448pp. £13.99. ISBN 9780954886318.

4795 Professional Golfers Association [USA]
www.pga.com
Site of the PGA of America, with news, tournament schedules, link to the PGA tour and sections for players on playing, improving and equipment, with golf club glossary. Glossary for beginners, golf etiquette and links to rules of the game; golf tips, features and find a (US) instructor facility.

4796 Ramblers Association [UK]
www.ramblers.org.uk
'Britain's biggest walking charity.' Works 'to encourage and support regular walking for health, leisure and transport in both urban and rural areas.' Walking information for beginners or experienced walkers. Practical advice, routes and statistics. Campaigns and countryside information. Postcode search facility with local clubs, weather, maps, etc.
- **Walking Britain** L. Johnson, ed. www.walkingbritain.co.uk. Personal website 'dedicated to the footpaths that cross the landscape', especially UK National Parks and Areas of Outstanding Natural Beauty. Articles, routes and walking advice. Search facility, product reviews, extensive collection of photographs and 'add a walk' feature. Maps for purchase.

4797 Royal & Ancient Golf Club of St Andrews
www.randa.org
The 'R&A is golf's world rules and development body and organizer of The Open Championship'. Site covers championships, golf development, equipment, course management and rules. International case studies; downloadable rules and documents. Best practice guidelines for course management. News, information about St Andrews and online shop.
- **The R & A golfer's handbook** R. Laidlaw   Macmillan, 2007, 960pp. £25. ISBN 9781405049351. Hardback annual review.
- **Rules of golf and the rules of amateur status 2004–2007** 30th edn 2003, 98pp. Free to download. www.randa.org/shop/productfiles/RoG2004.pdf. Available in various languages from R&A website, together with supporting documentation.

4798 Royal Yachting Association [UK]
www.rya.org.uk
UK 'national association for all forms of recreational and competitive boating, representing sailing, motor cruising, sports boats, windsurfing, inland boating, powerboat racing and personal watercraft'. Works at local, national and international levels. Details of activities, organization and regions. Advice for beginners, young people's section, course details and facilities directory.
- **RYA Knowledge Base** www.rya.org.uk/KnowledgeBase. Advice on boating abroad, buying and selling, disability, environment and technical issues, plus weather, statistics and 'ask the experts' facility. Racing Rules for purchase; downloadable background documentation.

4799 Rugby Football League
www.rfl.uk.com
'Rugby League is now accepted as one of the five major sports alongside cricket, football, rugby union and tennis.' Organizing body for the game of rugby league in the UK. Covers international and national leagues and cups together with the community game, including club resources and locator.

4800 Rugby Football Union
www.rfu.com
The RFU governs the game in England and aims to 'enable its successful development at all levels'. Site has news, results and fixtures, discussion forums and links to community rugby and the England team site. Corporate/legal informatio, competitions. There are a number of microsites such as the supporters' club and museum.
- **Community Rugby** www.community-rugby.com. RFU site for clubs and participants. Sections for schools, volunteers, club managers, coaches and officials, plus information for players, covering topics such as positions, fitness and equipment. Club finder. Extensive club management documentation.

4801 Soccer Training Info
www.soccer-training-info.com
'Soccer resource centre with tips on how to improve your

game', created by a group of former professional football players. Provides 'knowledge, advice, tips and encouragement'. History of the game and articles archive; sections on conditioning; skills and techniques; strategy and tactics; sports equipment. Video clips and blog.

4802 Society for American Baseball Research
www.sabr.org
Established in 1971, SABR's mission is 'to foster the study of baseball past and present and to provide an outlet for educational, historical and research information about the game'. Large number of committees, mailing lists and online projects. Publications include *The Baseball Research Journal* and *The National Pastime*. Link to OCLC's WorldCat. Members extranet.

- **Business of Baseball Committee** SABR committee website with 'historical documents, maps, polls, blogs, events calendar, and more'. Full access for SABR members only. Database of business and baseball-related references.
- **The Baseball Biography Project** http://bioproj.sabr.org. SABR project, 'an ongoing effort to produce comprehensive biographical articles on every person who ever played or managed in the major leagues, as well as any other person who touched baseball in a significant way'.
- **The Baseball Index** www.baseballindex.org. A SABR project, TBI is 'a free catalog to baseball literature. It encompasses books, magazine articles, programs, pamphlets, films, recordings, songs, poems, cartoons, advertising, or anything else that may be of interest to the baseball fan or researcher'.

4803 UK Athletics
www.ukathletics.net
National governing body for athletics in the UK, covering grassroots to elites. Sections for clubs, coaches, fans, kids, officials, teachers and volunteers. Includes information on getting started, world-class events, anti-doping, competition and events. Facilities guide, running track directory and strategy documents. Website accessibility options.

4804 USA Football
www.usafootball.com
'Independent non-profit organization whose purpose is to galvanize, support and promote the sport at all levels of amateur football.' History of American football, advice on setting up a league and sections on health and safety, officiating and coaching, each with contextual glossary.

Discovering print & electronic resources

4805 An athletics compendium: an annotated guide to the UK literature of track and field
T. MacNab, P. Lovesey and A. Huxtable; British Library 2001, 261pp. £10. ISBN 9780712311045.
The definitive guide to every book on athletics published in the UK between 1531 and 2000; contains an extensive review of the literature with comment on over 2000 books.

4806 The baseball bibliography
M.J. Smith 2nd edn, McFarland, 2006. 4 v., $150. ISBN 9780786415311.
Vol 1: A. Reference works. B. General works, history and special studies. C. Professional leagues and teams. Vol 2: D. Youth league, college, foreign and amateur/semi-pro baseball. E. Baseball rules and techniques. F. Collective biography. G. Individual biography, Aaron–Encarnacion. Vol 3:

G. Individual biography, Engel–Oxley. Vol 4: G. Individual biography, Oyley–Zwissig, journals, periodicals and magazines examined, index of names and subjects.

Digital data, image & text collections

4807 Association of Football Statisticians
www.11v11.co.uk
Football statistics website 'for football fans, statisticians and journalists alike'. 11v11 started as digitization of AFS library. Free access to history of football, photographs, obituaries and details of books. 'Today in History' feature.

- **The AFS Football Genome Project** www.11v11.co.uk/index.php?pageID=548. Professional football database. Includes 'the majority of international players and line-ups since 1870 for all countries'. As at August 2007, '270,000 matches, 46,000 players and 8,000 teams, with results going back to the earliest matches in the 19th century'. Full access for subscribers only.

4808 Athletics Data [UK]
www.athleticsdata.com
Free service of results and rankings regularly updated by *Athletics Weekly* magazine. Search by club, athlete, or ranking; search or browse results; browse fixtures and standards. Data 2005 onwards, apart from middle distance events (2001 onwards). Note that 'in due course a registration and login system will be created' for athletes and coaches.

- **gbrathletics** www.gbrathletics.com. 'Regularly updated (and free!) reference resource containing a wide range of British and International Athletics Statistics', now owned by *Athletics Weekly*. Some sections being transferred to Athletics Data website.

4809 Backcheck: a Hockey Retrospective
www.collectionscanada.ca/hockey
Digital project focusing on early history of ice hockey, using materials from the collection of Library and Archives Canada. Browse by theme, decade, photo or article or by general chronology, or use the search facility. Includes educational resources, books and links. Available in English and French.

- **Backcheck: Hockey for Kids** www.collectionscanada.ca/hockey/kids. 'Parallel site intended to interpret this material for a younger audience.' Available in English and French.

4810 Baseball Archive
http://baseball1.com
Established by sports writer Sean Lahman and described as 'the most complete set of baseball data available anywhere, with full statistics from 1871 to 2006'. Freely available in several formats. Site also includes sabermetrics, statistics, FAQ on and history of the game. Baseball Statistics System, requiring Access 2000 software.
Available for purchase in CD-ROM format ($15.95 plus $2.00 postage and packing).

- **The Essential Baseball Library** D. Nichols Free to view. http://baseball1.com/content/view/38/76/. Comprises Larry Ritter's 50-book Essential Baseball Library and SABR Review of Books Essential Library.

4811 Football club history database [UK]
www.fchd.info
'Attempt to give a brief statistical breakdown of the history of football clubs in England and Wales.' A to Z listing of

clubs by title; entries contain 'a seasonal summary of highpoints, league table information ... and then available cup information'. Compiled by enthusiast Richard Rundle. Useful bibliography. Complements AFS website.

Directories & encyclopedias

4812 A–Z encyclopaedia of ice hockey
P. Stamp and S. Roberts, eds
www.azhockey.com
A 'free access ice hockey resource, developed by *The ice hockey annual* and Graphyle Consultants for hockey fans worldwide' covering 'players, people, teams, leagues, competitions, awards, events, rinks, books, magazines, websites etc.' Information with embedded links and links to external websites.

4813 Encyclopedia of British football
R.W. Cox, D. Russell and W. Vamplew, eds Frank Cass, 2002, 400pp. £22.99. ISBN 0714652490.
'Over 250 entries focus on key organizations or individuals, famous clubs, major competitions, events, venues and incidents, institutions and organizations as well as key issues such as gender, racism, commercialization, professionalism and drugs, and alcohol and football.'

Keeping up to date

4814 Athletics
P. Matthews, ed. SportsBooks, annual. £18.95 [2007]. ISBN 9781899807499.
www.sportsbooks.ltd.uk/athletics.html [DESCRIPTION]
The major annual within the field, including biographies of 700 leading athletes country by country and exhaustive lists of performances.

4815 BritishSports.com
www.britishsports.com
Directory of British sports, with links to websites of governing bodies and national associations; regional associations and individual club sites. Includes jobs, newsletter, ticket purchase facility, online shop and events.

4816 The cricketers' who's who
C. Marshall, ed. Green Umbrella Publishing, annual. £16.99 [2007]. ISBN 1905828268.
Includes 'an entry for every single player to have represented a County in 2006 or is contracted for 2007'.

4817 The PFA footballers who's who
B.J. Hugman Mainstream Publishing, 2007, 480pp. £17.99. ISBN 9781845962463.
'(C)omprehensive review of the skills, achievements and statistics of all those who played in the Barclaycard Premiership and Coca-Cola Football League Championship and Divisions One and Two during the 2006–7 season. At the same time, it also takes into account each player's performances in the FA Cup, Carling Cup, Football League Trophy and European competitions, where applicable.'

Sports History

Introductions to the subject

4818 Athletics: a history of modern track and field athletics (1860–2000): men and women
R. Quercetani Sep Editrice, 2000, 430pp. £29.90. ISBN 9788887110234.
www.sepeditrice.com [DESCRIPTION]
Published with the support of the International Athletic Foundation, with each chapter covering a given period of time and recalling the facts and figures in their human, competitive and technical aspects, for both men and women.

4819 Landmarks in British sport
R.W. Cox Frank Cass, 2003, 112pp. £19.99. ISBN 9780714682990.
'Began as a Millennium project by the British Society of Sports History to identify the first 100, then 2000 most significant events in the history of British sport. Containing almost 3500 entries from 500 BC to 2000 it is the definitive chronology of British sport.'

Landmarks in the history of physical education
P.C. McIntosh See entry no. 4726

4820 Sport and the British: a modern history
R. Holt Clarendon, 1989, 396pp. £22. ISBN 9780192852298.
'This lively and deeply researched history – the first of its kind – goes beyond the great names and moments to explain how British sport has changed since 1800 and what it has meant to ordinary people. It shows how the way we play reflects not just our lives as citizens of a predominantly urban and industrial world, but what is especially distinctive about British sport. Innovators in abandoning traditional, often brutal sports and in establishing a code of "fair play", the British were also pioneers in popular sports and in the promotion of organized spectator events.'
'... an ideal introductory text ... The range and richness of the subjects are inviting to historians, and Holt supplies us with an indispensable vade-mecum.' (*English Historical Review*)

4821 Sport, economy and society in Britain, 1750–1914
N.L. Tranter; Economic History Society Cambridge University Press, 1998, 112pp. £10.99. ISBN 9780521576550.
Chapters are: 1. Author's introduction; 2. Growth or decline? The initial impact of urban-industrialization; 3. The 'revolution' in sport; 4. A conspiracy of the elites? 5. For health, prestige, or profit? 6. No place for women? 7. Agenda for research; Bibliography.
'Tranter has produced an important book. It should enable a wide range of teachers to introduce sports history to a cross disciplinary audience; an area of study that has often been trivialised, yet one that has been central to the fabric of British life since pre-industrialisation.' (*Journal of European Area Studies*)

4822 The story of sport in England
N. Wigglesworth Routledge, 2007, 196pp. £21.99. ISBN 9780415372640.
'Key themes and issues in the evolution of sport are examined, including Social structures, such as the division between amateurs and professionals; The growth of the popular press and the influence of television; The post-war

emergence of sports "welfarism" and "sport for all"; Globalization and commercialization.'

Dictionaries, thesauri, classifications

4823 Historical dictionary of African Americans in sport
D.K. Wiggins M.E. Sharpe, 2002, 400pp. £73.50. ISBN 9780765605764.
'Biographical entries for over 400 African American men and women involved in sports, as well as entries on tournaments, leagues, clubs, associations and other organizations and events that have featured prominently in the history of African American sport. The entries cover all professional and amateur sports, from the well known (and lesser known) personalities and events in baseball, basketball, football and track and field, to less examined areas such as golf, tennis, horse and sport car racing, fencing and many others.'

Research centres & institutes

4824 International Centre for Sport History & Culture
www.dmu.ac.uk/sportshistory
Based at De Montfort University, Leicester, and 'widely acknowledged as the leading centre for the study of sport history in the world, with the foremost historians in the field on its staff'. Details of staff publications, newsletter and research activity. Link to Arts and Humanities Research Council (AHRC) Sport History and Heritage Research Network.

Associations & societies

4825 International Society for the History of Physical Education & Sport
www.zen20110.zen.co.uk/SportHistWeb/SPORTS%20HISTORY/ishpes.html
'Umbrella organization for sports historians all over the world', promoting 'research and teaching in the area of physical education and sport'. Mailing list, conference details and multilingual online bulletin, available 1996 onwards.

Libraries, archives, museums

4826 Joyce Sports Research Collection [USA]
www.sports.nd.edu
Collection of sports materials at University of Notre Dame Library, Indiana, named after the Reverend Edmund P. Joyce. Extensive archive mainly ephemeral printed matter but also monographs, manuscripts, photographs, audiovisual material and memorabilia. Subject focus: modern American athletics, especially boxing, baseball, football, basketball and wrestling. Most material from 1935 to 1970. Specialized collections. Guides to the collection, digitized photographs and some full-text documents.

Portal & task environments

4827 British Society of Sports History
www.sporthistinfo.co.uk
BSSH aims 'to promote, stimulate and encourage

discussion, study, research and publications on the history of sport and physical education'. Comprehensive website maintained by Dr Richard Cox, with extensive links to sports history-related sites and details of theses and research. Details of publications, conferences and projects, including chronology of British sports history and encyclopaedia of British football. New site was annnounced for September 2007.
- **Index to current contents of sports history and related journals: A to Z**
  www.zen20110.zen.co.uk/SportHistWeb/SPORTS%20HISTORY/Current%20Contents/ccontent.html. Details of sports history-related articles in both specialist and general history journals, provided by BSSH. A to Z listing of journal titles. Some feature links to abstracts or full-text articles.
- **Index to sporting manuscripts in the UK R.W. Cox** .
  www.zen20110.zen.co.uk/SportHistWeb/Private/book4.html. One of many resources, both published and unpublished, compiled by Richard Cox and available from the BSSH website. Free to download; updates post-1993 on site. Includes name index and repository index.

4828 Jews in Sports Online [USA]
www.jewsinsports.org
Biographical and statistical information on more than 1000 amateur and professional Jewish athletes from baseball, basketball, boxing, chess, football, hockey, soccer, tennis, the Olympics and other sports. Compiled by the American Jewish Historical Society. Selected articles and extensive extracts from or full-text versions of related books (mainly US). Search facility.

4829 Sporting Chronicle
www.sportingchronicle.com
Sports news, results and fixtures for major sporting events in the areas of football, horse racing, Formula One motor racing, golf, American football and US baseball. Details of 'past and present sports winners and former sport champions'. Years vary by sport. Search facility, blog and site map. Maintained by sports journalist Richard Bevan.

Discovering print & electronic resources

4830 British sport: a bibliography to 2000
R.W. Cox Frank Cass, 2003. 3 v., £75.00 per volume.
Three-volume bibliography 'documenting all that has been written in the English language on the history of sport and physical education in Britain. It lists all secondary source material, including reference works, in a classified order to meet the needs of the sports historian'.
- **1. Nationwide histories** 200pp. ISBN 9780714652504.
- **2. Local histories** 312pp. ISBN 9780714652511.
- **3. Biographical studies of British sportsmen, women and animals** 176pp. ISBN 9780714652528.

4831 HickokSports.com
www.hickoksports.com
Potted histories and biographies covering a wide range of sports and sports people, with international coverage but focusing on the US. Created by former journalist and author, Ralph Hickok. Sports biographies, rules, sports glossaries, calendar of events, sports quotes and trivia, plus online stores. Continually growing.
- **Bibliography R. Hickok** Freely available.
  www.hickoksports.com/bibliog.shtml. Bibliograpy of sports history texts. Largely US-focused.

4832 **International sport: a bibliography, 1995–1999, including an index to sports history journals, conference proceedings and essay collections**
R.W. Cox, ed.   Routledge, 2004, 202pp. £75. ISBN 9780714652603.
www.zen20110.zen.co.uk/SportHistWeb/SPORTS%20HISTORY/bibsb.htm [COMPANION]
Planned regularly updated bibliography responding to the substantial growth in publications in this arena.

Digital data, image & text collections

4833 **LA84 Digital Archive**
www.la84foundation.org/5va/over_frmst.htm
Project 'to convert portions of its traditional library collection to digital format. The growing digital collection now contains more than 300,000 pages'. Titles are too many to list but include 'academic journals, scholarly books, popular sports magazines of the late nineteenth and early twentieth centuries and an extensive offering of Olympic publications'.
Formerly known as the AAFLA (Amateur Athletic Foundation of Los Angeles) Digital Archive.

Olympics through time
See entry no. 4718

4834 **The Sporting News**
www.paperofrecord.com/search_paper.asp?PaperId=834 [REGISTRATION]
Complete backset (1886–2003) of *The Sporting News*, a St Louis daily newspaper 'often referred to as the "Bible of Baseball" because of its extensive coverage of the sport', available from Paper of Record website. Freely searchable in five-year chunks. Thumbnail views available but registration required for full-text access.

Directories & encyclopedias

4835 **Biographical dictionary of American sports**
D.L. Porter, ed.   Greenwood Press, 2000. 3 v., $424.95. ISBN 9780313298844.
Profiles over 1450 baseball luminaries, including current stars, former major league players, managers, umpires, executives and Negro League and All-American Girls Professional Baseball League stars.
'Useful and enjoyable for baseball enthusiasts, this title is recommended for large sports collections and libraries serving a baseball-loving public.' (*Choice*)

4836 **Encyclopedia of British sport**
R.W. Cox, G. Jarvie and W. Vamplew   ABC-CLIO, 2000, 463pp. $47.50. ISBN 9781576073728.
An authoritative, one-stop overview of the history of sports in Britain from the earliest times to the present.
'... an excellent reference source ... Recommended for public libraries serving communities interested in British sports.' (*Choice*)

4837 **The encyclopedia of North American sports history**
R. Hickok   Facts on File, 2002, 594pp. $24.95. ISBN 9780816050710.
Arranged alphabetically, this encyclopedia has entries on modern and obsolete sports, topics of historical interest, key people, social issues related to sports, major awards and records, cities, stadiums and arenas, professional sports organizations, halls of fame and sports museums.

4838 **Encyclopedia of traditional British rural sports**
T. Collins, J. Martin and W. Vamplew, eds   Routledge, 2005, 301pp. £95. ISBN 9780415352246.
Provides a social, economic and political study of field sports and those other activities and customs labelled as rural sports, from the earliest of times to the present in all of the UK and Ireland.

4839 **History of Women in Sports Timeline**
www.northnet.org/stlawrenceaauw/timeline.htm
Part of the women's history resources produced by the St Lawrence County Branch of the American Association of University Women. Divided into periods, with emphasis on 1900 onwards. Details of notable events; US-focused. Not all embedded links active.

4840 **Sports in America**
Facts on File, 2004. 8 v., $240. ISBN 9780816052332.
www.factsonfile.com [DESCRIPTION]
'(H)istory of 20th-century American athletics that covers historical high points, scandals, records, championships and the rise of professional athletics with the unique slant of examining sports as social history.'

4841 **Sports in North America: a documentary history**
Academic International Press, 1992–2000. 8 v., $96.50 per volume.
www.ai-press.com/SportsDocs.html [DESCRIPTION]
'SPORTSDOCS for the first time documents the development of the spectrum of sports in the United States and Canada from colonial times to the present. The series demonstrates in firsthand, original ways the long-term relationships of sport, society and life.'
- **1 part 1. Sports in the colonial era, 1618–1783** T.L. Altherr, ed.   1996, 496pp. ISBN 9780875691886.
- **1 part 2. Sports in the new republic, 1784–1820** 1996, 469pp.
- **2. Origins of modern sports, 1820–1840** L.K. Menna, ed. 1997, 420pp. ISBN 9780875691367.
- **3. The rise of modern sports, 1840–1860** G.B. Kirsch, ed. 1992, 408pp. ISBN 9780875691565.
- **4. Sports in war, revival and expansion, 1860–1880** 1997, 412pp. ISBN 9780875691350.
- **5. Sports organized, 1880–1900** G.R. Gems, ed.   1996, 529pp. ISBN 9780875691480.
- **6. Sports and reform, 1900–1920** S.A. Riess, ed.   1996, 516pp.
- **8. Sports and the Depression, 1930–1940** D.O. Baldwin, ed. 2000, 501pp. ISBN 9780875692241.

Handbooks & manuals

4842 **A history and philosophy of sport and physical education: from ancient civilizations to the modern world**
R.A. Mechikoff and S. Estes   4th edn, McGraw-Hill, 2005, 415pp. £41.99. ISBN 9780072973020.
http://highered.mcgraw-hill.com/sites/0072973021 [COMPANION]
16 chapters in five sections: Section I. Ancient civilizations; Section II. From the spiritual world to the secular world: changing concepts of the body; Section III. The theoretical

and professional development of American physical education; Section IV. Historical and philosophical development of sport in America; Section V. A social and political history of the modern Olympic Games.

4843 The Victorians and sport
M. Huggins   Hambledon Continuum, 2007, 318pp. £12.99. ISBN 9781852855376.
Contents listed as: Sport in Victorian England; Sport, festivity and celebration; Conflicts; The media; Sportsmanship; Sporting stars; Rivalries; Global impact.

Sports Industry

leisure industries • sponsorship • sports equipment • stadiums

Introductions to the subject

4844 Fundamentals of sport marketing
B.G. Pitts and D.K. Stotlar   3rd edn, Fitness Information Technology, 2007, 440pp. $69. ISBN 9781885693785.
'(T)he most current, contemporary and indispensable book on sport marketing that is available.'

Leisure industries
K. Roberts   See entry no. 3607

4845 Sport in the city: the role of sport in economic and social regeneration
C. Gratton and I. Henry   Routledge, 2001, 322pp. £27.99. ISBN 9780415243490.
Five key areas are examined: Sport and urban economic regeneration; Sports events: bidding, planning and organization; Urban sports tourism; Sport and urban community development; Urban politics and sports policy.

4846 Sport marketing
B.J. Mullin, S. Hardy and W.A. Sutton   3rd edn, Human Kinetics, 2007, 552pp. $74. ISBN 9780736060523.
www.HumanKinetics.com/SportMarketing [COMPANION]
'(T)he latest version of the leading sport marketing text, directs students to a better understanding of the theoretical backbone that makes sport marketing such a unique and vibrant subject to study. The text has been thoroughly updated with a comprehensive ancillary package, new examples and perspectives from the field and the latest information about marketing in the burgeoning sport industry.'

4847 Sports development: policy, process, and practice
K. Hylton and P. Bramham, eds   2nd edn, Routledge, 2007, 288pp. £24.99. ISBN 9780415421836.
'This popular course text examines the roles of those working in and around sports development and explores how professionals can devise better and more effective ways of promoting interest, participation or performance in sport.'

Laws, standards, codes

4848 National Operating Committee on Standards for Athletic Equipment [USA]
www.nocsae.org

Based in the USA, the NOCSAE mission is 'to commission research on and, where feasible, establish standards for protective athletic equipment'. Includes documents on general and sport-specific standards for American football, soccer, baseball, hockey, polo and lacrosse. Useful FAQ, downloadable newsletter from 1998 onwards and summaries of research funded.

Official & quasi-official bodies

4849 SkillsActive [UK]
www.skillsactive.com
Sector Skills Council for Active Leisure and Learning, supporting employers in the sport and recreation, health and fitness, playwork, outdoors and caravan industries. Part of the Skills for Business Network (SfB), aiming to 'develop the skills that UK business needs'. Information on volunteering, workforce development, regional sectors and Sector Skills Agreement (SSA), plus case studies, research papers and publications (some members only).

- **SkillsActiveCareers** www.skillsactive.com/careers. Careers service with comprehensive guidance on entering the active leisure sector; advice on courses, qualifications, career pathways and transferable skills. Job profiles, case studies, interactive sport map and virtual careers advisor, plus news and regional factsheets.

Research centres & institutes

4850 International Center for Sports Studies
www.cies.ch
Private foundation, affiliated with University of Neuchâtel, created in 1995 in association with FIFA to encourage 'a closer collaboration between the sporting and academic worlds'. Specializes in law, sociology and sport economics, providing training, research and consultancy. Details of research projects, publications for purchase and courses. Site also in French.

4851 Motorsport Knowledge Exchange [UK]
www.msportknowledge.ac.uk
'Government-funded small cooperative of receptive and responsive institutions, involved … in motorsport education at a variety of different levels', led by Oxford Brookes University. Aims to sustain and improve 'worldwide competitiveness of the UK motorsport industry'. Course details, learning grid information, online racing games, careers guidance and downloadable industry and government documents.

4852 Sport Industry Research Centre [UK]
www.shu.ac.uk/research/sirc
Sport-related research centre founded in 1996, based at Sheffield Hallam University. 'The main focus of the centre's work is the use of applied economic techniques' in research on the sport and leisure industries. Details of publications and research programmes, including economics of sport, sports participation, major events, elite sport, volunteering and performance management.

4853 Sports Turf Research Institute [UK]
www.stri.co.uk
UK 'national centre for consultancy in Sports and Amenity Turf and a recognized world centre for research'. Information

about testing facilities, including disease, pest and weed guide. Details of training, advisory service and research areas. Full access to the site, including Turf Info sheets and the *International Turfgrass Bulletin*, is for subscribers only.

■ **Royal & Ancient Golf Club of St Andrews/STRI database of current research on golf courses**
www.stri.co.uk/24.asp. Search or browse database of research on golf courses which aims to 'identify research work being carried out on golf courses and related turf areas including construction, soils, grass selection, maintenance, pests and diseases, and golf course ecology'. Excludes North and South America.

4854 SportSURF [UK]
http://civil-unrest.lboro.ac.uk/sportsurf
The Sport Surfaces Research Forum at Loughborough University 'aims to stimulate an integrated multidisciplinary research response to address the problems associated with the interactions of sport players and the sport surfaces, for community and elite level across the full range of sports'. Details of activities and research plus downloadable newsletters and workshop presentations.
Parts of site under construction (August 2007), including research database.

Associations & societies

4855 Association of Play Industries [UK]
www.api-play.org
'Lead trade body within the play sector, representing the interests of the manufacturers, installers, designers and distributors of both outdoor and indoor play equipment and safer surfacing', aiming to improve the quality of play equipment and promote safer play. Database of published articles from January 2005 onwards, directory of members and technical guides for download. Members only section.

4856 Business in Sport & Leisure [UK]
www.bisl.org
Umbrella organization representing the interests of private sector companies in the sport, hospitality and leisure industry in the UK. Online resources include articles on leisure management, a newsletter and details of publications to order plus the downloadable *Active Annual* for 2006–7 and a list of members.

4857 European Network of Sport Science, Education & Employment
www.enssee.de
International non-profit association originally established in Luxembourg in 1989. From 1996, 'thematic network for research, training and the study of qualification and employment in the field of sport by the European Union'. Projects include EOSE, AEHESIS and EUROSEEN, covering PE, coaching, health and fitness, management, employment and e-learning in sport.

■ **European Observatoire of Sport & Employment**
www.eose.org. Aims to 'promote a dialogue between employment and education at the national and European level between public authorities, not for profit organisations, training providers, social partners and research organisations'. Details of projects and networks, downloadable newsletters and library of EOSE documents, some freely available.

4858 European Sponsorship Association
www.sponsorship.org
Formed by the merger of the Institute of Sports Sponsorship (ISS) and the European Sponsorship Consultants Association (ESCA) in 2003. Full-text industry White Papers and details of case studies, calendar of events, directory of ESA members. Mailing list. Members only area.

■ **Sportsmatch** www.sportsmatch.co.uk. UK government's grass-roots sports sponsorship incentive scheme for England. Managed by ESA. Separate Scottish and Welsh schemes.

4859 Federation of Sports & Play Associations [UK]
www.sportsandplay.com
National trade body for UK sports and play industries, formerly the Sports Industries Federation. Downloadable short factsheets from Croner Consulting on aspects of employment, tax, VAT and the law. Full access to resources for members only.

■ **SportsDATA** www.sportsdata.co.uk [REGISTRATION]. Full access for FSPA members only, but includes some free resources. Registration required.

4860 Federation of the European Sporting Goods Industry
www.fesi-sport.org
Represents 'the interests of some 1800 European sporting goods manufacturers before the European Institutions, other international sport federations and other associations'. Site features a large number of downloadable position papers and consultation documents, membership information and details of the various FESI working committees and their activities.

4861 Institute of Groundsmanship [UK]
www.iog.org
UK 'membership organization representing the whole of the grounds management industry and all those involved in it', including greenkeeping, horticulture, turfculture and the management of sports pitches, landscape and amenity facilities. Information on training and careers, events, online Technical Reference library for IOG members, details of funded research and online IOG directory in development.

4862 International Association for Sports Surface Sciences
www.isss-sportsurfacescience.org
An 'Association of technical experts involved in the investigation, development and testing of sports surfaces', comprising 'individuals, scientific institutes, testing laboratories, sports federations or public authorities'. Downloadable ISSS conference papers and publications on artificial turf, the Berlin Artificial Athlete impact test and other topics. Members' area.

4863 International Federation of Horseracing Authorities
www.ifhaonline.org
Founded in 1993, 'to promote good regulation and best practices on international matters'. Searchable racing, breeding and betting statistics database; online racing dictionary; links to members, industry, press and related sites. Results database. Downloadable International Cataloguing Standards and International Statistics report 2007. Members' area. Also available in French.

4864 International Sports Engineering Association

www.sportsengineering.co.uk

Forum for technical issues relating to sport for researchers and the sport and leisure industry. Searchable database of ISEA journal articles and conference papers for members. Electronic discussion list and database of members, some with areas of expertise given. Useful links include university courses, sports companies and research institutes.

- **Sports Engineering** Sheffield Hallam University, 1998–, qtrly. Free to members; £237 institutions (print only) [2007]. ISSN 13697072. www.sportsengineering.co.uk/journal.php. ISEA journal designed 'to fill the niche area which lies between classical engineering and sports science and … bridge the gap between the analysis of the equipment and the athlete'. Online version *Sports Engineering Online* covered 1998 to 2002.

4865 National Sporting Goods Association [USA]

www.nsga.org

US trade association for retailers, manufacturers and industry associates in the sporting goods industry, founded in 1927. Full access is for members only but summaries of publications and services are available. Some statistics on sports participation and consumer purchases available, industry news and range of newsletters. Link to NSGA Sporting Goods Buying Guide.

4866 World Federation of the Sporting Goods Industry

www.wfsgi.org

'World authoritative body for the sports industry', comprising industry suppliers, national organizations and sporting goods industry-related businesses and aiming 'to promote increased free and fair trade and improve the well-being of mankind through the practice of sports'. Downloadable themed annual handbook; report on restricted substances in sports footwear, clothing and accessories. Extranet for members.

- **CSR and the World of Sport: official international handbook 2007** 132pp. Free to download. www.wfsgi.org/pages/publications/hb07.pdf. Update of the 2004 handbook focusing on the issue of corporate social responsibility.

Portal & task environments

4867 Bicycle Helmet Safety Institute

www.bhsi.org

Programme of the Washington Area Bicyclist Association, 'acting as a clearinghouse and a technical resource for bicycle helmet information'. Access to a wide range of technical resources and articles on bicycle helmets, including design, maintenance, research and statistics, safety, laws, helmets for children, standards and teachers' section. Site map, topic listing and search facility. Also available in Spanish.

4868 Institute for Sport, Parks & Leisure [UK]

www.ispal.org.uk

Professional body representing the sport, parks and leisure industry, formed by merger of ILAM (Institute of Leisure and Amenity Management) and the NASD (National Institute for Sports Development) in 2006. Aims to provide education, training and CPD for the sport and leisure industry.

- **Information Hub** www.ispal.org.uk/info_hub.cfm. Range of current and archived publications, some free to download, including reports on: gender equity; race and ethnicity in leisure management; guide to careers in leisure. Abstracts from current articles, summaries of factsheets and advice for students. Access to full services for members only.

4869 Outdoor Industry Association

www.outdoorindustry.org

The US-based 'premier trade association for companies in the active outdoor recreation business', founded in 1989. Features information on US government policies, industry news and events, as well as downloadable social research and market research documents, presentations and information about industry standards.

4870 Sporting Goods Manufacturers Association [USA]

www.sgma.com

US-based international trade association of 'manufacturers, retailers and marketers in the sports products industry'. Wide range of research and industry reports on sports participation, the state of the industry and market segments: current reports for purchase (members discounted price or free access); archived reports downloadable upon registration. Sample reports freely available.

4871 Sports & Play Construction Association [UK]

www.sapca.org.uk

UK trade association which 'represents specialist constructors, manufacturers and suppliers of sports surfaces and related products and plays an important role in the promotion of high standards for sports facilities'. Searchable database of products, members and trade names. Technical guidance for members and for visitors upon registration, including glossary, presentations and information leaflets. Members' area.

Digital data, image & text collections

4872 Federation of European Sporting Goods Retail Associations

www.fedas.com

Represents the transborder trading interests of specialist sports retailers in Europe. Established FEDAS Standardization Organization to encourage commercial standards for electronic data interchange by using the FEDAS Product Classification Key, covering 5000 products. Complete table of classifications can be downloaded. Site available in multiple languages. Members' area.

4873 Sportdevelopment.org.uk [UK]

www.sportdevelopment.org.uk

A 'collection of resources for students about sports development in the United Kingdom' which is also 'designed to provide a distance learning and continued professional development resource for practitioners'. Contains 'ruff guides' as a starting point for students, plus extensive document library which can be browsed by title, author, date or topic, or searched via website search facility.

Website contents also available for purchase on CD-ROM (£49.99).

4874 World Stadiums

www.worldstadiums.com

Database of major sports stadiums throughout the world, past, current and future. Over 9500 in 223 countries listed (August 2007). Search by keyword such as sport or browse by location, tournament or capacity. Some architectural information and photographs.

Directories & encyclopedias

4875 Plunkett's sports industry almanac
Plunkett Research, annual, 500pp. $299.99 [2008 edn]. ISBN
159392089X.
www.plunkettresearch.com [DESCRIPTION]
Market research, business trends and statistics analysis, and
business development support.

Handbooks & manuals

4876 Sports marketing: a strategic perspective
M. Shank 3rd edn, Prentice Hall, 2005, 624pp. $126.67. ISBN
9780131440777.
'Organized around a framework of the strategic marketing
process that can be applied to the sports industry, this text
provides an appreciation for the growing popularity of
women's sports and the globalization of sport; a balanced
treatment of all aspects of sports marketing at all levels; an
introduction of the concepts and theories unique to sports
marketing and a review of the basic principles of marketing
in the context of sports; and comprehensive coverage of the
functions of sports marketing.'

4877 Understanding the leisure and sport industry
C. Wolsey and J. Abrams, eds Longman, 2001, 190pp. £31.99. ISBN
9780582381650.
12 chapters in three sections: 1. The leisure providers; 2. The
leisure and sports markets; 3. The management of leisure
and sport organizations.

Keeping up to date

4878 Deloitte Sports Business Group
www.deloitte.com/dtt/section_node/0,1042,sid%253D70402,00.html
Specialist UK-based team of consultants working in the
sports business, especially the football industry. Features
details of their business consulting and advisory services to
the sports industry, many with links to related case studies,
podcasts or business reports, some of which are free to
download; others can be ordered online. Registration
required to access Deloitte Football Money League 2007.

4879 Fitness Industry Association
www.fia.org.uk
A 'trade body promoting excellence and best practice within
the health and fitness sector'. Site under development
August 2007.

4880 Leisure Opportunities [UK]
Leisure Media Co Ltd, 1987–.
www.leisureopportunities.co.uk
UK job vacancies, training, tenders, shares, news and
property in the areas of sport, fitness, leisure, tourism,
hospitality, museums and the arts. Free e-mail subscription
on registration. Link to printed subscription version plus
other Leisure Media Company titles on sport and leisure
management.
Fortnightly print version. ISSN 09528210. £29.00 [2007]
- **Health Club Management** 1995–, 11 p.a. £39.00 print [2007].
  ISSN 13613510. www.health-club.co.uk. One of the stable of Leisure Media
  publications, as above.

4881 SportBusiness
www.sportbusiness.com
Commercial website supplying 'information, media and B2B
marketing services to the sports industry'. Search facility or
browse by events, marketing or media, or by sector, sport or
country. Business directory, conferences and jobs. Reports
for purchase (some free executive reports on request). Daily
e-mail news bulletin on registration; full access to magazines
to subscribers only (free trial issue).

Sports Law

Introductions to the subject

4882 Law and sport in contemporary society
S. Greenfield and G. Osborn, eds Frank Cass, 2000, 296pp. £26.99.
ISBN 9780714681245.
'As the commercialization of sport grows, the need for
proper regulation increases. In legal terms, sport is part of
the entertainment and media industries which are subject to
rapid change. This work brings together experts in many
fields to analyse these changes ...'

4883 Sport and the law
E. Grayson 3rd edn, Butterworths, 1999, 631pp. £61. ISBN
9780406905055.
Well established text, but now in need of update.

4884 Sports law
S. Gardiner [et al.] 3rd edn, Routledge, 2005, 724pp. £40.95. ISBN
9781859418949.
Firmly established as the market-leading textbook on sports
law, the third edition of this comprehensive and innovative
book provides a detailed examination of the legal issues
surrounding and governing sport.

4885 Sports law: an overview [USA]
http://straylight.law.cornell.edu/wex/index.php/Sports_law
Sports law entry from Wex, the public-access law dictionary
and encyclopaedia hosted by the Legal Information Institute
at Cornell Law School. Commentary and primary source
references covering sports law in the US. Links to relevant
full-text federal and state legal documents. Updated at least
annually.

Official & quasi-official bodies

4886 Court of Arbitration for Sport
www.tas-cas.org
Established in 1983, CAS provides a forum for the resolution
of international sports-related disputes from its
headquarters in Geneva, Switzerland and courts in Denver,
USA and Sydney, Australia. Code of sports-related
arbitration, mediation rules, ad hoc rules, recent case law,
history of the CAS and search facility. Presentation uses FAQ
format. English and French versions.

Research centres & institutes

4887   ASSER International Sports Law Centre
www.sportslaw.nl
Part of the TMC Asser Institute, the Hague, Netherlands, providing 'high quality research, services and products to the sporting world at large ... on both a national and an international basis'. Section on case law, full-text research reports mainly in Dutch or English, documentation centre covering variety of topics in international sports law. Bibliography, linking to Peace Palace Library.

- **Bibliography on sports law** www.ppl.nl/asser. Online database maintained by Peace Palace Library, The Hague, covering books, articles, reports and websites. Overview of topics shown on tag cloud; browse A to Z keyword listing or use search facility. Links to library catalogue record and full-text material where available.

4888   National Sports Law Institute [USA]
http://law.marquette.edu/cgi-bin/site.pl?2130&pageID=160
Based at Marquette University Law School, NSLI 'strives to be the leading national educational and research institute for the study of legal, ethical and business issues affecting amateur and professional sports from both an academic and practical perspective'. Publications include *Marquette Sports Law Review* (with index). Summaries of annual *Recent developments in sports law* downloadable 2003 onwards.

Associations & societies

4889   Australian & New Zealand Sports Law Association
www.anzsla.com.au
A 'non-profit organization dedicated to providing education, advocacy and networking opportunities on legal issues in sport to Australian and New Zealand sporting industries'; membership 'open to anyone with an interest in sport'. Details of events and extensive links but full access to resources, including papers, journals and literature database, for members only.

4890   British Association for Sport & Law
www.britishsportslaw.org
Main aim 'to assist the development of sports law as a legal discipline and provide a network for sports law practitioners, academics and sports administrators'. Details of events, useful links and tables of contents from *Sport and the Law Journal*, 2002 onwards. Members' area.

4891   International Association of Sports Law
http://iasl.org
Objective is 'the cultivation and the development of the Science, the research and the teaching of Sports Law and the institution of the Olympic Games'. Details of the many congresses, some with abstracts, but access to full-text papers and other resources for members only. Contents of issues of *International Sports Law Review: Pandektis*; most volumes for purchase.

4892   International Sport Lawyers Association
www.isla-int.com
A 'worldwide association of international, mainly European based sports lawyers, that was established under the laws of Switzerland'. Press releases, recent case law, events, articles and book details. Multilingual website; many documents only available in German.

4893   Sport & Recreation Law Association [USA]
http://srlaweb.org
US-based non-profit corporation, whose purpose is 'to further the study and dissemination of information regarding legal aspects of sport and recreation ... within both the public and private sectors'. Formerly the SSLASPA (Society for the Study of Legal Aspects of Sport and Physical Activity). Details of conferences, publications and list of legal resources. 'Teaching Tips' for members.

Portal & task environments

4894   Centre for Sport & Law [CAN]
www.sportlaw.ca
Canadian consulting company 'offering services and practical resources on legal and risk management issues'. Full-text articles organized by general topic such as violence, risk management, screening, doping and contracts, plus quarterly newsletter. Canadian focus. 'Information on this website is intended as general legal information and should not form the basis of legal advice or opinion.'

Discovering print & electronic resources

4895   International Sports Law
A. Burchfield
www.nyulawglobal.org/globalex/International_Sports_Law.htm
Online resource guide published on the GlobaLex website in 2006; available via the Hauser Global Law School Program, New York University School of Law. Annotated guide with hyperlinks covering governance, Olympics, CAS, anti-doping, human rights and other topics.

Handbooks & manuals

4896   Sport: law and practice
A. Lewis [et al.], eds   LexisNexis UK, 2002, 1145pp. ISBN 9780406945921.
'This is a major textbook on sports law in the UK and consolidates guidance across all the major practice areas of interest to sports lawyers. Written by a team of acknowledged and acclaimed experts, this comprehensive work is essential reading for solicitors and barristers practising sports law, as well as universities, governing bodies, sports agencies, clubs and commercial firms. The new edition is due in 2007.'

Keeping up to date

4897   International Sports Law Review
M.J. Beloff, ed.   Sweet & Maxwell, 2000–, qtrly. £378.00 [2007]. ISSN 14676680.
www.sweetandmaxwell.co.uk/details?prodid=6753&unitid=6753&search=&format=J&publisher=all&subject=all&from=401&to=450 [DESCRIPTION]
'This quarterly journal analyses current issues and developments in the practice of law as it affects sports business and sports-related litigation and is the only source of full sports law reports. Edited by a team of well known experts, it covers domestic and international developments in this fast-growing area.'

Sports Management & Policy

leisure industry • professional sport • recreation
management • sports economics • sports organizations

Introductions to the subject

4898 Contemporary sport management
J.B. Parks, J. Quarterman and L. Thibault, eds   3rd edn, Human
Kinetics, 2007, 520pp. $72. ISBN 9780736063654.
Contributions from 30 scholars and professionals provide 'an
excellent overview of the principles and possibilities in this
dynamic industry … The text is written at a reader-friendly
yet challenging level and will provide students with a solid
foundation in the field, allowing them to successfully
progress through their curriculum toward a career in sport
management.'

Economics of sport: an international perspective
R. Sandy, P.J. Sloane and M.S. Rosentraub   See entry no. 3602

Economics of sport and recreation
C. Gratton and P. Taylor   See entry no. 3603

**4899 Human resource management in sport and
recreation**
P. Chelladurai   2nd edn, Human Kinetics, 2006, 341pp. $59. ISBN
9780736055888.
16 chapters in four parts: Part I. Human resources in sport
and recreation; Part II. Individual differences in human
resources; Part III. Human resource practices; Part IV.
attitudinal outcomes.

4900 Leisure and recreation management
G. Torkildsen   5th edn, Routledge, 2005, 580pp. £30. ISBN
9780415309967.
Established text dealing with the theory of leisure studies as
well as the day-to-day practicalities of managing a recreation
facility.

4901 Managing public sport and leisure services
L. Robinson   Routledge, 2004, 193pp. £30. ISBN 9780415270779.
Contents: 1. The public sport and leisure context; 2. The
changing nature of public sport and leisure management; 3.
Managing public sport and leisure services; 4. Planning and
strategy development; 5. Human resources management; 6.
Financial management; 7. Performance management; 8.
Quality management; 9. The management of change; 10.
Best practice in public sport and leisure management.

4902 Sports management and administration
D.C. Watt   2nd edn, Routledge, 2003, 280pp. £32.99. ISBN
9780415274579.
Designed to help all those delivering sport to deliver it better.

Terminology, codes & standards

4903 Governance in Sport
www.governance-in-sport.com
Website originating from the 2001 European conference
entitled 'The Rules of the Game', organized by the EOC
(European Olympic Committee) and FIA (Fédération
Internationale de l'Automobile). Contains a statement of

good governance principles to be followed by sports
governing bodies (in English and French), key speeches and
the conference conclusions.

Laws, standards, codes

**4904 Professional sport in the European Union:
regulation and re-regulation**
A. Caiger and S. Gardiner, eds   Cambridge University Press, 2001,
368pp. £75. ISBN 9789067041263.
Eminent sports law scholars examine the relationship
between sport, business and policy.

Research centres & institutes

4905 Football Governance Research Centre
www.football-research.bbk.ac.uk
'Leading academic centre for the study of corporate
governance in professional football in the UK', based at
Birkbeck College, University of London. Contains extensive
number of full-text documents in library and research
sections, plus research project details and selected online
books. Details of conferences, seminars, courses and related
links.

Associations & societies

4906 Chief Cultural & Leisure Officers Association [UK]
www.cloa.org.uk
Represents strategic managers in UK local authorities or non-
profit-distributing trusts and those working in associated
areas such as health, education and social sectors and
coordinates the National Culture Forum. Details of events,
membership and current issues, which include downloadable
reports on topics such as asthma in swimming pools and
local government strategy documents.

4907 Fields in Trust [UK]
www.fieldsintrust.org
Formerly the National Playing Fields Association (NPFA), FIT
is 'the only independent UK wide organization dedicated to
protecting and improving outdoor sports and play spaces
and facilities'. Details of campaigns, downloadable policy
statements and responses to government, plus members'
area. FieldFinder database.

4908 Institute of Sport & Recreation Management [UK]
www.isrm.co.uk
The 'only national professional body for those involved
exclusively in providing, managing, operating and developing
sport and recreation services in the United Kingdom'. Details
of qualifications and training; research reports and
publications; downloadable policy statements, external
reference documents and selected 'information notes'.
Members' area with full access to ISRM journal *Recreation*
and to information notes.

4909 North American Society for Sport Management
www.nassm.com
NASSM's purpose is 'to promote, stimulate and encourage
study, research, scholarly writing and professional
development in the area of sport management – both

theoretical and applied aspects'. Details of conferences, courses, membership and the NASSM *Journal of Sport Management*.

Portal & task environments

4910 Sport Management Association of Australia & New Zealand
www.griffith.edu.au/school/gbs/tlhs/smaanz
Founded in 1995, SMAANZ aims 'to encourage scholarly enquiry into sport management related research and to provide the opportunity to communicate results from this research to the broader sport management community'. Details of conferences, membership and the SMAANZ journal, *Sport Management Review* (archived articles in LA84 Foundation digital archive).

Portal & task environments

4911 RunningSports [UK]
www.runningsports.org
Sport England service providing support for volunteers involved in running sports, in teams, clubs or community organizations. Aims 'to address key issues such as volunteer recruitment, retention management and motivation, club finances, links with schools and accessibility in sports clubs'. Members' and tutors' area. Downloadable Quick Guides on fund-raising, volunteer roles and other topics (require free registration).

4912 Sport in the European Union: two players – one goal?
http://sport-in-europe.com
Project of the Association of European Sport Studies. 'Besides the European Union's sport policy, the project deals with the common grounds between the field of sport and the European Union, the different forms and characteristics of sport and the specific sport structures of the 18 member states'. Overview of the EU structure; relevant treaties and declarations; background information on 24 EU countries.

4913 Sport, physical activity and renewal toolkit [UK]
www.renewal.net/toolkits/SportsToolkit
renewal.net was developed by the Department of Communities and Local Government 'to fulfil one of the commitments of the Government's National Strategy Action Plan for neighbourhood renewal'. The sport toolkit 'helps you to deliver effective sport, physical activity and renewal programmes'. Overview of problem, explanation and policy; case studies; research; guidance on designing and implementing sports projects.

Discovering print & electronic resources

4914 John Beech's Sport Management Information Gateway
J. Beech
www.stile.coventry.ac.uk/cbs/staff/beech/sport/index.htm
A 'starting point for British university students and others looking for sources relevant to coursework for sports management modules on Bachelor and Masters Degree programmes'. Focus on professional and sponsored sports, plus aspects of amateur sports such as retailing and equipment and the Olympics. Personal interest site maintained by John Beech, from Coventry University.

Handbooks & manuals

4915 The business of sport management
J. Beech and S. Chadwick, eds   Financial Times Prentice Hall, 2004, 528pp. £40.99. ISBN 9780273682684.
http://businessofsportmanagement.blogspot.com [COMPANION]
Nineteen contributed chapters covering a wide range of issues, organized into three parts: I. The context of sport; II. Business functions applied to sport; III. Sport management issues.

4916 The commercialisation of sport
T. Slack, ed.   Routledge, 2004, 335pp. £26.99. ISBN 9780714680781.
Examines five different aspects of the commercialization of sport: the sports industry; the public sector; the commercialization of 'amateur' sport; sport and television; and sports sponsorship.

4917 Game plan: a strategy for delivering Government's sport and physical activity objectives [UK]
Great Britain. Department for Culture, Media & Sport and Great Britain. Cabinet Office   2002, 223pp.
www.cabinetoffice.gov.uk/strategy
Major UK government report looking at: the state of UK sport in 2002; the benefits of physical activity; the vision for 2020; increasing mass participation; enhancing international success; hosting major events and improving the organization and delivery of sport in the UK.

4918 The global politics of sport: the role of global institutions in sport
L. Allison, ed.   Routledge, 2005, 194pp. £24.99. ISBN 9780415346023.
Examines the emerging global political issues in 21st-century sport, including the role and power of organizations such as FIFA and the IOC; the influence of US exceptionalism; the construction of global sports heroes; and tensions developing within traditionally 'alternative' sports in a global commercial culture.

4919 Managing environments for leisure and recreation
R. Broadhurst   Routledge, 2001, 359pp. £25.99. ISBN 9780415200998.
Contents: 1. The scope of leisure and recreation; 2. Histories of leisure and recreation; 3. The leisure and recreation web; 4. Benefits, costs and issues; 5. Attaching values; 6. Preparing to manage planning, from research to design; 7. Managing for the environment: the physical setting; 8. Managing for people: the socio-economic setting; 9. Managing future environments.
'Excellent ... this text is recommended to university libraries and to lecturers teaching in sport, recreation and leisure as well as tourism, as a valuable teaching and student resource.'
(*International Journal of Tourism Research*)

4920 Outdoor recreation management
J.J. Pigram and J.M. Jenkins   2nd edn, Routledge, 2005, 426pp. £28.99. ISBN 9780415365413.
Analyses leisure and outdoor recreation in terms of both their management and their wider importance to society.

4921 The politics of sports development: development of sport or development through sport?
B. Houlihan and A. White   Routledge, 2002, 250pp. £31.99. ISBN 9780415277495.
Traces the evolution of sports development in the UK in the context of broader shifts in sport and social policy. It explores the emergence of sports development from the early years of public policy for sport in the 1960s to the contemporary era.

4922 Transatlantic sport: the comparative economics of North American and European sports
B.C. Pestano, C. Ibrahímo and S. Szymanski   Edward Elgar, 2002, 222pp. £62. ISBN 9781840649475.
'Offers a comparative perspective on the economics of sport and highlights both the similarities and differences in the North American and European models of sport. It tackles policy issues, such as the organizing, financing and regulation of team sports alongside theoretical issues regarding income redistribution and competitive balance. It also evaluates the impact of sport and sports events on local communities and the wider economy providing a useful contrast of methods and results on the two continents.'

4923 Understanding sports organizations: the application of organization theory
T. Slack and M. Parent   2nd edn, Human Kinetics, 2006, 376pp. $62. ISBN 9780736056397.
'(G)round-breaking text ... (which) ... continues to give readers a strong foundation in organization theory and application of that theory by providing a real-world context to all its issues. It engages readers by providing opportunities to discover the theory in practice through use of profiles, case studies and examples of sport organizations in each chapter.'

Keeping up to date

4924 Sports Management Report [UK]
www.sportsmanagement.co.uk
Associated website of printed journal *Sports Management*, published by Leisure Media Company. News, events, jobs and free weekly e-mail service (registration required).
Printed magazine subscription £25.00 [2007]. 4 issues p.a.

Sports Nutrition
diet & physical activity

Introductions to the subject

4925 The complete guide to sports nutrition
A. Bean   5th edn, A. & C. Black, 2006, 292pp. £15.99. ISBN 9780713675580.
Includes maximizing endurance, strength and performance; how to calculate your optimal calorie, carbohydrate and protein requirements; advice on improving body composition; specific advice for women, children and vegetarians; and eating plans to cut body fat, gain muscle and prepare for competition.

4926 Sports nutrition
A.E. Jeukendrup and M. Gleeson   Human Kinetics, 2004, 424pp. $62. ISBN 9780736034043.
In-depth discussion of the science behind sport nutrition, including general principles, background and rationale for current nutritional guidelines.

4927 Sports nutrition
R. Maughan and L. Burke, eds   Blackwell Science, 2002, 200pp. £26.99. ISBN 9780632058143.
Practical supplement to *Olympic encyclopaedia of sports medicine* (q.v.), volume 7, *Nutrition in sport*.

Research centres & institutes

4928 Lucozade Sport Science Academy
www.thelssa.co.uk
Commercial site from GlaxoSmithKline promoting sports drink Lucozade Sport with sports nutrition and performance advice. Sports Nutrition Centre covering basic nutrition, energy, hydration, preparation, recovery, protein, supplements and climate. Glossary. Academy Toolkit includes animations and charts in zipped format. Abstracts from articles researching use of Lucozade products. Register for newsletter, its archive and e-mail science archive.
- **A Sporting Chance J.G. Morris and M.E. Nevill**   Sportnation, 2006, 34pp. Free to download. www.thelssa.co.uk/lssa/sportnation. Report from the Institute of Youth Sport about the relative age effect, published by Sportnation, a national sports thinktank supported by the LSSA. Executive summary or full report available.

Associations & societies

4929 Dietitians in Sport & Exercise Nutrition [UK]
www.disen.org
Interest group of the British Dietetic Association providing advice on nutrition for sport and exercise, for both athletes and the general public. Includes articles, recipes and details of publications, events and courses. Nutrition section covers fluids, alcohol, supplements, protein, fats and energy foods.

4930 International Society of Sports Nutrition
www.sportsnutritionsociety.org
Non-profit academic society dedicated to sports nutrition. Details of conferences, including PowerPoints of past presentations, international 'Find a Nutritionist' service, details of certification and other professional support. Information for members, newsletter and details of publications including the online ISSN journal.
- **Journal of the International Society of Sports Nutrition** BioMed Central, 2004–, 2 p.a. Free to download. ISSN 15502783. www.jissn.com. Official journal of the ISSN 'that covers various aspects of sports nutrition, supplementation, exercise metabolism, and/or scientific policies related to sports nutrition'. Volumes for 2004 to 2006 available from ISSN website.

4931 Sports Dietitians Australia
www.sportsdietitians.com.au
Australian professional organization for dietitians specializing in sports nutrition, providing 'up to date sports nutrition information based on sound scientific principles'. Factsheets on sports nutrition topics and information for specific sports. Product reviews of Australian food, sports drinks and

supplements. Listing of Australian sports dietitians; members' area. Nutritional information for children, with sport-specific booklets and a 36-page cookbook.

4932   Sports, Cardiovascular & Wellness Nutritionists
[USA]

www.scandpg.org

Section of the American Dietetic Association, dedicated to sports, cardiovascular and wellness nutrition, as well as healthy eating and treatment of eating disorders. Details of events, listings of SCAN dietitians, certification, career tips and members-only section. Bibliographies of books by members, sample issues of *Pulse* newsletter and links to web resources, including position stands.

■ **Sports nutrition: a practice manual for professionals M. Dunford**   4th edn, American Dietetic Association, 2006, 547pp. $69. ISBN 9780880914116. Four sections: sports nutrition basics; screening and assessment; sports nutrition across the life cycle; and sport-specific guidelines, plus 'at a glance' sport-specific information for 18 sports. Accompanying CD available.

Discovering print & electronic resources

4933   Fitness and Sports Nutrition
http://nirc.cas.psu.edu/fitness.cfm

Based at NIRC (Nutrition Information and Resource Center), Penn State University. Links to full-text online publications on sport and exercise nutrition, details of NIRC library materials and links to related websites, rated out of 25. Sections on general nutrition, nutrition for different age groups, food science and community resources. Searchable by keyword.

4934   International Bibliographic Information on Dietary Supplements Database
Office of Dietary Supplements

http://ods.od.nih.gov/Health_Information/IBIDS.aspx

Over 730,000 citations on dietary supplements from Medline, Agricola, Agris (FAO database) and CAB Abstracts and Health, 1986 onwards. Abstracts only. Search full database or sub-sets: Consumer Citations (less technical) and Peer Reviewed Citations. Alphabetical list of dietary supplement factsheets. Produced by the US National Institutes of Health's ODS and US Department of Agriculture's Food and Nutrition Information Center.

Handbooks & manuals

4935   Clinical sports nutrition
L. Burke and V. Deakin, eds   3rd edn, McGraw-Hill, 2006, 822pp. £37.99. ISBN 9780074716021.

Comprehensive reference that provides state-of-the-art sports nutrition information, coupled with advice on how to apply sports nutrition guidelines in a clinical and practical framework.

4936   Nutrition for health, fitness and sport
M.H. Williams   8th edn, McGraw-Hill, 2006, 574pp. £39.99. ISBN 9780071103336.

'This textbook provides the reader with thorough coverage of the role nutrition plays in enhancing one's health, fitness and sport performance. Current research and practical activities are incorporated throughout.'

4937   Sport nutrition for health and performance
M. Manore and J. Thompson   Human Kinetics, 2000, 514pp. $69. ISBN 9780873229395.

Designed to sort fact from fiction and help students and practitioners obtain the knowledge they need to give sound advice to athletes and active individuals.

Sports Participation

blind people in sport • disabled people in sport • participation in sport • women in sport • young people's sport

Introductions to the subject

4938   Exercise and young people: issues, implications and initiatives
L. Cale and J. Harris, eds   Palgrave Macmillan, 2005, 276pp. £19.99. ISBN 9781403902528.

'Explores the key issues, implications and initiatives associated with exercise and exercise promotion in young people, draws together the available evidence on young people's physical activity and fitness and explores how exercise can be promoted to young people in the contexts of the school and community.'

'... a readable, well-organised and invaluable reference book for those with an academic or personal interest in the area.' (*Times Higher Education Supplement*)

Terminology, codes & standards

4939   The Equality Standard: a framework for sport [UK]
www.equalitystandard.org

A 'framework for assisting sports organizations to widen access and reduce inequalities in sport and physical activity from under representative individuals, groups and communities especially women and girls, ethnic minority groups and disabled people', launched November 2004. Background information on the Standard and resources file covering above topics plus newsletter, legislation, policy and research documents.

Official & quasi-official bodies

4940   English Federation of Disability Sport
www.efds.net

National body responsible for developing sport for disabled people in England. Research includes full-text reports, mainly with regional focus. Guidance and advice, training support, the 20-page EFDS Sports Strategy 2007–2012, and information about the regions, each with their own projects, publications and resources.

■ **Disability Sport Events** www.disabilitysport.org.uk. EFDS sports events database; browse by date, region or sport. Includes links (some annotated) and publications on policy and procedures either to download or request by e-mail.

■ **Inclusive Fitness Initiative** www.inclusivefitness.org. EFDS initiative (IFI) supported by Sport England Lottery from 2001 to 2007, aiming to encourage the provision of accessible fitness facilities. Details of the Inclusive Fitness Mark quality mark accreditation scheme. Features UK postcode search for inclusive facilities.

4941 ParalympicsGB
British Paralympic Association
www.paralympics.org.uk
Body which prepares and trains Britain's team for the Paralympic Games (summer and winter). Details of rules, eligibility and classification of individual sports, plus summaries of past and forthcoming Games and other major events. Downloadable documents on hydration, nutrition and anti-doping (other formats, including Braille and large print, on request). Some sections for team members only.
- **Ability vs ability** www.abilityvsability.co.uk. British Paralympic pack for schools, aiming to 'raise awareness of the Paralympic movement; help young people appreciate more fully the nature of an inclusive society' and provide examples of sporting excellence in individual and team sports. Interviews with athletes; image bank of photographs and video clips; activities for young people; guidance for teachers and fact zone. Available in English and Welsh.

Research centres & institutes

4942 COMPASS
http://w3.uniroma1.it/compass
Project 'seeking the coordinated monitoring of participation in sports in Europe, jointly funded by the Italian National Olympic Committee, UK Sport and Sport England. History of the project; background methodology; national and cross-national data. Most data contributed 1996 to 2002. Pilot countries Czech Republic, Finland, Italy, Portugal, Spain, Sweden, Switzerland, the Netherlands and UK.

4943 Institute for the Study of Youth Sports [USA]
http://ed-web3.educ.msu.edu/ysi
Based at the College of Education, Michigan State University, ISYS aims to create a 'shift in the way America judges success in youth sports, placing youth development objectives ahead of winning'. Sections for coaches, parents, researchers and young people, including full-text documents. Left-hand menu colour can be hard to read.

4944 Institute of Youth Sport [UK]
www.lboro.ac.uk/departments/sses/institutes/iys
Research and development centre at Loughborough University for those 'with a common interest in the welfare, education, performance and development of young people participating … in sport and physical education'. Current and completed projects (some, including full documentation); Specialist Sports Colleges report (2004); School Sport Partnerships yearly reports 2004–6. Staff publications for purchase.

4945 National Center on Physical Activity & Disability [USA]
www.ncpad.org
Based at the University of Illinois at Chicago, NCPAD promotes exercise for everybody. Alphabetical list of conditions with exercise guidelines, links and references. Information on individual sports; research; health promotion (nutrition, wellness and programming). Downloadable clips from videos for purchase. Directories of programmes, organizations and suppliers, largely North American. Newsletter, forum and online shop. Access keys for easier navigation.
- **NCPAD: references** www.ncpad.org/refs/books. Extensive listing of references to books, articles, reports, videos, proceedings and theses, including abstracts and annotations. Use the left-hand menu to browse or search by type of publication or search the whole NCPAD site.

4946 Tucker Center for Research on Girls & Women in Sport [USA]
www.education.umn.edu/tuckercenter
Interdisciplinary research centre based at University of Minnesota. Explores 'how sport and exercise influence women's physical, psychological and social development', plus factors influencing 'girls' and women's participation in sports, recreation and physical activity'. Current and past projects, lecture series, downloadable newsletter and research resources, including website links and bibliographies on selected topics, most with abstracts.

Associations & societies

4947 British Universities Sports Association
www.busa.org.uk
Governing body for university sport in the UK. Organizes inter-university sports programme nationally and coordinates UK teams for the World University Championships and World University Games. Comprehensive information on participating sports; news and events; member contacts. Browse fixtures and results by institution, league, knockout or championship. Archived weekly mail-out and My Busa facility. Due to merge with University & College Sport in 2008.

4948 International Blind Sport Federation
www.ibsa.es
Based in Spain, the IBSA 'believe sport is the ideal means to promote the integration of disabled people in general and the blind in particular'. Sections on specific sports, including overview, rules, news, records, top athletes and competitions. IBSA documents, video clips and details of national federations. Available in English and Spanish.

4949 International Federation of Adapted Physical Activity
www.ifapa.biz
'International, cross-disciplinary professional organization of individuals, institutions and agencies supporting, promoting and disseminating information about adapted physical activity, disability sport and all aspects of sport, movement and exercise science for individuals of all abilities'. Events; online newsletter; AAPAR resource manual; adapted physical activity overview (including practice examples). Site accessibility aids and online translator.
- **Adapted Physical Activity Quarterly** Human Kinetics, 1984–, qtrly. $60.00 (individual) [2007]. ISSN 07365829. www.humankinetics.com/APAQ. Online ISSN 15432777. Official IFAPA journal. Tables of contents available from 2001; abstracts available from July 2003. Full-text access for subscribers or on pay-per-view basis.

4950 International Society for Aging & Physical Activity
www.isapa.org
International society 'promoting research, clinical practice and public policy initiatives in the area of ageing and physical activity'. Details of congresses, courses and events, an image gallery and annotated links. International Curriculum Guidelines for Preparing Physical Activity Instructors of Older Adults downloadable upon registration.

■ **Journal of Aging and Physical Activity** Human Kinetics, 1993–, qtrly. $60.00 individual [2007]. ISSN 10638652. www.humankinetics.com/JAPA. Online ISSN 1543267X. ISAPA official journal. Tables of contents and abstracts from 1993 onwards. Full-text access for subscribers or on pay-per-view basis.

4951 International Wheelchair & Amputee Sports Federation
www.wsw.org.uk
Formed by the merger of the ISMWSF (International Stoke Mandeville Wheelchair Sports Federation) and the ISOD (International Sports Organization for the Disabled) in 2004. Information about the IWAS World Games, individual sports, anti-doping policy and newsletter. Parts of site still under development as at August 2007.

4952 National Collegiate Athletic Association [USA]
www.ncaa.org
Purpose is 'to govern competition in a fair, safe, equitable and sportsmanlike manner and to integrate intercollegiate athletics into higher education'. Sports divided into spring, fall and winter as played in US higher education, not just athletics. Features full-text research reports, sport rules, athlete welfare, diversity programmes and statistics. Video clips.
■ **NCAA Sports** www.ncaasports.com. Official website for NCAA sports providing news, on-demand videos, broadcasting information and ticket purchase facility. Links to current and archived statistics, rankings and records.

Special Olympics
See entry no. 4713

4953 University & College Sport [UK]
www.ucsport.net
Mission is 'pursuit of excellence in the provision, management and development of sport in Higher and Further Education' in the UK. Contains clickable list of registered gyms; regional information; strategic plan covering 2003 to 2007. Merging with BUSA to form UK Universities Sport in 2008. Useful links, discussion forum, notice board and details of groups and committees, plus information about NASS and the HE Sport Network.
■ **National Active Student Survey** www.ucsport.net/NASS.asp. Developed to complement the Sport England Active People survey of 2006. Downloadable executive summary; full report available by e-mail or downloadable by members.

4954 WomenSport International
www.sportsbiz.bz/womensportinternational
Aims to 'encourage increased opportunities and positive changes for women and girls at all levels of involvement in sport and physical activity', on global basis. Details of research reports, conference summaries, advocacy case studies and WSI task forces on: sexual harassment; Female Athlete Triad; physical activity and health. Downloadable newsletter (1995–2002). Annotated links to related websites.

4955 Young Explorers' Trust [UK]
www.theyet.org
Charity established in 1972 providing advice on the running of safe and responsible expeditions for young people. Information on benefits of expeditions, YET grants and approvals system. Downloadable publications include YET newsletter; safe and responsible expeditions guidelines; good practice guidelines; guide to good environmental practice and beginnings of an expeditions manual.

4956 Youth Sport Trust [UK]
www.youthsporttrust.org
Registered charity supporting 'the education and development of all young people through physical education (PE) and sport'. Portfolio includes TOP programmes for ages 18 months to 18 years; PESSCL; Innovation and Development programmes encouraging sports participation. Short factsheets with background information. Online directory of companies supplying products and services to business and education sector.
■ **School Sport Xchange** http://ssx.youthsporttrust.org [REGISTRATION]. Resource for professionals in Specialist Sports Colleges and School Sport Partnerships with case studies, document bank and discussion forum. Requires registration.
■ **Talent Matters** www.talentmatters.org. Project of the Carnegie Research Institute, Leeds Metropolitan University, aiming 'to inform current efforts by the Youth Sport Trust to develop effective talent development practices in Physical Education'. Research reports, presentations and newsletter.

Portal & task environments

4957 Canadian Association for the Advancement of Women & Sport & Physical Activity
www.caaws.ca
Canadian organization launched 1981 to encourage women's sports participation and promote 'values of equity, inclusiveness, fairness and respect'. Covers gender equity, advocacy, leadership, physical activity and health, historical milestones, research and grants. Downloadable reports and documents by CAAWS. Extensive links include CAAWS programmes such as 'Mothers in Motion', 'On the Move' and 'VIEWS'. Also available in French.
■ **ACTive** www.caaws.ca/active. Canadian Strategy Framework and Action Blueprint for Girls and Women through Physical Activity and Sport, supported by CAAWS. Downloadable reports and 36-page workbook, links to further information, details of key strategy areas, success stories and mailing list. Also available in French.

4958 Child Protection in Sport Unit [UK]
www.thecpsu.org.uk
Collaboration between the NSPCC and UK Sports Councils to coordinate and support implementation of the 2000 National Action Plan for Child Protection in Sport. Some full-text reports; CPSU briefing papers. Sections for: parents, children, professionals, sports organizations and students/researchers, featuring useful books, articles and websites. Information on National School Sport Strategy, FAQ and UK sports governing body search facility. Keyword search facility.
■ **Strategy for safeguarding children and young people in sport** 20pp. Free to download. www.thecpsu.org.uk/Documents/SafeguardingStrategy.pdf. CPSU strategy document for the period 2006 to 2012.

4959 Disability Sports
http://edweb6.educ.msu.edu/kin866
Created largely by graduate students in the Department of Kinesiology, Michigan State University, for students studying adapted physical activity. Major revision 2002. Covers governance, international competitions, inclusion,

classification and other issues. Papers, abstracts and annotated bibliographies on disability and sport, including biomechanics, coaching, exercise physiology, psychology, sociology and sports medicine. Information on US disability laws. Study questions.

4960 European Women & Sport
www.ews-online.com/en
Aims to increase 'the involvement of women in sport at all levels', encouraging gender equality in education, training, participation, promotion, decision making and administration. List of contact persons throughout Europe. Large number of useful documents and reports, including declarations, conference documents, presentations, newsletters and media studies. Languages vary.

4961 Gender equity in athletics and sports
Feminist Majority Foundation
www.feminist.org/sports
Part of the site of the US-based Feminist Majority Foundation, which aims to promote the equality of women. Contains reports and background documentation on topics, including Title IX, sport and disability, empowering women through sport and women and the Olympics.
- **Empowering women in sports**
  www.feminist.org/research/sports/sports2.html. Publication of the Feminist Majority Foundation's Task Force on Women and Girls in Sports, originally produced in 1995.

4962 Gender Sport & Society Forum
www.gssf.co.nr
'Online project dedicated to scholars and students with an interest in social issues in gender and sport' – sport in the wider context of physical culture and pedagogy. Lists of relevant journals, bibliographies, information on conferences and recently published papers and texts (not up-to-date) and discussion group. Links to research centres, university courses and individual scholar websites.
- **Archives of GSSF@jiscmail.ac.uk: Gender Sport and Society Forum list** www.jiscmail.ac.uk/lists/gssf.html. E-mail discussion list, hosted by JISCmail list. Archives date back to May 2004.

4963 International Council on Active Aging
www.icaa.cc
Supports professionals and organizations working with older adults by providing information, resources and guidance on active ageing, retirement, fitness and well-being. Full access to site resources for members only; sample articles, journal issues and presentations freely available. Consumer section (US-focused). Professional resources include reports, links and details of courses, conferences and publications. Downloadable newsletter.

4964 National Blueprint: increasing physical activity among adults aged 50 and over [USA]
www.agingblueprint.org
Developed by Robert Wood Johnson Foundation as guide for US 'organizations, associations and agencies to inform and support their planning work related to increasing physical activity among America's aging population' in association with a large number of US organizations. Original report from 2001 and extensive supporting documentation, including active ageing tips, background information and progress reports.

4965 Play by the Rules [AUS]
Australian Sports Commission
www.playbytherules.net.au
ASC guidance on how to prevent and deal with discrimination, harassment and child abuse in the Australian sport and recreation industry. Sections for governing bodies, sports clubs, coaches and officials, participants, parents and young people, highlighting their rights and responsibilities. Australian court and tribunal decisions on equal opportunity in sport; state brochures and flyers; general guidelines for umpires and coaches.
- **Online training** www.playbytherules.net.au/site/online_training.jsp? [REGISTRATION]. Free online training courses on discrimination, harassment and child protection aimed at Australian coaches, administrators, umpires and referees, also participants and volunteers. Courses are short (two hour maximum), may be done in part or all at once, and use case studies. Requires registration.

4966 Sporting Equals [UK]
www.sportingequals.com
A 'national initiative working to promote racial equality in sport throughout England'. Established in 1998 as a partnership between Sport England and the CRE (Commission for Racial Equality). Information about the Racial Equality Charter and the Sports Equity Alliance, case studies and downloadable factsheets and research reports. Contextual site map.

4967 Transnational Perspectives of Women in Sport and Physical Culture
http://raw.rutgers.edu/womenandsports
Collection of resources celebrating the achievements of women in sport, including timeline of events to 2001; bibliographies on huge range of topics relating to women in sport and literature; short biographies of female scholars and their publications; film references; text of conference resolutions; and links to conferences and related websites.

4968 Women's Sports Foundation [USA]
www.womenssportsfoundation.org
US charitable organization aiming to 'advance the lives of girls and women through sport and physical activity', founded by Billie Jean King in 1974. Over 100 sports and fitness activities, with details of US organizations, books and videos. Section for athletes; US-focused career centre; issues include discrimination, participation, coaching, gender equity and Title IX ('Know Your Rights').
- **Women's Sports Facts and Statistics** , qtrly. Free to download. www.womenssportsfoundation.org/cgi-bin/iowa/issues/article.html?record=162. Compilation of largely US-based facts and statistics about women and sport.

4969 Womens Sports Foundation UK
www.wsf.org.uk
UK organization founded in 1984 to promote 'opportunities for women and girls in sport and physical activity – in all roles and at all levels'. Latest reports and quick links from the home page; downloadable research updates, factsheets, policy briefings, news, blog and details of regional groups. Completed WSF research can be browsed by topic, most easily located via the site map.
- **What works for women** www.whatworksforwomen.org.uk. WSF project which aims to encourage best practice in sports provision.

Directories & encyclopedias

History of Women in Sports Timeline
See entry no. 4839

Handbooks & manuals

4970 Inclusion through sports
R.W. Davis   Human Kinetics, 2002, 221pp. $29. ISBN 9780736034395.
'Learn how to use sport as the common element to build an effective physical education program that includes students with and without disabilities. *Inclusion Through Sports* is not merely a how-to for disability sport; it presents games and activities derived from six popular disability sports that will improve appropriate services to students with disabilities and broaden and enrich your curriculum for all students.'

4971 Sport and social exclusion
M.F. Collins   Routledge, 2002, 208pp. £28.99. ISBN 9780415259590.
'(P)resents the first comprehensive review of factors leading to exclusion from participation in sport in the UK. Structured around key excluded groups, such as the elderly, ethnic minorities, the disabled and rural communities, the book offers an important assessment of sports policy in contemporary Britain ...'

4972 Sport and women: social issues in international perspective
G. Pfister and I. Hartmann-Tews, eds   Routledge, 2002, 208pp. £25.99. ISBN 9780415246286.
Examines and compares the sporting experiences of women from different countries around the world and offers the first systematic and cross-cultural analysis of the topic of women in sport.

4973 Trends in outdoor recreation, leisure and tourism
W.C. Gartner and D.W. Lime, eds   CABI Publishing, 2000, 458pp. £55. ISBN 9780851994031.
Focuses on the issues and trends in outdoor, 'nature-based' recreation, leisure and tourism and explores the implications for public policy, planning, management and marketing.

Sports Psychology

applied psychology in sport • exercise psychology

Introductions to the subject

4974 Exploring sport and exercise psychology
J.W. Van Raalte and B.W. Brewer, eds   2nd edn, American Psychological Association, 2002, 561pp. $39.95. ISBN 9781557988867.
Provides an overview of applications, interventions and practice issues in this field. Features interventions for peak performance such as imagery training, hypnosis and goal setting. Also includes information about sport psychology services, education for becoming a sport psychologist, ethics and certification.

4975 Foundations of sport and exercise psychology
R.S. Weinberg and D. Gould   4th edn, Human Kinetics, 2007, 624pp. $79. ISBN 9780736064675.
Provides a thorough introduction to all aspects of the field. Topics covered include personality, motivation, arousal, stress and anxiety, competition and cooperation, reinforcement, group cohesion, leadership, communication, improving performance, imagery, self-confidence, concentration, exercise and well-being and children and sport. A useful text for students: clearly laid out with tables, examples and diagrams, chapter summaries, key terms and review questions.

4976 Sport psychology: a student's handbook
M. Jarvis   rev.edn, Psychology Press, 2005, 288pp. £14.95. ISBN 9781841695822.
A good introduction covering personality and sport, attitudes, aggression, social factors affecting performance, arousal and anxiety and motivation and skill acquisition.

4977 Sport psychology: concepts and applications
R.H. Cox   6th edn, McGraw-Hill, 2006, 532pp. £42.99. ISBN 9780071106429.
Twenty-seven chapters in seven parts: 1. Introduction; 2. Motivation of the athlete; 3. Arousal, attention and personality of the athlete; 4. Situational factors related to anxiety and mood; 5. Cognitive and behavioural interventions; 6. Social psychology of sport and exercise; 7. Psychobiology of sport and exercise.

4978 Sport psychology: contemporary themes
D. Lavallee [et al.]   Palgrave Macmillan, 2004, 336pp. £20.99. ISBN 9781403904683.
Provides an excellent overview of research in the main areas of sport psychology, including areas such as imagery, motivation, concentration, anxiety, expertise and teams. Each topic covers the history, background and theory and includes case studies and practical examples. Chapters are written by an international team of experts.

4979 Sport psychology: theory, applications and issues
T. Morris and J. Summers, eds   2nd edn, Wiley, 2004, 678pp. £24.95. ISBN 9780470800089.
Provides good coverage of relevant issues. The volume is in three parts: Theory and research includes chapters on mood, stress, motivation, self-confidence and team dynamics; Applications covers topics such as goal setting, anxiety, mental imagery and concentration; Current issues includes disabilities, children and the benefits of exercise.

Dictionaries, thesauri, classifications

4980 Sport and exercise psychology: the key concepts
E. Cashmore   2nd edn, Routledge, 2008, 480pp. £14.99. ISBN 9780415438667.
Forthcoming new edition: '120 entries cover such diverse terms as: Anger management; Attitudes and intention; Behaviourism; Exercise adherence; Kinaesthesia; Motor learning; Stimulus control.'

Associations & societies

4981 American Psychological Association, Exercise & Sport Psychology
www.apa.org/divisions/div47
Division 47 is the section of the American Psychological Association devoted to sports psychology. Maintained by the Center for Sport Psychology at the University of North Texas, the site features a full-text newsletter available from 2000 onwards, career information about the specialism and details of events. Members can access the APA members directory.

4982 Association for the Advancement of Applied Sport Psychology [USA]
www.aaasponline.org
AAASP Online provides information for coaches, athletes, students, parents, members, professionals and all those interested in applied sport psychology. Focuses on health psychology, performance enhancement/interventions and social psychology. Helpful information about the specialism; details of conferences and publications; guidance on certification.
■ **Journal of Applied Sport Psychology** Routledge, 1989–, qtrly. £72.00 personal print [2007]. ISSN 10413200. www.tandf.co.uk/journals/titles/10413200.asp. Online ISSN 15331571. Official AAASP journal; free to members. Abstracts online 2001 onwards. Online sample on registration.

4983 British Psychological Society, Division of Sport & Exercise Psychology
www.bps.org.uk/spex
Part of the British Psychological Society, DSEP was formed in 2004 to represent psychology professionals working in sport and exercise and promote its development. Details of the DSEP journal and other publications, including qualification and training routes in the UK.
■ **Sport and Exercise Psychology Review** 2005–, 2 p.a. Free to members. ISSN 17454980. www.bps.org.uk/spex/publications. DSEP journal. Back issues can be downloaded prior to February 2006 (as at August 2007); content pages of later issues viewable.

4984 International Society of Sport Psychology
www.issponline.org
A 'multidisciplinary association of scholars whose research interests focus on some aspect of sport psychology', devoted to its research, practice and development. Formed in 1965. Downloadable position statements on ethics, aggression, benefits of physical activity, the internet, anabolic steroids and accreditation. Members' access to ISSP newsletters.
■ **International Journal of Sport and Exercise Psychology** Fitness Information Technology Inc, 2003–. $70.00 individual [2007]. ISSN 1612197X. www.fitinfotech.com/IJSEP/IJSEP.tpl. Online ISSN 1557251X. Reduced price subscriptions for members. Archived articles also available on pay-per-view basis.

4985 North American Society for the Psychology of Sport & Physical Activity
www.naspspa.org
Multidisciplinary association concerned with development and advancement of the scientific study of human behaviour in sport and physical activity and seeking to 'improve the quality of research and teaching in the psychology of sport, motor development and motor learning and control'. Members' access to searchable directory and online

newsletter. NASPSPA official journal (see below) searchable back to 1979.
■ **Journal of Sport and Exercise Psychology** Human Kinetics, 1979–, qtrly. $78.00 individual [2007]. ISSN 08952779. www.humankinetics.com/JSEP. NASPSPA official journal; abstracts and contents can be browsed back to 1979. Online ISSN 15432904.

Handbooks & manuals

4986 Applied sport psychology: personal growth to peak performance
J.M. Williams, ed.   5th edn, McGraw-Hill, 2005, 647pp. £45.99. ISBN 9780072843835.
Comprehensive and practical guide to psychological concepts and theories as well as to strategies and techniques designed to help future coaches and sport psychologists cultivate peak performance and personal growth through recent advances in sport psychology.

4987 Applying sport psychology: four perspectives
J. Taylor and G. Wilson   Human Kinetics, 2005, 310pp. $52. ISBN 9780736045124.
'(M)ore than 50 contributors from around the globe make the study of sport psychology come alive. The four perspectives on each topic present a well rounded approach to understanding team and individual sport performance. Because readers are privy to a conversation of sorts taking place among these four key stakeholders, they will gain understanding from the varying perspectives, increase their knowledge and improve their interactions with clients.'

4988 Exercise psychology
J. Buckworth and R.K. Dishman   Human Kinetics, 2002, 330pp. $62. ISBN 9780736000789.
Provides an in-depth examination of the psychological antecedents and consequences of physical activity relationships, helping the reader to understand the mental health benefits of exercise as well as the thought processes behind the decision to exercise or not to exercise.

4989 Handbook of sport psychology
G. Tenenbaum and R.C. Eklund, eds   3rd edn, Wiley, 2007, 960pp. $120. ISBN 9780471738114.
Wide-ranging coverage, including motivation and emotion, social aspects, expertise, performance enhancement, exercise and health psychology, lifespan development, measurement and special topics such as gender, disabilities and drug use. Chapters are written by an international team of contributors.
2nd edn by R.A. Singer, H. Hausenblas and C. Janelle (2001)

4990 The psychology of physical activity
A.V. Carron, H.A. Hausenblas and P.A. Estabrooks   McGraw-Hill, 2002, 274pp. £46.99. ISBN 9780072849899.
'This is a ground-breaking and comprehensive text devoted solely to the discussion of exercise psychology. Exploring all areas of personal motivation, the benefits of exercise and the theories, pioneers and ongoing research, it prepares the exercise science professional for future career opportunities in the pubic and private sector.'

4991 Sport and exercise psychology: a critical introduction
A.P. Moran   Routledge, 2004, 347pp. £15.95. ISBN 9780415168090.
'(P)rovides the first textbook to combine an explanation of the theoretical foundations of sport and exercise psychology with critical reviews of contemporary research and practical suggestions for relevant independent research projects.'

Keeping up to date

4992 Athletic Insight: the Online Journal of Sport Psychology
Athletic Insight Inc, 1999–, qtrly. Irregular past publication, Freely available. ISSN 15360431.
www.athleticinsight.com
Online peer-reviewed journal providing 'a forum for discussion of topics that are relevant to the field of sport psychology'. Articles and reports of original research accompanied by reviews of research and literature. Free access to full text of current and back issues. Volumes can be browsed but no search facility. FAQ and new book details are included.

Sports Science

biomechanics in sport • exercise science • physiology of sport • sports medicine • sports skills

Introductions to the subject

4993 Acquiring skill in sport: an introduction
J. Honeybourne   Routledge, 2006, 142pp. £22.99. ISBN 9780415349369.
'This user-friendly, accessible text will enable new students to understand the basic concepts of sport skills acquisition. Each chapter covers important theoretical background and shows how this theory can be applied through practical examples from the world of sport.'

4994 Basic biomechanics
S.J. Hall   5th edn, McGraw-Hill, 2006, 544pp. £40.99. ISBN 9780071104319.
'This outstanding introduction to biomechanics uses the latest findings from the research literature to support and exemplify the concepts presented. Quantitative as well as qualitative examples of problems illustrate biomechanical principles; quantitative aspects are presented in a manageable, progressive fashion to make biomechanical principles accessible to all students, regardless of their mathematical skills.'

4995 The biochemical basis of sports performance
R. Maughan and M. Gleeson   Oxford University Press, 2004, 257pp. £24.99. ISBN 9780199269242.
www.oup.com/uk/booksites/biosciences [COMPANION]
The aim of this book is to introduce the student of sports science or exercise physiology to the biochemical processes that underpin exercise performance and the adaptations that occur with training. The focus is on skeletal muscle metabolism and the provision of energy for working muscles.

4996 Biomechanics of sport and exercise
P.M. McGinnis   2nd edn, Human Kinetics, 2005, 411pp. $72. ISBN 9780736051019.
'(I)ntroduces exercise and sport biomechanics in simple and concise terms rather than focusing on complex math and physics. With a unique presentation of biomechanical concepts supported with illustrations, the book helps students learn to appreciate external forces and their effects, how the body generates forces to maintain position and how forces create movement in physical activities.'

4997 Exercise physiology: energy, nutrition, and human performance
W.D. McArdle, V.L. Katch and F.I. Katch   6th edn, Lippincott Williams & Wilkins, 2006, 1184pp. $92.95. ISBN 9780781749909.
Integrates basic concepts and relevant scientific information to provide a foundation for understanding nutrition, energy transfer and exercise training.

4998 Exercise physiology: theory and application to fitness and performance
S. Powers and E.T. Howley   6th edn, McGraw-Hill, 2007, 624pp. £39.99. ISBN 9780071107266.
'Especially for exercise science and physical education students, this text provides a solid foundation in theory illuminated by application and performance models to increase understanding and to help students apply what they've learned in the classroom and beyond.'

4999 Foundations of exercise science
G. Kamen   Lippincott Williams & Wilkins, 2001, 352pp. $65.95. ISBN 9780683044980.
This entry-level text provides an overview of the human movement sciences, combining basic science principles with applications in exercise science.

5000 Fundamental principles of exercise physiology: for fitness, performance, and health
R. Robergs and S. Keteyian   2nd edn, McGraw-Hill, 2003, 512pp. £42.99. ISBN 9780071214070.
'(P)rovides basic and balanced information for the study of exercise physiology for the undergraduate introductory level student. It thoroughly examines both the immediate responses to, as well as the long-term benefits of, exercise.'

5001 Introduction to sports biomechanics: analysing human movement patterns
R. Bartlett   2nd edn, Routledge, 2007, 304pp. £29.99. ISBN 9780415339940.
Contents: 1. Movement patterns – the essence of biomechanics; 2. Qualitative analysis of sports movements; 3. More on movement patterns – the geometry of motion; 4. Quantitative analysis of movement; 5. Causes of movement – forces and torques; 6. The anatomy of human movement.

5002 Kinesiology: scientific basis of human motion
N. Hamilton, K. Luttgens and W. Weimer   11th edn, McGraw-Hill, 2008, 656pp. £40.99. ISBN 9780071106672.
'This introductory text provides undergraduate students with the basics of anatomy, physiology and the applications of kinesiology. It uses a qualitative approach with an easy-to-follow writing style. Theory is balanced with many sport and real-world applications to promote the integrated nature of kinesiology, including the anatomical and biomechanical concepts.'

5003 Motor control and learning: a behavioral emphasis
R.A. Schmidt and T.D. Lee   4th edn, Human Kinetics, 2005, 537pp. $79. ISBN 9780736042581.

'(A) comprehensive introduction to motor behavior. The authoritative text frames the important issues, theories, persons and research in the field in a reader-friendly way, allowing students to learn the most pertinent information in the field.'

'This book has been the mainstay of an entire field and clearly will remain so. (On the 3rd edn.)' (*Perceptual and Motor Skills*)

- **Motor learning and control: concepts and applications**
  R.A. Magill   8th edn, McGraw-Hill, 2006, 482pp. £42.99. ISBN 9780071106979. Another leading text in this field.

5004 Motor learning and performance
R.A. Schmidt and C.A. Wrisberg   4th edn, Human Kinetics, 2007, 416pp. $77. ISBN 9780736069649.

'(E)xpands on the fundamentals of motor performance and learning, providing valuable supporting literature and current research results in an accessible and engaging format.'

5005 Physiology of sport and exercise
J.H. Wilmore and D.L. Costill   3rd edn, Human Kinetics, 2004, 726pp. $85. ISBN 9780736062268.

21 chapters in seven parts: Part I. Essentials of movement; Part II. Energy for movement; Part III. Cardiovascular and respiratory function and performance; Part IV. Environmental influences on performance; Part V. Optimizing performance in sport; Part VI. Age and sex considerations in sport and exercise; Part VII. Physical activity for health and fitness.

Dictionaries, thesauri, classifications

5006 Dictionary of sport and exercise science
A. & C. Black, 2006, 256pp. £9.99. ISBN 9780713677850.

'An invaluable reference book for anyone interested in the fascinating world of sport, containing over 5000 terms relating to sport and sports science. Coverage includes anatomy, physiology, physiotherapy, biology, sports medicine, sporting rules and regulations, governing bodies, health and fitness and banned substances.'

5007 Oxford dictionary of sports science and medicine
M. Kent, comp.   3rd edn, Oxford University Press, 2006, 612pp. £15. ISBN 9780199210893.

'(P)rovides comprehensive and authoritative definitions of nearly 8000 sports science and sports medicine terms. All major areas are covered, including exercise psychology, sports nutrition, biomechanics, anatomy, sports sociology, training principles and techniques and sports injury and rehabilitation.'

Research centres & institutes

5008 Gatorade Sports Science Institute
www.gssiweb.com

US research and educational facility aimed at sports health professionals, established in 1988. Focuses on sports nutrition, exercise science and athlete performance. Sports Science Library contains articles on hydration; training and performance; medical conditions and sports injuries; nutrition and young people. Searchable by profession, sport or article type. Interactive tools include fluid loss calculator and 'deep body tour'.

Associations & societies

5009 British Association of Sport & Exercise Sciences
www.bases.org.uk

UK professional body for all those interested in sport and exercise science. Covers biomechanics, physiology, psychology and interdisciplinary issues; divided into three divisions: Education and Professional Development; Physical Activity for Health; and Sport and Performance. Course finder for undergraduates and postgraduates, details of accreditation, consultant finder and laboratory finder. Members' area.

- **A guide to careers in sport and exercise sciences**
  www.bases.org.uk/newsite/pdf/BASES%20Careers%20Guide.pdf. Developed in association with Human Kinetics.
- **Journal of Sports Sciences** Routledge, 1983–, monthly. £1654 institutional [2007]. ISSN 02640414. www.tandf.co.uk/journals/titles/02640414.html. Online ISSN 1466447X. Published on behalf of BASES, containing research reports, review articles and book reviews on many aspects of sport and exercise science. Special rates for individual members of BASES.

5010 European College of Sport Science
www.ecss.de

Aims to promote sports science at European level, covering all forms of human movement which promote physical fitness or mental well-being. Details of congresses and publications, including the *European Journal of Sport Science*.

5011 International Society of Biomechanics in Sports
www.twu.edu/biom/isbs

A 'forum for the exchange of ideas for sports biomechanics researchers, coaches and teachers', bridging the gap between researchers and practitioners, providing information and materials on biomechanics in sports. Details of annual symposia, the ISBS journal, mailing lists and full-text newsletter. Conference papers available by e-mail: five per annum free to members, carriage charge non-members.

- **Sports Biomechanics** Routledge, 2001–, 3 p.a. £57 personal [2007]. ISSN 14763141. www.tandf.co.uk/journals/titles/14763141.asp. Online ISSN 17526116. Journal of the ISBS; until 2006 published by Edinburgh University Press. Tables of contents available 2007 onwards.

5012 Sport & Exercise Science New Zealand
www.sportscience.org.nz

Professional body for sport and exercise scientists, practitioners and students in New Zealand. Searchable directory of SESNZ-accredited sports medics and health professionals; details of laboratories and publications, including *Guidelines for Athlete Assessment*, (introduction freely available; full guide members only). Downloadable research reports from 1992 to 2002 arranged by sport.

Portal & task environments

5013 The Athlete Project
www.athleteproject.com

US company giving athletes, coaches and others associated with athletics online information on performance and competing safely. Topics include sports medicine, strength and conditioning, exercise physiology, biomechanics, psychology, nutrition, pharmacology and coaching. Browse topics or check recent additions. Tips for athletes and equipment reviews. As at June 2007, site freely available. Discussion forums.

Discovering print & electronic resources

5014 Kinesiology Abstracts
Kinesiology Publications. Full online access $1500 [2006]. Indexed in SportDiscus. ISSN 15471284.
http://kinpubs.uoregon.edu/KinAbs.html
Produced since 1949 at the International Institute for Sport and Human Performance, University of Oregon. Abstracts from US and international theses and dissertations in human movement studies, downloadable in twice yearly editions. Divided into broad subject areas: dance, sports medicine, psychology, biomechanics and PE. Author, school and keyword index. As at August 2007, free coverage 1992 to 2005. Register to search online database; full access by subscription or individual purchase.
Formerly known as the Health, Physical Education and Recreation, Exercise and Sport Science Microform Publications Bulletin.

5015 SPOLIT
www.bisp-datenbanken.de
German database of abstracts from sports-related articles, including some in English. Choose 'Englisch' from the list marked 'Sprache' to search for English articles and abstracts only. Produced by the Bundesinstitut für Sportwissenschaft (BISp) in Cologne.

5016 Sportscience on the Net
www.sponet.de
SPONET database produced by IAT (Institut für Angewandte Trainingswissenschaft), Leipzig. Searchable database with links to full-text publications useful to sports scientists, coaches and athletes. Although searchable in both German and English, many but by no means all articles available only in German. Advanced search or browse by record tags, including keyword, document type, language, country, ISBN, author, date and title version.

5017 Teachers' Information Service
www.usfca.edu/ess/tis
Maintained by John Blackwell, University of San Francisco; now initiative of the International Society of Biomechanics in Sports. Provides collection of links for teachers of kinesiology and biomechanics. Coverage includes university courses, bibliography, tutorials and lesson plans, homework problems, laboratory exercises and links to journals, free software, associations and other relevant sites.

Directories & encyclopedias

5018 Olympic encyclopaedia of sports medicine
Blackwell Publishing, 1988–.
'The encyclopaedia of sports medicine is a multi-volume IOC Medical Commission publication, in collaboration with the International Federation of Sports Medicine. Each book is designed to present state-of-the-art information on current topics of specific clinical and scientific importance.'

▪ The young athlete H. Hebestreit and O. Bar-Or, eds   2007, 512pp. £90. ISBN 9781405156479. NYP. To replace vol. 6?.

▪ **1. The Olympic book of sports medicine** A. Dirix, H. Knuttgen and K. Tittel, eds   1988, 704pp. £75. ISBN 9780632019632.

▪ **2. Endurance in sport** R.J. Shephard and P. Astrand, eds   2nd edn 2000, 1008pp. £105. ISBN 9780632053483.

▪ **3. Strength and power in sport** P.V. Komi, ed.   2nd edn 2002, 544pp. £89.99. ISBN 9780632059119.

▪ **4. Sports injuries: basic principles of of prevention and care** P.A.F.H. Renstrom, ed.   1993, 512pp. £69.99. ISBN 9780632033317.

▪ **5. Clinical practice of sports injury prevention and care** P. Renström   2nd edn 1994, 744pp. £62.99. ISBN 9780632037858.

▪ **6. The child and adolescent athlete** O. Bar-Or   1995, 720pp. £79.99. ISBN 9780865429048.

▪ **7. Nutrition in sport** R.J. Maughan, ed.   2000, 704pp. £89.99. ISBN 9780632050949.

▪ **8. Women in sport** B.L. Drinkwater, ed.   2000, 680pp. £95. ISBN 9780632050840.

▪ **9. Biomechanics in sport: performance enhancement and injury prevention** V. Zatsiorsky, ed.   2000, 680pp. £89.99. ISBN 9780632053926.

▪ **10. Rehabilitation of sports injuries: scientific basis** W.R. Frontera, ed.   2002, 336pp. £79.99. ISBN 9780632058136.

▪ **11. The endocrine system in sports and exercise** W. Kraemer and A. Rogol, eds   2005, 648pp. £105. ISBN 9781405130172.

▪ **12. Tendinopathy in athletes** S. Woo, P. Renström and S. Arnoczky, eds   2007, 248pp. £69.50. ISBN 9781405156707. Excerpts available.

Handbooks & manuals

5019 ACSM advanced exercise physiology
American College of.Sports Medicine   Lippincott Williams & Wilkins, 2005, 704pp. $99.95. ISBN 9780781747264.
'Written by international experts in physiology, exercise physiology and research, ACSM's *Advanced Exercise Physiology* gives students an advanced level of understanding of exercise physiology. It emphasizes the acute and chronic effects of exercise on various physiological systems in adults and the integrative nature of these physiological responses.'

5020 Biomechanical basis of human movement
J. Hamill and K.M. Knutzen   2nd edn, Lippincott Williams & Wilkins, 2006, 575pp. $89.95. ISBN 9780781763066.
'(I)ntegrates basic anatomy, physics, calculus and physiology for the study of human movement. The book provides a uniquely quantitative approach to biomechanics and is organized into three parts: Foundations of human movement; Functional anatomy; Mechanical analysis of human motion.' The book includes motion analysis software.

5021 Biomechanics and biology of movement
B.M. Nigg, B.R. MacIntosh and J. Mester, eds   Human Kinetics, 2000, 488pp. $72. ISBN 9780736003315.
'Drawing on the expertise of 31 international researchers in biomechanics, exercise physiology and motor behavior, *Biomechanics and biology of movement* provides an integrated, multidisciplinary, scientific approach to understanding human movement. As a text, it uses an integrated scientific approach to explore solutions to problems in human movement. As a complete reference volume, it provides an overview of how energy and work, balance and control, load factors, fatigue and exercise interact to affect performance.'

5022 Biomechanics and motor control of human movement
D.A. Winter   3rd edn, Wiley, 2004, 325pp. £70. ISBN 9780471449898.
'Integrating a common set of data and analyses with reliable material on biomechanical techniques, this up-to-date edition examines techniques used to measure and analyse all body movements as mechanical systems, including such everyday movements as walking.'

5023 Biomechanics of the musculo-skeletal system
B.M. Nigg and W. Herzog, eds   3rd edn, John Wiley, 2007, 672pp. £65. ISBN 9780470017678.
Provides a comprehensive account of the mechanics of the neuro-musculo-skeletal system, with the contents organized: Introduction; Biological materials; Measuring techniques; Modeling.

5024 Essentials of exercise physiology
W.D. McArdle, V.L. Katch and F.I. Katch   3rd edn, Lippincott Williams & Wilkins, 2005, 753pp. Includes CD-ROM, $79.95. ISBN 9780781749916.
'(P)rovides excellent coverage of the fundamentals of exercise physiology, integrating scientific and clinical information on nutrition, energy transfer and exercise training.'

5025 Growth, maturation and physical activity
R.M. Malina, C. Bouchard and O. Bar-Or   2nd edn, Human Kinetics, 2004, 712pp. $75. ISBN 9780880118828.
The 2nd edition was 'expanded with almost 300 new pages of material, making it the most comprehensive text on the biological growth, maturation, physical performance and physical activity of children and adolescents.'

5026 Sports science handbook: the essential guide to kinesiology, sport and exercise science
S.P.R. Jenkins   Multi-Science, 2005. 2 v., £37.50 per volume. www.multi-science.co.uk/sports-science.htm [COMPANION]
An encyclopedic dictionary that is largely a 'review of authoritative reviews', with many references to key books and journal articles.
- **Vol 1.** ISBN 0906522366.
- **Vol. 2.** ISBN 0906522374.

5027 Textbook of work physiology: physiological bases of exercise
P. Åstrand [et al.]   4th edn, Human Kinetics, 2003, 649pp. $84. ISBN 9780736001403.
'(C)ombines classical issues in exercise and work physiology with the latest scientific findings. The result is an outstanding professional reference that will be indispensable to advanced students, physiologists, clinicians, physical educators – any professional pursuing study of the body as a working machine.'

Keeping up to date

5028 BioMechanics: the Magazine of Body Movement and Medicine
CMP Healthcare Media, 1994–, monthly. $47 [2007 outside US]. ISSN 10759662.
www.biomech.com
Monthly US 'news magazine dedicated to total body movement and medicine'. Articles peer-reviewed and focus on injuries, rehabilitation, pain management, diabetes, foot health and function analysis. Most articles from January 1996 archived and searchable by keyword; more recent issues can also be browsed.
Print copy free to selected US professionals on registration.

5029 Medicine and Science in Sports and Exercise
American College of Sports Medicine   Lippincott, Williams & Wilkins, 1969–, monthly. Online ISSN 15300315. $511 non-US individuals [2008], ISSN 01959131.
www.acsm-msse.org
Official journal of the ACSM (American College of Sports Medicine), featuring 'original investigations, clinical studies and comprehensive reviews on current topics in sports medicine and exercise science'. From 1996 onwards, abstracts freely available and searchable; sample issues and position statements from 1982 onwards available full-text. Other full-text articles for ACSM members, subscribers or pay-per-view basis.

5030 Sportscience
Internet Society for Sport Science, 1997–. Publication variable, Freely available. ISSN 11740698.
www.sportsci.org
Peer-reviewed electronic journal covering sports sciences research, originating from New Zealand. Search full-text articles or browse by volume or broad subject area: sports medicine, nutrition, statistics, technology, training and performance, or research resources. Discussion forum and link to older version of site (1997–1998). Beginnings of incomplete *Encyclopedia of sports medicine and science*.
- **Encyclopedia of sports medicine and science**
  www.sportsci.org/encyc. Although unfinished, contains a small number of articles by leading practitioners and researchers and nearly 300 articles in draft form with bibliographic references, added in 2002 but as yet unchecked.

MEDIA & INFORMATION

Media & Communications

'Media studies' has had difficulty establishing itself as a thoroughly respectable academic discipline; and 'Media and communication(s)' has hardly done better. We doubt that anyone these days underestimates the importance of the underlying phenomena with which the 'subject' is concerned in today's globally networked world. But whether this is a subject in its own right, or simply an amalgamation of elements of more proper, more rigorous intellectual pursuits (especially Psychology and Sociology in this volume – in which sections see much that complements the entries below): that will continue to be debated.

Fortunately, we do not need to decide here where we stand on the question. It is necessary to say only that we decided that there was a sufficiently distinctive corpus of reference material to permit treatment of 'Media & Communications' as a subject in its own right, emphasizing again its overlap not just with the two subject areas already mentioned, but also with much else in the Finance, Industry & Business section, as well as elsewhere in this Media & Information section.

In addition to the usual raft of types of reference resource found in any 'academic' subject area, there are two other types that need special mention. The first comprises the guides to media artefacts: newspapers, broadcasting agencies, etc. We have included some examples of those here – principally in the sections News & The Press, and Radio, TV & Film – but have been even more restrained in choosing exemplars than elsewhere in this text. Also, we have not covered here radio, television and film as art forms or entertainment: these will be covered in Volume 3; nor the more technical aspects of these and the other media, these having been treated in Volume 1.

The second special type of resource has the added difficulty that it is more than usually hazardous achieving a proper balance between the competing cultural, environmental, political, racial, religious, social, etc. facets of current global society, when choosing items to include. These are the resources principally referenced in the sections: Privacy, Freedom & Censorship; Media Watchers & Activists and Cyberculture. Attempts have been made to represent a range of current viewpoints in those sections. But a strong warning is needed – for this genre of literature – that it is even more critical than elsewhere in this volume vigorously to explore beyond the resources referenced here. Once one makes the effort, it is surprising (and sometimes disturbing) just how many different views are available in the public arena about the world of affairs: particularly, of course, in those resources accessible via the internet.

audience research • children & the media • communications • communications law • global communication • history of the media • mass communication • mass media • media literacy • media studies • regulation of media • semiotics

Introductions to the subject

5031 50 ways to understand communication: a guided tour of key ideas and theorists in communication, media, and culture
A.A. Berger   Rowman & Littlefield, 2006, 144pp. $23.95. ISBN 9780742541085.
'(F)amiliarizes readers with important concepts written by leading communication and cultural theorists ... Berger's clear explanations and examples surround this assortment of influential writing, walking the uninitiated through these sometimes dense theoretical works. His selections and commentary will challenge readers to reconsider the role of communication in our culture. This engaging, accessible book is essential for students of communication and anyone interested in how we communicate in a world of rapidly changing media.'

5032 Canonic texts in media research: are there any? should there be? how about these?
E. Katz [et al.]   Polity Press, 2003, 265pp. £15.99. ISBN 9780745629346.
Stimulating introductory volume which 'offers thirteen pairs of shoulders to stand on, the better to see the field of media studies. It will serve as an excellent teaching text for advanced students in communications and media and cultural studies.'

5033 Communication research: asking questions, finding answers
J. Keyton   2nd edn, McGraw-Hill, 2006, 416pp. £33.99. ISBN 9780073049502.
'This text covers basic research issues and both quantitative and qualitative approaches to communication research. The guiding principle of the text is that methodological choices arise from one's research questions and hypotheses; thus, the text focuses first on the research process and then discusses the methodological tools for understanding and conducting basic communication research projects.'

5034 Communication research: strategies and sources
R.B. Rubin, A.M. Rubin and L.J. Piele   6th edn, Thomson Wadsworth, 2005, 336pp. $58.95. ISBN 9780534564865.
Core US-based text providing 12 chapters organized into three parts: 1. Communication research strategies; 2. Communication research sources; 3. Communication research processes.

5035 The creation of the media: political origins of modern communications
P. Starr   Basic Books, 2004, 484pp. $16.95. ISBN 9780465081943.
'In this wide-ranging social history of American media, from the first printing press to the early days of radio, Paul Starr shows that the creation of modern communications was as much the result of political choices as of technological invention ...'
'Starr ... once again demonstrates his ability to treat a complex subject thoroughly yet succinctly.' (*Library Journal*)

5036 Mass media and society
J. Curran and M. Gurevitch, eds   4th edn, Hodder Arnold, 2005,
432pp. £19.99. ISBN 9780340884997.

First-rate, well established text whose 4th edition 'has been
fully updated and contains 13 new chapters on key topics,
ranging from post-feminism to war journalism as
entertainment. Above all, it offers a number of alternative
views on the changing role of the media in the era of
globalization, new communication technology, the 'war on
terror', the advance of women and increasing economic
inequality.'

■ **Media and communication** P. Scannell   Sage Publications, 2007,
303pp. £19.99. ISBN 9781412902694. Well reviewed more recent text
which 'traces the historical development of media and communication
studies. Media Studies itself has a short history but many antecedents, and
in this comprehensive and compelling book, Paddy Scannell sets out to
describe and analyse its formulation in North American and Europe'.

5037 McQuail's mass communication theory
D. McQuail   5th edn, Sage Publications, 2005, 616pp. £20.99. ISBN
9781412903721.

www.sagepub.co.uk/mcquail5 [COMPANION]

The leading textbook, organized as: Preliminaries
(Introduction to the book, The rise of mass media), Theories,
Structures, Organizations, Content, Audiences, Effects,
Epilogue (the future of mass communication). 40-page
bibliography.

■ **Mass communication** D. McQuail   Sage Publications, 2006. £475.
ISBN 9781412922418. 'Denis McQuail's major work in *Mass
communication* is another essential part of the Sage Benchmark series.
Drawing on both classic and contemporary sources, McQuail guides us
through the central defining papers that anchor this field. Taken together,
the four volumes will provide access to the key debates within the field and
all the main lines of research that have emerged.'

5038 The media: an introduction
A. Briggs and P. Cobley, eds   2nd edn, Longman, 2002, 520pp.
£25.99. ISBN 9780582423466.

Valuable collection of essays designed to introduce study of
the media.

■ **A social history of the media: from Gutenberg to the
internet** A. Briggs and P. Burke   2nd edn, Polity, 2005, 400pp. £16.99.
ISBN 9780745635125. Excellent, elegant survey. 'Avoiding technological
determinism and rejecting assumptions of straightforward evolutionary
progress, this book brings out the rich and varied histories of
communication media.' Extensive – and highly rewarding – bibliography.

**5039 Media now: understanding media, culture, and
technology**
J. Straubhaar and R. LaRose   5th edn, Wadsworth, 2006, 528pp.
(2008 Update also announced), $102. ISBN 9780534647087.
www.thomsonedu.com [DESCRIPTION]

Comprehensive US-based textbook with 16 chapters
structured into three parts: 1. Media and the information
age; 2. The media; 3. Media issues.

5040 Studying the media: an introduction
T. O'Sullivan, B. Dutton and P. Rayner   3rd edn, Arnold, 2003,
326pp. £17.99. ISBN 9780340807651.

Attractive, easily approachable, very colourful yet
authoritative text. Good bibliographies.

Dictionaries, thesauri, classifications

**5041 Communication, cultural and media studies: the
key concepts**
J. Hartley   3rd edn, Routledge, 2002, 262pp. £14.99. ISBN
9780415268899.

Good introductory survey, though now becoming dated in a
field notable for its often transitory terminology.

5042 Dictionary of media and communication studies
J. Watson and A. Hill   7th edn, Hodder Arnold, 2006, 337pp. £14.99.
ISBN 9780340913383.

Excellent compilation, regularly updated, good cross-
referencing, useful introductory Topic Guide listing the
entries under 26 broad headings. Appendix: A chronology of
media events.

5043 Dictionary of media studies
A. & C. Black, 2006, 261pp. £9.99. ISBN 9780713675931.

'Covering television, film, radio and theatre, the *Dictionary of
Media Studies* includes thousands of words and expressions
used in the media and entertainment industries.'

**5044 Encyclopedic dictionary of semiotics, media and
communications**
M. Danesi   University of Toronto Press, 2000, 400pp. $27.50. ISBN
0802083293.

'Semiotics, Media Studies and Communication Studies are
three closely interlinked fields. Briefly stated, Semiotics, the
science of signs, looks at how humans search for and
construct meaning; Communication Studies is concerned
with how meaning is conveyed; and Media Studies considers
the ways in which messages are transmitted and received.
This dictionary is designed to help students and general
readers unlock the significance of the terminology and
jargon commonly used in these fields ...'

■ **Open Semiotics Resource Center** www.semioticon.com. Useful
wide-ranging Site designed 'to provide innovative, responsible and reliable
knowledge in a variety of domains relevant to semiotics understood as the
multidisciplinary study of information, meaning, communication,
interpretation, sign systems and evolution, texts, interactions, organizations,
cultural and social transformations, sense-making and all other topics that
may emerge from future research, models and theories'.

Laws, standards, codes

5045 Blackstone's statutes on media law: 2007–2008
R. Caddell and H. Johnson, eds   Oxford University Press, 2006,
416pp. £15.99. ISBN 9780199205899.
www.oup.com/uk/orc/bin/statutes [COMPANION]

'(P)rovides a comprehensive collection of important
legislative provisions of UK, EC and international law
governing the print and broadcast media.'

■ **Communication law in America** P. Siegel   2nd edn, Rowman &
Littlefield, 2007, 636pp. $69.95. ISBN 9780742553873.
http://uhaweb.hartford.edu/PSIEGEL [COMPANION]. Engaging text covering all
the key aspects of the field.

5046 Communications Law Centre [AUS]
www.comslaw.org.au

Independent, non-profit, public-interest organization.
Excellent overviews of free speech defamation; broadcasting;
media ownership; journalism and media ethics; film and TV
industry; privacy; internet and online services; information

equity; and telecommunications. Each with extensive links to relevant legislation and other resources.

5047 EU competition law and regulation in the converging telecommunications, media and IT sectors

N.T. Nikolinakos Kluwer Law, 2006, 698pp. £119. ISBN 9789041124692.

'Of the major industries formerly characterized by a high degree of state monopoly control, telecommunications is proving to be increasingly susceptible to market failure. The fundamental causes of this difficulty, according to the author of this far-reaching analysis, are twofold: abusive behaviour of incumbents aimed at foreclosing competitors and the regulatory challenges posed by the technological convergence of the telecommunications, media and IT sectors. The answers, Dr. Nikolinakos shows with extraordinary rigour and detail, lie in the enforcement of specially-crafted competition rules and proportionate, targeted sectoral regulation ...'

5048 European Charter for Media Literacy

www.euromedialiteracy.eu

'The aims of the Charter are:

– to foster greater clarity and wider consensus in Europe on media literacy and media education;

– to raise the public profile of media literacy and media education in each European nation and in Europe as a whole;

– to encourage the development of a permanent and voluntary network of media educators in Europe, bound together by their common aims and enabled by their institutional commitment.

'The Charter has been developed out of an initiative/idea of the UK Film Council and the BFI [British Film Institute] by a Steering Group representing major institutions in a limited number of countries, who have each committed to ensuring support for Steering Group meeting costs for an initial three year period (2005–2008).'

5049 Media law

D. Bloy Sage Publications, 2007, 202pp. £12.99. ISBN 9781412911207.

UK-based volume 'designed to complement existing textbooks ... The tone and level of this guide makes it easy to follow and should prove invaluable in helping students construct assessed coursework.'

■ **Electronic media law R.L. Sadler** Sage Publications, 2005, 447pp. £45. ISBN 9781412905886. www.wiu.edu/users/mfrls [COMPANION]. '(C)overs First Amendment law, political broadcasting rules, broadcast content regulations, FCC rules for station operations, cable regulation, media ownership rules, media liability lawsuits, intrusive newsgathering methods, media restrictions during wartime, libel, privacy, copyright, advertising law, freedom of information, cameras in the court, and privilege'.

■ **Media law for journalists U. Smartt** Sage Publications, 2006, 326pp. £18.99. ISBN 9781412908474. 'A refreshing complement to more venerable textbooks. Indeed, being both reflective and accessible, it is arguably a better first resort for aspirant hacks.' (*Times Higher Education Supplement*).

Official & quasi-official bodies

Federal Communications Commission

See entry no. 5192

5050 Great Britain. Department for Culture, Media and Sport

www.culture.gov.uk

The UK Department 'responsible for Government policy on the arts, sport, the National Lottery, tourism, libraries, museums and galleries, broadcasting, creative industries including film and the music industry, press freedom and regulation, licensing, gambling and the historic environment.'

Consult the Reference Library, which 'includes everything published by DCMS, including information made available under our publication scheme and that requested under the Freedom of Information Act'.

5051 Information Society and Media [EUR]

European Commission: Directorate for Information Society & Media

http://ec.europa.eu/dgs/information_society

'DG Information Society & Media pursues an integrated approach to achieving the Information Society, encompassing an evolving regulatory environment which emphasises competition and lets the market decide on technology; a world-class research programme which pools Europe's resources for world leadership; and a range of programmes designed to promote wider use, demonstrate innovative technologies and ensure that the benefits are felt by all ... Each activity feeds the others holistically: EU regulation is developed in the light of cutting-edge research, for example, while both research and promotion help create the competitive, inclusive European economy foreseen by regulation.'

5052 International Clearinghouse on Children, Youth and Media

www.nordicom.gu.se/clearinghouse

Now financed by the Swedish government and UNESCO, a good portal to worldwide work in this arena, covering events, publications and databases. Special attention to media violence.

Ofcom

See entry no. 5193

United Nations Educational, Scientific & Cultural Organization

See entry no. 26

Research centres & institutes

5053 Center for Global Communication Studies [USA]

www.global.asc.upenn.edu

Research centre in the Annenberg School for Communication, University of Pennsylvania: 'A partnership for faculty and graduate student research and outreach on issues of media development, national identities and globalization'. Extensive website reflecting the work of an active centre: check-out the excellent site map to navigate.

5054 Center for Media Literacy [USA]

www.medialit.org

30-year-old body whose mission is 'to help children and adults prepare for living and learning in a global media culture by translating media literacy research and theory into practical information, training and educational tools for teachers and youth leaders, parents and caregivers of children.' Very good range of resources – the website being the most-referenced media literacy site of the web.

- **Media literacy W.J. Potter** 3rd edn, Sage Publications, 2005, 465pp. £39. ISBN 9781412909891. US-authored text which 'helps students develop strong knowledge structures about the media'.
- **Media Literacy Clearinghouse** www.frankwbaker.com. Rich personal interest site providing a very good gateway to the field.

5055 Center on Media & Child Health [USA]
www.cmch.tv
A joint venture of Children's Hospital Boston, Harvard Medical School and Harvard School of Public Health 'dedicated to understanding and responding to the effects of media on the physical, mental and social health of children through research, production and education … The CMCH Database of Research catalogs and cross-indexes the current body of research examining the relationship of media exposure to health-risk behaviors.' In addition to reviews of research, a good set of pages 'For Parents & Teachers', including 'Ask a Question' and 'Hot Topics'.

5056 College of Communication [USA]
http://communication.utexas.edu
Based at the University of Texas at Austin and 'the most comprehensive college of its kind in the country and one of the nation's foremost institutions …'. Rewarding website, well structured and, including extensive details of each of their major departments: Advertising; Public Relations; Communication Sciences & Disorders; Communication Studies; School of Journalism; Department of Radio-Television-Film.

5057 Communication for Social Change Consortium [USA]
www.communicationforsocialchange.org
'We are an international nonprofit organization working in developing and industrialized countries. Our goal is to build local capacity of people living in poor and marginalized communities to use communication in order to improve their own lives. We were chartered in June of 2003 in the United States to work globally as a registered public charity.'

Elegant website with regularly updated areas labelled 'Publications and Resources' and 'Body of Knowledge', as well as other useful material.

5058 Institute of Communications Studies [UK]
http://ics.leeds.ac.uk
Highly active Institute based at the University of Leeds, particularly notable for its wide range of affiliated Research Centres: Centre for International Communications, Centre for European Political Communications, Research Centre for Future Communications, International-Film.org, Jean Monnet European Centre of Excellence, and Louis le Prince Centre for Cinema, Photography & Television.

5059 Stanhope Centre for Communications Policy Research
www.stanhopecentre.org
Founded in 2002 and 'developed to provide a forum for open dialogue and scholarship related to media law and policy around the world. The Stanhope Centre is closely affiliated and receives institutional support from the Annenberg School of Communication at the University of Pennsylvania'. The Centre is now based at City University where it has good links with other parts of the University, including their Centre for

International Communications and Society, as well as with Centres and Institutes based elsewhere in the UK and overseas.

'Stanhope will continue to serve as a very unique and flexible organization that connects talented students, scholars, activists and policy makers from across the globe to creatively and critically think about important communications policy issues.'

Associations & societies

5060 European Communication Research & Education Association
www.ecrea.eu
'ECREA was established in 2005 as a merger of the two main European associations of communication researchers, the European Communication Association (ECA) and the European Consortium for Communications Research (ECCR).' Clearly laid-out and effective website gives access to good sets of resources covering News; Themes (especially extensive list); Networks (only one so far); Conferences plus a series of member-only pages. According to the Association's Objectives, its 'disciplinary focus will include media, (tele)communications and informatics research, including relevant approaches of human and social sciences'. The website provides an A–Z list of all its current members, giving their institutional affiliation.

Independent Media Arts Preservation
See entry no. 5204

5061 International Association for Media & Communication Research
www.iamcr.net
'(T)he worldwide professional organization in the field of media and communication research. Its members promote global inclusiveness and excellence within the best traditions of critical research in the field. Its objectives include strengthening and encouraging the participation of new scholars, women and those from economically disadvantaged regions, including researchers from African, Asian and South and Central American countries.'

Active organization with extensive range of sections (e.g. Gender and Communication, Emerging Scholars Network, Psychology and Public Opinion) and Working Groups (e.g. Digital Divide, European Public Broadcasting Policies, Post-Socialist, Post-Authoritarian and Intercultural Communication).

5062 International Communication Association
www.icahdq.org
'(A)n academic association for scholars interested in the study, teaching and application of all aspects of human and mediated communication.' Most valuable to non-members for its 23 Divisions and Interest Groups: see 'Sections'.

- **Council of Communication Associations** www.councilcomm.org. Umbrella organization for: American Journalism Historians Association; Association for Education in Journalism & Mass Communication; Association of Schools of Journalism & Mass Communication; Black College Communication Association; Broadcast Education Association; International Communication Association; National Communication Association.

5063 Media, Communication & Cultural Studies Association [UK]
www.meccsa.org.uk

'(R)epresents all who teach or research in [UK] Higher Education in media, communications and cultural studies, whether in arts, humanities or social sciences departments. This includes practice-based work as well as more "academic" disciplines.' Good website with list of members, access to details of work of its sections, discussion list, etc.

5064 National Communication Association [USA]
www.natcom.org

Leading organization of 'approximately 7700 educators, practitioners and students who work and reside in every state and more than 20 countries … (A) scholarly society and as such works to enhance the research, teaching and service produced by its members on topics of both intellectual and social significance.' Wide range of website resources, albeit not all parts recently updated, but also publishes ten academic journals and a newsletter, *Spectra*.

Libraries, archives, museums

National Media Museum
See entry no. 5216

Portal & task environments

5065 Alliance Online [AUS]
www.alliance.org.au

'The Alliance is the union and professional organization which covers everyone in the media, entertainment, sports and arts industries. Our 36,000 members include people working in TV, radio, theatre & film, entertainment venues, recreation grounds, journalists, actors, dancers, sportspeople, cartoonists, photographers, orchestral & opera performers as well as people working in public relations, advertising, book publishing & website production … in fact everyone who works in the industries that inform or entertain Australians …'

Good range of resources, especially representative of the prime focus of the organization.

5066 Communication Institute for Online Scholarship
www.cios.org [FEE-BASED]

Incorporated in 1990, to function as a parent organization for the set of online activities that had been initiated in 1986 as the Comserve service. Members have access to journal index data for more than 80 scholarly journals in communication, rhetoric and journalism through the CIOS online Journals Index service. The majority of the journals indexes are available to CIOS/Comserve associate members only. There is also access to the CIOS ComAbstracts database and the *Electronic Journal of Communication*, as well as to more than 4500 electronic files of relevance to communication professionals and students.

■ **Academic Serials in Communication** www.ascus.info. Service under development: 'Free and low-cost access to the communication field's literature is threatened by a corporate takeover of our professional societies' publishing. The ASCUS project, now gaining significant momentum, provides an exciting alternative. You can help by encouraging participation by the societies in which you participate …'.

■ **ComAbstracts** www.cios.org/www/abstract.htm. An OpenURL-enabled database of article abstracts, books, bibliographic records, and other sources of relevance to researchers, scholars, and students interested in fields related to human communication studies (mass communication, human interaction, rhetoric, health communication, communication and new media, journalism, communication history, etc.).

5067 Media InfoCenter
Northwestern University
www.mediainfocenter.org

Impressive and extensive portal developed and managed by the Media Management Center at the University. Good source of up-to-date news on the media industry, but much background information accessible also.

■ **Readership Institute** www.readership.org. Division of the Media Management Center which 'focuses on actionable research, field-testing of readership-building ideas and measurement of their success, and education and training for the newspaper industry on readership-building best practices'.

5068 Simba Information
www.simbanet.com [FEE-BASED]

'Serving the information needs of both traditional and new media organizations, we provide key decision-makers at more than 15,000 client companies across the globe with timely news, analysis, exclusive statistics and proprietary industry forecasts. Simba's extensive information network delivers valuable independent perspective on the people, events and alliances shaping the media and information industry. Our tightly focused editorial and marketing teams meet these needs through the publication of newsletters and market research reports, while our seasoned industry experts bring Simba's powerful information to life through consulting services.'

5069 Terra Media
D. Fisher
www.terramedia.co.uk

Impressive personal-interest site covering the history of media, particularly with reference to the UK: 'The core of the site is Chronomedia, a chronology of international media development with one page for each year from 1885. Years prior to that, for each of which there is less information, are grouped in small batches of five years between 1820 and 1884 or larger groupings before that.' But there is much else of value therein: e.g. an extensive review of the development and content of UK media laws.

5070 ZenithOptimedia
www.zenithoptimedia.com

Consultancy which is part of 'the world's largest media services group'. Notable here for its Marketer's Portal – offering innovative but well characterized lists of some 5000 links ('Daily Sites', 'Useful Sites', 'Category Sites', 'Media Sites', etc.) – as well as details of the company's range of Global Facts & Forecasts.

Discovering print & electronic resources

Communication Abstracts
See entry no. 761

5071 Internet for Media and Communication [UK]
J. Conolly; Joint Information Systems Committee
This is one of a national series of tutorials written by
qualified tutors, lecturers and librarians from across the UK.
It is part of the Intute: Virtual Training Suite, funded by JISC.
The resources covered are categorized: Organizations; Online
newspapers and news services; Electronic journals and
books; Articles, reports and guidelines; Bibliographic
databases; Library catalogues; internet gateways; Blogs,
wikis and e-mail discussion lists; Learning and teaching
materials; Job notices. The facility is nicely presented and a
good starting point for those new to the field.

5072 Online Communication Studies Resources
University of Iowa
www.uiowa.edu/~commstud/resources
The major academic institution based resource guide to
communication studies, produced by the university's
Department of Communication Studies within their College
of Liberal Arts & Sciences. Well structured and often
updated (though, as almost always with a large facility, not
as frequently as would be ideal). The main sections are:
General and Mixed communication; Advertising;
Communication studies/Digital media; Cultural studies; Film
studies; Gender, race and ethnicity in media; Health and
science communication; Journalism; Media studies; Political
communication and campaigns; Rhetorical studies, theory
and philosophy; Visual communication – visualrhetorics.
There are also lists of e-mail discussions (listserves) and of
journals and 'blogs of interest', as well as a search facility
and a section headed 'Online searching and information
gathering'. The best place to start if you do not know where
to start.

Digital data, image & text collections

Communication and Mass Media Complete
See entry no. 768

Directories & encyclopedias

5073 Encyclopedia of communication and information
J.R. Schement, ed.   Macmillan Reference USA, 2002, 1161pp. 3 v,
$460. ISBN 9780028653860.
www.galegroup.com/macmillan [DESCRIPTION]
Almost 300 articles arranged A–Z by title. Wide coverage
(e.g. Academia, careers in; Bush, Vannevar; Digital media
systems; Nonverbal communication; Religion and the media;
Telecommunications, wireless). Good for browsing around.

5074 Encyclopedia of international media and communications
D.H. Johnston, ed.   Academic Press, 2003. 4 v, £670. ISBN
9780123876706.
www.info.sciencedirect.com/content/books/ref_works [FEE-BASED]
The major reference work in the field, with authorship drawn
from across the world: very well presented and structured,
with excellent cross-referencing and definitions of
terminology: 'The "new information revolution" is upon us,
but few of us know how it got here. This remarkable new
encyclopedia provides detailed and comprehensive
treatments of media channels from medieval Muslim block
printing to personal websites of the internet, offering as good

a road map as there is to the myriad ways we communicate
and the equally complex impact those media have on our
societies. This reference work will be an invaluable resource
for students, journalists – to anyone who has wondered about
the ever-changing ways we find out about the world.' (Lisa
Anderson).

5075 History of the mass media in the United States: an encyclopedia
M.A. Blanchard, ed.   Fitzroy Dearborn, 1998, 752pp. £125. ISBN
1579580122.
'More than 475 alphabetically arranged entries covering
subjects ranging from key areas of newspaper history to
broader topics such as media coverage of wars, major
conflicts over press freedom, court cases and legislation and
the concerns and representation of ethnic and special
interest groups.'
■ **Sources in the history of mass communication R.A. Rabe**
https://mywebspace.wisc.edu/rarabe/web/resources.htm. Useful personal
interest site, regularly updated, mid-2007 containing approximately 3700
titles listed in some 50 categories. No links.

5076 International encyclopedia of communications
E. Barnouw, ed.   Oxford University Press, 1989. 4 v.
Now clearly dated, but an elegant work: a pleasure to use. In
Volume 4, the titles of the articles are grouped under 30
headings, including Communications research; Journalism;
Media; Photography; Print media; Radio; Television; and
Theories of communication.

Handbooks & manuals

5077 Assessing media education: a resource handbook for educators and administrators
W.G. Christ, ed.   Routledge, 2006, 600pp. £36.95. ISBN
9780805852264.
A volume providing guidelines for media educators and
administrators in higher education media programmes who
are creating or improving student-learning assessment
strategies. Two further volumes cover measurement
techniques and case studies.

5078 The business of media: corporate media and the public interest
D. Croteau and W. Hoynes   2nd edn, Pine Forge Press, 2006, 315pp.
£23. ISBN 1412913152.
Valuable overview with seven chapters in three parts: I.
Profits and the public interest: theoretical and historical
context; II. Industry structure and corporate strategy:
Explaining the rise of media conglomerates; III. Neglecting
the public interest: media conglomerates and the public
sphere. Useful Appendix 'Select online resources for studying
the media industry, media policy and media education'.

5079 A companion to media studies
A.N. Valdivia, ed.   Blackwell, 2003, 590pp. Blackwell Companions in
Cultural Studies series, £24.99. ISBN 9781405141741.
Very good and detailed, intending 'to provide a broad
overview to a generalist academic audience of the dynamic
interdiscipline of media studies ... For the purposes of *A
companion to media studies*, Media Studies and Mass
Communications will be used interchangeably. Another major
overlap in terms of this interdiscipline is the increasingly
close connection between Media Studies and the study of

Culture. Culture is not synonymous with Cultural Studies though often this is the form the overlap takes ...'

5080 The European Union and the regulation of media markets

A. Harcourt   Manchester University Press, 2005, 258pp. £14.99. ISBN 9780719066450.

Excellent, detailed study, full of data, arguing 'that although Member State governments have played a significant role in European policy-making, the EU is not just an arena where one can plot the interaction between different national actors and find a result. The same can be stated for globilization and technological change, which are salient, but not dominant factors. The book argues that the policy process is more dynamic and that EU institutions can be pro-active and make a difference ...'.

■ **Governing European communications: from unification to coordination M. Michalis**   Rowman & Littlefield, 2007, 368pp. $39.95. ISBN 9780739117361. Well reviewed text offering 'a single, comprehensive, and up-to-date account of telecommunications and television policies and regulation and their technological convergence'.

5081 Global communication: theories, stakeholders, and trends

T.L. McPhail   2nd edn, Blackwell, 2006, 357pp. £22.99. ISBN 9781405134279.

First-rate volume with detailed coverage of the major world players in the various media arenas, categorized as: American multimedia giants; Non-US stakeholders of global communications systems; Global broadcasters; Global news agencies; Media in the Middle East and North Africa; Global advertisers; International organizations. Forward-looking review of the continuing impact of the internet ending with 'Electronic colonialism theory' and 'World-system theory'.

■ **Bridging the gaps in global communication D. Newsom**   Blackwell Publishing, 2007, 153pp. £15.99. ISBN 9781405144124. 'Addresses an important subject that few other books do: how to communicate in the *global* media marketplace at both the interpersonal and public level.' 14 chapters in two parts: I. Global sources and systems of communication: concepts, economics, and politics; II. The cultural context in which information is received, interpreted, and understood.

5082 Handbook of international and intercultural communication

W.B. Gudykunst and B. Mody, eds   2nd edn, Sage Publications, 2002, 606pp. £85. ISBN 9780761920908.

Twenty-nine essays grouped in four parts: I. Cross-cultural communication; II. Intercultural communication; III. International communication; IV. Development communication. Good, detailed subject index, plus full author index.

5083 Mediamaking: mass media in a popular culture

L. Grossberg [et al.]   2nd edn, Sage Publications, 2006, 495pp. £25.99. ISBN 9780761925446.

Takes a 'unique approach to the study of mass communication and cultural studies by examining media as a whole – newspapers, books, magazines, radio, television, film – and their relationships with culture and society'.

Very well written US-based text having 13 chapters organized into 4 parts: I. Placing the media; II. Making sense of the media; III. The power of the media; IV. Media and the public life.

5084 Researching audiences

K. Schrøder [et al.]   Arnold, 2003, 422pp. £21.99. ISBN 9780340762745.

'Defines audience research within a theoretical framework of "discursive realism". Methodologically, we present and discuss four main approaches to audience research: media ethnography, reception research, audience surveys and experimental audience studies.' Good bibliography; detailed index.

5085 The Sage handbook of media studies

J.D.H. Downing [et al.]   Sage Publications, 2004, 629pp. £85. ISBN 9780761921691.

Valuable overview provided by leading group of US and international contributors within five interconnected areas: humanistic and social scientific approaches; global and comparative perspectives; the relation of media to economy and power; media users; and elements in the media mosaic ranging from popular music to digital technologies, from media ethics to advertising and from Hollywood and Bollywood to alternative media.

■ **The alternative media handbook K. Coyer [et al.]**   Routledge, 2008, 304pp. £18.99. ISBN 9780415359658. Forthcoming guide to 'Alternative Media', '... the term used to describe non-mainstream media forms that are independently run and community focussed, such as zines, pirate radio, online discussion boards, community run and owned broadcasting companies, and activist publications such as *Red Pepper* and *Corporate Watch*'.

Keeping up to date

5086 Media Bloggers Association

www.mediabloggers.org

'(A) nonpartisan organization dedicated to promoting, protecting and educating its members; supporting the development of "blogging" or "citizen journalism" as a distinct form of media; and helping to extend the power of the press, with all the rights and responsibilities that entails, to every citizen.' Well designed website gives a measured – and thus welcome – introduction to the sometime frenetic arena of 'blogging'.

5087 Media, Culture and Society

Sage Publications, 1979–, bi-monthly. $106.00 [2007]. ISSN 01634437.

http://mcs.sagepub.com

Approachable journal, not too technical for those relatively new to the area, good sets of book reviews. One of a wide range of Sage periodicals in the field of communication and media studies.

5088 MediaGuardian [UK]

http://media.guardian.co.uk

Well respected news on UK and overseas developments.

■ **The Guardian stylebook D. Marsh**   Atlantic Books, 2007. £14.99. ISBN 9781843549918. Leading guide to appear in new edition.

Journalism

editing • investigative journalism • law & journalism •
press freedom • print journalism

Introductions to the subject

5089 The American journalist in the 21st century: US news people at the dawn of a new millennium
D.H. Weaver [et al.]   Lawrence Erlbaum, 2006, 291pp. £19.95. ISBN 9780805853834.
Presents results from telephone surveys of nearly 1500 US journalists working in a variety of media outlets, updating similar study in the 1990s. Looks at demographic and educational backgrounds, working conditions and professional and ethical values of print, broadcast and internet journalists at the beginning of the 21st century.

5090 An introduction to journalism
C. Fleming [et al.]   Sage Publications, 2006, 245pp. £19.99. ISBN 9780761941828.
'The job of a journalist has changed dramatically over the past few decades with satellite links, 24 hour rolling news and the internet creating constant pressure for the latest updates. But for all that, the fundamentals of doing the job remain the same: it's about identifying a story, getting the interviews and delivering a balanced and interesting report.'
'The book does what it says on the label. It is punctuated throughout with useful and relevant quotes from working journalists – their opinions, tips and warnings – a technique that drives home the message and adds life and colour.' (*Times Higher Education Supplement*)

5091 Journalism: a critical history
M. Conboy   Sage Publications, 2004, 246pp. £19.99. ISBN 9780761941002.
Good, reflective, survey.

5092 Journalism: a very short introduction
J. Hargreaves   Oxford University Press, 2005, 176pp. £6.99. ISBN 9780192806567.
One of OUP's excellent series of subject Very Short Introductions: 'Is journalism the "first draft of history" or a dumbing-down of our culture and a glorification of the trivial and intrusive? In this intriguing book Ian Hargreaves argues that the core principles of "freedom of the press" and the necessity of exposing the truth are as vital today as they ever were.'
'Hargreaves has written a timely and disturbing account of journalism in peril.' (*The Times*)

5093 Journalism: principles and practice
T. Harcup   Sage Publications, 2003, 288pp. £18.99. ISBN 9780761974994.
Excellent practical inventory; very well structured and laid out; good index and selective list of 'some useful websites' (but whose links were last checked in 2003).

5094 Print journalism: a critical introduction
R. Keeble [et al.]   Routledge, 2005, 347pp. £18.99. ISBN 9780415358828.
First-rate overview, drawing together 'for the first time in a single volume a wide range of the elements of print journalism. The prime focus is on the practical skills, but the

treatment is always critical and placed within broader economic, historical and theoretical contexts'.

5095 So you want to be a journalist?
B. Grundy   Cambridge University Press, 2007, 358pp. £24.99. ISBN 9780521690492.
Chapters are: 1. Writing news; 2. Writing news for radio and television; 3. Writing for the reader; 4. Grammar; 5. Spelling and punctuation; 6. Subbing; 7. Reporting; 8. The law; 9. Knowing your rights; 10. Defamation; 11. Research and finding things; 12. Facts and figures, lies, damned lies, statistics and polls; 13. Questions and interviews; 14. Making your own newspaper; 15. Dangers, dilemmas, do's and don'ts; 16. News selection and news value.

Dictionaries, thesauri, classifications

5096 Key concepts in journalism studies
B. Franklin [et al.]   Sage Publications, 2005, 362pp. £16.99. ISBN 9780761944829.
Very good A–Z compilation explaining and elaborating the major terminology within journalism and related fields.

Laws, standards, codes

Law for advertising, broadcasting, journalism and public relations: a comprehensive text for students and practitioners
M.G. Parkinson and L.M. Parkinson   See entry no. 5188

5097 The law of journalism and mass communication
R. Trager, J. Russomanno and S. Ross   McGraw-Hill, 2005, 558pp. $96.25. ISBN 9780073213446.
Attractively presented comprehensive text, whose chapters are described: 1. The rule of law; 2. The First Amendment; 3. Disruptive speech: threats to social stability and personal safety; 4. Libel: the plaintiff's case; 5. Libel: defense issues and strategies; 6. Privacy in a global, mediated world; 7. Emotional distress, physical harm and other dangers; 8. Media and the courts; 9. Newsgathering for converging media; 10. Reporter's Privilege; 11. Advertising; 12. Broadcast, cable, DBS and internet regulation; 13. Offensive speech; 14. Special concerns about children and schools; 15. Intellectual property.

5098 McNae's essential law for journalists
T. Welsh, W. Greenwood and D. Banks   19th edn, Oxford University Press, 2007, 587pp. £18.99. ISBN 9780199211548.
www.oup.com/uk/orc/law/media [COMPANION]
The leading resource in the area with, new to this edition, a chapter 'The online journalist'. 'McNae's is endorsed by the National Council for the Training of Journalists as the essential text for students on journalism courses. It is the indispensable, complete and portable resource in the armoury of the practising journalist or editor; used in newsrooms, court rooms and at public meetings across the country.'
■ **Law for journalists** F. Quinn   Pearson Longman, 2007, 417pp. £18.99. ISBN 9780582823112. Designed more as an introduction for the non-specialist, but with a comprehensive coverage of all the key areas.

Research centres & institutes

College of Communication
See entry no. 5056

5099 Dart Center for Journalism & Trauma
www.dartcenter.org
'Global network of journalists, journalism educators and health professionals dedicated to improving media coverage of trauma, conflict and tragedy. The Center also addresses the consequences of such coverage for those working in journalism.' Very helpful series of Tipsheets and In-depth Resources. Excellent design.

5100 European Journalism Centre
www.ejc.nl
Independent institute based in Maastricht, the Netherlands. Access to extensive and highly rewarding sets of resources. Especially useful is the 'Media Landscape', with profiles of 35 European countries, each with coverage of such facets as: Written press; Audiovisual media; Digital media; Online media; News agencies; Media organizations; National media policies; Accountability systems; Main recent media developments; Prime sources for detailed information; Media resources. There is also a separate and very good Resources section' with nicely selected lists of items, each having a short helpful description. Finally, there is a daily updated 'Media News', covering the latest developments in European and international media. Overall, an excellent facility.

5101 International Center for Journalists
www.icfj.org
US-based organization which 'promotes quality journalism worldwide in the belief that independent, vigorous media are crucial in improving the human condition … ICFJ receives more than 75 percent of its funding from sponsoring foundations and agencies in the form of program grants and fees for its services. ICFJ's general operating support comes exclusively from the private sector in the form of contributions from individuals, news organizations, corporations and foundations.'
 ■ **International Journalists' Network** www.ijnet.org. Network published by the Center whose mission is 'to help connect journalists with the opportunities and information they need to better themselves and raise journalism standards in their countries. Hand-in-hand with that mission, IJNet strives to track media training and other assistance efforts in more than 150 countries, helping donors and organizers avoid duplication and learn about innovative programs around the world'. Useful section on media laws, categorized by country.

5102 International News Safety Institute
www.newssafety.com
'Non-governmental organization dedicated to the safety of journalists and media staff and committed to fighting the persecution of journalists everywhere. The Institute is a coalition of media organizations, press freedom groups, unions and humanitarian campaigners working to create a culture of safety in media in all corners of the world.' Extensive news service on worldwide developments.

5103 Knight Foundation [USA]
www.knightfdn.org
Funds under three headings: Journalism Program; Communities Program; National and New Initiatives. Details and links to wide range of funded projects.

 ■ **Knight Center for Journalism in the Americas**
http://knightcenter.utexas.edu. Professional training and outreach program for journalists in Latin America and the Caribbean. The Resources section covers journalism-related websites in the Americas, Spain and Portugal.

5104 Nieman Foundation [USA]
www.nieman.harvard.edu
Harvard University-based centre which produces *Nieman Reports*, a 'highly respected magazine of comment and criticism where current fellows, Nieman alums and leading journalists explore and examine the state of our craft'; also runs the Nieman Program on Narrative Journalism.
 ■ **Nieman Watchdog: questions the press should ask**
www.niemanwatchdog.org. 'The premise of watchdog journalism is that the press is a surrogate for the public, asking probing, penetrating questions at every level … The goal of watchdog journalism is to see that people in power provide information the public should have … There are already many very good journalism websites. Nevertheless, we think our function at NiemanWatchdog.org – suggesting questions the press should ask – sets us apart'.

5105 Philip Merrill College of Journalism [USA]
www.journalism.umd.edu
Based at the University of Maryland and of particular importance here for the quality of the resources it offers, while being one of leading schools of journalism within the US and having a very good website to match. 'The school's mission is simple: to produce the best possible journalists for the world's leading news organizations. Undergraduates are prepared for careers in newspapers, magazines, TV news and online media outlets through a program that incorporates rigorous courses in news reporting, writing, research, law, history, ethics and design into a traditional liberal arts curriculum. Master's students are immersed in intensive, one-year programs in print, broadcast and online journalism. And doctoral students are prepared for careers as media scholars, professors and critics.'
 ■ **American Journalism Review University of Maryland**, bi-monthly. $44. ISSN 10678654. www.ajr.org. Leading national magazine that covers all aspects of print, television, radio and online media.
 ■ **Casey Journalism Center on Children & Families**
www.cjc.umd.edu. Nonprofit, nonpartisan program of the College offering training for journalists covering children and families. Access to extensive resources.
 ■ **J-Lab: The Institute for Interactive Journalism** www.j-lab.org. Lively Center within the College which 'helps news organizations and citizens use new information ideas and innovative computer technologies to develop new ways for people to engage in critical public policy issues'.

Associations & societies

5106 American Journalism Historians Association
http://ajhaonline.org
'For purposes of written research papers and publications, the term "history" shall be seen as a continuous process emphasizing but not necessarily confined to the subject of American mass communications. It should be viewed not in the context of perception of the current decade, but as part of a unique, significant and time-conditioned past.' The AJHA Interest Groups are Early Americans; International; Women; Racial and Ethnic Media; and Senior Scholars.

■ **American Journalism** , qtrly. ISSN 08821127.
http://ajhaonline.org/journal.html [DESCRIPTION]. Articles, research notes, book reviews, and correspondence dealing with the history of journalism.

5107 American Society of Journalists & Authors
www.asja.org
Primarily concerned with the business of being a journalist and helping professional freelance writers advance their careers.

5108 Association for Education in Journalism & Mass Communication
www.aejmc.org
'(A) non-profit, educational association of journalism and mass communication faculty, administrators, students and media professionals. Founded in Chicago, Illinois, in 1912, AEJMC has some 3500 members around the world.' Good, selective links section with helpful annotations.

■ **Accrediting Council on Education in Journalism & Mass Communications** www2.ku.edu/~acejmc. '(T)he agency responsible for the evaluation of professional journalism and mass communications programs in colleges and universities'. The Student Information Center lists all currently accredited programs, with links to their websites, and there is a thrice-yearly Newsletter.

■ **Journalism and Mass Communication Abstracts** www.aejmc.org/abstracts. '(I)ncludes abstracts of dissertations and theses accepted for graduate degrees. The abstracts were prepared by the student authors and represent research theses. The abstracts of creative projects done to complete the graduate degree are excluded'.

5109 International Federation of Journalists
www.ifj.org
'(T)he world's largest organization of journalists. First established in 1926, it was relaunched in 1946 and again, in its present form, in 1952. Today the Federation represents around 500.000 members in more than 100 countries.' Useful overviews of key issues via the Subjects section: e.g. Author's rights; Freelance; Gender issues; Globalization. The Links section – including links to news articles and projects – is not the easiest to navigate and has variable quality, but can be useful for discovering non-mainstream activities.

5110 Investigative Reporters & Editors, Inc. [USA]
www.ire.org
'(A) grassroots nonprofit organization dedicated to improving the quality of investigative reporting. IRE was formed in 1975 to create a forum in which journalists throughout the world could help each other by sharing story ideas, newsgathering techniques and news sources ... The IRE Resource Center is a rich reserve of print and broadcast stories, tipsheets and guides to help you start and complete the best work of your career. This unique library is the starting point of any piece you're working on. You can search through abstracts of more than 23,250 investigative reporting stories without leaving the convenience of your Web browser!'

■ **National Institute for Computer-Assisted Reporting** www.nicar.org. NICAR, an IRE programme, in conjunction with the University of Missouri School of Journalism, maintains The Database Library, 'a library of databases containing government data on a wide array of subjects. Data include airplane service difficulty reports, storm events, FBI crime data, fatal highway accidents, problems with medical devices and federal contracts awarded to private companies. This is just a short list of the more than 30 datasets in the collection'.

5111 Journalism Education Association [USA]
www.jea.org
'The Journalism Education Association supports free and responsible scholastic journalism by providing resources and educational opportunities, by promoting professionalism, by encouraging and rewarding student excellence and teacher achievement and by fostering an atmosphere which encompasses diversity yet builds unity ... Among JEA's 2300 members are journalism teachers and publications advisers, media professionals, press associations, adviser organizations, libraries, yearbook companies, newspapers, radio stations and departments of journalism.'

Clear, pleasant website. The Resources section gives access to: the newsletter *Communication: journalism education today*; the *Scholastic Journalism Week*; the JEA Press Rights Commission; Standards for journalism educators; Other organizations (a particularly good 'links' list).

5112 National Association of Black Journalists [USA]
www.nabj.org
'NABJ is an association of journalists, students and media-related professionals that provides quality programs and services year-round to benefit black journalists worldwide.' It is a member of UNITY: Journalists of Color, Inc., 'a strategic alliance advocating fair and accurate news coverage about people of color and aggressively challenging the industry to staff its organizations at all levels to reflect the nation's diversity' (www.unityjournalists.org) – whose other members are Asian American Journalists Association, National Association of Hispanic Journalists and the Native American Journalists Association.

5113 National Lesbian & Gay Journalists Association [USA]
www.nlgja.org
'(A)n organization of journalists, media professionals, educators and students who work within the news industry to foster fair and accurate coverage of LGBT [Lesbian, Gay, Bisexual, Transgender] issues. NLGJA opposes all forms of workplace bias and provides professional development to its members.' Website provides access to the Stylebook Supplement on LGBT Terminology, 'intended to complement the prose stylebooks of individual publications, as well as the Associated Press stylebook, the leading stylebook in US newsrooms'; and to NLGJA's Journalists Toolbox, 'designed primarily to assist journalists who don't normally cover the LGBT community'.

5114 National Union of Journalists [UK]
www.nuj.org.uk
'We are among the biggest and best-established journalists' unions in the world, with 35,000 members. These members cover the whole range of editorial work – staff and freelance, writers and reporters, editors and sub-editors, photographers and illustrators, working in broadcasting, newspapers, magazines, books, on the internet and in public relations.' Much useful material, worth browsing around, e.g. searchable Freelance Directory; information about Press Cards; the NUJ Code of Conduct; the campaign Journalism Matters.

5115 Online News Association
Founded in 1999 'by several working members of the online press. ONA is open to journalists from around the world who produce news on the internet and other digital platforms and

to others with an interest in online news.' The most useful resources are only accessible to (fee-based) members; but ONA also sponsors CyberJournalist.Net, which has much freely available material.

■ **CyberJournalist.net** www.cyberjournalist.net. A lively, opinionated, and wide-ranging Site: very good for engaging with the industry's current preoccupations.

5116   Society for Editors & Proofreaders [UK]
www.sfep.org.uk
Professional organization based in the UK 'for editors and proofreaders – the people who strive to make text accurate and readable'. The SfEP Directory of Editorial Services provides contact information for more than 440 SfEP members plus details of the skills, subjects and services they offer. There is also a useful FAQ section plus a small links area.

5117   Society of Environmental Journalists
www.sej.org
'The mission of the Society of Environmental Journalists is to advance public understanding of environmental issues by improving the quality, accuracy and visibility of environmental reporting.' The Society offers a wide range and depth of services including EJToday 'our annotated and interactive selection of the day's most interesting environmental stories in print and on the air, including stories submitted by users of the site'; an intensive set of resources on Freedom of Information; and a very extensive set of links, with each section having a helpful overview. (The section 'Blogs and more' is particularly good.) In total, a first-rate resource.

5118   Society of Professional Journalists [USA]
www.spj.org
'Founded in 1909 as Sigma Delta Chi, SPJ promotes the free flow of information vital to a well informed citizenry through the daily work of its nearly 10,000 members; works to inspire and educate current and future journalists through professional development; and protects First Amendment guarantees of freedom of speech and press through its advocacy efforts.' Good sets of resources on Public and the Press, First Amendment, Freedom of Information, Ethics and Diversity. There is also a set of Blogs covering different sections of the Society's interests; and lists of Resources for students, freelancers, educators and international journalists. A very clearly laid-out website, easily navigated.

■ **JournalismTraining.Org** www.journalismtraining.org/action/home. A site managed by the Society for the Council of National Journalism Organizations (www.cnjo.org) and 'devoted to helping journalists everywhere find the training they need'.

■ **Quill** , 9 p.a. $72. ISSN 00336475. http://spj.org/quill.asp. 'For more than 90 years, Quill has been a respected and sought-after resource for journalists, industry leaders, students and educators on issues central to journalism'.

Portal & task environments

5119   Committee of Concerned Journalists [USA]
www.concernedjournalists.org
'(A) consortium of journalists, publishers, owners and academics worried about the future of the profession. To secure journalism's future, the group believes that journalists from all media, geography, rank and generation must be

clear about what sets our profession apart from other endeavours. To accomplish this, the group is creating a national conversation among journalists about principles.' Excellent range and depth of resources.

5120   Journalism.co.uk: the essential site for journalists
www.journalism.co.uk
Well organized site covering jobs, freelancing, events and awards and a good selective directory of annotated links within about a dozen categories.

5121   Journalism.org: Project for Excellence in Journalism: understanding news in the information age [USA]
www.journalism.org
The Project for Excellence in Journalism is now part of the Pew Research Center and offers a very good range of services labelled as: Numbers, data about the news media; Analysis, research studies, commentaries, background reports, articles, speeches; News Index; Daily Briefing; Journalism Resources, jobs, organizations, schools, tools, etc.

■ **The state of the news media: an annual report on American journalism** www.stateofthemedia.org. Major content uses standard template – Intro | Content Analysis | Audience | Economics | Ownership | News Investment | Public Attitudes | Conclusion | Charts & Tables | Roundtable – to report annually the current situation in newspapers, online, network TV, cable TV, local TV, magazines and radio.

Muckraker: Center for Investigative Reporting
See entry no. 5304

5122   PoynterOnline: everything you need to know to be a better journalist [USA]
www.poynter.org
Extensive and intensive gateway from the Poynter Institute in Florida covering news, careers, jobs, opinion pieces, training, events and so on. The Resource Center has a series of about 15 bibliographies, plus a good selective links section maintained by David Shedden, the Poynter Library Director. Included therein is a section Libraries with Journalism Resources: '(I)ncludes links to journalism libraries/research centers as well as other sites with journalism library resources. Bibliographers and subject specialists maintain many of the academic Web pages.'

Discovering print & electronic resources

5123   Journalism: a guide to the reference literature
J.A. Cates   3rd edn, Libraries Unlimited, 2004, 291pp. Foreword by James W. Carey, $70. ISBN 9781591580614.
Comprehensive source organized as: Introduction; Bibliographies and bibliographic guides; Encyclopedias; Dictionaries; Indexes and abstracts; Selected commercial databases; Selected internet sources; Biographical sources; Directories, yearbooks and collections; Handbooks, manuals and career guides; Stylebooks; Catalogs; Miscellaneous sources; Core periodicals; Societies and associations; Selected centers, archives and media institutes.
'Still the gold standard for journalism reference guides. Highly recommended for academic libraries supporting journalism programs' (Choice)

5124 The online journ@list: using the internet and other electronic resources
R. Reddick and E. King   3rd edn, Wadsworth, 2001, 288pp. ISBN 9780155067523.
Still useful for its very wide-ranging, logical organization.

Online newsgathering: research and reporting for journalists
S. Quinn and S. Lamble   See entry no. 5168

Digital data, image & text collections

5125 Annual surveys of journalism and mass communication [USA]
www.grady.uga.edu:16080/annualsurveys
Designed to monitor the employment rates and salaries of graduates of journalism and mass communication programmes in the USA.

Handbooks & manuals

5126 The future of journalism in advanced democracies
P.J. Anderson and G. Ward   Ashgate, 2007, 310pp. £19.95. ISBN 0754644057.
'What are the current problems, pressures and opportunities facing journalists in advanced democratic societies? Has there been a "dumbing down" of the news agenda? How can serious political, economic and social news be made interesting to young people? This book explores the current challenges faced by those working in the news media, focusing especially on the responsibilities of journalism in the advanced democracies ...'
'It combines journalistic clarity with academic research, and it is refreshingly different in not being narrowly insular. It is organised around a central quesiton – are changes in journalism serving democracy? – which gives the book a sharp edge' (*Times Higher Education Supplement*)

5127 Global journalism research: theories, methods, findings, future
M. Löffelholz and D. Weaver, eds   Blackwell Publishing, 352pp. £19.99. ISBN 9781405153324.
www.blackwellpublishing.com [DESCRIPTION]
Worldwide authors contribute to a major forthcoming work (2008) which 'offers a diversity of theoretical and methodological approaches for studying journalists and journalism around the world. It charts the opportunities and challenges facing journalism research in an increasingly global field.'

5128 Journalism: critical issues
S. Allan, ed.   Open University Press, 2005, 390pp. £19.99. ISBN 9780335214754.
Very good edited survey with the 27 chapters organized as: I. Journalism's histories; II. Journalism and democracy; III. Journalism's realities; IV. Journalism and the politics of othering; V. Journalism and the public interest.

5129 Lifting the lid: a guide to investigative research
D. Northmore   Cassell, 1996, 234pp. ISBN 0304331139.
Guide to all the types of source useful in investigative journalism, ranging from companies and other commercial organizations through voluntary sector bodies to the political

and international institutions and related bodies. Well written – with the underlying principles, though of course not necessarily the examples chosen, still valid today.

5130 Scholastic journalism
T. Rolnicki, C.D. Tate and S. Taylor   11th edn, Blackwell, 2007, 448pp. £29.99. ISBN 9781405144162.
'For more than 50 years, *Scholastic journalism* has served as a comprehensive textbook and guide for high school journalism students, teachers and advisors. This landmark 11th edition now includes updated information on the dynamic changes taking place in the field. It is the ideal textbook to teach students the basic skills of collecting, interviewing, reporting and writing in journalism.'

5131 Taking journalism seriously: news and the academy
B. Zelizer   Sage Publications, 2004, 286pp. £23. ISBN 9780803973145.
'How have scholars tended to conceptualize news, newsmaking, journalism, journalists and the news media? Which explanatory frames have they used to explore journalistic practice?' Erudite study, particularly notable for its extensive bibliography – divided into 'General sources' and 'Sources on journalism'.

5132 The universal journalist
D. Randall   3rd edn, Pluto Press, 2007, 256pp. £15.99. ISBN 9780745326559.
'This is a new edition of the world's leading textbook on journalism. Translated into more than a dozen languages, David Randall's handbook is an invaluable guide to the "universals" of good journalistic practice for professional and trainee journalists worldwide.'

5133 What are journalists for?
J. Rosen   Yale University Press, 2001, 338pp. $22. ISBN 9780300089073.
'American journalists in the 1990s confronted disturbing trends – an erosion of trust in the news media, weakening demand for serious news, flagging interest in politics and civic affairs and a discouraging public climate that seemed to be getting worse. In response, some news professionals sought to breach the growing gap between press and public with an experimental approach – public journalism. This book is an account of the movement for public journalism, or civic journalism, told by Jay Rosen, one of its leading developers and defenders ...'
■ **PressThink: ghost of democracy in the media machine**
J. Rosen   http://journalism.nyu.edu/pubzone/weblogs/pressthink.
Stimulating blog: 'I am a press critic, an observer of journalism's habits, and also a writer trying to make sense of the world. I am interested in the ideas about journalism that journalists work within, and those they feel they can work without. I try to discover the consequences in the world that result from having the kind of press we do. I call this blog PressThink because that's the kind of work I do. The title points to forms of thought that identify "journalism" to itself – but also to the habit of not thinking about certain things ...'.

Keeping up to date

5134 British Journalism Review
Sage Publications, qtrly. £36. ISSN 09564748.
www.bjr.org.uk [COMPANION]
'The *British Journalism Review* is designed as a forum of
analysis and debate, to monitor the media, submit the best
as well as the worst to scrutiny and to raise the level of the
dialogue. This website is designed to give you an idea of who
we are and what we publish. We hope it will appeal not only
to journalists, whether in newspapers, radio and television, or
online, but also to media academics and students and to
anyone who cares about communication ...'

5135 Columbia Journalism Review
Columbia University   1962–, 6 p.a. $29.70. ISSN 0010194X.
www.cjr.org [COMPANION]
Published by the University's School of Journalism and
offering 'a deliberative mix of reporting, analysis, criticism
and commentary'. This is supplemented by daily postings of
stories in the news. The Resources section has a very useful
'Who Owns What' profiling about 60 leading corporations
with detailed lists of each of their holdings. Much else of
value on the website: see the section Journalism Tools.

5136 eJournalist
Central Queensland University   2001, bi-annual.
www.ejournalism.au.com/ejournalist.htm
Published from the University's Faculty of Informatics and
Communication. A registered 'Open Access' journal
containing 'refereed articles on journalism, new media,
communications, graphics, websites and related issues. It
seeks to aid journalism and communications educators,
researchers and those concerned with media analysis'. The
University also offers comprehensive online journalism
courses through its eJournalism programmes.

5137 Jhistory
www.h-net.msu.edu/~jhistory
'A forum for discussion with professors, graduate students
and professionals debating and exploring journalism history
topics. The forum is free of charge and as easy to use as e-
mail. Members typically receive three or four messages a
day.'

News & The Press

circulations • journals • newsgathering • newspapers •
online news • periodicals • press • press complaints •
publishing • reporting

Introductions to the subject

**5138 Governing with the news: the news media as a
political institution**
T.E. Cook   2nd edn, University of Chicago Press, 2005, 313pp. $20.
ISBN 9780226115016.
US-based study arguing that 'the news media are in fact a
political institution integral to the day-to-day operations of
our government'.
'Provocative and often wise ... Cook, who has a complex
understanding of the relationship between governing and the
news, provides a fascinating account of the origins of this
complicity.' (*Washington Monthly*)

5139 A history of news
M. Stephens   3rd edn, Oxford University Press, 2007, 356pp.
£32.99. ISBN 9780195189919.
Well established volume, now structured into: Spoken news;
Written news; Printed news; Newspapers; Reporting; and
Electronic news – with the last having two chapters entitled:
'New technologies – improved means to an unimproved end'
and 'The information explosion – a surfeit of data'.

5140 News
J. Harrison   Routledge, 2006, 289pp. £15.99. ISBN 9780415319508.
Eclectic survey of 'news' within the series Routledge
introductions to media and communications. 'What I believe
to be its constituent features, its various manifestations and,
of course, its significance'. Focuses on the UK, but of wider
value.

5141 News and news sources: a critical introduction
P. Manning   Sage Publications, 2001, 262pp. £22.99. ISBN
9780761957973.
Excellent introduction to the 'sociology of news'. Very good
focus on the interactions between proprietors, corporations
and politicians. Extensive bibliography.

5142 News and the net
B. Gunter   Lawrence Erlbaum, 2003, 180pp. £42.50. ISBN
9780805845006.
Examines 'the growth of news production on the internet and
its implications for news presentation, journalism practice,
news consumers and the business of running news
organizations'. Good introductory overview of complex field.

**5143 News in a new century: reporting in an age of
converging media**
J. Lanson and B.C. Fought   Pine Forge Press, 1999, 339pp. $85.95.
ISBN 97807619850.
Wide-ranging and well presented. Delivers 'readable and
user-friendly chapters that are comprehensive without being
encyclopedic. Summary boxes help the hurried reader'.

Dictionaries, thesauri, classifications

**5144 The language of news: a journalist's pocket
reference**
J. Botts   Iowa State University Press, 1995, 216pp. ISBN
9780813824949.
'Individually, most dictionaries, academic grammars,
reporting textbooks, stylebooks and books on usage are
complete. But most aren't written for journalists. Few
combine grammar, language faults, usage, spelling, story
blunders and basic style references ...'

Laws, standards, codes

5145 Newspaper Licensing Agency [UK]
www.nla.co.uk
Established by UK national newspapers in 1996 and licenses
organizations to make paper and digital copies of newspaper
content.

5146 Organization of News Ombudsmen [USA]
www.newsombudsmen.org
List of members and well chosen list of 'Journalism Links'.

Official & quasi-official bodies

5147 Australian Press Council
www.presscouncil.org.au
Self-regulatory body for print media established in 1976 with two main aims: to help preserve the traditional freedom of the press within Australia and ensure that the free press acts responsibly and ethically. Well organized website with helpful pointers (though not all up-to-date).

5148 Press Complaints Commission [UK]
www.pcc.org.uk
'(I)ndependent body which deals with complaints from members of the public about the editorial content of newspapers and magazines. Our service to the public is free, quick and easy. We aim to deal with most complaints in just 25 working days – and there is absolutely no cost to the people complaining. The PCC received 3325 complaints in 2006 ...'
■ **Media Standards Trust** www.mediastandardstrust.org. A UK-based 'independent, not-for-profit organisation that aims to find ways to foster the highest standards of excellence in news journalism and ensure public trust in news is nurtured'. Especially useful in the context here for its Links section, structured: Analysis and debate; Campaigning groups; Citizen journalism; Existing initiatives; Industry organizations; Journalism schools; and so on. A good place to begin exploration of the field ....

Research centres & institutes

5149 Center for News Literacy [USA]
www.sunysb.edu
New centre announced September 2007 and 'designed to educate current and future news consumers on how to judge the credibility and reliability of news ... The Center will act as a resource center for universities across the US, develop curriculum for high school instruction and secondary teacher training programs and design conferences, seminars, lectures and workshops that will bring together scholars and journalists to explore issues related to the reliability of news from print, broadcast and the web'.

International News Safety Institute
See entry no. 5102

5150 Pew Research Center for the People & the Press [USA]
http://people-press.org
Leading research centre with five key foci: The people and the press; The people, the press and politics; The news interest index; America's place in the world; Media use.
■ **Pew Center for Civic Journalism** www.pewcenter.org. '(A)n incubator for civic journalism experiments that enable news organizations to create and refine better ways of reporting the news to re-engage people in public life'.

Associations & societies

5151 American Press Institute
www.americanpressinstitute.org
'The oldest and largest center devoted solely to training and professional development for the news industry and journalism educators.' Useful series of reports, especially focusing on the future of the news industry.

■ **Journalist's Toolbox** www.americanpressinstitute.org/pages/toolbox. Well laid-out and frequently updated, with, for each of some 100 topics, an opening 'Recent Additions to This Section'. Most links have a pertinent short annotation. There is a facility 'Sign up for our weekly newsletter and get updates on new sites and other resources'.

5152 International Women's Media Foundation
www.iwmf.org
'The IWMF's mission is to strengthen the role of women in the news media around the world, based on the belief that no press is truly free unless women share an equal voice.' Extensive website, not all parts recently updated, but much of value over wide arena.

5153 Newspaper Association of America
www.naa.org
'(N)onprofit organization representing the $55 billion newspaper industry. NAA members account for nearly 90 percent of the daily circulation in the United States and a wide range of non-daily US newspapers.' Extensive set of resources accessible from a well designed home page (though a number are only for members, or need log-in, or may not be recently updated): e.g. Nadbase: Newspaper Audience Database; VendorLinks Directory; Horizon Watching: Understanding the Strategic Forces Shaping the Newspaper Industry; etc. Check the good site map.

Online News Association
See entry no. 5115

5154 Periodical Publishers Association [UK]
www.ppa.co.uk
'PPA represents 80 per cent of the UK magazine market by turnover. Around 400 companies are currently in membership, representing around 2300 consumer, business and professional magazines. They also produce a large range of directories and websites in addition to organizing conferences, exhibitions and awards. A number of the larger companies also have TV and radio brands linked to their publishing interests.'
Clear, straightforward website with good sets of resources and up-to-date news on developments. There is a also a useful set of categorized and annotated links to related bodies.

5155 Publishers Association [UK]
www.publishers.org.uk
'(T)he leading trade organization serving book, journal and electronic publishers in the UK.' Useful website for gauging the state of the UK publishing industry – though significant portions of the information offered are only accessible to PA members.
■ **Directory of publishing: United Kingdom and the Republic of Ireland** 2008 edn, Continuum, 2007, 200pp. £100. ISBN 9780826499271. '(L)ists over 900 publishers in the UK and Republic of Ireland with full comprehensive entries including key contacts, fields of activity, annual turnover, overseas representation and parent/associated companies'.

5156 Religion Newswriters Association [USA]
www.rna.org
'RNA is the nation's only trade association for journalists who cover religion in the general circulation news media.' Helpful sections on: The Basics (e.g. do you need to be religious to report on religion?); Best Practices (e.g. 'remaining calm

amidst conflict'); Resources (numbers, experts, websites, books and yearbooks); A Roundup of Religions; Religion Outside the Box (e.g. spirituality); Issues for Reporters and Editors (e.g. revealing personal beliefs).

5157 World Association of Newspapers
www.wan-press.org
'Founded in 1948, the World Association of Newspapers groups 76 national newspaper associations, individual newspaper executives in 102 nations, 10 news agencies and 10 regional press organizations. It is a non-profit, non-government organization.' Good professional website, an excellent entreé to the world of newspapers. WAN publications include *Trends in Newsrooms 2007*; *World Digital Media Trends 2007*; *World Press Trends 2007*.

- **The Editors Weblog** www.editorsweblog.org. Set up in January 2004: 'It acts as a unique rendez-vous point for editors and senior news executives looking to learn about, be informed of, and participate in the monumental changes affecting journalism ... Our staff does the dirty work for you, reporting on the latest developments in the rapidly changing newspaper industry: more than 50 different sources from around the world are scanned every day. Usually, editors and senior news executives dedicate five minutes to reading The Editors Weblog, choosing to focus on one news or analysis among the six to ten postings we provide every weekday'.

Libraries, archives, museums

5158 Newseum: the interactive museum of news [USA]
www.newseum.org
To be based in Washington, DC – a project of the *Freedom Forum* – and 'will offer visitors an experience that blends five centuries of news history with up-to-the-second technology and hands-on exhibits'. Interesting, easily browsable website. The section Today's Front Pages displays over 500 newspaper front pages from 50 countries in their original, unedited form.

Vanderbilt Television News Archive
See entry no. 5219

Portal & task environments

5159 Associated Press
www.ap.org
'(T)he oldest and largest news organization in the world ... A not-for-profit cooperative, which means it is owned by its 1500 US daily newspaper members. They elect a board of directors that directs the cooperative ... On any given day, more than half the world's population sees news from AP. AP serves 1700 newspapers and 5000 radio and television outlets in the United States as well as newspaper, radio and television subscribers internationally ... The Associated Press employs some of the best and most experienced journalists in the world. Each is dedicated to the same standards – fairness, balance and accuracy. With a robust network of more than 3700 employees around the world, AP provides breaking news coverage and compelling enterprise pieces that can't be found anywhere else.'

In recent years, AP has branched from supply to the newspaper industry, creating for instance AP Broadcast, AP Digital and AP Images.

- **AccuNet/AP Multimedia Archive**
http://ap.accuweather.com/index.asp. 'Over two million photographs dating

back to 1826, more than one million audio sound bytes dating from the 1920's, two million Associated Press news stories from 1997, and a professionally produced collection of more than 45,000 maps, graphs, charts, logos, flags, illustrations, etc. are included. Updated with more than three thousand photos daily, the Archive is licensed for educational use exclusively through AccuWeather, Inc.'

- **The Associated Press stylebook (and briefing on media law)** N. Goldstein   Basic Books, 2007, 419pp. £10.99. ISBN 9780465004898. 'More people write for The Associated Press than for any newspaper in the world, and writers – nearly two million of them – have bought more copies of *The AP Stylebook* than of any other journalism reference. It provides facts and references for reporters, and defines usage, spelling, and grammar for editors ...'.

5160 Facts on File News Services
www.facts.com
'Facts On File was originally designed as a service for radio news journalists who needed fast, accurate access to fast-moving war-time events. But its print and online reference products today have come to be relied upon not only by the world's most respected media companies but also by public librarians – and the users they serve – government officials and millions of students, from elementary to graduate schools. Facts On File provides easily accessible information presented in a context that offers perspective but that is objective and also authoritative and timely.'

Media UK
See entry no. 5222

5161 PressDisplay.com
www.pressdisplay.com
Well crafted service providing integrated access to copy from 580 newspapers in 76 countries in 37 languages [in early September 2007]. 'PressDisplay users can only print full pages or individual articles using PressDisplay.com and PressReader. This is due to restrictions placed on PressDisplay by publishers who want to protect themselves from illegal distribution of their newspapers. With PressDisplay, publishers receive royalties on every paper read by our readers ...'

- **NewspaperDirect** www.newspaperdirect.com. 'Now, you can get your favorite newspaper anywhere in the world on the date of publication! Through the innovative technology of the NewspaperDirect global digital network, same-day editions of internationally-recognized newspapers are available in print and onscreen in their original layout'.

5162 Special Libraries Association, News Division
www.ibiblio.org/slanews
'(A)n international organization for print, Web and broadcast news librarians and news researchers, journalism and communications librarians, information professionals working with these materials and others interested in the role information plays in quality journalism.' Useful website with good links sections – though some parts need updating more frequently than at present. Good section on News Archiving; attractive PDF *Newsletter*; extensive list of Usenet news groups and e-mail lists.

Discovering print & electronic resources

Alternative Press Index
Alternative Press Center   See entry no. 70

5163   Alt-PressWatch
ProQuest.
www.il.proquest.com/products_pq/descriptions/alt_presswatch.shtml
[DESCRIPTION]
Database which 'showcases unique, independent voices from
some of our nation's most respected and cited grassroots
newspapers, magazines and journals. The database features
over 190,000 articles from more than 170 publications,
offering a wide range of unfettered, critical coverage of the
news.'

5164   Benn's Media
Hollis Publishing, Annual. 4 v: 1 UK; 2 – Europe (excluding UK); 3 –
North America; 4 – World, £413.00 [2007].
www.hollis-publishing.com/bennsmedia.htm [DESCRIPTION]
Over 100,000 media listings across four volumes, providing
more than 280,000 named contacts from over 208 countries
throughout the world. Attractively laid out, easy to use.
- **The all-in-one media directory** , annual. $165 [2007].
  www.gebbieinc.com [DESCRIPTION]. More than 24,000 US media listings,
  covering daily newspapers, weekly newspapers, radio stations, television
  stations, consumer magazines, trade publications, black press, black radio,
  Hispanic press, hispanic TV-Radio, and news syndicates.

5165   Brad [UK]
www.brad.co.uk/info [DESCRIPTION]
'Contains over 13,500 entries in the following sections: New
media 1752; Business press 5040; National newspapers
140; Television 197; Regional newspapers 2565; Radio 376;
Consumer press 3322; Out of home 181 … Brad is
continually researched and updated by our 25 strong
research team – in the space of a typical month we make
around 20,000 data amendments and update over half of
the 13,500 entries.'
*Available online or as a combination of online + book delivered 12 times
per year.*

**5166   Information sources for the press and broadcast
media**
S. Adair and S. Eagle, eds   2nd edn, Bowker-Saur, 1999, 242pp.
€88. ISBN 9783598244223.
Now dated, but gives a good, well written overview of the
field.

5167   News and Newspapers Online
University of North Carolina at Greensboro
http://library.uncg.edu/news
Excellent facility, covering over 3000 sources, with frequent
lists of recent changes. 'We have adopted these guidelines,
listed roughly in order of importance, to help us determine
which sites will be included: The news presented must be
based on facts, however truthful it may be … ; The news
must be current, preferably as up-to-date as the print
version; The news resource must provide free access to a
significant amount of content, rather than requiring payment
to get to anything at all; A significant amount of the news
must be full-text, not merely headlines or short summaries;
The link to the news resource must be reliable; The news
must be of general interest rather than specialized, focusing
only on business or computer news, for example; The news
resource should be Web-based or at least make use of
technologies that allow a user to access content within the
browser window; a good example of this is news published in
PDF that is accessible with a free browser plug-in application

… Preferably, the news resource should not require
registration.'
- **European Newspapers**
  www.netmasters.co.uk/european_newspapers. Clear, straightforward index
  of European national newspapers, but also of European search engines,
  directories and lists.

**5168   Online newsgathering: research and reporting for
journalists**
S. Quinn and S. Lamble   Elsevier, 2007, 208pp. £22.99. ISBN
9780240808512.
Recently announced guide designed to 'show you how to find
declassified governmental files, statistics of all kinds, simple
and complex search engines for small and large data
gathering and directories of subject experts. This book is for
the many journalists around the world who didn't attend a
formal journalism school before going to work, those
journalists who were educated before online research
became mainstream and for any student studying journalism
today'.

Digital data, image & text collections

**5169   International Federation of Audit Bureaux of
Circulations**
www.ifabc.org
A voluntary cooperative federation of industry-sponsored
organizations established in nations throughout the world to
verify and report facts about the circulations of publications
and related data.
- **Audit Bureau of Circulations** www.abc.org.uk. Free access to the
  circulation, distribution and attendance data for ABC certified magazines,
  newspapers, exhibitions and directories within the UK and Republic of
  Ireland.

Directories & encyclopedias

5170   Media directory [UK]
J. Gibson, ed.   Guardian, 2007, 544pp. £19.99. ISBN
9780852650592.
www.guardianbooks.co.uk [DESCRIPTION]
'Now in its fifteenth year, the essential handbook for media
professionals, journalists and students features
MediaGuardian's unrivalled industry analysis – plus more
than 13,000 up-to-date key contacts, including e-mail
addresses. MediaGuardian writers and industry experts
analyse the state of the media for 2007 – in press, TV, radio,
new media, global media, advertising, PR, media law, film,
music and more. This work covers updated media contacts
for every sector of the industry – including newspaper
editors, TV and film producers, radio stations, publishers,
record companies, agents, press agencies, lawyers and
more …'

**5171   Waterloo directory of English newspapers and
periodicals, 1800–1900**
North Waterloo Academic Press.
www.victorianperiodicals.com [DESCRIPTION]
The first electronic version was the Waterloo Directory of
English Newspapers and Periodicals, 1800–1900, Series 1,
on CD-ROM in 1994. It listed 25,000 titles, with the
convenience of electronic searching. A print edition in ten
volumes was published in 1998. The current online edition,

appearing in 2001 and since then greatly corrected and improved, contains all the data in both the Series 1 and Series 2 print editions.

Handbooks & manuals

5172 The magazines handbook
J. McKay 2nd edn, Routledge, 2006, 284pp. £18.99. ISBN 9780415371377.
Covers all aspects of magazine production, from obtaining copy through to delivering it to the consumer.

5173 News: a reader
H. Tumber, ed. Oxford University Press, 1999, 428pp. £23.99. ISBN 9780198742319.
Very good selection of classic texts, including Daniel Boorstin, Noam Chomsky and Stuart Hall.

5174 News narratives and news framing: constructing political reality
K.S. Johnson-Cartee Rowman & Littlefield, 2005, 361pp. $39.95. ISBN 9780742536630.
Wide-ranging, well written text with extensive bibliography. Detailed considerations of, for instance, the social construction of reality, news as narrative and personalized and confrontational news framing.

5175 The newspapers handbook
R. Keeble 4th edn, Routledge, 2006, 299pp. £16.99. ISBN 9780415331142.
Originally written because of concern at 'journalists and media theorists living in separate (and often antagonistic) "worlds"'; and concern at 'the narrow, Anglocentric focus of journalism education in many places ...' However, the book's main focus is on 'the basic skills of writing lively, coherent, accurate, engaging copy in a range genres.'

5176 Writing and reporting the news
J. Lanson and M. Stephens 3rd edn, Oxford University Press, 2007, 560pp. £32.99. ISBN 9780195306668.
US-based, highly comprehensive handbook, with 27 chapters organized into six parts, the first three concerned with Writing (I. The News; II. Leads; III. Stories) and the second three with Reporting (IV. Techniques; V. Coverage; VI. Specialized coverage). Six Appendices: Format; Style; Spelling and grammar; Analogies, metaphors and clichés; Ethics; Law.

Keeping up to date

5177 Editor and Publisher
VNU Business Publications, monthly. $99. ISSN 0013094X.
www.editorandpublisher.com
Covers all aspects of the North American newspaper industry, including business, newsroom, advertising, circulation, marketing, technology, online and syndicates.

5178 NewsNow
NewsNow Publishing.
www.newsnow.co.uk
Sophisticated service which 'monitors breaking news in 22 languages from the internet's most important online publications, including international, national and regional

titles, newswires, magazines, press releases and exclusively online news sources spanning 139 countries ... NewsNow is an online news aggregator. We don't write news ourselves; instead, we scan the internet for headlines and group them into convenient categories to make it easier for you to find the news you want.'

Radio, TV & Film

broadcasting • cable television • children & television • community radio • documentary • film • image • moving image • radio • television

Introductions to the subject

5179 Children and television: a global perspective
D. Lemish Blackwell, 2007, 272pp. £17.99. ISBN 9781405144193.
Good historical overview.
  ▪ **Children and television: fifty years of research** N. Pecora, J.P. Murray and E.A. Wartella, eds Lawrence Erlbaum, 2007, 389pp. £16.99. ISBN 9780805841398. Wide-ranging study with comprehensive bibliography whose full version appears on an accompanying CD-ROM.

5180 History of wireless
T.K. Sarkar [et al.] Wiley, 2006, 655pp. £34.50. ISBN 9780471718147.
Detailed, technologically intensive volume, useful for context.

5181 An introduction to television studies
J. Bignell Routledge, 2007, 368pp. £18.99. ISBN 9780415419185.
Revised edition of now standard UK-based introduction.

5182 A study of modern television: thinking inside the box
A. Crisell Palgrave Macmillan, 2006, 184pp. £18.99. ISBN 9780333964095.
www.palgrave.com/products [DESCRIPTION]
14 chapters in three parts: I. The foundations of modern television; II. Television genres; III. Television culture.

5183 Television: the life story of a technology
A.B. Magoun Greenwood Press, 2007, 232pp. $45. ISBN 9780313331282.
Covers 'the entire history of television from the early twentieth-century ideas of transmitting images by electromagnetic waves to the current issues involving HDTV' as well as 'the continuing importance of television in the lives of people across the globe'.

Dictionaries, thesauri, classifications

5184 BKSTS illustrated dictionary of moving image technology
M. Uren 4th edn, Focal Press, 2001, 350pp. £31.99. ISBN 9780240516325.
Attractive volume with over 3300 definitions covering film, television, sound and multimedia technologies.
  ▪ **BKSTS: The Moving Image Society** www.bksts.com. Mission is 'To encourage, sustain, educate, train and represent all those who are involved creatively or technologically in the business of providing moving images and associated crafts in any form and through any media'. BKSTS was originally the British Kinematograph Sound & Television Society.

5185 International dictionary of broadcasting and film

D.K. Bognár　2nd edn, Focal Press, 2000, 328pp. £37.99. ISBN 9780240803760.

http://books.google.com [DESCRIPTION]

Helpful overview of the book on Google Books – but omitting the main A–Z sequence of terms.

Laws, standards, codes

5186 Broadcasting, voice and accountability: a public interest approach to policy, law, and regulation

K. Duer [et al.]　University of Michigan Press, 2007, 416pp. $25. ISBN 9780472032723.

'Information on good practices in broadcasting policy is in demand in countries of every region – particularly in countries that are opening their economies, democratizing and decentralizing public service delivery. This book thus builds on a growing awareness of the role of media and voice in equipping people to better exercise their rights and hold leaders to account. It focuses on broadcasting because that is the medium with the greatest potential to reach and involve poor, illiterate populations – the most disadvantaged segments of society – in developing countries …'

5187 Descriptive metadata for television: an end-to-end introduction

M. Cox, E. Mulder and L. Tadic　Focal, 2006, 143pp. £20.99. ISBN 9780240807300.

Very useful guide covering What is metadata?; Types of metadata; Metadata schemes, structures and encoding; The impact of technology change on people and metadata processes; Identifiers and identification; Metadata for the consumer; Metadata in public collections.

5188 Law for advertising, broadcasting, journalism and public relations: a comprehensive text for students and practitioners

M.G. Parkinson and L.M. Parkinson　Lawrence Erlbaum, 2006, 528pp. £39.50. ISBN 9780805849752.

'Providing background to help readers understand legal concepts, this comprehensive communication law text includes an introduction to the legal system; covers legal procedures, structures and jurisdictions; discusses the First Amendment and electronic media regulations; and considers issues of access.'

Additional material includes coverage of Intellectual property law; Employment and agency law, with explanations of how these laws create obligations for mass communication professionals and their employees; Commercial communication laws; and Special laws and regulations that impact reporters, public relations practitioners and advertisers who deal with stock sales.

Official & quasi-official bodies

5189 Corporation for Public Broadcasting [USA]

www.cpb.org

'(A) private, non-profit corporation created by Congress in 1967. The mission of CPB is to facilitate the development of and ensure universal access to, non-commercial high-quality programming and telecommunications services. It does this in conjunction with non-commercial educational

telecommunications licensees across America.' Site provides useful overview.

5190 European Audiovisual Observatory: the information portal for the audiovisual sector

www.obs.coe.int

'Set up in December 1992, the European Audiovisual Observatory is the only centre of its kind to gather and circulate information on the audiovisual industry in Europe.' Easily navigable site offering good range of data and information and, naturally, particularly useful for comparative information across Europe (e.g. 'Sources of information on the television licence fee'). Quite an amount of detail in various databases offered via the site, for instance 'KORDA: database on public funding for the film and audiovisual sector in Europe'.

5191 European Broadcasting Union

www.ebu.ch

'(T)he largest professional association of national broadcasters in the world. The Union has 74 active members in 54 countries of Europe, North Africa and the Middle East and 44 associate members in 25 countries further afield. The EBU was founded in February 1950 by western European radio and television broadcasters. It merged with the OIRT – its counterpart in Eastern Europe – in 1993.'

Extensive inventory with very clear site map – though significant parts of the site are for members only. Nevertheless, much that is splendid (e.g. access to the PDF 115-page EBU Directory; the EBU News Archives).

5192 Federal Communications Commission [USA]

www.fcc.gov

'(E)stablished by the Communications Act of 1934 and is charged with regulating interstate and international communications by radio, television, wire, satellite and cable.' Site provides access to a mass of valuable information: particularly useful is the list of Major Initiatives, via which leads can be followed to 'Broadband', 'Children's television', 'Media and childhood obesity', 'Slamming', 'Voice over internet protocol' and so on.

5193 Ofcom [UK]

www.ofcom.org.uk

'Ofcom is the independent regulator and competition authority for the UK communications industries, with responsibilities across television, radio, telecommunications and wireless communications services.' Unfortunately, for this reviewer, not the most user-friendly of websites; but naturally worth persisting, the site map being of help.

- **Australia. Communications & Media Authority** www.acma.gov.au. Responsible for the regulation of broadcasting, radiocommunications, telecommunications and online content. Comprehensive website (though response time can be slow).
- **Canadian Radio-television & Telecommunications Commission** www.crtc.gc.ca. 'The CRTC is an independent agency responsible for regulating Canada's broadcasting and telecommunications systems. We report to Parliament through the Minister of Canadian Heritage'. Excellent website: exceptionally clear and responsive.

5194 Skillset: the sector Skills Council for the audio visual industries

www.skillset.org

Covers broadcast, film, video, interactive media and photo imaging: one of 25 such councils within the UK (see www.ssda.org.uk). Very good summaries of work across the sector, including standards, qualifications, research, strategy and so on.

5195 World Association of Community Radio Broadcasters
www.amarc.org
'AMARC is an international non-governmental organization serving the community radio movement. Its goal is to support and contribute to the development of community and participatory radio along the principles of solidarity and international cooperation.' Very extensive website giving access to developments worldwide. However, not the most intuitive of sites: try first the home page link AMARC WIKI – which gives access to a site map.

Research centres & institutes

5196 British Universities Film & Video Council
www.bufvc.ac.uk
'(R)epresentative body which promotes the production, study and use of film and related media in higher and further education and research. It was founded in 1948 as the British Universities Film Council.'
- **British Universities Newsreel Database** www.bufvc.ac.uk/databases/newsreels. Fascinating resource. The newsreels and cinemagazines have been gathered in five phases starting in 1969 and the database now contains 170,000 stories, a large collection of digitized documents, and web links to many of the films. But the site also provides access to details of a wealth of supporting material: books, videos, abstracts, links, talks, etc.
- **Moving Image Gateway** www.bufvc.ac.uk/gateway. 'Collects together websites that relate to moving images and sound and their use in higher and further education. The sites are classified by academic discipline, some forty subjects from agriculture to women's studies, collected within the four main categories of arts and humanities, bio-medical, social sciences and science and technology.
- **Society for Cinema & Media Studies** www.cmstudies.org. US-based 'professional organization of college and university educators, filmmakers, historians, critics, scholars, and others devoted to the study of the moving image'. Useful if somewhat limited website.
- **Television and Radio Index for Learning and Teaching: TRILT** www.trilt.ac.uk. 'The best source of UK television and radio data on the web … BUT only available to BUFVC members (including staff and students in BUFVC member institutions)'.

5197 Center for the Study of Popular Television [USA]
http://newhouse.syr.edu/research/POPTV
Centre located at Syracuse University 'providing scholarship, commentary and education in the areas of television and popular culture.' The Centre 'has an impressive archive of entertainment television programs, scripts and history' and 'also conducted an ambitious oral history project which includes videotaped first-person accounts from over 120 trailblazing luminaries on the founding and early days of television broadcasting'.
- **Journal of Popular Film and Television** Heldref Publications, qtrly. $59. ISSN 01956051. www.heldref.org/jpft.php [DESCRIPTION]. 'Articles discuss networks, genres, series, and audiences, as well as celebrity stars, directors, and studios. Regular features include essays on the social and cultural background of films and television programs, filmographies, bibliographies, and commissioned book and video reviews. Each year, the journal publishes one theme issue on such subjects as "Media literacy and education: The teacher-scholar in film and television" and "Fantastic

voyages: horror, fantasy, and science fiction/speculative cinema." In a field where most writing is hokum, *The Journal of Popular Film and Television* delivers solid, lively insights …'.

College of Communication
See entry no. 5056

POLIS
See entry no. 772

Associations & societies

5198 American Society of Media Photographers
www.asmp.org
'Promotes photographers' rights, educates photographers in better business practices, produces business publications for photographers and helps buyers find professional photographers. ASMP was founded in 1944 by a handful of the world's leading photojournalists and is recognized internationally for its leadership role. ASMP has over 5000 members, including many of the world's greatest photographers, in 39 chapters nationwide.'
Exemplary website. The site map is exceptionally well laid out and clearly indicates those areas of the site which are for 'Members Only'. For non-members there are a range of good resources and lists of links, as well as the services Find a Photographer and Find a Photo – the latter providing thumbnails of the results.
- **British Association of Picture Libraries & Agencies** www.bapla.org.uk. 'UK trade association for picture libraries and the largest organisation of its kind in the world. With over 400 member companies, it represents the vast majority of commercial picture libraries and agencies in the UK. Companies range from small specialists to multinationals, collectively managing in excess of 350 million images'. Helpful background information ('What is a picture library?' etc.); searchable A–Z list of members.

5199 Asia-Pacific Broadcasting Union
www.abu.org.my
'(F)ormed in 1964 to facilitate the development of broadcasting in the Asia-Pacific region and to organise cooperative activities among its members. It currently has over 160 members in 55 countries and regions, reaching a potential audience of about 3 billion people.' Extensive, well structured website providing useful entry to activity in the region.

5200 Association for International Broadcasting
www.aib.org.uk
'The only trade association for the cross-border broadcasting industry. It covers all sectors, with a growing worldwide membership, including television and radio broadcasters, satellite operators, manufacturers of studio and production equipment, transmission companies, news agencies and consultants.' Useful list of members with website links; news service; publications – including the *AIB Directory of Global Broadcasting*.

5201 British Film Institute
www.bfi.org.uk
Excellent website, concentrating on film as art, but with much else of great value about film in general. There is a clearly laid-out site map leading, for instance, to a Media Courses and Multimedia Courses Directory listing details of

over 6000 'courses across England, Northern Ireland, Scotland and Wales. Film courses, television courses, video courses, radio courses and web authoring courses are included'; and to a Moving Image Research Registry: a searchable database of some 600 'researchers and their research projects – based primarily at UK universities and colleges – relating to cinema, television and other moving image media'.

- **BFI National Archive** www.bfi.org.uk/nftva. '(O)ne of the world's greatest collections of film and television. The majority of the collection is British material but it also features internationally significant holdings from around the world … The archive contains more than 50,000 fiction films, over 100,000 non-fiction titles and around 625,000 television programmes'.
- **BFI National Library** www.bfi.org.uk/filmtvinfo/library. Offer a very good range of information services: for instance, the Films Links Gateway, providing 'a wide reaching but selective collection of websites available on the Internet, relating to film and the media both in the UK and internationally'.
- **Museum of the Moving Image** www.movingimage.us. New York-based and 'dedicated to educating the public about the art, history, technique, and technology of film, television, and digital media, and to examining their impact on culture and society. It maintains the nation's largest permanent collection of moving image artifacts, and offers the public exhibitions, film screening, lectures, seminars, and other education programs'.

5202 Broadcast Education Association [USA]
www.beaweb.org
'(T)he professional association for professors, industry professionals and graduate students who are interested in teaching and research related to electronic media and multimedia enterprises. There are currently more than 1400 individual and institutional members.'

Institutional membership directory; job openings; interest divisions (extensive list with informative descriptions); publications; research clearinghouse (with very useful inventory of research websites); syllabus project; other links.

5203 Cable & Satellite Broadcasting Association of Asia
www.casbaa.com
'Industry-based advocacy group dedicated to the promotion of multi-channel television via cable, satellite, broadband and wireless video networks across the Asia-Pacific. CASBAA represents some 110 Asia-based corporations, which in turn serve more than 3 billion people.'

Useful portal to developments in the region; good set of Industry News Links; member details; publications; and so on.

- **Broadcastpapers.com** www.broadcastpapers.com. 'Drawing on broadcast professionals, conferences and manufacturers, Broadcastpapers.com is a library of the latest ideas in broadcasting technology and business. A totally free resource, Broadcastpapers.com covers areas such as broadcast business, digital and analogue transmission, data services and interactivity, asset management, animation and FX, cameras and lenses, radio, audio and more …'.

5204 Independent Media Arts Preservation [USA]
www.imappreserve.org
'(A) nonprofit service, education and advocacy organization committed to the preservation of non-commercial electronic media. IMAP has grown from a New York-based consortium of arts organizations and individuals to a national resource for preservation training, information and advocacy.' Excellent entrée to the area, defined as 'time-based, non-commercial production incorporating video or audio, both analog and digital, including but not limited to: video art, audio art, new media and technology-based installation art; independent documentary and community media; and documentation of arts and culture.'

Good briefings in Preservation101; Cataloguing Project seeking 'to establish a compatible information system for independent media collections across broad geographic regions, among a wide range of arts organizations, artists and performers'; Online Resource Guide for Exhibiting, Collecting & Preserving Media Art.

5205 International Association for Media & History
www.iamhist.org
'(O)rganization of filmmakers, broadcasters, archivists and scholars dedicated to historical inquiry into film, radio, television and related media.' Very well laid out site: not a great amount of recent material, but what is there is useful.

5206 International Documentary Association
www.documentary.org
Mission is 'to promote nonfiction film and video around the world by: Supporting and recognizing the efforts of documentary film and video makers; increasing public appreciation and demand for the documentary; providing a forum for documentary makers, their supporters and suppliers.' Good starting point in this arena.

5207 International Federation of Film Archives
www.fiafnet.org/uk
'(B)rings together institutions dedicated to rescuing films both as cultural heritage and as historical documents. Founded in Paris in 1938, FIAF is a collaborative association of the world's leading film archives whose purpose has always been to ensure the proper preservation and showing of motion pictures. Today, more than 120 archives in over 65 countries collect, restore and exhibit films and cinema documentation spanning the entire history of film.'

Very well organized site, with especially effective Links sections.

- **FIAF Databases Online** www.fiafnet.org/uk/publications/fdbo_content.cfm. Contains the following databases: International Index to Film Periodicals; International Index to Television Periodicals; Treasures from the Film Archives; Bibliography of FIAF Members' Publications; International Directory of Film/TV Documentation Collections.

International Federation of Television Archives
See entry no. 5771

5208 National Alliance for Media Arts & Culture [USA]
www.namac.org
'(N)onprofit association whose membership comprises a diverse mix of organizations and individuals dedicated to a common goal: the support and advocacy of independent film, video, audio and online/multimedia arts.' Has searchable list with short descriptions of some 300 organizations active in the field. Also an extensive set of Hot Topics: 'NAMAC keeps you on top of burning issues in the field. Here you'll find recent articles, white papers, relevant links and a myriad of other resources relating to the most popular topics in the media arts.'

5209 National Association of Broadcasters [USA]
www.nab.org
'(T)rade association that advocates on behalf of more than

8300 free, local radio and television stations and also broadcast networks before Congress, the Federal Communications Commission and the Courts.' Access to extensive sets of resources (though website response time can be slow).

5210 National Cable & Telecommunications Association
[USA]
www.ncta.com
Principal trade association of the cable television industry in the USA. Clearly laid-out site with large section treating 'digital television'.

5211 RadioCentre [UK]
www.radiocentre.org
(F)ormed in July 2006 from the merger of the Radio Advertising Bureau (RAB) and the Commercial Radio Companies Association (CRCA). Its members consist of the overwhelming majority of UK commercial radio stations who fund the organization.' Enables good overview of the field of 'radio' in the UK – in conjunction with the sites referenced below.
- **Radio Academy** www.radioacademy.org. '(T)he professional body for the UK radio and audio industry. Founded in 1983, it represents the industry to outside bodies including government and offers neutral ground where everyone from national networks to individual podcasters can discuss the broadcasting, production, marketing and promotion of radio and audio services.
- **Radio Research Database Bournemouth University**. www.bufvc.ac.uk/databases/rrdb.html. '(A)ims to contain a record of all current radio-centred academic research in the UK, to assist all those researchers working in the new discipline of Radio Studies. The database is funded by the Radio Academy and managed by the Radio Studies Network'.
- **Radio Studies Network** www.radiostudiesnetwork.org.uk. '(F)ounded in December 1998 by lecturers and researchers to encourage sustained, lively and critical study and research in radio, and seek ways to improve its academic and cultural status'.
- **RAJAR** www.rajar.co.uk. 'RAJAR stands for Radio Joint Audience Research and is the official body in charge of measuring radio audiences in the UK. It is jointly owned by the BBC and the RadioCentre on behalf of the commercial sector. There are currently approximately 350 individual stations on the survey and results are published every quarter'.

5212 Radio-Television News Directors Association & Foundation
www.rtnda.org
Now with the by-line 'The Association of Electronic Journalists'. 'Membership with RTNDA is indispensable for every electronic journalist. We are the world's largest and only professional organization exclusively serving the electronic news profession and is made up of more than 3000 news directors, news associates, educators and students all engaged in the production of news for all media.' Good sets of regularly updated resources organized as Membership tools; Careers; Research; Best practices; Education; Supplier partners.

5213 Royal Television Society [UK]
www.rts.org.uk
'(T)he leading forum for discussion and debate on all aspects of the television community. In a fast changing sector, it reflects the full range of perspectives and views.' Especially notable for its Annual Lectures, but much else of value here, including details of the leading magazine *Television*.

Voice of the Listener & Viewer
See entry no. 5294

Libraries, archives, museums

5214 British Pathé
www.britishpathe.com
'British Pathé are one of the oldest media companies in the world. Their roots lie in 1890s Paris, where their founder, Charles Pathé, pioneered the development of the moving image. They were established in London in 1902 and by 1910 were producing their famous bi-weekly newsreel, the *Pathé Gazette* …
    'Welcome to Version 3.2 of the world's first digital news archive. Now you are here you can preview items from the entire 3500 hour British Pathé Film Archive, which covers news, sport, social history and entertainment from 1896 to 1970 …'

5215 Motion Picture and Television Reading Room [USA]
Library of Congress
www.loc.gov/rr/mopic
'The Library of Congress began collecting motion pictures in 1893 when Thomas Edison and his brilliant assistant W.K.L. Dickson deposited the Edison Kinetoscopic Records for copyright. However, because of the difficulty of safely storing the flammable nitrate film used at the time, the Library retained only the descriptive material relating to motion pictures. In 1942, recognizing the importance of motion pictures and the need to preserve them as a historical record, the Library began the collection of the films themselves. From 1949 on these included films made for television. Today the Motion Picture, Broadcasting and Recorded Sound Division (MBRS) has responsibility for the acquisition, cataloging and preservation of the motion picture and television collections. The Division operates the Motion Picture and Television Reading Room to provide access and information services to an international community of film and television professionals, archivists, scholars and researchers.'
- **Academic Film Archive of North America** www.afana.org. 'What is "academic film"? Of the over 100,000 educational films made in North America between the early 1900s and approximately 1985, many of the best were in the subject fields of art, history, social science, literature, and science. These we refer to as academic film, as opposed to those made in health, safety, civics, and other non-academic educational subject areas'.
- **Moving Image Collections: a Window to the World's Moving Images** http://mic.loc.gov. 'MIC documents moving image collections around the world through a catalog of titles and directory of repositories, providing a window to the world's moving image collections for discovery, access and preservation … MIC provides a technology base and informational resources to support research, collaboration, preservation, and education for archivists, exhibitors, educators, and the general public … MIC is a portal for integrating moving images into 21st Century education … MIC is a key access program of the Library of Congress's National Audio Visual Conservation Center.
- **National Film Preservation Board** www.loc.gov/film. 'The Foundation's primary mission is to save orphan films, films without owners able to pay for their preservation. The films most at-risk are newsreels, silent films, experimental works, films out of copyright protection, significant amateur footage, documentaries, and features made outside the commercial mainstream. Orphan films are the living record of the twentieth century. Hundreds of American museums, archives, libraries, universities,

and historical societies care for "orphaned" original film materials of cultural value. The Foundation will work with these film preservation organizations to preserve orphan films and make them accessible to "present and future generations of Americans"'.

5216 National Media Museum [UK]
www.nmpft.org.uk
'Welcome to the new website for the National Media Museum. In the past 23 years we have been the National Museum of Photography, Film & Television. We've changed our name because the world is changing and we need to keep pace and remain relevant ... 'Rich website giving access to good sets of resources.

5217 National Public Broadcasting Archives [USA]
University of Maryland
www.lib.umd.edu/NPBA
Good, straightforward website with comprehensive sections: About the archives; Research materials; Other resources. The core of the collection 'brings together the archival record of the major entities of non-commercial broadcasting in the United States'.

5218 University of Maryland, Library of American Broadcasting
www.lib.umd.edu/LAB
'(H)olds a wide-ranging collection of audio and video recordings, books, pamphlets, periodicals, personal collections, oral histories, photographs, scripts and vertical files devoted exclusively to the history of broadcasting.' Based at the University of Maryland.

5219 Vanderbilt Television News Archive [USA]
http://tvnews.vanderbilt.edu
'(T)he world's most extensive and complete archive of television news. The collection holds more than 30,000 individual network evening news broadcasts from the major US national broadcast networks: ABC, CBS, NBC and CNN and more than 9000 hours of special news-related programming ...'

Portal & task environments

5220 BBC
www.bbc.co.uk
The BBC's extensive and world-leading website has a full A–Z index whose entries can be restricted to 'Radio Only' or 'TV Only' and for each letter lists the 'Most popular pages'. Also of value in navigation is the section About the BBC – which has its own A–Z index.
- **Australian Broadcasting Corporation** http://abc.net.au. Includes a useful section Media Watch, which is 'Australia's leading forum for media analysis and comment. Conflicts of interest, bank backflips, deceit, misrepresentation, manipulation, plagiarism, abuse of power, technical lies and straight out fraud: Media Watch has built an unrivalled record of exposing media shenanigans since it first went to air in 1989 ...'.
- **Canadian Broadcasting Corporation** www.cbc.ca. Not the most intuitively structured website: navigate from 'Sitemap' on the Home Page.
- **PBS** www.pbs.org. US-based enterprise which 'serves 355 public noncommercial television stations and reaches nearly 73 million people each week through on-air and online content. Bringing diverse viewpoints to television and the Internet, PBS provides high-quality documentary and dramatic entertainment, and consistently dominates the most prestigious award competitions'.

5221 CNN.com
www.cnn.com
Engaging website, well organized. Includes Inside CNN Atlanta: 'This 55-minute behind-the-scenes tour shows you exactly what it takes to deliver the news available to over 2 billion people worldwide'. Also access to the associated news magazine *Time*.

5222 Media UK
www.mediauk.com
'The critically-acclaimed independent media directory for the UK. Listing websites, addresses, telephone numbers, live links and more for all areas of the online media, it's your one-stop media portal. Continually updated with 60 updates over the past week, we currently list 811 radio stations, 501 television channels, 1581 newspapers and 1892 magazines. Enjoy hundreds of live radio and television feeds from across the UK ...'

5223 MediaEd: the UK media education website
www.mediaed.org.uk
Site funded by the British Film Institute 'for teachers, students and anyone else who's interested in media and moving image education in primary, secondary, further and informal education'. Key pages are listed as: Media Studies resources – Reviews of resources for teaching Media Studies, Film Studies resources – Reviews of resources for teaching Film Studies, Film-making in the classroom – Advice on film language, getting started with digital video, equipment, classroom practice and training. Excellent selective set of links, classified into 14 sections.
- **Media Education Foundation** www.mediaed.org. '(P)roduces and distributes documentary films and other educational resources to inspire critical reflection on the social, political and cultural impact of American mass media'.

5224 National Public Radio [USA]
www.npr.org
'A privately supported, not-for-profit membership organization, NPR serves a growing audience of 26 million Americans each week in partnership with more than 800 independently operated, noncommercial public radio stations.'

5225 World Radio Network
www.wrn.org
'(A) leading broadcast and transmission company providing its worldwide clients with high quality, innovative and cutting-edge solutions for their broadcasting and telecommunications needs.' Site is an uncomplicated gateway to developments in radio broadcasting with a range of exemplar services.

Discovering print & electronic resources

Benn's Media
See entry no. 5164

Brad
See entry no. 5165

5226   Film and television: a guide to the reference literature

M. Emmons   Libraries Unlimited, 2006, 366pp. $40. ISBN 9781563089145.

Very good overview organized as: Introduction; Indexes and bibliographies; Dictionaries and encyclopedias; General film and television filmographies; National cinema; Genres; Formats; Studios; Portrayals; Filmmakers; Screenplays; Making films and television programs; Film and television industry; Fans and audience. Useful appendices cover subject heading and classification approaches of Library of Congress and Dewey.

'Emmons's passion for the large and small screen is evident in this annotated bibliography of reference sources, for which he personally examined and described over 1,200 resources ... An excellent guide for researchers. Highly recommended.' (*Choice*)

5227   Film and Television Literature Index

EBSCO.

www.epnet.com [DESCRIPTION]

Developed from the Film Literature Index and 'provides cover-to-cover indexing and abstracts for more than 300 publications and selected coverage of 300 more'.

5228   Gale directory of publications and broadcast media

143rd edn, Thomson Gale, 2008. $1000. ISBN 9780787696696.
www.gale.com [DESCRIPTION]

'This premier media directory contains thousands of listings for radio and television stations and cable companies. Print media entries provide address; phone, fax numbers and e-mail addresses; key personnel, including feature editors; and much more. Broadcast media entries provide address; phone, fax and e-mail addresses; key personnel; owner information; hours of operation; networks carried and more.'

Information sources for the press and broadcast media

S. Adair and S. Eagle, eds   See entry no. 5166

5229   Radio-Locator

Theodric Technologies.
www.radio-locator.com

'The most comprehensive radio station search engine on the internet. We have links to over 10,000 radio station web pages and over 2500 audio streams from radio stations in the US and around the world.' Good search facilities by format, country, etc. Formerly the MIT List of Radio Stations on the internet.

5230   The researcher's guide: film, television, radio and related documentation collections in the UK

S. Angelini, ed.; British Universities Film & Video Council   7th edn, 2006, 221pp. £19.99. ISBN 9780901299765.
http://joseph.bufvc.ac.uk/RGO/index.html [COMPANION]

Now lists details of 644 collections but in a new compact form 'thanks to our corresponding database, the Researcher's Guide Online, which provides the researcher with more extensive descriptions, collections details, illustrations and live web links. The RGO is constantly updated and now comes with the facility for collection owners to be able to add new records or amend existing ones.'

5231   Television program master index [USA]

2nd edn, McFarland, 2003, 302pp. $49.95. ISBN 9780786414925.

'Access to critical and historical information on 1927 Shows in 925 books, dissertations and journal articles ... New to this edition are journal articles, books devoted to only one show, dissertations and websites where more information about a particular television show can be found.'

'Absolutely invaluable.' (*American Reference Books Annual*)

5232   TVLink

Timelapse.com.
www.timelapse.com/tvlink

Good, simple, well categorized list of some 1000 film- and television-related websites. Short description of each site.

Digital data, image & text collections

5233   Arbitron

www.arbitron.com

'Arbitron Inc. (NYSE: ARB) is an international media and marketing research firm serving radio broadcasters, radio networks, cable companies, advertisers, advertising agencies, out-of-home advertising companies and the online radio industry in the United States and Europe. Through our Scarborough Research joint venture with The Nielsen Company, Arbitron also provides media and marketing research services to the broadcast television, cable, newspaper, out-of-home and online industries.'

Much of the data offered is naturally fee-based. But browse of the site offers a rewarding overview of both the industry itself and market and other research about the industry: checkout the detailed site index.

5234   BARB [UK]

Broadcasters' Audience Research Board.
www.barb.co.uk

BARB 'is responsible for providing estimates of the number of people watching television. This includes which channels and programmes are being watched, at what time and the type of people who are watching at any one time. BARB provides television audience data on a minute-by-minute basis for channels received within the UK. The data is available for reporting nationally and at ITV and BBC regional level and covers all analogue and digital platforms.' Significant data available free of charge; useful questions and answers section; good glossary of terminology.

5235   Baseline StudioSystems

New York Times Company.
www.pkbaseline.com

'(T)he world's pre-eminent provider of film and television information. Baseline's flagship product is The Studio System, a subscription database of premium film and television information. Combining real-time information updates with a sophisticated user interface, The Studio System is the industry's most powerful and reliable informational tool.'

5236   BBC Motion Gallery
BBC

www.bbcmotiongallery.com

'(O)ffers media professionals in advertising, commercials, television, film, interactive and corporate video production access to the world's most comprehensive collection of high-quality motion imagery for licensing and royalty-free usage worldwide. With more than 500 million feet of film and 600,000 hours of video, BBC Motion Gallery encompasses a wealth of content covering natural history, wildlife, news, locations, art, music, celebrities, culture, performing arts and more, including acclaimed programming produced in conjunction with Discovery and PBS.'

5237 Nielsen Media Research [USA]
www.nielsenmedia.com
Notable for its television ratings using People Meters, set-tuning meters and paper diaries: see the FAQ section. Extensive Glossary of Media Terms and Acronyms.

Directories & encyclopedias

5238 Encyclopedia of television
H. Newcomb; Museum of Broadcast Communications   2nd edn, Routledge, 2004. 4 v., £375. ISBN 9781579583941.
www.routledge-ny.com/ref/television [COMPANION]
'(B)uilds on the award-winning first edition that has been widely recognized and cited as the foremost reference work on the study of television. Incorporating almost 200 new entries and revisions of almost all of the original entries from the first edition, the second edition of the Encyclopedia not only focuses on the history and current state of television in today's society but looks to the future, exploring significant changes that have occurred in the economic, technological and regulatory contexts in which television is produced, transmitted and experienced.'
- **Museum of Broadcast Communications** www.museum.tv. 'Our mission is to collect, preserve, and present historic and contemporary radio and television content as well as educate, inform, and entertain through our archives, public programs, screenings, exhibits, publications and online access to our resources.' Currently building a new facility in Chicago, USA.

Media directory
J. Gibson, ed.   See entry no. 5170

Handbooks & manuals

5239 A companion to television
J. Wasko, ed.   Blackwell, 2005, 627pp. £95. ISBN 9781405100946.
www.blackwellreference.com/public [FEE-BASED]
31 chapters in 9 parts: Theoretical overviews; Television/history; Television/aesthetics and production; Television/the state and policy; Television/commerce; Television/programming, content and genre; Television/the public and audiences; Television/alternative challenges; International television/case studies.

5240 European television in the digital age: issues, dynamics and realities
S. Papathanassopoulos   Polity Press, 2002, 304pp. £16.99. ISBN 9780745628738.
Good comprehensive overview of long-term relevance, which 'attempts to describe the issues, dynamics and realities of West European television in the digital age by synthesizing the hard facts. It moves away from normative debates about what the audio-visual scene should be like and presents a detailed account of the contemporary television process,

focusing on digital TV and the rise of thematic channels in Europe.'

5241 Managing television news: a handbook for ethical and effective producing
B.W. Silcock, D. Heider and M.T. Rogus   Lawrence Erlbaum, 2007, 262pp. £22.95. ISBN 9780805853735.
'(P)rovides a practical introduction to the television news producer, one of the most significant and influential roles in a newscast ... (P)rovides a strategic approach to producing newscasts and serves as an in-depth guide to creating quality, audience-friendly newscasts working within the realistic limitations of most newsrooms.'

5242 The radio station: broadcast, satellite and internet
M.C. Keith   7th edn, Focal Press, 2006, 377pp.
www.elsevier.com [DESCRIPTION]
Latest edition of classic text covering all aspects of the radio industry.

5243 The television handbook
J. Bignell and J. Orlebar   3rd edn, Routledge, 2005, 340pp. £16.99. ISBN 041534252X.
One of the Media Practice series of handbooks intended as 'comprehensive resource books for students of media and journalism and for anyone planning a career as a media professional'. Extensive glossary and good index.

Keeping up to date

5244 Broadcasting and Cable [USA]
Reed Business Information, weekly. $199.99. ISSN 10686827.
www.broadcastingcable.com
'(T)he definitive news source on every aspect of the television industry: programming, finance, technology, regulatory and media trends. *Broadcasting & Cable* covers the entire spectrum of broadcast, cable, satellite, telco, multimedia, broadband and other emerging technologies and is the single most reliable source of industry news and information available.' Also useful Resources section.
- **Broadcasting and cable yearbook** Bowker, 2006, annual. $235.00 [2007 edn]. ISBN 9780835248495. www.bowker.com/catalog [DESCRIPTION]. '(I)ncludes profiles of 4,825 AM radio stations, 9,000 FM radio stations, and 2,180 television stations in the United States. A station's call letters, frequency or channel, address, telephone, fax, e-mail, Internet address, ownership, and programming format are all provided. Additionally, more than 1,100 Canadian radio and television stations are profiled, along with more than 5,100 industry service providers from law firms to engineers to industry associations, and more'.

5245 BroadcastNow
Emap Media.
www.broadcastnow.co.uk
The website for the leading weekly magazine *Broadcast*. News of current UK market behaviour, industry developments, government actions, etc.

5246 Journal of Broadcasting and Electronic Media
Broadcast Education Association   Lawrence Erlbaum, 1990–, qtrly. ISSN 08838151.
'Devoted to advancing research, knowledge and understanding of communication and the electronic media.'

5247 Radio Ink [USA]
Streamline Publishing, fortnightly. $199. ISSN 1064587X.
www.radioink.com
Popular but informative wide-ranging magazine whose 'annual subscription includes these popular issues: The 40 Most Powerful People in Radio; The Executive of the Year Issue; The Best Program Directors in America; The 25 Most Influential Women in Radio; The 20 Most Successful African-Americans in Radio'.

Privacy, Freedom & Censorship

censorship • digital freedom • electronic privacy • freedom of expression • freedom of information • freedom of the press • information ethics • information privacy • media ethics • privacy

Introductions to the subject

5248 Digital freedom: how much can you handle?
N.D. Batra   Rowman & Littlefield, 2007, 265pp. $28.95. ISBN 9780742555747.
'*Digital freedom* is an exploration of and meditation on the question: How much freedom does a person need? The question evokes Tolstoy's parable, "How much land does a man need?" Is freedom an acquired taste, much like one's love for symphony orchestra? Or, is it a necessity? After all, civilizations in the past have produced monumental works in all fields of human endeavor without as much obsession with individual freedom as we have today. *Digital freedom* explores these issues – including surveillance, intellectual property and copyright – from the perspective of an evolutionary, self-organizing social system. This system both creates and assimilates innovations and, in the process, undergoes reorganization and renewal.'

5249 Ethics for journalists
R. Keeble   Routledge, 2001, 168pp. £14.99. ISBN 9780415242974.
Good, short introduction to the issues from one of the UK's leading journalism academics.
■ **Ethics in journalism** R. Smith   6th edn, Blackwell Publishing, 2007. $49.95. ISBN 9781405159340. Announced latest edn of established text giving a US perspective.

5250 Ethics for the information age
M.J. Quinn   2nd edn, Pearson/Addison-Wesley, 2006, 484pp. £42.99. ISBN 9780321373342.
Well written text designed especially for technologists, but despite that (or perhaps because of that) of value more widely. The chapters are: Catalysts for change; Introduction to ethics; Networking; Intellectual property; Privacy; Computer and network security; Computer reliability; Work and wealth; Professional ethics.

Indoctrination U: the left's war against academic freedom
D. Horowitz   See entry no. 4520

5251 Privacy and the press
J. Rozenberg   Oxford University Press, 2005, 300pp. £14.99. ISBN 9780199288472.
Very well reviewed text. Chapters: 1. Confidence or privacy?;

2. Hello! OK?; 3. A free press; 4. Respecting private life; 5. Privacy and the press; 6. A chilling effect; 7. Responsible journalism.
'... a very good book, which once you start you cannot put down ... the research is meticulous and the book, whilst entertaining and readable, completely accurate ... I recommend this book to lawyers, journalists, politicians and those seeking to protect their privacy.' (*European Human Rights Law Review*)

5252 Speech, media and ethics: the limits of free expression
R. Cohen-Almagor   rev.edn, Palgrave Macmillan, 2004, 240pp. £17.99. ISBN 9781403947093.
In two parts, the second entitled 'Media Ethics, Freedom and Responsibilities' and having the chapters: Objective reporting in the media: phantom rather than panacea; Ethical boundaries of media coverage; Media coverage of suicide: comparative analysis; The work of the Press Councils in Great Britain, Canada and Israel: a comparative appraisal.
'The book is a welcome contribution to media ethics and the moral philosophy of free communication.' (*European Journal of Communication*)

Laws, standards, codes

Electronic Frontier Foundation
See entry no. 5322

5253 Freedom of speech
E.M. Barendt   2nd edn, Oxford University Press, 2007, 526pp. £27.95. ISBN 9780199225811.
'The only book to combine an analysis of the theoretical justification for the protection of free speech with a comparative study of how free speech has been enforced in courts worldwide ... The rich comparative treatment of six jurisdictions will aid practitioners dealing with questions on which little or no English authority exists ... Forward-looking analysis examines how free speech is applied in new contexts, including the internet, copyright protection and commercial speech.'
'It is one of the many virtues of this work that the various aspects of freedom of speech are kept constantly in play ... This book should be on the reading list of any student of the ideologies and manners of western liberal democracies.' (*The World Today*)

5254 Information privacy law
D.J. Solove, M. Rotenberg and P.M. Schwartz   2nd edn, Aspen, 2006, 1008pp. $108. ISBN 9780735555761.
Comprehensive work of cases and materials, organized: Introduction; Privacy and the media; Privacy and law enforcement; Health and genetic privacy; Privacy of associations, anonymity and identification; Privacy and government records and databases; Privacy and business and financial records; Privacy and place.
■ **The digital person: technology and privacy in the information age** D.J. Solove   New York University Press, 2004, 283pp. $18.95. ISBN 0814740375. A very well reviewed challenging text, e.g. 'This comprehensive analysis of privacy in the information age challenges traditional assumptions that breaches of privacy through the development of electronic dossiers involve the invasion of one's private space ... Solove drives his points home through considerable reconfiguration of the basic argument. Rather than casting blame or urging retreat to a precomputer database era, the solution is seen in informing

individuals, challenging data collectors, and bringing the law up-to-date.' (*Choice*).

5255   The law of privacy and the media
M. Tugendhat and I. Christie, eds   Oxford University Press, 2006. [Main Work and Second Cumulative Supplement], £195. ISBN 9780199283446.

'A specialist team of barristers from Five Raymond Buildings (the media, entertainment and human rights chambers) have come together to write this timely consideration of the rapidly developing law of privacy in England and Wales. The book considers how the law protects the publication of personal information without undermining the fundamental principle of freedom of expression.'

14 chapters in six sections, chapter titles including Data protection and the media; Privacy, copyright and moral rights; Freedom of information and newsgathering; Protection of journalistic material.

5256   Student Press Law Center [USA]
www.splc.org

The Center is 'an advocate for student free-press rights and provides information, advice and legal assistance at no charge to students and the educators who work with them.' Useful range of resources – especially relating to 'Student media'. There is a good, well thought-through Student Press Law Center Links Policy document.

5257   Your right to know: a citizen's guide to the Freedom of Information Act
H. Brooke   2nd edn, Pluto, 2007, 309pp. £13.99. ISBN 9780745325828.

Guide to the UK Act for non-specialists, with contents: Introduction; FOI in practice; Scotland; Laws of access; Central government; Intelligence, security and defence; Transport; The justice system; Law enforcement and civil defence; Health; The environment; Local government; Education; Private companies; Information about individuals.

Official & quasi-official bodies

Australian Press Council
See entry no. 5147

Press Complaints Commission
See entry no. 5148

5258   Representative on Freedom of the Media
www.osce.org/fom

The Representative 'observes media developments in all 56 OSCE participating States. He provides early warning on violations of freedom of expression and promotes full compliance with OSCE press freedom commitments'. A very well designed and presented website: a delight to use!

Research centres & institutes

5259   Center for Public Integrity [USA]
www.publicintegrity.org

Has the by-line: 'Investigative Journalism in the Public Interest'. The Centre 'is non-partisan and non-advocacy. We are committed to transparent and comprehensive reporting both in the United States and around the world ... (It) does

not accept contributions from corporations, labor unions, governments or anonymous donors'. Well presented details of current (and archival) Investigations, e.g. Campaign consultants; Collateral damage; Divine intervention, and so on; plus e-newsletters, videos, podcasts, RSS feeds and blogs. Much else of great value: for instance, the project entitled Well Connected, which tracks the players in telecommunications, media and technology.

5260   Electronic Privacy Information Center [USA]
www.epic.org

Established in 1994 'to focus public attention on emerging civil liberties issues and to protect privacy, the First Amendment and constitutional values'. Wide-ranging sets of resources with good access to details of other organizations concerned with privacy issues, particularly in the USA.

■ **Privacy Rights Clearinghouse: nonprofit consumer information and advocacy organization** www.privacyrights.org. Among other resources, the site provides access to an annotated list of online data vendors, divided into those which offer individuals an opt-out policy, and those that do not.

5261   MediaWise Trust [UK]
www.mediawise.org.uk

Formerly named PressWise, set up in 1993 by 'victims of media abuse' and supported by concerned journalists, media lawyers and politicians in the UK. 'We operate on the principle that press freedom is a responsibility exercised by journalists on behalf of the public and that the public have a right to know when the media publish inaccurate information.'

Access to in-depth resources about 'The Media' and children, conflict and trauma, diversity, health, etc. Very extensive Links area categorized into over 30 sections.

Associations & societies

5262   Campaign Against Censorship
www.dlas.org.uk

Originally founded in 1968 to assist writers, artists and others threatened by censorship and to campaign for reform of censorship laws; relaunched in 1983 with the object of promoting freedom of expression in all its forms and combating restrictions on that freedom and its exercise. Useful set of documents and links from that viewpoint.

5263   Campaign for Press & Broadcasting Freedom [UK]
www.cpbf.org.uk

Vigorous advocacy body: 'For over two decades we have worked for a more accountable, freer and diverse media.'

5264   Committee to Protect Journalists
www.cpj.org

'(A)n independent, nonprofit organization founded in 1981. We promote press freedom worldwide by defending the rights of journalists to report the news without fear of reprisal ... CPJ is funded solely by contributions from individuals, corporations and foundations. CPJ does not accept government funding.'

5265   Freedom Forum [USA]
www.freedomforum.org

'(A) non-partisan foundation dedicated to free press, free speech and free spirit for all people. The foundation focuses on three priorities: the Newseum, the First Amendment and newsroom diversity.'

- ■ **First Amendment Center** www.firstamendmentcenter.org.
  'Congress shall make no law respecting an establishment of religion, or prohibiting the free exercise thereof; or abridging the freedom of speech, or of the press; or the right of the people peaceably to assemble, and to petition the Government for a redress of grievances'.

5266 International Association of Privacy Professionals
www.privacyassociation.org
'Founded in 2001, the IAPP was established to define, promote and improve the privacy profession globally. The IAPP is committed to providing a forum for privacy professionals to share best practices, track trends, advance privacy management issues, standardize the designations for privacy professionals and provide education and guidance on opportunities in the field of privacy ... (T)he organization represents over 4000 members from businesses, governments and academia across 32 countries.'

Wide range of useful resources accessible via the website, including an extensive and valuable Privacy Policy statement.

5267 International PEN
www.internationalpen.org.uk
'International PEN, the worldwide association of writers with 144 Centres in 101 Countries, exists to promote friendship and intellectual cooperation among writers everywhere, to fight for freedom of expression and represent the conscience of world literature.'

5268 National Coalition Against Censorship [USA]
www.ncac.org
Founded in 1974 and 'is an alliance of 50 national non-profit organizations, including literary, artistic, religious, educational, professional, labor and civil liberties groups. United by a conviction that freedom of thought, inquiry and expression must be defended, we work to educate our own members and the public at large about the dangers of censorship and how to oppose them.'

Good source of resources: e.g. 'The Cyber-Library: legal and policy issues facing public libraries in the high-tech era'.

5269 Reporters Committee for Freedom of the Press
[USA]
www.rcfp.org
Created in 1970 'at a time when the nation's news media faced a wave of government subpoenas asking reporters to name confidential sources'. The Committee is a non-profit organization which operates solely on donations and the sale of publications. Nice, clear website provides access to a wealth of information: many publications are reproduced full-text with encouragement to readers to purchase their print equivalents.

Portal & task environments

5270 Article 19: global campaign for free expression
www.article19.org
'(A)n international human rights organization which defends and promotes freedom of expression and freedom of information all over the world. We take our name from Article 19 of the Universal Declaration of Human Rights ...'

Wide-ranging and in-depth site whose major sections of relevance here are entitled 'Overview' and 'Work' – each

having descriptions of the overall legal situation and of developments in the various regions of the world.

5271 Defence Advisory (DA) Notice System [UK]
www.dnotice.org.uk
'The DA Notice system is a voluntary code that provides guidance to the British media on the publication or broadcasting of national security information. The system is overseen by the Defence Press and Broadcasting Advisory Committee, a joint government/media body that approves the standing DA notices and monitors their implementation.'

Fascinating website structured into the sections: DA-Notices; Committee; History; Articles and speeches; FAQ; DA-Notice Secretary; The system; Records; Agenda.

5272 The Free Expression Policy Project: a think tank on artistic and intellectual freedom
www.fepproject.org
'The Free Expression Policy Project (FEPP), founded in 2000, provides research and advocacy on free speech, copyright and media democracy issues.' The site is notable for its extensive and well annotated list of links to websites which 'also have information about censorship, free expression, media policy, copyright and the public domain', as well as for useful sets of resources on the underlying issues.

5273 Index on censorship: for free expression
www.indexonline.org
'(F)ounded in 1972 by a dedicated team of writers, journalists and artists inspired by the British poet Stephen Spender to take to the page in defence of the basic human right of free expression.' Clearly laid-out website covers: News; Special reports; The magazine; Bookshop; Projects.

5274 Reporters Sans Frontières
www.rsf.org
'Reporters Without Borders is an association officially recognized as serving the public interest. More than a third of the world's people live in countries where there is no press freedom. Reporters Without Borders works constantly to restore their right to be informed ...'

Directories & encyclopedias

5275 Censorship: a world encyclopedia
D. Jones, ed.   Fitzroy Dearborn, 2001. 4 v, £350. ISBN 9781579581350.
Good overview presenting 'a comprehensive view of censorship, from Ancient Egypt to those modern societies that claim to have abolished the practice. For each country in the world, the history of censorship is described and placed in context and the media censored are examined: art, cyberspace, literature, music, the press, popular culture, radio, television and the theatre, not to mention the censorship of language, the most fundamental censorship of all. Also included are surveys of major controversies and chronicles of resistance.'

5276 Encyclopedia of information ethics and security
M. Quigley   Idea-Group Inc., 2007. ISBN 9781591409885.
www.galegroup.com [DESCRIPTION]
'The *Encyclopedia of information ethics and security* is an original, comprehensive reference source on ethical and security issues relating to the latest technologies. Covering a

wide range of themes, this valuable reference tool includes topics such as computer crime, information warfare, privacy, surveillance, intellectual property and education. This encyclopedia is a useful tool for students, academics and professionals.'

5277 Encyclopedia of privacy
W.G. Staples, ed. Greenwood Press, 2006. 2 v., $199.95. ISBN 9780313334771.
Excellent work providing some 225 alphabetically arranged entries written by more than 100 expert contributors.
'The entries range from a few paragraphs (Password protection) to several pages (Philosophical foundations of privacy), and each one includes a bibliography and cross-references. Topical and alphabetical lists of entries enhance the reference value of this volume. Especially useful are the numerous entries on court cases, with superb bibliographic references. The contributors are mostly law professors or other faculty and graduate students knowledgeable on the wide range of privacy issues ….[t]his work is an outstanding source containing many hard-to-find topics and bibliographic references ….[h]ighly recommended.' (*Booklist*)

Handbooks & manuals

5278 Freedom of the press: rights and liberties under the law
N.C. Cornwell ABC-CLIO, 2004, 355pp. $70. ISBN 9781851094769.
'An authoritative yet accessible analysis of the historical development and contemporary scope of press freedoms in America.'

5279 The history of information security
K. de Leeuw and J. Bergstra, eds Elsevier, 2007, 900pp. £100. ISBN 9780444516084.
Announced fascinating collection of readings, including 'Limitations on the publishing of scientific research' (J. Meadows); 'Semiotics of identity management' (P. Wisse); 'Intelligence and the emergence of the information society in eighteenth-century Britain' (J. Black); 'A history of internet security' (L. DeNardis); 'Munitions, wiretaps and MP3s: the changing interface between privacy and encryption policy in the information society' (A. Charlesworth).

5280 Invasion of privacy: a reference handbook
K.M. Keenan ABC-CLIO, 2005, 259pp. $55. ISBN 9781851096305.
'*Invasion of Privacy: A Reference Handbook* chronicles the most pressing privacy issues and dilemmas from around the world from the 17th century to today. Shocking accounts of government and corporate abuse liven discussions of controversial topics ranging from high-tech surveillance and the collection of personal data to bodily and sexual privacy. The internet, a platform for free speech now subject to calls for rigorous censorship and the global threat of terrorism in the post-September 11 era receive special emphasis.'
'Keenan achieves balance by presenting the varying points of view on the topic and manages to convey the essentials of a complex and timely subject. Highly recommended for most libraries.' (*Library Journal*)

■ **The right to privacy: rights and liberties under the law**
R.A. Glenn ABC-CLIO, 2003, 399pp. $70. ISBN 9781576077177. 'This brilliantly written and eminently readable introduction to the right of privacy as guaranteed by the US Constitution is written for upper-level high school and college students; however, its scholarly and well balanced research penned in both legal terminology and everyday English translation make it a suitable vehicle for all but the most advanced students of the topic …

strongly recommended for all high school libraries, undergraduate college libraries, and all but the smallest public libraries.' (*American Reference Books Annual*).

5281 The politics of internet communication
R.J. Klotz Rowman & Littlefield, 2004, 259pp. $29.95. ISBN 9780742529267.
A very comprehensive work treating the politics *of* the internet along with politics *on* the internet. After an introductory chapter 'Characteristics and development of the internet', there are five parts: I. Politics of internet access ('User base of the internet'; 'Impact of internet use'; 'internet access policy'); II. Political advocacy on the internet ('Cybercampaigning'; 'Party and group advocacy on the internet'); III. Government and media use of the internet ('E-Government'; 'Journalism and the internet'); IV. Legal and regulatory framework ('Fundamentals of cyberlaw'; 'Content regulation'; 'Domain Name law'; 'Piracy and privacy in cyberspace'); V. Global landscape of internet politics ('The internet in global democracies'; 'Walls and ladders in nations limiting political freedom'). Finally, a Conclusion: 'Net gain for democracy'.
Overall, an excellent survey.

Privacy in the 21st century: issues for public, school, and academic libraries
H.R. Adams [et al.] See entry no. 5472

Keeping up to date

5282 Free Press
www.freepress.net
'(A) national nonpartisan organization working to increase informed public participation in crucial media policy debates and to generate policies that will produce a more competitive and public interest-oriented media system with a strong nonprofit and noncommercial sector.
'We believe that a more democratic US media system will lead to better public policies – at home and abroad …'

5283 International Freedom of Expression eXchange: IFEX
www.ifex.org
'At its core, IFEX is made up of organizations whose members refuse to turn away when those who have the courage to insist upon their fundamental human right to free expression are censored, brutalized or killed. Comprised of 71 organizations – located everywhere from the Pacific Islands to Europe to West Africa – IFEX draws together a tremendously diverse and dedicated global community …'

Media Watchers & Activists

accuracy in the media • activism • alternative media •
blogging • democracy & the media • digital divide • global
media • internet politics • media activists • minority
media • misinformation in the media • violence in the
media

Introductions to the subject

5284 Blogging, citizenship and the future of media
M. Tremayne, ed.   Routledge, 2007, 287pp. £15.99. ISBN
9780415979405.
'When blogging first took off, the mainstream media (MSM)
poo-poohed it. Next, they started lifting its ideas and quoting
without attribution. Now the newspapers and broadcasters
have their own blogs and urge their readers to supply copy.
They have been turned around within about ten years ...
Mark Tremayne's collection of academic essays takes this
fact as a starting point and looks at the current state of
blogging as a cultural phenomenon ... What's certain is that
the print and broadcast media are losing their traditional
audience and power, the bloggers are gaining in strength and
number and journalism has a new force to be reckoned with.'
(Review by Roy Johnson on *Mantex* (www.mantex.co.uk) – an
excellent source of similar reviews ... and a rewarding blog
(http://mantex.blogspot.com)).

5285 Global activism, global media
W. de Jong, M. Shaw and N. Stammers, eds   Pluto Press, 2005,
224pp. £15.99. ISBN 9780745321950.
Brings together activists and academics in one volume, to
explore the theory and practice of global activism's relation
to all forms of media, mainstream and otherwise.

5286 The myth of media violence: a critical introduction
D. Trend   Blackwell, 2007, 139pp. £14.99. ISBN 9781405133852.
'(A)ssesses the current and historical debates over violence
in film, television and video games; extends the conversation
beyond simple condemnation or support; and addresses a
diverse range of issues and influences.'

Laws, standards, codes

**Broadcasting, voice and accountability: a public
interest approach to policy, law, and regulation**
K. Duer [et al.]   See entry no. 5186

Official & quasi-official bodies

**World Association of Community Radio
Broadcasters**
See entry no. 5195

Research centres & institutes

5287 Center for International Media Action [USA]
www.mediaactioncenter.org
'CIMA's work is funded through fee-for-service contracts and
collaborative fundraising, as well as direct philanthropic
grants ... This site can help you: build your media-activist

organization, campaign or project; learn from movement-
building research, perspectives and past gatherings; network
with other activists and educators; promote and share your
events, writings and activist tools for media justice, media
reform and communication rights. We can also provide
password-protected spaces for collaborative media activist
groups to share and store documents and other materials ...'

5288 Center for Media & Democracy [USA]
www.prwatch.org
'The nonprofit Center for Media & Democracy strengthens
participatory democracy by investigating and exposing public
relations spin and propaganda and by promoting media
literacy and citizen journalism, media "of, by and for the
people".'
- **SourceWatch** www.sourcewatch.org. '*SourceWatch* [a project of the
  Center for Media & Democracy] began as the 'Disinfopedia' in February
  2003. In January 2005 the name was changed to SourceWatch. Contributors
  are now working on 29,710 articles. In the last twelve months SourceWatch
  has served over 79 million pages to users ...'.

Electronic Privacy Information Center
See entry no. 5260

Associations & societies

5289 Association of Alternative Newsweeklies
www.aan.org
'(A) diverse group of 130 alt-weekly news organizations that
cover every major metropolitan area in North America ...
There are a wide range of publications in AAN. What ties
them all together are point-of-view-reporting; the use of
strong, direct language; a tolerance for individual freedoms
and social differences; and an eagerness to report news that
many mainstream media outlets would rather ignore.'

5290 Center for Digital Democracy [USA]
www.democraticmedia.org
The CDD 'is dedicated to ensuring that the public interest is
a fundamental part of the new digital communications
landscape. From open broadband networks, to free or low-
cost universal internet access, to diverse ownership of new
media outlets, to privacy and other consumer safeguards,
CDD works to promote an electronic media system that
fosters democratic expression and human rights.'
- **Digital destiny: new media and the future of
  democracy J. Chester**   New Press, 2007, 282pp. $24.95. ISBN
  1565847954. By the Executive Director of the Center: 'No other work as
  concisely and powerfully frames the democratic challenge that media policy
  presents. It is time people understood plainly just what is at stake. This
  book makes that understanding possible.' (Lawrence Lessig).

**5291 Committee for Accuracy in Middle East Reporting
in America**
www.camera.org
Founded in 1982, CAMERA 'is a media-monitoring, research
and membership organization devoted to promoting accurate
and balanced coverage of Israel and the Middle East.
CAMERA fosters rigorous reporting, while educating news
consumers about Middle East issues and the role of the
media. Because public opinion ultimately shapes public
policy, distorted news coverage that misleads the public can
be detrimental to sound policymaking. A non-partisan
organization, CAMERA takes no position with regard to

American or Israeli political issues or with regard to ultimate solutions to the Arab–Israeli conflict.'

Good example of this type of organizational resource. Extensive list of links: 'The above list is offered for informational purposes only. No endorsement of any political viewpoints should be inferred.'

5292 Community Media Association [UK]
www.commedia.org.uk
The Association 'is the UK representative body for the Community Media sector and is committed to promoting access to the media for people and communities. It aims to enable people to establish and develop community based communications media for empowerment, cultural expression, information and entertainment.' A very good gateway to activity in this area in the UK.

5293 Minority Media & Telecommunications Council [USA]
http://mmtconline.org
'(A) national nonprofit organization dedicated to promoting and preserving equal opportunity and civil rights in the mass media and telecommunications industries. MMTC is generally recognized as the nation's leading advocate for minority advancement in communications. We strongly believe that the breathtaking changes in communications technology and the new global forms of media partnerships must enhance diversity in the 21st century.'

■ **National Association of Minority Media Executives** www.namme.org. Formed in 1990 and 'the only organization of managers and executives of color working in both news and business operations, across all media-related fields, uniting diverse leaders across departments and across cultures'.

5294 Voice of the Listener & Viewer [UK]
http://vlv.org.uk
'(R)epresents the citizen and consumer interest in broadcasting and works for quality and diversity in British broadcasting ... VLV is the only organization in the UK speaking for listeners and viewers on the full range of issues which underpin the British broadcasting system: the structures, regulation, funding and institutions ... VLV has no connection with Mediawatch-uk, formerly known as the National Viewers' and Listeners' Association.'

Very good list of links to other organizations, covering regulators and other official bodies, VLV corporate members, programme feedback, other organizations with which VLV works, education links.

■ **MediaWatch-UK** www.mediawatchuk.org. 'We provide an independent voice for those concerned about issues of taste and decency in the media.' Good list of links and news service.

Portal & task environments

5295 Accuracy in Media: For Fairness, Balance and Accuracy in News Reporting [USA]
www.aim.org
'(A) non-profit, grassroots citizens' watchdog of the news media that critiques botched and bungled news stories and sets the record straight on important issues that have received slanted coverage.' Apart from the core content, has an interesting links section categorized by AIM quick links; Blogs; Conservative columnists; Conservative organizations;

Government/politics; News/talk media; Shopping; Think-tanks/misc.

5296 AlterNet: the mix is the message [USA]
www.alternet.org
'(A)im is to inspire citizen action and advocacy on the environment, human rights and civil liberties, social justice, media and health care issues. Our editorial mix underscores a commitment to fairness, equity and global stewardship and making connections across generational, ethnic and issue lines. AlterNet serves as a reliable filter, keeping hundreds of thousands of people well informed and engaged, helping them cope with a culture of information overload and resist the constant commercial media onslaught. Our aim is to stimulate, motivate and engage.'

5297 Citizens and governance in a knowledge-based society [EUR]
Community Research & Development Information Service
http://cordis.europa.eu/citizens
EU CORDIS programme 'intended to mobilise in a coherent effort, in all their wealth and diversity, European research in economic, political, social sciences and humanities that are necessary to develop an understanding of and to address issues related to, the emergence of a knowledge-based society and new forms of relationships between its citizens, on the one hand, and between its citizens and institutions, on the other.'

Committee of Concerned Journalists
See entry no. 5119

5298 Common Dreams News Center: breaking news and views from the progressive community [USA]
www.commondreams.org
'(N)ational non-profit citizens' organization working to bring progressive Americans together to promote progressive visions for America's future. Founded in 1997, we are committed to being on the cutting-edge of using the internet as a political organizing tool – and creating new models for internet activism.'

5299 Cursor
www.cursor.org
'Cursor's signature editorial feature is a media, politics and international affairs digest called Media Patrol that contextualizes and critiques the dominant narrative of major news organizations by adding other critical, independent voices published on the internet. This makes for a broader read on the news than is available from either mainstream or alternative media, while fostering a democratized media landscape where corporate and independent news sources have equal weight. And by, including commentary on the coverage, Cursor weaves together the story and the reporting of it.' Covers a remarkable range and volume of sources – the websites of each of which can be linked to.

5300 Digital Divide Network: knowledge to help everyone succeed in the digital age
www.digitaldividenetwork.org
A project of TakingITGlobal.org, which 'is an online community that connects youth to find inspiration, access information, get involved and take action in their local and global communities. It's the world's most popular online community for young people interested in making a

difference, with hundreds of thousands of unique visitors each month.'

ePolitix.com
See entry no. 1251

5301 Media Research Center: America's media watchdog
www.mediaresearch.org
'The Leader in Documenting, Exposing and Neutralizing Liberal Media Bias.' Well structured colourful website. Good list of links 'as an additional resource for information on various organizations which help expose or counter liberal media bias in the mainstream press'.

5302 MediaChannel
www.mediachannel.org
'(A) not-for-profit project of two established foundations: the UK-based OneWorld, publishers of the leading international supersite about human rights and sustainable development issues, www.oneworld.net; and The Global Center, a New York-based foundation that supports independent media ... MediaChannel has hundreds of national and international affiliated sites, including media-watch groups, university journalism departments, professional organizations, anti-censorship monitors, trade publications and many others. Content on the Website is drawn from this base of affiliated sites, which constitutes the deepest, highest quality database of media-related news and information online.'

MediaEd: the UK media education website
See entry no. 5223

5303 MediaMatters for America
http://mediamatters.org
'(A) web-based, not-for-profit, 501(c)(3) progressive research and information center dedicated to comprehensively monitoring, analyzing and correcting conservative misinformation in the US media.'

5304 Muckraker: Center for Investigative Reporting [USA]
www.muckraker.org
'At the Center for Investigative Reporting, we practise journalism that cares more about correcting injustice and abuse of power than making a profit. Unfortunately, investigative reporting – requiring long lead times and significant investment in people – is in short supply. Under increasing pressure to deliver higher profits for publicly traded media companies, editors and producers cut back on time and people first. The predictable outcome: a shortage of original, in-depth and risk-taking reporting and a citizenry deprived of the tools required to maintain a vibrant democracy and sound the alarm on injustice ...'

5305 Rhetorica [USA]
www.rhetorica.net
'(O)ffers analysis and commentary about the rhetoric, propaganda and spin of journalism and politics, including analysis of presidential speeches and election campaigns. This site features the Rhetorica: Press-Politics Journal web log, comprehensive news media links, a rhetoric textbook, a primer of critical techniques and information for citizens. The character of Rhetorica represents the purposes and canons of classical rhetoric.'

■ **Rhetoric Society of America** www.rhetoricsociety.org. Useful selective links list, plus collection of related organizations.

5306 STATS: Checking out the facts and figures behind the news
George Mason University
www.stats.org
'Our goals are to correct scientific misinformation in the media resulting from bad science, politics, or a simple lack of information or knowledge; and to act as a resource for journalists and policy makers on major scientific issues and controversies.' Clearly laid-out and highly informative site.

Discovering print & electronic resources

5307 The Left Index
www.nisc.com/factsheets/qli.asp [DESCRIPTION]
'The most comprehensive guide to leftist & radical media from around the world ... Many of the 774 sources indexed are unique; you won't find them indexed in API, the Reader's Guide to Periodical Literature or the Social Sciences Citation Index.'

Directories & encyclopedias

5308 Encyclopedia of media and politics
T. Schaefer and T. Birkland   CQ Press, 2006, 344pp. $140. ISBN 9781568028354.
'300 entries written by some 50 scholars and researchers in a wide range of fields, including political science; mass communication; television and radio; speech communications; public affairs; ethical studies; public opinion; technology; and journalism.'
   Very well presented volume ; small further reading list for each article; good subject index; useful summary of Communications in the USA covering press, news agencies, broadcasting and computing.

Handbooks & manuals

5309 Communicating for change: strategies of social and political advocates
J.P. McHale   Rowman & Littlefield, 2003, 251pp. $32.95. ISBN 9780742529731.
Chapters are: 1. Introduction: the importance of activist media use; 2. Face-to-face interaction; 3. Talking on the telephone; 4. Meeting in small groups; 5. Communicating at events; 6. Using paper; 7. Disseminating messages through mass media; 8. Connecting through computers; 9. Conclusion.
'The book is aimed to give practical tools to social activists, fund raisers, lobbyists, and other persons who want to have access to the inside of the mass media, in order to disseminate their messages. *Communicating for Change* is a well constructed book, following the same methodological structure in each of its eight chapters. Professional advocates and political advisers will find here some inspiring strategies for campaigns (or maybe ways to protect themselves from these aggressive methods). Scholars in media studies, political science, and students in associations will also find many case studies.' (*Political Studies Review*)

5310 Democratizing global media: one world, many struggles
R.A. Hackett and Y. Zhao, eds   Rowman & Littlefield, 2005, 328pp. $39.95. ISBN 9780742536432.
A major handbook, with remarkably wide coverage. After an introductory overview – 'Media globalization, media democratization: challenges, issues and paradoxes' – 13 chapters organized into three parts: I. Media globalization and democratic deficits: national and regional audits; II. Media and democracy in global sites and conflicts; III. Modalities of democratization.
'The book offers not only a nuanced and complex presentation of democratic media formations but also, and most useful, a possible model: i.e., regimes that have devised a multiple-media system that includes state, commercial, public, and community media, ownership, and control offer the most balanced and democratized communication. Highly recommended.' (*Choice*)

5311 Internet politics: states, citizens, and new communication technologies
A. Chadwick   Oxford University Press, 2006, 384pp. £25.99. ISBN 9780195177732.
'In the developed world, there is no longer an issue of whether the internet affects politics – but how, why and with what consequences. With the internet now spreading at a breathtaking rate in the developing world, the new medium is fraught with tensions, paradoxes and contradictions. How do we make sense of these? In this major new work, Andrew Chadwick addresses such concerns, providing the first comprehensive overview of internet politics ...'
'Well researched, timely and readable ... manages to impress both in its scope and its depth ... *Internet Politics* should be required reading for anyone attempting to understand the way in which the Internet affects our lives.' (*Journal of Information, Communication and Ethics in Society*)

5312 News: the politics of illusion
W.L. Bennett   7th edn, Longman, 304pp. £29.99. ISBN 9780321421616.
'Part of the 'Longman Classics in Political Science' series, this renowned book, known for a lively writing style, provocative point of view and exceptional scholarship has been thoroughly revised and updated, including up-to-the-minute case studies and the latest research.
'This favorite of both instructors and students is a "behind-the-scenes" tour of news in American politics. The core question explored in this book is: How well does the news, as the core of the national political information system, serve the needs of democracy? In investigating this question, the book examines how various political actors – from presidents and members of Congress, to interest organizations and citizen-activists – try to get their messages into the news.'

5313 Violence in the media: a reference handbook
N. Signorielli   ABC-CLIO, 2005, 263pp. £33.50. ISBN 1851096043.
Useful overview of complex arena.

Cyberculture

communication technology • culture & the media • multimedia • new media • semiotics

Introductions to the subject

5314 Communication technology update
A.E. Grant and J.H. Meadows, eds   10th edn, Focal Press, 2006, 374pp. £24.99. ISBN 9780240808819.
www.tfi.com/pubs/ctu/index.html [COMPANION]
'New communication technologies are being introduced at an astonishing rate. Making sense of these technologies is increasingly difficult. *Communication Technology Update* is the single best source for the latest developments, trends and issues in communication technology ...'

Digital freedom: how much can you handle?
N.D. Batra   See entry no. 5248

Digital nation: toward an inclusive information society
A.G. Wilhelm   See entry no. 5388

The internet galaxy: reflections on the internet, business and society
M. Castells   See entry no. 5391

5315 Introduction to media production: the path to digital production
G.A. Kindem and R.B. Musburger   3rd edn, Focal Press, 2005, 319pp. £34.99. ISBN 9780240806471.
Sound, comprehensive introduction – including writing for the internet. Chapters are: The production process – analog and digital technology; Scriptwriting; Directing – aesthetic principles and production coordination; Audio/Sound; Lighting; Camera; Recording; Design and graphics; The editing process; Visual editing; Sound editing; Animation and special effects; Distribution and exhibition.

The network society
D. Barney   See entry no. 5392

5316 New media: an introduction
T. Flew   2nd edn, Oxford University Press, 2005, 280pp. ISBN 0195550412.
Now a well established overview with wide coverage: ideal as an entrée to the whole field of 'cyberculture'. Its chapters are: Introduction to new media technologies; New media technologies: history and political economy; New media as cultural technologies; Virtual cultures; Digital media; Games: technology, industry, culture; Creative industries; Electronic commerce and the global knowledge economy; Online media and the future of education; Globalization and new media; internet law and policy.

5317 New media, old media: a history and theory reader
W.H.K. Chun and T. Keenan, eds   Routledge, 2006, 418pp. £15.99. ISBN 9780415942249.
Edited collection giving good introductory overview – if rather densely presented.

5318 Web studies
D. Gauntlett and R. Horsley, eds   2nd edn, Arnold, 2004, 327pp.
£16.99. ISBN 9780340814727.
www.newmediastudies.com [COMPANION]

A lively and un-pretentious overview, concentrating on the
cultural impacts of 'cyberculture'. 23 chapters in four parts:
I. Web studies; II. Web life, identities, arts and culture; III.
Web business, economics and capitalism; IV. Global web
communities, politics and protest.

'(T)his book aims to make theory accessible and puncture the
pretensions of those who'd have you swallow a dictionary before
you're allowed to comment. "Cyberculture," he says with
trademark mischief, "is a term whose useful potential has been
killed off by the staggering number of tedious things that have
been written about it." It's evident from the start that Gauntlett
wants to reclaim the territory for those who are using the net
creatively and exploring the possibilities it brings.' (HERO)

■ **Resource Center for Cyberculture Studies**
http://rccs.usfca.edu. Not an extensive Site; but worth citing as a concise
introduction to the field.

■ **Theory.org.uk: media/identity/resources and projects**
D. Gauntlett, comp.   www.theory.org.uk. Fascinating site – and full of
useful pointers: 'Established in 1997 … explores the complex connections
between media and identities, and tries to have a little fun …'.

Dictionaries, thesauri, classifications

5319 Cyberculture: the key concepts
D. Bell [et al.]   Routledge, 2004, 211pp. £14.99. ISBN
9780415247542.

'The only A–Z guide available on this subject, this book
provides a wide-ranging and up-to-date overview of the fast-
changing and increasingly important world of cyberculture.
Its clear and accessible entries cover aspects ranging from
the technical to the theoretical and from movies to the
everyday, including artificial intelligence; cyberfeminism;
cyberpunk; electronic government; games; HTML; Java;
netiquette; piracy.'

**5320 The dictionary of multimedia: terms and
acronyms**
B. Hansen   4th edn, Franklin, Beedle & Associates, 2005, 611pp.
$35. ISBN 1887902147.
www.fbeedle.com/14-7.html [DESCRIPTION]

2000 terms from multimedia, audio, video, networking,
animation and general computing. There is a more extensive
companion, Dictionary of computing & digital media, with 4000
terms.

Glossary of internet terms
M. Enzer   See entry no. 5394

Laws, standards, codes

**5321 Computer law: the law and regulation of
information technology**
C. Reed and J. Angel, eds   6th edn, Oxford University Press, 2007,
610pp. £35. ISBN 9780199205967.

First-rate, comprehensive work, with 12 chapters in five
parts: I. Commercial exploitation of information technology
products and services; II. Online commerce; III. Intellectual
property and related rights in information technology; IV.
Electronic privacy and access to information; V. Electronic
information misuse.

5322 Electronic Frontier Foundation [USA]
www.eff.org

'EFF is a nonprofit group of passionate people – lawyers,
technologists, volunteers and visionaries – working to protect
your digital rights. … EFF broke new ground when it was
founded in 1990 – well before the internet was on most
people's radar – and continues to confront cutting-edge
issues defending free speech, privacy, innovation and
consumer rights today. From the beginning, EFF has
championed the public interest in every critical battle
affecting digital rights …'

Research centres & institutes

Benton Foundation
See entry no. 5395

Berkman Center for Internet & Society
See entry no. 5396

5323 Center for Democracy & Technology [USA]
www.cdt.org

A Washington-based centre – 'Working for Democratic Values
in a Digital Age' – which receives funding from foundations,
corporations, international institutions and trade
associations, but accepts no government funding. Extensive
website, treating – among much else – a series of Issues:
free expression; consumer privacy; security and freedom;
digital copyright; standards and governance; international;
open government.

5324 Center for History & New Media [USA]
http://chnm.gmu.edu

'Since 1994 … has used digital media and computer
technology to democratize history – to incorporate multiple
voices, reach diverse audiences and encourage popular
participation in presenting and preserving the past. We
sponsor more than two dozen digital history projects and
offer free tools and resources for historians.'

Interesting site – though, as implied, more concerned with
'history' than with 'media'. But a good gateway to much of
collateral value.

5325 Stanford Persuasive Technology Lab
http://captology.stanford.edu

'The Stanford Persuasive Technology Lab creates insight into
how computing products – from websites to mobile phone
software – can be designed to change what people believe
and what they do. Yes, this can be a scary topic: machines
designed to influence human beliefs and behaviors. But
there's good news. We believe that much like human
persuaders, persuasive interactive technologies can bring
about positive changes in many domains, including health,
business, safety and education. With such ends in mind, we
are creating a body of expertise in the design, theory and
analysis of persuasive technologies, an area called
"captology" …'

Associations & societies

Minority Media & Telecommunications Council
See entry no. 5293

Online News Association
See entry no. 5115

Portal & task environments

Digital Divide Network: knowledge to help everyone succeed in the digital age
See entry no. 5300

5326 StreamingMedia.com
http://streamingmedia.com
'Streaming media technology enables the real time or on demand distribution of audio, video and multimedia on the internet. Streaming media is the simultaneous transfer of digital media (video, voice and data) so that it is received as a continuous real-time stream. Streamed data is transmitted by a server application and received and displayed in real-time by client applications. These applications can start displaying video or playing back audio as soon as enough data has been received and stored in the receiving station's buffer ... Our goal at streamingmedia.com is to provide industry professionals and corporations utilizing digital media technology with global real-time news, resources and information to help foster the adoption of streaming media technology and applications.'

Discovering print & electronic resources

5327 Cyberculture
http://dir.yahoo.com/Society_and_Culture/Cultures_and_Groups
There is a useful section for 'Cyberculture' in the Yahoo! Directory entry for 'Cultures and Groups'.

5328 Cyberspace
www.google.com/Top/Computers/Internet/Cyberspace
Google uses the term 'Cyberspace' in its Directory, with a sub-heading 'Culture'.

Directories & encyclopedias

5329 Berkshire encyclopedia of human–computer interaction
W.S. Bainbridge, ed.   Berkshire Publishing, 2004. 2 v, $295. ISBN 0974309125.
200 articles written by experts in a wide range of contributory disciplines. 'Designed to meet the needs of researchers and scientists as well as students, business and marketing professionals and interested non-experts.' The articles 'are accompanied by lively sidebars and a popular culture database of more than 300 novels, television shows and movies'.
'Each article is written for an educated layperson, but the bibliographies reflect the serious research behind the work. The use of quotes and sidebars to tell frequently humorous anecdotes related to the technology discussed makes these volumes fun to browse. The articles are particularly useful for professionals who suddenly encounter a new aspect of technology and want to learn a bit more about it. Buy this book for your own reference purposes, and recommend it to those in your library.' (*Online Magazine*)

5330 Encyclopedia of multimedia
B. Furht, ed.   Springer, 2006, 983pp. £291. ISBN 9780387243955.

www.springer.com [DESCRIPTION]
Significant focus on the technological aspects of multimedia with some 250 entries from worldwide experts. Each entry has definition of terms plus further reading.
Also available online: check via website.

Encyclopedia of new media: an essential reference to communication and technology
S. Jones, ed.   See entry no. 779

The internet encyclopedia
H. Bidgoli, ed.   See entry no. 5404

Handbooks & manuals

5331 Communication and new media: from broadcast to narrowcast
J. Harrison and M. Hirst   Oxford University Press, 2007, 420pp. £21.99. ISBN 9780195553550.
Lively, wide-ranging, up-to-date, forward-looking and highly readable. 'Using a political economy approach, the authors argue the era of mass communication – of broadcast communication to mass audiences – is over. In the digital age, the message is narrowcast to the audience, which is composed of individual citizen-consumers'.

5332 Critical cyberculture studies
D. Silver and A. Massanari, eds   New York University Press, 2006, 323pp. Foreword by Steve Jones, $23. ISBN 0814740243.
'Taking stock of the exciting work that is being done and positing what cyberculture's future might look like, *Critical cyberculture studies* brings together a diverse and multidisciplinary group of scholars from around the world to assess the state of the field. Opening with a historical overview of the field by its most prominent spokesperson, it goes on to highlight the interests and methodologies of a mobile and creative field, providing a much-needed how-to guide for those new to cyberstudies ...'

5333 Cybercultures: critical concepts in media and cultural studies
D. Bell, ed.   Routledge, 2006. 4 v., £525. ISBN 9780415343985.
'(A) historical contextualization and up-to-date overview of 'cyberculture' – a term understood as the cultural perspective on new information and communications technologies. Presenting a comprehensive account of the evolution, current forms, uses and theories of cyberculture, it brings together a wide range of case studies and thought to create a unique, broad-based resource.
    The four volumes are entitled: 1. Mapping cyberculture; 2. Thinking & doing cyberculture; 3. Cyberculture, cyberpolitics, cybersociety; 4. Identities & bodies in cyberculture.

5334 Handbook of new media: social shaping and social consequences of ICTs
L.A. Lievrouw and S. Livingstone, eds   updated student edn, Sage Publications, 2006, 475pp. £24.99. ISBN 9781412918732.
Excellent cross-displinary text successfully countering 'the "Balkanization" of new media studies that was dividing the field into dozens of specialized, non-communicating academic niches.' 22 chapters, organized into 3 parts: New media, culture and society; Technology, systems, design and industries; New media, institutions and governance.

5335 Handbook of semiotics
W. Nöth   Indiana University Press, 1995, 592pp. $55. ISBN 9780253209597.
An outstanding volume structured into eight sections: I. History and classics of modern semiotics; II. Sign and meaning; III. Semiosis, code and the semiotic field; IV. Language and language-based codes; V. From structuralism to text semiotics: schools and major figures; VI. Text semiotics: the field; VII. Non-verbal communication; VIII. Aesthetics and visual communication.

The information age: economy, society and culture
M. Castells   See entry no. 5405

The information society reader
F. Webster, ed.   See entry no. 5406

The internet and society: a reference handbook
B.H. Schell   See entry no. 5407

5336 Methods of historical analysis in electronic media
D.G. Godfrey, ed.   Lawrence Erlbaum, 2006, 420pp. £10.99. ISBN 0805851860.
Very useful edited collection covering a wide range of techniques and issues. Extensive bibliography.

The Oxford handbook of information and communication technologies
R. Mansell [et al.]   See entry no. 5408

The politics of internet communication
R.J. Klotz   See entry no. 5281

Keeping up to date

Convergence: the international journal of research into new media technologies
See entry no. 781

The Filter
Berkman Center for Internet & Society   See entry no. 5410

5337 First Monday
1996–, monthly. ISSN 13960466.
www.uic.edu/htbin/cgiwrap/bin/ojs/index.php/fm/index
Leading commentary: 'First Monday publishes articles on all aspects of the internet, including comments on trends and standards, technical issues, political and social implications of the internet and educational uses. Its focus is simply on interesting and novel ideas related to the history, current use and future of the internet.'

Journal of Broadcasting and Electronic Media
Broadcast Education Association   See entry no. 5246

Information & Library Sciences

Information & Library Sciences (ILS) covers the academic disciplines concerned with the representation, organization and communication of knowledge recorded in electronic or physical documentary forms, together with the related professional practices of Information Management, Librarianship, Records Management and Archives Administration found in a variety of organizational and social contexts. The arrangement of resources for this subject underlines the importance of the social and regulatory context of all types of information work, with sections on the Information Society and Information Policy placed near the start. It also highlights the current significance of Information Literacy and Knowledge Management as key areas of contemporary practice that cut across traditional professional boundaries.

The growing volume of publications and other resources related to ILS and its various sub-divisions has limited our coverage here to a highly selective sample, which aims to represent both traditional and emerging concerns in the discipline and its associated professions, but cannot claim complete or even comprehensive provision, in respect of either topics or types of resources. This selectivity applies particularly to our coverage of management-related topics and specialist library and information services, which is reflected especially in not being able to name individually the many different special-interest groups, e-mail discussion lists and other current awareness resources available to ILS practitioners around the world. Professional associations and networks play a central and fundamental role in defining and

shaping professional practice, but we have only been able to include the major players here, along with some of their sub-groups and a few of the smaller more specialized organizations.

Contemporary information work is critically dependent on Information and Communication Technology (ICT) and the pervasive role of technology is evident in the way that items with the words 'digital', 'electronic' and 'virtual' in their titles and annotations are distributed through all ILS sections and subsections. We have concentrated here on works specifically concerned with the application of ICT in the information, library, records and archives domains, placing these items in either the particular area of application or the section devoted to Library Systems & Technology, according to their focus. If you are looking for more general treatment of information technology and/or information systems, you will find a substantial section on this subject in *The New Walford* Volume 1, but may also identify some items of interest in the following Tools for Information Professionals section of the current volume.

The Tools section, as its title indicates, offers an array of resources selected to support information professionals in their work. It complements the ILS section by including both general reference works (such as resources likely to be helpful in answering enquiries) and works on other subjects considered particularly useful to information professionals, including some titles written specifically for the profession (notably texts on research methods in ILS).

information audit • information management • information policies • information profession • information strategy • information studies • librarianship • library profession • library work

Introductions to the subject

5338 Foundations of library and information science
R.E. Rubin   2nd edn, Neal-Schuman, 2004, 581pp. $65. ISBN 1555705189.
Comprehensive introduction which places librarianship in its broader context and identifies key issues for contemporary practice. Covers the information infrastructure, a services perspective on information science, information policy, information organization, library values, professional ethics, libraries as institutions and the library profession. Includes end-of-chapter references and selected readings on nine topics.
'As Victorian travelers once carried their Baedekers, MLIS students will now cart their Rubins ...' (*Journal of the American Society for Information Science*)

5339 Fundamentals of information studies: understanding information and its environment
J. Lester and W.C. Koehler   2nd edn, Neal-Schuman, 2007, 375pp. $65. ISBN 1555705944.
Accessible textbook intended to provide a broadly based introduction to the information field, covering information in society, fundamental concepts of information, information technology, information institutions, information professions, economics of information, regulation of information, information policy and information ethics. Announced new edition includes additional chapters on user behaviour and on information, power and society, with all other chapters updated and revised. End-of-chapter references, glossary and comprehensive index. Supported by companion website.

5340 Information management: a consolidation of operations, analysis and strategy
M. Middleton; Charles Sturt University   2002, 526pp. AUS$90. ISBN 1976938366.
Notable for its focus on the softer aspects of 'information management', defined: 'In this book information management is taken to be the organization of the institutional processes necessary for use of information, as well as organization of the information itself for effective

communication – whether directly or in recorded form.' Four parts: A. Overview; B. Organizational information management; C. Analytical aspects of information management; D. Administrative aspects of information management. Good use of graphics.

From the University's Centre for Information Studies

5341 Information strategy in practice
E. Orna   Gower, 2004, 163pp. £35. ISBN 0566085798.
Shorter, updated version of the author's classic text *Practical information policies* (2nd edn. Gower, 1999), aimed at newcomers to the field, particularly students and professionals lacking an information specialist background. Provides a step-by-step guide to developing and using an information strategy, starting with the conduct of an initial information audit, prior to formulating an organizational information policy and translating this into a practical information strategy. Prefaced by useful definitions and explanations of key concepts, such as knowledge, information, organizational information policy, information strategy, information management and knowledge management. Includes much new material offering practical insights gained by the author from her recent work in the field. Supported throughout with useful checklists, tables, diagrams and references. Includes index.

5342 An introduction to library and information work
A. Totterdell   Facet Publishing, 2005, 210pp. £29.95. ISBN 9781856045575.
Designed particularly for support staff, para-professionals and students: can be used as a self-development tool.

5343 Introduction to the library and information professions
R.C. Greer, R.J. Grover and S.G. Fowler   Libraries Unlimited, 2007, 208pp. $60. ISBN 9781591584865.
Approaches the functions of information professionals through models of communication theory, articulating their role of diagnosing the information needs of clients using information transfer theory. Discusses current trends and issues surrounding the role of a professional and the services to be offered.

5344 Messages, meanings and symbols: the communication of information
C.T. Meadows   Scarecrow, 2006, 264pp. $40. ISBN 9780810852716.
One of the leaders in the field provides a review of how the discipline developed and who were its major players. 'Communication in all its forms – be it print or electronic media, mass communication as well as person-to-person messaging, whether by mail, telephone, gesture, or e-mail – is thoroughly examined in this book, which can serve as either an introductory text to undergraduates in information science, an interesting read for the layman, or as a refresher for the communications professional.'

5345 Straight from the stacks: a firsthand guide to careers in library and information science
L.T. Kane   ALA Editions, 2003, 155pp. $36. ISBN 9780838908655.
Wide-ranging survey of the diversity of job opportunities now accessible to information and library science graduates.

Dictionaries, thesauri, classifications

5346 ASIST thesaurus of information science, technology and librarianship
A. Redmond-Neal and M.M.K. Hlava   3rd edn, Information Today, 2005, 272pp. Book with CD-ROM also available, $49.95. ISBN 1573872431.
Authoritative guide to the terminology of information science, technology and librarianship. The optional CD-ROM includes the complete contents of the print thesaurus together with Data Harmony's Thesaurus Master software, which allows users to add, change and delete terms and to learn the fundamentals of thesaurus construction while exploring the professional vocabulary of library and information science and technology.

5347 Dictionary of library and information management
2nd edn, A. & C. Black, 2006, 229pp. £9.99. ISBN 9780713675917.
'This comprehensive dictionary covers all aspects of librarianship and information and knowledge management. Designed to equip the trainee librarian or information management student with core industry terminology, this fully revised edition includes over 5000 terms connected with information management, classification, cataloguing and electronic knowledge management.'

5348 Harrod's librarians' glossary and reference book: a directory of over 10,200 terms, organizations, projects and acronyms in the areas of information management, library science, publishing and archive management
R. Prytherch, comp.   10th edn, Ashgate, 2005, 753pp. £110. ISBN 0754640388.
Established reference work, whose entries have been pruned, updated and expanded to reflect trends in the contemporary information environment. Tenth edition defines more than 10,000 terms, incorporating many revisions and additions related to developments in digital resources, electronic services, intellectual property and knowledge management. Also provides data on major libraries and information-related organizations in the UK and other countries.

5349 ODLIS – Online dictionary for library and information science
J.M. Reitz, comp.   Libraries Unlimited, in progress.
http://lu.com/odlis
Helpfully browsable collection of over 4000 terms having extensive hyperlinking throughout. Interesting section About ODLIS traces the history of the work and includes a useful and extensive bibliography of print and online tools used in its compilation.
- **Dictionary for library and information science** J.M. Reitz, comp.   Libraries Unlimited, 2004, 800pp. $50. ISBN 9781591580751. Print version of the dictionary, as at 2004.

Official & quasi-official bodies

Department for Culture, Media and Sport
See entry no. 5050

5350 Institute of Museum & Library Services [USA]
www.imls.gov
The primary source of federal support for the USA's 122,000 libraries and 17,500 museums. It is an independent federal

agency of the executive branch of the US government and the projected budget for 2008 is $271,246,000 – an increase of $24,102,000, or 9.8 percent, over the FY 2006.

5351 Museums, Libraries & Archives Council [UK]
www.mla.gov.uk
A non-departmental public body (NDPB), sponsored by the Department for Culture, Media & Sport, whose mission is 'to connect people and change lives through museums, libraries and archives'. Details of policy, programmes and publications and an extensive links section divided into 14 categories.

Research centres & institutes

5352 Center for the Book [USA]
www.loc.gov/loc/cfbook
Established in 1977 by the Library of Congress to promote books, reading, libraries and literacy. Clear, well designed website gives details of themes and projects, literary events, news, events and publications, and affiliates and partners. The last has an extensive and valuable A–Z listing of 'community of the book' national and international organizations and programs which 'have purposes and interests that relate to the basic mission of the Center for the Book'.

5353 Council on Library & Information Resources [USA]
www.clir.org
An independent non-profit organization primarily funded by US college and university libraries, but also by a small number of US-based corporate bodies. Its mission is 'to expand access to information, however recorded and preserved, as a public good', which it does through projects, programmes, meetings and publications. Reports cover a wide range of topics, such as strategies and tools for the digital library and perspectives on the evolving physical library. Many can be downloaded from the website. Also publishes a newsletter, *CLIR Issues* (6 p.a.). The Council also oversees the activities of the Digital Library Federation: 'a consortium of libraries and related agencies that are pioneering the use of electronic-information technologies to extend their collections and services'.

5354 Library & Information Statistics Unit [UK]
www.lboro.ac.uk/departments/dils/lisu
'LISU is an internationally renowned research and information centre for library and information services, based in the Department of Information Science at Loughborough University. We collect, analyse, interpret and publish statistical information for and about the library domain in the UK and undertake research and consultancy projects for a wide range of organizations.'

Site covers publications and current and past research projects, with a brief news and links service.

- **Average prices of British and USA academic books** , bi-annual. Well regarded LISU service based on data from over 12,000 UK and 30,000 US titles supplied by Blackwell's Book Services.
- **Public library materials fund and budget survey** , annual. LISU service describing in detail how UK public library services are faring and their plans for the future.

5355 UKOLN [UK]
www.ukoln.ac.uk
Centre of expertise in digital information management, providing advice and services to the library, information, education and cultural heritage communities. Primarily co-funded by JISC and the Museums, Libraries & Archives Council (q.v.). Its historical focus on bibliographic management has evolved to cover areas such as metadata standards, information architectures and digital repositories. Website provides access to project documentation, reports, presentations and other resources. Also publishes a magazine *Ariadne* (q.v.)

Associations & societies

5356 American Library Association
www.ala.org
'The oldest and largest library association in the world, with more than 65,000 members.' Organized into 11 membership divisions with either a sectoral or functional focus, including including the Association of College and Research Libraries, the Public Libraries Association, the Library and Information Technology Association and the Reference and User Services Association. ALA is very active in information literacy, intellectual freedom and library advocacy. Many guidelines, standards and other resources are available from the 'Professional tools' and 'Issues and advocacy' sectons of the website. The ALA Online Store [www.alastore.ala.org] provides access to a large range and number of books, periodicals and other library-related products, generally using the imprint ALA Editions.

- **American Libraries** , 11 p.a. $60 (North America); $70 (Foreign). ISSN 00029769. The official organ of the Association, but 'every opportunity shall be assured for expression of diverse views'. ALA members receive *American Libraries* as a perquisite of membership, but it is also available by paid subscription.
- **Booklist** , 22 p.a. $79.95 (USA); $95.00 (Outside USA). www.ala.org/booklist [DESCRIPTION]. 'For more than 90 years, *Booklist* magazine has been the librarian's leading choice for reviews of the latest books and (more recently) electronic media.' Reviews more than 500 reference books and electronic reference tools.

5357 American Society for Information Science & Technology
www.asis.org
Established 1937, now with membership of 'some 4000 information specialists from such fields as computer science, linguistics, management, librarianship, engineering, law, medicine, chemistry and education; individuals who share a common interest in improving the ways society stores, retrieves, analyses, manages, archives and disseminates information, coming together for mutual benefit'.

Sponsors a wide range of special interest groups, ranging from Arts and Humanities (AH) to Knowledge Management (KM) and Visualization, Images and Sound (VIS). Publishes the authoritative *Annual Review of Information Science and Technology* (ARIST), the highly regarded *Journal of Information Science and Technology* (JASIST, 14 p.a.), in addition to the *Proceedings* of its Annual Meetings and freely-available news *Bulletin* (6 p.a.). Also publishes monographs in association with Information Today.

5358 Aslib, the Association for Information Management
[UK]
www.aslib.com
Founded in 1924 as the Association of Special Libraries and
Information Bureaux, but currently using the strapline
Association for Information Management, Aslib's main
activities are training, recruitment and consultancy, though it
is still associated with several long-established journals now
published commercially, such as *Aslib Proceedings*, the
highly-regarded *Journal of Documentation* and *Program*
(covering electronic library and information systems). It
sponsors nine special-interest groups, notably the very active
Aslib Engineering Group. It also continues to publish a
magazine, *Managing Information*.
  ■ **Managing Information** , 10 p.a. £129. ISSN 13520229.
    www.managinginformation.com. Current awareness magazine carrytng
    'high-calibre features, top-level interviews, analysis and practical solutions
    all packaged in a readable and attractive style'. A modified version is freely
    available from its website as MI Lite.

**5359 Chartered Institute of Library & Information
Professionals** [UK]
www.cilip.org.uk
Formed in 2002 by the unification of the Institute of
Information Scientists (IIS, founded 1958) and The Library
Association (LA, established 1877). Special interest groups
cover library and information service sectors, including
government, health, public and university, as well as areas
such as library and information history, information services,
local studies, multimedia information and technology,
patents and trade marks.
  ■ **Career Development Group** CDG is especially committed to
    supporting newer entrants to the profession, including candidates working
    towards certified or chartered membership of CILIP and information and
    library science students. It provides a network of Candidate Support Officers
    and offers regular student conferences, in addition to organizing other
    events and publishing a journal, *Impact* (4 p.a.).
  ■ **Library + Information Update** monthly.
    www.cilip.org.uk/publications/updatemagazine [DESCRIPTION]. Editorially
    independent of CILIP and 'covers everything from policy issues, the political
    landscape or changes in technology to what you need to know for your
    personal professional development.
  ■ **UK eInformation Group** www.ukeig.org.uk. Formerly known as
    UKOLUG (the UK Online User Group), UKeiG provides a wide range of
    resources (factsheets, links) as well as a training and seminar programme
    and opportunities for online communication via an active discussion list,
    blog and wiki. Members can access the e-journal *eLucidate*.

**5360 European Bureau of Library, Information &
Documentation Associations**
www.eblida.org
'(A)n independent umbrella association of national library,
information, documentation and archive associations and
institutions in Europe ... In broad terms the strategy
continues to focus on issues of copyright and intellectual
property rights in order to promote and fight for libraries and
their central role in providing information and materials for
the European citizen. Developments in digitization, online
accessibility and issues of preservation also feature strongly
in the strategy, not least in regard to the European
Commission's focus in this area and the establishment of the
European Digital Library (EDL). To ensure the necessary
competence in this area EBLIDA has established an expert
group on digitization and online accessibility in 2007 ...'

  ■ **European Digital Library Project** www.edlproject.eu. 'Targeted
    Project funded by the European Commission under the eContentplus
    Programme and coordinated by the German National Library. The project,
    started in September 2006, works towards the integration of the
    bibliographic catalogues and digital collections of the National Libraries of
    Belgium, Greece, Iceland, Ireland, Liechtenstein, Luxembourg, Norway, Spain
    and Sweden, into The European Library'.

**5361 International Federation of Library Associations &
Institutions**
www.ifla.org
The main international body representing the interests of
library and information services and their users, with 1700
members in 150 countries. IFLA operates through more than
45 sections covering different library sectors and interests,
notable examples including Government Libraries, Public
Libraries, Reference & Information Services, Management &
Marketing, Information Literacy and Reading. It organises an
annual World Library and Information Congress, holds
professional meetings in different countries and publishes
IFLA Journal (4 p.a.), which is available from the website. The
page headed IFLA Electronic Collections links to an eclectic
set of library and information science resources, including a
list of quotations about libraries and librarians.

Libraries, archives, museums

British Library
See entry no. 56

GBV
See entry no. 57

Library & Archives Canada
See entry no. 58

Library of Congress
See entry no. 59

Portal & task environments

5362 UNESCO Libraries Portal
www.unesco.org/webworld/portal_bib
Within the Communication and Information Theme, a
collection of some 14,000 links to: Libraries; Professional
groups; Training facilities; Preservation and access initiatives;
Reference directories, portals, publications, blogs,
catalogues; Conferences and meetings; Librarianship
resources – each notable for their coverage beyond Europe
and North America.

Discovering print & electronic resources

**5363 Digital information in the information research
field**
T.D. Wilson, ed.   1999 -, In progress.
http://informationr.net/fr/freejnls.html
Lists more than 200 journals and newsletters which all
include at least a sample of papers or news items that are
freely accessible. Sites that simply provide the contents lists
of journals that are not freely accessible are not listed. Only
journals that still appear to be 'live' are included. Titles with

brief descriptions are listed A–Z; a subject guide provides access via c. 40 subject headings.

5364 International bibliography of bibliographies in library and information science and related fields
H. Sawoniak [et al.]   K.G. Saur, 1998–2002. 2 v., €820. ISBN 9783598111433.
Extensive work which 'covers a host of specialist fields related to librarianship such as library and information science, the book trade and publishing, reprography, book design, copyright law, the history of books, printing, writing and the alphabet, paper production and many other themes.' Two volumes published so far: V. 1 covers the period 1945–1978; V. 2 the period 1979–1990.

5365 Library and Information Science Abstracts
ProQuest, 1969–, 11 p.a. ISSN 00242179.
Currently abstracts over 440 periodicals from more than 68 countries and in more than 20 different languages. Mid-2007 contained over 300,000 records.

5366 Library Literature and Information Science
H.W. Wilson, 1921–, bi-monthly.
www.hwwilson.com/Databases/liblit.htm [DESCRIPTION]
Indexes English and foreign-language periodicals, selected state journals, conference proceedings, pamphlets, books and library school theses, plus over 300 books per year. Full-text articles from over a hundred select publications. An excellent service with good retrospective coverage.

Directories & encyclopedias

5367 The Bowker annual library and book trade almanac [USA]
D. Bogart, ed.   Information Today, 2007, annual, 850pp. $199.95. ISBN 9781573872898.
'As an on-the-job answer book, a statistical information resource, a planning and research guide and a directory and calendar, *The Bowker annual library and book trade almanac 2007* delivers the hard-to-find industry news and information you need.' Includes reviews of key current events, coverage of new legislation, a wide range of statistics, contact data for organizations and individuals, etc.

5368 Encyclopedia of library and information science
M.A. Drake, ed.   2nd edn, Marcel Dekker, 2003. 4 v. ISBN 082472075X.
www.dekker.com [COMPANION]
The major work in the field: over 400 articles written by experts; online version available; regular planned updating.

5369 International encyclopedia of information and library science
J. Feather and P. Sturges, eds   2nd edn, Routledge, 2003, 736pp. £140. ISBN 9780415259019.
600 entries written by 150 contributors recruited globally. 'Easily accessible to the less initiated, with extensive reference and reading lists for those interested in delving further … Highly recommended for information science and library school collections.' (*Library Journal*)

5370 World guide to library, archive and information science associations
M. Schweizer, comp.   2nd edn, K.G. Saur, 2005, 510pp. €168. ISBN 9783598218408.
Contains 633 comprehensive, updated entries for international and national organizations from more than 130 countries, arranged A–Z and providing contact data, including e-mail addresses and websites, officers, membership, goals and activities, publications and other organizational details. Includes multiple indexes to facilitate reference use.
■ **Professional associations in the information sciences**
http://slisweb.sjsu.edu/resources/orgs.htm. Lists more than 200 archive, computing, information science, library, media, and other related associations. Maintained by the San Jose State University's School of Library and Information Science.

5371 World guide to library, archive and information science education
3rd edn, K.G. Saur, 2007.
Announced new edition will update 1995 volume, providing full details of schools of library, archives and information science around the world, including information on programmes offered, professional accreditation, size of staff establishment and student intakes, in addition to contact data, including e-mail addresses and websites.
■ **World list of schools and departments of information science, information management and related disciplines** T.D. Wilson, ed.   1996–, in progress.
http://informationr.net/wl. Offers A–Z listing by country and then institution, offering access to websites at institutional, school/department and programme level, covering in c. 100 countries.

Handbooks & manuals

5372 Business information management: improving performance using information systems
D. Chaffey and S. Wood   Financial Times Prentice Hall, 2004, 662pp. £43.99. ISBN 9780273686552.
http://wps.pearsoned.co.uk/ema_uk_he_chaffey_bim_1 [COMPANION]
Comprehensive, extensively referenced textbook, containing 12 chapters organized in four parts: Introduction; Strategy; Implementation; and Management. Distinctive features include the holistic, problem-based treatment of information and knowledge management, which integrates information, systems and technology perspectives and the numerous real-world case studies drawn from the UK public and private sectors. Related web resources include searchable online glossary.

5373 Global librarianship
M.A. Kesselman and I. Weintraub, eds   CRC Press, 2004, 320pp. Originally published under the Marcel Dekker imprint, $159.95. ISBN 9780824709785.
'Studies the impact of libraries, social issues, education, the preservation of cultural heritage and economic development. Analyses the role of libraries around the world as leaders in global access to information in school, public, academic and multinational corporations. Demonstrates how libraries can serve their communities in the evolving digital environment. Considers how language barriers, national policies and the digital divide affect the free flow of information'.

5374 The information audit: a practical guide

S. Henczel K.G. Saur, 2001, 272pp. €68. ISBN 9783598243677.

Provides a comprehensive and systematic guide to planning, conducting and following through an information audit, supported by three case studies from Australian public sector organizations. Includes detailed advice on different methods, with more than 100 useful checklists, tables and figures, in addition to sample instruments and other documents for local adaptation. Concludes with a selected bibliography of 115 items and index.

5375 Information science in theory and practice

B. Vickery and A. Vickery 3rd edn, K.G. Saur, 2004, 400pp. ISBN 9783598440083.

Classic text which relates theoretical research and discussion to experimental studies of information processes and the practical environment of information provision. Covers information transfer, people and information, information retrieval, intermediaries and interfaces, information systems. Includes two maps of key writers in the discipline and index and an extensive set of references. For this edition a new chapter examines the effect of the internet on information science and librarianship.

5376 Practical information policies

E. Orna 2nd edn, Gower, 1999, 375pp. £62.50. ISBN 0566076934.

Although somewhat dated, this classic text remains the most comprehensive treatment of the subject and is particularly valuable for its clear definitions, articulation of principles, identification of critical issues and collection of 14 real-world case studies drawn from both public and private sector organizations. Provides a step-by-step guide to developing and using an information strategy, starting with the conduct of an initial information audit, prior to formulating an organizational information policy and translating this into a practical information strategy. Prefaced by useful explanations of key concepts, such as knowledge, information, organizational information policy, information strategy, information management and knowledge management. Supported throughout with useful checklists, tables, diagrams and references. A 'topic guide' provides a subject index to cases under c. 100 headings, allowing readers to select studies of special interest. Includes index. The author's latest thinking on this subject is captured in her more recent *Information strategy in practice* (Gower, 2004).

Keeping up to date

5377 Advances in library organization and administration

Elsevier, annual. £59.99 [2006 edn]. ISBN 9780762312979. www.elsevier.com/locate/series/alao [DESCRIPTION]

Useful series, worth bearing in mind.

■ **Advances in librarianship** Elsevier, annual. £57.99 [2006]. ISBN 9780120246304. 'The 30th volume of *Advances in librarianship* acknowledges changes in the profession over three and a half decades, while continuing a tradition of identifying new trends and innovations. The contributing authors were invited especially to celebrate the history of the past thirty-six years by reflecting, as appropriate, on advances made in their topic since the first volume of the series was published in 1970. The twelve chapters in this volume can be loosely grouped into four sections reflecting basic themes in librarianship: tracing issues in communication: relevance and freedom of expression; focusing on library services and resources; tailoring services to different user groups; and educating the

profession for the future. Together these offer a milestone in the retrospective view of advances in librarianship'.

5378 Annual review of information science and technology

B. Cronin, ed.; American Society for Information Science & Technology Information Today, annual, 816pp. $99.95 [41st edn, 2007]. ISBN 9781573872768.

www.asis.org/Publications/ARIST [DESCRIPTION]

An excellent publication: essential for keeping abreast of the field. Each volume comprises a series of extensive critical reviews of the literature: 'The range of topics varies considerably, reflecting the dynamism of the discipline and the diversity of theoretical and applied perspectives connoted by the rubric "information science and technology". While ARIST continues to cover key topics associated with "classical" information science (e.g., bibliometrics, information retrieval), the *Review* is expanding its footprint, prudently and selectively, in an effort to connect information science more tightly with cognate academic and professional communities.'

5379 Ariadne

www.ariadne.ac.uk

Free quarterly web magazine for information professionals in archives, libraries and museums in all sectors, which aims to keep the busy practitioner abreast of current digital library initiatives, as well as other relevant technological developments. It reports on programmes and services sponsored by the UK Joint Information Systems Committee, as well as developments in the field within the UK and internationally.

5380 British Librarianship and Information Work 2001–2005

J.H. Bowman, ed. Ashgate, 2007, 544pp. £75. ISBN 9780754647782.

Provides a literature-based overview of trends and developments in the field. Contains 32 chapters of c. 7,500 words by practitioners, consultants and academics, covering different types of libraries and areas of interest, including local studies, archives, education and training, research, library buildings, cooperation, marketing, information literacy, library management systems, cataloguing, classification, indexing and preservation.

5381 Cites and Insights: Crawford at large

W. Crawford Monthly. Free. ISSN 15340937.

http://citesandinsights.info

Good example of a single expert's view of current issues around libraries and their environments. 'My primary aims in Cites & Insights are to point people in interesting directions and encourage them to think about certain issues. If, after thinking about them, they come to different conclusions than mine, that's as it should be. (If I've obviously overlooked issues and facts, I trust readers to let me know – and I publish reader feedback when given permission and when it's at all feasible.)' Among much always interesting comment and opinion, includes 'Interesting and peculiar products' ('Gadgets and gizmos, but also truly interesting new products'); 'The library stuff' ('Annotated and argumentative citations of articles and other stuff directly related to libraries and librarians'); and 'Scholarly article access' ('Events and articles related to access, including Open

Access, alternative publishing models and institutional archives').

5382 D-Lib Magazine
Corporation for National Research Initiatives   11 p.a.
www.dlib.org
Very valuable 'solely electronic publication with a primary focus on digital library research and development, including but not limited to new technologies, applications and contextual social and economic issues'.

5383 Information Research Watch International
ProQuest, 6 p.a. ISSN 14701391.
www.csa.com/factsheets/irwi-set-c.php [DESCRIPTION]
'(R)eports new, ongoing and completed research in information and library science and related fields from around the world. Compiled from records supplied by the researchers themselves, the database gives access to information about current research prior to its appearance in the published literature, with details of researcher affiliation, research funding and funding bodies, duration, status of project and researcher contact information. The database currently contains over 8500 records from more than 70 countries stretching back over 20 years.'

5384 Information Today Inc.
www.infotoday.com
'Information Today, Inc. (ITI) is the publisher of *Information Today*, as well as other periodicals, books, directories and online products; and is the organizer of InfoToday and other prestigious conferences and exhibitions for the library, information & knowledge management community.' The company produces and organizes a wide range of valued events, publications and services in addition to the five noted below.

- ■ **Econtent: digital content strategies and resources**
  www.econtentmag.com [FEE-BASED]. 'Essential research, reporting, news, and analysis of content related issues (for) executives and professionals involved in content creation, management, acquisition, organization, and distribution in both commercial and enterprise environments.'
- ■ **Information Today** 11 p.a. $69.95 [2004]. ISSN 87556286. www.infotoday.com/it. US-based newspaper 'for users and producers of electronic information services'. Each monthly issue treats major developments in the industry by acknowledged experts – both in the public and private sectors. Useful are the sections Product News and Reviews and the various items entitled Report from the Field. The company produces and organizes a wide range of valued events, publications and services in addition to those noted in this entry. For more emphasis on UK and European developments, see the similar *Information World Review*.
- ■ **ITI Newslink** www.infotoday.com/newslink. Free weekly newsletter, with subscribers receiving each month a full-length issue with articles and reviews covering recent developments in the information industry.
- ■ **Online** , 6 p.a. $112. ISSN 01465422. 'Practical articles, product reviews and comparisons, case studies, and informed opinions about selecting, using, manipulating, and managing digital information products.'
- ■ **Searcher** , 10 p.a. $83.95 [2004]. ISSN 10704795. 'Targeted to experienced, knowledgeable searchers and combines evaluations of data content with discussions of delivery media.'

5385 Information World Review
11 per year. ISSN 09509879.
www.iwr.co.uk
Monthly (11 p.a.) news magazine with a particular focus on the European online information world. Provides news, features and comment from staff writers and industry

leaders. Includes interviews, case studies and company profiles, in addition to regular columns and book reviews.

5386 Library Journal
Reed Business Information, 20 p.a. $141 (USA); $221 (International Air Delivery). ISSN 03603113.
www.libraryjournal.com
'The oldest independent national library publication. Founded in 1876, this "bible" of the library world is read by over 100,000 library directors, administrators and others in public, academic and special (e.g., business) libraries.' Wide-ranging coverage; although overtly commercial, it includes lively – indeed, often pungent – comment on current developments and has many sections well worth browsing through, e.g. the book review section covers nearly 7000 books each year with hundreds of reviews of audiobooks, videos, databases, systems and software. Three Newsletters are available: Corporate Library Update, Library Hotline and Academic Newswire.
Subscription includes immediate access to all of the Library Journal web site, as well as the electronic newsletters.

5387 LIS-LINK: a general library and information science list for news and discussion [UK]
www.jiscmail.ac.uk/archives/lis-link.html
The major general-purpose list in the UK with – mid-2007 – some 800 subscribers.

Information Society

communities of practice • copyright • data protection • digital divide • digital rights • freedom of information • information behaviour • information ethics • information law • information literacy • information skills • intellectual capital • intellectual freedom • intellectual property • internet society • knowledge management • network society

Introductions to the subject

5388 Digital nation: toward an inclusive information society
A.G. Wilhelm   MIT Press, 2006, 161pp. £9.95. ISBN 9780262731775.
The Director of the US Technology Opportunities Program explains how inappropriate use of technology by public and private organizations will further undermine the position of disadvantaged groups, with adverse consequences for individuals, the economy and society. He makes the case for expanding access to computers and enabling people to gain the required digital literacy skills.
'Anthony Wilhelm has written a public policy manifesto for the digital age. His book lays out the social and economic case for bridging the digital divide, along with the policies required to achieve universal inclusion in our emerging information societies. *Digital Nation* is essential reading for anyone seriously concerned about the societal implications of the Internet.' (*William H. Dutton* (Director, Oxford Internet Institute))

5389 The impact of information on society: an examination of its nature, value and usage
M.W. Hill   2nd rev. edn, K.G. Saur, 2005, 340pp. €98. ISBN 9783598116483.
Solid text, giving a good overview of developments affecting information's impact on our lives.

5390 The information society: a study of continuity and change
J. Feather   4th edn, Facet Publishing, 2004, 220pp.
Now the standard introduction, covering the key issues which should be addressed in contemporary society: particularly 'in a world where data can be transmitted in a split second' and 'information can become a political tool, which can be abused as easily as it can be used'.
'This book presents a lucid and easily absorbed review of a complex and turbulent field ... a masterly, sweeping study [About an earlier edn]' (*Education for Information*)

5391 The internet galaxy: reflections on the internet, business and society
M. Castells   Oxford University Press, 2002, 292pp. £14.99. ISBN 9780199255771.
Based on the author's Clarendon Lectures in Management at Oxford University, this work provides a concise distillation of the insights of the leading thinker on the subject, drawing on his extensive research in the field (reported in his seminal three-volume work *The information age: economy, society and culture*, first published in 1996–1998).
'Thoroughly researched ... [and] truly global in scope. Castells provides balanced coverage of e-business and the new economy; the politics of the Internet, including privacy and freedom; and the geography of the Internet ... Highly recommended for academic libraries.' (*Library Journal*)

5392 The network society
D. Barney   Polity Press, 2004, 198pp. £14.95. ISBN 9780745626697.
Examines 'the social, political and economic implications of network technologies and their application across a wide range of practices and institutions ... Among the issues discussed are debates concerning the emergence of a "knowledge economy"; digital restructuring of employment and work; globalization and the status of the nation-state; the prospects of digital democracy; the digital divide; new social movements; and culture, community and identity in the age of new media.'

5393 Theories of the information society
F. Webster   3rd edn, Routledge, 2006, 317pp. £23.99. ISBN 9780415406338.
Excellent scholarly text, of particular value for its sceptical look at what thinkers mean when they refer to 'The Information Society'.

Dictionaries, thesauri, classifications

Cyberculture: the key concepts
D. Bell [et al.]   See entry no. 5319

5394 Glossary of internet terms
M. Enzer
www.matisse.net/files/glossary.html
Straightforward, freely accessible list – the definitions being particularly accessible to non-technologists.

Research centres & institutes

5395 Benton Foundation [USA]
www.benton.org
'The mission of the Benton Foundation is to articulate a public interest vision for the digital age and to demonstrate the value of communications for solving social problems. Current priorities include promoting a vision and policy alternatives for the digital age in which the benefit to the public is paramount; raising awareness among funders and nonprofits on their stake in critical policy issues; enabling communities and nonprofits to produce diverse and locally responsive media content.'
Excellent, clearly articulated website: Headlines (a daily news summary of the latest communications news); Topics (advertising, agenda, broadcasting, and so on); Initiatives (e.g. broadband benefits, media ownership). There is also a virtual library of 'Resources you can use'.

5396 Berkman Center for Internet & Society [USA]
http://cyber.law.harvard.edu
'The Berkman Center's mission is to explore and understand cyberspace, its development, dynamics, norms, standards and need or lack thereof for laws and sanctions. We are a research center, premised on the observation that what we seek to learn is not already recorded. Our method is to build out into cyberspace, record data as we go, self-study and publish. Our mode is entrepreneurial nonprofit.'
Another excellent website with wide-ranging access to a wealth of useful resources.

5397 Information Society Project
http://research.yale.edu/isp
'The ISP undertakes several initiatives each year and engages in a variety of activities that include awarding residency and fellowships to young scholars, organizing international conferences and events and providing advice and education to policy makers, business leaders, nonprofit organizations and the global legal community.'

5398 Institute of the Information Society [RUS]
www.iis.ru
'The Institute of the Information Society (IIS) is an independent research and service organization established in September 1998 by a number of professionals in the sphere of the information technologies, telecommunications and information policy, who were brought together by the common goal of developing the Information Society in Russia.' (Site includes English-language pages.)

5399 Open Society Institute Information Program
www.soros.org/initiatives/information
'(P)romotes equitable deployment of knowledge and communications resources – providing access to content, tools and networks – for civic empowerment and effective democratic governance.' The Program initiates projects in three focal areas: access to knowledge, including intellectual propety reform and open access to scholarly information;

civil society communication; and open information policy, including free expression on the internet.

5400   Oxford Internet Institute
www.oii.ox.ac.uk
Founded as a department of the University of Oxford in 2001, a centre for study of the societal implications of the internet. The website provides a very wide-ranging survey of current work relating to, for instance, everyday life; governance and democracy; science and learning; and shaping the internet.

Associations & societies

5401   Digital Divide Network
www.digitaldividenetwork.org
'(T)he internet's largest community for educators, activists, policy makers and concerned citizens working to bridge the digital divide. At DDN, you can build your own online community, publish a blog, share documents and discussions with colleagues and post news, events and articles.'

Portal & task environments

5402   Europe's information society
European Commission
http://europa.eu.int/information_society
Thematic portal using input from the EU Information Society and Media Directorate, but also from the Directorates for 'Education and Culture', 'Employment and Social Affairs', 'Enterprise', 'Regional Policy' and others as well as relevant European Parliament Committees. Examples of news items when the site was checked were: 'The winners of the European eGovernment Awards: The most outstanding digital public services in Europe'; 'Assessment of the economic and social impact of the public domain in the information society'; 'eContentplus Call for proposals 2007 – Guide for proposers just published'.

5403   Observatory on the information society
United Nations Educational, Scientific & Cultural Organization
www.unesco.org/cgi-bin/webworld/portal_observatory/cgi/page.cgi?d=1
Has the by-line: 'Monitoring the Development of the Information Society towards Knowledge Societies'. There are eight 'Directory Categories' (e.g. Access to information and knowledge; Information and communication infrastructure) each with sub-categories. It is also possible to search by types of information (e.g. national policies, associations, tools, periodicals). Access to much other information: worth browsing around.

Directories & encyclopedias

5404   The internet encyclopedia
H. Bidgoli, ed.   Wiley, 2003. 3 v, $750. ISBN 0471222011.
200 essays, starting with 'Active server pages' and ending with 'XBRL (Extensible Business Reporting Language): Business reporting with XML'. The chapter list by subject area has the section headings: Applications; Design, implementation and management; Electronic commerce;

Foundation; Infrastructure; Legal, social, organizational, international and taxation issues; Marketing and advertising on the web; Security issues and measures; Supply chain management; Web design and programming; Wireless internet and e-commerce: thus indicative of the very wide scope of the resource.

This is a well designed suite of volumes, pleasant to use and providing good state-of-the-art summaries of each topic covered – albeit now in some areas in need of update.
- **Internet Society** www.isoc.org. '(A) non-profit, non-governmental, international, professional membership organisation. Its more than 100 organisation members and over 20,000 individual members in over 180 nations worldwide represent a veritable who's who of the Internet community'.

Handbooks & manuals

5405   The information age: economy, society and culture
M. Castells   Blackwell Publishing, 2000–2003.
Updated editions of the author's seminal trilogy on the information age, which are rigorously researched, extensively referenced and still widely regarded as the most insightful and lucid commentary on the technological, social, economic and political dynamics transforming contemporary society.
'These three volumes provide a monumental and coherent account of the economic, social, personal and cultural changes that are occurring around the world in the age of computerisation. This is not, however, just another book proclaiming the information revolution. The conception of the work is vast, but it is performed with such clarity and comprehensiveness that one cannot imagine the work getting out of date for a very long time.' (*Times Higher Education Supplement*)
- **1. The rise of the network society** 2nd edn, 2000, 624pp. £20.99. ISBN 9780631221401.
- **2. The power of identity** 2nd edn, 2003, 560pp. £20.99. ISBN 9781405107136.
- **3. End of millennium** 2nd edn, 2000, 464pp. £20.99. ISBN 9780631221395.

5406   The information society reader
F. Webster, ed.   Routledge, 2003, 449pp. £24.99. ISBN 9780415319287.
'With a comprehensive introduction from Frank Webster, selections from Manuel Castells, Anthony Giddens, Michel Foucault and Christopher Lasch among others and section introductions contextualizing the readings, this book will be an invaluable resource for students and academics studying contemporary society and all things cyber.'

5407   The internet and society: a reference handbook
B.H. Schell   ABC-CLIO, 2007, 311pp. $55. ISBN 9781598840315.
Good historical overview of internet development: biographical sketches of 20 key figures (but an unfortunate mis-spelling of 'Berners-Lee' in the main body of the text); data and documents on US internet-related law; reference section comprising directory of organizations and of selected print and non-print resources.

5408   The Oxford handbook of information and communication technologies
R. Mansell [et al.]   Oxford University Press, 2007, 752pp. £85. ISBN 9780199266234.
'The production and consumption of information and communication technologies (or ICTs) are becoming deeply embedded within our societies. The influence and

implications of this have an impact at a macro level, in the way our governments, economies and businesses operate and at a micro level in our everyday lives. This handbook is about the many challenges presented by ICTs. It sets out an intellectual agenda that examines the implications of ICTs for individuals, organizations, democracy and the economy.'

A collection of interdisciplinary essays written by leading experts covering the influence and impact of information and communications technologies (ICT) on modern society. Organized around four key themes: the knowledge economy, organizational dynamics, strategy and design, governance and democracy, and culture, community and new media literacies.

Keeping up to date

5409 DigitalDivide Discussion List
Digital Divide Network
www.digitaldivide.net/community/digitaldivide
'(T)he official e-mail discussion forum for the Digital Divide Network. With approximately 10,000 members in more than 70 countries, the DIGITALDIVIDE list is the internet's premiere forum for discussing the digital divide. Membership is open to the public and all DDN members are encouraged to join ...'

5410 The Filter
Berkman Center for Internet & Society
http://cyber.law.harvard.edu
Monthly electronic newsletter which 'offers a unique take on today's most pressing internet issues through the eyes of leading experts, scholars and researchers'.

Information Literacy

Introductions to the subject

Brilliant books: running a successful school library book event
G. Dubber and E. Scott; School Library Association   See entry no. 5616

5411 Information literacy: a practitioner's guide
S. Andretta   Chandos, 2005, 208pp. £39. ISBN 9781843340652.
Provides a comparative evaluation of the relative strengths of the ACRL, ANZIIL and SCONUL models of information literacy (which are reproduced as appendices) and then provides two detailed case studies of teaching information literacy in a higher education setting, which focus respectively on the development of generic and subject-specific skills, also covering methods for diagnosing and assessing IL skills development. Includes a rich literature review and useful index.
'This book deserves a place on the shelves of any information professional striving to develop information literacy programmes in higher education, and would provide nuggets of inspiration for those in other sectors.' (*Legal Information Management*)

5412 Teaching information skills: theory and practice
J. Webb and C. Powis   Facet Publishing, 2004, 223pp. £39.95. ISBN 9781856045131.
This book blends theory and practice, with each chapter

having two parts: a section explaining the theories and principles, followed by case studies of successful approaches in each instance. A good introduction to an increasingly important facet of the information professional's job.

Laws, standards, codes

European Charter for Media Literacy
See entry no. 5048

5413 Information literacy competency standards for higher education
Association of College & Research Libraries
www.ala.org/ala/acrl/acrlstandards/informationliteracycompetency.htm
'*Information Literacy Competency Standards for Higher Education* provides a framework for assessing the information literate individual. It extends the work of the American Association of School Librarians Task Force on Information Literacy Standards, thereby providing higher education an opportunity to articulate its information literacy competencies with those of K-12 so that a continuum of expectations develops for students at all levels. The competencies presented here outline the process by which faculty, librarians and others pinpoint specific indicators that identify a student as information literate ...'
Widely used in the US and other countries.

5414 Information literacy standards for student learning
[USA]
American Association of School Librarians and Association for Educational Communications & Technology   ALA Editions, 1998, 56pp.
www.ala.org/aasl/ip_nine.html [COMPANION]
Developed by collaboration between the two bodies and widely adopted. The nine standards fall into three categories: information literacy, independent learning and social responsibility. The website provides a summary.

5415 The seven pillars of information literacy
Society of College, National & University Libraries
www.sconul.ac.uk/groups/information_literacy/seven_pillars.html
An influential model developed in the late 1990s and widely used in UK higher education. Different versions of the model are available for download. The seven 'pillars' are: 1. The ability to recognise a need for information; 2. The ability to distinguish ways in which the information 'gap' may be addressed; 3. The ability to construct strategies for locating information; 4. The ability to locate and access information; 5. The ability to compare and evaluate information obtained from different sources; 6. The ability to organize, apply and communicate information to others in ways appropriate; 7. The ability to synthesize and build upon existing information, contributing to the creation of new knowledge

Research centres & institutes

5416 Australian & New Zealand Institute for Information Literacy
Australian & New Zealand Institute for Information Literacy
www.anziil.org
Fee-based institutional membership organziation which 'supports organizations, institutions and individuals in the

promotion of information literacy and, in particular, the embedding of information literacy within the total educational process.' Useful, but not extensive, website.

■ **Australian and New Zealand information literacy framework: principles, standards and practice** A. Bundy, ed.; Australian & New Zealand Institute for Information Literacy and Council of Australian University Libraries   2nd edn2004, 52 p.a.. www.anziil.org/resources. Derived – with permission – from the ACRL *Information literacy competency standards for higher education*. The second edition incorporates changes resulting from user feedback. The document also includes contributions from leading IL practitioners, an account of how libraries used the 1st edition, and a selective chronology for 'information literacy' (1965–2003). Accessible as PDF file.

Center for Media Literacy
See entry no. 5054

Center for News Literacy
See entry no. 5149

5417 Centre for Information Literacy Research
www.shef.ac.uk/is/cilr
Based in the University of Sheffield, Department of Information Studies, website provides details of staff and student research projects and publications, as well as programmes and presentations for upcoming and past events. Also provides links to websites of strategic partners at Queensland University of Technology, Robert Gordon University and University of Strathclyde.

5418 Institute for Information Literacy
www.ala.org/ala/acrl/acrlissues/acrlinfolit/professactivity/iil/welcome.cfm
Established by the ALA Association of College and Research Libraries, the focus of the Institute is on helping librarians to become effective advocates, teachers and developers of information literacy. The website provides information about the Institute's purpose, structure, activities and publications, as well as links to related sites and publications.

Associations & societies

5419 IFLA Information Literacy Section
www.ifla.org/VII/s42/index.htm
IFLA body whose primary purpose is 'is to foster international cooperation in the development of information skills education in all types of libraries'. The Section has produced – on behalf of UNESCO – the International Information Literacy Resources Directory, incorporated in the portal InfoLit Global.

International Reading Association
See entry no. 4438

5420 National Forum on Information Literacy [USA]
www.infolit.org
Created in 1989 as a response to the recommendations of the American Library Association's Presidential Committee on Information Literacy. Notable here for providing access to a range of valuable resources: Annotated list of useful publications; News about the International Alliance for Information Literacy; link to Information Literacy Weblog; and so on.

5421 Society of College, National & University Libraries, SCONUL Working Group on Information Literacy [UK]
www.sconul.ac.uk/groups/information_literacy
Group of the UK Society of College, National and University Libraries which developed the 'Seven Pillars' model of information literacy (q.v.). Site provides useful links section and news of activities.

Portal & task environments

5422 The Big6: information skills for student achievement [USA]
M.B. Eisenberg and B. Berkowitz
www.big6.com
Lively website providing a wealth of resources relating to 'The Big 6' information skills for student achievement: 1. Task definition; 2. Information seeking strategies; 3. Location and access; 4. Use of information; 5. Synthesis; 6. Evaluation. The programme was developed by the two authors of the website in the late 1980s.

5423 Canadian Research Libraries Information Literacy Portal
Canadian Association of Research Libraries
http://apps.medialab.uwindsor.ca/crlil/wiki/FrontPage
Maintained as a wiki by information literacy librarians across Canada. Sections include Overviews of information literacy; Assessment of information resources; Canadian university IL initiatives; Conferences, workshops and professional development; Grants and funding opportunities; Discipline-specific IL; ICT literacy developments; IL instructional resources; IL standards and guidelines; Institutional IL programs and research projects; Institutions, organizations and committees; Listservs for IL.

5424 InfoLit Global
www.infolitglobal.info
Funded by the UNESCO Information Society Division and managed by the IFLA Information Literacy Section, this site incorporates a browsable and searchable database of publications, organizations, websites, events, toolkits, tutorials and other materials supporting advocacy, teaching and professional development, in addition to state-of-the-art reports on information literacy across the globe.

5425 The Information Literacy Website
www.informationliteracy.org.uk
UK-based site offering news, case studies, examples of best practice and freely available toolkits. Sections include Developing professional practice; Marketing IL; Research; Resources by subject; and Events. Research section covers funding opportunities, research resources, hints and tips and examples of current and past projects. Site also hosts the open-access *Journal of Information Literacy*.

Handbooks & manuals

5426 Building your own information literate school
C. Koechlin and S. Zwaan   Hi Willow Research & Publishing, 2003, 128pp. $40. ISBN 9780931510892.
Contains comprehensive and effectively presented guidance on both teaching and assessing essential information literacy

skills, covering not only finding, locating and sorting information, but also analysis and synthesis of information. Provides tips, worksheets and examples covering different subject areas and ability levels, from elementary to high school.

5427   Creating a comprehensive information literacy plan: a how-to-do-it manual and CD-ROM for librarians
J.M. Burkhardt, M.C. MacDonald and A.J. Rathemacher   Neal-Schuman, 2005, 174pp. $89.95. ISBN 1555705332.
Practical guide which covers all aspects of the planning process in addition to advice on content and structure. Includes planning worksheets; bibliographies on needs assessment, peer institution comparisons and marketing; and screenshots and URLs for plans produced by college and university libraries. CD-ROM enables customization of worksheets for local use.

5428   Information literacy: essential skills for the information age
M.B. Eisenberg, C.A. Lowe and K.L. Spitzer   2nd edn, Libraries Unlimited, 2004, 408pp. $50. ISBN 9781591581437.
Comprehensive and authoritative handbook, which outlines the evolution of the concept before providing detailed coverage of IL development in US elementary and middle schools, followed by discussion of US higher education. Key features include a thematic summary of IL research, reproduction of many key models and an 85-page annotated bibliography.
'A renowned expert on information literacy addresses history, economic importance, past and current research, theoretical underpinnings, and practical aspects. Global in scope.' (*Library Journal*)

Information literacy and the school library media center
J. Taylor   See entry no. 5629

5429   Information literacy and workplace performance
T.W. Goad   Quorum Books, 2002, 232pp. $93.95. ISBN 9781567204544.
A rare example of a text addressing the critical issue of information literacy in the workplace and its contribution to personal and organizational success in a knowledge-based economy. Examines several different dimensions of IL, including computer literacy, subject-matter literacy and learning how to learn, acknowledging the role of librarians in promoting IL.

5430   Information literacy instruction: theory and practice
E. Grassian and J. Kaplowitz   Neal-Schuman, 2001, 468pp. Includes CD-ROM, $65. ISBN 1555704069.
Provides a thorough and well structured blending of theory and practice. 18 chapters in five parts: I. Information literacy instruction background; II. Information literacy instruction building blocks; III. Planning and developing information literacy instruction; IV. Delivering information literacy instruction; V. The future of ILI. CD-ROM provides handouts for local use.
'Strongly recommended for librarians whose responsibilities involve teaching users how to access information of any kind.' (*Journal of the Medical Library Association*)

5431   Information literacy: a review of the research: a guide for practitioners and researchers
D.V. Loertscher and B. Woolls   2nd edn, Hi Willow Research & Publishing, 2002, 170pp. $30. ISBN 0931510805.
Reviews information literacy research from the library and educational domains, covering Australia and the UK, in addition to the US and Canada. A particular focus and strength is the extensive coverage of the many different models of information literacy developed to support teaching and learning in primary and secondary education.

5432   Integrating information literacy into the higher education curriculum: practical models for transformation
I.F. Rockman, ed.   Jossey-Bass, 2004, 260pp. $38. ISBN 9780787965273.
Contains nine extensively-referenced chapters contributed by information literacy practitioners from various types of higher education institutions. The authors use examples and case studies to discuss challenges and strategies for implementing IL programmes in HE. Key themes and topics covered include librarian-faculty partnerships and the development of IL in research settings.

5433   Looking for information: a survey of research on information seeking, needs, and behaviour
D.O. Case   2nd edn, Academic Press, 2007, 423pp. £42.99. ISBN 9780123694300.
The most comprehensive review of research in this area, citing more than 1110 references. Thirteen chapters are organized in five sections covering introduction and examples; relevant concepts; models, paradigms and theories; methods; research results and reflections. Chapters 11–12 review research by occupation and socio-demographic attributes. Includes glossary and author/subject indexes.

5434   Teaching web search skills: techniques and strategies of top trainers
G.R. Notess   Information Today, 2006, 368pp. $29.50. ISBN 9781573872676.
Notable for, including expert tips and advice from a range of leading practitioners. Covers: Understanding your audience; Instructional session goals; Online tutorials; Web search terminology; Organizing the training session; Creating workshop web pages; Presentation tips, tricks and shortcuts; Anecdotes, examples and exercises.

5435   Theories of information behaviour
K.E. Fisher, S. Erdelez and E.F. McKechnie, eds   Information Today, 2005, 431pp. $49.50. ISBN 157387230X.
Provides authoritative overviews of 72 conceptual frameworks for understanding how people seek, manage, share and use information in different contexts, prefaced by three introductory chapters by leading thinkers (Bates, Dervlin and Wilson). Descriptions cover origins, propositions, methodological implications, usage and links to related frameworks, supported by lists of authoritative references.

5436   Web-based instruction: a guide for libraries
S.S. Smith   2nd edn, ALA Editions, 2006, 263pp. $55. ISBN 9780838909089.
Comprehensive survey with a wealth of short sections organized into 8 chapters: 1. Setting the stage; 2. Library instruction on the web; 3. Design and development cycle; 4. Selecting project development tools; 5. Designing the user

interface; 6. Multimedia: using graphics, sound, animation and video; 7. Interactivity; 8. Evaluation, testing and assessment. An extensive Resources section is organized A–Z under some 50 headings.

Keeping up to date

5437 ILI-L: the Information Literacy Instruction Discussion List
http://lists.ala.org/wws/info/ili-l
Created in May 2002 as an evolution of the former BI-L (Bibliographic Instruction discussion list established in 1990), ILI-L is hosted by the American Library Association on behalf of the ACRL Instruction Section. With more than 4000 subscribers, this list generates a high level of postings on information literacy issues.

5438 The Information Literacy Land of Confusion
M. Lorenzen
www.information-literacy.net
Blog of US reference librarian, discussing library user education, library instruction, librarianship, information literacy and search engines.

- **LibraryInstruction.Com: the librarian's weapon of mass instruction** M. Lorenzen   www.libraryinstruction.com. This site contains library instruction lesson plans, articles about library instruction, a large library instruction bibliography (300 items organized in nine sections) and links to library instruction resources, as well as material relating to information literacy.

5439 Information literacy weblog
S. Webber and S. Boon
http://information-literacy.blogspot.com
The leading blog in the field, well structured with good use of photographs to enliven the text.

5440 LIS-INFOLITERACY: Information literacy and information skills teaching discussion list
www.jiscmail.ac.uk/lists/LIS-INFOLITERACY.html
Now a major discussion list, with currently almost 1200 subscribers.

Information Policy

Introductions to the subject

5441 Copyright: interpreting the law for libraries, archives and information services [UK]
G.P. Cornish   4th edn, Facet Publishing, 2004, 207pp. £29.95. ISBN 9781856045087.
User-friendly, well established text explaining the provisions of the UK Copyright Act and supporting legislation in quick and easy question-and-answer form. There is a detailed index and appendices lay out the statutory declaration forms and provide helpful lists of addresses and selected further sources of information.

- **Practical copyright for information professionals: the CILIP handbook** S. Norman   Facet, 2004, 194pp. £29.95. ISBN 9781856044905. Basic guide covering all the key areas.

5442 Copyright law for librarians and educators: creative strategies and practical solutions
K.D. Crews   2nd edn, ALA Editions, 2005, 176pp. $45. ISBN 9780838909065.
Accessible text with detailed coverage, based on the US environment. 18 chapters organized into five parts: The reach of copyright; Rights of ownership; Fair use; Focus on education and libraries; Special features. Good checklists in five appendices.

5443 Essential law for information professionals
P. Pedley   2nd edn, Facet Publishing, 2006, 278pp. £34.95. ISBN 9781856045520.
This text 'offers both a complete picture of the law as it affects information management and an exploration of the fundamental principles that underlie practice. It uses individual cases to illustrate legal principles and contextualize specific regulations'.

5444 A handbook of ethical practice: a practical guide to dealing with ethical issues in information and library work
D. McMenemy, A. Poulter and P.F. Burton   Chandos, 2007, 153pp. £39.95. ISBN 9781843342304.
Clear, well structured guide, which explains the nature of information ethics and provides an insightful comparative analysis of existing professional codes before offering a set of case studies presenting and discussing plausible ethical dilemmas related to four key areas: information services and supply, intellectual property, access and privacy and management. Also includes an excellent bibliography.
'... this sensible, shrewd, convincing book guides the reader through the subject clearly.' (*Library Review*)

5445 Information law in practice
P. Marett   2nd edn, Ashgate, 2002, 230pp. £57.50. ISBN 0566083906.
A very good overview – albeit now becoming somewhat out of date (though most of the underlying principles remain). Chapters are: Introduction; Protection of written works; Entertainment and related media; The work of the artist, designer and photographer; Electronic data; Patents and other industrial property; Copyright abroad; Transnational protection of intellectual property; Legal cautions for the information provider; The future; Appendices; Bibliography; Index.

5446 Librarian's guide to intellectual property in the digital age: copyright, patents, and trademarks [USA]
T.L. Wheery   American Library Association, 2002, 170pp. $38. ISBN 083890825X.
'An authoritative, quick reference for the thorny issues of copyright, trademarks and patents. With detailed explanations of the various types of intellectual property, how they differ, what they cover and how the protections affect library work and services to customers, this is a book you will turn to every day for answers.'
'Though called a librarian's guide, this book will be useful to anyone who wishes to understand the basics about copyrights, patents, and trademarks.' (*Reference & Research Book News*)

5447 Librarianship and human rights: a 21st century guide
T. Samek   Chandos, 2007, 200pp. £39.95. ISBN 9781843341468.
Discusses the library's role in supporting and promoting human rights, challenging the notion of professional neutrality as an acceptable response to present social and political agenda, by calling for positive action and identifying numerous strategies for librarians to consider in relation to contemporary concerns.

5448 Managing digital rights: a practitioner's guide
P. Pedley, ed.   Facet Publishing, 2005, 125pp. £39.95. ISBN 9781856045445.
Short, solid overview, with a particular focus on digital rights management.

Laws, standards, codes

5449 Copyright, Designs and Patents Act 1988: chapter 48 [UK]
HMSO, 1988.
www.opsi.gov.uk/acts/acts1988/Ukpga_19880048_en_1.htm
The full text of the Act, plus access to related information.

5450 Data Protection Act 1998: chapter 29 [UK]
Stationery Office, 1998.
www.opsi.gov.uk/acts/acts1998/19980029.htm
The full text of the Act, plus related information.

5451 Freedom of Information Act 2000 [UK]
Great Britain. Department for Constitutional Affairs
www.foi.gov.uk
Came into force January 2005; supersedes 'Code of Practice on Access to Government Information'. Under the Act, anybody may request information from a public authority which has functions in England, Wales and/or Northern Ireland. The Act confers two statutory rights on applicants:
    – To be told whether or not the public authority holds that information; and if so,
    – To have that information communicated to them.
- ■ **The Freedom of Information Act: FOIA** [USA].
www.gwu.edu/~nsarchiv/nsa/foia.html. Gateway to resources relevant to the law ensuring public access to US government records. 'FOIA carries a presumption of disclosure; the burden is on the government – not the public – to substantiate why information may not be released.'
- ■ **Your right to know: how to use the Freedom of Information Act and other access laws** [UK] **H. Brooke**   2nd edn, Pluto Press, 2006, 272pp. £13.99. ISBN 9780745325828. www.plutobooks.com [DESCRIPTION]. 'Even with my knowledge of Britain's secretive and undemocratic system of government, I found this book to be an eye opener. I will certainly be using the book myself.' David Shayler, former MI5 officer.

5452 Legal Deposit Libraries Act 2003: chapter 28 [UK]
Stationery Office, 2003.
www.opsi.gov.uk/acts/acts2003/20030028.htm
'A person who publishes in the United Kingdom a work to which this Act applies must at his own expense deliver a copy of it to an address specified (generally or in a particular case) by any deposit library entitled to delivery under this section ...'

Official & quasi-official bodies

5453 Copyright Clearance Center
www.copyright.com
'The largest licenser of text reproduction rights in the world, was formed in 1978 to facilitate compliance with US copyright law. CCC provides licensing systems for the reproduction and distribution of copyrighted materials in print and electronic formats throughout the world ... The company currently manages rights relating to over 1.75 million works and represents more than 9600 publishers and hundreds of thousands of authors and other creators, directly or through their representatives.'

5454 Copyright Licensing Agency [UK]
www.cla.co.uk
A non-profit company that licenses organizations for photocopying and scanning from magazines, books and journals. The site is especially valuable for its list of 'organizations that are concerned with or related to copyright and the creative industries'. The listing provides information on each of the organizations, including a summary of their role, contact details and links to their websites.

5455 Information Commissioner's Office
www.informationcommissioner.gov.uk
Independent supervisory authority reporting directly to the UK Parliament with an international role as well as a national one. Enforces and oversees the UK Data Protection Act 1998 and the Freedom of Information Act 2000. Also responsible for enforcing the Privacy and Electronic Communications (EC Directive) Regulations 2003.
    Rich website with a highly comprehensive range of online utilities and features.

See entry no. 5656

5456 UK Intellectual Property Office
www.ipo.gov.uk
The operating name of the UK Patent Office and the 'official government body responsible for granting Intellectual Property rights in the United Kingdom. These rights include Patents; Designs; Trade marks; Copyright.' Well structured website provides access to good sets of relevant resources.

5457 United States Copyright Office
www.copyright.gov
'The Copyright Office provides expert assistance to Congress on intellectual property matters; advises Congress on anticipated changes in US copyright law; analyses and assists in drafting copyright legislation and legislative reports and provides and undertakes studies for Congress; and offers advice to Congress on compliance with multilateral agreements, such as the Berne Convention for the Protection of Literary and Artistic Works.'
    Well organized sets of information: NewsNet is a 'free electronic newsletter that alerts subscribers to hearings, deadlines for comments, new and proposed regulations, new publications and other copyright-related subjects'.

5458 World Intellectual Property Organization
www.wipo.int
'Intellectual property refers to creations of the mind: inventions, literary and artistic works and symbols, names,

images and designs used in commerce ... (It) is divided into two categories:

'Industrial Property. Includes inventions (patents), trademarks, industrial designs and geographic indications of source

'Copyright. Includes literary and artistic works such as novels, poems and plays, films, musical works, artistic works such as drawings, paintings, photographs and sculptures and architectural designs.'

Among much other useful information, extensive website includes details of: Member states (currently 184); Treaties; Industrial property statistics; Publications (e-zines available). There is also an Intellectual Property Digital Library, as well as the WIPO Library – whose holdings are accessible through the United Nations Shared Cataloguing and Public Access System (q.v.) and which is also accessible to external researchers.

■ **Collection of laws for electronic access: CLEA**
www.wipo.int/clea/en. Bibliographic index of intellectual property laws and treaties in English linked with a full-text database available in English, French, Spanish.

■ **Collection of national copyright laws United Nations Educational, Scientific & Cultural Organization**.
http://portal.unesco.org/culture/en. Endeavours to provide access to national copyright and related rights legislation of UNESCO Member States. The collection currently comprises about 100 laws and is constantly being updated and completed.

Research centres & institutes

5459 Center for Intellectual Property
www.umuc.edu/distance/odell/cip/cip.shtml
Full title is The Center for Intellectual Property and Copyright in the Digital Environment, which reflects its prime focus. Extellent range of resources: a fine gateway to current preoccupations.

■ **The Center for Intellectual Property handbook K.M. Bonner [et al.], eds**   Neal-Schuman, 2006, 257pp. $85. ISBN 1555705618. Designed especially to help staff within educational institutions cope with the problems arising from use of digital content on and around campuses.

5460 Centre for Intellectual Property & Information Law
http://cipil.law.cam.ac.uk
Founded in 2004 within the University of Cambridge, replacing an 'IP Unit'. A range of resources is under development and there is already a useful worldwide list of 'Other academic centres for intellectual property'.

Associations & societies

5461 British Copyright Council
www.britishcopyright.org
'(E)stablished in 1965 and is a national consultative and advisory body representing organizations of copyright owners and performers and others interested in copyright in the UK. It lobbies the British Government, the European Commission and Parliament and international bodies such as the World Intellectual Property Organization on matters of copyright and related issues.'

Delightfully clear and intuitive website: an excellent entrée to work of the Council and related bodies.

■ **Authors' Licensing & Collecting Society** UK.
www.alcs.co.uk. '(R)epresents the interests of all UK writers and aims to ensure writers are fairly compensated for any works that are copied, broadcast or recorded'.

■ **Design & Artists Copyright Society** UK. www.dacs.org.uk.
'(T)he UK's copyright and collecting society for artists and visual creators. We exist to promote and protect the copyright and related rights of artists and visual creators'.

■ **Publishers Licensing Society** UK. www.pls.org.uk. 'PLS represents the interests of publishers in the collective licensing of photocopying and digitisation. Together with the Authors' Licensing and Collecting Society, PLS owns and directs the Copyright Licensing Agency and works in partnership with the Design and Artists Copyright Society'.

5462 Creative Commons
http://creativecommons.org
'We use private rights to create public goods: creative works set free for certain uses. Like the free software and open-source movements, our ends are cooperative and community-minded, but our means are voluntary and libertarian.' Site allows users to 'License your work' as well as 'Find CC licensed work'.

5463 IFLA Committee on Free Access to Information & Freedom of Expression
www.ifla.org/faife
Formed to defend and promote the basic human rights defined in Article 19 of the United Nations Universal Declaration of Human Rights. Useful sets of resources.

5464 Libraries & Archives Copyright Alliance
www.cilip.org.uk/professionalguidance/copyright
'(B)rings together the UK's major professional organizations and experts representing librarians and archivists to advocate a fair and balanced copyright regime and to lobby about the copyright issues affecting the ability of library, archive and information services to deliver access to knowledge in the digital age.'

Offers a range of resources and services: Advice and guidance; Consultation responses; Copyright forms and posters; Links; Books about copyright; Enquiries about copyright.

Portal & task environments

5465 IPR Helpdesk
European Commission
www.ipr-helpdesk.org
European Commission-sponsored programme run by University of Alicante and other bodies. It assists contractors carrying out EC-funded research and others in intellectual property rights issues. News, information and advice. Another more global objective of the action is to raise awareness of the European research community on IPR matters, emphasizing their European dimension.

5466 Liblicense: Licensing Digital Information
Yale University and Council on Library & Information Resources
www.library.yale.edu/~llicense/index.shtml
Provides a range of resources for librarians challenged with this complex field: model license; licensing vocabulary; bibliography; publishers' and authors' licenses; national site license inititatives; etc., as well as access to the Liblicense-L Discussion List.

Maintained by the University Library

Handbooks & manuals

Copyright for archivists and records managers
T. Padfield   See entry no. 5779

5467 Digital copyright
P. Pedley   2nd edn, Facet Publishing, 2007, 160pp. £34.95. ISBN 9781856046084.
'Examines how copyright applies in the electronic environment ... [and] asks whether digital content is treated differently than hard-copy material and if so how.

   The second edition, now in hard copy format only, includes a new chapter that takes an in-depth look at digital rights management, taking account of the All Party Internet Group's public inquiry findings, published in June 2006. It also offers a new section on copyright clearance for digital content; current examples of the penalties imposed for file sharing, piracy, counterfeiting; and more case law examples.'

5468 Freedom of information: a practical guide to implementing the Act
K. Smith   Facet Publishing, 2004, 186pp. £39.95. ISBN 9781856045179.
www.facetpublishing.co.uk/foi [COMPANION]
Strongly emphasizes the practical aspects of implementing the UK Freedom of Information Act 2000. Treats the issues from the point of view of the user of information resources, avoiding discussion of legal niceties where that is possible without oversimplification.

5469 Intellectual freedom manual [USA]
Office for Intellectual Freedom   7th edn, ALA Editions, 2005, 544pp. $52. ISBN 9780838935613.
www.ala.org/ala/oif/iftoolkits/ifmanual/intellectual.htm [COMPANION]
Now a core reference tool providing detailed guidance on the full gamut of complex issues within this field. The Companion website provides material that could not be published in the manual itself, as well as updating material between editions of the work.

5470 The law of libraries and archives
B.M. Carson   Scarecrow, 2007, 395pp. $65. ISBN 9780810851894.
www.wku.edu/~bryan.carson/librarylaw [COMPANION]
A valuable compendium focusing on the US environment: 'Legal concepts are explained in plain English so that librarians and archivists will be able to understand the principles that affect them on a daily basis.' Aims to equip information professionals with the knowledge and understanding to make informed choices and converse intelligently with legal specialists.

5471 Licensing digital content: a practical guide for librarians
L.E. Harris   American Library Association, 2002, 152pp. $45. ISBN 0838908152.
Introduction; Note to Canadian and other non-US readers; Quick-starter tips for a successful agreement; 1. When to license; 2. Demystifying the licensing experience; 3. Learning the lingo; 4. Key digital licensing clauses; 5. Boilerplate clauses; 6. Unintimidating negotiations; 7. Questions and answers on licensing; 8. Go license!. Appendixes: A. Section 107 of the US Copyright Act on Fair Use; B. Section 108 of the US Copyright Act on Inter-library Loan. Glossary. Resources. Index.
'Very useful for academic and public librarians or information professionals who are, or will be, licensing digital content, especially licenses that may require negotiation ... Well written and insightful' (*Portal*)

5472 Privacy in the 21st century: issues for public, school, and academic libraries
H.R. Adams [et al.]   Libraries Unlimited, 2005, 247pp. $40. ISBN 9781591582090.
Focuses on the US environment, but of value more widely. After a review of the underlying imperatives, treats privacy issues with respect to public libraries, K-12 school media centres, academic libraries. Concludes with a chapter on 'Privacy resources for educators and librarians' and a look at the future of privacy. Three useful appendices reproduce core documents in the area.

5473 Public internet access in libraries and information services
P. Sturges   Facet Publishing, 2002, 220pp. £39.95. ISBN 9781856044257.
Treats a now important aspect of library services, offering a step-by-step guide to developing an internet access policy, including guidance on controversial aspects such as surveillance and monitoring of use and software filtering and blocking. Appendices reproduce key internally developed and external documents.

5474 Staying legal: a guide to issues and practice affecting the library, information and publishing sectors
C.J. Armstrong and L.W. Bebbington, eds   2nd edn, Facet Publishing, 2003, 272pp. £49.95. ISBN 9781856044387.
Authoritative handbook, with contributions by leading experts in the field, which offers a practical guide to a wide range of legal issues. Aiming to make the law accessible, it alerts information professionals to the pitfalls surrounding such activities as publishing on the internet, direct marketing and doing business on the web.

5475 Who owns academic work?: battling for control of intellectual property
C. McSherry   Harvard University Press, 2003, 275pp. Originally published 2001, $16.95. ISBN 0674012437.
'Drawing on legal, historical and qualitative research, Corynne McSherry explores the propertization of academic work and shows how that process is shaking the foundations of the university, the professoriate and intellectual property law.'

   Introduction. 1. Building an epistemic regime; 2. An uncommon controversy; 3. "University Lectures Are Sui Generis"; 4. Metes and bounds; 5. Telling tales out of school.
'The book provokes much thought about issues that most academic scientists likely do not consider in much depth – copyright, patent and data ownership, and the "work-for-hire" exclusion of individual employee's rights in the US ... McSherry ably demonstrates that universities are going through a second revolution. Academics should be wary of what that revolution may bring.' (*New Scientist*)

Keeping up to date

5476 Deep Links: Noteworthy news from around the Internet
Electronic Frontier Foundation
www.eff.org/deeplinks
Lively comment on news items from the Foundation: 'Defending Freedom in the Digital World'.

5477 UK Freedom of Information Blog
Campaign for Freedom of Information
www.foia.blogspot.com
News and developments within the UK.

Knowledge Management

Introductions to the subject

5478 Knowledge management: an integrated approach
A. Jashapara   Financial Times Prentice Hall, 2004, 324pp. £39.99. ISBN 9780273682981.
Aims to integrate human resource, information systems and other perspectives on knowledge management. The text is organized around a KM cycle of five generic activities: discovering, generating, evaluating, sharing and leveraging knowledge. Key features include the discussion of historical perspectives, including the central function of libraries; substantial chapters on KM technologies and their configuration into KM systems; and the overview of intellectual capital frameworks. Illustrated with vignettes and case studies covering a range of organizations, numerous figures and tables. Includes glossary and index.

5479 Knowledge management: an integrative approach
M. Handzic and A.Z. Zhou   Chandos, 2005, 156pp. £35. ISBN 9781843341222.
Clear, concise introduction, which provides an effective synthesis of environmental forces driving KM and current thinking on the subject, before considering organizational enablers, the role of technology, knowledge processes and knowledge as an organizational asset. Provides good coverage of intellectual capital models, KM technologies and knowledge classification systems, with useful checklists, tables, mini case studies and end-of-chapter references.

5480 Knowledge management in organizations: a critical introduction
D. Hislop   Oxford University Press, 2005, 269pp. £28.99. ISBN 9780199262069.
Offers a critical review and analysis of key themes and debates surrounding knowledge management, drawing on examples from a wide range of organizations in the public and private sector. Topics covered include communities of practice, boundary-spanning processes, power and conflict, organizational culture, organizational learning and innovation dynamics. Final section examines knowledge sharing in network, multinational and knowledge-intensive organizations. Author has business/management school background.

5481 Perspectives on intellectual capital: multidisciplinary insights into management, measurement and reporting
B. Marr, ed.   Butterworth-Heinemann, 2005, 256pp. £44.99. ISBN 9780750677998.
Good state-of-the-art collection of articles providing a wide range of views from differing disciplines of what intellectual capital is and how it can be used, from their perspectives.

Dictionaries, thesauri, classifications

5482 KM Glossary
David Skyrme Associates, 2003.
www.skyrme.com/resource/glossary.htm
About 150 terms defined, with cross-references. Part of a Knowledge Connections portal whose content – as this glossary – has unfortunately not recently been updated.

5483 KM Terminology
European Committee for Standardization
www.cen.eu/cenorm
Part 5 of the *European guide to good practice in knowledge management* (q.v.). 'Summarises the key KM terms and concepts that users will find useful when navigating through the guide'.
  - **Knowledge management. Vocabulary: PD 7500:2003**
    British Standards Institution, 2003. £25. ISBN 058033340X. 145 terms defined: designed as a companion work to other BSI publications on knowledge management.

5484 Multilingual dictionary of knowledge management: English-German-French-Spanish-Italian
O. Vollnhals   K.G. Saur, 2001, 402pp. €120. ISBN 3598115512.
Well produced volume with 3400 entries and cross-referencing indexes between each of the languages. KM activities are divided into: Knowledge representation; Database technologies; Document management; Intelligent systems; Business applications.

Laws, standards, codes

5485 European guide to good practice in knowledge management
European Committee for Standardization   2004. CWA 14924.
www.cen.eu/cenorm
In five parts (the fifth being cited above): 1. Knowledge management framework; 2. Organizational culture; 3. Small- and medium-sized enterprise implementation; 4. Guidelines for measuring KM. All parts are downloadable as PDF files.

5486 Knowledge management: a guide to good practice
British Standards Institution   2001, 119pp. PAS 2001.
www.bsi-global.com [DESCRIPTION]
Prepared by staff from PricewaterhouseCoopers on behalf of BSI, in consultation with a panel of specialists which included strong representation from the library and information profession. The main sections are entitled: Why should organizations should care about KM? How should organizations approach KM? Benefits anticipated from investing in KM; and Moving towards a deeper understanding of KM. A detailed section-by-section contents list facilitates its use as a reference tool, and a novel feature at the front of the guide is the combined Glossary and Index of 35 key

terms. The main text provides checklists on key topics (eg topics to cover in a KM strategy, tasks and skills involved in KM roles) and annexes include diagnostic tools, references and a bibliography. Preface indicates this was intended to be the first of a series of guides, several of which have now been published (see below).

- **Guide to measurements in knowledge management** 2003. PD 7502:2003.
- **Knowledge management in the public sector: a guide to good practice** 2005. PD 7504:2005.
- **Linking knowledge management with other organizational functions and disciplines: a guide to good practice** 2005. PD 7506:2005.
- **Managing culture and knowledge: a guide to good practice** 2003. PD 7501:2003.
- **Skills for knowledge working: a guide to good practice** 2005. PD 7505:2005.

Research centres & institutes

5487 Centre for Knowledge Management [UK]
www.rgu.ac.uk/abs/centres
Launched at Robert Gordon University in Scotland in March 2000 'in response to the growing importance and development of the knowledge economy. The primary aim of the centre is to assist organizations in unlocking their untapped potential to achieve competitive advantage through the effective management of knowledge.' Among a range of activities, the Centre offers a Knowledge Management MSc, which is accredited by The Chartered Institute of Library & Information Professionals.

Associations & societies

5488 IFLA Knowledge Management Section
www.ifla.org/VII/s47/index.htm
Worth noting, although not very active between the annual meetings of IFLA. However, the Section does currently produce a useful twice-yearly Newsletter (available as PDF).
- **SLA Knowledge Management Division**
  http://units.sla.org/Division/dkm. This Special Library Association site is also worth citing, but gives access to relatively limited information.

5489 Special Interest Group on Knowledge Management
www.asis.org/SIG/sigkm
Group of the American Society for Information Science and Technology. Well designed reasonably up-to-date website provides access to good set of resources and list of activities.

Portal & task environments

5490 KMCentral
George Mason University
www.icasit.org/km/index.htm
'A dynamic central resource for practitioners and academics of all levels. The website includes materials that can be used for a general introduction to KM, overviews and links to KM technologies, emerging KM trends and best industry practices. A special section for KM Academics includes selected syllabi, recommended course textbooks and additional readings. Additionally the website highlights

books, articles, conferences, events and presentations from leading KM scholars. The website also facilitates communication and interaction between academics and practitioners through a list-serv.'

Sustained by the University's International Center for Applied Studies in Information Technology.

5491 Knowledge Management Specialist Library [UK]
National Library for Health
www.library.nhs.uk/knowledgemanagement
Very useful, wide-ranging gateway, part of the UK National Health Service's National Knowledge Service: 'The aim of this site is to provide the best available evidence and practical examples of health professionals successfully sharing and applying knowledge and experience to their daily activities. Research in this area is still in the early stages and for that reason, much of the current content has been selected from the business sector. However, the material available on the Knowledge Management Specialist Library has been chosen because the content can also be applied to the health sector.'

5492 WWW Virtual Library knowledge management
BRINT Institute.
http://brint.com/km
Extensive and rewarding gateway to data and information about KM businesses, processes, systems, technologies, etc. Registration needed for some facilities.

Handbooks & manuals

5493 Cultivating communities of practice: a guide to managing knowledge
E. Wenger, R. McDermott and W. Snyder   Harvard Business School Press, 2002, 284pp. $32.95. ISBN 1578513308.
Classic business-oriented textbook arguing that communities of practice – groups of individuals formed around common interests and expertise – provide the ideal vehicle for driving knowledge-management strategies and building lasting competitive advantage.

5494 Knowledge management: a strategic management perspective
S. Debowski   Wiley, 2005, 383pp. £30.99. ISBN 9780470805381.
Aims to present a comprehensive and practical model of KM for both students and managers in the field, drawing on diverse domains, including librarianship, IT, human resource management and business management. Organized in four parts: Knowledge influences; Knowledge foundations; Knowledge applications; and Knowledge enhancement and review. Draws on academic literature and real-world examples, including many from the public sector in Australia. A particular strength is the practical guidance offered in Part 3, which includes chapters on 'Developing a core knowledge framework', 'Developing and managing knowledge repositories' and 'Developing an effective knowledge service'. Includes glossary and index.

5495 Knowledge management: through the technology glass
M. Handzic   World Scientific, 2005, 280pp. £37. ISBN 9789812560247.
Discusses the potential and limitations of technology in knowledge management from a socio-technical perspective,

showing how both traditional and newer technologies can support the processes of knowledge creation, sharing, retention and discovery. Provides a categorization of technologies and their roles in KM, before detailed consideration of codification technologies, personalization technologies and integrated systems, supported by empirical research and case studies. Includes index.

5496   Knowledge management in theory and practice
K. Dalkir   Butterworth-Heinemann, 2005, 356pp. £31.99. ISBN 9780750678643.
Comprehensive textbook which provides an overview and synthesis of key concepts, models, tools and techniques. Key chapters cover the knowledge management cycle, KM models, knowledge capture and codification, knowledge application, the role of organizational culture, KM tools, KM strategy and metrics and the KM team. Author is based in an information and library sciences school, but offers a multidisciplinary perspective, drawing on real-world case studies, mainly from the private sector in North America. Includes an index and extensive glossary.
'... a book all managers and professionals should be given the opportunity to read. It provides much of the fundamental background for understanding KM and the food for thought to feed the discussions that need to occur in order for knowledge management initiatives to succeed and flourish.' (*ACM Interactions*)

5497   Knowledge management lessons learned: what works and what doesn't
M.E.D. Koenig and T.K. Srikantaiah, eds   ASIST/Information Today, 2003, 595pp. $44.50. ISBN 1573871818.
Contains 32 contributions from academic researchers and specialist practitioners, which are grouped into three large sections dealing respectively with strategy and implementation, content management and communities of practice, with smaller sections on organizational learning, competitive intelligence and cost analysis. A distinctive feature of the book is the 11-page 'road map' which complements the table of contents and index with a thematic overview of the contents arranged in 19 sections, allowing readers quickly to identify chapters dealing with topics of interest. Includes separate 10-page KM bibliography in addition to end-of-chapter references.

5498   Managing intellectual capital in practice
G. Roos, S. Pike and L. Fernstrom   Butterworth-Heinemann, 2006, 384pp. £19.99. ISBN 9780750679404.
Contents include What is intellectual capital and why is it important?; How to identify the organization's intellectual capital resources; Putting the intellectual capital resources to value-creating use; Valuing and measuring intellectual capital; Reporting on intellectual capital; Other applications of the intellectual capital approach.

5499   Managing knowledge: an essential reader
S. Little and T. Ray, eds   2nd edn, Sage Publications, 2005, 357pp. £24.99. ISBN 9781412912419.
Collection of 15 contributions from mainly academic authors, including many key figures in the field. Approximately half are edited versions of previously published journal articles, with the rest specially written for this volume or its previous edition. Part 1 covers key concepts, while Part 2, 'Knowing in practice', includes

several chapters with an explicit human resources focus. Includes index.

5500   Rethinking knowledge management: from knowledge objects to knowledge processes
C.R. McInerney and R.E. Day, eds   Springer, 2007, 358pp. £77. ISBN 9783540710103.
Contributed volume promoting a new area of study: knowledge processes. 'Knowledge processes go far beyond traditional information acquisition and processing by stressing the importance and creative potential of human expression, communication and learning for successful economic planning and meaningful personal and social existence.'

5501   The strategic management of intellectual capital and organizational knowledge
C.W. Choo and N. Bontis, eds   Oxford University Press, 2002, 748pp. £45. ISBN 9780195138665.
http://choo.fis.utoronto.ca/OUP [COMPANION]
A very good collection of 41 essays covering in turn: knowledge in organizations; knowledge-based perspectives of the firm; knowledge strategies; knowledge strategy in practice; knowledge creation; knowledge across boundaries; managing intellectual capital.
'An excellent overview of the range of theoretical perspectives and research undertaken to date ... One of the most useful aspects of the book is that the knowledge building blocks (or the history of intellectual capital) are described in a logical order, which helps the reader understand and interpret current thinking surrounding intellectual capital.' (*Managing Information*)

Keeping up to date

5502   SIG-KM E-mail Discussion List
Special Interest Group on Knowledge Management
www.asis.org/SIG/sigkm/ediscussion.html
E-mail list 'open to SIG-KM members and other interested parties to discuss knowledge management and related topics'.

Knowledge Organization

abstracting • authority records • book conservation • cataloguing & classification • collection development • content licensing • content management • digital libraries • digital preservation • digitization • electronic resource management • indexing • information organization • information retrieval • institutional repositories • internet searching • library acquisitions • metadata • ontologies • open access • preservation management • search engines • semantic web • subject analysis • subject headings • taxonomies • text retrieval • thesaurus construction • weblogs • website archiving • wikis

Introductions to the subject

5503   The content management handbook
M.S. White   Facet Publishing, 2005, 149pp. £44.95. ISBN 9781856045339.
www.intranetfocus.com/technology/cmhandbook.php [DESCRIPTION]
Well written text providing step-by-step guidance on the

specification, selection and implementation of content management system software for websites and intranets. The author is a leading consultant on intranet strategy, design and implementation.

5504 Information spaces: the architecture of cyberspace
R.M. Colomb Springer, 2002, 250pp. £42.50. ISBN 9781852335502.
'(A)imed at students taking information management as a minor in their course as well as those who manage document collections but who are not professional librarians.' After an introduction and an overview, the chapters cover: Describing information objects; Browsing: hypertext; world wide web; Structured documents: XML; Controlled vocabulary; Semantic dimensions; Classification in context; Large classification systems; Descriptors; Visualization; Archiving; and Quality. Each chapter concludes with: Further reading; Formative exercise; Tutorial exercises; Open discussion question.

5505 Ontologies: a silver bullet for knowledge management and electronic commerce
D. Fensel 2nd edn, Springer, 2004, 162pp. £27. ISBN 3540003029.
Introduces the notion of ontologies for the non-expert reader. Covers languages (XML, RDF) and tools and then surveys a range of applications. Appendix contains a very useful survey of the different groups of relevant standards: Ontology; Agent; Software engineering; WWW; Text, video and metadata; Electronic commerce (including web services).

5506 Organising knowledge in a global society: principles and practice in libraries and information centres
R. Harvey and P. Hider; Charles Sturt University Centre for Information Studies, 2004, 375pp. AUS$88. ISBN 1876938668.
Good, clear introduction covering all the key facets. 15 chapters in five parts: I. Overview; II. Bibliographic description; III. Subject access; IV. Bibliographic data exchange and management; V. Current issues in organizing knowledge.

5507 Organizing knowledge: an introduction to managing access to information
J.E. Rowley and R. Hartley 4th edn, Ashgate, 2008, 400pp. £25. ISBN 9780754644316.
Announced 4th edition of standard introduction to the subject (3rd edn, Gower, 2000). Contents are: Introduction. Part I. Structuring and describing: Knowledge, information and their organization; Formatting and structuring knowledge; Describing documents. Part II. Access: Users and interfaces; Subjects as access points; Classification and order; Further concepts and tools for subject access; Access through author names and titles. Part III. Systems: Knowledge organization systems; The evaluation and design of information retrieval systems; Organizing knowledge without IT; Management of knowledge systems.

Associations & societies

5508 International Society for Knowledge Organization
www.isko.org
500 members all over the world, from fields such as information science, philosophy, linguistics, computer

science, as well as special domains such as medical informatics. Useful publications.
■ **Networked Knowledge Organization Systems/Services: NKOS** http://nkos.slis.kent.edu. Group focusing on 'functional/data model for enabling knowledge organization systems such as classification systems, thesauri, gazetteers, ontologies as networked interactive information services for Internet description/retrieval of diverse information'.

Handbooks & manuals

5509 Content management bible
B. Boiko 2nd edn, Wiley, 2004, 1122pp. £26.99. ISBN 9780764573712.
A superb guide, clearly written and presented. 33 chapters in five parts: What is content?; What is content management?; Doing content management projects; The logical design of a CMS; Building a CMS. There is a companion website 'accessible only to owners of the book by entering specific facts from the book'.
■ **CMS Review** www.cmsreview.com. Links to the top CM sites in the world. Directories with descriptions of over 350 proprietary CMS, open-source CMS, and CMS services hosted at application service providers. Lists of 'CMS-Lite' products such as forums, news portals, weblogs, wikis, etc.

5510 Managing enterprise content: a unified content strategy
A. Rockley, P. Kostur and S. Manning New Riders Press, 2003, 565pp. £30.99. ISBN 9780735713062.
www.managingenterprisecontent.com [COMPANION]
Designed to provide a conceptual framework for understanding how to create and manage content that is to be repurposed for use in different media. Also aims to provide practical solutions to get a handle on content creation, repurposing, efficiency and cross-enterprise management.

5511 Ontological engineering: with examples from the areas of knowledge management, e-commerce and the semantic web
A. Gómez-Pérez, M. Fernández-López and O. Corcho Springer, 2004, 403pp. £55. ISBN 1852335513.
The title phrase refers to 'the set of activities that concern the ontology development process, the ontology life cycle, the methods and methodology for building ontologies and the tool suites and languages that support them'.

Detailed but approachable and well laid-out text covering theoretical foundations as well as practical procedures. 'We have paid special attention to the influence that ontologies have on the Semantic Web.' Each chapter ends with a well constructed 'Bibliographical notes and further reading'.

5512 The organization of information
A.G. Taylor 2nd edn, Libraries Unlimited, 2003, 417pp. $50. ISBN 9781563089695.
An excellent and impressive work. The major chapters are titled: Organization of recorded information; Retrieval tools; Development of the organization of recorded information in western civilization; Encoding standards; Systems and system design; Metadata; Metadata: description; Metadata: access and authority control; Subject analysis; Systems for vocabulary control; Systems for categorization; Arrangement and display.

'(A)n extremely well designed, structured, and articulated work, noteworthy for its clarity and usability. A fine contribution to the field of library and information science.' (*Booklist/Professional Reading*)

5513 Organizing knowledge: taxonomies, knowledge and organization effectiveness
P. Lambe   Chandos, 2007, 277pp. £39.95. ISBN 9781843342274.
Explains different forms of taxonomies (lists, trees, hierarchies, polyhierarchies, matrices, facets and system maps) and provides a readable step-by-step guide to planning and managing the development and implementation of an organizational taxonomy, drawing on case studies to show how taxonomies can help organizations to articulate and leverage their knowledge assets. Includes useful practical guidance on running a taxonomy project, but minimal coverage of the technological context and software aspects of taxonomy development.

5514 Searching for the concept, not just the word: a librarian's guide to ontologies and the semantic web
B. King and K. Reinold   Chandos, 2007, 200pp. £39.95. ISBN 9781843343189.
Explains the nature and function of ontologies and shows how concept maps can enhance users' search experiences by facilitating natural language queries and improving the effectiveness of information retrieval. Discusses software available for ontology building and likely future applications.

5515 Understanding digital libraries
M. Lesk   2nd edn, Morgan Kaufman, 2005, 424pp. £31.99. ISBN 9781558609242.
Full of useful detail over a wide canvas.

Cataloguing & Classification

Introductions to the subject

5516 Catskill
3rd edn, DocMatrix, 2003.
www.docmatrix.com.au/catskill.html
An excellent interactive multimedia product for Windows and Macintosh, designed to teach the use of Anglo-American Cataloguing Rules 2nd Edition (AACR2R) and MARC 21 coding. Available in web and CD-ROM versions.

5517 Classification made simple
E.J. Hunter   2nd edn, Ashgate, 2002, 147pp. £20. ISBN 9780754607953.
An ideal introduction for those new to the field.
'This book is a laudable contribution. The author has succeeded admirably in presenting the high science of classification in simple words and in meaningful examples. It is a valuable service to the classification discipline.' (*International Classification*)

5518 Essential cataloguing
J.H. Bowman   Facet Publishing, 2003, 216pp. £24.95. ISBN 1856044564.
Covers descriptive cataloguing and designed as a simple companion to the Anglo-American Cataloguing Rules (revised 2002 edition). Deals primarily with printed books, but includes many references to other formats. Step by step

guidance through the cataloguing process, covering description; access points; multipart works; headings for persons; headings for corporate bodies; authority control and uniform titles.

5519 Essential classification
V. Broughton   Facet Publishing, 2004, 324pp. £29.95. ISBN 9781856045148.
Clear overview of the major generic library classification schemes, with good coverage of the underlying principles supporting the differing schemes of classification: the enumerative scheme; the analytico-synthetic scheme; the faceted scheme. Especially suitable for those with no previous exposure to the field.

5520 Essential Dewey
J. Bowman   Facet Publishing, 2005, 150pp. £24.95. ISBN 9781856045193.
Engaging introduction to the most widely applied library classification scheme. Good use of examples based on real and imaginary titles.

5521 Essential thesaurus construction
V. Broughton   Facet Publishing, 2006, 296pp. £29.95. ISBN 9781856045650.
Systematic introduction to a complex arena for those unfamiliar with its details. Moves from 'What is a thesaurus?' through 'Why use a thesaurus?' to practical thesaurus construction and maintenance.

5522 Handbook of indexing techniques: a guide for beginning indexers
L.K. Fetters   3rd edn, FimCo Books, 2001, 128pp. $20. ISBN 9780929599052.
www.fettersinfo.com [DESCRIPTION]
Commendably concise volume, ideal for people who are new to indexing.

5523 MARC21 for everyone: a practical guide
D.A. Fritz and R.J. Fritz   ALA Editions, 2003, 240pp. $52. ISBN 9780838908426.
Good introduction for those new to MARC21: 'Packed with self-assessment tools, including quizzes, helpful tables and many examples of tags and subfields, this authoritative manual presents clear and practical guidance to get you up to speed and ready to apply MARC 21 to your catalog records'

5524 Metadata fundamentals for all librarians
P. Caplan   ALA Editions, 2003, 192pp. $48. ISBN 9780838908471.
First-rate work, with detailed coverage of fundamentals and linking more general use of 'metadata' to its use in library catalogues. These chapters are followed by discussion of specific metadata schemas – such as Dublin Core and EAD – ending with discussions of application of metadata systems in specific subject fields.
'This is an excellent introduction to metadata, with good examples, timely bibliographies of sources, and a very useful glossary of terms and acronyms.' (*Journal of Academic Librarianship*)

Laws, standards, codes

5525   Anglo-American cataloguing rules
Joint Steering Committee for Revision of AACR   2nd edn,
ALA/CLA/CILIP, 2005. Looseleaf text, £55. ISBN 1856045714.
www.aacr2.org [COMPANION]
'Since 1967, *Anglo-American Cataloguing Rules* has served
the profession with highly developed content standards for
cataloging the resources that come into your library. It is the
one-stop gold standard. AACR2 walks you through the
cataloging process with clearly defined rules and practical
examples representing standards that apply to any type of
resource and all metadata formats.'

     Published jointly by the American Library Association, the
Canadian Library Association and the Chartered Institute of
Library and Information Professionals. The website also gives
details of a *Concise AACR2* and a volume concentrating on
Cartographic materials.

**5526   Cataloguing distribution service: bibliographic
products and services**
Library of Congress
www.loc.gov/cds
Gateway giving access to details of the range of products
and services offered by the Library based on the Library of
Congress Classification and the Library of Congress Subject
Headings.
◼ **Metadata encoding and transmission standard: METS**
Library of Congress and Digital Library Federation.
www.loc.gov/standards/mets. 'The METS schema is a standard for encoding
descriptive, administrative, and structural metadata regarding objects
within a digital library, expressed using the XML schema language of the
World Wide Web Consortium'.
◼ **MARC standards Library of Congress**. www.loc.gov/marc. Products
and services based on the MARC formats, which are standards for the
representation and communication of bibliographic and related information
in machine-readable form.

5527   Dewey decimal classification and relative index
M. Dewey [et al.]   22nd edn, OCLC, 2003. 4 v., $375. ISBN
0910608709.
www.oclc.org/dewey [COMPANION]
The world's most widely used library classification system.
Website gives details of WebDewey, which 'enhances the
print updates with online delivery that is updated
continuously'; also of the *Abridged Dewey*.
◼ **Universal Decimal Classification** www.udcc.org. Detailed
classification scheme still being developed under the auspices of a UDC
Consortium but now not used widely in libraries. Nevertheless, the
publication by I.C. McIlwaine *The Universal Decimal Classification: a guide
to its use* (revised edn 2007) is of more general value.

5528   Dublin Core Metadata Initiative
http://dublincore.org
Mission is 'to make it easier to find resources using the
internet through the following activities: Developing metadata
standards for discovery across domains; Defining frameworks
for the interoperation of metadata sets; Facilitating the
development of community- or disciplinary-specific metadata
sets that are consistent with items 1 and 2.' The Initiative
created the Dublin Core metadata element set, a standard
for cross-domain information resource description where an
information resource is defined to be 'anything that has
identity'.

There is a helpful document 'Using Dublin Core',
accessible via the website.
◼ **The Dublin Core metadata element set**
http://dublincore.org/documents/dces. Description of the vocabulary of
fifteen properties for use in resource description. See also the international
standard ISO 15836:2003(E) at: ww.niso.org/international/SC4/n515.pdf :
'The simplicity of Dublin Core can be both a strength and a weakness.
Simplicity lowers the cost of creating metadata and promotes
interoperability (but it) does not accommodate the semantic and functional
richness supported by complex metadata schemes ...'.

5529   Encoded archival description (EAD)
Library of Congress and Society of American Archivists
www.loc.gov/ead
The XML markup language designed for encoding finding
aids – especially within an archival environment.

5530   Guidelines for authority records and references
IFLA Working Group on GARE Revision   K.G. Saur, 2001, 46pp. €34.
ISBN 3598115040.
www.ifla.org/VII/s13/garr/garr.pdf
Short, but very helpful document, recognizing on the one
hand that: ' ... "the IFLA goal of Universal Bibliographic
Control by way of requiring everyone to use the same form
for headings globally is not practical and is no longer
necessary". Such a statement was based on the fact that
"there are reasons to use the form of names familiar to our
end-users, in scripts they can read and in forms they most
likely would look for in their library catalogue or national
bibliography". But on the other hand that: "The new
principle, intended to preserve differences in authorized
forms for headings, must now coexist with the other one
related to uniformity of access, which is still one of the
catalogue's basic requirements in local or regional
environments."'

5531   Sears list of subject headings
19th edn, H.W. Wilson, 2007, 872pp. $145. ISBN 9780824210762.
www.hwwilson.com/print/searslst_19th.cfm [DESCRIPTION]
The classic list, especially designed for use in small and
medium-sized libraries. A 23-page document 'Principles of
the Sears list' states its theoretical foundations and offers an
introduction to subject cataloging in general.

Official & quasi-official bodies

5532   National Information Standards Organization
www.niso.org
Non-profit association accredited by the American National
Standards Institute (q.v.), which 'identifies, develops,
maintains and publishes technical standards to manage
information in our changing and ever-more digital
environment. NISO standards apply both traditional and new
technologies to the full range of information-related needs,
including retrieval, re-purposing, storage, metadata and
preservation.'

     The well designed website provides a Standards Quicklist
(all the standard numbers having the prefix ANSI/NISO Z39)
as well as information on standards in development, on trial,
at ballot, etc.; a section on NISO Initiatives (exchanging
serials information; thesauri; metasearch; ISBN); and access
to various white and briefing papers.

Associations & societies

5533 American Society of Indexers
www.asindexing.org
'(T)he only professional organization in the United States devoted solely to the advancement of indexing, abstracting and database building.' Useful guide to the notion of indexing; extensive A–Z index links to internal and external resources. Some parts of the site not recently updated.
- ■ **Indexer Locator** www.asindexing.org/custom/locator. Tool to help find an indexer.

5534 IFLA Cataloguing Section
www.ifla.org/VII/s13/index.htm
Active international group which 'proposes and develops cataloguing rules, guidelines and standards for bibliographic information taking into account the developing electronic and networked environment in order to promote universal access to and exchange of bibliographic and authority information'. It has responsibility within IFLA for the various types of International Standard Bibliographic Description, the influential *Functional Requirements for Bibliographic Records* and various other standards and documents in the field of bibliographic control.
- ■ **IFLA-CDNL Alliance for Bibliographic Standards** www.ifla.org/VI/7/icabs.htm. The National Library of Australia, the Library of Congress, the British Library, the Koninklijke Bibliotheek, and Die Deutsche Bibliothek have agreed to participate in a joint alliance together with the Biblioteca Nacional de Portugal, IFLA and CDNL to assure ongoing coordination, communication and support for key activities in the areas of bibliographic and resource control for all types of resources and related format and protocol standards'. Alliance formed 2004; action recently seems limited.

5535 IFLA Classification & Indexing Section
www.ifla.org/VII/s29/index.htm
'(F)ocuses on methods of providing subject access in catalogues, bibliographies and indexes to documents of all kinds, including electronic documents. The Section serves as a forum for producers and users of classification and subject indexing tools and it works to facilitate international exchange of information about methods of providing subject access.'

5536 Society of Indexers [UK]
www.indexers.org.uk
'The Society exists to promote indexing, the quality of indexes and the profession of indexing.' Clearly laid-out website; good resource section.
- ■ **Indexers Available** www.indexers.org.uk/InAvail/index.htm. Service for finding an indexer.

Discovering print & electronic resources

5537 Subject Analysis Systems Collection
www.fis.utoronto.ca/content/view/386/134
North American clearing house for subject classifications and controlled vocabularies in many different subject areas.

Handbooks & manuals

5538 Cataloging and organizing digital resources: a how-to-do-it manual for librarians
A.M. Mitchell and B.E. Surratt   Neal-Schuman, 2005, 219pp. $75. ISBN 1555705219.
First-rate handbook: particularly useful for its detailed description of MARC21-based processes, with both long and short examples.
'An impressive book ... It is difficult to think of what could have been overlooked in this useful volume ... It should be read by library directors, heads of technical services, catalogers, metadata librarians, and students. The professional bookshelves of every catalog department in every library currently buying or planning to buy electronic resources should contain a copy.' (*Technicalities*)

5539 Cataloging with AACR2 and MARC21: for books, electronic resources, sound recordings, videorecordings, and serials
D.A. Fritz, ed.   2nd edn updated, ALA Editions, 2006, 688pp. Binder-ready looseleaf pages, $68. ISBN 9780838909355.
Regularly updated text: e.g. 'The 2006 Cumulation brings the second edition up-to-date with the inclusion of the 2004, 2005 and 2006 updates'. Provides cross-references between the AACR2 and MARC21 standards in a clear, user-friendly fashion.

5540 Dewey decimal classification, 22nd edition: a study manual and number building guide
M.L. Scott   Libraries Unlimited, 2005, 348pp. $75. ISBN 9781591582106.
The new edition of DDC was published August 2003. This detailed study manual can be used as a reference for the application of Dewey, but is also suitable as a course text in Dewey.

5541 Indexing: the manual of good practice
P.F. Booth   K.G. Saur, 2001, 489pp. €110. ISBN 9783598115363.
Comprehensive manual covering the indexing of all types of media: books, serials, images and audio materials; electronic.

5542 Indexing and abstracting in theory and practice
F.W. Lancaster   3rd edn, Facet Publishing, 2003, 451pp. £39.95. ISBN 9781856044820.
Award-winning text, now with much wider applicability than when first published. Thorough coverage of indexing and abstracting in the digital environment. A model text.

5543 Indexing books
N.C. Mulvany   2nd edn, University of Chicago Press, 2005, 315pp. $45. ISBN 9780226552767.
The classic indexing text, radically updated: 'New to this edition are discussions of "information overload" and the role of the index, open-system versus closed-system indexing, electronic submission and display of indexes and trends in software development, among other topics.'

5544 Introduction to cataloguing and classification
A.G. Taylor   10th edn, Libraries Unlimited, 2006, 608pp. $50. ISBN 9781591582359.
A classic US-based text, with major revisions for this latest edition: 'The 10th edition incorporates the 2002 Anglo-American Cataloguing Rules, Second Edition (AACR2), MARC

21, the 22nd edition of Dewey Decimal Classification, current schedules of the LC Classifications, the latest Library of Congress Subject Headings and the 18th edition of the Sears List of Subject Headings. In addition, Taylor addresses such vital issues as FRBR (Functional Requirements for Bibliographic Records), FAST (Faceted Application of Subject Terminology) and the Semantic Web. The bibliography and glossary have also been substantially reworked. In fact, only the appendix, which covers arrangement dilemmas and filing rules, remains unchanged.'

5545   Library of Congress subject headings: principles and applications
L.M. Chan   4th edn, Libraries Unlimited, 2005, 549pp. $55. ISBN 9781591581567.
Well established, comprehensive guide. There is a good introduction to the scheme and its principles, followed by systematic coverage of the use of the scheme's tables. The latest edition has been revised to highlight the relevance of LCSH in the global electronic environment, including the use of FAST: Faceted Application of Subject Terminology.

5546   Manual of archival description
M. Proctor and M. Cook   3rd edn, Gower, 2000, 300pp. £50. ISBN 9780566082580.
Authoritative guide with excellent discussion of principles followed by detailed coverage of all types of material now likely to find their way into archival collections.

5547   Maxwell's guide to authority work
R.L. Maxwell   ALA Editions, 2002, 275pp. $55. ISBN 9780838908228.
www.alastore.ala.org [DESCRIPTION]
'Authority work is the linchpin of the library catalog. As the author puts it, "Without authority control, the burden is placed on the user to think of all the possible forms a cataloger might have used to give access in the catalog to a given author or subject." If a subject is not sorted by its authorized heading, then the library and its users and staff are left without a system and ultimately the cost of an unsatisfied user. From one of the preeminent experts in the field, this is the step-by-step guide for ensuring that your library and staff are creating and maintaining authority records with the end user in mind. Comprehensive and definitive, *Maxwell's Guide to Authority Work* is a must-have.'
■ **Maxwell's handbook for AACR2: explaining and illustrating the Anglo-American cataloguing rules through the 2003 update** R.L. Maxwell   4th edn, ALA Editions, 2004, 519pp. $68. ISBN 9780838908754. Now the standard guide. Systematic coverage of all the schedules with invariably helpful annotations.

5548   Thesaurus construction and use: a practical manual
J. Aitchison, A. Gilchrist and D. Bawden   4th edn, Europa, 2000.
An excellent work: clearly written and laid out. Coverage includes vocabulary control; specificity and compound terms; structure and relationships; auxiliary retrieval devices; thesaurus display; etc. Extensive bibliography.

Collection Development & Information Resource Management

Introductions to the subject

5549   Archiving websites: a practical guide for information management professionals
A. Brown   Facet Publishing, 2006, 238pp. £39.95. ISBN 9781856045537.
A now very important and difficult area which is well introduced in this text. The author has managed the archiving programme for the UK National Archives. Covers all aspects from the development of policy to delivery of archived content to users and includes good coverage of the key technical aspects.

5550   Building an electronic resource collection: a practical guide
S.L. Lee and F. Boyle   2nd edn, Facet Publishing, 2004, 174pp. £34.95. ISBN 9781856045315.
A good, helpful introduction. Five chapters: 1. Preliminary issues; 2. What is on offer? The electronic resources landscape; 3. E-books and e-journals; 4. What to buy? Assessing and acquiring the dataset; 5. Delivering the dataset. Glossary and select bibliography.

5551   Collection management: a concise introduction
J. Kennedy; Charles Sturt University   Centre for Information Studies, 2006, 144pp. AUS$66. ISBN 1876938137.
Good overview. Chapters are: 1. The changing collection management environment; 2. Formulating policy – the written collection development policy and alternative approaches; 3. Selection of hard copy and digital materials; 4. Acquisitions and licensing; 5. Evaluating the hard copy and digital collection; 6. Preservation and deselection; 7. Cooperation in collection management; 8. The future of collection management.

5552   Content licensing: buying and selling digital resources
M. Upshall   Chandos, 2007, 200pp. £39.95. ISBN 9781843343332.
Offers a wide-ranging guide to this key area of information resource management, examining licensing in different contexts from several perspectives. Covers books, journals and databases, supplied via aggregators and others. Reviews different models of licensing, methods of locating and retrieving content, technical and legal aspects and the implications for libraries.

5553   Digital libraries: policy, planning and practice
J. Andrews and D. Law, eds   Ashgate, 2004, 263pp. £52.50. ISBN 0754634485.
Provides a state-of-the-art review by international experts of digital library thinking and practice, drawing on UK and US national and institutional programmes and projects as case studies. Key areas covered include costs and funding, content and services, preservation and evaluation. The volume concludes with a forward look, highlighting technical concerns, such as interoperability and user interfaces and the role of digital libraries in learning. Includes and extensive bibliography and detailed index.

5554 Escholarship: a LITA guide
D. Shapiro, ed.; Library & Information Technology Association
2005, 79pp. $32. ISBN 0838983480.
Useful collection of essays about the ongoing efforts to create and support e-scholarship within the academy.

5555 The film preservation guide: the basics for archives, libraries, and museums
National Film Preservation Foundation   2004, 121pp. ISBN 0974709905.
www.filmpreservation.org/preservation/film_guide.html
Excellent publication, also accessible online as a full-text PDF. '(It) describes methods for handling, duplicating, making available and storing film that are practical for nonprofit and public organizations with limited resources. It traces the path of film through the preservation process and includes case studies, illustrations, charts, glossary, bibliography, vendor lists and index.'

5556 Introduction to digital libraries
G.G. Chowdhury and S. Chowdhury   Facet Publishing, 2003, 359pp. £34.95. ISBN 9781856044653.
Gives a good survey of the field – albeit with the details now somewhat dated. Key topics covered include digital libraries: definition and characteristics; features of some digital libraries; digital library design; digital library research; collection management; digitization; information organization; information access and user interface; information retrieval in digital libraries; digital archiving and preservation; digital library services; social, economic and legal issues; digital library evaluation; digital libraries and the information profession; trends in digital library research and development.

5557 Managing acquisitions in library and information services
L. Chapman   3rd edn, Facet Publishing, 2004, 150pp. £32.95. ISBN 1856044963.
Now the definitive text on procedures and practice in acquisitions. Covers the following aspects: pre-order checking; publishers and publishing; beyond the basic book; suppliers; ordering; out-of-the-ordinary ordering; when the orders arrive; budgets and finance; the way ahead.

5558 Managing preservation for libraries and archives: current practice and future developments
J. Feather, ed.   Ashgate, 2004, 181pp. £55. ISBN 9780754607052.
A good introduction to the field with detailed coverage of digital materials but also treating paper and sound recordings.

5559 Negotiating licences for digital resources
F. Durrant   Facet Publishing, 2006, 149pp. £39.95. ISBN 9781856045865.
Good introductory work, clearly written. Especially useful for its coverage of the skills and techniques of negotiation, whether in written or face-to-face scenarios.

5560 Open access: key strategic, technical and economic aspects
N. Jacobs, ed.   Chandos, 2006, 243pp. £39.95. ISBN 9781843342038.
www.eprints.org/community/blog/index.php?/archives/93-Open-Access-Key-Strategic-Technical-and-Economic-Aspects.html
[COMPANION]

This groundbreaking volume on the important concept of open access contains 20 contributions, representing different perspectives from leading thinkers, researchers and activists in the field, including Charles Bailey, Fred Friend, Jean-Claude Guedon, Stevan Harnad, Cliff Lynch, Andrew Odlyzko, Arthur Sale, Colin Steele, Peter Suber and Alma Swan. Almost all the chapters are (appropriately) available to download free of charge from the e-prints server at the University of Southampton.

5561 Preservation management for libraries, archives and museums
G.E. Gorman and S.J. Shep, eds   Facet Publishing, 2006, 206pp. £44.95. ISBN 9781856045742.
'Memory Institutions such as libraries, archives, galleries and museums all share concerns about preserving heritage, both material and documentary cultural artefacts in collections and new digitally-born material. The management of a wide range of traditional and new media formats creates a challenging environment for institutions. This new state-of-the-art collection offers guidance from a range of international experts on preservation methods for the sustainability of collections.'

5562 The preservation program blueprint
B.B. Higginbotham and J.W. Wild   ALA Editions, 2001, 151pp. $42. ISBN 9780838908020.
Argues that decentralizing preservation activities and integrating them into ongoing library functions will help preserve materials more effectively, efficiently and with buy-in from staff. Includes extensive resource guide and bibliography.
'This book serves as a reminder that collections are as central to a library as existence, mission, and purpose. Highly recommended for small to middle-sized libraries that sense a need for increased stewardship of their collections.' (*Library Journal*)

5563 Preserving digital materials
R. Harvey   K.G. Saur, 2005, 246pp. €98. ISBN 9783598116865.
Straightforward introduction covering principles, strategies and practices currently applied by librarians and record keepers. Includes a number of helpful case studies.

5564 Weblogs and libraries
L.A. Clyde   Chandos, 2004, 181pp. £39. ISBN 9781843340850.
Explains the origins and nature of blogs and blogging, their value as information resources and how to find them, before concentrating on their use in the library context. Reports findings of research on library applications and provides guidance on creating and managing library weblogs, with useful discussion of the many tools and hosting services available. Includes many practical hints and tips, references and links to additional sources of information.
'... this book provides a very useful introduction to weblogs and blogging both within the context of their use in libraries and for more general use.' (*The Electronic Library*)

5565 Wikis: tools for information work and collaboration
J. Klobas [et al.]   Chandos, 2006, 229pp. £39.95. ISBN 9781843341789.
Authored by an international team of writers, this book provides a comprehensive readable overview of wikis as information resources, with useful pointers to additional sources of material on the subject. Outlines the history,

development and uses of wikis and explains specialist terms before dealing with particular aspects, including finding and browsing tools; applications within ILS, business and education; technical options for developing and hosting wikis; and management issues relating to their implementation.

'... this book makes a valuable contribution to the field of groupware and collaborative knowledge construction ... contains lots of valuable tips and advice and provides a wealth of useful information.' (*The Electronic Library*)

Dictionaries, thesauri, classifications

5566 Bookbinding and the conservation of books: a dictionary of descriptive terminology
M.T. Roberts and D. Etherington   Stanford University Libraries, 1994. Scanned from 1982 edn with minor corrections.
http://palimpsest.stanford.edu/don/don.html
Online version of work now dated but still of considerable value – especially for those not professionally involved with bookbinding.

5567 Preservation and access technology: the relationship between digital and other media conversion processes: a structured glossary of technical terms
M.S. Lynn; Commission on Preservation & Access   1990.
www.clir.org/pubs/reports/lynn/index.html
'This document is offered as a *structured* glossary of terms associated with the technologies of document preservation, with particular emphasis on document media conversion technologies (often called "reformatting technologies") and even more particularly on the use of digital computer technologies. The Glossary also considers technologies associated with access to such preserved documents. Such a glossary is intended for communication among people of different professional backgrounds, especially since in recent years there has been a proliferation of such technologies and associated technical terms, technologies and terms that cut across many disciplines.'

Laws, standards, codes

5568 Recommendations for the storage and exhibition of archival documents: BS5454:2000
British Standards Institution   2000.
www.bsi-global.com/en/Standards-and-Publications [DESCRIPTION]
The recommendations mainly concern traditional materials, i.e. paper and parchment, but some guidance on more modern media is also given.

Official & quasi-official bodies

5569 European Commission on Preservation & Access
www.knaw.nl/ecpa
Independent body, based in the Netherlands and primarily funded by institutional subscriptions from European national archives and libraries. Notable here for its Gateway for Resources and Information on Preservation (GRIP) – which is 'a fully searchable database of information on preservation of the documentary heritage. It contains selected and annotated references to literature on preservation-related

topics, links to websites, projects, organizations and discussion groups'.

However, there is much else of value accessible via the site – e.g. the Preservation Map, which 'offers information on current preservation and conservation practice and policies in each European country'. There is also a useful news and events service.

Research centres & institutes

5570 Digital Curation Centre [UK]
www.dcc.ac.uk
'The purpose of our centre is to provide a national focus for research and development into curation issues and to promote expertise and good practice, both national and international, for the management of all research outputs in digital format.'

Well designed, rich website. Access to good range of briefing papers, technology watch papers, tools, standards and so on. There is also a very useful FAQ section covering questions from data creators, data curators and data re-users, as well as issues relating to freedom of information legislation and open source software and standards.

Library & Information Statistics Unit
See entry no. 5354

5571 National Preservation Office [UK]
www.bl.uk/services/npo/npo.html
Financed primarily by national archives and libraries within the UK and Ireland and located within the British Library, the Office 'provides an independent focus for the preservation of and continuing accessibility to library and archive materials held in the United Kingdom and Ireland'.
■ **Basic preservation guidelines for library and archive collections** A. Walker   2003. www.bl.uk/services/npo/pdf/basic.pdf. One of a range of useful guides produced by the Office: part of their Preservation in Practice series.

Associations & societies

5572 Digital Library Federation [USA]
www.diglib.org
A 'consortium of libraries and related agencies that are pioneering the use of electronic-information technologies to extend collections and services'. Within the structure 'Collect – Produce – Preserve – Use – Build' the attractive website provides access to a stimulating range of useful resources: an excellent place to start exploration of current work in this arena.

5573 Digital Preservation Coalition [UK]
www.dpconline.org
'The aim of the Digital Preservation Coalition is to secure the preservation of digital resources in the UK and to work with others internationally to secure our global digital memory and knowledge base.' Some useful sets of resources; but activity in recent years seems to have become less than earlier. However, worth noting is the Digital Preservation Discussion List, which – at the time of sampling – had 1109 subscribers and the excellent Handbook *Preservation management of digital materials*.

5574   IFLA Preservation & Conservation Section
www.ifla.org/VII/s19/index.htm
Rather inactive in recent years, compared to other IFLA Sections. But a useful pointer to international work in the field – including to that of the IFLA Core Activity on Preservation and Conservation.

■ **First, do no harm: a register of standards, codes of practice, guidelines, recommendations and similar works relating to preservation and conservation in libraries and archives** J. McIlwaine, comp.   2005, 79pp. Excellent inventory. The Section is planning to keep it up to date.

Portal & task environments

5575   Collections Link [UK]
MDA, Institute of Conservation and National Preservation Office
www.collectionslink.org.uk
'(A) collaboration of more than 20 national professional groups, bodies and associations who are responsible for providing advice and support to museums, archives, libraries and other collections-holding organizations. The aim of the service is to provide a single point of access to best practice in the care and management of collections.'

Is an active and lively service located within MDA and funded by the Museums, Libraries & Archives Council (q.v.): 'Although MDA is a museum-sector body and some of the resources make explicit reference to museums, the service has been designed and developed in conjunction with leading organizations across libraries and archives. Every effort has been made to provide resources that are equally applicable across all 3 domains and, indeed, any other context in which collections management is an issue – as it is for Local History Societies, cathedrals and private collectors.'

There are four main elements to the service: an online library of best practice guides and factsheets; a telephone and e-mail advisory service; a national database of training and skills development opportunities; and a commissioning fund to support the development of new resources.

■ **Benchmarks in collection care for museums, libraries and archives Museums, Libraries & Archives Council**.
www.collectionslink.org.uk/collections_care/benchmarks. '(A) self-assessment checklist to help you identify how well you are caring for your collections, give an indication of where and what improvements might be needed, and provide a practical framework for measuring future progress.' One of a range of valuable guides accessible under the rubric Care for my Collection.

5576   Conservation OnLine [USA]
Stanford University: Libraries
http://palimpsest.stanford.edu
Project of the University's Preservation Department: principally a full-text library of conservation information, but including also a service for 'Finding People' in the conservation and allied professions, as well as an extensive links list of 'Conservation resources at other sites'. Not the easiest site to navigate, but worth persistence.

Digital data, image & text collections

5577   US periodicals price index
B. Dingley   ALTCS (Association for Library Collections & Technical Services), annual.
www.ala.org/ala/alctscontent/serialssection/indexes/uspriceindex.htm

'Measure[s] changes in average US periodical prices in a historical context. The information provided here is of use to librarians who must prepare annual budget requests for serials, as well as those involved in analyzing serials pricing trends over a period of years.'

Handbooks & manuals

Building digital archives, descriptions and displays: a how-to-do-it manual for librarians and archivists
F.J. Stielow   See entry no. 5778

5578   Collection management for school libraries
J. McGregor, K. Dillon and J. Henri, eds   Scarecrow, 2003, 372pp. $54.50. ISBN 9780810844889.
Comprehensive treatment, with an Australian focus and organized: The information landscape; Introduction to collection management; Analyzing the environment; Policies for collection management; Selection and acquisition; Maintaining collection viability.

5579   Digitizing collections: strategic issues for the information manager
L.M. Hughes   Facet Publishing, 2004, 327pp. £39.95. ISBN 1856044661.
Valuable manual with ten chapters logically structured into two parts:
   Part I. Strategic decision making: Why digitize? The costs and benefits of digitization; Selecting materials for digitization; Intellectual property, copyright and other legal issues; Project management and the institutional framework; The importance of collaboration;
   Part II. Digitizing collections: Project planning and funding; Managing a digitization project; Digitization of rare and fragile materials; Digitization of audio and moving image collections; Digitization of text and images.

5580   E-journals: a how-to-do-it-manual for building, managing, and supporting electronic journal collections
D. Curtis   Neal-Schuman, 2004, 421pp. $75. ISBN 1555704654.
Extensive manual, organized as follows: Understanding electronic journals; Understanding users of online resources; Shifting library resources; Developing a collection of electronic journals; Trafficking in intellectual property: licensing and user authentication (an especially useful chapter); Ordering and receiving electronic journals; Delivering electronic journals and maintaining access channels; Supporting users and fostering the use of electronic journals; Analyzing electronic journal usage and evaluating services. Good set of appendices on records keeping.
'Excellent and well-written ... This book is a reliable source for all librarians to build, manage, and support electronic journal collections because it includes sound advice for libraries interested in starting the electronic journal collection and excellent tips for those libraries who have a good working collection but are facing problems.' (*American Reference Books Annual*)

5581 Fundamentals of collection development and management
P. Johnson   ALA Editions, 2004, 342pp. $62. ISBN 9780838908532.
Comprehensive guide offering a step-by-step approach to collection development and management. Draws on the latest research, with advice on allocating budgets, determining purchases, marketing collections, integrating digital and traditional resources and finding partners for cooperative collection development.

5582 Guide to licensing and acquiring electronic information
S. Bosch, P.A. Promis and C. Sugnet   Scarecrow, 2005, 120pp. $42. ISBN 9780810852594.
'This guide provides direction and suggestions for the selection, acquisition and licensing of electronic materials for libraries. The steps involved in the process of purchasing most of the existing electronic formats presently available are clearly delineated. Issues from policy concerns, through access and ownership, to licensing and the role of consortia are all covered.'

5583 Handbook on the international exchange of publications
K. Ekonen, P. Paloposki and P. Vattulainen, eds   5th edn, K.G. Saur, 2006, 158pp. €54. ISBN 9783598440182.
Treats the still-important processes involved in international exchange, within the context of the major technological and socio-economic changes that have taken place since the previous 1978 edn of this book.

How to build a digital library
I.H. Witten and D. Bainbridge   See entry no. 5743

5584 The institutional repository
R. Jones, T. Andrew and J. MacColl   Chandos, 2006, 247pp. £39.95. ISBN 9781843341383.
Discusses the concept of the institutional repository and provides commendably clear guidance on how they can be established, maintained and embedded into institutional practice. Considers technical, legal and administrative issues associated with capturing and storing material, with particular reference to the authors' experience with e-prints and e-theses. Clear diagrams and tables enhance the text, which is supplemented by appendices describing six major open source repository software platforms, contributed by their developers or user communities.
'... the seminal monograph on the topic.' (*Ariadne*)

5585 The Kovacs guide to electronic library collection development: essential core subject collections, selection criteria, and guidelines
D.L. Kovacs and K.L. Robinson   Neal-Schuman, 2004, 251pp. $125. ISBN 1555704832.
Comprehensive text. Consists of short sections covering both the principles of collection selection and management as well as providing lists of recommended core texts (as at 2003–4). The subject areas dealt with are characterized as: ready-reference; business; jobs and employment; medical; legal; biological sciences; physical sciences, engineering, computer sciences, technology; social sciences and education.
'Kovacs has provided a unique 'one stop' publication with everything you need to know about building an e-library.' (*Reference & User Services Quarterly*)

5586 Library web sites: creating online collections and services
A.P. Wilson   ALA Editions, 2004, 146pp. $38. ISBN 9780838908723. www.webliography.org/links.htm [COMPANION]
Good step-by-step text from expert in the field. Includes guidance on how to: manage content using database-backed web pages; brand the library's marketing and promote services online; integrate external content – licensed databases, library catalog and e-books – on to the site; conduct readers' advisory services online; keep the site fresh and updated using the editorial calendar tool; archive online resources.

5587 An ounce of prevention: integrated disaster planning for archives, libraries, and record centres
J. Wellheiser and J. Scott; Canadian Archives Foundation
Scarecrow Press, 2002, 288pp. $35. ISBN 9780810841765.
Good systematic work, organized into Disaster planning; The disaster plan; Disaster prevention planning; Disaster protection planning; Disaster preparedness planning; Disaster response planning; Disaster recovery planning for collections and records; Disaster rehabilitation planning for collections and records; Disaster recovery and rehabilitation planning for facilities and systems; Post-disaster planning.

5588 Preservation management of digital materials: the handbook
N. Beagrie and M. Jones, comps; Digital Preservation Coalition www.dpconline.org/graphics/handbook
Originally published in 2001, but now maintained online by the Coalition collaboration with the National Library of Australia and the PADI Gateway. There are (somewhat limited) navigation facilities though the wealth of content; but there is a helpful 'Change History'.

5589 Preserving archives
H. Forde   Facet Publishing, 2006, 320pp. £39.95. ISBN 9781856045773.
A major handbook written by the Head of Preservation Services at the UK National Archives. The key topics covered are: standards and policies of archive preservation; preservation assessment; understanding archive materials and their characteristics; managing digital preservation; archive buildings and their characteristics; managing archival storage; managing risks and avoiding disaster; setting up a conservation workshop; moving the records; exhibiting archives; handling the records; managing a pest control programme; using and creating surrogates; putting preservation into practice.

5590 Reference collection development: a manual
A.J. Perez, ed.; Reference & User Services Association   2nd edn, 2004, 80pp. $27. ISBN 0838982778.
'The manual is intended to serve as a guide for producing collection development policies for reference collections serving adults in academic and public libraries. The manual includes a checklist for writing a reference collection development policy; a model policy in outline, with illustrative examples; and a bibliography. By providing examples of existing policies from both academic and public libraries, the manual provides a unified procedure for developing a policy.'

5591 Selecting and managing electronic resources: a how-to-do-it manual for librarians
V.L. Gregory   rev. edn, Neal-Schuman, 2006, 139pp. $65. ISBN 1555705480.

Very good, short, concentrated text. Eight chapters: Collection development policies; Selection criteria and the selection process; Budgeting and acquisitions; Organization and access to electronic resources (by Ardis Hanson); Evaluation and assessment; Digital rights management and intellectual property; Preservation issues; The future of selecting and managing electronic resources.

5592 Weeding library collections: library weeding methods
S.J. Slote   4th edn, Libraries Unlimited, 1997, 240pp. $75. ISBN 9781563085116.

A classic text from one of the gurus of the field. Thorough coverage of this often neglected – but in reality often quite complex – arena.

'Slote leaves behind a magnificent testimonial to professional practice ... No library or librarian hoping to maintain a collection that is responsive to user needs and wants should be without a copy of this edition.' (*Library Acquisitions: Practice and Theory*)

Information Retrieval

Introductions to the subject

5593 A guide to finding quality information on the internet: selection and evaluation strategies
A. Cooke   2nd edn, Library Association Publishing, 2001, 216pp. £39.95. ISBN 9781856043793.

Although now seriously in need of updating, still a valuable resource for its sound underlying principles: 'Uniquely, it suggests a system of criteria and guidelines, developed through empirical research, for selecting and evaluating high-quality information resources. It also advises on devising checklists and rating schemes for numerically evaluating the quality of information.'

Associations & societies

5594 Special Interest Group on Information Retrieval
www.acm.org/sigs/sigir

SIGIR focuses on all aspects of information storage, retrieval and dissemination, including research strategies, output schemes and system evaluations. Holds four conferences annually, including a prestigious international conference on research and development in the field, in addition to conferences on Digital Libraries (with IEEE), Information and Knowledge Management, and Web Services and Data Mining. The *SIGIR Forum* consists of two freely available newsletter issues (June, December), which include short technical papers, book reviews and general information and a special issue containing the SIGIR conference proceedings, mailed to all members.

Handbooks & manuals

5595 The advanced internet searcher's handbook
P. Bradley   3rd edn, Facet Publishing, 2004, 272pp. £39.95. ISBN 1856045234.

Organized into three main parts, dealing respectively with mining the internet for information, becoming an expert searcher and the future. The latest edition of this highly regarded text includes detailed exploration of Google and AlltheWeb, in addition to new chapters on important areas such as searching the 'invisible web', weblogs and resource- or site-specific search engines. Includes numerous hints and tips throughout the text, pointers to additional useful resources and appendices offering helpful practical, technical guidance.

'... an invaluable guide to searching on the internet, whether it is read from cover to cover or merely dipped into when needed.' (*The Electronic Library*)

5596 The extreme searcher's internet handbook: a guide for the serious searcher
R. Hock   2nd edn, CyberAge Books, 2007, 326pp. $24.95. ISBN 9780910965767.
www.extremesearcher.com [COMPANION]

Good overview covering strategies and tools (including search engines, directories and portals) for all major areas of internet content. The companion site gives access to links for the sites covered in the handbook.

5597 Making search work: implementing web, intranet and enterprise search
M. White   Facet Publishing, 2007, 192pp. £39.95. ISBN 1856046028.

'Designed to help organizations to understand, specify and implement desktop, website, intranet and enterprise search applications, focusing on the practical aspects, rather than the theory of information retrieval.' Coverage includes the technology of searching; defining search requirements; usability of the search interface; developing the business case; selecting a search engine; and implementing a search engine.

5598 Modern information retrieval
R. Baeza-Yates and B. Ribeiro-Neto   Addison-Wesley, 1999, 544pp. £49.99. ISBN 9780201398298.

Well written comprehensive text approaching the subject from a computer science, as opposed to a user-centred, viewpoint.

5599 Text information retrieval systems
C.T. Meadow [et al.]   3rd edn, Academic Press, 2007, 371pp. £49.99. ISBN 9780123694126.
www.elsevier.com/wps/find/homepage.cws_home [DESCRIPTION]

Updated edition of classic text providing detailed coverage of all the elements which contribute to the success – or otherwise – of an information retrieval event.

Keeping up to date

5600 Search Engine Watch
D. Sullivan, ed.
http://searchenginewatch.com

Lively comment on current industry developments – though

many of the details only accessible to members. Emphasis on search engine strategies.

Libraries & Information Centres

academic libraries • children's libraries • college libraries • government libraries • health information services • learning commons • learning resource centres • legal information work • library buildings • local studies • map libraries • music libraries • national libraries • one-person libraries • public lending right • public libraries • reader development • readers' advisory services • reading groups • research libraries • specialist libraries

Introductions to the subject

5601 Countdown to a new library: managing the building project
J.A. Woodward   ALA Editions, 2000, 205pp. $55. ISBN 9780838907672.
A good place to start when faced with a new library building project: 'Packed with helpful checklists and worksheets, this "hard hat" book is an indispensable resource for learning how to "talk the talk' constructively with architects and builders; plan expertly for technology access; identify key building areas for security, electrical, HVAC, lighting, roofing and ADA requirements; and keep the project on track and on budget.'

Laws, standards, codes

5602 Access to libraries for persons with disabilities – checklist
B. Irvall and G.S. Nielsen; International Federation of Library Associations & Institutions   2005, 18pp.
www.ifla.org/VII/s9/nd1/iflapr-89e.pdf
Very good summary developed by the IFLA Standing Committee of Libraries Serving Disadvantaged Persons and covering physical access, media formats, service and communication. Appendix lists further resources.

Directories & encyclopedias

5603 American Library Directory
60th edn, Information Today, 2007, annual, 4138pp. $299.95 [2007–2008 edn]. ISBN 9781573872881.
http://books.infotoday.com/directories [DESCRIPTION]
'Profiles for more than 30,000 public, academic, special and government libraries and library-related organizations in the United States and Canada – including addresses, phone and fax numbers and e-mail addresses, network participation, expenditures, holdings and special collections, key personnel, special services and more – over 40 categories of library information in all.'

5604 The Aslib directory of information sources in the United Kingdom
K.W. Reynard, ed.   14th edn, Europa Publications, 2006, 1559pp. £370. ISBN 9781857433715.
Lists about 11,000 entries arranged A–Z by name, including

separate entries for branch/faculty libraries. Entries include year established, organization type and purpose, access arrangements and subject coverage. Also includes list of 10,000+ abbreviations and acronyms. Extensive index provides access by subject, place and personal name.

5605 Australian libraries: the essential directory
A. Bundy and J. Bundy, eds   8th edn, Auslib Press, 2007, 297pp. AUS$75.00 [2006/2008 edn]. ISBN 1875145613.
Comprehensive coverage of Australian libraries, plus a wealth of library-related information: library suppliers, library schools, library consultants, etc.
■ **Directory of Australian public libraries** A. Bundy and J. Bundy 7th edn, Auslib Press, 2006, 234pp. AUS$60. ISBN 1875145583. Full details of the national network of public lending libraries, State reference libraries and the National Library of Australia.

5606 Australian libraries gateway
National Library of Australia
www.nla.gov.au/libraries
Well designed free service which aims to be 'a "one-stop-shop" for information about Australian libraries – a tool for worldwide users, for both library professionals and the general public ... One of the differences between the Gateway and many other Library directories is that each ALG library has a password to update or amend information about itself, its services and collection via the Web. This means that many libraries are managing their information in the Gateway, thus ensuring that it is up-to-date and reliable. There are no charges associated with listing a library on the Gateway, nor any obligation for the listed libraries to provide any additional services to users of the Gateway.'

5607 International dictionary of library histories
D.H. Stam, ed.   Fitzroy Dearborn, 2001. 2 v., £150. ISBN 9781579582449.
'(P)rofiles more than 200 institutions from around the world, including the world's most important research libraries and other libraries with globally or regionally notable collections, innovative traditions and significant and interesting histories.'

5608 International directory of libraries for the blind
M. Nomura and M. Yamada, eds
http://ifla.jsrpd.jp
Simple, searchable listing.
Also published by K.G. Saur in 2000.

5609 Libraries and information services in the United Kingdom and the Republic of Ireland
L. Franklin and J. York, comps   Facet Publishing, 2007, 560pp. £44.95 [2007–2008 edn]. ISBN 9781856046213.
Lists over 3000 libraries in the UK, the Channel Islands, the Isle of Man and the Republic of Ireland, with contact names, addresses, telephone and fax numbers, e-mail addresses and URLs where appropriate. Covers public, education, government and special libraries, as well as key national and regional library agencies, professional organizations and schools of information and library science.

5610 Library world records
G. Oswald   McFarland, 2003, 238pp. $35. ISBN 9780786416196.
'Which university in the world has the largest library? What is the name of Europe's oldest public library? What year was the first CD-ROM book released? In what years were the first books in English, French, Spanish and Turkish printed? When

was the first major computer database released? What is the title of the largest book ever published? Where is the world's busiest public library? ...'

5611   The whole library handbook 4: current data, professional advice, and curiosa about libraries and library services
G.M. Eberhart   ALA Editions, 2006, 585pp. $42. ISBN 9780838909157.
'A one-volume encyclopedia of library history, demographics, folklore, humor, current events and popular wisdom. The new volume is organized in easy-to-find general categories, including types of libraries, the profession, people, materials, special users, operations, technology, promotion, issues and librariana.'
> ■ **Whole school library handbook** B. Woolls and D.V. Loertscher
> ALA Editions, 2004, 448pp. $50. ISBN 9780838908839. Modelled on *The whole library handbook* and directed to the school library media centre.

5612   World guide to libraries
W. van der Meer, ed.   21st edn, K.G. Saur, 2006. 2 v., €448. ISBN 9783598207693.
Lists 41,000+ entries from over 200 countries, arranged A–Z by country, then by nine library types: national, general research, university and college, school, government, ecclesiastical, corporate business, special, public. Entries include year established, important holdings and collection statistics.

Handbooks & manuals

5613   Checklist of building design considerations
W. Sannwald   4th edn, ALA Editions, 2001, 183pp. $48. ISBN 9780838935064.
Very good manual, well laid out, covering all facets of the exterior and interior of the library building.
'A must-have resource for library planners, librarians, architects, and all members of the design team, the work should help everyone involved to evaluate the current space, analyse each design element as it relates to space and function in the library, make decisions ranging from shelving finishes to technology equipment, and satisfy the requirements of the disabled.'
(*Australian Library Journal*)

5614   Libraries and learning resource centres
B. Edwards and B. Fisher   Architectural Press, 2002, 227pp. £60. ISBN 0750646055.
http://books.google.com [DESCRIPTION]
Attractively designed and produced book providing a good review of the architectural factors germane to library and learning resource centre buildings, both newly created and refurbished.

5615   Libraries designed for users: a 21st century guide
N. Lushington   Neal-Schuman, 2002, 247pp. $110. ISBN 1555704190.
An attractive text, with a good level of detail treating needs for both different types of material and differing types of library service.
'Logical, the writing style is readable, and the illustrations are clear and understandable ... A pleasure to hold and read.'
(*Reference & User Services Quarterly*)

Children's & School Libraries

Introductions to the subject

5616   Brilliant books: running a successful school library book event
G. Dubber and E. Scott; School Library Association   2nd edn, 2005, 62pp. £8.50. ISBN 1903446287.
Good, concise overview, covering funding, planning and publicity, finding authors and guests. Case studies; useful appendices. The Association publishes several similar short helpful publications, e.g.: *Fully booked!: reader development and the secondary school LRC* (2004); *Information matters: developing information literacy skills through the secondary school LRC* (2005); *Policy making and development planning for the primary school library* (2001); *Policy making and development planning for the secondary school LRC* (2003); *Shelf life, shelf matters: managing resources in the school library* (2001).

5617   Collection management for youth: responding to the needs of learners
S. Hughes-Hassell and J.C. Mancall   ALA Editions, 2005, 103pp. $38. ISBN 9780838908945.
Well focused text, clearly written, organized in the following sections: Changing expectations and models for practice; Collector behaviors; Policy as the foundation for the collection; Selecting resources for learning; Budgeting for maximum impact on learning; Collaboration from a planning perspective; Tools for learner-centered collection management.

5618   Fundamentals of children's services
M. Sullivan   ALA Editions, 2005, 255pp. $50. ISBN 9780838909072.
Comprehensive and stimulating text, with 22 chapters brought together into five parts: 1. Children's service and the mission of the library; 2. The collection; 3. Services; 4. Programming (story hours, book discussion groups; etc.); 5. Management, administration and leadership.

5619   Managing library services for children and young people: a practical handbook
C. Blanshard   Library Association Publishing, 1998, 203pp. ISBN 185604226X.
Core text, still of value, providing a comprehensive, well crafted review of the field.

5620   Managing your school library and information service: a practical handbook
A. Tilke   Facet Publishing, 2002, 293pp. ISBN 9781856044370.
'This book provides the school librarian with the skills, knowledge and competencies that are needed to make a school library effective in the 21st century. The school's organization and current learning and curriculum matters, are seen as equally important as the technical aspects of a school librarian's role. Linking all of these issues is management, either for a single-person unit or an organization with a large number of staff. The author uses case studies and comments from a wide number of British school librarians, thus drawing on a wide base of experience to provide a book that is relevant, informative, and, above all, thought-provoking.'

5621 New directions for library services to young adults
Young Adult Library Services Association   2nd edn, ALA Editions, 2002, 146pp. $35. ISBN 9780838908273.
Lively text tackling the challenges of helping 'libraries, with their communities, develop their teens into healthy, competent and caring adults'. Presents a holistic approach looking at policies, collections, programmes, services, technology, facilities, hours and human resources. Includes a series of valuable case studies.

Laws, standards, codes

5622 The CILIP guidelines for secondary school libraries
L. Barrett and J. Douglas, eds   2nd edn, Facet Publishing, 2004, 110pp. £22.95. ISBN 1856044815.
Prepared by editors for the Chartered Institute of Library & Information Professionals School Libraries Group. 'These Guidelines are the recommendations of CILIP for the effective management of secondary school libraries. They are primarily directed to those who manage school libraries – as practical guidance and as material for advocacy. They are also commended to the attention of headteachers, governors and all who are involved in the strategic management of education.'
■ **Children and young people: Library Association guidelines for public library services** C. Blanshard, ed. Library Association Publishing, 1997.

Official & quasi-official bodies

5623 International Board on Books for Young People
www.ibby.org
'(N)on-profit organization which represents an international network of people from all over the world who are committed to bringing books and children together ... (I)t is composed of seventy National Sections all over the world ... The National Sections are organized in many different ways and operate on national, regional and international levels. In countries that do not have a National Section, individual membership in IBBY is possible.'
Rich, well structured website with good site map, including links to the websites of each national section. A good starting point for international research in this field.

Associations & societies

5624 School Library Association [UK]
www.sla.org.uk
Founded in 1937 and an independent organization. Has a well designed and well structured website: a good place to start exploration of this area of library service. There is a particularly extensive and well categorized collection of links.

Digital data, image & text collections

5625 International Children's Digital Library
University of Maryland and Internet Archive
www.icdlbooks.org
Founded in 2002 and an online library 'designed to provide children aged 3 to 13 with an unparalleled opportunity to

experience different cultures through literature and an unequaled ease in accessing online books'. In 2005, the Library was awarded a five-year project funded primarily by the US National Science Foundation and the Institute for Museum and Library Services. The core aim is a collection of more than 10,000 books in at least 100 languages that is freely available to children, teachers, librarians, parents and scholars throughout the world via the internet.
Excellent website with many attractive features and superb use of graphics.

Directories & encyclopedias

5626 Children's book award handbook
D.F. Marks, comp.   Libraries Unlimited, 2006, 412pp. $40. ISBN 9781591583042.
An in-depth survey of 24 US-based children's and young adult book awards, in most cases providing an overview, biographical information on the namesake, timeline, award history and criteria and details of 2005 awards. There are useful suggested activties for students studying this area.

5627 The Newbery/Printz companion: booktalk and related materials for award winners and honor books
J.T. Gillespie and C.J. Naden, comps   3rd edn, Libraries Unlimited, 2006, 503pp. $75. ISBN 9781591583134.
Comprehensive guide to these influential awards for children's and young adult literature.

The whole library handbook 4: current data, professional advice, and curiosa about libraries and library services
G.M. Eberhart   See entry no. 5611

Handbooks & manuals

5628 Administering the school library media center
B.J. Morris   4th edn, Libraries Unlimited, 2004, 683pp. $55. ISBN 9781591581833.
Well established, comprehensive manual covering service development, staff, facilities, media selection, technology, programme administration, etc.

Collection management for school libraries
J. McGregor, K. Dillon and J. Henri, eds   See entry no. 5578

5629 Information literacy and the school library media center
J. Taylor   Libraries Unlimited, 2006, 148pp. $35. ISBN 9780313320200.
A very clear handbook, structured: What and why; Information literacy standards; Putting it all together: National, state and local standards; Planning for information literacy instruction; Collaboration with a purpose; Flexible scheduling; It's all about process; Setting the stage for learning; How did I do?: Assessment.
'Taylor's guidebook fulfills a need and adds a touch of inspiration as well. For newcomers, it offers a much-needed perspective; for veterans, it's a reminder of what school libraries are all about ...' (*School Library Journal*)

5630 **A place for children: public libraries as a major force in children's reading**
J. Elkin and M. Kinnell, eds   Library Association Publishing, 2000, 198pp. £49.95. ISBN 9781856043205.
Report of a British Library-funded research study offering a comprehensive analysis of children's literature, public library and children's library services. Offers detailed case study material and provides service criteria and performance indicators which can be used to inform future direction and policy decisions.

College & University Libraries

Introductions to the subject

5631 **The academic library**
P. Brophy   2nd edn, Facet Publishing, 2005, 233pp. £34.95. ISBN 9781856045278.
Useful text giving a good overview of the academic library in the 21st century. Covers the following key areas: the library in the institution; users of the academic library; the impacts and opportunities of ICTs; human resources; management and organization of resources; collection and access management; the academic library building; library systems and networks; specialist services; management and professional issues; performance measurement.

5632 **The academic research library in a decade of change**
R. Carr   Chandos, 2007, 236pp. £39.95. ISBN 9781843342458.
The former Director of Oxford University Library Services offers an overview and analysis of issues and challenges facing contemporary academic research libraries. Uses local and national examples to illuminate discussion of global concerns, such as changing user expectations, the role of library consortia, modernization of services, the future of the book and developments in e-science.

Laws, standards, codes

5633 **Guidelines for colleges: recommendations for learning resources**
A. Eynon, ed.   Facet Publishing, 2005, 70pp. £22.95. ISBN 9781856045513.
Guidance produced under the auspices of the CILIP Colleges of Further and Higher Education Group. At the heart of the Guidelines are ten recommendations that form the basic foundation of excellent learning resource services provision.

Associations & societies

5634 **Association of College & Research Libraries** [USA]
www.ala.org/ACRL
ALA's largest division, with more than 12,000 members 'representing librarians working with all types of academic libraries – community and junior college, college and university – as well as comprehensive and specialized research libraries and their professional staffs'. In 2002, the Association 'launched its Scholarly Communication initiative, with goals of creating increased access to scholarly information; fostering cost-effective alternative means of publishing, especially those that take advantage of electronic information technologies; and encouraging scholars to assert greater control over scholarly communications'. The website provides in-depth information about its work in this arena and related resources.
- **Choice** 1964–. $300 (Print, North America. Many other packages available, including online versions). ISSN 00094978. www.ala.org/ala/acrl/acrlpubs/choice [DESCRIPTION]. Subject expert reviews of significant current books and electronic media of higher education interest. Subscribers rate it highest among sources used to select materials for academic libraries. Some 7000 reviews/year: strong coverage of reference titles.
- **College and Research Libraries** $70.00 (USA). ISSN 00100870. www.ala.org/ala/acrl/acrlpubs/crljournal/collegeresearch.htm [DESCRIPTION]. Scholarly journal containing academic articles. Columns of the companion periodical *College and research libraries news* include: Washington Hotline, Grants and Acquisitions, People in the News, new publications, job advertisements, internet reviews and resources: full text of the last accessible online.

5635 **Association of Research Libraries** [USA]
www.arl.org
'Not-for-profit membership organization comprising the leading research libraries in North America.' Currently 123 members. The site provides efficient access to a very wide range of excellent resources relevant to the various ARL programmes: e.g. Copyright and Intellectual Property; Diversity; Library Support for E-Science – and is well worth browsing through.
   Particularly pertinent here is the section 'Scholarly Communication': 'One of ARL's strategic goals for 2005–2009 is the development of effective, extensible, sustainable and economically viable models of scholarly communication that provide barrier-free access to quality information. The ARL Office of Scholarly Communication works to create new models for scholarly exchange that build on the widespread adoption of digital technologies and networking for research, teaching and learning. At the same time, the program works to improve the traditional systems of scholarly exchange and increase the purchasing power of libraries and the terms and conditions under which content is made available.'
- **Coalition for Networked Information** www.cni.org. 'Dedicated to supporting the transformative promise of networked information technology for the advancement of scholarly communication and the enrichment of intellectual productivity.' 200 institutional members from academia, publishing, ICT, libraries.
- **Scholarly Publishing & Academic Resources Coalition** www.arl.org/sparc. Aims to stimulate the 'creation of better, faster, and more economically sustainable systems for distributing new knowledge. Especially in science, technology, and medicine'. Very good range of resources cited: almost all freely accessible full-text.

5636 **Canadian Association of Research Libraries**
www.carl-abrc.ca
30 university and national members. Useful gateway to current preoccupations in Canada.

5637 **Consortium of University Research Libraries** [UK]
www.curl.ac.uk
Consortium of UK university libraries with a national or international reputation plus the UK's legal deposit libraries and other major research information providers.
- **COPAC** www.copac.ac.uk. Free access to the merged online catalogues of 24 of the largest university research libraries in the UK and Ireland, plus the

British Library and the National Library of Scotland. Currently contains some 30 million records. Good search facilities.

5638 Council for Learning Resources in Colleges [UK]
www.colric.org.uk
'(A)n independent organization dedicated to enhancing and maintaining excellence in learning resources services in colleges throughout the United Kingdom and Ireland.' Useful news and links service.

5639 Council of Australian University Libraries
www.anu.edu.au/caul
40 institutional library members, all of whose whose parent institutions are full members of the Australian Vice-Chancellors' Committee. Simple but effective website provides access to a good range of resources. There is an extensive set of 'Links to other websites and documents' but unfortunately this needs more maintenance than it appears to receive at present.

5640 Society of College, National & University Libraries
[UK]
www.sconul.ac.uk
The body which primarily represents higher education libraries in the UK, though membership actually belongs to the libraries' parent institutions: 'All universities in the United Kingdom and Ireland are SCONUL members: so too are many of the UK's colleges of higher education. Also members are the major national libraries both sides of the Irish Sea.'

   Good, clear website. Particularly valuable is the section 'SCONUL hot topics', which at the time of sampling were: e-learning; e-research; information literacy; performance improvement; scholarly communications; and space planning. Also useful in gaining perspective are issues of the magazine *SCONUL Focus*, whose content is freely accessible via the site.

Directories & encyclopedias

5641 The directory of university libraries in Europe
3rd edn, Routledge, 2006, 478pp. £250. ISBN 9781857434019.
Libraries throughout Europe, arranged alphabetically by country, with contact details of chief librarians and other relevant staff, as well as areas of specialization, opening hours, entitlement to use the library, the size and composition of library holdings, online subscriptions and details of libraries' own publications.

Handbooks & manuals

Higher education in the Internet age: libraries creating a strategic edge
P.S. Breivik and E.G. Gee   See entry no. 4549

5642 Learning commons: evolution and collaborative essentials
B. Schader, ed.   Chandos, 2007, 200pp. $39.95. ISBN 9781843343127.
Traces the evolution of academic libraries from traditional library buildings through the information commons model to collaborative learning spaces, drawing on case studies from around the world. Discusses critical issues in planning and

creating the learning commons, including the characteristics of contemporary students, collaboration with key stakeholders and identification of the financial, human and technological resources required. Includes references, checklists, sample documentation and assessment tools to support implementation.

National Libraries

Introductions to the subject

5643 America's library: the story of the Library of Congress, 1800–2000
J. Conaway   Yale University Press, 2000, 226pp. $39.95. ISBN 0300083084.
Fascinating history of the Library, especially valuable for the attempt to treat the Library as a whole and place its position within American culture.

5644 Inside the British Library
A.E. Day   Library Association Publishing, 1998, 297pp. £49.95. ISBN 9781856042802.
The final part of a trilogy of books about the Library, the others being: *The British Library : a guide to its structure, publications, collections and services* (Library Association, 1988) and *The new British Library* (Library Association Publishing, 1994).

Laws, standards, codes

5645 British Library Act 1972: chapter 54
HMSO, 1972.
www.bl.uk/about/blact.html
The Act which led to the formation of the BL, including the transfer of the stock and services of the former British Museum Library.
  ■ **History of the British Museum Library: 1753–1973** P.R. Harris   British Library Publishing, 1998. £50. ISBN 712345620. The history from the founding of the Library until it became officially the British Library. Among the appendices is a list of well known persons who have used the reading rooms.

Associations & societies

5646 Conference of European National Librarians
www.cenl.org
'Members of CENL are the national librarians of all Member States of the Council of Europe. The conference currently consists of 47 members from 45 European countries.' Details of its projects and other activities plus a useful list of 'Related projects – past and present', including a link to the EC Digital Libraries Initiative project home page.

5647 IFLA National Libraries Section
www.ifla.org/VII/s1/index.htm
Produces a useful bi-annual newsletter and provides pointers to the work of related bodies, such as the Conference of Directors of National Libraries.
  ■ **National libraries of the world: address list**
  www.ifla.org/VI/2/p2/national-libraries.htm. 'A list of national libraries including those claiming this function but not having the actual title'.

Directories & encyclopedias

5648 Encyclopedia of the Library of Congress: for Congress, the nation and the world
J.Y. Cole and J. Aikin, eds   Bernan Press, 2005, 569pp. $125. ISBN 9780890599716.
'Describes, for the first time in one volume, the historical development of the collections, functions and services of the world's largest research institution – from its origins in 1800 to 2004.'

Handbooks & manuals

5649 National libraries: a selection of articles on national libraries
M.B. Line and J. Line, eds   Aslib, 1995, 303pp. £45. ISBN 0851423426.
A classic volume containing articles published between 1986 and 1994, supplementing two previously published volumes covering the post-war period (published in 1979) and the years 1977 through 1985 (published in 1987).

Public Libraries

Introductions to the subject

5650 Enrichment: a history of the public library in the United States in the twentieth century
L.A. Martin   Scarecrow, 1998, 205pp. $35.50. ISBN 9780810847545.
An elegant and enjoyable history, concentrating on the 20th century, but with a brief overview of developments in the 19th.

5651 Introduction to public librarianship
K. de la P. McCook   Neal-Schuman, 2004, 406pp. $59.95. ISBN 1555704751.
A good solid introduction, focusing on the US environment. Those new to the area should appreciate the historical context within which public libraries developed, before engaging with the details of policy and practice and their likely future in the 21st century. Two appendices cover selected readings and national statistics on public libraries.

5652 The public library in Britain 1914–2000
A. Black   British Library, 2000, 180pp. £30. ISBN 0712346856.
'Social historians and politicians have always made much of public libraries' contribution to the life of communities, but this study emphasizes the importance of their relationship with individual readers. Alistair Black argues that, despite the library's potential as a progressive force for furthering social growth and personal enlightenment, the conservatism of the authorities, their fear of revolutionary insurgency and a suspicion of mass culture resulted in a reluctance to reach the lower levels of society.'
    This book follows on from Black's earlier: *A new history of the English public library: social and intellectual contexts, 1850–1914* (Leicester University Press, 1996).

5653 Reading and reader development: the pleasure of reading
J. Elkin, B. Train and D. Denham   Facet Publishing, 2003, 241pp. £49.95. ISBN 9781856044677.
Notable for the depth of its underlying research, with case studies and interviews drawing on the wealth of experience of key players in the field. The book revolves around these themes: The reader; Reader development; Reading: a UK national focus; Reading: an international focus; Cultural and multicultural perspectives on reading; ICT and reader development; Special needs; and Reading and reader development research: the argument for quality. It ends with an overview and suggestions for future development.

Laws, standards, codes

5654 Public Libraries and Museums Act 1964: chapter 75 [UK]
HMSO, 1964, 22pp.
www.culture.gov.uk/what_we_do/Libraries/statutory_requirements.htm
The primary Act governing the activities of public libraries (and museums) in the UK. 'Legislation made prior to 1988 is only available in its original print format as before this date legislation was not produced electronically.' However, the website of the Department of Culture, Media & Sport gives a good summary of current statutory requirements, as well as details of the current Public Library Service Standards.
  ■ **Advisory Council on Libraries**
    www.culture.gov.uk/what_we_do/Libraries/ac_libraries.htm. 'Under the provisions of the 1964 Public Libraries and Museums Act, the Advisory Council on Libraries … provides advice to the Secretary of State "upon such matters connected with the provision of library facilities … as they think fit".' The composition of the Council is currently under review.

5655 The public library service: IFLA/UNESCO guidelines for development
P. Gill [et al.], eds; International Federation of Library Associations & Institutions   K.G. Saur, 2001, 116pp. €54. ISBN 9783598218279.
www.ifla.org/VII/s8/proj/publ97.pdf
An important publication, produced following worldwide consultation and 'framed to provide assistance to librarians in any situation to develop an effective public library service meeting the needs of their local community'.
Translations into other languages: www.ifla.org/VII/s8/news/pg01.htm

Official & quasi-official bodies

5656 Public Lending Right Registrar's Office [UK]
www.plr.uk.com
'Public Lending Right (PLR) is the right for authors to receive payment under PLR legislation for the loans of their books by public libraries. To qualify for payment, applicants must apply to register their books with us. Payments are made annually on the basis of loans data collected from a sample of public libraries in the UK. Over 23,000 writers, illustrators, photographers, translators and editors who have contributed to books lent out by public libraries receive PLR payments each year …'
  ■ **PLR International Network** www.plrinternational.com. Brings together those countries with established PLR systems and provides assistance and advice to countries interested in producing PLR schemes.

Research centres & institutes

5657　Centre for the Public Library & Information in Society [UK]
http://cplis.shef.ac.uk
Leading centre, whose members 'are available to carry out research and consultancy for public library services and for other information and advice agencies in the public and voluntary sectors. On-site courses covering most aspects of public library activities can also be tailor-made to meet the requirements of individual authorities and organizations.'

5658　Reading Agency [UK]
www.readingagency.co.uk
Formed in 2002 by merger of three smaller agencies, all of whom worked with libraries to promote reading. The Agency 'helps libraries develop and maintain new ways of working, share good practice, continue to raise standards and to publicise the excellent work they do'. Apart from information on the Centre's projects and promotional activities, there is an extensive Resources section on the website, categorized as reports, booklists, case studies, posters and leaflets, facts and figures, toolkits, checklists and activity ideas, and newsletters.

Associations & societies

5659　IFLA Public Libraries Section
www.ifla.org/VII/s8/index.htm
Not an especially active IFLA section, but worth referencing here.

5660　IFLA Reading Section
www.ifla.org/VII/s33/index.htm
A section of the International Federation of Library Associations & Institutions. Useful for pointers towards work in developing countries. Has sponsored the production of non-English language versions of the publication *Guidelines for library-based literacy programs*.

5661　Society of Chief Librarians [UK]
www.goscl.com/home.ikml
A local government association made up of the chief librarians of each library authority in England, Wales and Northern Ireland. Useful website for keeping abreast of developments in this arena in the UK.

Portal & task environments

5662　Designing libraries: the gateway to better library buildings
www.designinglibraries.org.uk
Initiative funded by the Museums, Libraries & Archives Council (q.v.) on behalf of the Department of Culture, Media & Sport, as part of the Framework for the Future programme; managed by the Chartered Institute of Library & Information Professionals.
　　Useful gateway: database of library buildings, toolkit, news, etc.

Directories & encyclopedias

Australian libraries: the essential directory
A. Bundy and J. Bundy, eds　See entry no. 5605

5663　UK public libraries
S. Harden and R. Harden, comps
http://dspace.dial.pipex.com/town/square/ac940/ukpublib.html
Excellent map-based guide to UK public libraries on the web, with some related links.

Handbooks & manuals

5664　The new planning for results: a streamlined approach
S.S. Nelson; Public Library Association　ALA Editions, 2001, 315pp. $58. ISBN 9780838935040.
Latest version of the US PLA strategic planning manual, which has been revised to provide a more compact guidebook within a reduced planning timeline. Six chapters offer step-by-step guidance on 12 planning tasks, supported by examples. Part 2 articulates 13 'service responses' to help libraries determine their distinctive approaches to serving the public. Parts 3 and 4 comprise a toolkit and workforms to support group work processes and compilation of planning data.

5665　Planning public library buildings
M. Dewe　Ashgate, 2006, 354pp. £60. ISBN 0754633888.
Authoritative and comprehensive guide to planning the creation, conversion and refurbishment of public library buildings, drawing on best practice and lessons learned from around the world. Key chapters cover: service point provision, size and shape; sustainability, safety, security and systems; planning, design and construction; and identity, communication and style. Illustrated throughout with case studies, plans and photographs, appendices cover UK and US building award programmes, bibliography and index.

5666　Public libraries in the 21st century: defining services and debating the future
A. Goulding　Ashgate, 2006, 387pp. £60. ISBN 9780754642862.
Analyses the impact of recent policy initiatives targeted at public libraries within the context of broader developments in the public sector environment within which they operate.

5667　Readers' advisory service in the public library
J.G. Saricks　3rd edn, ALA Editions, 2005, 211pp. $42. ISBN 9780838908976.
The latest edition of this well established text has been expanded and improved with: Easy ways to create 'read alike' lists, identifying what else is 'like' a favorite book; Practical guidelines for conducting the advisory interview so it's a comfortable exchange; Confidence-boosting tactics for drawing on reviews to make recommendations; Methods for incorporating nonfiction into the discussion; More resources and online tools.

5668　The reading groups book
J. Hartley　Oxford University Press, 2002, 232pp. £8.50. ISBN 9780199255962.
A good and interesting handbook – though the details are clearly now somewhat dated. Chapters are: 1. What is a reading group?; 2. Who belongs to reading groups?; 3. How

groups choose and what they read; 4. How groups talk; 5. The broader picture; 6. The reading group in the 21st century; Conclusion: the pleasures of reading together.

5669 Running book discussion groups: a how-to-do-it manual for librarians
L.Z. John   Neal-Schuman, 2006, 250pp. $55. ISBN 1555705421.
Helpful title in the publisher's series How-To-Do-It Manuals treating an increasingly important topic. Particularly useful are the discussions in Part III: 'Ten guaranteed crowd-pleasing book discussions'. Part IV has four Appendices summarizing the various resources used by book discussion groups.

Keeping up to date

5670 LIS-PUB-LIBS: UK Public Libraries
www.jiscmail.ac.uk/lists/LIS-PUB-LIBS.html
Active JISC list with over 1000 subscribers, mid-2007.

5671 PUBLIB
http://lists.webjunction.org/publib
Electronic discussion list began in 1992 and is one of the oldest and largest (over 5000 members) listservs in this area. Aimed at public librarians and those interested in public libraries, it concentrates on public library matters.

Specialist Libraries

Introductions to the subject

5672 The digital age and local studies
P.H. Reid   Chandos, 2003, 237pp. £39. ISBN 9781843340515.
Wide-ranging coverage of the field: useful for those involved with genealogical research.

5673 The role of the legal information officer
T. Harvey   Chandos, 2003, 190pp. £39. ISBN 9781843340478.
Aimed at new professionals and those new to the commercial sector, provides a basic introduction to the tasks and skills involved in legal information work. Includes discussion of know-how services and the role of professional support lawyers. Appendices include A week in the life of a legal information officer; Starting from scratch; and 20 tips for being a first-class legal information officer.

Associations & societies

5674 Special Libraries Association [USA]
www.sla.org
'Serves more than 12,000 members in 83 countries in the information profession, including corporate, academic and government information specialists.' Organized into 24 divisions representing subject interests, fields, or types of information-handling techniques, and including Advertising & Marketing; Business & Finance; Competitive Intelligence; Education; Government Information; Information Technology (with a range of sub-sections); Insurance and Employee Benefits; Knowledge Management; Leadership and Management; Legal; Military Librarians; Museums, Arts & Humanities; News; Social Science (with a range of sub-

sections); Solo Librarians. Most of these have their own sets of web pages providing lists of relevant events, people, organizations and resources.

  ■ **Competencies for information professionals of the 21st century** rev. edn, 2003, 17pp.
www.sla.org/content/learn/comp2003. An excellent overview of professional, personal and core competencies neeed by special librarians in the 21st century.

  ■ **Information Outlook** , monthly. ISSN 10910808.
www.sla.org/content/Shop/Information/index.cfm. Lively magazine: 'The editorial objective is to provide timely coverage of information management issues relevant to special librarians in a global environment. *Information Outlook* interprets the news and covers trends and issues that affect information professionals'.

Discovering print & electronic resources

5675 Local studies librarianship: a world bibliography
D. Dixon, comp.   Library Association Publishing, 2001, 265pp. £39.95. ISBN 9781856043076.
Comprehensive listing with international coverage of every aspect of local studies librarianship, including management, acquisition, cataloguing, promotion, conservation and preservation.

Directories & encyclopedias

5676 Directory of special libraries and information centers
34th edn, Gale, 2008. Includes mid-year supplement, $1210. ISBN 9780787696795.
'Covers thousands of special libraries and information centers associated with the general fields of science and engineering, medicine, law, art, religion, the social sciences and humanities, including international listings.' Separate geographic and personnel indexes provide access to profiled libraries by geographic region, as well as by the professional staff that are cited in each listing.

5677 Guide to libraries and information services in government departments and other organisations [UK]
P. Dale and P. Wilson, eds; British Library   34th edn, 2004, 192pp. £39. ISBN 0712308830.
'This comprehensive directory lists UK organizations which offer collections and services on your subject, identifying contacts, plus information on opening times and facilities and free and charged services. Librarians and information officers, students and academics, politicians and lawyers, pressure groups, local authorities and planners, journalists, companies, consultants: everyone who needs an answer to a specific question or access to information for detailed research will find this an invaluable book. Since the publication of the 33rd edition UK government departments have continued to float off constituent units which have become separate agencies and so a number of organizations now appear under new names or as separate entities. Elsewhere there have been many other reorganizations and mergers, which have led to changes of name. These are all reflected in this new edition. There is an organizational index and a subject index.'

5678 World directory of map collections
O. Loiseaux, ed.   4th edn, K.G. Saur, 2000, 541pp. €78. ISBN 9783598218187.
Now the standard tool in this field.

5679 World guide to special libraries
W. van der Meer and P. Schmidt, eds   7th edn, K.G. Saur, 2007. 2 v., €368. ISBN 3598222610.
Lists over 34,000 libraries under c. 800 subject headings. (Libraries may be included under more than one heading.) Includes subject-specialist national/central, faculty and institute libraries, as well as company, government and other traditional special libraries. Entries include year established, important holdings and collection statistics. Vol. 1 also lists national libraries, arranged A–Z by country.

Handbooks & manuals

BIALL handbook of legal information management
L. Worley   See entry no. 2812

5680 Exploiting knowledge in health services
G. Walton and A. Booth, eds   Facet Publishing, 2004, 274pp. £49.95. ISBN 9781856044790.
An excellent volume structured around three logical divisions: Part 1 looks at the context within which healthcare is delivered and examines the different users who have access to the knowledge base; Part 2 outlines the principles underlying the way health information resources and services are organized and managed; Part 3 discusses the skills required to use the knowledge base.
'If you have or aspire to managerial responsibility for health service information, buy it, read it, and apply its lessons [Review of predecessor to this work].' (*Health Information and Libraries Journal*)

5681 Handbook of information management
A. Scammell, ed.   8th edn, Routledge (for Aslib-IMI), 2001, 546pp. £60. ISBN 9780851424576.
'This is effectively the eighth edition of Aslib's flagship reference work, *Handbook of Special Librarianship and Information Work*, which has provided the seminal text on modern information theory, practice and procedure since 1957.'
26 useful chapters surveying the field as perceived at the start of this century.

5682 Local studies collection management
M. Dewe, ed.   Ashgate, 2002, 196pp. £55. ISBN 9780566083655.
Collection of essays aimed particularly at public librarians, but of value more generally.
'Book of the Month – September 2003 ... this is a well-written and comprehensive book on the management of what is an increasingly important collection in libraries. It is likely to be well received by specialist librarians and library managers ...' (*Managing Information*)

5683 The map library in the new millennium
R.B. Parry and C.R. Perkins, eds   Library Association Publishing, 2001, 267pp. £59.95. ISBN 9781856043977.
A very wide-ranging collection of essays providing an excellent overview of the state of the art at the turn of the century.

'... this book should be required reading for anyone interested in maps and map collections in the Western World.' (*Bulletin of the Society of Cartographers*)

5684 Music librarianship in the United Kingdom: fifty years of the United Kingdom Branch of the International Association of Music Libraries, Archives and Documentation Centres
R. Turbet, ed.   Ashgate, 2003, 252pp. £55. ISBN 9780754605720.
A splendid compendium: 16 chapters reveal the wealth of professionalism present and needed in music librarianship.
'... editor Richard Turbet has revealed a rich and productive history of music librarianship in the UK ... This book is a fascinating exploration not only into the history of the Association and its activities, but also into the history of music librarianship in the United Kingdom. It will serve as an important resource for ideas and best practices in the field.' (*Canadian Association of Music Libraries*)

5685 The new OPL sourcebook: a guide for solo and small libraries
J.A. Siess   Information Today, 2005, 427pp. $39.50. ISBN 9781573872416.
A guide for small and one-person libraries (OPLs) which, although authored in the USA, takes an international perspective. Its directory section lists important organizations, publications, vendors and suppliers, discussion lists and websites.

Library Operations & Organization

alerting services • chat reference services • digital reference services • disaster management • enquiry work • information marketing • information products • library administration • library automation • library fundraising • library marketing • library security • library systems & technology • reference interview • reference work • virtual reference services

Introductions to the subject

5686 Disaster management for libraries and archives
G. Matthews and J. Feather, eds   Ashgate, 2003, 236pp. £25. ISBN 9780754609179.
Edited set of articles giving very good overview of the area.
'In its combination of theory based on first-hand experience and lessons drawn from actual examples this book forms a very practical introduction to a topic which can elsewhere be obfuscated with jargon.' (*Ariadne*)

Portal & task environments

5687 Disaster control plan
M25 Consortium of Academic Libraries   rev. edn, Disaster Management Group, 2004.
www.m25lib.ac.uk/m25dcp
The M25 Consortium of Academic Libraries is a collaborative organization that works to improve library and information services within the M25 region surrounding London and more widely across the East and Southeast of the UK. This site is designed to provide a useful model for librarians and

archivists engaged in developing a Disaster Control Plan and in fostering a disaster management culture for collections in their care. Under each of four main headings (Prevention, Preparedness, Reaction and Recovery), the screen has a Commentary on the left-hand side and a Template on the right. The content can be downloaded. There is an extensive 'Disaster bibliography' and a list of 'Web-mounted disaster plans and other useful sites'. Overall, a good, helpful resource.

Discovering print & electronic resources

5688 Disaster planning and recovery
Special Libraries Association
www.sla.org/content/resources/inforesour/sept11help/disip/index.cfm
A site 'dedicated to the librarians who were killed or injured on September 11th, 2001'. Divided into articles, monographs, videos and websites. Regularly updated.

Handbooks & manuals

5689 Disaster response and planning for libraries
M.B. Kahn   2nd edn, ALA Editions, 2003, 152pp. $45. ISBN 9780838908372.
Organized as an extensive series of short sections, making it easy to explore this complex arena. Has a very wide coverage of the issues.
'From planning and preservation to response and recovery, here is a step-by-step process for development of a library disaster response plan in case of severe weather, fire, or other disasters. Essential reading, and well worth the price for checklists and forms alone.' (*Public Libraries*)

5690 Security in museums, libraries and archives: a practical guide
Resource   2nd edn, 2003, 182pp.
www.collectionslink.org.uk
Comprehensive handbook providing detailed guidance on all aspects of risk assessment, preventative action and operational procedures in relation to crime, fire and other threats. Eight sections cover: Security issues in museums, archives and libraries; General security guidance; Detailed guidance and operational procedures; Government indemnity scheme; Contingency planning; Security staffing; Audit and inventory; Equipment procurement; and Bibliography. Downloadable from the Collections Link website, where additional security factsheets are available.
'Resource' is now the Museums, Libraries & Archives Council (q.v.)

Information Products & Services

Introductions to the subject

5691 Chat reference: a guide to live virtual reference services
J.S. Ronan   Libraries Unlimited, 2003, 225pp. $50. ISBN 9781591580003.
Now somewhat dated, but still a good starting point for those new to live virtual reference services.

5692 Going live: starting and running a virtual reference service
S. Coffman [et al.]   ALA Editions, 2003, 182pp. $45. ISBN 9780838908501.
Chapters are: 1. Reference: the first one hundred years; 2. Getting started: designing virtual reference systems; 3. Managing virtual reference services; 4. Marketing virtual reference services; 5. Where do we go from here?
'This book will help one anticipate what's on the road ahead and avoid the dangerous curves. ... easy-to-read volume ... I would recommend *Going Live* for anyone undertaking a virtual reference project ... With this book and information from other perspectives, a smooth journey to "going live" is almost certain.' (*Reference & User Services Quarterly*)

5693 How LIS professionals can use alerting services
I. Fourie   Chandos, 2006, 178pp. £39. ISBN 9781843341284.
Discusses how library and information professionals can use web-based current awareness services (CAS) to enhance their service offer, career development, professional image and job satisfaction. Chapters cover the evolution of CAS; related environmental changes; the need to use information creatively, to 'make a difference'; the variety of alerting services available; personalization and self-knowledge and counteracting information overload.

5694 Introduction to reference work in the digital age
J. Janes   Neal-Schuman, 2003, 213pp. $59.95. ISBN 1555704298.
Seven chapters survey the key issues: 1. Reference, digital and otherwise; 2. Understanding users, communities and their needs; 3. Responding to information needs; 4. Technology; 5. The evolution of practice and the staff of the future; 6. Making it work: creating and institutionalizing a service; 7. Syncope: Play to our professional strengths; Begin by starting over; Final thoughts: All these things and more.

5695 Reference and information services in the 21st century: an introduction
K.A. Cassell and U. Hiremath   Neal-Schuman, 2006, 378pp. $65. ISBN 1555705634.
www.neal-schuman.com/reference21st [COMPANION]
Logically structured introduction with 20 chapters in four parts: Fundamental concepts; Introduction to major reference sources; Special topics in reference and information work; Developing and managing reference collections and services.

5696 Success at the enquiry desk: successful enquiry answering – every time
T.B. Owen   5th edn, Facet Publishing, 2006, 134pp. £24.95. ISBN 9781856046008.
Now classic text designed as a 'one-stop shop' for information professionals charged with answering user questions. Written in an engaging style, yet thorough and authoritative. An ideal introduction.

5697 Worlds of reference: lexicography, learning and language from the clay tablet to the computer
T. McArthur   Cambridge University Press, 1986, 230pp. ISBN 052130637X.
Rewarding, well written history. 20 chapters in six parts: Mind, word and world; The ancient world; The medieval world; The early modern world; The modern world; Tomorrow's world. The chapters 'Semantic fields and conceptual universes: the unshapeable lexis' and 'Shaping

things to come: the priests of High Technology' are particularly insightful – especially given that they were written 20 years ago.

Notes, references and related reading pp. 186–209; Bibliography pp.210–218; Index.

Associations & societies

5698 Reference & User Services Association [USA]
www.ala.org/RUSA
'Responsible for stimulating and supporting excellence in the delivery of general library services and materials to adults and the provision of reference and information services, collection development and resource sharing for all ages, in every type of library.' Lively Association who, for instance, have produced an extensive set of Reference Guidelines (e.g. 'Definition of a reference transaction', 'Guidelines for medical, legal and business responses', 'Professional competencies for reference and user services librarians', 'Guidelines for the introduction of electronic resources to users').

RUSA organizes the production of each year's *Outstanding Reference sources for small and medium-sized libraries*, among now a wide range of digitally-based innovative products and services. Its official journal is the *Reference and User Services Quarterly*.

Handbooks & manuals

5699 Conducting the reference interview: a how-to-do-it manual for librarians
C.S. Ross, K. Nilsen and P. Dewdney   Neal-Schuman, 2002, 175pp. $65. ISBN 1555704328.
After an introductory chapter, takes us through: Using the first 30 seconds to set the stage for the reference interview; Finding out what they really want to know; Moving beyond negative closure; Exploring special contexts for the reference interview; Performing the reference interview in an electronic environment; Establishing policy and training for the reference interview.

5700 Introduction to reference work
W.A. Katz   8th edn, McGraw-Hill, 2002. I. *Basic information services* $76.88; ISBN 9780072441079. II. *Reference services and reference processes* $79.06; ISBN 9780072441437.
www.mhhe.com/socscience/katz [COMPANION]
The longest-running US guide to reference work, whose first edition was published in 1969. Vol. 1 covers different types of reference resource, arranged in categories covering bibliographies, indexing and abstracting services, encyclopedias, dictionaries, ready-reference sources, biographical sources, geographical sources and government documents, with introductory chapters on the 'information highway' and 'electronic library'. Vol. 2 includes further discussion of internet resources, but is most useful for its chapters on the reference interview, search strategy, information literacy and reference policies. Student resources section of companion website provides occasional updates and chapter-by-chapter lists of links to online resources; also provides access to a new chapter on 'The internet community' planned for a new section on 'The public voice' in the next edition of vol. 2.

Readers' advisory service in the public library
J.G. Saricks   See entry no. 5667

5701 Reference and information services: an introduction
R.E. Bopp and L.C. Smith, eds   3rd edn, Libraries Unlimited, 2001, 617pp. $50. ISBN 9781563086243.
Although not updated for some time, this remains the most accessible and comprehensive textbook on the subject, which is interpreted broadly to include interlibrary loan, document delivery and user instruction, in addition to readers' advisory and enquiry work. It covers the concepts, theories and practicalities of reference services and sources today, though internet-related aspects are somewhat out of date. Part 1 includes an excellent chapter on 'The reference interview' in addition to covering topics such as search strategies, management and evaluation of reference services and training of reference staff. Part 2 includes a useful chapter on 'Selection and evaluation of reference sources', before considering nine different categories of information sources and their use.

Running book discussion groups: a how-to-do-it manual for librarians
L.Z. John   See entry no. 5669

5702 Understanding reference transactions: transferring an art into a science
M.L. Saxton and J.V. Richardson   Academic Press, 2002, 208pp. £59.99. ISBN 9780125877800.
Provides a detailed analysis of the question-answering process and methods of evaluating the completeness, usefulness, user satisfaction and accuracy of the information provided.

5703 The virtual reference librarian's handbook
A.G. Lipow   Neal-Schuman, 2003, 199pp. Includes CD-ROM. Foreword by Clifford Lynch, $85. ISBN 155570445X.
Very useful and practical guide. Three parts: The decision to go virtual; The process of moving to the virtual desk; Techniques for building a lively service.

Keeping up to date

5704 LIBREF-L
Kent State University
www.library.kent.edu/page/10391
Moderated discussion of issues related to reference librarianship, with over 2000 subscribers worldwide. The list was begun by the reference librarians in Libraries and Media Services, Kent State University in 1990 and continues to be managed as a team effort by librarians at Kent State and elsewhere.

5705 Project Wombat
http://project-wombat.org
E-mail discussion list for difficult reference questions. Membership is free and non-members may submit questions for discussion. Project Wombat continues the activity previously located on the Stumpers list (Stumpers-L, hosted by Dominican University) with some helpful new options.

Library Administration & Management

Introductions to the subject

5706 **An action plan for outcomes assessment in your library**
P. Hernon and R.E. Dugan   ALA Editions, 2002, 191pp. $55. ISBN 9780838908136.
Provides data collection tools for measuring both learning and research outcomes that link outcomes to user satisfaction. Includes detailed case studies. Appendix provides some recommended resources.

5707 **Effective financial planning for library and information services**
D. McKay   2nd edn, Europa, 2003, 114pp. £17.99. ISBN 9780851424644.
Clearly written guide to financial planning, with good definitions of financial terms and articulation of the key processes involved. Also provides tips on how to present your budget most effectively to secure funding.

5708 **Managing change: a how-to-do-it manual for librarians**
S.C. Curzon   rev. edn, Neal-Schuman, 2005, 129pp. $55. ISBN 1555705537.
Contains ten chapters dealing with different aspects of change, each with a 'Quick Check' list of key steps and questions, followed by 15 'change scenarios' (new for this edition), each with a set of questions intended as discussion points or coaching prompts. Offers good advice on forming a change task force, analysing resistance and evaluating progress, but neglects the key area of technological change, and has minimal indexing and no references.

5709 **Managing information services**
S. Roberts and J. Rowley   Facet Publishing, 2004, 242pp. £29.95. ISBN 9781856045155.
Gives a well written summary of the area. Key areas covered include management and managing organizations; people in organizations; human resource management; marketing and user relationships; quality management; finance and resources; environment and context; strategy and planning.

5710 **Marketing concepts for libraries and information services**
E.E. De Sáez   2nd edn, Facet Publishing, 2002, 224pp. £34.95. ISBN 9781856044264.
Coverage includes: what is marketing?; the corporate mission; marketing strategies for librarians and information professionals; the marketing mix; promotion and public relations; market segmentation; marketing research and market research; corporate identity and corporate image; the marketing plan. Ideal for someone new to the field.

5711 **Project management: tools and techniques for today's ILS professional**
B. Allan   Facet Publishing, 2004, 208pp. £32.95. ISBN 1856045048.
Divided into two main sections, dealing respectively with 'The project life cycle, systems and processes' and 'Projects and people', this book provides an accessible and well balanced introduction to the subject for people embarking on smallscale projects. Chapters are illustrated by case studies

from the literature and the author's own experience. There is useful coverage of the important process of bidding for funds and although some aspects of the text have dated (e.g. sources of project funding), the basic advice remains sound. 'For the practitioner who has been given a new project to undertake and needs some help and advice on where to start, this book would … be very valuable.' (*Journal of Librarianship and Information Science*)

5712 **Supervising and leading teams in ILS**
B. Allan   Facet Publishing, 2006, 224pp. £39.95. ISBN 9781856045872.
Practical guide aimed at team leaders and supervisors in library and information work, covering key areas such as communication, motivation, delegation and monitoring, delivering feedback, training and development, human resource management and managing difficult situations. Illustrated with examples taken from different ILS sectors and supported by checklists and self-development inventories.

Handbooks & manuals

5713 **Becoming a fundraiser: the principles and practice of library development**
V. Steele and S.D. Elder   2nd edn, ALA Editions, 2000, 138pp. $38. ISBN 9780838907832.
Provides the tools necessary for bringing librarians' development and fundraising skills up to the level necessary to lead an effective campaign.

5714 **Blueprint for your library marketing plan: a guide to help you survive and thrive**
P.H. Fisher and M.M. Pride   ALA Editions, 2006, 135pp. $50. ISBN 9780838909096.
Comprehensive text covering strategic plans, mining data, target markets, focusing resources, promotion and so on. Useful set of marketing plan worksheets as an Appendix.

5715 **Change management in information services**
L. Pugh   2nd edn, Ashgate, 2007, 230pp. £55. ISBN 0754646653.
Provides insights on change processes and guidance on implementing change, drawing on contemporary theory and real-world practices from organizational studies and information services. Topics covered include change theories, strategies and models; organizational metaphors and structures; teams and leadership in change management; the psychology of change and skills of change management. Includes case studies, explanatory diagrams and detailed index.

5716 **A comprehensive library staff training program in the information age**
A. Wood   Chandos, 2007, 357pp. £39. ISBN 9781843341185.
Provides guidance and resources to support training and development of library staff, covering areas such as training needs analysis, performance appraisal, personal development planning, curriculum vitae, learning styles, course development, informal methods and portfolio building.

5717   Delivering satisfaction and service quality: a customer-based approach for libraries
P. Hernon and J.R. Whitman   ALA Editions, 2001, 181pp. $45. ISBN 9780838907894.
Chapters are: 1. Understanding customer service; 2. Understanding service quality; 3. Understanding customer satisfaction; 4. The framework for improving service quality and customer satisfaction over time; 5. Developing and implementing a service plan; 6. Assessing and evaluating satisfaction; 7. Using computer technology to conduct surveys; 8. Analyzing survey results; 9. The challenges to being successful.

5718   Developing strategic marketing plans that really work
T. Kendrick   Facet Publishing, 2006, 192pp. £34.95. ISBN 185604548X.
www.facetpublishing.co.uk/websupport.shtml [COMPANION]
Following an introduction on marketing in the public library context, provides a step-by-step process to help public library staff research, plan and implement effective marketing strategies, with advice on key aspects such as segmentation, communication and project management. Appendix of 20 'fast-track templates' available to download from the web.

5719   Evaluating the impact of your library
S. Markless and D. Streatfield   Facet Publishing, 2006, 170pp. £39.95. ISBN 9781856044882.
www.facetpublishing.co.uk/evaluatingimpact [COMPANION]
Explains limitations of traditional approaches to impact evaluation and offers a new step-by-step model, developed by working with libraries in many different sectors. Provides detailed guidance on formulating success criteria, defining impact indicators and methods of collecting, analysing, interpreting and presenting evidence. The main text is prefaced with an explanation of key terms used and followed by an extensive set of references and index. The companion website provides evaluation tools and materials.

5720   Fundraising for libraries: 25 proven ways to get more money for your library
J. Swan   Neal-Schuman, 2002, 411pp. $75. ISBN 1555704336.
Based on US policy and practice, but many suggestions are applicable elsewhere. Part I has 8 chapters covering the fundamentals of fundraising, including writing grant bids, soliciting donations, selling goods and passive fundraising; Part II offers 25 'proven fundraising techniques', including deferred giving, annual campaigns, book fairs, direct mail, memorial gifts, special events and many others.

5721   Getting and staying noticed on the web: your web promotion questions answered
P. Bradley   Facet Publishing, 2002, 219pp. £39.95. ISBN 9781856044554.
Written by an expert in web technologies and their uses, this easy-to-read question and answer style handbook explains web promotion specifically as it relates to websites in the library and information world.

5722   Information marketing
J.E. Rowley   2nd edn, Ashgate, 2006, 228pp. £50. ISBN 0754644138.
The revised edition of this highly regarded work provides comprehensive coverage of marketing theories and techniques applied to an information and library services

context. Covers essential concepts such as marketing orientation, branding and customer relationship management, with useful focus on the challenges of marketing e-services, the role of customers in the service experience and the library brand. Includes extensive referencing and detailed indexing, enhancing its value as a reference resource.

5723   Leadership and learning: helping libraries and librarians reach their potential
L. Pugh   Scarecrow, 2001, 256pp. £32. ISBN 0810841460.
Provides a comprehensive overview of the literature on learning and library organizations, on the basis that librarians need to understand the theories behind both workplace learning and the organizational structures and attitudes supporting that learning. The arguments are supplemented by a series of case studies.

5724   Library and information center management
R.D. Stueart and B.B. Moran   7th edn, Libraries Unlimited, 2007, 492pp. $50. ISBN 9781591584063.
The latest edition of a classic text with wide-ranging and in-depth coverage. 20 chapters organized into seven sections: 1. Introduction; 2. Planning; 3. Organizing; 4. Human Resources; 5. Leading; 6. Coordinating; 7. Managing in the 21st century. Includes new chapters on marketing, team building and ethics; additional mini-cases and other activities; and updated references with more extensive international coverage. The misleadingly titled section on 'Coordinating' covers financial management and performance measurement.

5725   Library marketing that works!
S. Walker   Neal-Schuman, 2004, 257pp. Includes CD-ROM, $75. ISBN 1555704735.
Good, easily readable manual. Seven chapters in three parts: I. Strategic planning; II. Marketing planning processes; III. New directions in marketing. Two appendices summarize 'Marketing tools you can use'.

5726   Managerial accounting for libraries and other not-for-profit organizations
G.S. Smith   2nd edn, ALA Editions, 2002, 288pp. $65. ISBN 9780838908204.
Substantial and comprehensive work, especially valuable for the quantity and quality of its examples illustrating library-specific scenarios. Enables librarians to move from budgeting for and recording costs to relating those costs to mission-based business goals.
'... provides a thorough explanation of how the various costs incurred by libraries can be identified and then used ... appropriate for libraries in both the public and private sectors and essential reading for any librarian with substantial financial responsibility ... highly recommended' (*Feliciter*)

5727   Managing information services: a transformational approach
J. Bryson   2nd edn, Ashgate, 2006, 346pp. £28. ISBN 0754646343.
Thoroughly revised version of a highly-regarded text, which provides comprehensive treatment of the subject, but in a dynamic, engaging style, with good use of headings, charts and figures to define and illustrate key issues. Covers all the key areas, including strategic planning, corporate culture, leadership, managing people, accountability and service quality.

'… an excellent overview of the skills, competencies and knowledge required by today's library and information leaders … crammed with useful management tools and approaches and would be a useful addition to any information manager's bookshelf.' (*New Library World*)

5728 Managing outsourcing in library and information services
S. Pantry and P. Griffiths   Facet Publishing, 2005, 190pp. £34.95. ISBN 9781856045438.
Outsourcing of library and information services has presented many challenges. This work – illustrated by case studies – gives helpful guidance on how to achieve the best results.

5729 Measuring library performance: principles and techniques
P. Brophy   Facet Publishing, 2006, 242pp. £39.95. ISBN 9781856045939.
Authoritative and comprehensive guide to current thinking and practice, which draws on literature from the library and business management domains. Covers staff surveys, infrastructure assessment, benchmarking and standards, in addition to user satisfaction and input, throughput, output and impact measures. Appendices include a 40-page guide to data collection methods, supported by examples and sources of further information, followed by shorter sections on analysis of data and presentation of results. Includes index.

5730 Staff management in library and information work
P. Jordan and C. Lloyd   4th edn, Ashgate, 2002, 308pp. £62.50. ISBN 0754616517.
Comprehensively revised edition of the standard text in the field. Eight chapters cover: The working environment; Motivation and job satisfaction; Human resource planning; Job descriptions and person specifications; Recruitment and selection of staff; Staff appraisal; Staff training and development; and Staff supervision and interpersonal skills training. Offers both theoretical and practical perspectives, providing extensive lists of references and reproducing many examples of HR documentation from UK libraries.

5731 Strategic management of information services: a planning handbook
S. Corrall   Aslib/IMI, 2000, 364pp. £45. ISBN 0851423469.
Despite its age, this volume remains the most comprehensive treatment of the application of strategic management theory to information services practice. It offers practical guidance on all aspects of strategy development and implementation, supported by references to general management and library literature. Eight chapters cover planning paradigms, environmental appraisal, strategic focus, strategy formation, finance matters, achieving change, securing capability and managing flexibility. Key features include annotated suggestions for further reading and the extensive treatment of the financial processes of budgeting, costing and accounting, supported by a glossary of key concepts. Includes author and subject indexes.

Library Systems & Technology

Introductions to the subject

5732 Computers for librarians: an introduction to the electronic library
S. Ferguson and R. Hebels; Charles Sturt University   3rd edn, Centre for Information Studies, 2003, 332pp. AUS$60.50. ISBN 1876938609.
'(T)akes a top-down approach, starting with applications such as the internet, information sources and services, provision of access to information resources and library management systems, before looking at data management, computer systems and technology, data communications and networking and library systems development.'

5733 Introduction to imaging
H. Besser [et al.]; Getty Research Institute   rev. edn, 2003, 89pp. $22.50. ISBN 9780892367337.
www.getty.edu/research/conducting_research/standards [COMPANION]
Ideal short introduction. The revised edition 'expands on such fundamental issues as the different varieties and uses of metadata, the utilization of controlled vocabularies and digital preservation'. The Getty website provides access to much else of value in this arena.

5734 Library information systems: from library automation to distributed information access solutions
T.R. Kochtanek and J.R. Matthews   Libraries Unlimited, 2002, 287pp. $49. ISBN 9781591580188.
Suitable for those new to the field or requiring a refresher, 14 chapters are organized in four main parts: The broader context; The technologies; Management issues; and Future considerations. The technologies section covers integrated library systems, open systems, telecommunications and networking and standards, but not hardware. Management issues include planning, usability, the impact of technology on library services and systems administration, in addition to the authors' eight 'technology axioms'. The final section covers technology trends and digital libraries, concluding with a useful glossary and detailed index.

5735 Library technology companion: a basic guide for library staff
J.R. Burke   2nd edn, Neal-Schuman, 2006, 239pp. $59.95. ISBN 9781555705502.
http://techcompanion.blogspot.com [COMPANION]
Provides an excellent introduction for newcomers and a useful update for experienced staff. Seventeen chapters arranged in five sections deal with library technology basics, technology tools, applications, managing the technology environment and the future. The book reviews the history of library technology and identifies ten key developments, before considering the current situation. Coverage is broad, including blogs, flash drives, handhelds, laptops, MP3s, open source, podcasts, RSS, tablets, wi-fi and wikis, in addition areas such as adaptive/assistive technology, distance learning and virtual reference. Later sections cover security, troubleshooting, infrastructure and advice on technology planning. Also includes illustrative examples, resource lists and extensive glossary. A companion blog provides access to updated resources and materials.

'... Neal-Schuman *Library Technology Companion* will be useful for all library staff as well as for any librarians involved in developing guidelines and policies to implement and manage technology.' (*Journal of the Medical Library Association*)

5736 **Putting XML to work in the library: tools for improving access and management**
D.R. Miller and K.S. Clarke   ALA Editions, 2004, 205pp. $48. ISBN 9780838908631.
Good introduction to XML and its current and possible applications within the library environment.

Associations & societies

5737 **Library & Information Technology Association** [USA]
www.lita.org
Division of the American Library Association with a special interest in activities designed to promote, develop and aid the implementation of library and information technology. Website provides access to the LITA Blog, Wiki and Technology Electronic Reviews, an irregular publication offering reviews of print and electronic resources about information technology.

5738 **Multimedia Information & Technology Group** [UK]
www.mmit.org.uk
Special interest group of CILIP, with a focus on the acquisition, application and effective use of multimedia resources and appropriate technology in library and information services. Organizes meetings, publishes the journal *Multimedia information and technology (MmIT)* (online access restricted to members) and produces occasional factsheets, covering topics such as library systems suppliers and portals.

Portal & task environments

5739 **Library Technology Guides: Key resources in the field of Library Automation**
www.librarytechnology.org
Independent site offering comprehensive and objective information related to the field of library automation, enabling users to find information on products and companies and track developments in the field. Key sections include the company directory, bibliographic database, current news and data on systems used by US academic and public libraries. Maintained by Marshall Breeding, Director of Innovative Technology and Research for the Jean and Alexander Heard Library at Vanderbilt University.

5740 **oss4lib: open source systems for libraries**
www.oss4lib.org
Established at Yale Medical Library in 1999 and maintained by Dan Chudnov. The mission of oss4lib is 'to build better and free systems for use in libraries'. Provides listing of free software and systems designed for libraries and tracks news about open source projects and related areas.

5741 **Technical Advisory Service for Images** [UK]
www.tasi.ac.uk
A JISC-funded service providing advice and guidance to the UK's further and higher education community. A rich well designed and presented website provides excellent access to

advice, training, helpdesk, resources, glossary, image sites and a blog.

Handbooks & manuals

5742 **The complete RFID handbook: a manual and DVD for assessing, implementing, and managing radio frequency identification technologies in libraries**
D.M. Ward   Neal-Schuman, 2007, 274pp. $75. ISBN 9781555706029.
Provides advice on planning and implementing RFID, from the initial decision, through procurement and installation to marketing of new services and education of staff and users. Includes detailed information on both equipment (tags, readers, security gates, networks) and uses (inventory, self-check in and out, material handling and sorting, security). A companion DVD demonstrating existing library implementations can be used for management briefing and/or staff training.

5743 **How to build a digital library**
I.H. Witten and D. Bainbridge   Morgan Kaufman, 2002, 518pp. £38.99. ISBN 9781558607903.
www.greenstone.org [COMPANION]
Good coverage of content choice, user interfaces, markup and metadata, construction and delivery. Useful section on interoperability: standards and protocols (but now in need of update). The work is based on use of the Greenstone digital library software produced by the New Zealand Digital Library Project at the University of Waikato and which was developed and distributed in cooperation with UNESCO and the Human Info NGO.

5744 **Managing information technology: a handbook for systems librarians**
P. Ingersoll and J. Culshaw   Libraries Unlimited, 2004, 199pp. $50. ISBN 9780313324765.
Concise but comprehensive handbook for systems librarians and others with an interest in library technology, covering key areas of concern, including planning, staffing, communication, development, service and support, training, physical space and daily operations of the library systems function, concluding with a thoughtful look at current trends in technology. The book is clearly structured, facilitating use as a reference resource. Substantial appendix includes numerous references, charts and worksheets, suitable for local adaptation, as well as a detailed index.
'*Managing information technology* would be an asset to any systems librarian's office. The book accurately represents the primary areas of concern to today's library IT personnel and offers strong guidance for readers to consider viable solutions to their own local situations and settings ... systems librarians will find themselves returning to this handbook for guidance or suggestions well after their first read.' (*Journal of the American Society for Information Science and Technology*)

5745 **Planning for integrated systems and technologies: a how-to-do-it manual for librarians**
J.M. Cohn [et al.]   2nd edn, Neal-Schuman, 2001, 201pp. $65. ISBN 1555704212.
Inspired by the authors' landmark *Planning for automation* (2nd edn, Neal-Schuman, 1997), this comprehensive guide is intended for medium and small libraries of all types.
'Whether installing a system for the first time or replacing one, you'll find invaluable information and techniques for

assessing, acquiring, using and maintaining an automated system. A step-by-step section on selection and implementation covers everything from preparing RFPs and evaluating vendor proposals to negotiating contracts, testing and training.'

5746   Radio frequency identification handbook for librarians
C. Haley, L.A. Jacobsen and S. Robkin   Libraries Unlimited, 2007, 176pp. $45. ISBN 1591583713.
Identifies emerging trends with RFID technology and supplies information enabling the right questions to be asked and answered, such as 'Why should my library consider implementing RFID?'; 'What components make up an RFID system?'; 'How do I select a vendor?'; and 'How do I manage a barcode-RFID conversion project?'.

5747   Software for indexing
S. Schroeder, ed.; American Society of Indexers   Information Today, 2003, 275pp. $35. ISBN 1573871664.
Now somewhat out of date, but provides a good overview of still commonly used software tools for indexing, covering the major dedicated indexing programs, but also more specialized tools – including, for instance, voice recognition software.

5748   The strategic management of technology: a guide for library and information services
D. Baker   Chandos, 2004, 305pp. £39. ISBN 9781843340416.
Written by a former university librarian and director of information services, combines strategic management and information systems perspectives with case studies based on the author's personal experience of implementing technology in a higher education environment. Chapters cover strategic technology management, innovation and improvement, scenario planning, systems thinking and strategy implementation, illustrated with tables and diagrams throughout and rounded off with a concluding summary.

5749   Technology planning: preparing and updating a library technology plan
J.R. Matthews   Libraries Unlimited, 2004, 160pp. $50. ISBN 1591581907.
Organized around a possible structure for a library technology plan, explains different parts of the document and how they relate to each other. Chapters cover the purpose and need for a technology plan, the description of the library, challenges facing the library, emerging technologies, current technology environment, assessment of the current environment, evaluation of the library's website, recommendations and evaluation of the plan.

5750   Using open source systems for digital libraries
A. Rhyno   Libraries Unlimited, 2003, 176pp. $38. ISBN 9781591580652.
A practical and logical guide to using open source software to build digital libraries. Covers authoring and presentation tools; relational, object, XML and DL-specific databases; scripting languages; integration of digital libraries into the mainstream; and their long-term maintenance and preservation. Includes end notes, resource lists, a glossary and index.

5751   Wireless networking: a how-to-do-it manual for librarians
L. Alcorn and M.M. Allen   Neal-Schuman, 2006, 125pp. $65. ISBN 1555704786.
Explains why and how libraries should go wireless, covering technical issues such as equipment, standards, transfer rates and security, in addition to management concerns, including costs, planning and implementation. Appendices include a glossary of terminology, examples of policy documents and information on equipment manufacturers.

Keeping up to date

5752   Biblio Tech Review
www.ringgold.com/biblio-tech
Monthly news magazine from a commercial site providing news, analysis and comment on the library automation industry, together with an e-directory of suppliers of library products and services.

5753   Information Technology and Libraries
Library & Information Technology Association   qtrly. ISSN 07309295.
www.lita.org/ital
Refereed journal published by LITA. Includes material related to all aspects of libraries and information technology, including digital libraries, metadata, authorization and authentication, electronic journals and electronic publishing, networks, computer security, technical standards, futuristic forecasting, vendor relations, etc.

5754   Library Hi Tech
Emerald, qtrly. ISSN 07378831.
www.emeraldinsight.com
Refereed journal with a focus on computing and technology (broadly defined) for the library community. Journal issues are generally themed, allowing for extensive in-depth coverage and analysis of key areas.
- **Library Hi Tech News** Emerald, 10 p.a. ISSN 07419058. Related publication, issued 10 times a year, combines short features, conference reports, regular columns, news items and a diary of forthcoming events worldwide.

5755   LITA-L
www.lita.org/ala/lita/litahome.cfm
Discussion list sponsored by the Library and Information Technology Association (a division of the American Library Association) but open to anyone interested in the application of information technology to libraries and information services. Used to exchange information, ask questions and post employment opportunities and other announcements.

5756   On libraries, services and networks
http://orweblog.oclc.org
Weblog of Lorcan Dempsey, Vice President and Chief Strategist, OCLC Online Computer Library Center, covering topics such as library systems and technologies, library organization and services, distributed library environments, e-resources, digital asset management, knowledge organization and representation, metadata, etc. Site also provides links to his recent presentations and publications.

5757   **Program: electronic library and information systems**
Aslib, qtrly. ISSN 02640473.
www.aslib.co.uk/program
Refereed journal publishing material on all aspects of the management and use of information technology in libraries, archives and information centres, with a particular focus on the automation of library and information services, the storage and retrieval of all forms of electronic information and the delivery of information to end users. Also covers database design and management, networking and communications technology, the internet, user interface design, systems procurement and evaluation, user training and support.

5758   **Web4Lib**
R. Tennant, comp.
http://lists.webjunction.org/web4lib
Electronic discussion list for the discussion of issues relating to the creation, management and support of library-based world wide web servers, services and applications. Web4Lib is specifically aimed at librarians and library staff involved in world wide web management, but anyone is welcome to join the discussion. There are around 3400 subscribers worldwide and an average of 15–20 messages every day.

Records Management & Archives Administration

archival appraisal • digital archives • electronic records • museum archives

Introductions to the subject

5759   **Archives and archivists in the information age**
R.J. Cox   Neal-Schuman, 2005, 325pp. $85. ISBN 1555705308.
Comprehensive text starting with 'Why organizations need archivists' and 'Why organizations need archival consultants' through 'The archivist in the knowledge age: what have we become?' and ending with 'Putting it altogether: case studies of four institutional records programs'.

Archiving websites: a practical guide for information management professionals
A. Brown   See entry no. 5549

5760   **Ethics and the archival profession: introduction and case studies**
K.M. Benedict   Society of American Archivists, 2003, 90pp. $34.95. ISBN 9781931666053.
40 case studies cover nearly every facet of professional archival work.

The film preservation guide: the basics for archives, libraries, and museums
National Film Preservation Foundation   See entry no. 5555

5761   **First steps in archives: a practical guide**
ARLIS/UK & Ireland   2004, 45pp. £25. ISBN 0951967495.
Short, useful overview compiled by the Visual Archives Committee of the Art Libraries Society/UK & Ireland: 'This straightforward introduction to the key principles of archive work is designed for anyone whose collections include

archive material but who has no formal training in this area. It includes contributions from experienced archivists on the core subjects of acquisitions and appraisal, cataloguing, preservation, reader services and marketing, as well as a glossary of archive terms.'

5762   **Managing archives: foundations, principles and practice**
C. Williams   Chandos, 2006, 248pp. £39.95. ISBN 9781843343127.
A practical guide, aimed specifically at newcomers to the field, which covers the principles and purposes of records and archives; selection, appraisal and acquisition; intellectual organization and access; preservation and conservation of both paper and digital materials; and management of the service. Illustrated by examples representing different sectors and formats and supported by a bibliography arranged by subject to stimulate further reading.

5763   **Museum archives: an introduction**
D. Wythe, ed.; Society of American Archivists   2nd edn, 2004, 256pp. $62. ISBN 1931666067.
Wide-ranging collection of essays on the challenges within the 'museum archives' movement.

5764   **Organizing archival records: a practical method of arrangement and description for small archives**
D.W. Carmicheal   2nd edn, AltaMira Press, 2004, 104pp. Includes CD-ROM, $34.95. ISBN 9780759104402.
Explains the purpose of organizing records and provides step-by-step guidance, covering both manual and computer-based record-keeping. Introduces the basic terminology and theory of organization and how to avoid common pitfalls. Includes real-world examples, exercises and sample forms. Accompanying CD-ROM includes forms contained in the main text and also provides an Access database created for organizing archival materials.

5765   **Understanding archives and manuscripts**
J. O'Toole and R.J. Cox; Society of American Archivists   2nd edn, 2006, 255pp. $49. ISBN 9781931666206.
Excellent introduction for those new to the world of archives and manuscripts.

Dictionaries, thesauri, classifications

5766   **A glossary of archival and records terminology**
R. Pearce-Moses; Society of American Archivists   2005.
www.archivists.org/glossary
A first-class resource. This new edition targets 'a wider audience of anyone who needs to understand records because they work with them. It attempts to build a bridge between records, information technology and business communities by interpreting archival concepts for people in other disciplines, while at the same time explaining those other disciplines to archivists and records professionals.' Includes a very useful and extensive bibliography of over 300 items, the majority with URLs.

Laws, standards, codes

5767   **Describing archives: a content standard (DACS)**
Society of American Archivists   2007, 300pp. $49.
The standard 'officially approved by the Society of American

Archivists as an SAA standard in 2004, following review by its Standards Committee, its Technical Subcommittee for Descriptive Standards and by the general archival community ... DACS is an output-neutral set of rules for describing archives, personal papers and manuscript collections and can be applied to all material types. It is the US implementation of international standards (i.e., ISAD(G) and ISAAR(CPF)) for the description of archival materials and their creators'.

Encoded archival description (EAD)
Library of Congress and Society of American Archivists See entry no. 5529

Recommendations for the storage and exhibition of archival documents: BS5454:2000
British Standards Institution See entry no. 5568

Associations & societies

5768 ARMA International
www.arma.org
Access to an extensive set of resources. 'The association was established in 1955. Its approximately 11,000 members include records managers, archivists, corporate librarians, imaging specialists, legal professionals, IT managers, consultants and educators, all of whom work in a wide variety of industries, including government, legal, healthcare, financial services and petroleum in the United States, Canada and 30-plus other countries.' Formerly known as The Association of Records Managers & Administrators.

■ **Emergency management for records and information programs V.A. Jones and K.E. Keyes** 2001, 120pp. $44. ISBN 0933887981. 'Updated to better address electronic records, as well as salvage and recovery procedures, this essential guide will help you prepare for and recover from natural or manmade disasters. Its five sections provide a step-by-step guide through the essential phases of emergency management – prevention, preparedness, response, and recovery …'.

■ **The Information Management Journal** , bi-monthly. $95. ISSN 15352897. www.arma.org/imj/index.cfm. '(T)he leading source of information on topics and issues central to the management of records and information worldwide. Each issue features insightful articles written by experts in the management of records and information. Its goal is to advance the records and information management field's knowledge base and help satisfy the ever-changing educational needs of information management professionals worldwide'.

■ **Managing electronic records W. Saffady** 3rd edn, 2002, 198pp. $58. ISBN 1931786054. Classic text providing a comprehensive discussion of records management concepts and methodologies as they apply to electronic records.

5769 International Association of Sound & Audiovisual Archives
www.iasa-web.org
Established in 1969 to function as a medium for international cooperation between archives that preserve recorded sound and audiovisual documents. Has a number of specialist committees and regional branches – which can serve as good sources for further information.

5770 International Council on Archives
www.ica.org
'(T)he professional organization for the world archival community, dedicated to promoting the preservation,

development and use of the world's archival heritage. It brings together national archive administrations, professional associations of archivists, regional and local archives and archives of other organizations as well as individual archivists.'

■ **Ica-L** www.mailman.srv.ualberta.ca/mailman/listinfo/ica-l. Discussion list designed to facilitate communication between members of ICA, and to promote the international diffusion of professional news and materials.

5771 International Federation of Television Archives
http://fiatifta.org
'International professional association established to provide a means for cooperation among broadcast and national audiovisual archives and libraries concerned with the collection, preservation and exploitation of moving image and recorded sound materials and associated documentation.'

5772 Society of American Archivists
www.archivists.org
Now with almost 5000 members. Very active society whose members enjoy access to a wide range and depth of resources – many of which can be accessed by non-members. The Society publishes or sponsors significant publications, a number cited elsewhere here and including the bi-annual *American Archivist* and the bi-monthly *Archival Outlook*.

Libraries, archives, museums

National Archives
See entry no. 61

National Archives & Records Administration
See entry no. 62

Portal & task environments

5773 UNESCO Archives Portal
www.unesco.org/webworld/portal_archives
Designed as a comprehensive gateway to information for archivists and archives users. The Archives window covers government, academia and culture, and social life. The Resources window covers primary sources online, internet resources, education and training, and preservation and conservation. The Communities window covers associations, conferences, meetings and exhibitions, international cooperation, and others. The gateway seems not as frequently updated as would be ideal, but is worth exploration by those new to the field.

Directories & encyclopedias

5774 Archives Hub [UK]
www.archiveshub.ac.uk
'A national gateway to descriptions of archives in UK universities and colleges.' Covers over 80 institutions. Detailed subject search facility.

5775 British archives: a guide to archive resources in the United Kingdom
J. Foster and J. Sheppard, eds   4th edn, Palgrave, 2002, 815pp. $220. ISBN 0333735366.
Lists 1231 entries, including business archives, in addition to ecclesiastical, learned society, local authority, museum and university repositories. Entries cover historical background, major collections, finding aids, access and facilities. Includes annotated list of 57 useful organizations and useful publications (10 pp.) arranged in 19 sections. Indexes provide access by names of repository, organization, collection and subject.

Handbooks & manuals

5776 Archival appraisal: theory and practice
B.L. Craig   K.G. Saur, 2004, 224pp. €80. ISBN 9783598115387.
Good, clear summary of the techniques that can be used to appraise items for archive acquisition.

5777 Arranging and describing archives and manuscripts
K.D. Roe   Society of American Archivists, 2005, 180pp. $49. ISBN 9781931666138.
Definitive guide to arranging and describing archival materials.

5778 Building digital archives, descriptions and displays: a how-to-do-it manual for librarians and archivists
F.J. Stielow   Neal-Schuman, 2003, 229pp. $75. ISBN 1555704638.
Excellent step-by-step explanations covering planning the digitization project, understanding digitzed finding aids, creating effective web finding aids, and so on. Useful webliography – though of course now dated.

5779 Copyright for archivists and records managers
T. Padfield   3rd edn, Facet Publishing, 2007, 306pp. £34.95. ISBN 9781856046046.
Authoritative text by the UK National Archives copyright expert, covering regulations in the UK and other countries, with guidance on many contemporary problems and domains, including contractual assignments and licences; electronic signatures and declaration forms; digital rights management systems; software and databases; performers' and artists' rights; exhibitions; electoral registers; and magistrates' courts.

5780 Developing and maintaining practical archives: a how-to-do-it manual
G.S. Hunter   2nd edn, Neal-Schuman, 2003, 457pp. $65. ISBN 1555704670.
Award-winning text whose second edition was expanded to include crucial new information on digital records, encoded archival description (EAD), copyright issues, post-9/11 security concerns and international perspectives on these issues. Ideal for someone new to the field.

The law of libraries and archives
B.M. Carson   See entry no. 5470

5781 Managing archival and manuscript repositories
M.J. Kurtz; Society of American Archivists   2004, 255pp. $49. ISBN 1931666091.
Applies management theory and practice to the archives domain. Includes sample policy and planning documents to illustrate the principles discussed and provides useful overviews of selected readings to support each chapter.

5782 Managing electronic records
J. McLeod and C. Hare, eds   Facet Publishing, 2005, 202pp. £39.95. ISBN 9781856045506.
Edited collection providing a useful overview of research, theory and practice in the area.

5783 Managing records: a handbook of principles and practice
E. Shepherd and G. Yeo   Facet Publishing, 2003, 318pp. £39.95. ISBN 9781856043700.
An authoritative work giving thorough and detailed coverage of management of both paper and electronic records.

Manual of archival description
M. Proctor and M. Cook   See entry no. 5546

An ounce of prevention: integrated disaster planning for archives, libraries, and record centres
J. Wellheiser and J. Scott; Canadian Archives Foundation   See entry no. 5587

5784 Photographs: archival care and management
M.L. Ritzenthaler [et al.]   Society of American Archivists, 2006, 550pp. $84.95. ISBN 9781931666176.
Systematic and comprehensive manual, covering: Archival management of photos; History of photography; Preservation issues and techniques; Interpreting photographs; Legal issues; Digitizing; Using photographs in outreach and educational efforts.

Preserving archives
H. Forde   See entry no. 5589

5785 Privacy and confidentiality perspectives
Society of American Archivists, 2005.
Edited collection of essays exploring the legal, ethical, administrative and institutional issues and dilemmas surrounding the management of access to records containing personal information, drawing on the contributors' personal experience.

5786 Providing reference services for archives and manuscripts
M.J. Pugh   Society of American Archivists, 2005, 368pp. $49. ISBN 1931666121.
Well written and authoritative, especially useful for contrasting the differences between reference work within archives and within libraries.

5787 Selecting and appraising archives and manuscripts
F. Boles; Society of American Archivists   2005, 214pp. $49. ISBN 9781931666114.
This revised edition by a recognized authority in the field covers the theory and practice of selection and appraisal, combining a review of contemporary debate on the subject with practical guidance and advice on the selection process.

Keeping up to date

5788   Archives and Archivists (AandA) List
Society of American Archivists
www.archivists.org/listservs/arch_listserv_terms.asp
Sponsored by the Society, the A&A list is an open forum for
archivists on all topics relating to archival theory and
practice. The list is open to all individuals with an interest in
the archival profession and in the preservation and
promotion of archival materials. SAA membership is not
required for participation in the list.

5789   Archives-nra
www.jiscmail.ac.uk/lists/ARCHIVES-NRA.html
The UK discussion list for archivists, conservators and
records managers, which has more than 2000 subscribers.

5790   RECMGMT-L
www.arma.org/rim/listserv.cfm [DESCRIPTION]
The Records/Info Management Listserv is a free e-mail
listserv devoted to discussion of records and information
management. Its archives are located at:
http://lists.ufl.edu/archives/recmgmt-l.html

5791   RECORDS-MANAGEMENT-UK
www.jiscmail.ac.uk/archives/records-management-uk.html
The UK Records Management mailing list has more than
1000 subscribers and is used for the discussion of RM
theory and practice, with the mission of sharing knowledge
and expertise.

TOOLS FOR INFORMATION PROFESSIONALS

Tools for Information Professionals

Introductions to the subject

5792 Discovering computers: fundamentals
G.B. Shelly, T.J. Cashman and M.E. Vermaat   3rd edn, Cengage Learning, 2006, 552pp. $74. ISBN 1418843725.
www.course.com/catalog/product.cfm?isbn=1-4188-4372-5
[DESCRIPTION]
'Covers basic computer concepts [and] knowledge required to be computer literate in today's digital world; contains new Ethics and Issues boxes, updated Looking Ahead boxes, revised FAQ boxes, Web links, Companies on the cutting-edge and Technology Trailblazers in each chapter; engages students and teaches fundamental skills with Learn How To exercises, now, including a new video component; features a Discussion Forum on the Online Companion, connecting students everywhere using Discovering Computers: Fundamentals, Third Edition; enhances your learning experience by posting questions and thoughts on Chapter Review or Web Research exercises on the Online Companion.'

5793 E-learning and teaching in library and information services
B. Allan   Facet Publishing, 2002, 273pp. £34.95. ISBN 1856044394.
'Concentrates on ... the pedagogical approaches and models that can underpin uses of interactive network-based media and materials for learning'. Also examines the theory and jargon of pedagogy.
   'Written in an accessible style and includes a large number of "cookbook" examples that could probably be re-used by other professionals and institutions'. Focuses 'mainly on information-handling skills rather than other academic subject disciplines'.

5794 How to do research: a practical guide to designing and managing research projects
N. Moore   3rd edn, Facet Publishing, 2006, 192pp. £24.95. ISBN 9781856045940.
'Focuses on the day-to-day requirements of project managing a piece of research right through from the formulation of the initial idea, to the development of a research proposal and then to the writing up and disseminating of results.'
'As a guide to managing the research process and producing results it is a worthwhile companion to more comprehensive reseach methodology texts.' (*Australian Library Journal*)
'... this is a very useful book written in an accessible style that provides a succinct overview of the social research process and methods.' (LASIE)

5795 The internet under the hood: an introduction to network technologies for information professionals
R.E. Molyneux   Libraries Unlimited, 2003, 328pp. $40. ISBN 1591580056.
'Providing a clear and comprehensive introduction to network applications and concepts, this practical text covers the internet; IP addresses; network operating systems; routing; domain names; servers; file formats; and more. It also includes information about the economics of the internet, privacy, intellectual property and legal issues.'
'Molyneux provides a readable and often engaging primer for setting up your library, organization, or home office network ... a valuable guide for the information professional who either is new to networking or who seeks greater understanding of these technologies and their applications.' (*Public Libraries*)

5796 Introduction to patents information
S. Ashpitel, D. Newton and S. Van Dulken   4th edn, British Library Publishing, 2002, 143pp. £34. ISBN 712308628.
'A practical introduction to searching for patent information ... aimed at both the interested beginner and the more experienced user who can employ the guide as a reference tool. It explains how patent documents evolve and what they consist of; the numeration and structure of the patent documents of six major patenting authorities; and how to carry out subject searching, with an extensive appendix on major databases. There are many illustrations taken from the actual patent specifications.'

5797 Jump start your career in library and information science
P.K. Shontz   Scarecrow, 2002, 208pp. $31.95. ISBN 0810840847.
'Designed to help new librarians begin to manage a successful and satisfying career in the library and information science profession ... the book contains advice and anecdotes gathered from research and interviews with more than 70 information professionals in a variety of library-related careers. The book is written in a practical, easy-to-read style.'

5798 The library and information professional's internet companion
A. Poulter, D. Hiom and D. McMenemy   Facet Publishing, 2005, 200pp. £34.95. ISBN 9781856045094.
'This book will help information professionals to fully understand new internet technologies and applications in a workplace context and acts as a springboard to further sources of information.'

5799 Net crimes and misdemeanors: outmaneuvering web spammers, stalkers, and con artists
J.A. Hitchcock   2nd edn, CyberAge Books, 2006, 496pp. $24.95. ISBN 9780910965729.
www.netcrimes.net [COMPANION]
'Practical and easy-to-follow methods for dealing with spam, viruses, hack attacks, identity theft and other online dangers. A lifeline for both individuals and business Web users, the book covers a broad range of abusive practices and features dozens of firsthand anecdotes and success stories.'

5800 The semantic web: a guide to the future of XML, web services, and knowledge management
M.C. Daconta, L.J. Obrst and K.T. Smith   Wiley, 2003, 312pp. $35. ISBN 0471432571.
An easily read introductory overview with very good coverage of the semantic web as a concept, XML, web services, RDF (Resource Description Framework), taxonomies and ontologies. There is a helpful last chapter, 'Crafting your company's roadmap to the semantic web'.

5801 Web of deception: misinformation on the Internet
A.P. Mintz, ed.   CyberAge Books, 2002, 278pp. Foreword by Steve Forbes, $24.95. ISBN 0910965609.
'Intentionally misleading or erroneous information on the Web can wreak havoc on your health, privacy, investments, business decisions, online purchases, legal affairs and more. Until now, the breadth and significance of this growing problem for internet users have yet to be fully explored. In *Web of Deception*, Anne P. Mintz (Director of Knowledge Management at Forbes Inc.) brings together 10 information industry gurus to illuminate the issues and help you recognize and deal with the flood of deception and misinformation in a range of critical subject areas. A must-read for any internet searcher who needs to evaluate online information sources and avoid Web traps.'

5802 The weblog handbook: practical advice on creating and maintaining your blog
R. Blood   Basic Books, 2002, 208pp. $14. ISBN 073820756X.
www.rebeccablood.net/handbook [COMPANION]
Useful introductory guide: 'a clear and concise guide to everything one needs to know about the phenomenon that is exploding on the Web. [The author] expertly guides the reader through the whole process of starting and maintaining a Weblog and answers any questions that might pop up along the way, such as the elements of good Weblog design and how to find free hosting.'

5803 Your essential guide to career success
S. Pantry and P. Griffiths   Facet Publishing, 2003, 144pp. 2nd edn of *Your successful LIS career: planning your career, CVs, interviews and self-promotion*, £22.95. ISBN 9781856044912.
'Essential read for any information professional eager to prosper in the library and information environment of the 21st century. It offers guidance on managing every stage of your career, whether you are a new entrant to the profession wishing to know how to get a foot on the ladder, an information professional in mid-career wishing to progress, or a candidate for a more senior position needing a view of the current state of the profession.'

Terminology, codes & standards

5804 Unicode and multilingual support in HTML, fonts, web browsers and other applications
A. Wood
www.alanwood.net/unicode
First-rate personal interest site – a superb cornucopia, frequently refreshed and renewed.

Dictionaries, thesauri, classifications

5805 Acronym Finder
www.acronymfinder.com
'With more than 565,000 human-edited entries, Acronym Finder is the world's largest and most comprehensive dictionary of acronyms, abbreviations and initialisms.' Also provides access to *The Free Dictionary*: 'English, Medical, Legal, Financial and Computer Dictionaries, Thesaurus, Acronyms, Idioms, Encyclopedia, a Literature Reference Library and a Search Engine all in one!'

5806 The Guardian dictionary of publishing and printing
Guardian Unlimited   3rd edn, A. & C. Black, 2006, 320pp. £9.99. ISBN 9780713675894.
'This fully revised edition includes over 9000 words and expressions relating to the printing and publishing industry and allied trades. Topics covered are bookselling, typesetting, desktop publishing and design, copyright, editing, commissioning, contracts, rights, electronic publishing, papermaking, ink, printing and binding. Definitions are given in clear, simple English meaning that this dictionary is perfect for anyone wanting core terminology at their fingertips.'

5807 OneLook dictionary search
www.onelook.com
A delightful service to use: 'Think of this website as a search engine for words and phrases: If you have a word for which you'd like a definition or translation, we'll quickly shuttle you to the web-based dictionaries that define or translate that word. If you don't know how to spell the word, we'll help you do that too. No word is too obscure: More than 5 million words in more than 900 online dictionaries are indexed by the OneLook® search engine.'

5808 YourDictionary.com: the last word in words
www.yourdictionary.com
Access to more than 2500 dictionaries and grammars in over 300 languages. The section Speciality Dictionaries lists dictionaries and glossaries of specialized words in the English language, organized by subject area.

Laws, standards, codes

5809 ConsortiumInfo.org: the source for standard-setting news and information
Gesmer Updegrove LLP.
www.consortiuminfo.org
Excellent site maintained by Boston, USA-based law firm that specializes in representing technology clients. As well as extensive information about the current situation and developments in standards generally, focuses particularly on consortia: 'While standard setting has been an important

aspect of industrial society for over a hundred years, the formation of unofficial, fast-acting standard setting and promotional consortia is a more recent phenomenon. Given that the first wave of consortia was not formed until the late 1980s, the consortium process has only recently begun to be seriously studied.'

The Consortium and Standards List is a regularly updated annotated and worldwide list of several hundred such organizations; subject and geographical categorizations are available.

5810   CrossRef
Publishers International Linking Association
www.crossref.org

Mission is to be 'the citation linking backbone for all scholarly information in electronic form. CrossRef is a collaborative reference linking service that functions as a sort of digital switchboard. It holds no full-text content, but rather effects linkages through Digital Object Identifiers (DOI), which are tagged to article metadata supplied by the participating publishers. The end result is an efficient, scalable linking system through which a researcher can click on a reference citation in a journal and access the cited article. The service is operated by a non-profit, independent organization Publishers International Linking Association whose Board of Directors comprises representatives from AAAS (Science), AIP, ACM, APA, Blackwell Publishers, Elsevier Science, IEEE, Kluwer, Nature, OUP, Sage, Springer and Wiley.'

CrossRef has been a great success story. Late in 2003, it announced that 'it will drop its DOI retrieval fees for all members and affiliates starting in January 2004. This move gives all CrossRef users unlimited access to DOIs and is particularly significant for secondary publishers, as DOI links from citations and bibliographic databases to full-text are expected to increase greatly as a result'. Then early in 2004 we read that 'the 10 millionth DOI registered was … From the Japanese Society for Hygiene (and) among the other content types now included in CrossRef are the new Molecule Pages produced by Nature Publishing Group and the Alliance for Cellular Signaling.' By early April 2004, 300 publishers had signed up; and at the end of that month, there was the significant announcement of CrossRef Search, a collaboration with Google: 'Now, researchers and students interested in mining published scholarship have immediate access to targeted, interdisciplinary and cross-publisher search on full-text using the powerful and familiar Google technology … CrossRef Search is available to all users, free of charge, on the websites of participating publishers and encompasses current journal issues as well as back files. The results are delivered from the regular Google index but filter out everything except the participating publishers' content and will link to the content on publishers' websites via DOIs (Digital Object Identifiers) or regular URLs.' Nine organizations participated in the pilot, a mixture of professional society and commercial publishers.

Early 2005 CrossRef had 1408 participating publishers, 349 members, 34 affiliates, 6 agents and 490 library affiliates. There were over 15 million registered DOIs. C.f. the entry for Digital Object Identifier System.

■ **Distributed Systems A. Powell, comp.; UKOLN** .
www.ukoln.ac.uk/distributed-systems. Summary of range of projects which – inter alia – provides useful access to current work on OpenURL and related initiatives.

■ **OpenURL** http://library.caltech.edu/openurl. Being developed by National Information Standards Organization. Provides an architecture for context-sensitive reference linking in the web-based scholarly information environment. Now widely used since its introduction in 2002.

■ **Publishing requirements for industry standard metadata: PRISM** www.prismstandard.org. 'Defines an XML metadata vocabulary for managing, aggregating, post-processing, multi-purposing and aggregating magazine, news, catalog, book, and mainstream journal content.' Recommends use of existing standards such as XML, RDF, Dublin Core.

5811   Digital Object Identifier System
International DOI Foundation
www.doi.org

System for 'identifying and exchanging intellectual property in the digital environment … The DOI System provides a framework for managing intellectual content, for linking customers with content suppliers, for facilitating electronic commerce and enabling automated copyright management for all types of media … Several million DOIs have been assigned by DOI Registration Agencies in the US, Australasia and Europe … DOIs are names (characters and/or digits) assigned to objects of intellectual property (physical, digital or abstract) such as electronic journal articles, images, learning objects, e-books, images, any kind of content. They are used to provide current information, including where they (or information about them) can be found on the internet. Information about a digital object may change over time, including where to find it, but its DOI will not change.'

Excellent website: especially valuable are the FAQ section, the Glossary of Terms and the 169-page DOI Handbook which contains an extensive bibliography. C.f. entry for CrossRef.

5812   IMS Global Learning Consortium
www.imsglobal.org

'Develops and promotes the adoption of open technical specifications for interoperable learning technology … IMS specifications and related publications are made available to the public at no charge … No fee is required to implement the specifications.'

Some 50 contributing members come from every sector of the global e-learning community, including hardware and software vendors, educational institutions, publishers, government agencies, systems integrators, multimedia content providers and other consortia.

5813   International Digital Publishing Forum: international trade and standards organization for the digital publishing industry
www.idpf.org

Members consist of hardware and software companies, print and digital publishers, retailers, libraries, accessibility advocates, authors and related organizations whose common goals are to establish specifications and standards and to advance the competitiveness and exposure of the electronic publishing industries. Currently oversees two open international standards: the Open Publication Structure (OPS) and Open Container Format (OCF) used for the production and distribution of ".epub" file content.

5814   International ISBN Agency
www.isbn-international.org

Promotes, coordinates and supervises the worldwide use of the ISBN system – the standard numbering system for 'books, software, mixed media etc. in publishing, distribution and library practices.' Its Users' Manual can be downloaded as a PDF file; and there is also a description of the Directory.

■ **Publishers' international ISBN directory** 33rd edn, K.G. Saur, 2006/2007, 5914pp. €548. ISBN 3598215924 ISSN 09391975. www.saur.de/index.cfm?lang=EN&ID=0000012120 [DESCRIPTION]. 4 v. Edited by the Agency. CD-ROM version available.

5815 ISSN International Centre
www.issn.org

'The ISSN (International Standard Serial Number) is an eight-digit number which identifies periodical publications as such, including electronic serials. More than one million ISSN numbers have so far been assigned … It is managed by a world wide network of 77 National Centres coordinated by an International Centre based in Paris, backed by Unesco and the French Government.'

The new ISO standard, ISO 3297:2007, was completed in August 2007. ISSN Compact is a quarterly CD-ROM containing details of all currently assigned ISSNs plus a list of serial title word abbreviations: more than 54,000 words and their abbreviations in 70 languages. ISSN Online is the (fee-based) Web version.

5816 LLRX.com: law and technology resources for legal professionals
Law Library Resource Xchange LLC.
www.llrx.com

'Unique, free Web journal dedicated to providing legal, library, IT/IS, marketing and administrative professionals with the most up-to-date information on a wide range of internet research and technology-related issues, applications, resources and tools, since 1996.'

5817 Open Archives Initiative
www.openarchives.org

Develops and promotes interoperability standards that aim to facilitate the efficient dissemination of content. The Initiative 'has its roots in an effort to enhance access to e-print archives as a means of increasing the availability of scholarly communication'.

5818 Patent, trademark and copyright searching on the Internet [USA]
C.C. Sharpe   McFarland, 2000, 240pp. $39.95. ISBN 0786407573.

First five chapters concern patent laws and applying for a patent. Patent searching is in chapters 6–10. Limited to law and searching US patents and inevitably some internet sources have now changed. Likewise Part II on trademarks is restricted to the USA. No content on searching for copyright records. Appendices give copies of official forms and documents.

'A gem … a well-crafted and easy-to-use handbook.' (*Reference Reviews*)

5819 Understanding barcoding
B. Williams   Pira International, 2004, 428pp. £99. ISBN 1858029171.
www.pira.co.uk [DESCRIPTION]

Objective: to present enough information to help a range of readers understand barcoding in ways that suit each of their needs. Well designed and presented manual that progresses from four overview chapters in Part 1, through to Parts 2 and 3, which present eight chapters on the main codes, how they work and how technology is developing. Part 4 is more

detailed, for those who really need to understand the technicalities. Extensive glossary.

5820 Unicode
www.unicode.org

'Unicode provides a unique number for every character, no matter what the platform, no matter what the program, no matter what the language. The Unicode Standard has been adopted by such industry leaders as Apple, HP, IBM, JustSystem, Microsoft, Oracle, SAP, Sun, Sybase, Unisys and many others. Unicode is required by modern standards such as XML, Java, ECMAScript (JavaScript), LDAP, CORBA 3.0, WML, etc. and is the official way to implement ISO/IEC 10646. It is supported in many operating systems, all modern browsers and many other products. The emergence of the Unicode Standard and the availability of tools supporting it, are among the most significant recent global software technology trends.'

5821 Z39.50: International Standard Maintenance Agency
Library of Congress
www.loc.gov/z3950/agency

Links to information about Z39.50 resources and about the development and maintenance of Z39.50 (existing as well as future versions) and the implementation and use of the Z39.50 protocol. The standard specifies a client/server-based protocol for searching and retrieving information from remote databases.

Official & quasi-official bodies

5822 International Council of Museums
http://icom.museum

Non-governmental organization maintaining formal relations with UNESCO and having a consultative status with the United Nations Economic and Social Council. Financed primarily by membership fees, but supported by various governmental and other bodies. 17,000 members. Hosts the extensive Virtual Library Museums Pages and this, rather than the search engine on the site itself, is usually the best place to start a search for detailed information.

■ **Museums of the world** M. Zils, comp.   11th edn, K.G. Saur, 2004, 1277pp. €428. ISBN 359820616X.

Research centres & institutes

5823 Corporation for National Research Initiatives [USA]
www.cnri.reston.va.us

'Undertakes, fosters and promotes research in the public interest. Activities center around strategic development of network-based information technologies, providing leadership and funding for research and development of the National Information Infrastructure.'

Responsible for publication of *D-Lib Magazine*.

Associations & societies

5824 Association of American Publishers
www.publishers.org

Principal trade association of the US publishing industry, representing publishers of all sizes and types. Has active

Professional and Scholarly Publishing Division concerned about Open Access and other related politically charged issues.

5825 Association of American University Presses

http://aaupnet.org

125 members located around the world. Interesting and useful set of resources, including a scholarly publishing bibliography and descriptions of e-publishing initiatives among their membership.

Each year the Association works with the Public Library Association to recommend a list of notable books for public and high school libraries.

5826 Association of Learned & Professional Society Publishers

www.alpsp.org

'The international trade association for not-for-profit publishers and those who work with them; it currently has 272 members in 30 countries.' The site has an impressive list of Hot Topics (e.g. 'Developing Country Initiatives'; 'Linking'; 'Peer Review'; 'Science Citation Index'), with each topic being provided with Links to papers from the Association and other bodies. There are also many other good lists of sources of scholarly and scientific publishing related material, each regularly updated.

An excellent resource.

◼ **Learned Publishing** , qtrly. ISSN 09531513.

http://www.ingentaconnect.com/content/alpsp/lp [DESCRIPTION]. '*Learned Publishing* is the journal of the Association of Learned and Professional Society Publishers, published in collaboration with the Society for Scholarly Publishing. The journal is published quarterly in January/April/July/October. *Learned Publishing* is a major international journal, packed with the latest ideas and informed opinion to help you maximise new opportunities. The journal publishes 6–7 informed, topical articles in each issue plus reports on major initiatives and developments in the industry from around the world. Editorials, peer-reviewed research and other articles, personal views and book reviews cover all the major issues facing the world of academic publishing today. *Learned Publishing* is abstracted in *ASLIB Current Awareness, European Science Editing, Library and Information Science Abstracts and Sociological Abstracts*; fully covered in *Current Contents/Social and Behavioural Science* and the Institute for Scientific Information's *Social SciSearch* online database and *Research Alert* current awareness service; contents list indexed in the British Library Document Supply Centre's *Inside Information* database.'

5827 Association of Librarians & Information Professionals in the Social Sciences

www.alissnet.org.uk

A not-for-profit unincorporated professional society formed to 'provide opportunities for networking and self-development; offer a forum for communication; [and] create a network of cooperation and a forum for discussion about emerging issues in social science librarianship'.

◼ **ALISS Quarterly** , qtrly. £20. 'Designed for information workers and social scientists and offers a scholarly, but informal approach to a wide range of social science and information work related topics. Areas recently covered include: Knowledge Management, electronic regulation and professional development. Each issue also contains articles on information literacy.' Previously. published as *ASSIGNation*.

5828 Data Publishers Association [UK]

www.dpa.org.uk

Over 100 members, commercial and non-commercial. Full list of members giving addresses, key personnel, basic operating details (no. of employees, established, turnover, parent company), together with an A–Z list of the directories they produce, a valuable feature. Subject index. Useful source.

5829 EDUCAUSE: transforming education through information technologies [USA]

www.educause.edu

Non-profit association whose mission is 'to advance higher education by promoting the intelligent use of information technology. Membership is open to institutions of higher education, corporations serving the higher education information technology market and other related associations and organizations. EDUCAUSE programs include professional development activities, print and electronic publications, strategic policy initiatives, research, awards for leadership and exemplary practices and a wealth of online information services. The current membership comprises nearly 1900 colleges, universities and education organizations, including more than 180 corporations and more than 13,000 active member representatives.'

The Association has a good, interesting and current Resource Center including links to articles, books, conference sessions, contracts, effective practices, plans, policies, position descriptions and blog content. Early 2005, the 'Topical Resources' were categorized: Cybersecurity; Information systems and services; Technology management and leadership; Libraries and technology; Networking and emerging technologies; Policy and law; Teaching and learning.

◼ **EDUCAUSE Quarterly** qtrly. ISSN 15285324.

http://connect.educause.edu/eq/. '*EDUCAUSE Quarterly* includes articles (written by professionals in the field and peer-reviewed) that relate to planning, developing, managing, using, and evaluating information resources in higher education. Information resources encompass technology, services, and information. In general, *EDUCAUSE Quarterly* articles deal with the subject of campus information resources from a management point of view. The journal offers feature articles sharing campus experiences; columns dealing with current issues (including national policy issues and campus management issues); articles in the "good ideas" department, viewpoint pieces, and recommended reading.'

◼ **EDUCAUSE Review** , bi-monthly. ISSN 15276619.

www.educause.edu/apps/er/. 'The magazine takes a broad look at current developments and trends in information technology, what these mean for higher education, and how they may affect the college/university as a whole.'

5830 Foundation Center [USA]

www.fdncenter.org

'Mission is to strengthen the nonprofit sector by advancing knowledge about US philanthropy.' Its Online Librarian service was developed 'to respond to your need for factual information on foundations, philanthropy and other issues related to nonprofits and to assist with your fundraising research'. The Foundation Finder provides 'basic information about foundations within the universe of more than 70,000 private and community foundations in the USA'.

◼ **Foundation Directory**

http://fdncenter.org/learn/classroom/fdoguidedtour [FEE-BASED]. Instant access to information on thousands of grant makers and their giving interests.

◼ **Foundation Grants Index** http://fdncenter.org/marketplace [DESCRIPTION]. Records describing grants that have been awarded to non-profit organizations by the larger independent, corporate and community foundations (over 1000 in 1995) located in the USA. 1,157,705 records as of February 2004.

5831 Information Access Alliance [USA]
www.informationaccess.org

'Over the past two decades, increased concentration in the publishing industry has been accompanied by significant escalation in the price of serials publications, eroding libraries' ability to provide users with the publications they need. Nowhere does this seem more troublesome than in the market for scientific, technical and medical (STM) journals and legal serial publications where pricing, as well as marketing practices for electronic publications, threatens library budgets and ultimately the widespread availability of important writings to the public.'

The Information Access Alliance (IAA) is 'a joint initiative of leading US national library organizations to address problems in the scholarly and legal publishing markets, which are characterized by insupportably high prices, accelerating industry consolidation, and anti-competitive practices by some large publishers.'

- **The academic publishing industry M.H. Munroe**
www.ulib.niu.edu/publishers/. Useful review, early 2005 last updated June 2004, of ten leading STM publishing conglomerates: Blackwell; Bertelsmann; Candover and Cinven (Springer); Elsevier; Holtzbrinck; McGraw-Hill, Pearson; T&F Informa; Thomson; Wolters Kluwer.

5832 Institute of Translation & Interpreting [UK]
www.iti.org.uk

'Founded in 1986 as the only independent professional association of practising translators and interpreters in the United Kingdom. It is now one of the primary sources of information on these services to government, industry, the media and the general public.' ITI Subject Networks include Construction; Information technology; Medical and pharmaceutical; Patents; and Terminology. There is a free service that will help find a qualified provider of language services among the Institute's membership.

5833 International Federation of Classification Societies
www.classification-society.org

Federation of national, regional and linguistically-based classification societies; aims are to further classification research. Among other activities, the IFCS organises a biennial conference, publishes a newsletter and supports the *Journal of Classification*. For its communications it is starting to use the Class-L listserver, set up by the Classification Society of North America and currently with about 50 members.

5834 National Federation of Abstracting & Indexing Services
www.nfais.org

'Seeks to be recognized globally as the premier membership organization for groups that aggregate, organize and facilitate access to information.' Not a great deal on the site for non-members; but the descriptions of the work of the 50 or so members of the Federation give a good overview of current foci in this arena.

5835 Society for Scholarly Publishing [USA]
www.sspnet.org

Founded 1978. Good sets of website resources, including well laid-out, annotated and wide-ranging list of interesting

links. Also a useful calendar of forthcoming conferences, meetings, etc. Developing a professional services directory.

Portal & task environments

5836 Scholarly Societies Project
J. Parrott, ed. University of Waterloo
www.scholarly-societies.org

'Facilitating access to information about scholarly societies across the world since 1994.'

A superb facility. It is very well laid-out, with good search and display facilities; and the Guidelines for Inclusion in the Scholarly Societies Project are exceptionally clear: the focus is on societies with scholarly, academic, or research goals; preference is given to membership-based societies (in which a qualified person may apply to become a member); societies must have the URL of their website in standard domain-name format (with some exceptions noted); preference is given to societies of an international or national scope (again with some exceptions); any country; all languages; all academic subjects; societies must have a website if the society was founded from 1900 to the present.

Project entries include the society name, an English translation of the society name (if not originally in English), the URL and URL Stability Index of the website (if the society has a website), the language of the website, the subject pages in the Project where the website occurs, the founding year and notes about name changes (if any) and the geographical scope of the society. In October 2007 the Project was describing 4131 societies and providing access to 3804 websites.

Much other good information is provided: e.g. Creating a society website: recommendations – which includes helpful advice on keeping the URL as stable as possible.

Discovering print & electronic resources

5837 American reference books annual
S.G. Hysell   2007 edn, Libraries Unlimited, 2007, annual, 732pp. $125.00 [V. 38, 2007]. ISBN 1591585252.
www.arbaonline.com [FEE-BASED]

'Comprehensive, authoritative database for quality reviews of print and electronic reference works.

'ARBA 2007 consists of 37 chapters, an author/title index and a subject index. It is divided into four alphabetically arranged parts: "General Reference Works," "Social Sciences," "Humanities," and "Science and Technology." "General Reference Works" is subdivided by form: bibliography, biography, dictionaries and encyclopedias, government publications, handbooks and yearbooks and so on. Within the remaining three parts, chapters are organized by topic. Thus, under "Social Sciences" the reader will find chapters titled "Economics and Business," "Education," "History," "Law," "Sociology," and so on.'

- **Recommended reference books for small and medium-sized libraries and media centers S.G. Hysell**   Libraries Unlimited, 2007, 380pp. $70. ISBN 1591585260. Approximately 500 books selected as the best works for smaller libraries.

5838 CataList
www.lsoft.com/lists/listref.html

The official catalogue of lists based on LISTSERV, the e-mail list management software, originally developed in 1986 and the first e-mail list management software available. September 2007 inventoried over 50,000 public lists. Range of search options available, including viewing lists with more than 10,000 or more than 1000 subscribers; viewing lists by host country.

5839 China National Knowledge Infrastructure
www.global.cnki.net
'China National Knowledge Infrastructure is a key national e-publishing project of China started in 1996.' Coverage includes e-journals, newspapers, dissertations, proceedings, yearbooks and reference works.
- **Century journals** http://ckrd85.cnki.net/kns50/Navigator.aspx?ID=85 [DESCRIPTION]. 'Century Journals Project (CJP) selects the most important academic journals published in China and digitizes all issues since their very first issue up till 1993 in an effort to expand the China Academic Journals Full-text Database. The earliest journal dates back to 1915'.
- **China academic journals full-text database** http://ckrd85.cnki.net/kns50/Navigator.aspx?ID=1 [DESCRIPTION]. 'China Academic Journals Full-text Database (CAJ) is the largest searchable full-text and full-image interdisciplinary Chinese journals database in the world, covering over 8,460 titles since 1994 including 5,058 science and technology journals and 3402 social sciences and humanities journals by the end of 2007, article count reached over 25 million. The content is arranged into 10 series and 168 subjects for the convenience of academic research'.

5840 Directories in print: a descriptive guide to print and non-print directories, buyer's guides and other address lists of all kind [USA]
27th edn, Gale, 2007. 3 v., $720. ISBN 0787681970.
'The most comprehensive source in its field, *Directories in print* describes approximately 15,500 active rosters, guides and other print and nonprint address lists published in the United States and worldwide. Hundreds of additional directories (defunct, suspended and directories that cannot be located) are cited, with status notes, in the title/keyword index.'

5841 Directory of Open Access Journals
www.doaj.org
'Covers free, full-text, quality controlled scientific and scholarly journals ... [across] all subjects and languages. There are now 2832 journals in the directory. Currently 867 journals are searchable at article level.'

5842 Fulltext Sources Online
www.fso-online.com [FEE-BASED]
'Directory of over 35,000 full-text newspapers, journals, magazines, newsletters and transcripts from 30 aggregator products.'

5843 Fundamental reference sources
J.H. Sweetland   3rd edn, American Library Association, 2001, 612pp. $67.50. ISBN 0838907806.
'Completely updated and revised, this authoritative "reference on reference" features the best available materials in all media for general library collections. Credible and comprehensive, this handy manual outlines what it takes to easily locate, evaluate and select the best information sources for a wide variety of needs.'

5844 Genamics JournalSeek
www.journalseek.net
Database of journal information (not textual content), which

'presently contains 92871 titles. Journal information includes the description (aims and scope), journal abbreviation, journal home page link, subject category and ISSN. Searching this information allows the rapid identification of potential journals to publish your research in, as well as allow[ing] you to find new journals of interest to your field.'

5845 The Internet Public Library
www.ipl.org
The IPL is 'the first public library of and for the internet community [and] an experiment, trying to discover and promote the most effective roles and contributions of librarians to the internet and vice versa'. Provides a directory of human-edited and approved websites.

5846 The IPL's blog list
www.ipl.org/div/blogs
Excellent 'library-related' gateway to categorized lists of blogs plus much else of value about blogging. 'We only add blogs with substantive content and that we deem useful to those searching for information.'

5847 Lexicool.com: directory of bilingual and multilingual dictionaries
www.lexicool.com
Pleasant, easy-to-use site whose aim 'has been to create a complete and efficient search utility for linguists, especially translators and interpreters. The site is run by an international team of linguists and IT specialists based in France.'
    The efficient dictionary search engine has links to over 3500 bilingual and multilingual dictionaries and glossaries freely available on the internet, with each dictionary classified against about 60 languages (Afrikaans to Yiddish) and 20 subject areas. An e-zine lists new dictionaries and glossaries referenced at the site.

5848 Libweb: Library Servers via WWW
http://lists.webjunction.org/libweb
'Libweb currently lists over 7700 pages from libraries in 146 countries.' Content spans library sectors.

5849 Majordomo
Great Circle Associates.
www.greatcircle.com/majordomo
'Program which automates the management of internet mailing lists. Commands are sent to Majordomo via electronic mail to handle all aspects of list maintenance. Once a list is set up, virtually all operations can be performed remotely by e-mail.'

5850 Metacritic
www.metacritic.com
Provides 'access to and summarize[s] the vast amount of entertainment criticism available online'. Useful resource for critical information about film, video, music, games, books and television.
'Winner of the 2006 *BUDDIE* Award. The pre-eminent criterion for any aggregated database is its content. On this measure, Metacritic is unsurpassed. It gathers reviews from hundreds of respected and authoritative Web sites, including prominent newspapers (*Los Angeles Times*, *The Wall Street Journal*, *The Washington Post*, and dozens of other dailies), general magazines (*Entertainment Weekly*, *New Republic*, *The New Yorker*, *Newsweek*, *TIME*), Web journals (The Onion, Slate, Salon.com), and dozens of

special-interest publications, including *Booklist*, *Kirkus Reviews*, *Library Journal*, and many gamer magazines. Most of the reviews are full text. Those not available in full text have informative abstracts. All reviews have the Metacritic rating.' (*Information Today*)

5851 National Library Catalogues Worldwide
University of Queensland: Library
www.library.uq.edu.au/natlibs
'Lists national library catalogues alphabetically by country ... [and] aims to give all the information necessary to connect to the catalogue'.

5852 OAIster
University of Michigan: Library
www.oaister.org
'OAIster is a union catalog of digital resources ... [providing] access to these digital resources by "harvesting" their descriptive metadata (records) using OAI-PMH (the Open Archives Initiative Protocol for Metadata Harvesting)'.

5853 The Online Books Page
J.M. Ockerbloom, ed.
http://onlinebooks.library.upenn.edu
'Listing over 25,000 free books on the Web'. Contains only legitimate, free, full-text, well-formatted items.

5854 Open Directory Project
http://dmoz.org
'The largest, most comprehensive human-edited directory of the Web. It is constructed and maintained by a vast, global community of volunteer editors.' Submissions undergo editorial review and are therefore based on relevance to a given subject or category rather than usual search engine rating criteria. Significant numbers of sites under the Social Science area at www.dmoz.org/Science/Social_Sciences/

5855 Open J-Gate
Informatics India.
www.openj-gate.org
'An electronic gateway to global journal literature in open access domain ... indexed from 3000+ open access journals, with links to full-text at Publisher sites'. Includes access to more than 1500 peer-reviewed scholarly journals, links to one million+ open access articles, full-text links which are regularly validated, classification of journals in a three-level hierarchical system to provide for better relevancy in search results, table of contents browsing, and easy-to-use search functionality.

5856 Reference Reviews
Emerald, 8 p.a. £5795.29. ISSN 09504125.
www.emeraldinsight.com
'Choosing the most appropriate reference material can be a difficult decision for librarians and information service managers. With no guidelines to keep them on the right track, mistakes can prove costly. A subscription to *Reference Reviews* helps you to make informed decisions by offering comprehensive analyses of the latest and most significant reference material available today. Written for librarians by librarians, each in-depth review offers a comprehensive and unbiased appraisal by professionals who understand the criteria you use when purchasing a resource. Each issue also contains an editorial that outlines the key issues for reference librarians today and highlights some of the major

developments for the future. With the advent of the World Wide Web, *Reference Reviews* also provides a regular commentary on the wealth of resources and material available online in its internet Column. When using *Reference Reviews*, making key purchasing decisions has never been easier.'

5857 Repositories of primary sources
T. Abraham, comp.
www.uidaho.edu/special-collections/Other.Repositories.html
'A listing of over 5000 websites describing holdings of manuscripts, archives, rare books, historical photographs and other primary sources for the research scholar. All links have been tested for correctness and appropriateness.' Coverage is global.

5858 Scholarly electronic publishing bibliography
C.W. Bailey   University of Houston Libraries, 1996–, qtrly.
www.digital-scholarship.org/sepb
'This bibliography presents selected English-language articles, books and other printed and electronic sources that are useful in understanding scholarly electronic publishing efforts on the internet. Most sources have been published from 1990 to the present; however, a limited number of key sources published prior to 1990 are also included. Where possible, links are provided to sources that are freely available on the internet.'

Wide-ranging, valuable service – available by e-mail or as a weblog. Good selective directory of related websites. Search facility.

5859 The software encyclopedia: a guide for personal, professional and business users
2007 edn, Bowker, annual. 2 v., $440. ISBN 0835249115.
www.bowker.com/catalog/000103.htm [DESCRIPTION]
A 'comprehensive, easy-to-navigate guide filled with detailed information on micro-computer software. Listings of over 44,600 software programs from 4646 publishers and distributors are fully annotated to facilitate research and acquisition.'

5860 Specialist and technical dictionaries catalogue
Grant & Cutler.
www.grantandcutler.com/dictionaries
Lists of bilingual and multilingual specialist and technical dictionaries, as well as books of interest to translators and other language professionals, organized into 29 sections and produced by the UK's largest language bookseller.

5861 Syndic8
www.syndic8.com
Access to master list of over 100,000 syndicated news content feeds; reviews and pointers to syndicated tools and sites; much other useful information.

5862 Taxonomy Warehouse
www.taxonomywarehouse.com
'Created in 2001 as a valuable community resource, available free to users and vocabulary publishers to help organizations maximize their information assets and break through today's information overload ... Some interesting statistics about Taxonomy Warehouse: Over 660 Taxonomies; Classified by 73 subject domains; Produced by 261 publishers; In 39 languages; 65% produced in digital media; 100 directly licensable.'

5863 **Tile.net: the comprehensive internet reference**
http://tile.net
Inventories of e-mail newsletters and e-zines; Usenet newsgroups; computer products vendors; internet and web design companies.

5864 **The web library: building a world class personal library with free web resources**
N.G. Tomaiuolo   CyberAge Books, 2004, 440pp. $29.95. ISBN 0910965676.
www.ccsu.edu/library/tomaiuolon/theweblibrary.htm [COMPANION]
'This is an easy-to-use guide, with chapters organized into sections corresponding to departments in a physical library. *The Web Library* provides a wealth of URLs and examples of free material you can start using right away, but best of all it offers techniques for finding and collecting new content as the Web evolves.'

Digital data, image & text collections

5865 **Calisphere: a world of digital resources**
www.calisphere.universityofcalifornia.edu
'More than 150,000 digitized items – including photographs, documents, newspaper pages, political cartoons, works of art, diaries, transcribed oral histories, advertising and other unique cultural artifacts – reveal the diverse history and culture of California and its role in national and world history.'

5866 **Credo Reference**
Previously Xreferplus.
www.xreferplus.com [FEE-BASED]
Comprehensive online access to a number of reputable reference sets. 'Credo Reference enables users to find authoritative answers fast. It features content from hundreds of reference books in a broad range of subjects. CILIP/Nielsen BookData named Credo Reference, formerly Xrefer, an outstanding electronic reference work in 2003.'

5867 **ebrary**
www.ebrary.com/corp [DESCRIPTION]
E-book distribution software. 'Acquire integrated collections of eBooks and other content under a variety of ownership and subscription models. Distribute your own eContent choosing a business model that meets your needs.'

5868 **Eprints for digital repositories**
www.eprints.org
Dedicated to opening access to the refereed research literature online through author/institution self-archiving.

5869 **HighWire Press**
http://highwire.stanford.edu
'A division of the Stanford University Libraries, HighWire Press hosts the largest repository of high impact, peer-reviewed content, with 1065 journals and 4,422,368 full-text articles from over 130 scholarly publishers. HighWire-hosted publishers have collectively made 1,774,834 articles free.'
■ **Project MUSE** http://muse.jhu.edu. 'Project MUSE is a unique collaboration between libraries and publishers providing 100% full-text, affordable and user-friendly online access to over 300 high quality humanities, arts, and social sciences journals from 60 scholarly publishers … MUSE began in 1993 as a pioneering joint project of the Johns Hopkins University Press and the Milton S. Eisenhower Library at JHU.'

5870 **Index to theses** [UK]
www.theses.com
Listing over 500,000 theses, with abstracts, from British and Irish universities dating back as far as 1716. Significant collection, covering all subject fields. Highly useful gateway.

5871 **Internet Archive: universal access to human knowledge**
www.archive.org
'The internet Archive is building a digital library of internet sites and other cultural artifacts in digital form.' Free to access, the Archive allows users to track back to historical versions of a particular website. Extremely useful for examining changing trends in web design and web technologies.

5872 **JSTOR: the scholarly journal archive**
www.jstor.org
'JSTOR is a not-for-profit organization with a dual mission to create and maintain a trusted archive of important scholarly journals and to provide access to these journals as widely as possible. JSTOR offers researchers the ability to retrieve high-resolution, scanned images of journal issues and pages as they were originally designed, printed and illustrated. The journals archived in JSTOR span many disciplines.' The resource is not a current issues database, but an archive of back issues.

5873 **NetLibrary**
OCLC Online Computer Library Center
www.netlibrary.com
Comprehensive gateway to e-Book and e-Audiobook content. 'More than 100,000 titles and hundreds of global publishers already represent a comprehensive inventory of trade, reference and STM content.'

5874 **Networked Digital Library of Theses and Dissertations**
www.ndltd.org
International scope, providing information on Electronic Thesis and Dissertation (ETD) programmes as well as access to a variety of collections.
■ **VT ETDs from the Digital Libraries and Archives Virginia Tech**. http://scholar.lib.vt.edu/theses/. Access to over 10,000 electronic theses and dissertations from the organization hosting the Networked Digital Library of Theses and Dissertations.

5875 **ProQuest dissertations and theses**
www.il.proquest.com/promos/product/feature01_umi.shtml [DESCRIPTION]
Worldwide in scope, with over 2 million citations and 890,000 full-text PDF copies of dissertations and theses. PDQT also permits usage reporting on access to 24-page previews, enabling libraries to track popular items.
■ **Dissertation Express**
www.il.proquest.com/products_umi/dissertations/disexpress.shtml [FEE-BASED]. Offers delivery of unbound printed copies of dissertations and theses from a collection of 1.9 million.
■ **PQDT Open**
www.il.proquest.com/products_umi/dissertations/pqdt.shtml. 'Online repository of dissertations and theses published on an open access basis.' Newly launched, the list of material available is limited but due to expand significantly.

5876 Research Channel [USA]
www.researchchannel.org
A 'nonprofit media and technology organization that connects a global audience with the research and academic institutions whose developments, insights and discoveries affect our lives and futures.' Streams academic content both online and via cable television from collaborative institutions, including the Library of Congress, the University of Washington and John Hopkins University. 'The library houses more than 3000 full-length programs that are available 24 hours a day, seven days a week.'

5877 RSSxpress: RSS channel editor and directory [UK]
A. Powell
http://rssxpress.ukoln.ac.uk
Service to create, modify and register RSS news channels plus directory of RSS channels in the UK higher education and further education community, the UK cultural sector (galleries, libraries and museums) and in related organizations.

Directories & encyclopedias

5878 A.S.K. Hollis 2007: the directory of UK associations: the definitive guide to organisations representing a membership, a message and a mission
R. Sarginson and E. Canavan, eds   7th edn, Hollis Publishing, 2006, 935pp. £160. ISBN 1904193366.
www.hollis-publishing.com/ask.htm [DESCRIPTION]
'Over 6000 associations, pressure groups, unions, institutes, societies and more are profiled, representing every interest area from abrasives through to zoos, from industrial, professional and business sectors to government, charities and the consumer.'

5879 American national biography
www.anb.org [DESCRIPTION]
'Premier biographical work on people from all eras who have influenced and shaped American history and culture ... [with] profiles of more than 18,000 men and women from all walks of American life, from the well-known to the infamous to the obscure.'

5880 Annual register of grant support: a directory of funding sources
41st edn, Information Today, 2007, annual, 1500pp. $249. ISBN 9781573872928.
www.infotoday.com/books/directories/anreg.shtml [DESCRIPTION]
'Guide to more than 3500 grant-giving organizations offering non-repayable support.

'Organized by 11 major subject areas – with 61 specific subcategories – Grant Support 2008 is the definitive resource for researching and uncovering a full range of available grant sources. Not only does it direct you to traditional corporate, private and public funding programs, it also shows you the way to little known, non-traditional grant sources such as educational associations and unions.'

5881 The central register of charities [UK]
Charity Commission
www.charitycommission.gov.uk
'The Register holds comprehensive information about every registered charity in England and Wales.'

Can provide useful financial and other information about associations, societies, etc., officially registered as charities. There is a keyword search facility.
- **Britishcharities.com: the UK's definitive guide to charities** www.britishcharities.com. Subject categorization of charities: e.g. Animals and birds; Blind and partially sighted; Conservation and environment; Deaf and hard of hearing; etc.

5882 Councils, committees and boards – including government agencies and authorities: a handbook of advisory, consultative executive, regulatory and similar bodies in British public life
13th edn, CBD Research, 2004, 529pp. £163. ISBN 0900246952.
www.cbdresearch.com [DESCRIPTION]
Standard work giving access to details of some 2000 bodies.
- **Centres, bureaux and research institutes: the directory of UK concentrations of effort, information and expertise C.M. Edwards**   4th edn, CBD Research, 2000, 420pp. £125. ISBN 0900246855. 'Concentrations of effort and expertise, or which provide information to the general public and have "centre", "bureau" or "institute" in their names, specialising in areas ranging from acupuncture to whisky and from gerontology to organic farming'.

5883 Current British directories: a guide to the directories published in the British Isles
G.P. Henderson, ed.   14th edn, CBD Research, 2003. £165. ISBN 0900246936.
www.cbdresearch.com/CBD.htm [DESCRIPTION]
'2800 directories, yearbooks, guides, registers published in Britain in book, CD-ROM, internet and list formats – in fact any publication with directory information and in any field of activity.'

5884 Directory of British associations and associations in Ireland
18th edn, CBD Research, 2007, 879pp. Also available on CD-ROM, £215. ISBN 9780955451416.
www.cbdresearch.com/DBA.htm [DESCRIPTION]
The leading tool: 'Covers ALL aspects of life; it includes over 1500 trade associations, over 1350 professional bodies, over 800 learned societies; the remaining 3170 organizations fall into 19 separate categories such as art, education, farming, hobbies, medical, sports, etc.'

5885 Directory of European professional and learned societies
6th edn, CBD Research, 2004, 720pp. £147.50. ISBN 090024691X.
www.cbdresearch.com/DEPLS.htm [DESCRIPTION]
'Over 6000 European professional, academic, scientific and technical societies covering areas such as agriculture, astronautics, criminology and robotics.' Except for Great Britain and the Republic of Ireland, covers the whole of Europe, not just the EU.

5886 Directory of grant-making trusts
A. French, S. Johnston and D. Lillya, eds   20th edn, Directory of Social Change, 2007, 1016pp. In association with Charities Aid Foundation, £99. ISBN 9781903991794.
www.dsc.org.uk/acatalog/Grant_making_Trusts.html [DESCRIPTION]
'This comprehensive reference work covers 2500 grant-making trusts, with the potential to give collectively £3 billion a year. With fully updated information supplied by the trusts themselves, the entries include concise contact details, what is and what is not funded, type and range of grants made and examples of recent grants. The extensive indexes – by

geographical area, field of interest and type of beneficiary and type of grant – allow users to target the trusts that are most relevant to their needs.'

5887 Directory of museums, galleries and buildings of historic interest in the United Kingdom
K.W. Reynard, ed.   3rd edn, Europa Publications, 2003, 656pp. £150. ISBN 0851424732.
'Covers all types and sizes of museums; galleries of paintings, sculpture and photography; and buildings and sites of particular historic interest. It also provides an extensive index listing over 3200 subjects. The directory covers national collections and major buildings, but also the more unusual, less well known and local exhibits and sites.'

5888 Directory of research grants 2006
Oryx Press, 2006, annual, 952pp. $145. ISBN 1573566195.
'A treasure chest of information on more than 5100 current programs from 1880 sponsors, including US and foreign foundations, corporations, government agencies and other organizations. Find grants for basic research, equipment acquisition, building construction/renovation, fellowships and 23 other program types. Government grants include CFDA, NSF and NIH program numbers.'

5889 Government research directory [USA]
21st edn, Gale, 2007. $720. ISBN 0787684198.
'In this vital resource you'll find nearly 7600 research facilities and programs of the US and Canadian federal governments. Includes government sponsored or funded research projects from all US government cabinet departments, numerous independent agencies and Canadian government ministries. Entries are arranged by US cabinet department, independent government agency, or Canadian ministry. Also included are multiple access points through three indexes: subject, geographic and master.'

5890 International research centers directory
21st edn, Gale, 2007. $690. ISBN 0787684287.
'Access to more than 12,100 government, university, independent, nonprofit and commercial research and development activities in nearly 150 countries worldwide. Entries include English and foreign name of center, full mail and electronic address, personal contact, organizational affiliates, staff, description of research program, publications, services and more. Master, subject, personal name and country indexes are provided. Entries are organized into 17 subject sections with the sections grouped into 5 broad categories and have multiple access points through 4 indexes: subject, country, personal name and master.'

5891 Library resource guide: a catalog of services and suppliers for the library community [USA]
Information Today, annual.
www.libraryresource.com
Comprehensive database of library services and suppliers.

5892 The official museum directory
37th edn, National Register Publishing, 2006. 2 v., $315. ISBN 0872178110.
www.officialmuseumdir.com [DESCRIPTION]
US publication covering museums, historic sites, planetariums, technology centres, zoos, etc. of every size and type in all 50 states.

5893 Oxford dictionary of national biography
www.oxforddnb.com [DESCRIPTION]
'56,000 biographies of people who shaped the history of the British Isles and beyond, from the earliest times to the year 2003.' Limited amount of free content available on public pages, with the body of material available only to subscribers.

5894 Research centers directory [USA]
35th edn, Gale, 2007. Also published as *New research centers*, $800. ISBN 0787687758.
Reports on the programmes, facilities, publications, educational efforts and services of North America's leading non-profit research institutes. Includes more than 14,800 entries, organized into 17 subject sections.

5895 Trade associations and professional bodies of the UK and Eire
18th edn, Graham & Whiteside, 2005. $320. ISBN 186099430X.
Information on more than 3700 trade associations and professional bodies. There is also a companion *Trade associations and professional bodies of the continental European Union*: see website.

5896 Who's who
159th edn, A. & C. Black, 2007, annual, 2529pp. £145. ISBN 9780713675276.
www.ukwhoswho.com [DESCRIPTION]
'Published annually since 1849 and the first biographical book of its kind, [it is] among the world's most recognized and respected works of reference ... contain[ing] over 32,000 short biographies, continually updated, of living noteworthy and influential individuals, from all walks of life, worldwide. Approximately one thousand new entries are added every year.'
■ **Marquis who's who** www.marquiswhoswho.com [DESCRIPTION]. Originally published as *Who's Who in America*, the publication has grown 'to include the biographies of millions of leaders and achievers from around the world and from every significant field of endeavor'.
■ **World who's who** Routledge. www.worldwhoswho.com [DESCRIPTION]. 'Brings together current and hard-to-find biographical information on almost 60,000 of the most gifted, famous and influential men and women in all fields.' Also known as *International who's who*.

5897 World guide to foundations
M. Zils   3rd edn, K.G. Saur, 2004, 1200pp. 2 v., €418. ISBN 359822267X.
41,000 foundations in 115 countries. Two volumes: V. 1 Europe; V. 2 Africa/The Americas/ Asia and Oceania.

Handbooks & manuals

5898 Archival information [USA]
S. Fisher   Greenwood Press, 2004, 192pp. $69.95. ISBN 1573563897.
'This definitive guide shows novice and experienced researchers how to find archival information. It provides tips on how to use archival materials effectively and efficiently ... Topics covered include Government archives; Science and technology collections ... Also provided is an overview of the world of archives, including archival terminology, how to contact archives and archival etiquette.'
Series: How to Find It, How to Use It.

'The ability to find and use archival information is important in the research process, yet few works provide practical, succinct introductions to the process. Fisher's book does so, supplying for general researchers a useful guide to archival sources ... Recommended. All libraries.' (*Choice*)

5899 Basic research methods for librarians
R.P. Powell and L.S. Connaway   4th edn, Libraries Unlimited, 2004, 360pp.
http://lu.com/showbook.cfm?isbn=1591581036 [DESCRIPTION]
Covers specific research methodologies likely to be used by librarians: subject specific-rather than generic coverage of research methodology.

5900 Chicago manual of style
15th edn, University of Chicago Press, 2003, 984pp. Also available online (fee-based): http://www.chicagomanualofstyle.org/home.html, $55.
www.chicagomanualofstyle.org [COMPANION]
For this edition, 'every aspect of coverage has been examined and brought up to date – from publishing formats to editorial style and method, from documentation of electronic sources to book design and production and everything in between. In addition to books, the Manual now also treats journals and electronic publications. All chapters are written for the electronic age, with advice on how to prepare and edit manuscripts online, handle copyright and permissions issues raised by technology, use new methods of preparing mathematical copy and cite electronic and online sources.'

5901 Choosing and using a news alert service
R. Berkman   Information Today, 2004, 127pp. $79.95. ISBN 1573872245.
Comprehensive guide explaining how e-mail-based news alert services work and identifying, comparing and evaluating over two dozen free, inexpensive and fee-based alert services. 'A detailed appendix also compares specific news source coverage for the major news alert vendors.'

5902 Consider the source: a critical guide to 100 prominent news and information sites on the Web
J.F. Broderick and D.W. Miller   CyberAge Books, 2007, 416pp. $24.95. ISBN 9780910965774.
'An A-to-Z guide to the best and worst news and information sites, featuring 100 in-depth, critical reviews and a 5-star rating system.'

5903 Database design and development: an essential guide for IT professionals
P. Ponniah   IEEE Press/Wiley, 2003, 734pp. $94.95. ISBN 0471218774.
Indeed designed for more general IT professionals – rather than database experts. Comprehensive; well written; logically organized. A good introductory text.

5904 Evidence-based practice for information professionals: a handbook
A. Booth and A. Brice   Facet Publishing, 2004, 320pp. £44.95. ISBN 9781856044714.
'Divided into three parts: The Context for Evidence-based practice; Skills And Resources for Evidence-based Information Practice; and Using the Evidence Base in Practice. This last part explores each of the six domains of evidence-based librarianship identified in research, to

demonstrate the application of evidence-based information practice in a practical decision making context. These chapters with their associated Special Topics present concise summaries of evidence-based information practice within generic areas of work, together with practical examples of the application of evidence-based principles and methods.'

5905 First have something to say: writing for the library profession
W. Crawford   American Library Association, 2003, 141pp. $35. ISBN 0838908519.
'Proceeding matter-of-factly [this book] dissects what it really takes to write for library colleagues, countering traditional "received wisdom", while questioning the "powers that be". Whether you're on a tenure track and want your articles to offer more pleasure than pain, or just have something to share with colleagues, these suggestions will guide you in making both your writing and speaking inform, explain, illuminate, synthesize, reveal and entertain your audience.'

5906 Handbook of data management in information systems
J. Blazewicz [et al.], eds   Springer, 2003, 578pp. £123. ISBN 9783540438939.
'Provides practitioners, scientists and graduate students with a good overview of basic notions, methods and techniques, as well as important issues and trends across the broad spectrum of data management. In particular, the book covers fundamental topics in the field such as distributed databases, parallel databases, advanced databases, object-oriented databases, advanced transaction management, workflow management, data warehousing, data mining, mobile computing, data integration and the Web.'
Series: International Handbooks on Information Systems.

5907 The information professional's guide to career development online
S.L. Nesbeitt and R.S. Gordon   Information Today, 2001, 392pp. $29.50. ISBN 1573871249.
'A thorough why-to and how-to book, showing librarians how to use the Web for professional training, networking, job hunting and becoming known in the library community.'

5908 The information professional's guide to quantitative research: a practical handbook
P. Clayton and G.E. Gorman   Facet Publishing, 2003, 288pp. £39.95. ISBN 1856044734.
'Companion volume to the respected *Qualitative research for the information professional* [q.v.] ...
'Each chapter includes focus questions, an introduction to the subject matter, clear exposition of what are sometimes complex issues, scenarios set in a context relevant to the reader and suggestions for personal reflection and further activity and reading ...
'Key areas covered include the nature of information research; quantitative research design; choice of research methods; introduction to statistics; inferential statistics; reading and evaluating quantitative research; the research proposal; surveys; Delphi research; experimental research; content analysis; and reporting. This is an essential tool for all library professionals and information managers.'

5909 International libel and privacy handbook: a global reference for journalists, publishers, webmasters, and lawyers
C.J. Glasser, ed.   Bloomberg Press, 2006, 391pp. $95. ISBN 1576601889.
A nation-by-nation summary of libel and privacy law, written in straightforward language accessible to journalists and editors. The editor is media counsel to *Bloomberg News*: 'In lieu of royalties, the author and *Bloomberg News* will make donations to nonprofit organizations that support journalism and education'.

5910 Internet research: theory and practice
N.L. Fielden   2nd edn, McFarland, 2001, 205pp. $25. ISBN 078641099X.
'Provides useful information for anyone who wants to broaden the range and scope of their research tools or anyone who wants to increase their knowledge about what is available electronically.'
'Fills an important niche.' (*Library Journal*)
■ **Search engines handbook** N.L. Fielden and L. Kuntz   McFarland, 2002, 115pp. $25. ISBN 0786413085. Looks at the way search engines are put together, how they run, and how they locate information and display it. 'Should be required reading ... Most worthwhile ... Fluent and readable. This handbook is an absolute gem'. (*Voya*).

5911 IssueWeb: a guide and sourcebook for researching controversial issues on the web
K.R. Diaz and N. O'Hanlon   Libraries Unlimited, 2004, 304pp. $30. ISBN 1591580781.
'Provides instruction on techniques for researching controversial topics on the Web and evaluating Web information sources. Forty "Issue Briefs" include background on the topic, outline key controversies and suggest search terms for use in search engines and other databases.'
'They do an excellent job of taking readers through steps needed to evaluate each resource's value for the project, and then to put it all together with helpful instructions for citations and plagiarism avoidance ... This easy-to-use, easy-to-reference book is a godsend for those are able to incorporate controversial issues into their research instruction.' (*School Library Journal*)

5912 Keeping current: advanced internet strategies to meet librarian and patron needs
S.M. Cohen   American Library Association, 2003, 136pp. $38. ISBN 0838908640.
'Offers expert guidelines by: providing information strategies and tips and tools that are easy to use; uncovering methods that dig into the "invisible web" to bring to light sources not found by traditional search engines; revealing the pros and cons of website monitoring software; addressing ways to use weblogs and news search engines; exploring RSS (Rich Site Summary) feeds that bring content from multiple sites to your desktop; and evaluating the currency of these technological and informational tools.'

5913 Know it all, find it fast: an A–Z source guide for the enquiry desk
B. Duckett, P. Walker and C. Donnelly   2nd edn, Facet Publishing, 2004, 384pp. £32.95. ISBN 9781856045346.
'Designed as a first point of reference for library and information practitioners, to be depended upon if they are unfamiliar with the subject of an enquiry – or wish to find out more. It is arranged in an easily searchable, fully cross-

referenced A–Z list of around 150 of the subject areas most frequently handled at enquiry desks.
'Each subject entry lists the most important information sources and where to locate them, including printed and electronic sources, relevant websites and useful contacts for referral purposes. The authors use their extensive experience in reference work to offer useful tips, warn of potential pitfalls and spotlight typical queries and how to tackle them.'

5914 The librarian's and information professional's guide to plug-ins and other web browser tools: selection, installation, troubleshooting
C.M. Benjes-Small and M.L. Just   Neal-Schuman, 2002, 170pp. $65. ISBN 1555704417.
Examines dynamic web browser applications with recommendations on which plug-ins are suited to the library's needs and the needs of staff. Advises on how to make best use of office applications, image-viewing tools, sound enhancers, video players and more. Approximately 15 of the most essential plug-ins are discussed. Topics include system requirements; strengths and weaknesses; installation instructions; troubleshooting tips; and special benefits and applications for libraries.

5915 The librarian's career guidebook
P.K. Shontz, ed.   Scarecrow, 2004, 592pp. $45. ISBN 0810850346.
'Sage advice and career guidance is offered by sixty-four information professionals from diverse positions and workplaces. This practical guide addresses a wide variety of career issues. The advice is aimed at librarians in various stages of a career: prospective librarians, M.L.S. students and entry-level librarians, as well as experienced information professionals. Covers: Career options; Education; The job search; On-the-job experience; Professional development; Essential skills and strategies for enjoying your career.'

5916 The librarian's guide to writing for publication
R.S. Gordon   Scarecrow, 2004, 202pp. $39.95. ISBN 0810848953.
'Topics covered include, but are not limited to: queries and proposals; increasing your odds of publication; networking and collaboration; marketing and promotion; and the particular demands of authorship in an electronic environment. An appendix contains interviews with several library publishers and editors, covering the gamut of publication outlets.
'This is a one-stop guide for librarians at any stage of their publishing career.'

5917 The librarian's internet survival guide: strategies for the high-tech reference desk
I.E. McDermott   2nd edn, Information Today, 2006, 328pp. $29.50. ISBN 9781573872355.
Offers 'troubleshooting tips and advice, Web resources for answering reference questions and strategies for managing information and keeping current. In addition to helping librarians make the most of Web tools and resources, the book offers practical advice on privacy and child safety, assisting patrons with special needs, internet training, [and] building library Web pages.'

5918 Qualitative research for the information professional: a practical handbook
G.E. Gorman and P. Clayton   2nd edn, Facet Publishing, 2005, 282pp. £39.95. ISBN 9781856044721.
Very useful integrated manual on how to conduct qualitative

research, with an extensive coverage, including all aspects of work in this field from conception to completion and all types of study in a variety of settings from multisite studies to data organization. Content includes the nature of qualitative research; qualitative research design in information organizations; case studies in information organizations; laying the foundations for fieldwork in information organizations; beginning fieldwork and formulating a research plan; interviewing; group discussion techniques; historical investigation; recording fieldwork data; analysing qualitative data; writing research reports; evaluating qualitative research; and a new directory of global software applications.

5919 Research methods in information
A.J. Pickard   Facet Publishing, 2007, 352pp. £39.95. ISBN 1856045455.
Focuses on the needs of the information and communications community and 'guides the would-be researcher through the variety of options and possibilities open to them under the heading "research". The text has a practical focus, with examples and exercises to reinforce content, providing theory only for context.'

'It provides the student with sufficient knowledge of the research process to embark on their own empirical research leading to their dissertation with confidence. The exercises have been tried and tested over a number of years with undergraduate, postgraduate and research students and with practitioners.'

5920 Scholarly publishing: books, journals, publishers, and libraries in the twentieth century
R.E. Abel [et al.], eds   Wiley, 2002, 318pp. $34.95. ISBN 0471219290.
'Well rounded and accurate account of the amazing and unpredictable sequence of inter-related events experienced by the field of scholarly publishing in the 20th century.'
'Provides a unique view into the world of scholarly publishing ... There are no works that treat so thoroughly the history, current situation, and future prospects of scholarly publishing.' (*College & Research Libraries*)

5921 Teach beyond your reach: an instructor's guide to developing and running successful distance learning classes, workshops, training sessions and more
R. Neidorf   CyberAge Books, 2006, 248pp. $29.95. ISBN 9780910965736.
'A practical, curriculum-focused approach designed to help new and experienced distance educators develop and deliver quality courses and training sessions. [The author] shares best practices and examples, surveys the tools of the trade and covers key issues, including instructional design, course craft, adult learning styles, student-teacher interaction, strategies for building a community of learners and much more.'

5922 The translator's handbook
M. Sofer   5th edn, Schreiber, 2004, 420pp. $25.95. ISBN 1887563881.
'Includes chapters on the history of translation, sources of translation work and the quirks of translating in various languages ... More than half the book is composed of appendices, one more useful than the next. The first features 64 pages' worth of dictionaries and reference volumes for ...

64 languages. Others list agencies, organizations and companies likely to require translation work; information about translation courses and accreditation; and periodicals for professional translators.'

5923 XML: a manager's guide
K. Dick   2nd edn, Addison-Wesley, 2003, 298pp. £30.99. ISBN 0201770067.
Attractive introduction, each chapter starting with an executive summary. The last two chapters review, respectively, five XML applications for enterprises and for vendors.

Keeping up to date

5924 AllConferences.Com
www.allconferences.com
'A directory focusing on conferences, conventions, trade shows, exhibits, workshops, events and business meetings. This is a unique search directory that serves users looking for specific information on conference or event information; while at the same time provides services to the meeting planners, such as online registrations and payment processing.
    'The information ranges from specialized scientific, medical and academic conferences to all kinds of general events.'

5925 Annual Reviews
www.annurev.org
'Authoritative, analytic reviews in 33 focused disciplines within the Biomedical, Physical and Social Sciences. Annual Reviews publications are among the most highly cited in scientific literature.'

5926 Cafe con Leche XML News and Resources
E.R. Harold
http://cafeconleche.org
Excellent gateway to XML news, tutorials, recommended reading, specifications and development tools.

5927 Current Contents Connect
http://scientific.thomson.com/products/ccc [DESCRIPTION]
'A multidisciplinary current awareness Web resource providing access to complete bibliographic information from over 8000 of the world's leading scholarly journals and more than 2000 books.'

5928 The Data Administration Newsletter
R.S. Seiner
www.tdan.com
'This is a web-based newsletter, published by consultant Robert Seiner. It contains a range of articles on data management and related topics. It also has listings of conferences, jobs, companies and related Web pages. An archive and a search engine are provided.' An excellent, extensive compilation.

5929 DigitalKoans: what is the sound of one e-print downloading?
C.W. Bailey
www.digital-scholarship.org/digitalkoans
Weblog updated daily, providing commentary on copyright,

open access, scholarly communication and other digital information issues.

5930 FreePint

www.freepint.com

Website of the leading UK-based network of information researchers, with over 70,000 registered users globally. Entrée to a very wide range of useful news, comment and evaluation of information work. The FreePint newsletter is e-mailed free of charge fortnightly, each issue including – among much other interesting and relevant material – concise reviews of information resources in a specific sector.

5931 InterDok

www.interdok.com

Gateway to Directory of Published Conference Proceedings providing more than 280,000 references from over 60,000 sources.

5932 Internet Resources Newsletter

R. Macleod, C. Ure and C. Ferguson, eds; Heriot-Watt University
Heriot-Watt University, monthly. ISSN 13619381.
www.hw.ac.uk/libwww/irn

Very useful and interesting – and free of charge. Current sections are: Comment (including an eclectic 'News items of interest'); A–Z new and notable websites; Nice (websites): 'In the course of finding sites of interest for this Newsletter, we sometimes come across Websites which we feel deserve slightly more than a passing mention'; Press releases; Network news (principally UK); Recent internet books in the library (Heriot-Watt University); internet in print; Book reviews; Blogorama (News about weblogs, RSS, etc.); Get a life! Leisure time (in Edinburgh and Scotland).

  ■ **Pinakes** www.hw.ac.uk/libwww/irn/pinakes/pinakes.html. Colourful links to about 50 major subject gateways. ('As it became increasingly difficult to locate material in the Library of Alexandria, the poet Callimachus solved the problem by compiling a catalogue called *The Pinakes*'.).

5933 ResourceShelf: Resources and news for information professionals [USA]
G. Price
www.resourceshelf.com

Free daily electronic newsletter containing news and other resources of interest to the online researcher. Wide coverage, especially of US-based developments. Apart from news of movements and machinations in the online database industry, there are usually posted each day useful items in the sections Professional Reading Shelf and Resources, Reports, Tools, Lists and Full Text Documents. Well worth scanning regularly.

Topic Index

Title/Author Index

All numbers are entry numbers. Secondary entries are indexed to the entry number of the primary resource under which they appear. Titles of resources and names of corporate bodies are in bold type.

100% ME 4659
1040.com 3417
18 Doughty Street Talk TV 1960
18th century official parliamentary publications portal 1688–1834 1266
4S *see* Society for Social Studies of Science
50 ways to understand communication 5031

A

A.S.K. Hollis 2007 5878
AAA *see* American Arbitration Association
AAASP *see* Association for the Advancement of Applied Sport Psychology
AACS *see* Association for Applied & Clinical Sociology
AAF *see* American Advertising Federation
AAHPERD *see* American Alliance for Health, Physical Education, Recreation & Dance
AAN *see* Association of Alternative Newsweeklies
AAP *see* Association of American Publishers
AAPAR *see* American Association for Physical Activity & Recreation
Aarebrot, F.H.
  Handbook of political change in Eastern Europe **1381**
AARP *see* American Association of Retired People
AASL *see* American Association of School Librarians
AASW code of ethics 852
AAUP *see* Association of American University Presses
ABA *see* American Bar Association; Australian Bar Association
Abbot, P.
  Introduction to sociology **492**
Abbreviations and acronyms of the US Government 2060
ABC *see* Australian Broadcasting Corporation
ABC aerospace directory 3494
Abel, R.E.
  Scholarly publishing **5920**
Abercrombie, N.
  Penguin dictionary of sociology **500**
ABI/INFORM Dateline 4070
ABI/INFORM global 3901
Ability vs ability 4941
Abnormal and clinical psychology 397
Abnormal psychology 398
Abolition 2000 1789
Abraham, T.
  Repositories of primary sources **5857**
Abrams, J.
  Understanding the leisure and sport industry **4877**
Abridgement of New Zealand case law 2655

ABS *see* Association of Black Sociologists
Absolute returns 3121
Absolvitor 2732
ABU *see* Asia-Pacific Broadcasting Union
Aby, S.
  Sociology **538**
Academic Council on United Nations 1583
Academic Film Archive of North America 5215
Academic library 5631
Academic publishing industry 5831
Academic reading 4543
Academic research library in a decade of change 5632
Academic Serials in Communication 5066
Academic's handbook 4544
Academy blog 1241
Academy of Human Resource Development 4348
Academy of International Business 4049
Academy of Learned Societies for the Social Sciences *see* Commission on the Social Sciences
Academy of Management 3889
Academy of Management Journal 3889
Academy of Management Perspectives 3889
Academy of Management Review 3889
Academy of Marketing 4154
Academy of Marketing Science 4155
Academy of Social Sciences 45
Academy of the Social Sciences in Australia 45
Accardo, P.J.
  Dictionary of developmental disabilities terminology **997**
Access All Areas 3625
Access to libraries for persons with disabilities – checklist 5602
Accountable government 2012
Accountancy 3327
Accountancy Age 3328
Accountancy Direct 3321
Accountants World 3329
Accounting thesaurus 3312
Accounting trends and techniques 3322
Accrediting Council on Education in Journalism & Mass Communications 5108
Accuracy in Media 5295
ACE *see* Advisory Centre for Education
ACE electoral knowledge network 1439
ACEEEO *see* Association of Central & Eastern European Election Officials
ACEJMC *see* Accrediting Council on Education in Journalism & Mass Communications
ACGA *see* Asian Corporate Governance Association
Achievement and inclusion in schools 4574

ACHPER *see* Australian Council for Health, Physical Education & Recreation
ACICA *see* Australian Centre for International Commercial Arbitration
Ackermann, F.
  Practice of making strategy **4000**
ACL *see* Advisory Council on Libraries
ACMA *see* Australia. Communications & Media Authority
Acquiring skill in sport 4993
Acquisitions Monthly 3250
ACR *see* Association for Consumer Research
ACRL *see* Association of College & Research Libraries; Association of College & Research Libraries, Psychology/Psychiatry Committee
Acronym addiction 3583
Acronym Finder 5805
Acronym Institute 1774
ACSM *see* American College of Sports Medicine
ACSM advanced exercise physiology 5019
ACSS *see* Academy of Social Sciences
Action on Elder Abuse 1062
Action plan for outcomes assessment in your library 5706
Action research 100
Active living every day 4698
Active Living Partners 4681
Active Places 4622
Acts of Parliament concerning Wales, 1714–1901 2923
Acts of the Oireachtas 2566
Acts of the Parliament of the Commonwealth of Australia passed during the year 2454
Acts of the Parliaments of Scotland 1424–1707 2710
Acts of the Scottish Parliament 2711
Acts of the UK Parliament/Public General Acts and General Synod Measures 2761
Acts of Tynwald 2608
ACU *see* Autocycle Union
ACUN *see* Academic Council on United Nations
Ad Council 4220
Ad*Access 4238
Adair, S.
  Information sources for the press and broadcast media **5166**
Adams, B.N.
  Handbook of world families **646**
Adams, G.R.
  Blackwell handbook of adolescence **342**
Adams, H.R.
  Privacy in the 21st century **5472**
Adams, J.N.
  Bibliography of eighteenth century legal literature **2129**
  Bibliography of nineteenth century legal literature **2130**
Adapted Physical Activity Quarterly 4949
Addiction Search 975

Adflip 4239
Adler, G.
  Winning at service **3763**
Admap 4253
Administering the school library media center 5628
Administration yearbook 2007 2021
Administrative office management 3958
Adoption 1129
Adoption and Fostering 1174
Adult learner 4570
Adult psychopathology and diagnosis 421
Adults in higher education 4545
Adults learning 4559
Advanced accounting 3323, 3324, 3325
Advanced Institute of Management Research 3885
Advanced internet searcher's handbook 5595
Advanced modelling in finance using Excel and VBA 2952
Advanced Research & Assessment Group 1700
Advances in child development and behavior 356
Advances in Developing Human Resources 4348
Advances in experimental social psychology 395
Advances in library organization and administration 5377
Advances in management accounting 3340
Advertisers annual 4241
Advertising Age 4254
Advertising and Society Review 4231
Advertising Association 4221
Advertising Educational Foundation 4231
Advertising handbook 4248
Advertising Icon Museum 4228
Advertising Research Foundation 4222
Advertising self-regulation in Europe 4213
Advertising Standards Authority 4216
Advertising statistics yearbook 4221
Adviceguide 2783
Advisory Centre for Education 4499
Advisory Commission on Electronic Commerce 4031
Advisory Council on Libraries 5654
AECT *see* Association for Educational Communications & Technology
AEF *see* Advertising Educational Foundation
AEI-Brookings election reform project 1422
AEJMC *see* Association for Education in Journalism & Mass Communication
AEP *see* Association of Educational Psychologists
AERA *see* American Educational Research Association
AERADE 1722

E